INTERPRETATION of SCHIZOPHRENIA

Also by Silvano Arieti

AMERICAN HANDBOOK OF PSYCHIATRY
(*Editor-in-Chief*)

THE INTRAPSYCHIC SELF: FEELING, COGNITION, AND CREATIVITY IN HEALTH AND MENTAL ILLNESS

THE WORLD BIENNIAL OF PSYCHIATRY AND PSYCHOTHERAPY
(*Editor*)

THE WILL TO BE HUMAN

INTERPRETATION of SCHIZOPHRENIA

Second Edition

Completely Revised and Expanded

SILVANO ARIETI, M.D.

Crosby Lockwood Staples

LONDON

Granada Publishing Limited
First published in Great Britain 1974 by Crosby Lockwood Staples
Frogmore, St. Albans and 3 Upper James Street, London

ISBN: 0 258 97005 7

First published in the United States of America in 1974
by Basic Books, Inc.

TO THE MEMORY OF MY PARENTS

Dr. Elio AND Ines Arieti

Preface

Since the first edition of this book appeared in 1955, psychiatry has greatly expanded, as has the specific field of schizophrenia. When I look at the first edition, I realize how much I have learned in the intervening years, especially in psychodynamics, in schizophrenic cognition, and most of all in therapy. Although some basic orientations and salient points that were expressed in the first edition—for example, the psychodynamic mechanisms of childhood and adolescence, the structural analysis of schizophrenic thought and language, and the development of the catatonic process—remain valid, much has been added that permits a deeper understanding.

A new edition was long overdue. This volume has been almost completely rewritten. From the original volume I have retained the material that I consider still pertinent and illustrative, but I have expanded all parts of this vast subject. In order to give a more comprehensive character to the present work, I have also added new sections that may be useful to the beginner. These include the manifest symptomatology of the disorder, its sociocultural and epidemiological aspects, prevention of the psychosis, and genetic and other somatic studies.

Different parts of this work will have different relevance for various readers, in accordance with their predominant interest. The didactical presentation of psychotherapy in Part Seven has been particularly expanded. I have added many new ways of dealing therapeutically with psychotic problems, and I have included detailed reports of cases treated with intensive and prolonged psychotherapy. As in the first edition, especially in dealing with psychodynamics and psychotherapy, I have used a simple style shorn of almost all technical terminology. Some aspects of this subject have not been included, because I felt I did not have enough experience with them. Group and hospital milieu therapy have been omitted, and references to childhood schizophrenia have been reduced to a minimum.

This book is the result of thirty-three years of my life, spent to a large extent in studying and in treating schizophrenia. A third of a century, from the zest of age twenty-six to the maturity of fifty-nine, is a long time; but I believe it was spent in a worthwhile way. I often tell my students that to study schizophrenia deeply means to study more than half the field of psychiatry, because most problems pertaining to schizophrenia are connected with other psychiatric conditions as well. But, as I have tried to show throughout this book, the study of schizophrenia transcends psychiatry. No other condition in human pathology permits us to delve so deeply into what is specific to human nature. Although the main objective of the therapist of the schizophrenic is to relieve suffering, he will have to deal with a panorama of the human condition, which includes the cardinal problems of truth and illusion, bizarreness and creativity, grandiosity and self-abnegation, loneliness and capacity for communion, interminable suspiciousness and absolute faith, petrifying immobility and freedom of action, capacity for projecting and blaming and self-accusation, surrender to love and hate and imperviousness to these feelings.

To the persons mentioned in the preface to the first edition I could add a long list of people from various parts of the world who have stimulated ideas in me or given me material from patients. I shall mention only Drs. Hyman Barahal, Valentin Barenblit, William Bellamy, Henry Brill, and Giuseppe Uccheddu.

As I reflect on the difference between this work and the other one that has required a great deal of my time—the editorship of the *American Handbook of Psychiatry*—the following thought emerges. In the preparation of the *Handbook,* especially in the six volumes of the second edition, I endeavored, with the help of co-editors, to bring together a few hundred authors, specialists in the various fields. We all worked together in an effort to prepare a worthy representation of American psychiatry.

The present book, however, is the work of one man. Although I learned much from teachers, colleagues, and other writers, I paved my own way down the various avenues of this vast subject. I am pleased that I did not find it necessary to seek financial support from either taxpayer money or foundation funds. Thus, for the errors, as well as for the new insights expressed in these pages, I alone must be held accountable. Be lenient, reader, but not too much; for I was not alone in this thirty-three-year work. Always with me was the sufferer, who sooner or later gave me the gift of trust.

SILVANO ARIETI

New York, 1974

Acknowledgments

I wish to express my indebtedness to the publishers who have permitted the reproduction in this volume of long excerpts and/or illustrations from the following articles of mine:

"Special Logic of Schizophrenic and Other Types of Autistic Thought." *Psychiatry,* Vol. 11, 1948, pp. 325–338.

"The 'Placing into Mouth' and Coprophagic Habits." *Journal of Nervous and Mental Disease.* Vol. 99, 1944, pp. 959–964.

"Primitive Habits in the Preterminal Stage of Schizophrenia." *Journal of Nervous and Mental Disease.* Vol. 102, 1945, pp. 367–375.

"The Processes of Expectation and Anticipation." *Journal of Nervous and Mental Disease.* Vol. 106, 1947, pp. 471–481.

"Autistic Thought. Its Formal Mechanisms and Its Relationship to Schizophrenia." *Journal of Nervous and Mental Disease.* Vol. 111, 1950, pp. 288–303.

"The Possibility of Psychosomatic Involvement of the Central Nervous System in Schizophrenia." *Journal of Nervous and Mental Disease,* Vol. 123, 1956, pp. 324–333.

"Volition and Value: A Study Based on Catatonic Schizophrenia." *Comprehensive Psychiatry,* Vol. 2, 1961, pp. 74–82.

"Schizophrenic Thought." *American Journal of Psychotherapy,* Vol XIII, 1959, pp. 537–552.

"Hallucinations, Delusions, and Ideas of Reference." *American Journal of Psychotherapy,* Vol. 16, 1962, pp. 52–60.

"The Schizophrenic Patient in Office Treatment." Psychother. Schizophrenia, 3rd International Symposium, Lausanne, Switzerland, 1964, pp. 7–23. (Karger)

"Schizophrenic Art and Its Relationship to Modern Art," *Journal of the American Academy of Psychoanalysis,* Vol. 1, pp. 333–365. © 1973 by John Wiley & Sons.

Permissions for reproductions of illustrations were obtained from Dr. Hyman Barahal, Dr. Valentin Barenblit, Professor Jean Bobon, Dr. Enzo Gabrici, and Professor Giuseppe Uccheddu.

Contents

PART ONE

The Manifest Symptomatology and Other Basic Notions

PART TWO

The Psychodynamics of Schizophrenia

PART THREE

The World of Schizophrenia: A Psychostructural Approach

PART FOUR

A Longitudinal View of Schizophrenia

PART FIVE

The Somatic and Psychosomatic Aspects of Schizophrenia

PART SIX

Epidemiology, Transcultural Aspects, and Prevention of Schizophrenia

PART SEVEN

Psychotherapy of Schizophrenia

PART EIGHT

Physical Therapies of Schizophrenia

PART ONE

The Manifest Symptomatology and Other Basic Notions

CHAPTER

1

The Basic Questions

What is schizophrenia? How can it be recognized, interpreted, and treated? These basic questions are posed not only by the beginner in the field of psychiatry, but also by the professional who has spent the major part of his life treating psychiatric patients. A serious attempt will be made here to answer these difficult questions. Our long search will lead us in various directions. We shall not just collect and integrate what we know; we shall explore new areas and revisit old ones with new eyes. Even when definite conclusions will not be reached, we shall be aware that we have tried to broaden our views of man, of his suffering, and of his potentialities.

The basic questions we have posed imply that we cannot start our didactical journey with the standard procedure, that is, by defining our major theme. It is a formidable task to define schizophrenia unless we accept an unsatisfactory definition that consists of a list of the most common characteristics of the disorder. More appropriate definitions will be attempted several times in this book, after we have examined the subject from several perspectives.

Some authors consider schizophrenia an illness, others a syndrome, still others a mental mechanism or even a way of living. There is some truth in each of these views, and yet at closer analysis all of them prove to be unsatisfactory. The understanding or the clarity that they seem to offer reflect the facility of approaches that take into consideration only one or a few aspects of a complicated problem. Certainly schizophrenia is a way of living, but so is having a heart murmur, being a doctor, a nurse, remaining a bachelor, and so on. As we shall elaborate in other chapters of this book, the authors who call schizophrenia a way of living probably want to stress that it is a natural and enduring way of living, an appropriate response to certain environmental situations. This seems hardly the case to those who have witnessed the suffering that accompanies this special "way of living."

There are particular mental mechanisms in schizophrenia, but these have to be understood in their origins and consequences. Schizophrenia, of course, can be considered a syndrome; but again, which symptoms are the essential ones in a condition that presents itself in multiple ways? Moreover, what is the interrelation between the various symptoms? Could we say about schizophrenia something comparable in clarity to what we can say about diabetes, whose symptoms can be understood as consequent to a disorder of the carbohydrate metabolism?

Can we state that schizophrenia is an illness? If we follow the concepts of Virchow, or those derived from Virchow, which imply cellular pathology, an understanding of the pathological mechanisms, and the capacity to reproduce experimentally the condition, the answer is no. Apparently this negative answer is stressed by those authors who conclude that schizophrenia is not an illness, but probably only a special way of coping with life. Once more a semantic controversy complicates the issue. If we define disease as a state in which bodily health is impaired, we cannot at present call schizophrenia a disease because there is no uncontroversial evidence of bodily impairment. If by disease we mean an undesirable state of the subject, resulting in alterations of his basic functions, including the psychological, then schizophrenia is certainly a disease. Schizophrenia, as well as most mental illnesses or psychiatric conditions, does not fit the medical (especially Virchowian) model. This realization does not necessarily lead to the conclusion that the concept of schizophrenia or any mental illness is a myth. An alternative position is that the traditional medical model was built without taking psychiatry into consideration and does not include all the dimensions of human pathology. If we do change the traditional medical model, we can then call schizophrenia an illness. The big issues, however, remain untouched. What kind of illness? What is its nature?

Generally we consider schizophrenia a special type of illness (or disease or syndrome)—a psychosis. There are as many obscurities about the concept of psychosis as there are about the concept of schizophrenia, although the term *psychosis* refers to a broader category, to which schizophrenia belongs. As I expressed elsewhere (Arieti, 1973), psychosis is a term generally used to designate a severe or major psychiatric disorder. In theory and clinical practice the concept is more difficult to define because severity is not an inflexible characteristic and a certain number of cases diagnosed as psychosis may in fact be less serious from the point of view of the sufferer or of society than are some of those included in other psychiatric categories. The term *psychosis* is at times indistinctly equated with insanity. The latter term, when used legally or in popular language, suggests a person who is so incompetent that he may require special control or supervision. However, psychosis indicates not only actual or potential severity, but also connotes that an unrealistic way of appreciating the self and the world is accepted or tends to be accepted by the sufferer as a normal way of living. At any rate, typical psychotics who are not under treatment do not seem to know that there is anything wrong with them. This definition of psychosis lends itself to justified criticism because it implies that we know what is unreality or unrealistic.

This book will deal with the various biological and psychological approaches that have been applied to the problem of schizophrenia. It will pursue chiefly the psychological approach, which, in my opinion, has so far provided an understanding more significant than that provided by the other methods. Moreover, the practicing psychiatrist, even if he prefers physical methods of treatment, cannot help trying to understand the psychodynamics of the case and to practice some kind of psychotherapy.

All the methods that have been followed so far in this field have been rewarding to varying degrees. The simplest approach is the descriptive and taxonomic. With this method, the symptoms of the patients are recognized, described, and labeled. They are observed in their *manifest* aspect, that is, as they present themselves to a clinical examination without any physiologic or symbolic meaning being attached to them. Whereas this method was the only one at a certain stage in the history of psychiatry, it must today be considered as the initial and most elementary approach, even though it is still valuable. Contrary to old treatises of psychiatry, which dealt almost exclusively with this aspect of the disorder, this book will deal with it only in Chapters 3 and 4.

The dynamic approach initiated an era of greater and deeper understanding. The symptoms came to be interpreted as having a meaning; the symptomatology came to be seen as having a purpose and a genetic history as well, inasmuch as it could be related to the previous, predominantly early, life history of the individual. It is impossible to overestimate the value of the dynamic approach in schizophrenia and, of course, in psychiatry in general. Nothing could be more important from a psychotherapeutic point of view. One of the major parts of this book (Part Two) will be devoted to this dynamic interpretation, as a necessary preparation to psychotherapy, which will be dealt with in Part Seven. In the first chapters of Part Two (Chapters 5–8) we shall accompany the patient from birth to the onset of the psychosis. In the remainder of Part Two (Chapters 9–14), with the help of case histories, we shall examine the dynamisms occurring in the main types of schizophrenia, such as the paranoid, catatonic, hebephrenic, postpartum, and so forth. We shall be able to individualize patterns that tend to recur, that build to a crescendo of conflict and maladjustment, and that eventually lead to a disintegration of the defenses. This psychodynamic study will involve the patient in his intrapsychic life as well as in relation to his environment.

And yet we shall come to recognize that even this dynamic approach, in spite of the profound insights that it offers to the therapist, does not solve in its entirety the mystery of this mental disorder. Even when the symptoms are explained in their symbolic language, even when their motivation is understood, even when their relation to early life situations has been established, there is still a great deal that needs explanation. Why is the schizophrenic pattern so different from any other? Why have the symptoms such peculiar aspects? Why does the patient experience hallucinations and delusions? Why does he present word salad, catatonic postures, stereotyped activities, and so forth? Even if we accept the fact, and we do accept it, that the psychological traumata in schizophrenia were more violent and more destructive than in patients who develop psychoneuroses, we are not able, with a dynamic approach, to understand the formal structure of the symptoms. When a regressed schizophrenic replies, "White House," to the question "Who was the first president of the United States?" how is the disorder implicit in the answer to be interpreted? Bleuler would call the phenomenon a "loose association," but this term is more descriptive than explanatory. A dynamic approach clarifies the underlying motivation that has led to the selection or facilitated the occurrence of the process, but this approach does not explain the mechanisms of the process itself.

The first edition of this book (1955), pursuing some studies started in the early 1940s, pioneered an additional approach to schizophrenia. This approach, called structural or psychostructural, aimed at the understanding of the psychological structure, was developed independently and along different lines from the studies of Lévi-Strauss and preceded Chomsky's application of structuralism to other fields of inquiry. In this second edition the importance of the structural approach is reaffirmed and expanded.

In psychiatry the structural approach must be related to the dynamic; and the way in which dynamic factors use, exploit, and change the formal mechanisms must be determined.

The structural approach does not aim at a description, as the descriptive approach does, but at an understanding of the mechanisms of the psychological functions. This approach remains at a psychological level and is not necessarily concerned with, although it may lead to, studies of the organic basis of the psychic functions.

The dynamic and the structural approaches differ also in certain other respects. The structural approach emphasizes what patients have in common, and the common psychological mechanisms that they adopt. Although it does not do so exclusively, the dynamic approach studies predominantly what is specific in each case; the more specific are the elements studied, the more accurate and therapeutically useful they are. Both approaches must be used, because both are valuable. Every schizophrenic, like every man, is both similar to, and different from, other patients and men. Here again is that fundamental dichotomy—similarity and difference—on which all human understanding is based.

The psychostructural approach, which we shall study in Part Three, makes us enter into the world of schizophrenia. It reveals how the patient feels, thinks, acts, and relates, and how he experiences his own body, the inanimate world, art, work, the passage of time, and the looming of space. It focuses on those parts of the human being that are particularly human: symbolism, as expressed in imagery, language, thinking, interrelations; and volition, as expressed in choice and actions. The schizophrenic deformations will reveal themselves as psychodynamic conflicts that have assumed unusual and yet interpretable forms.

Whereas the dynamic approach remains predominantly a psychiatric study, the formal or psychostructural approach transcends the field of psychiatry. Excursions into other fields, such as anthropology, sociology, logic, aesthetics, neurology, and general biology, are necessary. The results obtained concern not only psychiatry, but all the sciences whose subject is the nature of man. Part Three will also disclose the influences of people who have made significant contributions in various fields—for example, Giambattista Vico, Hughlings Jackson, George Mead, Kurt Goldstein, Jean Piaget, Heinz Werner, and Susanne Langer.

The study of schizophrenia is not complete without taking into consideration the cases that proceed toward chronicity. Fortunately, these cases today are sharply decreasing in number. Although their response to treatment is by far inferior to that of recent cases, the psychiatrist must have some knowledge of them in order to understand the aspects of the schizophrenic phenomenon that are not revealed in less advanced cases. Part Four will be devoted to the longitudinal study of schizophrenia from the earliest to the most advanced stages. Many books on schizophrenia have failed to offer a detailed description and interpretation of the gradual progression of the illness. In Part Four, interpretation of some individual symptoms as well as of the whole phenomenon of regression will be offered.

The psychodynamic, psychostructural, and longitudinal approaches cover vast dimensions. Whatever they reveal seems *necessary* for the engendering and unfolding of schizophrenia. However, many psychiatrists doubt that these necessary factors are *sufficient* to cause or explain the disorder. Many researchers in the field have accumulated a vast amount of data, from the genetic code to biochemical changes. Most of the physiologic and organic changes reported in schizophrenic patients have been studied almost exclusively from the point of view of demonstrating the organic origin of this condition. In several, but not all, instances the possibility exists that these changes are only the result of the disorder. In some respects these changes may be psychosomatic, that is, they may be sequences of the primary psychological condition. Part Five of this book will be devoted to the somatic and psychosomatic study of schizophrenia.

Part Six will deal with the social, cultural, and epidemiological factors favoring the occurrence of the psychosis. This discussion will not be exhaustive, but will cover the material that is most pertinent to the practicing psychiatrist.

The first six parts of the book will reveal how our knowledge of schizophrenia has been vastly enlarged, even in the past few years, but they will also show that all the links have not yet been placed in the right sequence in the great chain of causes and effects. Final syntheses remain to be made. In spite of the incompleteness of our understanding, I think that the reader can approach Parts Seven and Eight, devoted to therapy, with a definite sense of optimism. Our understanding of the disorder is sufficient to permit a totally successful treatment of many patients and a marked amelioration in many others.

After a discussion of the choice of treatment, Part Seven will deal with psychotherapy. What has been learned predominantly from the dynamic and structural approaches, but also from all the other studies of schizophrenia, will be applied to psychotherapy. This is the method in which I have my largest experience, and so it will be described in greatest detail. The physical treatments, and in particular drug therapy, will be described in Part Eight.

Part Nine will reconsider the scope and extent of schizophrenia. Are such conditions as paranoia, child schizophrenia, and anorexia nervosa to be included in the great parameter of the disorder? After reexamining some theoretical concepts, I will attempt a recapitulation and synthesis of the basic concepts expressed in this work.

Before undertaking these studies, we shall review in Chapter 2 the evolution of the major concepts of schizophrenia, from the earliest formulations of the disorder to those preceding the publication of the first edition of this book.

CHAPTER

2

Historical Review of the Concept of Schizophrenia

A critical review of the changing concepts of schizophrenia will be attempted in this chapter. This review will not be a complete one; it will not include the pre-Kraepelinian conceptions, which now have only a historical interest; and it will omit entirely all those theories which have received transient and inconsequential consideration. The contributions published since 1955 will be discussed in the subsequent chapters of this book, in relation to the various aspects of the disorder. The contributions examined in this chapter are those of six authors who, in my opinion, are responsible for the evolution of the concept of schizophrenia from 1896 to 1955. These innovators are Kraepelin, Bleuler, Meyer, Freud, Jung, and Sullivan. A host of contributions, some of them very valuable, have been stimulated directly or indirectly by the works of these six men; and the reader who is interested may find an account of them elsewhere (Lewis, 1936; Bellak, 1948, 1957; Benedetti, Kind, and Mielke, 1957; Bellak and Loeb, 1969; Cancro, 1971, 1972).

Although our purpose here is to discuss six different views of schizophrenia, it is obvious that these views in respect to this condition reflect conceptions toward the entire field of psychiatry, or toward the human psyche, and therefore we cannot help in several instances to refer to other psychiatric areas. These six views have enlarged our understanding of schizophrenia almost exclusively in a psychological frame of reference. Some of the mentioned authors worked and theorized from an organic point of view also, but only their work in the psychological areas has retained significance. For instance, Kraepelin's hypothesis about metabolic-toxic disorders in schizophrenia did not produce the same repercussions that his clinical description of the psychological manifestations did.

In contrast with the relatively nonextensive work of these six authors is the immense amount of the work of countless researchers who have attacked the schizophrenic enigma from a predominantly organic point of view. These researchers have followed the assumption that in the study of schizophrenia, as in the study of other diseases in biology, one should follow Virchow's concept that any kind of pathology means organic or cellular pathology. Under the influence of this concept, which for a long time has dominated the whole field of medicine, researchers have examined every possible spot of the body of the schizophrenic patient from top to bottom, from the hair to the sexual glands, in a relentless attempt to find clues that would reveal the organic nature of this condition.

Even at present the organic studies of schizophrenia outnumber by far the psychological ones. The most important of them, or those that at least promise to open constructive avenues of research, will be discussed in Part Six.

Emil Kraepelin

Emil Kraepelin (1855–1926) was the first psychiatrist to differentiate from the mass of intramural mental patients that pathological entity which he called *dementia praecox*. He did so in 1896, although the name *dementia praecox* had already been used by Morel in 1860 and by Pick in 1891. Morel described his first case in a 14-year-old boy, and for him the word *praecox* meant that the demential state started early, or precociously, in life, in contrast to senile dementia, which occurred in old age. Kraepelin, too, following the observation of Hecker, used the term *praecox* to refer to the fact that the condition "seemed to stand in near relation to the period of youth." In Kraepelin's writings and in the Kraepelinian approach, however, the term *praecox* acquired, explicitly or by implication, an additional meaning: the state of dementia was supposed to follow precociously or soon after the onset of the illness. Thus even in the name of the disease, as used by Kraepelin, one recognizes his finalistic conception: the fundamental characteristic of the disease is its outcome, a prognostic characteristic.

The major contribution of Kraepelin was the inclusion, in the same syndrome, of catatonia, already described by Kahlbaum, hebephrenia, and "vesania typica," also described by Kahlbaum, characterized by auditory hallucinations and persecutory trends. After examining and observing thousands of patients, and seeing them panoramically in space and time, Kraepelin was able to discern the common characteristics in these apparently dissimilar cases. The characteristic that impressed him most was the progressive tendency toward a state of dementia. The other patients who did not have this tendency, like the manic-depressives, would be separated from the praecox group and subsequently would be recognized as having other differential symptoms also. Using this method of observation, Kraepelin could differentiate and define as dementia praecox a symptomatology consisting of hallucinations, delusions, incongruous emotivity, impairment of attention, negativism, stereotyped behavior, and progressive dilapidation in the presence of relatively intact sensorium.

In England, Thomas Clouston, in an impressive address that he delivered in 1888 as president of the Medico-Psychological Association, spoke of "adolescent insanities" and offered a description in many respects comparable to Kraepelin's. However, he did not separate the praecox cases from the manic-depressive, which at that time occurred quite frequently. Thus there is no doubt that Kraepelin deserves to be considered the first author who differentiated the disorder.

Once he defined this syndrome, Kraepelin tried his best to give an accurate description of it. Like a man working at a microscope, he described as many minute details as possible. His monograph *Dementia Praecox and Paraphrenia* (1919) remains until today the most complete description of the symptoms of the schizophrenic from a phenomenological point of view. The symptom is described and accepted as it is, with no attempt being made to interpret it, either physiologically or psychologically. Some symptoms (for instance, negativism) were described for the first time by Kraepelin.

Kraepelin also divided the patients into three groups: the hebephrenic, the catatonic, and the paranoid. Later, he accepted the differentiation of a fourth type, the simple, as suggested by other authors. He also separated from dementia praecox, a new nosological entity, "paraphrenia." In this syndrome, too, the outcome is the fundamental consideration: in spite of the progression of the illness, there is no decay of the personality. As to the etiology, Kraepelin considered dementia praecox an endogenous illness, that is, one not due to external causes. At first he thought it was due to organic pathology of the brain; later he felt that it might be due to a metabolic disorder.

The great merit of Kraepelin consists in his having been able to synthesize successfully the works of Kahlbaum, Morel, Wundt, and others, and to organize them in his own system. We cannot fully appreciate his influence until we read a book of psychiatry of the pre-Kraepelinian era and evaluate the confusing picture of psychiatry in those days. Today it is impossible, however, not to see the shortcomings of Kraepelin's conceptions of dementia praecox. The acceptance of the prognostic characteristic as the fundamental one cannot be considered a sound principle. First, as Kraepelin himself came to recognize, not all cases of dementia praecox end in dementia; as a matter of fact, some of them seem to make a complete recovery. Secondly, this finalistic or teleologic point of view is incompatible with the scientific method, which searches for the causes and not for the effects.

Although Kraepelin himself was probably unaware of this influence, this overall prognostic concept reinforced the popular fatalistic attitude toward mental illnesses and discouraged therapeutic attempts. Reading his monograph on dementia praecox, one cannot help admiring the accurateness of his description; however, his description is remarkable for its extension and completeness, not for its depth. The patient appears as a collection of symptoms, not as a person; or, if he appears as a person, he looks as if he belongs to a special species and thus should be differentiated from the rest of humanity and put into the insane asylum. The psychiatric hospital is a zoological garden with many differentiated species.

Kraepelin seems to see the patient as detached or to be detached from society. It never enters his mind that the schizophrenic may have been influenced by social forces, or may even be a product of society. Although his fundamental concept was the final outcome, that is, a temporal concept, he does not give a longitudinal picture of the patient. Except for the repeated mention of the fact that the patient decays progressively until he reaches a state of idiocy, we do not see in the Kraepelinian description different stages or any real movement, even toward regression. The patient is always seen in cross section.

It is often said that Kraepelin was more concerned with the structure of the psychic phenomena than with the content, that he was more concerned with how the patient thinks than with what he thinks. Undoubtedly he was not concerned with the psychological importance of the content of thought, but it seems to me that he was also not concerned with the real structure of patients' thoughts. A mere description of the symptoms is not a structural understanding.

When we examine the negative qualities of Kraepelin's conceptions, we are bound to be too harsh with him. It is really too easy for us to see what he did not see. Nobody would criticize Galileo for not knowing the principles of electricity. If we concentrate on what Kraepelin did not give us, in comparison to others like Freud or Bleuler, we are bound to minimize his accomplishments, which are immense.

Kraepelin may be viewed as the Linnaeus of psychiatry, in comparison to Freud, who may be viewed as the Darwin. But as Linnaeus and Darwin were necessary in the development of biology, so both Kraepelin and Freud were necessary in the development of psychiatry. A great deal of resentment toward Kraepelinian psychiatry, which may be noted in some psychiatric circles, is due, actually, not to an attempt to minimize Kraepelin's accomplishments, but rather to a displeasure with the tenacity with which his concepts have been retained, even long after more penetrating ones have been formulated. Zilboorg (1941) wrote that "the system of Kraepelin appears to have become a thing of the past as soon as it announced its own birth in 1896." In a certain way this is true, because Sigmund Freud published his first outstanding book in the same year. On the other hand, one may say that even today Kraepelinian psychiatry is the best known in the world. Thousands and thousands of patients are still viewed and classified as Kraepelin taught, and until the middle 1940s, in the United States, too, they were still labeled with the name *dementia praecox.**

* Bellak, who for many decades retained the role of reviewer of all the work done on schizophrenia, entitled his first work, published in 1948, *Dementia Praecox. The Past Decade's Work and Present Status: A Review and Evaluation.* In his subsequent books he used the word *schizophrenia.*

Eugen Bleuler

Kraepelin's contributions were not accepted without objections. Among the well-known psychiatrists who opposed most of his views were Ernest Meyer, Korsakov, Bianchi, Serbsky, and Marandon de Montyel.

Eugen Bleuler (1857–1930), a Swiss psychiatrist whose role in the history of psychiatry will remain an important one, accepted much of Kraepelin but revitalized the Kraepelinian concepts and revised them, making a strong attempt, though not a thoroughly successful one, to go beyond a purely descriptive approach.

In 1911 Bleuler published a monograph on dementia praecox that was the result of many years of study and research.* He renamed the syndrome "schizophrenia," implying that a splitting of the various psychic functions, rather than a progression toward a demential state, was one of the outstanding characteristics. He delivered a blow to the Kraepelinian concept of dementia praecox as a disease entity, inasmuch as he included in the schizophrenic group many syndromes that at that time no one was prepared to consider as being related to schizophrenia. He included in the schizophrenic group psychoses that arise in psychopathic personalities, alcoholic hallucinoses, prison psychoses, and cases of symptomatic manic-depressive psychoses. Furthermore, he thought that the largest number of cases of schizophrenia are latent cases; these patients are never hospitalized because the symptoms are not severe enough, but still they show oddities of behavior that are attributable to an insidious schizophrenic process. As several authors have remarked (Morselli, 1955; Stierlin, 1965, 1967), Bleuler also considered and humanized the concept of schizophrenia by pointing out that even normal persons, when preoccupied or distracted, show a number of schizophrenic symptoms, such as "peculiar associations, incomplete concepts and ideas, displacements, logical blunders, and stereotypes." He added that "the individual symptom in itself is less important than its intensity and extensiveness, and above all its relation to the psychological setting."

Bleuler classified the symptoms of schizophrenia in two sets of groups: the groups of fundamental and accessory symptoms and the groups of primary and secondary symptoms. The fundamental symptoms are not necessarily the primary ones; they are the symptoms that are present to an extent in every case of schizophrenia, whether latent or manifest. The accessory symptoms are those that may or may not occur. Among the fundamental symptoms Bleuler included the disorder of the process of association, which he considered the most important characteristic of schizophrenia, and also a particular type of thinking and behavior that he called autism. Among the accessory symptoms he included the acute manifestations of the psychosis, like delusions, hallucinations, catatonic postures, and so forth. Primary symptoms are directly related to the disease process; they are the necessary phenomena of the disease. The most important of them is again the association disorder. Secondary symptoms are caused by a combination of the action of the primary ones and the action of psychogenic factors.

* This classic work was translated into English only in 1950.

The most important contributions of Bleuler were those related to his study of the process of association and disturbances of the affective life, the concepts of autism and ambivalence, and his interpretation of negativism.

The disorder of the process of association, according to Bleuler, involves every aspect of schizophrenia. Whereas, on the one hand, Bleuler enlarged the concept of schizophrenia by making the Kraepelinian nosological entity less rigid and less specific, he tried, on the other hand, to individualize the essential mechanism of the schizophrenic process. He thought that it consisted of a loosening of the associations of ideas. This mechanism may range from a maximum, which corresponds to complete incoherence, to a minimum, which is hardly perceptible. He writes: ". . . single images or whole combinations may be rendered ineffective, in an apparently haphazard fashion. Instead, thinking operates with ideas and concepts which have no, or a completely insufficient, connection with the main idea and therefore should be excluded from the thought process. The result is that thinking becomes confused, bizarre, incorrect, abrupt. . . ." Bleuler described accurately the various degrees of this associative disorder and related symptoms such as blocking, elisions, logical errors, and so on, but he was not able to infer any underlying basic formal mechanism. He limited himself to the formulation that these symptoms were the result of a loosening of associations. As far as their motivation was concerned, Bleuler accepted Freudian mechanisms quite often. Blocking was seen by him as an exaggeration of repression. He felt that psychological complexes might explain the combinations of ideas in a condensed or bizarre pattern. He accepted the Freudian concept of unconscious motivation and of symbolism, especially in explaining hallucinations and delusions. He thought that delusions result, not from a defect in logic, but from an inner need. At the same time, he expressed the opinion that it was not enough to explain everything with dynamic processes.

Bleuler went further than Kraepelin; he wanted to explain symptoms in respect to their psychological content as well as their structure. As to the content, he accepted Freud's explanations. He realized, however, that these were not enough; and although he was not able to formulate clearly what was missing in the Freudian approach, it is obvious that he searched for a structural or formal explanation of the symptoms, that is, he would have liked to have known why the symptoms have specific manifestations in schizophrenia. He tried to solve the problem by assuming that the structural defect involved always the loosening of associations; but he could not go beyond this point, and therefore his formal studies remained as descriptive as Kraepelin's. Although he might have been influenced by Wernicke's "concept of sejunction," Bleuler did not attempt to give an anatomical interpretation of the symptoms. On the other hand, because he could not explain everything with Freudian mechanisms, he could not dismiss the idea that schizophrenia might be due to an underlying organic disease. In his book he mentions the possibility that mental causes produce the symptoms, but not the disease. He states that the disease process may be due to some kind of toxin, as is rheumatism. Thus, Bleuler himself is a good example of that ambivalent attitude which he was the first to describe; he expresses the feeling that schizophrenia is a psychogenic disorder, and yet he cannot dispel the idea that it may be organic in origin.

This concept of ambivalence, which Bleuler first described in psychotics, has since played an important role in psychiatric thinking, not only in reference to psychotics, but also in reference to neurotics and normal human beings. By ambivalence Bleuler meant the simultaneous occurrence of two opposite feelings for the same object, such as in the case of the husband who both loves and hates his wife. He found this symptom in every schizophrenic and thought that the most marked form of it was inherent in catatonic negativism. Shortly after the publication of his major book, Bleuler became less ambivalent and, as Stierlin (1967) put it, grew "defensive about his Freudian leanings." He strongly reiterated that only symptoms may come about in the ways described by Freud and Jung, but the illness itself was probably the result of organic causes, as Kraepelin had postulated (Bleuler, 1913*b*).

Bleuler thought that the affective disorders that occurred in schizophrenia were not primary but secondary. He was one of the first to note that when the patients' complexes were involved, the feelings of the patients were normal or even exaggerated. He also noticed that patients who appeared completely apathetic were capable of complete or partial recoveries. He saw the apparent loss of affect as due to repression.

The concept of autism is another of Bleuler's major contributions. He used this term to refer to a certain tendency to turn away from reality, accompanied by a certain type of thinking. Autistic thinking, according to Bleuler, as opposed to logical thinking, does not represent occurrences in the outer world and their associations; as a matter of fact, it excludes many external and internal facts. The autistic patient tends to live in a world of fantasy, where symbolization is used constantly. Autistic thinking is not bound by the laws of logic and reality. "It is unlogical and permits the greatest contradictions with the outer world and in itself." By failing to take into consideration the facts of reality it becomes "dereistic." The autistic person identifies wishes or fears with reality. "The fear of having enemies is for his autistic thinking identical with the fixed conviction that they exist." Autistic thinking flourishes particularly in schizophrenia, but it may occur even in normal situations: for instance, in children when they play; in subjects that are not sufficiently accessible to our knowledge and our logic, such as religion, love; or wherever the emotions "obtain too great a significance" (Bleuler, 1913*a*).

Undoubtedly it is to Bleuler's credit that he defined and described this type of thinking, which is so different from what is generally called logical thinking. However, it must be remembered that fundamentally Bleuler has given us only a description of it. Here again it should be stated that he accepted Freudian interpretations in regard to the content; from a formal point of view, he limited himself to saying that this type of thinking was not logical. He felt that his concept of autism nearly coincided with Freud's concept of autoerotism and with Janet's "loss of the sense of reality."

As far as negativism is concerned, Bleuler thought that it could not be explained solely as a motor phenomenon (1912*a*, 1950). He was inclined to consider it as a psychological attitude. The patient considers all stimuli coming from the environment as hostile and disturbing, and therefore he tries to block them off. This psychological interpretation allows for the explanation of negativism as being expressed only at times toward certain persons. As was mentioned before, Bleuler saw the negativistic attitude as being related to the ambivalent attitude. He also felt that intellectual negativism might be based on a general tendency of ideas to associate with their opposites.

Thus we may summarize the contribution of Bleuler as follows:

1. He saw the schizophrenic syndrome, not as a progression toward dementia, but as a particular condition characterized mainly by a disorder of association and by a splitting of the basic functions of the personality.
2. He enlarged the boundaries of what should be included under this syndrome.
3. He differentiated a new subtype, the simple (or simplex) type, using the name and some of the concepts already partially advanced by Weygandt (1902) and by Diem (1903).
4. He emphasized that affectivity is not absent in schizophrenia, and that it plays a more important role than it was then thought.
5. He attempted not only to describe the symptoms, but to explain them. As to their psychological content, he accepted Freud's contributions. From a formal point of view, his efforts have remained unfulfilled.
6. He gave psychiatry the concepts of autistic thinking and of ambivalence.
7. He enlarged the psychiatric terminology by coining the following well-accepted terms: schizophrenia, depth psychology, autism, ambivalence, and dereism.

Adolph Meyer

Adolph Meyer (1866–1950), a Swiss physician who came to the United States in 1892, was for several decades the leading American psychiatrist. Schizophrenia was one of his major interests from the beginning of his career (Lief, 1948; Meyer, 1906, 1910, 1912*a*, 1912*b*). Meyer was dissatisfied with the role given to heredity and autointoxication in the etiology and pathogenesis of dementia praecox. He felt that perhaps the psychological factors to which laymen and old schools of psychiatry had given so much importance in the past should be reconsidered.

Kraepelin had given an accurate description of the disease after the onset. Meyer advocated that the patient be studied "longitudinally"; from the beginning of his life, all the factors that might have contributed to the mental condition should be searched and examined. Meyer thus became convinced that dementia praecox was the result of an accumulation of habit disorders or faulty habits of reaction. The individual who is not able to cope with the problems and difficulties of life, and who is confronted with failure after failure, may tend toward what Meyer called substitutive reactions. At first these new habits appear as "trivial and harmless subterfuges," such as day dreaming, rumination, decrease of interests, and so on, but later they become harmful, uncontrollable, and tend to assume definite mechanisms, like hallucinations, delusions, blocking, and so forth. These anomalous mechanisms, according to Meyer, are partially intelligible as substitutions for "efficient adjustment to concrete and actual difficulties." Meyer felt that it was possible to formulate the main facts appearing in the history of most cases as a "natural chain of cause and effect." He saw dementia praecox as "the usually inevitable outcome of (1) conflicts of instincts, or conflicts of complexes of experience, and (2) incapacity for a harmless constructive adjustment."

Meyer called his concept "dynamic," inasmuch as it implied a longitudinal interaction of forces; he also called it "psychobiological," inasmuch as it considered the psychological as well as all the pertinent biological factors. He renamed the disorder *parergasia,* which etymologically means incongruity of behavior. This term, however, has not been accepted outside of his school.

An unbiased critic may find great merits and great pitfalls in Meyer's concepts. The greatest merit lies in his having reaffirmed the importance of "mental" or psychological factors in the etiology of schizophrenia. The longitudinal aspect of the process of maladjustment, before it reaches psychotic proportions, had not been adequately stressed before by any other school, except the psychoanalytic. In other respects, however, Meyer's formulations remain vague and inadequate in explaining any specific characteristics of schizophrenia. Accumulation of faulty habits and of repeated failures may already indicate some preexisting abnormality, either organic or environmental. Meyer explains the progression of the habit deterioration as caused by the gradual substitution of increasingly inferior and distorted material. Finally, the distortions are so great that they become full-fledged schizophrenic symptoms. The role that anxiety plays in this process is not clearly apparent from his writings. Furthermore, how and why these faulty habits lead necessarily to schizophrenia, and not to other psychopathological reactions, remains unexplained. Meyer seems to believe that there is only a gradual or quantitative difference between faulty habits and clear-cut schizophrenic symptoms. He seems to consider the faulty habits only as the expression of maladjustment at a realistic level; he does not stress enough the point that what he calls substitutive habits often have a symbolic or nonapparent meaning. Moreover he does not emphasize that schizophrenic symptoms have an archaic or primordial aspect that is lacking in prepsychotic faulty habits.

In addition, although some schizophrenic-like or symbolic manifestations may appear as faulty habits in everybody's life, a constellation of them, as is found in schizophrenia, seems typical or characteristic enough, even from a qualitative point of view. The faulty habits that we may find in human beings are innumerable, but the schizophrenic symptoms, from a formal point of view, are strikingly similar in every patient. The patients do not appear only as caricatures or exaggerated expressions of their prepsychotic personality; the greatest number of their characteristics have undergone a drastic metamorphosis and have been channeled into few definite patterns. In other words, if a substitution of faulty habits occurs, it is because they are substituted by schizophrenic symptoms. Meyer's interpretation of schizophrenia as a substitution of faulty habits is therefore not an interpretation. In addition, those faulty habits found in the history of many schizophrenics are found also in the history of many psychoneurotics.

Meyer is correct in considering schizophrenia a progressive pathological adjustment; however, from his writings one does not learn when a patient with faulty habits is to be considered an overt schizophrenic. It may be asserted that the faulty habits of the schizophrenic disclose some kind of malignancy that is not present in the faulty habits of the neurotic. This concept had led many psychiatrists to make an accurate search for those latent schizophrenic symptoms that seem to be psychoneurotic traits. A pseudoneurotic type of schizophrenia has even been described (Hoch and Polatin, 1949). Because many of these patients do not move toward either a more or less psychotic condition, it remains for the individual observer to classify them in one way or the other.

No doubt this search for latent schizophrenia in apparent psychoneurotics has resulted in the early diagnosis of many schizophrenics. However, this tendency is perhaps exaggerated in some sectors and for some time may have had a deterrent effect as far as therapy is concerned. In fact, until the early 1940s a diagnosis of schizophrenia discouraged a psychotherapeutic approach, which Meyer himself usually found "negative and rarely clearly positive" in these cases (Meyer, Jelliffe, and Hoch, 1911).

Summarizing, we may state that Meyer's major contribution was his emphasis on a longitudinal study of the patient and on the reaffirmation of the importance of the psychogenic factors. His approach must therefore be considered a partially dynamic one. Its dynamism is somehow stunted by the fact that the early environmental factors, acting during the childhood of the patient, do not receive the proper stress, and by the fact that its symptoms are more or less considered from a realistic, that is, nonsymbolic, point of view. The dynamic psychoanalytic point of view not only is more complete, but actually preceded the psychobiological one historically.

Although Freud was born before Meyer, and some of the main psychoanalytic concepts preceded those of the psychobiological schools, we have disregarded chronological order and have discussed Meyer before the founder of psychoanalysis. Conceptually, in fact, Meyer does not go as far as Freud and seems to provide a bridge between the Kraepelinian–Bleulerian points of view and those which follow a fully psychodynamic approach. Moreover, in the first few decades of its existence, psychoanalysis devoted itself almost exclusively to the psychoneuroses, so that the psychobiological approach had an opportunity to gain a respectful place in the study of schizophrenia.

Sigmund Freud

Whereas the German schools of psychiatry had been interested mainly in the psychoses, the French schools centered their interest on the study of the psychoneuroses. Sigmund Freud (1855–1939), himself an Austrian, after spending one year in Paris at the school of Charcot, felt the influence of the French school of psychiatry more than of any other. Thus we find that throughout his life he paid only secondary attention to the study of the psychoses. Freud's influence on psychiatry as a whole, however, is of such magnitude and of such a revolutionary nature that even the field of psychoses had to be totally reviewed in the light of his contributions.

Because of his special interest in the psychoneuroses, Freud was predisposed to see the psychoses, not as clinical entities completely unrelated psychologically and etiologically to the psychoneuroses, but, on the contrary, as having the same basic functions and mechanisms. This point of view was already a fundamental innovation in a psychiatry that insisted on individualizing nosological entities.

In one of his first psychoanalytic papers (1894), written nine years before the first dynamic interpretations of Adolph Meyer, Freud first described how unbearable ideas may give rise to hallucinatory psychoses. The unbearable idea is rejected by the ego, but the attempt to reject it is not successful. The idea comes back as a hallucinatory wish-fulfillment. The girl who could not accept the fact that she was not loved by a certain man, in her delusional system saw him and heard him near her.

In another early paper (1896), Freud gave the dynamic interpretation of what seemed at first to be a case of chronic paranoia, but which later was recognized as a case of the paranoid type of dementia praecox. In this paper, for the first time in the history of psychiatry, the term *projection* was used, and this mental mechanism was explained. Freud found that in this case, too, as is common with neurotics, the nucleus of the psychical mechanism was repression. However, in this case repression of self-reproach is "projected" onto others who thus become the persecutors.

In another paper of paramount importance (1911) that reported Schreber's case, Freud described other projection mechanisms. He showed that the rejection of a homosexual wish accounted for the persecutory complex. The proposition "I (a man) love him (a man)" is not accepted by the patient, who wants to deny it with the contradictory proposition "I do not *love* him, I hate him." "I hate him," by projection, becomes transformed into "He hates me." Thus from a homosexual wish a delusional idea is formed.

According to Freud, in erotomania the mechanism is the following. The patient, who does not want to admit attachment to a man, forces himself to think, "I do not love him—I love her" (that is, "I do not love a man, I love a woman"). By projection, "I love her" becomes "She loves me." Delusions of jealousy in women have a similar mechanism. "It is not I who love women, but he (my husband) who loves them." In every case the delusion is a defense or an attempt to deny the homosexual wish.

It is only with his paper on narcissism (1914) that Freud applied his libido theory to the interpretation of schizophrenia and could integrate the other psychoanalytic concepts in the interpretation of this psychosis. Contrary to Kraepelin, Bleuler, and Meyer, Freud felt that the essential characteristic of schizophrenia was the change in the patient's relationship with people and "the other objects" in his environment. Other psychiatrists had already noticed that the schizophrenic is remote and disinterested in other people. Freud interpreted this withdrawal as withdrawal of libidinal cathexes. What other authors consider affective disposition for the various components of one's life and environment was for Freud cathexis, that is, an investment of energy or libido. When the libido is withdrawn from the environmental objects (or rather from the mental representations of these objects), we have a state of narcissism. Decathexis (or withdrawal of libido) in the schizophrenic psychosis has the role that repression has in psychoneurosis. Now the withdrawn libido is directed into the self. When the ego becomes hypercathected, the result is megalomania. When the body becomes hypercathected, the result is hypochondriasis. Freud believed that all cases of schizophrenia start with either megalomania or hypochondriasis. The libido, which in other conditions withdraws to less primitive points of fixation, in schizophrenia withdraws to a narcissistic level. A narcissistic regression that entails regression of ego functions ensues.

Most schizophrenic symptoms, including thought disorders, have to be interpreted as impairment of ego functions and expression of the resurgence of the primary process. The primary process is a way of functioning of the unconscious, as well as of mental life in early childhood, before the system preconscious comes into being (see Chapter 15). According to Freud, in schizophrenia there is an attempt at restitution; that is, an attempt to invest again with energy (or to recathect) the objects that have been decathected. Hallucinations and delusions are interpreted by Freud as attempts to reestablish contact with the world, to reinvest energy in the environment. In other words, in psychosis there is not only loss of reality, but also remodeling of reality (1924*b*). Psychosis, whether in paranoia or dementia praecox, substitutes something for what it denies; the symptom is not only regressive, but also restitutional. Catastrophic delusions of cosmic magnitude, like the experience of the "end of the world," often found in these patients, are withdrawal of libido. Things become indifferent or irrelevant and may appear ruined or dissipated. The delusion formation is interpreted as an attempt at recovery, a process of reconstruction, inasmuch as it is a method used to recapture a relationship, though a distorted one, with the world.

At first Freud thought that the schizophrenic regression is the result of strong instinctual demands with which the ego is not capable of coping. Especially in his early theories, there is a neglect of the role played by the ego and superego in determining the disequilibrium that brings about the disorder. However, in his book *The Ego and the Id* (1923), Freud wrote that neurosis is the result of a conflict between the ego and its id, whereas psychosis is the analogous outcome of a similar disturbance in the relation between the ego and its environment (the outer world). In the paper "Neurosis and Psychosis" (1924*a*), he wrote that whereas in neurosis the ego, in virtue of its allegiance to reality, suppresses a part of the id, in psychosis the ego, in the service of the id, withdraws itself from a part of reality. In other words, the ego accepts part of the id.

Freud also never fully evaluated the role of anxiety in schizophrenia. His second theory of anxiety, which would have helped him greatly in this attempt, was formulated in 1926, after he had already written his works on the psychoses.

Any attempt to give an adequate account of the importance of Freud's contributions to the field of schizophrenia remains somewhat unfulfilled because the whole psychoanalytic theory would have to be repeated, each part of it having a direct or indirect relevance.

Many of Freud's theories have to be discarded. It is not true that schizophrenic regression is caused only by instinctual demands. Even such orthodox Freudians as Arlow and Brenner (1964, 1969) recognize how little importance Freud gave to the ego and superego. The withdrawal of libido to the narcissistic level can hardly explain in itself the specific characteristic of schizophrenia. On the other hand, the concept of regression as a return to earlier levels of integration is acceptable to many authors if it is separated from the concept of libido. The concept of regression has replaced that of deterioration in schizophrenia. The patient returns to infantile or archaic levels of integration because he is unable to function at a higher level. These levels, however, are not necessarily representative of earlier levels of sexual development, as Freud thought. The most prominent ego psychologist of the orthodox Freudian school, Hartmann (1953), added to Freud's concepts by postulating that schizophrenia is due to a failure to neutralize sexual and aggressive energy.

It is also not true that all schizophrenic psychoses start with megalomaniac or hypochondriacal syndromes. The thought disorders of the schizophrenic cannot just be labeled regressive aspects of ego functions without further analysis. On the other hand, the whole psychodynamic interpretation of schizophrenia can benefit immensely from concepts developed by Freud in reference to other subjects. Perhaps of all the contributions of the founder of psychoanalysis, the most important in relation to schizophrenia is the concept of symbolization. According to this concept, the symptoms are no longer accepted at a phenomenological level, but as substitutes for something else that they symbolize. The repressive forces of the ego transform the symptoms in such a way that they are no longer recognizable to the patient as attempts to fulfill objectionable wishes. The study of symbols, which Freud made in his masterful book on dreams (1901), was later extended, especially by Jung, to the field of schizophrenia. Symbolization is possible in most cases through the use of the primary process.

Freud's important concepts such as those of the unconscious, repression, and transference have a great value when they are applied also to schizophrenia. Rather than to attempt in this book a too sketchy account of their significance, the reader is referred to the usual textbooks of psychoanalysis and especially to the writings of Fenichel (1945), Drellich (1974), Greenson (1974), and Freud himself (1938). It is important, however, to mention here that the significance of these concepts in schizophrenia is somewhat different from that derived from their application to neuroses. For instance, the unconscious decreases in extension in schizophrenia as a consequence of a partial return to consciousness of what is generally repressed in psychoneuroses and under normal conditions. The concept of transference is applied by Freud to schizophrenia in a negative way. According to him, all the libido in the schizophrenic is withdrawn from external objects; and therefore no transference, no attachment for the analyst, is possible. The result is that the patient is scarcely accessible to analytic treatment. This idea of Freud's discouraged many therapists from attempts to treat schizophrenics, although, as Fromm-Reichmann wrote (1952), Freud hoped that future modifications of the analytic technique would make schizophrenics, too, amenable to treatment.

Freud was the first author who really succeeded in explaining the content of this psychosis in psychological terms. He was also the first to disclose in a convincing manner the importance of psychological factors in the etiology of this condition. He did not limit himself, as Meyer did, to the interpretation of the symptoms as faulty patterns, but also uncovered their symbolic meaning.

Freud was also successful in explaining, at least partially, the formal aspects of several symptoms, such as projections. His concept of regression remains a fundamental one in the field of schizophrenia. However, the excessive importance that he gave to sexual frustrations as the cause of the regressions did not permit him to give enough consideration to the patient's total interpersonal relations.

Carl G. Jung

Of the psychoanalysts who departed from Freud, Carl G. Jung (1875–1961) was the first to make outstanding contributions to the field of schizophrenia. His book *Psychology of Dementia Praecox* was written in 1903, nine years before his break with Freud (American edition, 1936). In this book Jung described the importance of the autonomous complex. Certain French authors, in particular Charcot and Janet, had already postulated that a series of ideas, removed from consciousness, maintain a more or less independent existence. Janet attributed the phenomenon to the so-called *abaissement du niveau mental*. Jung added that the dissociation of this autochthonous group of ideas was dynamically determined. Word association tests convinced him that the dissociated ideas were emotionally charged and that the defense mechanisms that isolated them were the same as those described by Freud in hysterical patients.

Jung felt that delusions, hallucinations, and other schizophrenic symptoms were due to the activity of the complex, which could not be under the control or correction of consciousness. He criticized those theories that interpreted the apparent incongruity between the ideational and affective functions of the schizophrenic as due to psychic ataxia (Stransky, 1903). The *belle indifference* of hysterics is a reaction to oversensitiveness; why not accept the same mechanism in dementia praecox? He thought, however, that the hysterogenic complex causes manifestations that are reparable, whereas the effects of dementia praecox are not. He thought also that possibly the emotional disturbance in dementia praecox engenders an anomalous metabolism or toxin that injures the brain in a more or less irreparable manner, so that the highest psychic functions become paralyzed.

Jung is thus the first author to conceive of the possibility of a psychosomatic mechanism in schizophrenia. According to him, it is not an organic disorder that produces the psychic disorder; on the contrary, the emotional disorder produces an abnormal metabolism that causes physical damage to the brain. This fact is particularly interesting in that, for the first time, the nervous system itself is considered the victim of a psychosomatic disorder. Jung, however, considers this possibility as a mere hypothesis and does not exclude the idea that a change of metabolism may be primary, as Kraepelin suggested. On account of this metabolic disorder, the last accidental complex may become "clotted" or "curdled" and thus determine the content of the symptoms.

Jung stated that the "essential basis of our personality is affectivity." Thought and action are only "symptoms" of affectivity. Affectivity is the dynamic force of the complex, which may occupy the whole mental field and disturb many of the ideational processes. Jung referred to the disturbances as he noticed them in his experiments on associations, but he did not give a complete explanation of the formal mechanisms of schizophrenia. According to him, the autonomous complex disturbs the concentration of the patient and paralyzes all other psychic activities. Recognizing that the psychological mechanisms of dreams are closely related to those of dementia praecox, he wrote, "Let the dreamer walk about and act as though he were awake and we have at once the clinical picture of dementia praecox."

In a paper originally published in 1908 he stated that some unknown factor of predisposition may produce a nonadaptable psychological function that can develop into manifest mental disorder (1917). In its turn, the mental disorder may determine organic degeneration with its own progression of symptoms. In the same paper he wrote that there is overwhelming proof that a primary psychological fault in function exists from the time of childhood. He also added that borderline cases of dementia praecox had been restored to normal life with analytic treatment.

In a 1913 paper Jung differentiated his psychological types, formulating a concept that was to have great importance in psychiatric thinking (1920, 1933). His first thoughts about a psychological classification actually originated from his effort to compare hysteria and dementia praecox in every possible way. He felt that whereas in hysteria one always finds an "extrovert personality," as he called it, with an exaggerated emotivity and psychic energy directed centrifugally, that is, toward the environment, the opposite is true in dementia praecox. In dementia praecox the psychic energy is centripetal, that is, directed away from the environment and toward the self, the emotivity is decreased, the personality as a whole is what he called "introvert." These early studies of Jung stimulated a subsequent series of studies of the personality of the schizophrenic. Others, like Kretschmer, added a physical counterpart to Jung's psychological description. According to Kretschmer the introvert has an asthenic and the extrovert a pyknic constitution (1934).

Another of Jung's concepts that was important in his interpretation of schizophrenia was his hypothesis of the collective unconscious (1921). Jung was very much impressed by the similarity of myths all over the world in spite of geographical, historical, and racial differences. He explained this similarity as the manifestation of a general or collective unconscious that stores the primordial images or *archetypes* that have been deposited there as a result of numerous recurrences of identical situations. Thus our personal psyche rests on a deep impersonal psyche. Jung thought that it was not enough to interpret the symptoms of the patient, as Freud did, from the information derived from the detailed personal history of the patient, but that it was necessary to go beyond. For instance, a person's image of parents cannot be attributed only to his childhood memories of his parents. The images of father and mother acquire a stronger value and intensity on account of the archetypical parental image stored in our collective unconscious.

Jung minimized the effect of culture and society on the individual psyche. Some of the patterns that he attributes to the collective unconscious are the effect of the impact of culture on the individual. The individual's image of his mother is not only the result of what he thinks and feels about his own mother on account of his memories of her, but also the result of what culture teaches him that mother is.* Certainly in pathological conditions, and especially in schizophrenia, archaic modes of thinking and feeling resurge. However, only the formal mechanisms, or rather the propensity for those formal mechanisms, may be attributed to nonacquired factors. We may call these factors functions of our nervous system or of our collective unconscious, as we wish. The content and the motivation of those emotions and thoughts, however, to a large extent originate in the environment of the individual, that is, in the family and in his culture. The explanations of symptoms go beyond the study of the personal history of the patient and the environment to which he was exposed. Jung is right in this respect; however, what is not explained by personal and environmental factors is the *formal* aspect of the symptom, or the psychological structure.

Jung's theoretical formulations force one to attribute more importance to congenital or hereditary factors than to environmental ones. Nevertheless they have not led to major therapeutic errors. In certain cases, therapy may solve psychological problems no matter whether we think they are due to the collective unconscious or to social forces. Thus, the Jungian approach has helped many psychotics, and especially borderline cases (Baynes, 1949).

In a paper read in 1939 at the Psychiatric Section of the Royal Society of Medicine, Jung reiterated some of his previously expressed ideas and added a few others. He criticized the concept of latent psychosis. A latent psychosis is nothing else than the possibility that an individual may become temporarily mentally ill at some period in his life. The existence of unconscious material in his mind proves nothing. Such material is found in neurotics, artists, poets, and normal people. According to Jung, "The possibility of a future psychosis has nothing to do with the peculiar contents of the unconscious mind. But it has everything to do with the question whether the individual can stand a certain panic, or the constant strain of a psyche at war with itself." Jung states that the psychosis is generally interpreted from two points of view, either as a primary weakness of consciousness or as an "inordinate strength of the unconscious." He believes that the second theory

* Jung has taken into consideration the effect of cultural factors, but only in the engendering of the *analogues*. The analogue is an equivalent of the archetype, after culture has modified its appearance. Jung's archetype, however, is not just a formal structure; it has also a content that is determined by the collective unconscious (1959).

"cannot be easily dismissed, since it is not unthinkable that the abundant archaic material could be the expression of a still existing infantile, as well as primitive, mentality. It could be a question of atavism." He adds, "I seriously consider the possibility of a so-called *development arrêté,* where a more than normal amount of primitive psychology remains intact and does not become adapted to modern conditions."

Jung's contributions to other fields are too extensive to be reported here. The reader is referred to the original works of Jung as well as to the writings of Jacobi (1943) and Henderson and Wheelwright (1974). Jung's major contributions to the study of schizophrenia can be summarized as follows:

1. He was the first to apply psychoanalytic concepts fully to schizophrenia. He described the existence of the autochthonous complex in this condition and felt that affectivity was the dynamic force of the complex.
2. He was the first to see the possibility of psychosomatic involvement of the central nervous system in schizophrenia, although he did not formulate his concept in these words.
3. He attempted a description of the basic personality of the schizophrenic, which he identified with the introvert type, and contrasted it with the personality of the hysteric, which he identified with the extrovert type.
4. He advanced the theory of the collective unconscious. According to him, many symptoms of schizophrenia were the reproductions of the archetypes deposited in our collective unconscious.
5. He thought that schizophrenia was due to unusual strength of the unconscious and that an abnormal number of atavic tendencies did not adjust to modern life. With this last point, Jung seemed to reaffirm the importance of congenital factors and to minimize greatly the role played by environmental or interpersonal forces.

Harry Stack Sullivan

Harry Stack Sullivan (1892–1949) is the American psychiatrist who has made the most valuable contribution to the understanding of schizophrenia in a psychological frame of reference.

The full evaluation and assessment of this man in the history of psychiatry have not yet been accomplished. Even in the short period since his death, his appreciation has undergone various changes. His greatest merit consists of having added the interpersonal dimension to the field of psychiatry. More than any predecessor, he has shown that one becomes a person mainly by virtue of relations with other human beings and not by means of inborn instinctual drives. He is actually the first author to offer a deep and convincing *psychodynamic* interpretation of schizophrenia. Freud had already indicated that the essential characteristic of this psychosis is the change in the patient's relationship with the environment. But whereas Freud attributed this change to a withdrawal of libidinal energy, Sullivan attributed it to difficulties originating in interpersonal relations. According to him, the psychiatrist must be more concerned with what goes on between people than with the intrapsychic. As a matter of fact, according to him nothing that is psychodynamically or psychotherapeutically significant is intrapersonal or intrapsychic; everything evolves from the individual's relations with other people, especially people with whom he has lived in his childhood, his parents or parent-substitutes, whom Sullivan calls "the significant adults" in the individual's life. Everything is interpersonal; all our thoughts and fantasies deal with people, either real or imaginary.

One might say that every type of dynamic psychiatry is interpersonal. Is not Freud, for instance, studying what goes on between parents and children when he describes and interprets the Oedipal situation? This is true only to a limited degree. Freud focused his attention, not on the interpersonal relations, but on the fight of the individual against his instincts. The parents are seen by Freud mostly as a source of sexual strivings that the child has to inhibit. In his early writings, Sullivan too, under the influence of Freud, gave considerable attention to these sexual strivings and stressed sexual maladjustment as the precipitating factor of neuroses and psychoses. Later, however, he came to recognize the importance of the parent-child relationship in its totality. Sexual difficulties may enter, under exceptional circumstances, as the cause of the abnormal interpersonal relations. Generally they are the effect, not the cause, of a poor parent-child relationship. The child has needs that require the cooperation of others, generally the significant adults, for their satisfaction. An interpersonal process that may bring about insecurity is thus necessary.

According to Sullivan, the attitudes of the parents determine the responses of the children. The personality, or the "self," of the child is built from "reflected appraisals," that is, appraisals coming from the parents. The anxiety of the mother, or her anger or disapproval, brings about discomfort and anxiety also in the child. He may be badly hurt in the course of the development of his self-esteem; he may dissociate from consciousness what is unpleasant, and throughout his life may resort to "parataxic distortions." By parataxic distortion Sullivan meant distorted interpretation of an interpersonal situation. The distortion is due to the fact that the patient identifies the other person involved in the relation with somebody else, or with a person who exists only in his fantasy. If the parataxic thinking is not corrected, the patient will obtain less and less "consensual validation," that is, less and less recognition from others of the validity of his statements. This lack of recognition will increase the difficulty of the interpersonal relations.

A complete examination of Sullivan's contributions and theories will not be attempted here. Some of his concepts will be illustrated in Part Two of this book. For a more thorough understanding of his impact on modern psychiatry, the reader is referred to other works (Mullahy, 1948, 1949, 1952, 1967, 1968; Thompson, 1950, 1952*a;* Witenberg, 1974). The works of Sullivan himself have finally all been published, most of them posthumously (1953*a,* 1953*b,* 1956, 1962, 1964). In this section only some of Sullivan's contributions to the field of schizophrenia will be considered.

Unpleasant "uncanny" experiences, which occur in childhood because of poor maternal care, determine in the child a tension state that eventually changes into a state of great anxiety. The associations that are connected with disapproval and anxiety become connected in a conceptual construct and are personalized as the "bad-me." The child tries to dissociate these experiences from his consciousness; they become "not-me processes."

In the initial phase of schizophrenia there is a failure of the dissociative process, and a state of panic occurs. A disorganization of the personality takes place, and the early uncanny experiences come back to the surface. The patient perceives a terror, which reproduces the primitive formulation of the *bad* mother. According to Mullahy (1967), for Sullivan the bad mother is a "complexus of impressions" of the mothering one by the infant resulting from her interference with the satisfaction of needs and "her association with the induction of anxiety." For Sullivan schizophrenia is a disorder of living, disorder that may consist of one episode, a series of episodes, or a whole life.

An issue which is very important in Sullivan's theory and nevertheless was minimized until recently is the role of the adolescence period in the engendering of schizophrenia. Although the early Sullivanians stressed the importance of childhood, adolescence too was deeply studied by Sullivan and was given an important role in the psychodynamics of the disorder. The repeated blows to self-regard that occur in this period of life are just as important as the uncanny experiences of early childhood. The sequence of events that leads the patient from the state of panic to a full-fledged symptomatology was dynamically and very vividly illustrated by Sullivan in *Conceptions of Modern Psychiatry* (1953). In that book he described the resurgence of what was dissociated, more from the point of view of the subjective experience of the patient than from the point of view of the observer. In all the writings of Sullivan, even in those that deal with abstract conceptions, the patient is seen, not as a clinical specimen, but as a person who cannot relate to his fellow human beings without a hard struggle. When the patient is examined or treated by Sullivan, he is no longer alone in his subjective world; Sullivan shares his suffering and sees his frightening vision of "reality." In the therapeutic situation Sullivan was not predominantly an *observer* but, as he put it, a *participant*.

Sullivan also pointed out that in the "paranoid solution" there is not only on the part of the patient an attempt to project, but also to *blame* the environment. Contrary to some extreme positions of later psychiatrists, who consider the blaming of the environment a completely justifiable act on the part of the patient, Sullivan deemed this tendency pathological and hoped to abate it with therapeutic intervention.

In his first paper on schizophrenia (1924), he stated that the foundations of his work and his concepts of this disorder are pluralistic, but that he accepted three conceptions particularly in the interpretation of his data. The first is the postulate of the unconscious, as formulated by Freud. The second is the teleological vitalist hypothesis of hormic energy. The third is "the genetic hypothesis of mental structure and functions, which implies a vital sequence of experience."

In this paper Sullivan wrote that "the disorder is one in which the total experience of the individual is recognized." He acknowledged the eruptions of primitive functions of thinking, and, even in this first paper, he mentions the fact that there is a profound alteration of the sentiment of self-regard. He criticized Bleuler's formulation of the disorder as based on impairment of the association of ideas and reached the important conclusion that the primary disorder in this illness is one of *mental structure*. He wrote that the mental structure is dissociated in such a way that "the disintegrated portions regress in function to earlier levels of mental ontology."

Although in this important paper he expressed regard for the works of Lévy-Bruhl, Jung, and Storch and referred more than once to the appearance of primordial or archaic concepts, Sullivan tried to explain the schizophrenic symptomatology as a return to infantile and fetal mental functions exclusively. In other words, according to him there is no necessity for accepting the notion of phyletic regression of mind structure. The phenomenology is subsumed in the "ontogenetic psychology." Although, to my knowledge, Sullivan was the first psychiatrist to speak of *mental structure* in a formal nonorganic sense, his predominant interest in the dynamics of schizophrenia prevented him from conceiving that some of the phenomena, even from a formal point of view, are determined by factors that transcend the history of the patient. Thus, already in this first paper his conceptions were diametrically opposite to those of Jung.

Sullivan was not clear, however, in his understanding of the schizophrenic mental *structure* to which he referred. From a dynamic point of view, his first paper is a good forerunner of the great contributions he was to make later. We have already mentioned his realization of the alteration of the sentiment of self-regard in the schizophrenic. He also outlined in this paper simple therapeutic procedures: there should be no free associations; the patient should be asked simple questions; the psychotherapist should have recourse to primitive forms of thought exchange.

In a subsequent paper, Sullivan (1925) stated that according to his experience, the complex etiology of the disorder invariably culminated in a situation in which the sexual adequacy of the individual, according to his own ideals, was acutely unsatisfactory. In the same paper he wrote that there is no good reason for believing that all or most of that which is not fairly accessible to awareness is sexual. He felt, however, that many things, particularly undeveloped impulses that finally escape inhibition, may acquire a sexual coloring.

In another paper, Sullivan (1929) wrote that after thirteen years of study of schizophrenics, his conclusion was that the existing interpretations of this disorder were misleading. He felt that the current researches, such as genetic, organic, and psychoanalytic, had been inadequate. The schizophrenic has to be seen as a total person. Prenatal and childhood environmental factors are very important. He reminded the reader of the peculiarity of the parents of the schizophrenics and stated that psychiatrists have usually noted that they cannot secure a good history of a schizophrenic from his mother. He regarded schizophrenia as a condition characterized by (1) "regressive preponderance" in implicit fantasy life; (2) a "regressive preponderance" of overt irrational activity, like ritualistic and magical behavior; and (3) an extraordinary preponderance of motivations that normally receive only occasional expression. He stated that this concept of schizophrenia implies a genetic-evolutionary view and eliminates all considerations of duration of the process and of the outcome. The problem of motivation was the fundamental one. In the history of every case that he studied, he found a point at which there occurred "a disaster to self-esteem." This event often was experienced as a state of *panic*.

Sullivan's contributions to the field of schizophrenia can be summarized as follows:

1. He demonstrated that schizophrenia, as well as any other psychiatric condition, is engendered by poor interpersonal relations, especially parent-child relations. In doing so, he opened up new vistas and included psychiatry in the realm of social sciences. His achievement in this field has not been contrasted by two limitations that, for sake of objectivity, must be taken into consideration. First, even he, the creator of the theory of psychiatry as the field of interpersonal relations, felt that the chronic insidious cases of schizophrenia must be organic in nature. This idea, however, to my knowledge was never elaborated and was lost in the midst of Sullivan's great contributions. Secondly, although Sullivan made a social science of psychiatry, he did not study the overall sociological forces that derive from the structure of our society and that, by acting upon the individual, may predispose him to mental illness. Undoubtedly Sullivan had been exposed to the anthropological and sociological influences necessary for such a study (Sapir, George Mead, Benedict, and others); as a matter of fact, in the last few years of his life he devoted himself to the psychiatric study of international relations. It is to be assumed that if untimely death had not interrupted his work, he would have expanded his interpersonal approach to include the impact of society as a whole on the engendering of psychiatric conditions and of schizophrenia in particular.

2. More than any of his contemporaries, Sullivan felt that schizophrenia could be treated psychotherapeutically. He made the psychotherapeutic treatment of the schizophrenic the primary work of his life.

CHAPTER

3

The Manifest Symptomatology

I

General Remarks

The symptomatology of schizophrenia assumes a large number of clinical forms. Whereas the early psychiatric books dealt almost exclusively with the description of the various types, more recent ones have minimized the importance of the clinical picture. It has been repeated quite often that schizophrenia is like a dream, and in dreams what counts is the meaning, not the manifest content. But just as there is now a revival of interest in the manifest aspect of the dream, there is a renewed concern with the manifest symptomatology of schizophrenia. Psychiatrists realize more and more that it is not only the psychodynamic content and meaning themselves that count, but also how they appear in the clinical picture. On the other hand, in a book prepared in our times, it would be impractical to cover all the possible details of all the clinical varieties, including the most rare ones. Moreover, we know now that the historical climate of a particular era and specific sociocultural factors influence in multiple ways even the manifest symptomatology.

In what follows I shall present first a general description of the disorder, and then shall discuss the various types.

II

General Description of the Disorder

The patient, generally a young human being (from the time of puberty to his early thirties) but less commonly at any other age of life, starts to show unusual behavior. Some unconventional traits may have appeared even earlier, but they remained almost unnoticed. Now they have become conspicuous, although at times they still retain a plausible explanation. Some important decisions seem strange, although again in some cases justifiable. For instance, a college student may drop out of school suddenly. A worker may feel that the boss or the other workers are unfair to him, are not well disposed toward him, or are disrespectful: they want to get him in trouble, represent him in a bad light, or give him a difficult assignment, or they dislike him for some special reasons. In some cases the patient refuses to go to work or becomes preoccupied with seemingly unimportant matters. The anomalies eventually become striking, at times in a slow, insidious, gradual way; at other times more acutely. As we shall study in greater detail in Part Two, the prepsychotic personality of the patient in some cases blended almost imperceptibly with the manifestation of the illness, so that it is impossible to determine with accuracy when the onset occurred.

In some cases the illness starts with a period of confusion, excitement, and agitation. The patient seems to be eager to make contacts, to reach all the people he knows, to reconnect himself with what seems to him an escaping world. He searches for something that he cannot find. But he does not even know that he searches. He wants to be active, manifests an intensified hunger for life, for experience, but his confusion is more prominent than his search. His excitement may become pronounced, his speech may lose coherence, and the abnormality becomes obvious.

In other cases the patient becomes concerned with hypochondriacal preoccupations or with some aspect of his physical appearance. Again, whereas his complaints at first seem to have some plausibility, soon they reveal themselves as somatic delusions.

In many cases the patient seems less interested in life than he used to be and seems to concentrate on some specific problems. He starts to think that certain things are related to him or have a special meaning (*ideas of reference*). For instance, if he met a particular person on the street, it was because that person had to spy on him. Events seem to occur not by chance or at random, but because they are preordained. Thus, if he happened to think about a certain subject and then he sees that particular subject mentioned in the newspaper, on television or radio, or in the movies, he does not consider this fact as a mere coincidence, but something to be looked upon with suspicion. Suspiciousness of others increases. They look at him in a peculiar way; they make fun of him and may even talk behind his back. He is under the influence of obscure external agencies. "They" make him experience peculiar sensations; "they" make him think in a way that is alien to his way of thinking; "they" make him act in a way over which he has no control. Finally the patient gives some definite interpretations to facts and things that are not supported by the observations made by other people. The house is wired; dictaphones are hidden to register the patient's thoughts; poison has been put in the food; telepathic or hypnotic experiments are done on him. These are false beliefs, or *delusions;* they are generally of negative character, inasmuch as they seem to convince the patient that some people or outside forces want to persecute him, injure him, or at least watch him or plan some future disturbance. There is somebody who controls, or wants to control, his actions or thoughts. The patient receives special messages, often transmitted in secret codes. Words used by people acquire special meanings, appear to him to be puns or alliterations. Some patients discover puns all over; others give special interpretations to some gestures of people they come into contact with, and even to casual or accidental sounds. At a later stage, however, these delusions may become pleasant in content and even grandiose. The patient is a queen, a millionaire; a great actor is going to marry her. The patient may believe that he has made a great invention or has discovered the secret of the universe or a philosophical system that will explain the essence of life. It is he now who can control by telepathic or hypnotic means other people, the weather, the stock market, the population explosion.

The perceptual functions of the patient seem altered, too, as he sees or hears things in a distorted way. The world, or the environment, appears to him strange or at least unusual. Things and persons have a different aspect and relate to him in a way that is different from the previous one. People may change dimensions and appear unusually large or small. Also, movements may be perceived differently; the rhythm of life has become too fast or too slow. At times things are misidentified (*illusions*). Persons are misidentified for others. Strange resemblances are observed. An old man on the street looked exactly like the patient's grandfather (maybe he is the grandfather's twin brother, whose existence was unknown to the patient).

As frequent as, and in some cases more frequent than, illusions are *hallucinations,* or perceptions occurring without any object or stimulus in the external environment being responsible for them. In many cases hallucinations are preceded by, or occur together with, the feeling that one's thoughts have become audible, that they can be heard by people standing nearby or even in distant places. In a very large number of cases the patient hears voices that accuse him of being a spy, a homosexual, or a murderer, and yet nobody is there to say these things. Hallucinations involve every sense, the auditory being as a rule the most common throughout the course of the disorder. In the early stages, however, especially in very acute cases, visual hallucinations may be as numerous as auditory ones. Hallucinations involving smell, taste, and touch are much less frequent. Olfactory hallucinations, generally related to one's body, are relatively frequent in mild cases that do not require hospitalization.

In addition to this content of thought that is definitely psychotic in character, the patient may manifest other symptoms that seem neurotic, especially at the beginning of the illness: tiredness, insomnia, headache.

At times the general behavior of the patient seems normal and the only apparent symptoms are the abnormal ideas. In the majority of cases, however, the general behavior strikes the examiner as much as the content of thought. The patient may disclose mannerisms, grimaces, purposeless acts, stereotyped motions, and impulsive gestures. In addition, in the catatonic type there are particular symptoms to be described later.

In some cases the patient behaves in a way that is in striking contrast with his previous habits. Whereas before he was shy sexually, now he becomes daring and given to unconventional behavior. He may even make sexual advances in the most inappropriate and unacceptable ways. Whereas before he was submissive or self-effacing, he may become querulous, antagonistic, even belligerent. Many patients are unable to pay attention when people address them. They repeat the same question as if they had not heard the answer already given.

The mood and the affective sphere in general are altered. The patient may appear angry, highly emotional, suspicious, cynical, and so forth, especially when he refers to his delusional complexes; as a whole he is somewhat inadequate emotionally. Often the emotional tone does not seem appropriate to the present situation. Often a blunting of affect, ranging from a relative coldness to complete apathy, can be detected.

A type of symptomatology that occurs frequently (although much less frequently than in previous decades) is that of the patient who has completely lost interest in his surroundings and seems to be withdrawn into himself. He is often described as being "in a shell," in his own world, as if he had lost not only his understanding of, but also his interest in, reality. When he presents this picture of withdrawal, he is generally underactive. His activities are reduced to a minimum and are often performed in a routine, stereotyped manner. Often he has to be pushed to do things. He may be so unwilling to act that he may become neglectful of his personal appearance. A deterioration in his habits of living is more or less apparent.

The speech and language of many patients show peculiar characteristics, which will be examined in other chapters. If certain questions are asked, the patient seems *evasive* because he does not answer them directly. At times he seems to beat around the bush—he says something related to what was asked but not exactly what was requested. For instance, to the question "Who is the President of the United States?" he may reply, "White House." At times he uses impressive, abstract words, but in an empty or inappropriate way. Often his speech is characterized by the intrusion of apparently extraneous elements. In advanced cases it may be difficult to understand what the patient tries to convey. His sentences consist of a sequence of words that seem unrelated to one another (*word-salad*). At times certain words are used repeatedly in a stereotyped manner (*perseveration*); the patient may use other words that do not appear in the dictionary, words that he has coined by condensing or putting together usual words (*neologisms*). In many cases the patient is unable to talk (*mutism*), or able to do so only after overcoming a great resistance (*blocking*).

The sensorium and the intellectual functions are not seriously impaired. Orientation, memory, retention, attention, grasp of general information, calculation, and so forth, may seem disturbed in many cases. The disturbance is actually the result of the other symptoms described and may disappear once these symptoms disappear. What seems impaired from the beginning is only an ability for very abstract thought, as we shall study in subsequent chapters. Even this symptom, however, is reversible.

Insight, that is, realization of being in an abnormal condition, is absent except in mild or initial states.

The description so far given is only an approximation of what is observed in individual cases. In the midst of the multiform aspects, the characteristic that stands out in almost every case is the fact that the patient is not what he used to be. His whole relation with the world, himself, and others has undergone a drastic change. In some cases the change has been so gradual that people in daily contact with him have not become aware or alarmed, but people who have not seen him for a long time or who do not know him realize at once that there is something unnatural in the way he relates to people and to himself. Almost every patient goes through an incipient or early stage, during which a change has occurred, but no disorganization of the personality has manifested itself to more than a minimal degree. In many cases the disorganization proceeds to advanced stages and may progress indefinitely.

III

Taxonomy of Schizophrenia

The schizophrenic syndromes have been classified in various ways. Traditionally, four major types have been recognized: the paranoid, the hebephrenic, the catatonic, and the simple. The *Diagnostic and Statistical Manual of Mental Disorders* of the American Psychiatric Association (1968) differentiates other types and gives a number to each condition: the latent (295.5), the residual (295.6), the schizo-affective (295.7), the childhood (295.8), and the chronic undifferentiated type (295.99).

In this chapter we shall proceed with a brief description of the traditional four major types. Then we shall describe the atypical forms. The childhood type will be studied in Chapter 44.

IV

The Paranoid Type

Patients suffering from the paranoid type constitute the majority of cases diagnosed as schizophrenic. They are by far more numerous than the other types; but the percentage has varied according to geographical and historical contingencies and the prevailing diagnostic criteria of the local psychiatric profession.

The cases generally classified as paranoid present, fundamentally, the picture described in the previous section. They also present some characteristics of their own. First of all, in a larger percentage of cases the onset of the psychosis occurs later in life than in the other types. Although many cases of this type occur even as early as the time of puberty, they are found even in the fourth and fifth decade of life. The older the patient, the more difficult it will be to decide whether his symptomatology is a schizophrenic one or one that is better classified as paranoid state or paranoia (see Chapter 4).

Paranoid patients are as a rule more intelligent than the other schizophrenic patients, although all levels of I.Q. are found. From the beginning of the illness, patients may seem suspicious and bound to misinterpret things and events in a way derogatory to themselves. The underlying feeling about oneself is immediately lost and transformed into a symptomatology where *projection* occurs (that is, attributing to others a negative feeling about the patient). For instance, a patient may consider himself clumsy and ridiculously inadequate. He develops the impression that people are laughing at him. The impression soon becomes certainty. He is sure they think he is no good and inadequate. But to be no good and inadequate means to be homosexual. That is why they refer to him as a "she." The patient, for instance, heard co-workers saying, "She is not doing her work as she should." They used the word *she* because they think the patient is not a man.

The phenomenon of *spreading of meaning* is common. A particular meaning is given to many things, because reality or the environment is reinterpreted to fit the basic idea of the patient.

Not only does the patient claim that the others accuse him of the traits he himself does not like in himself, but he eventually ascribes to others the characteristics he cannot accept in himself. Whereas he started by being suspicious, he soon becomes sure that other people plot or conspire against him. He sees or collects the alleged evidence. He may assume the bitter, angry, antagonistic, defiant attitude of the person who is unfairly victimized, or the attitude of the submissive person who wants to be helped, but does not know what to do because "strange things are happening."

The content of thought of these patients is characterized by ideas of reference and delusions, even more than in other types of schizophrenia. Although the delusions are unsystematized in the majority of cases, they are more systematized than in the hebephrenic type and may be quite well systematized at the beginning of the illness. In American patients, the delusions are almost always persecutory in content, especially at the beginning of the illness. Syndromes characterized by grandiose delusions from the onset of the illness were more common in the past.

Whereas at the beginning of the illness the patient presented many neurotic features, these traits soon do not retain the salient role. What emerges is the delusional content, as delusions invade progressively the psyche of the patient. They may be persecutory, grandiose, hypochondriacal, ideas of being transformed, accused, influenced, hypnotized, controlled, or poisoned, or being made the victim of experiments, and so forth.

In a considerable number of cases the delusions become *systematized;* that is, the patient does not accept them as unrelated beliefs, but rationalizes them or explains them more or less logically in relation with the rest of his life or with what he observes in the world. A definite delusional system may be built around the idea that the patient is persecuted because of his ideology, philosophy, or religion. He may build a system of beliefs and then attempt to give this system an apparently plausible scientific, philosophical, or theological structure.

Delusions may have all types of content. It is impossible to enumerate all the facts and things they refer to. They reflect the patient's familial, cultural, and social conditions. At times this cultural influence is manifested in a paradoxical way. For instance, whereas religion as a whole has less influence in the life of people today than in previous eras, I have seen recently an increase in grandiose delusions with religious content. The delusion of being Jesus Christ is common both in Christian patients and in Jewish patients living in predominantly Christian countries. The delusion of being Moses occurs in both male and female Jewish patients. The delusion of being Saint Paul, the Virgin Mary, Saint Peter, and so forth, is also fairly common. Contrary to what is written in popular books of psychiatry or common jokes, I have never seen a patient claiming to be Napoleon Bonaparte.

Delusions of jealousy (beliefs that the spouse is unfaithful) are also quite common, especially later in life. They are, however, more frequent in those conditions generally called paranoid states, involutional paranoid states, and paranoia.

The paranoid type may present itself in a subtype called *monosymptomatic*. That is, at a manifest level, the illness is detected by the presence of only one delusion, generally of persecution, whereas the rest of the personality remains apparently intact. Many of these isolated delusions, like, for instance, the idea of being able to influence the weather, are harmless. Other, fortunately very rare, monosymptomatic delusions are dangerous and lead to the so-called unmotivated crimes. They lead to murder of the father, mother, or even a series of unknown persons. As we shall see in Chapter 4, these delusions are difficult to recognize and the differential diagnosis from psychopathic personality may be doubtful in some instances.

Hallucinations, especially auditory ones, as a rule are common in the paranoid type of schizophrenia. They may be totally absent in cases in which the personality is fairly well preserved and the delusions well systematized.

The progression of the illness may be rapid and may lead to advanced regression in a short period of time; as a rule, however, the majority of paranoid patients regress less rapidly than the other types, and many of them remain indefinitely at a stage of illness that is not much advanced. Paranoid patients remain in better contact with the environment and may adjust better to hospital routine. Often their activities can be channeled into useful work. On the other hand, their suspiciousness, ideas of reference, and delusions may make them antagonistic, rebellious, and even violent. Escapes from hospitals and homicidal impulses, at times successful, are more common in this group. Detailed reports of clinical cases of the paranoid type of schizophrenia will be presented in various chapters of this book. At this point we shall use a simple example, to be considered only from the point of the manifest symptomatology.

George is a 22-year-old male, the second of two siblings in a middle-class family. Although described as high-strung throughout his life, he never showed gross abnormalities of behavior. During college, however, he found the scholastic work increasingly hard. He finally decided to quit school and to accept a job as a salesman, but he found that this occupation too was not satisfactory. He appeared different to the members of his family, who thought he was probably worried about his working conditions. He appeared distressed and absent-minded and soon grew very peculiar. He became increasingly preoccupied with certain thoughts, which he revealed to his parents and sister. On hearing the word *home,* he understood *homo;* if he heard the word *fair,* he felt *fairy* was the word really meant. He became more and more convinced that people thought he was homosexual. When he saw groups of people in his neighborhood, he was sure that they were talking about him. He often "heard" them talking about him and making accusations. He became more and more preoccupied, upset, unable to attend to his work. He became somewhat neglectful of his appearance, oblivious of the many usual aspects of life, and more and more involved in thoughts of being accused, spied on, spoken of, ridiculed. In a few weeks it became impossible for him to hold his job, and he quit voluntarily. A few days later he became increasingly restless and finally agitated. The psychiatrist who was consulted recommended hospitalization.

V

The Hebephrenic Type

The hebephrenic type of schizophrenia is often difficult to differentiate from the paranoid. The most striking difference consists of a more rapid disintegration. The symptoms start generally in adolescence or early youth insidiously and with a progressive course. The content of thought is characterized by many poorly systematized, poorly rationalized, and in many cases completely disorganized delusions. Grandiose delusions are more common than in the paranoid type. Also much more common are hypochondriacal ideas, preoccupations with the body image, and kinesthetic delusions. It is not rare to find a patient who thinks that he has lost his bowels or that his heart has changed place, his brain has melted, and so forth. Hallucinations are common and, more frequently than in the paranoid type, are pleasing in content.

The mood may be slightly depressed; more often it is one of apathy and detachment, interrupted now and then by an apparently humorous or jocular attitude. The patient often smiles in situations that seem completely inappropriate. For instance, a question may evoke an incongruous smile instead of a verbal answer. Language disorders are prominent, especially in cases of rapid regression. Word-salad, clang associations, and neologisms are very common.

The dilapidation of personality is soon evident. The neglect of personal habits becomes more pronounced and the patient has to be taken care of. The patient often exhibits a childlike attitude and behavior, an infantilism that is not ingratiating, but rather grotesque or grossly incongruous.

We may distinguish two subtypes. In the first there is a progressive and lasting regressive behavior, with paucity of hallucinations and delusions and frequent occurrence of bizarre acts. In the second subtype, we have a relatively acute course, with many features similar to those of the paranoid type. The following case belongs to this second subtype.

Gladys was a $17^1/_2$-year-old white girl attending high school. Both her parents had psychotic depressions, from which they recovered with the help of shock treatment. Gladys's familial surrounding was characterized by parental conflicts, usually bickering over money matters. Gladys was the third of three children. The other two never received any psychiatric treatment and were described as well adjusted.

Gladys had always done well in school; but, before consultation, she became apprehensive, her marks fell down, and she became afraid to do her homework. When she was seen in consultation, she was in a state of great excitement. She said that soon she would have to take the examinations, and she was not prepared. She did not know anything. She constantly repeated the same questions: "Should I go to school? Shall I pass the examinations?" but no reassurance would help her. She continued to ask the same questions incessantly. Apparently she seemed in good contact, because she seemed alert and emotionally alive; actually, nothing that the examiner said registered. No delusions or hallucinations were elicited.

During the night, however, Gladys became more excited, expressed suicidal ideas, and was hospitalized. At the time of her admission she was extremely confused, hyperactive, and resistive. At times, when she was asked a question, she seemed unable to speak spontaneously, but would occasionally utter small whimpering sounds, moving her lips as if to pronounce words, but being unable to do so.

The second day after her admission she began to masturbate in the presence of other patients and also to pick at the skin of her face. She was restless, agitated, and screamed a great deal. At other times she sat on one chair in her room and stared vacantly out the window. She refused to eat and had to be tube fed. At other times she laughed in an incongruous way, was flighty, and talked in an apparently joyful mood, although what she was saying often was completely incoherent.

A few weeks later she occasionally expressed the idea that she was in a concentration camp where the Russians had allegedly put her. Later, when she was given electric shock, she misidentified one of the nurses who was leaving the room, believing that this nurse was her mother.

The members of the staff thought she was not suitable for psychotherapy. She was given a course of electric shock and then one of insulin, but there was no improvement in her condition. On the contrary, she seemed to regress rapidly. Later she was treated with large doses of Thorazine. She became more accessible and responsive to psychotherapy. She left the hospital six months after admission, apparently free of the serious symptoms. She remained, however, somewhat flighty and tended to joke in a rather inappropriate way. After her discharge she started long-term psychotherapy. A gradual, slow improvement followed.

VI

THE CATATONIC TYPE

Catatonic schizophrenia, more than any other type, presents characteristics of its own.

After a certain period of excitement, which may even be absent in many cases and which is characterized by agitated, apparently aimless behavior, the patient slows down, reaching sooner or later a state at times of almost complete immobility. The patient may become so inactive as to be unable to move around and take care of his physical needs and must be confined in bed (*catatonic stupor*). The patient in this condition cannot dress or undress himself and does not have the initiative to feed himself or to talk in the presence of other people, even if questions are asked of him. He seems completely paralyzed. At other times the patient is not so intensely affected, but his activities are still reduced to a minimum. He is not really paralyzed. What is disturbed is his faculty to will. He cannot will and therefore cannot will to move. At times he is very obedient and suggestible, because he follows the will of someone else. For instance, if a patient is told, "Show me your tongue; I want to prick it with a pin," the patient may obligingly comply. The examiner may put the body of the patient in the most awkward positions, and the patient will remain in those positions for hours. This is the phenomenon of *flexibilitas cerea* ("waxy flexibility"). At other times the patient puts himself in an awkward, uncomfortable, or statuesque position and remains in that position until he is put to bed and then resumes the same position the following day (see Figure 1). A phenomenon that seems opposite to this suggestibility but is instead related to it is *negativism*. Instead of doing what he is requested to do, the patient does the opposite. For instance, if he is told to show the tongue, he closes the mouth tightly or turns the face away. If he is told to stand, he assumes a reclining position, and so forth. In many cases a few activities remain, but they are carried out in a routine, stereotyped manner. Any spontaneous or new activity is abolished. There are striking exceptions, however. In contrast to the usual immobility, the patient repeatedly performs some actions that have a special meaning or purpose to him. Thus a patient interrupted occasionally his immobility when he initiated a suicidal attempt. Another patient, a 22-year-old girl, would periodically completely undress herself irrespective of the presence of patients and members of the staff of both sexes.

Delusions and hallucinations are present in many cases. They cannot be elicited, however, because, until he improves, the patient cannot communicate with the examiner. Often these delusions and hallucinations are of a general and cosmic quality—"The world is being destroyed." Attempts to talk to the patient often elicit other symptoms. Echolalia is prominent—that is, instead of answering the questions, the patient repeats the questions. At other times the answers are monosyllabic; at still other times neologisms are numerous. The handwriting manifests a peculiarity of style that is even more pronounced than in other types of schizophrenia. The general behavior is characterized by mannerisms, grimaces, and bizarre acts.

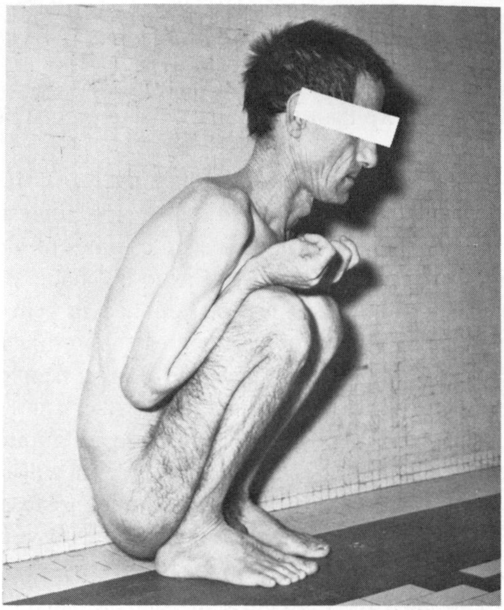

FIGURE 1. A 43-year-old catatonic patient admitted to the hospital at the age of 18. After a short period of excitement, he assumed statuesque or awkward positions. Insulin, ECT, and drug therapy had no favorable results. He has maintained the position shown in the picture for several years and resists change. However, he allows the attendant to dress him daily and to accompany him for a walk in the hospital's park. On returning to the ward he disrobes himself and resumes this awkward position.

Anthony is a 24-year-old male who, in the past few weeks, had been brooding excessively about his life. He did not feel well, but did not know how to explain his malaise. No hallucinations or delusions were elicited. There was an urge to make contact with people, while on the ward, but there was also a sense of disappointment. One morning a few days after his arrival, he was found in a statuesque position, with his legs contorted in an awkward position. Attempts to talk to him were of no avail. He acted as if he could not hear or see anything. His face was completely deprived of any mimic play and did not reveal any emotion. A few days later he could talk a little bit, but in an echolalic way. For instance, to the question "What is your name?" he would reply, "What is your name?" He had to be taken care of, and spoon feeding was necessary.

VII

THE SIMPLE TYPE

Simple schizophrenia almost never occurs in an acute manner. The beginning is slow, insidious, and generally goes back to a time preceding puberty. The major changes, however, occur after puberty, when the family realizes that the patient is not up to par in spite of the expectations that at an earlier age he had evoked in people. The patient becomes quite inactive and limits his life as much as he can. He refuses to go out, to go to school or to work, and gradually his life becomes very restricted. When he talks, there is no looseness of ideas or illogical sequence of thought, as in other forms of schizophrenia, but rather *poverty of thought*. The patient is able to talk only about a few concrete things, abstract notions being eliminated. Careful examination of thought processes reveals an impairment of abstract thinking.

Hallucinations, delusions, ideas of reference, and other obvious symptoms are absent. In spite of the absence of these obvious symptoms, the behavior of the patient remains odd, inappropriate, insufficient to the demands of life, and his affect is inadequate. Unless hospitalized or successfully treated, the patients remain a burden to their families. When no family is available, they run the risk of becoming hoboes or prostitutes or of being exploited by organized crime.

Mary is the older of two sisters. The father was an alcoholic who died when Mary was a child; the mother died when the two sisters were in their teens. Although Mary had never appeared very bright, her inadequacies became more evident after the death of her mother. At that time she became even more dependent on her sister. Mary had several jobs, but could not fulfill them adequately. She was repeatedly fired, or she herself left the job because she felt the work was "too much for her." She refused the few invitations to go out with young men and restricted her life to a minimum. Finally it was agreed that her sister would go to work and she would attend to the care of the household. But even that became "too much for her." She would remain idle for hours and hours and showed no interest in anything. Her conversation was reduced to a few words. She had to be told what to do, even in relation to her personal needs. Finally the sister decided to hospitalize her. At admission she appeared neat and tidy and able to take care of herself and accepted hospitalization without protest. On the contrary, it was a relief for her to be away from the world, where she had to make so many efforts. No hallucinations, delusions, or ideas of reference were elicited. During the interviews with the physician, her answers were literal, concrete, and not commensurate with her education. The patient's life was reduced to a few stereotyped acts. The nurses and attendants could not persuade her to do more than a minimum amount of work on the ward. When her sister visited her in the hospital, she seemed to sink into a mild state of depression.

VIII
Ill-Defined or Controversial Types

In addition to the four classic types, which we have just described, and the atypical types, which we shall examine in the next sections, many psychiatrists acknowledge the existence of ill-defined types. Some of them have been included in the *Diagnostic and Statistical Manual of Mental Disorders* (DSM) of the American Psychiatric Association; others appear in personal classifications.

In the DSM-1 a *latent type* is described as a category "for patients having clear symptoms of schizophrenia, but no history of a psychotic schizophrenic episode.'' It is difficult to see how a syndrome showing ''clear symptoms'' could be considered *latent*. This term, originally used by Bleuler, was reserved for cases not presenting clear symptoms. As a matter of fact, the guide continues to characterize this category in this way: ''Disorders sometimes designated as incipient, prepsychotic, pseudoneurotic, pseudopsychopathic, or borderline schizophrenia are categorized here.''

Many practitioners include in this category patients who seem to be *potential* schizophrenics. In other words, no definite symptoms are detected, but the clinician has the impression that the patient is so sick as to become psychotic in the near future. Thus, the diagnosis is in many cases impressionistic. As we shall see later on, many patients who seem to have all the requisites and potentials for schizophrenia never develop the disorder.

Probably in the latent category are to be included the cases that Hoch and Polatin in 1949 called *pseudoneurotic schizophrenia*. Under this name these authors described a syndrome whose symptoms are not usually considered characteristic of schizophrenia. The diagnosis is made on the subjective evaluation of the constellation of symptoms. The patients present ''pan-anxiety'' and ''pan-neurosis.'' That is, ''an all-pervading anxiety structure . . . does not leave any life-approach of the person free from tension.'' By ''pan-neurosis,'' the authors meant that the patients do not have only one or two neurotic manifestations, but that ''all symptoms known in neurotic illness are often present at the same time.'' Gross hysterical mechanisms, vegetative dysfunctions such as poor sleep, anorexia, vomiting, and palpitations, phobias, obsessions, and compulsions may all be present. The neurotic manifestations shift constantly, but are never completely absent. ''A considerable number of these patients have short psychotic episodes or later become frankly schizophrenic.''

Cantor (1968) suggests the term *occult schizophrenia* for all ill-defined forms of schizophrenia, including the pseudoneurotic. By occult he means ''concealed, hidden, not immediately known, perceivable only by investigation, and 'covert' rather than overt.'' Although Cantor is correct in stating that some symptoms are occult, we must continue to regard them as part of the manifest symptomatology, that is, of the constellations of symptoms as they appear at first clinical approach and not in their symbolic or psychodynamic meaning.

The DSM-2 guide lists also the chronic undifferentiated type of schizophrenia (295.90), ''for patients who show mixed schizophrenic symptoms and who present definite schizophrenic thought, affect, and behavior not classifiable under the other types of schizophrenia.'' In my experience, many psychiatrists use this diagnosis in absence of definite delusions, hallucinations, or catatonic symptoms. At times it is a question of individual preference to use this diagnosis rather than the simple or hebephrenic type.

A classification that has been accepted by a considerable number of psychiatrists in the United States is one that divides schizophrenia into two major types: reactive schizophrenia and process schizophrenia (Kantor and Herron, 1966; Higgins, 1964, 1969). The reactive type is a relatively mild syndrome, in spite of an often acute and pronounced flourishing of symptoms. Anxiety is obvious, and precipitating factors are easily found. In the process type, precipitating factors are not ascertainable; the onset is gradual or insidious, the prognosis poor.

The underlying assumption in this classification is that the reactive type is determined predominantly by psychological factors, whereas the process type is determined by organic ones. This apparently plausible distinction is generally made *post hoc:* patients who recover or who are understood psychodynamically are called reactive; those who do not are called process. The word *process* conceals either ignorance or therapeutic failure.

I have never accepted this distinction, which, moreover, is applicable only to a moderate percentage of cases, not to the many that seem to belong to a state intermediary between the reactive and the process. Higgins (1964) wrote a first article in which he accepted this classification. In a second article (1969), after reviewing the literature of 205 publications on the subject, he wrote: "The previous review [1964] concluded on the optimistic note that 'Although the evidence to date is far from unequivocal, it would seem . . . that process-reactive schizophrenia is a justifiable classificatory principle. . . .' At this date the writer is somewhat less certain of the future of the concept. It sometimes seems that for every study supporting the efficacy of the concept two nonsupportive ones can be cited."

Nevertheless, Higgins could not reject this classification because, "Despite the problems surrounding the concept, it continues to permit reduction of schizophrenic heterogeneity with sufficient frequency to ensure its continued and broadened application." I cannot go along with the last remarks. Certainly "reduction of heterogeneity" is to be welcomed, but only when it is valid. I believe that the more intensely we study the cases of the so-called process type, the more evident becomes the effect of serious psychological factors. These factors did not affect the patient with an obvious impact, but were slow and hidden in their relentless and insidious course.

Classifications conceptually related to the process-reactive classifications are those of Langfeldt (1939, 1969), who separated the schizophrenic from the schizophreniform, and of Robins and Guze (1970), who distinguish two separate illnesses, one with good prognosis and the other with poor prognosis.

IX

Atypical Forms of Schizophrenia

Atypical and rare types of schizophrenia have also been recognized. *Childhood schizophrenia* (or schizophrenia, childhood type, 295.8) is perhaps the most important of these atypical forms, and yet it is even doubtful that this condition is related to adult schizophrenia. Because we devote a section of Chapter 44 to this disorder, no report of it will be made here. *Schizophrenia, schizo-affective type* (295.7) is characterized by recurring episodes that present a mixture of schizophrenic and manic-depressive symptomatology. For instance, the patient may present ideational content with delusions, ideas of reference, and hallucinations that seem typically schizophrenic, and yet at the same time show other symptoms, such as a mood of depression accompanied by ideas of guilt and self-accusation or a mood of elation with a grandiose overtone. Until 1955, at least in the United States, the prevailing type of schizo-affective psychosis was characterized at the beginning of the illness by a predominance of manic-depressive traits. In the long run, however, the symptomatology assumed a typical schizophrenic aspect, indistinguishable from the classic types of schizophrenia. If the illness was characterized by several psychotic episodes, generally every successive attack was closer to typical schizophrenia and more distant from manic-depressive psychosis. Since the late 1950s we have seen a reverse in the sequence of the symptoms. What was predominantly a schizophrenic syndrome assumes more and more the symptomatology of manic-depressive psychosis, especially of depression. Many authors (for instance, Roth, 1970; Miller and Sonnenberg, 1973) have reported the frequency of depression following or accompanying acute schizophrenic episodes (Spiegel, 1973).

For accuracy's sake we must add that the term *schizo-affective psychosis* was coined by Kasanin (1933) to connote acute psychoses characterized by "emotional turmoil with a distortion of the outside world." Later the nomenclature of the American Psychiatric Association included the schizo-affective psychoses as a subgroup of schizophrenia.

Schizophrenia in old age, at times called late schizophrenia, is a condition that is accepted by a few. Many psychiatrists exclude this condition, because they feel that a relatively young age is necessary for the occurrence of this psychosis. Young age, however, does not seem to be as important as Kraepelin and his contemporaries thought. Relatively frequently we encounter patients in old age who do not show the organic symptoms characteristic of senile or arteriosclerotic psychoses, but rather a paranoid symptomatology characterized by delusions of persecution. (The patient is poisoned, robbed, deprived of his property, and so on.) If these patients were younger, there would be no doubt in classifying them as cases of the paranoid type of schizophrenia. However, many feel that old age is a very important factor in these cases. These patients were able to avoid the psychosis throughout their lives; their defenses were not broken until the changes due to old age occurred. Therefore, many psychiatrists prefer to diagnose these patients as suffering from "a paranoid type of senile psychosis." The problem is still debatable. If we study the history of these patients, we discover that many of them have made only a limited adjustment throughout their lives. Most of them have had suspicious, withdrawn personalities. A great many of them never married. Somehow they managed to escape an acute breakdown until old age. Old age presents new problems of adjustment, at the same time that it produces lesions in the nervous system that make the person less responsive to the new demands of adjustment. Deterioration and regression are much slower in these paranoid forms than in typical cases of senile psychosis. Impairment of orientation, memory, recall, intelligence, and so forth, are much less marked, and in certain cases not appreciable.

In addition to these paranoid cases characterized by delusions of persecution, other cases present delusions of grandeur or delusions and hallucinations with very bizarre content that somehow bring comfort rather than grief to the patient. Thus I remember a black man almost 70 years old, not regressed or deteriorated, who imagined that a beautiful Chinese woman was visiting him every night. He had vivid visual hallucinations. A woman who became sick after the age of 65 had fantastic delusions of transformation into animals. She also felt that she was the queen of Hungary and that the hospital was her royal palace. These senile pictures generally resemble those found in the second stage of schizophrenia (see Chapter 23). I feel that for a very long time schizophrenia was a potentiality in these patients and became an actuality when old age occurred.

Generally the subject of schizophrenia in old age has interested the German authors more than those writing in English. Janzanik (1957) differentiates a late schizophrenia (*Spätschizophrenien*), which occurs in the fifth and sixth decades of life, from old-age schizophrenia (*Altersschizophrenien*), which occurs in the seventh and eight decades.

Most authors agree that old-age schizophrenia is a rare condition. Manfred Bleuler (1943), in a study of 126 cases of late schizophrenia, found five patients that developed the disorder after the age of 60. Giberti, De Carolis, and Rossi (1961) found only two patients who developed the illness after the age of 60 in a study of 362 adult schizophrenics of various ages. Schizophrenia in old age has been studied also by authors who were particularly concerned with the possible hereditary aspect of the problem (Kay and Roth, 1961; Bacciagaluppi and Serra, 1963).

Postpartum schizophrenia is a schizophrenic syndrome occurring in the mother after childbirth. The *Diagnostic and Statistical Manual* of the American Psychiatric Association discourages the diagnosis of psychosis with childbirth (294.4), stating that any type of psychosis may occur during pregnancy and the postpartum period. Although cases of all types of schizophrenia occur postpartum, they have a psychodynamic of their own, which we shall study in Chapter 13.

Schizophrenia accompanying other diseases presents diagnostic problems. Not infrequently we see schizophrenic symptomatologies with patients presenting the serology of general paresis, or epilepsy, Huntington's chorea, postencephalitic conditions, multiple sclerosis, pernicious anemia with nervous complications, cerebellar atrophies, and so on. Although in some of these cases the crippling effects of the organic disease may have increased the anxiety of the patient and released a potential schizophrenia, most psychiatrists feel that in the majority of these cases an organic diagnosis should be preferred.

Propfschizophrenia is a form occurring in a small minority of mental defectives, generally at the moron or borderline level. It is characterized by paranoid episodes with delusions and hallucinations, which may be followed by slow regression.

X

Changing Aspects of Schizophrenia

The symptomatology of schizophrenia does not remain the same in different eras, countries, and cultures. Although the variations are not such as to make recognition of the disorder impossible or difficult, they are noticeable, even during the span of the career of a psychiatrist. Perhaps the marked changes that have occurred in the sociocultural environment in the last few decades have affected the symptomatology and made the changes more conspicuous than in other times.

During the thirty-three years of my experience with schizophrenics, I have seen the following changes. Whereas *withdrawal* used to be by far the predominant feature in most incipient cases of schizophrenia, the incidence of this characteristic has decreased. Many more patients now than in the past present an active restlessness, uncoordinated activity, or psychopathic traits. One of the most striking changes is in the sexual area. Whereas the schizophrenic used to be markedly inhibited in his sexual behavior, now he often has an active sex life or attempts to have one, even in conditions where such behavior is not expected or is grossly inappropriate. In previous times most patients inhibited or repressed their sex life to such an extent that they were considered by Rado and Daniel (1956) to be *unhedonic;* that is, they were considered unable to experience pleasure, sexual or otherwise. Now many of them tend to follow heterosexual, homosexual, or exhibitionistic impulses. Even in classes of people where such behavior was the least expected, striking examples occur. Thus, a young Protestant minister, previously well balanced, at the onset of the disorder started to make homosexual advances in the most obvious manner. A previously well-mannered young man studying to be a rabbi started to touch or lean on girls who would pass by or sit next to him in buses or subways. Sexual exhibitionism and activity of all sorts that was previously a rare occurrence in psychiatric hospitals have now become much more common.

Another changing characteristic is the age of onset of the illness. Until 1955–1960 many psychiatrists were discovering that, contrary to earlier reports, schizophrenia was occurring at a more and more advanced age. This finding was to some extent due to the fact that many cases diagnosed in the past as paraphrenia, paranoid conditions, paranoia, paranoid type of involutional psychosis, alcoholic psychosis, and so forth, were recognized more and more as cases of schizophrenia. Since 1960 an opposite phenomenon has been observed: an increasing number of patients are becoming ill at a young age, especially in adolescence and early youth. As far as the intensity of the symptoms is concerned, many psychiatrists, especially those who are in private practice and do not work in psychiatric hospitals, report that they see many patients with symptomatology so mild as not to require hospitalization or drug therapy. These are not latent cases in the sense described by Bleuler, but patients who are actively psychotic, although their symptoms are few and not pronounced. It is difficult to determine statistically whether this increase in mild cases is more apparent than real. The explanation that comes to mind is that today, with the greater understanding of psychiatry and with increased psychiatric facilities, many patients who, because of the relative nonseverity of their symptoms, would not have been recognized in the past, are easily diagnosed now. Whether the increase in these mild or *oligosymptomatic* cases is real or apparent, the fact remains that the psychiatrist in private practice today is bound to see a large number of them and therefore must be able to recognize them. Of course, we do not include in this group patients whose symptomatology has become less marked on account of drug therapy.

In addition to the change in the intensity of symptoms, there is also a quantitative change in the percentage of the various types of schizophrenia, a change that is apparent especially to psychiatrists who are associated with hospitals. Until a few decades ago there was not too marked a difference in the incidence of the hebephrenic, paranoid, and catatonic forms (with the simple type trailing); now many admitting psychiatrists feel that the paranoid type is by far the most common among the four classic types. The psychiatrists who accept the varieties "latent" and "chronic undifferentiated" now classify with these terms a large number of seriously disturbed people who do not fit into other categories.

It is relatively easy to understand the decline in the number of hebephrenics, because possibly many cases previously diagnosed as hebephrenic were paranoid with rapid disintegration. Timely intervention would have arrested them at a paranoid level. More difficult to explain is the decline of full-fledged catatonic patients, who until twenty-five years ago were much more common. From colleagues working in small hospitals we hear that the admission of a catatonic patient with typical symptoms, such as stupor and waxy flexibility, has become almost a rarity.

I have described (Arieti, 1959) what I have called *oligosymptomatic,* or very mild, cases of schizophrenia, which are much more easily recognized since the early 1950s. It must be understood that when we refer to oligosymptomatic cases, we are not speaking about borderline cases. A borderline case, as we generally use this term today, is that of a patient who, although presenting a symptomatology so serious as to be classified between the neuroses and the psychoses, generally is not psychotic, does not act as a psychotic, and most probably will never become fully psychotic. The mild cases that are going to be described are considered psychotic.

The Paranoid Type

No definite delusions or hallucinations are found in the oligosymptomatic form of the paranoid type. The patient, however, is suspicious and antagonistic, and a *paranoid flavor* characterizes his conversation. Often his parents, siblings, or in-laws are the object of his distortions in thinking. Allegedly, these relatives or other persons are trying to hurt the patient, to spoil his reputation, and so forth. Even what the therapist says to the patient is misinterpreted, as the patient often clearly gives it a special twist. This tendency to misinterpret, at first limited to dealings with relatives, later spreads to employers and co-workers, so that finally it becomes impossible for the patient to maintain his occupation. If the patient is not treated, full-fledged episodes, with definite delusions and hallucinations, may occur.

The Hebephrenic Type

In the oligosymptomatic form of the hebephrenic type, the patient complains a lot about physical ailments. Often he attributes the responsibility for his troubles to previous physicians who allegedly have treated him badly. At times there is an incongruous euphoria. Odd ideas, either of reference or semigrandiose, creep in. There is an apparent lack of anxiety.

The Catatonic Type

There are no motor disorders in the oligosymptomatic form of the catatonic type, but the activities of the patient are reduced to a minimum. The patient takes an enormous amount of time to do simple things. To get dressed or undressed may require two or three hours, and it becomes a real ordeal. The patient refuses to leave the house. When he goes out, he arrives at his destination extremely late. Occasionally, almost catatonic episodes occur. There is no catatonic immobility, but the patient is confined to bed for several days, refusing to get up in spite of absence of physical illness. The patient may improve completely, only to develop a full catatonic attack a few years later.

The Simple Type

The simple type is the most common among the oligosymptomatic forms. Contrary to the classic simple type, the prognosis is good if intensive psychodynamic therapy is instituted. The patient manifests anxiety much more frequently than in the classic type. At times a diagnostic difficulty consists in differentiating this type from the oligosymptomatic catatonic. Like the catatonic, the patient does not want to go out of the house or seek employment and tells you that he "cannot do it." Activities are reduced to a minimum and are extremely slow. The sleep rhythm is altered. Often he sleeps during the day and stays up until very late at night or the early part of the morning. In quite a few cases he becomes overconcerned with his appearance or with his weight. He may go into periodic eating sprees that alternate with periods of almost total starvation. The differential diagnosis from anorexia nervosa is debatable in some cases.

It is often difficult to determine to which one of the classical types of schizophrenia these mild cases belong. Often one gets the impression that they are mixed or undifferentiated and that the effort made to recognize in them a particular type is mostly due to our desire to adhere to the traditional terminology.

XI

The Course of Schizophrenia

A striking characteristic of schizophrenia is the great variability of its course. Some patients recover from an acute attack in only a few hours, days, or months, whereas others remain sick for the rest of their lives. Some undergo a cyclical course characterized by episodes occurring in a fundamentally vulnerable personality. Some recover from the acute attacks, but retain a residue or deficit. Those who remain permanently ill may show an arrest of the disorder at a certain stage, whereas others undergo a slow but progressive regression. Even the onset of the disorder presents various aspects, as we have already mentioned. Ey, Bernard, and Brisset (1967) distinguish four types of onset: (1) the insidious and progressive; (2) the acute; (3) the cyclic; and rarely (4) the monosymptomatic.

I have differentiated (1955) four different stages of regression in patients (fortunately now in sharply decreasing number) who undergo a complete course of the illness.

Most of the patients seen by psychiatrists in private practice belong to the first or initial stage. Even if the patients are undergoing a second or third attack, they generally belong in the first stage, because modern types of treatment prevent them from progressing further. After the third attack the patient tends to advance rapidly to subsequent stages. Statistics vary considerably as to the frequency of recurrences. The first stage of regression extends from the time the patient starts to lose contact with reality to the full formation of the characteristic symptoms of schizophrenia. The patient may retain great anxiety and restlessness. He seems either to fight his illness and want to return to reality or to fight the external world in an attempt to vindicate his symptoms. There is great variation of symptoms in this period, except in case of the catatonic patient, who may exhibit all the catatonic characteristics from the very beginning. Some catatonic patients, however, may change into a paranoid picture and vice versa.

Although a detailed description and interpretation of the four stages of schizophrenic development will be presented in Part Four, here is a summarization of the overt symptomatology.

The first stage is characterized by the presence of anxiety and lack of a certain equilibrium, in spite of the presence of typical psychotic symptoms. This first stage can be divided into three phases:

1. A phase of *panic*—when the patient starts to perceive things in a different way, is frightened on account of it, appears confused, and does not know how to explain "the strange things that are happening."

2. A phase of *psychotic insight*—when he succeeds in "putting things together." By devising a pathological way of seeing reality, he is able to explain his abnormal experiences. The phenomenon is called "insight" because the patient finally sees meaning and relations in his experiences, but the insight is psychotic because it is founded on mental processes that occur only in a state of psychosis.

3. A phase of *multiplication of symptoms*—when symptoms become more and more numerous as the patient vainly attempts to use the symptoms to solve his conflicts and remove his anxiety.

The second, or advanced, stage is characterized by an apparent acceptance of the illness. All the classic symptoms are present, and they do not seem to bother the patient as much as before. Life has become more and more restricted and lacks spontaneity. Routine and stereotyped behavior are outstanding.

In the third, or preterminal, stage many symptoms seem to have burned out, and, because all the types of schizophrenia resemble one another so closely, it is often difficult to distinguish a paranoid from a catatonic. At this stage, primitive habits such as hoarding useless objects and decorating oneself in a bizarre manner are conspicuous. This stage generally occurs from five to fifteen years after the beginning of the illness, but it may occur sooner or later.

In the fourth, or terminal, stage the behavior of the patient is even more impulsive and reflexlike. Primitive habits are replaced by even more primitive ones. Hoarding of objects is substituted by food grabbing, and later by ingestion of small objects, whether they are edible or not (*placing-into-mouth* reaction).

Later, during the fourth stage (although in some cases even at a much earlier stage), many patients present what appear to be perceptual alterations. They seem insensitive to pain, temperature, and taste, although they still react to olfactory stimuli. This anesthesia is the cause of many accidents (for instance, burning oneself by sitting too close to a radiator).

CHAPTER

4

The Diagnosis and Prognosis of Schizophrenia

I

DIAGNOSIS

Typical cases of schizophrenia are easy to diagnose. Difficult to diagnose are those belonging to that ill-defined group that includes so-called latent cases, borderline, character disorder, quasi-psychotic psychopaths, severe personality difficulties, and so on. The diagnosis made in these cases is apt to reflect more the classificatory criteria of the psychiatrist than the symptomatology *per se*. Even in a typical case the diagnosis may be difficult if the patient has been interviewed only once or twice on a consultation basis.

The first rule to be adopted in diagnosing schizophrenia is that an individual symptom or even a few symptoms should not be considered absolute proof of the condition. The constellation of symptoms should be evaluated in the general picture or gestalt they generate. Even symptoms that seem typical, like auditory hallucinations, delusions, or language disorders, should not be considered to be absolute proof of the psychosis, because they may occur in other organic or functional conditions. Very often, seriously disturbed, but not psychotic, adolescents are often mistaken for schizophrenics.

In Chapter 3 we mentioned the changing aspects of the symptomatology of schizophrenia. We shall mention now a changing trend in diagnosing schizophrenia. Whereas until 1955–1960 the diagnostic ability of a psychiatrist was measured by his skill in recognizing the largest number of previously undetected schizophrenics, the trend is now reversed. It has gradually been recognized that the diagnosis of schizophrenia is made too frequently, especially in the presence of serious psychopathology. The competency of the psychiatrist is often measured by his ability to rule out from the classification *schizophrenia* many patients who present a schizophrenic-like symptomatology.

Differential Diagnosis from Psychoneuroses

Differential diagnosis from psychoneuroses, easy in typical cases, is made difficult by the fact that neurotic symptoms may have preceded schizophrenia or may actually be present. When the personality as a whole undergoes a rapid decline or maladjustment, one must think of the possibility of a schizophrenic outcome, even though the previous symptomatology was neurotic. For instance, sudden scholastic decline, dropping out, or any drastic transformation of character should be viewed with suspicion.

When hysteria was much more common than it is now, schizophrenia used to be confused with it. It is possible that patients diagnosed in former times as hysterics were suffering from schizophrenia. Hysterical attacks occur more frequently in people with an extrovert personality and are characterized by conversion syndromes. The symptomatology is easily influenced by certain persons in the immediate environment and responds easily to hypnosis.

Typical obsessive-compulsive psychoneurosis is easily distinguishable from schizophrenia. The examiner must keep in mind, however, that many patients who develop schizophrenia go through an obsessive-compulsive stage. In some cases this neurosis gradually blends into schizophrenia. Obsessive thoughts in preschizophrenics or schizophrenics are more general in character; they may progressively invade the whole life of the patient. Moreover, they have some characteristics that are more frequent than in neurotic obsessions—they have a particular meaning even at a conscious or manifest level, and this meaning has a spreading quality. For instance, the patient may either count, look at, or avoid a particular number; but the number has a contagious meaning. A patient felt she had to avoid number 8. She started to decompensate after the death of her grandmother, who died on September 8 at eight o'clock in the evening. The patient expected something bad to happen on the eighth day of any month. Up to this point the symptoms could be classified as a superstition or as a neurotic symptom; but soon the patient started to hate every number that included 8 (18, 28, 800, and so on) and brooded over the special foreboding meanings of these numbers. Eventually she developed acute delusional thoughts and experienced hallucinations.

Similarly, a typical phobic syndrome is easily distinguishable from schizophrenia. When the patient is afraid of dogs, horses, crossing streets, squares, or bridges, and special uniforms, it is easy to make the diagnosis of psychoneurosis. However, there are symptoms intermediary between phobias and delusions. In typical neurotic phobias the patient intellectually knows that his fears are unfounded; seemingly the phobigenic element is an animal, object, event, or situation. If the phobigenic object is a human being, it is because he wears a special uniform, like a nun or a policeman, or has a special job, like a doctor or a dentist. However, in phobic syndromes that are close to schizophrenia, the patient is not sure of the irrationality of his fears. Not always, but often, the fears involve human beings. For instance, a patient expects a man to come out of the closet and strangle her.

Some phobias and obsessions that are *mistaken* for delusions occur in women who believe they may hurt, even kill, their child or children. Especially if these fears occur postpartum, they are likely to be mistaken for delusions as part of a postpartum psychosis. However, every psychiatric symptom, including phobias and obsessions, can occur postpartum. The existence of such fears in women who have just given birth is not sufficient to warrant the diagnosis of schizophrenia.

Differential Diagnosis from Manic-Depressive Psychosis

The diagnosis is easy in typical cases. Severe thought disorders, like illogical remarks, incongruous statements, bizarre delusions, or ideas of reference, are rare in manic-depressive patients. When delusions occur, they are consequent to the mood with which they are congruous. For instance, a patient suffering from psychotic depression may feel guilty for having committed alleged crimes, but this thought is part of a self-incriminating attitude. An elated manic patient may believe he is a millionaire. Manic excitement may be confused with that occurring in many schizophrenics. The excitement of the manic is sustained as long as the manic phase lasts, whereas that of the schizophrenic is more acute and inconsistent. A catatonic excitement in particular may be confused with a manic state. However, in the manic state the mood is more congruous; the actions, although grandiose, are less inappropriate. The anger of a manic patient, when he feels hindered or misunderstood, may be confused with the paranoid attitude of the schizophrenic. However, it generally lacks the suspiciousness, the innuendos, or the carefully conceived persecutory framework of the paranoid patient.

Hallucinations occur very rarely in manic-depressive psychosis. They do not have the distinct perceptual quality that they have in schizophrenia. They are clearly related to the mood of the patient, and they occur at night, very seldom during the day.

A catatonic stupor may be mistaken for the depressive stupor occurring in severe depression. In the catatonic stupor there is no overt depression and no history of it.

The history of the patient is, of course, very useful. It may reveal a cyclical course typical of manic-depressive psychosis. On the other hand, it may reveal whether or not the present depression has followed a schizophrenic attack. In some cases in which the differential diagnosis is impossible to make because of the presence of both types of symptomatology, the diagnosis of schizo-affective psychosis is resorted to, as we have seen in Chapter 3.

Differential Diagnosis from Psychopathic Personality

Differential diagnosis from the psychopatic personality is important, often not only for medical reasons, but also for legal ones. From a medical point of view, the diagnosis is important because drug therapy based on tranquilizers, the type commonly used in schizophrenia, should not be given indiscriminately to psychopaths. Some psychopaths, in fact, under the action of medication, may lose any anxiety or restraint and may give vent to psychopathic behavior. The diagnosis is important legally because, notwithstanding some controversial points of view, psychopaths are considered responsible for their actions by the law, whereas schizophrenics generally are not.

The differential diagnosis is easy in the presence of typical schizophrenic symptoms, like delusions and hallucinations. It is difficult when it is based only on the behavior of the patient. In fact, *antisocial behavior* may be the result of both schizophrenia and psychopathic condition. In the psychopathic personality the antisocial action has an easily recognizable aim: stealing, sexual gratification, revenge, and so on. Even when it could be demonstrated that the action had an unconscious symbolic meaning (for instance, stealing was a symbolic way to recapture the love of mother that a sibling had stolen from the patient), the fact that the patient was also motivated at a conscious level and obtained or sought to obtain gratification at a conscious level is indicative of the likelihood of psychopathic personality. On the other hand, if the antisocial behavior appears bizarre, absurd, and apparently unmotivated, the likelihood is that we are dealing with a schizophrenic psychosis, at times of a monosymptomatic type.

Differential diagnoses from paranoia and anorexia nervosa will be discussed in Chapter 44.

Differential Diagnosis from Organic Conditions

Many organic conditions have to be differentiated from schizophrenia, and all of them have to be taken into consideration by the examiner. We shall start with the two that in recent years have been most frequently encountered in clinical practice: minimal brain damage and drug-induced syndromes.

Youngsters suffering from conditions variously called minimal brain damage, minimal cerebral dysfunction, hyperkinesia, may be difficult to differentiate from child schizophrenia or adult schizophrenia. Approximately half the patients who presented these conditions in childhood are sufficiently recovered by the end of adolescence to escape psychiatric attention. A considerable number of them, however, continue even later in life to manifest constant or periodic excessive motor activity, at times slightly inappropriate behavior caused by restlessness, by the need to move, or by lack of attention, and delay in the normal development of intellectual and emotional maturity. On account of their excessive mobility, these patients were difficult to take care of in childhood, caused disruption of family life, and fostered conflicts inviting rejection. Because of the strained relationships with their parents and because they have been left behind scholastically and otherwise even though they at times had unusual potential endowment, they present deep feelings of inadequacy. This symptomatology is sometimes wrongly interpreted as regressive and as indicative of an insidious development of schizophrenia. Of course, schizophrenia may occur in these patients, too, perhaps because of the mentioned superimposed psychological difficulties. However, this is the exception, not the rule. Generally if they are properly recognized and are treated symptomatically in a family that understands the problem of the patient, these patients do well later in life and may regain the lost ground.

History of hyperkinesis in childhood, presence of restlessness, absence of delusions, hallucinations, ideas of reference, and realization that a tendency toward maturity exists, although manifested with considerable delay, will lead to the correct diagnosis. Unfortunately, amphetamines, Ritalin, or similar products used diagnostically in children because of the prompt therapeutic effect in these conditions cannot be used in older patients, because they are not so effective later in life and may promote addiction.

The differential diagnosis between schizophrenia and psychoses due to drug abuse has recently become necessary. The use of lysergic acid diethylamide (LSD) may bring about clinical pictures similar to schizophrenia, during the immediate reaction to drug intake as well as in conditions caused by a prolonged adverse effect of the drug. In the presence of a history of LSD intake, the diagnosis is easy. Visual hallucinations, with red, yellow, and blue predominating, occur much more frequently than in schizophrenia. There is an uncertain sense of wonderment, which may be unpleasant or pleasant to the point of conferring an aesthetic and mystical quality. The patient may feel that he has reached the absolute, the universal, the sublime, that he has come to understand God. There is difficulty in focusing on objects, but there is a sharpened sense of hearing. Auditory hallucinations are very rare. The pupils are dilated, and the reflexes are exaggerated. There is increased muscle tension and slight incoordination and ataxia. The reappearance of overt psychotic symptoms, seemingly schizophrenic long after the intake of LSD, may lead to a wrong diagnosis. Panic, or at least strong anxiety, often accompanies these recurrences.

Chronic users of LSD may be difficult to distinguish from schizophrenics. They may appear sloppy, dull, and with a flattened facial expression. They may present unusual mannerisms, like unusual motions of the tongue. Memory disturbances, slow thinking, difficulty in organizing ideas and in reaching conclusions suggest organic impairment. These patients, however, are socially more adequate than schizophrenics who are regressed to the point of showing equal disorganization in thinking. Generally they are able to give an account of the beautiful original trip experience (Blacker et al., 1968). Many authors have reported the longlasting adverse effects of LSD (Fink et al., 1966; Ungerleider et al., 1968). Diagnostic difficulties arise when one suspects that the LSD experience has precipitated a potential schizophrenic psychosis. I have seen many patients in whom I felt that a potentiality for schizophrenia would have never reached clinical actualization if LSD had not been used. Similar symptoms, simulating schizophrenia, although less pronounced than those caused by LSD, are seen after use of mescaline and psilocybin (Hollister, 1968).

Amphetamine-induced psychosis is to be suspected in paranoid states accompanied by tachycardia, mydriasis, anorexia, loss of weight, and aggressive behavior, occurring especially in those groups that are likely to use drugs. Ellinwood (1967) has reported an accurate description of amphetamine psychosis. Visual hallucinations are the most common. Thinking disorders and body schema distortions are indistinguishable from those occurring in schizophrenia. Because five of the twenty-five patients whom Ellinwood treated continued to experience psychotic symptoms long after amphetamine withdrawal, he suspected an underlying psychotic process. He did not know whether amphetamine contributed permanent effects to the psychotic process. I have seen the disappearance of psychotic symptoms after withdrawal of the drug in all patients who had not shown psychotic symptoms prior to the addiction.

Moderate marihuana use does not produce conditions likely to simulate schizophrenia. However, I have seen many patients presenting acute schizophrenic episodes after excessive use of marihuana or a combination of marihuana and hashish. My impression was that the excessive use of these drugs had actualized a potentiality for schizophrenia. Whether the disorder would have eventually materialized even if the patient had made no use of marihuana or hashish is a matter of speculation.

Other organic conditions to be ruled out are epilepsy, brain tumors, general paresis, Huntington's chorea, mental deficiency, alcoholic hallucinosis, and several neurological syndromes.

Epilepsy presents no differential diagnostic problems when there is history of grand mal or petit mal attacks. The relations between schizophrenia and epilepsy will be discussed in more detail in Chapter 30. Here we shall mention that occasionally so-called twilight states of psychomotor equivalents are confused with schizophrenic behavior. However, they are generally of shorter duration and are accompanied by a state of disturbed consciousness. Schizophrenic behavior may coexist with epilepsy. It is a controversial issue whether these patients should be considered as suffering from epilepsy with schizophrenic symptomatology or from coexistence of schizophrenia and epilepsy.

Like many other psychiatrists, I have seen a considerable number of cases presenting at times a seemingly typical schizophrenic syndrome, episodic or of short duration, in patients who had dysrhythmia of the temporal lobes, especially the right. Often these patients present also attacks of depression, more prolonged than in schizophrenia, and unpleasant behavior. They are belligerent, antagonistic, rebellious, without presenting, in the majority of cases, a clear or definite picture of psychopathic or antisocial behavior. Violent behavior and suicidal attempts, however, occasionally occur. When some of these patients hallucinate, they seem to be aware that they do so.

I am reluctant to make the diagnosis of schizophrenia when psychotic behavior occurs in patients who have dysrhythmia in the temporal lobes. These patients show no psychotic symptoms between psychotic episodes. However, some peculiarity of character may persist.

Petit mal attacks may be confused with schizophrenic blocking phenomena, but they occur suddenly and are of shorter duration.

Mental deficiency may be mistaken for the simple type of schizophrenia, or confused with Propfschizophrenia. Generally, in mental deficiency the defect was apparent in childhood, whereas in the simple type of schizophrenia and in Propfschizophrenia the disorder manifested itself at or after puberty.

Occasionally we see patients who are diagnosed as schizophrenics who presented symptoms from birth other than those of child schizophrenia. These youngsters cannot be considered mental defectives, as some of them have an I.Q. as high as 120–130. Their behavior is unusual, given to irritability, anger, and occasionally to aggressive impulses. They cannot be considered cases of minimal brain damage, as the picture is different and more striking. If they had pyramidal or extrapyramidal symptoms, they would be immediately recognized as cases of birth injury, but the neurological examination does not reveal gross pathology. The electroencephalogram is also negative. They often present minimal incoordination of movements and some visual difficulties, like refractive errors, stabismus, and poor visual motor perception. Many of them present speech defects, such as dysarthria or dysphasia. I personally call these patients cases of intermediate brain damage, that is, with a pathology intermediate between minimal brain damage and usual cerebral palsy. The factors which operated at the time of birth and immediately afterwards either passed unnoticed or were soon forgotten. They might have been anoxia, the use of forceps, or traumata occurring during the passage of the head through the birth canal. Because of the peculiarity of their behavior, especially their appearance, and because of the unusual way of talking, these youngsters are the object of ridicule from their peers. When they complain that people are talking about them, or laughing at them, there is more than an element of truth in these statements, which are mistaken for delusional and lead to the wrong diagnosis of schizophrenia. Rehabilitation, milieu therapy, and sedation rather than depth psychotherapy are necessary.

Brain tumors, especially in the frontal lobes, but in all so-called silent areas, may simulate schizophrenic symptomatology. At times there is a decay of the personality and deterioration of behavior in absence of neurological symptoms. Ideas of reference may also occur. However, a history of seizures and headaches and marked change in memory, attention, recall, or reasoning ability should make the examiner suspect an organic syndrome, and recommend a neurological consultation, X ray of the skull, and an electroencephalogram. In doubtful cases, a pneumoencephalogram may be indicated. Brain tumors misdiagnosed as cases of schizophrenia were much more common in past times when these diagnostic methods were not available. Figure 2 shows the brain of a patient who died after twenty-seven years of hospitalization. In the hospital she lived a vegetative existence. Prior to her hospitalization, she had complained of headache and had had two epileptic seizures. These symptoms were ignored because when she entered the hospital, she showed apparent schizophrenic symptoms, and no neurological

A

B

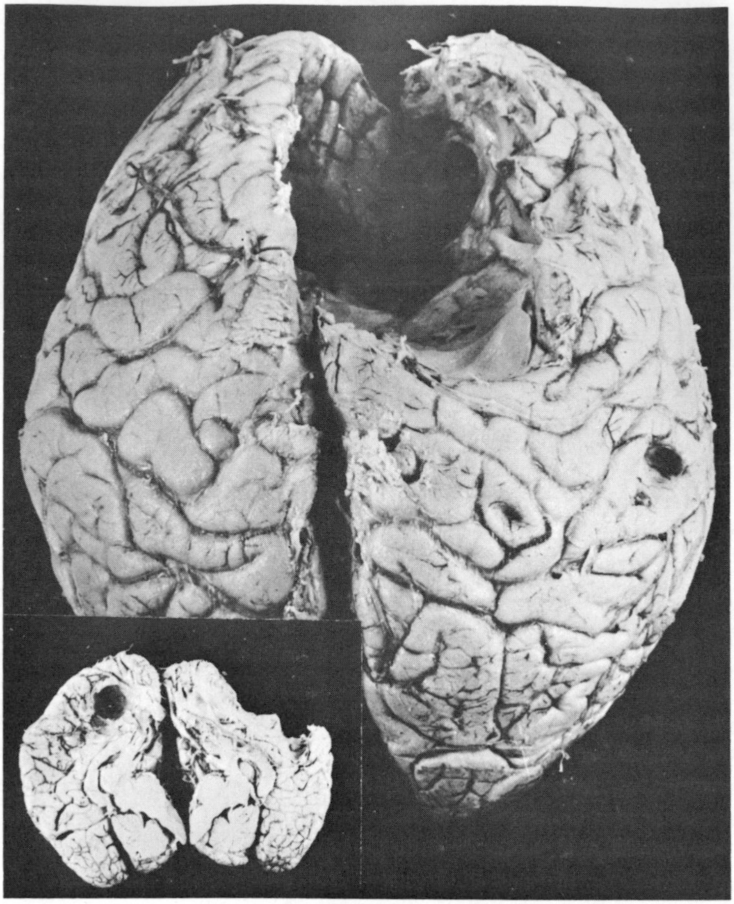

FIGURE 2. (a) Brain of a patient hospitalized for 27 years under the diagnosis of the hebephrenic type of dementia praecox. The brain is seen dorsally after a huge encapsulated fibroblastic meningioma and a small one have been removed. The larger tumor had replaced most of the right frontal lobe and, to a lesser degree, the left frontal lobe. (b) The same brain after the hemispheres have been separated. Notice the extension of the destruction of the normal tissue in the right hemisphere. The tumor extended from the right hemisphere toward the left frontal lobe, producing a well-defined cavity.

signs were recognized. Strangely, during her twenty-seven years of hospital life, no epileptic seizure was observed. She appeared to be a typical regressed hebephrenic.

Early arteriosclerotic and presenile psychoses may be confused with schizophrenia, particularly when at first they manifest a paranoid symptomatology. The age of the patient, the presence of arteriosclerosis, and changes in the sensorium lead to the correct diagnosis. As we shall see in greater detail in Chapter 30, some aphasic patients show language and thought disorders that are at times difficult to distinguish from those of regressed schizophrenics. In these cases again either the history of schizophrenia or of the organic condition that caused the aphasia will lead to the correct diagnosis.

When general paresis was a common disease, many patients were misdiagnosed as suffering from schizophrenia, especially when they did not present the typical grandiose mood, and dysarthric and ocular signs. In the rare cases occurring today, the history of syphilis and the serological and spinal fluid examination lead to the diagnosis.

Cases in which a schizophrenic or schizophrenic-like symptomatology accompanies a neurological condition are generally classified as psychosis with other cerebral conditions, such as encephalitis, degenerative disease of the central nervous system, and so forth.

Some cases of Huntington's chorea start with paranoid syndromes. In the beginning the choreiform movements may be mistaken for schizophrenic mannerisms and grimaces. The history of the occurrence of other cases of this hereditary disease in the family, especially when a history of previous generations is taken, will lead to the proper diagnosis.

Catatonic conditions are occasionally superimposed on organic syndromes. I have seen a few cases in which the patient was hemiplegic as a result of cerebral hemorrhage and totally immobilized by a superimposed catatonic condition. These cases present the most unusual combination, because the neurological symptomatology is covered by the catatonic symptomatology. Catatonic syndromes associated with organic conditions or suspected organic conditions, especially in children and adolescents, have been reported by several authors (Relfer and D'Autremont, 1971; Bemporad and Dunton, 1972). A rare syndrome that may be confused with catatonic schizophrenia is akinetic mutism, described by Cairns and associates (1941) in patients having lesions near the third ventricle. These patients cannot move or talk, but generally have other neurological symptoms and are affected by hypersomnia.

Alcoholic psychoses, especially alcoholic hallucinosis and alcoholic paranoid state, should be considered in the presence of an apparently schizophrenic syndrome in patients with history of alcoholic habits. In some psychiatric hospitals it is customary to diagnose as suffering from alcoholic paranoid state or alcoholic paranoia patients who drink excessively and who present intense jealousy and delusions of infidelity concerning the spouse. I have seen the same syndromes in many patients who abstained from alcohol completely, and therefore I am almost always reluctant to diagnose these patients as suffering from an alcoholic paranoid state.

At times, delusions, ideas of reference, and auditory hallucinations occur in patients suffering from myxedema. The condition may simulate schizophrenia. The thickened edematous skin, the puffiness of the hands and face, especially around the eyelids, the large tongue, the obesity, the occasional deafness, low basal metabolism rate, diminished iodine uptake, and hypercholesteremia lead to the diagnosis. At times it is difficult to distinguish a psychosis due to myxedema from myxedema arising in patients already schizophrenic (Easson, 1966).

In untreated pernicious anemia, all kinds of psychiatric syndromes have been reported (Bowman, 1935), but in my experience paranoid conditions are the most frequent (Ferraro, Arieti, and English, 1945). The underlying illness leads to the diagnosis. The same could be repeated in reference to pellagra.

Confused with schizophrenia are those acute toxic-infective-exhaustive conditions, which are often referred to in Europe as Meynert's amentia. In addition to a general paranoid background, they show a fluctuating impairment of consciousness varying from mild confusion to complete disorientation. If an infection underlies the condition, fever is often present. The delirium, however, may persist after the febrile period. Thinking is disconnected, and hallucinations are predominantly visual. Specific infections may produce deliriums similar to schizophrenia. I have described them in the case of cerebral malaria (Arieti, 1946).

Differential Diagnosis from Miscellaneous or Unclassifiable Conditions

Occasionally cases of Ganser syndrome are confused with cases of schizophrenia. The Ganser syndrome occurs generally, but not exclusively, in prisoners who want to escape indictment. The patients often seem to have sustained memory losses. They appear bewildered, confused, and give answers reminiscent of the metonymic distortions of schizophrenics. For instance, they may say that a cat has five legs. When they are asked to identify objects, they give the name of a related object. For instance, upon being shown a spoon, the patient may say it is a fork. The history of the indictment and the need to escape responsibility by resorting to voluntary or to unconsciously produced mental deficiency and the rapidly occurring memory loss lead to the diagnosis of Ganser syndrome (Arieti and Bemporad, 1974).

A condition which in some cases is confused with schizophrenia is Gilles de la Tourette's disease. The patient presents jerking movements of the face and other parts of the body which resemble schizophrenic grimaces and mannerisms. Some patients also present coprolalia (impulsive use of profane words) or make unnatural guttural sounds. A history dating the first symptoms back to childhood, and the absence of definite schizophrenic symptoms, establishes the diagnosis. However, I have seen cases of Gilles de la Tourette's syndrome in patients who subsequently developed a definite schizophrenic psychosis or in patients who were apparently in remission from a schizophrenic psychosis. Thus the picture is often confusing. It is possible that at least in some cases a connection exists between the two conditions. Differential characteristics from such controversial or exotic conditions as *bouffée delirante,* Capgras' syndrome, and *latah* will be discussed in Chapter 32.

Another condition which is to be differentiated from schizophrenia is the autoscopic syndrome, or Lukianowicz syndrome (Lukianowicz, 1958). The syndrome consists of the delusional experience of a double. The double is not a person from the patient's environment but the patient himself. The patient sees a person who looks exactly like himself, talks, dresses and acts as he does. Quite often this double seems exactly like a mirror image of the patient. He generally appears in gray, or black and white, like images in dreams. Many patients experience the phenomenon only in the evening, at night, or at dawn. Although occasional instances of autoscopic syndrome have been reported in schizophrenia and in depressions, the phenomenon is generally not connected with these conditions. The majority of cases occurs in patients suffering from migraine and epilepsy (Arieti and Bemporad, 1974).

Strangely enough, a condition which occasionally makes some people suspect schizophrenia is *gullibility*. On rare occasions scared parents consult psychiatrists because their youngsters profess to believe in such things as flying saucers, interplanetary communication, reincarnation, communication with ghosts, etc. The possibility that such thoughts may be delusional has to be taken into consideration. However, it will be easy to determine that the would-be patient has been influenced by some special subculture groups or by what he has read in newspapers or books, or has seen in science fiction, movies, or television.

Gullibility may be the result of disparate conditions. Among the most common are the need to belong to, or to be accepted by, a group at any cost; or a state of anxiety and insecurity which hinders critical faculties and promotes suggestibility and indoctrination. Less frequently a limited intellectual endowment is responsible for credulity. On the other hand, gullibility may even be a quality necessary for creativity. Creative people tend to keep an open mind to even hard to believe possibilities in order to let their thinking and imagination roam along new patterns. They dismiss the incredible idea only when it was definitely been proven wrong (Arieti, 1966*a*).

Two other differential diagnoses, to be made generally in relation to legal implications, are *malingering* and *temporary insanity*. Malingering is to be considered in the presence of a history of psychopathic personality, especially in people who wish to avoid military service or a jail sentence. The patient who does not develop a Ganser syndrome will have great difficulty in simulating schizophrenia. The malingerer makes a conscious effort to produce the symptoms, at the same time that he tries to portray spontaneity. But the spontaneity arouses suspicion when the total picture does not fit the recognizable diagnostic categories. Faked delusions are not part of a delusional system as the patient could not fabricate such a system rapidly enough after having committed the crime. In the psychotic the delusion fits the personal history, or the psychodynamic mechanisms; in the malingerer the delusion is often an isolated symptom. Stereotypy, bizarre behavior, is occasionally simulated. Again, the examiner must evaluate the totality of the picture. Catatonic mutism is very seldom simulated since the nonpsychotic has great difficulty in enduring mutism for a protracted period of time.

Temporary insanity, or isolated episodic psychotic dyscontrol, is a condition of more than doubtful existence. It is supposed to be manifested by irrational, often antisocial or illegal action, carried out by a person who prior to that act did not present any history of mental abnormality, and after the act revealed no psychiatric symptoms upon examination. Defense lawyers would like to believe that their defendant was temporarily insane when he committed the incriminating action. I myself have seen several patients who committed crimes during episodic exacerbations of psychosis. The so-called temporary insanity was part of an epileptic, schizophrenic, or manic-depressive condition which had not been recognized prior to the crime. After the crime there was often a period of remission. However, the whole history of the patient betrayed the presence of a subclinical or intermittent, but not "temporary," psychosis, in the sense used by lawyers.

Many psychiatrists, in diagnosing schizophrenia, avail themselves of the help of clinical psychologists. Especially projective tests like the Rorschach may provide valuable information that is not available or deducible from the manifest symptomatology. Thus the value of these psychological tests is particularly high at the beginning of treatment. Because this book is aimed predominantly at the psychiatrist, clinician, and therapist, no description is given here of any psychological test. For a valuable discussion of the application of psychodiagnostic techniques to the differential diagnosis of schizophrenia, the reader is referred to the excellent book by Weiner (1966).

II

Prognosis

The prediction of the outcome of schizophrenia when the psychiatrist has been able only to observe the manifest symptomatology has been a matter of great interest since the early contributions of Kraepelin and Bleuler. Many authors have studied the prognosis of schizophrenia from a purely statistical point of view, without any consideration for the symptomatology. Typical of this type of research is the work done by the Finnish authors Niskanen and Achté (1971), who have studied the outcome of first admissions for schizophrenic psychoses in Helsinki in 1950, 1960, and 1965. The percentage of patients who recovered or were socially recovered after a period of five years was 59 percent of the 1950 patients, 68 percent of the 1960 patients, and 64 percent of the 1965 patients. The findings also suggested that the proportion of those who were in need of hospital treatment after a period of five years decreased steadily: 22 percent of the 1950 patients, 14 percent of the 1960 patients, and 10 percent of the 1965 patients.

Most authors, however, have done a different type of research. They have tried to determine the prognosis by virtue of the characteristics of the manifest symptomatology, with the implicit understanding that the treatment to be administered later would improve the prognosis. Thus the majority of psychiatrists today do not agree with Bleuler, who stated that he or his contemporaries had "not discovered any correlation between the initial disease symptoms and the severity of the outcome of the illness" (1950, p. 261).

Typical of the group of authors who tried to predict the prognosis from the symptomatology is Vaillant (1967). He listed six criteria that indicated a good prognosis: (1) Psychotic depressive heredity. (2) Symptoms suggesting a depressive psychosis. (3) Onset within six months before the fully developed illness. (4) Presence of precipitating factors. (5) Absence of a schizoid personality. (6) Confusion or disorientation. As a rule, the recovered schizophrenic presented symptoms suggestive of an affective psychosis and often possessed a heredity positive for psychotic depression.

In the first edition of this book I stated that although no one can be absolutely sure what course a given patient will follow, a certain group of symptoms and factors tend to occur more frequently in patients who recover; on the other hand, other symptoms and factors tend to occur in patients with a poor outcome. In this second edition I can reaffirm that certain characteristics to be mentioned shortly have a prognostic significance even when they are studied merely in their manifest aspect.

The *onset* of the illness is prognostically important. The more acute the onset, the more favorable is the prognosis, especially if characterized by a state of confusion. This criterion is not absolute. Every psychiatrist has observed very acute cases that were not followed by recovery or improvement.

The *obvious occurrence of specific precipitating factors* (like loss of employment, broken engagement, childbirth) indicates a good prognosis. As we shall study in more detail in Chapter 8, the necessary occurrence or presence of these factors for the engendering of the psychosis indicates that the personality has a relatively better chance of reintegrating once these factors are removed. They also indicate that the underlying or more obscure part of the etiology was less prominent in these cases.

Conscious anxiety is an important indication of good prognosis. Its presence indicates that more severe mechanisms of the psychosis are not present or have not eliminated the presence of this emotion. By being distressing, anxiety invites the patient to continue his search and possibly to return to reality. However, if the anxiety increases in spite of the treatment, more severe mechanisms of regression may develop. For instance, the hebephrenic may become more grandiose and disconnected, the catatonic more immobile. When the paranoid is forced by his anxiety to search for an increasing number of logical defenses, he may remain ill for a long period of time or permanently.

Thus anxiety may work in two ways. But without anxiety, no improvement is possible. Of course, we should not confuse the decrease in anxiety due to improvement with the decrease in anxiety due to progression of the illness. The latter is accompanied by more and more detachment from reality, whereas the opposite occurs in the former.

The type of prepsychotic personality is prognostically important. The *stormy* type indicates a more favorable prognosis, the *schizoid* type a less favorable one (see Chapters 6 and 7). Recent studies have confirmed this statement by concluding that a good ''premorbid personality'' generally indicates good prognosis and shorter hospitalization (see, for instance, Harrow, Tucker, and Bromet, 1969).

A *general attitude of defiance or compliance* is also another important prognostic characteristic. If the patient is compliant toward therapists and nurses, the chances of his recovery are much greater than if he is defiant (Seitz, 1951). This is particularly true about the paranoid. The patient who defies the therapist, wants to demonstrate at any cost the veracity of his allegations, and is uncooperative and unwilling to submit to the suggestions of the therapist has a more guarded prognosis. He wastes his energies in the fight to retain his psychosis.

The *general affective condition* is also important. The presence of depression improves the prognosis. As we have already discussed, at times the depression is so marked that the syndrome has been diagnosed schizo-affective, or a differential diagnosis from manic-depressive psychosis has been difficult. The schizophrenic depression is not necessarily accompanied by a conscious feeling of unworthiness. The more adequate or richer the affective behavior is, the better is the prognosis.

A *state of hopelessness, not accompanied by congruous depression,* is an ominous prognostic sign.

The *content of the delusional or hallucinatory material* has important prognostic value. The more the patient projects toward others and exonerates himself, the more severe is the psychosis. If, on the other hand, he believes that he is persecuted because he is somehow guilty or responsible, the prognosis is better. The prognosis is much better if the delusions concern feelings of guilt and responsibility. But here again the diagnosis may be uncertain, wavering between schizophrenia, manic-depressive psychosis, or schizo-affective psychosis. At times, the differential characteristics and the prognosis are difficult to evaluate, as, for example, when the delusions follow a schizophrenic pattern and the depression and the feeling of guilt present a manic-depressive picture. The following example is typical of this combination.

The patient was a 32-year-old chemist, the youngest of five children. After the death of his father, which occurred when the patient was 3 years old, he was raised in an orphan asylum, where he stayed until puberty. He was a very shy, submissive person, fearful of authority, who gained some kind of security through intellectual achievements. In his youth he had been too shy to date girls; occasionally he would visit a prostitute. At the age of 30 he met a rather energetic woman who became interested in him and persuaded him to marry her. It is doubtful whether he ever loved her. He considered her physically unattractive and domineering. But still, she was the only woman who had ever paid any attention to him. Two years after the marriage, the wife became sick with a rather serious arthritic disorder, which made her appear even more unattractive to him. One day the patient was sent by his firm to a distant city on a business commission. While he was sitting in the lobby of his hotel, he was approached by a prostitute who proposed that he invite her to his room. He agreed. They had intercourse, after which he promptly dismissed her. After she left, he started to worry. She had had a funny look on her face. Maybe she was sick. Maybe she had infected him. He became so disturbed that he returned to New York City sooner than he had planned. He visited his physician to find out whether he could detect any sign of infection. The physician did not find any pathology. A few days later the patient thought he saw some peculiar spots on his penis. This time he was sure he had syphilis. He visited two or three specialists who reassured him that he had no venereal disease. A blood Wassermann was taken and was found to be negative. Two weeks later he noticed some peculiar pimples on his wife's face, and he also heard that a neighbor's child, whom he had caressed on the street a few days before, was sick in bed. He became convinced that he had infected his wife and this child with syphilis. He also noticed that the workers in his firm showed some peculiar pimples on their faces, and he was almost sure that he had spread the infection to the whole company. He was not absolutely sure of all his apprehensions, but he was "almost" sure, and he tried to rationalize his anxiety. For instance, every two weeks he would take a new blood Wassermann. Although all of them were negative, he was not sure that he was not syphilitic. He had read in a book that the Wassermann reaction is accurate only in 98 percent of the cases. After all, he might belong to that 2 percent showing inaccurate results. He was very depressed and felt extremely guilty. He connected several events with his delusions. For instance, he had read in the paper that two or three people had committed suicide. These people lived in a part of New York City that was crossed by a subway line that he used to take. He thought that maybe he had infected these people by touching them or by using the same seats. These people had contracted syphilis from him and consequently had committed suicide. He was very depressed and was so preoccupied with these thoughts that he had to stop working. He was seen by several psychiatrists who differed as to the diagnosis. Two-thirds of the group who had seen him emphasized the delusional system and favored the diagnosis of schizophrenia. One-third pointed out that the patient was very depressed, that he had strong feelings of guilt, and that the delusions were not projected, but somehow introjected, as regards, for example, his feelings of responsibility for the increase in the number of suicides. They felt the depression was congruous with the tremendous feeling of guilt and favored the diagnosis of the depressed type of manic-depressive psychosis. The patient had two or three psychotherapeutic sessions, during which the hostility for his wife came to the fore. But the awareness of this hostility increased his feelings of guilt also. Because it was not possible to arrange a prolonged psychotherapeutic treatment, the majority of physicians who examined him recommended shock treatment. After the first treatment a striking symptomatic improvement was noted. The delusions lost their strength, and after the fourth or fifth grand mal seizure, the patient was no longer delusional. This apparently excellent response to electric shock confirmed the opinions of those who had diagnosed the case as one of manic-depressive psychosis. Two years later, however, the patient manifested open symptoms again. His mother had died of a cerebral hemorrhage, and again he thought that she had died because he had infected her with syphilis. A person who worked in the same firm also had died of apoplexy, and the patient felt responsible for his death too.

I could not treat this patient, and I do not know what has become of him. Unfortunately, this case could not be explored or treated dynamically in spite of the excellent possibilities. It has been briefly reported here as an example of the fact that delusions of guilt have a better prognosis and a better response to any type of treatment, at least as far as the single attack is concerned.

There are, however, other delusions connected with guilt and responsibility that do not have a good prognostic meaning. They are seen in the hebephrenic type of schizophrenia especially. For instance, a patient felt that if he went swimming in a pool or in the ocean, he would impregnate all the women who were in the water. Therefore he did not go swimming, because he did not want to be responsible. This patient had been told by his mother that he had been responsible for all her sicknesses, which had started from the time she was pregnant with him. Her "being pregnant with him" had symbolically become his act of "impregnating mother," and it aroused feelings of guilt. He did not want to repeat his original sin. By thinking of his own original sin, however, he magnified his power; he had the power to impregnate many women, and in a psychotic way he compensated for the inferiority feeling that his mother had engendered.

Hebephrenics and catatonics at times feel that they are, or may become, responsible for all the evils of the world. In these delusions, the feeling of power is more obvious than the feeling of guilt, which may not be apparent.

If the delusions involve members of the family, such as the spouse or the parents, generally there is an arrest of the illness, or very slow regression, but the probability of final recovery, without recurrences, is not enhanced or reduced.

The *state of insight* has important prognostic value. Opinions differ on this point, mainly because the word *insight* has been given several meanings. The "psychotic insight," to be described in Chapter 22, has a negative prognostic value. When the patient feels that he fully understands what is behind the strange things that happen to him, the prognosis tends to be unfavorable.

The insight the patient may have about the symbolic meaning of his symptoms generally has a negative prognostic value. The repressive forces are all destroyed, and the patient is in immediate contact with the sources of his disturbances. Of course, an exception is the symbolic insight that is acquired through treatment, because in this case the anxiety is also progressively removed.

The insight that makes one aware of being sick is, on the other hand, a good prognostic sign. It is reminiscent of the insight that the dreamer has when he is about to wake up from a dream and realizes that what he experienced was a dream, not reality. This type of insight has a particularly good prognostic value if it occurs after a period in which it was absent.

There are also patients who are generally in a borderline condition, with occasional outbreaks of transitory psychotic symptoms. These patients are usually aware that they are sick; at times they go as far as to diagnose themselves as cases of schizophrenia. In this case, the insight does not have a good prognostic value as far as complete recovery is concerned; however, it somehow seems to indicate that the process of regression is prevented or at least slowed up.

The *ability to pretend, or to lie,* is a good prognostic sign. Delusional life is reality for a patient, not pretension. When he is questioned about his delusions, he cannot deny them or lie about their existence, even when he knows that admitting them will have an unfavorable result, such as the rejection of his demand for discharge from the hospital. He cannot lie or pretend because he cannot shift to an imaginary assumption.* The denial of delusions, which are so real to him, requires a power to abstract or to shift to a set of facts that from his point of view are unreal. At times, when he knows that admitting his truth would mean being kept in the hospital, he will try to be as evasive and defensive as possible, but he will not actually lie. When the patient is able to lie about his delusions, he is in the process of recovery. He will not have to lie for a long time, because the delusions will soon disappear.

This inability of the schizophrenic to lie should not be confused with the inability to lie that is present in certain obsessive-compulsive patients. The latter cannot lie, not because they cannot shift to an imaginary assumption, but because they feel compelled to tell the truth in order to ward off guilt and anxiety.

* Schizophrenics treated even with moderate amounts of tranquilizers often reacquire the ability to lie.

Finally, the *acceptance of one's illness, or resignation to being sick,* has an ominous prognostic meaning. This trait belongs more properly to the second or advanced stage of schizophrenia. Other prognostic criteria have been considered by Rennie (1941) in an accurate statistical analysis of one hundred schizophrenics who recovered.

PART TWO

The Psychodynamics of Schizophrenia

CHAPTER

5

First Period: Early Childhood and Family Environment

I

Introductory Remarks

The *beginning* of the manifest symptomatology of schizophrenia, described in the previous part of this book, represents also an end—the end of a nonpsychotic but special personal history that started much earlier, in some cases even at the moment the patient was born. This history has to be studied not merely as a sequence of events, but in its developmental impact and multiple interconnections. In other words, it becomes the subject of a study of psychological forces, a *psychodynamics*. I do not imply that psychological forces cease to exist once the manifest symptomatology begins. They only change channels and mechanisms as they become conveyed predominantly through psychotic symptoms. In Part Two we shall discuss the psychodynamics of the life of the patient prior to the psychosis, as well as during the initial psychotic stage.

A characteristic unique to the human race—prolonged childhood with consequent extended dependency on adults—is the basis of the psychodynamics of schizophrenia. What occurs at any subsequent age is also relevant and may bring about the decisive turns of events that trigger the psychosis. The childhood situation, however, provides preparatory factors that have a fundamental role inasmuch as they may narrow the range of choices of life directions, thwart the possibility of compensation, determine basic orientations, and facilitate abnormal sequences of events.

A psychodynamic understanding of any human being and, in our particular case, of a person who will eventually suffer from schizophrenia, requires that we study the following:

1. The world which the child meets.
2. The child's way of experiencing that world, especially in its interpersonal aspects.
3. The way the child internalizes that world and the effects of such internalization.
4. The ways by which the sequence of later experiences weaken, reinforce, distort, neutralize, expand, or restrict the effects of the early experiences.

Prolonged childhood implies a prolonged state of physical, emotional, and cognitive immaturity with which the child meets the environment, experiences it, and internalizes it. The function of internalization requires some explanation. Starting from approximately the ninth month of life the baby retains in his psyche the mental representations of the persons who are involved with him and of the events or situations that occur in his small environment. These mental representations, usually called *inner objects,* will constitute more and more his psychological life. This inner life, or inner reality, may represent, substitute, distort, enrich, or impoverish the reality of the external world. It becomes the essence of the individual.

Inner reality is the result of a constant reelaboration of past and present experiences. Its development is never completed throughout the life of man, although its greater rate of growth occurs in childhood and adolescence. It is based on the fact that perceptions, thoughts, feelings, actions, and other psychological functions do not cease to exist completely once the neuronal mechanisms that mediated their occurrence have taken place. Although they cannot be retained as they were experienced, their effects are retained as various components of the psyche.

Although this inner life, or inner self, has an enduring life of its own, it should not be considered a closed system. It has many exchanges with the environment. Psychodynamics thus involves the study of the intricate interplay and mutual dependence between interpersonal relations and inner life. In other words, it implies the study of what is interpersonal as well as intrapsychic in the individual. In this chapter and in the following ones we shall at times focus on the patient's inner life; at other times we shall focus on his environment, especially the family environment, in order to show how the two aspects of his life interrelate. This alternation may appear in some cases as a strident contrast, but it is by correlating the two aspects of the human psyche that we can reach an adequate psychodynamic understanding.

I have found it useful to divide the psychodynamic development of schizophrenia into four periods, of which only the last one can be considered psychotic.

The first period extends from birth to approximately the time when the child enters grade school. The second period covers late childhood, or that period which in Freudian literature is referred to as the latency period. The third period generally starts around the time of puberty, but it may start much later. The fourth period starts with the beginning of the psychosis.

The present chapter will deal with the different phases of the first period.

II

The First Few Months of Life

During the first six or seven months inner life is rudimentary. The psychology of the baby to a large extent can be understood in terms of simple physiological mechanisms, immediate interpersonal contacts, and what Piaget calls sensori-motor intelligence. The baby probably has a primitive kind of identity that includes his motor behavior, the awareness of his body and his contacts with the immediate external world. Although the baby is already able to experience many events inside and outside his body, the parts of the central nervous system that permit the retention of images and the recall of past experiences have not yet matured. He functions at a sensori-motor level.

Like the newborn of many species he is helpless and dependent on parental care for survival. He has certain needs, like food, sleep, rest, warmth, and contact with the body of mother, that must be satisfied. When these needs are met, a state of *satisfaction* occurs. The lack of satisfaction of these needs brings about a state of discomfort that may be designated as tension, deprivation, or a relatively simple state of anxiety similar to the one that is also experienced by subhuman animals in similar conditions.

More complicated events, however, do take place even in the life of the few-month-old baby. The contact with the mother, for instance, acquires a great significance already from birth. The nursing situation is not just a mechanical nipple-in-lips situation, or just a gratification of appetite or of a sucking need, but includes the experiencing of a primitive, presymbolic, immediate empathic tenderness of the mother. It is important to stress that although abnormalities may already exist at this age in the baby and in the relation with his mother, they are not those that are directly responsible for a subsequent adult schizophrenia. This point is emphasized because in spite of abundant evidence to the contrary (Fromm-Reichmann, 1952; Arieti, 1955; Lidz et al., 1965), some authors continue to consider the schizophrenic disorder to be a "fixation at the oral stage." Certainly some abnormal conditions occurring in the first few months of life may lead to other abnormalities that in their turn may be schizophrenogenic. The baby may be in a state of altered homeostasis, discomfort, or deprivation, but does not experience a state of conflict, either intrapsychic or interpersonal. Among the possible deprivations, we must underline the absence of a tender human being. Some authors (Spitz, 1945, 1965; Bowlby, 1951, 1960) have described severe psychopathology, like depression, in the first year of life, following separation from mother. It is doubtful that this "depression," no matter how unpleasant and disturbing, is the same syndrome as the depression of the adult. The infant cannot conceptualize such ideas as abandonment, death, irreparable loss, and hopelessness, and therefore cannot experience the feeling that leads to a depression. A relation between maternal deprivation in the first few months of life and adult schizophrenia is even more uncertain. In my many years of clinical experience I have ascertained only one case in which this relationship existed—namely, a girl who sustained probably great deprivation when the parents left for an extended vacation when she was 9 months old. This girl subsequently developed separation anxiety, school phobia, and, by the time of puberty, a very schizoid personality bordering on simple schizophrenia. Because this is the only case of this type, it is not statistically significant, even in the range of my experience. Moreover, this girl underwent this deprivation when she was 9 months old; and I am referring here only to the first 7 or 8 months of life.

However, if a child has been exposed to a depriving environment in the first few months of life, the probability is great that he will be exposed to an adverse or schizophrenogenic environment after the ninth or tenth month. The reverse, however, is not true. Many parents of schizophrenics were able to fulfill more or less adequately their parental role when the child was a baby, a completely dependent entity not yet showing signs of autonomy. The baby, as a matter of fact, may have been treated with constant and scrupulous care, and with some kind of tenderness and concern, as a pet or a doll. In these cases no serious difficulties arise until later when the child becomes an autonomous individual in his own right, with wishes and wants that are discordant from those of the parents. It is at this stage that motherhood may become defective.

A different observation made in a minority of cases is worthy of consideration. Some relatives of schizophrenics have reported that there seemed to be something wrong with the child from the very moment of birth. The baby appeared nervous, would cry all the time, had feeding problems, and so on. Later, but still in early childhood, he was a child impossible to take care of. "Even a saint could not have been able to take care of him." Again it is impossible to determine whether these characteristics of the child originated in the child or were a reaction to the anxiety or hostility of the mother. It could very well be, however, that some children deviate slightly from the normal. They are irritable, cry excessively, and have difficulties in adapting to environmental situations. Whereas the average mother is able to adjust to these deviations of the child, the mother of the future patient is not. She becomes increasingly alarmed and anxious and responds to her anxiety, not with greater care, but with poor motherhood. A vicious circle, or a two-way stream results. Most probably the majority of these so-called impossible children are children with minimal brain damage and are consequently hyperkinetic (see Clements, 1966; S. Levy, 1966; Werry, 1968). Fortunately the majority of these children outgrow their symptoms or at least ameliorate them later on. It could be, however, that a certain number of them elicit in the mother a state of anxiety and despair that in its turn may affect adversely the child, even with schizophrenogenic effects.

For the vast majority of cases of adult schizophrenia it is more important to study what happens to the child during and after the last quarter of the first year of life. Contrary to what happens in other species, the human child continues to be dependent on others; moreover, from now on he will require not only satisfaction of needs but also a feeling of *security*. We owe to Sullivan (1953*a*) the differentiation between satisfaction and security.

The capacity to experience security or to suffer from the lack of it requires a degree of psychological organization that is more complicated than that occurring in the first few months of life. The relations with the adults who take care of the child are very important in this respect. Thus, at this point we shall interrupt the study of the child, and we shall take into consideration the family of which he happens to be a member.

III
The Family Environment

The reader must be aware that the studies of the family of the schizophrenic patient were made after the patient became sick and in most cases had grown to be an adult. The assumption is made that the study of how the family is at the time of the illness, together with the past history, may give us an adequate picture of how the family environment was during the time preceding the psychosis. This is, however, only an assumption. All in all, some conclusions may be justified, but the degree of accuracy is questionable. This is the only type of inquiry that was done so far. Thus, although this chapter is devoted to the very early environment of the future patient, most of the characteristics we are going to describe pertain even more to the family of the patient as it was in subsequent periods. There will be here, therefore, some chronological irregularities in our exposition, which are due to the present status of our knowledge of this matter.

Among the experiences that psychiatrists very vividly remember about their residence training are their first encounters with members of the family of the schizophrenic. It is relatively easy for the trainee to conclude that this family is not a happy one, and that its unhappiness is not merely connected with the patient's present illness. It could be traced back to the formative years of the patient. This unhappiness, although aggravated at times by realistic situations (poverty, physical illness, disappointments of various kinds), is as a rule grounded in personality factors. The disharmonious marriage of the parents looms prominent among these factors. As we shall see later in greater detail, the marriage is unhappy not only because of the incompatibility of the parents, but also because their personal difficulties, rather than being ameliorated by compensatory mechanisms, were aggravated in the process of living together. In families of nonschizophrenics, marital unhappiness is also very common, but it is not allowed to interfere so diffusely or so deeply with the upbringing of the children. For instance, the unhappily married mother may genuinely learn to expect life fulfillment in motherhood. Although this compromise is not satisfactory, it may be of some value, especially when supported by the prevailing cultural or societal mores. It does not remove all psychological difficulties of the children, but may prevent the most serious ones.

The atmosphere of unhappiness and tension, although all pervading and pronounced in the family of schizophrenics, in many cases is not apparent to the casual observer, because an attempt is made by all concerned to conceal it not only from the external world, but also from themselves. At times it is almost totally repressed and replaced by psychological insensitivity. The psychiatrist in training learns also to recognize the anxiety-ridden parents who are motivated by a strong unconscious guilt feeling. These parents exert pressure on the physician, trying to get reassurance from him that everything possible is being done to restore the patient's health. Often the doctor wishes to alleviate this guilt feeling and tries to reassure the parents—"You should not feel responsible; schizophrenia is a mysterious disease; it can happen to everybody." But the parents are generally not reassured.

In a vague way, or in the form of a feeling that cannot be very well verbalized and therefore gives the impression of being irrational, they sense that they have played a role in their child's illness. These guilt feelings often lead parents to irrational actions. In a vain attempt to undo what they feel they have done, they may take the patient home from the hospital in spite of obvious contraindications. Consequently the activities of the family are thwarted or actually paralyzed, and care of minors at times is curtailed because of the enormous amount and unusual kind of care that a very ill person requires at home.

At other times it is obvious to the young psychiatrist that a great deal of love for the patient existed, but that this love had not been utilized by the patient because it was mixed with a great deal of anxiety.

These rather simple clinical observations made by several generations of psychiatrists have rightly been considered insufficient to evaluate the family of the patient. Thus many authors have tried to go more deeply into this matter. One group of authors has studied the family by means of the treatment of the patient himself, that is, they relied greatly on how the patient portrayed his own family. Another group of authors, starting with the pioneer work of Theodore Lidz, has studied the family of the patient independently.

The first group of authors has concluded almost unanimously that the mother is the main dynamic factor in the genesis of the child's future psychiatric condition. Some of these authors have followed Fromm-Reichmann (1948) in referring to the mother of the patient as "schizophrenogenic." They have described her as overprotective, hostile, overtly or subtly rejecting, overanxious, cold, distant, and so forth. Because of these characteristics she was unable to give herself to the child and was unfit for motherhood. Sometimes she tried, but she did not know how. John Rosen referred to her perverse sense of motherhood. In the writings of a large number of authors she was described as a malevolent creature and was portrayed in an intensely negative, judgmental way (Sullivan, 1953*a,* 1964; Rosen, 1962, 1963; Hill, 1955; Limentani, 1956; Bateson et al., 1956; Lu, 1961; Lidz, et al., 1965). Reichard and Tillman (1950*a*) quote in addition to their own research a long list of works in which this negative parenthood was illustrated.

Searles (1958) is in a small minority in finding something positive in the relationship between the schizophrenic and his mother.

As already mentioned, a second group of authors wanted to determine whether the picture of mother and father given by the patient could be confirmed by studying the family. Alanen (1958) studied a hundred mothers of schizophrenic patients and found that more than one-half of these mothers were suffering from personality disorders that were, in his opinion, more severe than psychoneurotic. Many of these mothers presented near-psychotic and schizoid traits. Alanen described an attitude that he called *the schizoid pattern of interpersonal relationship*. He wrote:

> Such an attitude is characterized especially by a tendency to domination, which does not have any understanding for the child's own needs and feelings; but often at the same time also to powerful possessiveness, which all is quite particularly likely to suppress the child's possibilities to develop into an independent person and to tie him up to an authority which is inimical to his own self. In many cases one had to assume that the root of such an attitude was an anxious, ambivalent hostility which the mother felt toward her child, and in the generation of which, in turn, the hardships the mother herself had met during her life and especially in connection with her marital conflicts, had contributed their effect.

Alanen added that it often seemed "as though the mothers had made their children experience as doubled the frustrations they themselves had experienced."

Lidz too has confirmed the patient's negative appraisal of his mother.

The father of the schizophrenic patient has also been studied by Lidz and his associates (1957*b*). Whereas previous authors had emphasized the weakness, aloofness, and ineffectiveness of the father in the paternal role, Lidz and associates describe him as insecure in his masculinity and in need of great admiration for the sake of bolstering his shaky self-esteem. Not infrequently he was found paranoid or given to paranoid-like irrational behavior and just as impervious as his wife to the feelings and needs of others.

Mostly because of the influence of the pioneer work of Ackerman (1954, 1958), the family has come to be studied as a unit, or a constellation, having an impact on the future patient that is greater than the sum of the effects of the individual members. For instance, it is not just the attitude of the mother toward the child that has to be taken into consideration, but also how the attitude of the mother affects the whole family, and how the result of this attitude toward the whole family indirectly affects the child. Vice versa, it is also important how each member of the family interacts with each other, and how, in consequence of this interaction, each one, or most of them, or all of them will act toward the individual child. In other words, we are not dealing exclusively with relatively simple one-to-one relationships. More complicated multiple interactions take place. To give a concrete example, the mother is not just the mother of little John, but is also the person who, while she is dealing with John, is affected by the father, by the other children individually, by the whole family, and by John himself. All these intricate relations are difficult to disentangle and study separately. By definition, they cannot be completely separated. Jackson (1967*b*) made the pertinent observation that families of schizophrenics are not disturbed in the usual sense attributed to this word, nor are they disorganized. On the contrary, the schizophrenic family is more highly organized than the normal family, in the sense that "such a family utilizes relatively few of the behavioral possibilities available to it." According to Jackson, the bizarre, maladaptive behavior of the family is an indication of a restriction of the behavioral repertory that does not allow variations or other rules to be followed.

Many authors have described special family constellations in schizophrenics. In the first edition of this book I have described one family constellation, which I frequently encountered in two varieties (Arieti, 1955). The first was when a domineering, nagging, and hostile mother, who gives the child no chance to assert himself, is married to a dependent, weak man, who is too weak to help the child. The father does not dare protect the child because of fear of losing his wife's sexual favors, or simply because he is not able to oppose her strong personality. By default, more than by his direct doing, he has an adverse effect on the child.

Occurring less frequently in the United States, but still frequently enough, is the second, opposite, combination: a tyrannical or extremely narcissistic father is married to a weak mother, who has solved her problems by unconditionally accepting her husband's rules. These rules do not allow her to give enough love to the child or to be considerate enough of his affective requirements. In these families, the weak parent, whether mother or father, becomes antagonistic and hostile toward the children because she (or he) displaces her (or his) anger from the spouse to the children, as the spouse is too strong to be a suitable target.

Lidz and associates (1957*a*) also described this type of family constellation and gave it the name *marital skew*. At the same time, they described what they called *marital schism* (Lidz et al., 1957*a*). They found that in this case the role of each spouse in the family cannot be well established and that no attempt is made by them to complement or to help each other. There is no possibility of getting together and no reciprocal understanding, cooperation, mutual trust, or confidence; instead, there is only rivalry, undercutting of worth, threat of separation, and enrollment of the children's support against the other. Each partner is disillusioned with the other: the husband sees the wife as a defiant and disregarding person who also fails as a mother; the wife is disappointed because she does not find in her husband the father she expected for her child. It is in this background that the family becomes split into two factions by the overt marital schism of the parents. Generally the children belong to one side of the schism or to the other and have to contend with problems of guilt because of their divided loyalty.

I have found other frequent constellations. One of them consists of a family in which each member is intensely involved with the others. Each member experiences not just a feeling of competition with the others, but an extreme sense of participation, reactivity, and sensitivity to the actions of the others, often interpreted in a negative way. In these cases the members of the family want to help each other, but because of their neurotic entanglement, anxiety, distrust, and misinterpretation, they end up by hurting one another. They remind one of some plays by Chekhov or other authors in which the limitations of the characters' personalities and their morbid involvement with one another lead gradually to disaster.

I have observed also a different type of family, which is almost the opposite, or perhaps a reaction formation, of the one described. The family can be compared to an archipelago. Each member lives in emotional isolation and communicates very little with the others, in spite of physical proximity.

Other authors have reported different patterns of abnormal interaction. For instance, according to Wolman (1966) the following situation occurs. Normally intraparental relationships are mutual, that is, they are characterized by giving and taking. The parental attitude is *vectorial,* which means giving and protecting. The child's attitude is characterized by taking. According to Wolman, in the family of the schizophrenic neither father nor mother is vectorial. The mother requests love from the child and the father assumes the role of a (1) sick, (2) prodigy, (3) rebellious, or (4) runaway child. The father competes with the child, who is forced to assume a protective hypervectorial attitude toward the parents. The child worries about his parents and is terror stricken. This emotional disturbance leads to schizophrenia, which Wolman renames *vectoriasis praecox.*

In evaluating these families in a general way, Lidz and Fleck (1964) wrote of the possibilities of something being fundamentally wrong with the capacities of the "parents to establish families capable of providing the integrative development of their offspring." They spoke more specifically of three categories of deficiency: (1) poor parental nurturance; (2) the failure of the family as a social institution; and (3) inadequate transmission of the communicative and other basic intrumental techniques of the culture. Lidz and co-authors (1958) speak also of the irrationality of the parents being transmitted directly to the patient. Some delusional or quasi-delusional conceptions of the parents are reported by these authors as accepted by the patient, without further elaboration, just as happens in *folie à deux* (see Chapter 11). As a matter of fact, Lidz speaks of *folie à famille* in the family of the schizophrenic.

An important problem that has interested authors who have studied family processes in schizophrenia is the persistence of these abnormal interaction patterns (Mishler and Waxler, 1968). An outsider is generally inclined to believe that if a pattern of living leading to undesirable results has been formed in a family, the pattern would be corrected and equilibrium restored. The opposite, however, occurs in the family of schizophrenics. The same unhealthy "homeostasis" at times lasts decades. Haley (1959) writes:

> If a family confines itself to repetitional patterns within a certain range of possible behavior, then they are confined to that range by some sort of governing process. No outside governor requires the family members to behave in their habitual patterns. . . . When people respond to one another, they govern, or establish rules, for each other's behavior. . . . Such a system tends to be error-activated. Should one family member break a family rule,

the others become activated until he either conforms to the rule again or successfully establishes a new one.

Many authors see the future schizophrenic as assuming in the family structure the role of scapegoat, or as a responsible ally of one parent. This role maintains the pathogenetic interaction patterns of the whole family. Searles (1958) and Wolman (1966) believe that the child maintains the morbid role because he loves mother and wants to give to her. He believes that without him she would be in a disastrous situation.

As I shall illustrate in various parts of this book, I believe that circular patterns are created that not only maintain the abnormal pathogenetic family structure, but also make it worse and more rigid.

IV

Conclusions about the Family of the Schizophrenic

I shall offer now my own evaluations and conclusions about the above findings. Some readers will recognize that in some aspects my points of view have changed since the first edition of this book was published.

1. The findings described in the previous section indicate that turbulent conflict, tension, anxiety, hostility, or detachment generally existed in the family of the patient since his formative years. However, we must be aware that these findings cannot be subjected to statistical investigation. It is often an enormous task to evaluate qualitatively or quantitatively the psychological disturbance existing in a family. One must keep in mind that a minority of authors (for instance, Waring and Ricks, 1965) have found the above described specific family constellations less frequently among schizophrenics than in control studies.

2. It is common knowledge that similar family disturbances exist even in families in which there has not been a single case of schizophrenia within the two or three generations that could be investigated.

3. It is not possible to prove that the adult schizophrenics studied in family research were potentially normal children whose lives were warped only by environmental influences.

4. The only point of agreement of most authors who have studied schizophrenic patients psychodynamically is that *in every case of schizophrenia studied serious family disturbance was found*. Unless biases have grossly distorted the judgment of the investigators, we must believe that serious disturbance existed.

5. This conclusion is important. It indicates that although serious family disturbance is not *sufficient* to explain schizophrenia, it is *presumably a necessary*

condition. To have differentiated a necessary, though not sufficient, causative factor is important enough to make this factor the object of our full consideration.*

6. I have revised the concept of the so-called schizophrenogenic mother. We have seen that the mother of the schizophrenic has been described as a malevolent creature, deprived of maternal feeling or having a perverse sense of motherhood. She has been called a monstrous human being. At times it is indeed difficult not to make these negative appraisals, because some of these mothers seem to fit that image. Quite often, however, an unwarranted generalization is made. The mother of the patient is not a monster or an evildoer, but a person who has been overcome by the difficulties of living. These difficulties have become enormous partly because of her unhappy marriage, but most of all because of her neurosis and the neurotic defenses that she built up in interacting with her children. Moreover, we must take into account the fact that the studies of these mothers were made immediately preceding the era of women's liberation. In other words, it was a period during which the woman had to contend fully, but most of the time tacitly, with her newly emerged need to assert equality. She could not accept submission any longer, and yet she strove to fulfill her traditional role. These are not just social changes; they are factors that enter into the intimacy of family life and complicate the parental roles of both mothers and fathers.

We must add that this was the time when the so-called nuclear family, an invention of urban industrial society, came into its full existence. The nuclear family consists of a small number of people who live in little space, compete for room, for material and emotional possession, and are ridden by hostility and rivalry. The home is often deprived of educational, vocational, and religious values. The nuclear family is frequently destructive not only for the children but for the parents too.

In the last fifteen years I have compiled some statistics that differ from what other authors have reported and what I myself described in the first edition of this book. Although personal biases cannot be excluded, and the overall figures are too small to be definitive, I have reached the tentative conclusion that only 25 percent of the mothers of schizophrenics fit the image of the schizophrenogenic mother.† Why then have so many different authors generalized to all cases what is found in a minority of apparently typical cases?

Of course there is the possibility that I have not recognized what was not apparent. However, it is hard for me to believe that later in my psychiatric work I have grown insensitive or less aware of the intangible and subtle dynamics. Re-

* Some readers may wonder why we call this factor *presumably* necessary and not just necessary. The reason is two-fold: (1) statistical evidence is very suggestive of causal connections, but the number of cases seriously studied is a minority of all cases of schizophrenia, and (2) because we cannot give a statistically convincing empirical proof, we would like to give a logical explanation of how the psychodynamic conflict leads to the disorder. Again this explanation, given in Chapters 7 and 8, is convincing and presumably correct, but it still contains gaps in strict logic that leave it open to criticism.

† I actually would be more inclined to say that only 20 percent correspond to this image, but I have included doubtful cases and conceded a maximum of 25 percent.

peated observations have led me to different tentative conclusions. As we shall see in greater detail in Chapter 38, schizophrenics who are at a relatively advanced stage of psychodynamically oriented psychotherapy often describe their parents, especially the mother, in negative terms. Therapists, including myself, have believed what the patients told us. Inasmuch as a considerable percentage of mothers have proved to be just as they were described by the patient, we have considered this percentage as typical and have made an unwarranted generalization that includes all the mothers of schizophrenics. The therapists of schizophrenic patients have made a mistake reminiscent of the one made by Freud when he came to believe that neurotic patients had been assaulted sexually by their parents. Later Freud realized that what he had believed as true was, in by far the majority of cases, only the product of the fantasy of the patient. The comparison is not exactly similar, because in possibly 25 percent of the cases the mothers of schizophrenic patients have really been nonmaternal, and we do not know what percentage of mothers of nonschizophrenics have been nonmaternal.

If this conclusion is correct, we must inquire why many patients have transformed the image of the mother or of both parents into one that is much worse than the real one. As we shall see later in the sixth section of this chapter, the answer to this problem will be provided by the intrapsychic study of the patient, especially in his early childhood.

V

Early Development

In order to understand the abnormalities in the development of the future schizophrenic, it is important to present a brief account of some developmental aspects in normal early childhood.*

Toward the end of the second section of this chapter we saw that in order to continue to grow normally after the first nine–twelve months, the human being needs, in addition to a state of satisfaction, a state of security. Before the others acquire "a significant" or symbolic importance, the life of the child is governed almost entirely by simple psychological mechanisms.

Things are taken for granted by the infant; they are expected to occur, as they have occurred before. After a certain stimulus (hunger, for instance) a subsequent act (the appearance of the mother's breast) is expected. Later the child comes to feel that all things in life are due to others or depend on others. It is up to mother to give him the breast, to keep him on her lap, to fondle him. The child learns to see everything in a teleologic way—everything depends on the will or actions of others. But together with the feeling that everything depends on others, there is also the feeling that people will do these wonderful things. In other words, the

* For the preparation of this section, I had to draw liberally from previous writings (Arieti, 1957*a*, 1965*c*, 1967, 1971*a*).

child expects these wonderful things to happen; he trusts adults. At first, of course, these feelings of the child are vague and indefinite. Because the child is deprived of the use of abstract words to describe these phenomena, his expression of these feelings remains at a primitive level. We may describe them as diffuse feelings, postural attitudes, physiological preparation for what is expected, nonverbal symbolism, and so forth. Security does not consist only of removal of unpleasant emotions or removal of uncertainty, but also of pleasant anticipation, a feeling of well-being, a trust in people and in things to come. Year-old children experience security in their contacts with the mother if she is not anxious, hostile, or prevented by other causes from mothering the child.

This feeling of security, at least in its early stages, corresponds to what Buber (1953), Erikson (1953), and Arieti (1957*b*) have in different contexts called trust or basic trust. Basic trust or security is a feeling that is elicited in proximity to some other human beings. Although occurring in connection with various interpersonal relations, it is experienced intrapsychically. As we shall see later, security starts to be fully experienced later in childhood, when higher cognitive processes permit reflected appraisal and the building of self-esteem. The need for security will remain constant throughout the life of the individual, although it will assume different aspects in different ages.

In a subsequent phase the child also expects approval from others. That is, the child expects the significant adults to expect something of him; the child *trusts* that the adults will *trust* him. In other words, there is a reciprocal trust that things are going to be well, that the child will be capable of growing up to be a healthy and mature man or woman. The child perceives this faith of the mother and accepts it, just as he used to accept the primitive responses to the usual stimuli. He finally assimilates the trust of the significant adults, and he *trusts* himself (Arieti, 1957*b*). Thus, things will no longer depend exclusively on others, but also on himself.

This feeling of trust in oneself and this favorable expectancy, which at first is limited to the immediate future, becomes extended to the immediate contingencies of life and then expands into a feeling of favorable anticipation as far as a more or less distant future is concerned. A basic optimism, founded on basic trust, is thus originated. Security then will consist of all these feelings. If we consider this feeling of security or basic trust in its more social or interpersonal aspect, we may state that its interpersonal counterpart is what can be called a state of *communion.**

This atmosphere, first of satisfaction, then of security and communion (at least with the mother), facilitates the introjection in the child of the symbolic world of the others. It is this introjection that actually permits the emergence and the growth of the self, especially the introjection of the attitudes, feelings, verbal symbolisms, and so forth, emanating from the mother.

* Precursors of communion existed also in the sensori-motor period, and are generally called symbiosis or parasitism. These terms indicate one aspect of the contact or the extreme dependency. Communion implies the possibility of sharing the joy of being together.

Using Buber's useful terminology and conceptions, we may say that an I-Thou relationship exists. Psychologically, this means that without others and trust in them there would be no I, no development of the self.*

It is toward the end of the first year of life, generally from the ninth month, that through internalization the child starts to build an inner life, or psychic reality, which is a counterpart to the external reality with which he is involved. Internalization occurs first through cognitive mechanisms belonging predominantly to what Freud called the primary process, and later more and more to what Freud called the secondary process. Freud originally described the primary process as it occurs in dreams. He called this process "primary" because according to him it occurs earlier in child development, and not because it is more important than the secondary. The secondary process develops later and employs the usual normal cognitive processes of the adult awake mind. Whenever complex recognition, differentiation, deduction, and induction are used, the secondary process is necessary.

Both primary and secondary processes use symbolic cognitive mechanisms. Contrary to more primitive nonsymbolic methods, like simple learning directly associated with perceptions or with what is immediately given, the primary and secondary processes open up a symbolic world to the child, that is, the representation of what is absent, potentially absent, or imagined.

The child continues to participate in the world through nonsymbolic ways, like simple or direct learning derived from perceptions, conditioned reflexes, and so forth. Soon, however, he develops symbolic mechanisms, the most primitive of which constitute what I have called primary cognition. They are images, endocepts, and paleologic thinking.† Except in pathological conditions, these primitive mechanisms are replaced and overpowered by more mature secondary processes. They occur also in normal adult life, but it is difficult to find pure forms of them in adults or even in children if they are normal.

The image is a memory trace that assumes the form of a representation. It is almost an internal reproduction of a perception that does not require the corresponding external stimulus in order to be evoked. The image is indeed one of the earliest and most important foundations of human symbolism, if by symbolism we mean something that stands for something else that is not present. From now on cognition will rely also on what is absent and inferred. For instance, the child closes his eyes and visualizes his mother. She may not be present, but her image is with the child; it stands for her. The image is obviously based on the memory traces of previous perceptions of the mother. The mother then acquires a psychic reality not tied to her physical presence.

Image formation introduces the child into that inner world which I have called fantasmic (Arieti, 1967). The image becomes a substitute for the external

* Buber's I-Thou expression corresponds approximately to Sullivan's me-you expression.

† For a more elaborate analysis of images, endocepts, and paleologic thinking, see *The Intrapsychic Self* (Arieti, 1967).

object; it is a primitive inner object. In a considerable number of children the image is eidetic; that is, particularly vivid, almost indistinguishable from perception. The predominant use of images, especially eidetic ones, may cause in young children what Baldwin (1929) called *adualism,* or at least difficult *dualism:* that is, an inability to distinguish between the two realities, that of the mind and that of the external world. This condition may correspond to what orthodox analysts, following Federn (1952), call lack of ego boundary.

Another important aspect that very young children may retain from the sensorimotor level of organization is the lack of appreciation of causality. The child cannot ask himself why certain things occur. He either naïvely accepts them as just happenings, or he expects things to take place in a certain succession, as a sort of habit rather than as a result of causality or of an order of nature. The only phenomenon remotely connected with causation is a subjective or experiential feeling of expectancy, a feeling that is derived from the observation of repeated temporal associations.

The endocept is a mental construct representative of a level intermediary between the one characterized by the prevalence of images and the one characterized by language. It derives from memory traces, images, and motor engrams. Its organization results in a construct that does not tend to reproduce reality and that remains at a nonrepresentational, preverbal, and preaction level. It is just a disposition to feel, to act, to think and is accompanied by a vague awareness and at times undefinable, diffuse emotions.

Paleologic thinking occurs for a short period of time early in childhood, from the age 1 to age 3. It is a way of thinking that seems illogical according to adult standards or normal logic. As we shall see in greater detail later, it is based on a confusion between similarities and identities. A salient part or characteristic that two persons or objects have in common is enough to make them appear identical, or belonging to the same category or class—formation of primary classes (Arieti, 1963*b*). All pictures of men are ''daddies'' because they look like daddy.

Normal maturation controls the inhibition of these primitive forms and enhances the replacement by mature or secondary forms of cognition. That young children have greater difficulty in dealing with objects similar to those already known to them, than they do with objects completely unknown, has been recently confirmed by Kagan (1972), who formulated the discrepancy principle. As a result of the infant's encounters with the environment he acquires mental representations of events, called schemata. Events that are moderately different from an infant's schema (or discrepant events) elicit longer spans of attention than either totally familiar events or totally novel events. For instance, in one experiment the child was shown a two-inch orange cube on six separate occasions. The infant was shown either a smaller orange cube (a discrepant event) or a yellow rippled cylinder (a novel event). Kagan reports that infants between 7 and 12 months old became excited by the discrepant small cube, whereas they were not disturbed by the appearance of the novel rippled cylinder. Discrepant objects or events are similar. A tendency exists in children to overcome the problem of how to deal with similar events by reacting to them as if they were identical (paleologic structure). Normal maturation regulates the inhibition of all these primitive forms of cognition as well as their replacement by mature or secondary forms.

Young children soon become aware of causality and repeatedly ask "why." At first causality is teleological: events are believed to occur "because" they are willed or wanted by people or by anthropomorphized forces.

We should not conclude that young children *must* think paleologically; they only have a propensity to do so. Unless abnormal conditions (either environmental or biological) make difficult either the process of maturation or the process of becoming part of the adult world, this propensity is almost entirely and very rapidly overpowered by the adoption of secondary process cognition. Moreover, children may still deal more or less realistically with the environment when they follow the more primitive type of nonsymbolic learning that permits a simple and immediate understanding. In secondary process cognition the individual learns to distinguish essential from nonessential characteristics and develops more and more the tendency to put into categories subjects that are indissolubly tied to essential characteristics.

The randomness of experience in early childhood is more and more superseded by the gradual organization of inner constructs. These constructs continuously exchange some of their components and increase in differentiation, rank, and order. A large number of them, however, retain the enduring mark of their individuality. Although in early childhood they consist of the cognitive forms that we have described (images, endocepts, paleologic thoughts) and of their accompanying feelings, they become more and more complicated and difficult to analyze. Some of them have powerful effects and have an intense life of their own, even if at this stage of our knowledge we cannot give them an anatomical location or a neurophysiological interpretation. They may be considered the very inhabitants of inner reality. The two most important ones in the preschool age, and the only two that we shall describe, are the image of mother and the self-image.

Before proceeding we must warn the reader about a confusion that may result from the two different meanings given to the word *image* in psychological and psychiatric literature. The word *image* is often used, as we did earlier in this section, in reference to the simple sensorial images that tend to reproduce perceptions. With this term we shall now refer also to those much higher psychological constructs or inner objects that represent whatever is connected with a person. For instance, in this more elaborate sense, the image of the mother would mean a conglomeration of what the child feels and knows about her; even more specifically, the result of the *structure* that he gives to what he feels and knows about her. Although each child creates structures and patterns in a selective, individual way, certain similarities occur in the structures of all children because of the similarities of the biological endowment and of the interpersonal situations.

In normal circumstances the mother as an inner object will consist of a group of agreeable images: as the giver, the helper, the assuager of hunger, thirst, cold, loneliness, immobility, and any other discomfort. She becomes the prototype of the good inner object. At the same time she will become the representative of the

"Thou," the other human being without which, to follow again Buber, there would be no "I." There is no I without Thou. The mother becomes the most important Thou, but also the prototype of any other Thou, any other fellow human being who, in his essential human qualities, will be modeled after her. If a state of communion is established, the I and the Thou do not lose their individuality in the act of being together. Their being together adds, does not subtract. The negative characteristics of mother play a secondary role that loses significance in the context of the good inner object, the good Thou.

Much more difficult to describe in early childhood is the self-image. This construct will be easier to understand in later developmental stages. At the sensorimotor level, the primordial self probably consisted of a bundle of relatively simple relations between feelings, kinesthetic sensations, perceptions, motor activity, and a partial integration of these elements. At the image level the child who is raised in normal circumstances learns to experience himself not exclusively as a cluster of feelings and of self-initiated movements, but also as a body image and as an entity having many kinds of relations with other images, especially those of the parents. Inasmuch as the child cannot see his own face, his own visual image will be faceless—as, indeed, he will tend to see himself in dreams throughout his life. He wishes, however, to be in appearance, gestures, and actions like people toward whom he has a pleasant emotional attitude or by whom he feels protected and gratified. The wish tends to be experienced as reality, and he believes that he is or is about to become like the others or as powerful as the others. Because of the reality value of wishes and images, there results what psychoanalytic literature has called a feeling of omnipotence.

In the subsequent endoceptual and paleologic stages the self-image will acquire many more elements. However, these elements will continue to be integrated so that the self-image will continue to be experienced as a unity, as an entity separate from the rest of the world. The psychological life of the child will no longer be limited to acting and experiencing, but will include also observing oneself and having an image of oneself.

In a large part of psychological and psychiatric literature a confusion exists between the concepts of self and of self-image. In this section we shall focus on the study of the self-image. Also in a large part of psychiatric literature the self and the consequent self-image are conceived predominantly in a passive role. For instance, Sullivan has indicated that the preconceptual and first conceptual appraisals of the self are determined by the relationships of the child with the significant adults. Sullivan (1953*a*) considers the self (and self-image) as consisting of reflected appraisals from the significant adults: the child would see himself and feel about himself as his parents, especially the mother, see him and feel about him. What is not taken into account in this conception is the fact that the self is not merely a passive reflection. The mechanism of the formation of the self cannot be compared to the function of a mirror. If we want to use the metaphor of the mirror, we must specify that we mean an activated mirror that adds to the reflected images its own distortions, especially those distortions that at an early age are caused by primary cognition. The child does not merely respond to the environment. He integrates experiences and transforms them into inner reality, into increasingly complicated structures. He is indeed in a position to participate in the formation of his own self. His own self acquires a structure.

The self-image may be conceived as consisting of three parts: *body image, self-identity,* and *self-esteem*. The body image consists of the internalized visual, kinesthetic, tactile, and other sensations and perceptions connected with one's body. The body and also the actions of the body on the not-self are discovered by degrees. The body image eventually will be connected with belonging to one of the two genders. Self-identity, called also personal identity or ego-identity, depends on the discovery of oneself not only as continuous and as same, but also as having certain definite characteristics and a role in the group to which the person belongs.

Self-esteem depends on the child's ability to do what he has the urge to do, but is also connected with his capacity to avoid doing what the parents do not want him to do. Later it is connected also with his capacity to do what his parents want him to do. His behavior is explicitly or by implication classified by the adults as bad or good. Self-identity and self-esteem seem thus to be related, as Sullivan has emphasized, to the evaluation that the child receives from the significant adults. However, again, this self-evaluation is not an exact reproduction of the one made by the adults. The child is impressed more by the appraisals that hurt him the most or please him the most. These partial salient appraisals and the ways they are integrated with other elements will make up the self-image.

Before concluding this section I must mention that a large part of the psychiatric literature of psychodynamic orientation has made the error of seeing not only the child but also the adolescent and young adult as completely molded by circumstances, a passive agent at the mercy of others, either parents or society. Although these environmental forces are of crucial importance, we should not forget other factors. The person, even at a young age, is not a *tabula rasa,* or a sponge which absorbs whatever is given him, without he himself adding an element of individuality and creativity to what he receives and thus contributing to his own transformation. As we shall see in several parts of this book, the individual will never reproduce the experiences of childhood as an historian would; he always transforms and recreates, in favorable or unfavorable ways. Some of the authors who study the effect of the family and of the environment on the future patient do so in a crude way, as if they were describing a rapport of simple linear causality. It would be like studying the intake of food but not the functions of the digestive system and the metabolic processes of the body. The following sections of this chapter, as well as Chapters 6, 7, and 8, will show how much more complex the unfolding of psychopathology can be.

VI
Psychodynamic Development in the Early Childhood of Schizophrenics

The child who is being raised in the family environment that we have described in the third section of this chapter often tends to participate as little as possible in the unpleasant reality. He tends to be by himself, and thus aloofness favors an overdevelopment of fantasy or life of images. On account of the negative characteristics of the environment, few are the images that have pleasant connections and that induce the child to search the corresponding external objects. The result is that inner life in these children is mainly disagreeable at this level of development. Images become associated with others and spread an unpleasant affective tonality to all inner objects.

We may state that in these children an unbalance exists between external and internal psychological processes. The child escapes from the external life and lives preponderantly in his inner life, but the inner life is not pleasant either. A certain number of children perhaps succeed in escaping this dilemma, and eventually in escaping psychosis, too, by reverting to the antecedent sensorimotor level of development. They become hyperkinetic. They indulge in actions, even if not very coordinated or goal-directed, rather than in inner life. For reasons that still remain to be determined, only a minority of children can avail themselves of this defense. Moreover, it could be, as we have already mentioned, that these hyperkinetic children had undergone minimal brain damage at birth and that the psychological factors only accentuated the pathology.

The most important inner object at this age is the image of the mother or of the mother-substitute. The inner object of the mother is not a photographic representation of the real mother, but a transformation of it in accordance with primary process cognition. We have seen that in normal circumstances, or even when the disturbance was only of moderate intensity, the child tends to build a positive or benevolent image of the mother. The future schizophrenic, however, does not build this benevolent maternal image in early childhood. He finds himself having to relate to a mother who, because of her perfectionism, excessive anxiety, or hostility, exposes him to overwhelming scolding, criticism, and nagging. At other times a detached attitude makes the mother appear remote, inaccessible, ungiving, perhaps inimical. Even though the mother may have positive characteristics and may even love the child and try her best, the future patient becomes particularly sensitized to one or all of four fundamental negative characteristics: anxiety, hostility, detachment, unpredictability. The child becomes particularly aware of these negative characteristics because they are the parts of mother that hurt and to which he responds deeply. He ignores the others. His use of primary process cognition makes possible and perpetuates this partial awareness, this original part-object relationship, if we use Klein's terminology. The patient who responds mainly to the negative parts of mother will make a whole image of mother out of these negative parts, and the resulting whole will be a monstrous transformation of mother.

Thus the image of mother as an inner structure is radically different from that built by the child raised in normal circumstances. Later this negative image may attract other negative aspects of the other members of the family or of the family constellation as a whole, so that the mother image will be intensified in her negative aspect. Mother becomes the malevolent mother of the psychiatric literature, and her image becomes the malevolent image: an inner structure that, in a latent or unconscious way, may persist for the lifetime of the patient.

If, at this time, the child could possess the vocabulary of the adult, he would call the mother barbarous, bitter, bloodthirsty, brutal, callous, cold-blooded, cruel, demonic, devilish, diabolical, envious, evil-minded, faithless, false, ferocious, hardhearted, harsh, hateful, hellish, ill-disposed, ill-natured, implacable, infernal, inhuman, maleficent, malicious, malignant, maligning, merciless, relentless, revengeful, ruthless, satanic, sinister, stony, unfeeling, unkind, and so forth. These names, which I put in alphabetical order, actually have been used by several adult patients at a certain stage of psychotherapy to describe their parents, generally the mother. The mother image, as the representative of the other—that is, of any other human being and of the interpersonal world—becomes a negative Thou. A normal I-Thou relationship, in Buber's sense, cannot exist. The child will have difficulty in accepting the others, whom he models after the mother. The Thou is too threatening and is a carrier of too much anxiety. This is the beginning of the schizophrenic cleavage, this never complete acceptance and integration of the Thou, of that part of the self that originates from others. Unless deprived of its emotional import or potentiality, this Thou tends to remain unintegrated or to become dissociated, like a foregin body that is easily externalized later in life in forms of projections and hallucinations.

This vision of mother is somewhat understood by the mother, who responds to the child with more anxiety. The mother expresses her anxiety in the form of hostility toward the child, who, in his turn, will be even more adversely affected. He will respond with behavior that will be more objectionable to the parent. Furthermore, the mother most of the time feels guilty for her hostility, and this guilt feeling increases her anxiety. A circular process of ominous proportions originates, which produces intense distortions and maladaptations.

In the case of girls, a typically Freudian Oedipal situation may facilitate the development of the bad image of the mother. A rivalry with the mother for father's love may help the future patient to see mother in a bad light. In the cases in which the malevolent image of mother is formed, two tendencies may develop. The first is an attempt to repress from consciousness the reality of the mother-patient relation, but, as we shall see shortly, this task cannot be easily achieved. The second tendency is to displace or project to some parts of the external world this type of relation.

Rosen (1962, 1963) uses the concept of "early maternal environment" to explain the whole psychodynamics of the schizophrenic psychosis and, later, the characteristics of the psychotic symptomatology. For Rosen, whatever impinges upon the child is experienced as related to mother. Whatever has to do with mother, according to Rosen, gives special shape to the appreciation of the world.

Rosen seems to believe in the reality of the intense perverse motherhood of the patient's mother. He does not seem to be aware of the transformation and intensification of her negative traits that we have described in this section. In other words, Rosen accepts the experiential mother as the real mother, just as the patient does.* When patients in psychoanalytically oriented therapy lose the overt paranoid symptomatology and discuss at length their mother, they tend to reexperience her as they did during the first psychodynamic period studied in this chapter; and many therapists have accepted their patients' version of facts.

In the majority of cases the inner object of the father consists also of negative, although less intense, characteristics. The future schizophrenic feels that both parents, in different ways or in similar ways, have failed him. In a minority of cases the parental roles are inversed, and what we have described in reference to the maternal image pertains to the paternal and vice versa. At this stage of our knowledge we cannot positively state why future schizophrenics develop this negative, malevolent image of the mother. We have seen that in only approximately 25 percent of the cases does this inner image correspond to the real mother. Why are 75 percent of schizophrenics transforming the image into a much worse one? We can postulate only hypotheses. Further studies are necessary. Time factors and cyclical recurrences have to be considered. For instance, each child has to be disapproved and criticized at times, but the good mother will permit the child to recuperate between one punishment or criticism and another and will not cause too strong or too frequent psychological unpleasure. No matter how critical, the average mother will not inflict on the child an inner feeling of worthlessness. Similarly, the average mother in some cases may not be able to prevent herself from preferring children other than the patient, or may not be able to abstain from making promises she will never keep. Nevertheless, she is able to give to the child the feeling that he too counts and is never forgotten. Myriads of intangible little factors are already operating early in life, and the scientifically minded researcher who would like to calculate the algebraic sum of them and determine whether the result is positive or negative is doomed to be frustrated.

It could also be that because of biological predispostion to be taken into consideration later in this chapter and also in Part Six of this book, the future schizophrenic experiences much more intensely a phenomenon that occurs in every living animal organism. Inasmuch as painful characteristics or negative parts of complex stimuli generally hinder adaptation, they are more dangerous from the point of view of survival; thus evolution has favored a stronger response to them. We react more vigorously to pain than to pleasure, and to sorrow more than to joy. This stronger response to the negative may involve also the early interpersonal relations, especially in the future schizophrenic.

The difficulties in accepting and integrating the Thou are manifested by the reluctance of children raised in a disturbed environment to acquire the language and ways of the surrounding adults and by the emergence of autistic ways and

* Lidz (1969) is not less definite than Rosen in characterizing the mother of the schizophrenic. Lidz speaks of the "engulfing parent, who arouses homicidal impulses or provokes incestuous fears."

expressions such as neologisms. Autistic tendencies exist even in normal children to a minimum degree, but they are more pronounced in pathological conditions, generally when the child is afraid of the first interpersonal relations. Unless the child develops child schizophrenia, these autistic tendencies are outgrown, and the individual acquires the use of verbal symbols learned from others. However, a propensity to lose the symbols of the others and to return to one's private autistic ways will persist.

We must take into consideration now the other important inner object—the self-image. The future patient, raised in the circumstances that we have described in the third section of this chapter, tends to see himself, not in the way he appears to others or as the parents have appraised him, but in a much worse condition. We can repeat here what we have said about the mother image. The child does not respond equally to all appraisals and roles attributed to him. Those elements that hurt him more stand out as salient elements and are integrated disproportionately. The self-image thus, although related to the external appraisals, is not a reproduction of them, but a caricature of them. The grotesque representation of the self that future patients already form at this early age would stupefy their parents if they were aware of it. According to my own observations, it would stupefy approximately 80 percent of them, who never consciously or unconsciously wanted to inflict it on the children. It may remain as an inner structure, which, in a latent or unconscious way, may persist for the lifetime of the patient.

The body image does not generally correspond to the actual physical appearance. The child may perceive himself as little, feeble, helpless, and distorted. As many authors have described, quite often the preschizophrenic child has also some indecision as to what his sex is going to be.

Some uncertainty about sexual life exists in normal children, too, even in children older than those studied in this chapter. This frequent uncertainty has various causes. First of all, our cultural mores make difficult any frank conversation about sex between parents and children. Consequently many children who have no access to other sources of information will retain a distorted or fragmentary knowledge of sexual life. Secondly, it is difficult to explain "the facts of life" in a simple language that young children would understand. Thirdly, the parents feel with some justification that it is difficult to talk about sexual matters without arousing some feelings that cannot be satisfied. In children who tend to become schizophrenic in adult life, the uncertainty about sexuality is of a different nature. It concerns the sex and gender identity. Some of these children do not know what their sex is going to be. Although they know that they are boys or girls, they are not sure that they will maintain their sex throughout their lives. Boys may lose a penis; girls may grow one. Although even normal children or children who later develop less serious psychiatric conditions occasionally have these thoughts, in the preschizophrenic they assume the form of serious and disturbing doubts. In many cases the doubts are related to the fact that children somehow connect a sense of hostility coming from others with their belonging to a given sex. If they were girls instead of boys, or boys instead of girls, they think their parents would be more pleased with them. If the most disturbing parent is of the opposite sex, the child would like to be of the same sex as this parent, so that he could resist him or her better.

In my opinion, the most common cause of sexual or gender uncertainty is the fact that the child who feels rejected by both parents tends also to reject both parents and therefore has difficulties in identifying with either one of them. I have not found fear of castration to be an important or frequent cause of the anxiety that leads to schizophrenia. Even the most orthodox Freudian analysts have found that the early psychic traumata in cases of schizophrenia are not related to the Oedipus complex. However, in families or cultural environments where sex is strongly expressed or repressed, the Oedipal situation may in certain cases increase the already existing anxiety and make the occurrence of schizophrenia more probable. The child attributes his sexual desires to his being bad.

A combination that I have found in some preschizophrenic girls is the following. Since early childhood, the girl has felt rejected by the mother, who, in rejecting her, rejected herself. The same mother had a different attitude toward "her boys." Later, the girl was afraid of closeness to the father because of her incestuous strivings. She rejected the father or managed to be rejected by the father in order to escape her sexual desires. In this situation, too, the preexisting relation with the mother is the most important factor, and has sensitized the girl to such a degree that she is not able to cope with her incestuous feelings.

Self-identity and self-esteem in the age period that we are considering are difficult to study. Future schizophrenics at this age do not see themselves as occupying a definite role within the family. They perceive themselves as being unliked and unwanted. Some of these children have a definite feeling of being bad, but others are not even sure of being bad, because they may change and improve. Paradoxically, they would feel less insecure if they could see themselves consistently bad, without any uncertainty about their role or image.

Guilt and feelings of worthlessness may already be very pronounced in the preschool age. They are generally attributed to parental authority, and in classic psychoanalysis are considered expressions of a harsh, tyrannical superego. The following mechanism often occurs. The child nourished some hostility for the parent, but he could not accept this hostility, and he projected it to the parent. Thus the parent was endowed not only with his own hostility, but also with the child's hostility and appeared doubly harsh and punitive. By introjecting this primitive attitude the child developed a strong sense of guilt and increased the "badness" of his own image.

Even normal children occasionally have the feeling that adults know their thoughts or steal their thoughts (Erikson, 1940; Kasanin, 1945; Piaget, 1948). In the preschizophrenic child this impression is enhanced by the fear that the parents may know the feelings of hostility he harbors for them and by the anticipation of consequent punishment. Other aspects of cognitive immaturity, which are easily outgrown in normal children raised in normal circumstances, complicate the picture. Adualism, or inability to distinguish inner from external reality, is retained longer than usual. Inasmuch as life of images in these children is predominantly unpleasant, the result is a negative appraisal of the world. Whereas the normally raised child learns to take things for granted and acquires fundamental optimism and basic trust, children described in this section live in a state of ominous expectancy. They will experience what Laing (1960) has called ontological insecurity. Later these children will be more and more under the impression that whatever occurs is brought about by the will of those unpleasant clusters of images that represent the parents, especially the mother.

VII

The Building of Early Defenses

The child that we have described is in a very distressful situation. Parents are experienced as grotesque inner images or are paleologically transformed into terrifying fantasy figures. The self is also seen as a deformed, grotesque, worthless creature, or as a presumably bad person.

What we have just expressed is a translation into adult language of what a child age 2, 3, or 4 experiences. Actually he does not have the vocabulary necessary for expressing these feelings and emerging ideas. He often mediates these experiences through endocepts (or preverbal structures). This possibility is beneficial because endocepts are not representations and are not generally acutely traumatic. However, the child must resort to other defenses. The inner objects are very painful, and he cannot bear them. If these inner constructs were allowed to become connected with an increasing number of ramifications and implications, they would increase their potentiality and would devastate the psychological life of the child. This is probably what happens in childhood schizophrenia (see Chapter 44). One of the major defenses consists in separating from consciousness (or dissociating) the emotional impact of these constructs. A massive repression ensues. In the majority of cases the child who has at first to contend with the image of the malevolent mother succeeds in repressing it from consciousness. At a conscious level he succeeds in transforming the malevolent Thou into a *distressing* Thou. The Thou is still distressing, but it has lost the power to demolish the patient to an enormous degree.

In order to understand better what occurs in the transformation of the maternal image in the preschizophrenic, we must stress that different transformations occur in cases where less serious pathology is involved. In conditions that lead to psychoneuroses, or character disorders, the child who suffers on account of his relations with the rejecting parent, generally the mother, tries desperately to preserve a good image of the parent, and he often succeeds, at times to a very pronounced degree. He wants to feel that the parent is good.* If mother is punitive and anxiety arousing, it is not because she is bad but because he, the child, is bad—mother is right in being harsh and strict with him and showing how bad he

* The tendency to preserve the "lovableness" of mother and the consequences of such tendency have been considered by Suttie (1952) in a different frame of reference.

is. The child who is raised in this environment and wants to maintain the image of the mother as a benevolent person tends therefore to accept her negative appraisal of him. By accepting this negative appraisal, he develops the self-image of the bad child, that is, he considers himself inadequate and bad, and has little self-esteem.

The preservation of the good image of the parent is made possible by the removal from consciousness of the most unpleasant traits of the parent. Thus, the child will have two images of the parent: the good image, which is conscious, and the bad image, which will remain unconscious. The good parental image appears in myths, legends, and dreams as God, the fairy, the magic helper, the protector. The parental bad image appears as the witch, the stepmother, the bad man, and so forth.

Why does the child need to preserve the image of the good parent? In early childhood the parent, generally the mother, is the person who connects the child with the environment; she is the Thou, the representative of the interpersonal world. The child must accept her in order to fulfill his inborn potentialities for full maturation and socialization. If she is not good, his need and desire to accept the world will be thwarted, and certain tendencies toward autism and arrested socialization will manifest themselves. In the cases in which the mother is not the almost exclusively important adult, this need to preserve her good image is not so strong.

There are other reasons for wanting to preserve the image of the good parent. It is more tolerable for the child to think that he is punished by the good parent because he deserves to be punished than to think that he is unfairly punished. If he is punished although he is not bad, he will have a feeling of despair; the situation will seem to him beyond remedy, hopeless. Maybe he is so horrible and worthless that he must be punished even without being bad. Some children actually force themselves to do "bad things" in order to be bad because they want to be punished for something that they have done rather than for nothing. By being "bad" they preserve the self-image of the bad child. In addition, if mother is good, the child thinks that she will love him even if he is bad.

In the majority of the cases where schizophrenia will eventually occur, the transformation of the parental image into a benevolent one does not take place. At a conscious level the Thou remains distressing, although not malevolent. The child, however, retains hostile feelings for the parents. Moreover, the characteristics of the internalized parents are generalized to some extent to all women or to all adults.

The "I," that is, the self-image, is also altered. The negative attributes of the self are to a large extent repressed. Also, the child no longer sees himself as hated, falsely accused, or the target of hostility. He continues, however, to see himself as weak. The "bad" me is transformed into the "weak" me. The child will see himself as a weakling in a world of strong and distressing adults.

In a minority of cases of schizophrenia the child is able to retain the good maternal image that he built before the end of the second year of life, when the mother could still relate to him with care and some devotion. In these cases the child tends to continue to act like a baby or to manifest strong regressive tendencies toward babyhood. He learns to remain a dependent person. If he is still a baby, if he is completely taken care of and has no will of his own, mother will be good to him. Mother then will appear again not only as good, but also as omnipotent, and the child will tend to maintain a parasitic attitude. Any real or symbolic separation from mother is capable of producing great anxiety even much later in life. I have found these tendencies to a more or less pronounced degree in several preschizophrenics and schizophrenics, but in my experience they are not the most common or the usually predominant trends in the psychodynamics of schizophrenia.

CHAPTER

6

Second Period: Late Childhood

I

The Abnormal Dialogue

In spite of the anomalies, dreariness, and intense turmoil of the first period, relatively few children succumb to child psychosis. The psyche has many resources, and in the majority of cases the child enters *the second period.* Although primary process mechanisms continue to function in these children for a period of time longer than in normal circumstances, the primary process is eventually overcome and to a very large extent is replaced by secondary process mechanisms. The latter are easily accepted, as they seem to offer solutions to many of the patient's problems. The child learns the language of the community as well as the prevailing ideas, mores, and modes of thought. The prevailing of secondary process mechanisms similar to those of the surrounding adults does not imply, however, that normal relatedness is established between the future patient and the members of his family. There is an abnormal dialogue between the child and his parents and siblings. No language of basic trust, no taken-for-granted acceptance, no easiness of communication exist, but rather lack of clarity of meaning, excessive contradictions, unexpressed or distorted emotions, suspiciousness or at best very pronounced cautiousness. Many authors have done much research to elucidate the disturbed communications in the family. For instance, Bateson and associates (1956) have advanced the so-called double-bind theory, by which to a large extent they explain etiologically schizophrenia. Although the situation that they describe may be applied to any age of the patient, it is particularly in late childhood that it is thought to take place.

The ingredients for a double-bind situation are described as follows:

1. Two or more persons. One of them is the patient. The authors write, "We do not assume that the double bind is *inflicted by the mother alone,* but that it may be done either by mother alone or by some combination of mother, father, and/or siblings." (Italics added.)

2. Repeated experience.

3. A primary negative injunction, expressed in two forms: (a) "Do not do so-and-so, or I will punish you," or (b) "If you do not do so-and-so, I will punish you."

4. A secondary injunction that conflicts with the first at a more abstract level and like the first is connected with punishment or threat to survival. The posture, gesture, or tone of voice may convey this more abstract message.

5. "A tertiary negative injunction prohibiting the victim from escaping from the field."

6. The complete set of the first five ingredients is no longer necessary when the patient has learned to perceive the world in double-bind patterns. "Almost any part of a double-bind sequence may then be sufficient to precipitate panic or rage."

Following are some examples from the original articles by Bateson and associates. The mother tells the child, "Pull up your socks." At the same time, her gesture implies, "Don't be so obedient." In this situation the child receives the message, "Pull up your socks," but if he does so, he is too obedient. The other message says, "Don't be so obedient," but if he does not obey, he will incur mother's disapproval. In colloquial expression he is damned if he does it, and he is damned if he does not. To use the authors' own words, "If he solves a problem of human relationship at the level at which it is apparently offered, he will find himself in the wrong at some other level."

Another example taken from Powdermaker (1952) and used by Bateson and associates is the following: An aunt comes to visit, and the little niece sees her. This aunt could not tolerate children, but mother has told the child, "Auntie loves you." The child is thus exposed to a double bind. Should she be bound by the message coming from mother, which says, "Aunt is a loving creature," or by the message coming directly from the aunt, which seems to declare in an obvious manner, "I detest children"? These are two different external binds, or at least an internal and an external one. The child has an external message that tells her she should respond with kindness to the aunt and an inner message that tells her that she should respond with anger to the aunt.

Bateson and associates state that double-bind situations provoke helplessness, fear, exasperation, and anxiety in the individual. According to them, the schizophrenic early in life was exposed to a great many double-bind situations. The eventual psychosis may be viewed as a way of dealing with double-bind situations. At times the psychotic masters the situation by shifting to the metaphorical field; more often he himself becomes an expert in setting double-bind situations. The authors admit that the double-bind situation may be seen as ambivalence, in Bleuler's sense, but as a special ambivalence inasmuch as it is not merely indecision between multiple possibilities, but a circular process, or a feedback mechanism. For instance, in one of the above examples the resolution of being kind to the aunt brings about in the child an automatic negative impulse that may also lead to the expression of anger. But the expression of anger brings about its negative impulse, which will compel the child to be kind. And so on, back and forth.

Let us examine the three postulates of Bateson and associates: (1) that schizophrenia may be the result of excessive double-bind situations in childhood; (2) that the psychosis is a way of dealing with the environmental double-bind situations; (3) that the schizophrenic himself learns to use a large number of double-bind situations.

My criticism of the first postulate of Bateson is that every man, normal, neurotic, and future psychotic, was exposed in childhood and later to double-bind situations (Arieti, 1960). Double-bind situations are a characteristic of life, not of schizophrenia. However, in the childhood of future schizophrenics, the double bind may have often been used, *together with many other mechanisms,* in a way that elicited insecurity and a distorted view of the world. We must emphasize, however, that double-bind situations represent not necessarily pathology, but the complexity of human existence. If we were called upon to deal, not with double binds, but only with single messages, in a sort of reflex or conditioned reflex manner, life undoubtedly would be much simpler and would offer much less anxiety, but it would not be human life; it would be unidimensional life. Culture itself exposes the individual to many double-bind situations, or, if we want to use the traditional way of expressing the mechanisms, to conflictful situations. For instance, it teaches us to be sincere and truthful and at the same time to respect the dignity of the individual, including that of an undesired relative who unexpectedly comes to visit us. It is not always easy to do so. The human being, however, is generally equipped to face highly complicated processes. He has been amply provided by nature with alternative neuronal patterns for this purpose. It is true that many pathological situations involve double binds, but it is also true that they may involve other highly complicated mental mechanisms. To mention another possibility: the ability to anticipate the future, which has the normal purpose of protecting us from forthcoming danger, may actually become the source of anxiety, despair, and suicide.

The healthy child learns to use these processes and to apply them to any difficult situation that is part of his social life, including those similar to the one set up by the visiting aunt. But for the child who is to become schizophrenic, the double bind is not only a double bind; it is also one of the many carriers of hostility and anxiety coming from the interpersonal environment. Being exposed to an atmosphere of excessive anxiety or hostility and not to an atmosphere of basic trust, he is ill equipped to handle many difficult situations, including double-bind situations. This general atmosphere to which he is exposed may be the primal source of his difficulties. Undoubtedly his consequent inability to handle these complicated situations increases his anxiety and hastens the breakdown. In conclusion, it is not the double-bind mechanism *per se* that is pathogenetic, but rather the use of it in a pathogenetic situation. The pathogenetic situation is often one of maternal hostility or maternal anxiety made worse by futile attempts, in the form of messages, to deny the rejection or the anxiety.

Foudraine (1961) and Watzlawick (1963) doubt that I do justice to the double-bind theory. Watzlawick (1963) puts me together with other authors critical of the theory (Ackerman, 1960; Bruch and Palombo, 1961) on the ground that we have overlooked what in the original paper was defined as the "tertiary negative injunction prohibiting the victim from escaping from the field." Actually, many nonschizophrenogenetic stress situations involve a double bind with a tertiary injunction that prevents escaping: Consider, for instance, the situation of divided loyalty, as in the case of the soldier during the Civil War who had to fight in the Confederate Army and yet believed in the ideals of the Union Army. He could escape from his field, but not from his conflict, no matter whether he would fight for the South or for the North.

What is probably quasi-specific in the double-bind situation described by Bateson and associates is the fact that at least two of the three injunctions come from the same source (generally the mother or mother-substitute). But again, as the mother is for the child the great teacher and the main representative of the world, she has to collect in herself and to transmit to the child the different points of view of the world. Moreover, as Festinger (1957) has illustrated in his theory of cognitive dissonance, each person retains many inconsistent points of view, and this diversity of points of view is transmitted to the other, in spite of attempts to deny it to oneself and others.

The normal child learns to tolerate ambivalence, plurality of dimensions in interpersonal relations, including cognitive dissonance. It could be that the future schizophrenic is not able to tolerate this plurality, either because it appears to him too threatening or because he is ill equipped biologically with *a priori* structures that handle such pluralities.

The second assertion of Bateson and associates is that the psychosis equips the patient to handle double-bind situations by escaping into metaphorical language. But the truth is that the language of the schizophrenic is not metaphorical for the patient himself (see Chapter 16). The third point made by the authors is that the schizophrenic himself learns to use a large number of double-bind situations. It is true that schizophrenics use a large number of *disturbing* double-bind situations. In addition to learning the methods from the significant adults, after the onset of the psychosis, they use schizophrenic cognition. Consequently they condense several levels of mental integration, with the result that their statements have several concomitant meanings, just as the dreams of every person do.

Some other authors (Lidz et al., 1965; Wynne et al., 1958, 1963) have described ways of thinking and of communicating in the parents of the schizophrenics. These authors indicate that the patient learns these ways as a child ordinarily learns a specific language from his parents. Although this point will receive more consideration in Chapter 8, it is pertinent to make a few preliminary remarks about this important question. There is no doubt that the family's disturbed communication has a great deal to do with the pathology of the patient, but not in the direct connection of causality that has been described by some authors.

The dialogue of the family is disturbed, but not yet necessarily in a schizophrenic way. It has a definite adverse effect on the future patient, but only in a psychodynamic, affective way, because of its disturbing, undermining impact, not because it directly transmits to the future patient specific formal modalities of language and thinking. The peculiarities that the parents may transmit may already be considered pathological, but not yet psychotic. Something else is necessary to transform peculiarities of communication into psychotic structures.

II

The Emerging Personality

At this point we must stress again that psychodynamics should not be confused with the whole etiology. What happened in the first period and what has been described in the first section of this chapter is a set of preparatory factors that (to repeat what we said at the beginning of Chapter 5) narrowed the range of choice, thwarted the possibility of compensation, determined basic orientations, and facilitated an abnormal sequence of events. These factors had an adverse effect, but in themselves did not constitute all the necessary prerequisites for schizophrenia.

Let us assess the child who has gone through the first period. First of all, he has to repress a large part of his life, which is very unpleasant, and this repression (or dissociation of uncanny experiences, as Sullivan would say) exacts a great toll on his psychological resources. The child will have difficulties in identifying with the significant adults. Nevertheless he will be able to build up some kind of less undesirable self-image, including identification with one sex rather than the other. Sexual confusion or homosexual tendencies are repressed, and the child's identification with his own sex is achieved. However, this patched-up self-image and these identifications are not deeply rooted in the core of his being. They are more superficial reflections of how he feels people deal with him, rather than a well-integrated vision of the self. Obviously this child not only is not able to live in, but even to approach, what we have called a state of *communion* with others. He has to learn special ways of relating to people that will constitute an important part of his basic personality structure.

Before describing what occurs in preschizophrenic persons, we must examine what occurs in average circumstances. Three major types of relating are found in normal persons, generally in various degrees and combinations. These three types begin to differentiate in the second year of life, but develop greatly in late childhood and may be retained for the whole life of the individual. In children who have been raised in an anxiety-producing environment and develop psychoneuroses or character neuroses these three types become more pronounced and rigid, and generally one of them acquires supremacy over the others, imparting a special style on the whole personality. We can recognize that in these situations one of two basic emotions (anxiety and anger) and one of two types of motor behavior (withdrawal or approach) prevail. We have then three major combinations: (1)

anxiety and approach, (2) anger and approach, and (3) anxiety and withdrawal. In some cases, this third combination consists of anxiety, anger and withdrawal. In other words, the presence of anxiety and anger does not make the child reject or dislike the world, but rather teaches him that the world is not a garden of roses. Furthermore, even roses have thorns. Thus, cautious anxiety, defensive anger, or moderate withdrawal are in order in many situations. A moderate withdrawal should not be confused with genuine indifference, which may be the attitude we have toward something that we neither like nor dislike.

The anxious or angry child who anticipates parental disapproval or punishment nevertheless aims at obtaining parental love and affection. A frequent method by which he tries to obtain this love is by complying with his parents' requests and denying his own wishes. He may see that there is no other way out, that the parents, although "good," never yield; he may obtain love or approval and therefore maintain some self-esteem only at the price of compliance. The child becomes a compliant person (anxiety and approach).

Other children find out, instead, that their parents, although "good," yield only if they continue to cry or to have temper tantrums, if they insist and argue for what they want. They learn from experience that the fight will be rewarded. They develop an aggressive, hostile personality. It could be that a constitutional predisposition makes these children prone to experience rage more intensely than fear (anger and approach).

Other children learn that the best way to avoid fear, anxiety and anger is not by complying or by fighting (parents will not give in to these methods), but by keeping away from their parents as much as possible by maintaining an emotional or physical distance. They develop an aloof, detached personality (withdrawal following repression of anxiety and/or anger).

An important defense thus consists in developing one of these types of personality (compliant, aggressive, or detached) or a mixture of them. Horney (1937, 1943) was the first to describe these three types of personality and to understand fully their consequences in the whole life of the individual. She called these three types of relating: (1) moving toward people; (2) moving against people; and (3) moving away from people. As far as I know, however, she did not mention that the specific type of personality is the result of the combination (or prevailing of some) of four psychological variables (anxiety, anger, approach, withdrawal) and the specific type of parental behavior.

The preschizophrenic who has already been so battered by life does not have all the choices that we have described in building up a basic personality, a self-image, and in preserving a sense of self. As we shall see later in this chapter, he will develop one or the other of two types of prepsychotic personality.* Like the other types that we have described, these two types expand in late childhood, but may be retained for the lifetime of the individual. What is described in the follow-

* The possibility is not excluded that other types of preschizophrenic personality will be recognized in the future.

ing two sections may apply also to later ages. Additional characteristics occurring in adolescence and adulthood will be described in Chapter 7.

The reader must also keep in mind that these two types of personality (schizoid and stormy) are not found exclusively in prepsychotics. To a mild degree they occur in a large percentage of people. Furthermore, even when they are very pronounced, they do not make a psychotic decompensation necessary. They narrow further the range of possibilities and facilitate abnormal sequences of events.

III

The Schizoid Personality

The child who has been raised in the previously discussed environmental conditions often learns that complying, as the person who "moves toward people" does, or being aggressive and hostile, as the person "who moves against people" does, does not pay. His parents may not accept either compliance or hostility. He must move away from people and must become a detached personality. The massive repression that he had to sustain toward the end of early childhood probably predisposes him to this detachment. He does not develop just a detached personality as many people do, but a special variety of it, generally called the *schizoid personality*. He is very far indeed from the state of communion described in Chapter 5.

The schizoid personality is a character armor that will protect the child in his increasing contacts with the world. The schizoid personality will continue to transform the malevolent Thou into a less disturbing agent, the distressing Thou, or to be more correct, the *distressing other*. The designation "other" in the third person implies distance. The schizoid personality defends the self from the distressing others who constitute the family and the world. It is a set of defenses built as reaction to chronic danger, not to immediate fear; it provides tepid responses to poorly expressed states of anxiety and anger. By detaching himself emotionally the patient will avoid the pain connected with the attacks on his self-esteem. Furthermore, it will be easier for him to tolerate the inner images, which, although not as unpleasant as those of the previous period, are still disturbing. I am referring especially to the images of the parents, as distressing others, and to the image of himself as the "weak me." The hostility for the parents produces less guilt feeling, and the image of the self, at first at least, produces less decrease in self-esteem. The intense relatedness among the members of the family, which was often present during the first period, is now in many instances replaced by distance and coldness.

The schizoid appears aloof, detached, less emotional than the average person, less concerned and less involved. Actually, at an unconscious level he continues to be very sensitive, but he has learned to avoid anxiety and anger in two ways: (1) by putting physical distance between himself and situations that are apt to arouse these feelings and (2) by repressing all emotions. This physical distance is maintained by avoiding interpersonal relations or refraining from actions that will evoke an unpleasant reaction in other people. Often, when the schizoid person is in the latter stages of his childhood, he would like to be a participant or a doer, but he still remembers from early childhood that action does not pay because it provokes a storm of intense and threatening emotional responses in the surrounding adults. Anticipation of actions means anticipation of a repetition of these emotional storms. The patient therefore becomes underactive. In some cases the parents have actually encouraged him not to do things; doing nothing meant being a good child, "because" what the child did was "always bad." The patient may grow older with a deeply rooted pessimism about the outcome of his actions.

A characteristic of the schizoid person is the difficulty he has in looking into the eyes of the person who is with him. The schizoid child, and even more so later on the schizoid adolescent and young adult, may look elsewhere or make only fleeting eye contact. Eye contact not only makes him aware that another person is there, but that that person looks at him. As long as the other person does not look at the patient, the other may be experienced as an object. As soon as he looks, he becomes an older person, an intruder, almost an inquisitor. The glance is a threat. Sartre has given great consideration to eye contact in his book *Being and Nothingness* (1969). However, what Sartre attributes to every human being seems to me characteristic only of the schizoid (and later, even more of the schizophrenic). According to Sartre, even though the other who looks at the individual may not be aggressive or reproaching, the individual feels dispossessed. Sartre believes that the individual feels he is for another; feels the shame of not being for himself. Sartre attributes to everybody an encounter with the other that is lived as a conflict or a state of anxiety. I believe that in a state of communion, of basic trust, or at least of absence of anxiety, the child or the youngster does not have the experience of being invaded and possessed by the glance of others, for instance, of the good mother or of the good friend. On the contrary the glance of mother is an act of love, is reassuring, and has the flavor of a caress, an embrace.

In several instances schizoid patients seem to be relatively active. On close observation they reveal, however, that they do things because they cannot resist the pressure of somebody who pushes them, generally the parent. More often than not, this parental pressure is exerted, not directly, but in a subtle way. Rationalized or actually experienced as a desire to help the child, a parental invasion of the child's personal prerogatives takes place. Ironically, many of these parents boast about their liberality and noninterference in their children's lives. The children protect themselves from this parental invasion with further detachment.

Contrary to what the compliant person does under parental pressure, the child who has developed a schizoid personality prefers not to comply. And yet, to the observer, he quite often gives the impression of being extremely compliant. Actually he complies in a perfunctory way. He goes through the motions of the imposed act, but without being emotionally involved. In order to avoid anxiety, he becomes a person *uncommitted* to what he is doing or to what he is participating in. We must remember that if the patient succeeds in experiencing himself as being emotionally uninvolved, it is because his resentment and hostility are deeply repressed. Should he later become schizophrenic, the resentment and the hostility may be displaced toward nonparental figures, who may become the persecutors.

The person who develops a compliant personality has much less difficulty than the schizoid, because the former learns to accept emotionally the values of his parents. Of course, at a deep level of unconsciousness he may also retain the bad image of them and not accept them. Only later in life, or if he undergoes psychotherapy, may he dethrone his parents. The compliant person complies in order to please; the schizoid complies in order not to displease. The schizoid is often partially aware of the conflict between himself and his parents. The character armor of indifference will remove to a great extent the unpleasantness of the conflict, but will not succeed entirely in repressing the awareness of the conflict itself. The schizoid character armor will remove the consciousness of anxiety to a large extent, but will never confer on the patient the feeling that he is really wanted, approved, and accepted.

Often the schizoid acquires a certain insight into his personality. He recognizes that his detachment is a very unsatisfactory solution and indeed he is justified in feeling that way. The compliant person and the aggressive person find some kind of solution, although at a high price. The compliant person gets approval, whereas the aggressive person generally manages to get at least some kind of substitute for what he really wants. The schizoid reaches a pseudosolution by denying a great part of his life, but by doing so he may make the part of his life that he continues to live more awkward and unstable. His unconscious hostility and resentment increase; his emotional and social isolation are never complete enough to protect him entirely from anxiety; on the other hand, he harbors secret desires to reconnect himself with the emotional and social life from which he has tried to detach himself. Somehow he senses that he does not live the full reality of life.

His lack of emotion is not due to simple repression of feelings; it is also a reaction formation to too much sensitivity, not only to the sensitivity of the preceding intense relatedness to the parents, experienced during the first period, but also to the sensitivity that still exists at an unconscious or preconscious level. The dreams or fantasies of the schizoid often reveal great emotional potentialities; they are very dramatic and have great intensity of feelings and vivacity of actions. They transport the patient into an adventurous life, and often into storms of affect.* With his actions, on the other hand, the schizoid person tries to be as static as possible. Often, if he acts, he will be very impersonal and will try to avoid communication by direct contact.

A 9-year-old schizoid girl used to write letters to her parents in which she would explain what she did not dare to tell them directly. Even when they are older, these schizoid patients prefer to write letters, rather than make telephone calls, and even when they write, they do so in a cold, formal, businesslike man-

* It is worth mentioning that often, although not in all cases, when the schizoid patient tells a dramatic dream to the therapist, he does so with his usual detached, uninvolved attitude—as if the dream was experienced by another hypothetical person.

ner. In his schoolwork, the schizoid learns much more from a book than from the direct presentation of the teacher. Written material conveys meaning to him much better than spoken material, because a direct interpersonal experience is eliminated.

In conclusion we may state that the schizoid person experiences life as a danger to his own self. He succeeds in preserving his self, as an entity, by diminishing his contacts with life. The schizoid person does not want to withdraw to the symbiotic existence of the first year of life, which we have described in some patients. According to Guntrip (1968), he wants to go further back, to return to the womb (for safety, not for pleasure). The schizoid pattern of living is a compromise, because return to the womb is impossible. The compromise is a halfway-house position, according to Guntrip: neither in life nor out.

The later vicissitudes of the schizoid person will be discussed in Chapter 7. At this point we have to take into consideration some important issues.

The distressing other may realistically be distressing, just as the malevolent you (Thou) may have really been malevolent. As a matter of fact, we find that in the majority of cases the image of the distressing other is often closer to reality than the image of the malevolent you was. However, the image of the distressing other does not correspond to reality when the patient sees every adult, or many adults, as modeled after this image. This is an unwarranted generalization, an application to most adults of what has become an *a priori* structure. Whether the image is in some cases a faithful reproduction of the surrounding adults or not, the adults are categorically experienced as distressing others.

The distressing others thus come to exist in their external reality and remain powerful inner objects as well. They exist as offenses and as defenses: offenses because they still determine fear, detachment, and withdrawal; defenses because their distressing quality does not elicit the devastating anxiety of the first period and permits some healthy developments or at least some compromises.

Melanie Klein, Fairbairn, Guntrip, and myself give great importance to inner objects, although we use different interpretations and frames of reference. External relations are also important and contribute to the maintenance or alteration of their inner counterpart.

The following outcomes are to be taken into account.

1. The schizoid person in childhood and later in life appears to others as having at least some of the following characteristics: being detached, cold, peculiar, suspicious, arrogant, condescending, and cocky. Thus the interpersonal world will not be able to interact with ease with a schizoid person. A state of tension, distance, mistrust, and misinterpretation is likely to occur that will reinforce in the patient his schizoid attitude. That is, he will continue to envision his being with others as a chronic, unspoken, moderate state of danger or surrounding hostility, from which he has to continue to defend himself.

2. Because of the experiences and habits acquired during the first period, the patient is predisposed to interpret the world in a way that confirms his unconscious

premises, unconscious presuppositions, and general way of seeing reality. Thus he uses the attitudes he evokes in others in order to reinforce his schizoidism.

IV
The Stormy Personality

The second type of prepsychotic personality is what I have described and designated as "stormy personality" (Arieti, 1955).

Not all preschizophrenics find in the schizoid detachment a protection from the injuries caused by the early interpersonal relations. The children who develop a stormy personality try all types of attitudes and try them to an extreme degree in their attempts to find a *modus vivendi,* a compromise with the significant adults. They try detachment as well as compliance and hostility. They have to try all possible means of defense, because none of them is effective in removing the existing anxiety. This uncertainty about the way of dealing with others is enhanced by the inconsistency of the parents. Thus, the early environmental situation promotes in them a capacity to change their attitudes toward life repeatedly. The changes may be slow or abrupt; more often, they are sudden, violent, and drastic. The distressing you they have to contend with is not just distressing, but unpredictable and inconsistent. It does not become a distressing other, but unless detachment is present, remains a *you.* The members of the family are still experienced as close, perhaps manifesting that pseudomutuality that Wynne and associates (1958) have described.

When children with stormy personality are observed for a short period of time, they give the wrong impression of being compliant, aggressive, or detached. But sooner or later we discover that this behavior is a maneuver adopted in specific situations. They have learned to change rapidly, and without conscious realization of what they are doing, in accordance with what the situation requires.

The child who develops a stormy personality has a greater difficulty in preserving a sense of self than does the schizoid person. Like the child who develops a schizoid personality, he could not properly identify with either of his parents, and his sex and gender identity were in many cases not well defined. However, even more than the schizoid child, he was uncertain about the role that the parents and siblings assigned to him in the family. He could not make out what *he* meant to each of the surrounding persons, especially adults, but also siblings. He felt *inconsistently unwanted,* the meaning of his identity or presence in the home remaining not well established, unless connected with overt rejection. As we have seen, no general attitude toward others (either of compliance, aggressiveness, or detachment) could become well established. This uncertainty about the role attributed to him is due not only to the fact that the parents were inconsistent and torn by opposite feelings, like hostility and a sense of duty. It is due also, and perhaps predominantly, to the fact that the child tried to deny the role he felt the parents were attributing to him. He was too frightened to become aware of something that was presumably bad. He also was inclined to believe that the parents considered him "bad," but he did not want to see himself consistently in that light; it would be too devastating to his self-esteem. Somehow he felt he was not accepted, but he was not sure that he would be rejected entirely. He vacillated between all possible points of view. He saved some self-esteem, but at the expense of a stable sense of self-identity.

Whereas the schizoid person succeeds in preserving his self by decreasing the intensity of his contacts with people, the stormy person retains his willingness to explore life. He does not consider himself weak to the extent of withdrawing forever. But no matter what psychological maneuvers he uses, he succeeds only in grasping tastes of life. Whatever gives him some pleasure seems unretainable and flies away.

In an attempt to retain what they occasionally get, some patients use methods that are more characteristic and abnormal than those so far illustrated. Some of these stormy youngsters go to the extent of assuming temporarily the personality of the most important adult they are dealing with: mother, father, older sibling, and so on. This is not, however, a real identification, as it is in the case of normal children. It is something superficially superimposed, which shows gross distortions and at times to a degree resembles caricature or pantomime.*

Laing (1960) has designated all these maneuvers of the patients as "the false-self" system. He does not distinguish between schizoid and stormy personalities, and most of his observations concern the schizoid person.

The assumption of this personality or false-self system is a defensive maneuver. The youngster succeeds in most instances in avoiding tragic consequences. Obviously he does not come out of this turmoil intact. He will harbor serious doubts about his personal significance and self-worth. But at least he has succeeded in preserving his self as an entity, as a unity. We must stress that vicious or circular patterns are developed in the life of the stormy individual. The family members, too, consider the patient unpredictable and respond with varying behavior, which reinforces the child's inner images of the family members.

V

Later Developments

In the case of both the schizoid and the stormy child, the psychological picture seems much improved toward the last phase of childhood. The family has learned to live less inadequately with the patient, who is now less immature, less dependent, or less demanding. Although the child's earlier basic impressions and feel-

* In non-Western countries a syndrome known by the name *latah* or by several other designations occurs frequently. It is applied to patients who imitate gestures, acts, and words of other people in a pantomime fashion (Arieti and Meth, 1959). In rare instances I have seen pre- and post-schizophrenic stormy personalities who resemble *latah* patients.

ings about the world will linger, he is to a considerable extent able to alter them. These modifications are generally useful, even though at first they may seem to have an adverse effect. For instance, we have seen that if the mother has been an inadequate parent, deprived of maternal feelings, the child may during the first part of his childhood assume, at an unverbalized level, that mothers are all this way—that is how the world is. Later he discovers that the mothers of his schoolmates and playmates are not like his own mother and that he likes those mothers more. Still later he discovers that culture or society, as a whole, represents, or even takes for granted, an image of mother that is much better than that of his own mother. At first impression one would think that the child will suffer when he discovers this discrepancy. Certainly it would be better if such discrepancy did not exist, and to a certain extent he does suffer.

However, he reacquires some hope in life. He becomes more and more aware that the family does not constitute the whole world. He thinks that he will discover the world at large in the future. More and more he appreciates the importance of the future in one's life, and he builds hopes for his own future.

Although the family is not in this second period as important in eliciting psychopathology as it was in the first period, its role cannot be minimized. It is still inadequate in providing what is needed or, even less, in compensating for what occurred previously. Some of the trends described in the first and second periods could be corrected at least partially if the child were exposed to some healthy influences, like close relations with friends and distant relatives. Unfortunately, in several cases the parents of future schizophrenic patients did not encourage extrafamilial social intercourse, and what has been described as the "ingrown family" or nuclear family has resulted. Compensatory interpersonal contacts were lacking, and the children were dependent for psychological development on their unfit parents, even more than children usually are dependent on parents.

The ingrown or nuclear family, although it has been encountered somewhat less frequently since the end of the 1950s, is still very common in some parts of big cities where families live in isolation in their own small apartments. In too many instances no feeling of neighborhood develops in spite of close proximity. Ingrown families are also found among people who live in real geographical isolation, for example, on farms, islands, isolated hamlets, boats, and so forth (see case of Geraldine, Chapter 40). It occurs less frequently in small towns or villages where communal life is rich and warm. The difficulties of the second period are, relatively speaking, not overwhelming. In the majority of cases the individual succeeds in building up adequate defenses and in adjusting more or less to life, and the psychosis never occurs.

CHAPTER

7

Third Period: Adolescence and Early Adulthood

I

Further Aspects of the Prepsychotic Personality

Because the early experiences have made the future patient awkward socially, clumsy in his activities, and somewhat inadequate in coping with life in general, his defects become more evident in adolescence and later, when he has to deal with a greater range of situations. We shall first examine adolescents and young adults who had developed a schizoid type of personality in childhood. Most of them will retain this type of personality, whose traits will be even more marked and obvious. Many of these youngsters appear markedly detached, as if something unnatural and strange divided them from the world.

In spite of this apathy and aloofness, little signs can be detected in them that indicate how their original sensitivity is ready to erupt to awareness. One of these characteristics is their lack of a sense of humor. They cannot stand a joke or anything humorous said about themselves. Sensitized as they are to environmental hostility, they see in the joke a pungent remark made against them. In this interpretation they are right, because many jokes and humorous remarks have an element of hostility (Freud, 1938; Arieti, 1950*b*). However, this element of hostility is so mild that it is not only tolerated, but often perceived as a pleasant teasing by the normal person. For the schizoid, a joke is a serious rebuff. For the same reasons, schizoids are poor losers at play. Defeat is another proof of their inadequacy and increases their already strong reluctance to do things with others or to share experiences.

Most of these schizoid persons develop other defenses or protections, which consist of unusually drastic actions or habits at a reality level, rather than *obvious* symptoms. The schizoid may enter a monastery, where he will be away from the dangers of life; he may join the Army, where he will be forced to respect authority; he may select some kind of work where he has to display no initiative whatsoever. In a considerable number of cases he may devote himself more and more to religion. In the belief and practice of religion he will try to get the comfort that he could not find elsewhere. Religion and God are the good parents, whom he substitutes for the bad parents. They are the parents who accept even the inadequate and worthless children. The patient is unwilling to submit to the authority of his parents, but may respect the authority of God. He is not able to relate to people, but is able to develop some kind of relatedness to God. People do not give love, but God does. In some cases this escape into the church is a protection that may delay the psychosis. On the other hand, if in the association with organized religion the patient does not come into contact with some human beings and receive warmth and comfort from them, he may receive no help at all. Abstract concepts often do not provide what he needs. Some religious conceptions may slip into real delusions. On the other hand, because they seem so distant from daily reality, they may make unrealistic developments unnecessary. From a practical point of view, the religious fervor may push the patient in two directions. The patient may retain the religion of his parents, but may become much more involved in it than they were, or the patient may change his religion. By converting to a new religion, he fulfills several goals: (1) he rebels against his parents; (2) he tries to find in the new religion a solution to his problems, which he thinks cannot be solved if things remain unchanged; and (3) he tries desperately to make some satisfactory interpersonal relationships, though they have to be in a very unusual form (convent, missionary work, mystical group, and so forth). Generally, the change in religion occurs from the more rational and abstract religion to the more mystical.

In some cases the schizoid person may alter his general behavior in order to become a member of a marginal or fringe group: a beatnik, a bohemian, a hippie, a marginally social person. In other words, his detachment from the type of life in which he grew up urges him to become attached and committed to a different life that does not require conforming. Moreover, he feels finally accepted by a group. The group requests from him less of a sense of responsibility and duty than society at large.

We must keep in mind, however, that most marginally social people never develop a schizophrenic psychosis. They remain marginally social for the rest of their lives or eventually return to a more accepted style of living.

A common defense among schizoid persons is that of decreasing their needs to an almost unbelievable extent. Many of them live alone in furnished rooms, away from social contacts of any kind, except those that are absolutely necessary. As we have already mentioned, fantasies, sexual or otherwise, replace their need for action. The fantasies often involve objectives that cannot be attained; therefore, any possibility of action is removed. When they are confronted with a situation requiring some action, they convince themselves that it is not necessary or worthwhile to act. They are able to work, but they do not let any emotion enter into their activities. Often they select a type of work that is impersonal and may be performed without any emotional involvement, for example, mathematics.

On the other hand, the schizoid, at some time during his life, may even become concerned over his lack of feelings. In spite of his detachment he knows that his life is dull and gray. He would like to become emotionally involved, but he cannot. At times he feels that he must pretend to have feelings and is afraid that people may "see through" him and recognize that he has no emotions. Actually, once he is successfully treated, he will discover not that he has pretended to have feelings, but the opposite, that he has pretended to have no feelings. Psychotherapy is difficult, first because of this lack of conscious feeling, and second because when the patient becomes aware of his feelings, he is afraid to bring them up. He fears that they may be used against him to demonstrate how bad he is. He is still afraid that feelings would bring about rebuff, anxiety, and attacks on his self-esteem.

Adolescents with a stormy personality continue to be unable to build a relatively stable self-image. As we have seen in Chapter 5, they are the persons who, in childhood, could not build up the self-image of the bad child, but only the image of the *presumably* bad child. They also cannot establish an adequate sense of self-identity. We do not refer only to sex or gender identity. We mean also that the patient is not able to answer certain fundamental questions that he asks himself. Who is he and what do his family, acquaintances, and society at large expect from him? And if he ever finds out what others expect from him, would he be able to live up to these expectations? Even more crucial is the question of what he expects of himself. These questions are not asked in a general, abstract, theoretical, or philosophical sense. Philosophical questions of this kind are normal occurrences in bright adolescents and young adults. The preschizophrenic, and especially the stormy person, is concerned with these problems in a more concrete way and in reference only to his own specific interpersonal and social situations. When we say that he asks himself these questions, we do not necessarily mean that he literally asks them of himself, although that may also happen. Often these questions and the inability to answer them remain at a nonverbal level, as a feeling of drifting aimlessly, a feeling of not being able to find oneself.

In both the schizoid and the stormy personalities self-esteem and self-identity are impaired, but self-identity is more impaired in the stormy personality. The schizoid person is to a certain degree more certain of his own identity, because he has accepted, at least to some extent, the self-image of the bad child. He resorts to detachment to defend himself; he becomes an inconspicuous follower, a wallflower, an isolated person. But the stormy person cannot compromise in that way. He is forever busy searching for his role, although he does not meet with success.

He still tries to "reach" people, although he is hurt every time he tries. He still harbors ambitions, although he becomes increasingly discouraged.

The difficulties increase as the patient's inability to find his place extends beyond the family circle and involves a larger number of peers, acquaintances, and the community in which he lives. What role does he play with them? What do they think of him? When later he enters the working world, the same uncertainty creeps in as inability to find himself as a member of a certain profession or trade. These feelings are further increased by the competition that he senses all around him. Although feelings of this kind are experienced by neurotics, too, they are much more pronounced in those prepsychotic individuals who have a stormy personality.

As already mentioned in Chapter 6, patients with stormy personalities often are compliant to a degree of extreme submissiveness; at other times they are aggressive and hostile; more seldom, they withdraw into an ivory tower of complete detachment. When they are not detached, they are very anxious; anxiety governs their lives. They are like schizoid persons who have been deprived of the protection of the schizoid defenses. They are, therefore, very vulnerable; every little event has the power of unchaining a crisis. The life of these persons in general is a series of crises.

In some instances these patients do not show sudden changes in character, but appear almost constantly either submissive or aggressive. Their submissiveness and pseudocompliance, to which we have already referred, may turn into obsequiousness or may become a caricature. Their aggressiveness consists mostly of loud manners void of results. Rather than to bring some relief, these attitudes provoke more anxiety and precipitate additional crises.

These patients often live in an atmosphere of catastrophe and doom. Still, they show an extreme resiliency, as mentioned before, and seem able to recover strength, spirits, and good humor easily. Generally, however, they do a poor job in covering up the underlying unrest with this gay, shallow, and effervescent attitude. When they are in a relatively good mood, they harbor grandiose fantasies and even paranoid tendencies. They are going to be great and successful, if they are just given a chance. They are going to get married to wonderful persons, and so forth. They like extremes only. For them, everything is black or white. Acceptance means devotion and love; nonacceptance means utter rejection and hate. There are no nuances in their lives. If the therapist accepts them, he must give all of himself to them. If they feel that the therapist rejects them, they go into a state of despair or detachment.

The changes in mood and attitudes do not relieve these patients. They often resort to excessive use of drugs and alcohol. The crises they go through often weaken them progressively. These crises are frequently precipitated by little happenings, magnified by the patients, who unconsciously see in them symbolic reproductions of the original situations that produced anxiety. At other times, the crises are really precipitated by critical situations that arise as the anxiety of the patients forces them to inappropriate actions (marriage, love affairs, absurd jobs, and so forth). Things do not just happen to them, as they seem to happen to schizoid persons. The patients seem to search actively for a meaningful way of living. They actually live a stormy life, in a certain way comparable to the life that appears in the dreams of schizoid persons.*

Many schizoid or stormy persons never develop a psychosis. They retain a prepsychotic personality during their entire life, unless, of course, timely therapy or unforeseen circumstances direct them toward a different type of adjustment.

Some of these people increase the abnormality of their behavior so that many psychiatrists consider them preschizophrenics, latent schizophrenics, borderline schizophrenics, or even "psychotic personalities without psychoses." Most of them succeed in living a socially permissible, though inadequate, life. However, in many cases the schizoid or stormy character structures eventually no longer constitute adequate protection. The difficulties become more apparent the more the patient proceeds toward adulthood, for several reasons. The school situation, the increasing sexual desires, and the search for a position in a competitive world put his character armor to serious strain. The defenses that the patient was able to mobilize earlier in life used to be fairly efficient when he had to contend exclusively or predominantly with his family. Now he feels he has to deal with the world at large. In spite of his emotional detachment the schizoid person resents the fact that both the family and society demand that he relinquish his detachment and withdrawal—a request that he cannot fulfill. His schizoid defenses not only do not protect him, but actually handicap him when social pressures compel him to do things in spite of his withdrawal. He feels "pushed around." He does things haphazardly and halfheartedly and cannot exploit his full potentialities. The reduction of spontaneous activity confers on him a certain awkwardness and inappropriateness. His lack of experience in dealing with people increases his fears. When he succeeds in evading his schizoid attitudes and in doing things, the old sensitivity tends to come back, and tremendous anxiety is experienced. The early uncanny experiences, which the patient has forgotten, continue to alter, or to give a particular coloring to, his present experiences. The persons he has to deal with are, symbolically speaking, other parents, and he has never learned to deal adequately with parents. The world appears to him to be populated by millions of authorities, ready to criticize him. Symbolically, every interpersonal situation is a reproduction of the old parent-child relationship; a compulsive attitude quite often compels the patient to make this reproduction more similar to the original situation than is actually required. The competitive spirit of our society, where everybody is supposed to assert himself or to show how good he is, makes his predicament worse. Handicapped as he is, it is no wonder that he fails. Any additional failure increases his feeling of inadequacy and predisposes him to subsequent failures. The series of failures and disappointments that Adolph Meyer was the first to describe takes place. The patient undergoes a progressive maladaptation and needs to withdraw into a stronger armor, with more defensive mechanisms.

This progressive maladaptation has many different aspects and courses. At

* In an article published in 1962, Greene expands and clarifies my concept of the stormy personality.

times, although it is very pronounced, it is not noticed by the superficial observer. On the contrary, the lack of emotional involvement and the slow tempo confer a certain poise on the individual that may even be appealing to some who do not recognize the underlying unrest. In other cases an insidious maladaptation leading to schizophrenia may become apparent even to the superficial observer, but only in some areas. For instance, the scholastic record may reveal a steady decline. The patient was a good student in grammar school, less than average in high school, and could not function at all in college.

The stormy personality continues to try to make contacts with the world, but without success. The pleasant reality he continues to crave continues to elude him. People see him more and more as a bizarre person who will never accomplish anything in life; he is indeed labeled a failure. This appraisal becomes obvious to him, or at least is suspected.

We may conclude that for both schizoid and stormy patients the intrafamily difficulties of the earlier periods continue to exist at later ages, although in a different context and with social implications. The sense of distance, the lack of communication, the incomprehension, the unrelatedness between the patient and the others increase, although in stormy patients this situation is often not immediately recognized. The family drama or the social drama involving the patient and his milieu becomes more intense. Let us remember, however, that as long as this drama remains an interpersonal or social one and is not internalized in abnormal ways, schizophrenia is not present. In order to lead to schizophrenia the drama must injure the self very much and must become a drama of the self.

II

The Injury to the Self

Before determining how the self is injured, we must discuss an area of cognitive life, namely, conceptual life. We shall restrict our discussion to what is of particular relevance to the understanding of schizophrenia.

In my view, the conceptual part of the psyche is not a conflict-free area, nor merely a vehicle to mediate necessarily more primitive conflicts, but to a large extent it is the originator or transformer of the conflicts themselves. Human conflicts, both intrapersonal and interpersonal, go far beyond instinctual deprivation and cannot be experienced without intricate conceptualization. What may prove most pathogenetic are not instinctual impulses or instinctual deprivations, but *ideas:* the cognitive part of man, which has been badly neglected in psychiatry. Freudian psychoanalysis, too, has either ignored the power of the idea or, when it could not ignore it, has attempted to transform it into a quantity of sexual libido.

As Vygotsky (1962) has illustrated, conceptual thinking starts early in life, but it is in adolescence that it acquires prominence. Conceptual life is a necessary and very important part of mature life. Some people, however, make an exaggerated use of concepts. They rubricize, tend to put things into categories, and forget individual characteristics. For these people the Platonic universals become the real things. Some adolescents who later become schizophrenics tend to select the formation of concepts and categories that have a gloomy emotional load, and these classes and categories are given an absolute, exceptionless finality.

Previous endoceptual experiences are now verbalized in negative contexts. Individual memories that had escaped repression continue to bother the patient no longer as individual facts, but as concepts. Their emotional tonality is extended to whole categories and clusters of concepts that become complexes. Specific events, scenes, memories, like the creaking voice of the mother, the arrogant gesture of the father, the smoky and smelly kitchen, the dark living room, the disagreeable anecdotal happenings, are interconnected in a dreary web of feelings. Let us take again, as an example, the concept of mother, to which I referred in earlier chapters. We have seen how in the prepubertal period the earlier concept of mother, derived from the individual experiences, undergoes improvement because of the acquisition of the image of mother provided by the culture. The child had thus actually been able to overcome the formation of a primary process generalization and no longer included all mothers in one category. He became able to resist making this suggestible induction, and the subsequent deduction that each mother was a bad mother because each belonged to the same category. But now because of his unsuccessful dealings with the world, the future patient has come to the conclusion that all adults, and consequently mothers, are not loving creatures. They are also fakers, like his own mother.

From a psychiatric point of view, perhaps the more important aspect of this expansion of conceptual life is the fact that the image of the self from now on will consist mostly of concepts. The image of the self varies through the ages. After several transformations in adolescence it consists of remnants of previous images, but predominantly of concepts.

The concept-feelings of personal significance, of self-identity, of one's role in life, of self-esteem now constitute a great part of the self. The self of the future schizophrenic will consist of concepts that have adverse emotional components.

Because of his adverse experiences the preschizophrenic continues to change in a negative way the image of the self. We have seen that in spite of his detachment the schizoid person has maintained and reinforced the image of himself as the bad child. But at a certain age, to be bad acquires the meaning of being incapable, inadequate, worthless, and even guilty for being so. The stormy person, in spite of his desperate attempts, will never find a reliable meaning for his existence. He will reach the point when he can no longer trust life as a possible source of pleasure or self-fulfillment.

This worsening of the self-image is to a large extent determined by the patient's new orientation toward time. We have seen that in the second period the future acquires importance and some optimism remains. In many cases the importance of the future and a sense of optimism are retained for a part of adolescence and young adulthood. In order to feed his present self-esteem and maintain a less inadequate self-image, the young individual has, so to say, to borrow from his expectations and hopes for the future. "One day it will happen," he secretly says to himself. But eventually he starts to doubt this belief. "Life is going to be bad," he says to himself. He also comes to feel that life is not necessarily bad for everybody, but that it is going to be bad for him. Eventually he may conclude that his life is going to be bad because he is bad or worthless. He feels that if he has always done wrong, it is because there is something wrong with him; if he has not been loved, it is not because love does not exist in this world, but because he is not lovable. The authorities that populate the world are malevolent toward him, and with good reason. He must hate himself more than anybody else hates him. His self-esteem undergoes the most injurious attacks. To some extent he protects the image of the external world, as he protected the images of his parents (see Chapter 5), but at the expense of having an unbearable self-image.

This devastating self-image in its turn compels the patient to change his conceptual understanding of other matters, and these changes in their turn will do further damage to the concept of the self. Let us examine again the example of the concept of mother. We have seen that often, after puberty, the patient generalizes and sees all mothers as bad and insincere. Later he develops another concept of mothers that has a more ominous effect than the previous one, even if it remains unverbalized. He comes to believe that no matter what woman would be his mother, even the best, she would be a bad mother for him because he himself is so undeserving and so bad that he elicits badness in others who try to be close to him.

III

Psychosexual Conflicts

Before proceeding with the course of events that lead to the disorder, we must examine more accurately the sexual life of the future patient from the time of puberty.

Sexual life is important also in the psychodynamics of schizophrenia, but not in a relation of simple and direct causality. Psychological difficulties connected with the boy's first ejaculations and the onset of menstruation in the girl as a rule are not directly involved with the psychodynamics of schizophrenia. To be more specific, the possible revival in girls of an archaic fear of castration and the fear of eventual castration in boys who masturbate or who have wet dreams do not play an important role in the development of the disorder. Sexual deprivations, anomalies, or lack of sexual control may facilitate the occurrence of a psychosis only when they affect injuriously the self-image.

We have already mentioned that one of the most common sexual difficulties consists of the inability on the part of the future schizophrenic to establish a definite and stable sexual identity. Although the occurrence of this difficulty cannot be evaluated statistically with accuracy, I would roughly estimate that it is one of the most common, if not the most common.

In the second period of development, as described in Chapter 6, the young individual succeeded in hiding the sexual uncertainty transmitted from the first period and reached some kind of sexual identity; but, as we have already mentioned, this identity was not deeply grounded and was later easily shaken by the events of life. The unfavorable dealings with the world reinforce in the patient the feeling that he or she is not really a man or a woman. He sees himself in an ambiguous position.*

Next in frequency among the sexual difficulties of the preschizophrenic is homosexuality, both in its latent and overt forms. Until not too long ago in psychoanalytic theory latent homosexuality was considered the major etiological factor of paranoia, paranoid states, and paranoid types of schizophrenia. This conception was first expressed by Freud in his report on the Schreber case (Freud, 1911).

Some confusion still exists about the meaning of "latent homosexuality." This term does not mean that homosexuality is not practiced. It means that the patient is not aware of his own homosexual orientation. Even a person who does not have homosexual relations may be aware of his homosexual tendency. In this case he has a manifest form of homosexuality. The latent homosexual has become aware since early life of the extreme hostility with which society views this type of sexuality. Homosexuality thus becomes unacceptable also to him. The patient consequently makes strong efforts to repress his own wishes or to divert them into other areas. To a large extent this repression is successful. Sooner or later, however, the patient can no longer repress these wishes. In Chapter 8 we shall see that irrepressible sexual desires may injure very much one's concept of oneself.

In my experience, as well as in that of many other psychiatrists, the importance of homosexuality in the etiology of all paranoid disorders has been exaggerated. There is nothing specific in latent homosexuality *per se* as a cause of psychosis. Homosexuality in several cases leads to psychological decompensation only because it engenders a great deal of anxiety in the patient who is no longer able to repress this "unacceptable" sexual orientation. In a hypothetical homosexual society, or in a society that would not discriminate against homosexuality, this psychosexual conflict would not exist or would not have the power to lead to a psychosis.

I must also stress that, according to my clinical findings, not only latent, but also overt, homosexuality has a role in the psychodynamics of several cases of schizophrenia. Here again social ostracism rather than homosexuality *per se* is the pathogenetic factor. I could not obtain relevant data for comparing the incidence of overt homosexuality in schizophrenics and in the general population, and therefore I am not in a position to say whether a difference exists. In the cases of overt homosexuality the psychological difficulty emerges not from the effort to repress the sexual urge, but from the effort to suppress it. The patient eventually succumbs to the desire, although according to my findings somewhat later in life

* After the onset of the psychosis, this lack of definite sexual identity becomes manifest in the overt schizophrenic symptomatology. The different gender identity that the patient may assume and his drawings of human figures with characteristics of both sexes are expressions of this psychosexual conflict.

than nonschizophrenic homosexuals. The patient may become an impulsive or compulsive homosexual, and consequently he may be in constant conflict with society.

Most probably the early identity difficulties that predispose the patient to homosexuality are related to those that predispose him to schizophrenia. However, there are some justifications for believing that homosexuality as an organismic organization, even if psychological in origin, preceded the formation of a definite self or of self-image. In late childhood and adolescence, cognitive processes make the patient realize the social implications of homosexuality, and the self-image may be unfavorably affected.

A third common cause of psychosexual conflict in the prepsychotic is the feeling of inadequacy as a sexual performer. This feeling is usually part of a general feeling of inadequacy. However, the general feeling of inadequacy is reinforced by the concept of the self as sexually inadequate, and a vicious circle originates.

In my experience these feelings of sexual inadequacy in the preschizophrenic do not originate from castration threats or from brooding over the size or shape of one's genitals. These preoccupations are generally a pretext, or a particular channeling of a previously existing feeling of inadequacy.

Sexual indifference or lack of concern about sexual life is also found in a certain number of preschizophrenics. This detachment from what pertains to sex is generally part of the schizoid type of relating. Originally it was a defense against an anxiety-provoking environment, but subsequently it becomes part of one's life pattern. Still, some schizoid persons retain strong interest in sexual matters and repeatedly masturbate. At times indifference for sexual matters occurs at the onset of the psychosis. According to Rado, "anhedonia" or pleasure deficiency, including deficiency in experiencing sexual pleasure, is an inherent characteristic of the preschizophrenic and schizophrenic. According to my findings, these patients prove to be able to experience pleasure fully once they have overcome their psychological difficulties (see Chapter 37).

If the future psychotic feels inadequate as a sexual performer, he feels even more inadequate as a sexual partner and as a love object. Feeling undesired sexually and unloved are experiences injurious to the self, but feeling unlovable and undesirable is even a more devastating emotion. In other words, what is particularly damaging is not the idea that the patient does not obtain love or sexual gratification *now*. It is the idea that his constitution and personality make it impossible for him ever to elicit love or sexual desire.

These unbearable feelings at times compel these patients to impulsive behavior aimed at proving at least a minimum of sexual adequacy. Patients become promiscuous in order to reassure themselves that they can be accepted as sexual partners.

Another psychosexual conflict of the preschizophrenic, which used to be common in the past, is now rather rare. It consists of the fear, on the part of the patient, of succumbing to his or her own heterosexual desires, at times with undesirable partners, with partners objected to by the families, or in ways not sanctioned by society. This conflict occurs in adolescents or young adults brought up in puritanical, Victorian, or very religious cultures. A greater acceptance of sexuality or even of masturbation as a sexual relief has caused an almost complete disappearance of this conflict, even in the preschizophrenic.

Summarizing, we can make the following statements about sexual conflicts in the preschizophrenic:

1. These conflicts are not specific and may occur also in persons who never become psychotic. Only uncertainty about sexual identification seems to be considerably more common in the preschizophrenic.

2. In relation to the psychodynamics of schizophrenia, sexual life is not important in itself, but only insofar as it may affect injuriously the self-image. Either because the patient sees himself as a sexually inadequate person, or a homosexual, or an undesirable sexual partner, or lacking sexual self-control, or having no definite sexual identity, he may develop a devastating concept of himself. Moreover, in the case of lack of definite sexual identity, there is a continual draining of the resources of the person who strives toward self-identity.

IV

The Prepsychotic Panic

The efforts made by the patient either to change his relation with the world or to adapt his self to the inner and external difficulties have not resulted in effective protection. To some extent the conclusion is reached, consciously or unconsciously, that the future will not redeem the present or the past. It is when the patient comes to believe that the future has no hope, that the promise of life will not be fulfilled, and that the future may be even more desolate than the present that the psychological decline characteristic of this third period reaches its culmination. He feels threatened from all sides, as if he were in a jungle. It is not a jungle where lions, tigers, snakes, and spiders are to be found, but a jungle of concepts, where the threat is not to survival, but to the self-image. The dangers are concept-feelings such as that of being unwanted, unloved, unlovable, inadequate, unacceptable, inferior, awkward, clumsy, not belonging, peculiar, different, rejected, humiliated, guilty, unable to find his own way among the different paths of life, disgraced, discriminated against, kept at a distance, suspected, and so on. Is this a man-made jungle created by civilization in place of the jungle to which primitive tribes are exposed? The answer lies in the understanding of a circular process. To a large extent the collectivity of man, in its historical heritage and present conditions, has made this jungle; but to a large extent the patient, too, has created it. Sensitized as he is, because of his past experiences and crippling defenses, he distorts the environment. At this point, his distortion is not yet a paranoid projection or a delusion in a technical sense. It is predominantly experienced as anguish, increased vulnerability, fear, anxiety, mental pain. Now the patient feels not only that the segment of the world that is important to him finds him unacceptable, but also that as long as he lives, he will be unacceptable to others. He is excluded from the busy, relentless ways of the world. He does not fit; he is alone. He experiences ultimate loneliness; and inasmuch as he becomes unacceptable to himself, he also becomes somewhat alienated from himself. It is at this point that the *prepsychotic panic* occurs.

A schizophrenic panic has been described by Sullivan (1953*a*). Sullivan considered it the outcome of injury to self-regard. He also described it as disorganization, terror, perception of danger, need to escape. He explained it as "an acute failure of the dissociative power of the self," that is, of the mechanisms that keep unpleasant memories in repression. In my opinion, it is preferable to distinguish the prepsychotic panic from the psychosis. I consider the prepsychotic panic much more than "an acute failure of the dissociative power" and of injury to self-regard, although it includes these processes. It is at first experienced as a sort of strange emotional *resonance* between something that is very clear (as the devastating self-image brought about by the expansion of the secondary process and of the conceptual world) and something that is unclear and yet gloomy, horrifying. These obscure forces, generally silent but now reemerging with destructive clamor, are the repressed early experiences of the first period and their transformations in accordance with the laws of the primary process. In other words, either because of their strength or because of their inherent similarity to primary process experiences, the ineluctable conceptual conclusions reached through secondary process mechanisms, and their emotional accompaniment, reactivate primary process mechanisms and their original contents. These resurging mechanisms reinforce those of the secondary process, because they are in agreement with them, and the result has dire proportions and consequences. It is this concordance, or unification of the primary and secondary processes, that (1) reawakens the primary process and (2) completes and magnifies in terrifying ways the horrendous vision of the self. In the totality of his human existence, and through the depth of all his feelings, the individual now sees himself as totally defeated, without any worth and possibility of redemption. In the past he had undergone similar experiences, but they were faint; now they are vivid. They are vivid even though they are not verbalized and occur in a nonrepresentational, almost abstract form. They include experiences that cannot be analyzed or broken down into pieces of information and yet are accompanied by increasingly lugubrious feelings. At times a drastic change is experienced dramatically; the patient may wake one morning and feel he cannot get up from bed and go to work or to school. Everything seems useless, meaningless, or frightening. He cannot accept life or himself anymore. He does not dare express these feelings in words. In many cases he would not be able to do so. Nevertheless, in some circumstances he tries to appeal for help. This occurs not too seldom in youngsters who are away in camps or colleges. These appeals are often misunderstood. Occasionally an almost "magic encounter" occurs with a person who is able at once to reach psychologically a patient; in other words, this other person is able to relate to him, to change his secondary process vision of the world, and to arrest the psychosis (see Chapter 22).

CHAPTER

8

Fourth Period: The Psychosis

I

The Onset

In most cases only one solution, one defense, is available to the psyche that has undergone the inner and outer assaults described in the previous chapters: to dissolve the secondary process, the process that has brought about conceptual disaster and has acquired ominous resonance with the archaic primary process. It is at this point that the fourth, psychotic, period begins. It covers the whole psychosis, from its onset to termination. I divide this period into four stages, which will be described in Part Four. In this chapter the discussion will be limited to the initial stage of the psychosis, which is the most important from a psychodynamic point of view. We shall examine in detail the psychodynamic significance of the acute paranoid attack, which lends itself more to a didactical presentation. We must keep in mind, however, that the psychosis may assume many different forms. Also, the prepsychotic panic and the psychosis may blend gradually and slowly, by almost imperceptible steps. At times the gradual changes are so minimal that neither the patient nor his relatives are aware of them. An acquaintance, however, who has not seen the patient for a long time generally recognizes the transformation at once.

When the secondary process starts to disintegrate, it loses control of the primary process, which becomes prominent. The patient acquires nonlearned, nonimitated habits that will constitute his schizophrenic ways of dealing with the world and himself. They are archaic and to a large extent unpredictable ways. They have the flavor of myths and primitivity. They finally do change the unbearable concepts into hallucinated lions and tigers, and mother and father into persecutors or kings or fairies. In other words, the individual now evaluates some aspects of the external world and reassesses some of his past experiences in accordance with the modes of the primary process. The formal characteristics of the dissolution of the secondary process and the return of the primary process will be studied in Part Three.

During the prepsychotic panic, the patient had, so to say, protected the world from blame and to a large extent had considered himself responsible for his own defeat. Now he externalizes again this feeling. He senses a vague feeling of hostility almost in the air. The world is terrible. A sensation of threat surrounds him. He cannot escape from it.

The psychosis starts not only when these concept-feelings are projected to the external world, but also when they become specific and concrete. The indefinite feelings become finite, the imperceptible becomes perceptible, the vague menace is transformed into a specific threat. It is no longer the whole horrible world that is against the patient; "they" are against him. No longer has he a feeling of being under scrutiny, under the eyes of the world; no longer a mild sense of suspiciousness toward his unfriendly neighbors. The sense of suspiciousness becomes the conviction that "they" follow, watch, influence, or even control him. The conceptual and abstract are reduced to the concrete, the specific (Chapter15). The "they" is a concretization of external threats; later, "they" are more definitely recognized as FBI agents, neighbors, or other specific persecutors. Whereas often during the third period the patient felt that millions of authorities were justified in having the lowest opinion of him, now he feels that a few malevolent, powerful people are unfair toward him and cause him troubles. There is thus a return to a situation similar to the one he experienced in his childhood, when he felt that a few powerful people were responsible for his difficulties; but now there is a displacement in his attributing the responsibility. In the majority of cases, not the parents but other people are considered the wrongdoers. This displacement permits, even during the psychosis, a partial repression of the bad image of the parent. In many cases the displacement is later extended to a whole category of persons who are identified with the original wrongdoers. But whether a whole category of people, or a few persons, or only an individual, is seen as the persecutor or persecutors, such people are experienced as persons, as malevolent Thou or malevolent you. The malevolent you, who had been transformed, introjected, tamed, and transformed into a distressing other, is now extrojected, projected, appears strong, often in the most unusual, fantasied forms. At times the patient refers not to a person as the persecutor, but to a machine, rays, telepathy, electricity, with the tacit or manifest understanding that these means are used by some malevolent human beings.

The patient often experiences some phenomena that convince him that something is done or ordained against him. He is the victim of a plot. He is accused of being a spy, a murderer, a traitor, a homosexual. He hears hallucinatory voices that repeat these accusations. He is unhappy, fearful, often indignant.

At first impression one would think that the development of these symptoms is not a defensive maneuver at all. The patient is indeed suffering. It is not difficult to recognize, however, that the externalization (or projection) and the reduction (or concretization) of some of the psychodynamic conflicts into these psychotic symptoms prove to be advantageous to him. As unpleasant as it is to be accused by others, it is not as unpleasant as to accuse oneself. It is true that because of the cognitive transformations, to be studied in Chapter 16, the accusation assumes a specific form. For instance, the projected feeling of being a failure does not appear as a belief of being accused of being a failure, but of being a spy or a murderer. These accusations seem worse than the original self-accusations, but are more easily projected to others. The patient who believes he is accused feels falsely accused. Thus, although the projected accusation is painful, it is not injurious to the self-esteem. On the contrary, in comparison with his prepsychotic state, the patient experiences a rise in self-esteem, often accompanied by a feeling of martyrdom. The person who is really accused now is not the patient, but the persecutor who is accused of persecuting the patient. What was an intrapsychic evaluation of the self now becomes an evaluation or an attitude of malevolent others who reside in the external world. No longer does the patient consider himself bad; the others unfairly think he is bad. The danger, which used to be an internal one, is now transformed by the psychosis into an external one. *In this transformation actually lies the psychodynamic significance of the paranoid psychosis.* Guilt feeling is eliminated. In some cases pleasant self-images that were not allowed to exist are now recaptured and often assume a grandiose, distorted, grotesque appearance.

The delusion of persecution is not just a projection and a concretization. An unpleasant part of the self-image is restituted, brought back to symbolic equivalents of the people who originally appraised the patient in a way that, rightly or wrongly, was experienced as destructive and undermining. Inasmuch as this appraisal was experienced in this negative way, it became an important constituent of the negative self-image. In the psychotic period the rest of the self no longer accepts that part of the self-image.

An incomplete form of this mechanism is found in some neurotic, borderline, prepsychotic, and also psychotic patients. In these cases the patient continues to accuse, hate, and disparage himself at the same time that he thinks that other people have the same feelings toward him. Thus, there is a partial projection to other people of the feelings that the patient nourishes toward himself, but there is no repudiation of this self-accusatory component of his psyche, that is, of the self-image of the bad child. In these instances the mechanism of projection, which is arrested before it reaches full proportions, consists of the fact that people in general are experienced as authorities and are identified with the parents. It does not consist of a return to others of the derogatory self-image. In some of these cases the emotional disturbance to which the patient is subjected is terrific. The *you* is experienced both outside, in the external world, and inside, in the psyche of the patient. If the emotional pressure continues or increases, the patient may find relief only in a psychotic attack, which will remove *the internal you,* that is, the unpleasant image of the self.

In some cases the transition between the third and fourth period is not so clear or definite as we have described. Frosch (1964) has illustrated a lifelong psychotic character without definite psychosis, and, as we have already mentioned, Hoch and Polatin (1949) reported cases with a permanent pseudoneurotic symptomatology. At times the sequence of events takes an insidious, slow course that is hard to delineate. We really do not know when the psychosis started. These are the cases that received most attention from Adolph Meyer, who saw the process as an indefinite deterioration of habits (see Chapter 2). At other times we do not have definite psychotic symptoms, but only oddity of behavior reminiscent of what Bleuler called latent schizophrenia (Chapter 2). In some cases the patient (more frequently a woman) presents a symptomatology that is halfway between a phobic psychoneurosis and a delusional psychosis. The patient has several fears, fo instance, of being attacked at night. Somebody may come while she sleeps and strangle her or kill her in various ways. Psychodynamic studies soon reveal that these fears are concrete representations of the more complicated fear of life that the patient is experiencing.

Since the first edition of this book was published in 1955, we have witnessed in the United States a marked increase in cases of schizophrenia occurring in adolescence and early adulthood, from the age of 13 to 23. In contrast to previous decades, psychiatric hospitals have recently admitted a large number of young patients. We must assume that the present cultural climate in the United States facilitates the occurrence at an early age of that conceptual attack to the self that brings about resonance and unification with primary process experience. To follow the sociologist Riesman (et al., 1950), the culture has recently become more and more other-directed. The models are the peers and the contemporaries, not the older generations or the heroes of the past. The conceived ideals are considered less distant and are expected to be more quickly attained. Consequently, the despair in the self occurs earlier in life.

This consideration and others reveal that there is a strict relation between the psychodynamics of the individual case and the sociocultural environment. The events that we have described in this chapter, as well as in Chapters 5, 6, and 7, are either facilitated or inhibited by sets of sociocultural circumstances that will be studied in detail in Part Six.

II

Different Views of the Psychodynamic Meaning of the Psychosis

Some psychiatrists interpret the psychosis, not as a negative or pathological phenomenon, but as a positive development that reveals truths to fellow men and opens new paths toward greater moral values. We must devote a few words to these conceptions, which recently have acquired some popularity. In several writings, the Finnish psychiatrist Siirala (1961, 1963) discusses what he considers the prophetic value of many apparent delusions of schizophrenics. Siirala sees the patient as a victim and as a prophet to whom nobody listens. He sees the therapist as a person who has the duty to reveal to society the prophecies of these patients. These prophecies would consist of insights into our collective sickness, into the murders that we have committed for many generations and that we have buried so that they will not be noticed (1963). He feels that schizophrenia emerges out of a common sort of sickness, a sickness shared by the others, the healthy.

In Laing's opinion schizophrenia is not a disease, but a broken-down relationship (1967). The environment of the patient is so bad that he has to invent special strategies in order "to live in this unlivable situation." The psychotic does not want to do any more denying. He unmasks himself; he unmasks the others. The psychosis thus appears as madness only to ordinary human beings, who have the limited vision of the secondary process. Not only the family but society at large with its hypocrisies makes the situation unlivable. Echoing in a certain way Szasz (1961), Laing goes to the extent of saying that the diagnosis of schizophrenia is political, not medical.

I agree with these authors only to a limited degree. In my opinion, the schizophrenic, especially the paranoid, in both his prepsychotic and psychotic stages, behaves and thinks as if he had a psychological radar that enabled him to detect and register the world's hostility much more than can the average person. Must we assess this characteristic as a positive value that we can share or as manifestation of illness? To discuss whether the paranoid is delusional or a prophet is like discussing whether a dream represents irrationality or the "real reality." The dream is very true as an experience and may indeed reveal a message that is not easily heard when we are awake, but dreams transmit the truth in a fictitious way. Although hostility exists in the world, the psychotic's version of it is pathological. Although the hostility is related etiologically to the psychosis, other predisposing factors also enable it to become related. Although the hostility is an operating psychodynamic factor, other important psychodynamic factors are involved.

We must be aware of the possibility that the patient has positive values upon which the psychosis inflicts a transformation. If we remove the delusional overlay we may retrieve the values in their original purity. In our psychodynamic inquiries we discover that the patient was exposed to hostility in his family. Moreover, as we shall see in Part Six, studies of social psychiatry reveal that the parents, too, were the object of adverse social circumstances that predisposed them to poor parenthood. However, in my opinion we cannot conclude that the schizophrenic psychosis is a normal reaction to an abnormal situation, as the mentioned authors imply. In my opinion it is *an abnormal way of dealing with an unfavorable situation.* The psychosis cannot be called just a rebellion to a prior unlivable situation. The prior situation may have been so unfavorable as to be experienced as unlivable, but the rebellion is abnormal and also hardly livable. In other words, we must not stop at an analysis of the environment that the patient met, especially in childhood. This is number one in our list of inquiries, but only number one. We must also study the particular way in which the future patient experienced the environment, the particular ways by which he internalized it, and the particular ways by which this internalization led to subsequent instability and finally to the psychosis.

It is true that schizophrenia reflects sociocultural factors in many respects. It is also true that from the study of it we may learn new values. The same statement, however, could be repeated for every human situation that is not strictly biological. For instance, if we analyze a murder that has been committed, we soon discover that the whole cause of it is not restricted to the murderer's intent, but that society, too, shares some responsibility, Moreover, paraphrasing Siirala, we may say that not only our present society is responsible, but all previous generations of men who directly or indirectly have influenced our lives so that murders are possible in our time. In the same way, each case of schizophrenia is representative of those human situations in which something went very wrong in the act of becoming part of society or in the act of consensually validating one's emotions, behavior, and symbols with those of one's community.

However, this is different from assuming that the schizophrenic is directly concerned with the sickness of society or that the sickness of society is directly or solely responsible for the schizophrenic syndrome.* Although the paranoid schizophrenic may borrow the scenario of the society-oriented person, his suffering can easily be recognized as a personal one and as different from that of the philosopher, the prophet, the innovator, the revolutionary, the dissenter.

Contrary to Laing's conceptions, in by far the majority of cases we cannot consider the patient in his predominant characteristics as an asserter of truth, a remover of the masks. The patient tells us his experiential truth, which often contains some truth about the evils of the world. This partial truth must be recognized by the therapist and must be acknowledged and used in treatment (see Part Seven). Its import must be neither ignored nor exaggerated. If we ignore it, we become deaf to a profound message that the patient may try to convey. If we exaggerate it, we also do a disservice to him. We may admire the patient for removing the masks, for saying what other people do not dare to say, for how much he accepted and how much he rejected, for the supreme effort to adjust to a nonadjustable situation, and for going down to defeat rather than to deny his self.† But we must also recognize that the fragments of truth he uncovers assume grotesque forms, and that he will apply these grotesque forms to the whole world, so that whatever insight he has achieved will be less pronounced and less profound than his distor-

* This point of view is related to what some philosophers call the theory of "internal relations." According to this view, "The world is rational in the specific sense that every fact and event is connected with its context, and ultimately with every other fact and event, in a way that is logically necessary" (Blanshard, 1967). For instance, the fact that Richard Nixon is president of the United States is connected with the fact that Columbus discovered America and that the United States is part of our solar system.

Unless we adopt in psychiatry, too, the theory of internal relations, we must consider and evaluate only the factors that are necessary, nonreplaceable, and specific determinants of the phenomena that we are studying.

† See, for instance, the case of Geraldine (Chapter 40) and, to a lesser degree, the case of Gabriel (Chapter 9).

tion. And his distortion not only has no adaptational value, but is inimical to any form of adaptation even within a liberal community of men.

The psychotic outcome is thus only a pseudosolution. Therapists and patients alike must come to the recognition that the environmental circumstances are responsible for the disorder, not in a simple relation of direct causality, but because in different stages of the patient's development they facilitated intrapsychic mechanisms that later permitted the psychosis to feed on itself. It is too simple and too naïve to join the patient in blaming solely the environment. The psychosis does not represent any longer an external drama; it is predominantly an inner drama and inner metamorphosis. As a matter of fact the main defensive aspect of the psychosis is the transformation of an intrapsychic danger into an external one.

Another view of the psychodynamic meaning of the psychosis is that the psychosis merely represents irrationality directly transmitted from the parents to the patient. This point of view, which we have already referred to in Chapter 5, was presented in 1958 by Lidz and collaborators. It was later expressed again by Fleck (1960), Wynne and Singer (1963), and Jackson (1967*a,b*). This irrationality is said to be learned by the patient in a way similar to the way a child learns special habits or some patterns of living from his parents. Here are some examples.

Fleck (1960) described a patient, Dollfuss, who presented bizarre and peculiar psychotic behavior, delusions, ideas of reference, and hoarding of food. Like his father he was preoccupied with strange mystical religions and would seclude himself for hours in the bathroom as his father had also done.

D. D. Jackson (1967*a*) reported the following example. A young paranoid patient says very little except for the following sentence, which he often repeats: "It's all a matter of chemistry and physics." The interviewer asked the parents what they thought about their son's illness. After a long silence the mother said, "Well, we don't know anything about it. It's just a matter of chemistry and physics to us." The father and the patient then repeated in a low tone, "Yeah, just a matter of chemistry and physics." But to think that schizophrenia is a "matter of chemistry and physics" is not necessarily schizophrenia irrationally transmitted from parents to children. Even a large number of psychiatrists share this belief. Wynne and collaborators go even further than Lidz and Fleck. They believe that not only irrational content but even an abnormal way of thinking is learned by the patient from the members of the family. The patient has learned to think in a diffuse, fragmented, or amorphous way.

I understand how easy it is to be persuaded by this interpretation. A female patient hears a voice calling her a prostitute. But we know from her history that the mother would really call her "a whore" just because she was wearing lipstick.

The mother of a young paranoid male schizophrenic may be a hostile, suspicious person, whose vision of the world is one permeated by pessimism, distrust, and hate: the world is a jungle; people are ready to cheat you. If you want to survive, you must be careful and be prepared to defend yourself. This point of view is not necessarily psychotic. It may even be called a philosophy of life, which may very well be transmitted to the world. However, when the son of this mother not only sees the world as hostile, but starts to think that people are plotting to kidnap him or to poison him, he goes further than the mother. To the irrationality of the mother he has added his psychotic, autistic, primary process twist.

The error some authors make is *not* simply in seeing a connection between the irrationality of the patient and that of his parents. *Obviously such connection exists*. These authors err when they confuse psychodynamics (or content) with the form (psychological structure). The irrationality of the schizophrenic is not transmitted from generation to generation by means of simple mechanisms, in the way that language, manners, or mores are transmitted. Direct transmission is not a mechanism that can explain the characteristics of schizophrenic thinking, delusional ideas, hallucinations, and so on. If the parents of the schizophrenic would present the same irrationality and would use the same forms of cognition as the patient, they themselves would be recognized as schizophrenics, but they are not, except in a relatively small percentage of cases. They may be peculiar, odd, eccentric. Certainly their children may adopt their peculiarities, but they are not to be diagnosed schizophrenic simply because they learn these peculiarities. To the extent that they do, they may also be eccentric, but not schizophrenic. Schizophrenia is not learned, although it may be acquired by virtue of certain relations with parents and the family. The family affects the patient psychodynamically, so that eventually under the stress of conflicts the secondary process mechanisms weaken or disintegrate, primary process mechanisms acquire predominance, become the media that carry the conflicts, and the psychosis occurs. Certainly psychotic symptoms reflect or echo the family conflicts, just as a dream may reflect family conflicts. Family conflicts could never explain the characteristics of dreams, for example, reduction of ideas to visual images, special way of thinking, confusion of reality with imagination, and so on.

In one of the just mentioned examples, the mark of schizophrenia was not that the patient had been told by the mother that she behaved like a prostitute: this may be part of the dynamics. The mark of schizophrenia was that the mother's accusation in this case (and not in that of other patients with similar history) was transformed into a hallucinatory voice.

Not only the family, but also society and culture may inflict on the individual peculiar habits, false beliefs, myths, prejudices, and schizophrenic-like modes of thinking. To the extent that the individual learns these peculiarities from the culture and even accepts them as normal and rational, he is not psychotic. He becomes a concern to the sociologist and anthropologist as well as to the psychiatrist.

Culture and society, like the family, remain important psychodynamic factors because they do affect the psychodynamics of the family and of the sense of self. Thus indirectly they may contribute greatly to the engendering of mental illness (see Part Six). It is because I have seen how many times these issues have been misunderstood that I have thought it necessary to devote to them more than a few words.

Needless to say, the misunderstanding of how the familial or social environment affects the patient does not detract from the high value of the contributions to the study of the psychodynamics of the family of the schizophrenic that such authors as Lidz, Jackson, Wynne, Fleck, and others have made.

A point of view that, in some respects, seems opposite to the one just considered must also be avoided, namely, the view that family relations operate only by triggering off potential psychotic symptoms in genetically predisposed individuals. Again the mechanisms are not so simple. Disturbed family relations are not just predisposing or precipitating factors. They become intensely connected with the personality and psychological structure of the individual patient. They are intertwined with the development and psychotic denouement. They do not act just as cold weather does in reference to pneumonia and malnutrition in the case of tuberculosis. The interplay is much more complex.

III

Relevance of Late Precipitating Events

For the sake of clarity we have omitted from our discussion the importance of some external events that have occurred shortly before the prepsychotic panic or the onset of the psychosis.

The importance of these events deserves careful study. There are many cases of schizophrenia in which the prepsychotic panic or the onset of the psychosis occurs without having been preceded by any particularly significant external event. On the other hand, other cases occur after such events as marriage, childbirth, loss of a position, accident at work, automobile accident, traveling, flunking examinations, striking of a new friendship, quarrel with one's boss or with coworkers, changing apartment, and so on.

In the majority of these cases it is easy to recognize that the precipitating event would not have had the power to engender the state of panic and the psychosis if the ground had not been prepared by the circumstances that we have described in Chapters 5, 6, and 7.

However, we cannot dismiss altogether the significance of the precipitating event. Here again we have another manifestation of the interplay between two categories of factors: the external and the internal. The authors who divide schizophrenia into the process and reactive types acknowledge the importance of the precipitating event only in the reactive type.

Let us examine now some of these precipitating events. In most cases it is easy to recognize that the occurrence of a specific event suddenly put the patient in a position in which he had to face a challenge that he thought he would not be able to cope with. Even the very schizoid person at times is not able to avoid challenges. As we have mentioned before, in spite of his detachment he harbors secret desires of experiencing feelings again and of making excursions into life. Occasionally, in a rather uncautious manner, he takes active steps that are completely incongruous with his previous attitude. More often, however, he lets himself be pushed by the events.

A schizoid young woman may be induced by her mother to get married, although she is psychologically unprepared for that step. The husband, actually selected by the mother, may be experienced as another parent who will evoke the old childhood anxiety.

A schizoid man, who has lived in a single room of a boardinghouse for many years, practically in isolation, may come in contact with another tenant, an aggressive, domineering woman. By her aggressive methods, she may succeed in overcoming his shyness, and then later in convincing him to marry her. Sexual urges or desire to comply with the expectations of society may induce the patient to accept the marriage proposal. After the marriage, the patient's anxiety is apt to increase because he finds in the wife a replica of the image he once had of his parents. He will make serious attempts to adjust to the spouse's new way of living, but he will find that task insurmountable. Because of what he considers blatant proof of his failure in living, he can no longer hide from himself the feeling of worthlessness that he has been able to check up to that point in life.

The intimacy of marriage is often very threatening for the patient, because it tends to reproduce situations similar to those that have caused him intense anxiety in his childhood.

Another frequent occurrence that may precipitate the panic is the unexpected development of a friendship or of some social contact with a person of the same sex. Strangely enough, the patient succeeds, for the first time in his life, in establishing a more meaningful interpersonal relationship, but homosexuality, which had been repressed for so long on account of the social ostracism connected with it and on account of the patient's rejection of the parent of the same sex, threatens to come to the fore again and causes deep anxiety. This development is often referred to in the literature as homosexual panic. Disappointments in love may be especially traumatic in those women (now diminishing in number) who seek their identity only by living for a man, or in marriage. The security of a love relation compensates for the instability that permeates their lives. The challenge here is how to be able to face life again after such disappointment. The challenge constituted by childbirth will be discussed in detail in Chapter 13. Acute catatonic attacks are often precipitated by sudden and difficult decisions the patient has to make (Chapter 10).

The person with a stormy personality will be forced even more than the schizoid to face the challenges of his inappropriate actions, which bring about additional precipitating events.

In a large number of cases the event seems so minor as to be hardly conceived as the precipitating event of such a serious occurrence as the psychosis. For instance, the patient had a minor automobile accident, lost her pocketbook, changed his apartment, has been dismissed from a very insignificant job. In these cases we must be aware of two possibilities: (1) the apparently insignificant event has the power to reactivate a very significant and traumatic event in the early life of the patient (see case of Laura, Chapter 11; (2) although not related to specific past events, the episode transcends itself in psychological significance; *it fits the patient's particular vulnerability*. For instance, a small accident on the job may be interpreted as the final proof of the patient's utter inadequacy. In other words, to the distressing reality of the event, in itself not overwhelming, additional traumatic force is added symbolically. And it is the symbolic part that is overwhelming.

We are often confronted with an opposite set of factors. Very extenuating and taxing external or realistic events not only do not precipitate a schizophrenic psychosis, but at times seem even able to prevent it. Conditions of obvious danger, as they occur in time of war, national defeat, and adversities that affect the whole community, do not *per se* precipitate schizophrenia. They may elicit anxiety and psychological disorders, but do not necessarily hurt the sense of self. In some conditions, like state of war or military defeat, a feeling of solidarity or common destiny and the absence of personal responsibility for what is happening may even be helpful to the self-image.

The psychiatrist must carefully differentiate two types of anxiety, the one that signals an external danger and the one that signals an internal one. Only the latter is important in the psychodynamics of schizophrenia. As a matter of fact we have seen that one of the important psychodynamic aspects of the psychosis is that of transforming an inner danger into an external one. This transformation occurs also in many dreams, but not in all of them. The dream, more than the psychosis, accepts injury to the self. It may even "train" the dreamer to accept the danger or to find ways to solve it (see Chapter 39).

CHAPTER

9

Patients Studied through Family Members

In this chapter, we shall begin to study individual cases. We shall start, not with the direct study of schizophrenic patients, but with an evaluation of the dynamic factors operating in their lives, as they appear from the treatment of a close relative. As a matter of fact, the schizophrenic patient to be reported in detail in this chapter was never seen by me, nor discussed in supervision with other colleagues. This seemingly unorthodox procedure has a definite purpose: to illustrate how much in some instances we can learn about the psychodynamics of schizophrenia from the special perspective of a close member of the family. Thus, although this procedure can be included in the framework of family studies, it has the additional advantages of an intensive individual psychotherapy. The distortions and unilateral views of the family member who was treated were carefully considered, analyzed, and corrected when recognized.

We shall also discuss in this chapter, in reference to a specific family, a problem that has puzzled many psychiatrists: even when the environment has been very adverse, most of the time only one of the siblings develops schizophrenia.

This chapter will illustrate that the parents and the family environment are the same for all the siblings in name only. The parents, in their feelings and in their conscious and unconscious attitudes, are different for each child. They may elicit a very destructive pattern of events in one child, and a less destructive one or one that is not destructive at all in another child. Siblings, in their attitudes and feelings, are also different toward one another or toward the parents, so that actually for each member of the same family the play of interpersonal forces is different. Of course, from a genetic point of view, too, the parents are different for each child, because they transmit to each of them a different set of genes. However, at this stage of our knowledge, we cannot assert that the different genetic endowment in siblings denies the importance of the variety of the psychodynamic contingencies to which they were exposed.

The information reported in this chapter was obtained from Peter, a severely neurotic patient with some schizoid traits, who was the brother of Gabriel, a full-fledged schizophrenic. After the cases of the two brothers have been presented individually, some comments will be made concerning both of them and their family.

Peter

Peter * was a 23-year-old male of Jewish extraction, born in Central Europe. After the German invasion of his native land, his family moved to a South American country, where they have resided since then. Peter started to complain of nervous symptoms about a year prior to the beginning of psychiatric treatment. After trying every kind of physical treatment in South America, the parents felt that a trip to the United States would do him some good. In the United States Peter continued to be distressed by his symptoms and consulted a physician, who advised him to see a psychiatrist.

During the first interview, the patient appeared morose and preoccupied. He could hardly speak English and expressed himself mostly in Spanish. He said that he perspired all over, had repeated attacks of diarrhea, could not sleep, and felt always tired and tense. These symptoms abated somewhat when he was not in the company of others. He added that when he was very tense, his nose would first become clogged, then red and swollen. He was worried lest people would see this disfiguration of his face. He also said that he felt guilty over the death of his brother Gabriel, who had been affected by schizophrenia and had recently committed suicide. Peter felt that maybe he too was affected by an organic disease of the brain, and that maybe "a bad heredity ran in the family." He was very disturbed.

Psychotherapy was recommended, and Peter agreed to it. For many sessions the main topic was the patient's parents. The mother, 43 years old, was described by Peter as a fearful person who had no confidence in herself. Although she was well educated and spoke many languages, she always claimed that she did not know anything and did not want to participate in any discussion. When the family moved to South America, she was afraid to make social contacts to such a point that she had not succeeded in making a single friend in the new country. When she was introduced to people, she blushed and was so nervous that she could not even pronounce her own name. Peter felt he could never confide in her. To use his own words, he never heard one thing from her that he liked to hear. Talks between mother and son would usually end in fights. She criticized everything he did: his work, his girl friends, his attitude toward his father, and so forth. She also never praised him. When he was a child, she hit him repeatedly; during the beat-

* All names of patients in this book are fictitious and identifying data have been altered.

ings he would smile at her in defiance. She put him to bed at half-past six every evening until he was 6 years old.

Peter never experienced any feeling of closeness for his mother; on the contrary, he always had contempt for her. In the beginning of the treatment he thought that maybe he loved her, but then he felt that he really did not. It was difficult for him to make such an admission, for he experienced guilt feelings for not loving her. He had forced himself to love her because a child should love his mother, but no real warmth or love had existed between them. Peter did not remember, except in very rare instances, having been kissed or hugged by his mother. She had been equally cold and distant, or even more so, toward Gabriel.

Peter's mother had always been unhappy, more so after the death of her second child. Peter knew that his grandmother had treated her badly, and that she had married his father to escape from her parents. At first she did not care for her husband, but finally she "adjusted" to him. Now mother was the father's most powerful ally in any controversy between him and the patient.

Peter's father, 51 years old, had played the most important role in Peter's life. According to the patient, he was a mechanical genius. In Europe he was a farmer, and mechanical engineering was his hobby; but in South America he had gone into the business of building machines for farmers. With little means, he had built marvelous machines and had had a few new agricultural implements patented.

Peter's father had peculiar habits. He got up at six o'clock in the morning, worked the whole day without any relaxation, and went to bed at six o'clock in the evening. He ate in bed, spoke to his wife about business for a few minutes, and then went to sleep. He was also as fearful as the mother was, but in a different way. Ever since Peter was a baby, he had heard his father say that they had to be careful, because "People are bad. They are ready to cheat you and steal from you if you are not careful enough." Peter's father cultivated no friends. His only interest was to save money. "Save, save; save everything in every way" was his motto. For instance, when he brushed his teeth, he used the minimum amount of tooth powder. Peter was proud of his father because he knew that to save was a good thing. Another of his father's mottoes, which he liked to hear when he was a child was, "Foolish people make shit of gold; wise people make gold of shit." Peter's father would also praise wise people who were able to overcome the innumerable adversities of life. Peter listened to him with great admiration and was always convinced that his father was right. His father never told him, "You have to do so-and-so," but he merely said, "I did so-and-so," and that was enough. The paternal examples were an unbreakable code of behavior for Peter.

Father had been very considerate of Peter since the day he was born; he seemed to concentrate his attention on him and to neglect Gabriel. He used to tell Peter many stories, whose purpose, Peter thought, was only entertainment. But, as Peter discovered during treatment, his father, with his stories, had been constantly seeking admiration from the child. His father would say that many of the stories were episodes from his own life. Peter remembers that when he was 4, his father had already told him of his adventures during the war against Russia. He had many scars on his arms and would exhibit them and say that they were the results of wounds sustained in fighting against a large number of Russians. Peter would listen in ecstatic reverence, but, at the age of 6, he heard from an uncle that his father had never been in the war. Later he even found out that his father had been a deserter, and for several years during the war had hidden himself in a cellar. Peter was ready to excuse his father, feeling that he had to lie to "undo the truth," and preserve the honor of the family. The other stories that his father used to tell him concerned children who had been massacred in wars; some were about gypsies who had stolen children and had cut their throats with a sharp knife, after which the children had died a slow death, having been in agony for hours and hours. Father used to tell Peter these stories while he was sitting on his lap and would often simulate a cutting knife with his hands, laughingly saying, "We have to *schecht* * this child."

The stories that Peter's father told emphasized the evilness of life. The world was terrible; Peter had better be careful and stay near his father for protection. Father, or a paternal figure, was the hero and the protector, who would solve all the problems. For instance, Peter's father would often mention how he had eliminated the economic difficulties of his own parents by working hard since he had been a child. What a good child he had been, and what a wonderful man he had become! In Peter there was a strong desire to emulate him, but at the same time he experienced anxiety because he felt that he would not be able to be a good child, according to his father's standards. His father never seemed to be satisfied; he often complained of how much the family was making him suffer; too much money was spent, too little work was accomplished, and so on. He never seemed to be pleased and never praised Peter or any other members of the family. Moreover, he often made impossible demands. Peter remembers that once when he was 4½ years old, he went for a walk with his father in the country. They came to a narrow brook. Father wanted to go to the other side of this brook, but because there was no bridge, he decided to pick Peter up and throw him over to the other side on the grass. However, he did not succeed in doing so, and Peter fell into the middle of the brook and got all wet. For a second the child was scared and looked at his father. There he was, laughing. Why did father laugh? Peter thought he did so to reassure him; but was it really so? During the treatment, Peter realized that there had always been a double meaning in what his father did. That was what had confused him more than anything else.

Peter's father also had had the habit of simulating William Tell. He used to ask Peter to hold a piece of wood in his hand, and then he would shoot at the wood with a real gun from a distance of a few yards. While this was happening, Peter's mother would be infuriated and would scream from the window of the house, horrified at the possibility of an accident. The patient felt that his mother was a despicable coward who did not want to give him a chance to prove his courage and heroism to father.

Much later, when Peter was working for his father on a farm, and was using

* Jewish word for "cutting" or "slaughtering."

a big agricultural machine, the little finger of his right hand got caught in the teeth of a large cogwheel. The wheel was moving only in one direction so that it was not possible for the finger to be freed unless the whole machine was dismantled. Peter decided immediately to keep the machine moving even if it meant losing a finger. He tolerated the pain very well as the machine was amputating the last phalanx. After receiving first aid, he left the farm and ran to his parents' home, proud of himself, hoping that he would receive admiration for his heroic gesture. But even then he was disappointed. His parents did not seem to be pleased.

At other times the patient would expose himself to dangers in the jungle, hunting snakes and other wild beasts in an attempt to obtain recognition from his father. The few times that he got recognition, his anxiety was not relieved because he felt that now he had a bigger task; that is, he had to retain that level of attainment. He felt that the demands on him would increase. He was therefore always in a state of self-perpetuating anxiety caused by a feeling of nonfulfillment. In his own words, he was "running after an escaping goal, like a child runs after the moon." This anxiety, which originated in relation to his father, increased with his contacts with other persons, whom he experienced as father substitutes.

The father never paid enough attention to Gabriel, who never admired him as Peter did. Somehow, the father did not seek as much admiration from the second child.

Apparently Peter was not fully aware of his own anxiety and state of unhappiness. He lived with a modicum of stability, conferred on him by the security he obtained in trying to fulfill his father's demands. But, to use his own words, "To sustain myself on father was like sustaining myself on quicksand . . . but even quicksand is better than nothing. Without that quicksand there would have been only emptiness."

The situation remained about the same until an important event occurred in the family. At the end of World War II, a cousin, Miriam, and her husband, Leo, arrived from Europe. Through the good offices of Peter's father, they had been able to obtain a visa to immigrate to South America. After their arrival, it was decided that Peter and Leo would go to a farm owned by the father to work together. Father was enthusiastic about the farm and told them that they could become millionaires. It was agreed that Leo would get one-half of the profit, Peter one-fourth, and his father one-fourth. Peter started to work with great enthusiasm and hope. They had to chop away the wild vegetation of the jungle, cut the trees, seed new plants, remove stones, build cabins, and so on. Leo, Peter, and a group of natives worked an average of sixteen hours a day. But the father was never satisfied. Now and then he would come from the city to inspect and would always have a great many criticisms to make. Because it was new land, not yet cultivated, he had to invest money. He resented that and was incapable of waiting for the results. Father started to talk against Leo, telling Peter how lazy Leo was, what a bum he was, how incapable he was of fulfilling his obligations.

But now, for the first time in his life, Peter had been exposed to close contact with another adult and could no longer accept the derogatory attitude of his father.

Leo seemed to be a very nice man. Peter often compared him with his father and could see how much better Leo was. Leo knew how to enjoy life; he knew how to work, but also how to play. He would talk, not about money or work exclusively, but also about sports and women. A friendship grew between the two. Peter discovered a new world; he came to know that a different life existed and realized that his home had been a "living grave." At the same time he was torn by conflicts. Maybe father was right. Leo was too self-indulgent; maybe he could think about trivial things because he was a mediocre man, not a genius like father.

Three months after they had started to work, Leo told Peter that his father wanted to change his verbal agreement and give Leo only one-third of the profit. Peter became very indignant and went to the city to argue with his father. It was the first time in his life that he opposed his father. Violent verbal fights resulted. Father told mother, "Peter is not our son; he is Leo's son." Peter tried to persuade his parents to change their opinion of Leo, but it was not possible to convince them. He went on working for a while with Leo, but the altercations continued. This situation deteriorated rapidly, so that the work on the farm had to be stopped, and the farm was sold.

From that time on, Peter's symptoms became manifest. He became aware of a state of anxiety whenever he had to perform a task. When in company, he was afraid that his nose would become swollen. Often he was tormented by acute pain in his chest and stomach. He would perspire conspicuously.

During the course of treatment, Peter improved gradually. Many months were devoted to the analysis of his relations with his parents. Whereas in the very beginning he had claimed that he loved his father and mother, later his real feelings for them became obvious. He had fantasies in which he imagined that he was quarreling with his parents. At first these fantasies occupied all of his free time. All his thoughts had only one purpose, namely, to show his parents that they were wrong. He also realized that his actions always had one of two purposes, either to fulfill his father's expectations or to prove that he was wrong. In order to act, he would have to give himself an order: "Do this, do that; you don't do well enough." He recognized that these were the words of the incorporated father. Every action was loaded with anxiety. He had many dreams that repeated almost the same scene. He was doing something wrong; his father was dissatisfied, but ostensibly seemed to approve. In the dream Peter had the feeling that his father did not mean to approve and felt worse than if he had openly disapproved.

He had recurrent dreams in which sharks appeared. One of these typical dreams is the following: Peter is in the ocean, riding on the back of a shark. There are many other sharks in the water, so that it is safe to be on the back of one of them. The shark he is on goes up and down, in and out of the water, producing in Peter a fear of drowning.

Another of the dreams is the following: Peter is pushed into the water by an invisible force. In the water he sees many sharks devouring human beings. A shark comes toward him. At first he is afraid, but then he sees that the shark is smiling and is going to kiss him. Peter laughs, and also kisses the shark, but has the feeling of degrading himself.

Peter remembers that he has had dreams about sharks since the age of 4, at which time he liked the company of Irving, a much older cousin, who would tell him stories. His father did not want him to stay with Irving; he would say, "Don't stay near him; I don't like him. We don't know him well enough. He may be a bad man. He may even have syphilis." Peter remembers that his father would say the same thing about any person with whom he would associate. He was apparently jealous and wanted Peter's admiration only for himself.

One day Irving explained about sharks to Peter. "Sharks are animals who seem very tame and nice; but finally in a treacherous way they come near you and eat you up." After that, Peter's feelings for Irving changed. He felt distant from him; he felt that his father had been right, and that maybe Irving had syphilis. He could not understand why his feelings changed, but in the course of treatment he realized that he had unconsciously identified the shark with his father, and that he had wanted to reject this identification, which Irving, with his talks, had made possible. In the dreams, Peter realized, father is an evil shark, but a protecting one who defends him from the other sharks who populate this horrible world. At the same time this protecting shark causes anxiety too (jumping up and down, in and out of the water, indicating uncertain approval). In order to survive, he has to debase himself, to kiss the shark, to submit himself to the horrible father.

During treatment Peter acquired gradual understanding, and the intensity of anxiety decreased. The psychosomatic symptoms all disappeared. In situations which represented an unusual task for him, however, the anxiety tended to recur. When treatment was terminated, he had integrated better socially, but was still uncertain about the future. He went out with girls and had successful sexual relations. He still had the tendency to lean on strong people, whom he accepted as authorities. He had intellectual insight about his dependent attitude, and succeeded in controlling it to a certain extent. He was able to immigrate to the United States with a permanent visa, but he was uncertain what his definitive residence would be. Two or three years after termination of treatment he wrote to me from a distant town, notifying me that he would return to South America.

Gabriel

This is the story of Gabriel as it was reconstructed from the information obtained during the treatment of Peter.

Gabriel was born two and one-half years after Peter. The mother's attitude toward Gabriel was the same as toward Peter; she was a cold and hostile person whose main role was a punitive one. On the other hand, the father's attitude toward Gabriel was vey much different from the one he had toward Peter. Gabriel and his father did not seem to care for each other. In the beginning of treatment, Peter felt that Gabriel never had had much interest in their father; but later on he discovered that their father had had no interest in Gabriel. He seemed to have had his needs satisfied by the admiration and love that he received from Peter and did not seem to have needed Gabriel. He was much cooler toward the second child. Gabriel would seldom come to listen to his father's stories and did not show any admiration or enthusiasm for him. In return, his father gave him practically no affection. A different pattern was thus established, one of detachment. The very few times that the parents showed consideration for Gabriel, they did not evoke a satisfactory response. On the other hand, the attitude of Gabriel toward Peter was different. Gabriel was rather shy and had difficulty in making friends. He wanted to lean on Peter for companionship, but Peter resented that and was not willing to please him. Peter was jealous of his friends; he had the feeling that Gabriel wanted to steal them from him and used to tell him to find his own friends. Gabriel sometimes wanted to play "cops and robbers" with Peter and his friends, but he was not good enough. Peter used to make fun of him and would often refer to his funny ears, which would greatly embarrass Gabriel.

Peter felt that Gabriel did not belong in his company and used every possible means to show that Gabriel was inferior to him. He remembers that up to the age of 12 Gabriel used to cry loudly for long periods of time. He would cry in fury, and Peter would make fun of him. Whenever Gabriel went to his father to complain about his brother, the father would scold Peter, but not in a forceful way. Peter knew that his father did not mean to punish him and therefore was not fearful. Gabriel soon used to forget the fights with Peter, and after a short time would go to his brother again for companionship; he wanted to follow Peter, as Peter's own shadow did, but he was almost always rejected.

Gabriel showed no enthusiasm for anything; he was quiet, spoke very little, and often nobody knew that he was there. He would never ask for toys and never got anything. The father used to say that Gabriel was not even interested in toys; when Peter got the toys and Gabriel tried to touch them, however, he was rebuffed by Peter. There were moments, nevertheless, when Peter and Gabriel understood each other and enjoyed their mutual companionship. The very few times that Peter fought with his parents, he sought out Gabriel and felt love for him. Gabriel was glad to be on Peter's side and give him support.

In school Gabriel was a very good student. The teachers would say that he learned much better than Peter. He was particularly good in writing and drawing. At home he was a very obedient child; he would never rebel. Both Peter and Gabriel complied, but in a different way. Peter's was an active compliance, Gabriel's a passive one. Peter participated actively and was emotionally involved with what the parents expected of him, because he expected a reward or praise from them. Gabriel obeyed blindly, without openly objecting, but without enthusiasm. Often he would not even say a word. He seemed to be interested only in playing chess and showed remarkable aptitude for that game from early childhood.

When the parents decided to immigrate to South America, their disinterest in the children increased. They were concerned about their own future, were extremely anxious, and had long discussions about their plans for South America. Peter tried to add some words to the discussions, to show approval for his father's plans, but Gabriel took no part. If he did, no attention was paid to him anyhow. He was like a shadow, always present and, in a certain way, always absent, unable to separate himself totally and unable to participate. On the ship to South America, Peter made some friends. Gabriel did not, but he followed his brother, only to be repulsed again with, "Go away, don't follow me; find your own friends."

At the age of 13, Gabriel started to do less well in school than he had before. One of the teachers remarked that he used to be such a good student and that now he was much less attentive and diligent. The mother began to be a little concerned and wanted to find the cause for this; the father did not care. At times, in Gabriel's presence, the parents used to discuss what to do with him because he was not good in school. In these discussions he would listen without giving any opinion. He transferred to a business school, but after a year it was decided to have him moved to an agricultural boarding school, with the hope that he would do better there. He remained there until he was 15½. He visited the family only twice during the time he attended that school. The second time he came home, he had grown tall and looked like an athlete. After supper, the two brothers went for a walk. Peter asked, "Tell me something about your girls." Gabriel did not answer; then, suddenly, as Peter repeated the question, he said, sighing, "You don't know what is happening there." Peter asked, "What's happening? Tell me; I am your brother." Gabriel replied, "I cannot tell you." Later he mumbled something about experiences with prostitutes. A few months later Gabriel came back unexpectedly. He had a peculiar expression on his face and smoked one cigarette after another. Suddenly he said, "I don't want to be in the school anymore. I am tired of being without money. I want to work."

After that, he worked in a few places, but without success. The parents became more alarmed and more critical of him. The father bought a small farm near the city and told him, "Gabriel, this farm is for you." From that day on, however, Gabriel was showered with much advice from his father and mother. They would always tell him what to do or not to do on the farm. He had no right to change anything or to give any orders. He was very tense and insecure, but he would never complain. He talked less and less. He wanted to plant according to the instructions he had received from the school, but his mother would interfere and even tell him in which order he had to plant the vegetables. Gabriel had difficulty in expressing himself, could not argue, and yielded to his mother's relentless pressure.

One day Gabriel suddenly said, "I don't want to go to the farm anymore. It is too far." The parents exploded. "What? Who do you think we are? Millionaires? We are still working for you. We worked hard to buy you this farm." Peter joined in this criticism. Gabriel was considered a parasite, the black sheep of the family. He walked around the house, smoking incessantly, writing his name on sheets of paper, and reading pornographic books.

The father bought another farm where Gabriel could stay without the necessity of commuting, but his work did not improve. Gabriel gave wrong orders to the workers, who made fun of him. He would barter his food for their cigarettes. Once a month he would go to the city to see his parents. He was sloppy, did not shave, would laugh occasionally without cause. He used to beg for cigarettes. Occasionally he would pick up cigarette butts from the street. He would go for long walks alone. He used to play chess with Peter at night, and he seemed to enjoy that. Peter had the impression that Gabriel liked to stay with him, in spite of the fact that Peter had sided with their parents in criticizing him for not working. Gabriel was told, "The Nazis used to kill people who did not work. Now you are here, free, and you don't want to work." After these long sessions, Gabriel would smile and mumble some words. Once, during lunch, he suddenly stood up, with tears running down his cheeks, and with a convulsive voice told his father, "I know what you want to do to me. You can't. You will see what I'll do." Then he went out of the room, crying loudly. A few days later he started to say that the radio was broadcasting news about him— that his father had given the radio station orders to talk about him.

One day Gabriel sold a gold watch and his coat at a ridiculously small price. When he was asked by his parents why he had done so, he replied, "I thought that at least these things belonged to me and that I could do what I wanted with them." Even at this point the parents did not consider the possibility of having him treated; on the contrary, they would mention the possibility of sending him to a psychiatric hospital as a threat. "You do a foolish thing once more and we shall send you to the insane asylum."

After Gabriel had been away from home for a period of twenty-four hours, a psychiatrist was finally consulted. During the examination, done in the presence of the whole family, Gabriel spoke incoherently about trains and "locomotives." He divided the word *locomotive* into *loco* and *motive*. *Loco* in Spanish means "crazy." "He wonders about the motive that drives him crazy," said the psychiatrist. He made the diagnosis of schizophrenia and recommended hospitalization. Gabriel was hospitalized in a private mental hospital, where he received a series of shock treatments. After two months he was discharged, though no improvement was made. When he came home, his hostility toward the parents increased. He would call his mother "poisonous snake"; to his father he would often say, "One day I'll show you what I shall do." He did not show any hate for Peter; he continued to follow him and to play chess with him. Peter continued to lecture him, asking him, "Why do you laugh in that silly way?" Once Gabriel replied, "Don't be a fool; don't you see, it is my nerves; it is not my fault."

After a few months Gabriel was hospitalized again in a public psychiatric hospital. He was there only three months. He was very unhappy and begged the parents to take him out. His father used to tell him, "How can I take you out? You will do the same foolish things again." When Peter visited him, Gabriel begged him to stay a little longer. He used to talk about his delusions. He would often say that in the hospital there was a pilot who had come down with his plane. He wanted to die, but he could not die. They beat him in the hospital; he had no peace. The father finally yielded and took Gabriel home. At home he walked aimlessly and talked to himself. In the evening he used to play chess with Peter. By this time he played very badly. Occasionally, in some moves, he would show a spark of brilliance reminiscent of the way he used to play, but then with wrong moves he would spoil the game.

Gabriel was sent to a doctor for vitamin injections. One morning there was an argument with his father. He wanted to go to another doctor he knew, not the one his father had selected. He did not want vitamins any more. His father and mother again coerced him to go, saying, "It is good for you; you need the injections." Gabriel went. When he came back, he said he wanted to go to the farm and left for the country. When he arrived there, a girl who was working on the farm said, "Here comes the 'loco.' " Gabriel went into a room where a rifle was kept, took it, and aiming it at his frontal region, shot himself. He died instantly.

This account of Gabriel's illness is a very incomplete one. It gives us only what Peter observed at a behavior level. No access to Gabriel's inner experiences has been possible. However, if we add to this account what we have learned from Peter about the parents, we are in a position to reach some understanding.

The cases of these two brothers are enlightening because they reveal how the different attitudes of the parents are related to the different illnesses in the two children: a severe psychoneurosis in Peter, a fatal schizophrenia in Gabriel.

The attitude of the mother did not show great variation in relation to one child or the other. This woman, who had married to escape from the tyranny of her own mother, found herself tied to a man she detested. Seeing herself trapped and too weak and too afraid to fight a husband with a strong-willed personality, she gradually succeeded in deceiving herself. She became able to believe that her husband was a good man, and she learned to submit to all his wishes. Unconsciously, of course, she was full of hostility toward this man, hostility that was discharged on the defenseless children. She went to the extent of allying herself with her husband whenever a disagreement arose between the father and children. Overcritical, petulant, and at the same time detached, she gave the children neither love nor support.

There is enough evidence from what we know about this family to make us deduce that the attitude of the mother was a very important psychogenetic factor in the illness of the children, both because of what she did and of what she did not do. However, it is the different role that the father played in the life of the two children that could explain the diverging patterns that their illnesses assumed. In my experience, this father is one of the few parents who comes close or even surpasses the picture of the schizophrenogenic parent portrayed in some psychiatric literature. We have enough proof that he had very pronounced narcissistic and sadistic traits. The role commonly attributed in psychiatric literature to the mother was in this instance played by the father. As we have seen in several of the little episodes reported, in relation to both Peter and Gabriel the father used that double-bind type of communication that Bateson and collaborators were later to describe in detail (1956). In the context of the disturbed personalities of father and mother and of the family climate that they created, father's communications, with their multiplicity of understandings, meanings, and implications, were difficult for the sons to handle. Peter tried to cope with them although with great anxiety; Gabriel did not even try.

Although maladjusted to a marked degree, the father managed to survive by succeeding in manipulating the lives of the people around him, and by creating his little neurotic world in which he could satisfy his own mental aberrations. He succeeded in overwhelming the personality of his wife to such a point that, though she detested him, she became his faithful servant and ally; he made Peter a tool with which to fulfill his tremendous desire for admiration and completely ignored Gabriel, who was thus exposed only to hostility or to indifference.

The father showed great interest in Peter, but of what kind, and for what purpose? Was that a genuine love, based only on the interest of the child? By depicting the whole world as a horrible and dangerous place, populated only by criminals (the sharks), the father enormously increased Peter's dependency on him. The father became the hero, the savior, the only one who would rescue him from the dangers. His desire for admiration and for being worshipped like a god were thus fulfilled. The price Peter had to pay for such protection was his complete submission to the paternal authority. That was an impossible task, because his father's demands were insatiable and unattainable. Peter was constantly afraid that he could not fulfill the requests of his father and that his father would punish him. The father, too, symbolically became a shark; he might punish Peter by withdrawing what little love he had offered him, a love that was very little and not genuine, but the only love available to Peter in his whole life, and therefore extremely valuable. The father's interest was demonstrated, not by manifestation of affection, but by continuous stimulation toward fulfillment of goals that quite often could not be attained. Peter could have detected, through these manifestations of pseudolove, the underlying hostility and narcissism if this need for love had not blinded him.

Peter's anxiety, which originated from his relationship with his father, spread to all persons who had authority, and finally to everybody. Every human being became an irrational authority, a shark, who would reject him or actually injure him unless he showed either superhuman ability or extreme compliance or obliging self-destruction (as in the case of the mutilation of his finger).

The security that he obtained by living as he did was only partial, and in a certain way this renewed his anxiety, repeating a vicious circle. As he himself put it, he felt that he was living on quicksand, but that without that quicksand there would be nothing else, only emptiness.

Gabriel did not get even that quicksand. By concentrating on Peter, the father's narcissistic requirements were satisfied in a certain way. He obtained enough admiration from the elder, very compliant son. It was not necessary for him to spend energy and renew the same effort with Gabriel when he was born. Thus he showed no interest, not even pseudointerest, in Gabriel, although at the same time he asked for strict compliance from him too. Gabriel did comply, but as we have already mentioned, in a different way from Peter. Peter believed in his father, wanted to comply because he would get something in return, even though very little, and tried to accept his father's wishes and his conception of the world. Gabriel complied passively, went through the motions of the requested acts, and in order to do so had to learn to detach himself. This detachment was a necessity for him, the only possible defense, because it would have been too painful not to be detached. The adults were insufferable people; it was better not to be involved with them. This detachment, at the time, was very realistic; but for him it somehow became a boomerang because it made his father even more detached from him. The father would say that Gabriel was not interested in anything, not even in toys; why, then, should he bother with him, why should he tell him stories, buy him things, spend time on him, and so on? A self-perpetuating vicious circle was thus established. Furthermore this detachment did not abate the parental bad images. As we have seen, Peter also retained a conscious bad image of the mother, but had repressed entirely the bad image of the father. Gabriel, on the contrary, retained in consciousness the bad images of both parents.

Unfortunately we do not have as much detailed information about Gabriel as we have about Peter, but we know enough to be able to picture him in his years of development in a very unhealthy atmosphere. He had no chance to assert himself; his will was always crushed by his parents, who were not able to give him anything except material care. Since early childhood he made strong attempts to cope with the situation by detaching himself, but that defense finally proved inadequate. His adolescence was a crescendo of frustration, anxiety, and injury to self-esteem. The only person who theoretically could have saved Gabriel from the psychosis was Peter. In fact, we have seen how many times Gabriel had tried to get close to him. He needed him desperately, but was almost always rebuffed by Peter too. Peter was too sick himself, too deprived, too worried about complying with his parents' demands, too much in need to assert his superiority in respect to a weaker person like his brother, to be able to help him.

When the first symptoms of the psychosis occurred, these symptoms were interpreted as manifestations of laziness and rebelliousness. Even when the illness was already at an advanced stage the parents did nothing about it. This attitude, of course, cannot be attributed to ignorance. Both parents were well-educated people; they could not see, as usual, because they could not accept the facts. They remained as blind as they had always been to any psychological manifestations. When the illness was advanced, Gabriel asserted himself in a psychotic way. He sold things that belonged to him. He undersold them, but they were his; by underselling them, he proved that he could do what he wanted. In his delusional system, his father was the persecutor; he had given orders to the radio station to talk about him. There was no displacement of the original wrongdoer, as occurs in the majority of cases, and not even partial repression of the bad image of the father. He identified himself with the pilot of the plane that had fallen down, a man unable to live and fly and yet unable to die. He felt that people were torturing him.

After his discharge from the hospital, Gabriel gave several indications that he wanted to kill himself. No steps were taken to remove the weapons from his surroundings, however, and he finally killed himself. His last act was a liberation for himself and a revenge against his parents.*

* The reader may be interested to know that approximately fifteen years after termination of Peter's treatment, while traveling in South America, I unexpectedly went to visit him. I found him well adjusted, a happy husband and a proud father. He was well established professionally. The mother had in the meantime died. The relation with the father had much improved. Peter received me enthusiastically, with warmth, devotion, and festivity, almost as if the president of the United States had gone to visit him.

CHAPTER 10

Study of Catatonic Patients

As we have seen in Chapter 3, the manifest symptomatology of catatonia has characteristics so specific as to make some psychiatrists consider this condition a separate illness, unrelated to the other types of schizophrenia. These specific features are the motor phenomena, which have made several authors think of the possibility of a neurological disorder based on an organic pathology or on some kind of intoxication, such as the one produced by bulbocapnine in experimental animals (DeJong, 1922; and Baruk, 1930*a,b*).

From a psychodynamic point of view, the understanding of catatonic schizophrenia is controversial. Very few cases have been studied psychodynamically. In three recent books on schizophrenia (Searles, 1965, Kantor and Herron, 1966, Shulman, 1968) no psychodynamic study of catatonia is presented. Rosenfeld (1952*b*) has made an interesting report on a case of catatonia; however, the catatonic syndrome is considered there to be incidental and is not studied specifically. Recently Will (1972) has written an insightful report of a case, which I have discussed (Arieti, 1972*b*). The occasional reports that have appeared in other recent publications are fragmentary. Catatonic patients are mentioned in passing or in reference to other patients.

The psychodynamic study of these cases is hindered by several difficulties. The first is the rarity of these cases. Whereas in the past catatonic patients were quite numerous, now they have drastically diminished in number. The second difficulty lies in the manifest symptomatology, which lends itself to a psychodynamic study much less than do other types of schizophrenia. The typical patient is mute, or almost. One of the ways to obviate this second difficulty is to study patients who are not typical from the point of view of the manifest symptomatology, and this is what I have done. The first two cases reported in this chapter had, in addition to catatonic symptoms, many distinct obsessive-compulsive features. The third case is that of a patient who discussed his catatonic episode with me long after it had occurred. I am aware of the criticisms to which these reports expose themselves. And yet the fact that the atypical clinical picture of these patients made them available to psychodynamic inquiry seems to outweigh the fact that they were not typical. As a matter of fact, their study seems to indicate that a typical psychodynamics of the catatonic type of schizophrenia can be differentiated. As to the reliability of reports, as those of the third case, the doubts are partially mitigated by the genuine flavor of the patient's account, as the therapist experiences it.

In spite of the relative rarity of catatonic patients, it is important for the psychiatrist to become acquainted with what is known of their psychodynamics in order to increase his skill in treating this condition, which is one of the most distressing occurring in human beings. Moreover, no matter how strong is our desire to help these suffering patients, the study of catatonia will soon transcend our therapeutic devotion. The psychodynamic and formal processes of catatonia are intimately related to the problems of human will and its intermediary role between motivation and overt behavior.

I have also made another clinical observation connected with the disappearance of catatonic patients, which later studies must confirm or deny. Whereas cases of full-fledged catatonic syndrome have become very rare, we now frequently see patients who have been for days or weeks in almost complete immobility and inactivity, lying in bed, or closed in the bathroom, and so on. Although these patients lack the typical catatonic features, and some of them must be considered as suffering from simple schizophrenic withdrawal, some may be recognized as aborted forms of catatonia.

The catatonic syndrome cannot be fully explained in terms of psychodynamics. The reader will have a much greater understanding of this multiform problem after having studied the formal mechanisms of catatonia in Chapter 17.

Sally

Sally was a 23-year-old Jewish married woman who lived in a small town in the vicinity of New York City. She was referred by a psychiatrist who had attempted electric shock therapy. After shock treatment, the patient seemed to make some improvement, but the symptoms returned very shortly. Psychotherapy was tried for a few months, with no appreciable results. The psychiatrist felt that the patient should try another therapist and referred her to me.

The first time she came, she was accompanied by her parents, who gave the following history: The apparent beginning of the illness occurred a few days after her marriage, when the patient was 22. During the honeymoon the patient had been anxious and disturbed, and had wanted to go back to her parents' home. When she returned and went to her new apartment, she became increasingly distressed by obsessions. She gradually became slower in her motions and finally lapsed into a catatonic stupor. She had to be dressed, undressed, and spoon fed, and she defecated and urinated in bed. She was unable to move and hardly answered questions; often she answered in monosyllables. The striking feature in this case, however, was that this catatonic state was not constant. The patient occasionally was able to move freely, especially outside her own home. However, when she was not in a catatonic posture, she was distressed by obsessional symptoms, which will be described later.

When I saw the patient for the first time, she gave me the impression of a typical catatonic. She was asthenic, very much undernourished and pale, and maintained the same posture throughout the interview; the mimic musculature of the face was practically paralyzed, except for an apparently incongruous smile, which appeared now and then. She gave the impression of being totally flat emotionally. Contrasting with this picture, however, was her ability to talk in my presence. She spoke rather fluently and expressed herself very well, but her speech was cold and rigid, without emotional inflections.

Sally gave me an accurate description of her symptoms. When she was not in a catatonic state, she had the impression that small pieces or corpuscles were falling down on her body or from her body. She preferred not to move, because she was afraid that her movements would cause small pieces to fall. She had to reassure herself constantly that pieces were not falling down, and she had to check herself constantly in an obsessive way. If she moved, even if she made the smallest movement, she had to think about the movement, dividing it into small parts to reassure herself that each part of the movement had not been accompanied by the falling of small bodies. This task was terrific; it kept her in mortal fear of any movement and compelled obsessive thinking from which she could not escape. She used to ask her relatives to help her do the searching for her, to reassure her that no bodies were falling down.

In the beginning her relatives refused to give in to her symptoms. When she felt unable to satisfy the obsessions and became overwhelmed by them, she lapsed into a catatonic stupor. Later on, at the suggestion of the first psychiatrist who treated her, the relatives were much more tolerant. They did a great deal of looking for her, and consequently she was not in a stupor so often; but if she was not in a stupor, she was extremely compulsive, always looking around or asking other people to look for her. Even when she could move, she tried to reduce her movements to a minimum because each motion would entail a tremendous amount of compulsive looking and thinking. Therefore, everything had to be done for her; she had to be dressed, undressed, fed, and even wiped when she went to the toilet. If other people did these things for her, the movements that were necessary for these activities were not "so much" her "responsibility." She spent most of her time in bed and was fed only once every twenty-four hours.

The following is a brief description of the family background and personal history as obtained later on from Sally herself. Her mother was a seemingly warm person, very much interested in the welfare of the patient. She was, however, overprotective, overbearing, and domineering. With the pretext of helping the patient, and giving good advice when it was needed, she did not allow Sally to develop the capacity to make a choice. Sally's mother was always choosing for her; until Sally was in her teens she was not allowed to cross the street alone, for fear of the traffic; when the other children were going to a picnic or ice skating, and Sally wanted to join them, her mother would never let her go: "It is better to listen to Mommy; those activities are dangerous and must be avoided." Sally was even told what friends to have. When she was older and wanted to go to art school or take dancing lessons, her mother was very discouraging; she believed that those things were not practical. If Sally needed to buy clothes, even after her marriage, her mother wanted to be consulted in their selection. A few times Sally had bought a dress by herself and had been strongly criticized. The mother had rigid norms for everything. For instance, when the gas had to be turned on, the flame had to be of a certain size. If Sally made it a little higher or lower, she would incur her mother's disapproval. The mother also had always put tremendous emphasis on cleanliness. She was not very religious, but kept a strictly "kosher" home.

Sally constantly felt under pressure from her mother, always believing that her mother must be obeyed, that her advice must be good, even if unpleasant, and must be followed.

Sally's father was different from her mother in that he was not domineering, but weak. Sally felt that although he had the same point of view as the children quite often, he always supported her mother in her requests, maintaining a united front with her. The father was too weak to oppose the strong-willed mother and always yielded to her wishes. Sally, therefore, had even more contempt for him than for her mother; he was the one who could help her, and instead he was her mother's ally in crushing her desires. Sally experienced a sense of suffocation and pressure when her parents were around. Her only happy time had been at night when everybody was in bed. Then she could feel free to do what she wanted. But even then her freedom did not last long. Soon she would hear the voice of her mother saying, "Sally, it is late. Go to bed." To prolong this time of solitude, she would take long baths and showers. She remembers, however, that quite a few times, when she purposely prolonged her baths, she had the impression that her mother came into the bathroom and stabbed her in the back with a dagger. If the water was running from the faucet, making noise, she was particularly afraid her mother could come in, and she would not even hear it. But she knew that this was just a fantasy, and she tried to dispel it, although some fear remained.

The patient had two siblings, a sister and a brother, who were older. She had never been close to them. Living with the parents was an aunt, her mother's sister, who had been married a few years before, but had gotten a divorce a few weeks after her marriage. At the time of the divorce the aunt had not sold her new furniture, but had put it in storage to be used again if the opportunity arose. This detail is relevant, as we shall see later.

At the age of 18, Sally had started to go out with a young man named Robert, with whom she very soon became infatuated. Robert was different from her parents; he was intellectual, spoke about science, the arts, and especially about modern art. They would go to museums together. For Sally, he represented the artistic and intellectual life of New York City, in contrast to the life of the small town where she lived. Sally and Robert had satisfactory sexual relations.

As soon as they had started to talk about marriage, Sally's parents had begun a campaign against Robert. He was not the man for her. He was not practical enough; he was a dreamer. At first Sally tried to resist her parents, but it was too great a strain and created too much suffering for her. Soon she became convinced that Robert was not the man for her, and she severed the relationship. A year later she met another young man, Ben, who became interested in her. Ben lived in the same town as she and had the same views about life that her parents had. Her parents liked him very much and encouraged her to marry him. She became convinced that that was a good thing to do, and she agreed to marry him. The wedding was soon arranged. Because the couple did not have much savings, Sally's parents felt that they could use the aunt's furniture, which was still new, although it had been kept in storage for several years. Sally did not like the idea, but she and Ben soon realized that this was the most practical thing to do, because the aunt was generous enough to give them the furniture. Sally agreed to accept her aunt's furniture, with one exception. The aunt had a painting that Sally did not like at all. That painting was not to enter her new home.

The parents told her that they would fix up her new apartment while she and her husband were honeymooning, and that they would find everything ready when they returned. During the honeymoon Sally did not feel well, and the newlyweds returned sooner than they had anticipated. When they walked into their apartment, Sally's parents were arranging the furniture, and what were they doing at that moment? They were hanging the painting that Sally detested over the headboard of the bed. When Sally saw that, she became very distressed. When I asked her to explain why she disliked the painting so much, she said, "It was an old painting, representing French aristocrats in wigs; it was a traditional painting, so different from modern art." In other words, the painting symbolized for her the life of her parents and of Ben, in contrast to the life with Robert.

Soon Sally became afraid that she would not be able to fulfill her duties as a wife, that she would not satisfy Ben's expectations. She became slower and slower in her actions and was unable to do the work in the house. The parents became worried and asked her and Ben to come to live with them so that Sally would not have to take care of the apartment. In her parents' home Sally became worse and gradually fell into a state of catatonia.

Later on, when Sally could explain her symptoms, she said that she could not move, because if she moved, she felt guilty, inasmuch as she was always afraid of doing the wrong thing. Later, when she resorted to compulsions, this feeling of doing the wrong thing was at least partially removed, if she could assure herself that she was accurately following her compulsive ritual. The compulsive ritual consisted of reassuring herself that bodies had not fallen. In going back over her movements in her thoughts, she followed this formula: "Do, feel, done, on, off, see, hear, think, and what else." This formula meant that she should think or revisualize in her mind what she had done, how she had felt, what she should have done, whether or not anything was on her, whether or not anything had fallen off, what things she had seen, what sounds she had heard, what thoughts she had had. "What else" stood for a final mental checkup.

All these symptoms, including the tendency not to move at all, were much more marked in the presence of her parents and Ben. Even in the first few months of treatment, the patient became aware, after discussion of many small episodes, that her symptoms had something to do with her feelings, especially the feelings of guilt and resentment toward her parents and Ben. She was able to understand this relationship when she was reassured that she did not have to feel guilty with the therapist, and was willing to accept his support. She realized that she was afraid to act, because no matter how she acted, she would incur the disapproval of her real mother, or the disapproval of the mother that she had incorporated. When she would snap out of immobility, she could do so only with the protection of her ritual. Her ritual was not only a protection against guilt, but also a retaliation against her relatives. She realized that when she was particularly angry at her parents or Ben, her ritual increased and produced a disturbance for the whole family. They had to take care of her, and do the looking for her, no matter how reluctant they were to do so. This was the only way she was capable of expressing anger.

Although Sally acquired this degree of insight early in treatment, she could not refrain from indulging in her symptoms. Thus, it became obvious to me that no improvement could be expected from the treatment alone; her living conditions reactivated her anxiety and made it necessary for the symptoms to occur. Therefore, I decided that it would be better for her, at this stage of the treatment, to be in a situation where she did not need to feel guilty and resentful. Five months after the beginning of treatment, arrangements were made for Sally to live with a social worker, who would devote herself entirely to the patient.

When Sally went to live with this social worker, whom we shall call Barbara, a dramatic change occurred in the condition of the patient. For the first time since the beginning of the illness, she started to do things by herself. Barbara gave her progressively more difficult tasks, which the patient was able to undertake, with some effort. Thus she started to dress and undress, and to do a little work in the house. It was necessary to give her a great deal of praise. In the beginning, she felt that Barbara was a great friend; they were two girls living together in mutual friendship. Her entire outlook toward life changed. The necessity of resorting to her ritual decreased, and there was a progressive reawakening of her emotions. Her face was no longer masklike, but responded emotionally to the surroundings. She also started to eat by herself and gained a lot of weight. This state of affairs, however, did not last very long. After a few weeks, Sally began to think that Barbara was making too many demands on her, that she was not patient enough with her slowness, that she was pushing her even more than her own mother had. Possibly there was some truth in these allegations. Although Barbara was an excellent social worker who had undergone intensive psychoanalytic treatment, and who had a great deal of understanding for psychiatric patients, perhaps she was not the best person to work with someone like Sally. Being a very active person, Barbara experienced some kind of frustration at Sally's slowness.

Sally herself decided to return to her parents, called up her husband, and insisted that she be taken back immediately. When she returned to her parents' home, there was some relapse, but the symptoms were not as severe as they had been. It was obvious, however, that Sally was retrogressing, especially in the presence of her parents. It was then arranged that a young woman psychologist, Rhoda, would visit her in her parents' home every weekday, from early in the morning until half-past five, when Ben came home from work. In the company of this psychologist, Sally continued to improve and was able to accept and fulfill bigger and bigger goals. Whereas she had not been able to assert herself with Barbara, whom she had felt obligated to obey, no matter how reluctantly, she was able to reveal her anger to Rhoda, whenever she felt the latter had slighted her. She felt like a peer of Rhoda, and a feeling of warm friendship developed. Rhoda was able to avoid becoming a mother-substitute; but, by praising Sally a great deal, as one would do with a little child, she gradually built Sally's confidence in herself, confidence that she had never had. Sally became willing to do things and dared to accept bigger and bigger goals. Occasionally, tendencies to misinterpret and the desire to put Rhoda into a mother's role again occurred. During treatment these tendencies were worked out.

Both a prolonged relationship with a healthy human being and psychotherapy with the psychiatrist were necessary. One of the purposes of the treatment was to examine this new, healthy, interpersonal relationship and to see to it that the old patterns of the patient did not force her to misinterpret it and spoil it. Sally became progressively more assertive and dared to ask questions and to disagree. After a year of treatment, she was able to leave her parents' home and to have her own apartment with her husband. She started to take piano lessons and showed considerable interest and talent in playing that instrument. Her relations toward her husband improved to a great extent as she progressively became aware of the fact that she identified him with her mother and acted toward him almost exactly as she had acted toward her mother. Many of the bad qualities that she had projected on him were the result of this identification. She also learned to consider herself, not as a shadow of her mother, but as a person living in her own right.

After two years of treatment the patient was able to secure a position as a saleswoman.

Sally continued to come for treatment, and there was progressive improvement. At a certain stage of therapy she felt that she had never been so well. The illness, in spite of the symptoms ranging from catatonic immobility to distressing obsessions and compulsions, made her a different person. She finally was able to free herself from those conditions, which she never accepted. Her interests in various aspects of life expanded and she was able to sustain these interests, not only without shame or guilt, which she had formerly, but with confidence and inner feeling of satisfaction.

Richard

Richard was a 23-year-old white, Protestant, single, unemployed male who sought psychiatric treatment a few months after his discharge from a state hospital. His immediate problem was that he had a tremendous desire to commit himself to the state hospital again. He remembered the time he spent there with great pleasure. He felt that in the hospital he had spent the best time of his life; he had had nothing to worry about, everything had been taken care of for him, he had been able to work, and had had no difficulty in getting along with people. When he expressed to his family his desire to return to the hospital, they became worried and encouraged him to seek private treatment. Richard himself had had this intention, but the family had previously discouraged him from doing so.

The following is a brief family and personal history as it was obtained from the patient himself in the course of treatment. The father was born in Europe. After a few years spent in the United States, he returned to his native country, where he married and had two children. He returned to America with his family a few years later, against the wishes of his wife. In Europe he was a farmer, but in this country he worked as a cook and kitchen helper and a waiter. He was described by the patient as a very quiet man, submissive, and entirely dominated by his wife. He had little contact with his children, because he worked at night and slept during the day. The mother was described as a very unhappy person, hypochondriacal, and a constant nagger. She was always complaining of pains and aches and had undergone several operations. She had always been dissatisfied with Richard. He remembered violent scenes that had occurred in his childhood. His mother was utterly disgusted with him when he did not want to obey her. She would even spit at him, kick him, and throw dishes and other objects at him. She never praised him, but nagged him constantly. If he turned on the radio, it was to the wrong program; if he looked for a job, it was always for the wrong job, and so forth. His mother used to tell him that he had been a pest since his birth, and that when he was an infant he had always cried, causing her terrific headaches.

During the course of treatment, Richard realized that the marriage of his parents was a very unhappy one. His mother was taking out on the children, and especially on Richard, who was the eldest, the resentment that she had toward her marriage. When there were open arguments between the children and the mother, his father usually was not there because he was working; on the few occasions when he was present, he would offer only a very weak defense for the children. Richard remembered that when he was a small child, once at the age of 5 and another time when he was 8, his mother went to the hospital for operations, and he was taken to a children's shelter. He retained a very happy memory of the two times spent in the shelter, which he considered the best experiences in his childhood. He was very unhappy when he had to go back home. Later in his childhood and in early adolescence, he became very religious and had the intention of becoming a minister. He used to pray quite often; he prayed to God to let him win a ball game, have a girl friend, be successful on a job, and so on.

In high school, Richard was an average student. After graduation from high school, he was drafted into the army, where he felt unhappy because the other enlisted men bragged about their sexual exploits and he was not able to offer anything in that field. After his discharge, he wanted to enter some kind of musical career, but gave up the idea because it did not offer financial security. He had several jobs, for example, as a delivery boy, elevator man, and hospital helper. He could not keep a job for any length of time because he was very sensitive to criticism and was always afraid that he would not satisfy his bosses.

Richard remembered this period, after his discharge from the army, as one of the worst in his life, even worse than his childhood. Throughout his life he had been very sensitive and had always taken things too much to heart, but after his discharge, when he was supposed to do things on his own and show what he was able to do, his sensitivity increased. He was "eating his heart out" for unimportant reasons; any, even remote, anticipation of disappointment was able to provoke attacks of anxiety in him. He could never be indifferent or detached, but was very much involved in everything. After his discharge from the army his life had become a series of crises.

Approximately two years after his return to civilian life, Richard left his job because he became overwhelmed by these feelings of lack of confidence in himself, and he refused to go look for another one. He stayed home most of the day. His mother would nag him that he was too lazy and unwilling to do anything. He became slower and slower in dressing and undressing and taking care of himself. When he went out of the house, he felt compelled "to give interpretations" to everything he looked at. He did not know what to do outside the house, where to go, where to turn. If he saw a red light at a crossing, he would interpret it as a message that he should not go in that direction. If he saw an arrow, he would follow the arrow interpreting it as a sign sent by God that he should go in that direction. Feeling lost and horrified, he would go home and stay there, afraid to go out because going out meant making decisions or choices that he felt unable to make. He reached the point where he stayed home most of the time. But even at home, he was tortured by his symptoms. He could not act; any motion that he felt like making seemed to him an insurmountable obstacle, because he did not know whether he should make it or not. He was increasingly afraid of doing the wrong thing. Such fears prevented him from dressing, undressing, eating, and so forth. He felt paralyzed and lay motionless in bed. He gradually became worse, was completely motionless, and had to be hospitalized.

In the state hospital, Richard was diagnosed as a case of schizophrenia, catatonic type, and electric shock treatment was recommended. He remembers that prior to the shock treatment, even in the hospital, he had to interpret everything that occurred. If a doctor asked him a question, he had a sudden impulse to answer, but then feared that by answering he would do the wrong thing. He tried desperately to find signs that would indicate to him whether he should answer or not. An accidental noise, the arrival of another person, or the number of words the questions consisted of were indications of whether he should reply or not.

Being undecided, he felt blocked, and often would remain mute and motionless, like a statue, even for days. He had always been more or less afraid of being with people because he did not feel strong enough to take their suggestions or to refuse them; in the hospital such fear increased.

After shock treatment, which consisted of a series of twenty-one grand mal seizures, the patient felt much better. He found in the hospital an environment that he liked very much, one in which he was not afraid. He became very friendly with other patients, helped them, liked his doctors, followed their guidance, and participated in occupational therapy classes; when he was in the process of doing things, he was not tortured by the previous horrible anxiety. In the hospital he was told what to do by authorities whom he was willing to accept. He improved so rapidly that the doctors wanted to discharge him. He begged them not to do so, because he was very happy there, much happier than outside; but after many delays they discharged him nevertheless. Outside the hospital, his difficulties tended to return, and therefore he sought treatment.

For many reasons, this patient presented several difficult problems in the therapeutic situation. First of all, he was exposed again to the influence of the family. His mother was nagging him to find a job. The same acrimonious scenes were going on between the constantly disapproving mother and the patient. The economic conditions of the family were such that it was impossible for Richard to live by himself, or to have an additional person, as Sally did, who would work with him.

Although Richard was afraid to do things, his "stormy personality" pushed him again to act a great deal and try new things, in spite of his fear. He would go out quite often; he was eager to start friendships with girls, but later he would feel extremely frustrated and rejected by them, at the least provocation. Although he was afraid to have sexual relations, he would proposition girls who he knew were virgins and modest and then would feel painfully rejected when they did not accede to his request. He worked as an attendant in a general hospital, and there he was afraid that the nurse in charge of the ward did not like his work. He was very active and ambitious in spite of his fears and anxiety. Thus, he decided to register in a school of music, where his tuition would be paid by the government under the GI Bill of Rights. At school his difficulties greatly increased. At first he did not know which instrument to choose; later he felt that the teachers were dissatisfied with his work and were not friendly enough. At the same time, his mother was criticizing him for his interest in music and his lack of practicality. His anxiety increased in the same proportion as the wish to be back in the state hospital.

One afternoon, when he was supposed to be in my office for a session, I received a telephone call from an admitting physician of the state hospital, who told me that the patient had entered the hospital again on voluntary admission. He stayed in the hospital a few months. This time he was not as satisfied as he had been the previous time; when he was discharged again, he did not return for psychotherapy. He decreased his ambitions and was able to make a subliminal adjustment. The therapy of this patient was not entirely successful, although it prevented the occurrence of another catatonic attack.

John

John * was an intelligent professional man in his thirties, Catholic, of European background, who was referred to me because of his rapidly increasing anxiety—anxiety that reminded him of the anxiety he experienced about ten years previously, when he developed a full catatonic episode. Wanting to prevent a recurrence of the event, he sought treatment.

The following is not a complete report, but only a brief history of the patient and a description of his catatonic episode, as it was reconstructed during psychotherapy.

The patient was one of four children. The father was described as a bad husband, an adventurer who, although a good provider, always caused trouble and home instability. The mother was a somewhat inadequate person, distant from the patient. One of his sisters is said to have led a very promiscuous life since youth. John was raised more or less by a maternal aunt, who lived in the family and acted as a housekeeper.

Early childhood memories were mostly unpleasant for John. He recollected attacks of anxiety going back to his early childhood. He remembered also how he needed to cling to his aunt; how painful it always was to separate from her. The aunt also had the habit of undressing in his presence, and this caused him to have mixed feelings of sexual excitement and guilt. Frequently he would experience pain in his stomach, for which there was no apparent reason. Between the age of 9 and 10 there was an attempted homosexual relation with his best friend. During his prepubertal period he had strong desires to look at pictures of naked women, and occasionally he would surreptitiously take some pornographic books or magazines from his father's collection and look at them. Fleeting homosexual desires would also occur occasionally. He masturbated with fantasies of women, but he had to stimulate his rectum with his fingers in order to experience, as he said, "a greater pleasure." Among the things that he remembered from his early life were also obsessive preoccupations with feces of animals and excretions in general of human beings. He had a special admiration for horses, because "They excreted such beautiful feces coming from such statuesque bodies."

In spite of all these circumstances, John managed to grow more or less adequately, was not too disturbed by the dealth of his aunt, and did well in school. There were practically no dates with girls until much later in life. After puberty he became very interested in religion, especially in order to find a method to control his sexual impulses. The possibility of becoming a monk was considered by him several times. When he finished college, at the age of 20, he decided to make a complete attempt to remove sex from his life. He decided also to go for a rest and summer vacation to a farm for young men, where he would cut trees, enjoy the country, and be far away from the temptations of the city. On this farm, however, he soon became anxious and depressed. He found out that he resented the other

* This case was originally reported in a separate publication (Arieti, 1961*a*).

fellows more and more. They were rough guys, they used profane language. He felt like he was going to pieces, progressively. He remembers that one night he was saying to himself, "I cannot stand it any more. Why am I in this way, so anxious for no reason? I have done no wrong in my whole life. Perhaps I should become a priest or get married." When he was feeling very badly he would console himself by thinking that perhaps what he was experiencing was in accordance with the will of God.

Obsessions and compulsions acquired more and more prominence. The campers had to go chopping wood. This practice became an ordeal for John because he was possessed by doubts. He was thinking, for instance: "Maybe I should not cut this tree because it is too small. Next year it will be bigger. But if I don't cut this tree, another fellow will. Maybe it is better if he cuts it, or maybe I should do so." As he expressed himself, he found himself "doubting, then doubting his doubts, and finally doubting the doubting of his doubts." It was an overwhelmingly spreading anxiety. The anxiety gradually extended to every act he had to perform. He was literally possessed by intense terror.

One day, while he was in this predicament, he observed another phenomenon that he could not understand. There was a discrepancy between the act he wanted to perform and the action that he really carried out. For instance, when he was undressing, he wanted to drop a shoe, and instead he dropped a big log; he wanted to put something in a drawer and instead he threw a stone away. However, most of the time there was a similarity between the act that he had wanted and anticipated and the act he actually performed. The same phenomenon appeared in talking. He would utter words that were not the ones he meant to say, but were related to them. Later, however, his actions became more and more disconnected. He was mentally lucid and able to perceive what was happening, but he realized he had no control over his actions. He thought he could commit crimes, even kill somebody, and became even more afraid. He was saying to himself, "I don't want to be damned in this world as well as in the other. I am trying to do good and I can't. It is not fair. I may kill somebody when I want a piece of bread."

Fear had by now become connected with any possible movement. The fear was so intense as to actually inhibit any movement. He was almost literally petrified. To use his own words, he "saw himself solidifying, assuming statuesque positions." However, he was not always in this condition. As a matter of fact, the following day he could move again and go to chop wood. He had one purpose in mind: to kill himself. He remembers that he was very capable of observing himself and of deciding that it would be better for him to die than to commit crimes. He climbed a big tree and jumped down in an attempt to kill himself; but he inflicted upon himself only minor contusions. The other men, who ran to help him, realized that he was mentally ill, and he was soon sent to a psychiatric hospital. He remembers understanding that he was taken to the hospital and being happy about it—at least he was considered sick and not a criminal. But in the hospital he found that he could not move at all. He was like a statue of stone.

There were some actions, however, that could escape this otherwise complete immobility; namely, the actions needed for the purpose of committing suicide. In fact, he was sure that he had to die to avoid the terror of becoming a murderer; he had to kill himself before that would happen.

During his hospitalization, John made seventy-one attempts at suicide. Although he was generally in a state of catatonia, he would occasionally have impulsive acts, tear the straitjacket to pieces, and make a rope with it to hang himself. Another time he broke a dish in order to cut the veins of his wrist with some pieces of it. Other times he swallowed stones. He was always put under restraint after a suicidal attempt. However, he could understand everything that was going on. As a matter of fact, his acuity in devising methods for committing suicide seemed sharpened.

When he was questioned more about this long series of suicidal attempts, John added that the most drastic attempts were actually the first ten or twelve. Only these attempts could really have killed him. Later the attempts were not very dangerous, like, for instance, swallowing a small object or inflicting on himself a small injury with a sharp object. When I asked him whether he knew why he had to repeat these token suicidal attempts, he gave two reasons. The first was to relieve his feeling of guilt and fulfill his duty of preventing himself from committing crimes. But the second reason, whose full meaning he discovered during psychotherapy, was even stranger. To commit suicide was the only act that he could perform, the only act that would go beyond the barrier of immobility. Thus to commit suicide was to live, the only act of life left to him.

The patient was given a course of electric shock treatment. The exact number could not be ascertained. He improved for about two weeks, but then he relapsed into catatonic stupor interrupted only by additional suicidal attempts. While he was in stupor, he remembers a young psychiatrist saying to a nurse, "Poor fellow, so young and so sick. He will continue to deterioriate for the rest of his life." After five or six months of hospitalization his catatonic state became somewhat less rigid, and he was able to walk and to utter a few words. At this time he had noticed that a new doctor seemed to have some interest in him. One day this doctor told him, "You want to kill yourself. Isn't there anything at all in life that you want?" With great effort the patient mumbled, "Eat, to eat." In fact he really felt hungry because on account of his immobility he could not feed himself properly and was spoon fed poorly. The doctor took him to the patients' cafeteria and told him, "You may eat anything you want." John grabbed immediately a large quantity of food and ate in a ravenous manner. The doctor noticed that John liked soup and told him to take even more soup. From that day on John lived only for the sake of eating. He gained about sixty pounds in a few weeks. When I asked him why he ate so much, was it because he was really so hungry, he said: "No. That was only at the beginning. The pleasure in eating consisted partially in grabbing food and putting it into my mouth." Later it was discovered by the attendants that John not only ate a lot, but also that he hoarded food in his drawers and under his mattress.

John continued to improve and in a few months he was able to leave the hospital. He was able to make a satisfactory adjustment, to work, and later went to a professional school and obtained his Ph.D. degree. As a whole he has managed fairly well until shortly before he decided to receive psychotherapy. Important, however, for our topic are the following additional details. Two years after recovering from the psychotic episode he noticed an incoordination of movements and fear of this incoordination would occur when he was anxious. He had to force himself to win against this resistance to moving; but the movements, to use his own words, "were pasty." Up to a short time prior to psychotherapy, when he would undergo fits of anxiety, he would often think of inanimate objects, like iron, wood, and so on—things that cannot move and cannot feel anxiety.

These three cases confirm some pathological developments described in Chapters 5, 6, 7, and 8 and disclose additional factors frequently encountered in catatonic schizophrenia.

We have many details about the unhappy childhood of Sally and Richard and the unhealthy atmosphere in which they were raised. In both cases the mother was the parent experienced as actively destructive, whereas the father was a weakling who was unable to compensate for the mother even to a minimal degree.

In both cases the patients complied with their mother's wishes, not really because they wanted to. Contrary to what happens in the person who develops a compliant neurotic personality, these two patients never accepted their mothers' way of living. They did what the mother wanted at all times, but they secretly rebelled. Richard was so unhappy when he was with his mother that he remembers the time spent in the children's shelter as the best in his childhood. Later on, when he wanted to go back to the state hospital, he tried to repeat the same situation, to go away from his mother, from the place where he had to be active and was therefore subject to criticism. In other words, going to the state hospital was not only an escape from his mother, but also an escape from action: we may say that it was a partial catatonia. At the same time, going to the hospital meant going to an omnipotent overgenerous mother who would take care of him completely; a mother who corresponded to the image of the good mother that he had possibly conceived when he was a baby.

One finds that in cases of catatonia, more than in the other types of schizophrenia, the parents not only have imposed their will on the reluctant pseudo-compliant children, but also have made it difficult for the children to develop the capacity to will, and therefore, to a certain extent, the capacity to act according to their own wishes. These children are unable to accept their environmental conditions, and at the same time they are unable to fight them. The situation that produces the least anxiety in them is one of *ostensible acceptance,* that is, compliance in spite of themselves. If, on the other hand, they act according to their own wishes, they are either afraid or they feel guilty. Their ability to will, to make a choice, will always remain impaired. They will always experience indecision and ambivalent attitudes. If these patients make their own decisions, they feel that the mother will be angry or that the action will turn out to be wrong, and they will feel responsible for the failure. The ambivalent attitude is due to the conflict between their own wish, which they do not *dare* to accept, and the parental wish, which they do not *want* to accept. Later on in life, when the parents are not physically present, the incorporated image of the parents (the Freudian superego) continues to argue against the patient's own wishes. One of the frequent methods by which they try to solve their difficulties is by giving up their will and making themselves completely dependent on another person, a symbolic omnipotent mother who will do everything for them. At times the omnipotent good mother is represented by an organization or institution (army, religious order, and similar organizations).

Our third patient, John, wanted to become a monk, put himself entirely under the protection of God, and in this way remove sex and other evil impulses from his life. John, however, never actualized this idea.

If the patients cannot find this kind of solution, and their difficulties of living pile up, the inability to make decisions, to will, to act, will also increase. The patients will try to protect themselves from anxiety in any possible way; one frequent method, such as was used by our three patients, is to resort to compulsive rituals. The ritual sanctions the actions. If the ritual is not enough to eliminate anxiety, catatonia will occur and will abolish action. The anxiety that the patients experience at first in performing certain specific actions, which they think would be disapproved by the real parent, or by the incorporated image, is generalized later to every action. All actions that are willed by the patients may arouse in them either guilt or fear and are therefore eliminated. This process of generalization is responsible for the state of catatonic stupor. The patients may allow themselves to undergo movements imposed by another person or may obey even absurd requests because they do not will them and therefore are not responsible for them. However, the patients may remain in a state of waxy flexibility, because they cannot will any change in the position of their bodies.

This generalization of the anxiety to every possible action would not take place, however, and would not precipitate the catatonic stupor if there were not a general return to a primitive mechanism of willing and acting that attributes to the person who wills a feeling of responsibility and guilt. This mechanism, which will be discussed in Chapter 17, is generally repressed, but is reactivated by the anxiety of the patient.

As I said before, the state of catatonia, by eliminating actions, removes any guilt or fear connected with them. One of the fears that has not as yet been considered, but that is present in almost every catatonic, is the fear of his own hostility. The action he contemplates may be a violent action against the parent or parent-substitute. Another fear, which I have found several times in European patients, but less frequently in Americans, and which has been frequently described by other authors, is the fear that each and every movement has a sexual meaning. This is probably what happened to John at the beginning of his acute psychotic episode. It is obvious that this patient underwent an overpowering increase in anxiety when he went to the camp and was exposed to close homosexual stimulation. His early interpersonal relations had subjected him to great instability and insecurity and had made him very vulnerable to many sources of anxiety. This anxiety, however, retained a propensity to be aroused by, or to be channeled in, the pattern of sexual stimulation and inhibition. His psychological defenses and cultural background made the situation worse. John could not ignore completely that part of the self that is variously called social self, conscience, or superego, nor could he go against his cultural-religious background, as his philandering father and promiscuous sister had done. Sex was evil for him, and homosexuality much more so. As a matter of fact, homosexual desires were not permitted to become fully conscious.

When he was about to be overwhelmed by the anxiety while at the farm, at first he tried again, as previously in his life, to find refuge in religious feelings. But as those feelings proved to be insufficient protection, he resorted to obsessive-compulsive mechanisms. The anxiety that presumably was at first connected with any action that had something to do with sexual feelings became extended to practically every action. This extension was not just the result of primitive generalization (see Chapter 17), but also was due to the fact that John had noticed a lack of correspondence between the act, as anticipated and willed, and the act as it was performed. For instance, he was afraid he could kill somebody when he wanted to cut a piece of bread. The significance of substituting actions with analogic ones will be discussed in Chapter 17. Every action of John's became loaded with a sense of responsibility. Every willed movement came to be seen by him, not as a function, but as a moral issue. Every motion was considered not as a fact but as a value. This primitive generalization of his responsibility extended to what he could cause to the whole community. By moving he could produce havoc not only to himself, but to the whole camp. It became thus his moral responsibility to inhibit every movement. John's feelings are reminiscent of the feelings of cosmic power or negative omnipotence experienced by other catatonic patients who believe that by acting they may cause the destruction of the universe. John had to choose immobility.

In many cases of catatonia the stupor is not complete. Through the barrier of immobility passage is allowed to actions that represent obedience to the will of others or have special meaning for the patient. This selectivity for certain actions should be convincing proof that catatonia is a functional condition, not an organic disease. It is a disorder of the will, not of the motor apparatus.

In the case of John the actions necessary for the suicidal attempts were allowed to go through. Incidentally, these suicidal attempts in catatonics, accompanied by religious feelings and eventually by stupor, have often led to the wrong diagnosis of the depressed form of manic-depressive psychosis. Kraepelin (1919) described suicidal attempts and ideas of sin in catatonics, but did not give to them any psychodynamic significance. What is of particular interest in John's case is the fact that the suicidal act eventually became the only act of living. It is not possible here to examine in greater detail the encounter of John with the doctor in the hospital. Often the influence of a powerful and at the same time benevolent person has this rapid therapeutic effect on catatonics. The fact that the doctor gave John permission to eat as much as he wanted is important. The only previously possible act (killing oneself) was replaced with one of the most primitive acts of life (nourishing oneself). In Chapter 25 we shall describe the placing-into-mouth habit in regressed schizophrenics. In slightly less regressed patients we find the hoarding habit (Chapter 24), a stage John went through in his progress toward recovery. In acute cases of catatonia we often find symptoms and stages appearing in other types of schizophrenia after many years of regression.

On the other hand, in other cases of acute catatonia the patient lapses into complete stupor without going through the usual previous stages. For instance, Cecile, a married European woman in her late twenties, fell into a state of complete immobility a few minutes before she was supposed to board a taxi that would take her to the airport. She was supposed to go to Europe, where her husband had gone a year before. The trip would put her in a position to face him after she had become pregnant from another man and had had an illegal abortion. The situation that the patient wanted to avoid was to pretend faithfulness. Such pretension was more guilt producing than having been unfaithful, something that was terrifying.

The cases of John and Cecile reveal that a profound sense of guilt and a consequent threat to an acceptable self-image can be elicited by events in the sexual area. Here again we must realize that some events of sexual life (even in deviant forms like homosexuality) are schizophrenogenic, not in themselves, but because of their significance for some patients and the previous vulnerability of these patients. In the cases of Sally and Richard sex played only a minor role.

The connection between sexuality and catatonia has been reported by other authors. Ferenczi (1950) mentioned a patient who spontaneously explained to him that with all his catatonic postures and movements he was seeking to defend himself from erotic sensations in the various parts of his body. In the same article Ferenczi reports another patient, whom he strangely considered a case of paranoid paraphrenia. The patient, a talented young artist, had become interested, to a fanatic extent, in Ostwald's natural philosophy, which preaches that one should accomplish as much as possible with as little expenditure of energy as possible. This patient went to extremes in following this philosophy. At first he made exact plans for the day, allotting a definite time for every kind of bodily and mental activity. Later he felt that he ought not to perform any work at all except thinking. He requested that his relatives respect his absolute rest during his mental work. In his efforts to work "with the most favorable coefficients possible" he neglected the common tasks he was supposed to attend to. With the excuse of acting in the most economic way, he gave up acting altogether. Finally he lay inactive for hours in peculiar positions, which Ferenczi regarded as catatonic postures. We have in this case a progressive withdrawal from action, in the beginning rationalized with ideas taken from a philosophical system, then followed by compulsions and finally catatonic symptoms.

It is important to understand the symbolism of the obsessive-compulsive rituals that in many cases precede catatonic symptoms. In the case of Sally, the ritual about making sure that small pieces had not fallen down may be interpreted in various ways. At a superficial level it represents the compulsive necessity to obey her mother again. Sally's mother was concerned about cleanliness to a punctilious degree. What a calamity if she were to discover some dust in a remote corner of the house! Only by making sure that she was complying with her mother's wishes could Sally move. On the other hand, those little bodies may represent parts of the bodies of the relatives for whom she had so much hostility. She wanted to reassure herself that the parts of bodies did not fall down. At an even deeper level the little pieces may mean the world that was falling down. She had come to the realization that she had given up everything; the world she expected to live in was going to pieces. She saw herself only as a shadow of her mother, as a desire of her mother. There is also an additional possibility: toward the end of the second year of treatment, she began to use the phrase, "feeling like falling to pieces" when she was confronted by a difficulty. At this time, however, she was able to overcome her difficulties. It could be that earlier in her illness her symptoms were only a concrete representation of her subjective feeling of falling apart, of disintegrating as a willing person. Only by lapsing into a catatonic stupor could she avoid this catastrophe.

Why did Sally and Richard become sick at the time they did? In the case of Sally, the interpretation is easier. By marrying Ben, she saw herself as being compelled to give up her own individuality and to live as her mother wanted her to for the rest of her life. Ben was a symbolic mother who was able to reactivate the old anxiety at a time when the patient, after a series of disappointments, was least able to cope with it.

In the case of Richard we see a progression of events leading to the psychosis. He did not have a schizoid personality, but rather a stormy one, although not typical. He was very sensitive and tried to protect himself by escaping from action, withdrawing, and avoiding the guilt, the feeling of responsibility, and the anticipation of rebuff. On the other hand, he did not accept the withdrawal and made excursions into life that progressively increased his anxiety and his feeling of hopelessness. In the case of Sally, the marriage was the important culminating factor that precipitated the psychosis. In the case of Richard, no final precipitating factor could be found, but there was a long chain of causes and effects that progressively reactivated the childhood anxiety.

Before concluding this chapter we must mention that some of the psychodynamic mechanisms are related to sociocultural factors (see Part Six).

At this point we shall only mention that Bastide (1965) has tried to correlate the concepts expressed in the first edition of this book (1955) with some of the findings by Sanua (1962). Bastide stresses that my findings indicate that catatonic patients were overprotected children, because they could not act sufficiently on their own and their parents had made all important decisions for them. Bastide feels that paranoid patients were not overprotected, but rather rejected. Sanua found that children were overprotected more frequently by Jewish parents and rejected more frequently by Protestant parents. These facts would explain, according to Bastide, why Sanua also found a greater incidence of catatonics among Jews and of paranoids among Protestants.

In my opinion overprotection alone is not sufficient to explain the psychodynamics of catatonia. However, overprotection that is not accompanied by permissiveness, but on the contrary, and in a self-contradictory way, is heightened by an extreme sense of responsibility for one's actions, may predispose a person to this type of schizophrenia.

CHAPTER

11

Study of Paranoid Patients

The paranoid type of schizophrenia presents many aspects for clinical exploration and study. The rich variety of its manifestations and the complexity of its psychodynamic patterns will be the object of various parts of this book.

In Chapter 8 we have already studied the formation of delusions at the onset of the psychosis. As an introduction to the psychodynamic analysis of paranoid schizophrenia a relatively simple case will be presented in this chapter. Then some comments will be made on this case and on paranoid patients in general. More difficult cases, presenting new dimensions, will be studied in Part Seven in relation to psychotherapy. The structure of paranoid mechanisms will be discussed in detail in Parts Three and Four.

Laura

Laura was a 40-year-old married woman. A few weeks prior to her first examination, her husband had noted restlessness and agitation, which he interpreted as being due to some physical disorder. A physician who was consulted prescribed a tonic. Later Laura started to complain about the neighbors. A woman who lived on the floor beneath them was knocking on the wall to irritate her. According to the husband, this woman had really knocked on the wall a few times; he had heard the noises. However, Laura became more and more concerned about it. She would wake up in the middle of the night under the impression that she was hearing noises from the apartment downstairs. She would become upset and angry at the neighbors. Once she was awake, she could not sleep for the rest of the night. The husband would vainly try to calm her. Later she became more disturbed. She started to feel that the neighbors were now recording everything she said; maybe they had hidden wires in the apartment. She started to feel "funny" sensations. There were many strange things happening, which she did not know how to explain; people were looking at her in a funny way in the street; in the butcher shop, the butcher had purposely served her last, although she was in the middle of the line. During the next few days she felt that people were planning to harm either her or her husband. In the neighborhood she saw a German woman whom she had not seen for several years. Now the woman had suddenly reappeared, probably to testify that the patient and her husband were involved in some sort of crime.

Laura was distressed and agitated. She felt unjustly accused, because she had committed no crime. Maybe these people were really not after her, but after her husband. In the evening when she looked at television, it became obvious to her that the programs referred to her life. Often the people on the programs were just repeating what she had thought. They were stealing her ideas. She wanted to go to the police and report them. At this point the husband felt that the patient could not be left alone, and after a brief telephone conversation with the family doctor, a consultation with me was arranged.

When I saw Laura, she repeated all her allegations to me. She was confused, agitated, and afraid. Everything seemed to have a hidden meaning, but she did not know how to put all these meanings together. She was very distressed and unwilling to explain. If the husband or someone else doubted the validity of her beliefs, she would become infuriated.

Laura was hospitalized the same day. In the hospital several attempts were made by the members of the staff to treat her psychotherapeutically, but to no avail. As a matter of fact, it seemed that every such attempt made her worse. The patient was in a state in which every interpersonal approach would increase her anxiety to an enormous degree and would promote the development of defensive paranoid symptomatology. For instance, she manifested paranoid attitudes toward every nurse who took care of her. Inasmuch as a non–anxiety-producing interpersonal relationship could not be established, the staff agreed to treat her with electric shock therapy.* She received four electric shock treatments, during the last of which she sustained a minor fracture of a lumbar vertebra. It was felt, then, that insulin therapy should be instituted. After fifteen comas, the patient seemed to be free of overt symptoms, was discharged from the hospital, and came to my office for treatment, as previously agreed. At this point she was no longer afraid of contacts. On the contrary, she was eager to come for treatment, although she was a little resentful about telling her past. She realized that she had had a nervous breakdown and attributed it to her present difficulties with her husband. In the course of the treatment she was able to give an adequate account of her past history.

Laura was born in Vienna, Austria, of Jewish parents. Her father, a painter, died while fighting in World War I. She did not remember him, but from a picture

* Drug therapy was not yet in existence when this patient became ill.

her grandmother had once shown her, she knew that he was a handsome man. Her mother remarried soon, even before the end of the war, and went to live with her second husband in a small town in Germany. The early period in the life of the patient is somewhat confused. She saw her youth, from as early in her childhood as she can remember to her late teens, as a sequence of changes of residence back and forth from Germany, where her mother lived, to Austria, where her maternal grandparents were. It was not absolutely clear to the patient, in the beginning of treatment, why she had had to move so many times, perhaps once every six months. She remembered later, however, that she was not happy living with her mother. Her mother was interested in her own personal affairs, but not in the child. Laura remembered her stressing the fact that she was sending her daughter to the best nursery schools and other schools since she was very little. Later the patient came to realize that this was a device her mother used not to have her around. Laura's mother was not very affectionate, and yet always blamed the patient for not being affectionate toward her. She used to say, "I buy you clothes, toys, and still you give me no affection." Still, when Laura would try to kiss her mother and sit on her lap, her mother would say, "Don't be silly." Her mother's attitude was so inconsistent that Laura did not know what to do. Most of the time, however, she preferred not to show any signs of affection because she was afraid that her mother would think she was not sincere. Thus, she gave the impression of being cold and distant.

Her mother would also accuse her of lying. The patient did not remember what specific lies her mother accused her of, but she did remember that she was accused several times. Laura remembered her disagreeable voice saying, "This child is lying." She felt unjustly accused and was very unhappy. She was very obedient, but she obeyed only in order not to be accused, not because she felt that her mother's instructions were right. She often expected to be accused. Whenever she was accused, she felt guilty, even if she had not done anything. At the same time, she had a feeling of repulsion for her mother.

Laura liked to have pets. Once she had a dog, and another time guinea pigs. On one of her returns from Vienna, she found out that the dog had died. She became very depressed about it, asked her mother about the death of her dog, and was given many contradictory explanations. Her mother told her once that the dog had had a heart condition and had died of a heart attack; another time, that he had run away; still another time, that the animal had contracted a terrible disease and had to be destroyed. According to Laura, her mother forgot each time what she had told her before about the dog. The result was that she knew that her mother had ordered the dog destroyed, against Laura's wishes.

The guinea pigs also disappeared one day, and the mother said that they had just died of a "sunstroke." Laura felt that her mother had ordered them killed because it was too much trouble to have them in the house.

Her stepfather, according to Laura, was a nice man, but he was disinterested in her. Her mother, also, was much more interested in him than in the child. Every time she was in Germany, Laura felt unhappy; she wanted to go to live in

Austria with her grandparents. Sometimes she even threatened suicide if she were not sent to Vienna. When she was in Vienna, she would feel better, but she was not happy there either. Her grandmother was relatively tolerant, but her grandfather would often say, "This is not your home. Children must stay with their mothers." When she was sent back to Germany, the same cycle would begin again. Moreover, the German children considered her a foreigner, a stranger, and she felt alone.

Laura's desire was to become independent and leave home as soon as possible. Throughout her childhood she attended dancing schools, and she became a professional dancer at the age of 20. In the meantime, her mother and stepfather moved to South America, and soon they stopped corresponding with her. Laura did not know whether they were still alive. Her grandparents died, and she continued her theatrical career. She was very successful and was booked for vaudeville theaters in many European countries, but she performed mostly in Germany. Her occasional encounters with men were not too important.

It was during one of her tours in Germany that Laura met her husband. He was a French tourist, a businessman, who became interested in her acting. He would often go to Germany from France just to see her. He overwhelmed her with his consideration and interest, and Laura felt that she liked his attention. She had some qualms about leaving her theatrical career and marrying him, but finally she decided to do so. They were married and went to live in a small provincial town in France where the husband's business was. Laura felt like a stranger immediately; she was in an environment very different from her own and was not accepted by his family. There were realistic grounds for her feelings. They considered her a foreigner and could not forgive her for having been a dancer, and not a "regular girl." She spent a year in that town and was very unhappy. She felt that when there were arguments or controversies, her husband always took the side of his family and never took her part.

Finally, because of the uncertain political situation in Europe, Laura and her husband decided to immigrate to the United States, along with her husband's sister. Laura did not get along well with her sister-in-law and again felt that her husband showed favoritism toward his sister.

The years spent in America had not been easy ones. Laura and her husband had not been happy together. They had different points of view about many things, and the gap caused by their different backgrounds was never closed. Laura's husband became more and more intolerant of her attitude and started to neglect her. Nothing would irritate her more than his lavish attentions to his sister. They had no children, and Laura again showed interest in pets. She had a dog to whom she was very devoted. The dog became sick and partially paralyzed, and veterinarians felt that there was no hope of recovery. The dog required difficult care, and her husband, who knew how she felt about the animal, tolerated the situation for several weeks. But finally he broached the problem to his wife, asking her, "Should the dog be destroyed or not?" From that time on Laura became restless, agitated, and depressed. As we know, her symptoms became progressively worse until the time of her hospitalization.

This case is not too difficult to understand. The childhood of this patient was bad enough to produce excessive anxiety, and to give her the feeling that she was not wanted and not loved. It is interesting that although Laura's mother was unwilling to give her care and affection, she blamed the child for not loving her. The patient felt guilty, probably on account of the hostility she had toward her mother. She felt that when her mother accused her of lying, she referred to her hostile thoughts rather than to her actions. Actually the mother was the one who lied. The example of the dog indicates that Laura had realistic reasons for becoming suspicious and anticipating hostility from the surrounding adults. At the same time, the mother was suspicious of her. Laura was not criticized for her actions, as people who become catatonics generally are, but for her intentions. She had to defend herself by anticipating these false accusations. At times she would deny them; at other times she would accept them because her guilt about her own feelings of hostility did not allow her to reject them.

Laura's suspicious personality was determined by the actions of her mother, whose inconsistencies provoked uncertainty and anxiety in her. She was very badly disappointed by her mother; she trusted her, and her trust proved to be unfounded. There is enough here to establish the basis for a paranoid personality. In other words, certainly Laura's mother had given her sufficient reason to become suspicious, ready to anticipate rebuff and to defend herself from possible accusations. On the other hand, Laura developed the habit of focusing on the bad qualities of her mother, magnifying them and overpreparing herself for attack. It could be that a few so-called white lies, similar to those told by many parents with the intention of pacifying their children, were interpreted by Laura as irrefutable evidence of her mother's mendacity and propensity for subterfuges. A vicious circle that perpetuated mistrust and abnormal sensitivity was thus created.

However, the patient probably could have compensated for the anxiety of her childhood if fortunate circumstances in her later life had helped her. In fact, not everything was negative or destructive. She received a more than tolerant attitude and possibly some love from her grandmother. Her stepfather did not seem to resent her. In addition, Laura was able to find a field, classical dancing, in which she could express herself, and from which she received acclaim and gain in self-esteem. Her marriage, however, was an unfortunate event. At the same time that it deprived her of her theatrical career and artistic expression, it placed her in a situation where she again felt anxious and unwanted. Going to France, a foreign country, to live in a small town was like going once more to Germany after one of her visits in Vienna. Her mother-in-law and sister-in-law were other women in authority, ready to find fault with her actions, but mostly with her intentions. A woman coming from the theatrical world was not to be trusted. Her husband also vacillated in his attitude and favored his family too much.

The situation did not improve in America. The patient felt more frustrated and disappointed. She had no interest in motherhood, possibly because the example of motherhood she had seen in her own mother was not an inspiring one. Her discontent and anxiety increased. These problems were accompanied by the realistic difficulties that the patient and her husband had to face in settling in the

United States. Furthermore, living with her husband was a constant threat to her already unstable security. He was more and more critical of her, as her mother had been. She oscillated between believing him and increasing her self-image of the bad, worthless person, and repudiating him and defending herself from the accusations.

When the dog became sick and the patient's husband proposed having it destroyed, she identified the present situation with the one that had occurred with her dog in her childhood, which had caused her so much distress. She experienced horror. If nobody would be left to love her, if even the dog would be taken away, she would certainly feel alone, unloved, unlovable. A reactivation of the bad self-image that she had formed in early childhood and of all the unpleasant sensations undergone in that period took place (Chapter 8). But that unspoken, unverbalizable horror did not last long: a psychotic solution was found. It was not true that she was worthless. The truth was that her husband was against her and what was dear to her. But even this idea could not be maintained. She displaced the threatening role from her husband to other persons, generally women, who could better be identified with her mother. The neighbor was reading her thoughts, as she once felt that her mother had done. The neighbor was doing even more: she was making a recording of her words and thoughts. Finally, there was a wide generalization when she thought that people were accusing her, that even the television programs were referring to her.

This case is fairly typical, and it reveals the basis for a selection of the paranoid pattern rather than the catatonic or hebephrenic. The factors which predispose to the paranoid type are the following. The important adults in the childhood of paranoids do not criticize the patients for their *actions;* they generally *accuse* the patients for their *intentions* or for *lying*. The child learns to defend himself, either by anticipating these accusations and therefore becoming anxious and suspicious, or by developing a facility for rationalizations. He has to find almost a legal or technical way to protect himself from insinuations and accusations.

Various trends may develop. The patient may become a submissive person who, although suspicious and living with the anxiety of being attacked, hurt, or accused, feels some guilt at the same time. As a matter of fact, he often oscillates between feeling misunderstood, guilty, inadequate, and "not good," and feeling unjustly accused, the victim of lies. He is generally compliant and fairly cooperative. These cases generally are benign and respond well to therapy.

In other cases, the desire of the patient to defend himself predominates; there is a certain pride and complacency in the way the patient defends himself from the accusers. Rationalizations and pseudological defenses are built up. Some of these patients may never become psychotic in a manifest way; on the contrary, their tendencies to find legal reasons for protecting themselves or accusing others may be channeled successfully into certain professions. At times their hostile allegations, based on half-truths and on distortions, may meet with popular favor and may help their careers. When they become psychotic, these patients are generally defiant and resistant to treatment. One of these types of paranoids is the "querulous paranoid.'' He feels that injustices have been perpetrated on him, and he resorts to the law to defend himself. When he is defeated, he does not surrender but appeals as many times as the judicial system permits. With his pride in his knowledge of the law and his fanatic belief in his rights, he acquires at times almost a grandiose and manic flavor. Sometimes the diagnosis of manic-depressive psychosis with paranoid trends is made. French writers (Serieux and Capgras, 1950) call the querulous paranoids *maniaques raisonnants*. According to Mayer-Cross (1950), this type is not as common in England as it is in Germany. He states that the difference in incidence may be due to the fact that the Common Law does not elicit this type of reaction the way the codified system does; or that it may be due to the fact that the pathological nature of these reactions is not as easily recognized in England as in Germany. In my own experience, I have found that this type of paranoid is not rare in the United States. I have come in contact with several cases.

Other patients, instead of focusing their attention on their pseudorational defenses, seem to sense or magnify any kind of hostility in the environment. At times this hostility is real and is caused by the attitude of the patient; at other times it is just a mild hostility that accompanies many actions of normal people. The paranoid is sensitized to this hostility; he magnifies it and generalizes it. He feels *pushed around,* pressured. The pressure that, as a child, he experienced as coming from the malevolent, hostile, and inconsistent parent is now generalized to a great part of humanity. In some of these cases any interpersonal relationship increases the anxiety and enhances paranoid developments. This tendency may make psychotherapy very difficult or impossible.

Because classic psychoanalytic literature has stressed so much the importance of latent homosexuality in relation to paranoid states, we shall discuss again here what we have mentioned in Chapter 8 in reference to this topic. Latent homosexuality is a relatively frequent factor, but not a necessary one, in paranoid conditions. It leads to paranoid conditions, not because it is an inherent part of the paranoid process, but because homosexuality engenders a great deal of anxiety in many people. The latent homosexual tries to deny his own homosexuality because this form of sexuality is not accepted by society. In certain situations, however, as when he encounters a person to whom he is particularly attracted, he cannot deny his feeling to himself. He feels that he is succumbing to his impulses, and in order to avoid doing so he may resort to psychotic denial. The loved person becomes the persecutor, as Freud illustrated in Schreber's case. The patient no longer accuses himself of any homosexual desires, but other people do accuse him of awful things, as, for instance, of being a spy. The parents or their symbols enter the picture again; they accuse him of being a ''bad child.'' He is bad, he is homosexual, he is a murderer, a spy. All these accusations are emotionally equivalent. It is generally assumed today, although with insufficient evidence, that no homosexuality, even at a latent state, would have originated if the patients had had healthy interpersonal relationships with their parents or parent-substitutes (Bieber et al., 1962). Not all persons who deny homosexuality become paranoids; not all paranoids are latent homosexuals. Furthermore, in a society where this form of sexuality would be more acceptable, there would be fewer persons who, on account of these latent leanings, would develop the intense anxiety which leads to psychosis.

As already mentioned in Chapter 8, uncertainty about one's own sexuality and a general sexual maladjustment, rather than a clear-cut homosexual pattern, are the psychosexual pictures more frequently found in the paranoid.*

Under the paranoid classification are to be included the cases of *folie à deux* or *folie à trois*. In these instances we have the simultaneous occurrence of two or three cases of paranoid conditions in the same family or household. The situation is generally the following. The first one to become sick is usually a person with a strong, overbearing, arrogant personality. He is able to make the spouse, a child, a brother, a sister, or a friend living on the same premises accept his own delusional system. The recipients are generally weak, submissive persons who find it easier to accept the ideas of the donor, even if they are psychotic, than to fight them. The unshakable conviction of the donor, as well as the anxiety that a rejection of his authority would provoke in the recipients, makes the latter accept his delusions. Of course, the recipients must be predisposed by their own psychological difficulties (such as an extreme state of dependency, and so on) to accept the psychotic burden of someone else. Gralnick (1942) has made an accurate dynamic study of these cases. The prognosis is good for the induced cases if they are separated from the donor and receive adequate therapy. Layman and Cohen (1957) reported the history of two brothers who developed *folie à deux*. Dawson and Burke (1958) reported the cases of a husband and wife whose joint delusions met the intrapsychic needs of both. It is questionable whether we could speak of real schizophrenia in the recipient.

* Other authors (Klein and Horwitz, 1949; Tyhurst, 1957) have experienced similar doubts about the necessity of the association homosexuality-paranoid condition.

CHAPTER

12

Study of Hebephrenic Patients

In Chapter 3 we learned that the hebephrenic type of schizophrenia manifests itself in two main forms:(1) as a syndrome immediately characterized by marked regressive features, with restitutional symptoms playing a minimal role; (2) as a syndrome in which the paranoid defenses failed to arrest the process, which proceeded toward a rapid regression.

In this chapter the case of a patient suffering from this second form of hebephrenic disorder will be illustrated. This report will focus on the more recent precipitating events rather than on the early environmental factors.

Ann

Ann was a 26-year-old, white, Catholic, married woman who was brought to the hospital for observation while having an acute mental disturbance. Her illness began a week and a half prior to admission. The patient had been going dancing frequently with her sister. About this time she had met a young man, Charles, at the dance hall, and they had danced together. One evening she came home from dancing and told her mother that she was going to give up her husband Henry, marry Charles, go to Brazil with him, and have twenty babies. She was talking very fast and saying many things, several of which were incomprehensible. At the same time she also told her mother that she was seeing the Virgin Mary in visions. She then went to her mother-in-law and told her to take back her son Henry, because he was too immature. The following day Ann went to work and tried to get the entire office down on their knees with her to recite the rosary. A few days later, her mother took her to a priest, whom she ''told off'' in no uncertain terms. She finally spit at him. A psychiatrist was consulted, and he recommended hospitalization.

Part of the following information was obtained from various members of the family, because the patient was too disturbed on admission. Ann was born in the United States to parents of French lineage. She was the second of four siblings, having a brother six years older and two younger sisters. Her birth was not planned. The relationship between Ann and her father is not known well. The family can recall that the father was very fond of Ann and apparently had never punished her, leaving any discipline to the mother. When the patient was 4½ years old, her father died as a result of pneumonia. He is described as having been an easygoing, quiet, friendly person. He was about thirty years older than the mother and was 60 when he died.

The mother was 54 years of age at the time the patient became ill. She tried to be friendly and pleasant, but rambled in her talk. She seemed somewhat confused and displayed a rather shallow affect, particularly when discussing serious matters. The physician who interviewed her in reference to the patient had the impression that she herself was psychotic and possibly affected by a mild form of schizophrenia. When she attempted to put into writing what she considered important aspects of her daughter's history, she disclosed some scattering of thought processes. She felt that at the time of her pregnancy with the patient she had gone to see a horrifying film about a man trapped in a burning building. She suggested that this prenatal influence might have played a part in the patient's present illness.

The mother was the disciplinarian in the family, although she never resorted to actual physical punishment. What she would mete out was a stern look and a hand upraised as if to strike, but she never did strike. She was very strict in the patient's training. She was always very prudish about sexual matters and never discussed them with Ann. Shortly after the father's death, an uncle (a brother of the father) came to live in their house, but he would not have much to do with the patient. Ann's older brother seems to have been the most serious-minded member of the family. He would frequently take care of the patient in her early years, but saw less and less of her as she grew older. The younger sisters played a minor role in Ann's life.

Ann graduated from high school and from a school for commercial art. She was a very persistent student, very punctual in her study habits, and even in her early childhood showed a talent for drawing and painting. Following her studies in commercial art she obtained several jobs which were not commensurate with her ability. She even did factory work.

The patient apparently had been kept fairly ignorant of sexual matters until the age of about 17, when her older brother explained to her in a didactic manner "the facts of life." She began to menstruate when she was about thirteen and apparently became very anxious at this time. She went to her mother for an explanation of what had occurred and was reassured. The patient had had several acquaintances throughout her life, but no deep friendships. In the whole household a deep religious atmosphere prevailed. At the age of 18 she met a man ten years her senior with whom she became infatuated. They went out on frequent dates, but this man was inducted into the army. The patient then began going out with Henry, the younger brother of the inducted man, who was a year younger than Ann.

They became engaged shortly thereafter and went out together frequently until their marriage, which took place three years prior to Ann's hospitalization. There had been no premarital relationships. During married life they indulged more in mutual masturbation than in regular intercourse. They seemed to enjoy this form of sexuality. Regular intercourse was practiced once every two or three weeks. The husband often became irritated at the patient for her apparent joviality during sexual relations. On a few occasions, while he was on the point of having an orgasm, Ann would crack jokes, upset him, and prevent him from continuing. This would result in arguments afterwards. Married life was considered a boring routine by both Ann and Henry. There was very little conversation between them.

Family life became more and more monotonous, and Ann had to resort to outside activities to have some fun. A year prior to the onset of the illness she had had the desire to go out West, where her father had lived, and to find out from his relatives facts about his life, which she had never known. She went there and visited his grave, but did not learn much about his life.

Ann's disappointment in Henry increased. They had nothing in common; she was artistically inclined, whereas he had only an ordinary, conventional outlook toward life. It was at this time that she started to go dancing and then met Charles. Her interest in him increased, but she knew that she was married and that a divorce was not compatible with the precepts of the Catholic church. Her conflict grew and put her in a state of great agitation. A few days before she became openly disturbed, she wrote a long letter to a priest. Here are some excerpts from this letter:

Dear Father L.,

I have to start out with the most daring words that I could ever tell a priest or anyone.

I have no right to wear a wedding ring.

It's most peculiar that when you become an *adult* in the eyes of *God* you can begin to see *NOT* with your own but *HIS* vision—and be able to tackle life's problems (sufferings) in only *one* way which is his order.

For all my years, I went into this marriage as a skeptic and knowing and not knowing, mind you, that I didn't love my about to be husband.

When a person is at peace with himself and knows he's done his best he can sleep.

I can't feel this way and remain married to Henry. It is no marriage, but self-inflicted torment on my part. I know that God didn't mean it to be this way. If Henry and I cannot *grow* together in marriage the way it should be, we have nothing but emptiness.

I look at Henry with my newly found values of life and see a great big cold handsome person. One that represents my old values. He is only cold to me because he has always sensed that I don't love him. (I could never put this into words before.) I know that if I could learn to love him, I would never have another complaint. He is that good! I can't bear the thought of him being hurt. *It* hurts. What looks right in the eyes of this world is not what is right at all.

People get so used to living their own narrow, inhibited life ("nobody's going to tell me what to do'' attitude), they never get along with the right time—and they can't see it. It's wrong for themselves because it can *only* be done with God's help.

Speaking of interpretation I have only been able to come to my drastic conclusions through the Blessed Virgin Mary's reaching God for my betterment. How I would like to be able to say *our* betterment—Henry's and mine. I can't.

I know all my answers now—as I repeat through Mary's intervention. For three years I couldn't live without a struggle. I didn't have much religion then but because of my struggle and not being able to reach Henry I turned to it—my now greatest value in life.

I have found the greater your struggle for truth—no matter how low or miserable—the greater your reward.

Rather than cross the sex boundary from which you cannot return—I have crossed into a spiritual intellect world that knows no turning back unless all my beliefs and *present* values are wrong. In that case I belong in insane asylum. (And many would say, ''Ha, I always thought so.'')

How can I ever have children or *ever* begin to live in marriage if *I* with these thoughts do not possess love. I have no foundation. All my great building which I have in my power is to no avail without love as the basis.

In a nutshell, I violated God's law of marriage! It has taken three years for me to be beaten into submission. This is my case, it is for you, as a priest, to tell me whether or not I am married!

Nobody can go against God's law, otherwise they suffer unnaturally so. (This is what happens to nonbelievers—the poor souls.) Just the way he can make your cross lighter (for it shall always be there) with your *full* cooperation so is suffering made *worse* than sin (if such a thing can be) without his help.

These three years served only as a means of helping me to grow up. It furthered everything about *ME* (which sounds so selfish). The good Lord knows how many times I could not express myself but only feel that gap between Henry and I. Why did I feel so selfish all the time *knowing* what a good guy Henry is with his being so unselfish? Why couldn't I take intercourse? Why was I so lopsided in my mind as to make jokes at a *serious* time like that and hear Henry's exclamation of ''No cooperation''—''I've done my part,'' ''What's the matter now?'' ''What's wrong with you?'' For three years *we* lived like this. Just like two kids on a perpetual date always parallel with each other—never coming together.

For the first time in my life I *feel* that I have become an adult. Marriage was instituted for adult people that *know* what they are doing—not kids. Why doesn't the church put out a questionnaire that states DO *NOT* marry if not for love? Know what you are doing—scare people. I'd say the church is so lax on this issue, it *takes for granted* that its pets will do the right thing. The church is strict on divorce. Fine but it should BE *MUCH* stricter BEFORE entering marriage.

Why can't people know that religion with all its binding laws is what makes a man free—no longer a slave to himself but a sincere natural person?

Faith is the answer.

How does a person acquire it?

Dependence on God through Mary.

I'm the luckiest person in the world. I used to possess blind faith. It is not so blind any longer. It makes a lot of sense. I humbly thank God and Mary for it.

You, a priest, is next in line—for who else would understand and not consider me off the beaten path but on it.

Ann, however, did not have the courage to mail this letter. Instead she went to her mother, hoping to find in her comprehension and advice. She told her that Henry was a wonderful guy, but that she could not live with him and was going to leave him. Her mother told her that she absolutely could not leave him, that the church would not permit it. When, for the first time, the mother heard the name of Charles and of Ann's love for him, she became very upset and said, "You can't do this. What God joins together no man separates. God doesn't want you to separate. That's the devil." Then the mother kissed Ann, and Ann returned the kiss. Later Ann went to see her mother-in-law, became increasingly disturbed, and the events that led to her hospitalization took place, as has already been noted.

When the patient was first seen in the ward by the examiner, she was dashing around the room, singing and laughing. She was markedly agitated; frequently she would cry one minute and then laugh in a silly, impulsive manner, or suddenly slump over and become mute. Her speech would be incoherent at one time because she mumbled and at another time she would shriek very loudly. She would be irrelevant, or circumstantial, and she frequently rambled, her thoughts being completely unrelated to one another. Her affect would vary from extreme liability to complete flatness. She was hallucinating in auditory and visual spheres quite vividly. She was saying:

I was judged insane and others felt that this was the place for me. I am too weak. You look to me like Uncle Joe, and he is so far away. He knew how much I loved him. We could always get along. I never meant to be disobedient to you. The darn son of a bitch, you couldn't smile at me. You are the Pope and I must be obedient to the Pope. He is the only one I must be obedient to. You didn't flinch when I said "son of a bitch." You are trying to help me. All the others are different. That I can't fake in your presence, my Lord. You will understand me as my friends didn't. Russia is the only Catholic country. Russia is to the rest of the world what God is to the Pope.

Later the patient became more agitated and required strong sedation. Her illness seemed to proceed toward more advanced disintegration. She laughed in an inappropriate manner, and her whole behavior appeared silly. She was restless, confused, and talked to imaginary persons. Her productions consisted of word-salads and clang associations. During the therapy session, however, she acted calmer and maintained a fairly relevant conversation. During painting sessions on the ward she would frequently smear herself deliberately with fecal-colored paints. Frequently she would make loving gestures at other patients, particularly blacks, and would hug and kiss them.

During the therapy sessions she appeared friendly and seemed to like the therapist. However, her productions were still disconnected. One day she said to the therapist, "We have come to a draw. This is the end of the line. You are a man and I am a woman. You are a Jew and I am a Catholic. We both like music." The patient seemed to have some anxiety about her friendship for the therapist, and therapy was therefore conducted on the ward. When her mother was mentioned, she would refer to her as the "Blue mother." About a month and a half after admission, the patient became more negativistic, refused to enter therapy sessions, and was extremely hostile toward the therapist and other authority figures about her. She was, however, very friendly toward the patients. Frequently she would smear food over her body. She told the nurse on the ward that she might be pregnant, because she had had intercourse with a fellow. Around this time the patient began to urinate and defecate in bed. When questioned about this, she stated that the nurse did not bring her a pan and she could not control herself. Shortly thereafter the patient became very disturbed on the ward; she would take her feces and smear them on the walls, attempting to draw murals. She would run around the ward laughing, screaming, and acting in an incongruous manner. Two months after admission, it was felt that the patient should receive shock therapy in addition to psychotherapy. She was given a series of fourteen electric shocks, which was completed three weeks later.* At this point the patient seemed much quieter and friendlier, developed amnesia of her earlier behavior on the ward, and would speak in a fairly relevant and coherent manner. She was no longer inappropriate or silly. She apparently did not hallucinate but occasionally seemed to have some ideas of reference and vague ideas of persecution.

Therapy was continued for a few weeks in the hospital. During this time Ann became more and more lucid and was able to verbalize her conflicts about her marriage. She was soon discharged from the hospital, and private therapy with another physician not connected with the hospital was instituted.

In this case we shall limit the analysis to the acute episode. Why did it occur? Of course the early environmental factors are important in this case, too. We know that Ann's father died when she was only 4½ years old, and that thereafter she was exposed exclusively to the influence of her mother. We do not know much about the mother, but what we know does not seem constructive, from the patient's point of view. At the time of Ann's illness, her mother also seemed psychotic, and possibly had been for a long time. The fact that she married a man thirty years older than herself seems to reveal an unusual oddity. Her ideas about prenatal influence seem to be due more to a certain paranoid frame of mind than to ignorance. When Ann was in the most critical situation of her life, at the time when she wanted to leave her husband, and went to her mother for support, the latter was not able to help her at all. On the contrary, she reinforced Ann's religious conflicts.

The patient had an ambivalent attitude toward her mother. Not only was her mother the person whom she sought during her marital crisis, but possibly the black patients whom she hugged and kissed during her psychotic attack were concrete symbols of her "blue mother." She liked them, but at the same time they were blacks and, according to social prejudice, were inferior, like her mother. Mother was blue in her mood; they were dark in their skin color. Her feelings for her mother were bound to be frustrated because her mother disappointed her again

* Patient's illness occurred prior to the development of drug therapy.

and again, even at the most crucial moment in her life. The real "blue mother" for her was probably the Virgin Mary in heaven, to whom she addressed her prayers and on whose love she relied in periods of distress. After disappointments in her artistic career, the patient had rushed into marriage with Henry and had found herself disillusioned again. The letter that she wanted to send to the priest is an excellent document of her state of mind at that time. She seemed to have remarkable insight about her situation. However, paranoid ideation was developing already. She tried to solve her conflicts with the help of the church, but she could not go against the church. She felt that the priest to whom she wrote would be able to help her. The church, God, and the Virgin Mary (all symbols of good parents) would be able to help her. Rather than divorce Henry and marry Charles (that would be tantamount to adultery in her religious conceptions), she tried to immerse herself in religious feelings and to obtain the approval of the church.

"Rather than cross the sex boundary from which you cannot return—I have crossed into a spiritual intellect world that knows no turning back unless all my beliefs and *present* values are wrong. In that case I belong in an insane asylum." The spiritual intellectual world of the church could not help her. The church could not make her love Henry and could not declare that she was not married. She understood this, and therefore did not send the letter to the priest. Instead, she made an attempt again to seek help from her real parent, her mother, and again she was disappointed. She had to turn back, and, as she had mentioned in her letter, she turned toward insanity. At a time when she had a great challenge to meet, she found herself unable to cope with the challenge; nor was she able to find anybody who would understand her and help her. Her values were integrated in the framework of her religion, and in this particular circumstance her religion could not help her. Although at the beginning of the attack she manifested paranoid conceptions as concretizations of religious concepts, an arrest at a paranoid level was not sufficient to allay her anxiety. Harboring paranoid delusions still would mean being part of a "spiritual intellect world" from which she had to turn back also. Her escape had to be more pronounced, and therefore it reached hebephrenic proportions. Her words became incomprehensible most of the time; her behavior was that of acute regression, but it was not antagonistic. Therapy with a male physician did not decrease the anxiety, and the staff decided to submit her to shock treatment. With this type of treatment, the anxiety about the recent developments in her life was eliminated; she became accessible to psychotherapy and was able to reintegrate.

Much more difficult to study psychodynamically and to treat is the first variety of hebephrenic schizophrenia, in which an insidious beginning with no restitutional symptoms forms the basis of the symptomatology. In this eventuality, it may be difficult to distinguish hebephrenic from simple schizophrenics. As a matter of fact, a mixture of these two types may be found in some patients. Frequently, in the development of the simple type of schizophrenia, in addition to poor child-parent relationships, I have found another dynamic factor. The patient has had to compete with a younger sibling who, on account of superior intelligence or of favoritism from the parents, has had a better chance to develop. The patient abandons the fight; he not only accepts the younger sibling's supremacy, but wants to remain in an inconspicuous role and refuses to grow psychologically. He may remain in the shadow of the sibling and may obtain some security as long as he does not try to compete with him.

CHAPTER

13

Postpartum Schizophrenic Psychoses

I
General Remarks

Postpartum schizophrenic and schizophrenic-like psychoses must be considered in a larger frame of reference that includes all psychiatric conditions occurring after childbirth. The relations between pregnancy-labor-puerperium and the occasional occurrence of psychiatric conditions must be investigated.

The question occurring to many psychiatrists is whether pregnancy, labor, puerperium, lactation, and so on, produce an organic alteration in the mother sufficient to cause concomitant psychiatric disorders. Such alterations would be mediated through an endocrine disequilibrium. Hamilton (1962) believes that there is conclusive evidence that late postpartum syndromes are associated with diminished secretory activity of the thyroid gland. He believes that the adrenal gland, too, particularly through its production of certain corticosteroids, may be involved in postpartum syndromes, especially those that occur early in the puerperium. A postpartum involution of the pituitary is also considered responsible for the disorders. All these interpretations are hypothetical and not conclusively confirmed. As a matter of fact, previous authors have reported opposite findings, for instance, hyperactivity of the thyroid gland.

Another point of view sees the postpartum syndrome as resulting from special metabolic processes occurring during pregnancy. As a matter of fact, psychoses do occur more frequently in patients who had eclampsias and other toxic conditions. Another possibility is that the labor acted merely as a physical stress situation, eliciting mechanisms similar to those occurring in so-called combat psychoses or in those psychoses that follow surgery. Still another possibility is that the labor merely precipitates a latent psychosis that may have existed for a long time.

It is my belief that a certain number of psychiatric conditions occurring postpartum must be included in the category of toxic-exhaustive delirium. In the presence of a psychiatric condition occurring after birth, the psychiatrist must first of all evaluate whether he is in the presence of a postpartum delirium. All the other conditions that are not deliriums must be considered to a large extent psychogenic. Common postpartum conditions are: schizophrenia in all its varieties, psychotic depression, mild depressive attacks (postpartum blues), obsessive-compulsive psychoneurosis, phobias, hypochondriasis, anxiety states. This vast variety of clinical syndromes would seem at first to indicate that childbirth is only a precipitating event. Actually, the more we study each case psychodynamically, the more we realize that the experience of giving birth to a child was an episode of such magnitude as to require a complete psychological readjustment on the part of the patient. Chertok (1969) writes that maternity appears to be an integrative crisis in women's psychosexual development. The assuming of the maternal role involves the revival of the structuring conflicts that have marked the mother's personal history and molded her identifications. Chertok adds that "childbirth is the 'end'—at least a temporary one—of this crisis, and also frequently its culminating point. The way in which it is experienced depends upon the woman's whole past history; at the same time, it is exposed to the hazards of a crucial moment in time and may have a directive effect on the future." These words seem to be even more pertinent in relation to women who develop psychiatric conditions after childbirth. I believe that the revival of the structuring conflicts at times necessitates psychopathological developments. The psychopathology is the result of the interplay of the conflicts of the patient and of the psychological defenses that she can build up. Childbirth was thus an essential factor in the engendering of the disorder.

It is a common belief that postpartum conditions are less common today, and as a matter of fact, there are many fewer reports about these conditions in the current psychiatric literature than in the literature of a few decades ago. A recent good article from the point of view of the manifest symptomatology and statistics is by Protheroe (1969).

In my opinion this belief is not correct. Perhaps postpartum deliriums and full-fledged psychoses are less common because prenatal care and medical assistance during labor and puerperium have improved. However, less pronounced conditions are, in my opinion, very common, and schizophrenic and affective psychoses are not rare.

Childbirth affects many women in different ways. As a matter of fact, under close psychodynamic examination, various psychiatric disorders that occur long after the birth of a child reveal themselves to have started as early as three days after the birth of the child, although nobody suspected so. After the birth of the child the woman was requested to make adjustments of which she considered herself incapable. The particular childbirth that was followed by a psychiatric disorder is the one that required the woman to reevaluate her feminine identity (Shainess, 1966).

Psychoses due to childbirth are reported differently by various authors (see also Hamilton, 1962). According to Davidson (1936), schizophrenia and manic-depressive psychosis each constituted 30 percent of postpartum psychiatric disorders. For Boyd (1942), manic-depressive psychosis constituted 40 percent; schizophrenia, 20 percent; deliriums, 28.5 percent; psychoneuroses, 6 percent. Strecker and Ebaugh (1926) reported 34 percent deliriums; 36 percent manic-depressive; 26 percent schizophrenia. Protheroe (1969), in England, reported almost twice as many cases of affective psychoses as compared with schizophrenic psychoses. It is worth considering that these data were collected in periods when manic-depressive psychosis and deliriums occurred (or were diagnosed) much more frequently than today. Possibly a higher incidence of schizophrenia would appear in more recent statistics. On the other hand I have noted, much to my regret, that even in very reputable psychiatric centers women who presented postpartum neuroses were freely diagnosed as being affected by postpartum schizophrenia. Many obsessive women who presented the fear that they were going to hurt or neglect the child were diagnosed as schizophrenic. The occurrence of obsessive-compulsive psychoneurosis and of phobic syndromes is quite common after childbirth.

There is no doubt that full-fledged postpartum psychoses are very rare in some countries. Some prominent European obstetricians have not seen even one case. Because the diagnosis is very easy, this discrepancy cannot be attributed to diagnostic difficulties. Cultural reasons probably play an important role. In some countries motherhood strengthens the woman's self-image, no matter how severe are her conflicts and the psychological adversities to which she was subjected.

II

Symptomatology and Psychodynamics

Almost without exception there are no symptoms of postpartum schizophrenic psychosis in the first two days after the birth of the child. In the majority of cases symptoms develop from the third to the fifteenth day. The largest incidence is on the sixth day. We have already mentioned that although in some atypical cases mild symptoms or a different outlook toward life and oneself could be traced back to a period as early as the third day, the symptomatology may not become manifest until a few weeks or months later.

The prodromal symptoms are restlessness, exhaustion, irritability, rapid change of mood, and insomnia. These symptoms may pass unnoticed, because the patient at this stage is not able to verbalize how she feels. People who take care of the patient generally attribute these symptoms to the stress of having given birth. Soon, however, the symptoms become more prominent. The patient becomes suspicious, confused, makes statements that are not understood, and seems concerned over inconsequential matters. Finally she expresses definite delusions and responds to voices; in very acute cases her speech becomes a real word-salad. The majority of cases seem to fit into the paranoid type of schizophrenia; but the hebephrenic and catatonic types or a mixture of the three is also relatively commonly observed.

The fact that there is an interval between the labor and the onset of symptoms seems to be strong evidence that the psychiatric syndrome is not the result of physical exhaustion caused by the labor. As a matter of fact, in most instances it is in the first or second day after birth that the patient has the possibility of recuperating strength. By the third day she is no longer concerned with her physical condition and for the first time she has the possibility of looking at herself in a new way. *Now she is a mother* (or in the case of a multipara, she is a mother again). She has to face all the meanings of this event. How is she able to cope with the challenge? What does it mean to be a mother (or a mother again)?

Various psychological conflicts recur frequently in women who develop postpartum schizophrenic psychosis. In most cases these various conflicts are confused, interconnected; and it is impossible to disentangle one from the other. The patient in most cases is not able to verbalize them. In only a minority of cases is the patient able to express her conflicts before the psychosis occurs, or later after the psychotic episode is over. For expository reasons these conflictful areas will be reported separately here in the order of frequency in which they have appeared in my experience. I must stress that the experience of any single practitioner in this area is limited and that therefore this order of frequency is subject to revision when larger statistics become available.

In the first group of conflicts, the patient presents a sudden insecurity about fulfilling her role as a mother. She feels she cannot take care of the baby. She would like "to send him back" if possible because he complicates her life immeasurably. She wants to run away, leave her home, her husband, her baby. At other times she alternates between thinking that she does not love the child and thinking that she loves the baby very much, but is not able to take care of him. Often she feels guilty, worthless, not even capable of being a mother. However, contrary to what happens in patients who develop a postpartum depression, guilt feelings and need for approval do not play the most important role. The most important conflict is the feeling of inadequacy, of not being able to cope with the challenge of motherhood. In almost all the cases that follow in this group, the patient identifies with her mother, whom she considered a bad mother, and with the child, who will be the victim of another bad mother. She relives the anxiety of her former relationship with her own mother (see also Fromm-Reichmann, 1950). I believe it is not due to chance that I have seen postpartum psychosis occur more frequently when the baby was a girl.

The patient does not want to be a bad mother, as her mother was, but now, in the presence of the sudden fact of being called to be a mother, she feels she will be as her mother was. As we mentioned before, she would like to escape from the predicament, but she knows that she cannot. She cannot send the baby back, nor can she run away. She cannot communicate these feelings to anybody, and therefore she cannot be reassured. As a matter of fact she herself cannot face these thoughts. And yet these thoughts become more tormenting. They reactivate the feelings of inadequacy and terror that she once experienced in her life (see Chapter 7); she becomes confused, and her thinking becomes incoherent, paranoid.

The second cluster of conflicts, which is more frequently found today than in the past, has to do with the acceptance of motherhood and the acceptance of the baby. The patient resents being a woman, if being a woman means being a mother, like the female of every animal species, and renouncing a career or an individual life, as only the male of the human species can enjoy. The patient cannot find her identity in the traditional role of woman. Being a mother means being no longer attractive, as the body was deformed by the pregnancy and labor and eventually will be by nursing. It means also renouncing forever any possibility of finding a role in life that is congruous with what the patient expected of herself—to have an independent role, to be creative, to be an actress, a dancer, a business woman. She may be jealous of the baby because of the affection and love the husband will have for the baby. Now she will be tied, chained to the house; she will not be able to walk out of the house when she wants. The intruder is there. She wishes she could turn the clock back.

She is very ashamed of these feelings. She could not communicate them to anybody. If she was not able to accept the baby, others would consider her a monster. She cannot accept the fact that she cannot accept being a mother or that she cannot accept the baby as a new member of the family. At the same time she is afraid the baby will suffer. In these cases, too, the patient did not find inspiration toward motherhood from her own mother, for whom she had hostile feelings and with whom she did not want to identify.

Her anxiety increases rapidly. If she does not see a way out of her predicament, she will lapse into prepsychotic panic followed by a full psychosis.

A third important group of conflicts focuses on the patient's marriage and relation with her husband. She does not accept this marriage or her husband; but now that she has a child from him, she feels stuck. What is she now to do? Some authors (Astrachan, 1965; Kaplan and Blackman, 1969) have given much attention to the attitude of the husband as an important dynamic role in postpartum psychosis and have minimized the two previous situations that we have discussed. It is true that if the husband fails to satisfy the heightened dependency requirements of his generally dependent wife, the situation becomes more precarious.

Other situations may occur after childbirth that are unacceptable to the patient or that injure further her already weak self-image. In the presence of a psychodynamic life history that predisposes to schizophrenia, these conditions may precipitate a postpartum psychosis. Zilboorg (1928, 1929) has tried to interpret these conflicts in a Freudian frame of reference. He believes that childbirth represents castration to the patients and that the psychotic reaction is due to a recrudescence of the penis envy. Zilboorg thinks that for postpartum psychotic women the child has "more the value of a lost male organ than anything else." Zilboorg's patients, too, experienced an inadequate motherly relation to the child. It is for this reason that Zilboorg believes they turned to masculinity. Occasionally I have observed a rekindling of dormant homosexual tendencies in women who underwent psychiatric complications after childbirth.

It is interesting to evaluate why some women develop postpartum psychosis after the first birth, others after subsequent births. Deutsch (1945) found postpartum psychosis more frequently in multiparae and interpreted this finding with the hypothesis that it is more difficult for emotionally deranged, schizoid women to preserve their psychic balance when the maternal relationship must be spread to several children than when it is concentrated on one child. In my experience postpartum psychoses occur more frequently after the first birth than after each subsequent labor. It is only when we take into consideration all subsequent births together versus first births that these psychoses seem more frequent in multiparae. Postpartum psychoses occur also very frequently in women who had previous schizophrenic episodes. As a matter of fact, we can surely state that pregnancy is a hazard in women who had previous psychotic attacks that were not followed by a complete recovery or by a successful and prolonged psychodynamic psychotherapy. The challenge of motherhood may disturb again the tenuous equilibrium.

When postpartum psychoses occur after subsequent births, we must believe that the previous births had prepared the ground, but only now the patient cannot accept herself or her motherhood, her ability to be a mother, an irreparable renunciation of her own hopes, or an irrevocable marital tie.

We must stress again that the challenges presented by childbirth would not unchain a psychosis if the previous circumstances of the life history of the patient and her crippling, rather than protecting, defenses had not prepared the ground. Other factors in the family situation are important in the dynamics of the psychosis. In typical cases the family is unable to help the patient at all. The family involved in this special situation generally consists of three people in addition to the patient, and these three people are perceived by the patient as strangers or enemies.

The first person is the baby, who is seen, not as a source of joy, love, hope, inspiration, motivation, and so forth, but as a source of anxiety. With his presence and demands he will reveal the patient's failure as a mother, her ungiving qualities. He will condemn her to be a female in a subordinate role or tied to an unloved husband.

The second stranger is the mother of the patient, who, as in the past, is incapable of reassuring her daughter. As a matter of fact, she seems to scold the patient for her failure to be a mother, and, paradoxically, she herself seems to the patient to be the prototype of bad motherhood.

The third stranger is the husband, who is also caught in a situation he does not know how to cope with. Although he tries to control himself, he cannot comfort or express sympathy for the wife, who is not able even to be a real woman, a mother for his child. Instead of sympathizing with her he bemoans his destiny for having married such a woman.

Although the mother and husband try most of the time to conceal these feelings, the real feelings are conveyed to the patient. We must specify, however, that in a certain number of patients falling into the first category the husband is not seen as a stranger or inimical; only the mother is. The husband's indirect fault is to have fathered the child. However, later the husband may even be perceived as a savior or redeemer (see case of Priscilla in this chapter).

As we have mentioned, generally a period of prepsychotic panic is followed by a very acute schizophrenic episode. Generally the more acute the psychosis, the more difficult it is for the patient to be aware of, or to be able to give an account of, her conflicts. Some patients become acutely ill long after the birth, even months after. And yet when they are studied psychodynamically, we succeed in tracing the disorder back to its beginning a few days after the birth. The patient may have felt depressed, or euphoric, or restless, or always on the go, almost in a manic frenzy, always looking for something to do, or particularly talkative, anxious, and so on. However, these characteristics are not so pronounced as to make the relatives foresee the imminence of a psychosis.

In other cases patients never become acutely psychotic. In them it is easier to recognize a whole gamut of postpartum disorders, which range from quasi-delusional states where the distortion never reached full psychotic dimensions to simple psychoneuroses.

When an obsessive pattern prevails, the patient is afraid of hurting the child—she may harm him with a knife, drop him, feed him the wrong food, and so forth. These obsessions are concrete representations of the patient's indefinite fear of harming the child by not being a good mother. These obsessive-compulsive or phobic mothers must be distinguished from really psychotic mothers in whom a potential (although not common) danger of filicide really exists.

Two patients will be presented in the remainder of this chapter. The first suffered from an acute postpartum psychosis of the paranoid type of schizophrenia; the second experienced a condition in which a full-fledged psychosis was not reached, but was averted by timely therapy. Although the second case may not technically be considered a postpartum psychosis, it is presented here as representative of those more numerous cases in which, in my opinion, there is an intermediary state between psychosis and other postpartum psychiatric conditions.

Priscilla

Priscilla was 23 years old when she first came for a psychiatric consultation. When I first saw her, she was an attractive red-haired young woman in a state of excitement. She came accompanied by her husband, who told me that the patient had given birth to a girl approximately a month earlier. In the last few days she had become increasingly incoherent, restless, and seemed in a state of pain and agitation. According to the husband, she had been preoccupied with the number 3, had looked in shop windows to find dolls with red hair, and would repeatedly state that her little daughter Sara, to whom she had just given birth, was not a virgin. She was particularly impressed by the fact that Sara, too, had red hair as she had. I tried to convey a message of reassurance, but to no avail. The patient could not listen, became increasingly irritated, and no possibility was found of establishing with her any sort of relatedness. She was agitated, her actions were aimless or inappropriate, and the possibility of her hurting herself or others was not remote. Hospitalization was recommended. Following hospitalization the patient became worse; her speech consisted of word-salad. Only occasionally was it possible to establish some contacts and to listen to her delusional statements. For instance, a few days after she was admitted she developed an infection in one of her fingers. The terminal phalanx was swollen and red. The patient told me several times, "This finger is me." Pointing to it she said, "This is my red and rotten head." She did not mean that her finger was a symbolic representation of herself, but in a way hard to understand, really herself or an actual duplication of herself.

A history of the patient was soon obtained from her mother. The mother said that Priscilla was born in podalic position after a difficult labor that lasted twenty-two hours. She was born at half-past ten in the evening, but her birth was not recorded officially until the following day because the placenta was not expelled until three hours later. It was a natural birth in the sense that no anesthetic was used and also a dry birth because the membranes broke before the mother entered the hospital. Priscilla weighed seven pounds at birth and was born with very sore buttocks, which cleared up by the time she was 3 weeks old. She was breast fed until she was 9 months old. Priscilla sucked her thumb. At a doctor's suggestion, when she was over a year old quinine was applied to it so that the unpleasant taste would discourage the sucking. Shortly after quinine was used, Priscilla became constipated and had a violent bowel movement that caused a small tear in her rectum. The mother did not become aware of this at first. However, Priscilla resisted having bowel movements, as it was later assumed, because they were painful to her. She was taken to a doctor, who found the tear practically healed. However, Priscilla's fear for bowel movements continued for some months. According to her mother, this was the only time during which Priscilla had been unhappy. According to her, Priscilla had been a happy, friendly child and adolescent, and her life had been uneventful from a medical point of view until the present illness.

The patient got married a year and a half prior to her hospitalization, and a few months later she became pregnant. Pregnancy was normal. However, while in labor, it became evident that a Caesarian was necessary. The operation and convalescence were normal. The patient returned home from the hospital with the baby, apparently in perfect condition. However, the husband remembered in retrospect that two or three days after her return, Priscilla became increasingly dissatisfied, intolerant, and even suspicious of the woman hired to help her as a nursemaid. This woman was eventually fired. Another woman was hired, but the patient became rapidly intolerant, resentful, and suspicious of her too. The patient became excitable and restless, but it was on December 10 that she became obviously psychotic. The exact date is remembered because, as we shall see, it possibly had a special meaning for the patient.

We have already mentioned that after a psychiatric consultation the patient was hospitalized. Because she was extremely disturbed and because no contact or relatedness could be established, a course of electric shock treatment was recommended, with the understanding that as soon as she would be accessible to psychotherapy, she would be referred back to me for ambulatory treatment.* While in the hospital the patient continued to be disturbed. She was irrational, almost always delusional, and occasionally hallucinated. She offered typical examples of schizophrenic thinking. For instance, she would, on a few occasions, hear the voice of Benjamin, a former college teacher of hers, for whom she had had an infatuation. She insisted that Benjamin was a painter, although there was no evidence for such a statement. Later, during one of my visits to the hospital, she told me that the name Benjamin was connected in her mind with being a painter because "being a painter reminds me of colors and colors remind me of the biblical story of Joseph, who had a coat of many colors." When she was questioned about the fact that the biblical story concerns Joseph and no Benjamin, she said, "True, but Benjamin was Joseph's preferred brother."

With a course of shock treatments the patient cleared up somewhat. After a period of confusion and loss of memory she appeared more coherent and less deluded. She would, however, occasionally continue to hallucinate. Her references to her daughter were delusional. The fact that Sara, too, had red hair seemed to be a source of either preoccupation or reassurance. The patient gradually became capable of expressing anxiety about her ability to take care of the baby. Only when she was told that Sara would be taken care of by the paternal grandmother, who lived in a different city, did the patient seem reassured and expressed desire to go home.

The patient was discharged after approximately four weeks of hospitalization and came regularly to the writer's office for treatment. She acquired a good relation with the therapist, the obvious symptoms disappeared rapidly, and in the course of a few months she became capable of giving an adequate history of her life, which is summarized in what follows.

The mother of the patient was described as a detached person who lacked warmth or capacity to understand children. Priscilla had a vague recollection that when she was a very little girl, mother was nice and loving; but the more she grew up, the more detached and embittered mother became. Mother could not accept her developing a will of her own. The relation between mother and daughter became a battle for power—was mother allowed to rule without being questioned or not? Patient's dislike for the mother became more and more intense. Priscilla remembered that once she cried a lot, and mother gagged her so that she would stop crying. What actually happened is hard to determine, but this was the patient's recollection. Priscilla remembered another episode, which had remained vivid in her mind. Once, when the patient was 8 and the father had been away on a long trip that lasted several months, the mother was cutting meat with a knife. The patient had the impression that mother was pointing the knife toward her and cried, "Don't point the knife at me." She remembered also that she wrote to her father about the fact that mother had done this, but father made no reference to the episode when he answered the letter. During the treatment Priscilla realized that the mother had no intention of hurting her when this episode occurred, but the

* Drug therapy was not yet commonly used at the time this patient became ill.

very fact that she could entertain such thoughts revealed what an atmosphere of suspiciousness and fear prevailed in the household, especially between mother and daughter. The situation was made worse by the fact that, on account of the father's occupation, the family had to move quite often. It was exceptional rather than usual for the family to stay in the same location for more than a year. Priscilla thus could not make intimate friends and had to rely on her family for companionship and stimulation. The fact that father would also go away on long business trips and leave Priscilla alone with her mother made the situation still worse.

When Priscilla grew up, she noticed that mother, who was usually so reserved, would become overly friendly with some men; and the idea occurred to her that perhaps her mother was unfaithful to her father. She could never find evidence for such doubt, so that even when treatment ended, Priscilla was still debating whether the mother had really been unfaithful to her father, although this matter, by then, did not seem so significant and had lost the power to disturb her.

When the patient was 7 years old, her mother gave birth to a boy who had some congenital defects that caused his death a few days later. The boy was born on December 10, and the reader will remember that it was on an anniversary of this birth that the patient became acutely ill. The baby seemed to be a beautiful red-haired boy. Mother and father became so disturbed over his death that they decided not to have other children. As a matter of fact, the whole subject of the birth of this boy became taboo; nobody was supposed to talk about it. However, the mother would occasionally say that in the future she would have another child, and jokingly she would say to Priscilla, "You will get married, and you and I will have a child together," meaning "Each of us will have a child at the same time."

Even in later years the relation between Priscilla and mother did not improve. Mother apparently had no faith in Priscilla, no trust that she would be able to find a husband, and she would occasionally say to her, "I don't want you to become an old maid like these undesirable creatures that we know [some acquaintances who were not married]. If you cannot get a husband, I will find one for you." The mother perhaps wanted to help, but her way of doing so was deleterious to Priscilla's self-esteem.

The relation with father was more rewarding although ambivalent. Priscilla remembered loving him very much. He was warmer, sociable, and kind and considerate toward Priscilla. However, Priscilla could not forgive him, not only for his long trips, but also because when he was home, he was very submissive to mother. He would never contradict mother; on the contrary, he would always give in.

There is no doubt, according to Priscilla, that father has always been faithful to mother. Since Priscilla became an adult, the father seemed to be obsessed with the phenomenon of prostitution: how prostitutes are allowed to circulate freely in the big cities that he visited because of his business. According to Priscilla, her father, in spite of finding this matter an object of frequent conversation, has never been a customer of these women, but gained some kind of vicarious pleasure by observing them from a distance and remembering them.

When Priscilla went to college and left home, she felt liberated. She was a good student and soon became popular on the campus. However, she refused to go out with the few red-haired young men who asked her out "because they were like brothers."

While she was preparing for her master's degree, she met the man who, a year later, became her husband. Courtship and marriage had been happy. Mutual understanding and reciprocal enrichment developed soon between husband and wife. The parents, on either side of the family, lived in distant cities and did not interfere.

When Priscilla was about to give birth, however, her mother came to help her. During psychotherapy Priscilla mentioned that her mother's arrival made her irritable, anxious. Mother appeared worse because the anxiety about the oncoming birth added to the usual lack of comprehension between the two of them. After all, mother had had a difficult birth at the time Priscilla was born, and the second child was born with fatal congenital defects. Priscilla remembered that she herself was afraid of giving birth to an abnormal child. When she came back from the hospital, mother was there intending to help her; but her mere presence and her wishes or advice would make Priscilla furious. She remembered that at first she was suspicious of the two women who worked as nursemaids, but that subsequently they became confused in her mind with her mother. Her hostility and resentment came to be expressed toward all older women—incidentally, even toward her obstetrician, who was a woman. As we have already mentioned, she became much more confused on December 10, and she did not remember what occurred later, during the whole acute stage of her disorder.

If we try now to interpret the case dynamically, we are in a position to draw some conclusions about some aspects of the case and to advance some hypotheses about others. We could easily dismiss the second and third types of psychodynamic conflicts, which we have illustrated earlier in this chapter. Priscilla did not reject the woman's role and was eager to have children. Also, she was not rejecting her marriage. Her relation with the husband was good. As a matter of fact, this case was different from the majority of postpartum psychoses, because the husband was not experienced as a stranger, but as a reassuring person, one who was very close to the patient. His presence and help were very propitious and hastened the patient's recovery. It seems obvious that Priscilla's condition has to be interpreted as being precipitated by an identification with her mother, for whom she harbored intense hatred. If she would be like her mother, she would be a bad mother, unable to take care of the child in the proper way. Priscilla rejected her mother, and yet, because of the special conditions of isolation in which she found herself in the formative years, mother was the only adult with whom she could identify. More than anything else it was her becoming a mother that would make her become like her own mother. Consequently Priscilla's daughter would hate her as Priscilla hated her own mother. Thus there was a double identification on the part of Priscilla. The fact that the newborn was a girl and had red hair made the identification with the child easier. When mother arrived from a distant city for the purpose of helping when the birth was due and expressed her old anxiety in connection with childbirth, she reactivated Priscilla's original anxiety. At first Priscilla developed obsessive-compulsive symptoms, like preoccupations with numbers; but soon these symptoms were insufficient to arrest the anxiety and were replaced by delusional ones. Mother's old statement, "You and I shall have a child together," probably continued to have an impact on her psyche. Priscilla was afraid that Sara would be a deformed child as her brother had been. As she explained later, her fear that Sara was not a virgin meant that she was born with an imperfection—lack of virginity. The presumed imperfection was given a sexual coloring.

The other important issue that transcends the postpartum psychosis concerns the relation between Priscilla and her mother. The possibility exists that the account or interpretation of this relation, as given by Priscilla herself, does not correspond to facts, but is only an exaggerated distortion or caricature of what actually took place. The mother probably was rigid, very anxious, and lacking in warmth, but not necessarily that terrible human being that Priscilla described during treatment. The gagging episode has to be taken with more than a grain of salt. Moreover, Priscilla herself eventually recognized her distortion concerning the episode of the knife. Why then had Priscilla the need to see her mother in that negative way? We know that very early in life there seemed to be a warm feeling between mother and daughter. This case would seem to indicate that an Oedipal attachment to the father predisposed the patient to focus on the negative qualities of the mother and to build a monstrous whole out of these qualities (see Chapter 5). It is also important to notice how more benevolent and excusing was Priscilla's attitude toward her father. For instance, there was no question that, contrary to what she thought about her mother, she believed in her father's marital faithfulness, in spite of his trips and talks about prostitutes.

Priscilla recovered quickly from her psychotic episode but continued psychotherapy until a second pregnancy was completed. When the present report was written, she had recently given birth to a third child. The second and third childbirths were normal in every respect. Priscilla is leading a normal and happy life.

Mary

Mary, a married woman of Italian extraction, Catholic, was 29 when she started psychotherapy. She was of asthenic constitution, rather attractive, had a delicate expression on her face, and was somewhat reserved in her manner. When I first saw her, she told me that she was tense, nervous, incapable of tolerating her condition. She could not sleep and had to force herself to eat. She also said that she had had no troubles until she gave birth to twins three months previously. Since then she had felt unhappy, depressed, and did not know why. She was afraid she was not able to take care of the two newborn boys at the same time that she had to take care of her older child, a girl who was 3 years old. She said that about a month and a half after she gave birth, she had a strange experience—to use her own words, "a shock of some sort"—after which she saw things differently. She was in the process of taking care of the twins, changing their diapers in the living room. Her mother was in the same room, sitting on the couch. All of a sudden Mary had the sensation that something had happened: time was standing still; time had ceased to go on. There would be no tomorrow, no yesterday, but only now. It was Monday, and she felt that Tuesday would never come. She was confused and afraid that she was going out of her mind. She was frightened, would not talk to anybody, would not explain to her mother that strange sensation. As a matter of fact, she had never expressed that sensation to anybody before she revealed it to me. Even to me she could not explain very well what she meant with the words, "Time stood still." I did not press the point because I felt that at this stage of her illness questions would frighten her and would promote the crystallization of uncommunicable impressions into definite delusions. I tried instead to reassure her. She was not going out of her mind; her life was really difficult, having to take care of three little children without help from anybody. I felt that somehow I had established emotional contact.

In the following sessions, Mary spoke more freely. She said that her life was not a happy one. When she married her husband, she thought she was in love with him, but later she realized he was intellectually inferior to her by far and that there was no spiritual kinship between them. Also, he was not able to hold a job, had gone into business for himself, and lost all his capital. He had no ability to comfort her in any way.

Later she spoke at length about some characteristics that in a certain way had patterned her way of living. She told me that at every moment in her life she felt she had to do something. She had to follow a routine, a schedule, constantly; she had to do things in a prearranged order. The obligation to do things started from the moment she got up in the morning to the moment she went to bed at night. To be specific, when she got up, she had to prepare breakfast, take care of the babies, clean the kitchen, then take care of the older child, then make the bed, then take care of the babies, and so on, for the whole day. The whole day was an endless series of obligations. At times she felt frightened at the idea of going through this routine again. The endless series of things she had to do seemed impossible to face; and yet if she did not initiate the series, she felt very guilty. To counteract this feeling of guilt she started to do things and went on with her work. At times she was caught in an ambivalent feeling or attitude. She was afraid to start or to continue the series, and she stood motionless for some time; but finally the feeling of guilt was stronger and put her into motion again. She said that she never did things because she wished to do them, but only because she had to do them. She was moved only by guilt and a feeling of obligation. As a matter of fact, she had the impression that many times she did not even know how to wish or what to wish, or even what a wish was. At other times, she felt that she wished to do certain things, for instance, to go to the movies, but she felt guilty and she did not go. If she did something that she wished to do, the action had to be initiated by somebody else. For instance, her husband had to tell her to go to the movies. This, however, happened very seldom. At other times she felt that she must wish to do certain things that she must do. But in reality she knew very well that it was a must, not a wish. For instance, she felt she should wish to love her twin babies, and she should wish to do things for them, to change their diapers, to feed them, and so on. But she knew she was fooling herself. She did not want the babies; the pregnancy was an accident.

When she found out that she would give birth to twins, she was almost overwhelmed by fear, but she tried to deny the fact by not thinking about it or by not believing that she would really have twins until they were actually born. When they were born, and the unbelievable fact that she had given birth to twins had occurred, she oscillated between two different feelings. Even then the birth of the twins appeared to her unreal. At other times she felt instead that the twins were there, in their physical reality, and that her task with them was tremendous. The endless series of things she had to do seemed to spread immensely and to overpower her. Then she would have a feeling of despair, anxiety, panic.

At this time we analyzed carefully these feelings. Where did they come from? She could trace them back to her early childhood, in relation to her mother. Her mother was always there to tell her what to do. Any initiative on the part of the patient was discouraged. If she was doing anything on her own, her mother was there with her anxiety to warn her that she would do the wrong thing. In order to protect herself from sharing her mother's anxiety and in order to remove her feeling of guilt, she had to do what the mother wanted. If she did what mother wanted, mother's nagging was eliminated. Her whole life thus became almost an uninterrupted series of actions imposed by mother.

Mary's father was a tyrannical man, a drunkard. He had always been oblivious of the psychological needs of the family, although he provided somewhat for their financial and physical needs. He detested his wife and often he would drown the unhappiness of his life in alcohol. Mary was afraid of him, especially when he was drunk. She remembered that once when she was about 12, she saw her father drunk, naked, with his penis erect and in the act of masturbating. She remembered her childhood as a very unpleasant part of her life. The family had to move many times, either because the rent was not paid and they were evicted, or because the parents got into trouble with the neighbors.

In her late teens and early twenties she was very unhappy. Once for about a week or two she stayed in bed, without moving or doing anything. She felt depressed. To get up and do things was an ordeal and she preferred to remain in bed. A doctor was called and said there was nothing physically wrong with her. Until she got married, she had odd jobs and did most of the housework in her parents' home. In her early twenties she fell in love with a man who soon appeared unreliable, and she left him. Later she met her future husband, and the couple were soon married.

Space limitations prevent reporting many other facts about the life of this patient, as well as the later developments during her therapy. We shall evaluate her condition, especially in relation to childbirth.

First of all, was this patient in a state of panic at the time of the first consultation? Were some of her conceptions, like the one about time, full-fledged psychotic symptoms? My point of view is that at the time I first saw her, Mary still had some contact with reality and was able to test it. Even in her ideas about time she had elements of doubt. In her different versions of her unusual experience concerning time, most of the time she did not actually say that time had stopped, but rather that she felt *as if* time had stopped. At other times she said that in the moment when that terrifying experience took place, something happened in her mind; maybe she was becoming crazy.

My feeling is that in this case the state of prepsychotic panic that occurred after childbirth and that was more prolonged than usual did not develop into a full psychotic state. She developed instead peculiar sensations of unreality for which she still had an element of doubt. This doubt, however, was not too strong. She was in an intermediary stage between panic and psychosis. I feel, however, that if the patient had not come for treatment at this point, she would have become a full-fledged psychotic. What type of psychosis? Probably the catatonic type of schizophrenia. We have seen in Chapter 10 that catatonic patients often have a psychodynamic history similar to Mary's history. In early childhood they do not develop normal capacity to choose, to wish, and to will what they wish. If things happen in their life that all of a sudden increase their anxiety, especially if the anxiety is related to actions, tasks, choices, and so forth, they may develop a catatonic condition. Sometimes in their life they go through periods of inactivity that seem to be forerunners of their later catatonic condition. We must remember that Mary, when she was in her late teens, could not move out of bed for two weeks, although there was no sign of physical illness. Often these prodromal attacks of catatonia are mistaken for hysteria.

Was Mary's condition related in any way to the birth of the twins? In my opinion it was. It is true that the patient came for therapy three months after the twins were born, but we know that her condition started with the birth of the twins and culminated with the experience about the stopping of time, which occurred a month and a half after the birth. Throughout her life she had been able to maintain a certain equilibrium. Even the unhappiness of her marriage and the birth of the first child did not disturb this equilibrium, but the birth of the twins was too much. Her overwhelming feeling of duty, of having to do things as the mother wanted, was reactivated. Actions frightened her; and yet actions were imposed on her in an expanding number. The twins were there and demanded thousands of actions. The husband not only did not help her, but increased her irritation and discomfort and, with his criticisms, increased her feelings of guilt and inadequacy. On one side we may assume that she felt incapable of coping with the challenge—she would not be able to live up to what was expected of her. On the other side she wanted to reject her role as a mother and wife. Her own mother, with her own example, had not inspired her to become a mother. She did not want the life she was living. We must consider her case as a mixture of the first two types of psychodynamic mechanisms described earlier in this chapter.

Predisposed as she was by the dynamic history of her life, one could have expected that Mary could have developed a full catatonic attack. We know that many catatonic developments are accompanied by feelings of cosmic destruction. The world will collapse, the end of the universe is approaching. In Mary's case, the world was not ending; time was ending. We may thus interpret Mary's ideas as related to catatonic cosmic delusions. In Chapter 16 we shall see that schizophrenic patients present alterations in their conception and perception of the passage of time. However, Mary did not present an altered conception or perception of time. She had delusions or quasi-delusions about time.

In his book *The Two Faces of Man* (1954), Meerloo subscribes to the usual interpretation of the orthodox psychoanalytic school that time is often used as a symbol of father. In Greek mythology the god of time is Cronus, the god who devoured his children. This interpretation is a suggestive one, but it can hardly explain Mary's picture. Mary's father played an important destructive role in the family, but we cannot attribute to his influence the fact that the patient's troubles became much worse after the birth of the twins.

It seems to me that there is a connection between Mary's preoccupations about time and her preoccupations about movements, actions, things she had to do. Her feeling that time had stopped seems to me a concrete representation of her inner feelings. She intuitively realized that she was not living as an independent individual. She had no desires, and her time was not filled with things she wished to do; therefore her time was not really hers—it belonged to her position of mother and wife. But she did not want to be a mother, she did not want to be a wife. Time thus was not moving for her; it was still.

When this impression first occurred to her, she was in the living room with her mother on one side, the mother who always told her what to do, and with the twins on the other side, the twins who expected what she felt unable to give. The three of them submerged her as an independent person. As usual, the husband was not there to help. Had he been there, he too would have made demands. As she said later, there was nothing for her to look forward to. It was the end of her time, if by time we mean a dimension in which we wish and will.

CHAPTER

14

Averted Schizophrenia: Relation between Psychosis and Psychoneurosis

In the previous chapters of Part Two we have studied the profound psychodynamic importance of the patient's life history. And yet one is often impressed by the fact that schizophrenia has not occurred in certain individuals in spite of what seemed to the psychiatrist the most unfavorable environmental circumstances. Certainly we cannot dismiss the importance of the genetic components, which in these cases might have had protective values. Nevertheless, the adverse environmental situation itself deserves further study. First of all we have to repeat here what we already mentioned in Chapter 8, that conditions of obvious external danger, as in the case of wars, disasters, or other adversities that affect the collectivity, do not produce the type of anxiety that hurts the inner self and do not in themselves favor schizophrenia. Even extreme poverty, physical illness, or personal tragedies do not necessarily lead to schizophrenogenic conflicts unless they have psychological ramifications that hurt the sense of self. Even homes broken by death, divorce, or desertion may be less destructive than homes where both parents are alive, live together, and always undermine the child's conception of himself.

After ruling out these cases, many remain where, in spite of situations very destructive to the inner self, schizophrenia has not occurred. We shall use the term *averted schizophrenia* to describe a situation where all the ground seemed to have been prepared psychodynamically for a schizophrenic psychosis, and yet the psychosis never occurred. We shall omit from our present discussion those patients who became acutely ill, were already on the brink of the psychosis or in a state of prepsychotic panic, but escaped the psychosis because of prompt therapeutic intervention. In this chapter we are going to discuss patients in whom a slow psychodynamic development that appeared directed toward a schizophrenic outcome was diverted, arrested, or slowed down.

At times fortunate external circumstances have compensatory or remedial effects valuable enough to prevent the disorder. The presence of a beneficial person may be enough to change the pathogenetic potentiality of the environment. A grandmother, a teacher, a maid, an older sibling, or an aunt may have given the patient enough affection and created enough self-esteem to compensate for the deficiencies of the parents. At times, some fantasy to which the patient has clung tenaciously may have replaced a good parent. For example, a very neurotic patient that a colleague of mine reported on at a meeting was a child of divorced parents. Until he became an adult, he lived with his mother, who hated him. In childhood he had a fantasy that his father, who had gone to live in a distant part of the country, still loved him. One day the father would come back and rescue him from the distressing situation. Although this fantasy was irrational, at the same time it had a strong reassuring quality that possibly saved the patient from a worse mental disorder. Although it was fundamentally a passive fantasy, in the sense that it gave the feeling of being rescued by another human being, nevertheless it enabled the patient to hope and provided an incentive for helping himself in the present.

The point of the actual value of the fantasy *per se* is debatable. One may ask why the patient was capable of creating such a fantasy. Here again circumstances helped. The paternal grandmother, although not a loving person herself, would often mention the father and his alleged great deeds, with the implication that one day he would come back. Thus the grandmother was not able to give much love, but at least she gave hope to which the child could cling.

At times, under the influence of a newly made acquaintance or of some cultural ideology, the patient changes his expectations from life, accepts some aims more commensurate with his ability, and therefore avoids traumatic challenges.

At other times, psychosis is avoided by means that are unacceptable or less acceptable to society. For instance, the potential schizophrenic may be accepted by a fringe or asocial group. The acceptance by the group or the diminished demands that life makes because of the adoption of the group's habits may prevent an otherwise unavoidable decompensation. Some women avoid the psychosis by becoming a prostitute, or working in burlesque or in underground criminal groups. In those capacities they find some fulfillment, a role, and feel capable of exerting some power. If they are removed from those occupations, they may become psychotic.

In numerous cases schizophrenia is avoided because the patient succeeds in developing sufficient psychoneurotic defenses (hysterical, phobic, obsessive-compulsive mechanisms, and so on). It is only in this respect (in that a neurosis may protect from a psychosis) that the idea of an antithesis between psychoneurosis and schizophrenia may be upheld. If the character neurosis or the psychoneurosis does not protect the patient sufficiently, a full-fledged psychosis may follow. There are no intrinsic psychological qualities in psychoneuroses, character neuroses, and psychoses that would make one of these conditions eliminate the other. They are all abnormal compromises that are created to deal with certain distressing factors. If the neurotic compromise is not sufficient, the schizophrenic one may follow. In many cases, however, the neurotic compromise is sufficient. In other cases, which are increasing in number, timely psychiatric treatment prevents the psychosis.

Three case histories will be presented in this chapter. In the first two, the character neurosis and the psychoneurotic symptoms protected the patients from the psychosis, in spite of very adverse early environments. In the third case the psychosis seems to have been averted by treatment only. In the first case one can see that from early life the patient followed a definite psychoneurotic pattern and that the question of schizophrenia never arose. In the other two cases, instead, quasi-schizophrenic manifestations were already in evidence and the psychosis was averted by a narrow margin.

Louis

Louis came for treatment with the following complaints: "I think I am falling out of love with my wife. I love my wife very much, and yet I feel I am going to desert her or that something will happen which will make me separate from her." He was overanxious, weepy, trembling, and his voice was unsteady in spite of an effort to control it. He added that these ideas came to him all of a sudden while, in the company of his wife, he was seeing a movie starring Ingrid Bergman. He mentioned also that two years previously he had had a fear that he was going to kill everybody, especially his wife. He was also afraid that his father would die.

The patient was a 37-year-old printer, Jewish, of asthenic constitution, who looked a little older than his age. His father was 65 years old, was born in Europe, and owned a stationery store. The father always had put emphasis on work and education, had been a good provider, but had not spent much time with the children. He was never satisfied. If a child's grade was 95 at school, he would say, "Even marks like 100 are made for people." The only time he spent with the children was at the dinner table from five to six o'clock, at which time he would always emphasize school and intellectual accomplishments. He never played with them or showed them any affection.

Louis was extremely afraid of his father. The latter would often beat him on account of his poor scholastic achievements and would say, "You will grow up to be a taxi driver; you will never be a professional man." These words appeared almost prophetic for the patient, who is the only one in the family who did not become a professional man. At the same time that he was afraid of his father, Louis admired him, thought that he was very intelligent, always right, and that his predictions would come true. The father was always worried and anxious and somehow was able to impart his anxiety to Louis. Whereas the father was a tyrant in respect to the children, he was completely submissive toward the mother.

The mother was a rather energetic business woman, who had always been disinterested in the family. She spent most of her time in the store. At four o'clock she would go home to prepare supper for the family, but at five o'clock she would go back to the store and would return home late at night with her husband. The children were left alone; occasionally one or another of the neighbors was asked to keep an eye on them.

The family consisted of six children, Louis being the second oldest. A sister six years older than Louis was the favored child. She worked hard in the store, and the parents seemed to appreciate her. Louis was envious of her and used to incite the other children against her. The third child, Roy, was two years younger than the patient, and Louis had the impression that Roy was ashamed of him. Roy, a good student, was sociable, had nice friends, and made a better impression. Though Louis was older, he always felt inferior to Roy; he felt that Roy did not want to introduce him (such a shy, scared-looking, and shameful brother) to his friends.

The other three siblings did not play a very important role in the life of the patient. All of them, however, appeared to him to be better than he, to be preferred by the parents, and somehow to have a disparaging attitude toward him.

The atmosphere at home was very tense and insecure. Louis felt that he could almost never obtain the approval of his parents. At the age of 14 he had to leave school because he was falsely accused of stealing a knife. He did not have the courage to defend himself in front of the teacher, and he was considered guilty. He could not face the class again and refused to go back to school. His parents did not insist that he go because they were discouraged by his poor academic achievements. Louis grew up with the idea that he was the black sheep of the family, that he was not only the most stupid member of the family, but very stupid—"not even intelligent enough to go to school," his father said. Louis tried to compensate for his scholastic failures by doing a lot of work in his parents' store, carrying heavy packages, doing everything he was asked to do, and so on. He never rebelled, but felt that no amount of work that he did was enough to redeem him in the estimation of his parents. He felt inferior, hardly tolerated, and tried to make himself as inconspicuous as possible in the family. He would never talk for fear of being ridiculed. Later he was afraid to associate with young men and especially with girls. He never had premarital sexual relations.

When Louis left his native city and came to live in New York, through friends he met a girl who became interested in him. He was pleased by her attention, and they were married. This woman actually offered love to Louis, who accepted it enthusiastically and reciprocated. However, she always tried to mother and dominate him in a more or less subtle way. As has already been mentioned, when Louis came for treatment about ten years after his marriage, he had developed the idea that he was falling out of love with his wife. After a few sessions he admitted that he was afraid he was going to kill her. He was also afraid that his father was going to die.

During the first year of treatment, the family situation was explored. The parents, who in Louis's eyes were "very good and nice parents," were dethroned, and he eventually was able to trace back his excessive anxiety to his childhood. He would still insist, however, that his marriage was perfect and that his wife was a superior woman. During the second year of analysis, he came to the realization that he resented being dominated by his wife, whom he saw as a new parent. Domination was the price he had to pay for her love. When this situation was understood and he was able to express his resentment, he became more anxious for a while. Gradually, however, he became more assertive, less resentful, and lost the fear of killing her. He became able to accept her love and to reciprocate it in a genuine way.

Toward the end of the second year I felt that the treatment was successfully progressing toward a solution. And yet at the beginning of therapy, when I was not aware of many factors, I had been rather pessimistic, wondering why this patient, although very sick, was not even sicker. With an early atmosphere as threatening as his, with parents apparently so oblivious of their children's needs, with additional difficulties coming from the siblings, with such a desire to make himself inferior and inconspicuous, with this lack of self-esteem and despair of pleasing his parents, I felt that the patient could very easily have developed a schizophrenic disorder. The more I understood the dynamics of this case, however, the more I realized that this case could not develop into schizophrenia.

Several months after the beginning of treatment, the patient said that he was still suffering from a disturbing symptom that he had not mentioned to me as yet because he was too ashamed of it. He had peculiar food habits. There were many foods that he could not eat. These foods, which he excluded from his diet, did not follow any apparent pattern. He had never eaten some of these foods, not because he did not like them, but merely because he did not want to eat them. He was not even aware of any anxiety or fear associated with the act of eating them. He assumed that they were very good, but he could not make himself eat them because he had never eaten them before. He could not explain the origin of this habit, which was very distressing and led to embarrassing situations when he was invited to dinner at his friends' homes and refused almost everything. His wife had to comply with his absurd likes and dislikes and could never prepare some of the foods that she liked. He later remembered that this peculiarity had existed since his childhood. No matter how severely he was punished for refusing to eat, he would not eat the "forbidden" foods. On this point he did not comply with his parents' wishes. His mother had to go to the trouble of preparing special foods for him every day so that he would not starve. During the course of treatment Louis gradually realized that his motivation was the following: he was forcing his mother, who was reluctant to do anything for him, to do this, at least to prepare special food for him. He forced her to do this extra work, which she was very reluctant to do. This may be interpreted as a manifestation of hostility and retaliation on his part. Certainly there was a big component of hostility in this attitude, but at the same time Louis got the feeling that he was not completely neglected, forgotten, or allowed to die of starvation; his mother was doing something for him, too; she did love him; she gave him care and love as she did the others. This compulsive habit thus prevented him from developing that feeling of utter despair, of complete emotional isolation, that is harbored by the person who feels completely unloved and unlovable. That is why he had to cling to this habit so tenaciously; it was proof that he, too, got something, some love, from others. But he was not aware of the motivation of this habit, which therefore became a symptom. When he got married, he maintained the symptom, which served the same purpose. After the symptom had been interpreted to him and he had already accepted the fact that he was really loved by his wife, and when he had learned to assert himself even with her, the symptom disappeared.

One may conjecture that until the patient was psychologically prepared for an interpretation, this neurotic symptom had a useful purpose; without it the patient would have been much sicker. We may postulate that either intuitive choice or a combination of fortuitous circumstances made the patient select this protective neurotic defense. However, it would be erroneous to go so far as to think that without this protective neurotic symptom the patient would have developed schizophrenia when, after his marriage, his difficulties with his wife reactivated the old anxiety. In fact, there are other indications in this case that schizophrenia was not likely to occur. But first, let us reconsider this symptom of not eating certain foods. The mother actually allowed this symptom to exist. It is more than doubtful that the patient would have died of starvation if he had not been given the special foods. Sooner or later he would have eaten the food that the others ate. Somehow Louis felt that his mother would respond to such a threat. On certain occasions his mother would respond, would do things only for him. In other words, he could "reach" his mother, although with neurotic mechanisms.

In addition, the general attitude of this patient is not the one found in the person who becomes schizophrenic. It is true that as a child he was withdrawn and tried to make himself as inconspicuous as possible; however, even when he separated himself from the others in a physical sense, he was very much involved emotionally in the interpersonal relationships of the family. He did not become apathetic or unemotional; the opposite is true. He was always emotionally involved. Furthermore, although he felt rejected, he tried, in spite of his skepticism, to gain the approval of his parents. He complied excessively, as when he helped them in the store. He did not comply in a passive way, in order not to displease them, but in an active way, in order to regain the affection that he had allegedly lost on account of his poor scholastic achievements. Thus he developed a fundamentally compliant personality, not a schizoid or stormy one. Finally, he never doubted the values of his parents; at a conscious level he always felt that his parents were right and good, especially his father. A certain degree of identification with his father was possible.

Other factors played a role. Either because he considered his father's prediction as ineluctable, or because he chose to do so, Louis did not compete with the rest of the family and accepted himself as the only nonprofessional person in the family. Contrary to what happens in other less fortunate young people, he did not sustain repeated attacks to the self-image on account of this difference in status. Finally, the marriage with a woman who accepted him fully helped him considerably. When he temporarily felt dominated by his wife (who was not the ideal like Ingrid Bergman), his equilibrium was temporarily threatened. Treatment was able to restore the equilibrium.

Anthony

Anthony was a 32-year-old mathematician, single, Catholic, of asthenic constitution. He complained that while he was preparing for some examinations for his Ph.D. degree in mathematics, rather suddenly he felt unable to do his work. He felt that he could not cope with the situation any longer. The problems appeared insurmountable to him. He had not as yet finished his thesis, in spite of his recognized ability in mathematics. At his age, when he should have been married, his relationships with women had been very few. He had never had sexual relations. He had always found excuses for not going out with girls; he was too busy, he had no money, and so on. In social situations he felt very tense and awkward. He was afraid that people would see the gold filling in one of his teeth and therefore consider him maimed. He was also very much afraid to eat in front of people. He felt that while he was drinking a cup of coffee or a glass of water his hand would shake and people would notice and make fun of him. At times after eating he had attacks of nausea. A few times he had vomited after eating in the company of other people.

While working for over two years on his thesis, Anthony would always find difficulties that would delay the completion of the work. Finally he decided to change to another college and write another thesis. He also had other symptoms. When he went to a high building, he was afraid of falling; if he was in the lobby of such a building, he was afraid that the building would fall on him. He felt very dissatisfied and lonely.

Anthony was the second of four children of poor Sicilian immigrants. The first child died when the patient was very young. The other two children were also boys. The father of the patient was an illiterate laborer. At home he spoke his native language, not having been able to learn English in spite of having lived in the United States for about forty years. He had never been very close to the patient or to the other children. He seemed to have shown some interest only in their scholastic achievements. He was not cruel, but apparently disinterested. He was never home, and in later years he had taken to drink and quite often came home intoxicated.

The mother was described as a very ignorant and very domineering woman. She was ignorant to such a point that she believed in the flatness of the earth. She had never praised the patient; she never seemed satisfied either with her husband or with Anthony. She seemed less antagonistic toward the other two children, and Anthony always had felt as though he were the most disliked person in the family. His mother always told him what to do. To be with her at mealtimes was particularly unpleasant, because she would take that opportunity to make one criticism after another of him. His table manners were not good, he had not helped her enough with the housework, he had done so many things wrong. His mother was also very strict about the children's observance of all the rites of the Catholic church; she made sure that no one transgressed, and she sent the children to a Catholic school, directed by nuns. Guilt and sin were concepts always present in the teachings of that school. The atmosphere at home and in school was intensely colored by this religious feeling; life was just a preparation for death; the only purpose of living was the salvation of the soul. The patient remembered his very intense feelings and ideas about religion since childhood. He recalled an extraordinary experience that he had at the age of 12, when he looked up at the sky and felt that a voice was reaching him, saying, "You must become a priest." He interpreted this voice as a message from God. He never had a similar experience either before or after that one. He staggered; he was perplexed and astonished, but decided not to tell his mother or anybody else what had happened. He wanted to enter a Catholic seminary, but his parents discouraged him. After that experience he worried for months. He was afraid to look up at the sky for fear of receiving messages again. At the time this event occurred, he felt that the future was dissolving because he did not want to become a priest, but that he had to obey God. He felt sure that God wanted him to become a priest; however, he felt that as long as he did not get married, he could always postpone becoming a priest, and would eventually become one. When he was an adolescent, he felt that one of the reasons for not going out with girls was the knowledge that he had the mission from God to become a priest, in spite of his desire not to do so. Even at the beginning of treatment, when the patient was 32, doubts about this religious experience remained. Even then Anthony felt that it was a genuine religious experience. "If such things exist, if people receive messages from God, then this was one of those instances," he would say.

Anthony also had obsessions that were religious in content. Before Holy Communion one is not supposed to eat. He was afraid that some nasal drip or swallowing of his saliva would constitute eating and therefore make him unsuitable for Holy Communion. He was also afraid of committing sins in the interval between confession and Holy Communion, when one is supposed to remain pure. These sins were sinful thoughts about his mother, which consisted of believing that his mother wanted to get rid of him and put poison in his food. Often he did not want to eat his meals, fearing that his mother had poisoned them. He felt ashamed of these ideas; a good son should not have such thoughts about a loving mother. Twice he revealed these thoughts to the priest during confession. The priest agreed that those were sinful thoughts.

The patient remembered some fantasies that recurred during his late childhood and adolescence. He was the slave of a cruel queen. This queen would make him do degrading things, such as washing her feet, kneeling in front of her, and doing many humble forms of work. He would always obey, gladly, to please the queen at any cost.

The patient remembered some sex talk among the boys in grammar school, but during adolescence he never spoke about sexual matters. Attainment of sexual gratification was considered by him absolutely beyond the realm of possibility and very sinful. He had started to masturbate at the age of 28, as far as he remembered.

At school the patient had always been a very good student. During World

War II, he had been deferred from service because of the position he had as a mathematician. After the war he resumed his studies toward a Ph.D.

The personality of this patient has to be described in more detail. He had always cultivated very few friends and had spent most of his time by himself, avoiding social contacts as much as possible. At the same time he felt lonely and ashamed of being alone. He had always found pride and comfort in intellectual achievement. At the beginning of treatment he felt quite lost when, during the session, he was requested to say just what came to his mind. He wanted to follow an outline, or at least be given a topic. Often he would ask for a book where he could learn what to talk about during the session. The inability to prepare in advance for the therapeutic hour was very disturbing to him. When he was asked to describe a certain feeling that he was experiencing, he would beg the therapist to give him a list of possible feelings so that he could recognize the one that he was experiencing. He had to anticipate the direction in which the therapist or the treatment was aiming, and as a result he had difficulty in making contact with the present feeling. In other words, he felt completely at a loss when he had to do something spontaneously. He had acquired a certain degree of security by doing everything as it should be done, according to a certain routine. Everything had to be planned or known in advance. He would often point out the superiority of the mathematical method as compared with the therapeutic. This psychological attitude also had some repercussion on his mathematical views. For instance, he did not accept quantum theories because they leave room for unpredictability and uncertainty. In the beginning he was disappointed that the therapist, after knowing his symptoms, had not been able to classify him properly, and thereafter follow the most economic and efficient methods to elicit the other symptoms and the causes. He felt that the therapist should be able to classify him in a certain category and by doing so know everything that was to be found in him.

Although many other interesting facts concerning this patient have to be omitted, we are now in a position to understand several processes that have occurred in his life. Again we have an unhappy childhood. The father, with his detachment, the mother, with her hostility, were both destructive. One wonders whether or not the events described by the patient, such as hearing the voice of God and being afraid of being poisoned by his mother, were full-fledged schizophrenic symptoms. Feeling so rejected and hopeless about obtaining his mother's approval, the patient needed to believe that God had accepted him and wanted him to be a priest. Maybe God in heaven was a substitute for his emotionally distant father, from whom he wanted, but could not get, a message of love and encouragement. God would accept him if he became a priest and stayed away from women, that is, from his mother. In an environment permeated by religion, such as the one in which Anthony was raised, the idea of having a mission from God is not necessarily a delusion. It must be admitted, however, that the anxiety and distress of the patient must have been very intense if they caused him to develop this nonrealistic belief. Whether the experience was a real hallucinatory one or not cannot be fully ascertained. An uncertain belief in the reality of this experience remained until the patient was at a fairly advanced stage of treatment.

As for the fear of being poisoned, we have to remember that it occurred only at mealtimes. During these times Anthony's mother used to shower her nasty criticisms on him. To be near her during lunch or supper was an ordeal. In a metaphorical sense she poisoned his food. In the symptoms, this metaphor was changed into a concrete act; mother might actually have poisoned his food. Even in this case, however, the patient was doubtful; most of the time he felt that it was not true and felt guilty for having such a belief. Later in his life, when the symptomatology changed and followed a more psychoneurotic picture, he felt extremely anxious during meals, especially if he ate in company. He attributed the anxiety to his bad table manners and fear of criticism. Again, symbolically, the people who watched him were mother-substitutes, who saw how worthless he was. From the time of adolescence, many of these ideas disappeared; the patient improved, and in certain areas, like the scholastic, he made a good adjustment. One wonders why this situation, which in early life seemed oriented toward a schizophrenic breakdown, took a turn for the better and changed into a less serious one.

If we reexamine the childhood, we see that already there were elements more typical of the psychoneurotic than of the schizophrenic pattern. The patient never lost the desire to please his parents. The recurrent fantasy about the cruel queen indicates his desire to placate his cruel mother at any cost. In other words, he had not become hopeless about obtaining her approval. He was concerned about obtaining this approval, no matter what it entailed, and therefore there was no emotional detachment. The fantasy about receiving the order from God to become a priest is also something of the same nature. In the fantasy of the queen he is the slave who has to do horrible things to please her; in the fantasy of God he has to become a priest and keep away from women. It is true that he has to submit reluctantly, but at the same time he has been chosen by the queen as the servant, and by God as his minister. In a certain way he has been accepted and approved. We see indications that he will develop not a completely detached personality, but elements of a dependent, compliant character that will play an important role in his makeup.

The desire to gain the approval that his siblings had already obtained gave him the stimulus to go further in life than they did, and to become the most educated, and the most advanced, professionally, in his family. He chose the field of mathematics, which requires very little emotional involvement, and in which every step necessarily follows the previous one and can be predicted. He also developed schizoid traits, characterized chiefly by removal of spontaneity. Any spontaneous act might incur the disapproval of his incorporated mother. If he did what he was "supposed to do," he would remove anxiety. He had removed sex entirely from his life; he had no respect for his emotions, which he tried to repress all the time. At the age of 32, he wanted to look for a wife because at that age a man "should" marry. This combination of a compliant and schizoid personality protected the patient from the anxiety that could have engendered a schizophrenic psychosis. By removing spontaneity, he became withdrawn and apathetic; but by doing what he should do all the time he manifested his willingness to comply with the authority in his family and in his society. This mixture of very pronounced compliant and schizoid personalities protected the patient from psychosis. However, it impoverished immensely his life. Were he to relinquish these defenses, he might still become a victim of psychosis.

Arthur

Arthur was a 25-year-old white man who sought psychiatric help because of an apparent lack of emotions, obsessive ideas, compulsions, occasional stuttering, and "peculiar thought disorders." The "peculiar thought disorders" were the symptoms that distressed him most. He did not know how to explain them and attributed them to a serious mental disease. He noticed that often normal thinking was impossible for him because it was replaced by a strange form of thinking that he recognized as abnormal. This disorder occurred not only while he was thinking, but in talking and reading. Here are some examples taken verbatim:

"I see in the paper 'Camera Fotoshop' and I read 'Campo Formio,' which is the name of a peace treaty. I see 'Triumph' and I read 'Truman.' While walking on the street I saw a girl with a button on her blouse on which a word was written beginning with a large *F*. I immediately read it as 'Frustration' but on coming closer I saw it was 'Fieldston,' the name of a school. When I meet people who have a certain appearance and manner, a name will often flash into my mind and I will think of this name each time I see the person subsequently. The name 'Higinio' flashes into my mind whenever I see a certain fellow whom I recently met. He is short, and the black hair on his head sticks up like a porcupine's. All this seems to me to be so much more appropriately expressed by the name 'Higinio' than by his actual name. . . .

"Once I saw a letter on my uncle's desk in which were the words 'Lyon's velvet.' I immediately thought that the letter must have come from England. The fact that the letterhead and the stamp showed it to have been sent by an American firm did not cause the feeling to vanish; the facts, on the contrary, seemed inappropriate because they contradicted what I somehow felt should be the truth. Now the word 'Lyon's' rather suggests England to me; it seems an English rather than an American name. There is a chain of restaurants in London called 'Lyon's restaurants.' Moreover, I have always associated the manufacture of textiles, such as cotton and velvet goods, with England. So I had a definite feeling that the letter must have come from England and been written by an English firm. . . .

"When I lie in bed at night or early in the morning, long strings of words, many of which are meaningless, will pour into my mind. These appear to have a meaning sometimes. Other times completely meaningless sentences come up; for instance, 'Spain for a half-inch sword.' "

At the beginning of treatment, the patient described other experiences that had a disturbing effect on him. He generally took a bus to come to my office. At times when he got off at the stop nearest my office, he had the impression that the other people who got off at the same time were also coming to see me. He recognized the unreality of such an idea and did not *believe* that the other people came to my office, but he had a *momentary feeling* that they were doing that. Occasionally, when he was riding in buses or subways, if he saw people talking, he had the feeling that they were talking about him. He realized almost immediately that it could not be so, and actually he did not think that they were talking about him, but for a fraction of a second he had that feeling.

The patient also complained of emotional indifference and apathy. He used to say repeatedly that he had lost all his emotions. He could not become involved in anything. When he had to do something, he was going through the motions of what he had to do without any emotional participation. Life appeared colorless to him. He could not force himself to do anything; he just wanted to be left alone. On account of this thought disorder and apathy, he could not concentrate on his studies. He had intended to get his M.A. in mathematics, but had to give up the idea. He would not go out with girls because it was too much of an effort to ask for a date. Never in his life had he had sexual relations. He would go into parks and become sexually aroused at the sight of girls lying on the grass.

Arthur was born in England. There was no history of mental or nervous disorders in his family. The father had died about ten years before of cancer. The patient did not love him; as a matter of fact, he had experienced relief when he died. Arthur remembered attempts he had made during his childhood to get close to his father. His father used to take him to restaurants or to movies occasionally and would tell him stories. However, whenever the patient started to feel a little warmer toward him, his feelings were generally changed by his father's subsequent nagging attitude. Arthur felt that it was better not to allow himself to get close to him and never confided in him.

During adolescence, Arthur's father appeared to him as a tyrant who was always after him, like a policeman, to investigate whether he had masturbated or not. If the patient had a pimple on his face, or was pale, the father would say that these were signs of masturbation and that terrible things would happen to him. Because the patient had actually masturbated, he felt guilty; he felt that his father could read "through him" and was afraid that he would develop serious diseases. He was also afraid of actual punishment from his father.

The patient hardly remembered how his mother appeared to him during his early childhood; he rarely saw her, because he was almost always cared for by a governess. He did not remember having been caressed or kissed by his mother, or having done anything with her in his early years. For several years he was taken care of by a governess who later developed the paranoid type of schizophrenia. Later on, when the parents came to the United States, they could not afford maids, and Arthur had more contact with his mother. At the same time, however, he had the impression that his mother was much more concerned with his sister, who is his only sibling and four years younger than he. Arthur considered his mother a very weak person. She was not tyrannical, like his father; however, when the latter bitterly criticized and punished Arthur, she never came to his defense, but was always on his father's side. After the father's death, when Arthur was 15, his mother tried to get close to him, but it was too late. Somehow the patient did not trust her.

Arthur remembered both parents, from his early childhood on, with a sense of annoyance or disgust. Being near them was unpleasant. He felt that they were ugly; he even had the impression than an awful odor emanated from their bodies. He had to obey all the time, to avoid his father's punishment; he never put up a fight. He tried rather to detach himself from them. To use his own words, he felt that "Those adults were intolerable naggers who never understood you. Why bother to defend yourself?" He did not play much with children of his own age and stayed by himself most of the time. He had vivid fantasies that persisted throughout adolescence and kept him busy when he was alone. In his mind he had constructed an imaginary world made up of countries of different periods in the recent or remote past, which he had learned about in history.

Ever since childhood he had also been disturbed by obsessive thoughts. The following is a verbatim description of some of them:

"I was very impressed by religion from an early age, and my obsessions consisted of horrible ideas about Jesus Christ, that he was unclean, or that I should urinate or excrete upon him or upon his mother. I also had similar thoughts about God, and often I would fantasy that God or Jesus or his mother would perform similar defiling actions upon one another. I also remember compulsions to fill all my pockets and to perform all kinds of actions an even number of times. For instance, if I spilled some soup by accident and was reprimanded by my parents, I would nevertheless feel obliged to repeat the act in order to make an even number."

From the time that he was 16, Arthur fell in love periodically with girls. These loves were never manifested. For one reason or another these girls were unattainable, or he imagined that they were unattainable (they lived in different cities, were of a different religion, and so on). These unmanifested loves were so intense that they caused relatively important changes in his life. For instance, while he was attending college, he took courses that were unnecessary in his curriculum, wasting time and energy, only because the girl he loved was taking them. He had always been an excellent student, but in the last few years there had been a decline in his scholastic achievements, and finally he had had to interrupt his studies.

Many other things could be said about this interesting patient, especially in relation to treatment. However, we have to limit ourselves to the consideration of what is relevant to the subject of this chapter. Here again is an example of an unhappy childhood. The early uncanny experiences had been very well repressed by the patient, who had very little recollection of the role played by his parents during his early childhood. He did not succeed, however, in repressing entirely the bad images of his parents, for whom he always had hostile feelings. He remembered his past life from the age of 5 or 6. Reality was so unpleasant that the child had to isolate himself emotionally. He did not dare to put up a fight; it was useless to fight the adults; the best thing to do was to disregard them. He justified his detachment perhaps by visualizing them even worse than they were. While he was detaching himself, he was also preserving the individuality that he had been able to acquire. At the same time these difficulties with the significant adults in his early life did not help him to become an integral part of the social world in which he had to live.

He was living in his own world, a world made up of fantasies. As will be further discussed in Part Three, this detachment gave momentum to autistic tendencies, which were retained by the patient up to the time he came for treatment. Even during the second year of treatment, autistic tendencies, represented mostly by thought disorders, tended to come back when he was faced with a situation that provoked strong anxiety.

By detaching himself from his parents, Arthur succeeded in finding a more or less stable equilibrium. He became aloof, reserved, and pseudocompliant. After puberty, however, the situation changed. His father, with his own obsessive thoughts about sex, did not allow him to be aloof and detached. This attitude increased the patient's hostility toward the father and stimulated further detachment. After the death of his father, Arthur was confronted with new problems: guilt about having wished his death, inability to gratify his sexual urges, and feelings of inadequacy when he attempted to establish social relationships. His mother could not help him. Although she was finally willing to get closer to him, he was somehow afraid of her "smothering" attitude and he had to reject her.

The situation deteriorated to such a point that the picture presented by the patient when he came for treatment consisted not of just a strong or very rigid schizoid personality. Especially in anxiety-arousing situations many autistic phenomena were occurring. Some of them did not seem of too serious significance. He read "frustration" instead of "Fieldston" on the button pinned on the girl's blouse. Girls represented frustrations to him, or his frustrated attempts to love. Everything that was associated with England, where he spent his childhood, was charged with great emotional tone for him. Thus, when he read Lyon on a letter found on his uncle's desk, he thought that the letter came from England. Some other symptoms gave almost a schizophrenic appearance to his condition. For instance, he had pseudoideas of reference, tendencies toward neologisms, and psuedo-word-salad phenomena. I use the prefix *pseudo* here because these experiences were not accepted by the patient as reality, but were immediately recognized as abnormal manifestations. It was only the preservation of the ability to test and disprove their reality, however, that distinguished them from full-fledged schizophrenic symptoms. The formal structure of the symptoms was the same as in cases of schizophrenia. The patient also presented some symptoms of depersonalization. He did not experience emotions; at the same time, he was aware of his emotional bluntness and was afraid of developing schizophrenia, the symptoms of which he had read in psychiatric books, which he had studied avidly.

Indeed, Arthur was very close to schizophrenia, and it is a fair guess that if he had not come for treatment at this point, the psychosis would have developed.

Many psychiatrists, I am sure, would have diagnosed this case as schizophrenia. The typical background for a schizophrenic psychosis was present: experience of being rejected by both parents; development of a strong schizoid personality with great propensity for autistic phenomena; inability of the patient to defend himself from the increasing difficulties after puberty, in spite of the rigidity of the schizoid personality. There were also, however, some favorable signs, which may explain why the patient did not develop a psychosis. First, his father's attitude toward him was ambivalent and he did make some effort to reach him. The patient, however, did not trust these efforts and preferred detachment. Later he felt that if only he could abstain from masturbation or from sexual desires, he could obtain acceptance from his father. The sexual urges were very strong, however, and he had a feeling of hopelessness about being able to suppress them. A second relatively favorable sign was the fact that from early childhood this patient protected himself, not with detachment exclusively, but also with compulsive symptoms. Although some of them could have had the purpose of retaliating against the parents (spilling the soup twice), they also protected him from anxiety.

The treatment of this patient has been long and laborious. He was in therapy for eight years, but he made steady progress. There was an affective reintegration, and he soon became aware of his anxiety, especially in social contacts with the opposite sex. The autistic phenomena entirely disappeared. He was able to resume his studies and to secure an important position as a mathematician.

The writer had the unusual opportunity of having followed these three patients for more than twenty years. In fact, he maintained some contact with them after termination of treatment. Was schizophrenia really averted by them during this long part of life?

Let us start with Louis, the first patient reported in this chapter. Approximately fifteen years after termination of treatment, Louis called me and asked for a consultation. His mother was dying of a serious disease, and he felt anxious, guilty, almost as if he were responsible for her condition. His old anxiety was reactivated. Apparently the hostility he once had for her had not been completely solved. A few sessions were able to restore the state of health. There were no signs of schizophrenia. Louis has been able to work steadily all these twenty years and to live harmoniously with his wife.

As to Arthur, he got married shortly after termination of treatment. He has been able to retain important professional positions, but continues to have hypochondriacal preoccupations. No thought disorder of any kind has reappeared.

In comparing the cases of Louis and Arthur, it seems obvious that whereas in the case of Louis there were strong indications that he would never develop a psychosis, in the case of Arthur the psychosis was very near. Some would think that perhaps it was already active in a slow, insidious way. It seems likely that a full-fledged psychosis was averted by a narrow margin through therapeutic intervention.

The case of Anthony is more complicated. He stopped regular treatment shortly afterward, but for a few years maintained irregular and insufficient contacts with me. Professionally he did well. He was able to obtain his Ph.D., secured a position as a teacher of mathematics in a college, did important research, and wrote papers that were promptly accepted for publication. Personal life has not been equally successful. While he was coming regularly for treatment, he was able to improve his social contacts with women. He was never able to establish a deep or very meaningful relationship. When he stopped treatment against advice, his social contacts decreased, and there was a marked accentuation of his schizoid traits. He stopped entirely going out with girls. He wrote some papers that were rejected. Because he was sustaining his self-esteem on his academic achievements, this was a serious defeat. He followed in his father's footsteps and started to drink. In a few years he became an alcoholic. Nevertheless he was able to teach and retain his position. A few years later when Anthony called me for consultation, I found Anthony in a state of delirium tremens with visual and tactile hallucinations, including the typical ones of small animals. The patient quickly recovered from this episode and seemed to be improved as far as his alcoholic habits were concerned. However, it is difficult to predict the ultimate prognosis as far as his addiction is concerned. He moved to another city, where his family lived. He continued to teach mathematics in a college.

The case of Anthony is interesting from a nosological point of view because he experienced early in life what were questionable psychotic symptoms. Do alcoholic psychoses tend to occur in people who are close to schizophrenia or potentially (or latently) schizophrenics? We know that some authors have postulated a close relation between schizophrenia and alcoholic hallucinosis. Anthony, however, presented a delirium tremens syndrome.

In spite of all these complications and psychiatric difficulties we may say that Anthony, too, averted schizophrenia or at least typical schizophrenia. He remained a great psychiatric challenge.

PART THREE

The World of Schizophrenia: A Psychostructural Approach

CHAPTER

15

The Break with Reality

In Part Two we have studied the psychogenic factors that lead to a schizophrenic disorder. We have seen how an extreme state of anxiety, originating in early childhood, produces a vulnerability that in many instances lasts for the whole life of the individual. We have seen how desperately, even heroically, the patient attempts to maintain contact with reality, to survive, and to grow. However, in dealing with new threats in adolescence and adult life, his defenses become increasingly inadequate. Confronted with overpowering anxiety, the patient finally succumbs, and the break with reality occurs. In other words, when he cannot change the unbearable vision of himself any longer, not even in prepsychotic ways, he has to change reality. But reality cannot change, and he has to change himself again in order to see ''reality'' in a different way.

In this part of the book we shall examine the mechanisms with which the patient attempts to envision life in a less frightening manner. He will enter the world of schizophrenia. The psychotic transformation will enable him to experience himself and the environment in strange, unique ways, often not susceptible to consensual validation. And yet the mechanisms that he resorts to now are available to every human being; they are part of his human nature. As a matter of fact, even normal people use some of these mechanisms when they make errors, especially in conceptual formation or in the understanding of concepts. However, what is an exceptional error for a normal person may not be an error for the schizophrenic but a way of thinking which guides his life. All this implies that the mechanisms by which the patient experiences reality and himself in a different way are predominantly cognitive mechanisms.

In Part Two we have seen that psychodynamic studies are chiefly concerned with the emotional life of the patient. At a human level, however, only the most primitive emotions do not depend on cognition, although they too become interconnected with cognitive processes (see Chapter 7 of this book; also Arieti, 1967, 1973). The cognitive process may be unconscious, automatic, or distorted, but it is always present. As it is true that no human activity is completely deprived of emotions, because emotions accompany us everywhere and to a great extent determine our lives, it is equally true that there are no naked emotions—emotions are always accompanied by some kind of cognitive process. By cognitive process is meant some kind of organized mental activity, by virtue of which an understanding of the situation involved is attempted. Emotions, however, have the power to distort the cognitive processes, just as cognitive processes distort old or create new emotions (Arieti, 1967). The most pronounced distortions occur in schizophrenia.

In neuroses the distortion occurs to a much lesser degree. But more important than the degree of the distortion is the recognition that such distortion occurs. In the neuroses such recognition on the part of the patient exists, or if it does not exist, it may relatively easily gain consciousness through psychotherapy. It is not so in schizophrenia. Let us take, for example, the case of an obsessive patient who has the obsession that if he does not wash his hands three times at each meal, his children are going to become sick and will die. This patient fully recognizes the absurdity of such an idea. It is true that a power stronger than himself will continue to compel him to wash his hands three times, but he has retained sufficient logical power to recognize the unreal nature of such an obsession. Usual psychoanalytic therapy will help in explaining what unconscious emotional factors have determined this symptom. Instead, in the case of a deluded schizophrenic patient, who thinks that he is the king of Egypt, let us say, usual analytic procedure may also uncover the unconscious emotional factors that have determined this delusional idea. It will not explain, however, why such an idea is accepted as reality by the patient, in spite of the most complete contradictory evidence. In other words, it does not explain what change has occurred in the cognitive powers of the patient to make him no longer able to test reality. To limit ourselves to saying that "the ego of the schizophrenic is weak and disintegrating under the stress of the emotions" is to cover the complexity of the problem with a semantic screen. We must make an effort to understand why the disintegration has that particular aspect, why it deprives the patient of the power to test reality.*

* The above concepts are expressed in the psychiatric literature at times with different terminology. Whereas in psychoneuroses the symptomatology is called dystonic, in schizophrenia it is called syntonic: that is, integrated with, or not denied by, the rest of the personality.

I

General Views of Schizophrenic Cognition

Several interpretations have been proposed. The simplest and probably the most naïve is the hypothesis that there are two types of thinking, rational and irrational, and that the schizophrenic adopts the irrational.

This point of view has not been subjected to scientific analysis. First of all, any ''irrationality'' is not whimsical or completely at random, but retains some organization and direction. Even mechanisms conducive to error can be understood. Secondly, this hypothesis does not explain how the schizophrenic can accept irrationality in spite of contradictory evidence. How can he believe that he is the king of Egypt? Obviously he can believe so because he is irrational. But this is a pseudoexplanation that attempts to explain in terms of what has to be explained.

A second interpretation is that offered by Goldstein (1939, 1943*a*). According to this author, whereas the normal human being has two attitudes toward the world, the abstract and the concrete, the schizophrenic has only or predominantly the concrete.

These two attitudes, according to Goldstein, are not acquired, but *a priori;* that is, they are inherent in human nature. They are two ways of adapting to the world. When he is in a concrete attitude, the individual is bound to the immediate experience or to the specific stimuli to which he is presently exposed. In the abstract attitude, man transcends what is specific, immediate, particular. He is oriented toward a category, a class, a general meaning, and detaches himself (that is, *abstracts* himself) from the given experience.

According to Goldstein, the abstract attitude is basic for the following abilities: (1) to assume a mental set (frame of reference) voluntarily; (2) to shift voluntarily from one aspect of the situation to another; (3) to keep in mind simultaneously various aspects; (4) to grasp the essential of a given whole and to break up a given whole into parts and to isolate these parts; (5) to generalize—that is, to abstract common properties; (6) to detach the ego from the external world.

We owe a great deal to Goldstein, because he has opened a new path of fruitful inquiry. There is no doubt that in many instances schizophrenics characterize themselves by being specific, concrete, and unable to transcend the particular situation or set. We must recognize, nevertheless, that Goldstein's formulations are incomplete and suffer from the fact that originally he worked only with brain-injured patients. Life, experienced only or predominantly at a concrete level, is a reduced life, but not necessarily a psychotic one, or a life that has sustained a psychotic loss of reality. A brain-injured patient with cortical lesions may not be able to understand difficult mathematical or philosophical problems, but he may remain in the realm of a limited reality. Goldstein himself states that the concrete attitude is a realistic attitude. Even a subhuman animal, which does not possess the ability to conceive categories, concepts, or platonic universals, lives in a limited, but nevertheless realistic, world. Goldstein too realizes that the concreteness of the schizophrenic is not the same as that of the brain-injured patient, but he interprets the difference simply as the result of different levels of concreteness. This explanation is not satisfactory. We find different degrees of concreteness in various organic defects and also in mental deficiencies, but these conditions are not necessarily accompanied by psychosis. As a matter of fact, the organic defect, although limiting greatly human potentialities, may eliminate the psychoses, as, for instance, in some forms of psychosurgery. In the adoption of the concrete attitude Goldstein does not recognize psychodynamic factors that have a compensatory purpose or a symbolic meaning. The only purpose Goldstein recognizes is that of avoiding a decompensation, or what he called "the catastrophic situation" that he described in patients suffering from organic brain injuries. Although Goldstein was very much influenced by Jackson and by Vigotsky, he did not accept the developmental approach of these two authors.

In my opinion the phenomena studied by Goldstein in schizophrenia do not represent a reduction of the psyche to a concrete level, but a *process of active concretization*. By active concretization I mean that the psyche is still capable of conceiving the abstract, but not of sustaining it because the abstract is too anxiety provoking or too disintegrating. We must remember that abstract ideations are not lost by the schizophrenic. If they were lost, the patient would not have schizophrenogenic anxiety. The abstract ideations, however, are transformed by the psychotic into concrete representations. For instance, a paranoid had the delusion that his wife was putting poison in his food. He actually felt that his wife disturbed, spoiled, "poisoned" his life. Thus the abstract poisoning became a concrete and specific one; a concept was transformed into an object, a chemical poison, after the inner turmoil had been projected to the external world.

We may actually interpret the whole schizophrenic cognitive transformation from a general point of view as a process of active concretization. However, the reader must realize that this explanation is not complete. We must determine and study the different modalities by which this active concretization takes place.

Another group of authors interprets schizophrenic cognition as characterized by dedifferentiation (that is, loss of distinction of parts within any system) or regression (that is, return to earlier and less mature functioning or behavior). It is easy to recognize the affinity between the concepts of concretization, dedifferentiation, and regression. Ultimately all the psychiatric theories postulating regression (or similar concepts) are derivatives of Darwin's theories, through the intermediary concept of dissolution advanced by the neurologist J. Hughlings Jackson (1932). Regression or dedifferentiation are often considered as development or evolution in reverse: the direction is from higher to lower levels of integration.

According to Jackson's principle, in neurological and mental diseases the functions that are the last to develop are the first to be lost. In every disease we have two kinds of symptoms: (1) negative: the loss of high functions (in Goldstein's theory, loss of abstract attitude); (2) positive: the emergence of supremacy of the functions of the level that remains intact (in Goldstein's theory, the concrete attitude).

Freud too was influenced by Jackson in postulating the concept of regression. In schizophrenia the libido would revert to the narcissistic stage (see Chapter 2).

As we shall see several times in this book, an author who has inspired many psychiatrists, including myself, is the psychologist Heinz Werner, with his comparative developmental approach. According to Werner, in psychopathological conditions cognitive structures that are characteristic of previous stages of development emerge. Development means unfolding in time of forms or structures. Three types of development can be distinguished. The first is the phylogenetic, or the unfolding of a psychological mechanism or form through the evolution of the species. The second is the ontogenetic, or the unfolding of a mechanism or form through the maturation of the individual. The third is the microgenetic. Because this type is less known than the previous two, some words of explanation are required.

Microgeny, as illustrated by Werner (1956), is the immediate unfolding of a phenomenon, that is, the sequence of the necessary steps inherent in the occurrence of a psychological process. For instance, to the question, "Who is the author of *Hamlet?*" a person answers "Shakespeare." He is aware only of the question (stimulus) and of his answer (conscious response), but not of the numerous steps that in a remarkably short time led him to give the correct answer. Why did he not reply, "Sophocles" or "George Bernard Shaw"? How did he reach the correct answer? There are numerous proofs that the answer was not necessarily an established and purely physical or neuronic association between *Hamlet* and Shakespeare, but that an actual unconscious search went on. In fact, if the same question is asked of a mental patient (either affected by cerebral arteriosclerosis or by schizophrenia in a stage of advanced regression) or of a person who is very sleepy or drunk or paying little attention, he may reply, "Sophocles" or "George Bernard Shaw." These are wrong but not haphazard answers, inasmuch as they refer to playwrights. The mental search required by the answer had at least reached the category of playwrights. The numerous steps that a mental process goes through constitute its microgenetic development (Arieti, 1962*c*).

These three types of development—phylogeny, ontogeny, and microgeny—unfold in time, although with great variation in the quantity of time. The length of this span of time ranges from periods as long as geological eras in the case of phylogeny to periods as short as fractions of a second in microgeny. What is of fundamental importance is that the three processes tend to use the same structural developmental plans. We do not mean literally that microgeny recapitulates ontogeny and that ontogeny recapitulates phylogeny, but that there are certain formal similarities in the three fields of development and that we are able to individualize schemes of highest forms of generality that involve all levels of the psyche in its three types of development. It is equally important to recognize the variants of the same overall structural plans.

As I wrote elsewhere (Arieti, 1967), the two aspects of the psyche, the organization of forms (a logical order) and the threefold development (a temporal order) are equally important. Inasmuch as one tends to permanence, the other to change, a double functionality that constitutes a main characteristic of the psyche results.

Throughout this part of this book we shall illustrate how cognitive forms belonging to early stages of the three types of development reappear in schizophrenia.

There is finally another possibility that must be taken into consideration for the purpose of understanding schizophrenic cognition: namely, that the patient thinks in an abnormal way simply because he wishes to do so. This possibility may prove to be not as absurd as it may seem at first consideration, at least in some cases. Some patients, during the period of preschizophrenic panic, are able to evaluate in a conscious way what they consider the failure of their existence and to predict the unfulfillment of their life promises. The ways of thinking that in the past would occasionally emerge to consciousness and then be immediately rejected because they were unrealistic have now a very strong seductive appeal. The patients may choose to embrace them. Once they embrace these thoroughly, they can no longer dismiss them.

I believe that although this hypothesis cannot possibly explain the psychotic transformation, it may contain elements of truth. In some schizophrenics and preschizophrenics, and especially in incipient schizophrenics, there are periods during which the patient seems to understand both the world of reality and the world of psychosis and to be able potentially to choose between them. This possibility, as a matter of fact, will be stressed at a certain stage of psychotherapy (see Chapter 37). We must still explain, however, why abnormal thinking is available and what kind of structure this abnormal thinking has.

II

The Principle of Progressive Teleologic Regression

I feel that schizophrenic cognition is not illogical or senseless, but that it can be interpreted. The schizophrenic patient adopts cognitive mechanisms that are different from those used by human beings generally. He does not think with ordinary logic, but follows different structural organizations that lead to deductions different from those usually reached by the healthy person. The schizophrenic is similar to a man who would solve mathematical problems, not with our decimal system, but with another hypothetical system, and would consequently reach different solutions. In other words, the schizophrenic interprets and consequently experiences the world in ways that differ from those of the normal man. In this part of this book we shall study the particular psychological structures that impose on a schizophrenic a psychotic existence. These structures, which are potentially available to every human being, become the prevalent ones in the schizophrenic condition. Healthy persons do not ordinarily adopt these structures, except in dreams, in particular situations that will be described later, in occasional errors, and in some specific social and collective manifestations. This different faculty of experiencing and interpreting the world follows what Freud called the primary process (see Chapter 2). In reference to cognition, Freud restricted his study of the primary process to two essential mechanisms—displacement and condensation—which are described in Chapter 7 of his book *The Interpretation of Dreams* (1901). Later Freud connected the theory of the primary process to the libido theory and did not pursue the study of schizophrenic cognition.

Whether we accept the view that the schizophrenic adopts a concrete attitude or a less differentiated type of thinking or one that follows Freud's primary process or Werner's early phases of ontogenetic and microgenetic developments, the patient is almost unanimously recognized as using a less mature kind of cognition.

The characteristic of reverting to less mature mechanisms is a quite common occurrence in pathology. For instance, in diseases of the heart, when the sinoauricular node is injured, the more ancient auriculo-ventricular bundle takes over its functions. This is as true in psychopathology as it is in general pathology.

Reverting to the use of less mature forms of development means what in psychoanalytic terminology is generally called regressing. Regression, a term introduced by Freud to indicate a return to earlier stages of libido (see Chapter 2), will be used in this book to indicate an unusual and intensified availability of psychological mechanisms and forms that are more typical of earlier developmental stages.*

As we have already mentioned, J. Hughlings Jackson's concept of neurologic dissolution, which is a precursor of the concept of regression, is too mechanistic and deterministic when applied to psychiatry.† It does not help us to understand psychiatric conditions from a psychodynamic point of view. It does not indicate that regression (or its equivalents) has a psychodynamic meaning, a purpose.

I have tried to formulate the dynamic occurrence of the phenomenon of regression in the form of the following principle: if, in a situation of severe anxiety, function at a certain level of psychological integration cannot take place or does not bring about the desired results, a strong tendency exists toward functioning at lower levels of integration in order to effect those results (Arieti, 1955, 1967). I have called this the principle of teleologic regression. We must clarify that teleologic regression is not the only mechanism occurring in psychopathology, but one of many. However, because a special variety of it, more properly called *progressive teleologic regression,* plays such an important role in schizophrenia, we have to study it in detail.

First of all, we have to stress again that the anxiety that brings about regression in the pathology of schizophrenia is not just any type of strong anxiety, but the anxiety that, directly or indirectly, injures the self-image and is experienced as an inner danger (see Chapter 8). The strong anxiety apparently has the capacity to

* Bieber (1958) and Szalita (1958) have similarly criticized the Freudian concept of regression of libido. Bieber stressed that what we call regression is availability of generally unused mechanisms. For Szalita it means a lower level of functioning.

† Jackson's ideas today have undergone revisions (Livingston, 1962). The nervous system is no longer seen exclusively as a series of horizontally organized centers. In addition to the horizontal organization, there are vertical organizations between the different centers. The concept of interaction has been replaced by the concept of transaction: no longer linear or simple relations, but multiple relations between the different parts of the nervous system.

disintegrate the high levels of functioning, but the psyche does not cease to function; it reintegrates at lower levels.

The reader should note that the word *tendency* is used in the formulation of the principle of teleologic regression. In other words, this principle is not like a physical law, which must operate without exceptions. There is just a propensity toward its occurrence, but it may not occur, as, for instance, in cases where something unexpected intervenes.

By resorting to lower levels of integration, the psyche turns again to methods that were discarded when new methods had been adopted. In one aspect (and *one* only) it is a repetition of history in reversed chronology. This happens not only to human beings, but to animals as well. Mowrer (1946) has demonstrated this principle in rats with a very ingenious experiment. The animals learned to protect themselves from an electric current by sitting on their hind legs. Later the rats learned a much better way; they discovered how to turn off the current by pressing a pedal. When this habit was well ingrained, it replaced the previous one. Later the pedal too was charged with electricity, and the rats had to face another shock if they continued to press it. At this point they went back to the method of sitting on their hind legs. Thus they reverted to the earlier and inferior method.

When experimental animals have learned to solve a problem with the mechanism of insight and, for some reason, can no longer solve the problem with this method, they revert to the method of trial and error. In other words, there is a tendency toward a reversed hierarchy of responses, from the highest to the lowest.* The words *regression* and *teleologic* are used for the following reasons: *regression,* because less advanced levels of mental integration are used; *teleologic,* because this regression seems to have a purpose, namely, to avoid tension, stress, and anxiety by bringing about the wanted results. As a matter of fact, studies in abnormal psychology have revealed innumerable instances in which the mind in distress does not necessarily follow scientific thinking (events are the effects of previous causes), but rather teleologic thinking (events have a purpose). Thus, dreams, hallucinations, symptoms, delusions, and so on, seem to have a purpose, even though they themselves are the results of previous causes.

More often than not, of course, thinking that follows the principle of teleologic regression does not effect the desired results, but yet it will decrease the anxiety, at least temporarily. Legends and myths frequently reveal the adoption of this principle. For instance, the Jews, as described in the Bible, had reached that high cultural level that permitted them to worship an abstract God. When, however, they were under the stress of anxiety caused by the sudden disappearance of their leader, Moses, they reverted to the worship of the Golden Calf. When Moses reappeared and the anxiety was relieved, they went back to the cult of the abstract God. Similar regressive tendencies have also occurred innumerable times in human history in special social situations. For instance, if diplomatic discussions do not bring about certain results, much more primitive methods, such as wars,

* The emphasis here, however, is given not to the response in a behavioristic way, but to the central process that is responsible for the response.

paranoid attitudes toward minorities, and persecution of them, may be resorted to.

It is evident that in these conceptions we have a mixture of deterministic and teleologic explanations. Determinism is the all-embracing concept that has been adopted in science—causes determine effects. In teleologic explanation the fact or event that is being studied is seen as having a purpose, is envisioned as useful or agreeable to the individual, and it is because of its purpose that it occurs. The fact that a patient cannot function at a high level can be interpreted deterministically no matter whether the disturbance is organic or psychological in origin. The difficult fact to explain is how the psyche comes to use purposefully the lower-level mechanisms that are released and available again.

As I had opportunity to state in greater detail elsewhere (Arieti, 1967), since the work of Claude Bernard the usefulness or adaptational value of a pathological mechanism was recognized not only in psychiatric conditions, but in the whole field of medicine. In infectious diseases, for instance, fever occurs as a reaction to the invasion of foreign proteins. This reaction can be interpreted in accordance with deterministic causality. Fever, however, seems to have a purpose: to combat the invasion of foreign proteins. Here the organism seems to follow a purpose, or teleologic causality. Only organisms that are able to build up adequate defenses can survive and transmit such a possibility genetically. Thus the defenses, from a human point of view, do acquire a purpose.

We have already mentioned that in schizophrenia teleologic regression has distinctive features. First of all, it is determined by that special type of anxiety that we have described. Secondly, it is progressive. The term *progressive* here means that the regression does not tend to stop at a certain level, but proceeds to lower and lower levels unless treatment is instituted or unforeseeable fortunate turns of events occur. The situation is thus different from that occurring in other psychopathological conditions. For instance, the typical phobic patient, too, undergoes a regression. He may have a phobia that prevents him from crossing streets, and this may stand for his abstract fear of life. He may become worse, and become afraid also of crossing squares, leaving his home, crossing bridges, and so on. The symptoms, however, remain phobias. Why regression should tend to proceed in untreated schizophrenia is a subject that will be discussed in Chapter 26. The progressive teleologic regression brings about the process of active concretization that we have described earlier in this chapter.

CHAPTER

16

The Cognitive Transformation

I

Minor and Not Necessarily Psychotic Alterations

In many cases of schizophrenia the disorder does not manifest itself, at least in its initial stages, with obvious symptoms. Some cognitive alterations may appear to be within the normal range or not distinguishable from those occurring in neuroses and character disorders. Usual psychological tests may also fail to show evidence of cognitive impairment. However, people who knew the patient well can recognize the difference in him. His attitude toward life has changed. Some ideas become predominant and repetitious, almost as if the whole predicament of the patient hinged on them. For instance, a patient may repeatedly and strongly state that if men would respect women, all troubles in life would disappear. Although there may be some reality in what the patient says, the tenacity, recurrence, or stubborn quality of this predominant idea shows that the patient uses it for another purpose. The idea or problem, as formulated by the patient, takes the place of what bothers him in life in general; it becomes a specific and concrete representation of the patient's predicament. We have here already the process of active concretization (Chapter 15).

Another mechanism that is common also at the onset of schizophrenia is the mechanism of projection or externalization; this does not yet take the form of delusions and hallucinations, but is an attributing of one's difficulties to the external world, or to some segments of the external world. Like many people who are not considered mentally ill, the schizophrenic who is not acutely ill may in the initial stage blame his relatives, his boss, or his co-workers for all his troubles. This is, of course, a protective mechanism. If the source of his trouble is external, he may hope to change it by changing his behavior, and moreover will relieve himself of the responsibility.

Another characteristic shared by the schizophrenic, the neurotic, and the normal person is rationalization. The term *rationalization,* introduced in psychoanalysis by Jones (1938), means an attempt to provide a logical justification for actions or ideas that are directed by an emotional need. This attempt is made by resorting to explanations that, although not valid, seem correct and plausible because they succeed in hiding their illogicality and real motivation.

Let us examine the rationalization of a normal person. A professional man who intended to attend a lecture did not fully realize that that evening he would have preferred to remain home with his family and relax. He looked out the window, saw that it was raining, and said, "The weather is bad. It is wiser to stay home." In this way, not he but the weather became responsible for his not attending the lecture.

A mildly neurotic patient was suffering from feelings of rivalry for his brother, who was a singer. The patient used to warn his brother in a paternal and affectionate tone of voice, "Don't sing so often at clubs and private parties. You will ruin your voice!" This was a correct recommendation. The singer had also been told by many experts that he should not strain his voice with too much work. Actually the motivation of the patient in repeating this recommendation was a different one: he was jealous of the consideration and honor that the brother was receiving when he sang and wanted to prevent them.

In Chapter 9 we saw that the patient, Peter, rationalized his father's saying that he had been a hero during World War I, although actually he had been a deserter. According to Peter, his father had to say this in order to remove all doubts about his participation in the war, and by so doing, he was saving the honor of the family. His brother Gabriel, when he was already psychotic, sold a gold watch and some other valuable objects for a few cents. When he was questioned about it, he justified himself with the following rationalization: "These things were mine. Can't I do what I want with my things?" He switched the problem from the advisability of the act to the permissibility of the act in an attempt to justify it.

Another example will show that rationalizations are common in cases of advanced or moderate schizophrenic regression. A woman who was born and raised in a South American country in a well-to-do family, came to the United States in her early twenties, after having completed her college education. While in the United States she married an American citizen, from whom she had a child. When I first saw her, she was in her middle thirties, had been sick for several years, and showed signs of regression. She appeared apathetic, except when she was talking about her husband, for whom she nourished bitter resentment. She would repeatedly say that her husband was a bad man and that she always knew it. When she was asked why she married her husband if she knew he was such a bad man, she replied, "The wedding ceremony took place in this country. When the priest asked me if I wanted to marry my husband, he spoke in English and I did not understand him. I said, 'I do.' If he had spoken in Spanish, my own language, I would have never agreed to marry such a man." This rationalization would be facetious if it were not pathetic. It would be logical if it was not based on illogical premises. The patient obviously understood the question at the wedding ceremony and replied, "I do," in English. Moreover she spoke English fairly well, even at the time of her wedding. Her rationalization, however, cannot be interpreted just at face value as an attempt to justify herself or to disavow her responsibility or to make her marriage almost illegal. There was much more than that in this apparently absurd rationalization. The years spent in the United States had a flavor of unreality for her, or at least there seemed to be an atmosphere of fogginess and confusion. These years were characterized by a series of unfortunate events, which culminated in her unhappy marriage. Only life prior to her coming to the United States, that is, that period of her life when she was speaking Spanish, made sense to her. In her mind thus what was confused or unclearly motivated or directly or indirectly led to mental pain became associated with the English language. Again, following our theoretical framework, we could say that the patient resorted to active concretization. She reduced the uncertainty and fogginess of her North American life to a linguistic difficulty. Again this symptom, a rationalization, is not just a technical device to avoid responsibility; it is also and predominantly an expression of her whole life history, of her whole tragedy, of the difference between the peace or apparent peace of her early life and the turbulence or apparent turbulence of her married life.

In a way comparable to the work of the fine artist and of the poet, a little episode, or a single symptom like a rationalization, becomes representative of a much larger segment of reality.

But let us examine again the examples of nonpsychotic rationalizations that we have reported. We cannot take even them literally. In the example of the professional man, the bad weather, the storm, and his going out at night may be for him symbolic of the hard professional competitive world where you always have to keep abreast, where you have challenges to meet. Staying home is being protected, being with one's wife, or with mother, or in mother's womb, whatever level of interpretation is more suitable to the specific case. The rationalization of the professional man represents a dilemma between the two types of life he has to cope with.

The rationalization of the mildly neurotic patient who was jealous of his brother repeated the compulsive effort to assert his supremacy in relation to his sibling. Peter's need to consider his father a venerable authority compelled him to resort to almost a fantastic rationalization. In the case of his brother Gabriel, the reported rationalization about underselling his watch was different from what his words conveyed. In a latent way Gabriel was saying to his parents, "I had to become crazy in order to assert myself. You never let me do what I wanted. Now I can."

Under subtle examination we recognize the difference between the rationalizations of the nonpsychotic and those of the psychotic. The rationalization of the professional man could stand on its own merit. People at times do stay home because of the bad weather. The rationalization of the mildly neurotic patient had also some validity. Experts had recommended that his brother should not strain his voice. In these cases there is thus a concordance between the obvious reality, although a superficial reality, and the psychodynamic reality that is suppressed. That is, the professional man can stay home for both reasons, because of the weather and because he does not want to meet the challenge of the professional life; the mildly neurotic patient can give his recommendation to the brother for both reasons, because he is jealous of him and because the experts too had made that recommendation. In the case of Peter, and much more so in the case of Gabriel, the rationalizations maintain a very minimum of plausibility: the farfetchedness of their rationalizations seem to be proportional to the severity of their disorder.

In the rationalization of the South American woman there was no congruence or concordance between the external or superficial reality and the psychodynamic. The rationalization becomes plausible only if we understand what is suppressed, substituted, or concretized, if we know the complicated experiences the patient went through. From the examples given, and from others reported later in the book, it is evident that an attempt is almost constantly made by the human being, even when he is schizophrenic, to maintain an element of plausibility. Contrary to what is believed by some, most human beings cannot accept anything that seems irrational to them. The need for rationality is as powerful as the need to gratify the irrational motivation. This need for rationality is always underestimated by people who see the human being as dominated by instinctual drives. If the concept *instinct* is to be retained, the instinct toward rationality (including reason and rationalization) has also to be acknowledged.

If rationality is never completely abandoned, a certain level or type of rationality, however, is often lost, especially in situations of severe anxiety or emergency. The rationality seems at times to have declined to such an extent that it can no longer be recognized. This will be true to an even greater extent in the processes that we shall discuss later in this chapter. However, and here we cannot avoid marveling at the multiform aspects of the human psyche, every irrationality has its own rationality; the illogical element is a plausible part of a logical gestalt. To refer again to the examples given, the professional man's reluctance to attend the lecture is part of his life dilemma; the remark of the mildly neurotic patient is part of his major battle in his young life; the absurd assertion of Peter is part of his crusade to save his respect for his father; the twisted reply of Gabriel is a desperate cry for assertion; the ludicrous remark of the South American woman was her terminal chance to attenuate a life defeat.

Prior to the manifest onset of the psychosis, as well as during many stages of its course, many patients present a disturbance in attention. In quite a large number of patients (but by no means all) there is inability to keep attention fixed for any length of time. They may hear what is said to them, but they do not register the meaning of the words. Many patients do not notice what is happening in their surroundings, no matter how important it is, or, when they do notice it by way of exception, they do not follow it. Dodge and Diefendorff (quoted by Kraepelin,

1919) reported that patients do not usually follow a moving pendulum continuously, as normal persons do, but intermittently and with hesitation. There is often on the part of many patients awareness of all stimuli, without capacity to filter or to screen them out and to focus only on certain aspects voluntarily selected. In other words, the schizophrenic often loses the faculty that Schactel (1954) called focal attention.*

Disturbed attention and distractibility, carefully described long ago by Kraepelin (1919) and Bleuler (1950), have recently received renewed consideration (McGhie and Chapman, 1961; Silvermann, 1964, 1967; Chapman, 1966; McGhie, 1966, 1972; Livingston and Blum, 1968; Blum, Livingston, and Shader, 1969; Neale and Cromwell, 1972). Shakow (1963) concluded: "It is as if, in the scanning process which takes place before the response to a stimulus is made, the schizophrenic is unable to select out the material relevant for optimal response. He apparently cannot free himself from the irrelevant among the numerous possibilities available for choice." Shakow, however, like Wichowicz and Blewett (1959), reported that the inability to attend selectively to stimuli is confined to the hebephrenic group. Paranoid schizophrenics show little evidence of this disorder.

I believe that although the impairment of selective attention is an important symptom to be related to others, its importance should not be exaggerated. Only a few of the cognitive disorders of the schizophrenic can be based on this impairment. For instance, one can hardly believe that a patient thinks he is Jesus Christ just because he has difficulty in selective attention. Equally unsatisfactory is the Freudian school's interpretation of this phenomenon of impaired attention as shifting of libido.

There are also other alterations of attention, first described by Kraepelin (1919), that deserve consideration. The attention of patients is often rigidly fixed for a long time, so that they stare at the same point or continue the same line of thought for a long time, in a stereotyped manner, or do not allow interruption of their work or talk. At times they deliberately turn away their attention from things or thoughts toward which they are attracted (negativism?); at other times they are forcibly or irresistibly attracted to focus their attention on certain objects or thoughts (obsession? compulsion? perseveration?).

A disturbance in attention is very marked in many varieties of organic brain disease, which present syndromes quite different from schizophrenia.

* Schactel defines focal attention as characterized by five aspects: (1) it is directional—that is, it does not concern the total field; (2) it is directed at a particular object; (3) it takes hold of the object and aims at its active mental grasp; (4) each act of attention consists not of one but of several renewed approaches; (5) it excludes the rest of the field.

II
Paleologic Thought

Delusion is one of the most common characteristics of schizophrenic cognition. This term generally designates a false belief that is considered true by the patient in spite of what to most human beings appears incontrovertible proof or evidence of its invalidity.

Various are the mechanisms by which this false idea is conceived. In many cases we can recognize that it came to be because the patient followed a special cognitive structure, a logic that is constituted differently from that of the normal man. The phylogenetic origin of this logic will be discussed in a subsequent section. However, it is important to say that because in a developmental theoretical framework this logic seemed to be a precursor of our normal secondary process logic, it was called *paleologic* (from the Greek *palaios,* "ancient and old").* The usual logic of the normal human being, who uses secondary process cognition, is generally called Aristotelian, because Aristotle was the first to enunciate its laws.

Again we must stress that our study of paleologic thought patterns is within a psychodynamic frame of reference. The patient adopts paleologic thought in accordance with the principle of teleologic regression. He does so in order to escape anxiety that would be disastrous to his inner self and to his conception of himself. As long as he interprets reality with Aristotelian logic, he is aware of the unbearable truth, and the state of panic persists. Once he sees things in a different way, with a new logic, his anxiety decreases or changes in character. This new logic either will permit him to see reality as he wants to, or will offer him at least a partial pseudofulfillment of his wishes.

The adoption of the paleologic way of thinking occurs in all types of schizophrenia, to a minimal degree in the simple type, and to a maximum degree in the hebephrenic. However, even in the hebephrenic, not all thinking follows paleologic modalities. Islands of logical thoughts remain, but they are more and more overwhelmed by the paleological way of thinking. In the paranoid type, especially in incipient cases, the patient reverts to paleologic thinking only when he deals with his own conflicts and complexes. He retains the capacity to think with Aristotelian logic when he deals with non–anxiety-arousing content. At times he does more than that. As we shall see later in detail, he uses Aristotelian thought to support the conclusions reached with paleologic thinking.

Before going into the study of the structure of paleologic thinking a question of terminology must be clarified. The reader may be confused by the use of the words *logic, logical, rational, cognitive,* or *intellectual* to indicate thoughts or actions that appear irrational and illogical. In a more liberal sense than usually done, Von Domarus (1944) and myself (Arieti, 1948) have used the word *logic* for any type of mental organization, not immediately given or structured like a perception, but moving or striving toward an understanding, irrespective of the validity of this

* Lévy-Bruhl used the term *prelogical* for the method of thinking that he found in primitive societies. Von Domarus used the term *paralogical,* which is a term usually adopted by professional logicians.

understanding. There are different types of organization of cognitive processes. The paleologic type of organization is archaic or incomplete in comparison to the Aristotelian. The schizophrenic patient, when he thinks in a typically schizophrenic way, uses non-Aristotelian cognitive organizations.*

What may seem to be forms of irrationality are instead archaic or not commonly used forms of rationality. As a matter of fact, we shall find more and more in the present study that cognitive organization is always present. As I have already mentioned, it is as difficult to escape from some type of intellectual organization as it is to escape from emotions. Even the most nonsensical, bizarre, and irrational thoughts have some kind of cognitive organization. When we understand the type of cognitive organization and its content, it becomes possible to translate pathological thought into Aristotelian thought. Even the word-salad of the schizophrenic is not just a bizarre, whimsical *sequence* of words. When we understand it, we discover that is a *consequence* (see the seventh section of this chapter).

Paleologic thought patterns are to a great extent based on a principle enunciated by Von Domarus (1925, 1944). Von Domarus, as a result of his studies on schizophrenia, formulated a principle that, in a slightly modified form, is as follows: whereas the normal person accepts identity only upon the basis of identical subjects, the paleologician accepts identity based upon identical predicates. For instance, the normal person is able to conclude, ''John Doe is an American citizen'' if he is given the following information: ''Those who are born in the United States are American citizens; John Doe was born in the United States.'' This normal person is able to reach this conclusion because the subject of the minor premise, ''John Doe,'' is contained in the subject of the major premise, ''those who are born in the United States.''

On the other hand, suppose that the following information is given to a schizophrenic: ''The president of the United States is a person who was born in the United States. John Doe is a person who was born in the United States.'' In certain circumstances, the schizophrenic may conclude: ''John Doe is the president of the United States.'' This conclusion, which to a normal person appears delusional, is reached because the identity of the predicate of the two premises, ''a person who was born in the United States,'' makes the schizophrenic accept the identity of the two subjects, ''the president of the United States'' and ''John Doe.'' Of course, this schizophrenic has an emotional need to believe that John Doe is the president of the United States, a need that will arouse anxiety if it is not satisfied. He cannot think that John Doe is the president of the United States if he follows Aristotelian logic; thus, following the principle of teleologic regression, he abandons Aristotelian logic and follows Von Domarus's principle.

A patient thought that she was the Virgin Mary. Her thought process was the following: ''The Virgin Mary was a virgin; I am a virgin; therefore I am the

* The difficulty that some people may experience in calling some psychopathological processes ''intellectual'' or ''logical'' is in a certain way similar to the difficulty that some philosophically minded people experienced in calling the unconscious mechanisms discovered by Freud ''psychological.'' They thought that a necessary characteristic for a psychological phenomenon was that it be conscious; without consciousness a phenomenon could not be psychological.

Virgin Mary." The delusional conclusion was reached because the identity of the predicate of the two premises (the state of being virgin) made the patient accept the identity of the two subjects (the Virgin Mary and the patient). She needed to identify herself with the Virgin Mary because of the extreme closeness and spiritual kinship she felt for the Virgin Mary, who was her ideal of feminine perfection. At the same time the patient had the need to deny her feeling of unworthiness and inadequacy.

A patient, quoted by Bleuler (1913), thought that he was Switzerland. How can one explain such a bizarre thought? Even at the time of Bleuler, Switzerland was one of the few free countries in the world, and the patient had selected the name of this country for the concept of freedom with which he had the impelling need to identify himself. "Switzerland loves freedom, I love freedom. I am Switzerland."

Following are a few more examples. In Chapter 13 we have reported the case of Priscilla, the red-haired woman in a postpartum psychosis who developed an infection in one of her fingers. The terminal phalanx was swollen and red. She told the therapist a few times, "This finger is me." Pointing to the terminal phalanx she said, "This is my red and rotten head." She did not mean that her finger was a representation of herself, but, in a way incomprehensible to us, really herself or an actual duplicate of herself. Another patient believed that the two men she loved in her life were actually the same person, although one lived in Mexico City and the other in New York. In fact both of them played the guitar and both of them loved her. By resorting to a cognition that followed the principle of Von Domarus, she could reaffirm the unity of the image of the man she wanted to love.

Slightly different is the example of a new patient who, while waiting for the first time in the waiting room of my office, saw in a magazine an advertisement with the picture of a nude baby. He remembered that he too, when he was a small child, had a picture of himself taken in that way, and "the bastard" of his father had not too long ago threatened to show that picture to the patient's girl friend. Seeing that picture in my waiting room, he thought, was not a fortuitous coincidence. The patient presented the phenomenon commonly found in schizophrenics of seeing nonfortuitous coincidences all over. The terrible coincidences for which there was no explanation were pursuing him relentlessly. The phenomenon of the coincidences is related also to the principle of Von Domarus. A coincidence is a similar element occurring in two or more instances at the same time or after a short period of time. The patient tries to find glimpses of regularities in the midst of the confusion in which he now lives. He tends to register identical segments of experience and to build up systems of regularity upon such identical segments. At times the alleged regularity that the identical segments suggest gives sustenance to a complex that, although by now disorganized, still retains a strong emotional investment. At times automatic emphasis on similarity gives rise to special types of delusional thinking. For instance, a patient had some difficulties at work just prior to his developing a psychotic attack. During his illness he believed that many people in the street looked exactly like those who worked in the firm where he was employed. He felt that his co-workers must have many brothers and sisters or even identical twins who were there to disturb him with their presence. He saw a young man who looked like a girl he used to go out with. He immediately thought that this man must be the girl's brother, although he knew that she had no brother. When the patient improved, he still reported to the therapist his strong tendency to associate people and things with others, because of some similarities. However, he was able to resist the tendency and did not reach the stage of abnormal identification.

Any person who has a characteristic in common with an alleged persecutor, like having a beard or red hair or wearing a special dress, may become the persecutor, or a relative of the persecutor, or somehow associated with the persecutor. From all these examples it is easy to recognize that many patients at this stage indulge in what I have called an orgy of identifications. A French psychiatrist, Gabel (1948), independently discovered the same phenomenon in schizophrenia and called it a hypertrophy of the sense of identification.

The mechanisms or successive steps of paleologic thinking are not necessarily known to the schizophrenic, who automatically thinks in this way, just as the normal person automatically applies the Aristotelian laws of logic without even knowing them. For instance, a schizophrenic patient thinks, without knowing why, that the doctor in charge of the ward is her father and that the other patients are her sisters. A common predicate, a man in authority, leads to the identity between the father and the physician. Another common predicate, females in the same position of dependency, leads the patient to consider herself and the other inmates as sisters. At times, the interpretation of this type of thinking requires more elaboration. For instance, a patient of Von Domarus thought that Jesus, cigar boxes, and sex were identical. Study of this delusion disclosed that the common predicate, which led to the identification, was the state of being encircled. According to the patient, the head of Jesus, as of a saint, is encircled by a halo, the package of cigars by the tax band, and the woman by the sex glance of the man.

At times paleologic thought is even more difficult to interpret because the principle of Von Domarus is applied only partially; that is, some partial identity among the subjects is based upon partial or total identity of the predicate. For instance, a person who is conceived of by a schizophrenic as having a quality or characteristic of a horse may be thought of with a visual image consisting of part man and part horse (see Chapter 20). In this case, one subject, the person, is partially identified with the other subject, the horse, because of a common characteristic—for instance, strength.

It is well known how frequently similar distortions and condensations appear in hallucinations and drawings of schizophrenics. Similar conceptions appear in mythologies of ancient peoples and of primitives of today. As a matter of fact, anthropologic studies may disclose to the careful reader how often the principle of Von Domarus is applied in primitive thinking. Numerous studies, outstanding among which is the one by Storch (1924), have emphasized the similarities between primitive and schizophrenic thought, but the common underlying principles of logic that rule this thought have received no mention. Werner writes:

> It is one of the most important tasks of the developmental psychology to show that the advanced form of thinking characteristic of Western civilization is only one form among many, and that more primitive forms are not so much lacking in logic as based on logic of a different kind. The premise of Aristotelian logic that, when a thing is A it cannot at the same time be B, will not hold true for the primitive. . . . A Congo native says to a European: "During the day you drank palm wine with a man, unaware that in him there was an evil spirit. In the evening you heard a crocodile devouring some poor fellow. A wildcat, during the night, ate up all your chickens. Now, the man with whom you drank, the crocodile who ate a man, and the wildcat are all one and the same person" (Werner, 1957, Congo incident quoted from Lévy-Bruhl).

Obviously a common characteristic or predicate (having an evil spirit) led to the identification. Werner rightly states that "this kind of interpretation is rooted in an altogether different mental pattern, a differently constituted faculty of conception, from that exhibited by the scientifically thinking man." He adds that this primitive mode of thinking is neither illogical nor prelogical. It is logical in a different sense. Werner, however, does not attempt to enunciate the principles of a different logic. He does not add that for the primitive *A* may be *B* if *A* and *B* have only a quality (predicate) in common, although in his outstanding book, *Comparative Psychology of Mental Development* (1957), he gives numerous examples proving this fundamental fact. It is not necessary to give other examples here. The reader may be convinced of the universality of Von Domarus's principle, just by reading a book of anthropology. The student of myths, legends, folklore, traditions, fairy tales, and so on, will also be impressed with the same findings.

Young children, too, have the inclination, although not the necessity, to think in accordance with Von Domarus's principle. Levin, who compares schizophrenic thought to that of young children, concludes that the patient, as well as the young child, "cannot distinguish adequately between a symbol and the object it symbolizes" (1938*a*). For example, a middle-aged schizophrenic, speaking of an actor whom she admired, said, "He was smiling at me." The patient had seen, on the cover of a magazine, a picture of the actor in the act of smiling. Thus she had confused a picture of the actor with the actor himself. Levin reports that a 26-month-old child, drinking milk while looking at the picture of a horse, said, "Give milk to the horse." At 25 months, the same child, looking at a picture of a car, tried to lift the car from the picture and said to his father, "Daddy, get car out!" For the child the pictured object was real. Levin is correct in his observations. However, he has not seen them in the light of Von Domarus's principle. What appears to us as a symbol of the object for the schizophrenic or for the child is not necessarily a symbol, but may be a duplication of the object.

Levin makes other exceptionally interesting observations that do not receive complete interpretation, however, and he is led to the conclusion that infantile and schizophrenic concepts "are the result of amusing mixtures of relevant and irrelevant." For instance, he reports that a child, 25 months old, was calling "wheel" anything that was made of white rubber, as, for example, the white rubber guard that is supplied with little boys' toilet seats to deflect urine. The child knew the meaning of the word *wheel* as applied, for example, to the wheel of a toy car. This child had many toy cars whose wheels, when made of rubber, were always of white rubber. Thus he came to think that the word *wheel* included not only wheels, but also anything made of white rubber. Levin concludes that this example "shows how associations of the most ephemeral nature are permitted to enter into a concept when the child is too young to appreciate the non-essentiality." In view of what has been said before, it is obvious that an identification had occurred because of the same characteristic—white rubber.

In my experience, children have a propensity to indulge in paleologic thinking especially from the age of 1½ to the age of 3½ or even 4. Thus, children around 2 years of age, if shown a picture of a man, will quite often say "Daddy," and if shown a picture of a woman, will say "Mommy," no matter whom the pictures represent. A girl, 3 years and 9 months old, saw two nuns walking together, and told her mother, "Mommy, look at the twins!" She thought that the nuns were twins because they were dressed alike. The characteristic of being dressed alike, which twins often have, led to the identification of the nuns as twins.

The foregoing does not imply that young children or primitive societies of today *must* think paleologically. They just have a greater propensity to do so than adult Western man. This greater propensity should not be interpreted as proof of inferiority; it is based on reasons that will be discussed in the following sections. We shall discuss here instead another point of more direct importance to the psychiatrist, the application of Von Domarus's principle to the understanding of the structure of dreams. It will not be difficult to recognize the same organization or structures after a translation of the cognitive content into images has taken place in the dream.

Freud has shown that a person or object *A* having a certain characteristic of *B* may appear in the dream as being *B* or a composite of *A* and *B*. In the first case there is identification; in the second, composition. The whole field of Freudian symbolism, from a formal point of view, is based on Von Domarus's principle. A symbol of *X* is something that stands for *X*, but also something that retains some similarity with *X*—a common predicate or characteristic. Thus, a snake or a fountain pen may symbolize a penis because of the similar shape; king may symbolize father on account of the position they both enjoy; a box may symbolize a vagina because both a box and a vagina are apt to contain something in their cavities, and so on. The wife of a dreamer appeared in a dream as having the physical appearance of the dreamer's boss. The two persons were identified in the dream because the dreamer was concerned with a predicate common to both of them (their domineering attitude). The boss was selected as a symbol because it was more tolerable for the dreamer to be dominated by his boss than by his own wife. A male patient, obsessive-compulsive, had the obsession that he was homosexual, or that he was going to become homosexual. Once he would be known as homosexual, all women would reject him. He had the following dream. He was resting, lying on a couch, when a beautiful woman appeared and told him, "I like vinegar too!" He was pleasantly surprised and woke up. The dream made no sense to him. I asked him what came to his mind when he thought of vinegar. He replied, "Something bitter and disgusting." Then I asked him what came to his mind when he thought of something bitter and disgusting. He replied, "Homosexuality." Thus it is obvious that in the dream vinegar and homosexuality were identified because they had the common characteristics of being bitter and disgusting. The beautiful lady who appeared in the dream was telling him in paleologic language, "I like you even if you are homosexual." Thus the dream was a reassuring one; it removed the anxiety about being rejected by women.

Another patient, 18 years old, also an obsessive-compulsive with schizoid traits, was a devout Catholic who wanted to become a theological student and be ordained a priest. At the same time he struggled very hard against his sexual instincts. He had the following dream. He was undressing a young woman with sexual intentions, when suddenly he realizes her vagina looks like an umbilicus. He wakes up. In his associations, the patient remembered that when he was a child, he believed that children were born from the umbilicus. Thus, in the dream, vagina and umbilicus are identified because they are thought of by the patient as organs having the common characteristic of giving birth to children. The dream serves a purpose; the vagina is seen, not as a sexual organ, but solely as an organ that gives birth to children. The patient, after having been stimulated sexually, tries to make a reconciliation with the precepts of the Catholic church, which considers the sexual organs as organs of reproduction rather than as organs that give carnal pleasure.

One may conclude that Von Domarus's principle, or the first principle of paleologic thought, gives an important clue not only to the understanding of the schizophrenic way of thinking, but also to the understanding of the mechanisms of dreams and of some infantile and primitive thinking. However, Von Domarus's principle and the other paleologic laws that will be mentioned shortly do not explain these phenomena dynamically, but only formally. In other words, the study of paleologic thought may explain the essential structure of this type of thinking, without taking into account the content of thought. The content of thought varies with the various emotional factors, which can be studied fully only by psychodynamic procedures. The study of formal mechanisms reveals *how* we think and feel. The study of dynamic or psychoanalytic mechanisms reveals *what* we think and feel and *why* (content and motivation).

Although the purpose of this book is to expound only what pertains to schizophrenia, it is not possible to avoid references to other conditions, normal or pathological, when different types of cognition are studied. Thus, in this section we could not help calling to the attention of the reader the tremendous role played by Von Domarus's principle in all non-Aristotelian thinking, a role that transcends by far the schizophrenic process. Von Domarus formulated this principle in connection with schizophrenia in 1925. This formulation permitted the linking of this type of cognition to the phenomenon of Freudian symbolism and to primary process cognition in general. Von Domarus himself, however, did not see this connection; it was several years after his discovery, in 1947–1948, that my research indicated this relationship.

III
Further Discussion of the Structure of Paleologic Thought

The study of Von Domarus's principle in schizophrenia, as well as in other instances that have been mentioned, requires more consideration of the predicate that determines the identification. In fact, it is obvious that the predicate is the most important part in this type of thinking. In Aristotelian thinking only identical subjects are identified. The subjects are immutable; therefore, only a few (and the same) deductions are possible. In paleologic thinking, on the other hand, the predicates lead to the identification. Because the predicates of the same subject may be extremely numerous and because one does not know which one will be chosen by the patient in the process of identification, this type of thought becomes bizarre, unpredictable, individualistic, and often incomprehensible. For instance, in the example quoted from Von Domarus, the characteristic of being encircled was the identifying quality. Each of the three subjects that were identified—Jesus, cigar boxes, and sex—had a potentially large number of predicates, but the patient selected one that was completely unpredictable and bizarre. The Congo native, quoted by Lévy-Bruhl, chose the characteristic "having an evil spirit" in order to identify the man, the crocodile, and the wildcat, thus giving the European the impression that his reasoning was bizarre, unpredictable, and illogical.

The predicate that is selected in the process of identification is called the "identifying link." Why a certain predicate, out of numerous ones, should be selected as the identifying link can be found out only by the study of the emotional factors involved. In other words, emotional factors may determine which one of the predicates will be taken as the identifying link. It is obvious that if John Doe thinks that he is the president of the United States because he was born in the United States, he must wish to think so. His emotional needs direct him toward the selection of that predicate, being born in the United States, out of many other possibilities. If a patient thinks that she is the Virgin Mary, just because she is a virgin, she must have a strong urge to identify herself with the Virgin Mary.

The emotional factors operating in paleologic thinking are, of course, the same as those described by Freud in *Psychopathology of Everyday Life* (1938), and by Jung in *Psychology of Dementia Praecox* (1936) and in his works on word associations (1910, 1918). However, a study limited to the consideration of emotional factors will not explain the formal manifestations of this type of thinking. Conscious or unconscious emotions are only the directing motivation of thoughts that, in accordance with the principle of teleologic regression, acquire a paleologic mold. It is thus obvious that the principle of teleologic regression operates only inasmuch as Von Domarus's principle permits a psychodynamic selection of the predicate.

Von Domarus's principle indicates two aspects of schizophrenic cognition that only apparently are contradictory: on one side, it defines this type of cognition as having a definite structure; on the other side, it explains why cognitive conclusions reached by schizophrenics are so different from one another as to be unpredictable and thus make it impossible to talk of a schizophrenic language. The second characteristic is caused by the fact already referred to that the same subjects have many predicates, and we do not know which one is for psychodynamic reasons used by the patient in order to reach the identification. The result is that schizophrenic verbal productions, in spite of some common recognizable characteristics, often differ more from one another than they differ from verbal productions of normal people.

Because predicates will be discussed again when we examine the disturbances of thought-associations in schizophrenics, it is important that we define them accurately. A predicate is, by definition, something that concerns the subject. One is accustomed to recognizing as predicates abstract or concrete qualities of the subject or something that in a certain way is contained in the subject—for instance, the characteristic of being white, honest, attractive, big, small, of having a tail, and infinite other possibilities. These are called *predicates of quality*. There are, however, other characteristics that paleologically are conceived of as pertaining to the subjects and, therefore, are considered predicates, although they are not contained in the subject—for instance, the characteristic of occurring at a certain time or a given place. These are the *predicates of contiguity*. For instance, if a patient accidentally ate a certain exotic food on a day in which he had a pleasant experience, he may dream of eating that special food again, because he wishes to revive the pleasant experience. The special food and the pleasant experience are identified in the dream because they happen to have been perceived at the same time. The identifying link in this case is a *predicate of temporal contiguity*. The predicate of contiguity may be not only temporal, but also spatial. For instance, a patient may dream of being in his summer home in the country. A woman he loves lives near his summer home. The summer home and the loved woman are identified because they both are located in the same place. In this case the identifying link is a *predicate of spatial contiguity*. In many other cases the identifying link is a mixture of predicates of the two different types, quality and contiguity.

If the identifying link is a predicate of quality, it will be relatively easy to understand the meaning of what the patient expresses. What are referred to in psychoanalytic literature as universal symbols are generally objects whose identifying links are predicates of quality. If the identifying link is an accidental predicate of contiguity, obviously the symbol may be specific for the individual, and many details concerning his life history may be necessary in order to understand its meaning. For instance, only the patient mentioned could identify the girl he loved with his summer home in the country.

If we take into consideration again traditional logic and its four laws of thought—law of identity, law of contradiction, law of excluded middle, law of sufficient reason—we may easily conclude, as we shall soon see, that the first three are annulled by Von Domarus's principle.* Before comparing paleologic

* The fourth law of thought, the law of sufficient reason, was formulated not by Aristotle, but by Leibniz twenty centuries later. However, for the sake of simplicity, it will be considered here together with the other laws of traditional logic, with which it is usually associated.

logic with Aristotelian logic, however, I wish to point out that I am not necessarily implying that Aristotelian logic is the model of correct thinking in *an absolute sense*. This implication would require long philosophical discussions that are inappropriate here. I am aware of the criticisms that have been made of Aristotelian logic at different times. I have used Aristotelian logic as a system of reference because it is most commonly accepted as representative of normal thinking. It is only in this relative sense that the effect of Von Domarus's principle on the first three laws of Aristotelian logic is examined. The physician or psychologist who is unfamiliar with the subject of logic need not worry. This discussion will be brief and simple.

The law of identity says that *A* is always *A*, never *B*. Now, according to Von Domarus's principle, *B* may be *A*, provided *B* has a quality of *A*. The law of contradiction states that *A* cannot be *A* and not be *A* at the same time and place. Now, if the patient follows Von Domarus's principle, he may see *A* as *A* and at the same time as *B* (that is, non-*A*), if he concentrates on a quality that *A* and *B* have in common. The law of excluded middle says that *A* must be *A* or not be *A;* there cannot be an intermediate state. In its tendency to condense several subjects, paleologic thinking seems to neglect this law of excluded middle. Things are often seen as a composite of *A* and *B*. For instance, in schizophrenic drawings one often sees a human figure who is half man and half woman. The person represented in the drawing may be conceived by the schizophrenic as having a characteristic of the opposite sex. Also the emotional difficulty the schizophrenic has in identifying himself with one sex may be revealed formally by his nonadherence to the third law of thought. Similar composition (that is, abolition of the third law of thought) occurs quite commonly in dreams. The neologisms of the schizophrenic are due to composition of different verbal symbols.

The philosopher Vico, who published his major works at the beginning of the eighteenth century, advanced similar ideas about the origin of mythological figures, for example, satyrs and centaurs (1725). He wrote that the ancients, being unable to abstract the same property from two different bodies, united the bodies in their minds. Vico explained mythological metamorphoses in a similar way. If the subject acquires a new property that is more characteristic of a second subject, the first subject is conceived as transformed into the second. For instance, if a woman who used to travel or to change in many ways finally stopped at a certain place, and no further change occurred in her life, in the myth she might appear as transformed into a tree. Even today angels are usually represented with wings because they are supposed to be in the sky (heaven) like birds. Vico's interpretation of myths may be applied also to dreams and to schizophrenic thinking.

The study of Von Domarus's principle can also explain other peculiarities of thought in schizophrenia and in dreams. For instance, it is not too difficult to understand how in these types of thinking, the part may symbolize the whole and the whole may symbolize the part. In fact, according to Von Domarus's principle $A = A + B + C$, because the two terms of the equation have a part *A* in common. Therefore, in dreams and schizophrenic delusions we find that a person, either the patient or another person, may be identified with a part of himself, so that he may at the same time be symbolized by (identified with) several people, each of them having a quality that he has.

Von Domarus's principle often leads to delusions of identification of the patient with another person. The formal mechanism is the following: "If *A* can be identified with *B* because they have a common quality, it will be sufficient for me to acquire a quality of the person I want to be identified with in order to become that person." The deluded patient discovers in himself a quality possessed also by a hero, a saint, or a general and then identifies himself with the person with whom he shares that given quality. Other deluded patients try to acquire identifying qualities or confer them on others. A paranoid schizophrenic wanted her child to become an angel. Because angels are nourished only by "spiritual food," she did not feed her child for a few days—that is, until her relatives became aware of her acutely developed psychosis.

The converse of Von Domarus's principle is also applied in paleologic thinking, as well as in primitive and infantile thinking. If A has not a given quality of *A'*, *A* cannot be *A'*. I will mention again one of the interesting examples given by Levin (1938*b*). A bright 6-year-old boy asked Levin whether twins are always boys. He replied that they may be either boys or girls, or a girl and a boy. When the child heard that twins may be a girl or a boy, he asked with surprise, "Then how could they wear the same clothes?" Levin concludes that the child had seen identical twins dressed alike, and that his concept of twins included an irrelevant detail, identity of raiment. If we apply Von Domarus's principle in reverse, the mental mechanism seems to be the following: "Twins have a common quality, identical raiment. If two persons have not or cannot have identical raiment, they cannot be twins!"

Not all delusions can be explained by Von Domarus's principle because many are based only on the Freudian mechanisms of projection, or because they imply other paleologic rules that we have not yet examined. Some of the more complicated mechanisms of delusions will be examined in Chapters 18, 19, 38, and 39.

I shall mention one here that implies both projection and Von Domarus's principle. Why may the person who is loved homosexually become, in the delusional system of the patient, the persecutor? The mechanism may be as follows: This man produces something very disturbing in me and causes me a lot of misery. He must be a persecutor. The persecutor and the loved person are identified, because they both have the quality of producing in the patient a very disturbing reaction; homosexual love and hate themselves are identified, because they produce the same disturbing effect in the patient. The patient, of course, prefers to think that the person involved is a persecutor and harbors hate, not love, for him because in this case he will not feel guilty of the socially unacceptable homosexuality.

Another important occurrence of Von Domarus's principle, which will be mentioned again when therapy is discussed, is found in the transference situation, not only in psychotics, but in neurotics as well. The analytic situation appears to the patient as a repetition of the relationship with his own parent, not only because he has the emotional need to repeat the relationship, but also because the two situations have several characteristics in common. Later the patient will realize that the relations are not the same (he was deceived by Von Domarus's principle), and the transference will evolve toward a more fruitful development.

Paleologic thinking can be interpreted with formulations that are apparently different from Von Domarus's principle and yet refer to the same phenomena. We may, for instance, state that the cognitive faculty of the schizophrenic organizes classes or categories that differ from those characteristic of normal thinking. For normal persons *a class is a collection of objects to which a concept applies*. For instance, Washington, Jefferson, Lincoln, Roosevelt, Truman, and others form a class of objects to which the concept "president of the United States" applies. In paleologic thinking *a class is a collection of objects that have a predicate or part in common* (for instance, the state of being virgin); *by virtue of having such predicate or part in common, these objects become identified or equivalent*. Whereas the members of a normal class (arrived at by secondary process cognition) are recognized as being similar (and it is actually on their similarity that their classification is based), the members of a paleologic class (arrived at by primary process cognition) become equivalent; that is, they are freely interchanged (for instance, the patient becomes the Virgin Mary). Not only do they all become equivalent, but one of them may become equivalent to the whole class.

It is easy to understand why it is so. In primary classification only the common element counts; all the rest is not important or not noticed or not responded to fully by the organism. The common element is the predicate, which the psyche experiences deeply.

Many authors have stressed the fact that schizophrenics do not use the same categories as other people. Generally this characteristic has been interpreted as a desire on the part of the schizophrenic to reject the ready-made categories offered by society. Of course, societies, too, differ in the way that they segment (or interpret) the world into categories. The similarities among the various societies, however, are also many and are based on the same fundamental principles according to which the human mind experiences the world. Neither sociocultural difference nor the desire to reject the categories of one's society are sufficient explanations of schizophrenic thinking. We shall return to this topic in the thirteenth section of this chapter and in Chapter 18. Although it is true that the schizophrenic is not eager to accept the categories of society, it is also true that he uses special ways of organizing his experiences. The schizophrenic seems either to break the rules of categorization or to use inappropriate categories, or to think "intracategorically," that is, in the midst of categories used by people in general. We may interpret this phenomenon as due to the fact that schizophrenic concept formation does not follow normal logic, and does not accept cultural ready-made concepts, but instead it resorts to the formation of primary classes. Some of the consequences of this type of thinking will be studied in Chapter 18.

The important mechanisms of displacement and symbolization (one thing standing for another), like a box standing for a vagina and a stick standing for a penis, as described by Freud in connection with dreams, are from a cognitive point of view to be interpreted as manifestations of the formation of primary classes. However, Freud did not investigate further these primitive (or primary process) mechanisms from the point of view of cognition. For Freud primary and secondary processes came to be considered primarily not as two different ways of thinking, but as two different ways of dealing with cathexis. Whereas the secondary process binds the libido firmly, the primary process allows it to shift from one investment to another (Arlow, 1958). Inasmuch as this shifting would easily occur from realistic and appropriate objects to unrealistic and inappropriate ones, the primary process would become an irrational mode of functioning.

This point of view leaves many unexplored aspects, especially those that pertain more closely to cognition. What is ignored in these studies is that this alleged shifting of libido requires the existence of alternative cognitive elements. The psyche must have available mental representations of various objects to which the cathexis could be shifted. Furthermore, if the libido is shifted to another object, this shifting or displacement is due, not to chance, but to a cognitive relation between the original object and the substitutes, that is, to an immediate mental grasping of a similarity or relation between the object and the substitute. For instance, if in dreams the cathexis is shifted from the vagina to a box, this shifting is not casual, but is due to a special type of cognition that first is able to represent mentally a vagina and a box and secondly sees a special relation between the function and shape of the vagina and of the box, so that the latter can replace the former. In Freudian theory the displacement is not due to the formation of primary classes.*

IV

Teleologic Causality

It was mentioned in the previous section that the first three laws of thought of traditional logic were eliminated by Von Domarus's principle. Paleologic thinking does retain something similar to the fourth law, the law of sufficient reason: we must assume a reason for every event. We say something "similar" to the fourth law because actually the methods by which a reason for, or a cause of, an event is searched for by the paleologician are different from those used by the normal person. The paleologician confuses the physical world with the psychological one. Instead of finding a physical explanation of an event, he looks for a personal motivation or an intention as the cause of an event. Every act, every event, occurs because it is willed or wanted, either by the person who seeks an explanation or by another person or by something that becomes personified. In other words, causality by logical deduction, often implying concepts involving the physical world, is replaced with causality by psychological explanation, that is, by *teleologic causality*. Teleologic causality is valid in many instances; it determines most

* In *The Intrapsychic Self* (Arieti, 1967, Chap. 7) I have described how primary classes precede the secondary in phylogeny and ontogeny.

actions of men. It is the explanation that many historians give to certain social events, and that psychologists and novelists give to personal occurrences. For example: This man drinks *because* he wants to quench his thirst; I read this book because I want to learn Spanish; Caesar went into politics because he wanted to satisfy his ambition. All these "becauses" mean *for the purpose of.* The purpose is carried out by a will.

Often in common thinking and as a rule in scientific procedures *because* has a different meaning. It means *on account of* (generally on account of a previous fact). For instance, the water became ice because of (on account of) the lowering of the temperature. This explanation is called *deterministic causality.*

The difficulty of the schizophrenic, especially of the paranoid schizophrenic, is that to support his delusions he resorts exclusively, or almost exclusively, to explanation by teleologic causality. Everything that occurs is interpreted by him as due to the will of a person. If a person is killed, if a storm occurs, if the wind blows, it is so *solely* because somebody wants it so. This method of interpreting events is much more primitive than the one by logical deduction. Piaget has described this method very well in young children (1929, 1930, 1948). Children examined by him in Switzerland thought that God made the thunder in the sky, that Negroes were made the way they were because they were naughty when they were little and God punished them, that there were a great and a little Salève Lakes because some people wanted to go into the little one and some into the great one. Werner reports other examples (1957). A 5-year-old boy thought that in the evening it got dark because people were tired and wanted to sleep. The same child thought that the rain was due to the fact that the angels swept the heavens with their brooms and lots of water. The intentions are ascribed first to other people, then to things. The moon follows the child; the sun goes up in the sky; the rivers run. An animistic and anthropomorphic conception of the world originates. Things become animated; they either have a will of their own or are moved by the will of somebody. The same conception of psychological causality is found by many anthropologists in primitive cultures.

Man living in a primitive society has the need for explanation just as civilized man has. The need for explanation is one of the basic needs of the human race and is to be found in every member of *Homo sapiens.* However, man living in a primitive culture is entirely satisfied when he can think that some person, or a personified entity, is responsible for an event. The moral point is not more important than the causal link; it is the *only* aspect taken into consideration, because *to be responsible for an event means to be the cause of the event.* The concept of impersonal force is a scientific abstraction which requires a much higher level of thinking (Arieti, 1967). Many magic practices of primitive societies consist of attempts to change or modify the will or intentions of the people who are responsible for (are causers of) the event. Study of myths reveals the same thing. If Ulysses is wrecked, it is because Poseidon, the god of the sea, is angry at him. If the Greeks are afflicted by epidemics, it is because Phoebus wants to punish Agamemnon. Anthropological and mythological examples of projected teleological causality could be multiplied indefinitely. The reader who is particularly interested is referred to Vico (1725), Lévy-Bruhl (1910, 1922), Werner (1957), and Kelsen (1943).

In dreams, too, events are engendered by wishes, intentions, or psychological motivations. Paranoiacs and paranoids interpret almost everything as manifesting a psychological intention or meaning related to their delusional complexes. If the nurse looks at the patient in a special way, if a certain food is given at a certain meal, if a certain noise is heard, and so on, each of these things has a special meaning. They are willed by other persons in that specific way for reasons that involve the patient. In many cases, practically everything that occurs is interpreted as willed by the persecutors of the patient. In many other cases, especially when the delusions are not well organized, the patient does not even ask himself why the alleged persecutors commit these acts against him. He simply accepts the fact that they do so, that those acts are willed by somebody. If those acts were not willed, they could not occur. Of course, in these ideas of reference, two mechanisms are at play: not only is there the belief that each event is willed, but also the belief that each event has a special reference to the patient himself.

In *The Intrapsychic Self* (Arieti, 1967, Chap. 7) I have discussed the emergence of teleologic causality in children. I wrote that "before the child has acquired the ability to speak, he can already sense some kind of vague intentionality in the surrounding adults. For instance, he understands in a primitive way that it is up to Mother to feed him, to keep him on her lap, to fondle him. Through imagery he can even expect these things to happen and he anticipates them." However, this vague intentionality cannot be abstracted or conceived as a causal factor or as an act of will until the child can use words to represent people and actions and to detach them from the total situation in which he finds himself. When he acquires a rudimentary language, he learns to interpret everything in a teleologic way: everything depends on the will or actions of others. The child makes a generalization and comes to conceive of everything in nature as a consequence of will. In some instances it will be very difficult to relinquish such a belief later. However, school and life in general in a civilized world will help the child to proceed to the order of deterministic causality; and in most cases the transition will be rapid because the child is offered ready-made concepts and social systems of symbolism with which it will be relatively easy to grasp new concepts of causality.

In certain stages of schizophrenia, especially of the paranoid type, teleologic causality again reacquires the upper hand and deterministic causality plays a minor role, especially in the cognitive structures of the patient's delusions, ideas of reference, and other symptoms.

V

Reverse Inference and Pseudoabstraction

A characteristic of schizophrenic thinking is its reverse order of progression. In normal cognition the human being moves from description to inference. When we interpret a descriptive statement, or even a perception, we make an inference. For instance, if we see a large quantity of smoke and smell an odor of burning material, we infer that a fire is taking place. As Korzybski (1933) has pointed out, the descriptive levels (perceptual and apperceptual levels) are not the level of inference. If a person evaluates, or responds to, an inference as he would respond to a description, he beclouds whatever evidence there is to support the inference. The inference is already made, and it influences the observation. For instance, a paranoid has the idea that somebody plots to poison him. He sees a glass of water prepared for him on the dinner table. Influenced as he is by his premise, he "sees a cloudiness" in the water. He tastes the water and "discovers" in it a peculiar "metallic" taste, a sure indication that the water has been poisoned.

In these cases of schizophrenia the patient is able to foresee the conclusions of his reasoning because it is the anticipated conclusion that retrospectively directs his train of thought. In other words, in the process of demonstrating something, the patient chooses only those possibilities that lead to the conclusion he has anticipated and wished. For instance, a 49-year-old patient had the delusion that a certain man she knew was going to divorce his wife and marry her. The wife of this man was a respectable, attractive, blond young woman who had just given birth to a baby. According to my patient, who had an unconscious homosexual attachment for her, this woman was ugly, had already undergone the menopause, and had been a prostitute. How could the patient sustain her beliefs in the face of such contradictory evidence? We shall not take into consideration here the motivation of her thinking, that is, the fact that unconsciously she wanted to reject her homosexual desire. We are interested here only in the formal mechanism of her delusional ideas. Consciously, the patient needed to reach the conclusion that the man was going to divorce this woman and marry her. She needed to believe that this woman was unworthy of the love of this man. According to the patient, therefore, the woman was extremely ugly, but being a prostitute, she had learned to dissemble her appearance, as all prostitutes do; she was a brunette, in fact, but had bleached her hair. She had already undergone the menopause, but she had been visiting a famous obstetrician who had given her hormone therapy so that she could conceive. As a matter of fact, the patient saw this woman on the same street where this famous obstetrician resided. It is obvious that the patient could anticipate the deductions of her thoughts, because it was the conclusion itself (impossibility for the man to love that woman) that retrospectively directed, and consequently distorted, her reasoning. The delusional premise was supposed to be an inference; but it was organized by the mind in advance, and therefore was not an inference but a delusional premise that acted as a reversed inference and stimulated the patient to collect the alleged evidence that was necessary to sustain the inference (that is, the delusion).

Inference before description is not pathognomonic of schizophrenia. In fact, we find many examples of this type of wrong thinking in nonschizophrenics. In his writings, Korzybski wanted to show how to avoid this error as well as others. However, whereas this erroneous thinking is easily corrected in the normal person, it will persist in the schizophrenic as long as the motivation or its understanding have not been altered by therapy.

In all these delusional processes we can distinguish two important factors. The first is the need or the wish to believe the delusion. Such need or wish is very strong because it is closely integrated with the whole psychodynamic history and structure of the patient. To believe in the reality of the delusions becomes, especially for the paranoid, the purpose or meaning of his life. Second, the patient must feel able to demonstrate to himself, and in many cases to others, that there is a logical foundation for what he believes. As we have repeatedly stated in Part Two, the feelings of the patient about himself and his world would be more threatening without the delusions. If, after having studied the patient psychodynamically, we would ask the question, "What would be the person's situation without the delusion," the answer would be, "Worse." The reason for the delusion lies in its intentionality. A person becomes delusional when he cannot visualize other alternatives.

In order to infer, either in the proper or in reversed order, the person must be capable of so-called seriatim functions (Morgan, 1943). By seriatim functions is meant the organization or synthesis of skilled acts or thoughts into an orderly series. High species, like monkeys and apes, are capable of simple seriatim functions, but in men this ability is much more developed. The number of acts or thoughts that may occur in a given sequence may increase to a tremendous degree. Seriatim functions imply ability (1) to anticipate a goal and (2) to organize and synthesize acts or thoughts in a given temporal series.

In the beginning of schizophrenia, seriatim functions and ability to foresee the future are retained. The early paranoid who has delusions of persecution or of jealousy is able to foresee the future and direct his thoughts in logical, chronological patterns that lead to the foreseen delusional deductions. He retains a great emotional capacity in connection with his complexes, and at times is so apparently logical as to be considered lucid. Later he becomes less logical, less capable of organizing his thoughts in a logical series. The seriatim function disintegrates, and he is less able to foresee the future and the deductions of his reasoning; his delusions become related to the present time and not to the future, their content is not persecutory but more or less grandiose, and their emotional tone is shallower. Later his thinking presents definite scattering, his delusions are connected with the immediate present, and are of a definitely expansive type. "I *am* the Virgin Mary," "I *am* the emperor of China." He accepts his delusions as indisputable, immediate reality, no longer caring to demonstrate logically their validity. As a matter of fact, he would not even be able to attempt such a demonstration.

In some cases, at times even at the beginning of the illness, but more often in chronic cases, patients seem not to have undergone a process of active concretization and even speak in an abstract manner. At times their style is definitely pretentious and pompous. They may use big words that do not refer to concrete or material things but to abstract concepts. Some of these patients, although only grammar or high-school graduates, begin to use big, philosophical, theological terms that generally are used by people with more education. Some psychiatrists (for instance, Barison, 1934) have been led to the conclusion that the patients have increased their capacity for abstract thinking. It is true that in these cases the patient attempts to escape from the reality of life by plunging into abstract conceptions. However, he really does not succeed. If we ask him to explain what he means with these big words, he will not be able to do so. He will use other big words that will accentuate the feeling of confusion. Actually the patient again concretizes: his confusion and the mysteriousness of the events that he perceived in a diffuse, unclear way become represented or concretized by him in the use of big, abstract words whose meaning he does not even know, or whose meaning he knows only with not too close approximation. Various German authors have very appropriately called this characteristic "talking on stilts." Examples of these pseudoabstractions will be given in Chapter 23.

Bumke (1924) has pointed out that some very beautiful examples of talking on stilts have been attributed to Don Quixote by Cervantes. For instance, "The profound sense of the absurd which exhibits itself to my senses shakes my reason in such a way that I carry an ambiguous chagrin on your beauty"; "The high heavens, in which your divinity divinely lives with the stars, have aroused the honorability of the honor with which Your Highness is honored."

VI

Time and Space

We must distinguish between experience of time and conception of time. Both of them may be altered in schizophrenia in various ways. The existentialists and phenomenologists have given much importance to the experience of time (Minkowski, 1933; Jaspers, 1946). The patient may experience time as standing still (see case of Mary, Chapter 13). Awareness of time may disappear completely, and so the patient lives in a timeless world. Time may seem to pass with excessive rapidity or, on the contrary, very slowly. On other occasions time seems chaotic, intermittent, interrupted, confused, without future or past. This altered experience is the result of alteration in the psychostructure of the patient.

The conception of time reflects more closely the cognitive changes. We must remember that the only possible experiential or subjective tense is the present. The human mind, however, is capable of transporting to the present chronologically remote events, thus permitting, in a symbolic way, the revival of the past and the anticipation of the future. Past and future become not only conceptual constructs but also emotional experiences.

The ability to anticipate the distant future is one of the last achievements in evolution. Infrahuman animals do not possess this faculty. Experiments with delayed reactions have disclosed that even the highest species of mammals cannot keep future events in mind for more than a few minutes (Harlow, Wehling, and Maslow, 1932; Hunter, 1913). They can foresee only the very immediate future—that is, only the immediate reaction to a stimulus, or the outcome of their reaction to a stimulus, if the stimulus was present not longer than a few minutes previously. Prehuman species may be called "organisms without a psychic tomorrow." Cattle go to the slaughterhouse without feelings of anxiety, being unable to foresee what is going to happen to them. In humans the ability to anticipate the distant future begins in about the second year of life. At that stage of development, the child becomes able to postpone immediate pleasure for some future gratification. In other words, it is when the ability to anticipate is developed that the "reality principle" originates.

Phylogenetically, anticipation of the distant future appeared when early man no longer limited his activity to cannibalism and hunting, which were related to immediate present necessities, but became interested in hoarding and, later, in agriculture in order to provide for future needs. It was in this period that culture—that is, knowledge to be used in future times or to be transmitted to future generations—originated. A person who mentally was able to conceive only the present time would aim only toward what Sullivan calls "satisfaction." A person who is able to prospect the future as well aims also toward what Sullivan calls "security."

In a paper written some years ago, I discussed the importance of the role of this ability to prospect the future in the engendering of the type of anxiety that is due to lack of security (Arieti, 1947). I pointed out that the neuroses experimentally produced in animals are the result of a state of tension (or short-circuited anxiety); they are not the much more complicated neuroses involving the anxiety that is due to lack of security. Although the animal may remain neurotic or maladjusted after the experiment, the actual state of discomfort is determined by the *presence* of the external disturbing stimuli, or of their equivalents. In other words, the reaction of the animal is temporarily tied to the experimental stimulus; the fear of danger always involves the present time or the immediate future. In human anxiety, however, there may be a temporal lapse between the anxiety-precipitating stimulus and the dreaded event, and the anxiety may last even when such an external stimulus is removed. Actually, in humans the external stimulus is replaced by an inner stimulus, which is symbolic of the external, is retained in the mind, and may even be unconscious. Anticipation of the future is thus impossible without the ability to symbolize. In *The Intrapsychic Self* (Arieti, 1967), I have discussed the role of language in the conceptualization of the future and remote past.

In schizophrenia there is a tendency to abandon the faculty of anticipating the future; one finds in this condition what I have called "restriction of the psychotemporal field.'' The temporal orientation of the patient gradually becomes limited to the present time. Balken (1943), in her study with the Thematic Apperception Test, found that the schizophrenic does not distinguish between past, present, and future. According to her, the schizophrenic, in the attempt to ''relieve the tension between the possible and the real,'' clings ''desperately and without awareness to the present.'' In early schizophrenia, however, and especially in the paranoid type, the patient is still able to concern himself with past and future. Some delusions, especially with persecutory content, may involve the future rather than the present. In the preceding section we have seen that many delusions required *organized* thinking or seriatim functions. The patient must thus be able to anticipate inferences either in the proper order or in reverse order. However, the more advanced is the regression, the more restricted to the present is that patient's ideation.

Wallace (1956) found that future time perspective is ''influenced by the schizophrenic process to such an extent that both the length of the future time span and the organization of its contents are significantly reduced for a sample of schizophrenic patients as compared to a group of normal controls.''

Dahl (1958) found that some hospitalized patients are able to give the year of their birth and the current year correctly but will not give their correct age. A psychological factor rather than lack of arithmetical ability is responsible for the phenomenon. According to Dahl the unpleasant awareness of having spent so many years in mental illness becomes unacceptable. The patient uses paleologic thinking: ''I was *X* years old when I was adjusted. I am adjusted now; therefore I am *X* years old.'' One patient stated, ''I have lost so much time here [in the hospital], I am putting myself back.''

Occasionally, in advanced stages of hebephrenic and paranoid types of schizophrenia, delusions seem to imply anticipation of the future, but it is not really so. For instance, a patient had the delusional idea that for her the calendar was always one day in advance. When for the rest of humanity it was Tuesday, February 13, 1946, for her it was Wednesday, February 14, 1946. This delusion is only superficially connected with anticipation of time and has a symbolic meaning that is related to the present.

In dreams, too, the situation is lived in the present; we may remember past events, but we never project ourselves into the future. Although the dream may be the symbolic manifestation or fulfillment of a wish for a future event, the dreamt action is always in the present. The dreamer may worry about an imminent but not a distant danger.

What is the purpose of this restriction to the present that we find in dreams and, as a progressive tendency, in schizophrenia? Obviously it is the elimination of the anxiety that is injurious to the self-image (see Chapters 7 and 8). In Chapter 7 we showed how a deep injury to the self is involved with future conceptualization and anticipation. The patient who lives in the present and the dreamer may still experience fear and anxiety, but it is of a different and less traumatic type.

In addition to the restriction to the present we find in schizophrenia a general tendency to conceive of, or refer to, time in concrete representations. Minkowski

(1958) reported a typical example. For his patient, the future was blocked, because the certainty of a terrifying and destructive event dominated that patient's entire outlook. The present also was experienced in a monotonous and uniform way. He experienced the days in the following way: "On Monday the silver was polished; on Tuesday the barber came to cut his hair; on Wednesday the gardener mowed the lawn," and so forth. In other words, days were represented by virtue of a concrete happening (temporal events). Although the patient's whole life was altered as a consequence of his illness, new meanings with concrete expressions were found.

Experience and conception of space in schizophrenia have also received much more consideration from the phenomenological and existential schools than from any other. Binswanger described in the schizophrenic the *gestimmter Raum,* an experience of space that is determined by one's feeling: space with an atmosphere or emotionally colored space (reported by Jaspers, 1946).

Objects may appear to the patient smaller (micropsia), larger (macropsia), or larger on one side than the other (dysmegalopsia).

A frequent experience is one of anxiety in the face of space and escape into a restricted or very definite space, like the corner of a room. Some patients seem to grasp for what they can touch and see; they cannot stand emptiness, even on a piece of paper. This feeling often obliges them to write on sheets of paper up to the border, without leaving any margin or space unwritten.

VII

Language in Schizophrenia

Language and its relations with thought processes are so characteristic in schizophrenia as to lead in typical cases to a prompt diagnosis. In the most pronounced cases, schizophrenic language appears obscure or utterly incomprehensible. Some authors go to the extent of interpreting the lack of clarity of schizophrenic language as an effort on the part of the patient to hide from others, or even more probably from himself, the anxiety-provoking content of what he has to say. He does not want to communicate. These authors see in the schizophrenic speech the same mechanism that Freud saw in dreams: an attempt to hide the manifest content. Although this may be the case, we must pursue the problem further, as Freud did in his study of dreams.

In this section we shall consider those alterations that are closely related to paleologic thinking, as described in the second and third sections of this chapter. In the eighth section we shall describe more pronounced language alterations.

Before discussing schizophrenic language in detail we shall define three terms used in this context: connotation, denotation, and verbalization. The first two are traditionally used in the field of logic; the third has been introduced by the author. Let us take, for instance, the term *table*. The connotation of this term is the meaning or definition of the term; that is, the concept *article of furniture with flat hori-*

zontal top, set on legs. The denotation of the term is the object meant; that is, the table as a physical entity. In other words, the term *table* may mean table in general or it may mean any or all particular tables. Every term has both these aspects. It means certain definite qualities or attributes and also refers to certain objects or, in the case of a singular term, to one object that has those qualities. The connotation refers to the whole class of the object, without any reference to a concrete embodiment of the object.

I have proposed to call *verbalization* a third aspect of the term; namely, the term as a word, or phonetic entity, or phoneme. Thus the term *table* may be considered from three aspects: its connotation, when one refers to its meaning; its denotation, when one refers to the object meant; its verbalization, when one considers the word as a word; that is, as a verbal expression independent of its symbolic value.* We can also more simply state that the connotation is a thought, the denotation a thing, the verbalization a word.

Now it is possible to formulate a second important principle of schizophrenic cognition. Whereas the healthy person in a wakened state is concerned mainly with the connotation and the denotation of a symbol but is capable of shifting his attention from one to another of the three aspects of a symbol, the schizophrenic tends to become more concerned with the denotation and the verbalization and experiences an impairment of his ability to connote. In view of this principle, two important phenomena have to be considered in the schizophrenic's use of language: first, the reduction of the connotation power; second, the emphasis on the denotation and verbalization. In a general way these phenomena reproduce in reverse some stages of language that I have described elsewhere (Arieti, 1967, Chaps. 7, 8).

Reduction of Connotation Power

For the person who thinks paleologically, the verbal symbols cease to be representative of a group or of a class; they are representative only of the specific objects that the patient is considering at the moment. For instance, the word *cat* cannot be used as relating to any member of the feline genus, but only in reference to a specific cat, like "the cat sitting on that chair." More often there is a gradual shifting from the connotation to the denotation level.† This gradual regression is apparent if we ask a moderately regressed schizophrenic to define words. For instance, the following are some words that a schizophrenic was asked to define, and her replies:

Q. Book.
A. It depends what book you are referring to.

* Different terminologies are used in the various types of semantics. In Ogden's and Richards's semantics (1947), connotation is the reference, denotation the referent, and verbalization the symbol.

† The statement made by many logicians that there is an inverse ratio between connotation and denotation does not hold true if the problem is considered from a psychological point of view. In other words, a decrease in the connotation power is not accompanied by an increase in the denotation power and vice versa. Many logicians, too, have criticized this concept of inverse ratio because objects (denotation) can be enumerated, but qualities and meanings cannot be measured mathematically.

Q. Table.
A. What kind of table? A wooden table, a porcelain table, a surgical table, or a table you want to have a meal on?
Q. House.
A. There are all kinds of houses, nice houses, nice private houses.
Q. Life.
A. I have to know what life you happen to be referring to—*Life* magazine or the sweetheart who can make another individual happy and gay.

From the examples, it is obvious that the patient, a high-school graduate, is unable to define common words. She cannot cope with the task of defining the word as a symbol of a class or a symbol including all the members of the class, like all books, all tables, and so on. She tries first to decrease her task by attempting to break it into little pieces, that is, by limiting her definition to special subgroups or to particular members of the class. For instance, she is unable to define the word *table* and attempts to simplify her problem by asking whether she has to define various subgroups of tables—wooden tables, surgical tables, and so on. In the last example, she wants to know whether I am referring to one of two particular instances, *Life* magazine or the life of the sweetheart. This reply, which reveals impairment of connotation power, is also complicated by the emphasis on the verbalization, as will be demonstrated in the following section.

Other patients, when asked to supply a general or categorical definition, reply by giving specific embodiments of the definition. A patient who was asked to define the word *chair* said, "I sit on a chair now. I am not a carpenter." Another patient answered the same question with, "A throne." He restricted the meaning to this particular type of chair because of a connection with his delusions. He believed that he was an angel and was sitting on a throne in heaven. At times these definitions reveal not only a constriction to one or a few specific instances of the class, but also the prominence of bizarre associations. Correct but uncommon definitions are also given. For instance, a patient who was asked to define the word *bird* replied, "A feathered fowl." Another patient answered, "A winged creature."

The psychologist Goldman (1960) has experimentally confirmed the decrease of connotation power in schizophrenics.

Anthropologists have noted often a similar inability to formulate or use words or concepts that include whole classes on the part of primitive people. For instance, Steinen (1894) reports that primitive people of Brazil have a group of expressions for different species of parrots, but the generic term *parrot* is lacking in their language. Smith (1878) reports that the Australian aborigines have no class names such as *bird, tree,* or *fish,* but on the other hand they have special terms for particular species of birds, trees, and fishes.

The philosopher Cassirer (1946, 1953, 1955, 1957) described very well the difficulty or inability of the primitive mind in connoting. He emphasized that when the concept is separated from the class, the single experience remains isolated, loses expansion, but acquires emotional concentration or "intensive compression." The immediate sensible experience increases in power. The universe of the schizophrenic, of the primitive, and of the child is closer than that of the normal adult to the immediate perception, to the phenomenological world, and so reflects an extreme subjectivity.

According to Langer (1949) many of the psychological phenomena that caught Cassirer's interest arose from Kurt Goldstein's psychiatric work on cases of cerebral damage caused by physical accidents. In later studies Goldstein (1943*a*) dealt with this decrease of the connotation power in schizophrenics also. In the color-sorting test, one of Goldstein's patients picked out various shades of green, but in doing so he named them—peacock green, emerald green, taupe green, bright green, bell green, and baby green. He could not say that all of them might be called green. Another patient of Goldstein said in the same situation: "This is the color of the grass in Virginia, this is the color of the grass in Kentucky, this is the color of the bark of the tree, this is the color of the leaves." The words used by the patients in naming colors belonged to a definite situation. "The words," Goldstein wrote, "have become individual words, i.e., words which fit only a specific object or situation." In other words, the meaning or the connotation of the word includes not a class but only à specific instance. There is, therefore, a definite restriction of the connotation power.* Goldstein called this phenomena expressions of "concrete attitude." This tightness to the denotation prevents the schizophrenic from using figurative or metaphorical language, contrary to what it may seem as at first impression.

It has been stated by Benjamin (1944) that the schizophrenic is unable to interpret proverbs correctly. He will always give a more or less literal interpretation of them. Figurative language increases the use of the term, which acquires an unusual denotation and connotation. If one says, "When the cat's away, the mice will play," a normal listener will understand that by *cat* is meant a person in authority. A schizophrenic patient gave the following literal interpretation of that proverb: "There are all kinds of mice, but when the cat is away, the mice take advantage of the cat." In other words, for the schizophrenic the word *cat* could not acquire a special connotation.

The inability of the schizophrenic to use metaphorical language is also revealed by the following replies of a patient who was asked to explain what was meant when a person was referred to by the names of various animals, for instance:

Q. Wolf.
A. Wolf is a greedy animal.
Q. Fox.
A. A fox and a wolf are two different animals. One is more vicious than the other, more and more greedy than the other.
Q. Parrot.
A. It all depends on what the parrot says.
Q. Peacock.
A. A woman with beautiful feathers. By the way, *Woman* is a magazine.

* Many logicians, on the other hand, would say that the connotation is increased. This point of view is psychologically incorrect.

Many beginners in the field of psychiatry get the impression that schizophrenic language and thought are highly metaphorical and poetic. In reality it is not so. This impression is due to misinterpretation of the phenomena that were explained above in terms of Von Domarus's principle. For instance, a schizophrenic will be able to *identify* a man with a wolf on account of a common characteristic, greediness, but he will not be able to accept the concept *wolf* as a symbol of greedy men. Two different mechanisms are employed. In the first instance, a very primitive paleologic mechanism is necessary; in the second instance a high degree of abstraction is at play. The schizophrenic uses metaphors out of necessity, not for aesthetic reasons. The artist may exploit archaic processes to intensify the emotional tone of his expression, but at the same time he will retain the power of abstraction that has been lost by the schizophrenic and that has not been sufficiently used by the primitive.

Now a question may occur to the reader. If these reversions to primitive mechanisms have a teleologic function in psychopathology, what is the purpose of this loss of connotation power in the schizophrenic? This is an important point. The answer, however, requires knowledge of other aspects involved, and these will be taken into consideration in Chapter 19.

Emphasis on Denotation and Verbalization

When the word has lost its connotation power, its denotation and verbalization acquire greater significance. The word, disrobed of its connotation, in a certain way remains isolated from a logical context but increases its emotional tone, acquires more subjective value, a uniqueness that is connected with the subjective sensorial image of the individual. In other words, it becomes much nearer to the perceptual level. Ideas are, therefore, quite often expressed with words which describe sensory images. Storch (1924) has described this phenomenon in schizophrenia at length. One of his patients spoke of "a heap of truth," another of an "idea" as being "smaller than a flea," and so on. Often the attempt of the patient to stress the denotation is frustrated. Since the patient conceptualizes things in a different way, he tends to misidentify them and therefore cannot denote them accurately. He may misidentify himself, others, and objects. The misidentification is due to the adoption of non-Aristotelian primary classes. His way of denoting is similar to that of children who have not yet acquired the ability to conceptualize properly and who, therefore, follow a paleologic structure of thought. We have already mentioned, for instance, children around two years of age who say "mommy" if shown a picture of a woman, no matter whom the picture represents. Between the right and the wrong denotation there is a paleologic relation. At other times, the patient does not misidentify but fails to identify with accuracy. Because of his semantic difficulty he cannot properly name the people he speaks of and refers to them with the pronoun "they"; for instance, "they are after me." This use of the pronoun is not the usual one and is typically schizophrenic; in normal speech the use of the pronoun is correct and economic when it replaces a well-known subject. If we talk about Italians, we say, "they are opera lovers; they prefer Chianti wine to Beaujolais.'' The schizophrenic often uses the pronoun because he cannot identify the subject in a specific way. The ''they'' maintains a sense of indefiniteness and mystery.

In many cases, when the connotation value is diminished or lost, the attention of the schizophrenic is focused on the verbalization or on the word merely as a word or a purely phonetic entity. The loss or diminution of the socially established semantic value (*semantic evasion* or *loss*) is accompanied by increased value of the verbalization (*formal pregnancy*). When this happens, several different situations may ensue.

1. Often mental processes occur that are stimulated only by verbalization.
2. The verbalization becomes the identifying link in identifications.
3. The verbalization becomes confused with the whole or part of the denotation; that is, the word and its characteristics may be taken as identical with the thing and its characteristics.
4. Ideas associate not because of their meaning but because of the phonetic quality of the words by which they are represented. Words also associate for phonetic reasons.
5. The assonance, and other phonetic qualities, are invested with special semantic meaning.

As an example of the first possibility, I shall mention a patient whom I examined during World War II. During the examination, she told me that the next time the Japanese would attack the Americans it would be at Diamond Harbor or Gold Harbor. When she was asked why, she replied, ''The first time, they attacked at Pearl Harbor; now they will attack at Diamond Harbor or at Sapphire Harbor.'' ''Do you think that the Japanese attacked Pearl Harbor because of its name?'' I asked. ''No, no,'' she replied. ''It was a *happy* coincidence.'' Note the inappropriateness of the adjective *happy*. It was a happy coincidence for her because she could prove thereby the alleged validity of her present paleologic thinking. Her train of thought was stimulated by the words *Pearl Harbor*. A literal connotation was given to the word *Pearl,* and this aroused in the patient associations with precious stones. Often the verbalization is exploited to fit a certain delusional or referential framework. For instance, every time a patient heard the words *home* and *fair,* he thought they were the slang words for homosexuals, *homo* and *fairy*. He was preoccupied with the problem of sexual identification and believed that people were subtly referring to his alleged homosexuality. The similarity between these words would not have been noticed or seized upon had the patient not been so preoccupied.

A patient thought he was Jesus Christ. When he was asked to explain the reason for his belief, he replied, ''I drink Carnation milk. I am incarnated.'' Another patient heard some employees in her office saying that ''Attention should be paid to O.B.'' She immediately thought they were referring to her: O.B. would stand for *old bag* or for *obstetrics,* thus implying or unfairly accusing her of being illegitimately pregnant. She had repressed the fact, well known to her, that in the firm there was an *Order and Billing* department and that the initials *O* and *B* had always been used to refer to the work of that department.

The second possibility that we have mentioned merely states the application of Von Domarus's principle with the verbalization as the identifying link. Different things are identified because they have names that have a common characteristic. The identification is particularly prone to occur if the names are homonymous. Two otherwise different things are identified, or considered together, because they have the same phonetic or written symbol. In one example mentioned above, the patient put together *Life* magazine and the life of the sweetheart. Another schizophrenic had the habit of wetting her body with oil. When asked why, she replied, "The human body is a machine and has to be lubricated." The word *machine,* applied in a figurative sense to the human body, had led to the identification with man-made machines.

Another patient felt that when people were using the word *candies* they were referring to her former boyfriend. She was on a diet and had *given up* eating candies, just as she had previously *given up* her boyfriend. The predicate "having been given up" led the patient to identify candies and boyfriend and to assume that other people would make a similar identification, at least in the verbal expressions that represented the two subjects. It is obvious that for the schizophrenic the term may be not a symbol but a characteristic, a quality, or a predicate, or a whole duplication of the object that is symbolized. The identification due to similar or common verbal expression is based not only on Von Domarus's principle, but also on the emphasis on the verbalization and the decreased importance of the connotation.

Proper names are often the objects of similar processes. A patient whose name was Marcia, and who knew Italian, thought her name meant that she was rotten (in Italian *marcia* means "rotten" in the feminine gender). Another patient whose name was Stella felt that her name indicated that she was a fallen star. Because they are so involved with verbalization, patients often discover puns all over and feel that these puns are used purposely to annoy them. Actually quite often the patients themselves, because of this unusual capacity to concentrate on the verbalization, become very skillful in making puns.

These two mechanisms, application of Von Domarus's principle and emphasis on the verbalization, are quite often used by normal adults in jokes and witticisms. Some of the examples mentioned above, such as the patient who was wetting her body with oil, or the patient who gave a special significance to the initials O.B., have definite comical characteristics. The important point, however, is that what is comical for the healthy person is taken seriously by the schizophrenic. In other publications I have described in detail the use of paleologic thinking in wit (Arieti, 1950; 1967, Chap. 20). Freud (1938), in his important monograph on wit, described many mechanisms involved in the technique of witticisms and compared them to the mechanisms in dreams. He did not compare them, however, to schizophrenic expressions.

The emphasis on verbalization also appears in many dreams, as revealed first by Freud (1960) in his book on dream interpretation. The following is one of the numerous examples he gives. C. dreams that on the road to *X* he sees a girl bathed in a white light and wearing a white blouse. The dreamer had begun an affair with a Miss White on that road. The following example from a patient of mine is also instructive. The wife of the patient dreamt that she had intercourse with Mr. X., a friend of the family. Motivated either by guilt or hostility, she revealed this dream to her husband, my patient. The patient was hurt, but he did not say anything because, after all, ''It was only a dream.'' The following night the patient dreamt that his wife was unfaithful to him, but to his great surprise the man she had relations with in the dream was her own brother. The patient, in the dream, was thinking: ''After all, it is not so bad. It is true that she had intercourse, but only with her brother. Sex with a brother does not count.'' The patient did not know how to explain the dream, but suddenly it occurred to him that Mr. X.'s first name was Carl, the same name as that of his brother-in-law, who had had relations with his wife in the dream. Thus it seems that in the dream Mr. X. and the brother-in-law were identified because they had the same name, Carl. The dream reported by the wife apparently hurt the patient very much. By the identification that occurred in his own dream, his anxiety was diminished because, ''Sex with a brother does not count, cannot be too pleasant.''

The third possibility mentioned concerns the tendency of the verbalization to become part of the denotation, when the connotation has been lost; that is, the schizophrenic sees the verbal symbol as part of the thing that is symbolized. Cassirer, too, has noted that in primitive thinking there is an essential identity between the word and what the word denotes. The word is not a mere conventional symbol, but it is merged with its object in an indissoluble unity. Thus word magic originates. The word denoting an object acquires the same property of the object and may be substituted for the object when the latter is not available. The name of a god is as powerful as the god himself. Werner and many other authors have reported identical observations.

Piaget (1929) has observed that children, too, experience names as fused in the objects they denote. Piaget asked children not older than 6, ''Where is the name of the sun?'' and he elicited the following responses: ''Inside! Inside the sun!'' or ''High up in the sky!''

The fourth possibility that we have mentioned occurs when words or ideas associate merely because of the phonetic quality of the verbal symbols. These are so-called sound associations. A schizophrenic wrote the following clang associations: ''*C,* see, sea,'' ''*Y,* why, *Y.*'' Another patient wrote: ''Chuck, luck, luck, buck. True, two. Frame! Name! Same! Same! Same! Same!''

At times series of words, associated because of their similar verbalization, retain a general sense of meaning, reminiscent of what I have called primary aggregation (see Arieti, 1967, Chap. 7). For instance, the patient quoted earlier who defined chair as throne, wrote the following ''prayer'' which he used to recite every morning: ''Sweetness angel, gentle, mild, mellow, gladness, glory, grandeur, splendor, bubbling, babbling, gurgling, handy, candy, dandy, honor, honey, sugar, frosting, guide, guiding, enormous, pure, magnificent, enchanted, blooming plumes.''

In addition to words that he felt were applicable to the divinity and to angels (and he thought he was an angel, too), he often selected words because of their assonance or because in addition to a specific meaning they had an assonance. The last case is represented by ''blooming plumes'' that winged angels have. It is evident that the meaning that this prayer had for the patient derived from the phonetic structures of its verbal components. In comparison to usual prayers this one manifested a semantic loss or evasion for the usual reader but acquired a particular one for the patient on account of its many series of assonances. The following list does not include all of them:

1. an*gel, gen*tle
2. *m*ild, *m*ellow
3. *gl*adness, *gl*ory, *gr*andeur
4. gra*nd*eur, sple*nd*or
5. bu*bbl*ing, ba*bbl*ing, gur*gl*ing
6. h*andy,* c*andy,* d*andy*
7. *ho*nor, *ho*ney

Finally we must mention that at times the proper denotation of a word is lost and another one is given that is suggested by the verbalization. For instance, a patient was shown a pen and was asked to say the name of the object shown. He replied, ''A prison.'' The word *pen* elicited in him the idea of *pen*itentiary.

In some rather unusual cases the emphasis on the verbalization compels the patients to express themselves in rhymes or poetry. Some poetic tendencies of some patients will be studied in the following section.

VIII
Very Severe Thought and Language Disorders

In the previous sections we have seen how the schizophrenic adopts a special logical organization in order to reach some conclusions. However, the disturbances in his thought processes may extend beyond the loss of Aristotelian logic and the adoption of paleologic thinking, and the effects may be more pronounced. They involve even the simple, normal associations of ideas, to such an extent that scattering of thoughts, dissociation, and word-salad are commonly observed. In Chapter 2 we have mentioned how much importance Bleuler (1950) attributed to the disorder of associations of ideas. According to him these disturbances range from a maximum, which corresponds to complete confusion, to a minimum, which is hardly noticeable. The disease ''interrupts, quite haphazardly, single threads, sometimes a whole group, and sometimes even large segments of the thousands of associative threads which guide our thinking.'' According to Bleuler, ''The most important determinant of the association is completely lacking—the concept of purpose.'' Bleuler adds:

> . . . Thinking operates with ideas and concepts which have no, or a completely insufficient, connection with the main idea and should therefore be excluded from the thought-process. The result is that thinking becomes confused, bizarre, incorrect, abrupt. Sometimes, all the associative threads fail and the thought chain is totally interrupted; after such ''blocking,'' ideas may emerge which have no recognizable connection with preceding ones.

Bleuler's conceptions were incomplete and preliminary in character. It is regrettable that his lead was not pursued and that the study of associations of ideas in the schizophrenic has been neglected. This neglect is largely a reflection of prevailing trends in psychiatry and psychology. Psychiatric studies that deal *exclusively* with environmental factors cannot consider the severe formal disorders of thinking and language, such as those described in this section. In the field of psychology an excessive fear of so-called mental atomism has prevailed for many decades and has made many psychologists disregard this important aspect of mental life.* It is true that the problem is still obscure; and that maybe even the phrase ''association of ideas'' is wrong. When we say that ideas associate, we refer only to the last stages of a very complicated microgenetic process. Not only do we not know the neuronal mechanisms involved, but we do not know even the different psychological steps that lead to the associations. The state of our ignorance is disturbing, but it is not a justification for ignoring the phenomenon. The phenomenon of association cannot be denied. It is one of the most important, perhaps the most important, of psychic life.

A two-minute observation can convince anyone that ideas do associate. I see my old grammar school and think of my childhood; I hear somebody mention the name of Beethoven, and I think of an acquaintance of mine who is a musician. I study my own thoughts or those of my friends, and I see that ideas do not occur at random, but that there is always a connection between them, no matter how petty and trivial this connection may be. It is because such power of association is so important and so general that we are so impressed and baffled by the schizophrenic, who seems to have lost it partially or totally.

Before we study the phenomenon in schizophrenia, let us examine very briefly how ideas associate in normal individuals.

When a person thinks logically, he organizes his thoughts according to a pattern or structure that leads toward an end or conclusion. If, however, he relaxes and lets his thoughts come up spontaneously, without exerting any selection or direction, ideas that seem to acquire consciousness for their own sake and not for any distant purpose will come to him. Conversation in casual social gatherings often consists of thoughts occurring in this way. If we study these thoughts, we see that even they follow one another according to certain rules. They do not come at random, but they are determined rationally. We do not find irrationality, but

* There are, of course, exceptions; for instance, Robinson (1932).

psychological determinism. One idea is determined or caused by the occurrence of a previous one. Idea *B*, which follows idea *A*, is associated in some way with *A*. It is because of this association that *B* may occur, and not because of chance. Even at this simple level thinking follows some kind of organization.

What are the ways by which ideas associate? Although some authors have described or subdivided more types, ideas are generally considered as associating in two ways: by contiguity and by similarity.*

The *law of contiguity* states that when two mental processes have been active together or in immediate succession, one of them on recurring tends to elicit the recurrence of the other. For instance, if I think of a rose, I may think of its color or odor, or of the garden where I saw it; if I think of New York, I may think of the Empire State Building or of the Hudson River; if I think of fire, I may think of smoke, or of the danger of being burned, and so on.

The *law of similarity* states that if two mental representations resemble each other, that is, if they have one or more characteristics in common, the occurrence of one of them tends also to elicit the occurrence of the other. For instance, when I think of the Empire State Building, I may think also of the Eiffel Tower, because they are both high constructions; when I think of Beethoven, I may also think of Mozart, because they are both composers.

The *associative link,* that is, the element that makes two ideas associate, is either the fact that they originally occurred in the same place or at the same time or in succession or the fact that they have a quality in common. Using our own terminology, we may state that two ideas associate by contiguity if they have a common predicate of contiguity. Two ideas associate by the law of similarity if the associational link is a predicate of quality.

In normal people there are also differences in the way ideas associate. As James described in his *Principles of Psychology* (1950), the association by similarity is the higher form of association and is generally found in larger percentage in gifted individuals. The association by contiguity is found in everybody, but occurs more often in nongifted individuals than in gifted ones.

In schizophrenia, we find a gamut of disturbances in association of ideas. Contrary to what Bleuler wrote, the first disturbances consist of the more frequent occurrence of ideas connected only by the laws of association. In some nonsevere conditions we find that schizophrenics talk without logical direction; their thoughts are connected, one with the other, by the simple laws of association. The disturbance may be minimal and hardly noticeable; at other times the patient seems to wander in various directions. The ideas, however, are still connected, but the lack of logical continuity reveals the extent of the mental disintegration, such as in the following passage from a letter of Margaret, a schizophrenic patient:

Dear Dr. Arieti,

It Is Because I Am So Passionate That They Brought Me Here.

Doctor Webster Asked Me Why I Was Brought Here And I Couldn't Answer Without A Certain Hesitation, But Now I Know, I Know Now:

* Law of contrast is often added.

I'm Too Passionate!
That's Why I Can't Get A Job.
You Had The Wrong Diagnosis
Take This For Instance:
Look Up The Word Passions In The Encyclopedia (A Masterpiece Of A Word) And In The Dictionaries. Don't Get Cerebral Meningitis In Your Studies
But You Will Find That There Is A Difference Between The Passions of Jesus of Bethlehem And The Passions Of Blue Beard
Between The Passion Of Misplaced Sympathies And The Passions Of Suicidal Thoughts.
Are You Passionately In Sympathy With Your Great Poet Dante, Doctor Arieti?
And I Am In Passionate Admiration Of The Works of Molière, The French Troubadour.
And There Is The Passion Flower
And The Passion Plays of Oberammergau.

The patient wants to convey the idea that she was hospitalized because she was too passionate. She is not mentally sick. A wrong diagnosis was made. Soon, however, Margaret becomes involved with the meanings of the word *passion* and loses the main point. We see here that the laws of association are respected, but that there is no logical or directed thinking, and therefore no apparent purpose. This disturbance resembles the flight of ideas that we find in the manic patients. The resemblance, however, is only superficial. In the manic, the push to talk is so strong that he has no time to think and cannot adopt logical rules. In the schizophrenic, the lack of logic is not due to this pressure, but to a withdrawal from logic. In addition, in the flight of ideas of the manic, stimuli that elicit associations come from the outside environment much more frequently than they do in the schizophrenic. An object, color, or event in the immediate environment may lead to numerous associations.

In all schizophrenic writings or verbal productions we must not stop with examining the lack of logical continuity and the specific formal characteristics. Whenever possible we must examine also the content, the schizophrenic's conscious or unconscious attempt to convey a meaning in spite of his difficulties, and the distortions in the meaning. As we shall see again in Part Nine, this type of examination will be very useful in psychotherapy, even in regressed patients.

Now if we reexamine Margaret's letter, we find that it had a meaning. The patient wanted to assert once again that she was not mentally ill; the wrong diagnosis was made. At the time Margaret wrote this letter, she was in a state of fairly advanced regression. She had been hospitalized for a few years and gave the impression of being apathetic or at least shallow emotionally. She did not appear so in her writings, which had a strong emotional impact. Her trouble, she states vehemently, is not mental illness but being "too passionate." In her letter she soon deflects the direction of her thinking and focuses on the meaning of "passionate," so difficult a word that the study of it may harm one's nervous system (she warns: Don't develop cerebral meningitis over the study of this word). In common everyday language the words *passion* and *passionate* refer to strong sexual desire; and inability to control such desire could be considered the origin of the patient's trouble. But the patient transcended this meaning: sex was extended to the whole realm of passions, that is, of strong emotions. The word *passion* itself becomes "a masterpiece." The patient lists the sublime passion of Jesus Christ as well as the criminal one of Blue Beard; the pain that comes from having put affections in the wrong place and that which comes from suicidal thoughts; the emotion from the experience of poetry and art.

Thus a second examination of this letter shows that this patient is aware of many things, although in an unclear or peripheral form of consciousness. The extent of her feelings and the gamut of her intellect, as well as the results of experiences before and during the illness (misplaced sympathies, suicidal thoughts) come through in spite of the mental disintegration. The meaning is conveyed not by logical progression of thought, but by the totality of the thoughts. No matter how disconnected, the letter conveys a tone, an atmosphere, "a sphere of meaning" similar to what we find in primary aggregations (to be discussed later in this section).

When the schizophrenic process advances, ideas still tend to associate by similarity, but by a similarity that is connected with the verbalization, rather than with the connotation. In other words, the *associational link is a predicate of verbal quality*. Two things or ideas are associated because they have the same phonetic or written symbols.

The patients quite often seem to forget the meanings of the word, and concentrate exclusively on the verbalization. They have a predilection for phonetic similarity. Many of them devote time to writing prose or poems that appear very odd. No purposeful thought is recognizable, except occasionally. Ideas follow one another by the laws of association, or for the purpose of maintaining rhythm (verbal similarity). Stereotyped expressions associate easily, because repetition or identity is the highest degree of similarity.

The following poem was written by a hebephrenic woman. She had pleasant delusions: for instance, she believed that she was growing feathers and becoming a bird, "because" she wanted to fly away from the hospital. She wrote me this poem when she heard that I was transferred to another division of the hospital:

Dear Dr. Arieti,

Brilliant to the sky,
Why you are far away
The spirit comes so nigh
While you are far away
Ah woe to the sad tiding
That you are not residing
Under the same roof
As our friends of the ebony hoof
Would take you out in flight
And drive you quite aloof
And would carry you in spite

Of the fact that you are so light
  In your tender golden head
  Like a hollow round your head
I'd send you a dozen horses
Nay a gross
  Only to keep you awhile
  As extended as the Nile
    Happy in your bile
Only you are far away
And the mares are gray.

With the increase in occurrence of paleologic thought, there is a decrease in the number of associations by similarity, a process that occurs because the patient develops an increasing tendency to identify rather than to abstract. For instance, the normal person is able to place in one category, Hannibal, Julius Caesar, and Napoleon because he may abstract from each of these three subjects the quality of their being great military men (Arieti, 1950*a*). A person who thinks paleologically would be unable to abstract this quality from the whole of the subjects and would tend instead to identify Hannibal with Julius Caesar or with Napoleon, in agreement with the principle of Von Domarus. *Association by similarity has been replaced by identification by similarity.* If we remember what we have discussed in the second section of this chapter we may conclude that the formation of primary classes (that is, the tendency to identify objects that have a predicate in common) prevents or impairs *association* by similarity. But association by similarity, which requires ability to abstract, is an absolute prerequisite for Aristotelian logic. The paleologician gradually loses the general ability to associate by similarity although he still retains the ability to associate by similarity of verbalization and by the law of contiguity.

Whereas in the early stages of the disorder the use of primary classes was limited to the complexes of the patient, in more advanced stages it expands to larger areas of thinking. For instance, if you ask a patient, "What is the capital of France?" he may reply, "London." London and Paris are identified because they are both capitals. To the question, "Where are you?" the patient may answer, "In a church." Churches and hospitals are identified because of many characteristics in common, such as being buildings for many people, or places where people are helped, and so on. These examples show that the patient is still able to organize up to the rank of categories, but these categories have not yet fully reached the rank of being secondary classes; their members are equivalent as London is with Paris. If some patients are asked the date of their birth, they give a wrong date, but a date whose first two numbers are the same as those of the actual date. For example, a patient born in 1911 gave the date of birth as 1923, a patient born in 1917 gave the date of birth as 1988. Of course, even in these simple cases, the dynamic desire to deny reality or to make no contact with the examiner should not be overlooked. However, in these instances, too, we should not consider only the motivation, but also the psychotic ways by which the motivation is carried out.

When the schizophrenic process becomes even more advanced, a further complication occurs. Not only ideas that might associate by similarity, but also ideas that associate by contiguity are no longer just associated, but paleologically identified. One idea or thing may be substituted for another that occurred at the same time or place or was learned at the same time or place or that belongs to the same context.

For instance, a very regressed hebephrenic patient was asked the following question: "Who was the first president of the United States?" She replied, "White House." Although George Washington actually did not even live in the White House, White House had for her the same significance as George Washington. The idea of president of the United States was in her mind associated with White House. Each element of this context (anything usually associated with presidents of the United States) had the same value as any other elements and might have replaced any other element of the same context. At her level of regression, one part of a context cannot be separated or abstracted or distinguished any more from any other part of the same context or background. To associate George Washington with White House is a normal mental process that may occur to anyone, let us say, during a word association test. The anomaly here is not that the two subjects, George Washington and White House, are associated, but that they are identified and substituted for one another.

Cameron (1938) has studied the same phenomenon, which he calls "metonymic distortion," pointing out the fact that the distortion consists of the use of an approximate but related term for the more precise definite term that normal adults would use. For instance, one of his patients said that he had "menu" three times a day instead of meals. Cameron describes this phenomenon very well when he writes that "the schizophrenic attributes a false equivalence to several terms or phrases which in the normal person might belong to the fringe of his conceptual structures." The patient strikes "not at the bull's eye" but at the periphery of the target. Cameron's formulations are important but tend to remain descriptive because they do not imply that the underlying process is the tendency toward progressive identification.

Another phenomenon that Cameron (1938, 1939, 1947) has studied in advanced schizophrenia is what he calls "asyndetic thinking." At the level of language behavior this disorder manifests itself as a juxtaposition of elements, without adequate linkage between them. It should be mentioned here that such juxtapositions are identical with those that Freud has described in his study of dreams. In my opinion there is not only a juxtaposition of elements but also a juxtaposition of meanings. Certain sentences are as confusing as photographic films that have been exposed several times. The superimposed images and meanings, however, have some connection in the mind of the patient. Often the word that, as we have mentioned, is representative of an enlarged context is taken to represent another context of which it is also a part, and the two contexts become superimposed. Schizophrenic thought often bristles with different planes of meaning and is, as I call it, *multifocal,* because it has to focus at the same time on different meanings with their different objective situations.

Werner (1957) wrote that whenever development occurs, it proceeds from a state of relative globality and lack of differentiation to a state of increasing differentiation, articulation, and hierarchic integration. In schizophrenia there is a return to the primitive stages where differentiation is still rudimentary. At the stages that we are discussing, disparate elements agglomerate to form "primary aggregations." Although primary aggregations do not have a definite holistic organization, we can find in them a loose, general, or what Werner called "spheric" meaning.

In the example given earlier concerning the patient who said "White House" instead of "George Washington," when asked, "who was the first president of the United States," the primary aggregation had to do with the presidency of the United States. Many primary aggregations, however, have a much more primitive organization. They seem like strange agglomerations of disparate things put together as in a collage. At other times they may be recognized as embryonic structures from which logical concepts eventually emerge. In some cases they may even embrace a field that at higher levels of cognition corresponds to highly abstract ideation.

How a primary aggregation is formed is difficult to say. Often the grouping of the elements is naturalistic, reproducing the contiguity found in the external world or the chronological continuity of some experiences. For the occurrence of these phenomena in primitive cultures see Werner (1957); in other instances see Arieti (1967, Chap. 7). As mentioned, an important characteristic of the primary aggregation (at least of its most primitive forms) is that any element of it becomes equivalent to another element or may replace the whole.

When we consider all the phenomena described in this section, we are no longer surprised that the language of regressed schizophrenics becomes so obscure. When one thing is substituted for another thing that it resembles or that is a different part of the same context or background, the result is incomprehensible. These tendencies to identify segments or fragments, which are usually only associated in large contexts, explain the so-called word-salad that has so far remained incomprehensible. I repeat here that what I call "identification" of segments or fragments actually may not be identification or effort to identify so much as it may be the result of an inability to separate or dissociate a part or to distinguish any of the parts of a whole. For practical purposes, or from the point of view of the observer, there is an identification of all the parts of the whole with one another or with the whole. In some cases this tendency progresses toward identification so rapidly that a word may come to replace or represent bigger and bigger contexts, so that finally the language of the patient is impoverished to the point of being reduced to relatively few words or stereotyped expressions. As Sullivan wrote, in the stereotypy there is "an impractical concentration of meaning in the expression" (1953*a*). The same stereotypies mean many things, just as the crying of a baby does. In word-salad this impoverishment has not reached the point of reducing the language to a few words, but the elements of the sentences, being replaced for others in a unique selection, make up sequences of words that a listener cannot understand or can understand only with great difficulty. It is debatable whether the patient himself understands what he is saying. This point will be examined when we shall discuss the therapeutic situation (Chapter 36). In some other cases, however, even when the most pronounced forms of stereotypy and impoverished language are found, it is possible to trace some diffuse, global, or spheric meaning. Let us take as an example the following writing of a very regressed schizophrenic:

Do I see cake Do I do the reverse of acting
Yes Do I feel sensually deceived
thoughts in mental suggestion in increase of
senses in suggestion
senses deceptive
in in deception deception deception
deception
vanilla lemon as lemon vanilla as the beginning
of in in suggestion suggestion suggestion
suggestion of the suggestions as the
beginning of in suggestion
lemon vanilla as susceptibility of the
reason as lemon as in in suggestion
suggestion suggestion suggestion of
the suggestions
insuggestion
iv
DoIseeIdo in sugget

This is a typical example of word-salad and sterotypies. The first impression we get upon reading it is that it is utter nonsense. We are also impressed by the repetition of some words. Let us try, at least, to grasp the spheric meaning. The patient is preoccupied with a phenomenon that he cannot understand: are his senses reliable, or does he undergo mental suggestion? The world he is experiencing is chaotic, fragmentary, uncertain. Almost all the things he observes lead him to two alternative conclusions or symbols that have become prominent to the point of embracing everything else: sense deception or mental suggestion. In other words, is he the victim of his own senses, which deceive him, or is he undergoing mental suggestion, coming either from himself or from the external world? Almost everything comes to be perceived in terms of these two stereotyped concepts: deception and suggestion. He undergoes strange phenomena. "Do I do the reverse of acting?" That is, "Do I do the opposite of what I would like to do?" However, a few things remain like islands of reality and are not yet submerged by the invading ocean of deception and suggestibility. "Do I see cake?" he asks himself; that is, something tangible, concrete. And later he sees lemon and vanilla, colorful and pleasant objects that stand out in the sea of confusion expressed by abstract words. Mental suggestion seems to win out over sense deception. The patient seems to recognize that the trouble is suggestion; and as a matter of fact, the repetition of the word suggestion has a suggestive quality.

The disorders that we have examined in this chapter do not cover the whole gamut of schizophrenic language and thinking disorders. Other important characteristics will be studied in Chapters 19 and 23.

The previously mentioned neologisms, which are due to composition of different verbal symbols, at times reach extremely bizarre representations in advanced cases. Vetter recently (1968) reviewed the literature on neologisms. One of the most interesting studies made in the United States on schizophrenic neologism is the one by Forrest (1969). He described the case of a 43-year-old ''schizophrenic savant'' who, except for the three and a half years from age 39 to 42, had spent his entire life in institutions. The patient submitted a list of ninety newly coined words, with their definitions. Here are some examples:

1. Spec'tro-tav'to-ro-ta'tion: Circling in every way, as with checkers or a bat in baseball.

2. Tav'to-tac-ta'tion: A touching that repeats. Getting communication, talking with somebody. Touching with hands is sometimes pleasant when somebody loves me.

3. Su'-per-skel'e-ton'i-za'tion: Being higher than the span of the George Washington Bridge (coined when a patient was first allowed on the tenth floor of the N.Y. State Psychiatric Institute from which the bridge can be seen).

The average length of the patient's coinages was seventeen letters, almost double the nine-letter average of entries in Webster's New Collegiate Dictionary. The patient's longest word consisted of fifty letters: semicentiosteophotoseismophysiopleopolycomputation.

IX

Hallucinations and Related Phenomena

Hallucinations represent a common and important characteristic of schizophrenia. Although they indicate that the disorder is very active and already able to inflict profound alterations, they do not necessarily imply a bad prognosis. On the contrary, when they are present from the very beginning, they suggest that the psychosis is likely to have an acute and reversible course. Hallucinations, however, occur in the majority of patients in all stages of the illness. Many theories have been advanced to explain this complex phenomenon. A book that may be considered a classic and that reviews all the old theories is Mourgue's *Neurobiologie de l'hallucination* (1932). More recent studies on the subject are reported by West (1962*a*). In this section hallucinations will be examined predominantly from the general point of schizophrenic cognition presented in this book.

Hallucination is an apparent perception of an external object when no such object is present. The stimulus that elicits the seeming perception is an internal one; that is, it comes from within the individual himself. Inasmuch as what is perceived in the hallucinatory experience purports to portray or mirror an aspect of external reality, the perception is false.*

Hallucinations as Personal Experience

There are many modalities by which hallucinations are experienced. However, in the typical case we may distinguish three phases. The first consists of the very first time the patient experiences a hallucination. In some cases he may give little importance to the phenomenon, but in others he undergoes a sudden, profound, and shaking experience. He hears a powerful voice, or sound, with a message directed to him, only for him, a message which is related to his whole psychological being. In several cases it is the response of the patient to this first experience that determines the course of the illness. Although badly affected and frightened, the patient may say to himself, "What I perceive is not true; it is only my imagination." If he is able to respond in that way, he still has the power to resist schizophrenia. Unfortunately, in the majority of cases the patient, because of antecedent psychological conditions, is more indignant than frightened, and more in a receptive mood than a refractory one. Instead of thinking, "This is not a real voice," he says to himself, "The voice is real, but what it says is false." In quite a few cases the patient makes a complete psychological readjustment. "What does it mean that I hear this voice? Why do they say these things about me?" He concludes, "I am accused. I am persecuted. They talk behind my back in a disparaging, insulting manner."

After this early experience the patient proceeds to a second phase, during which he expects to have hallucinations, and indeed he has them. This second stage will be further explored in Chapter 37, where we shall discuss the therapy of hallucinations.

In the third phase, hallucinations have become such a familiar phenomenon and their occurrence so frequent that the patient accepts them as an important part of his life.

Psychological Content

The psychophysiologic mechanism that mediates schizophrenic hallucinations cannot be considered independently from their content. Although the content will

*Because several authors define hallucination as a sensation, it may be useful to define some terms whose meaning is generally assumed as known. By *sensation* is meant the effect of a stimulus when it acts upon one of our sense organs. Sensation is the first effect of the stimulus. It does not imply any recognition of the stimulus, that is, any association with past experiences.

By *perception* is meant recognition and understanding of the sensation. For instance, when I see a book, not only do I see it, but I also know that I see it and know it is a book.

By *image* is meant an inner reproduction of sensations and perceptions, even when the stimuli that produce the latter are absent (see Chapter 5). The concept of image should not be confused with the concept of *engram* or *template*. With the latter terms many neurologists designate a neuronal pattern of complex movement or of an acquired skilled act.

be reexamined later, it must be considered briefly at this point. For instance, to repeat examples already given in this book, a patient sees himself as a rotten person, and he develops the olfactory hallucination that a bad odor emanates from his body. Another patient felt that his wife was making his life miserable. He develops a gustatory hallucination: every time he eats food prepared by his wife, he experiences a peculiar taste in his mouth, probably "because of the poison she put in the food."

It is obvious from these examples that concepts that have to do with the patient's complexes become transformed into perceptions: the rotten personality becomes the rotten body that smells; the way the wife treats the patient becomes poison. As some of the conflictful thoughts of people become transformed into visual perceptions in dreams, so some of the conflicts of the patient become transformed into perceptions, predominantly auditory ones. In other words, the concept is not sustained any longer as a concept; it has acquired a lower form. However, as we have already mentioned, the phenomenon cannot be interpreted as just a return to a concrete level. In fact the mentioned patient is still able to conceive the abstract idea—feeling that he is a rotten person; but such an emotionally loaded concept cannot be sustained at its proper level and is immediately and actively translated into a concrete form. What seems symbolic to the psychiatrist is actually a concretization.

Viewing this mechanism as a process of active concretization (see Chapter 15) is a fruitful approach but does not provide a complete understanding of the problem unless we clarify how this concretization takes place. The mechanism requires a profound alteration: the adoption of a form of primary process cognition. Let us consider again the patient who felt at first that his wife was poisoning his life and who later experienced the delusion that the wife poisoned his food. If we examine this concretization, we realize that the concrete form is not a random occurrence but is related to the abstract form. The two concepts (poisoning of life and poisoning of food) are members of a secondary process (logical) class whose concept is "causing the destruction or warping of the patient's life." The patient, however, tends either to eliminate the concept of the secondary class or to transform the secondary class into a primary class, so that the poisoning of life becomes equivalent to the poisoning of food (see the third section of this chapter). The abstract is eliminated and the more concrete member of the class emerges.

Thus, again, although the patient is able to conceive the abstract and to make a connection between the abstract and concrete elements that together form a secondary class, the secondary class is transformed into a primary one and remains represented by a concrete member. In other words, the first few stages of this process of concretization still require abstract conceptualization.

The Perceptualization of the Concept

The phenomenon of perceptualization of the concept consists of two aspects: the regressive and the psychodynamic (or restitutional). The regressive implies the transformation of a mental representation into a lower one. The psychodynamic reduces the conflict to a percept or to a specific thing; thus the anxiety of the patient is restricted to a smaller and less disturbing area of ideation.*

We must now examine more closely the problem of the perceptualization of the concept.

Hallucinations consist of a process that is at a higher level than the perception. The stimulus that elicits them is an internal mental process. This mental process, by engendering the hallucination, is regressing to the lower level of the perception. Many writers have for a long time debated and continue to debate the question of whether hallucinations are images that have acquired a special intensity and strength, or whether they are perceptions. Many people believe that they are merely intense images. However, the closer one examines patients, the more one becomes convinced that they actually experience perceptions. Patients do not think that they "hear voices," but they actually hear them, just as the dreamer does not think that he sees things, but actually sees them, although not through his eyes. The hallucinating person does not distinguish real voices from hallucinations.

In the light of our general interpretation of the schizophrenic process, it is not difficult to understand hallucinations. They were originally thoughts or images that have changed into perceptions. The level of perception is phylogenetically and ontogenetically lower than the levels of verbal thought, and lower even than the level of images. Images, stored in our memory, may be used by hallucinations, but they are reproduced with the modalities of perception.

As our thoughts at times descend from the Aristotelian to the paleologic level, and within the paleologic level to more or less primitive sublevels, so they may descend further to the level of images and even to the level of perceptions. Hypnagogic hallucinations, which are phenomena occurring to some people as they are falling asleep, are often recognized as images, that is, they are between the level of images and that of perceptions. It seems useless, therefore, to continue to argue as to whether hallucinations are intensified images or perceptions. They are mental processes, usually occurring at higher levels of integration, which use some of the mechanisms of perceptions, although they do not originate from the peripheral sense organs.

* The perceptualization of the concept is a relatively well known phenomenon in psychopathology. Since Lelut (1846) wrote that "the hallucination is the transformation of a thought into a sensation," this phenomenon has been described in many ways, but a complete interpretation is still lacking. Silberer (1909, 1912), influenced by Freud, reported a method of eliciting certain symbolic hallucinatory phenomena. Once, while he was lying on a couch, he was thinking of a very difficult abstract subject when an image automatically occurred to him that was a concrete symbol of what he was thinking. After this experience, Silberer learned to elicit voluntarily these quasi-hallucinations, which he reported in detail. Here is an example given by him: he is thinking about something but, pursuing a secondary consideration, he departs from the original theme. A hallucination occurs: he is mountain climbing. The mountains near him conceal the farther ones from which he came and to which he wants to return. Silberer called these phenomena autosymbolic. They were not real hallucinations because Silberer knew that they did not represent phenomena of external reality. They were abstract constructs that manifested themselves in concrete forms.

When we study the terminal stage of schizophrenia, we shall see that the disintegrating process goes beyond the perceptual levels and regresses even to the stage of sensation (Chapter 24).

Images and hallucinations are elaborations of stored sensorial and perceptual material. Therefore, there cannot be images without present or past perceptions. For instance, if the dreamer thinks about himself, he sees himself in the dream as a concrete image or physical entity, not as an abstract concept symbolized by the pronoun "I." However, because for anatomical reasons nobody can see his own face, the dreamer cannot recall the visual image of his face. This explains why the dreamer sees himself in the dream, but not his face. In dreams and hallucinations, the individual may perceive things that actually do not exist; in these cases, the images are made up, in a creative way, with elements that were actually perceived from the external world.

People who are deaf-mute from birth cannot experience auditory hallucinations. I have treated a schizophrenic deaf-mute who pretended that she was hearing people talking about her. Actually, by "hearing" she meant that she had the impression people were talking about her, as she inferred from the movements of their lips and from their general attitude. This patient was able to read and write; and her writing presented disconnected thoughts and the other verbal characteristics found in schizophrenics who are not deaf-mutes.

I have had no experience with schizophrenics who are congenitally blind, but I am inclined to believe that they cannot experience visual hallucinations. Gutheil (1951) wrote that blind people whose defect is congenital or acquired at an early age, dream with images derived from tactile and kinesthetic sensations. Kimmins (1937) wrote that children who have become blind before the age of 5 do not see in dreams, but that children who become blind after the age of 7 do "see" in their dreams.

The following question about both dreams and hallucinations may occur to the reader. If dreams and hallucinations are translations or regressions of thoughts to a perceptual level, how is it that in dreams and hallucinations the person not only hears and sees, but talks and thinks? This is due to the fact that there is no complete regression to the perceptual level. The concomitant occurrence of phenomena that belong to different mental levels is one of the most common characteristics of human psychopathology. Especially in schizophrenia, it produces a very bizarre clinical picture. In many cases, one may find symptoms belonging predominantly to one level, but a mixture always occurs. Thus a patient, for instance, may usually adopt the Aristotelian type of logic when he talks, but at times he may hallucinate and therefore regress to a perceptual level. The voices he hears use a paleologic mode of thinking. This mixture, this splitting of the person at various levels, is the most specific characteristic of schizophrenia and fully justifies its name.

The perceptualization of the concept is the most specific characteristic of hallucinations. Before this stage of complete perceptualization is reached, intermediate stages may be experienced. I have already mentioned hypnagogic hallucinations. Other intermediate stages occur frequently. For instance, an Italian patient who had two acute psychotic episodes, with delusions and hallucinations predominantly religious in content, experienced the following phenomena. Between the two psychotic episodes, when he was able to live outside the hospital and to attend to his work as a barber, he was hearing a voice inside himself expressing his thoughts. Every normal person can hear his own thoughts, because thoughts are generally expressed internally by auditory verbal images, but it was obvious from the description given by the patient that the perceptual quality of his thoughts was increased. He himself recognized that the voice was his own; as a matter of fact, he knew that the voice was expressing his own thoughts in Italian, whereas the clients and other people around him were talking English. This phenomenon is very common in schizophrenics. Often the perceptual quality of the patient's thoughts is so pronounced that he is afraid that people around him will hear them. Because he has no control over the content of his thoughts, and they can be heard, he feels embarrassed. When the process is more advanced, he still recognizes that the thoughts are his own, but on account of their perceptual character he feels that people are repeating them verbally. He has the impression that it is he who thinks, but that people around him pronounce the thoughts. They "steal" his ideas. These phenomena are generally called *écho de la pensée*. When the process advances further, the patient does not recognize his thoughts as his own and projects them completely to other people.

Another important question, which brings us back to a comparison with dreams, must be asked. Why are hallucinations predominantly auditory perceptualizations and not visual ones as in dreams? We may advance only hypotheses on this interesting problem. The sense of vision originates very early in the phyletic scale. Even protozoans possess a rudimentary organ of vision (the eyespot in the flagellate euglena). In fishes, the sense of vision already is very similar to that of men. This cannot be said for the sense of hearing. One has to go as high as the class of birds on the evolutionary scale to find an organ similar to the human cochlea.

In dreams, when the most rest is desired, it is natural that only the more primitive sensory phenomena should occupy the major role. The tactile and olfactory senses are more primitive than the visual, but they do not play such an important role in human symbolism. Of the important human senses, the visual and the auditory, the visual is the more primitive. Auditory images probably require more elaboration, which is not compatible with the state of sleep.

Another important fact may be that when the individual sleeps, all external visual perceptions are eliminated, and the centers that elaborate them are free for other activities. When the patient is awake and hallucinates, the visual centers are occupied by external perceptions. True, one may say that the auditory centers, too, are occupied by auditory external perceptions, but not in such a dominant manner. We know, for instance, that when an electroencephalogram is taken, the patient is asked to close his eyes because visual perceptions are very disturbing. Noises do not produce so much disturbance.

Auditory perceptions are less primitive than the visual and are more apt to become used first when thought processes regress to a perceptual level. In addition, one's thoughts are generally experienced as an inner language, as a conversation with one's self, consisting of verbal auditory images.*

In trying to explain the psychophysiological mechanism that is responsible for the hallucinatory phenomenon, many authors have found inspiration in the works on sensory deprivation that have followed the pioneer experiments done at McGill (Heron, Bexton, and Hebb, 1953; Bexton, Heron, and Scott, 1954; Heron, Doane, and Scott, 1956) and by Lilly (1956). These researchers have found that when the human subject is put into a state of sensory isolation, at first a hunger for stimulation is experienced, then indulgence in reveries occurs, finally the reveries assume a perceptual quality and become hallucinations, predominantly or exclusively of the visual type.

Although Heron, Bexton, and Hebb deserve the credit of having been the first to report hallucinatory phenomena produced with experimental sensory deprivation, similar phenomena have been reported by people who underwent sensory deprivation caused by unusual circumstances, for instance, by polar explorers (Courtald, 1932; Byrd, 1938; Ritter, 1954), by solitary sailors (Slocum, 1901), and by people in forced confinement (Burney, 1952).

Some observations reported by Hebb (1954) indicate that some of the mechanisms operating in schizophrenic cognition occur also in the visual hallucinations of those undergoing sensory deprivation. Hebb reports that one subject during an experiment tried "to see" some objects suggested by the experimenter, but he succeeded only approximately. For instance, "one subject, trying to visualize a pen, saw an inkblot; or, trying to visualize a shoe, saw a ski boot." In other words, things were substituted for others or identified with others with which they had a resemblance or similarity: objects were made equivalents to other members of the same categorical class, or equivalent to others with which they had spatial or temporal contiguity (see the third section of this chapter).

West (1962*b*) has been responsible for many of the findings on the subject of sensory deprivation and has advanced his own theory of hallucinations and dreams. According to him effective sensory input ordinarily serves to inhibit the emergence into consciousness of previously recorded percepts. If effective sensory input is impaired, recorded perceptual traces are released and emerge. According to West, effective sensory input may be impaired in three ways: (1) absolute decrease or depatterning; (2) input overload, or "jamming the circuits"; (3) de-

* Some authors (Seitz and Mohlholm, 1947) feel that auditory hallucinations are more frequent in people who have a predominantly visual form of imagery. The tests used to determine whether subjects have a predominantly visual or auditory imagery are not to be trusted entirely, because they ignore the verbal representations that accompany the images, even visual ones. For instance, if the patient responds to the stimulus "ringing of the telephone" by saying, "I can imagine seeing it, but I can't hear it ring," he has a response using a visual image, but at the same time internally he hears his thoughts, expressed by verbal auditory images, stating that he sees the phone. Auditory verbal images are, therefore, almost always present, even when they are accompanied by visual images. Because of the tremendous importance that language plays in human thinking, auditory images are almost always used in mental processes, even when visual images occupy the predominant role.

creased psychological contact with the environment through the exercise of mental mechanisms (dissociation).

West believes that if at the same time that the input is decreased, there is sufficient internal arousal of the brain (through the reticular formation of the brain stem) to permit vivid awareness, the released perceptions may be dynamically organized and reexperienced as fantasies, dreams, or hallucinations. In my opinion, the theory advanced by West and other authors who see similarities between hallucinations and phenomena occurring during sensory deprivation explains a facilitating mechanism that occurs in many situations. We have already mentioned that in the state of sleep we have a physiological sensory deprivation. The occipital cortex is not bombarded by external stimili. In schizophrenia, too, we have some kind of psychological isolation. Stimuli from the external world reach the patient, but he is much less aware of them. They do not affect him very much, receive a superficial registration, and are not elaborated in higher mental constructs.

It is questionable whether the schizophrenic is confronted by an "input overload," even in acute cases of the psychosis. In many cases, an overload is only apparent. For psychodynamic reasons the stimuli become so powerful and so disturbing as to appear not only qualitatively, but also quantitatively, overpowering.

I must repeat that I find it difficult in schizophrenics to consider hallucinations independently from their content. The schizophrenic process tends to give a concrete or close-to-perception form to the disturbing conflict. Hallucination is one of these forms. If there are conditions that make the occurrence of hallucinations easier, the phenomenon will be more likely to occur. It is not enough to say, as West does, that the perceptual traces become dynamically organized. This dynamic organization is an integral and necessary part of the process itself. As we shall see in Chapter 37, during psychotherapy we discover that the content of the hallucination almost always, perhaps always, represents or refers to a crucial part of the patient's personal predicament.

At the end of the nineteenth century and beginning of the twentieth, theoreticians were very much influenced by the then emerging studies on cerebral localization and advanced relatively simple hypotheses about hallucinations. A review of these theories goes beyond the scope of this chapter. I shall limit myself to a brief retrospective look at Tanzi's theory (1909), which is representative of the theories popular in Europe and the United States during the first two decades of this century. Tanzi thought that the hallucination is an idea that comes possibly from the centers where memories are stored and, by a route that is the reverse of what normally occurs, goes back to the perceptual centers, and becomes a hallucination. The retrograde regression is an anatomical, or if we want, a neurophysiological interpretation of the phenomenon of regression or of the perceptualization of the concept. Today, of course, we cannot interpret regression with these simple retrograde neurophysiological mechanisms, and yet Tanzi's theory may one day be proved to contain grains of truth. It could be that in pathological conditions, when the highest centers cannot function either because of organic or psychogenic conditions, a reintegration of the whole nervous system occurs, so that some lower centers take over some of the functions of the higher centers.*

Our troubles are not over with this hypothesis, because we have to individualize which and where are the "lower centers" that allegedly would take over the functions of the higher centers. A quick assumption would be to think that they are what Orton (1929) called the arrival platforms, that is, the borders of the calcarine fissure, Heschl convolutions, and the postcerebral gyrus (with other contiguous small areas of the parietal cortex and small portions of the precentral gyrus). But we know, for instance, from cases of brain tumors that hallucinations do occur even when these arrival platforms are diseased or entirely removed. They must be mediated at higher levels, for instance, those represented in the occipital lobe by area 18 or 19, in the temporal lobe by area 42, or perhaps in large parts of the temporal lobes where, according to Penfield (1952) and others, images are stored. I do not imply that the hallucinatory phenomenon would be mediated exclusively in the areas where images are stored. Higher levels are needed, too, to conceive the concept and in many cases to formulate it in a verbal form; but such high levels do not sustain the processes that are soon channeled or directed in these centers where images are stored or reproduced. Alas! This explanation is not entirely satisfactory either, because we know that hallucinations are not images, but they have the subjective characteristics of actual perceptions.

Projection to the External World

We come now to another important characteristic of hallucinations: projection to the external world. This quality is present in dreams also. In fact, the dreamer believes that the dream actually takes place outside himself. We have seen that in those phenomena that precede hallucinations, projection at times does not occur. For instance, patients may hear their own thoughts in almost a perceptual form, and yet they recognize that what they hear are their thoughts. Generally, however, typical hallucinations are projected to the external world.

The phenomenon of projection may also be interpreted in two ways, the dynamic and the formal. Dynamically the individual projects, or experiences as not belonging to his own self, everything that is painful or that may cause anxiety, and that originated from others. He wants to put distance between himself and the phenomenon that is experienced as unpleasant. Most important, as we have seen especially in Chapter 8, is the possibility of attributing to the external world the delusional content of the hallucinations.

Formally, one must remember that projection takes place also in the normal phenomenon of perception. Perception of an external stimulus actually takes place internally in our cortical centers. However, the perception is projected outside and is experienced as a reproduction of the external environment. We are aware of the stimuli hitting us from outside, but we are not aware of the externalization of the

* This neurophysiological interpretation may apply, of course, not only to hallucinations but to all the other mechanisms of active concretization, which are even more difficult to localize (see Chapter 30).

perception into the outside world. This externalization coincides with what is known to us as a realistic status of the environment. Whether it is so, or whether some philosophers are correct in denying that perception reproduces external reality, is a problem that need not be discussed here. This externalization or projection, which occurs normally in perception, occurs also in hallucinations. Inasmuch as the hallucination is experienced as a perception, the process of externalization is an implicit, necessary, concomitant characteristic.

Difficult Corrigibility of the Experience

We come now to another characteristic of schizophrenic hallucinations: the difficult corrigibility of the experience or the inability of the nontreated patient who hallucinates to recognize that the hallucination is a false perception having no foundation in reality. It is conceivable for us to imagine that if a normal person were to hallucinate, he would be able to realize, by testing himself in other ways, that the hallucination is false. This happens actually in the few nonpsychotic persons who occasionally have hallucinations, but it does not happen, as a rule, in the schizophrenic. For instance, a medical student experienced the following phenomenon. While he was preparing for an examination, for a few days prior to the test he was cramming in a furious way for days and nights. He had strong anxiety lest he not complete his preparation. In the town where he lived, there was a tower with a bell that rang each hour on the hour. The day before the examination this person heard the bell ringing every few minutes. He realized that the bell would not ring so often; he knew that it rang only each hour, and when he asked other people, he accepted as true the fact that they were not hearing the bell ring. He realized then that he was hallucinating, although he was not able to distinguish the hallucinated sound from the real one, and he understood that this phenomenon was due to his anxiety. He was afraid that the time would pass too quickly and that the day of the examination would arrive before he had finished his preparation.

Schizophrenics who are recovering start to doubt the reality of their hallucinations in the same way that the dreamer in the process of waking up starts to realize that the dream was a dream. Generally, however, the schizophrenic has no insight into the pathological nature of his hallucinations. Again we have to invoke a dynamic as well as a structural mechanism. From a dynamic point of view, we know that the patient needs to believe the reality of the hallucination. From our study of the structural mechanisms, we know that he interprets his own experiences with the means that he has at his disposal. When he hallucinates, his thoughts regress to the perceptual level, and it is only with the means available at that level, that is, with his perceptions, that he evaluates what happens to him. The level to which he regresses predominates over the higher ones.

Since the first edition of this book was published, there has been an important change in my evaluation of this symptom. I spoke then of the incorrigibility of the hallucinatory experience and of the inability of the patient to recognize the unrealistic nature of the hallucination, unless, of course, he recovers. As we shall see in Chapter 37, I no longer believe this to be true. With a psychotherapeutic procedure that I have devised, many patients are able to recognize the unreality of the experience.

Nonschizophrenic Hallucinations

Hallucinations occur in many psychiatric conditions, and the reader is referred to the usual textbooks of psychiatry for a complete differential diagnosis. Generally in the United States the presence of an incorrigible hallucination is not considered consistent with the diagnosis of neurosis. In states of panic or great fear, corrigible hallucinations may occur. Freud reported that hysterics may have occasional hallucinations. Hallucinations have also been reported in disturbed, but not necessarily psychotic, children (Levin, 1932). Hallucinations of all kinds, but especially visual, occur in many organic disorders of the central nervous system, such as brain tumor, cerebral arteriosclerosis, senile psychosis, presenile psychosis, general paresis, encephalitis, cerebral malaria, toxic deliriums of various kinds, and so forth. In alcoholic hallucinosis the hallucinations are auditory and are difficult to distinguish from schizophrenic ones in the absence of adequate history. In delirium tremens they are predominantly visual and represent animals such as snakes and rats. Haptic hallucinations of vermin crawling over the skin are also frequently seen, but these are probably often based on paresthesiae.

Recently it has become quite important, because of their frequent occurrence, to distinguish drug-induced hallucinations from schizophrenic ones. Lysergic acid diethylamide (LSD) and mescaline are frequent causal agents. These hallucinations are generally a visual phantasmagoria. Many consist of amazing, unrealistic colors in kaleidoscopic arrangements. Other differential characteristics from schizophrenic visual hallucinations are:

1. Whereas schizophrenic hallucinations generally contrast with a visual environment that is normal, drug-induced hallucinations are accompanied by distortions that occupy the whole visual field, or the whole perceived environment.
2. Whereas schizophrenic hallucinations are generally seen with the eyes open, drug-induced hallucinations are more readily seen with the eyes closed or in poorly lighted surroundings.

Some psychiatrists have discussed whether noncorrigible hallucinations occur in normal people or normal circumstances. According to Freud's theories, reaffirmed by Rapaport (1951), hallucinations are a normal phenomenon in babies. These theories assert that the hungry baby hallucinates that he is sucking the breast of the mother when the breast is not available, and the hallucination quiets him down. According to Rapaport this is the beginning of human thought.

Of course it is impossible to ask babies whether they hallucinate or not, but I must say that I have some doubts about it. Mothers and fathers know that the baby cries and cries when he is hungry; he is a realist; not hallucination but a realistic cry will bring back the maternal breast. It is hard to imagine how such an unrealistic mechanism would permit the survival of the human species. Furthermore, we have seen that hallucinations are not mediated in the primary sensory areas. They must thus be mediated in areas that are not yet myelinized and therefore not yet functioning during the first few months of life.

Hallucinations occur also as mystical experiences in religious people who are not reputed to be mentally ill. This problem is not of as much practical importance in the United States as it is in other countries, but nevertheless it deserves to be studied for its theoretical aspects. Not only do we read in biographies of saints, prophets, and other religious leaders that they underwent what seem to us hallucinations, but we also hear about similar phenomena occurring today in some people living in environments permeated by very intense religious feelings. Are these people schizophrenics?

It is my conviction that they are not. Obviously there are many hospitalized and nonhospitalized schizophrenics who have hallucinations and other symptoms with religious content, but they are easily distinguishable from the religious or mystical people I am referring to. But if these people are not psychotic, what interpretation must we give to the hallucinatory phenomena? Certainly we do not need to subscribe to a supernatural interpretation. First of all, how do we distinguish these religious hallucinations from those occurring in schizophrenics?

1. They are predominantly visual; that is, they have mostly the aspect of apparitions. If there is an auditory component, it is as a rule secondary to the visual.
2. In their content they often involve old people, parent-substitutes; but they are benevolent parents who guide the person to whom they appear.
3. Their content is gratifying in a manifest way.
4. They give the person who experiences them a marked rise in self-esteem and a sense of his being or becoming a worthwhile and a very active person. He has been given a mission or a special insight, and from now on he must be on the move, must be doing something important, more important than his own life. Although the message is often an order, the subject does not generally feel that he is the victim of tyranny or a passive agent, but rather that he has been chosen to perform something of stupendous proportions.

The whole personalities and behavior of the people who experience these hallucinations are not such as to warrant the diagnosis of psychosis. Mystics are fanatical, but not in the same way as the paranoid. They lack the bitterness or resentment or the calm resignation and disdain of the unjustly accused. They show instead a serene and yet active optimism, like that of people who have been blessed by the love of a good mother. Moreover, the hallucinatory and delusional experiences of the schizophrenic are generally accompanied by a more or less apparent disintegration of the whole person.

My impression is that, influenced by environmental factors, these people can easily put themselves into a state of autohypnosis during which they have intense religious experiences. During the self-induced hypnotic state, archaic mechanisms or primary process mechanisms come to the surface. But these archaic mechanisms do not undergo schizophrenic distortions. They adapt themselves to the general state and environment of the individual and can actually evoke insight that would not be possible in normal conditions—insight that is in contrast to the conventional attitudes and ideas of that particular historical and geographical situation. In *The Intrapsychic Self* (Arieti, 1967), I present classical examples of religious hallucinations.

X

Adualism

A phenomenon that could be subsumed from many of the schizophrenic phenomena examined in this chapter is *adualism*. This term, used also by Piaget (1929), was introduced by Baldwin (1929) in his studies of young children. Adualism means lack of dualism, that is, lack of the ability to distinguish between the two realities, that of the mind and that of the external world. This condition corresponds to what orthodox analysts, following Federn (1952), call lack of ego boundaries. Many of the phenomena, such as hallucinations and delusions, that have been described in this chapter are confused by patients with events or things in external reality. At more advanced states of the illness more complicated symptoms occur. For instance, a schizophrenic may remember and visualize a scene in which people who played an important role in his childhood, and who are now dead, come to visit him in the hospital. As soon as he has these thoughts, he sees the dead people in the hospital visiting him. Actually, he is misidentifying some fellow inmates as these visitors. Emotionally loaded thoughts are transformed by the schizophrenic into actual things or events, and the events of the inner life and of the external world become parts of one and the same reality. Whatever is experienced tends to become true by virtue of the fact of being experienced.

Adualism is very common in various degrees in all stages of schizophrenia, and at times is prominent even in the early stages.

If we ask severely ill schizophrenics to explain why they believe their strange ideas in spite of lack of evidence, they do not attempt to demonstrate the validity of the ideas. They do not resort to paleologic thinking, as less regressed patients do. Almost invariably they give this answer: "I know," meaning, "I know that it is so." The patient's belief is more than a strong conviction; it is a certitude. Something that he knows or something about which he has some thoughts becomes equivalent to something that exists, almost as if the patient would actualize the tenets of the idealistic school of philosophy.

Even in the early stages of schizophrenia, the patient is unable to lie about his delusions unless he is recovering or is under drug therapy. To lie requires the ability to visualize what does not exist, an abstract function no longer at the patient's disposal. The delusions are absolute reality for him, and he cannot deny them.

The wish-fulfillment quality of the psychopathological mechanism reaches its culmination when merely to experience a wish becomes equivalent to its actualization. Motivational factors induce the patient to indulge in pleasant thoughts and images, but it is his total cognitive state that permits him to equate images and thoughts with reality. As a matter of fact, he also experiences anxieties and fears as if they were presently actualized in the real world.

XI

Perceptual Alterations

Perception is the basis for higher cognitive processes. Many authors agree that perception is altered in schizophrenics, but few of them evaluate and interpret this alteration in the same way. Some authors find in perceptual alterations support for an organic etiology. For instance, Mettler (1955) thought that the corpus striatum does not function normally in schizophrenics, who consequently have perceptual difficulties and are not able to establish normal contact with reality. Mettler's hypotheses have not been confirmed.

Size-constancy has been studied by many investigators in schizophrenia. By size-constancy is meant the possibility of perceiving a familiar object as of a standard size, in spite of the fact its distance from the observer varies. Some authors, like Bruner (1951), who anticipated an attempt on the part of the schizophrenic to defend himself from the intruding stimulation of the external world, predicted that such withdrawal would cause lower size-constancy in schizophrenics. Rausch (1952), however, found a higher degree of constancy in schizophrenics. Many of these psychological studies have led to inconclusive results. I agree with Rausch (1956) that symbolic value exerts more influence on the perceptual judgments and alters the results.

In many, but not all, cases of acute schizophrenia, the patient experiences an increased acuity of perception. Noises seem louder, colors are more pronounced and are often compared to technicolor seen in movies. This increased intensity of perception at the beginning of the illness is generally well remembered by patients who experienced it. For instance, a patient told me that the day of his acute breakdown he woke up in the morning at the sound of the alarm clock. That ring seemed tremendous in volume to him, almost deafening, and would never end. In this and similar cases it is again difficult to separate the perceptual alteration from the dynamic symbolism that is connected with it. For that patient, it could be that waking up and facing that particular day meant again facing unbearable failure and defeat.

On the other hand, there may be in incipient schizophrenia a lack of balance between the perception *per se* and the subsequent cognitive elaboration of the perception. In this case the cognitive elaboration may be decreased and the perceptual intensity increased. In very advanced stages we find marked perceptual alterations generally in the direction of perceptual defect. We shall discuss them in Chapters 24 and 25.

At this point I shall describe a phenomenon that I have observed in acutely ill patients and in some derivative forms in the chronic patient (Arieti, 1961*a*). Many patients go through periods during which they are unable to perceive wholes. The disintegration of wholes is gradual. At first the patient must divide big or complex wholes into smaller unities. For instance, patients looking at nurses, attendants, and physicians cannot see them as persons, but they perceive only parts of them—a nose, right or left eye, arm, and so on. A female patient who had undergone an acute episode with dangerous excitement described in detail to me the experiences she had while she was in a seclusion cell. She remembered that she could not look at the whole door of the cell. She could see only the knob or the keyhole or some corner of the door. The wall too had to be fragmented into parts. Some other patients who were able to remember the acute episode told me how at first wholes or big unities were divided into the smaller units of which they were composed. Later, however, as the psychomotor excitement increased, even the smaller unities were divided into smaller fragments. Similar pronounced fragmentations probably occur in states of acute confusion, such as some toxic-infective deliriums, and in some very bizarre, almost entirely forgotten dreams of normal people. One of the reasons why the phenomenon has not been described in the literature in reference to schizophrenia is the difficulty most patients encounter in remembering it. These amnesias are at least partially determined by the fact that disintegrated wholes or fragments have no names or do not correspond to schemata of previous experiences, similarly perhaps to what according to Schactel (1959) occurs in childhood amnesias.

Many years ago (1941–1945) I noticed the fragmentation of wholes in drawings of very regressed patients. At that time I did not understand the phenomenon and unfortunately did not preserve those drawings, with one exception, which is reproduced in this book (Figure 20).

In this case, whereas prior to her illness Lucille was able to draw very well, from the beginning of the psychosis her drawings started to show the usual schizophrenic bizarreness.* Later, when the illness was quite advanced, the disorganization became extremely marked. For instance, when she wanted to draw a profile, she could not finish it. Parts of the profile were disconnected; furthermore, some of these parts were repeated several times, conferring a confusing appearance to the whole drawing.

Some patients have reported to me that during the acute episode they were aware that they were losing perception of wholes and were making conscious efforts to reconstruct these wholes, but the attempts were only partially successful. At times the parts that replaced the missing ones were not appropriate, and distorted wholes resulted.

Bemporad (1967) did experiments with four groups of patients by using four pseudo-isochromatic plates for testing color perception, manufactured by the American Optical Company. Three cards showed a number made up of different-sized dots against a field of dots of contrasting colors. The fourth card was unambiguous, showing a clearly defined number against a field of contrasting color. It

* The drawings of Lucille will be examined in detail in Chapter 20.

was hypothesized that nonschizophrenic patients would automatically respond to the numbers (wholes) at first and then mention the dots.

The acute schizophrenic group showed almost exclusive fragmentation of perception with response to part rather than whole percepts. This fragmentation occasionally persisted to the fourth card, which did not lend itself to part perception. The chronic and recovered groups correctly identified a greater number of whole percepts than did the acute group, but the majority also fragmented the card data. These groups also showed more than twice as many incorrect whole responses as the acute group.

Bemporad concluded that in many schizophrenic patients there is an automatic fragmentation of perceptual wholes followed by an instantaneous reintegration according to primary process, rather than secondary process, principles of cognition. Because of my previous publications on this topic, Bemporad kindly named this finding "the Arieti effect."

Can this difficulty of the very ill schizophrenic be interpreted as a return to a primitive stage of perception, perhaps to a stage of "primary aggregation" in which wholes are not yet organized and in which elements of fragments may reappear in isolation? There is presumptive evidence, coming from various sources, that this is so.

Under the influence of the gestalt school, psychology has been dominated by the idea that objects are apprehended as wholes. This point of view is now gradually recognized as incorrect. It was the result of the fact that perception was studied as it occurs in the secondary process and in a state of full consciousness. The study of early ontogeny and microgeny reveals that objects are first perceived as parts and that only subsequently are they perceived as wholes or gestalts. However, in microgeny part-perception is very rapid and remains unconscious, so that we are aware only of whole-perception, or of the gestalt, which becomes the dominant one in the early stages of the secondary process. Riesen (1947), in mammals raised in darkness, and Von Senden (1960), in adult humans who were operated on for congenital cataracts and were learning to see, have demonstrated how part-perception preceded the whole-perception of the object. A serial apprehension of the parts preceded perception of the whole. The shortest time in which a congenitally blind person approximated normal perception of wholes was about a month.

In the psychoanalytic literature, Klein (1948) has given great importance to the apprehension of partial object in infants. According to her, objects that are perceived (or introjected) are at first partial objects. For instance, the mother is seen as several disconnected parts, often only as a breast. Theoretical formulations of Hebb (1949) also postulate that part-perception precedes whole-perception.

Impressive evidence comes also from neurologists who have studied cases of visual agnosia. The literature is abundant, but, according to my own knowledge, no report is so accurate and pertinent to the present topic as that by Alexandra Adler (1944, 1950) on the disintegration and the restoration that occur in visual agnosia. Adler described, among other things, the alteration in visual perception that occurred in a 22-year-old woman who was injured in the famous fire at the Coconut Grove nightclub in Boston on November 28, 1942. At first she was totally blind; after two days she could distinguish white from dark but could not recognize colors. She presented also a picture of a pure subcortical visual alexia, Wernicke type. The diagnosis of lesion of the brain, probably caused by carbon monoxide fumes, was made. After her injury this woman was no longer able to perceive wholes. She had to add part by part in order to reconstruct wholes and recognize objects. Often the patient recognized parts and guessed the rest. She could not recognize the numbers 2, 3, 5, 6, 8, and 9 because she could not recognize the direction of the curves of which these figures were composed, but she was able to recognize 1, 4, and 7 during the second week of her illness because she could guess where a straight line was going. Because this patient recognized objects ''by tracing the contours, by adding the parts and by making conclusions from all she had perceived, she had to take more time than did the normal person, who recognizes all the parts, in the main, simultaneously'' (quoted verbatim from Alder [1944] except for change from present to past tense).

Some neurologists (Brain; Nissl von Mayendorf; Poppelreuter, cited by Adler, 1944) had suggested that a patient's inability to perceive the whole might be caused by a defect in the visual fields. Some controversy, for instance, arose in the interpretation of a famous case, described by Goldstein and Gelb (1920), of a man whose brain was injured during combat in World War I. This man lost the capacity of recognizing by a simultaneous act of visual perception the whole of a figure or the gestalt. Golstein (1939, 1943*b*) and Adler herself, supported by observations made by other authors, could disprove the interpretation that a defective visual field might be involved. The conclusion reached is that in certain pathological conditions wholes cannot be perceived, only parts. A tendency exists, however, to reconstruct wholes, at times inappropriate ones, only loosely related to the original.

Important corroboration can also be obtained from the experimental works of Pritchard, Heron, and Hebb (1960, 1961). They confirmed the findings of previous authors that movements of the eyeballs are necessary for normal perception. If the eye movements are made impossible, and an image is thus stabilized on the retina, an abnormal, presumably primitive form of perception occurs. Pritchard and associates have attached to the eyeball itself a special device consisting of a contact lens and an optical projector. With this device the image remains fixed on the retina and does not move with the movements of the eyeball. The authors found that with this procedure a complex image, such as the profile of a face, may vanish in fragments with one or more of its parts fading independently. Some fragments remain in perception. This fragmentation seems to correspond to the original part-perception and, if we compare perception to thinking, to the fragmentation of the primary aggregation. For some fleeting periods of time parts may remain aggregated, but they do not form wholes. In tachistoscopic and other subliminal experiments often parts only are registered (Werner, 1956). Some parts, which in subliminal experiments were apparently not perceived, were registered instead, as demonstrated by the fact that they appeared in subsequent dreams. Fisher and his associates (1954, 1959, 1960, 1963) have done interesting work in this respect by continuing and expanding work originally devised by Pötzl and co-workers (1960, 1971).

Another important phenomenon appears in acute schizophrenia, tachistoscopic experiments, visual agnosias, stabilized images, and so on. When the primary aggregation is broken and fragmented, there is a spontaneous effort on the part of the subject to reaggregate and possibly to reform wholes. If we want to anthropomorphize, we could say that it is almost as if these parts or fragments were searching for wholes to which to belong.

But the new wholes (whether they appear in experimental perceptions or in dreams, as in Pötzl's and Fisher's experiments) are unrealistic or only loosely associated wholes and correspond to the primary categories that we have described in the microgeny of thought. We cannot talk of categories, however, in the phenomenon of perception, which is probably precategorial. An appropriate name for this phenomenon may be "primary awholism."

This new formation of wholes may give some encouragement to the gestalt psychologists, who may see in it an urge toward a gestalt. The phenomenon may be called "primary gestalt." Let us remember, however, that this phenomenon is secondary to the primary aggregation and follows mechanisms similar to those occurring in the formation of the primary categories.

We have already discussed the formation of distorted wholes in schizophrenia. Adler (1944, 1950) has described the reading and perceiving of related words in her patient suffering from visual agnosia, and similar phenomena have been reported in many aphasias. Pritchard (1961) with his method of the stabilized image, reported also that when entire words were presented to the subject, the partial fragmentation of letters caused different words to be perceived (for instance, the word *beer* was perceived *peer, peep, bee, be*).

We may conclude thus that what appears to us normal perception, involving wholes, is only the ultimate stage of a complicated mechanism. This microgenetic mechanism occurs in the normal subject in a fraction of a second, and the subject is aware only of the terminal stage, that is, when he perceives wholes as wholes. In some pathological conditions, neurological or schizophrenic in nature, perception becomes arrested at one of these pregestaltic stages. The phenomenon is further complicated by reconstructive efforts leading to incorrect reproductions, similar in meaning to Freud's restitutional symptoms.

XII
The Biological Basis of Schizophrenic Cognition

We shall continue the trend of thought developed in the previous section by resorting to other biological sciences. We shall now deal, not with perception, but with the response that follows perception.

Ethology and animal psychology give many examples of animal responses that can be interpreted as responses to parts and not to wholes. Tinbergen (1951) has illustrated some very interesting mechanisms; for instance, certain fish, like the sticklebacks, react only to the red color on the bellies of competitor male fish that invade their territory. The color red elicits in the sticklebacks a given fighting behavior toward males of the same species. Because they react blindly only to a part of the total environmental situation and neglect the other parts, they make what seem to us mistakes. For instance, artificial red objects placed by the experimenter elicit the same fighting response. All of us are familiar with similar examples. Moths are attracted only by light and may burn themselves to death by flying into hot electric bulbs. Flypaper, which was used until not too long ago to kill flies, exploited part-perception. Flies reacted only to the sweetness of the paper and were caught by its stickiness and killed.

It would seem thus that early in phylogeny the organism reacts predominantly or compellingly to a *releasing element* or to a part, and only in a very weak fashion to the rest, which is experienced as undifferentiated or as a nonorganized aggregation of parts. It could also be that at very primitive levels there are no such things as parts and wholes, but only releasing elements.

Actually this problem cannot be separated from the problem of the response to the part versus the response to the whole. In nature there are two ways of responding: to the part (or to the releasing element) and to the whole (Arieti, 1967). Each of these two types of responses is generalized; that is, the organism tends to respond in the same way to different exemplars of the same stimulus, whether the stimulus is what we consider a part or a whole.

Generalization is a process applicable to a plurality of stimuli: a plurality of what seems to us parts or a plurality of what seems to us wholes. Generalization of responses to a plurality of objects, which have only a part in common, will eventually lead, at the level of thinking, to the formation of primary classes. Generalization of responses to wholes leads eventually to the formation of secondary, or logical, classes.

Elsewhere (Arieti, 1967, Chap. 4) I have described how the first type of generalization corresponds to Pavlov's generalization of responses. The second type of generalization corresponds to the Pavlovian technique for discrimination. I have also shown how responding to parts and not to wholes gives rise to the phenomena described by Klüver (1933, 1936) about equivalent stimuli, that is, about stimuli that appear to human beings to be very different from one another and yet evoke the same response in some animals. In effect, part-perception and response to a part belong to the primary process, whereas whole-perception and response to a whole belong to the secondary process.

The Pavlovian technique of conditioned reflexes may give us some other very interesting evidence about responding to a whole and responding to a part. Pavlov's technique has shown that the cortex is able to fuse separate individual stimuli and to produce a unitary response. Best and Taylor (1939), reported an example of simultaneous stimuli acting upon the same analyzer. An alimentary conditioned reflex was established to a chord of three tones of equal intensity but of

85, 256, and 786 cycles per second. Later each tone caused a response even when sounded separately. The responses to the different tones were approximately equal.

Here again, if we consider the combination of three tones as a whole and each individual tone as a part, we may conclude that the dog can be conditioned to respond to a whole as well as to a part. However, in the dog at least, the equivalence of the parts of a compound stimulus occurs when the partial stimuli act upon the same analyzer. If different parts of the cortex act as analyzers, only one component in isolation is effective.

In Chapter 5 we discussed Kagan's work (1972) with infants, who have greater difficulty in dealing with similar (discrepant) objects thant they do with dissimilar ones. The child tends to react to the discrepant object as if it were identical to a familiar object. In other words, there is a tendency in the child toward Pavlov's generalization of responses, rather than to discrimination of responses. If we remember our discussion of paleologic thinking and substitute the word *whole* for the word *subject* and the word *part* for the word *predicate,* we are in a position to make interesting correlations. In primary cognition, the person who thinks paleologically identifies not on the basis of identical wholes, but on the basis of identical parts. Similarly the animal or man who perceives according to primary, primitive, Pavlovian generalization of responses, or by means of pregestaltic forms of cognition, responds to the part and not to the whole.

At this point it is possible to see a parallel between part-perception (and also conditioned response to a part-stimulus) and paleologic thinking (or the formation of primary classes). It is also possible to see a similar parallel between whole-perception (or conditioned response to a compound stimulus) and Aristotelian thinking (or the formation of secondary classes). It seems that at the levels both of perception and of thinking, the human mind can, at least potentially, operate with the two forms of generalization that we have discussed. What in primary perceptual generalization is the *releasing element* corresponds to what in paleologic thinking is the *identifying predicate*.

Following Werner's comparative approach and my own psychostructural approach we can individualize recurrent patterns of organization in different levels of cognition and recognize the phylogenetic precursors of Von Domarus's principle. In several writings (Arieti, 1962*c,* 1965*b, c*) and especially in *The Intrapsychic Self* (Arieti, 1967) I have made an attempt to show the evolutionary struggle between the perception and/or conception of a whole and the perception and/or conception of a part.

Neither Von Domarus's principle nor pregestaltic perception can explain all the multiform facets of schizophrenic cognition. However, they show two very important and common characteristics of this cognition.

XIII

Schizophrenic Thinking in Everyday Life and Everyday Thinking in Schizophrenia

We have described schizophrenic thought disorders as having a certain degree of specificity. And yet many people remind us that schizophrenic thinking is present in everyday life and that common everyday thinking is present in schizophrenia, except perhaps in the most regressed cases.

There is truth in these assertions. However, we must clarify the extent of this truth and its implications.

Even normal people do not adopt the most mature ways of thinking. *Some* normal persons, but more frequently neurotic and borderline patients, follow what I have called *spontaneous organization*. Spontaneous organization of thinking is not directed by a search for logical consistency or for consensual validation but by a tendency to satisfy wishes and to give to these wishes an apparently logical sustenance by resorting to primary process cognition. This, of course, is reminiscent of schizophrenia. The hidden motivation is easily uncovered by psychotherapy. The following is an example.

The patient is a 19-year-old girl whose mother died two years previously and whose father married again. The patient lives now with the father and stepmother, but she hates her stepmother. Whatever involves the stepmother is misinterpreted or seen in a peculiar slant. Quite often the patient interprets paleologically whatever the stepmother says or does. In other words, the spontaneous organization of the input coming from the stepmother is predominantly organized according to the rules of primary process cognition. The inner need to hate the stepmother is stronger than the respect for the demands of reality, and the patient succumbs to the seduction of the spontaneous organization. For instance, the stepmother gave the patient a dress, but the patient interpreted the gift as an attempt to placate her; moreover the stepmother bought her something that she knew the patient would not like. We may interpret the case in terms of old rivalry with her real mother or, in Freudian terms, as an unresolved Oedipal situation. In fact, the patient did not accept entirely even her own mother when the latter was alive. The patient eventually repressed the original situation, accepted the demands of reality, and soon even loved her own mother. However, when the mother died and the father married again, the old situation was revived. Now the patient could more freely allow the spontaneous organization of the primary process to affect the interplay with the new rival for her father's affection. She was not bound to the stepmother by deep respect and filial love. The spontaneous organization covered only the area of rivalry for the stepmother. As a matter of fact, the patient had no rivalry whatsoever for the stepsister, a child of the stepmother's first marriage.

After dinner the patient often had gastric discomfort. She believed that her indigestion was caused by the stepmother, who thoughtlessly prepared foods that the patient, with a delicate stomach, could not digest.

The patient did not consider her attitude toward the stepmother to be abnormal, but on the contrary, realistic, natural, appropriate; in other word, syntonic. This lack of insight does not necessarily indicate that the patient was schizophrenic. As a matter of fact, after relatively short treatment the patient got well. We must distinguish two types of syntonic symptoms. In both cases the symptoms are accepted as realistic by the patient. However, in nonpsychotic conditions the symptom, even if accepted by the patient, is not fully or deeply integrated. For instance, although this girl felt that her feelings toward the stepmother were justified, she knew that the rest of her life and whatever she knew about her father and stepmother were at variance with her feelings. The patient had not gone through an elaborate reconstruction of her constellations of thoughts in order to believe that her stepmother was evil. She had not reached paranoid structuralization. When her inner needs were explained to her, her hostility diminished and finally the symptoms dropped. For instance, the idea that the stepmother thoughtlessly prepared meals that she could not digest cannot be considered similar to the delusion of a patient mentioned earlier in this chapter who thought that his wife was poisoning his food. As a matter of fact, when it was pointed out to the girl that it was not the food that made her sick but the fact that she had to have dinner with a person whom she did not accept in her parental role, she accepted the explanation and the symptom soon disappeared.

Similar use of spontaneous organization and of primary process mechanisms occurs in everyday life in presumably normal or quasi-normal persons. It also occurs in those conditions described by Horney (1950) that do not correspond to the classic psychoneuroses of the official classifications and nomenclatures and are nevertheless neurotic conditions.

The normal or would-be normal young bride may be suspicious toward her mother-in-law and may misinterpret some of her remarks in a paranoid-like fashion; the tired and irritated worker may give a special meaning to the attitude of his boss and may assume what may seem a referential point of view. In slips of the tongue all of us may create neologisms or make unpredictable puns. These phenomena occur in everyday life, but they do not make a schizophrenic gestalt. They are like little islands of primary process or immature cognition that are still controlled or checked by the predominant secondary process. Some of them have even been described by Freud in *Psychopathology of Everyday Life* (1938).

The presence of primary process cognition in everyday life is stressed by some theoreticians who minimize any distinction between schizophrenic and nonschizophrenic conditions and by a group of people who would in this way strengthen their belief that the schizophrenic way of thinking is transmitted environmentally from generation to generation. In my opinion these points of view are fundamentally wrong and are based on the fact that more importance is given to the similarities between the conditions that are compared than to the differences between them. In typical psychoneuroses the symptoms consist mostly of primary process mechanisms, but the symptoms are rejected by the secondary process, which is still the recognized ruler of life.

In character neuroses and in those conditions described by Horney the secondary process prevails, but to a large extent it is used to defend structures formed originally by spontaneous organization. Life is consequently impoverished. In schizophrenic psychoses and in dreams the primary process prevails.

Once again, in agreement with Freud, we must stress that the primary process is present in the psychological life of every human being, whether normal, neurotic, or psychotic, and is not a characteristic of schizophrenia. In schizophrenia, however, its presence has three distinctive features:

1. It involves a larger segment of life than in the nonschizophrenic.
2. At least in its pathological manifestation, it is not corrected, neutralized, or rejected by the secondary process. On the other hand, it resists or overpowers the influence of the secondary process.
3. Except in rare cases, it is not harmoniously integrated with the secondary process to form a creative product (see Chapter 20, and also Arieti, 1967, Part Three).

Other people who find ''schizophrenic'' thinking in everyday life make another confusion. For them every irrationality is schizophrenic in nature. This mistake is reminiscent of that made by those psychiatrists who believe that any irrationality found in the family of the schizophrenic is schizophrenic irrationality (see Chapter 8).

Also the irrationality, found in the culture, with few exceptions, is not schizophrenic in origin. Moreover, the acceptance of cultural irrationality does not make a person schizophrenic when such irrationality is not subjected to subsequent transformation and is accepted directly from one generation to another or from other members of the same generation. A great deal of irrationality is transmitted by such methods as psychological habituation, indoctrination, brain washing, imitation, acceptance on faith, and so on, and is not caused by schizophrenia. For instance, staunchest Nazis may believe that Jews are evil and must be eliminated. The acceptance of this belief is not a delusion; morally, and in its practical effects, it is infinitely much worse than a delusion. It is cultural in origin and because of special techniques devised by society, like coercion, falsification of truths, impossibility of ventilation, and so forth, it is transformed into an introject. The reverse is also true. If some members of a minority that has suffered from persecutions for many centuries feel persecuted when they are not, their thinking is obviously not valid; their misinterpretation, however, is not necessarily or technically delusional. It may be a state of habituation that may be overcome much more easily than a delusion, and with different methods (see also Ziferstein, 1967).

Similarly, when we hear or read that in some islands in the Pacific or in some remote Indian or African tribes all the members of the tribes have a paranoid and delusional attitude toward other people or groups of people, we cannot conclude that these natives are schizophrenic. It would also be a misnomer to call the culture itself schizophrenic. Myths, ceremonials, rituals, ideas transmitted from generation to generation and taken for granted as true, may seem to us delusional, although we have our own, not less irrational beliefs and traditions. They are learned from society. As long as they are accepted by the individual from the external world, they become part of his psychological content; they are not products of his own alleged schizophrenic process.

When we come specifically to study the family and not the general culture, we find that in addition to the cultural irrationality there is some irrationality transmitted in every family from parents to children and between siblings. We have seen that in disturbed families, like those of schizophrenic patients the amount of irrationality is greater (Chapters 5 and 8).

The presence of everyday thinking and even of the most correct or valid Aristotelian thinking in schizophrenia is undeniable. Especially in incipient or mild forms of schizophrenia abnormal ways of thinking are relegated to conflictful content or to a few delusional ideas.

XIV

Relation of Schizophrenic Thinking to Autism and to Mythical Thinking of Cultural Origin

Two types of thinking that show similarities to the schizophrenic are those usually called "autistic" and "primitive."

In the previous sections of this chapter the terms *autism* and *autistic* have been purposely avoided, although they are commonly used in connection with schizophrenia. In their psychiatric dictionary Hinsie and Shatsky (1950) defined autism as

> a form of thinking, more or less genuinely, of a subjective character; if objective material enters, it is given subjective meaning and emphasis. Autism generally carries with it the thought that the material is derived from the individual himself, appearing in the nature of day-dreams, phantasies, delusions, hallucinations, etc. The content of thought, in other words, is largely endogenous. In classical instances of autistic thinking, such as occurs in schizophrenia, the unconscious sphere makes the largest contribution to autism.*

It is obvious that the terms *autistic thought* and *paleologic thought* are applied to the same phenomenon. Autism, however, is more a descriptive term. In fact, Bleuler, who made the original contributions on autistic or dereistic thinking, limited himself to a description of it (see Chapter 2). Paleologic is more a structural term; it means that autistic thought uses a paleological type of logic. Thus, both terms are useful; autism refers generally to a particular type of thinking; paleologic refers to the type of logic that is used in that type of thinking.

Of course, when definitions of autistic thought are formulated now, they should not be limited to a description; they should stress the fact that the main formal characteristic of this type of thinking is its foundation upon a non-Aristotelian logic, which has been designated as paleologic.

* This definition has not been changed in the more recent edition of this dictionary by Hinsie and Campbell (1960).

Bleuler (1913*a*) spoke of the occurrence of this type of thinking not only in schizophrenia, but also in healthy adults "when the emotions obtain too great a significance," and in normal children during play activities. When children identify themselves with Superman, let us say, or the bogeyman, or their parents, or when they play with toys, acting as if the toys were the things they represent, they seem to think paleologically. It is questionable, however, whether they really do so; children know that they play; they do not *believe* the reality of their games, they *make believe*. Undoubtedly, such a propensity for make-believe is related to their facility to accept paleologic thinking, but to make believe is no proof of the necessity to think paleologically. Children voluntarily and playfully revert to paleologic thinking, just as does the artist or the person who makes humorous remarks (Arieti, 1950*b*, 1967).

True autistic thought occurs in children at a very early age, when they think with paleological logic. (Several examples of this kind of thought were given in previous sections of this chapter.) The occurrence of autistic thought in young children is not a necessity, but only a propensity. Although even perfectly normal children may have autistic manifestations between the age of 1½ and 3, the occurrence of such manifestations, even at that age, and their persistence afterwards, is much commoner in children who cannot relate well to the people with whom they live. If the child is well integrated, this propensity to autism is almost automatically overcome. If there are emotional difficulties between the child and the significant adults, autistic tendencies are more frequent. As will be discussed at greater length in Chapter 19, if anxiety-laden situations arise that interfere with the process of socialization, this autistic propensity of the child is enhanced to a pathological degree. Its most serious manifestations are found in the condition that Kanner originally described and designated as "early infantile autism" (1944, 1946, 1949). After Kanner, the term *autistic,* when applied to children, was used to designate severe psychopathology (for instance, in Mahler (1968) and Bettelheim (1967, 1970). Child psychosis will be discussed in Chapter 44.

The difference between the concept of autism and that of paleologic thinking is even more obvious when one takes into consideration so-called "primitive thinking." We have already discussed several examples of thinking in primitive cultures, which indicate the frequent occurrence of a paleologic logic. And yet, primitive man cannot be called autistic; as a matter of fact, and here is the fundamental fact that has to be stressed, the opposite seems to be the case. The primitive who thinks paleologically often does so not in order to be subjective and individualistic, but so that he may comply with the mores of his society. By using paleologic conceptions, he does not withdraw behind an autistic barrier, as the schizophrenic does, but, on the contrary, he becomes more intimately a part of his tribe.

The reference that I have made in previous works to the frequent instances in primitive cultures of paleologic thought similar to that of the schizophrenic has caused some criticism (Mead, 1958; Henle, 1962). It is the same kind of criticism that has been made of the works of Lévy-Bruhl, Storch, Werner, and others. Some of my concepts have been interpreted as implying the intellectual inferiority of certain non-Western people, a fact that many modern American anthropologists have convincingly disproved. Obviously, never have I implied any inferiority. In Western societies, too, manifestations of paleologic thinking are abundantly found, even in our time (Arieti, 1967). In his admirably scholarly book *The Waning of the Middle Ages* (1924), Huizinga clearly described the prevalence of this type of thinking in medieval Europe, although, of course, he did not use the word *paleologic*.

I shall try to explain in this section that the frequency of paleologic thinking in some societies neither implies that their individual members are mentally inferior, nor calls into question the moral and spiritual equality of man. Although this book is concerned with a psychiatric problem, I shall not evade this important issue, which belongs more properly to anthropology, sociology, social psychology, and social psychiatry. Three problems require a solution and demand discussion:

1. If paleologic thinking appears as a cultural manifestation or in collective or social functions, why should it be considered pathological in certain instances, or less desirable than Aristotelian thinking?
2. Why does paleologic thinking appear more frequently in some cultures than in others: to be specific, in some non-Western cultures more than in the Western ones? How is it that many examples of primitive thought are taken from non-Western peoples living today?
3. Even if the presence of paleologic thinking is to be attributed to cultural factors and is shared by the collectivity, must we not ultimately find its origin in a special way of functioning of the human mind?

There seems to be no doubt that paleologic thought is less differentiated than the Aristotelian. It consists of primary categories or classes, which have a simpler organization than the secondary ones (see the third section of this chapter). It is much less reliable and induces errors and the perpetuation of these errors that could be avoided with Aristotelian thought. Unless we revise our philosophical concept of progress, we have to consider Aristotelian thought as being superior to the paleologic. The achievements in which humanity takes pride could not have been attained if the paleologic method of thought had been the prevalent one. The tendency of such thought to occur in early childhood, in a dream-state, and in pathological conditions, when our higher mental functions have not yet developed or cannot be used, indicates irrefutably that it is a way of thinking that does not require our highest levels of integration.

Primitive thinking occurs in every culture. The difference in quantity of paleologic thinking between Western and non-Western culture is more apparent than real. Most anthropologists who have reported such instances were Western men who were more prone to detect paleologic thinking in other cultures than in their own. It is very difficult to detect illogical thinking in the cultural, social, and religious manifestations to which we are accustomed, and whose truths or values we take for granted (see Arieti, 1956, 1967, and the thirteenth section of this chapter). Often the culture itself imposes paleologic conceptions and habits on the individual, even though the individual is capable of high forms of thinking and behavior.

Some anthropological evidence seems to indicate, however, that although the quantitative difference is not as great as it seems at first impression, a difference exists between one culture or society and another. On the other hand, anthropologists have stressed the fact that the individual native is capable of thinking with Aristotelian logic even in his own environment. It is only when he wishes to comply with the mores of the culture, especially in situations that have a social significance—such as magic, religion, initiation rites, marriages, war, and so forth—that he accepts paleologic conceptions.

Lévy-Bruhl, too, in speaking of "primitive" mentality in inferior *societies,* has been misunderstood. He wrote about the presence of paleologic mentality only in social situations, not in the individual. It is true that he considered some societies to be inferior, but only the societies, not the individual. Many anthropologists, as well as philosophers like Cassirer, have overlooked this important distinction that Lévy-Bruhl made.

There is an intrinsic conservative or static quality in every culture on account of which cultural elements are perpetuated and transmitted as they are. The more abundant is the paleologic thinking in a culture, the more difficult it is for the culture to get rid of it. For instance, Cro-Magnon men paleologically identified red powder with blood and therefore with life. They used to sprinkle the corpses of relatives with ochre in the hope that this color would restore them to life. From evidence turned up at different excavations, this practice seems to have persisted for at least 20,000 years, long after everyone should have been convinced of its futility. Cro-Magnon men lived probably between 10,000 to 80,000 years ago. They were an evolved race of men, not much different from ours. Although the percentage of their paleologic thinking may have been greater than ours and the persistence of such thinking longer, they were also capable of thinking logically. As a matter of fact, they have left ample proof of their higly symbolic and Aristotelian thinking.

An individual who, at a young age, is transposed to a different culture may lose completely the paleologic ways of the original culture and acquire the ones of the new culture. There is also a tendency in every culture, although generally weaker than the opposite one, toward demythization, or the abandonment of paleologic and other types of primary process cognition.

Some historical, social, and geographical factors have helped Western culture to get rid of primitive thinking faster than other cultures have done. Some of these factors are: the abstract thinking of the Hebrew religion and of religions that derive from it; Platonic and Aristotelian philosophy; Greek mathematics and Euclidean geometry; expansion of mathematics and sciences. These factors, as powerful as they are, have by no means completed the process of demythization; in some respects they have increased it. To complicate the process further is the fact that myths and primary process thinking are not without value. We know that some myths convey basic truths (Vico, 1725) and that primary process thinking is necessary in most forms of creativity (Arieti, 1967).

Again, what we have so far discussed does not explain how paleologic or other types of primitive thinking are acquired by a given culture. Obviously it must originate from the minds of one or several men and be accepted by the collectivity, because of its magic, reassuring, sociopolitical, religious values.

Once more I repeat that the prevalence of this type of thinking in some cultures does not make individual people belonging to that culture potentially or actually inferior or superior. Often culture detracts, arrests, handicaps, delays, or distorts the potentiality of the individual man. This is a very high price that some individuals have to pay for belonging to a given culture. On the other hand, if we could compare quantitatively what any culture adds or subtracts from the potentiality of the individual, the balance would probably be on the positive side. I regret that some great men of the stature of Kurt Goldstein have misinterpreted my writings and attributed to me conceptions that are actually alien to my way of thinking and repulsive to my spirit. In one of his last writings Goldstein (1960) wrote that I assume that the behavior of "primitive people" shows inferior mentality and is an expression of a prelogical state of mind. Never have I implied that the use of an inferior type of thinking by *Homo sapiens* is necessarily based on biological inferiority (1955). I would be ashamed of such a concept. As I have expressed, ". . . Every existing man who is in a state of health and more than three years old is at least potentially capable of thinking in accordance with the Aristotelian laws of thought" (1963*b*).

Like Goldstein I believe that some cultures make larger use than others of non-Aristotelian thinking. Possibly some styles of life, with some religious, social, economic, and technical organizations, are more susceptible than others to a type of thinking.

The problem that we may posit, and that must remain at a purely hypothetical level, is whether a now-extinct presapiens species was once forced by the level of their biological endowment to think paleologically and whether it was possible for such species to evolve to conceptual man. No presapiens species of hominids exists today.

Goldstein does not believe in the possibility of man evolving from earlier species. In the same article (1960) he writes, "How could . . . the symbolic function—so characteristic for man—develop from a capacity level which gives only the possibility for thinking and acting in 'sign' relations?" Goldstein perhaps accepts literally the biblical version of the creation of man and rejects a Darwinian interpretation. If we accept the evolutionary point of view in biology, and correspondingly a comparative developmental approach in psychology, we have also to accept the notion that intermediary stages of psychological integrations existed between *Homo sapiens* and presapiens species.

Prehuman species had indeed a type of cognition that was not symbolic. Animals are capable of learning. They respond to stimuli and to signs, which are signals of these stimuli. Although their understanding of the universe is limited, they retain a grasp of reality, and it is difficult for them to escape from reality. When an animal responds to a sign, as for example when a cat responds to the odor of a mouse, he is a realist. The cat does not let his imagination confuse him.

The odor is there, therefore, the mouse is there. At the level of signs, mistakes are difficult and rare, unless artificial situations are devised by men to confuse the animal. However, when species evolve and are capable of images, paleosymbols, and paleologic thinking, together with a greater vision of reality, there is a greater facility of escaping from reality and plunging into error (Arieti, 1967). If presapiens species of men existed that had not reached a connotational, secondary process, Aristotelian degree of cognition, they lived in danger. One may wonder how these primitive species were able to survive or evolve into others if their actions were determined *exclusively* by a system of thinking, like that of the primary process, that appears so unrealistic to us.

When a new state of evolution brings with it new challenges that make species survival very difficult, two possibilities present themselves: either the species perishes or a mutation (in this case Aristotelian or secondary process thinking) that insures survival occurs. Presapiens hominids had at their disposal a way by which they could live more or less safely and realistically: by relying purely on (or regressing to) their presymbolic or sign levels; that is, by being guided exclusively by stimuli and signs. However, whenever they indulged in paleologic thinking, they put themselves in a dangerous situation. Eventually *all* the species that could not sufficiently overcome this type of thinking perished; no one has been left on earth. Thus, although the appearance of symbolic thinking was an evolutionary improvement that led to what is specifically human in man, it was a dangerous improvement because at first it emerged in the form of paleologic thinking. Secondary process thinking probably did not occur abruptly by the sudden occurrence of a mutation, but possibly was the result of a slow, tremendously difficult, and improbable convergence of minor positive mutations.

Modern anthropologists believe that the earliest human races appeared on this planet several million years ago. Even if we accept the view of conservative anthropologists who believe that man appeared on earth only one or two million years ago, we still have to explain why civilization originated only about 10,000 years ago, and the so-called historical period, of which we have more definite knowledge, only 5,000 years ago.

The long delay in the development of civilization was due to two facts. The first, purely hypothetical fact is that presapiens races, which lived from 500,000 or to 900,000 years ago, for example, *Pithecanthropus erectus* and *Paleoanthropus Heidelbergensis,* or others that lived two or three million years ago, had not yet reached a secondary process form of thinking. Secondary process thinking probably emerged between *Pithecanthropus* and Neanderthal man. This period covers at least several hundred thousand years. Whether some of the last races of *Pithecanthropus* were already capable of some secondary process thinking, we do not know. We do not even know whether the progression toward conceptual thinking was gradual or by jumps. Even if it proceeded by jumps, these jumps were probably numerous and small, and in their sequence presumably could have given the impression to an imaginary observer of a slow and apparently continuous change.

The second fact, also hypothetical, is that when *Homo sapiens* (or other races) equipped with secondary process thinking appeared, the use of primary process thinking in collective organization was overwhelming. We have already stressed that any society and culture imposes ways of thinking on the individual, even if he is capable of higher levels of cognition. We must realize, however, that not only culture or society impose primitive ways of thinking. Primitive ways have also a strong appeal to the unconscious or to the less evolved part of the individual psyche.

XV
Critical Review of Various Theories of Schizophrenic Cognition

We shall conclude this long chapter with a review of important theories of schizophrenic cognition. Space and time limitations will compel us to make a selection of the many works on this subject. Whenever some contributions of different authors have already been discussed in this book, the reader will be referred to previous chapters. When some authors have followed the lead of a previous writer or continued in the same line of research, they will be mentioned after the original writer and not necessarily in chronological order.

Eugen Bleuler is the first important author to study thought disorders in schizophrenia and has influenced all subsequent students of this subject. His contributions have already been discussed in Chapter 2.

Alfred Storch is, after Bleuler, chronologically the first author to make important research on this topic. In 1922 he published in Tübingen, Germany, his book on schizophrenic thinking; it was translated and published in the United States in 1924. Storch was a pupil of the comparative psychologist Heinz Werner and of the genetic psychologist Kruger. His work is more descriptive than interpretative. When he interpreted, he generally illustrated the similarities between primitive and schizophrenic thought. He did not differentiate the special structures that underlie or sustain these types of thought. He stressed that in the schizophrenic as well as in primitives, emotions are expressed as if they were vivid sensorial experiences. In schizophrenic ideation, the sensorial image occupies the center of consciousness and replaces the abstract idea. The ideas of the schizophrenic have no definite limits, are diffused, and overlap. The world of objects does not consist of separate or distinct things, but of diffused and disorganized complexes. The consciousness of one's own person as an entity is also defective. The ego is divided into many compartments that are projected to the external world, as it happens in dreams of normal persons.

In the second part of his book Storch emphasized some specific analogies between the magic world of the primitive and the delusional world of the patient, especially such delusional complexes as cosmic identification, sense of rebirth, and mystic ecstasy.

Storch referred to a prelogical thinking of the patient but did not define its rules. He recognized that the schizophrenic patient is not compelled to think prelogically. He may return to a normal way of thinking. This return, however, is made difficult by the fact that the emotional currents find more adequate expressions in prelogical forms.

Lev Vygotsky was a first-rate Russian psychologist who unfortunately died at a young age after having devoted only ten years to scientific research. Vygotsky was much more interested in the development of normal cognitive processes than in schizophrenia. Nevertheless his contribution is of primary importance because many other authors, in particular the Russian Luria and the Americans Hanfmann and Kasanin (1942), have applied his ideas and his methods to the study of schizophrenia. With the use of a test that is a modification of one devised by Ach, Vygotsky (1934) tried to demonstrate that the schizophrenic returns to a mental level that precedes that of the adult. In this test, Vygotsky used blocks of various sizes, shapes, and colors, which could be classified in various categories when the patient discovers the principle in accordance with which the blocks are divided. The most elementary classifying levels are colors and shapes, but the normal individual soon realizes that these classifications are not the right ones and eventually discovers the principle of the correct classification. The schizophrenic patient finds the solution with great difficulty. Vygotsky interpreted the results as indicating a dysfunction of abstract or conceptual thinking. Following Vygotsky, Luria, Kasanin, and Hanfmann also concluded that the schizophrenic thinks in a concrete, realistic way, in a context where things have more a personal than a symbolic value (Kasanin, 1944*a, b,* 1945).

Kurt Goldstein was a very prolific and creative writer whose contributions have already been taken into consideration in this book (Chapter 15). He developed the organismic approach in psychiatry (Goldstein, 1939, 1959). He had the great merit of having pointed out that when the schizophenic uses schizophrenic thinking, he adopts the *concrete attitude*. Whereas some of his concepts or their derivatives have been accepted by many authors, including myself, they have been rejected by others. At times the criticism is merely semantic. Some authors (for instance, Gabel, 1962) object to the word *concrete,* as used by Goldstein. They feel that Goldstein uses it in a pejorative sense, whereas the word *concrete* (especially in the French language) is usually associated with the meaning of being positive, realistic, valid, and reliable.

I find the following shortcomings in Goldstein's concepts:

1. He stresses more the similarities than the differences between patients with brain injuries and schizophrenics.
2. He sees the adoption of the concrete attitude as a way to avoid anxiety and "catastrophic reactions." This interpretation is true, but not complete. He does not show that the concrete representation is generally symbolic of the abstract.
3. He lacks appreciation of the historical element. The effect that history of humanity or personal history has on the individual is hardly taken into account. The individual is seen purely in a biological or neurological frame of reference, that is, as "an organism."

Norman Cameron, already mentioned in section VIII of this chapter, has made important contributions, which have been continued by a large number of authors. According to him (1938, 1939, 1967) schizophrenic thought has the following characteristics:

1. It is asyndetic; that is, it has few causal links.
2. It is metonymic; that is, it lacks precise terms and uses words with approximate meaning. For instance, a patient instead of saying that he had three meals a day said he had "three menus."
3. It presents interpenetrations; that is, parts of a theme intrude with others with which they are not related.
4. It presents overinclusions; that is, includes material with which there may be only peripheral connections.
5. It presents requests to change the conditions with which problems are solved in order to justify the errors.
6. It presents incongruity between acts and words.
7. It presents ineffectual change of generalizations and hypotheses in the attempt to find solutions.
8. It presents disorganization rather than organic deterioration.

Of all the characteristics of schizophrenic thought described by Cameron, overinclusion is the one that has received the greatest consideration. Some authors believe that if the patient's thinking is overinclusive, that is, if it comprehends more than it should, schizophrenic thinking cannot be considered concrete, as Goldstein, Vygotsky, Arieti, and others interpreted. One of the most tenacious advocates of this point of view is Payne (Payne, 1958, 1961, 1972; Payne, Matussek, and George, 1959). According to Payne schizophrenic thought disorder is due to inability to develop and maintain a normal set. Normal mechanisms of inhibition would be broken down. Ideas distantly related are thus included in thoughts. Similarly the patient is unable to disregard perceptual stimuli that most people ignore, and perception too becomes overinclusive.

In my opinion, there is no contradiction between "overinclusive" in the sense used by Cameron and Payne and the meaning of "concrete." "Overinclusive" means inability to *exclude* the nonessential and to abstract the essential. The nonessential related to the essential by a whimsical or peripheral similarity, is included in the new category formed by the schizophrenic. In other words, overinclusion implies a defect in the formation of Aristotelian, or secondary, classes (see the third section of this chapter). The formation of more restrictive categories (or higher classes) requires increased power of abstraction (increased intension and not exclusion). For instance, if a schizophrenic is asked to continue the following series, "dog, cat, horse, lion, tiger, leopard, cow, donkey, elephant, fox, . . ." and he adds "spider, sparrow, bluefish," we should not conclude that he has a higher power of abstraction because he includes in the series several types of animals. Obviously he was not able to abstract from the examples given to him the category "mammals." His overinclusions are proofs of his inability to grasp an abstract idea. This inability of the schizophrenic is related to stimulus generalization, as Mednick (1958) thinks, or to increased equivalence of stimuli (Klüver, 1933, 1936), or to what I have called primary generalization (Arieti, 1967, Chap. 4).

In other words, schizophrenic generalization tends to be at the level of nondifferentiation; it is not the type of generalization that follows the Pavlovian technique of discrimination. (See also the twelfth section of this chapter.) Thus, contrary to what Payne and other authors believe, overinclusion is not the converse of concreteness but an expression of it. This point of view has also been reaffirmed by Sturm (1965).

In a recent book, Lidz (1973) gives more consideration to schizophrenic thinking, to which he now gives an important place in his revised theory of schizophrenia. Lidz is mentioned again at this point because he fundamentally accepts Cameron's concept of overinclusiveness. But, Lidz adds, this overinclusiveness is egocentric. The parents of the patient are egocentric inasmuch as they are unable to recognize that the other person has different feelings, needs, and ways of experiencing. In order to adapt to the parents' needs, the patient becomes egocentric by being parent-centered. "His feelings of being central to his parents' lives lead to feelings of being central and important to everyone, including God." This egocentricity of the patient leads him to "cognitive regression," specifically to "an intercategorical realm" of thinking. In other words, the patient becomes particularly preoccupied with material that lies between categories. It is not very clear how Lidz puts together egocentricity and overinclusiveness. The "overinclusiveness" that leads the patient to believe that many events refer particularly to him may be egocentric, but that is quite different from the overinclusiveness that makes him believe, for instance, that pencil and shoe belong to one category because they both "leave traces" (example from Polyakov, 1969). Vygotsky and Goldstein have very well demonstrated with the tests that they used that this inability to form acceptable categories appears in attempts to solve problems that require abstract thinking and is not necessarily associated with egocentricity. For my interpretation of the phenomenon see the second, third, and twelfth sections of this chapter. I wish to reiterate, however, that especially in incipient schizophrenia, abnormal cognition appears only in the symptoms or in thoughts related to the patient's conflicts.

Eilhard Von Domarus has been mentioned so often in this book that any additional reference to his very important contribution is unnecessary here. However, because most readers know little about the life of this author, I shall give here some biographical data.

Von Domarus was born in Germany into a family that descended from Swedish nobility; they had emigrated to Germany presumably when King Gustave Adolph invaded Europe. Von Domarus obtained his M.D. degree in Germany; then he was awarded a fellowship to continue his studies in philosophy in the United States at Yale University. An enemy of Nazi tyranny, he never returned to Germany after Hitler came to power. Von Domarus was a person completely dedicated to scholarship and to professional life. He died, a bachelor, in 1958.

Born a Protestant, he later in life embraced the Vedic Indian religion. His major focuses of interest were the application of logic and anthropology to psychiatry. In death he proved a philanthropist by leaving almost his entire estate to the Association for the Advancement of Psychotherapy.

F. Barison is an important author who has made a strong impact on the European, and especially Italian, literature. Beginning with his first work in 1934, he has consistently differed from the authors who see schizophrenic thinking as concrete. According to him, both the content and the form of patients are more abstract than those of normal persons at least in the initial stages of schizophrenia. The schizophrenic uses abstract nouns in place of words that refer to concrete objects or ideas. According to Barison, the patient thinks in this abstract way, not in order to beautify his speech or to seek an aesthetic effect or to impress his listener, but in order to repair the dissociative tendencies of his thinking (Barison, 1934, 1948, 1949). For a discussion of Barison's point of view the reader is referred to the fifth section of this chapter. We have already concluded that schizophrenic language and thought at times assume pseudoabstract form and content.

Sergio Piro has intensely and extensively studied schizophrenic language and thought. His recent book (1967) is a mine of information and is strongly recommended to all those who can read Italian. It has a thirty-five-page international bibliography. Piro has been strongly influenced by Barison, but he has been able to transcend the latter's conceptions. He is a bitter critic of such authors as Goldstein and Von Domarus and of any other author, including myself, who believes that in the schizophrenic there is an impairment or diminished use of the capacity to abstract. At times the disagreement is purely semantic; at other times it is due to misunderstanding or to the fact that the emphasis has been put on a particular aspect of the vast subject. For instance, he again attributes to Von Domarus and myself the idea that primitive people must think paleologically. But neither Von Domarus nor I have ever made that statement. He writes that "primitives would with justification feel offended by Von Domarus's hypothesis." But Von Domarus has never made that hypothesis. The reader is again referred to the fourteenth section of this chapter where not the individual use but the collective normal use of paleologic thinking is described, not only in reference to so-called "primitive cultures" but also to our own.

In spite of these inaccuracies and misunderstandings, Piro's book is an important work, and his personal contribution needs to be studied. According to Piro, there is a *semantic dissociation* in schizophrenia. He believes that this dissociation is linguistic and does not refer to thinking *per se*. For him dissociation means loosening of the connections between the verbal sign and its cognitive and emotional meaning. The word is no longer applied to the original semantic structure (or meaning). In the usage of normal persons as well as patients, every sign (or word) has a *semantic halo*. By this term Piro means that in normal persons, too, words do not have only a regular definite meaning but also a certain extension of meaning that allows a certain ambiguity and indetermination in their use. Normally, the more abstract is the level of the word, the more extended is its semantic halo. According to Piro, in the schizophrenic there is an abnormal restriction or increase of the semantic halo. However, he refers to the phenomenon as fluctuation of the semantic halo rather than as increase or decrease.

Piro has described several types of "semantic dissociation, dissociation, dispersion." According to him, this semantic dissociation is not to be confused with Bleuler's loosening of associations of ideas. Also it does not presuppose an organic deterioration or a functional regression, but it is a "global human condition." What Piro is saying is that verbal signs, as used by the schizophrenic, mean more to them than they do to normal people; they may also mean less or may have a different meaning entirely. Of course, we do agree to all this. But the fundamental issue is how to explain this fluctuation of the semantic halo. We have explained it by assuming that the schizophrenic does not always succeed in forming Aristotelian categories. The adoption of primary process cognition prevents him from forming normal categories, especially when the content is involved with his conflicts.

Ignacio Matte-Blanco is a Chilean author who has done considerable work on the logic of schizophrenia. As he mentioned personally to me, he was not aware of the works of Vygotsky, Von Domarus, and myself when he carried out his studies.

Matte-Blanco (1959, 1965) believes that the schizophrenic abandons Aristotelian logic and adopts that of the unconscious system. He believes that he has found the principle that rules the unconscious; he calls this the principle of symmetry. The principle is the following: "The unconscious system accepts the converse of a relation as identical with the relation; in other words, it deals with the relations as if they were symmetric."

Matte-Blanco gives, among others, the following example: If John is the father of Peter, the converse is that Peter is the son of John. But for the schizophrenic patient, if John is the father of Peter, Peter is also the father of John. Peter and John become symmetric.

I have infrequently found this anomaly in schizophrenic thinking. When I found it, it could be interpreted with Von Domarus's principle and with the application of primary classes. John and Peter have the common predicate of being related or relatives. Thus they become equivalent and interchangeable.

Matte-Blanco gives another example. A patient says, "I smoke myself." According to Matte-Blanco the proposition "I smoke a cigarette" becomes for the patient, by virtue of the principle of symmetry, "The cigarette smokes me." Matte-Blanco does not realize that the patient identifies with the cigarette because in his conceptions both he and the cigarette consume themselves.

Loren J. Chapman alone (1958, 1960, 1961) or with collaborators (1964, 1965) wrote a series of important papers on schizophrenic cognition. In the paper published in 1964 Chapman and co-workers advanced "a theory of verbal behavior in schizophrenia." According to these authors words have varieties of meaning and meaning responses. The meaning responses vary in strength: the interpretation of words by normal persons reflects the use of the weaker as well as the stronger meaning responses. On the other hand, schizophrenics' misinterpretations arise from the fact that they abide only by the strongest meaning responses. The following is an example given by the authors:

> The schizophrenics often said things like, "You can ride on a bicycle and you can ride in a wagon, so they mean the same." Normal persons would say something like, "You can ride on both a bicycle and in a wagon, but a bicycle has two wheels and a wagon has four, so they don't really mean the same." These responses suggested that schizophrenics do not weigh simultaneously the several different aspects of meaning in order to answer appropriately the question at hand, but instead answer by using a more limited number of aspects of the meaning."

I have difficulty in understanding why Chapman and co-workers cannot interpret their findings in light of Von Domarus's principle. It is obvious that what they call the strongest meaning is a partial meaning, that is, a predicate. Moreover, it is the predicate that has been selected for a psychodynamic reason, that is, because of the response that it elicits. For instance, bicycle and wagon have many predicates, but the predicate with which patients are psychodynamically involved is "riding vehicle." In this case this chosen predicate may elicit the strongest response in both normal subjects and patients. In many other examples, however, the strongest psychodynamic response is unusual and is determined by the special conflicts and history of the patient.

Russian authors (for instance, Zeigarnik, 1965) have tried to follow Vygotsky's work, but have not been equally successful. Polyakov (1969) found that schizophrenics select unusual attributes (what we call predicates). For instance, requested to find a pairing attribute between pencil and shoe, a patient said, "Leaves traces." Required to find a common attribute between clock and river, a patient said, "Moves along a closed circle." It is obvious that all this could be interpreted as formation of primary classes (see the second and third sections of this chapter).

Recently Reed (1970) has reviewed several theories about schizophrenic thinking. He concludes by repeating the frequent observation that "much of what is found in schizophrenic thought, speech, and writing also occurs in normal people." He suggests that what is typical in schizophrenic thought is not a qualitatively abnormal mechanism but rather a quantitatively abnormal way of using normal mechanisms. The abnormality may result from varying degrees of "information deprivation" and also from a failure of some "filter mechanisms" to separate what is relevant information from what is irrelevant.

Wynne and collaborators (Wynne et al., 1958; Wynne and Singer, 1963; Singer and Wynne, 1965) have carried out many interesting studies on the relation between thinking disorders in schizophrenia and family dynamics. According to Wynne and co-workers the style of interpersonal action in the family of the schizophrenic is connected with his cognitive development. Wynne and Singer found four main characteristics in the family of the schizophrenic: (1) inability to pay attention—this inability of the parents would trigger a similar disturbance in their children, who in turn could not concentrate their attention on certain actions that have a subjective meaning or aim; (2) inappropriate cognitive and affective distance or closeness between members of the family; (3) sense of purposelessness; (4) pseudomutuality.

In other works Wynne and Singer (1963) and Singer and Wynne (1965) divided the disturbances of schizophrenic thinking into two categories: fragmentation and amorphousness. Fragmentation corresponds to Bleuler's loosening of associations. Amorphousness corresponds to a state of dedifferentiation, or early developmental stages in Werner's sense. It is doubtful that what Wynne and coworkers describe in the parents of schizophrenics are *typical* characteristics of schizophrenic thinking. We have already referred to the distinction between what is abnormal but not yet psychotic in the members of the family of the schizophrenic (see Chapter 8). We have also stressed how important it is to separate what is psychodynamically significant but not yet psychotic, and what instead undergoes the psychotic transformation (Chapter 8).

CHAPTER

17

Disorders of Gesture, Action, and Volition

I

Introductory Remarks

The behavior of the schizophrenic patient is usually described as bizarre, odd, peculiar, strange, in many cases unpredictable, or vice versa, predictable and stereotyped. These descriptions are appropriate, but refer only to the manifest symptomatology at a behavioral level.

The manifest behavior of the schizophrenic patient was studied in Chapters 3 and 4. Habitual patterns of regressed patients will be studied in Chapters 23, 24, and 25. The present chapter, in an attempt to go beyond overt behavior, will cover topics of great practical relevance, such as unusual actions, self-mutilation, suicide, and homicide, and issues of fundamental practical and theoretical importance, like the disorder of the will, especially in catatonic patients.

We shall study separately gesture, action, and volition. By *gesture* we mean a motion of the body (or of parts of it) that expresses a special psychological state of the individual. By *action* we mean a purposeful or meaningful behavior, even if the purpose or meaning is not known to the subject. Behavior becomes action when it is connected, consciously or unconsciously, with some symbolic processes. Action has a content that reflects the psychological condition of the subject and a form or structure that reflects a state of normality or pathology. *Volition* is the process of choosing and of initiating, continuing, actualizing, interrupting, or terminating the chosen action. Volition deals with actions. However, when we study action *per se,* we refer to its form and content. When we study volition, we refer to the process of choosing and putting into effect the action.

These three functions (gesture, action, and volition) undergo alterations in schizophrenic patients. At times the alterations are so inconspicuous as to be recognized only with difficulty even by the expert. At other times they are so obvious, especially in catatonic patients, as to leave no doubt about the diagnosis.

II
Gesture

Among the many functions of the human body there is that of presenting the person to other people. The body, with its movements, tone, postures, becomes a vehicle of communication, a language. We shall avoid discussing here whether these bodily changes are intended to constitute a language or whether they are spontaneous activities that express a meaning to the observer, even though the individual may not intend to express it. Usually the gestures of the body are used in dance, pantomime, all theatrical arts, and are represented in the visual arts. They can be profitably studied in psychiatric patients too. Petiziol and Sanmartino (1969) have devoted an entire book to the expressions and gestures of mental patients. The schizophrenic, especially the chronic schizophrenic, seems to have a special style of gestures. At times a schizophrenic or quasi-schizophrenic style is recognizable also in preschizophrenics and, temporarily, in people who are close to, but succeed in averting, schizophrenia.

Mannerisms, affectations, repetitions of movements, especially in particular situations, are schizophrenic and, less frequently, preschizophrenic characteristics. Even more characteristic is the presence of new and unusual movements and peculiar mimic expressions, such as grimaces, movements of the head, shaking of parts of the body, twitching, and so forth. Bobon (1955) has coined for them the name "neomisms," thus indicating that they are related to neologisms and neoformisms. At times an abundance of movements, reminiscent of what is observed in extrapyramidal syndromes, is observed while the patient talks. In some cases the movements and motions seem uncertain, definitely not wanted, and indicative of a search for the required behavior. At other times, especially as the illness advances, the unusual movements become more stereotyped. The repetition seems to eliminate accessory details and to reduce the motion to the essentials.

The theatrical aspect of patients' motions has been remarked by many authors. Are the patients eager to communicate something new, unusual, not easily expressed? In spite of what seems to be the case in certain instances, the patient does not assume a special expression for the purpose of hiding his feelings. He has no poker face. However, the peculiar motions may stand for a combination of contrasting feelings, fusions of ideas, and identifications that are similar to those appearing in his verbal language. For instance, the movement of an arm may not be in accordance with the movement or posture of the trunk or of the legs. Perhaps the patient tries to represent at a motor and muscular level something that cannot be written or spoken and that has no standard symbolic expression. Perhaps the peculiar movement and gesture are ways to express and partially mitigate the patient's pain. He may want to assume a role that does not exist in common life. Some authors do not see only theatrical characteristics in the attitude of the schizophrenic but a surrealistic style of life (Roi, 1953; Barison, 1948).

Manneristic theatricality, stereotypes, and neomisms are three characteristics that often contrast with one another. Most of the time a meaning can be found in them that is valid only for the patient involved. On the other hand, some special movements recur in several patients. One of them is *twiddling,* or rapid shaking of one or more of the fingers. Several authors, but in particular Bettelheim, have described twiddling also in autistic children. Bettelheim writes: "In lieu of an unbearable reality he [the autistic child] creates a private one whose visual appearance he controls through the speed of his twiddling" (1967). Other primitive habits to be differentiated from mimic activity will be discussed in Chapters 23 and 24.

III

Action

Stereotyped action will be discussed in Chapter 23. Here only unusual action, which may be found in all stages of the illness, even the initial ones, will be considered.

It will always be possible to find a meaning in a patient's unusual action that transcends the action itself and is representative of his general psychopathology. Action has to be differentiated from gesture or expression, inasmuch as it is aimed at producing a change that is not limited to the appearance of one's body. A pathological action may indicate (1) decontrol or disinhibition, and (2) putting into effect actions, orders, or thoughts suggested by special cognitive processes, such as "active concretization," delusions, hallucinations, paleologic thinking, and so on.

Among the purely disinhibited actions are those that have an obvious or indirect sexual content. At the onset of the illness the patient may give vent to unrestrained sexual urges, being unable to inhibit them as he used to. At the beginning of schizophrenic episodes several male patients who came to my attention had what they called an irresistible impulse to touch or bump into girls who would walk by on the street. When the patients were hospitalized, they had the urge to touch with sexual intentions female patients and nurses. Some patients in the initial stage of the illness do not refrain from masturbating or exhibiting themselves in public places or on the wards of the hospital. Raping is rare; but promiscuity is relatively frequent in both sexes.

If the illness advances, however, sexual activity other than masturbation decreases and eventually becomes by far less pronounced than in normal persons. In a certain number of patients excessive masturbation persists even when the patient has reached the advanced, preterminal, and terminal stages of regression. It seems almost as if masturbation has remained one of the few (or perhaps the only) means of experiencing at least a part of life. We find, however, marked differences in hospitalized patients as far as sexual life is concerned. Often these differences are related to the period of time when the observation was made and to the type of hospital administration. In the years 1941–1945, when I was working in Pilgrim State Hospital (New York), sexual activities among chronic patients were relatively rare. In later years in psychiatric hospitals in general these activities have become more common. Again it could be that the policy of restrictiveness or permissiveness, which varies according to time and place, is one of the factors responsible for the difference. In recent years it has also become a practice in many hospitals to have patients of both sexes reside in the same wards. In addition to increased difficulty in controlling sexual urges, desire to defy or to seek power are reasons for increased sexual activity. The eventual marked decline in sexuality in patients who continue to regress must be considered as partially due to hospitalization, lack of stimulation, detachment, and so on. Contrasting with the decreased activity in overt sexual life, however, is the persistent and occasionally even increasing role of sexual symbolism in the delusions and ideas of reference of some chronic patients. In these cases, sex symbols, often expressed in unusual and bizarre ways, refer to life in general and not only to sexual activity.

The process of *active concretization* can be easily recognized in many apparently senseless and bizarre actions of patients. A professional man, after a long history of apparent neurosis and maladjustment, manifested psychotic behavior all of a sudden. He exposed himself nude to relatives. While he was walking on the street, although accompanied by his father, he insisted on walking on the edge of the sidewalk in a conspicuous and ridiculous manner. Later in the treatment the meaning of these bizarre acts could be established. His exhibiting himself in the nude meant showing others how he really was, in spite of the fact that he could not express himself verbally. When the therapist asked him why he walked on the edge of the sidewalk, he replied, "I was in danger; my condition was unstable." Apparently he had to translate his feeling of danger and instability into a physical situation, which could be more easily controlled. In fact, he obviously succeeded in walking on the edge of the sidewalk without falling by carefully placing one foot after the other, but he had not been so successful in the journey of life. This patient, like many others who indulge in this bizarre type of action, did not know the meaning of his actions when he was carrying them out, but he was able to retrieve the meaning later at an advanced stage of therapy.

Another patient used to go into stores and put the light on and off repeatedly, to the consternation of all people who were there. At a time when he felt powerless, this act gave him a feeling of power and reconnected him with the world that was escaping him.

Reitman (1951) reported a patient who thought that as a private in the army he had a dog's life. While on a parade he disclosed his manifest outbreak of schizophrenia. He suddenly went on all fours and started to bark. His thought "I am treated like a dog," became, "I am a dog," and consequently he acted as a dog.

Many regressed patients have the habit of staying most of the time either in a corner of a ward if they are hospitalized, or of a room if they are living at home. In some cases they do not actually stay in a corner, but they always remain close to a wall, away from the center of the room. They also cannot express verbally the reason why they are reluctant to move to other parts of the room. In many cases the patients, by resorting to the process of active concretization, feel that the walls protect them from the threatening feelings, from the ineffable hostility and danger that they sense all around. In some other cases the patients seem to treat the walls as their friends, the only friends they have. A patient standing in a corner is "in the company of two friends," the two walls. He would feel too threatened by friendship with human beings.

Another recurring symptom, even in patients who are not regressed, is the *scream*. At times unexpectedly, or after a period of acute disturbance, the patient explodes into a loud, horrifying scream, a symptom that for centuries has been represented in literature as a symbol of madness. The scream stands for the life-long whimpering that was never heard. From patients who later were able to verbalize their feeling, I have learned that the scream is a protest. The scream means, "Stop, stop, surrounding malevolent forces. Don't overcome me, don't drown me. I want to live, I am alive, I scream" (Arieti, 1963*a*).

A certain number of hospitalized patients have a record of repeated bizarre behavior. Some smashed furniture, others broke mirrors into pieces, threw jewelry into the toilet, burned rare books or other valuable objects, rang fire alarms, threw plants and other solid objects out of the windows, and so on. Some of these actions, like, for instance, throwing the marriage ring into the toilet, have an obvious meaning. Others have been interpreted merely as acts of rebellion against the mores of the established society, the habits of the family, parental authority, and so forth. In quite a large number of these actions we can detect a more subtle symbolic meaning, one that is expressed through active concretization. The clinician must always remember that the bizarreness of an act is not sufficient to warrant the diagnosis of schizophrenia. The bizarre act has to be evaluated in its meaning and in the context of the whole symptomatology. Nonpsychotic people also occasionally perform bizarre actions.

Self-mutilation is a socially unacceptable alteration of the body inflicted by the individual upon himself. It is carried out by actions that aim at cutting off, removing, destroying, maiming, or impairing one or more parts of the organism. Phillips and Alkan (1961*a, b*) have found this practice in 4.29 percent of a hospital population. The female patients constituted 6.10 percent, and the male patients 2.17. Thus nearly three times as many females as males engaged in self-mutilation. The authors did not classify the patients, but probably most of them were chronic schizophrenics.

A large number of these patients want to substitute a physical pain for an emotional one. Perhaps in these cases we may consider again the self-mutilating act as a concretization or an embodiment of the mental anguish. The patient, however, does not succeed in obtaining what he wants because the physical pain is considered less disturbing than the mental one, and so the act is repeated. A few patients, in the course of treatment, told me that they used to hurt themselves because the pain then became real. They wanted to escape from what they vaguely perceived as unreal pain.

In many cases the self-mutilating act has a more specific symbolic meaning. Castrations play a prominent role (Hemphill, 1951). By cutting, or burning, or injuring in any way the arms, legs, fingers, toes, penis, and testicles, often male patients want to castrate themselves in order to punish themselves or because "they prefer to belong to the other sex." I have found that self-inflicted injuries to testicles and penis are not necessarily castration attempts but symbolic expressions of preoccupation with birth, being born, being one's parents' real son, or the father of one's children, and so on. At times these acts of self-mutilation carry out commands received from auditory hallucinations. At other times they are determined by delusional beliefs.

Fenichel (1945) compares the self-castrations, as they occasionally occur in catatonic conditions, to the "auto-castrations" performed by religious fanatics, who, by such radical denial of their active sexual wishes, try to regain "peaceful unity with God," that is, an extreme passive submissiveness, less a feminine nature than an early infantile "oceanic" one.

According to Szasz (1957*b*), in self-mutilating schizophrenic patients the ego needs "to bring the body up to date, so to speak, in order that it correspond to the psychically amputated (new) body image. Since the body part was already lost from the point of view of the experiencing ego, its removal is unaccompanied by pain."

In some cases it is difficult to believe that the patient is telling us the truth when he reports an act of self-injury, and he may be considered as expressing somatic delusions. For instance, Kraft and Babigian (1972) reported the case of a woman who came to a psychiatric emergency room because of pain from needles in her arms. Her history suggested that she was experiencing somatic delusions as part of her chronic schizophrenic condition. Radiological studies showed actual multiple needles in her left arm due to past episodes of self-mutilation.

The clinician is warned again that an act of self-mutilation is not in itself pathognomonic of schizophrenia. It may be ritual, or the result of very unusual motivation as it was in the case of the patient Peter (Chapter 9). At times these self-mutilating patients are diagnosed as suffering from psychopathic personalities, like the one described by Phillips and Alkan (1961*b*), or character neuroses, and so on, but it seems evident that all these patients are at least quasi-psychotic or potentially psychotic. The actions of these patients seem to take the place of delusions.

Suicide is another important possibility that has to be taken into serious consideration in schizophrenics, too, and not only in patients suffering from depression. Rennie (reported by Warnes, 1968), in a follow-up study of 500 schizophrenics admitted to a mental hospital from 1913 to 1923, found that 11 percent of those who had died, had died as a result of suicide. Suicide ranked third among the causes of death after tuberculosis and respiratory infections. A study reported by Wilson (1968) showed that two-thirds of psychiatric patients who had received hospital treatment and who had committed suicide were schizophrenic and chronically ill. This incidence is not as high as it seems, considering that the majority of hospitalized chronic patients are schizophrenics. Although the majority of authors agree that successful suicide is most common among persons suffering from psychotic depression, they also agree that it is relatively common in schizophrenics (Lewis, 1933, 1934; Jamieson, 1936; Norris, 1959).

Statistics on suicide among schizophrenics are unreliable. Too many variables are involved—the severity of surveillance in hospitals, the policy of admission and discharge, and the difference in the incidence of schizophrenics who are hospitalized or treated in the community. There seems to be no doubt, however, that the incidence of suicide among schizophrenics is considerably higher than the incidence in the general population (which is approximately 15 in 100,000). Warnes (1968) reports that the incidence of suicide in institutions is twenty-eight times higher than it is among the general population. For recent studies on the subject the reader is referred to the works by Warnes (1968) and Wilson (1968).

The increased liberality with which patients are treated in hospitals, the practice of psychotherapy, and the large use of drug therapy, with quick amelioration of symptoms, indirectly increase the possibility of suicide—an increased risk that in the large context of the overall benefits of modern treatment has to be accepted. Worthy of consideration are the words of Bleuler, which appear at the very end of his major work (1950, pp. 488–489). He believed that the surveillance to which the schizophrenic patient is subjected "awakes, increases and maintains the suicidal drive." He added, "Only in exceptional cases would any of our patients commit suicide if they were permitted to do as they wished. And even if a few more killed themselves—does this reason justify the fact that we torture hundreds of patients and aggravate their disease?"

Wilson's (1968) five-factor psychosocial evaluation showed that schizophrenic suicidal patients were characterized by "lack of constructive plans for the future, high chaotic energy levels, and general isolation."

I classify suicides of schizophrenics into three categories, according to the dominant psychopathology:

1. Disinhibition of masochistic trends, not necessarily connected with conscious depression.
2. As part of a depressive syndrome or of depressive episodes superimposed on the schizophrenic syndrome feelings of hopelessness, melancholia, unworthiness, inner disintegration, and so on.
3. As acting out of commands or ideas suggested by the delusional ideas, hallucinations, new ways of thinking, and so forth.

In my experience the third group is the largest. However, in many cases the suicidal act is the result of a combination of these three factors (see, for instance, the suicide of the patient Gabriel, described in Chapter 9).

In a considerable number of patients we find a history of suicidal attempts prior to the onset of the illness. Reichard and Tillman (1950*b*) postulated that suicide, as well as homicide, is an attempt to defend oneself from the psychosis.

Berk (1950) found that suicidal schizophrenics are immature, less emotionally controlled, self-absorbed, and have greater difficulties in heterosexual relations than nonsuicidal schizophrenics.

Criminality is much less prevalent among schizophrenics than among psychopaths, alcoholics, and drug addicts (Guze, Goodwin, and Crane, 1969). These authors found the combined prevalence of criminality among schizophrenic and depressed patients not very different from that expected in the general population.

Homicide is not as common among schizophrenic patients as some people believe. Guttmacher (1960) stressed the fact that homicide is a very rare phenomenon among schizophrenics. He stated, "When one considers the great prevalence of this disorder, the tens of thousands of cases that exist, and the few homicides committed by schizophrenics and other types of psychotic individuals, there is no cause for alarm." On the other hand, there seems to be no doubt that schizophrenia is more common among murderers than among the general population. A study by Cole, Fisher, and Cole (1968) found that 18 percent of women who had committed murder were psychotic (usually paranoid schizophrenic), but they were not considered legally insane. Guttmacher wrote, "Whenever a former inmate of a psychiatric hospital commits a homicide, there is likely to be raised a hue and cry, demanding that such things stop." Guttmacher added that until we have "an absolute and permanent cure for all psychotic patients, such an occasional tragedy must necessarily be perpetrated by discharged patients. The only sure way to prevent them would be to keep all psychiatric hospital patients in permanent custody, an act the impracticality of which would only be surpassed by its inhumanity. There must be this irreducible minimum of such cases. If none ever occurred, we could conclude that discharge policies were too strict."

Nivoli (1973) has recently completed a study of the "schizophrenic murderer" which could be considered fundamental to the subject. According to him the murders committed by schizophrenics imply greater violence and body mutilation than those committed by nonschizophrenics. The crimes generally involve more than one victim. The average age of the patient is 29 and he comes from a family living in social anomie; if he is married, his first victim is generally his wife. In many cases, he has asked for help or implicitly requested that he be put in a position in which he could be prevented from committing the crime. However, he was ignored or not believed. The offense is not so much the result of a well organized delusional system, but of decontrolled hostility, or of a sense of fear. In some cases, he had asked to be helped to move away, either to escape a delusionally conceived danger or the urge to commit the crime. He does not seem to have guilt feeling or sorrow for the victim. Often he denies that his victim is dead and may continue to write letters to him.

Theoretically a schizophrenic patient, especially if mildly sick, could commit a crime that is not in any way motivated, caused, or facilitated by the illness. In other words, it is conceivable that the nonsick, still integral part of the patient dictated and actualized the murder. Schipkowensky (1938, 1967), a Bulgarian psychiatrist who has made a careful study of homicides committed by schizophrenics, calls this group "intelligible homicides." He writes that the influence of the schizophrenic process cannot be found in these cases. He reported three such cases—two patients killed for money and one in self-defense. The author adds that patients may commit also "murders of liberation" in order to eliminate a hated member of the family. These murders committed by schizophrenics seem identical to those committed by psychopaths, and epileptic and healthy persons, and are not necessarily related to the schizophrenic condition. Actually there is no way to ascertain that the illness did not motivate or facilitate the murder. The other possibility—that is, that the illness had a great deal to do with the murder—seems much more probable, especially from the study of the cases that have come under accurate psychiatric examination.

Schizophrenic murders can be divided into many categories. As in the case of suicides, these categories are artificial. A case that would fit into only one of the categories would be unusual. The homicide may be:

1. A disinhibition of strong hostile trends preexisting in the prepsychotic life of the patient.
2. An effort to prevent the psychosis, or an exacerbation of the psychosis, or to defend against overwhelming attacks of anxiety.
3. A symbolic suicide.
4. An order from hallucinations or delusions, or an act necessitated only by the distorted thinking processes of the patient. This fourth category can be divided into subgroups, as we shall see.

When the psychiatrist studies psychodynamically cases belonging to the first category, he realizes that in addition to the "disinhibition" made possible by the illness, there was a preexisting strong aggressive or hostile trend. Guttmacher (1960), for instance, described the case of a patient who was raised in the most unusual way by a strict, peculiar, stultifying, punishing father who did not allow freedom and individuality. The patient had three sisters, who also appeared to Guttmacher as eccentric. As a matter of fact, when the patient eventually slew both parents, the sisters seemed untouched and apathetic. One of them, when she discovered the bodies of the murdered parents, went to notify the authorities; then she returned to the barn and milked the cow. The patient told Guttmacher, "I couldn't take it any more. It seemed like he was always trying to punish me. I thought of using this knife that I did use." The patient said that no voice or compulsion had ordered him to kill his father. He had not drunk alcohol that day. When he was asked why he also killed his mother, he gave the following explanation: "I did not want my mother to know her son had done it. She was sick; she had a bad heart. . . ." The patient had shown in the last few months several peculiarities, and the father had contemplated having him examined by a psychiatrist. Apparently the onset of the illness released his control and permitted him to act in accordance with his hostility toward his father.

The second category, to which belong schizophrenics who commit crimes in order to overcome an oncoming or already existing psychosis or an overwhelming anxiety, has been described by Wertham (1937) and Reichard and Tillman (1950*a*).

Wertham writes that the crime is "an expression of the fight on the part of the patient for safe-guarding of the personality. One gains the impression that the violent act in these cases prevents the developments that would be far more serious for the patient's health. The overt act seems to be a rallying point for the constructive forces of the personality." What the patient undergoes in these situations is called by Wertham *catathymic crisis*. Reichard and Tillman (1950) seem to have been influenced by Wertham. Reichard and Tillman write: "Murders and suicides which lack an adequate motive may represent an attempted defense against the outbreak of a schizophrenic psychosis in which the ego seeks to protect itself from disintegration by discharging the unassuageable anger through an act of violence." Other authors believe that the murderous acts are attempts to channel anxiety into intense motor activity. They culminate in aggression toward a significant figure in the life history of the patient. Guttmacher (1960) does not subscribe to these interpretations inspired by Wertham's work. He writes that the concept of the murderous act as a defense against the psychosis is interesting, but its validity is difficult to establish. Defense mechanisms are generally habitual methods of response, whereas the schizophrenic act of violence is used generally once. He is inclined to believe that many of the schizophrenic homicides are "short-lived psychic decompensations in vulnerable persons" because of great external or intrapsychic stress. He discusses these cases in a chapter devoted to the "temporarily psychotic murder," because many of these patients seem to have been psychotic only for a short period of time. When they come to trial at times there is little or no evidence of psychosis. For legal reasons it is very important to determine whether they were psychotic or not when they committed the crime. The evidence of the temporary psychosis is lacking unless the patient wrote psychotic letters or was witnessed in psychotic manifestations during the episode. Guttmacher connects these patients with those described by Menninger and Mayman (1956). These two authors have described patients whose actions suggest the influence of a psychosis and yet did not present evidence of psychosis at the time of the examination or later. Their crimes seem to be the result of unmotivated, silly, impulsive, perhaps automatic behavior.

The third category consists of schizophrenic patients who committed a homicide that was a symbolic suicide. Again we owe to Guttmacher the best report of such cases. He mentions, among others, a schizophrenic mother who had been quite promiscuous sexually and who killed her 13-year-old daughter when she found out that she too had become promiscuous. In these cases the patient identifies with his victim; or, in other words, he projects to the victim that part of himself that he wants to reject and destroy.

The fourth category, which is the most numerous, includes all the murders that are committed as a result of complicated delusional thinking or under the order of hallucinations. Needless to say, in addition to the manifest motivation that is related to delusions, ideas of reference, and hallucinations, there is often an underlying psychodynamic that only in some cases can be understood.

Schipkowensky (1967) reported that the prevailing manifest motivations for schizophrenic crime are defense and sacrifice. Both motivations are inspired by a common goal: "rescue," of the patient or of the family, nation, state, party, and so on, as well as of some ideologies. Delusions of jealousy are also common motivational factors. A patient reported by Schipkowensky killed his physician, a young woman, who was allegedly stealing his sexual potency and transmitting it to the patient's brother. Another patient reported by Schipkowensky killed his cook, who was believed to be attempting to poison the patient and his neighbors. Schipkowensky reported three mothers who killed their babies (one, 1 month old) in order "to save themselves." He reported also ten cases of patients who killed their parents. The larger of his groups included fifteen patients who killed their wives under the influence of delusions of jealousy. Schipkowensky collected also a group of four schizophrenics who attempted to kill their physicians, but only one of them (already mentioned) succeeded. In the other three cases the physicians were seriously wounded.

Stierlin (1956) has probably made the most extensive inquiry of cases of aggression committed by mental patients residing in seventy-three psychiatric hospitals. Fifty-four (or 6.9 percent) of 773 acts of aggression were directed against physicians, and in five cases death resulted. In 719 cases (or 93.1 percent) the aggression was directed against nurses, attendants, and others, and resulted in eleven deaths. Of the patients involved in these crimes, 60 percent were schizophrenics.

Schipkowensky devoted a great deal of attention to the sacrificial or, in general, symbolic meaning of some schizophrenic crimes, reminiscent of ancient rites. He described in detail the interesting case of patient N., whose crime was inspired by a dream. The patient dreamt of a monster who would destroy the whole world. On awakening, "N. assumed the role of St. George." He obeyed a voice that told him, "Get up and shoot." He killed a 19-year-old girl, a cousin of his wife.

Contrasted to the harmful or bizarre acts which have been reported in this chapter are the amazingly appropriate actions, manifestations of sudden reintegration of the ego, which occasionally occur in some regressed schizophrenics. I shall mention as an example a woman in her 30's who came for treatment after an acute schizophrenic episode which was followed, as well as preceded, by chronic milder symptomatology, with ideas of reference, delusional thinking, and many distortions. In her life situation as well as during the sessions, she could not go beyond a very narrow range of interest and preoccupation. She spoke almost constantly about the little injustices that her mother-in-law and sister-in-law perpetrated against her and the alleged ineffectiveness of her husband in protecting her. Although there was an element of truth in her allegations, this truth was lost in a web of distortions and petty preoccupations. She had three little children, and it happened that one day one of them was playing with matches and started a big fire which, in a few minutes, involved and destroyed the whole house, an isolated home in the suburban area. The patient, who was in the garden when the fire started, entered the home, saved her three children, important documents and money, then called the firemen and the police. When they arrived, the whole house had burned, but she had been able to rescue the whole family, as very few normal people would have been able to do in similar circumstances. Many persons in similar cases are overwhelmed by panic and do not live up to what the situation demands. Many therapists have heard similar examples from their patients.

How is this contrasting behavior to be explained? I believe that when a piece of reality is perceived by the patient very clearly and with strength, it may succeed in bypassing the schizophrenic ideation. Finally reality, no longer connected with the patient's habitual cognitive processes, impinges strongly upon him. The perception of the danger and the very adequate response constitute a short-circuited mechanism which contrasts with the usual thought processes. Unfortunately these special actions are the exceptions. Ordinarily the personal mode of thought obliterates the distinction between the real and unreal, and abnormal action results.

IV

Volition

Volition, or the capacity to choose and to carry out the choice, is a topic that has not received much consideration in American psychiatric and psychological literature. Recently, however, three books have been written on the subject (Farber, 1966; May, 1969; Arieti, 1972*a*). On the other hand, volition, as an object of study, has a long tradition in French and German psychiatric literature (see, for instance, Ribot, 1899; Bostroem, 1928; Ach, 1935; Blondel, 1939; Boutonier, 1951).

Volition, like the phenomenon consciousness, does not lend itself easily to scientific study. Moreover, a great part of the scientific world, so involved in the concept of determinism, denies the existence of free choice altogether. The psychoanalytic schools (especially the classic Freudian, but also most of the neo-Freudians) have contributed to this neglect by denying the importance of the will and accepting the existence of motivation as the universal psychological determinant of action. According to this point of view, every act is motivated (or caused) by a wish or drive. Thus, it is not the will that determines which action is chosen, but rather the motivation (conscious or unconscious) or the strongest of the possible contrasting motivations. If motivation removes the possibility of free choice, then the only act of free will would be one that is not motivated. But an act that is not motivated at all is not performed voluntarily by any human being—it is automatic. In *The Will To Be Human* (Arieti, 1972*a*) I clarify how will may enter into the phenomenon of motivation. A will-motivated action may be consistent or not with a wish-motivated action. Certainly conscious or unconscious motivation *per se,* is very important, but so is the mechanism that either actualizes or inhibits the motivated action.

As I discussed elsewhere (Arieti, 1967), mature volition requires several steps: (1) the evaluation of several alternatives; (2) the choice of one alternative; (3) the planning of the chosen alternative; (4) the will (or determination) to carry out the chosen and planned alternative; (5) the inhibition of the envisioned but not-willed forms of behavior; (6) the execution of the chosen behavior.

The first three steps are more cognitive processes than conative ones. They are not exclusively cognitive, however, because they have an emotional counterpart and are always influenced or promoted by conscious or unconscious motivation, or by multiple and conflictful motivations. To discuss the first three steps is beyond the purpose of this chapter. We would have to repeat a great deal of what we discussed in Part Two.

It is with the fourth step that conation is added to cognition. As Terzuolo and Adey (1960) wrote, our physiological knowledge of willed movement is very meager. These authors added that none of the known neurophysiological data can account for the initiation and arrest of movement, nor for the purposive changes made in the course of a movement on the basis of previous experience. There is considerable proof that starting or stopping of motor activities takes place through the pyramidal fibers in the primary motor area. However, information has already been integrated in other neural centers before executive orders are transmitted to the motor area.*

The last three steps in the mechanism of volition require special consideration in this chapter. We shall discuss them especially with regard to catatonic patients. Although catatonic patients have become much less numerous in the last two decades, I think that this topic continues to be of greatest interest, and its study by every psychiatrist is imperative for three reasons: (1) it throws important light on the whole schizophrenic process and on the phenomenon of will as a human function; (2) it cannot be excluded that, although rare today, catatonic patients may become common again in a not too distant future; (3) although rare, catatonic syndromes occur, and the psychiatrist must recognize them and understand them in the light of the knowledge that is available. A comparative developmental approach will be pursued here.

As we have already mentioned in previous chapters, the symptomatology of catatonia consists not of motor disorders but of will disorders. The patient cannot move, not because he is paralyzed, but because he cannot *will* to move. If an action would merely be a motion, the patient would be able to move freely, but human action is connected with meaning and choice.

Just as symbolism includes an elaborate transformation of what the posterior human brain (temporal, occipital, and parietal lobes) receives from the external world, willing and acting include the elaborate transformation of motor impulses, which take place in the anterior brain (frontal lobes).

Although steps four, five, and six occur in a fraction of a second in most initial actions, they require complicated mechanisms and various possibilities. The first clear-cut manifestation of willed action is the inhibition of the reflex response. The toilet-trained baby is a clear example of this inhibition. Because of rectal dis-

* The neurophysiology of the inhibitory mechanisms that permit choice has been reviewed by Diamond, Balvin, and Diamond (1963).

tention, he has the impulse to defecate, but he learns to inhibit the response and to control his sphincters by using cortical mechanisms. The child has the neurological capacity to resist defecation, but he must not want to defecate. If the child chooses not to defecate, although it would be pleasant to do so, it is because he wants to please his mother. Thus, even in the first volitional acts, which imply choices, a new dimension enters: the interpersonal (the you). From a philosophical point of view it seems almost a contradiction in terms: the first acts of volition are acts of obedience, or of submission to the will of others. Choice, this new portentous tool that emerges in phylogenesis with the human race, in the early ontogenetic stages requires support from others before it can be exercised independently. At the same time there is an equally important change in the mechanism of motivation: no longer is motivation involved only with pleasing the self, but also with pleasing others, or at best with pleasing the self through pleasing others.

Whereas infrahuman animals *react* to events, men *act*—that is, they have a choice as to what to do, or at least they act in the belief that they have a choice as to what to do. One of the first facts of life that primitive men become aware of is their ability to will. Men understood this fact long before they grasped the concept of physical causality, that is, the concept that a given physical event is the cause of another event. As a matter of fact, as has been mentioned in Chapter 16, in primitive societies every event is considered to be caused by the will of men or anthropomorphized beings (gods, animals, rivers, and so on). We have also seen how the person who caused the event was in primitive or ancient societies considered to be responsible for the event. Responsibility and causality were interconnected. If an event was harmful (and in a primitive society that can hardly protect itself from nature, many events are bound to be harmful), the person deemed responsible for the event was considered guilty. The concept of *guilt* and *cause* are confused in many primitive languages. Even in early Greek, the word *aitia* (from which is derived the English word *etiology*) means both guilt and cause. For the primitive, to do is to be potentially guilty, because, after all, you could not know the event that will follow what you are doing. The event might even have an effect on the whole tribe; its repercussions might be enormous, like an epidemic or drought. Kelsen (1943) has well illustrated the relation between *to do* and *to be guilty*.

How do primitive men act in order to diminish their feeling of guilt? They refrain from acting freely; they perform only those acts that are accepted by the tribe. For any desired effect, the tribe teaches the individual what act to perform. Ritualism and magic thus originate. The life of primitive man is not as free as many philosophers and romantic writers believe. It is completely regulated by an enormous number of norms and restrictions. The individual has to follow the ritual for practically everything he does. By performing the act according to ritual, primitive man removes the anxiety that arises from the expectation of possible evil effects. The ritual ensures that the effect will be good.

Now, if we translate the foregoing into psychiatric terminology, we may state that an extreme state of anxiety is alleviated by the adoption of an enormous system of compulsions. What would happen if the primitive would not follow the ritual? He would be overwhelmed by tremendous anxiety, not only because he is afraid of being punished by the tribe, but also because he feels guilty or responsible for his free acts. He may seek punishment or remain anxious. If the anxiety is intolerable and as intense as panic, he may eliminate action entirely. Actually that happens very seldom; the man living in a primitive culture faithfully follows the ritual.

From a certain point of view, the history of humanity, subsequent to the primitive period, can be seen, in spite of many detours and regressions, as a gradual movement toward freedom, that is, toward less reliance on the support of the group and toward individual will. This act of liberation from the influence or suggestion of others has its ontogenetic representation in the negativistic stage of children, who, for a certain period of early childhood, refuse to do what they are told to do. By disobeying, they practice their newly acquired ability to will; but they do so by resorting to a primitive method of willing—namely, by resisting.

A comparative developmental approach thus discloses that the unfolding of volition, which in its mature form consists of six steps, goes through the following developmental stages:

1. Negative volition, consisting of the capacity and conative efforts to resist reflex responses or other automatic responses.
2. Volition with compliance to mother, or tribe, or ritual, or volition accompanied by anxiety and/or guilt.
3. Volition by resisting compliance, anxiety, and/or guilt.
4. Independent positive volition. This fourth stage will permit the unfolding of the six steps of mature volition.

This is, of course, a simplified scheme. In normal human beings, all possible types are found, but in pathological conditions we find a preponderance of immature types and partial or total loss of others. For instance, in neurotic persons we find excessive compliance to others; in obsessive-compulsives it is compliance to ritual. In catatonic patients we find the most regressive forms.

V

Volition in Catatonics

The dynamic studies reported in Chapter 10 indicate that people apt to become catatonic are those who in their early childhood were prevented from developing confidence in their own actions and reliance on their capacity to will. The parents or parent-substitutes predisposed these patients either not to will or to follow parental decisions. When the patients later had to make their own choices, they found themselves unable to act; if they acted, they were criticized and made to feel guilty. Thus in catatonia, the typical schizophrenic childhood struggle with the significant adults is connected particularly with the patient's actions and choices. The fear of action becomes panic. The catatonic state is a way to remove action in order to remove the panic connected with the willed action. Sometimes this panic is generalized. When it is extended to every action, the patient may lapse into a state of complete immobility (stupor). Let us reconsider the cases of the patients reported in Chapter 10. When Richard was in a state of extreme anxiety and in the process of developing a catatonic attack, he presented the following strange phenomena. More and more he realized that it was difficult for him to act. He did not know what to do. He did not know where to look, where to turn. Any motion that he was inclined to make appeared to him as an insurmountable problem because he did not know whether he should make it or not. This problem presented itself when any act was to be performed; it was an exasperating, horrible experience. The overwhelming fear of doing the wrong thing, which would either hurt or disappoint him, possessed him to an increasing degree. Therefore he preferred not to eat, not to dress, not to wash himself. He preferred to be motionless, almost paralyzed, to lie in bed or on a chair for a long time. However, before he developed the symptoms of immobility, when he realized that it was becoming increasingly difficult for him to do things and had the feeling that he was lost, or was losing himself, he tried desperately to hold on to something. That something was, to use his own word, ''magic.'' For instance, when he was walking and would see a red light, that was interpreted by him as a sign that he should not go ahead; God was guiding him and was telling him to stop. If he saw an arrow, he would go in the direction of the arrow. He felt that he *must* go in that direction. If he discovered no signs, a terrific hesitation tortured him. When he was motionless, he had to ''interpret'' everything. Every occurrence seemed to have a special reference to him and was an indication of whether he should do the thing he wished to do or not. When he was asked questions, he tried to answer, but an accidental noise or other occurrence was interpreted by him as a possible sign or order for him not to respond. The number of words the question consisted of was interpreted as a possible sign not to answer. Even before he had become so sick, he had tried to find signs for guidance. One day he saw a girl working in a hospital, an indication to him that he should work in that hospital. As the anxiety increased, his reliance on these signs did not help much, and he gradually sank into a complete catatonic stupor.

In this case I have related these experiences almost verbatim, as given by the patient. Very few patients are able to recollect the experiences of precatatonic panic as well as this patient did. I was very fortunate indeed to be able to recapture them from him. They are dramatic and frightful experiences of tremendous emotional intensity and often completely forgotten by the patient. At times, the patient who senses that he is sinking into stupor because he is afraid to act tries to prevent this by becoming overactive and submerging himself in a manic-like sequence of aimless acts. This is the so-called catatonic excitement that precedes or follows the catatonic stupor. During this period of excitement the patient acts in the opposite way, that is, as if he were not concerned at all with responsibility or as if he would defy previous concepts of responsibility. He may become homicidal, suicidal, and destructive. Indeed, the catatonic excitement is one of the most dangerous psychiatric occurrences, more dangerous by far then the manic excitement.

Now, let us reexamine the case of Richard in view of our knowledge of the mechanism of volition accompanied by guilt. We have seen that because of the traumatic environment of his early life, whenever Richard was in the act of doing something, he would be possessed by anxiety. Mother was always there, either in her physical reality or as an incorporated image, to tell him that he was doing the wrong thing. When the difficulties in living, which were described in Chapter 10, further increased his anxiety, the problem of acting became even more difficult. Action automatically produced either guilt or at least further anxiety. In other words, the patient was in the same predicament as was primitive man, when he was first confronted with this new and portentous weapon, the choice of action. Like the primitive, he tried to protect himself by resorting to neurotic compromises, compulsions, and obsessions, which correspond to ritual and magic.

If the prepsychotic patient knows what to do, if a sign is given to him, he will not feel guilty or anxious. The future will be controlled, he feels, the effect may be foreseen, the result will be good. Often, however, this compromise or defense is not sufficient, either because the anxiety is too overpowering or because the patient is not able to find enough signs, that is, is not able to fabricate compulsions quickly enough. He is actually in a much worse situation than the primitive. The tribe protects the primitive by giving him all the signs he needs (magic and ritual), but the patient has to fabricate all of them by himself at an increasing speed, and the more acute the spell of anxiety is, the more difficult it is for him to do so. He has only one other resort, the last, with which to escape anxiety: not to act. He will not act and will fall into catatonic stupor.

This sequence of events also explains why many catatonic attacks occur acutely or semiacutely. If the anxiety does not increase in an acute manner, there is the possibility of building a compulsive defense, which may prevent the psychotic breakdown. But, before interpreting other psychotic symptoms and the relations between catatonia and obsessive-compulsive psychoneurosis, it may be useful to reexamine briefly the case of Sally.

As in the case of Richard, Sally grew up in an atmosphere of over burdensome parental interference. Her fear of doing the wrong thing was always present. She either did what her mother wanted or had to face anxiety. However, after her marriage, when the anxiety increased to a tremendous degree, the fear became uncontrollable. We have seen how, at other times in her life, she resorted to compulsive defenses. After her marriage, with the precipitation of events, she sank into a catatonic stupor. Like Richard, she was able to describe what happened. She was afraid to make any movement. Any movement she made might be wrong. For that reason, she could not dress herself, get up from bed, eat, and so forth. If she were dressed by others, and if she were spoon fed, the responsibility would rest on others. Even talking was an action, and she wanted to avoid it as much as possible. This catatonic condition lasted for a while, but later, when she was less insecure, she was able to transform the catatonic symptoms into compulsive ones. If she acted in a special way, that is, by examining every movement and seeing that pieces of herself were not falling off, she might be allowed to act. She might do a few things, but at the expense of tremendous ritual. Each small trivial act had to be made licit by the application of the ritual. This was so cumbersome, however, that she often preferred absolute immobility to the action. That is why, during the first few months of treatment, the patient alternated between compulsive activities and catatonic postures.

From both these cases one sees that there is a major difference between the primitive and the patient. Whereas the primitive has the support of authority (the tribe) and therefore may indulge in the ritual with a certain facility, the patient does not have such support. In the case of the patient, the authority (parents) is generally the one that predisposes the patient to revert to the stage of introjected guilt. This explains why obsessional neuroses are absent in primitive societies (Carothers, 1947, 1951). The culture itself is obsessive-compulsive. "It is only when the individual stands alone and must develop his own ethical code that this neurosis can develop." In the ten years spent in Kenya as a psychiatrist, Carothers never saw a single case of obsessional neurosis. He did see, however, thirty-two cases of catatonia. We do not know the dynamics of those cases. One may venture to guess that the culture did not protect them any longer with the ritual and that they protected themselves with a catatonic armor, just as people in our culture may do.

What has been mentioned explains other characteristics encountered in cases of catatonic schizophrenia. In order to avoid anxiety and guilt, the patient cannot will any act, but he may passively follow orders given by others, because the responsibility will not be his. Thus, if somebody tells a catatonic, "Show your tongue, I want to prick it with a pin," the catatonic may show his tongue in a very submissive way. This blind acceptance is due to the complete substitution of someone else's will for his own. Waxy flexibility, or the retention of uncomfortable body positions in which the patient is passively put, can also be explained in this way. When the patient is put in a given position, the will or responsibility of someone else is involved. If he wants to change positions, he has to will the change, and that will engender anxiety or guilt.

Quite often the reverse seems to occur. The patient will resist the order or will do the opposite. This is the phenomenon of negativism, which has baffled many investigators. As we have learned from Richard and Sally, the resistance is due to the fact that often the patient feels the responsibility for an act, even when it is ordered by somebody else. It is true that he is ordered to act, but he himself must will to move. Therefore he resists. Bleuler (1912, 1950) thought that one of the reasons for external negativism has to be found in the autistic withdrawal of the patient into his fantasies, which makes every influence acting from without a comparatively intolerable interruption. According to this interpretation, the patient wants to be left alone or wants to be unaware of all stimuli emanating from the outside world because they are unpleasant. This undoubtedly is the impression the observer receives; but if we try to decatatonize early catatonics with injections of sodium amytal, we may convince ourselves that in many cases this interruption of stimuli from the external world does not take place, even if the patient wishes so.

The patient who comes out of the stupor is able to give an accurate account of the events that occurred or of the words which were spoken in his presence when he could not move or talk. This indicates that, in spite of appearances, the attention toward the external world is preserved and that only actions are blocked because only actions are willed. The phenomenon of negativism will be considered again further on in this section.

Formerly, psychiatrists used to say the most disturbing things about diagnoses and prognoses in the presence of catatonic patients, thinking that they could not pay any attention to what was said (Arieti, 1973). It is true, however, that in several instances, the attention of the patient is withdrawn from his surroundings because the patient cannot *will* to pay attention. In numerous other cases the catatonic pays attention to his surroundings, but his interpretation of the external world is unrealistic and paleologic.This is particularly true in cases that present mixtures of catatonic and hebephrenic features. On the other hand, in the typical catatonic the perception of the external world is well preserved. Psychiatrists who have worked in institutions for many years know of several examples proving this to be so. We know that in the case of fire in hospitals, catatonics suddenly move, start to run, or even help others. It is equally true that some others preserve their catatonic state and perish in the flames. In many psychiatric hospitals, we hear anecdotes about unpredictable and very appropriate behavior and actions of catatonic patients. Many years ago I heard this small but significant episode; its authenticity has been guaranteed to me by a reputable psychiatrist. In a state hospital, resident psychiatrists, instead of attending to their duties, were playing cards in the vicinity of a patient who had been in a complete mute catatonic stupor for many years. From a window the patient saw the director of the hospital coming toward that ward. He was reputed to be a strict man, and the positions of the doctors would have been jeopardized had he caught them playing cards. All of a sudden, the patient shouted, "The director is coming." The doctors immediately stopped their game. From that moment on the patient resumed his catatonic silence, which he kept for many more years, possibly until his death. I believe that this episode might have really happened. That the patient was able to see the director and visualize the disastrous consequences for the doctors is not surprising to me. I have been convinced that the perception of the external environment is normal in many catatonics; at times it is even sharpened because, being unable to respond, they concentrate on perceiving, a process of which they remain fully capable. Withdrawal, as a protection against unpleasant influences of the environment, is more typical of the hebephrenic. The catatonic withdrawal is a retreat from action and from will, rather than from the environment, but because the environment forces him to will, the catatonic may withdraw from it also. The abovementioned episode is remarkable, however, because the patient, under strong and unusual emotional stress, became able to talk.

The inability to act also covers any manifestation of emotion, so that quite often the observer gets the impression that the patient is apathetic. Occasionally, however, a little movement or sign discloses the emotional involvement that is present in some cases at least. I remember the case of a young man who had been hospitalized for many years in Pilgrim State Hospital. He was in a state of complete immobility, confined to bed, was wetting and soiling, and had to be tube fed. Every time I was feeding him tears would drop from his eyes. This sign of his emotional life was enough to demonstrate that behind this armor of immobility he could still feel and suffer. It is possible, however, that, especially in very pronounced cases, the patient is never aware of the fact that it is the fear of movement that immobilizes him. He may sink into the stupor and remain in it without knowing the psychological processes that have determined it. He may have learned to react to stimuli with inactivity and to repeat the mechanism automatically. As the schizophrenic process proceeds, the patient bypasses the stage at which his will has to be exercised and regresses to a lower, apparently more active stage, where he merely reacts in reflex or short-circuited ways that do not involve his will centers. Echolalia may be explained in terms of such a regression.

In less advanced cases, one clearly sees the involvement of the will. For instance, as an answer to an order, the patient starts a movement, but then stops, as if a counter-order had prevented him from completing the movement. Having decided to obey, he is then afraid to will the act involved, and so he stops. At times there is a series of alternated opposite movements. For example, if one asks the patient to reach for an object, he starts the movement and then stops, many times in succession, giving the impression of performing a cogwheel movement, similar to that observed in postencephalitic patients affected by muscular rigidity. Incidentally, this resemblance to postencephalitic patients is superficial; the cogwheel phenomenon in the catatonic has nothing to do with muscular tone but has to do with an alternation of volition. For instance, a patient who reaches for an object may become afraid of willing that act in the middle of the movement; he then decides not to perform the act and arrests his arm. But to decide not to perform the act is also a volition. The patient becomes afraid of it and starts to make the movement again. To do this is also a volition, and he is again afraid. This series of attempted escapes from volition may go on for a long time; it is a horrifying experience, which only a few patients, like Richard, are able to remember and describe. In a personal communication, Prof. Christian Müller (1962), of Lausanne, Switzerland, told me that one of his patients had been condemned by the Nazis to be executed but was saved just before going to the executing squad. Subsequently this patient underwent a catatonic episode. Later the patient was able to tell Prof. Müller that the experiences he underwent when he was in a catatonic state were by far more painful and terrifying than that of expecting to be executed by the Nazis. Ferenczi (1950) wrote that catatonia is really a cataclonia, a high-frequency alternation of activating and inhibitory impulses.

A mixture of obedience and disobedience often appears in the actions of catatonics. For instance, if we ask a patient to close his eyes, he may close them, and at the same time will turn his face in the opposite direction. More than once Bleuler has compared this resisting negativistic attitude of the catatonic to a sexual attitude, especially that of the woman who resists sexual overtures. He also feels that often the negativism of the catatonic has a sexual connotation. I am not convinced that this is true. It seems to me that a somewhat similar motivation causes the resistance in the catatonic and in the woman—namely, fear of guilt versus a desire to act. In our culture sexual indulgence, especially at the time of Bleuler, is often connected with guilt. The woman feels she must resist and not act, because if she does act, she will feel guilty. At the same time, she wishes to yield in order to gratify her sexual needs; therefore, there is an alternation of acceptance and resistance. At times, she puts on an act to convince her partner and herself that she cannot be considered responsible, inasmuch as she made some resistance. Many women enjoy fantasies of being raped. If they are raped, they have sexual gratification without the feeling of responsibility.

In our society unconscious feelings of guilt often induce acceptable ways of avoiding action. The hermit, the anchorite, and the person who goes into a convent choose for themselves a life as deprived of action as possible. Some, though by no means all, of these persons want to avoid the guilt that would accompany their ordinary activities, especially the joyful ones. Often they remove their unconscious guilt not only by escaping from actions, but also by indulging in ritual, that is, in sanctioned or sanctified actions. They do this, for instance, when they join religious orders. These people act as if they were condemning themselves to a metaphorical and partial catatonia or to a social obsessive-compulsive psychoneurosis. Society treats those who have been found guilty similarly. By putting the culprits in jail, it limits their actions. An artificial catatonia is imposed on them. We remember that Richard, when he was over the catatonic attack, still wanted to escape from actions of life by committing himself again to the state hospital. The catatonic's fear of action at times becomes personified, projected externally, and perceptualized in the form of voices that tell the patient "no" when he is about to perform an act.

At times the patient does not limit himself to avoidance of what he is supposed to do but resists actively; at times he even does the opposite. This active or willed disobedience is sometimes present in the normal person and in the negativistic child, as if the unwillingness to obey or to follow the order would automatically engender an opposite action of resistance. We have seen that in the development of volition, resistance enters at least twice: first, as a resistance to automatic or reflex response; second, as a resistance to the influence of mother, ritual, or group. Among the various disorders of volition found in catatonia there is apparently regression to negative (or resisting) volition.

In Chapter 10 we discussed a third important case—John. We have seen how in this patient any action became a moral issue. However, there was an additional feature in John's case, which made it unique: analogic action became a substitute for the intended action. For instance, when he was undressing, he wanted to drop a shoe, and instead he dropped a big log. When he wanted to put something in a drawer, he threw a stone away. Thus, at times the action was similar or analogic to the one intended; at other times dissimilar or opposite.

The disorder seems to have involved one of the first three steps in the development of volition. Perhaps step three is involved: the planning of the chosen alternative. In John's case the engram for the chosen action was at times substituted by one that was similar. In other words, two actions became psychologically equivalent because they were similar or had something in common. The similarity between these regressive conative phenomena and paleologic cognition is impressive. It seems to indicate that the same basic formal psychopathological mechanisms apply to every area of the psyche. Unfortunately, no case similar to John's has been described in the literature, and any interpretation must remain purely hypothetical. Some neurological studies of motor integration by Denny-Brown (1960) may be helpful. The analogic movement may be viewed as a "release" of "dedifferentiation or loss of restriction to specific attributes of adequate stimulus." Very important in the case of John was also the fact that some actions escaped the catatonic barrier: those needed for carrying out the suicidal attempt.

As a matter of fact, in practically every catatonic some actions escape the impairment of the will: for instance, those necessary to put one's own body in uncomfortable positions that obviously have acquired for the patient a symbolic meaning (see Figure 1, p. 40).

Some relations between obsessive-compulsive psychoneuroses and catatonia must be further discussed.

It is not to be assumed that every obsessive-compulsive is potentially a catatonic. Some obsessive-compulsive symptoms are present in practically every human being as defenses against anxiety. There are infinite quantitative gradations from the normal to the catatonic. Many cases are definitely arrested at one of these numerous stages. Sudden and intense exacerbations occur in the person who is to become catatonic. If the process is very acute, a catatonic stupor may ensue without apparently having been preceded by a compulsive stage. There are undoubtedly many similarities between the obsessive-compulsive personality and that of the catatonic. The difficulty in making decisions, the occasional obstinacy in maintaining one's opinion, the going back and forth between two alternate dispositions or points of view, such as aggressiveness and submissiveness, pleasing oneself or somebody else, dirt and cleanliness, order and disorder, the feeling of command coming from within, as contrasted with commands from outside, and so on, are all obsessive-compulsive symptoms reminiscent of catatonic negativism.

Fear of uncertainty (of the effect) is also a characteristic common to both catatonics and compulsives. Even a remote possibility that the dreaded event may occur arouses anxiety, as if that possibility might immediately materialize. For instance, the patient cannot feel *mathematically sure* that he will not become infected if he does not wash his hands three times before eating. Many obsessive-compulsives actually become mathematicians in their search for that absolute certainty that allegedly is the only thing that can confer security. As was mentioned before, other obsessives become very religious and submerge themselves in ritual. The greater the fervor or the anxiety, the more extensive is the inclusion of ordinary acts in the ritual. Some neurotics find a guide for their behavior in the study of numbers or astrology, as an escape from uncertainty. Many obsessive-compulsive patients would like advice from their therapists on what to do. They want to know what they are *supposed* to do in every circumstance. They want to follow a schedule, a routine. They dread *spontaneity,* which means, as the etymology of the word implies, acting according to one's will. Some of them feel guilty if they do what they wish to do; therefore, they never do what they wish, and they comply with authority. Other patients spend their lives going through the formality of situations without becoming at all involved in them. They become extremely conventional, or automatic, in order to escape the anxiety and the guilt of spontaneous actions. The catatonic is much more afraid than the obsessive, because he is deprived of the ritual. The uncertainty of what may happen if he puts into effect the wrong volition reduces him to immobility.

Bleuler (1950) and other authors have found obsessive-compulsive behavior in patients who later became catatonic. It is equally true, however, that in many obsessive-compulsives who later become schizophrenic, the psychosis assumes a predominantly paranoid or hebephrenic symptomatology. The projected type of causality and other paleologic mechanisms play more prominent roles in their symptomatology.

Although we have emphasized the role of the fear of parental disapproval in the psychodynamics of the future catatonic, we must stress that such fear is not the same as the fear of action of the person who has already become a catatonic. The fear of action of the catatonic is much more intense, having acquired an archaic form; later it is disconnected from the fear of the authority, and it becomes fear of the action itself. Some patients develop for a certain period of time a mixed feeling of fear and power, which we may call a feeling of *negative omnipotence*. They feel that if they move, the whole world will collapse or all mankind will perish. Together with a feeling of cosmic power they have a feeling of cosmic responsibility. Finally, the fear of the action itself becomes unconscious and is followed by an automatic state in which the patient has entirely given up the function to will and performs only automatic or reflex acts. Thus, one can conclude that the dynamic and the formal mechanisms very clearly are connected in catatonia.

Since Kahlbaum differentiated catatonia (1863), there have been numerous attempts to explain catatonia as manifestation of a primary physical disease of the brain. Kahlbaum himself thought that catatonia was due to edema of the brain (1874). Some authors have tried to explain the syndrome as a disease of the cortical motor centers, others as a disease of the basal ganglia. The fact that postencephalitic patients, in their attitude, posture, and lack of action, resemble catatonics very much has reinforced the belief that catatonia is primarily an organic disease. In 1921 DeJong began a series of investigations aimed at comparing the effects of bulbocapnine on animals with the symptomatology of human catatonia (1922). DeJong and Baruk (1930*a, b*) as well as many other authors, found that when bulbocapnine is administered to animals, a clinical picture follows that is characterized by loss of motor initiative, maintenance of passively impressed postures, maintenance of posture against gravity, resistance to passive movements, and variations of muscular forms.

I am not going to attempt a complete refutation of these organic theories of catatonia here. As far as the early theories are concerned, they have been confuted very well by Bleuler (1950). As to bulbocapnine, Ferraro and Barrera (1932), in a monograph on the subject, describe their experiments with cats and monkeys, showing the superficiality of the resemblance between catatonia and bulbocapnine intoxication. They found that the manifestations of bulbocapnine occur even in animals deprived of the whole cerebral cortex and have no psychic components whatsoever.

CHAPTER

18

Changes of the Body Image

I

THE BODY IMAGE

Disturbances of the body image in schizophrenia have been stressed by some authors and neglected by others. They do not occur in every patient, but in some they cause intense preoccupation. In some patients the distortion of the body image becomes the focal point of the psychotic transformation. The body image can be studied from three different points of view: (1) as a body schema, or a neurological engram; (2) as a percept, or, in a more general way, as an experience; (3) as a concept, which is altered by the delusional ideation or at least by the psychodynamic conflict of the patient. Perhaps in almost all cases there is a mixture of at least two of these aspects.

The body image as a schema is a notion first developed by Head (1920). He interpreted the body schema, not just as an integration of past sensations and perceptions, but as a unity integrated in the cortex. The body image would consist of postural schemata dealing with position, movement, and space. Reviewing all the neurological knowledge in reference to organic disorders responsible for an alteration of the body image, Critchley (1953) concluded that in these conditions "the parietal lobe of the non-dominant hemisphere would obviously be identified as the locus which comes most frequently under suspicion." Schilder (1953) emphasized that the body image, even as a schema, is subject to continuous change and rebuilding. Individual experiences are constantly integrated with the body image.

The body schema is difficult to distinguish from the body percept if we concentrate on the physiological aspect of the body image. The body, however, can be considered as a very rich experience. I could examine my own body merely as an object, like many others existing in the world. The body becomes only an object of my observation. On the other hand, my own body may be me, or at least part of me. My body belongs to me; it is in me, in my possession. The authors who use the German phenomenological terminology distinguish a *Leib,* or body for me, from *Körper,* or body in itself, an object (Cargnello, 1964).

The experiences that make up the body image are not only subjective experiences originating exclusively in the individual. Schilder (1935) stressed the importance of interpersonal and environmental factors, such as social relations and morality, in the building of the body image.

The body image as a cognitive construct consists of many ideas, referring to one's own body, associated with various emotions. The body may be conceived in the following ways:

1. As the self, or as most of the self, or as the representative of the self. It confers identity, not only in relation to sex, but also in relation to the whole person. Although the body, as a lived experience, gives a sense of continuity of the self to the individual, such continuity is conceptualized as a self, or identity of the self.
2. As a carrier of sexual feelings, or as a sexualized object. Again in this case the concept is connected with the experience.
3. As a means to relate to others.

In discussing what he called ego-feeling, Federn (1953) distinguished between body scheme, body image, and bodily ego. He wrote, "The body scheme represents the constant mental knowledge of one's body; the body image is the changing presentation of the body in one's mind. Throughout the changes, the bodily ego is the continuous awareness of one's body. Image, scheme, ego, all three are themselves not somatic but mental phenomena."

II
Patients' Experiences of Their Own Body

It is common clinical experience to treat schizophrenic patients who have distorted ideas about their own bodies. The face is the most common cause of complaint and preoccupation. A 23-year-old girl described her experience as follows: "I look at myself in the mirror, and it is not really me that I see. I don't have any definite image of myself, but many different ones, all of them horrible to me. I look like a man." She demanded that plastic surgery be done on her. Some patients demand plastic surgery to change the look of their eyes, ears, nose, face, head, legs, breasts, and so on. They have the idea that their arms are shrunken, legs expanded, eyes dislocated. Kinesthetic delusions of any kind are very common. Some patients are *dysmorphophobic,* that is they are afraid that their body is going to change appearance. Typical hypochondriacs instead have the conviction of having a bodily illness.

Some authors have followed accurate procedures to investigate more deeply these clinical findings. Weckowicz and Sommer (1960) studied the patient's reaction to his reflection in a large three-paneled mirror. They found that schizophrenic patients, when compared with nonschizophrenic controls, underestimated the size of the distinct parts of their bodies. With a different technique, Burton and Adkins (1961) obtained different results. They found that schizophrenics have the tendency to overestimate some parts of their bodies, especially those parts that "have a libidinal and interactional charge."

De Martis and Porta (1965) repeated the tests of Weckowicz and Sommer and added new ones in a study of sixty patients and twenty control subjects. Six patients did not recognize themselves in the mirror; many saw more than three images; twenty-six saw their own limbs decreased in size or completely absent.

Faure (1971) has vividly described some phenomena experienced by some patients: the fluctuation of the self-image and the insecurities about the limits of one's own body. According to Faure some patients see in their own photographic picture "a possibility of occult influences susceptible of hurting them"; some others see in their pictures "a second presence of themselves." The picture acquires an autonomous existence.

III

INTERPRETATION

For a more detailed interpretation of the disorders of the body image in psychiatric conditions the reader is referred to the writings of Schilder (1935), Kolb (1959*a, b*), Lukianowitz (1967).

Weckowicz and collaborators have intensely studied perceptual constancy in schizophrenia (Weckowicz, 1957; Weckowicz, Sommer, and Hall, 1958; Weckowicz and Sommer, 1960). They believe that some of the changes in the perception of one's own body can be attributed to "a breakdown in perceptual constancy." Many other authors do not share this point of view. We know, however, that with the administration of LSD both normal persons and schizophrenics overestimate the size of their heads (Liebert, Wapner, and Werner, 1957). De Martis (1964) and De Martis and Porta (1965) do not believe that the body schema is altered in schizophrenics. De Martis (1964) interprets the alterations in the body image as belonging to one of the following four categories:

1. Symptoms of hypochondriac nature, similar to those found in neurotics. These symptoms are symbolic in their content.
2. Manifestations of depersonalization to be interpreted as intermediary stages toward either full delusional thinking or toward the reintegration of the psyche.

3. Kinesthetic delusions.

4. Global disorders of soma-psyche integration, secondary to loss of libidinal investment. "The body appears as a disarticulated structure, with unclear boundaries, confused in the most pronounced cases with external reality."

In a review article Kolb (1959*b*) asks, among others, the following questions:

> Is this maldevelopment [of the body image] the consequence of disturbances in the communicative process between mother and child or, to put it another way, does the interaction between the mother's and the child's bodies, the mother's attitude and feelings as they are conveyed to the child in the very earliest times, lead to a disturbance in the capacity of the cortex to evolve a stable concept of the body, as well as altering later concepts of the body? If this is the case, what are the peculiarities of the mother-child relationship which contribute to the evolution of the disordered body-ego complex in the schizophrenic child? Is it that these children were not fondled enough, were not handled consistently, or were handled in a manner which produced such variables of sensory and emotional arousals that the cortex failed to integrate a stable body image?

Kolb's questions have not yet been satisfactorily answered.

The original psychoanalytic theory (reviewed by Fenichel, 1945, and also by Arlow and Brenner, 1964) is that the patient has turned his interest (cathexis) from the outside world to the body. Because of this change many somatic processes that are usually unconscious reach consciousness. The somatic symptoms are symbolic and use a body language, in which a sexual meaning predominates. Fenichel summarized the view of classic psychoanalysis in the following way: "Many schizophrenics begin with characteristic hypochondriacal sensations. The theory of hypochondriasis, which maintains that organ cathexis grew at the expense of object cathexis, makes this early symptomatology intelligible. The beginning of the schizophrenic process is a regression to narcissism." See also the section on Freud in Chapter 2.

Szasz (1957*b*) advanced another hypothesis within the framework of classic psychoanalytic theory. He does not believe that bodily feelings reduplicate ego-experiences characteristic of infancy or childhood. In the prepsychotic stage there is fear of object loss. A trauma, like a mourning reaction, may actually precipitate loss of objects. Then "the ego takes the body as the only remaining object to which it can relate (with more or less safety). The body now functions as an object vis-à-vis the ego, just as personal objects did heretofore" (Szasz, 1957*b*). In simple language, at the beginning of schizophrenia there would be a change of interest from interpersonal relations and the world at large to one's own body. This change certainly occurs in many patients, but by no means in all of them. This interpretation explains increased *interest* in one's body, but it does not explain the distortions of the body image.

In my opinion, attributing one's own difficulties to the body is another instance of concretization. The psyche is no longer involved with its abstract, complicated, interpersonal, and symbolic processes; the body is "blamed." It is safer to concentrate one's interest on one's body and to overlook the anxiety originated with the world at large.

Selvini (1963, 1970) has described how in anorexic girls the body becomes the persecutor. It is the "fault" of a part of the body that the patient is in a predicament. For instance, her face has changed, and she is unappealing to men.

I have found that the parts of the body that have more meaning in interpersonal contacts (the head, the face, the eyes, the hands) are the most frequently involved in delusions. Some patients try to remove their difficulties by changing their body images. They request plastic surgery, in order of frequency, on their nose, face, breasts, or legs. Plastic surgeons must be very careful to recognize this type of schizophrenic from normal persons who request plastic surgery. In fact, many of these patients (generally, but not exclusively, female) are not satisfied after surgery. They may intensify their delusions about the part of the body that underwent surgery or may shift the delusions to other parts of the body. In some cases they may even involve the surgeon in their delusional system. (The surgeon is a persecutor: he has made the patient's body worse.)

Often the delusional change in the body image indicates metaphorically what the patient thinks about himself: the body is little, deformed, looks like a man's body instead of a woman's body, or vice versa. The body smells; is too short or too tall; the penis and testicles are too small; the vagina is either too big or too little; the breasts are also too big or too small; the hair is falling. The brain is melting; something happened that destroyed a part of the brain. The sight has changed so that the patient cannot see things properly or cannot focus on any particular object. At times there is an element of truth in the complaints of the patient (for instance, about the nose or the breast), but the significance of the condition is exaggerated to an enormous degree. At times the patient may have a real psychosomatic condition (like a vasomotor rhinitis; constipation), but he adds to it a delusional structure. Often the complaints have no basis in reality at all and seem ridiculous to others.

Some authors (for instance, Meth, 1974) have reported among Chinese and Indonesians a phobic condition called *Koro*. The patient becomes fearful that his penis will disappear into his abdomen and he will die. I have seen in schizophrenics a related delusion (that the penis or testicles have already entered into the abdomen), at times because of some medical treatment allegedly received from unscrupulous doctors. The patient is not afraid to die but to lose his masculinity. Generally the patient with this or similar delusions is afraid of being homosexual, of being considered homosexual, or of having lost his potency.

As a rule, delusions about sexual organs and functions are accessible to psychotherapy with good results, because they lead easily to analysis of many problems. On the other hand, I have found that delusions concerning brain, face, and nose are very resistant to any type of therapy. The patient seems to have focused all his concern on that part of the body and clings tenaciously to his belief.

CHAPTER

19

The Retreat from Society

I

General Remarks

Almost every schizophrenic retreats from society to a mild, moderate, or pronounced degree. The patient seems to live in a shell, or in a world of his own, or behind what has been called an autistic barrier. Before reviewing the various theories on schizophrenic desocialization and presenting my own interpretation, I shall briefly describe the overt characteristics of the withdrawal. First of all the reader must be reminded of what was referred to in Parts One and Two. Whereas the schizophrenic withdrawal was once observed in almost every case of schizophrenia, it is less frequent now. In an increasing number of patients a different phenomenon occurs, especially at the onset of the psychosis: almost an intense desire to make contacts with people, to talk, to communicate, to be seen and noticed. However, even in this group of patients enduring or very meaningful relationships are not established. The patient continues to feel alone and unfulfilled. His repeated efforts to establish contacts do not relieve his discomfort.

The most pronounced forms of withdrawal are found in patients who had a prepsychotic schizoid personality (see Chapters 6 and 7). As a matter of fact the withdrawal seems to be an exaggeration of that personality. The patient communicates with visible effort. He prefers to be by himself, to replace with his inner experiences the actions that require a social exchange. If he is addressed, he resents even simple questions as if they were intrusions or attacks. He indulges in an extreme degree of privacy, so extreme that nobody, even his roommate, his closest relative, or his best friend can touch it.

In every schizophrenic there is an impairment of the ability to communicate with others and to share experiences with others. The most pronounced and obvious forms of this desocialization are seen in regressed patients in back wards of state hospitals. This impairment is even more pronounced than would seem from a superficial examination of the patient's behavior. For instance, in a state hospital where one sees many schizophrenics working together, one may get the impression that they actually cooperate and divide their labor in some kind of organized manner. Actually the organization comes from a nonschizophrenic supervisor. It is true that the patients work together, but in a physical sense only, inasmuch as they work in the same place. Each one works independently. A group of schizophrenics in reality is not a group; it is a number of separate individuals. At first one gets the opposite impression; they are just a bunch of schizophrenics who are similar to a herd of cattle. This impression is far from the truth; they seem to have lost their individuality because they cannot communicate or transmit their individual feelings and ideas. If they talk, the formal characteristics of their utterances give the listener an impression of uniformity that is only apparent. Their ability to share experiences is so disturbed that they cannot spontaneously initiate any plan with any other human being. There are exceptions: at times friendships are possible between patients who are not too regressed or who are on the way to recovery. In many of these cases, however, one is a nonschizophrenic patient. Alcoholic and organic patients do not lose the ability to socialize as much as the schizophrenic does.

The extent of the process of desocialization and inability to plan together in chronic schizophrenics who do not receive any kind of therapy is revealed in the following observation. During World War II, when there was a serious shortage of manpower, the attendants at state hospitals were reduced to a minimum. The shortage in Pilgrim State Hospital, where I worked, was so acute that, at times, at certain hours during the night, a single attendant had to take care of several wards. Many patients, especially paranoids, often plan to escape. A single patient who tries to escape is easily overcome by the generally robust attendant. If two patients, however, were to cooperate, they could easily overcome the attendant, grab his keys, and escape. But even that degree of cooperation, between two people, is impossible for full-fledged schizophrenics who receive no treatment, not even drug therapy. Even a group of two, in the sense of two people planning and sharing common experiences, is impossible for them. That is why it was possible to keep patients from escaping even when the attendants were so few in number.

An amusing short story by Edgar Allan Poe, "The System of Doctor Tarr and Professor Fether," in which the staff of a private mental sanitarium is overcome and kept in captivity by a well-organized group of patients, is hardly believable. When we read in the newspapers that mental patients have rebelled or mutinied, we may easily conclude that these patients are psychopaths (generally detained because they are allegedly criminally insane), not psychotics. Of course, a group of schizophrenics may also escape if they are helped by nonschizophrenic persons. This ability to plan together and to share experiences is impaired even when the general intelligence of the patient is preserved.

What has been said so far is merely a description of this characteristic of schizophrenia. Now an attempt must be made to understand it. The explanation that the schizophrenic is like the schizoid person (Chapter 6) and tries to cut all communications because he experiences anything coming from outside as hostile, unpleasant, threatening, and harmful is correct, but it does not account for all the facts. The schizophrenic is not a hermit who withdraws from this unpleasant world. The hermit retains his ability to communicate and to share experiences. The patient undergoes a process of desocialization that, although motivated by the desire to withdraw from anxiety-ridden societal experiences, is something more profound than the actualization of this desire.

II

Reviews of Theories on Desocialization

The phenomenon of desocialization in schizophrenia has been interpreted in many ways. We have seen in Chapter 2 that Freud considered the change in the patient's relationships with persons and other objects as the most important characteristic of dementia praecox. He interpreted this withdrawal as a withdrawal of libidinal cathexes from the mental representations of the objects when the instinctual drives become unmanageable. In other words, the patient would decathect the surrounding world and become interested only in his body or his self. This interpretation does not make clear why some patients do not present the phenomenon; nor does it explain how the desocialization or would-be decathexis is actually carried out.

Fairbairn (1952) understood the inadequacy of Freud's libido theory in the interpretation of withdrawal. For Fairbairn, libido is not a thing in itself, but the object-seeking drive of the primary ego. He did not believe that the patient withdraws his cathexes because he has difficulty in controlling libidinal impulses in his object relationships. Fairbairn thought that the schizoid patient has an infantile, undeveloped, weak ego. He escapes from all the bad objects, whether they are external or internal. Fairbairn rejected Freud's division of the psyche into id, ego, and superego and pointed out that Freud's view is based on a dualistic separation of energy (id) and structure (ego and superego), which is Newtonian and Helmholtzian, but not in accord with modern scientific theories (see also Guntrip, 1961, 1966, 1968, 1973). Although Fairbairn's theory of object relationship is an advancement over the original libido hypothesis, his account of internal objects remains nebulous. They are described as very active entities, in a dynamic sense, but what they consist of is never specified. Fairbairn interpreted regression as an advanced type of withdrawal, which is reached when the schizoid state becomes very pronounced. The realities of the day are experienced as intolerable because the bad objects are projected into them. According to Fairbairn, psychotic conditions, like myths and dreams, represent flight back into the womb.

Szasz (1957*c*) has also advanced an interesting theory of schizophrenia, which is related to the concepts of Melanie Klein and Fairbairn. Szasz believes that schizophrenia is largely the result of a deficiency in internal objects, or deficiency of introjected objects. Having introjected so few objects, the patient has no models to use in his life. He is awkward and inadequate; no wonder that, when he leaves home and goes to college for the first time, he may develop a schizophrenic break.

In my opinion the concept is more plausible in the simple type of schizophrenia, in child schizophrenia, and possibly in those cases that start in early adolescence. It is difficult, however, to accept this concept for all cases of schizophrenia, especially for those in which the psychosis occurred later in life. In these cases the patient was not deficient in models or in symbolic interchanges with adults. The patient did internalize higher constructs that consist mostly of symbolic cognitive media and accompanying affects. In many cases the patients, especially those with a stormy personality, were able to have an intense life with participation of internal and external objects.

The important difference from the normal person is that these internal objects cannot be taken as examples or models because they carry within themselves the anxiety of the early interpersonal relations. Instead of being useful examples, they make life appear dreadful and difficult. These internal objects are finally projected into the external world.*

American psychiatrists and psychologists have tried to interpret the phenomenon of schizophrenic desocialization from a sociological point of view. They have been influenced by the philosophy of John Dewey and George Mead, who studied the human mind in its relation to society.

Ernest Becker (1962) has developed a theory that is related to Szasz's and to George Mead's behavioristic view of meaning. For Becker, schizophrenia is due to a deficiency, *not* of internal objects, but of what he calls external objects. According to Becker meaning can be built up only "by behavior transactions with external objects." The individual, in growing up, finds dependable responses by reducing problematic situations to habitual ones. In other words, he organizes behavior by building external objects. External objects are "organized behavioral responses to specific situations." According to Becker the schizophrenic is unable to reduce problematic situations into habits, in converting the multiplicity of experience into meaningful objects. His answers to the basic problems of life "never become meaningful because no pattern of dependable behavioral response can be organized around them."

Becker is right in assuming that the patient is unable to find dependable responses. The schizoid as well as the stormy patients have not been able to find adequate responses because of the preexisting symbolic interpersonal difficulties—not considered by Becker—that have handicapped him. The psychotic will substitute for these dependable responses his own, individualistic abnormal habits.

* This theory of Szasz seems difficult to reconcile with his other theory that we examined in Chapter 18 (Szasz, 1957*b*). According to this theory the schizophrenic loses interpersonal objects and becomes interested mainly in his body. But it is obvious that one may *lose* only what he previously had.

The two American psychiatrists who made great contributions to the understanding of this process of socialization are Harry Stack Sullivan and Norman Cameron.

We have already discussed Sullivan's contribution at great length. We have seen how his whole concept of psychiatry is based on the process of socialization. According to him, the self is created by the ensemble of the social relations that the child has with the significant adults in his life, by the reflected appraisal of these significant adults. If these interpersonal relations are unhealthy and create an excessive amount of anxiety, the psychological development is disturbed and the process of socialization is altered. This sequence of events may lead to schizophrenia.

Sullivan's concepts are of great value but do not explain the whole problem. Although it is true that an altered relatedness to others in childhood may engender that other altered relatedness to others that we call schizophrenia, this interpretation does not explain the formal characteristics of this condition.

Norman Cameron (1947, 1951) thinks that, to a very large extent, the symbolic behavior of adults is socially derived. Individuals with socially inadequate development progressively fail to maintain a level of intelligible communication. They have the tendency to separate themselves from their community and to indulge in their own private thinking, which does not require conformity to the thinking of others. Through a process of progressive desocialization, they replace the social language habits with personal, highly individual habits. In these people, the social community, which is a realistic interpretation of the interactions of the individuals with others, is replaced by the pseudocommunity. This pseudocommunity is a behavioral organization that the patient has built up out of his distorted observations and inferences. Here he sees himself generally as the victim of some concerted action. Because the paranoid does not reveal his suspicions to others, the suspicions continue to build up and organize in the pseudocommunity. When he finally voices his beliefs, they are already so established in rigid patterns of thinking that they cannot be removed. The negative response that he elicits in others, when he finally expresses his delusions, reinforces his belief that he is being persecuted. The autistic community, according to Cameron, is a behavioral organization consisting of imagination "in a fantasied context." The autistic community may be replaced by disorganization, which consists of fragmentary and chaotic behavior.

Cameron's formulations have the following merits:

1. They recognize the magnitude of the role society plays in abnormal behavior.
2. Not only do they give a good description of the progression of the disorder, but they explain how previous stages engender or favor the subsequent ones.
3. They recognize the important role that desocialization plays in schizophrenia to a greater extent than other formulations.

On the other hand, they have shortcomings. From a dynamic point of view, Cameron does not give an adequate account of the early experiences that interplay between parents and children or of the importance that the feelings of the parents have in the process of socialization of the children. From a formal point of view, he describes but does not explain the characteristics of the autistic and disorganized behavior. As was mentioned before, the only thing that is explained is how the disorders favor a progression toward further disorganization.

III
Symbolization and Socialization in a Developmental Frame of Reference

The point of view presented in this book is that the process of desocialization parallels a concomitant process that occurs in the patient's inner reality. In Chapter 5, and to a lesser extent in Chapter 6, we have outlined the development of this inner reality, mostly from the point of the formation of inner objects and inner images. In this section we must give particular consideration to the function of symbolization, which is strictly related to the process of socialization.

The capacity to symbolize, or to create symbols, is one of the most outstanding functions of the mind. For a more comprehensive exposition of the processes of socialization, and acquisition of roles and symbols, the reader is referred to books of sociology, social psychology, and semantics. Here we shall study only those phylogenetic and ontogenetic aspects of these processes that may lead to a better understanding of schizophrenia.

From a very broad point of view, symbolization may be defined as *transformation of experiences*. Sense data are not accepted by the mind as they are but are taken to mean something else. Rudimentary forms of symbolization are also present in animals; they begin in the phyletic scale as early as the conditioned reflex does, because they require something like the conditioned reflex. For instance, through repetition in the course of the experiment, the sound of a bell causes a dog to expect food and to secrete gastric juice. The sound of the bell becomes a *sign* of the forthcoming food. The bell is not food, and yet it indicates food. The sign thus stands for something else, which is present or about to be present in the total situation. It is part of a whole, which is selected to represent either the whole present situation or other parts of the present situation.

Men, too, use many signs. The physician sees a rash on the skin of the child and knows that this rash is the sign of chickenpox. But, more frequently, men use things that stand for something else, even when this something else is not present. When I say, "George," the word *George* substitutes for the person George, when George is not present. Thus the word *George* is not necessarily a sign of the person George, but is more often *a symbol* of the person George. People know it and know of one another that they know it.

Perhaps the greatest difference between the psychic functions of animals and men is that whereas animals are not capable of symbols, men are. The use of symbols expands our lives to an enormous degree, because we may replace things with others, to an indefinite degree. No human endeavor is conceivable without symbols. The reader is referred to the excellent book by Langer, *Philosophy in a New Key* (1942).

The problem to be considered here is the following: why is the human mind capable of symbols? Is this ability due only to a more evolved nervous system or to being together with other human beings? Both factors are necessary. Twenty dogs, who are conditioned to a bell, react to the sound of the bell individually, without any communication about the forthcoming food taking place among the dogs. Each dog reacts individually, his secretions of gastric juice being independent or, for practical purposes, almost independent of the secretions of the other dogs. But if we mention the word *George,* and we all understand that we are talking about the person George, an agreement must have been reached between us. We all agree that the word *George* is a symbol of the person George. An interpersonal process has taken place, as a result of which the word *George* has become the symbol of the person George. Thus, verbal symbolization requires an interpersonal relationship. We must not only have the ability to exchange experiences and information between us, but also we must be together so that we can actualize these exchanges. This description probably seems to be only an elaboration of the obvious, but what may seem extremely easy was, on the contrary, one of the most dramatic, difficult, and eventful steps in evolution, the change from the sign to the symbol.

We have seen in Chapter 5 that images are the most primitive forms of symbols of which the human psyche is capable. Although these images may be enriched tremendously by social relationships, they may exist even without them. They have peculiar characteristics. They are very private, original, fleeting, flexible, and mutable. Two persons do not seem to have the same image about the same object; the same person has different images of the same object at two different moments. Through images we live in our own individualistic world. It is a symbolic world because it stands for an external world, and yet it is very close to sensation and perception and therefore has a primitive emotional tone.

Do animals have images? This question is hard to answer; they probably do, especially images of an olfactory nature. They seem to dream, and if they dream, they must do so with some kind of images. However, animals do not seem to have the capacity to evoke or reproduce images when they want to, and of course they are incapable of expressing them to others. Men, too, have great difficulty in communicating images. In the history of evolution, it was only when men acquired verbal symbols that they became capable of communicating their images. The process of socialization enables man to translate his inner private images into symbols that he can transmit to others. Without socialization, however, even his inner private images would be reduced to a minimum because most of his inner life is also determined by his relationships with other people. Social contacts stimulate symbols that may undergo a process of individual imagery and then may be translated into more social symbols.

Let us now examine the transformation of the private image into a social symbol. The comparative psychologist Kellogg (1933) reports that his little chimpanzee, Gua, was so attached to him that whenever he left the house, she became very despondent. She would go into a tantrum of terror and grief. If, however, he gave her his coverall at the time of his departure, she seemed placated, showed no emotional displeasure, and carried the coverall around with her as a fetish. As Langer points out, this fact is extremely important. This is probably one of the first manifestations of high symbolization of which animals may be capable. The coverall represented the master. However, it was more than a symbol of the master; it replaced the master. It acquired the property that the master had in that it would satisfy the ape emotionally just as he did. In other words, it was a symbol, but it was a symbol that was identified with the object it symbolized. Possibly the ape was able to evoke the image of his master at the sight of the coverall, or the coverall reproduced the image of the master plus coverall, or the ape really accepted the coverall not as a coverall, but as an emotional equivalent of his master. At the present stage of our knowledge it is impossible to be sure which of these possibilities is the correct one. We might even say that master and coverall were possibly identified according to Von Domarus's principle or a precursor of that principle.

Let us assume, theoretically, that at the same time that Kellogg trained Gua, he had trained two other chimpanzees, with potentialities similar to hers. When Kellogg would leave, maybe the second chimpanzee would find comfort, not at the sight of his coverall, but at the sight of one of his tools. In fact, it is difficult to believe that the second chimpanzee would have selected the coverall as a symbol of Kellogg. Obviously there were some incidental events, specific in the life of Gua, that caused her to choose the coverall as the symbol of her master. For similar reasons, the second chimpanzee would be comforted at the sight of a tool, and the third chimpanzee, let us say, at the sight of Kellogg's pipe. Thus, we have three chimpanzees who use three different things as symbols of the master. These symbols are private, individual symbols that are valid only for the subject who uses them. They are qualities or parts of a whole which they symbolize. So the coverall, the tool, and the pipe are parts of whole situations. This type of symbol is not a social symbol. It is valid only for one individual, because each individual uses a different predicate (part-quality) as symbol of the object that is symbolized.

Let us assume, again, a theoretical situation in which three hominids, that is, members of species lower than *Homo sapiens,* are together after the departure of their mother. One of the three hominid children sees a stone that is always used by the mother. Like Gua, he is sad at the departure of his mother, but is consoled when he sees the stone. He is excited, makes a gesture with his hands, one implying happiness, and emits the sound "ma-ma" similar to the babbling of children. The other two hominid children are there, and in a sudden flash of illumination they understand that the stone, the gesture with the hands, and the sound "ma-ma" mean mother to the first child. A great event has happened in the world! The symbol that was individual is communicated to the second and third hominids and will mean the same thing to them as to the person who pronounced it. It becomes a verbal symbol, a social symbol, something that is shared, something that they have in common. From then on, when the first hominid wants to express the idea of mother, he will use either the stone or that particular gesture of the hands or the sound "ma-ma." The others will respond to these signs as he does. By using them he will evoke in himself the same response that he evokes in others. The stone as a symbol of mother will originate fetish magic, so common in primitive people.

The gesture is a kind of language that is still quite prevalent in primitive cultures and has by no means disappeared in Western culture. For the sake of simplification we shall omit consideration of the fetish and the manual gesture and concentrate on the verbal concomitant.

The first hominid says "ma-ma" and the others understand "mother." They surrender their own individual symbols and accept "ma-ma" as a symbol of mother. Each of them, by saying "ma-ma," evokes in the other the same thing that he evokes in himself, or, vice versa, he arouses in himself the same response that he arouses in the others. The symbol "ma-ma" eventually will replace the stone and the manual gesture.

The symbol "ma-ma" has a definite denotation: mother. It will also have those syncretic qualities so well described by Werner (1957). It may even be used as a verb to mean things we have *to do* to please mother. The symbol "ma-ma" will do other wonderful things. It will orient the mind of the hominid to replace the image or visualization of mother with a verbal symbol. It will substitute for the individual fleeting images something that from this time on will be common to others and less temporary. Something that has a tendency to fade away is replaced by something else that has a definite form. It permits thinking of mother, not only in the present situation when mother is there, but also of a mother in the past, and a mother in the future. Thus the verbal symbol widens the horizon of the mind, which from now on will be able to reproduce the past and envisage the future. No longer will it be, like the mind of animals, restricted to the present (see Chapter 16).

By accepting the verbal sign "ma-ma," the hominids, however, have to give up many things. They have to give up their individual symbols; they have to suppress the images that are so near to their sensations; and they have to lose part of the direct sensuous contact with the phenomenon. They gain acceptance in a social world that will multiply the symbols to an enormous degree.

To repeat, what has been described would not have occurred without a first interpersonal contact, as a result of which a symbol was grasped not only by the person who uttered it, but by at least one other living creature. When the first hominid of our hypothetical example said "ma-ma" and meant mother, the symbol "ma-ma" was not yet language. It became language when the second hominid interpreted it as a symbol of mother. The first hominid, in turn, understood that the second hominid had interpreted it as a symbol of mother. In other words, one hominid could not have created even a rudimentary language of one word. At least two persons were necessary to make the transition from the level of private symbols to the level of verbal symbols.

There are several corroborations for these assertions. Children learn language not only because they have the potentiality to learn it at a certain stage of their development, but also because they have interpersonal contacts. Deaf children do not learn how to talk, not because there is something wrong with their vocal equipment. In spite of their perfect neurological and laryngeal equipment, they become mute because they cannot receive the verbal symbols coming from other persons. Helen Keller (1951), the amazing woman who was blind and deaf since early childhood, in her autobiography gave a very good description of her acquisition of verbal symbols in spite of her defects. As a cool stream of water flowed over one of her hands, her teacher spelled the word *water* into her hand, at first slowly, then rapidly. With a flashing thrill, Miss Keller realized that the letters *w-a-t-e-r* spelled on her hand meant that "wonderful cool something" *for her teacher;* and from then on, *for her too,* that "wonderful cool something" was represented by that combination of letters. Miss Keller described the episode as a momentous experience. Finally she had a medium through which she could communicate with other people. The barrier of isolation, which blindness and deafness had erected, could be demolished by her entrance into the level of verbal symbols, that is, by the fact that an interpersonal contact with her teacher at the level of verbal symbolism was made possible.

Before that wonderful experience with the water, Miss Keller had other kinds of symbols that were more primitive. For instance, she had signs. The fragrance of the flowers made her understand that she was in the garden. She also had images, made up mostly of kinesthetic, olfactory, and gustatory elements. In addition, she had private symbols, because she was able to anticipate events. She said that she felt during this period as if invisible hands were holding her while she was making frantic efforts to free herself. Even before she was able to understand social symbols from her teacher, she had experienced emotional and social experiences with her parents and friends. However, no high social integration was possible until she acquired the use of verbal symbols.

To summarize the foregoing, in addition to signs, which they have in common with animals, human beings have three types of symbols:

1. Images.
2. Private symbols, which from now on will be called *paleosymbols*.
3. Social (or verbal or common or communicable) symbols.

The signs that exist also in subhuman animals and in human babies in the first few months of life permit a type of nonsymbolic learning that may be quite realistic, accurate, and goal fulfilling. A cat, which responds to the odor of a mouse, is a realist. The cat does not let his imagination confuse him. The odor is there; therefore the mouse is there. At the level of signs, mistakes are difficult unless artificial situations are devised by men to confuse the animal. Signs do not pretend to stand for something that is not there; they are indicators of something that is there or of something that is seen as part of a whole that is there. At the level of signs, mental life is very limited, is narrowed to what is here now, but mistakes are difficult.

Complications start with the symbolic type of cognition. The less differentiated type of symbolic cognition is what I have called primary cognition, or the cognition of the primary process. It includes images and paleosymbols. The endocept, which we have referred to in Chapter 5, is not a symbol. It is perhaps only a potential symbol or a symbol trigger; in fact it is not representative, not externalizable, and it is unconscious or dimly conscious. Images are present in animals to a very rudimentary degree. If they exist in animals, they seem to be evoked only by external stimuli, not by internal ones, except possibly in the state of sleep. Images usually stand for things that are not present. They attempt to reproduce a sensorial picture of what is absent, but memory is defective, and the individual's experiences interfere and tamper with the reproduction. The image is so fleeting that it cannot be reproduced twice in the same way. It cannot be experienced by anybody except the person who has it, and it is strongly influenced by concomitant emotions. Consequently it has a quality of indefiniteness; it is inaccurate and unverifiable.

When the image is externalized, or when an external act of the individual or an object replaces the image, we have the paleosymbols. The paleosymbols possibly exist in apes but are more characteristic of immediately prehuman and human species. In paleosymbols, the image may be substituted by an external object, gesture, or a sound. But these externalizations are chosen arbitrarily by the individual. Therefore they may lead to fatal errors. If the ape continues to react to the coverall as she reacted to the master after the master dies, she may also die of starvation. The paleosymbols enlarge mental life, because they allow for the thinking of things that are not there; but they are apt to lead to mistakes. The object that is taken as a symbol, or the manual gesture or the uttered sound, is not a reproduction of the thing that is symbolized. Furthermore, at the early stages of this level, the individual still has the tendency to confuse the paleosymbol with the object symbolized or to see the paleosymbol as part of the symbolized situation in the same way that the sign was. The paleosymbol is more definite than the image, but it is also highly individual, subjective, emotionally loaded, and unverifiable. When the social level is reached, the paleosymbols invade the social life also. As a matter of fact, it would seem that every verbal symbol was a paleosymbol before it became a socialized or verbal symbol. The struggle that the individual had to undergo in evolving from the paleosymbol to the social symbol was no less strenuous than the struggle to evolve from the image to the paleosymbol. This struggle has not yet ended. We are still motivated by paleosymbols to a considerable degree. The struggle for survival that the primitive races had to undergo was the result of the mistakes to which these paleosymbols and their use in paleologic thinking led (see Chapter 16).

Signs permit the experience of fear, that is, an emotional reaction to the perception of an immediate actual danger. They also permit the experience of a certain type of anxiety, which may be called short-circuited anxiety, that is related to the fact that the individual is unable to react to two simultaneous confusing stimuli or to satisfy a need or to discharge the tension caused by his propensity to react when under the influence of a certain stimulus. As I have indicated elsewhere (Arieti, 1967), I prefer the term *tension* for this type of short-circuited anxiety.

Signs, however, do not allow for the experience of anxiety that is due to the anticipation of a future danger, the most common form of anxiety in human beings. Images, paleosymbols, and symbols are necessary for this type of anxiety.

The foregoing discloses the limitation of studying psychopathological processes in animals with the purpose of elucidating the psychopathology of human beings. The psychopathology of animals is the psychopathology of signs, of the conditioned reflex, or of short-circuited anxiety. The psychopathology of human beings is predominantly a pathology of images, paleosymbols, and symbols. Therefore, to study psychoneuroses or psychoses in animals would be the same as to study cerebellar dysfunctions in invertebrates. Invertebrates have no cerebellum. In saying this, I am not denying the value of the experiments carried on by such people as Masserman (1943), Mowrer (1946), and other prominent researchers in this field. These experiments do have value inasmuch as they illuminate basic processes of psychic life, as for instance, regression, instincts of preservation (reaction to fear), and anxiety caused by simultaneous conflicting stimuli or by inability to satisfy needs. These experiments, however, disclose only the pathological mechanisms at the level of signs, and we know that this level is the one least involved in human psychoneuroses and psychoses.

The social symbols are exclusively human. They imply an initial process of socialization, and in turn they make social integration possible. A much higher degree of accuracy, predictability, and verification becomes possible with them, as they will become to an increasing degree ruled by the laws of secondary process cognition. A continuous expansion of social symbols has taken place since the acquisition of the first word. The history of humanity is the history of its social symbols. With this process of expansion, a process of increasing abstraction and complex socialization occurred. With new symbols, social relations become more and more interrelated as man acquires new roles: he is a human being, a parent, a child, a spouse, a neighbor, a friend, an enemy, a buyer, a taxpayer, a seller, and so on indefinitely. Man has to acquire an increasing number of roles, and he has to integrate all of them and still remain the same person. Even simple concepts have a long history of their own. In our hypothetical example we have discussed three hominids who agreed on the meaning of the verbal symbol "ma-ma." At the beginning "ma-ma" had only a denotative characteristic: it indicated a mother. Before the word *mother* became the representative of the concept "female parent," a tremendous development was necessary. Mother, as an idea, had to go through many preconceptual stages, some of which were probably organized in accordance with the law of the primary process. For a discussion of the evolution from rudimentary to conceptual language the reader is referred to *The Intrapsychic Self* (Arieti, 1967).

When the child is ready for the acquisition of language, he is handed it as a tool ready to be used, a product of the largest part of human history. It is true that the young child is only gradually exposed to the complexities of language; nevertheless he is taking a very accelerated course about words and concepts that took humanity at least a million years to develop.

It is not the purpose of this book to give an account of the development of the processes of symbolization and socialization, as permitted by secondary process cognition. Semantics and sociology deal with this subject. Also, for a detailed comparative development of primary cognition the reader is referred elsewhere (Werner, 1957; Werner and Kaplan, 1963; Arieti, 1967). Another complicating point, however, has to be mentioned. This is the overlapping of the levels of symbolization. Whenever a higher level is reached, the previous one does not cease to exist. These levels overlap in both directions, from the lower to the higher, and from the higher to the lower. The first direction is easily understood. Although man uses verbal symbols predominantly, he retains signs, as is evident when he looks at the clouds to see if it is going to rain. He has images, as when he thinks about things that are not present, and also paleosymbols, most of which are used, however, in his private fantasies, dreams, artistic productions, and neurotic symptoms. The other direction in which the levels overlap is somewhat more complicated. For instance, although the process of socialization, with integrated social activities, could not have taken place without the acquisition of the third symbolic level, mental activities connected with social situations now invade the levels of the paleosymbols or private fantasies, the images, and even the signs. An arrow indicating the direction of traffic on a street is a sign, but a highly socialized one. By far the majority of our images, fantasies, dreams, and so on, involve social situations almost all of which could not have originated without the acquisition of the third symbolic level. Man is a highly social animal, and this socializing attitude does not wish to be confined to the level at which it originated but expands in both directions. When it moves toward more primitive levels, let us say, even to the level of signs, it should not be confused with those superficial social tendencies of which animals too are capable. On the contrary, its expressions are always highly symbolized.

Before the acquisition of language, the child has already acquired nonverbal social symbols of the highest levels. Gestures, attitudes, actions, and feelings already have an interpersonal meaning.

When the child is ready to learn language, he learns that some of the sounds evoke a certain response in the adults around him; he then learns to evoke in himself the same response that these sounds elicit in others. Personal babbling is given up and gradually is replaced by verbal symbols. However, individual tendencies are strong at this age. In many children there is a tendency (generally termed autistic) to name an object or a person with a special sound that the child himself has invented. Parents generally notice that certain sounds or words that are not part of the official language are used by the child to mean certain things.

These paleosymbols used by young children are either created from the original babbling or are made up with badly reproduced verbal symbols. Children, however, learn very soon to repress these autistic or paleologic or paleosymbolic activities and adopt the social symbols learned from adults. It must be noted that a strong autistic tendency, even in a very young child, is a sign of some kind of disorder in his process of socialization. Children who use a great many autistic expressions are children who cannot integrate well socially. When one hears many autistic expressions in a child, one should look for some kind of difficulty between the child and his parents, generally the mother. The child is so unwilling to accept the symbols of the rejecting mother that he resorts more than other children to his own individual symbols. However, unless the child develops child schizophrenia, he sooner or later accepts the symbols of the adults. Even a schizoid type of personality does not prevent the incorporation of symbols. The same thing could be repeated for thinking and formation of concepts. In every child between the age of 1½ to 3½ there is an individualistic tendency to think in accordance with the laws of the primary process. We have seen in Chapter 16 examples of normal children who used paleologic thinking with the adoption of Von Domarus's principle. This tendency is soon overcome by the logical or secondary process thinking of the surrounding adults. In normal circumstances the primary process is overcome and is relegated to the dream world. We stress again the fact that in some families, as well as in some cultures, there is much more paleologic or irrational thinking than in others. Persons living in these families and cultures accept this type of thinking as normal. Inasmuch as this paleologic or irrational thinking is transmitted directly from the family or from the culture, it is conveyed with secondary process media and pertains to the secondary process. It should not be confused with primary process content of intrapsychic origin (see Chapter 16).

IV

Desocialization and Inner Reality in Schizophrenia

We have already mentioned that the process of desocialization takes place because of a concomitant process occurring in the patient's inner reality. The difficulty the patient experiences in dealing with other human beings and with the world in general is the external counterpart of what goes on inside himself. As we saw in Part Two, inner life and external life are constantly interrelated: abnormal external relations early in life trigger intrapsychic mechanisms that disturb the inner life. In its turn a disturbed inner life causes alterations in relating to others. A vicious circle thus originates.

We have seen in Chapter 6 that the prepsychotic patient assumes one of the types of altered relatedness that we have designated as the stormy and schizoid personalities. These types of personalities prevent *communion* and security and bring about peculiar, or at least ill-at-ease, ways of interacting with people. These mechanisms, however, are not psychotic. The psychosis most of the time occurs when the patient adopts a paleologic way of thinking, uses paleosymbols more and more, and drops—at times gradually, at other times acutely—common symbols. By giving up common or socially shared symbols he desocializes himself. Although he may still use common symbols predominantly, the symbols that are involved in his delusions and more intensely experienced by him are his own paleosymbols. We have seen in Chapter 16 that many of the symbols used by the patient are often distortions of social symbols. As long as the patient uses private symbols, at least for the life situations that are most important to him, he cannot integrate socially. However, even the most regressed schizophrenic will retain expressions, words, and ways that belong to the interpersonal world. A total abandonment of what is obtained from others is not possible.

When we have taken into consideration common symbols, for the sake of simplification, we have considered only verbal symbols, but even gestures and motions are being desocialized by the schizophrenic, and they become mannerisms, grimaces, and stereotyped movements whose meaning society does not understand. The patient is no longer an integral part of society. Society requires a symbolic integration of individuals and cultural heritage, that is, the ability on the part of a group of people to understand and organize and give roles to one another in accordance with common symbols. Desocialization, as part of the loss of contact with reality, is not just a physical separation from others or even an emotional detachment. It is also a relinquishing of common ways of experiencing the world and relying on his own individualistic one. It is giving supremacy to inner life, but not the inner life of the philosopher, hermit, or dedicated man who escapes from the amenities of the world or commonplace ideas. It is an inner life that follows the rules of the primary process.

I do not mean that the schizophrenic loses the understanding of the meaning that the society in which he lives gives to the common symbols. In several cases, especially when the illness is very advanced, this is actually the case, but it is not necessarily so. In the majority of cases the schizophrenic retains the intellectual understanding of these symbols, but to him they are emotionally remote; they are like foreign bodies and do not arouse in him the strong reactions that his own paleosymbols do. Therefore, the schizophrenic, especially at the beginning of the illness, may still retain a capacity to socialize, or to check somehow the process of desocialization, but this will only be at the expense of a strenuous intellectual effort. Thus we have that frequent picture of the schizophrenic who succeeds in partially relating to other people through his intellectual functions, but who is emotionally distant and desocialized.

Following one of the comparisons already used, the withdrawn schizophrenic is not simply an anchorite. He is desocialized, not only because of his desire to escape from society like the anchorite, but also because he lives in a symbolic world that is not shared by any society. Perhaps he may be compared somewhat with a person who, in order to become an anchorite, inflicted some kind of sensory aphasia on himself.

The process of desocialization of the schizophrenic does not operate only in the sense of a loss of common symbols. There is also a tendency to reject or to divest the self of those attitudes, roles, and tendencies that became part of the self and that were reflected from others. In other words, a great deal of what was introjected in the process of the development of the self is not only rejected, but also projected, or given back to the persons who originally gave it to the self. An example will explain what I mean. The nagging, scolding attitude of the parent is originally introjected by the child in a distorted and exaggerated form. The child will then acquire a critical, condemnatory attitude toward himself, or what we have called the self-image of the bad child (Chapter 5). When the patient becomes psychotic, this attitude is projected, or given back to a parent-substitute, an authority, or a person paleologically conceived as a persecutor, because he seems to have one of the persecuting traits of the parent.

It seems to me that this explanation increases our present understanding of the mechanism of projection. Projection is not only an attributing of an idea to others; it is a giving back, a restitution of an unpleasant part of the self to the others, to the people who are experienced as having built that part of the self. That part of the self is given back because it is unpleasant. The rest of the patient's self is not going to accept it any longer. The person does not accept self-condemnation any longer as a part of the self; condemnation now comes from the persecutor. He does not hate himself anymore; somebody else hates him. This mechanism is greatly complicated and made obscure by the fact that what is given back is not returned to the people who were experienced as the original givers, but to persons who symbolize them. As we have seen in Chapter 8, the distressing others are often experienced in indefinite ways. "They" are against the patient; "they" plot against him; "they" talk about him. The indefinite persons thus become more personal and more direct forms when they become experienced and identified as, for instance, the Nazis, the FBI agents, and so forth.

Valentin, a patient of mine who developed mild and transient psychotic episodes at the age of 32, is quite typical of a very numerous group of patients. When he was not psychotic, he presented a rather detached, shy, aloof, timid character. In his early childhood, he had the feeling that his parents had unjustly accused him. Later this feeling changed into a deep feeling of self-accusation. He was the bad boy who was causing so much trouble to his parents. A feeling of guilt and inadequacy persisted in spite of the fact that he had acquired a predominantly detached personality. During the psychotic episodes these feelings of guilt, self-hatred, and unworthiness disappeared. He had the idea, however, that agents of the FBI were after him, unjustly accusing him of having participated in subversive activities.

Some patients have the feeling that some alleged persecutors control their thoughts. Again, these alleged persecutors are symbolically the parents or the parent-substitutes who were once experienced as controlling the patient, forcing him to think, that is, to view the world, as they wish, as opposed to the way the patient wishes to see it. On a concrete, almost perceptual, level, the patient reexperiences what he experienced in his early life.

The schizophrenic's belief in the existence of persecutors and enemies implies, one might say, that he makes contact with people and experiences some sort of social integration. That is true to a certain extent. The schizophrenic is capable of functioning at several levels at the same time. When he functions at a social level, it will be easier for him to do so if he sees only a disturbing, condemnatory society around him, because originally he had to adjust to an emotionally similar society in his childhood. In the process of projection he does not use mechanisms derived only from the social level, but also mechanisms as low as the perceptualization of concepts. He hallucinates and hears the voices of the persecutors.

At the same time that the patient rejects these incorporated attitudes from himself, by projecting them back, another process is taking place. The patient feels free to attribute to himself those attitudes and roles that he wished to give to himself in the past, but could not, because of the checking influence of the surrounding world. Those fantasies about himself that he had when he was young, fantasies that had to be repressed or discarded because they were unrealistic in dealings with others, have the tendency to come back. Now they are accepted by the self, but these attitudes toward oneself are very rich in paleosymbols and use a paleological logic. The patient becomes a millionaire, a king, an inventor. Although these attitudes belong to the paleosymbolic level, they have been influenced to a large extent by the level of the common symbols, because without common symbols there would be no concepts of millionaires, kings, and so forth.

Nevertheless, it is possible to recognize that what occurs is an autochthonous or asocial expansion of the self (what some authors call a hypertrophy of the ego) that is due to the attributing to the self of attitudes and roles that are originated by the self itself. These attributes are permitted to expand after the unpleasant attitudes, originally introjected from others, are rejected and projected. That is why the persecutory stage of the paranoid form of schizophrenia is, in some cases, followed by a stage characterized by delusions of grandeur. At first these attributes and roles the patient gives to himself show the influence of the common symbols, or, in other words, of the social level. However, the further he regresses from the social level, the more personal and bizarre these roles become. Whatever smacked of punishment and threatened the self-image is rejected, and delusional grandeur is permitted to flourish.

Some schizophrenics—a relatively small percentage of them—seem to develop a system of grandiose delusions without having gone through the persecutory stage. If these patients had been accurately examined at the beginning of their illness, before they were hospitalized, the examiner would have discovered a persecutory stage of short duration, lasting perhaps a few hours or a few days, or presenting a mild, or even clinical, symptomatology. The important problem is to determine why in these patients the persecutory stage was of such transient or mild type. Most probably these patients cannot find a psychotic equilibrium in a persecutory system. They must bypass this stage in accordance with the teleologic essence of the illness, just as some other patients cannot find an equilibrium at a paranoid level and must proceed toward hebephrenic dilapidation.

The symptoms of cataclysmic catastrophe that many patients experience, like the feeling that the world has come to an end, must be considered as a subjective interpretation of expanding desocialization.

Delusions of negation have often been described in the European literature (Jaspers, 1946; Callieri, 1954; De Martis, 1965, 1967). The end of the world and the twilight of heaven have arrived. All people, all men, are involved; the patient has a tremendous task to accomplish. According to some authors (Rubino and Piro, 1959) the painful changing of reality seems to express the vacillation of the significant ties of the various aspects of reality and the loss of the unity of the ego. The *Weltuntergangerlebnis* seems to express the extreme degree of estrangement from the world. Other authors (for instance, De Martino, 1964) find in these delusions echoes of the apocalyptic themes which are part of the major religions or have recurred in the literature. In my interpretation, things that lose their meanings are destroyed in their symbolic entity. At the same time there is an attempt to rebuild. The feelings of ecumenical influence that some patients experience may be due to the attributing of subjective meanings to everything that surrounds them. Everything around becomes in meaning part of the patient, who consequently may feel he is expanding to a cosmic magnitude.

This implies, of course, that this process of desocialization may be arrested, slowed down, or made more bearable by these restitution phenomena. Patients may remain indefinitely at a level of desocialization in which restitution phenomena are predominant. In many cases, however, the schizophrenic process progresses to a point where it is obvious that desocialization means not only enrichment with schizophrenic symptoms, but also general impoverishment. As we have mentioned when we were discussing the overlapping of levels, many symptoms continue to exploit material belonging to levels from which the patient has predominantly withdrawn. Paleosymbols, for instance, are never pure expression of the paleologic level. When the patient says she is the Virgin Mary, she uses common symbols in a paleologic way. It is because paleosymbols are not pure, but retain remnants of the social level, that we are able to understand them. If it were not so, it would be almost impossible to understand schizophrenia. But as the illness progresses, even the invasion of social symbols at a paleosymbolic level decreases, and the degree of the mental impoverishment of the patient manifests itself in its appalling grandeur. The more he divests himself of common symbols, the more difficult it is for the patient to take the roles of other people and the roles that he felt others assigned to him. This impoverishment reveals how much of man is actually made of social life. When what was obtained from others is eliminated, man remains an insignificant residue of what he used to be.

Previously it was assumed that the more desocialized the patient is, the more he loses the benefits of his interchanges with society. This is true, but it is not all; he loses more than that. By desocializing he loses a great part of himself. This loss is compensated to a minimal degree by the individualistic restitution symptoms, but this compensation is inadequate and in many cases transitory. To be alone, as the schizophrenic is, does not mean only to be without others, but to be less of himself. The meaning of loneliness, as experienced even by normal people and by neurotics, may be fully understood, in my opinion, if we think of the tragic effect of desocialization in schizophrenia. Loneliness means fear of losing oneself partially or totally. This meaning reveals itself fully in the panoramic dimensions and in the intensity of the schizophrenic devastation; but the ghost of loneliness that also haunts normal people may include, to a minimal degree, some of the qualities of these extreme and ultimate consequences.

This brings up another problem. The schizophrenic is *alone* in the world, even in "the world" of his own making; but is he *lonely?* Recovered schizophrenics have stated that they felt terribly lonely when they were sick, and there is no ground for thinking that this is a retrospective falsification. However, the fear of interpersonal relations was even greater than loneliness. It is one of the major tasks of psychotherapy to make such fear less powerful than the desire to establish ties with fellow human beings.

CHAPTER

20

Creative Activities of Schizophrenic Patients: Visual Art, Poetry, Wit

I

Introduction and Historical Review

When the pain is so intense that it no longer has access to the level of consciousness, when the thoughts are so dispersed that they are no longer understood by fellow men, when the most vital contacts with the world are cut off, even then the spirit of man does not succumb, and the urge to create may persist. The search, the appeal, the anguish, the revolt, the wish, may all be there and can be recognized in the fog of the emotional storm of the schizophrenic patient and within the crumbling of his cognitive structure.

Of all the creative activities of the schizophrenic patient, painting is the one that has been studied the most, and we shall devote the bulk of this chapter to this subject. Because the literature on this topic is immense, we shall limit a review of it to the works that are the most significant in a historical frame of reference.

Max Simon (1876, 1888) is reputed to be the first psychiatrist to have made a systematic study of drawings of mental patients. He described five major types of art work, each related to a different syndrome. He also remarked on the similarity between the art of the insane and that of children and primitive people. In 1880 the Italian psychiatrist Cesare Lombroso wrote "On the Art of the Insane." He attempted to understand the conflicts of the patient, stressed again the similarity between psychotic and primitive art, and noticed the importance of sexual symbolism.

Fritz Mohr made the next important contribution. He devised drawing tests, which he used as diagnostic aids (1906). He also attempted to interpret the patients' artwork. For instance, he recognized expressions of obstructions of the will in catatonic patients. Hans Prinzhorn utilized the previous approaches to psychotic art, which he called "the psychiatric," "the folk-lore," and "the psychoanalytic" (1922). He felt that the work has to be studied with an aesthetic approach and should be seen also as an expression of the whole personality. He felt that although the psychoanalytic approach may be useful in unraveling the patient's conflict, it is of little value in studying creativity *per se*. Other important works on the subject were written by Schilder (1918), Morgenthaler (1921), and Pfeifer (1925).

Delgado (1922) found the artistic material of the psychotic patient very rich in sexual symbolism and useful for the psychological understanding of the patient. Pfister (1923) criticized Delgado and stated that sexual content is rare in the art of the psychotic.

Nolan D. C. Lewis (1925, 1928) was the first American author to make important contributions on this subject. He interpreted the symbolism of the visual productions in accordance with psychoanalytic principles. He gave particular importance to the "death wish" that is "so artfully concealed that the producer is not aware of its existence." He also stressed the recurrence of the "evil eye": the "all-seeing eye" of God, the male parent, or the analyst or a combination of all three as the central theme in many drawings of patients of both sexes, all ages, and all nationalities.

Karpov (1926) emphasized that some symptoms may appear in the artistic production before they occur at a clinical level. Vinchon (1926, 1950) also stressed that the psychological disturbance may appear in the artistic production before the onset of the psychosis.

The well-known French psychiatrist Henri Ey (1948) classified the artistic productions of the mentally ill into four categories: (1) aesthetic forms that have nothing to do with the mental disorder and are simply juxtaposed; (2) aesthetic forms modified by the illness; (3) aesthetic forms of pathologic projection; (4) aesthetic forms immanent in the delusional ideas.

Margaret Naumburg (1950) has done important work on schizophrenic art from the point of view of its meaning in psychotherapy. In her accurate reports about two schizophrenic girls, Naumburg demonstrated how the symbolic forms expressed their life history, their conflicts, and their solutions. In the course of therapy the patients abandoned gradually stereotypy and archaic forms and assumed an increasing freedom of expression. Naumburg feels that art therapy increases the patients' awareness of their conflicts and their ability to verbalize them.

Francis Reitman (1951, 1954) has made important studies of schizophrenic art. He believes that its peculiarities and special features depend primarily on the cognitive abnormalities of the patient. According to him the similarities, emphasized by some authors, between modern art and schizophrenic art are only apparent or superficial. He wrote that whereas the work of normal artists reveals a deliberate restructuring of reality into complex patterns or relations of form and color, the work of schizophrenics discloses a general lack of structure, a disintegration of perceptual relations, and a dissolution of concepts. Whereas in the painting of modern artists the radical alteration is one of reorganization, in the work of schizophrenics it is one of disorganization. Reitman feels that there is an interconnection between art and conceptual thinking, but he does not illustrate how the various alterations in cognition are responsible for the characteristics of psychotic art.

Dax (1953) did interesting experimental studies of psychiatric art. He compared the representations of ancient Egyptian gods to the composite figures of schizophrenics. He gave particular importance to the meaning of the eye in the paintings of patients. He thought that it is not sufficient to interpret the eye in association with guilt feelings or an "eye of conscience" or "the eye of God" or an "all-seeing eye." He compared the importance of the schizophrenic eye symbolism to that of the ancient Egyptians. In ancient Egypt the eye had five main symbolic meanings: (1) the eyes of the sun and the moon; (2) the sacred eye; (3) the eye of sacrifice; (4) the eye of immortality; (5) the evil eye.

A very important book on psychopathological art was written by Volmat (1955). Not only does this author give an accurate account of the literature, but he also reports on the international exposition of psychopathological art that took place in Paris in 1950 on the occasion of the first world congress of psychiatry. Volmat's book contains reproductions of 169 works and analyzes the main points of view of the various authors who did research on this subject. Volmat concluded that in his artwork the patient expresses himself and his illness totally.

II
General Remarks about Schizophrenic Art

According to some statistics reported by Volmat, only 29 percent of psychiatric patients paint spontaneously. It is impossible to ascertain the observation reported by some authors that schizophrenics paint more frequently than normal persons. Whether this is true or not, it is certain that the habit of painting noted in many schizophrenics contrasts with their general inactivity and lack of involvement with the things of the world. Many hypotheses have been proposed to explain the phenomenon. Some people believe that the boredom of years spent in hospitals triggers off even a modest talent that has remained dormant for many years. This hypothesis does not explain why schizophrenics would not relieve boredom in other ways. Another hypothesis explains the habit as a search for what the patient has lost in life. Psychological loss and emptiness would promote in the patient the urge to compensate or restore. But again, why to restore in this way? It seems to me that the most important reason resides in the nature of the schizophrenic process itself. On one side, the regression makes primary process cognition reappear with renewed availability of unused forms On the other side, we have the rekindling of fantasies and motivational impulses, never realized in life, now searching an actualization on paper or on canvas, just as in the majority of patients they find actualization in delusions and hallucinations.

The motivational impulses may be wishes that were never fulfilled or even expressed because of their primitive, shameful content. They may be fantasies that were repressed because they were unrealizable and frustrating. However, in my opinion, attributing to the schizophrenic a primitive, infantile, or purely sexual motivation is a common mistake. Whereas sexual expression has recently reached a degree of frequency never reached before in the visual art of normal people of the Western culture, schizophrenic art seems more and more concerned with different aims. It would be equally incorrect to say that schizophrenic art ignores sex. What counts is not only the specific nature of the motivation, but how the motivation is artistically realized and how pathology appears through the realization. In the last two decades several psychiatrists have noted that there are changes in a large number of art works of schizophrenics. In addition to those rigid, schematic, and stereotyped works, which used to be reported in textbooks of psychiatry, we see now an increasing number of confused, irregular, freedom-seeking products. Whether these changes are the result of drug therapy, psychotherapy, art therapy, a difference in the climate of hospital life, or a combination of all these factors is difficult to ascertain.

From a broad point of view we can make the following generalization: schizophrenic art is the result of a struggle between motivational impulses and the specific schizophrenic cognitive media available to the patient. The sudden availability of primary process forms and the disinhibitions of wishes and aspirations become substitutes for the technique, skill, and commitment that many patients never had before they became ill.

The artwork has another practical purpose for the patient. The schizophrenic experiences the world in fleeting, fugitive ways that are not only different from the ones he perceived prior to the psychosis, but also from those perceived at different stages of the illness. His world tends to be in constant and turbulent metamorphosis. Like many symptoms of the schizophrenic, painting is an effort to adjust to the new vision of reality, to crystallize it, to arrest it, or to delay further changes. This is one of the reasons why many paintings done by regressed schizophrenics show not only metamorphosis, but also an extreme static quality.

In typical cases, which do not recover, we see the following sequence of phases:

1. The eruption of the conflict and the supremacy of the wish prevail without sufficient correction by the secondary process. The correction is insufficient to make the work acceptable to other people. During the first phase it is often difficult to distinguish artwork of schizophrenics from that of nonschizophrenics. It depends on evaluating whether the correction of the secondary process was sufficient or insufficient, and this evaluation may be arbitrary.

2. A gradual disintegration of the mechanisms of the secondary process and

obvious emergence of those of the primary process, reflecting paleologic ideation, take place.

3. A crystallization of primary process mechanisms occurs in more rigid and stereotyped forms.

4. A disintegration of primary process mechanisms also occurs.

In patients who recover, the process does not go beyond the second phase. Eventually secondary process mechanisms succeed in repressing or, hopefully, in integrating or solving the conflict.

The principle of active concretization, discussed in Chapter 15, occurs also in fine art and in schizophrenic art. In fine art a concrete representation may stand for the abstract—a flower may stand for the beautiful, the portrait of a smiling girl may stand for youth and happiness. In art of normal people it is through the medium of the primary process that the abstract concept emerges. In psychopathological art, as in dreams of normal people and in delusional thinking, the consciousness of the abstract rapidly decreases and may be completely lost. What remains is the concrete representation.

The principle of Von Domarus, which we have described in Chapter 16, is applied quite often in schizophrenic artwork. In many cases it is applied only partially; that is, some partial identity among the subjects is based upon an identification of a part, generally identity of a form, detail, visual appearance, shape. In these cases we have no total identification; instead, *fusion* or *condensation* of two or more subjects is quite characteristic. Other mechanisms of primary process cognition deal with mannerisms, stereotypes, repetition of forms, and so forth. Many of these mechanisms are also used in normal art, but whereas in normal art they are harmoniously matched by the secondary process, in schizophrenic art they remain incongruous.

III

Content and Conflict

In some artworks what strikes the observer most is not the presence of regressive forms but an unusual content or the manner in which the conflict is represented. These works are generally done by patients at the beginning of the illness or, if they had been ill for a long time, by those who had not undergone advanced regression. In some of these patients, nontypical schizophrenic features were also present, like psychopathic, depressive, or involutional features.

Figure 3 is a drawing made by Pauline, who was in the first stage of schizophrenia and whose work showed what I consider the first phase of artistic pathology. Pauline is aware of the major conflicts in her life, although she is not aware that the inability to solve them makes her frail, reactivates an ancient anxiety, and precipitates her illness. Pregnancy is obviously the theme. The abdomen of the woman protrudes and the fetus is represented in various positions. Worth noticing is the fact that the head of the woman does not appear; it seems to be covered or perhaps replaced by an elongated object that may stand for the right arm, for the head, for a torch, or for a brush. The similarity to a brush leads me to the second picture (Figure 4), which actually was made by the patient one day before the first one.

Figure 4 reveals that the woman feels fragmented under the weight of her major problem: is she going to fulfill her desire to be a painter? We see again here the paleologic confusion among arm, torch, and brush because of the similar shape of these objects. The brush, which is her life torch, fell to the floor. Important to notice is that the palette bears a striking resemblance to the womb in the left part of the previous picture: the various colors, ingredients for her creativity, remind us of the fetus in the various positions. Her head, covered by her hair, is similar to the brush.

The following drawing (Figure 5), also made the day before the first one was made, was entitled by Pauline: "The Awakening of a Dream." No longer is it the dream or daydream of being a painter. With the eye that feels and cries, the ear that listens, she tries to put herself together. Her big breast and belly, and the torch-hair-brush, indicate that she is selecting motherhood.

When we compare Figures 3 and 4, we see how Pauline's conflict—between being a painter and being a mother, the war between the palette and the womb—was represented in visual forms, to a considerable extent, through the application at a visual level of Von Domarus's principle. Her life drama finds a visual expression that, although partially affected by pathological mechanisms, is still acceptable and elicits in the normal observer consensual validation, shared feeling, compassion, and so on. We recognize that the womb has won and that the palette has been defeated; but it was a pyrrhic victory. At this level the conflict of the patient and its artistic representation still evoke a response, the pathos becomes ethos.

A case described by the Belgian psychiatrist Bobon (1957), and later in greater detail by Bernard and Bobon (1961), reveals very well the importance of content. Gaston, the son of a violent alcoholic father and a mother who was irritable and overprotective, developed catatonic schizophrenia. A few years later, while he was a patient in a hospital for the chronically ill, it was accidentally discovered that he would spontaneously draw when he had a pencil. On pages of newspapers or odd bits of paper he drew a kind of stereotyped monster, which he called "the rhinoceros." For several years his numerous drawings and paintings were endless variations on the theme of the rhinoceros. A better contact was established by discussing his drawings, and the patient during psychotherapy was able to recall an episode he had forgotten. At the age of 13 he had seen a movie representing a jungle populated by wild beasts, hunters armed with rifles, and especially by striking rhinoceroses. According to Bernard and Bobon the rhinoceros is the image of power and implies also an image of powerlessness. The power is the angry, furious father, as well as any kind of irrational force in the world. The powerlessness is the powerlessness of the patient, who has to face such evil power. According to Bobon the powerlessness is experienced not only as inferior-

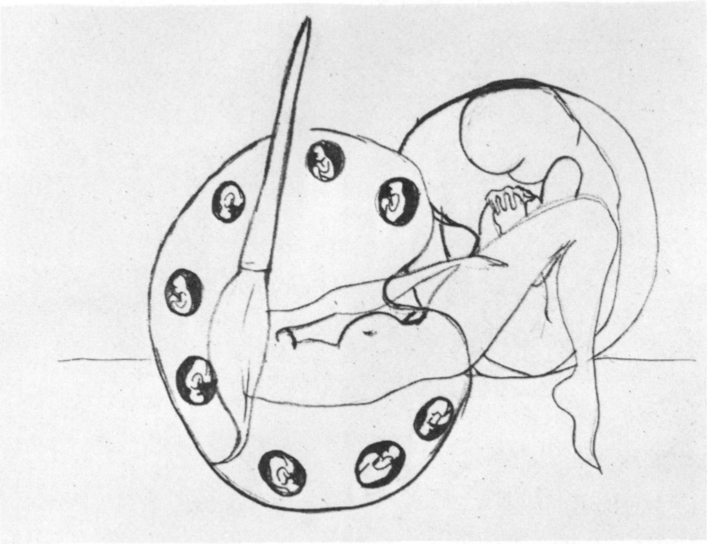

FIGURE 3

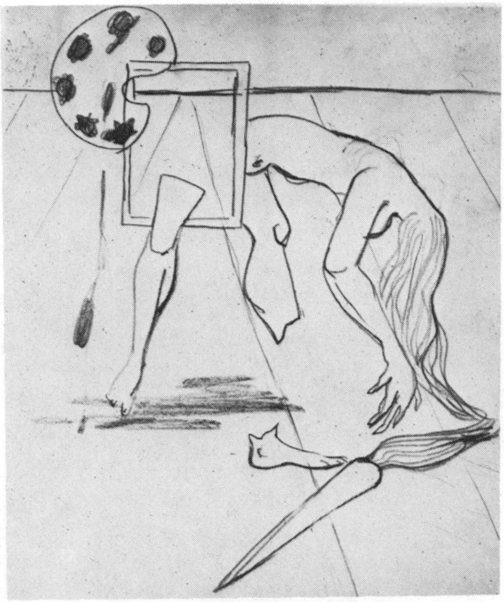

FIGURE 4

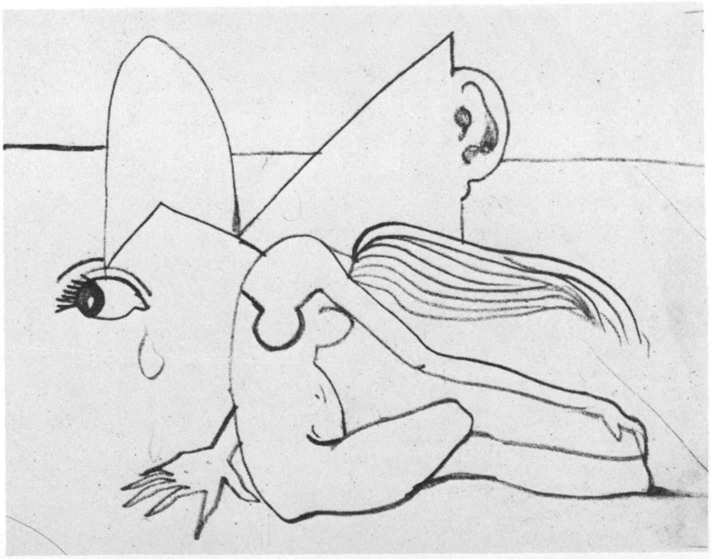

FIGURE 5

Explanations for each picture are given in the text

FIGURE 6

FIGURE 7

FIGURE 8

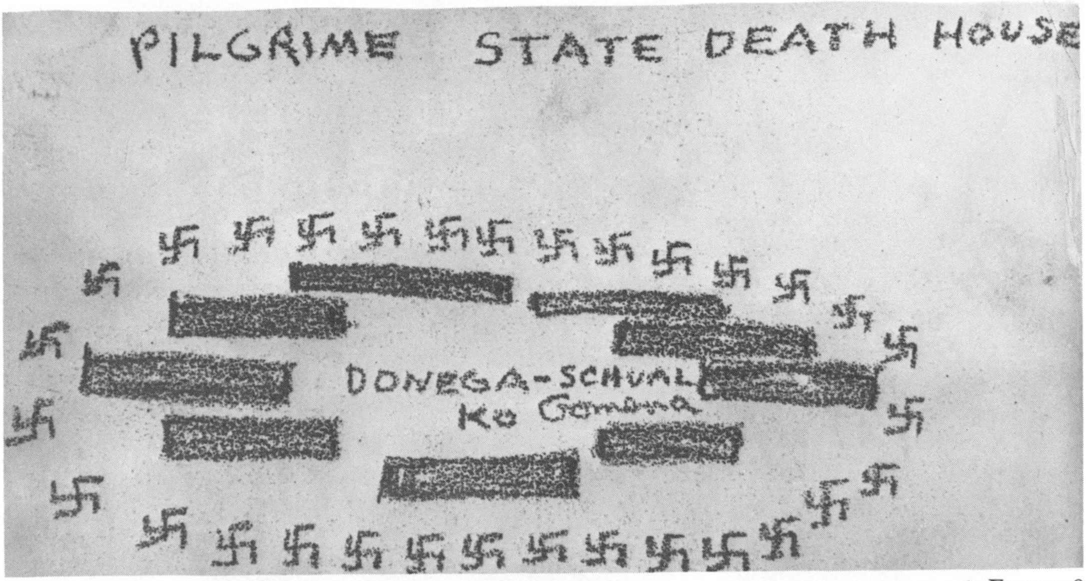

FIGURE 9

FIGURE 10

FIGURE 12

FIGURE 11

Explanations for each picture are given in the text

Explanations for each picture are given in the text

FIGURE 13

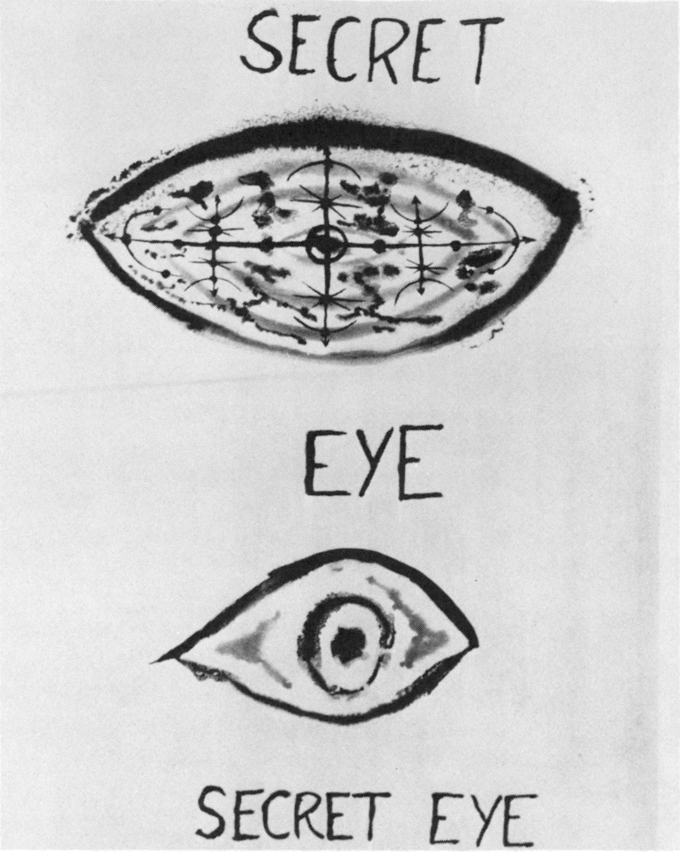

FIGURE 14

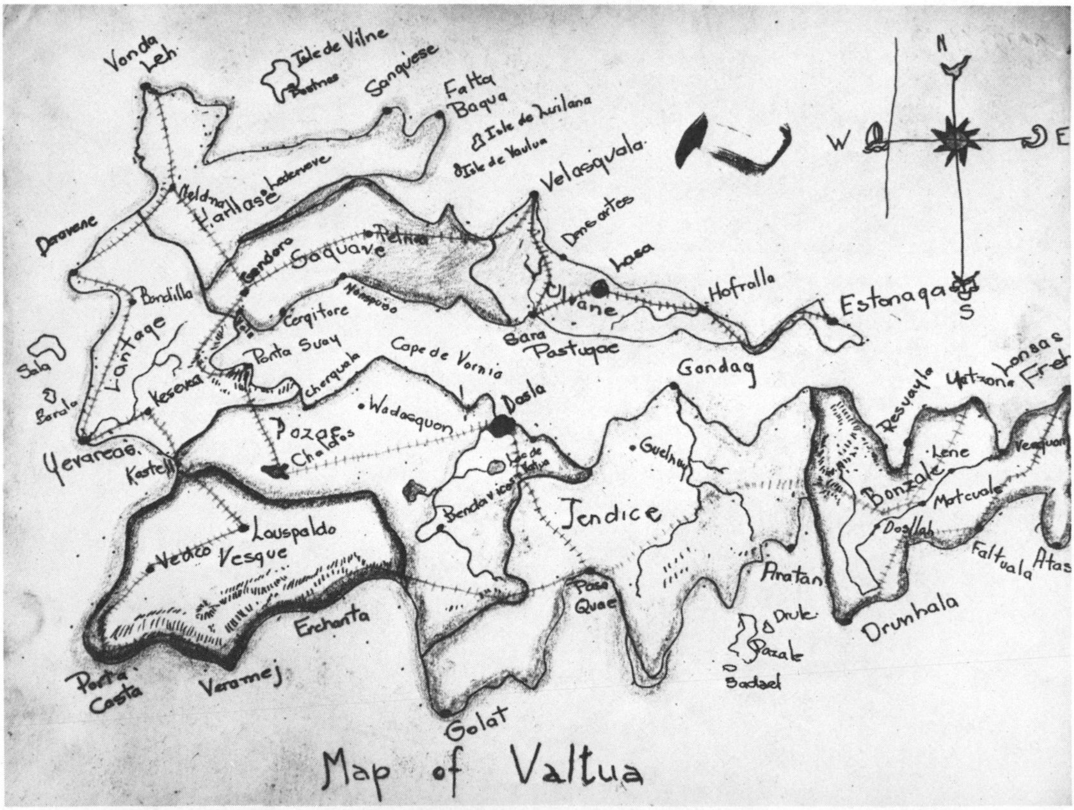

FIGURE 15

FIGURE 16

FIGURE 17

FIGURE 18

FIGURE 19

FIGURE 20

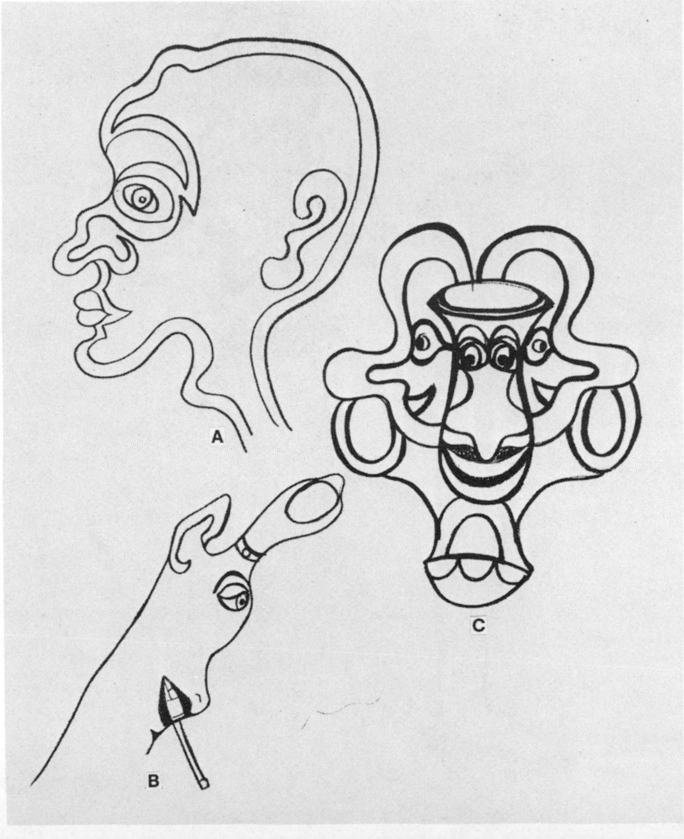

FIGURE 21

Explanations
or each picture
are given in
the text

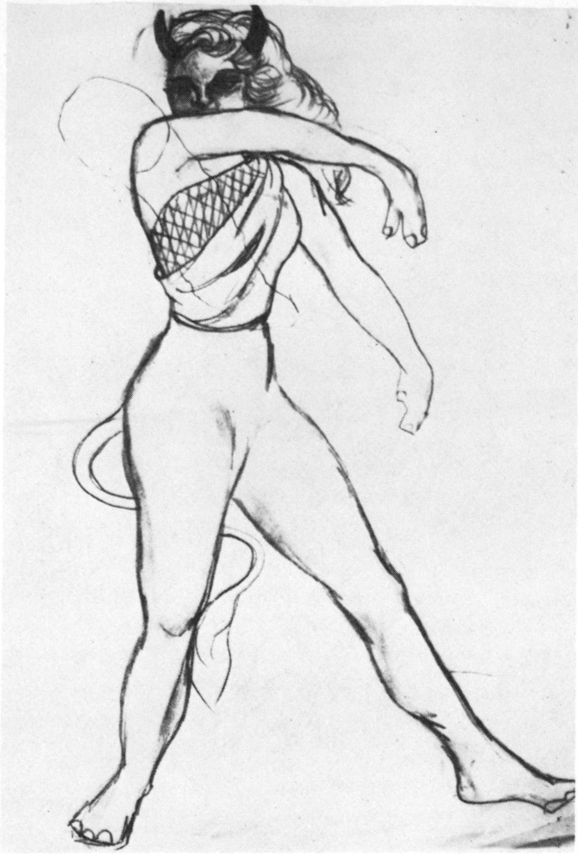

Figure 22

Explanations
for each picture
are given in
the text

Figure 23

FIGURE 24

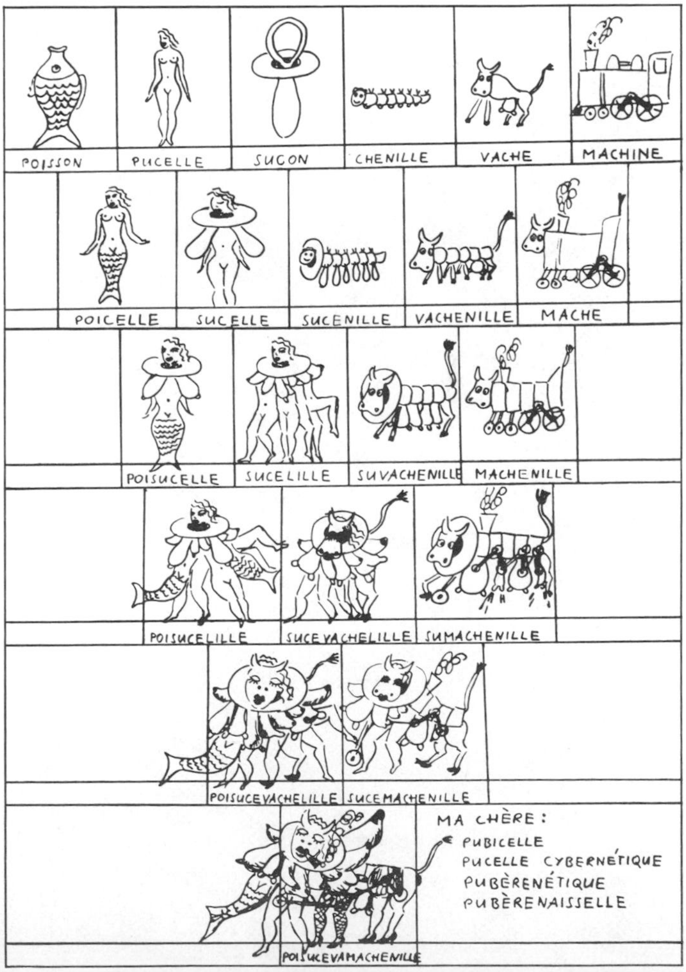
POISSON
PUCELLE
SUCON
CHENILLE
VACHE
MACHINE
POICELLE
SUCELLE
SUCENILLE
VACHENILLE
MACHE
POISUCELLE
SUCELILLE
SUVACHENILLE
MACHENILLE
POISUCELILLE
SUCEVACHELILLE
SUMACHENILLE
POISUCEVACHELILLE
SUCEMACHENILLE
MA CHÈRE:
PUBICELLE
PUCELLE CYBERNÉTIQUE
PUBÈRENÉTIQUE
PUBÈRENAISSELLE
POISUCEVAMACHENILLE

FIGURE 25

FIGURE 26

FIGURE 27

FIGURE 28

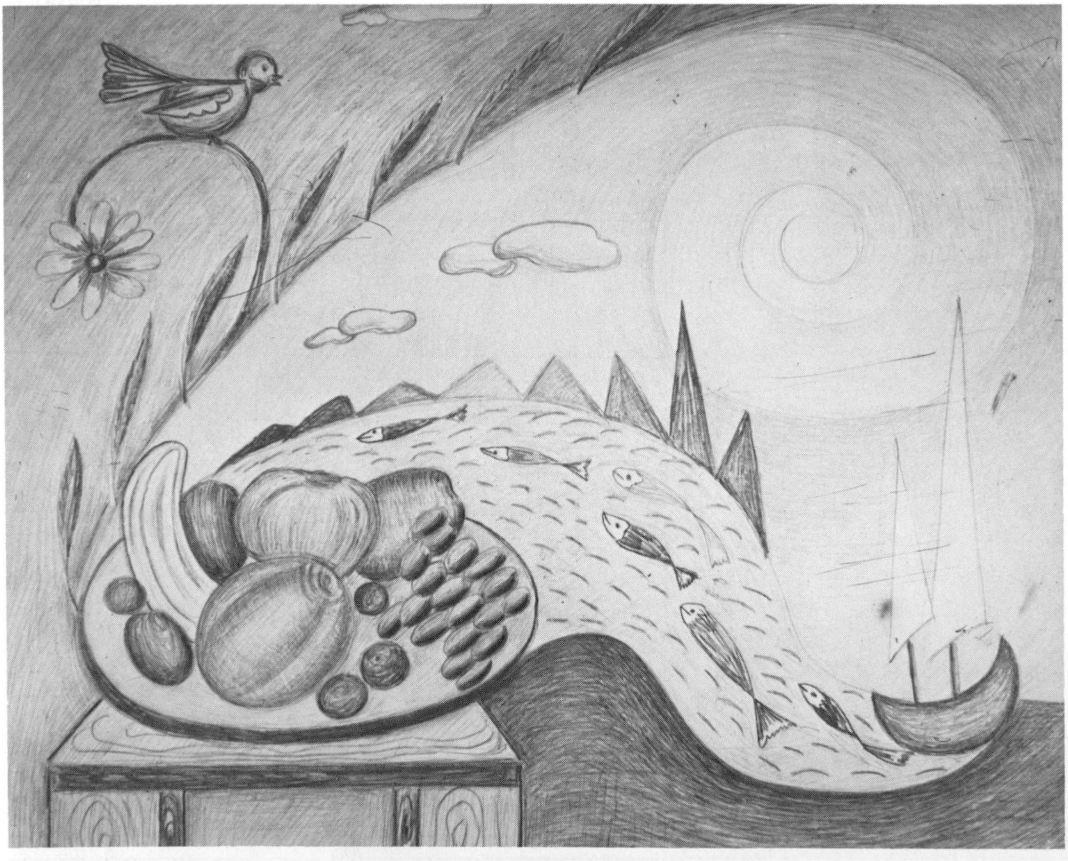

FIGURE 29

FIGURE 30

FIGURE 31

Explanations
for each picture
are given in
the text

FIGURE 32

FIGURE 33

FIGURE 34

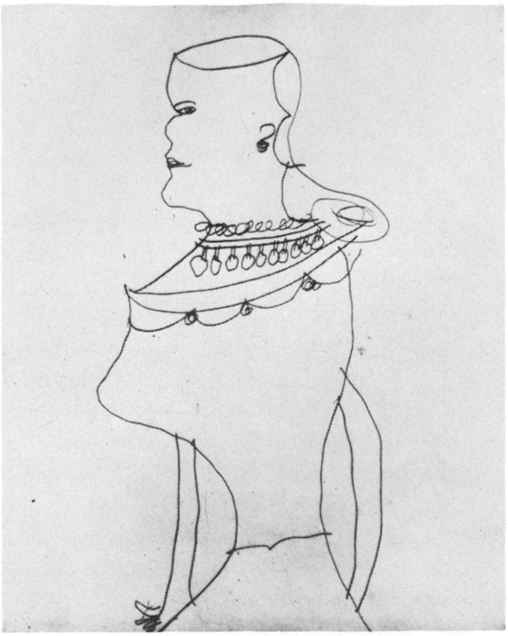

FIGURE 35

Explanations
for each picture
are given in
the text

FIGURE 36

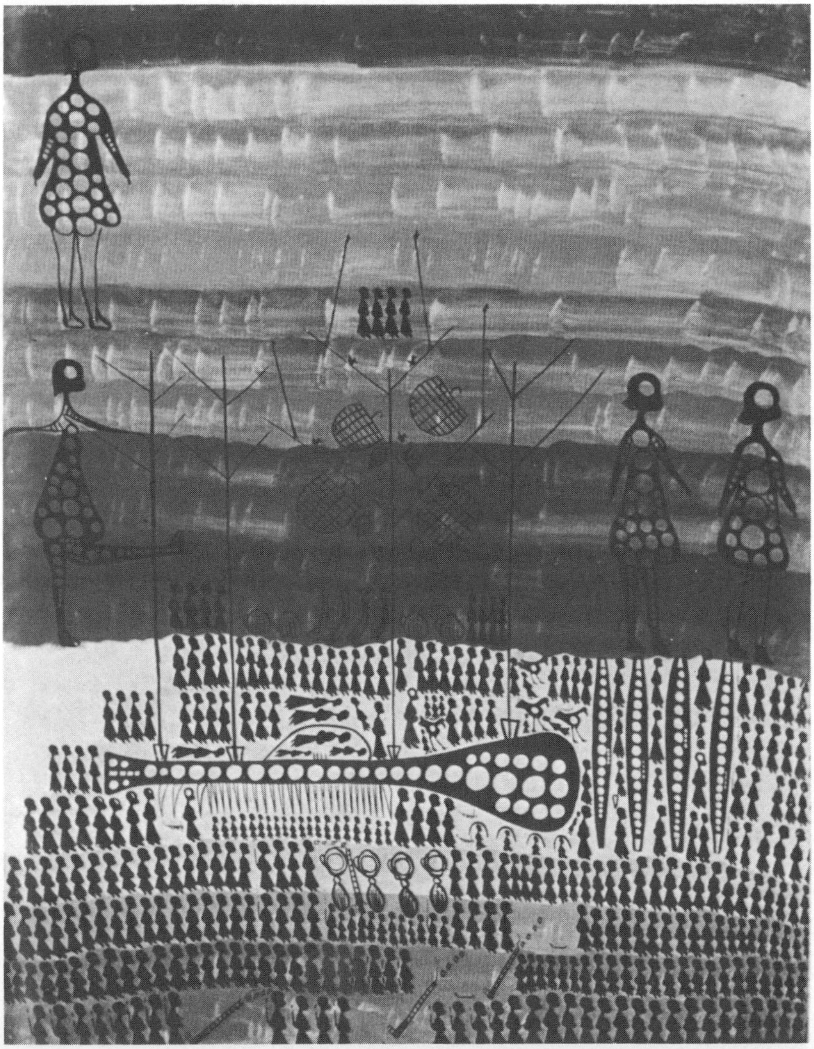

FIGURE 37

FIGURE 38

FIGURE 39

FIGURE 40

Explanations for each picture are given in the text

FIGURE 42

FIGURE 41

Explanations
for each picture
are given in
the text

FIGURE 43

ity but also as guilt for being inferior. However, Gaston was able to externalize his complexes the day he took a pencil and started to draw. Incidentally, Gaston's artistic activity anteceded Ionesco's famous play *Rhinoceros*. Moreover, Gaston had never seen Salvador Dali paintings where parts of rhinoceroses appear. The turbulent rhinoceros, which used to be an inner object, was externalized, and Gaston acquired calm and relaxation. However, during subsequent years strange things happened. The drawn rhinoceros became the depository of anxiety. Under injections of sodium amytal Gaston became talkative and was able to say that after completing a picture of the rhinoceros he became afraid of it. The picture became invested with the meanings and intentions that Gaston had attributed to a real rhinoceros. It became empowered with real physical power. The patient soon stopped drawing and since then lapsed again into a vegetative, motionless, empty life, which possibly will continue ineluctably.

Bernard and Bobon wrote that the rhinoceros became a speech, "the clue to a morbid system," that permitted an understanding of the patient. We must be grateful to the authors for this remarkable report; but we must also ask ourselves what went wrong. This form of expression, which at first seemed to help the patient, in the long run did not help at all. The patient became afraid of what at first appeared a psychological defense. He had to escape from the rhinoceros as he had once from the real father. This is unfortunately what happens when the schizophrenic psychosis is not successfully treated. What is probably intended to be a defense with restitutional qualities proves to be more disturbing and to cause further regression. The tragic drama of the schizophrenic is thus repeated. The fugitive from reality seeks refuge in a new world, to a large extent of his own creation. But in unfortunate circumstances his fantasy world is more threatening than the one he escaped from.

In the case of Gaston, therapy apparently did not succeed in depriving the rhinoceros of his power. My own hypothesis is that the therapist tried to be good and maternal, but like Gaston's real mother, revealed himself to be weak and ineffective in comparison to the rhinocerontic father.

Figures 6, 7, and 8 are paintings done by a 32-year-old man, a commercial artist who became depressed and finally delusional. He never had auditory hallucinations but frequently had visual ones. He claimed that he was seeing angels and that every night before falling asleep Jesus Christ appeared to him. He painted many hours every day and would repeatedly say that he could paint with closed eyes, as God guided his hands. Figure 6 shows no gross distortions. There is a desire to change nature, to improve on it in a way that is still acceptable to the observer. The house, the trees, the land constitute an ensemble where hope can still sojourn.

Figure 7 shows where the hope comes from: Christ and the church. A woman is going there, and this may indicate some problems in sexual identification of the male patient, who was not married.

Figure 8 shows a more unrealistic scene. A Freudian observer may find forms reminiscent of penises, vaginas, and pubic hair. The whole is acceptable: hope is still there, as represented by the rainbow and the nice home. After long hospitalization and with old age already approaching, the patient was discharged on custodial care.

The case of Sheila is completely different. Her father, an alcoholic, deserted the family shortly after the patient's birth. The mother died when the patient was 2 years old. Sheila was taken care of in several foster homes, but because of her behavior she was admitted to a psychiatric hospital at the age of 10 under the diagnosis of primary behavior disorder. In her childhood and youth she repeatedly lied, stole, and destroyed property. She was hospitalized several times. As an adult, she was diagnosed as suffering from the mixed type of schizophrenia, later changed to the catatonic type. Her life has been characterized by repeated episodes of disorderly behavior and by suicidal attempts that necessitated her hospitalizations. During each of her hospitalizations she appeared at first haughty, disdainful, evasive, overactive, tangential, and disconnected in her speech, at times even in catatonic withdrawal. However, shortly her behavior would improve, she would be discharged from the hospital, and after intervals of various lengths she would become acutely ill again. With a few striking exceptions, most of her finger paintings do not disclose schizophrenic characteristics but a turbulent, angry, ferocious personality. She would often sign her paintings and drawings not with her name but with the following phrase: "Drawn by EVERYONE frightened by the Devils." Noteworthy is the word *everyone;* that is, not just she, but anyone of the millions who populate the world and are frightened by the devils. Society and the hospital are among the devils. They become a Nazi society. Pilgrim State Hospital is a death house (Figure 9). The dollar sign, symbol of the capitalistic United States, becomes a swastika (Figure 10). If this world is a world of the devil, a Nazi world, she is better off saying good-bye to the world and committing suicide. In Figure 11, which shows a falling woman and falling flowers, she says, "Nice knowing you," to the world she intends to leave. Paradoxically she has one thing in common with the Nazis—a strong hate for the Jews. In Figure 12 she portrays what she never had: maternal love bestowed to a little girl. In her delusional thinking she believes that the Jews are responsible for the deprivation that she sustained. Actually Jewish people tried to help Sheila, but because of her conflicts she mistrusted them. She was not able to accept any warmth. Often the hand offered to help her met with the bite of her revenge and fury. It is this attitude of mistrust, determined by the early circumstances of life, that makes therapy with patients like Sheila extremely difficult. However, her psychotic episodes did not bring about regression. In some of her distortions one could see some metaphorical representations of society that many nonschizophrenics can share.

Some themes recur frequently in schizophrenic art. One of them is the theme of the eye (Figure 13). The eye symbolizes the world, or the other, any person other than yourself, the other human being who is there not to commune with you but to watch. And to watch means to scrutinize, to blame, to condemn, to reject you, and to destroy your sense of self-regard, your privacy, and your human dignity. The main part of the other is not his penis or her vagina but the eye: not an eye that cries, unless it portrays the eye of the patient himself, as in the case of Pauline. It is not the eye that loves, embraces, and protects, like that of a good mother, but a cruel eye that follows you and pierces you. It is Big Brother's eye, the persecutory secret eye.

IV
Progression of Illness as Revealed by the Artwork

It is important in some cases to study the psychodynamics and the progression of the illness as it is revealed by works of art done by the same patient at different times. The following case lends itself to such inquiry.

While she was an adolescent and not yet ill, Lucille drew maps of imaginary countries. Figure 14 shows the map of the imaginary land of Valtua. This habit of drawing maps of imaginary countries is not necessarily psychotic or prepsychotic (Gondor, 1963). It is also found in bright and creative children and adolescents, although it often denotes a certain detachment or schizoidism, discomfort with reality, and indulgence in fantasy life. Just prior to her illness Lucille's drawings portray also a desire to plunge into life, to give to it accentuated pageantry (Figure 15).

Lucille portrayed also a desire to escape into a fairy-tale world different from her reality. In Figure 16, castle and ships, friendly waves, sirens, and moons are put together to signify a world without anxiety, a place where we too, like the girl on the ship, would like to land. But the patient did not land there. Figure 17, made at the beginning of the illness, portrays already the patient's conflict. Woman is the protagonist. The theatrical setting discloses the drama of woman, as lived by the patient. Woman appears in various poses that reveal grace and beauty in the majesty of the stage of life. But let us look at the two couples in the center of the picture. Strangely, each couple does not consist of a woman and a man, but of two women: one more energetic, not fully dressed, and another one typically feminine in a beautiful evening gown.

The illness progresses, as shown by Figure 18. Here athletic women have incongruously masculine physical characteristics. Now the desire to be a man can no longer be repressed by the patient, who had tried to fight her own homosexuality. At this point Lucille ceases to be an artist and becomes a schizophrenic patient. There is here no artistic blending of femininity and masculinity, no artistic synthesis and reintegration but bizarre concretization and schizophrenic fusion, which the observer is not going to accept. The illness progresses and the sexual orientation manifests itself, not as it does in common homosexuality, but in schizophrenic forms. The patient desperately tries to rebuild the image of woman, but let us see what happens. Figure 19 is a typical schizophrenic drawing. Bizarreness in the formalism, regularity in the irregularity, mannerism and distortion are seen in what is supposed to be a woman, or Woman. Again the left arm and hand, which are often symbols of homosexuality, appear bigger than the right heterosexual arm. The hebephrenic illness progresses and dilapidation occurs. Figure 20 shows that the patient is no longer able to form wholes. The profiles of women are hardly recognizable. Woman has now undergone advanced schizophrenic fragmentation. The patient can no longer be helped. She is totally smashed by the weight of her psychological problem; she had searched for a solution but had found none—no mythical country of Valtua, no fairy land, no women's liberation.

And yet our imagination wanders in the realm of theoretical possibilities. Had Lucille been helped by psychotherapy to accept her problem, had she revealed her secret to her mother and father, had society not shown her that intolerance and shame were connected with the intimate part of her individuality, had the hospital been a therapeutic community and not a forced confinement, had her therapists (of whom I was one) not been so young (we too were in our twenties, were residents in psychiatry, and were not yet trained psychodynamically), she might have uplifted the burden that crushed her tender spirit.

A case in which this transformation or deterioration of forms occurred in a period of a few hours has been described by Crahay and Bobon (1961). These authors described the case of Octave, who developed an acute and severe schizophrenic episode that required five months of hospitalization. The authors have since followed the patient for seven years and consider him recovered.

When Octave was 7 years old he saw his father for the first time. His father had returned home after having been a prisoner of war for a few years. His father died when Octave was 11 years old, and so Octave knew his father only for about four years. With the death of his father he lost somebody "with whom he could talk." He witnessed then with great distress a metamorphosis of his mother. She became "a sort of man," and at the same time a person who sacrificed herself to help her children. Octave became a student of architecture. At the age of 18 he became acutely ill. During the episode he was incoherent and claimed he was soon going to marry a girl whom he had occasionally seen at the railroad station. During a session that took place during the acute stage of the illness, he made some drawings that reproduced the experience he had dramatically lived.

The following is a summary of the episode, as reported by the authors. What is in brackets has been added by me. The report discusses thirteen drawings made by the patient, which were selected from a total of thirty.

The subject of the woman first appears in a dozen distinctly erotic nudes, skillfully drawn in black pencil with artistic excellence. Then the graphic is gradually disconnected from the real object: the woman is completely transformed into a violently red-colored, ambiguous, bisexual being, loaded with culpability and aggressiveness. [She appears devilish; her feet having an animal-like or demonic form.]

The succeeding drawings [representing a male figure; perhaps the patient himself, having, however, big breasts like a woman], where red and black alternate, progressively deviate from naturalistic representation. The human being is dislocated, dismembered; only a huge eye, a greedy mouth with enormous teeth, and fingers resembling these teeth (paramorphism) remain. The general form retains a certain dynamism but becomes more and more schematized, geometrized, and destructurized, and finally disintegrates into a complete scrawl, the result of an almost pure motor outburst. [To me the last drawing seems to reproduce a swastika: a nude human being has been actually transformed into the

Nazi emblem, possibly the symbol of evil. Remember that the father of the patient had been taken prisoner during World War II, presumably by the Germans, and had died a few years after his return.] At this moment the patient is in a condition of extreme agitation; he is anxious and semi-confused; speech is incoherent, and he has to be isolated. The drawings, in their succession, are particularly expressive and eloquent; they do not only depict the preferred contents of the usual pathologic condition but also convey the progress of a depersonalization crisis, where reality, first experienced as controlled imagination, gradually becomes disorganized and dehumanized in the abstract and finally dissolves up to the point of disappearing. The drawings also raise the problem of the formal modifications of spontaneous artistic expression in relation with the distortions of the patient's experience.

We must at this point mention that the mobilization of the primary process form of expression often starts before the illness manifests itself clinically as schizophrenic in nature. We have already mentioned that Karpov (1926) and Vinchon (1926, 1950) reported that the pathological art may occur before the onset of the overt psychosis. Patient Henriette may illustrate this point. She came for therapy at the age of 19 at the request of her family. She had dropped out of college and felt no motivation to go to school or to work. For several months she had as a boy friend a psychopath who used and pushed drugs, would occasionally steal, and eventually died of an overdose. Henriette occasionally helped him to get out of trouble at her own risk. Henriette's identity was made more difficult by the fact that she had an identical twin sister. Like her twin sister, she felt rejected by both parents and was unable to relate to anybody except her sister. Her only satisfaction was in drawing and painting. She was unusually intelligent and deep in her feelings, but she felt she could not sustain any psychological effort. She would always yield to immediate pleasure or a quick solution. When she first came for therapy, she seemed at first oriented more toward a psychopathic pattern of behavior. She would often draw or paint flowers that appeared to be distortions of real ones, even though they were similar to natural flowers. The patient used to say that she wanted to create and not reproduce reality.

To remove her from her boy friend the parents sent her to live in another city, and she interrupted therapy. On her return a few months later, she was much worse. Although not clear-cut, schizophrenic symptoms were evident; quasi-schizophrenic symptomatology was prominent. She would say that occasionally in the subway she felt *as if* people were talking about her or looking at her. She knew it was not so, but nevertheless the experience made her uncomfortable. In the subway she would see people who looked like other people she knew, and often she had them confused. She had to go through the trouble of seeing whether these people were really the people she knew or not. These symptoms were indications that primary process cognition (like projection, confusion of similarity for identity, and so forth) would threaten to come to the surface. However, as a whole she managed to maintain a fairly integrated ego and did not appear schizophrenic to anybody except the therapist. It is in her artwork that pathology clearly appeared. After a long period during which she painted unrealistic flowers, she painted geometrical, simple designs, either as a form of relaxation, or perhaps to preserve some regularity in her disorderly experience of life. At the same time she painted different subjects in unusual ways, for instance, repulsive faces (Figure 21). Figure 21B was supposed to represent a hand; but what was intended to be a finger looked like a hat and inspired the patient to make a head out of a hand. Figure 21C represents a vase, which is also a head. In the ears of the central face she saw other faces. We have here again the irresistible need to succumb to similarity. The orgy of similarity, however, does not introduce her to an artistic transformation of reality. Whatever comes from reality is made worse and is magnified in its negative aspects. She portrays a world of repulsive ugliness from which she wants to escape. This world is made worse by her illness, and she finds herself trapped in it. After the marriage of her twin sister, on whom she depended so much, Henriette became worse. She felt threatened, isolated, incapable of fulfillment. She interrupted therapy again and had a full-blown psychotic episode, with delusions and hallucinations that were grandiose and religious in content. The episode lasted six months.

V

Crystallization of Primary Process Mechanisms

The previous examples have shown how even the schizophrenic who draws or paints for the first time in his life may immediately find at his disposal an emerging personal style and a new technique. At first the style is mixed with the ones he observed in his cultural background. Relatively soon, however, as the detachment from the environment increases and the illness progresses, regressive forms prevail and give to the art product its characteristic pathological aspect. Finally the work of art becomes crystallized in typical schizophrenic forms. Even the motivation to draw a specific object seems overpowered by the laws of schizophrenic cognition.

In some of the examples given there was a complete application of Von Domarus's principle. For instance, in the case of Gaston, the father was identified with the rhinoceros because of his terrifying quality. In the case of Pauline, the palette was identified with the womb because of similar shape and similar creative possibility. But the most characteristic feature of schizophrenic art is a partial application of Von Domarus's principle. Some partial identity among the subjects is based upon partial or total identity of a predicate or a part. In these cases, we have no total identity but fusion or condensation of two or more subjects. Figures 22 and 23 are drawings made by a female patient with unresolved homosexual conflicts. She sees herself as a devil. The tail and the snake are phallic symbols.

The condensation assumes more bizarre forms when no unity is reached; that is, when the different subjects, although fused together, fail to identify with one another or to converge into a unity. The disparate elements do not produce a harmonious combination but a bizarre product (*une bizarrie*), as in Figure 24. We shall focus on the central and main part of the picture. Because they are all strong, an ancient warrior, a horse, a mythical bird, mountains, and people are partially identified and fused. The patient wants to convey an ideal of grandeur and strength.

Somehow the artist fails to convince us; his inner world does not evoke in us a sense of participation. However, although no universal chord is struck, the work is not without merit. We sense in it the presence of mysteriousness and grandeur. We would be willing to accept the mysteriousness and grandeur, but not the pathology that is connected with it. What is private here, what pertains only to the artist's way of seeing the world, is more prominent than what elicits collective resonance. The patient has failed to convince us, because he has not been able to control the eruption of primary process mechanisms. Their emergence was so strong that the various elements of the work of art became fused, in spite of the fact that such fusion was unacceptable to mental mechanisms that follow the secondary process.

Schizophrenics soon learn the technique of fusing together numerous subjects, and the results at times are the most strange and the most unpredictable. Figure 25, reproduced with permission from a work by Bobon and Maccagnani (1962), shows how with the progressive fusion of six original words and images (the fish, the girl, the nipple, the caterpillar, the cow, and the steam engine) the patient produced an amazing list of neologisms and neoformisms. Here Von Domarus's principle and primary process mechanisms reach extreme supremacy, and the result is completely unacceptable to the secondary process of the normal observer.

But this is not always the case. In the following illustration (Figure 26), the fusion is almost acceptable and may be considered not schizophrenic condensation but creative synthesis. The patient was a 30-year-old woman who, during her psychosis, thought her husband was the Messiah, she the Virgin Mary, and her child the Holy Ghost. It is relevant to mention that she was a teacher of art and always felt in competition with her husband, who was a painter. She felt alone, in spite of the fact that she was married and had a child. She reminds me of a patient of Frieda Fromm-Reichmann's who, as I have reported elsewhere (Arieti, 1969), walked with a finger extended and the other fingers flexed over the palm of her hand. Fromm-Reichmann did not interpret this gesture as others would have. For her, the extended finger was not a phallic symbol, nor did it indicate penis envy. It meant, "I am one: alone, alone, alone!"

It is easy to understand why I was struck by the similarity with Fromm-Reichmann's patient. What does the drawing represent? A finger? A hand? An arm? A female body? It is all of them in a creative fusion. The fusion portrays unity: being one and alone and walking in the spiral world. Will she be able to walk in the circular paths? The spiral threads interfere between her legs and perhaps will not permit the woman to go ahead. But more than that. Looking closely, one can see that the path of life seems to originate from her, like a tail of an animal above the buttocks. At a certain point it reaches the hand, and the hand holds it, almost to control it and direct it. But the whirl of life forms something like a cocoon or a cage, and she becomes a prisoner. Thus she recognizes that she is sick; she points out that she is sick, alone, and isolated.

But let us continue our analysis. The extended finger, which represents her and says that she is alone, says something else. It is pointed toward somebody else; it seems to say "You." The finger thus says, "I" and "You." Probably it says in a paranoid way, "You, the other, did this to me." But we would be poor therapists if we would stop at this manifest content. We must interpret it in an additional way: "You, you, fellow human being, must help me, you, you must." This is the message she was sending. Her message was heard. The spiraling life that imprisoned her in a cage of autistic solitude was transformed by therapy into a place where she could commune with people.

In Chapter 16 we have seen that when schizophrenic regression goes beyond the level of Von Domarus's principle, objects and their mental constructs are no longer identified or fused, but put together to form "primary aggregations."

In language the primary aggregation assumes the form generally called "word-salad." In artwork it is represented by drawings and paintings that portray strange agglomerations of disparate objects. Figure 27 was made by the same patient who made the drawing shown in Figure 24. The patient is now at a more advanced stage of illness. We cannot call the drawing shown in Figure 27 a collage, because it lacks cognitive or aesthetic unifying principles. In Figure 27, as in Figure 24, expressions of grandeur recur in visual forms: cathedrals, castles, mountains, high stairs to be climbed. The patient wants to escape from the world of mediocre reality but somehow does not convince us to be his companions.

As the schizophrenic process continues, condensations and primary aggregations become more and more fragmented. Many phenomena of progressive disintegration occur. It is important to emphasize, however, that the tendency toward progressive fragmentation of units is resisted with some defenses similar to those that occur in patients' thinking processes. These defenses slow down the process of disintegration and confer to the work of art some typical schizophrenic features. They are all related. The most important are mannerism, ornamentation, simplification or stylization, stereotypy, spatial alteration, overfilling, and infantilization. Mannerism is perhaps the most typical. "Manneristic" generally means excessive adherence to style or to the influence of another school or artist. But the mannerism of the schizophrenic comes from inner sources, resembles that of other schizophrenics, and seems to have the purpose of filling an empty life with formalisms and decorations. In some cases the formalism and stylization are almost acceptable, as in Figures 28, 29, 30, and 31. Stereotypies and archaic features are evident in Figures 30 and 31.

In other cases the results are less acceptable, although at times the technique is vaguely reminiscent of that used in some forms of modern art. Figures 32, 33, 34, and 35 illustrate typical schizophrenic formalism and stylization.

Stereotypy is an attempt to arrest the flux of the world. Reality escapes and has to be stated and restated many times, as in Figure 36, which is reproduced with permission from the collection of Enzo Gabrici.

In the state of flux in which the patient sees the world, it is difficult for him to register natural spatial perspectives. Each element or part may be abstracted from the rest. Actually this is not real abstraction but the most concrete way of seeing the world. For instance, in Figure 37 each fruit is conceived, perceived, and drawn by itself, with no respect for spatial relation with the other objects.

Some writers, for instance Billig (1957, 1968), speak of transparence, or X-ray pictures, in such cases as when the schizophrenic draws the interior of the house and the facade at the same time. Again it is not a question of X rays or of transparence but of disregard for spatial interrelations. Like the painter of modern art, the patient represents what occurs in his mind by association and not in accordance with the law of geometry.

An additional characteristic of many schizophrenic artworks is infantilism. Infantilism may appear in the content, as it does in Figure 38, where the watermelons are as big and abundant as the patient's desire to eat them. It may manifest itself in regression to infantile forms, as it does in Figure 39, which shows how an adult patient represents his family.

VI

Artwork of Patients Suffering from Schizophrenic-like Toxic Psychoses

Difficult to recognize as nonschizophrenic are works of art made by patients suffering from toxic psychoses, especially as a consequence of mescaline and LSD. The picture shown in Figure 40 was made by a patient recovering from toxic psychosis, probably due to LSD. He said, however, that he made this drawing under the influence of the psychedelic world.

The next three pictures (Figures 41, 42, and 43) were made by a patient who, after recovering from alcoholism, became addicted to amphetamines, turbine hydrate, marijuana, heroin, morphine, and nutmeg. He stated that he never took LSD but claimed that people gave it to him. He had many delusions of persecution. He thought people wanted to kill him. In his despair he attempted suicide by stabbing himself in the neck, chest, abdomen, and arms. Figure 41 portrays the theme of being buried alive after the long, descending journey of life. In the coffin he would not be able to see the sun and the stars. Figure 42 repeats the paranoid theme of the evil eye, which watches, condemns, persecutes, and traps poor people. The persecutory eye becomes a spider in whose web fly-people are caught. Here we have again the phenomenon of the double vision: the eye becomes a spider. Figure 43 shows an improved outlook. The person who is provided with a benevolent eye is now a domestic animal—donkey or horse—representing the patient. The animal is able to bear the big burden of life.

As a rule of thumb we may state that in psychosis caused by drugs the conflicts of the person and paranoid ideation are similar to those appearing in schizophrenic psychoses. However, the artwork shows a sense of completeness and integration uncommon in regressed schizophrenics.

VII

Relation of Schizophrenic Artwork to Primitive, Ancient, and Modern Art

From the pioneer works of Simon (1876, 1888) and Lombroso (1880) to those of Kretschmer (1934), schizophrenic works of art have repeatedly been compared to those of primitives and ancients. Kretschmer referred to what he called ''imaginal agglutination'' in the mythology and art of ancient Egypt, India, and Greece. In those cultures we can find many examples of composite figures, such as centaurs, sphinxes, fauns, griffins, sirens, and so forth. Egyptian deities were often represented with heads of snakes, frogs, or other animals. In Christian art, too, angels are represented as human beings having wings like birds.

Stylization, geometrical simplification, bilateral symmetry, repetition of forms vaguely reminiscent of schizophrenic productions prevailed also in Egyptian, African, and Indian sculptures.

It is also worthwhile to compare schizophrenic art to the modern art of Western culture, which also departs from objective reality and opens up new worlds. It has been said that the modern artist relies for inspiration not on external reality and outer space but on his unconscious inner space. Not only does he allow inner conflicts to come to the surface—the conflicts that other people would suppress, repress, or disguise because they are not acceptable to society—but also the forms of the primary process that are rejected by the logical mind. This topic is too vast to be treated adequately in this book. Certainly the similarities are striking, especially in expressionistic and surrealistic painters. A comparison between surrealism and schizophrenia has been made by several authors (for instance, Roi, 1953).

The case of Salvador Dali is one of the most typical. Not only do his paintings afford an opportunity for a study like the present one, but his own writings on the subject are very illuminating. Dali referred often to his own paranoia and wrote, ''. . . all men are equal in their madness . . . madness constitutes the common basis of the human spirit.'' I believe that what he calls ''the common basis of the human spirit'' is the primary process; it is not Plato's universals but the fantastic universals that Giambattista Vico described. Dali seems to have access to the mechanisms of the primary process more than many other painters. One of these mechanisms is the phenomenon of the double image. An image suggests, or turns into, a second and possibly a third one, instantly or after some contemplation.

Let us take, for instance, a drawing by Dali of a hamlet, a copy of which the author owns. The picture portrays a group of homes, a small village, protected from predatory birds: the rest of the world. A tree in the middle beautifies this little oasis of love and harmony. But if we view the picture in its totality it represents not a hamlet, but man himself. We may also distinguish the vertebral column, the trunk, ribs, arms, and legs. Man is identified with the hamlet because of the similar shape; each part of the hamlet is identified with a similarly shaped part of man. Some observers may also see a phallus in the act of ejaculation.

Here Von Domarus's principle is applied visually. We do not deal with identical predicates, but with visually similar parts that lead to the identification. The result is that man is identified with his habitat or with his social nature. This phenomenon of the double or third image occurs frequently in Dali's works—for instance, in such a well-known painting as *Apparition of Face and Fruit Dish on a Beach*. The mysteriousness of the metamorphosis, as made possible by the primary process, is appreciated by Dali, who does not consider the phenomenon as merely a game. He suggests that the hidden image may be reality itself. In "La Femme Visible" he wrote, "I challenge materialists . . . to inquire into the more complex problem as to which of these images has the highest probability of existence if the intervention of desire is taken into account" (quoted by Soby, 1946). Dali correctly believes that paranoiacs (but of course in this category he includes also paranoids) have "a special capacity for the recognition of double images inasmuch as their disordered minds are hypersensitive to hidden appearances, real or imagined." *

If we think of some of the schizophrenic drawings referred to in this chapter (the palette that becomes a womb, the eye that becomes a spider), we must agree with Dali. Is Dali paranoiac? Is he paranoid? Not in a legal or clinical sense. As he expresses himself in his writings, he has "his own paranoia." I interpret his words as meaning that he has a unique accessibility to the primary process. Generally people who have such accessibility are psychotics who partially or totally have lost contact with the secondary process. But Dali is exceptional in that he retains complete contact with the secondary process, so that the secondary process is able to control the primary. This control is well demonstrated in his paintings, which disclose an overall pattern of exactitude, superimposed on an absurd content. The almost photographic exactitude that gives an aspect of reality to many of his paintings not only strikingly contrasts with the absurd content but also mingles with it in an unparalleled way. Thus Dali maintains an aesthetic distance that the schizophrenic does not possess. On the one hand, he seems to be an explorer of a primary process land who comes from a country where the secondary process reigns; but, on the other hand, we know that this primary process land is Dali's own psyche. Dali explores himself as an artist does, not as a scientist. What we experience in his paintings is not scientific or old-fashioned clinical distance but aesthetic distance in the sense that no matter how naked the primary process is, it will still permit the hand that holds the brush to be guided by the secondary process.

I believe that psychiatry owes a debt of gratitude to Salvador Dali. By making available in pictorial medium "madness . . . as common basis of the human spirit" he has reasserted the universality of the primary process and has shown

* In an introductory paper, Weckowicz (1960) has reported that schizophrenic patients performed much worse than normal persons (but better than organic patients) in the test devised by Gelb and Goldstein (1920) that requires recognition of hidden figures. At first this would seem to indicate that schizophrenic patients have less accessibility to primary process. It is not really so. The test requires secondary process mechanisms. The patient may have easier access to his own primary process and create or discover his own similarities. The capacity to discover the hidden pictures created by secondary process mechanisms of other people is certainly a function of the secondary process, and it is mostly (but not exclusively) impaired in organic conditions.

that schizophrenic madness has intrapsychic origin. Psychodynamic forms transmitted by the environment trigger the mechanisms of the primary process and become mediated or channeled by them.

Of course, imitations of primary process may be carried out through the secondary process, by imitators and second- and third-rate artists. Culture itself may adopt primary process ways and use them as secondary process cultural characteristics; but this important topic will be the object of a future study. I shall simply mention that permissiveness toward the unique, the original, and the irrational, which has become so prominent in some avant-garde segments of society today, makes it more difficult to distinguish schizophrenic art from nonschizophrenic art. Just as delusional or irrational myths have been accepted by many societies throughout the course of history, some forms of art may accept pure expressions of primary process and disregard those of the secondary. However, not only in Dali but in all great artists we find no disregard for the secondary process, nor disharmony between primary and secondary process; instead we discover fusion. These matchings or special harmonious combinations of the primary and secondary processes constitute what I have called the tertiary process. In *The Intrapsychic Self* (Arieti, 1967) I have described the various ways by which these matches and combinations occur in various fields of creativity, such as wit, poetry, religion, and science.

In modern art we find that the artist plunges much deeper than usual into the primary process, as in the case of Dali. But no matter how deeply he plunges, the artist resurges to attune his work with the secondary process. Thus what at first seems to be a private experience receives a collective consensus. The artist allows himself to be alone and lonely, but only to a degree that facilitates the emergence of his own individuality, not to a degree that necessitates desocialization. He makes the details merge into a unity, the parts into a whole, and forces the concrete to become the incorporation of the abstract.

In conclusion I wish to express the opinion that schizophrenic art teaches us basic facts and basic values that transcend schizophrenia. The basic facts are the primacy of the primary process as a universal human phenomenon and, in particular, its emergence and role in the tertiary creative process.

The basic values concern the bond between those human beings who achieve the pinnacles of creativity and those human beings who are seriously ill and in some cases locked in back wards of psychiatric hospitals. Great artists and the mentally ill are shaken by what is terribly absent in our daily reality, and they send us messages of their own search and samples of their own findings. The schizophrenic cannot send us the message of peace and beauty of a *Mona Lisa* or a *Birth of Venus,* and very, very seldom is he able to transform his personal need into a spiritual vision. Often we have a hard time retrieving in his work even a trace of aesthetic pleasure. And yet, in some of his works, we hit unsuspected treasures of concentrated meanings. In some others we can get to share the worldwide threat, the unmitigated sorrow, the secret despair, the childish wish, and the hopeless concern, even if expressed by the secret eye (Figure 13), the watermelon bonanza (Figure 38), or the enigma of mixed sexuality (Figures 17 and 18).

VIII

Poetry

Poetry is a form of creativity that appears relatively frequently in schizophrenic patients. It has not received as vast consideration as visual art for several reasons: (1) it is less frequent; (2) it is less conspicuous; (3) it blends often imperceptibly with other language and thought characteristics of the psychotic.

Relatively few are the reports in the literature. Noteworthy from the point of view of psychodynamic content is the case of Harriet, an 18-year-old schizophrenic girl whom Naumburg (1950) studied particularly in relation to her visual art. The themes of death and rebirth that appeared in Harriet's paintings were also present in her poems, which did not show schizophrenic characteristics. Harriet recovered. A second case reported by Naumburg is that of a 25-year-old girl who was particularly interested in visual art and wrote poems that revealed a well-integrated and deep-feeling person. Poems of patients have been reported by Fromm-Reichmann (in Bullard, 1959) and other authors in the context of psychodynamic studies only. Grassi (1961) studied the poems written in Italian by a 29-year-old paranoid patient. Although these poems showed the characteristic language and thought disorders of the schizophrenic, some fragments of them retained intense aesthetic beauty. Grassi pointed out that some characteristics, like lack of adherence to such things as grammar, syntax, and punctuation were not an attempt on the part of the patient to follow the schools of modern poetry but were indications of schizophrenic disintegration. The content of the poems belonged more to the romantic era than to modern poetry. The patient also wrote some poems in a new language, a pseudo-French that was actually Italian with some added characteristics of the French language.

Forrest (1965, 1968) has made an accurate study of schizophrenic poetry. Forrest sees many similarities between real poetry of the best-known poets and the language and poetry of the schizophrenic patient. He agrees that not only the psychodynamic need is important in schizophrenic productions, but also the adherence to a paleologic rule. The schizophrenic and the legitimate poet "bring to the words the authority of a phonetic order." Forrest states that there are several differences between normal poets and schizophrenics who write poetry:

1. The normal poet is still able to distinguish the word from the object represented by the word.
2. "The poet is a master of language, and the schizophrenic, even more than everyone else, is a slave to language. . . . The poet's purposes are triumphant in language, but the schizophrenic's purposes are often lost in or originate in language, to a greater degree than most people's."
3. The patient has difficulty in distinguishing levels of abstraction and differentiating concrete from abstract.

In previous writings (Arieti, 1955, 1966*a*) and especially in Chapter 21 of *The Intrapsychic Self* (Arieti, 1967) I have discussed relations between schizophrenia and poetry. Any reader who is interested in the relation between primary process and literary creativity is referred to that chapter. Here I shall mention only a few of the main points.

What was said previously in this chapter about visual art could be repeated in relation to poetry. Schizophrenic poetry discloses a struggle between psychodynamic content that searches for expression in artistic actualization and the specific linguistic media that are available to the patient. Inasmuch as the normal poet, too, uses cognitive media that derive from the primary process, the similarities between his poetry and schizophrenic productions are impressive. On closer analysis the observer soon realizes, however, that whereas the poet integrates primary process mechanisms with those of the secondary process, to achieve a tertiary process product, the schizophrenic most of the time cannot. Whereas the poet is aware that he substitutes the abstract with the concrete, the patient is not. The metaphor is not a metaphor for the patient. Like the delusional patient, the poetic patient lives a metaphorical reality. Some forms, usually considered poetical devices, like rhyme, rhythm, alliteration, assonance, onomatopoeia, repetition, homonyms, and similarities of verbalization are used by the schizophrenic, too, whether he intends to write poetry or to speak in prose.

We have seen in Chapter 16 that in schizophrenic cognition there is an emphasis on verbalization, emphasis that manifests itself in various forms. When the disintegration is moderate, we can still recognize a motive and a content.

The following poem was written by the same patient who wrote the poem reported in Chapter 16.

MOUNTY

Oh Mounty Of The Circus
In Cap And Balloon Dress
How Strangely You Resemble
The One That I Adore
The Feelings You Reveal
Or A Secret you Conceal
  Always Envelope
  Always Caress
The Man Of Sacred Lore
The One Who Is My Husband.
Toss At Me Your Playful Balls
With Cauliflowers Applaud Me
Knife Thou Me Against The Walls
And With Pies, Dear, Land Me
  That Through Thee
  I Might Find Him
  The Man That I Adore
  The Man Who Is My Husband
  Oh Mounty Of The Circus.

The poem is difficult to interpret, and the patient could not explain it. The thought disorder and the schizophrenic formulations (like starting every word with a capital letter) are recognizable. In other poems the patient praised the man of the circus who does wonderful things. In this poem she seems to identify him with a member of the Royal Canadian Mounted Police. If the two of them, or the best qualities of the two of them, including "the playful balls," were combined, they would make "the one that she adores," the imaginary husband.

In more advanced regression or in acute psychosis no sustained attempt is made to retain a content. The verbalization and the phonetic effect take over, replacing any other consideration, as in the following poem written by an 18-year-old boy:

I think a little
even a chittle
if don't mittle
on the tittle
in the middle
of a diddle
of a kiddle
in my middle
don't you taddle
or I'll saddle
then good bye
good bye.

The patient, once he recovered from the attack, during which he had grandiose religious delusions, said that he wrote the poem in reference to his brother, who used to tell on him, so that he (the patient) was punished and made to feel responsible (saddle). Neologisms and paralogisms abound here.

In his important contribution, Forrest (1965) wrote that the schizophrenic's utterances do not necessarily originate in his emotions or in meanings. They need not be determined by intrapsychic factors, but rather by the exigencies of his language, by relationships, and by verbal characteristics that inhere in the language that he uses.

It is true that the patient, like the poet, finds inspiration from the language; however, he goes further. He creates neologisms. His need to focus on the verbalization at the exclusion of the connotation comes from an intrapsychic mechanism. To take into consideration again the last example, the English language may have given the possibility to the patient of using certain words, but when he wrote

I think a little
even a chittle
if don't mittle
on the tittle

the supremacy of intrapsychic primary process mechanisms cannot be doubted. Contrary to the real poet, he did not bother to find agreement with secondary process mechanisms. The patient gave exclusive consideration to rhyme and assonance and disregarded meaning, or consensual validation. As already mentioned in reference to severe language disorders; semantic evasion is accompanied by accentuated phonetic formalism.

When the patient becomes more regressed, his ''poetic'' productions become so disorganized that they cannot be distinguished from word-salad.

Much more important for prognostic reasons as well as for gaining insight into the nature of the creative process is the study of poems, and of linguistic productions in general, of recovering patients. As I described in *The Intrapsychic Self* (Arieti, 1967), some recovering schizophrenics retain a greater accessibility to the primary process than normal persons and are nevertheless in a position to use the secondary process. Reports of such cases are rare because the examiner has to see them during a special transitional stage that lasts a short time and is easily missed if not looked for.

Such a patient was Rosette, a 13-year-old schizophrenic girl who was admitted to the hospital following an acute psychotic episode in which she experienced hallucinations, delusions, and ideas of reference. Three days after admission, during a routine mental examination, she was asked to explain the difference between character and reputation. She replied, ''Character is your personality. Reputation is stamped on and can never be erased. Your reputation is a bed, and when you get in, you can't get out of it. Character is like a bedspread which can be taken off, or character is like dirt on a sheet which, if you wash it, can be removed.'' The patient was asked to define the word *despair*. She answered, ''Despair is like a wall covered with thick grease, and a person is trying to climb up this wall by digging his fingers in. Down below is a deep, bottomless pit. Up at the top of the wall on the ceiling is a big, black spider. I have been in this deep pit during the past year, but now I am climbing up a rope, trying to get out of it.''

When Rosette was asked to tell the difference between idleness and laziness, she said, ''Both have to be present for one to be present. You have to be idle to be lazy, but you don't have to be lazy to be idle. When you're idle, you are living physically, but not really living. Laziness is when you give up.'' When she was asked the difference between poverty and misery, she replied, ''Poverty is poor; misery is agony.''

It is very unusual for a 13-year-old to express herself with such depth. She was not physically mature for her age; on the contrary, she looked younger than 13. Although bright, she did not give the impression of being exceptionally intelligent. And yet her expressions often revealed that uncommon faculties were at her disposal. Her definitions of character, personality, and despair are not those to be found in a dictionary. She did not explain the concept or the connotation of these three words. She defined them by transforming the concept into a constellation of perceptual images. Webster's defines despair, for example, as loss of hope—an accurate but also circular and prosaic definition in comparison with that of the patient, who resorted to a sequence of vivid images: the wall covered with thick grease, the person who tries to climb up and digs his fingers in, the bottomless pit, the black spider. The girl's definition is a poetic definition; so are her definitions of character and reputation.

Was Rosette's illness at least partially responsible for her ability to translate concepts into images? Most probably. She was in that rare condition where both primary and secondary processes are accessible and can be coordinated. We know that some poets, artists, as well as some preschizophrenics and addiction-prone people have tried to obtain similar states by alcoholic intoxication or the use of opium, marijuana, mescaline, LSD, or other drugs. Mescaline or LSD may also produce mental conditions reminiscent of the one experienced by Rosette. The trouble with these artificially induced conditions is that they either do not regress sufficiently to a primary process level, or, if they do, they lose the use of the secondary process or the capacity to coordinate it artistically with the primary.

The particular state of Rosette permitted her to change from a language of classification (or of concepts) to a language of experience, for instance, when she gave definitions of character and despair. Her language was certainly not based on classifications or ideas prevailing in her social environment. In addition to visual imagery, other aesthetic characteristics were recognizable in the statements of this girl. One was the emphasis on verbalization, which appeared, for instance, when she explained the difference between idleness and laziness. As she started to define the words, she had the idea, which she later discarded, that idleness and laziness are correlational terms—that is, one cannot exist without the other (for example, the words *husband* and *wife*). Bertrand Russell, in his *Introduction to Mathematical Philosophy,* calls this a one-one relation. How much more beautiful is the girl's definition: "Both have to be present for one to be present." The contrast between the words *both* and *one* and the repetition of the words *to be present* confer aesthetic qualities on her expression.

This girl actually contradicted herself almost immediately when she stated correctly that "You have to be idle to be lazy, but you don't have to be lazy to be idle." Here again the repetition of the same words gives rhetorical emphasis. In the rest of her reply, "When you're idle, you are living physically, but not really living," she achieved an aesthetic effect by repeating the word *living,* which assumed a different meaning. "Really living" meant to her a full living, one not compatible with idleness, which permits living in a vegetative way. When she was asked what the difference is between poverty and misery, again she gave an artistic definition. The usual dictionary definitions are "state of being poor" for poverty and "state of great distress" for misery. Rosette includes these definitions in hers, but offers much more: she succeeds in accentuating the contrast between poverty and misery. *Poverty* is a *poor* word in comparison with *misery,* which has much stronger affective associations, evoked by the word *agony*.

It is not enough to conclude that this girl had greater accessibility to the mechanisms of the primary process. We must recognize that she was also able to make good selections among the various possibilities offered by her primary process and that she could coordinate them with secondary process mechanisms.

Another patient, a 35-year-old poet, occasionally experienced quasi-schizophrenic episodes that were elusive in nature; often it was difficult to determine whether she was in a psychotic state or not. At times her poems almost resembled schizophrenic word-salad; at other times they had a genuine beauty. They were nevertheless always difficult to understand, like much of contemporary poetry.

At the beginning of this woman's treatment she used to speak of human beings as worms, and she wrote poems in which they were represented as worms. Her ideas could have been accepted at a metaphorical level except that she insisted that people really were worms. It was impossible to determine whether the statement was made in a metaphorical sense or not. There was a flavor of literalness in her remarks; even if she meant "worms" metaphorically, there was a resolute attachment to this metaphor, as if it literally represented reality. Her expressions seemed to me to belong to an intermediary stage, hard to delineate, between metamorphosis and metaphor. As her condition improved, she wrote poems in which the metaphorical meaning of the word *worm* could no longer be doubted.

IX

Comedy and Wit

Occasionally the patients' remarks appear witty, just as their appearance and demeanor do. But we must remember that what appears comic or witty to us is not so for the patient, who means literally what he says, expresses, or does. We cannot therefore speak in these cases of real creativity. We have already mentioned the patient who had the habit of wetting her body with oil. Asked why she did so, she replied, "The human body is a machine and has to be lubricated." The word *machine,* applied in a figurative sense to the human body, had led to her identification with man-made machines.

A creative process is not involved in what this patient said. She did not know that her explanation was witty; she meant it literally. Her delusional remark is witty only for us. Apparent witticisms of schizophrenics have been reported in the literature. These witticisms generally result from paleological identifications or from extreme literalness, which follows reduction of the connotation power and emphasis on verbalization.

One of Levin's (1938*a*) patients believed that she was in a ward for blacks. Asked why she thought so, she replied, "Because I was brought here by Miss Brown" (the nurse who had accompanied her to the hospital). A patient of Bychowski (1943), asked where her husband was, replied, "On our wedding picture."

The already mentioned tendency to see puns all over makes patients discover real puns, not seldom sexual in content. Such words as "soft, hard, big, small" are often interpreted as referring to the penis and seem to be used in a witty frame of reference.

There is indeed a similarity, based on the common use of the primary process, between witticism, comic, as acts of creativity, and schizophrenic thinking (see *The Intrapsychic Self,* Arieti, 1967).

CHAPTER

21

Emotional Change and Expansion of Human Experience

I

Emotional Impairment and Desymbolization

Acutely ill patients as well as many others who, although not acutely ill, do not progress beyond the first or initial stage (see Chapter 22), are in a state of emotional turmoil, especially if they had a prepsychotic stormy personality.

When the disorder follows a course of progressive decline, the emotional impairment manifests itself in a different way. The patient seems indifferent to his surroundings; no usual emotional expressions appear on his face. He reacts weakly to both good news and bad news, or he may not even react at all. In many cases there is a great discrepancy or incongruity between the retention of the intellectual faculties and the loss of affective responses. At an advanced stage of the illness the patient seems to have completely lost the capacity to feel. The picture is even more complicated. At times some affect is retained but appears inadequate or inappropriate. The patient is overly concerned about what may seem trivialities to the observer, whereas he may remain indifferent to something of the greatest importance. Even more amazing is the fact that patients who had ostensibly lost their capacity for affect regain it to a considerable extent, or entirely, for a brief period of time or permanently.

How can all of these manifestations be explained? The easiest way to explain them is by again invoking the mechanism of repression. The patient wants so much to avoid all these unpleasant feelings that he has to dissociate them from consciousness. In other words, the schizophrenic would react or continue to react as he did when he was a detached person, aloof and schizoid, except that he does it in an even more pronounced manner. The schizophrenic, like the schizoid, wants to deny the emotional impact of the external world, because it is too unbearable and irreconcilable with his inner world. All of this is true, but not explanatory. Again, we should not confuse the dynamic mechanisms with the formal ones that occur at the same time. Even the orthodox Freudian school has been unable to explain this emotional blunting with the phenomenon of repression as it occurs in neurotics, and has formulated the concept of decathexis.

Some repression occurs in schizophrenics too, especially in incipient or nonregressed cases. Some paranoid patients must repress a great deal in order to formulate delusional systems that appear removed from the original conflicts. However, the majority of authors and clinicians agree that in many schizophrenics not only is there less repression than in psychoneurotics, but also some material ordinarily repressed in the neurotic and normal person tends to come back to consciousness in this psychosis. The mechanism of repression does not seem to function too well in schizophrenia. The patient has tried to use it before becoming psychotic, especially if he had a schizoid prepsychotic personality, but he has failed. He has to use different mechanisms now. To attribute the blunting of affect to the phenomenon of decathexis (or withdrawal of libido) is an attempt to explain a psychological phenomenon with concepts borrowed from physics.

When the repressed content comes to the surface and reproduces the traumatic effect, it undergoes a symbolic transformation. This symbolic transformation, of course, occurs also in neuroses, but not to such a pronounced degree as in schizophrenia. In addition, in schizophrenia it involves the experience of the external world much more than in psychoneuroses.

Alterations of emotional responses are to a large extent implicit in the other mechanisms that we have taken into consideration. The conflict of the person who is or will be a schizophrenic does not revolve around primitive emotions; this conflict concerns affects that depend for their occurrence on high cognitive processes. We have repeatedly stressed in this book the importance of the idea and of the secondary process in the psychodynamics of this psychosis. When the patient loses or alters his common symbols and thus desocializes himself, he will no longer have an adequate or usual emotional reaction to the common social symbols (see Chapter 19). In other words, he does not *repress* the emotions and *decathect* the world; he *cannot experience* it as he used to. It is true that in the past he may have tried with a schizoid armor to experience the world in a less frightening manner, to become less involved with it, or to repress its emotional impact. When he becomes psychotic, however, he goes further: he desymbolizes himself, that is, he transforms the common symbols into paleosymbols. He loses many conventional emotions or emotional reactions that society expects from him and replaces them with other emotions that appear bizarre and inappropriate to us, only because we cannot share them. The patient, however, does experience emotions when he uses paleosymbols. The following is an approximate comparison. If a Western man went, let us say, into a Buddhist temple while a religious ceremony was taking place, this man probably would watch the ceremony almost as an anthropologist would; that is, with some kind of cultural interest but with emotional detachment. The other people in the temple, if they could forget that their visitor was a Western man, would think that his emotional involvement was inappropriate. That man would not seem to be touched at all by the holiness of the ceremony, would not respond emotionally to its symbols. The schizophrenic is in a similar situation, or rather in a much worse one because he has lost the ability to transport himself artificially into a set of values other than his own. However, when the patient is in his own symbolic world, he may react with very deep emotions. We know how distressed the patient feels as a result of alleged persecutions. Retention of these emotional responses is prognostically good because it means that the patient has not regressed beyond a predominantly paleosymbolic level.

Even more than the psychoanalytic, the existentialistic school has been concerned with the patient's ability to experience the world in a unique, individualistic way. All psychodynamically oriented psychiatrists believe that we must uncover the meaning and the mechanism of the private way of experiencing life. The existentialists, however, are right in reminding us that we should not forget the experience as it is actually lived by the patient. The patient's suffering is real, and the impact of the experience, with its horror, uniqueness, and immediacy, should always be stressed in psychotherapy.

At this point we cannot omit the explanation of an apparent contradiction, which may have puzzled the reader. The reader might think: the author states that the schizophrenic is extremely individualistic, does not want to accept society, and wants to retain his unique paleosymbols and his unique paleologic way of thinking. Because the author also describes the *laws* of paleologic thinking and paleosymbols, which apply to all paleologic or paleosymbolic thought, is not that a contradiction? Is he not talking again of formality, which applies to all people regressed to a certain level, and not of individuality and uniqueness? Is he not changing the universals of Aristotelian logic and of the common symbols to the universals of paleologic thought and paleosymbols? How is that to be reconciled with the assumption of "uniqueness"? *

There is some truth in this allegation, because there cannot be any content without some kind of formal mechanism, and any kind of formal mechanism is subject to laws. Perhaps the works of the abstract painters come closest to being expressions of a content without form, but some form exists in their works too.

However, one could say without hesitation that one's originality and individuality, as far as the formal structure is concerned, are better expressed by primary process mechanisms, and for various reasons. First of all, there are many of them, and the schizophrenic and the artist may use any or several of them. Secondly,

* Similar objection was made by Benedetto Croce (1947) to the theories of the philosopher Vico. Croce wrote that in his conclusions about the studies of ancient people, Vico had replaced Plato's universals with "phantastic universals" (corresponding approximately to our paleologic mechanisms of the primary process).

paleologic thinking, to a great extent, is based on Von Domarus's principle. Now this principle is, or appears to our Aristotelian minds to be, a principle or a law; actually, it gives the greatest possible freedom to the individual. A subject may have an infinite number of predicates; it is up to the individuality of the person to select the predicate for the identification (see Chapter 16).

It is true that we view schizophrenics as being similar to one another, and we are able to detect common symptoms in them. It is because of these common symptoms that we are able to recognize them. Actually their realm of originality exceeds by far that of the normal man. Paradoxically they seem similar to us because they are original and because they do not use our methods of thinking. They are similar in their difference from us, just as all Chinese may appear similar to Caucasians. Being unable to understand the originality of the content of their expressions and actions, we tend to emphasize the frequent occurrence of the few formal mechanisms that we understand. Paradoxically, it is by adopting *universal* forms that the individuality of the patient, with its specific dynamic determinants, is allowed to emerge.

In later stages the patient seems to lose emotions even for the complexes with which he was paleologically concerned.

II

Enlargement of Human Experience

We have so far described the world of schizophrenia as an impoverished one relative to that of the normal man. This conclusion seems obvious even to the casual observer, and yet from time to time some authors have expressed a voice of dissent. They assert that the schizophrenic experience could actually enrich life. In Chapter 8 we have seen that according to Laing the schizophrenic knows the truth better than other people. According to Siirala (1961, 1963) the patient is a prophet to whom nobody listens; he is a dissenter who does not accept the evil of the world. Again we have to separate what is a true possibility from the exaggerations and idealizations of some authors. Certainly many unusual and even troublesome experiences of the human being, like going to war, may have positive aspects. They may strengthen the individual and add dimensions to his personality, provided he comes back alive and not maimed physiologically or psychologically. If a patient recovers completely from schizophrenia, he may be a fuller and better-integrated person, but what a price to pay in suffering and risk!

In spite of its mysteries and potentialities the world of schizophrenia is not to be recommended as a place where one can escape from the human predicament, or as a method with which to achieve truth and wisdom or to enhance one's spiritual aims. This statement is a truism and would not be expressed here, except for the fact that it has recently been challenged or replaced by confused points of view. The confusion derives from the fact that some schizophrenic experiences, once detached from the whole picture, can be definitely seen as an enlargement and enrichment of human life. In *The Intrapsychic Self* (Arieti, 1967) and in other works now in preparation, I stress that, relative to the average person, the schizophrenic has easier access to the rich sources of the primary process, and I illustrate how these sources may enlarge his human experience. However, as a rule the patient is unable to exploit his potentialities. He cannot harmonize what comes from the primary process with the requirements of the secondary process. Unless recovery occurs, the incongruities resulting from such discordancies lead to bizarreness, isolation, and psychological impoverishment.

There is no doubt, however, that some specific or isolated characteristics of schizophrenia can be considered highly positive. The patient is not a revolutionary, a dissenter, or a philosopher; but in his process of desocialization severe and often valid criticism of society is implicit. In his paranoid attitude he becomes particularly sensitized to the surrounding hostility. From his protestations we may learn many sociological truths, generally hidden from the average citizen, and we may learn to recognize everyday hypocrisies which we meekly accept as ineluctable facts of life (see also Chapter 39).

In Chapter 8 we have mentioned that Siirala sees the schizophrenic as a prophet to whom nobody listens. Whereas for some time I have been recalcitrant to Siirala's view, I believe that now I understand him better; and some of his ideas seem to me, in a partial sense, acceptable. We can find some similarity (certainly not identity) between many schizophrenics and the prophets of the Old Testament. The biblical prophets were people extremely sensitive to evil, or surrounding hostility, as well as to society's callousness to evil.

The extreme individualism of the schizophrenic, his use of paleosymbols, the expanded capacity for symbolism, his paleologic thinking permit an enlargement of the human experience, can open new horizons and lead to new paths of feeling and understanding. The new combinations of ideas and feelings may result in higher syntheses or altered states of consciousness. From the histories of the patients that we have already discussed in detail and those that will be reported later in this book, we have learned to recognize the depth and the extension of the private experience. However, there is no doubt that in reporting them as a psychiatrist I have emphasized mostly the pathology and the suffering and have not paid enough attention to the enrichment of human existence. Although I hope to deal in greater length with this topic in a future publication, I wish in the rest of this chapter to give some consideration to this aspect of schizophrenia.

Perhaps the reader will remember that earlier in the book (Chapter 16), in order to show the impairment of connotation power, I reported the answers given by a regressed schizophrenic patient who had been for several years in a state hospital. A high school graduate, she gave typical examples of schizophrenic thinking and language when she was asked to define words. Many years later I went over the records of the same patient and looked at them with different eyes. Some of her answers which had appeared to me only typical of a regressed schizophrenic disclosed additional meanings. I asked her to define life, and she asked me in return whether I meant *Life* magazine or the life of the sweetheart. She thus used homonyms in schizophrenic style, but couldn't she have also meant, in her own individualistic way, "You ask me, a high school graduate, to define what even Linnaeus and Darwin would not be able to do?" When she was asked to explain what the word "tongue" meant, she said, "Tongue is what you chew with, if you have something to chew." She referred, of course, to her poverty in her early life. On another occasion she said, "A fool is a fool when a fool calls a fool a fool." I considered this sentence as indicating the schizophrenic tendency to repeat the same word. But didn't the patient perhaps refer to the fact that I was a fool if I thought that she was a fool because she was a mental patient?

Another time, in the midst of a session, she said something apparently irrelevant: "When a rose grows, if that rose should grow, it grows to the top." Did she perhaps mean that life will flourish and bloom to its utmost, if not prevented or warped, as hers was?

During another interview she said, "In order to acquire charm, should I eat *charm* or read *charm?*" Of course, Charm was a brand of candy, and *Charm* was also a magazine. Was this just a schizophrenic pun or did she mean "To become acceptable must I accept eating, receiving, reading what you suggest?"

During another session, after a statement that she made, I asked her "Why?" She replied, "Why is a silly question because Y is a crooked letter. It should be who. Who is the why." I asked her what she meant when she said "Who is the why." She went on to say that "There are several why's that depend on who," that is, on people. People are the cause of any event, question, problem. This was one of her recurring themes. As a matter of fact, when, during a discussion of her delusions of persecution, she was asked the question, "Why do they hurt you?" She replied, "I don't say why, I say who." In other words, behind a why there is a who, a human will, a human motivation.

On another occasion she spoke about people. She said, "People are not people. If people were people, things might prove to be more beneficial for the people." I asked then, "Aren't people people?" She replied, "There are all kinds of people." I asked her, "What do you mean by people?" She replied, "Persons of quality." Now the first sentence became clearer. If people were persons of quality, things in general would be more beneficial for everybody.

These examples disclose that in some cases what appears unusual, illogical, imaginary, or exclusively the result of psychosis, should be seen not only in the restricted sense of being outside of reality but also of being an expansion of reality. This point of view is indeed close to one of the major tenets of the surrealistic school of art and literature. (See also Chapter 17; Barison, 1948; Roi, 1953) Surreality includes the real and the unreal, comprehends both categories into an enlarged universe, which is expanded for better or for worse.

Perhaps it is appropriate to remind the reader here that the founder of the surrealistic movement in literature was a French psychiatrist, André Breton, who, at a crucial stage in his life, abandoned psychiatry and became a poet. Although very much indebted to Freud, André Breton opposed some views of Freud both in his writings and during his personal meeting with the founder of psychoanalysis (Breton, 1932; Breton and Eluard, 1930). Whereas Freud made a sharp distinction between the external world and psychic reality, as well as between the rational and the irrational which should be relegated to the id, Breton wrote that the psychotic comes closer to the great secrets of life and offers a reservoir of mental health to those who are restricted by a routine rationalism (Balakian, 1970). Like the painter Salvador Dali (see Chapter 20), Breton believed that absurdity is not just absurdity but an enrichment of reality or a super-sense of reality. The transfiguration of the dream, the delusion, the hallucination, are not deformations but an enrichment of life.

My position is that *in some cases* they can be a great enrichment. Together with the greatest errors and greatest impoverishments I have at times found great truths and enrichments inherent in psychosis, truths and enrichments which transcend the parochialism of time and space.

I don't want to be misunderstood. These new insights or expansions of reality do not deal only with great universal problems or concepts but also with the humble, little, daily circumstances of life, of ordinary people. In Chapter 37 we shall see how this expansion of awareness may come through the phenomenon which I have called punctiform insight. It may come also through apparently absurd rationalizations. In Chapter 16, section I, we have seen that the psychotic rationalization is an effort on the part of the regressed schizophrenic to justify, in a way seemingly so inappropriate or childlike to the point of being humorous, a position or an attempt to escape from a serious predicament. As I showed in Chapter 16, behind this absurd rationalization is often hidden the real voice of the patient, a personal truth which wants to be heard. But the environment is deaf and a specifically thunderous way of expressing it had to be found. I shall close Part Three with one more such example. In 1946, when I was working at a clinic of the Veterans Administration and I was examining veterans who had had psychiatric casualties during World War II, I had the opportunity of seeing a young man who had been in the Pacific theatre of operation. From his medical records I learned that he was a grammar school graduate, a shoemaker by profession, who, for reasons beyond his comprehension, found himself catapulted into the Pacific, fighting an enemy of whose existence until then he had not even been aware. He did not like to be there, had an acute psychotic episode, and was recovering in a military camp.

In the camp he seemed fairly contented; kept busy repairing the shoes of the servicemen, and did not seem eager to reach a full recovery and go into action again. To the medical officer who examined him, he said, "I devoted half of my life to repairing shoes; I am a good repair man; that is all I like to do; I can't be a soldier; I'd be happy again repairing shoes." Apparently the medical officer was not satisfied and asked the patient if he thought this was sufficient contribution to the war effort. The patient replied, "Sure, when the fellow who wears one of the shoes I repaired kicks a Jap in the face, he will know something hit him; that's my contribution." Is this just a facetious rationalization of a still partially psychotic person or also the genuine belief of a poor man who somewhat hesitantly, somewhat vaguely, but also strikingly and originally, tells us "I don't want to be here. I am not a soldier. Do you understand that I am not a soldier? I am a shoemaker! I am a shoemaker! I am a shoemaker!"

PART FOUR

A Longitudinal View of Schizophrenia

CHAPTER

22

The First, or Initial, Stage

I

Introductory Remarks

In the previous parts of this book, schizophrenia has been examined in its manifest symptomatology, psychodynamics, and formal psychological structure. We shall now study the psychosis from the point of view of its progression, meaning progression toward regression. Of the four outcomes of schizophrenia (recovery, improvement, arrest, regression), only regression will be considered here. Although Kraepelin himself gave great significance to the progress of the illness, to such a point that all his concepts about this condition were influenced by it, this progression itself has not been studied longitudinally.

The difficulty in studying schizophrenia from a longitudinal point of view is implicit in the long duration of the illness. Many psychiatrists focus their attention on the initial stages, which respond better to any type of treatment. On the other hand, psychiatrists working in state hospitals do not see the prepsychotic or early psychotic stages. Even Meyer's longitudinal approach was not complete inasmuch as it studied the patient from his birth to the onset of the psychosis but did not study in detail the progression of the illness after its onset. Another difficulty in the longitudinal study of schizophrenia is its multiform clinical course, not comparable to that of any other known disease or condition. In fact, the same stage of regression that is reached by a patient in a period of a few days or weeks may be reached by another patient in a period of over half a century. A third difficulty consists of the fact, so well known, that different levels of regression do not appear in any case in pure culture; each case presents a mixture of several stages. It is only by artificial abstraction that we may reconstruct the individual stages.

Kraepelin spoke of progressive *deterioration*. Although he considered this characteristic of schizophrenia the fundamental one, he could not go beyond a descriptive approach because he did not use the Freudian concept of *regression*. Therefore he emphasized the type of symptomatology rather than the stage of the illness. It was more important for him to distinguish the three types—catatonic, hebephrenic, and paranoid—than to attempt to individualize any stage. Later he added the simple type, after Bleuler. As was seen in Parts Two and Three of this book, these divisions in the four types were accepted in the present study, not purely from a descriptive point of view, but also because they indicate the prevalence of specific dynamic and formal mechanisms. However, I feel that it is also important to divide the illness into four successive stages: the initial, the advanced, the preterminal, and the terminal. The separate study of these stages further clarifies the intricacies of the disorder.*

In this part of the book we shall accompany the patient from the initial stage of the overt psychosis to the terminal stage. As he progresses from one stage to the following, he will be seen less and less in an interpersonal context and more and more in isolation, wrapped in his own symptoms, generally within the walls of the psychiatric institution. Those interpersonal relations that were of so much significance when we studied the prepsychotic stages lose importance when the patient succeeds in finding the path of progressive regression. The interpersonal relations of the past continue to act through the distortions they still engender, but the impact of new relations is diminishing progressively. That is not what we want, of course. If the few remaining interpersonal relations were studied and corrected, as done by Stanton and Schwartz (1949*a, b*), or if the patients were exposed to a kind of "milieu therapy," as suggested by Rioch and Stanton (1953), it would become less likely that patients would follow the pattern described in this part of the book. The author hopes that soon the conditions described in Chapters 23, 24, and 25 will be things of the past, because the patients will not be allowed to go beyond the initial stage of the disorder. At the present time we must admit that these conditions occur and that we must face and study them in order to combat them more efficiently.

In this chapter we shall discuss only the initial stage of the disorder, which, as we have seen in Chapter 8, can start in numerous possible ways. In many cases, the beginning is slow and insidious, and it passes unnoticed. This is almost always the case in the simple type. On the other hand, in the other three types, the beginning may be either slow, acute, or very acute. We shall examine here only acute cases, which lend themselves better to didactical purposes.

* The reader is reminded not to confuse *period,* as defined in Chapter 5, with *stage*. All the stages of schizophrenia belong, from a psychodynamic point of view, to the fourth, or psychotic, period.

II
The Onset of the Psychosis: Sequence of Early Substages

Many patients go through the substage of prepsychotic panic that we have described in Chapter 7. In a large number of patients this prepsychotic panic slips almost imperceptibly into a real psychotic stage. The patient may have some ideas that absorb him entirely, some fantasies and fears that may become delusions, some reluctance to act that may become withdrawal or even catatonic stupor. The following case shows some of these features.

At the time of the psychotic episode Fred was a 31-year-old, single, professional man engaged in research work in a university. The patient's father was a successful businessman. Fred had always felt distant from him, had always considered him as a man of action, not of thought, as a man rigid in his ideas, conventional, and authoritarian in imposing his will on the rest of the family.

Fred's mother was described by the patient as a submissive person who always did what the husband wanted. Although she had never been cruel or antagonistic toward her only child, no real closeness had ever developed between them. Her overprotectiveness, and also her ostensive agreement with the father, who was looking askance at Fred's peculiarities and unconventionalities, kept the patient distant from her, too.

Fred's peculiarities were his habit of remaining alone for prolonged periods of time, his reluctance to cultivate friends and acquaintances or to celebrate holidays, birthdays, and other family gatherings, and his almost exclusive preoccupation with study and research. These peculiarities made it difficult for Fred and his parents to live together. Since his teens they almost always lived apart, Fred in university towns, the parents in New York City. Fred's contacts with girls were very few. His extreme shyness prevented him from seeking romantic companionship. He had, however, a relatively close relation with a rather aggressive woman, Rose, who initiated the friendship. Normal sexual relations occurred, but after a year and a half Fred and Rose broke off because he refused to marry her. Since then there had been no other relations with women. He felt inadequate and unattractive and feared establishing contacts with women.

In one field, however—his professional work—Fred always did much better than the average person. He was working in a theoretical field, and the papers he wrote were well received.

Sometime in spring, while he was involved in a certain piece of research, he became aware of new avenues of investigation to be explored in relation to his work. This complication would require a great deal of time, he thought. On the other hand, he knew that the professor, the chief of his department, wanted the work finished before summer vacation. Fred's anxiety about finishing his research increased. He worked on it without rest. He would skip meals, would not shave for days, would not leave his room except for some meals in a luncheonette or to visit the professor every two weeks and report on his work. He would work through the whole night, feeling that he could concentrate better during these silent hours. He would go to bed at dawn and would get up at two o'clock in the afternoon to resume his work. On the other hand, he became worried about other things that he had neglected for the sake of saving time. He had not filled out his state income tax return; his car, parked in the street, needed repairs and new license plates, and he had done nothing about it. His fountain pen was broken, and, because he could not go to buy a new pen, he was writing with pencils only.

Physically he did not feel well; he was run down. The work seemed to offer great promises, but somehow the solution of it eluded him. He caught a cold and developed a fever. While he was lying in bed, he noticed that some fantasies would occur. These fantasies concerned his former girl friend Rose. At the beginning he felt he could stop these fantasies. He wanted to stop them because they were not pleasant. But, as he put it, a morbid curiosity got the best of him, and he continued for hours and hours to indulge in them. They concerned Rose and him, visiting an amusement park, going into the trailers of gypsies, and seeing a puppet show held in one of these trailers. While the puppet show was going on, he realized that the puppets gave him the optical illusion of distance, an enormous distance. All of a sudden he woke up from the fantasy. He told himself, "This is not a daydream; this is schizophrenia. I'd better stop it." But then the idea occurred to him that he could indulge in the fantasies because he had just proved to himself that he could stop them whenever he wanted. He is back then in the daydream. He is still at the puppet show in the trailer. He is sitting on a chair. He wants to get up, but he cannot. All of a sudden he sees that Rose pretends to operate the show, to make the puppets dance. He loses his temper; he is angry. He wants to go out. He yells, but he cannot move. Finally he succeeds in getting up, but feels that he is ill, extremely ill. He tells the owner of the trailer that he understands those optical illusions. The puppet show is not an innocent performance, and he is going to expose him.

The fantasy seemed to stop at this point. Fred told me later that it was more than a fantasy. Although he knew that he was imagining things, these fantasies were perceived by him as vividly as if they were real. He did not remember what happened the following day. Later, however, he felt very sick, almost unable to move. He felt he was in the same way, or almost, as he had imagined himself to be in the fantasy, when he wanted to move and could not. As he put it, the impulse to move was not delivered to the hand or to the part of the body he wanted to move. The wish to move, now, was like the experience of a person who dreams and wants to wake up from the dream but cannot. At the same time he was still worried about the things he had to do: the paper, the income tax, the car, the license, the fountain pen. In the midst of his immobility he was overwhelmed by what seemed an avalanche of things he had to do. He felt confused; he could no longer understand things well. However, certain things started to appear strange. The place where he lived began to look peculiar to him. In reality that place had always been peculiar; it was an isolated house on a big lot in a slum that was undergoing demolition. The newspapers had reported from time to time that some crimes had been committed in that area. The house where the patient lived was one of the last scheduled to be demolished, was run as a boardinghouse, and was inhabited by peculiar people. On one floor there was a couple who were deaf-mutes and another couple who were maimed. On another floor there were some entertainers who practiced their songs the whole day and left the door open. Confusion and noises were going on all the time. While confined at home, Fred succeeded during the day in moving around the apartment. One day he looked out and saw policemen passing by. The fleeting idea occurred to him that maybe they were looking for somebody who had committed a crime and that they would accuse him. For a few days, he also had a terrific pain in his testicles. He had the impression that a putrid odor was emanating from his nose. He was extremely anxious about everything. He felt that the house, too, was smelling peculiar and that maybe there was a leak in the gas pipe. He had a terrific headache, felt that he was possibly drugged or that he had undergone a hemorrhage in the brain. He did not have any definite idea of what was going on. He knew, however, that he was sick, terribly sick, and terribly alone. Finally he decided that he had to see the professor. With a superhuman effort he left the room and went out of the house. On the way to the institute he felt almost unable to move. He had to give himself orders, as one usually gives to another person: "Go. Turn. Go ahead. Go in this direction." Only by doing that was he able to reach the institute. When he arrived there, he walked into the office of the professor and said, in a hesitant voice, "I am sick, maybe drugged." He was dirty and unshaven. From his appearance, expression, and voice, the professor understood immediately what was going on. He replied in a friendly, reassuring voice that he would accompany him to see the doctor on the campus. The doctor recommended consulting a psychiatrist. The professor accompanied Fred to the psychiatrist, who made the diagnosis of an acute psychotic episode, with hallucinations and delusions in formation, but no violence or agitation. The professor called up the family in New York, and it was decided that the patient would fly immediately to his parents, who would have him treated by a psychiatrist as soon as possible. The professor accompanied Fred to the airport, and he flew to New York.

When he arrived in New York, everything seemed to him in vivid color, like in technicolor movies. He felt better already, and the terrific experiences that he had undergone the previous days seemed to be disappearing. When I saw him the following day, he was still somewhat confused and unable to concentrate, but at the same time he was recovering. He was able to explain the abnormal experiences he had had, and he seemed rapidly to reacquire a grasp on reality. In the following weeks we were able to analyze what had happened to him.

His deep insecurity, which originated early in life, was only partially compensated by the security that he was gaining in his academic work. The need for this security was such that everything else had to be sacrificed for the sake of this academic achievement. At the same time academic life permitted him to hide and maintain his schizoid personality. Any act of living that required closeness with others was for him more difficult than was his difficult research work. A rapid deterioration in his habits of living could be retraced when, during the treatment, we analyzed the years prior to his psychotic episode. Later the insecurity invaded the area of his work, which had previously remained immune to anxiety. He had new ideas about his research that he could not demonstrate as valid, and at the same time he thought the professor wanted the paper ready at an early deadline.

The anxiety increased enormously and finally produced a state of panic in which all the conflicts related to the other aspects of his life came again to the foreground. Thus in the fantasy about the puppet show, it was Rose, the domineering girl friend and his only girl friend, who was running the show, moving the puppets. He was like a puppet himself, manipulated by Rose, or a paralyzed man who cannot move. The image of himself, unable to move from the chair, represented, at a concrete level, his feelings of passivity. The fantasy about the optical illusion of distance was a concrete representation of his inner knowledge that the emotional distance, the detachment, was an illusion: he must live closely to someone.

It is interesting to consider the precipitation of events. Everything is confused, strange, frightening; he develops some paranoid tendencies. He has vague ideas, suspicions, is scared, knows that he is sick. His perceptions are distorted or intensified. He tries to make sense of the various impressions, like the police, the crime, the smell, but cannot. In other words, he tries to reach what later in this chapter we shall call "psychotic insight," but fortunately he cannot. What happens instead? He has a real insight. He must see the professor. He succeeds in overcoming partial catatonic tendencies and goes to the professor. This man, who had threatened him with the deadline, was sympathetic, understanding, showed real concern, went out of his way. Fred did not feel alone any more; the needed encounter had occurred.

As he told me later, it was from the very moment he saw the professor that he started to feel better, that the delusional trends became weaker. The professor also did something else that showed unusual courage. He allowed the patient to come alone to New York by plane. Few people would have dared to do so. The professor could have been seriously criticized for allowing a person so sick to fly alone. On the other hand, Fred told me later that such a move from the professor helped him tremendously. It meant that the professor still had confidence in him, somebody trusted him. He was not hopelessly lost. We may ask ourselves where the professor got this courage. The professor intuitively understood that Fred could be trusted to fly alone, a feeling that we shall take again into consideration when we study psychotherapy (Chapter 36).

When Fred reached New York, the beneficial encounter was continued with psychotherapy. He recovered completely from the acute episode and continued in his scientific career.

The case of Fred is a very interesting one from a didactical point of view. Although we do not want to deal with the topic of psychotherapy in this chapter, I shall mention that this case indicates that in some cases schizophrenia can be immediately reversible at its onset if the proper interpersonal encounter occurs.

In many other cases, although the patient is recognized as requiring psychiatric treatment, no definite prepsychotic panic or state of emergency is noticed prior to the psychosis. The schizophrenic episode seems to be precipitated by an apparently insignificant episode.

I mention here the case of a veteran whom I saw only three times after his return from World War II. He had great difficulty in readjusting to civilian life and was uncertain as to whether he should reenlist in the army or not. He was engaged to be married, but had no position. At the end of the second session he felt that he did not want any more treatment, and I was not able to persuade him to continue. He felt that his only difficulty was the lack of an occupation and that once he found a job every difficulty in his life would be solved. One of the reasons given for discontinuing treatment was that he had to go out of town to visit wealthy and prominent relatives who probably would offer him a good position. There were no psychotic symptoms at this time. Three months later I received a telephone call from his wife. She said that the patient was very ill and that I must see him immediately. The patient and his wife came to my office. I saw the wife first, who gave me the following history. She and the patient had been married a month previously. His relatives had not kept their promises, but the patient had had several odd jobs, and "everything seemed to be all right." Two days previously the patient had secured a position as a bus driver. The very morning that she called me, her husband had had a minor accident; his bus had collided with a car. No one was hurt, but the car was damaged. The damage would probably amount to two or three hundred dollars. She said that since the time of the accident, which had occurred about seven hours previously, the patient had been excited, restless, and had talked nonsense. The night before, they had talked about their future plans and had been very happy. The wife was pregnant, and they had been talking about the expected baby. According to the wife, the husband had shown no abnormality whatsoever. The trouble started all of a sudden after the accident. When I saw the patient, he was restless and excited. He recognized that something very important was disturbing him, but he was not able to say what it was. During the interview my phone rang twice. Each time he thought that some people were calling me concerning him. They must be after him. They must know where he is. Because he heard the voice of a woman at the end of the line, he assumed that it was the voice of his aunt. She was talking to me about him. He did not know what was happening. Everything was confused, strange, and moving. The following are some of his statements, taken verbatim: "The world is going very fast; it keeps spinning on an axe [sic], but keeps going. If the people of the world are going a little faster, they try to go with the world, and they shouldn't. It is my desperate opinion that the people are rushing slowly and slowly and when they reach a certain point they start to realize that they are going fast or slow, and they cannot be judges of the world as it is spinning. The world has changed, is going fast, keeps going, going. I couldn't keep up with it."

I recommended immediate hospitalization. The patient was hospitalized in a veterans hospital, received shock therapy, and I heard later that he had made a seemingly complete recovery. Because I had seen this patient only three times, I was not in a position to make an adequate dynamic evaluation of the case. After returning from the army, he had made an attempt to adjust to civilian life. The old personal difficulties, which were not manifested as long as he was in the army, made this adjustment difficult. At the same time that his difficulties increased, the demands made on him complicated the situation. He felt that as soon as possible he should marry the girl to whom he had been engaged for a long time and who had waited for his return. His relatives disappointed him, and his dependency on them was frustrated. Finally he secured a good position as a bus driver, and two days later had an accident. He thought that probably he would lose his position, and this belief reinforced his deep feeling of worthlessness. Whether he unconsciously provoked the accident, we are not in a position to say; of course, such a possibility exists. After the accident he broke down. The accident was to him the proof of his inherent inadequacy, especially because he gave so much importance to having a job. Almost all his security was precariously founded on his having a position. Now nobody would have any confidence in him. The relatives were right in not trusting him with a job. He was hopeless; he was not able to keep pace with life.

This case shows how a simple event, which can symbolically fit the vulnerability of the patient, may induce or unchain a psychosis, when the necessary ground is ready for it, of course. Because we know so little about this patient, we cannot understand the fundamental issue, that is, why he was so vulnerable that even the accident, in itself not a serious one, was capable of eliciting a major mental disorder. This case is nevertheless valuable for didactical purposes because it shows that a few hours after the clear-cut onset of the acute attack, the schizophrenic symptoms were already very pronounced. The patient's thoughts were disorganized. He saw the world in a different way, going fast, so fast that he could not cope with its movements. The abstract feeling of inadequacy was concretized in his not being able, in a physical sense, to keep up with the movements of the world. The accident with the car probably provided the idea of the movement. Ideas of reference were already in full swing, and paranoid concepts were developing. He already saw things in a different, confusing way, and was making an attempt to reinterpret reality.

Less acute onsets occur when the patient feels unable to satisfy excessive compulsions and falls into a state of panic. In several cases, some ideas that seem plausible acquire predominance in the patient's mind, so that he is not able to pay attention to other things or to answer questions that are not directly related to the problem he is thinking about. He feels confused and experiences vague feelings of discomfort. The conscious problem that worries him seems to possess him entirely. He wants reassurance very badly, but he is not capable of being reassured. Pertinent answers to his questions are almost not heard. He repeats the same question many times, and he is depressed and seems to suffer a great deal.

At times he succeeds in overcoming this state of torment, especially if fortunate circumstances occur, as in the case of Fred. The patient may snap out of this state and go back to his usual condition. At times he may feel better for a few hours or days, but then the panic returns, even stronger than before. He has the feeling that something terrible is happening to him. Maybe he is becoming insane. A little later he feels that people think he may be insane. He has the feeling he is losing a battle, an unknown battle. He becomes more and more discouraged. His confusion and fright become greater and greater; they overcome and submerge him, like big waves. Things seem peculiar, funny, have acquired a different perceptual quality and an obscure meaning. At times he finds himself indulging in some fantasies, which he himself recognizes as false, and yet they are so vivid that they seem real. He tries to find explanation for all this, but he cannot.

Even at this point the patient may snap out of the confusion and return to his previous condition. On the other hand, if the fear increases, he may rapidly become unable to do things, to decide, to act, and more or less acutely he will lapse into a catatonic stupor. If the confusion increases, he may fall into a hebephrenic excitement. In many cases the patient feels that people are acting out a play to confuse him. The world becomes a big stage.

At other times, after a period of confusion, the patient feels that everything is clear. All of a sudden he experiences a flash of understanding. The light has come back. Things that appeared confused and obscure have a meaning, a purpose. He feels exceptionally lucid. He understands everything now; the strange events were not accidental, but purposely arranged. Somebody, somewhere, is after him, against him. From now on, and for a long time, the patient will try to demonstrate logically what seems evident to him. He develops the phenomenon that I have called *psychotic insight.* The psychosis is now well established in a paranoid pattern.

Why should we call this phenomenon psychotic insight? Insight means a sudden discovery of relationships and meanings between different things and facts. Certain things that before appeared to the patient as disconnected and unrelated are now seen as parts of a whole. But the insight is psychotic because only the patient sees these connections. To use his own words, he "puts two and two together"; he is able "to assemble the various pieces of a jigsaw puzzle." But only he is able to detect the puzzle. He is able to see the world in a different way because he adopts new ways of thinking. He abandons secondary process cognition and adopts the primary process mechanisms that we have described in Part Three. He feels that he has never thought as clearly and effectively as now. Such an impression is occasionally conveyed to the layman.

It is important to stress that the patient often does not acquire the new regressive ways of interpreting reality without first putting up a fight. When this new way of thinking lurks in the background and threatens to come to the surface, the patient tries to resist it at first. He feels a struggle within himself that is experienced as an "attempt to resist a tendency to give in." The patient is, however, afraid that sooner or later he will succumb. Succumbing in a certain way seems a pleasant temptation because it would seem to relieve the state of confusion. Stein (1967) described similar experiences in the patient who becomes psychotic: his effort to resist the seduction of the psychosis and finally his possible *initial consent* to the sense of becoming psychotic. Stein writes, "Now, even though he has this sense of utter powerlessness or of being a passive observer of his own destruction, he still from time to time makes abortive attempts to resist dying, just as a drowning man who cannot swim nevertheless struggles frantically."

When the patient finally succumbs and has psychotic insight, the opposite process occurs: he searches actively for this corroborative perceptual evidence. If a noise is heard, if the neighbor uses a special word, if a strange man is walking up and down in the street, all this is corroborative evidence that what he thinks is true.

At other times this psychotic insight manifests itself in a different way. The patient does not attempt to demonstrate the validity of his ideas. "He knows"; that is enough. His knowledge comes from an inner, unchallenged certitude that does not require demonstration. "He knows." The "psychotic certainty" is something that impresses the examiner very much. For instance, a patient, a young woman who had been for three days in a state of confusion, panic, and acute delusional ideation, was examined by a psychiatrist who addressed her in this way: "Mary, I want to know about the confusion and insecurity that you have been in lately." She replied, "I prefer to talk about the security and certainty *of today*. Everything is clear to me."

The following case clearly illustrates the initial substages of the illness. I saw this patient just once for a checkup about five years after he had recovered from an acute attack. At the time of my examination he seemed to have made a satisfactory adjustment, he was happy, and he did not remember anything about the acute episode that he had experienced while he was in military service. The adjustment, satisfactory in every area that was considered, made me feel optimistic from a prognostic point of view.

The history of this patient revealed that while he was in the service during World War II he had made unsuccessful attempts to be discharged on the basis of hardship for the family. Shortly afterward he developed an acute episode characterized by hallucinations and delusions. He misidentified people and felt that through television "they" were keeping track of his movements. He had somatic complaints and was argumentative. He received a course of electric shock treatments, developed amnesia for the episode, and made an apparently complete recovery. A few days after the onset of the psychosis, he wrote a letter to his family that described the beginning of his attack very well. Here are some excerpts from his letter:

> . . . I entered the hospital and was admitted in Ward 1 for feet trouble, or better to cure a "wart" as they call it on my right foot. Well, to my surprise on the tenth day that I spent there the doctor made such a grin to me, that it finally dawned on me that I was there not for feet but for mental observation, the feet must have been just an excuse of which I was ignorant until then. When I discovered that, my first thought was to get out of the place; finally on the 12th day I was allowed to leave and it was Saturday. As I got out, the first breath of air that I inhaled made me feel as though I came out of a prison. At any rate, while waiting for the bus two fellows that I knew . . . picked me up and brought me to my squadron . . . they left me in front of my barrack and left; looking up, I saw that everybody was dressed and were going to the ramp on parade. . . . I sat waiting for the parade to be over. When they finally came back my first thought was to go to the orderly room to ask about a furlough which I had been waiting from week to week. The next thing I remember at 12 o'clock I had to report on the line for duty which I did. There, to my surprise I felt out of place, fellows spoke to me but it didn't make much sense to me. I remember I got a splitting headache, at that time all the aeroplanes were gone cross country, there were very few left on the line. I went back to my squadron all puzzled and yet I was unable to figure it out.

The following day I went back on the line. They put me to work, but to my amazement I realized that I had forgotten to do the simplest things on an engine. Everybody looked at me with some sort of sneer. Then I was asked to stand fire guard on a plane; a certain sergeant . . . asked for a loan of $5 and another fellow asked for a loan of $2 to whom I gave. At night I heard lots of planes warming up engines on the ramp, everything seemed to be very noisy, cars coming and going and motorcycles. Everything in my surroundings seemed very strange, it just didn't make any sense. I used to go to the general hall almost afraid of everything. In the barrack one evening I heard some real beautiful music which I enjoyed very much, yet to my eyes everybody didn't seem very friendly.

The following morning I was made room orderly, cleaned all the barrack downstairs and upstairs; for some reason I knew that everybody thought I was crazy, I sat on the stoop and tried very hard to hold myself from crying. I cleaned the barrack extra just to show them I wasn't crazy and that I was as normal as others.

One night or perhaps in the early morning I felt as though my brain came back to me, it felt like little particles of sand going back in its place. The airplanes were still going on the ramp and I began to think. I try to find out what it was all about. All of a sudden I thought that the two extremes, too much quiet in the hospital and too much noise on the line, were the cause of it all. I got dressed and I went right back to the hospital and tell them what my trouble was. There to my surprise they didn't pay much attention to my saying and I went back to the squadron. On the way to the hall I thought some more and having in mind the expression of the doctor in the hospital, that noise of the aeroplanes which I don't think had ever heard before, it stroke my mind that it was no longer an accident but had been done purposely. I remembered this sergeant . . . ask me on the line if I wanted a discharge; well, then I put 2 and 2 together and I no longer thought but knew that the reason for the entire affair was just for that. In reality I was always preoccupied about home, my wife and child although they were in my father's house, yet that thought of me being in the army while many other married men were out really discomforted me. I wished I was out myself. . . .

Then I found myself in Room #6; here too I heard lots of noise, my mind has been on and off; I got to the point where I believed in many things, autos coming and going, birds, especially one to signify my wife, another to signify my penis, etc., etc., etc. Here I have seen my father and mother and two sisters, seen my wife twice; once on Oct. 12 a date which I shall not forget; my mind wasn't my own and I didn't even move to meet her. From Room #6 I was moved in back of the ward, then I had a fight with a sergeant and am presently under guard."

This letter remains an accurate document of the sequence of the events at the beginning of the psychosis. Because the distortions are not pronounced, they permit an easy understanding of the early development of the psychosis. Being in the armed forces caused the patient a great deal of apprehension and reinforced his anxiety. He had made attempts to be discharged and had not succeeded. Of course, we do not have any preceding history of the patient, and therefore we do not know why he was psychologically vulnerable. Obviously he could not accept being away from his wife and child and could not adjust to army life. The anxiety became intolerable and overwhelmed his defenses. His letter describes very well the dreamlike atmosphere of the first few days of the psychotic attack. It reminds one of Kafka's novels.

During these first few days things started to appear funny, peculiar, confused, dreamlike to him. When he reported for duty, after being discharged from the ward, he felt out of place; what people said made no sense, and they seemed to look at him in a sneering manner. Everything appeared changed, everybody was unfriendly; he was afraid and felt that people thought he was insane.

After this first impression of confusion, bizarreness, and apprehension, the patient progressed to another stage. He felt that his brain was "coming back" to him. Things that were happening were no longer accidental but had been done *purposely*. He put "two and two" together, and everything became clear to him. The feeling of being insane was discarded; he acquired, as in a flash, psychotic insight. He was able to fit things together.

Thus we can recognize a sequence of phases: first, a period of intense anxiety and panic; second, a period of confusion, when everything seems strange and crazy; and third, a period of psychotic insight. When this psychotic insight occurs, the external world is understood according to a new system of thinking, which, of course, follows the motivational trends of the patient.

In the catatonic type of schizophrenia, the phase of psychotic insight is replaced by the catatonic state.

After this beginning of the psychosis, the usual symptoms of schizophrenia flourish: hallucinations, delusions, ideas of reference, catatonic posture, and so forth. The patient has now lost the battle for the supremacy of his logical thinking. If he follows the catatonic pattern it is because he is overwhelmed by fear of actions. If he follows the hebephrenic path, he is swayed by the unconscious forces that will make him resort to paleologic thinking. If he selects the paranoid way, it is because he mobilizes the remaining conscious and logical forces in the service of his unconscious. That is, he will use the logical forces to corroborate and to sustain feelings and ideas that are emotionally determined and paleologically conceived. In the well-systematized paranoid, both the logical and paleological systems (or, if we prefer the original orthodox Freudian terminology, both the ego and the id) are at the service of the psychosis.

This *logical reinforcement* of delusional and paleological material at times reaches fantastic heights. Even in the beginning of the illness, the patient tries to give a logical appearance to phenomena that he experiences and that he himself recognizes as illogical. If he hears voices and does not know how the voices may reach him, he tries to explain the phenomenon by believing that hidden radios or loudspeakers transmit the messages. Hidden dictaphones or "wired" rooms record everything he says, does, or even thinks. In past centuries psychotics explained their hallucinatory phenomena in terms of magic, sorcery, spiritism, and so forth, or, in other words, in terms that could have been acceptable in those days. In the hebephrenic type this need for apparent logicality is absent or greatly diminished. The patient accepts the delusional material without being concerned with the demonstration of its validity.

The symptoms of the first, or initial, stage of schizophrenia have already been described and discussed in this book. At this point we have to stress that although the psychosis is now in full swing and the primary process has taken over some of the functions that were under the domain of the secondary process, the psychotic state is not yet crystallized. A fight against the secondary process is in most cases visible. Anxiety is either present or can be easily mobilized. A spontaneous return to a prepsychotic level is not likely; and yet even a state of psychotic equilibrium is not reached, in spite of the symptoms. The symptoms may change, not only toward more or less regression, but also from one of the four major types to another. Thus, occasionally we see sequences of this kind occurring. A patient who in the beginning of the psychosis has a paranoid symptomatology may all of a sudden change into a catatonic state. Subsequently he may become decatatonized and will exhibit paranoid symptoms again. These changes indicate that the patient searches every possible pattern in order to escape anxiety, and, unless fortunate circumstances take place, these changes are not necessarily hopeful signs.

In many patients, but especially in paranoids, the symptoms are such as to elicit unfavorable reactions in others, which, in turn, will increase the anxiety of the patient. A vicious circle is thus established.

The classification of schizophrenia into acute and chronic cases, which many psychiatrists adopt, has nothing to do with belonging to the initial stage or not. Obviously, when the patient has reached the second, third, or fourth stage, he may be called chronic in spite of occasional remissions and even recoveries. However, he may remain chronically ill at the first stage, too, although this happens less frequently. It goes without saying that every effort should be made to prevent the patient from proceeding from the initial to subsequent stages.

CHAPTER

23

The Second, or Advanced, Stage

I

Crystallization versus Disintegration

The second, or advanced, stage of schizophrenia is reached when the symptoms seem crystallized, to have assumed a fixed and definite form. The secondary process has been definitely defeated in some areas of the psyche, and the primary process reigns, undisputed, at least within the realm of the symptomatology. A certain equilibrium seems to have been reached; the patient seems to have accepted, at least to some extent, his illness, and anxiety seems decreased or even absent.

The reader must have noticed how many times the word *seems* has been used. The use of this word has been deliberate, because the mental status of the patient is not really one of immobility, crystallization, or decrease of anxiety, in spite of the appearance. Certainly most symptoms have typical primary process characteristics and recur indefinitely; but no equilibrium is really obtained. The patient seldom finds a compromise, and the symptomatology, although defensive, does not compensate for what was lost. Thus the symptoms become additional causes of maladjustment and decompensation, and the decline continues in the direction of further regression. Typical of this stage, however, is the effort to stop the decline, to retain whatever grasp is possible on the escaping reality and to maintain at least the paleologic understanding of the world. Outbursts are less frequent. In some patients the delusions and the hallucinations have lost a great many of their unpleasant qualities. Persecutory trends may still dominate the scenery, but somehow they have lost any convincing aspect. They are stereotyped and are not accompanied by appropriate affect. Most patients do no seem to be disturbed any more by threatening voices. On the contrary, some of them hear voices that bring them comfort. In some of these cases the delusions of persecution have been replaced by delusions of grandeur.

Unless there is stereotyped thinking, thoughts appear more disconnected and abound in paleologic mechanisms or even more primitive processes such as word-salad.

However, as already mentioned, in many patients the disintegration process is slowed down, and in some cases arrested, by the tendency to stereotype all thoughts and activities or to reduce them to a mere routine. Hospitalized patients repeat the same activities every day with little variation. They sit in the same place in similar postures and talk in the same way. They avoid more and more any unpredictable situation or any spontaneous response.

Stereotypies require further consideration. From a formal point of view we may distinguish in them two major elements: (1) the repetition of the act; (2) the rigidity of the act, which allows minimal variation or none at all. The acts are stylized, occasionally assuming the form of an archaic ritual, gesture, or dance. Stereotypy has been interpreted psychodynamically by many authors. Fromm-Reichmann (1942) believes that "the seemingly meaningless and inappropriate stereotyped actions of schizophrenics are meaningful, as are the rest of their communications. They serve to screen the appropriate emotional reactions that are at their bottom. . . . They are a means of defense against non-acceptance and rebuff." De Martis and Petrella (1964) have made an accurate study of patients who presented stereotypies and have found many meanings in them:

1. Tendency to overcome destructive anxiety.
2. Wish to reestablish contact with vanishing external reality.
3. Need for defense and for masking oneself toward inner experiences that are felt as dangerous.
4. Reductive process, on account of which a vital and complicated situation becomes implemented in its most significative and syntactic form.
5. Regressive structuralization, through which terrifying inner experiences find autistic forms. These autistic forms may appear poetic or jocular.

In simpler words, we may say that stereotypies have a form and a content, may be defensive and regressive at the same time, are ways of detaching from society and yet of maintaining some contact with the external world. Their main characteristic is the reduction of a complicated life to a pattern of a few stylized movements or actions. The pattern is preserved and used as an outlet for many complicated conflicts.

The writings of patients in the second, or advanced, stage of schizophrenia disclose typical characteristics. Many patients have the habit of writing letters that help greatly in the understanding of the disorder. When integration of the personality and paranoid fervor are retained, the writings of these patients continue to express anger, an attitude that they are the victim of planned persecution and inhumane injustice. This intensely expressed content contrasts with the formality, the mannerisms, the interminable length of some writings, and the repetition, at times taking place for years and years. At first, one is inclined to interpret this repetition from an exclusively psychodynamic point of view. The patient realizes that his message is not heard by people who remain hostile and deaf to his claim and lament. In the prepsychotic period of his life, the patient really found himself in situations in which his psychological needs and feelings in general were not acknowledged. The fact that the staff of the hospital or the family do not take seriously these messages certainly reinforces the need to repeat them. The patient sends his letters first to the doctors in charge, then to the director of the hospital, then to the commissioner of mental health, then to the governor of the state, and then to the president of the United States, or to all these people.

A letter like the following one is touching:

Aug. 2, 1941

President Roosevelt
White House
Washington, D.C.

My dear President Roosevelt:

I am herewith inclosing copy of letter written to the Agriculture Milk Program and to which I have not received a reply.

Please be advised that I have 6 children at home badly in need of milk—three of my children attend the Tuberculosis clinic at Bellevue as they are very undernourished

Since I know that you are very interest in the welfare of the children in this country, I take the liberty of placing this matter before you hoping that your usual kindness will find a way to replace the milk that my children have been deprived of for these last 2 months

Respectfully Yours
A. B.

However, this patient wrote about ten letters a day, all of which were identical or almost identical to the one reported. Note the characteristic infrequent use of the period.

When regression is advanced, especially toward the end of the second stage, it becomes obvious that in addition to whatever need is there to transmit the message, the stereotyping tendency is used as a defense against the paleologic transformation, mutability, and fragmentation of the psychological world of the patient. He makes "stills" of what constantly changes, and he wants to retain tenaciously "these still pictures" as something on which he can sustain himself. The feeling of being victimized, ignored, mortified is the only thing that is experienced with some clarity and that helps the patient not to be overwhelmed by the flux and fragmentation of his mental processes. The undeniably unpleasant characteristics of institutional life, however, often give him to some extent some justification for his feelings.

Following are texts of telegrams that the patient Rudolph F. wanted the nurse to send in his behalf.

TELEGRAM

September 8, 1938

Franklin D. Roosevelt, President, Hyde Park, L.I.
Herbert H Lehman—Governor, Albany NY
Dept of Mental Hygiene, Albany NY
Fred C Munder, District Attorney, Riverhead, L.I.
Holland T Breiner Smithtown L I
Mrs. Porass—c/o The Jop Estate, Smithtown, L.I
They have locked me up again and will compel me to be shaved by the same barber who almost blinded me by infecting my eyes with syphi-gonnorrhea germs.

Please help me at once

Rudolph F.

Collect
3:20 pm

TELEGRAM

President Franklin D Roosebelt [sic]
Hyde Park L.I

Wont you please come to the aid of a helpless innocent man who is being destroyed step by step in Kings Park State Hospital. Have been unjustly locked up again and my life is in danger.

Rudolph F.

Collect
Same telegram to
Gov Herbert H Lehman
Albany

TELEGRAM

Sept 8, 1938

[Names of four friends]

Wont you come to the aid of a helpless innocent man whose life is being destroyed step by step in Kings Park State Hospital. Have been unjustly locked up again and my life is in danger.

Rudolph F.

Telegram
Collect

TELEGRAM

To [friend]

They are again attempting to harm me. Please come and help me at once

Rudolph F.

Collect

Some paranoid patients succeed in controlling the stereotyping tendency and in maintaining logical structure. Nevertheless, the bizarreness and the weakening of the thought processes are evident, as in the following "legal affidavit" written by a patient who signed his name as "America."

Affidavit

LEGAL The undersigned is being detained "here" Illegally under misrepresentation (criminal slander) The motive—We will mention only the principal reason. Having specolated "on easy" possibilities of criminal exploitation public enemies have caused through corruption a cloud to sorround a life and by so doing try to hide the honorable talented upright sane qualities, of a social giant Life

MEDICAL It behoove's you to know that I am sound and one hundreth per cent Clean healthy ((Wasserman test)) blood test indicate 100 per cent perfection quality Purity.

URGENT The writer has a Sacred Mission to perform, to give the american Social structure

will

a chance to know the Truth. I demand my release and go my way. It save you The shame of being mixed up with these public enemies parasites who are criminally. . . . fooling you I am an American able bodied cabable of earning a good and honest living I am within my own rights I believe in Law and ORDER and in the sacred rights of man enbodied in Constitution and seth forth in the Bill of Rights of the U. States of America Are you an American? then release an Innocent man

Signed America

What follows is the beginning of a five-page letter written by a patient to Dr. Tiffany, who was the director of Pilgrim State Hospital. Dr. Tiffany is addressed as His Royal Majesty, and the whole letter seems to have a humorous quality. A criticism of the hierarchic organization of the hospital is undeniable; however, the patient meant literally what could have been a jocular protest.

To His Most Royal Majesty and Excellence
King Nebuchadnezzar Tiffany,
King of Persia and Media and the Isles Roundabout,
Most Worshipful King of Kings, Ruler of All the World, *and* the P.S.H.
At His Royal Palace in Babylon, L.I.
(or Brentwood, or thereabouts!)

Your Most High and Mighty Majesty:

I most humbly beg to record the receipt of your verbal reply to my communication of yesterday,—sent by your Majesty's special Ambassador and Minister Plenipotentiary, the Honorable Sir Lang, M.D.

I had asked for your kind permission to depart from this Royal Castle of Yours wherein I am now kept a prisoner, and I made my application in writing as per information from your Royal officer at the Capital of this your Royal Province, Nova York, at Albany.

I understand that I cannot be permitted to leave on account of my Mental Condition, and I presume this is the Court Order referred to

(in)

(in)

the communication from Albany, as per His Royal Majesty Emperor Frederick the 1*st* Parsons, that I *must be* released within ten (10) days after notice in writing. Or perhaps again my admittance to Your Royal P.S.H. Palace was not according to proper rules and procedures? You see it is so long since I left all Courts and Court-manners and Kings and Nobilities behind me in the old Province of Your Majesty, Sweden, that I am very much bewildered as to the proper procedures and ettiquette in this World Empire State and Nation.

Perhaps I should still await Your Majesty's Royal Court Order in writing, properly signed and sealed by Your Majesty's Royal Chamberlain? It would hardly seem quite fair, to me, to require me to make my request in writing and not get a similar answer, in writing. Particularly when we consider the poor Condition of my somewhat Crippled-up right arm and hand. I have earnestly wished to get away from this eternal letter-writing business but it seems I am doomed to keep it up until I have drawn my last breath.———

The grandiosity and bizarreness of this patient appear also in Figure 44, which reproduces a letter in which he calls himself Prince A. and asks the staff of the hospital to allow him to deliver a lecture on the subject sex as cause of mental illness. Notice the play on words and on letters *c, s,* and *x*.

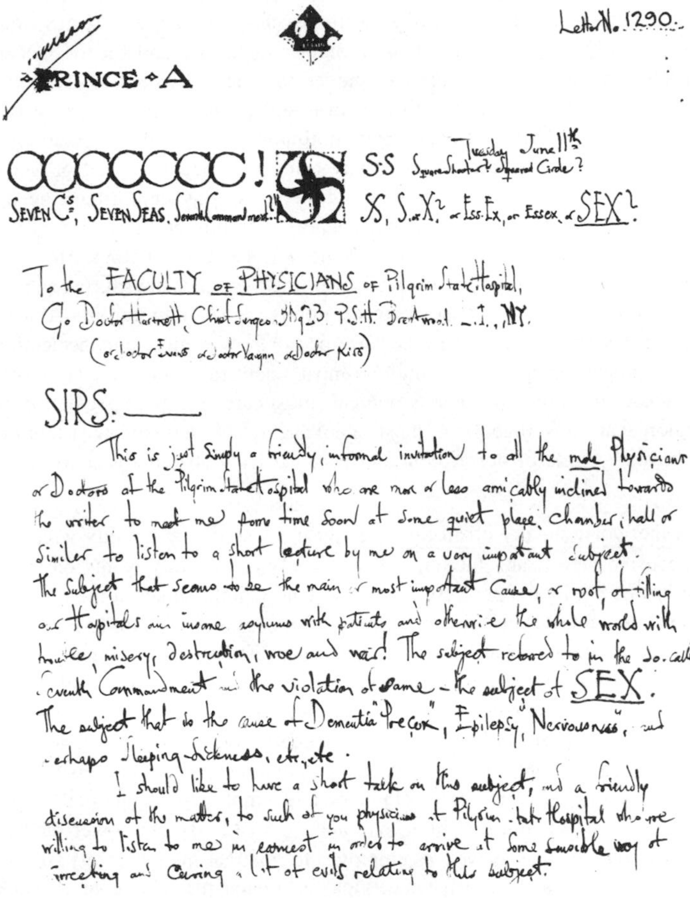

Letter No. 1290.

Mission

PRINCE A

CCCCCCC! S·S Square Shooter's Squared Circle? Tuesday June 11th

SEVEN C's, SEVEN SEAS, Seventh Commandment!? S, S. or X?, or Ess. Ex, or Essex, or SEX?

To the FACULTY OF PHYSICIANS of Pilgrim State Hospital,
C/o Doctor Hartnett, Chief Surgeon, Bldg 23. P.S.H. Brentwood, L.I., N.Y.
(or Doctor Evans or Doctor Vaughn or Doctor Kirs)

SIRS:——

This is just simply a friendly, informal invitation to all the male Physicians or Doctors of the Pilgrim State Hospital who are more or less amicably inclined towards the writer to meet me some time soon at some quiet place, chamber, hall or similar to listen to a short lecture by me on a very important subject. The subject that seems to be the main or most important Cause, or root, of filling our Hospitals and insane asylums with patients and otherwise the whole world with trouble, misery, destruction, woe and war! The subject referred to in the so-called Seventh Commandment and the violation of same — the subject of SEX. The subject that is the cause of "Dementia Precox", "Epilepsy", "Nervousness", and perhaps Sleeping-Sickness, etc., etc.

I should like to have a short talk on this subject, and a friendly discussion of the matter, to such of you physicians at Pilgrim State Hospital who are willing to listen to me in earnest in order to arrive at some sensible way of correcting and curing a lot of evils relating to this subject.

FIGURE 44. Explanation in the text.

The following letter, reported in its entirety, depicts well the climate of persecution.

Dear doctor (you, to whom I have given this letter): I am extremely sorry to say that I am now at Kings park state hospital for the insane, building D, ward 16, at Kings park, Long Island, N.Y. I have been at Kings park state hospital since April 5, 1934. I am a perfectly sane man who is imprisoned most unjustly and for no reason whatsoever, in the most detestable insane asylum. I am the victim of the worst injustice and the most unbearable conditions. my being here is the worst sin, the worst mistake and the worst crime. nobody has the right to keep me here at all. Here is my story. The tenants who were living directly beneath us, where I used to live with my family (parents, brother and sisters), were talking to me telepathically, daily, continuously and invisible from their home and while I was at home. I was absolutely a slave and I was not able to avoid hearing or receiving mentally from them. They annoyed me extremely because they talked to me mentally. when I was at home, I did not teach telepathy to any member of my family. my mother did not believe that telepathy was true and consequently she thought that I was imagining that the tenants were talking to me telepathically and, because of that, she had me sent, suddenly, to Kings park state hospital after I was kept four days at the psychopathic ward of Kings County hospital at Brooklyn, N.Y. If it was not for my mother's ignorance and for the fact that I did not teach her telepathy at home, I would have never been here. I would have surely become a successful business man instead of rotting in an insane asylum under the most unbearable conditions and suffering, daily, extremely and continuously and without cessation, day and night and always liable to become insane at any time or to become blind or to die at any time. ever since I have been here, my mother and the rest of the family, have been coming, asking and begging doctor K., the doctor under whose direction building D was, to let them take me home but he always refused. His attitude was most astounding. He should have discharged me from Kings park state hospital from the very first day during which I came under his direction but he was most unconscientious, most unmoral, most wicked. etc beyond words or description. I am here because doctor K was most unconscientious, most irrational, most unreasonable, most unmoral, most unethical, most unjust, most unrighteous, most wicked, most biased, most tyrannical, most careless, most neglectful, the worst liar, most demoniacal, most diabolical, most satanical, most unhuman, most inhumane, and most insane beyond words or description and because I am absolutely controlled in mind and body

<u>My slavery is the worst slavery of all times</u>. Even if I was insane nobody would have had the right to keep me here if any member of my family or anybody wants me out of here. And I am not insane but I am a perfectly sane man who is imprisoned in the most detestable insane aylyum most unjustly and for no reason whatsoever and my family wants me out of here. not only am I sane but also I am more intelligent and moral than many sane people. Furthermore I was always working, earning my living and saving money and I was never a burden on anybody. The inmates, here, hate me extremely because I am sane and they always do their best to keep me here. They succeeded wonderfully and that is why I am here. In order to keep me here, (1) they talk to me telepathically, continuously and daily almost without cessation, day and night. (Inmates and employes talk to me telepathically, daily, and continuously without cessation, day and night) (2) By the power of their imagination, they force one another as well as employes to mistreat me extremely, daily, continuously and in every way and to strike me, kick me punch me, choke me, knock at me,

cause extreme pain in various parts of my body and to harm me in every way. (I have been struck, kicked, choked, punched over two thousand times most unjustly and for no reason whatsoever. I have been struck on my eyes many times for no reason whatsoever. I have been kicked strongly on my testes and many times and for no reason whatsoever. My health has been ruined because of strokes and other conditions, They strike me or kick me or choke me or punch me, daily. My ribs and bones have become crooked because of that) (3) By the power of their imagination and daily and continuously, they create extreme pain in my head, brain, eyes, heart, stomach and in every part of my body. Also by their imagination and daily and continuously, they lift my heart and stomach and they pull my heart, and they stop it, move it, twist it and shake it and pull its muscles and tissues. By the power of their imagination and daily and continuously, they dilate my pupil and iris and they pull the veins, muscles and tissues of my eyes. At any time, they will surely burst my pupil and iris. (4) By their imagination and daily and continuously, they force one another to knock at me their hands fists, feet and anything they could hold and, by their imagination, they send the noise and sound to my head, brain, temples and teeth. By their imagination and telepathy and daily and continuously, they force one another to talk orally and to send their voices to my head, forehead, temples and heart. (5) By telepathy and imagination, they force me to say orally whatever they desire, whenever they desire and as long as they desire. I never said a word of my own. I never created a thought or image of my own. (6) By their imagination and their bodily mouvents, they scare me continuously and by their imagination, they move the blood violently in every part of my body (7) By their imagination and daily and continuously, they absolutely control the motion and mouvement of my body and every part of it. (8) When they force me to talk to anybody, they control, by their imagination and telepathy, the speech and behaviour of that person. (9) Also when a person talks to me, they control that person as well as myself. (10) By the power of their imagination and every night, they force me to sleep and awake as many times as they desire and they create my dreams and they tell them to me. (11) By their imagination, they prevent me from writing whenever I desire and, when they let me write, I have to write very slowly and, while I am writing, they create extreme and continuous pain in my fingers and in every part of my hand. (12) By their imagination, they force employes to put me in the strong room most unjustly and for no reason whatsoever and to torture me in it. They also do everything possible to prevent me from getting out of Kings park state hospital. Furthermore I am suffering daily, extremely, and without cessation, day and night, because they are continuously creating extreme pain in my eyes, brain, heart, and in every part of my body. What I am undergoing here is worse than the torments of hell itself. The situation is absolutely uncontrollable and irremediable. I must get out of here at once or I will surely become insane or blind or I will surely die. please save me from insanity or blindness or death. please discharge me from Kings park state hospital as soon as possible during today or tomorrow and I swear by God that I will give or send you five hundred dollars, or any sum which you desire as high as one thousand dollars, as a reward for that and within three days after my discharge and I thank you most cordially. Gain my gratitude for life as well as that of my family.

R. A.

Following is the beginning of a sixteen-page letter with again a pervading feeling of persecution.

1952

Sir;

During my 82:8 stay, I was numerous times, savagely and absolutely un-necessary assaulted . . . . . cures . . . . . treatments . . . . . . strait-jacketings, etc., by head X.

My lower (bridge) teeth broken; Two pairs of eyeglasses damaged$_x$

Searched practically every day$_x$ The following were maliciously seized from me, by head X. . . . on the silly, flimsy pretenses: "excessive baggage":—

My Dimes Savings Bank book deliberated wrested from me and torn into shreds, before my eyes . . . . by head X$_x$ I didnt compliment head X$_x$ I blew my top$_x$ Kerplunko . . . I was rear ended onto the floor$_x$

The passbook's cover design, with
its 1-280-850 . . . . . . the DSB (photo
engraved) branch building, imprint
. . . . . . a blind person
could sense its
nature's contents
and wouldn't mutilate and confiscate
it as "EXCESSIVE BAGGAGE"!

I complained to my doc., about it$_x$ He merely snickered and gave me the brush$_x$
To speak to the doc., I first asked head X. "No"$_x$
I lay in wait$_x$ The next time the doc. was in X's office, I over rode the outer guard and dashed in. The doc brushed-me-off$_x$ Results: my fanny again floor-collided. . . . by head X$_x$

From then on X's atrocious brutualities towards me were tough going!
My eyeglasses case (container) confiscated
"pencil sharper; also eraser, "
"cigarette roller Bugler machine"
and other essential personal
properties frisked from me
as "EXCESSIVE BAGGAGE"

I certainly DID REPULSE these dirty, bastardly tactics of head X!

Following is the beginning of a seven-page letter that discloses new formation of paranoid ideas.

Dear Sir:

I have this day, at about 4:30 pm discovered another plot to harm me by violence.

At supper time, as I was standing at the end of the corridor, near the door which leads down to the Dining Room, looking out of the window, with my backe turned, I heard a movement behind me. I looked around quickly and found a patient had just seated himself on a chair behind by backe. In his hand he had a long, sharp pointed weapon, with a handle on it made of wire. As he heard me turn he quickly put it into his inside coat pocket.

I asked Spirit, who had of course also seen it, what the man was doing with such a dangerous weapon. Spirit replied it was to protect me.

As I have found Spirit to be fraudulent, lying and treacherous on many occasions in the past I immediately made up my mind to report the man and have the weapon taken away from him. I told the first attendant I met on the way down about it. His name is McMahon and he was standing at the foot of the stairs. I told him I would point out the man to him as all the men came down. Although this man was nearest the door to the stairs leading down to the Dining Room, and should have been one of the first men to reach there, and although I waited until all the men in my ward came down, I was unable to show him to the attendant, as apparently Spirit had warned him not to come down.

Contrasting with the deep sorrow, anguish, and sense of injustice that appear in these letters, the patients who wrote them often appeared calm, detached, apathetic.

Many patients in the second stage of the illness have a style that seems pretentious, pseudoabstract, or ''on stilts,'' as described in Chapter 16. The pseudoabstraction at times approximates word-salad, as in the following letter.

Pilgrim State Hosp
West Brentwood
Long Island
Bldg 30 War8
State Hosp. Insane
USA.
1———2
2———1

Hon. Staff Doctor's
Dept Office.
State Hosp. Insane.

Honorables:
At the presents
past on hour future and the beginnin off the life every Doctor's on the capacity that have have to be sure off the buisness life and made it on confortables act on insuerance capacity acts at the moral mentaly on good Health. I'm my self I think any way for the true and give and all together the best onsuerds by ward for my inteligence to resolve a - problen that one plus one is one them I my self think iff it is true or I mistake later I have to correct. Know at this presents moments I don't have to say anything and I don't have a word only on the same hared one and the same word have the ansuerd's (Liberty on free). Just only that I have an warred too. Anything more for my self I needed. I would like to have that consideration for finish and take a rest and to have a good time because many thing at my recuerments life. I made you at your self this propotion. To give me and oportunity to apraff me a hoadcard for the few time that I won to stay here If you wanted to aproff me this allright and good too. Them when I resired I give you the thanks no for ever but for the presents mannen ts' allright and very good for all and pleasure with your's.

E. R.

Grandiose paranoid systems are more frequent in the advanced stage than in the first. They often retain a scientific or impressive aspect. Neologisms and mixing of words, designs, and ornamentations occur in many writings of patients in the advanced stage. Figure 45 reveals many neologisms. It also portrays five spoons, which stand for the five members of the family to which they are respectively assigned.

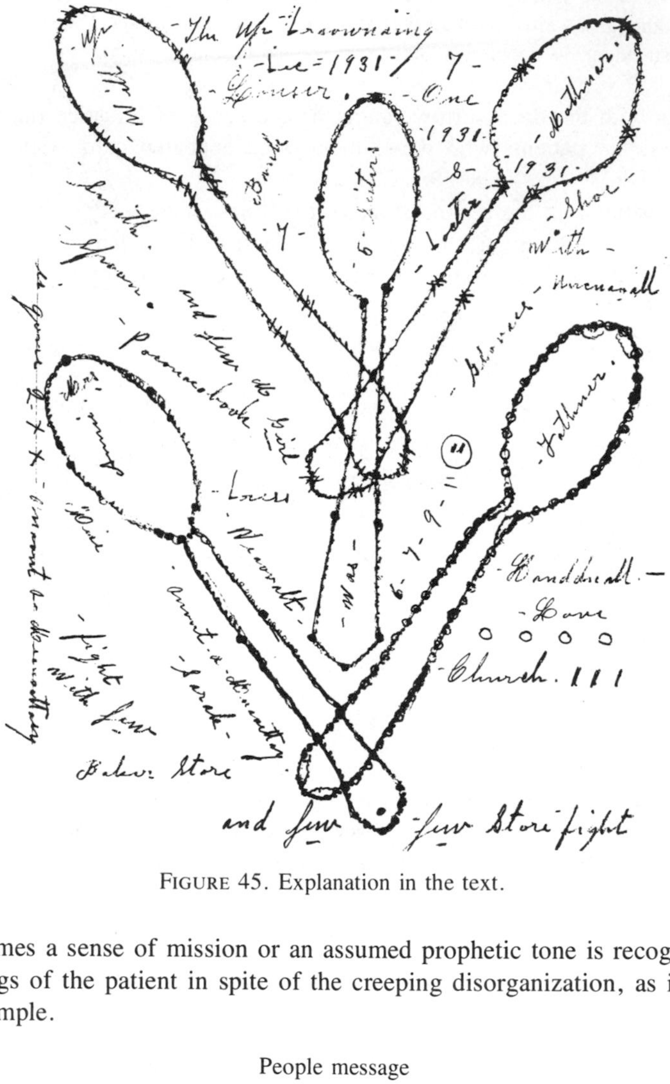

FIGURE 45. Explanation in the text.

At times a sense of mission or an assumed prophetic tone is recognizable in the writings of the patient in spite of the creeping disorganization, as in the following sample.

People message

God let me see how its done and I want the
people, public and Court people to get and know how
its done, to save humanity human life through out
the nations Europe's plight and Russians' plight and

all and America's human life plight are all the
same slave bond through film actors camera men
doing evil poison fog hypnotic put on the human
life
pray that it can get be push through for world
to know.
This is the living truth and facts
faith
circulars only to here from Mary Reen
cant work for wages or health until people kown
how its done

The more the illness advances, the more disorganized the language and the writing become, so that often complete incoherence results. Life becomes increasingly monotonous. Although some paranoid patients continue for many years to make their protests in writing, a large number of them give the impression of not being disturbed by institutional life as one would expect. Although their lives become narrower and narrower, they do not seem to be bored. As a matter of fact, they never yawn. Boredom is an emotional state of which they do not seem capable. Boredom eventually would produce anxiety. Sexual life continues to decline except for a certain group of patients who masturbate repeatedly.

Catatonics in the second stage, however, are a little more active. Waxy flexibility is often replaced by stereotyped minimal activity. The patients are less rigid and allow themselves to perform some movements. It seems almost as if at this stage the four classic types of schizophrenia (simple, paranoid, hebephrenic, and catatonic) have acquired a much more similar symptomatology. At this stage it may be difficult to differentiate a paranoid from a hebephrenic. Paranoids, however, reach the second stage of regression much later than hebephrenics. In many instances they remain indefinitely at the first stage.

As was noted before, a group of patients seem contented and, at least when they harbor grandiose delusions, proud of themselves. They seem to have achieved what they wanted, that is, they have acquired self-esteem and removed anxiety. But can we accept this appearance as corresponding to the inner state of the patient? We have seen that in the first stage an attempt to remove anxiety was made by accepting psychotic mechanisms. We have also seen, however, that in the first stage, even at a superficial symptomatological level, anxiety was retained.

Once the patients have selected the path of schizophrenic regression and desocialization, they tend to continue to follow that path. The process of desocialization is like quicksand; in most cases, it actually increases the anxiety of patients, especially when they feel pressured to resocialize but find themselves deprived of the necessary tools.

In the second stage of schizophrenia, anxiety is less visible. One could say that the illness has been a good transformer, has transformed anxiety into psychotic symptoms. Theoretically, however, we have to assume that anxiety is still there, at least potentially, to perpetuate the illness. In fact, if there were no anxiety, the patients would tend to recover. That is what happens in some cases; but in the majority of cases anxiety still exists in actuality or potentiality. Any tendency toward normalization reactivates anxiety, and the patients therefore maintain the psychotic symptoms. Actually, any attempt toward recovery, even the slightest one, presumably produces great anxiety, because by becoming psychotic the patients have given up many of the means (powers of abstraction, and so on) that equipped them to fulfill social demands. They are in a situation similar to the one described by Goldstein (1939, 1943*a*) in organic cerebral cases. The patients are afraid to go into a ''catastrophic reaction''; their tendency, therefore, is to do the opposite, to follow the path toward more stereotyped activity and desocialization. Any anxiety-producing demands may push them further toward regression.

The situation is a vicious circle. What should be a defense in the majority of cases makes the patients more helpless and vulnerable, a circumstance similar to that which occurs in some organic diseases.

It is interesting to determine how patients who have been sick for many years remember or evaluate the onset of their illness. De Martis, F. Petrella, and A. M. Petrella (1967) have examined fifty female patients who had been hospitalized for a period ranging from three to thirty years. They obtained the following results:

1. Eight patients denied ever having been sick, or they attributed their hospitalization to persecution.
2. The thirty-five patients who gave psychological explanations did so in a stereotyped, repetitious way. Ten of them attributed their original hospitalization to exhaustion; three to overwork; four to menstrual troubles; eight to fright.
3. Reference to a physical illness was frequent. Headache, lack of appetite, and loss of weight were often mentioned as causes of hospitalization.
4. Reference to psychological traumas was much more frequently made by patients who originally were hospitalized for a brief period of time and became chronically ill outside the hospital.
5. Explicit magical interpretations of the onset of the illness were present in only three cases.

In their accurate work, De Martis and co-authors found in patients in the second stage of schizophrenia a level of mental suffering that was unsuspected and that contrasted with the apparent flatness of affect and degradation of the personality.

A related kind of work was made by Brooks, Deane, and Hugel (1968). Although the sixty-eight patients whom they studied were described as being in remission and in a rehabilitation aftercare clinic, they were labeled chronic schizophrenics and had been sick for a period ranging from eight to twenty years. The authors concluded that:

1. For all sixty-eight subjects the schizophrenic experience was a horrible, nightmarish one.
2. The basic schizophrenic experience seemed to vary little or not at all in relation to clinical manifestations or the individual's style of communicating this experience. Patients belonging to various subtypes that could be clearly diagnosed

as paranoid, catatonic, simple, hebephrenic, schizo-affective, and undifferentiated showed no difference in the nature or reporting of their inner experiences. According to the authors, their findings would support a unitary view of schizophrenia as a disorder.

A certain number of patients in the advanced stage of schizophrenia were, until not too long ago, particularly conspicuous for the antisocial character of their symptoms. In large hospitals like Pilgrim State Hospital, entire buildings, or at least entire wards, were used only for patients who had shown aggressive or violent behavior, who would destroy all their clothes and walk naked, would repeatedly try to escape, would smash windows, would be incontinent of feces and urine, and would smear feces. Many patients were kept in straightjackets for long periods of time. The management of these wards was an arduous job. These places smelled like stables, and some of them were reminiscent of the illustrations for Dante's *Inferno*. Fortunately these scenes belong to the past. In 1968 I visited and spent some time in Pilgrim State Hospital after an absence of twenty-two years and could gladly witness to the disappearance of these tragic pictures. This behavioral improvement is to a large extent the result of drug therapy. Although I rejoiced at the fact that the *antisocial* overt symptoms had disappeared, I could notice to my regret that the *asocial* symptoms of the advanced stage of schizophrenia had been touched only to a minimal degree by the use of drugs. The thought disorder, the stereotyped behavior, and the decrease in life experience still dominated the picture.

II

The Advanced Period of Schizophrenia and Institutional Life

Is the institutional life to which most patients in the advanced stage are subjected at least partially responsible for the symptomatology?

The following questions are often posed:

1. Is hospital life changing an acute into a chronic condition?
2. Is the symptomatology of the hospitalized chronic schizophrenic partially caused by hospital life?
3. Does hospital life perpetuate the symptomatology?
4. Traditional institutional life is unsatisfactory and would have an adverse effect even on normal persons. Is it not likely that it may have even a worse effect on the vulnerable schizophrenic who is in a state of advanced regression?

These questions or problems are not necessarily related.

Several authors have attempted to demonstrate that hospital practices tend to transform an acute into a chronic schizophrenic, or to make the chronic worse or permanent. Macmillan (1958) wrote:

> Many of the symptoms which we had formerly regarded as due to the psychosis were in fact due to the restrictions which we had imposed on the patients, and disappeared with the removal of these restrictions. . . . The resentment and feeling of injustice which certification causes in the mind of the patient is intense, and it lasts for many years. When patients are in a state of emotional upset, when their self-confidence is already seriously undermined and disturbed, to deprive them of civil rights depletes that stock of self-confidence even more at this critical phase of their life. One can hardly imagine anything more likely to upset them.

Hunt (1958), also believes that much disability in mental illness is not part of the illness itself but is artificially superimposed, the result of the rejection on the part of society of the deviant individual. Lehrman (1961) wrote: "Since there is usually insufficient staff to help the patient to see the healthy aspect of his incorrect rebellious behavior, he begins increasingly to see life as presenting a choice only between punishable defiance and relatively painless apathy. The latter response tends often, in consequence, to be chosen."

Ludwig and Farrelly (1966) maintain that in psychiatric hospitals a situation "is unwittingly created whereby patients find it difficult to relinquish their identification as chronic patients and to adopt more socialized values and attitudes." These two authors have aptly given the name of "code of chronicity" to the complex of traditional attitudes and consequent behavior found in chronic hospitalized patients, as well as in the staff.

Kantor and Gelineau (1969) have made a profound study of how the interaction of five specific mechanisms in the patient and of five social mechanisms in a typical ward for chronic patients operates to support and maintain chronic schizophrenia. The mechanisms in the patient are the following:

1. *Injury patterning*. Because of his life history, the patient evolves into a recurrent pattern of injury: expectation of injury anew and the fulfillment of the expectation. The process operates circularly and becomes a fixed pattern.
2. *Fear patterning*. Unable to leave the field, the patient adopts a fixed pattern of existential despair.
3. *Flight patterning*. The patient learns to avoid the pain of anxiety by withdrawing.
4. *Distorted language patterning*. The future chronic schizophrenic develops a system of unintelligible and unpredictable communication.
5. *Role-loss patterning*. The patient is shifted from a civilian role to that of being a hospitalized schizophrenic.

The five social mechanisms that meet the personality patterns and with them make schizophrenia a chronic condition are:

1. Rituals of degradation. Attendants recurrently humiliate patients.
2. Mechanisms that differentiate states and establish social distance between personnel and patients.
3. Rigid social controls. Absolute authority over the patients is used to administer a range of rewards and punishments.

4. Insulation from the demands of other institutional systems, such as the family, psychiatric staff, visiting or voluntary outsiders.

5. Constriction of role set. The patient's role set is reduced to a constellation of a few role partners: the other patients, the attendants, and the physician, but only to a greatly reduced degree.

According to Kantor and Gelineau three types of patients ensue as a result of the interaction of these personality and social factors: the stormy rebel, the quiet conformist, and the autistic recluse. The names of these types suggest their prevailing type of behavior. Kantor and Gelineau write that these three types of patients

> make different demands on their environment; and each elicits a different response set from the system. These response sets, though selective, are limited by the inflexibility of the ward structure and culture. Indeed, what makes such a ward an improper place for schizophrenics (or anybody) is its staff members' selective insensitivity to the varying needs of its patients. It thwarts the rebel's desperate attempts at self-integration, it encourages the conformist's martyrdom, and it ritually mutilates the recluse's already mangled concept of self.

Goffman (1961) has reported in detail the conditions, experiences, and behavior of the chronically mentally ill in mental institutions. He has dramatically portrayed the process of mortification that the patient undergoes in traditional mental hospitals. The hospital disrupts those actions that give the person the feeling that he has some command over his world and consequently a sense of self. He cannot indulge in those actions that confer self-determination. While the process of mortification goes on, the patient learns how the privilege system works:

1. House rules are defined.
2. A small number of clearly defined rewards or privileges are held out in exchange for obedience. The patient actually builds up a world around these minor privileges.
3. Punishment is inflicted on those who break the rules.

Goffman has described four types of adaptation to institutional life:

1. Patients who withdraw.
2. Patients who follow the "intransigent line" by challenging the institution and flagrantly refusing to cooperate with the staff.
3. Patients who adopt "colonization." Like good colonists the patients adapt to the environment.
4. Patients who are "converted." The inmate takes over the official view of himself and tries to act out the role of the perfect inmate.

Now if we compare the types presented by Goffman and by Kantor and Gelineau, we see great similarities: Goffman's withdrawing patient corresponds to Kantor-Gelineau's autistic recluse. Goffman's intransigent patient corresponds to Kantor-Gelineau's stormy rebel; Goffman's colonist-convert patient corresponds to Kantor-Gelineau's quiet conformist. Goffman's fourth type is, in my opinion, a variation of the third.

Following Horney (1945, 1950), in Chapter 6 of this book, I divided normal and neurotic people according to three types of prevailing personality: (1) detached, or moving away from people; (2) aggressive, or moving against people; (3) compliant, or moving toward people. Thus it seems to me that what Goffman and Kantor and Gelineau have done is to describe the chronically psychotic counterpart or version of these three basic types of personality. Institutional life reinforces and makes come back to the surface a basic or predominant type of personality. If the type of personality is detached, it will probably change into schizoid during the prepsychotic stage and withdrawn during the psychotic period and hospitalization. If the patient in the prepsychotic stage of life has what we have called a stormy personality, he may, during the chronic psychotic period, reveal more the detached, aggressive, or compliant component of his psyche. According to which one of these three major characteristics he will disclose, he will be classified in one or the other categories proposed by Goffman and by Kantor and Gelineau.

The problem, posed by many authors, of whether hospitalization itself makes acute patients become chronic is an important one, but one that is difficult to examine with equanimity and fairness. A consideration to be made is that the schizophrenic patient, whether hospitalized or not, elicits in others a set of responses that in their turn reinforce his beliefs and symptomatology (see Chapter 19). Deviant behavior in general elicits negative feelings in the environment, and these negative feelings reinforce the experience of estrangement, low self-esteem, or the feeling of being victimized and persecuted.

It is true, however, that many institutions were organized when their only function was custodial care: to keep these people away from society, where they can be harmful to themselves and others or create a public scandal. Therapy was not even contemplated. Several institutions, fortunately in decreasing number, still suffer from the fact that they continue to follow a type of organization whose only purpose was custodial care. These organizations succeeded in preventing these people from having *antisocial* or suicidal behavior but did not help them to overcome their *asocial* behavior. As a matter of fact the institution itself, by separating people from the community, diminishing their realm of activities, and organizing the sets of rules and disciplines that Goffman and others have illustrated, has actually fostered in the patient an asocial style of life. The private, paleologic, autistic functions have not been combated but have been allowed to flourish. The patient has tended to become more distrustful, more passive, more withdrawn.

Contrary to its effect in the first stage of schizophrenia, drug therapy has a therapeutic effect toward the antisocial but not the asocial symptoms of the patient in the second stage of the illness. Modern types of milieu and social therapy, like the therapeutic community and the types of milieu therapy suggested by Stanton and Schwartz (1949*a, b*) and by Rioch and Stanton (1953) have done much to change drastically or at least to ameliorate these conditions.

CHAPTER

24

The Third, or Preterminal, Stage

I

Introductory Remarks

Whereas the first stage of schizophrenia has been intensely studied by many psychiatrists from a dynamic point of view, and the second stage has been studied in great detail by the early descriptive authors, the third and fourth stages have been relatively neglected.

This neglect, even by those authors who limit their studies to a description of the symptoms, may seem difficult to understand, because almost the majority of patients in advanced stages of regression are hospitalized. The classical symptoms of schizophrenia, however, are no longer prominent in these stages, so that many observers may have felt that the patients did not present symptoms worth reporting. They have described these patients as approximating more and more a vegetative existence. Very little more than similar generalities is mentioned in the literature. The result is that even from a simple, descriptive point of view, relatively little is known about these patients.

When I was working in Pilgrim State Hospital, I had an opportunity to study these very regressed patients, and I felt that such study could eventually reveal important information. As I reported in a previous contribution (Arieti, 1945*b*), I gave the name "preterminal" to a stage that is rather difficult to delimit or to differentiate. This stage occurs generally from five to fifteen years after the beginning of the illness but may occur sooner or later.

In this phase of the illness, hallucinations and delusions have disappeared or cannot be elicited. In some cases they are still present, but they are completely disorganized and deprived of any apparent emotional charge. The patients present severe disintegration of thought processes, so that their ideas are conveyed to the examiner with great difficulty.

In this stage, it is difficult to distinguish a catatonic from a paranoid. Now the different types converge toward one another even more than they do during the second stage. Although all the types of schizophrenia may pass through the preterminal stage, in a large group of cases belonging to this phase we find a predominance of patients previously diagnosed as affected by the paranoid type. This preponderance may be due to the fact that paranoid patients remain at this level a longer time or even indefinitely without regressing further. Hebephrenics and catatonics, on the other hand, regress sooner to the terminal stage.

The reason why patients of the four classic types seem more alike during this phase is that most of the obvious symptoms have disappeared. On account of the absence of many symptoms, these patients are at times discharged from the hospital, if a suitable nondemanding environment is found. They manifest what Lewis (1944) calls ''improvement by regression.'' It would seem as if in these cases the illness had really been able to achieve its purpose. A little more than the most superficial examination, however, reveals that these patients are very sick. Not only is the impairment of their thinking very marked, but they also present peculiar habits, which are typical of this stage.

These habits are numerous but probably many of them have escaped the notice of observers. Often, in fact, institutionalized patients learn to conceal them very well. Examples of some habits are picking of the skin, pulling out of the hair, and performance of rhythmic movements. Particular attention will be given in this chapter to two habits that, in my opinion, are the most common—the hoarding and the self-decorating habits.

II

The Hoarding Habit

The hoarding habit is the practice of collecting a more or less large number of objects, generally of limited size and generally of no practical use. The objects that, in the course of my investigation, were found to have been hoarded by the patients were papers of any kind—old letters, toilet paper, pages of newspapers, and so on—pieces of wood, stones, leaves, sticks, soap, spoons, strings, rags, hairpins, old toothbrushes, wires, cups, feathers, cores of fruit, stale food, feces, hair, pencils, pens, combs, small boxes, cardboards, and other things. Until she was discovered, one patient used to carry a large number of teaspoons, which she had taken from the dining room, hidden in her bosom. Another patient had collected a large number of her own feces, and still another had collected 117 prune pits in a stocking. Another patient preferred to hoard her daily ration of food rather than eat it. She eventually had to be tube fed. Less regressed patients, whose habits have been developed more recently, may collect objects that have some symbolic or actual use—letters, pictures, recent papers. However, their subsequent behavior discloses that they do not collect these things with the purpose of using them, but just for the sake of collecting them. Not only do they not use these objects, but they start to hoard other things that have no use whatsoever. Some patients start to develop this habit by collecting and wrapping objects of the same kind in separate bundles. Later, however, they no longer continue to divide them and keep them separately according to their kind; instead they put them all together.

The patients collect these objects in their pockets, in bags or boxes, in their stockings or socks, and not infrequently in their shoes. Female patients very often hide them in their bosom or in other parts of their body. Many carry the entire collection with them always as if it were an important part of their person. Others collect the objects under their beds, pillows, or in other relatively hidden spaces. Some patients put paper and other objects wherever they can find a hole. One patient had made a hole in the lining of a mattress and had put into it an enormous quantity of toilet paper and other trash.

When the patients become more regressed and approach the terminal stage, they start to use the cavities of their own bodies as deposits for the hoarded material. Male patients frequently deposit small objects in their external auditory canals or in their nasal cavities. Female patients resort to their vaginas. In my series, seven patients had the habit of placing objects in their vaginas. One of them had put into her vagina a small metal cup, two handles of teaspoons, several small pieces of soap, and a little rag, by the time this practice was discovered. Another patient used to hoard small objects in her oral cavity, but she did not eat them. During her meals she would remove the objects and then put them back in her mouth afterward. In a few cases, the patients had resorted to their somatic cavities only when they were deprived of their bags or pocketbooks.

In my opinion, this hoarding habit is extremely frequent among regressed patients, but the extent of its incidence cannot be easily evaluated because nurses and attendants try to prevent it. In fact, if the patients were permitted to hoard as many things as they were inclined to, the large quantity of garbage and trash that they would collect would interfere with the hygienic management of the hospital wards. The repression of this tendency is a real problem of administrative psychiatry.

Although I have observed and studied this habit in patients of both sexes, I was able to do statistical investigations only in female services. I collected a series of sixty-four patients presenting this habit, although for the reasons mentioned above the actual number of patients having the hoarding tendency probably was many times as large. Forty-eight (75 percent) of the patients were diagnosed as cases of schizophrenia. The other sixteen were diagnosed as follows: involutional psychosis, paranoid type (1); paranoid condition (2); manic-depressive psychosis (4); alcoholic psychosis, paranoid type (1); cerebral arteriosclerosis (3); psychosis due to epilepsy (4); general paresis (1). Such variety of psychiatric entities denies the specificity of this habit. It could be that, at least in some of these sixteen cases, the initial diagnosis, made many years previously, had not been the correct one. In fact, at the time of this investigation their condition, at a clinical level, was in no way different from that of an advanced schizophrenic regression. I am inclined to think, however, that the hoarding habit is not pathognomonic of advanced schizophrenia, but that it may be found in all the conditions that bring about a state of regression. As a matter of fact, several years after I had reported the original investigation of this habit in schizophrenia, I observed similar, although much less pronounced, hoarding tendencies in several very old non-psychiatric patients who were institutionalized in a home for the aged. The fact remains, however, that schizophrenia is the most common condition that brings about a regression to the level of the hoarding habit.

Within the schizophrenic group, twenty-nine patients (60.42 percent) were of the paranoid type, nine (18.75 percent) were hebephrenic, seven (14.58 percent) were of the simple type, and one (2.08 percent) was of the mixed types. The group of paranoid patients was by far the largest and becomes even more outstanding if we add to it the other four patients diagnosed as paranoid but not schizophrenic (involutional psychosis, paranoid type; alcoholic psychosis, paranoid type; and paranoid condition).

In addition to the statistical and diagnostic importance of the hoarding habit, there remains the problem of its psychological meaning. Attempts to obtain information directly from the patients were unsuccessful. The majority did not answer inquiries; they reacted only by smiling in an apparently incongruous manner. Several gave evasive replies. Only a few attempted to give a logical explanation. The patient who had filled the mattress with toilet paper said that she had done it so as to be ready in case she developed diarrhea. Another patient replied, "I use what God has given me." It appears to me, however, that such practices give a certain amount of pleasure to the patients. As a matter of fact, when they are deprived of their collections, they are obviously displeased and sometimes resist and resent these hygienic steps. They are not as resentful as one would expect, however, considering the constancy and apparent zeal that they often show in this collecting tendency. It is hard to estimate whether relatively more pleasure is derived from the act of collecting or from keeping the collection; probably pleasure is derived from both of these actions.

Textbooks of psychiatry do not mention this habit, which is common in advanced schizophrenia. However, occasional instances have been reported in the literature. For example, Staercke (1920) described a paranoid patient who had the habit of collecting corks, and Abraham (1927) reported the case of a psychotic patient who used to collect stones.

In the orthodox psychoanalytic literature, the habit of collecting is interpreted as an expression of the anal character. Abraham (1912) and Jones (1938) have described the same hoarding habit in neurotics presenting anal traits. In these cases, however, the habit occurs in a much less accentuated and bizarre form than I have observed in the preterminal stage of schizophrenia. Abraham (1927) describes persons who "collect bits of paper, old envelopes, worn-out pens, and similar things, and cannot get rid of these possessions for long periods of time."

I shall not refrain from calling this habit anal, if the use of such a word is for the sake of common understanding. However, in my opinion, this habit has nothing to do with the anus or with sexual pleasure. I am inclined to think instead that it is a primitive or archaic habit that is found at a certain level of mental integration. The child's ability to retain feces, in spite of the urge to defecate, may require a level of mental integration that corresponds to the level of the hoarding habit.

Primitive levels of cognition, starting with the paleologic, lead to transformation or mutability of inner objects as well as of external objects. As I have described in this book (Chapter 16) and in *The Intrapsychic Self* (Arieti, 1967, Chap. 7), the patient who thinks in accordance with primary process cognition tries to go beyond the particular, but his attempts lead him not to Platonic universals but to transmutability. If things change according to the wishes of the patient, he acquires a feeling of grandiosity and even omnipotence. If the patient believes that things change contrary to his wishes, anxiety increases again, in spite of the regression.

Like the primitive man, the patient tries to counterbalance the transmutability of the inner reality by plunging into external reality; that is, by collecting and possessing. The volume and plurality of external objects will be the best antidote to the uncertainty of the inner objects, because what is familiar by volume and plurality will be less likely to transmute. Its existence is less likely to be doubted.

In human phylogenesis, hoarding became prominent when human beings ceased to be interested only in the present, that is, in activities connected with immediate needs, such as finding food and eating it immediately. When *Homo* became *sapiens,* he started to think and worry about his future needs and collected food in order to prevent famine. Anthropologists have often reported that primitive people used to hoard food in holes made in the earth. Man abandons the most primitive state of savagery when he becomes a food gatherer. In the schizophrenic, however, the habit seems inappropriate, like a shallow or sham reproduction of the utilitarian activity of the habit of the primitive. The schizophrenic seems to hoard in order to possess; the objects he collects have no intrinsic value; they are valuable only inasmuch as they are possessed by the patient. The patient seems almost to have a desire to incorporate them, to make them part of his own person, and puts them in his mouth, nostrils, vagina, anus, and so on.

The hoarding habit of the regressed schizophrenic can be interpreted in accordance with Fairbairn's theories of object relations. To my knowledge this connection has not been made in the psychoanalytic literature. The regressed patient has lost so many object relations that he is now in the position of making the last effort to maintain some of these relations, no matter how concrete, inadequate, and inappropriate they are. The useless objects that the patient collects are very useful to him: they represent the last vestiges of his object relations; they replace the important relations he once had; they maintain some ties with the external world. By counterbalancing transmutability they permit the maintenance of some enduring inner objects. By collecting and controlling real objects, the patient sees some correspondence between external and internal objects, correspondence that is very defective in interpersonal objects. Kanner (1944) has described similar preoccupation with inanimate objects in children suffering from infantile autism.

The possibility has to be discussed as to whether the hoarding habit is an artifact, a result of prolonged hospitalization. I have mentioned that I have observed this habit also in homes for the normal aged, although to a much milder degree. Any incarceration and hospitalization may impoverish the human being of human contacts, of the things of the world in general, and may bring about symptoms of regression. However, I am convinced that the schizophrenic process has an important role to play in the institution of the hoarding habit. I have sometimes seen this habit in nonhospitalized patients kept home and also in some regressed schizophrenics, most of them belonging to the simple type, who had never been hospitalized or officially diagnosed as schizophrenics. The famous case of the Collier brothers may be interpreted in this way. Some patients whom I have seen in consultation, and who had not previously been recognized as suffering from schizophrenia, had filled their rooms with old newspapers and other discarded material.

Goffman (1961) stresses that the habit of collecting exists in all prisoners. According to him, in an environment that deprives the individual of almost everything, collecting enables one to retain a minimum of privacy. It becomes a secondary modality of adjustment in the "underlife of the institution."

Petrella (1968) has followed my original works (Arieti, 1945*a*, 1945*b*, 1955) and has added new dimensions to the understanding of the hoarding habit. He has studied the relation between the patients and the nurses and attendants who want to deprive the patients of their "valuable property." The relational cycle between patient and nurse may lead to frustration and further regression. Although Petrella too attributes to the psychosis itself the largest responsibility for this regressive habit, he stresses the following environmental factors, which push the patient toward this and other regressed forms of behavior: (1) real frustrations; (2) impossibility of finding and retaining private space; (3) the rule, more or less explicitly formulated, against keeping personal objects; (4) the rigid distribution of roles to staff, personnel, and patients.

Whatever interpretation one gives to this hoarding habit (libido at anal stage, primitive level of integration, institutional, cultural, or interpersonal influence, or a mixture of all these interpretations), the fact remains that this tendency is a manifestation of advanced schizophrenic regression, although not a pathognomonic one.

III

The Self-Decorating Habit

Another habit that recurs especially during this stage of regression is the self-decorating habit. As a rule it is observed in patients who are slightly less regressed than those presenting the hoarding habit, patients who are at what may be considered the beginning of the preterminal stage. Though in my experience this habit has been observed to be less common by far than the hoarding habit, it is generally better known because it meets the eye more easily. For reasons that I was unable to determine, but that make one think of complementary social factors, I observed this habit more frequently in black patients. The habit consists of the primitive use of small objects or stains for decoration of one's body. Pieces of paper and rags are cut into several bands, and bracelets, rings, necklaces, and belts are made with them. Many, predominantly female, patients paint their faces in a conspicuous, ridiculous manner. Many patients of both sexes adorn themselves by placing buttons, stamps, small boxes, corks, or coins on their chests.

The same objects that are hoarded by other, more regressed patients are sought by these patients and are valued only for decorative purposes. It is therefore possible, though by no means proved, that the self-decorating habit is also connected with the hoarding habit.

A normal person cannot see any decorative value in this practice, which appears not only inartistic but often disfiguring and ridiculous. Such is obviously not the impression of the patient. Although he seems apathetic to his environment, he is interested in decorating his body. When he is asked why he decorates himself in such a manner, he often denies any decorative purposes. A female patient said that she used paper bracelets "to cover her own arms." Another one replied that she used necklaces "to tie her neck." These practices, although not to be confused with other artistic activities of schizophrenics (see Chapter 20), retain some aesthetic value for the patients and represent primitive artistic tendencies. Anthropology teaches, in fact, that similar habits of self-decoration are probably expressions of primitive artistic tendencies. Bracelets, necklaces, and other small objects were commonly used by both sexes during the Paleolithic period. The practice of painting the body was also common among the cave dwellers (MacCurdy, 1926).

But what are the meaning and purpose of this practice? Desire to increase appeal, self-satisfaction in producing the artistic objects, or aesthetic admiration of oneself? In schizophrenics this habit seemingly does not have any practical or social purposes, but possibly it offers a certain kind of satisfaction through the making of the ornamental objects or through self-admiration. The fact that the patient denies the purpose of improving his appearance is not a proof that such aim does not exist.

By analogy, one might be tempted to interpret art as originating not for utilitarian purposes but exclusively for the pleasure of the artist. Some interesting observations reported by Boas (1927) would seem to corroborate this point of view. This well-known anthropologist noted that the rawhide boxes of the Sauk and Fox Indians were made of a piece of hide that was carefully and skillfully ornamented according to a definite plan. When the boxes were made, the hide was folded and the pattern, which had required so much work, was completely lost. This author gives other examples to illustrate that when materials originally made with patterns were used for practical purposes, the patterns were disregarded. He reaches the conclusion that the previous work seems to be done only for the satisfaction of the maker.

Although my observations would lead to similar interpretation, I think it would be hazardous to reach such a conclusion from my findings on schizophrenics. The fact that a habit has not obvious environmental value in schizophrenics does not prove at all that its equivalents at a phylogenetic or ontogenetic level had no social value. The schizophrenic process engenders a resurgence of primitive habits, which often appears to us a shallow or an exclusively formal reproduction of what happened in ontogenesis and phylogenesis. These habits seem worthless to us because they do not have the same utilitarian purpose that they had originally. It is an error on the part of the observer to look for the same purpose. However, these habits must indeed have a purpose. Even the schizophrenic, in spite of his withdrawal, has a need for activity. No matter how regressed he is, he needs some feeling of power, which is more or less gratified by actions and performances. He tends to act, therefore, and in the easiest possible way, in a manner that does not bring about anxiety. He tends to act in accordance with the mechanisms that correspond to the level or levels to which he has regressed. Moreover, the characteristics and restrictions of hospital life add to the peculiarity of these habits.

I am sure that other primitive habits of the preterminal period have escaped my attention. It is to be hoped that in the near future people in daily contact with regressed patients will publish their observations.

As far as the hoarding and the self-decorating habits are concerned, they will be examined again, and their interpretation will be continued, after the description of the terminal stage. It is important to add here, however, that like the asocial habits of the second, or advanced, stage, the primitive habits of the third, or preterminal, stage have not been markedly influenced by drug therapy. After an interval of twenty-two years (from 1946 to 1968) I visited the wards of Pilgrim State Hospital, where I had made my original observations and studies, and could reconfirm the very frequent occurrence of these habits.

CHAPTER

25

The Fourth, or Terminal, Stage

I

Primitive Oral Habits

We have now come to the fourth, or last, stage of schizophrenia during which a new set of phenomena occurs. Some of the symptoms appear no longer as predominantly psychological but neurological. It seems as if the disorder has reached a level where psychology and neurology coalesce. The indefinite quality of some of the symptoms leaves ample space for speculation and makes their study difficult.

How and when does this last stage start? It is well known that decreased activity is one of the most common characteristics of progressing schizophrenia, though not a constant one. This motor reduction often interferes with the dietary requirements of the patient to such a point as to bring about a state of malnutrition, anemia, and, occasionally, avitaminosis. This inactivity, which is a part of the schizophrenic withdrawal, is noted throughout the long years of progressing regression and is interrupted only by occasional and transitory partial remissions. In patients who continue to regress indefinitely, however, a more or less sudden increase in motor activity is noted at a certain point. As a rule such an increase is not transitory but lasts for the lifetime of the patient, or until a physical illness neutralizes its effects. It is when this partial increase of motor activity takes place that what I call the terminal stage begins.

In the patients whom I observed and whose clinical records I studied, the terminal stage started any time from seven to forty years after the onset of the illness, but it probably may start even sooner, or later. The increase in activity is only relative, because the patients somehow remain underactive in comparison with normal subjects. Their actions, which are now more numerous, appear sharply reactive or impulsive; they are reactive to certain habitual situations, which will be taken into consideration shortly, or impulsive, inasmuch as they appear to be due to sudden internal stimulation. The patients may be impulsively destructive, assaultive, and much more violent than previously. At this stage of the illness they do not seem able to experience hallucinations or to elaborate delusions. Verbal expressions are either completely absent or are reduced to a few disconnected utterances.

The most striking changes, however, are noted in the dining room. The patients who had always eaten so little as to have reduced themselves to a state of malnutrition now seem to have a voracious appetite (bulimia) and often gain a considerable amount of weight. The nurses often report that these patients have the habit of stealing food. In reality, closer observation reveals that the concept of stealing is not implied in the actions of these patients. They cannot prevent themselves from grabbing food at the sight of it, so that they are better termed *food grabbers*.

Observations in the dining room reveal other interesting habits. A few of these patients show preference for certain foods. No matter how many kinds of food are in the dish, they always grasp and eat the preferred food first. They do not alternate the various kinds, as normal adults do, but only when they have entirely finished the preferred food do they start to eat the others. Similarly, if they show several degrees of preference, they first eat the food that is the first choice; when this is finished, they eat the second choice, and so on. If there are desserts, these are generally eaten before anything else. It seems that the patients are obliged to react first to stronger stimuli. The preference for a certain food is not shown by all patients who are food grabbers. On the other hand, such preference is maintained only for a brief period after the acquisition of the food-grabbing habit. After this period the patients seem to eat with avidity any kind of food. *Whatever belongs in the category of edibility elicits equal and prompt reaction.* Another characteristic that is often observed is the extreme rapidity with which these patients eat (tachyphagia). In a few minutes these food grabbers may finish the rations of several patients if they are not prevented from doing so. Often they do not leave any remnants of food in the dish but clean the plate with the tongue.

The patients may remain indefinitely at this level, which is characterized by the food-grabbing habit, but the majority progress more or less rapidly to a more advanced level of regression characterized chiefly by what I have termed the habit of "placing into mouth." At this level the category of edibility is no longer respected. Whereas the patients had previously distinguished themselves by grabbing food and food only, now they manifest the habit of grabbing every small object and putting it into the mouth, paying no attention at all to the edible or nonedible nature of it. If they are not restrained, these patients pick up crumbs, cockroaches, stones, rags, paper, wood, clothes, pencils, and leaves from the floor and put them into the mouth. Generally they eat these things; occasionally they swallow them with great risk. Many patients, however, limit themselves to chewing these nonedible objects and finally rejecting them. When they eat or swallow dangerous materials, such as an inkwell or a teaspoon, they are erroneously considered suicidal. Closer observation reveals, however, that the idea of suicide is not implied in the action. They simply react to a visual stimulus by grasping the object and putting it into the mouth. They act as if they were coerced to react in this way. It is as though they were especially attracted by small, three-dimensional stimuli that seem to be distinguished from the background more distinctly than usual.

On the autopsy tables of state hospitals it is a relatively common experience to find spoons, stones, pieces of scrap iron, wood, paper, cores, and other objects in the stomachs or intestines of patients who died while they were in the fourth stage of schizophrenia.

As a typical example, the case of A. R. will be mentioned briefly. This patient entered Pilgrim State Hospital in October 1933 at the age of 32. On admission he had delusions and hallucinations but was fairly well preserved. The diagnosis of dementia praecox, paranoid type, was then made. Subsequently he showed a steady downhill progression in his mental condition. He became negativistic, mute, manneristic, and idle. He had the habit of wetting and soiling and required a great deal of supervision. On frequent occasions it was necessary to tube feed him. He did not show any interest in his surroundings, appearing completely withdrawn and living an almost vegetative existence. In the dining room, however, he showed great interest, grabbing food and eating in a ravenous manner. On December 31, 1939, he died of acute intestinal obstruction. At autopsy fourteen spoon handles were found in his colon and two spoon handles and a suspender clasp in his stomach. In the terminal ileum there was a rolled piece of shirt collar, which was the cause of the obstruction. The collection of foreign bodies in the stomach of this patient is very modest in comparison with that found in many other patients.

The grasping and ingestion of the objects may be accompanied by a quick movement, as a prompt reaction to a visual stimulus, or by a slow movement, apparently not accompanied by any emotional coloring. If the patients are under some mechanical restraint, they may try to reach the objects directly with their mouths.

It is also not rare to see some patients grasping their own feces, chewing them, and eating them, at times with great pleasure and satisfaction (coprophagia). These coprophagic patients may put everything indiscriminately into their mouths and incidentally their own feces, but this situation is rather exceptional. As a rule, they show a marked discrimination in putting into their mouths specifically their own feces. Other patients often smear themselves with their own excrement.

Are these habits only manifestations of purposeless behavior of demented patients or are they determined by deeper causes? I feel that the latter viewpoint is correct and that a genetic approach may help explain these habits.

In fact, it is possible to interpret them not as newly acquired habits but as behavior manifestations of lower levels of integration. The food-grabbing habit reminds one of what is generally observed in cats, dogs, monkeys, and other animals. The animal is coerced to react to the food at the sight of it. The food does not stand for itself but is what Werner (1957) calls a "thing of action." It is a "signal thing," the sight of which leads immediately to a fixed action (Werner, 1957). The animal cannot delay the reaction or channel the impulse into longer integrative circuits. Similarly, other habits previously described disclose the same syncretic characteristics encountered in more primitive organizations. It is well known that when monkeys, dogs, cats, and other animals are given different items of food at the same time, they eat first the preferred food (for instance, meat in the case of the dog, or banana in the case of monkeys), and only when the entire portion of the preferred food is finished do they start to eat the other foods. They cannot alternate the various kinds but are coerced first to react to the strongest stimulus. Similarly, a child between the age of 3½ and 4, if not prevented, eats first the preferred food, and only when he has finished it does he eat the others.

When the patients become even sicker, this integration of the stimuli is even more primitive, so that they react to edible and nonedible objects in the same way, by grasping them and putting them into the mouth. The category of edibility is no longer respected.

This habit of regressed psychotics has some points in common with what is generally observed in children approximately 6 months to 2 years old. When confronted by objects of a certain size, children of this age grasp these objects and attempt to put them into the mouth. There is no discrimination made between edible and nonedible objects; the baby places in his mouth anything that comes within his reach and licks, sucks, or eats it. "If the object is too heavy or cannot be grasped with the hand . . . the infant brings his mouth close to the object and licks or, in the case of clothing or bibs or blankets, sucks at it" (Kanner, 1942). Rugs, cotton, leaves, worms, wool, wood, stones, and paper are eaten or at least put into the mouth. "The objects eaten are the objects accessible; accessibility and not 'craving' or 'appetite' governs their selection" (Kanner, 1942).

All parents have observed this particular behavior when their children have reached this age and attribute it erroneously to various causes. Most of the time they attribute it to incipient teething or to increased appetite. Generally the people in charge of the child remove the object from the child's mouth with their own hands, fearing it may be swallowed. But the child, if let alone, will test the object and often reject it if it is not edible or if it has an unpleasant tast. Only relatively seldom is the object swallowed with serious consequences. It seems almost as if taste discrimination, or at least oral discrimination by means of the sensory properties of the oral cavity, supersedes the visual one. In pathological conditions this habit persists to age of 3 or even 4 and is erroneously called perverted appetite, or pica.

In a series of papers Klüver and Bucy (1937, 1938, 1939) described interesting observations on trained monkeys after the extirpation of both temporal lobes. The extirpation included Brodmann's areas 22, 21, 20, area 19 being left untouched. The removal of both lobes constantly caused typical manifestations, whereas the ablation of only one lobe or of an entire lobe and a part of the other did not bring about characteristic results.

The authors found that the monkeys, after this surgical treatment, showed an irresistible tendency to grasp anything within reach. They placed the grasped object in the mouth, bit it, touched it to the lips, and finally ate it if it was edible. If inedible, the object was rejected. All objects, edible or not, were grasped indiscriminately. Every one of the monkeys manifested this particular type of reaction, environmental changes having apparently no influence at all. It seemed as if all previous learning had no influence whatsoever on their behavior. As a matter of fact, the established reactions to visual and weight differences were superseded by the constant grasping and placing-into-mouth reaction (called by the authors "oral tendencies"). In addition, it seemed to the observers as if the animal were "acting under the influence of some compulsory or irresistible impulse. The monkey behaves as if forced to react to objects . . . in the environmental stimulus constellation." It seemed to be dominated by only one tendency, namely, the tendency to contact every object as quickly as possible, any visual object immediately leading, whenever possible, to a motor response.

A different kind of forced ingestion of inedible objects is reported in another field of investigation. Members of primitive tribes are in the habit of eating some inedible substances (geophagy). They are almost forced to eat these objects, because they cannot avoid eating them when they see them. This habit is highly discriminatory for a certain substance in a given tribe but retains almost a compulsory characteristic.

The above-mentioned examples, taken from different fields of investigation, have some features in common, namely, the picking up of objects from the immediate environment and the placing of them in the oral cavity, with no discrimination as to their nature and no consideration of the fact that they are not edible. These actions, in all the cited instances, have a more or less compulsory characteristic.

It could be objected that such similarities are only apparent or very superficial, and that we ourselves disclose paleologic thinking in connecting these various instances. Somebody else could emphasize the differences in the situations taken as examples. For instance, the geophagic habit found in some tribes may be part of a ritual and may be exclusively cultural in origin. On the other hand, in all the other cases that we have mentioned, the differences may be due to various factors acting contemporaneously with the common factor, which may be an expression of a certain level of development. The differences could be explained without difficulty. The precise movements of the monkey contrast with those of the child, because the monkey has acquired voluntary movements very well, whereas the child, whose nervous system is not yet completely myelinized, has not.

Unlike the child, the bitemporal monkey of Klüver and Bucy can indefatigably continue to grasp every object, to react repetitiously in this way to every visual stimulus. This reaction is probably due to the fact that the damage or the lack of cerebral areas causes the animal's hyperactivity or the state of "being forced by the stimulus," similar to that which is observed in human cases with extensive cerebral defects (Goldstein, 1939). The fact that regressed schizophrenics presenting the described behavior grasp objects not in such number and not with such rapidity as the Klüver and Bucy monkey, or not at every opportunity, as the child, may be explained if we take into consideration the other aspects of the schizophrenic picture. The withdrawal and the emotional impairment of the schizophrenic may be responsible for such difference.

Klüver and Bucy give an interesting preliminary interpretation of some behavior characteristics of their bitemporal monkeys, in considering the latter as "psychically blind," or suffering from visual agnosia. Because in their tendency to approach their mouths and place all objects in them "without hesitation" the animals show no discrimination, no preference for food or for learned reactions, and no ability to concentrate on particular objects, the authors consider these monkeys to be psychically blind. If I have understood correctly, these authors come to the "psychic blindness" conclusion in view of the fact that the animal, after the removal of both temporal lobes, grasps and uses each object indiscriminately, even though it had learned before the operation to distinguish the objects and use them discriminately. But is that behavior really due to "psychic blindness" or to that "compulsory or irresistible impulse" that forces the monkey, as well as the child, and at times the regressed schizophrenic, to grasp any object within reach? It could be, in fact, that the need to respond immediately does not permit any cognitive elaboration of the stimulus, beyond the most primitive sensoperceptual experience.

We must direct our attention to the fact that the ability to appreciate differences in lightness, size, shape, distance, position, and movement is not reported to be impaired in these monkeys. Therefore, we can reach the conclusion that the only bodies that are not "recognized" are the bodies with a definite, sharp, three-dimensional shape. Although the forced placing-into-mouth reaction of these monkeys is not explained by assuming the presence of visual agnosia, it cannot be disproved that the monkeys are really in a certain way psychically blind. As a matter of fact, in a certain sense even the child of one or two years of age may be considered partially psychically blind. The visual stimuli often do not lead the child to recognize the objects; his visual perceptions are still partially agnostic. By means of the mouth, more than by his eyes, the 1-year-old child explores what is still unknown to him. Werner (1957) states: "The mouth is the primitive means of knowing objects, that is, in a literal sense, through the grasping of the objects. The spatial knowledge of an object results from a sucking in on the thing through the mouth and a consequent tactual discovery and incorporation." However, the child apparently grasps the objects and puts them into his mouth not in order to know them, but under a certain kind of primitive impulse. It happens that in doing so he starts to know the objects, and this behavior has beneficial results for him.

The demented schizophrenic in the terminal stage of regression may also be considered, in a certain way, partially psychically blind because the visual stimuli of the objects do not elicit cognitive and affective associations concerning their inedibility and the relative danger of putting them into his mouth and eating them. However, one must consider the theoretical possibility that the patient is conscious that these objects are inedible, but that he cannot inhibit the impulse to grasp them. Such a possibility cannot be ruled out. We may, however, advance the hypothesis that this behavior of children, bitemporal monkeys, and regressed schizophrenics is a primitive way of reacting, which is characteristic of a certain level of development and is inhibited or transformed by higher centers. In other words, we may be dealing with one of those responses in which a short-circuiting takes place between the functions of reception and those of reaction instead of the usual response with participation of the higher centers. These reactions are intermediate between reflexes and voluntary acts, having some characteristics of compulsory acts. The placing-into-mouth reaction seems to belong to a much lower level than the archaic mechanisms described in other chapters, but it seems to be at a higher level than, for instance, the grasp reflex. The grasp reflex is found in infants from 1 to 3 months of age and in adults with lesions of the frontal lobes, although this reflex does not always appear as a true reflex but frequently as a prehension attitude implying some voluntary action. Schilder (1931), however, considers the taking of objects into the mouth ''at least as primitive as grasping.'' This placing-into-mouth reaction is apparently not caused by any agnosia but seems to belong coincidentally to a level at which high apperceptions elaborating visual stimuli are not yet possible. This primitive reaction may have its early origins even in low vertebrates. It may have some connection with the feeding response of amphibians, reptiles, and birds, animals in which the temporal lobe is represented only by the hippocampal area. Although its main purpose in phylogenesis is to contact food, it certainly is also a means of recognizing objects, especially in those animals whose visual centers have not reached a high degree of development.

Taking into consideration the coprophagic habit, the fact is worthy of mention that such behavior is usual in healthy apes. In 1940, while working in the Laboratory of Primate Biology of Yale University, directed by Robert Yerkes, I had the opportunity to observe the frequency of such a habit in the chimpanzees kept in captivity. Yerkes (1943) reported that the causes, controls, and prevention of coprophagy among captive chimpanzees have been searched carefully but with discouraging results. He felt that the hypothesis that coprophagy is induced by dietary deficiency finds no support in the inquiries conducted in his laboratories and concludes that this behavior is determined by complex underlying factors.

Köhler (1925) had previously described such peculiar behavior of primates. He reported that out of the many chimpanzees studied by him only one did not indulge in coprophagy. He states that the habit of smearing the excrement is also frequent among chimpanzees. Such habits have not been observed in healthy monkeys. In mental patients this behavior is observed especially among catatonics and hebephrenics. Although it is a sign of advanced regression, it is not as malignant as the ''oral tendency'' described here, and probably belongs to a less primitive level. As a matter of fact, catatonics who have eaten feces or smeared themselves occasionally gain a temporary remission (Chrzanowski, 1943) or even an apparently complete recovery (personal observations).

II
Perceptual Alterations

The patients may remain indefinitely at a level characterized chiefly by the oral habits described above or may progress to a more advanced phase that is characterized by apparent sensory alterations.

Because of the lack of cooperation and communicability of these patients, such alterations cannot be studied with the usual neurological technique, but much stronger stimuli, not ordinarily used, or observation of the patient's reaction in certain special situations must be resorted to. Therefore only gross alterations are reported here, and no claim to accuracy is made (Arieti, 1944*a,* 1945*a,* 1955).

It seems as though the patients who have reached the terminal stage are insensitive to pain. They appear analgesic not only to pinprick but to much more painful stimuli. When they are in need of surgical intervention and require sutures in such sensitive regions as the lips, face, skull, or hands, they act as though they cannot feel anything, even in the absence of any anesthetic procedure. Many times when I was working in Pilgrim State Hospital, I sutured wounds caused by violent and assaultive behavior without eliciting any sign of pain or resistance. Some patients seem to feel some pain, but far less than normal persons would. Only exceptionally is there a local withdrawal. The same anesthesia is noted for temperature. The patient may hold a piece of ice in his hands without showing any reaction. Pieces of ice may also be placed over the breast, abdomen, or other sensitive regions without eliciting any reaction or defensive movement. Such patients also appear insensitive when the flame of a candle is passed rapidly over the skin. They may sit near the radiator, and, if they are not moved, they may continue to stay there even when, as a result of close contact, they are burned. This state of insensitivity is, in my opinion, one of the chief causes of the large number of burns occurring in wards for regressed schizophrenics.

One may be induced to interpret this lack of responsiveness to pain and temperature stimuli, not as true anesthesia, but as an expression either of catatonic inactivity or of a certain kind of "inner negativism." Repeated observations, however, have led me to the conclusion that such an interpretation is not valid. Patients who show anesthesia for pain or temperature stimuli are not, as a rule, inactive; on the contrary, they show the aforementioned relative increase in activity that, together with the apparent anesthesia, is responsible for numerous accidents. The possibility that these patients do not react to dangerous sensations on account of inner negativism in my opinion is also untenable because many such patients do not show other signs of negativism. The phenomenon of negativism, although not absent at this stage of the illness, is much more commonly observed in patients who are at a less advanced stage of regression. On the other hand, the possibility that pain and temperature sensations are perceived, with only the affective components of such perceptions being lost, must be taken into consideration and will be discussed later. In a small number of patients this apparent anesthesia or hypesthesia for pain and temperature stimuli is only transitory. Even patients who have been insensitive to heat for several months to some extent may reacquire capacity to perceive pain or temperature sensations or both. Occasionally, striking changes occur at brief intervals. However, I have the impression that some degree of hypesthesia is always retained. Partial hypesthesia is also found in many patients who have not yet reached the terminal stage. Tactile perception does not seem impaired in these patients. Tendon and superficial reflexes are not only present but often increased. The corneal reflexes are also present. On the other hand, many, but not all, of the patients who present anesthesia for pain and temperature stimuli seem also to have lost the sensation of taste. When they are given bitter radishes or teaspoons of sugar, salt, pepper, or quinine, they do not show any pleasant or unpleasant reaction. They do not spit out the unpleasant substances as quickly as possible, as do control mentally defective persons or deteriorated patients with organic disease; instead they continue to eat the entire dose without hesitation. Some of them seem to recognize salt but do not object to pepper or quinine. Others react mildly to quinine but not to pepper or salt.

In contrast to this lack of reactivity to pain, temperature, and taste stimuli is the normal reaction to strong olfactory stimuli. Patients who do not react at all to such stimuli as flames, pieces of ice, and suturing, react in a normal way when they smell such things as ammonia and strong vinegar. They withdraw quickly from the stimulus with manifest displeasure. Such a reaction strikes the observer, inasmuch as many other strong stimuli from other sensory fields do not bring about any response or bring about only a mild reaction. It seems as though the phylogenetically ancient olfactory sense can better resist the schizophrenic process. However, the schizophrenic patient does not seem to make use of these olfactory sensations as well as he can, probably on account of his general withdrawal.

The aforementioned phases of the terminal stage (phases characterized by the food-grabbing habit, the placing-into-mouth habit, apparent anesthesia for pain, temperature, and taste sensation, and preponderance of the olfactory sense, respectively) do not always occur in the order given. A number of patients, especially but not exclusively those of the paranoid type, remain indefinitely at a less advanced phase. In others two stages of the illness overlap. For instance, a few patients who have the food-grabbing habit may retain the capacity to hallucinate. Other food grabbers may already have anesthesia for pain and temperature stimuli, and so on. However, the order described is the one in which I have most commonly observed appearance of the symptoms. Occasionally a patient may improve and return to a less advanced phase or stage. Intravenous injections of sodium amytal do not produce any perceptible change in the picture of the terminal stage of schizophrenia.

Although statistical conclusions are difficult on account of this overlapping of symptoms, I have the impression that the number of patients presenting the habit of grabbing food or placing objects in the mouth is large in services for patients in the terminal stage. The number of patients presenting some hypesthesia for pain, temperature, and taste sensations is also large. On the contrary, patients presenting total anesthesia for pain and temperature sensations are relatively few.

Several authors have reported altered perception of pain in cases of early catatonia, and Bender and Schilder (1930) have discussed this subject in relation to the capacity to acquire conditioned reflexes. In my experience, the hypesthesia found in patients with early catatonia is generally not so severe as that observed in patients who have reached the terminal stage and often is not detected if, instead of pinprick, one uses stronger stimuli. Anesthesia for temperature and taste stimuli is even more rare in patients with early catatonia and is not comparable to that encountered in very regressed patients originally diagnosed as suffering from the various types of schizophrenia. However, the possibility is not denied that the nature of the phenomenon may be the same. In many of the textbooks of psychiatry no mention is made of this analgesia encountered in some deteriorated schizophrenics. Bleuler (1950), however, reported that an analgesia, sometimes quite complete, occurs in schizophrenia not too rarely. He stated that this anesthesia is responsible for the fact that the patients readily injure themselves.

In agreement with the observations of Bender and Schilder on patients with early catatonia, I am inclined to believe that the real sensation of pain and temperature is not lost in patients in the terminal stage. The fact that the corneal reflexes are always retained may be a proof of it. However, these patients seem to be unaware of the pain and temperature stimuli and do not show any emotional reaction to them. They seem to be unable to perceive the stimuli. In other words, the rough sensation may be present but remains isolated and is not elaborated to the perception and apperception levels. The patients are unable to recognize the emotional and cognitive value of the pain and temperature stimuli and therefore are unaware of the possible dangers that they at times imply. For this reason they often hurt themselves. These patients, for all practical purposes, have agnosia and may be compared to persons with sensorial aphasia who hear spoken language without understanding it.

Is this loss of nociceptive perception only an exaggeration of the general schizophrenic emotional indifference? Probably the basic mechanisms responsible for these derangements are related, but for all practical purposes these terminal patients are better described as having agnosia and may be termed "psychically analgesic" and not apathetic only. They fail to perceive pain and temperature sensation, not only from an emotional but from a cognitive point of view. That is the reason that they so often hurt themselves if they are not under constant supervision. At present it is a controversial problem whether these phenomena are due to loss of emotional capacity or to loss of perception of pain and temperature sensation.*

The fact that taste perception is often lost or impaired in these analgesic patients and that the olfactory perceptions are preserved instead is also important to

* The relation between emotional indifference and agnosia has been taken into consideration by Von Monakow and Mourgue (1914, 1928), who observed impairment of emotions in aphasic persons. The same authors considered the possibility that asymbolia may be due to disturbances in the affective sphere.

The findings by Penfield and Rasmussen (1952) prove that pain and temperature sensations are retained even when the cortical areas that supersede these sensations are completely removed. These findings make interpreting the pain and temperature anesthesia of the schizophrenic even more difficult.

consider. The association of taste and pain asymbolias points to the conclusion that taste should be included among the general somatic sensations, as investigations by Boernstein (1940*a, b*) and by Shenkin and Lewey (1944) seem to prove. The striking survival of smell perceptions, which are phylogenetically very old, may induce one to think that the archipallium is less affected than the neopallium by the schizophrenic process. The olfactory sense, which is the dominant sense in lower vertebrates, in some regressed schizophrenic patients seems to reacquire a position of predominance among the senses, not because of increased acuity, but because of impairment of perceptions of stimuli coming from other sensory fields. However, contrary to what is found in lower vertebrates, these schizophrenic patients do not take as much advantage of the olfactory sense as they could. It is interesting to observe that the sense of smell in schizophrenic patients is not involved even in short-circuiting reactions, whereas it was involved in the monkeys of Klüver and Bucy.

CHAPTER

26

Recapitulation and Interpretation of Schizophrenic Regression

In the previous chapters of Part Four we have seen the long and multiform course of schizophrenia, from the initial to the terminal stage. We shall try now to recapitulate what we have reported in detail and to interpret the factors that in many cases make this regression unavoidable.

We have seen how an uncoped-with state of anxiety and vulnerability, whose roots are to be found in early childhood, makes the patient enter the first stage of the disorder. In the first stage archaic mechanisms that are dormant in every human being become again available to him. The patient resorts to them when any other method of decreasing the anxiety that injures the inner self and of maintaining his own individuality has failed. In the first stage the patient is still struggling between the world of reality and the world of his symptoms. He is not *completely* regressed to any particular level and is still experiencing anxiety.

In the second stage, this fight between reality and illness is over. There is no apparent emotional turmoil. One feels that the patient has more completely regressed to a lower level. Paleologic thinking and desocialization prevail. The patient seems to have accepted his illness; but the illness does not seem to have accepted the patient at this stage and seems to require further regression. How is this to be explained?

Throughout this book it has been maintained that when the dynamic factors compel the patient to develop schizophrenic symptoms, there is a regression. We have to remind the reader of what was discussed in Chapter 15. The regression is purely functional in the sense that discarded mechanisms become available again. However, the patient, even in a purely functional way, cannot *integrate* at lower levels. Biologically, psychologically, and socially he is not fit to integrate at a level that is not originally his own. What he will undergo is a *regression,* but not an *integration* at a lower level. Perhaps an example from biology will clarify this issue. Lower animals, who do not have a cerebral cortex, are integrated at a noncortical level of development. For their kind of life, they do not require a cerebral cortex. But a higher animal without a cerebral cortex does not function like a healthy animal of noncortical species. He is in a pathological condition, because his whole organism, each part of it, was integrated at a level that required the cerebral cortex.

No matter how much the schizophrenic regresses, he cannot become a healthy infant, he cannot become a presapiens man, he cannot become a chimpanzee. Children, ancient men, and apes are totally integrated at their respective levels; the schizophrenic is not. He will not even be able to exploit the reduced potentialities of the levels to which he regresses. For instance, we have seen that when in the terminal stage many sensory perceptions are impaired, the patient cannot exploit the ancient olfactory sense as much as he potentially should be able to, because his total organism, like the organism of every man, is not organized for the prominence of this sense. In other instances, it is true that he will repeat compulsively actions and habits of the levels to which he regresses, such as the hoarding habit, or placing-into-mouth habit, and so forth. These habits, however, have lost their original purposeful meaning and are not integrated with the rest of the life of the patient. No matter how much the patient regresses, he will always be disintegrated. This process of disintegration is enhanced by another phenomenon that, as we have seen, occurs repeatedly. This phenomenon consists of the fact that when a higher level is out of function or does not function properly, several lower levels are disinhibited at the same time and interfere with one another. The schizophrenic patient is thus obliged to operate at several levels at the same time. This adds to the confusion, and increases the disequilibrium and the disintegration. But disintegration is not a state that nature accepts. Then how does the patient defend himself from it? With further regression. The same mechanism is repeated all over again. Regression engenders further regression.

The patient has reached the third stage when his voluntary life is much impoverished and certain primitive habits acquire prominence. The prominence of these primitive habits reveals a marked reorganization of the psyche in its relation to external and internal objects. External objects do not exist any longer in themselves, as objects of contemplation, and the concepts that constitute their corresponding inner objects are gradually being destroyed by the prevailing of primitive cognition.

The hoarding habit has, among others, the important purpose of counterbalancing transmutability and of retaining some inner objects in an evanescing world. When the patient regresses further, he shows a tendency not only to collect these objects, but also to make them become part of himself by putting them in the natural cavities of his body (vagina, mouth, anus, auditory canals, and so on).

When he regresses further and reaches the terminal stage, he does not grasp the objects any longer for the purpose of collecting them but in order to ingest them. He places them indiscriminately in his mouth, no matter whether they are edible or not.

Examining these phenomena in a longitudinal section, one is induced to believe that one habit is just a continuation or transformation of the other; first, the objects are collected, then an attempt is made to incorporate part of them, finally they are totally incorporated by ingestion. We have here a bizarre reproduction in reverse of phenomena that occurred in phylogenesis. Object relation becomes more and more primitive. Symbolic processes are bypassed, and the residual and habitual relations with the world assume the structure of primitive stimulus-response mechanisms. Low species grasp or pick up only what they eat or use right away. The newborn baby is concerned with activities that involve his mouth; only much later will he become interested, not in ingesting objects, but in collecting them.

At the terminal stage of the illness many patients also show those quasi-neurological alterations that we have described in the previous chapter. These alterations indicate a regression to a level where even many of our common perceptions do not exist. At this level the organism is able to experience some sensations only when they are deprived of perceptual elaborations.

From the preterminal to the terminal stages there is a progressive decrease of the processes involving apperceptions and perceptions. The actions of the patient are responses that are less and less meditated, and more and more primitive, almost like reflexes. Finally it seems as if some of the sensory stimuli are not even perceived or recognized, although they are experienced as sensations. Are these perceptual alterations a further step of teleologic regression, the final unique outcome of a progressive self-perpetuating regression? It would seem so. The patient seems compelled to escape from perceptions, and he functions like a person suffering from psychic agnosia.

What is the relation between the reported observations on regressed schizophrenics and the libido theory promulgated by Freud? The oral tendencies seem to be manifestations of what Freud calls the oral stage, and the hoarding tendencies seem to be manifestations of what Freud calls the anal stage. I do not think it necessary to interpret schizophrenic regression in accordance with the libido theory. The phenomena observed in the schizophrenics are not due to an arrest of sexual energy but to a functional return to lower levels of integration. The crucial points are the availability and refunctioning of different hierarchical levels.

The oral tendencies of the newborn infant are biologically determined. As Thompson (1950) puts it, the newborn infant is chiefly a mouth. At birth the most mature part of the cortex is that which presided over the functions of the oral cavity. Erotic pleasure, if it exists at all, is incidental. The pleasure that the baby and the regressed schizophrenic attain with their oral tendencies derives from the relatively few functions that they are capable of at their level of integration.

The desire to collect without incorporating the objects requires a much more differentiated neurological apparatus. It requires, among other things, the ability to anticipate the future. The perceptual alterations described in the previous chapter are also difficult to explain with the libido theory.

In summary it seems to me that all these manifestations, among which are those that are called anal and oral, are symptomatic not of an arrested sexuality but of lower levels of functional integration that have lower psychological and, at times, neurological organizations. At each of these levels, when they appeared originally in phylogenesis, a mature sexual development could be reached; but when regression occurs, sexuality cannot integrate well to lower levels, for the reasons mentioned in this chapter.

At this point we must conclude that if the first part of this book has helped the reader to consider schizophrenia as a syndrome, the second part as a psychodynamic process, and the third part as the adoption of a special psychological structure, this fourth part has illustrated another dimension, which can be observed only when the disorder is not cured or arrested: namely, regression, viewed as a movement toward less and less differentiated mechanisms and forms. Schizophrenia appears again as an entity and a process.

PART FIVE

The Somatic and Psychosomatic Aspects of Schizophrenia

CHAPTER

27

Heredity and Constitution in Schizophrenia

I

Introductory Remarks

The organic studies of schizophrenia outnumber by far the psychological ones. The quantity of these works and the variety of directions that they have taken reveal that no breakthrough has been made. Even in fields like genetics and biochemistry where some evidence of the organic nature of schizophrenia has been collected, the results are unclear and controversial. Some approaches popular in the 1920s and 1930s have been totally abandoned and would seem absurd today, for example, the studies that investigated the supposed tubercular origin of schizophrenia or an etiologic connection with rheumatic fever. The constitutional, cardiovascular, endocrinological, and neuropathological researches have lost ground. On the other hand, the genetic, biochemical, and neurophysiological approaches have gained support.

I have not engaged in research designed to find organic changes in the somata of schizophrenics. Nor can I review even a large part of published works on the subject; there are simply too many of them. Only those works will be mentioned that retain a promising outlook or that had an important historical role at a certain period, since schizophrenia was recognized as a psychiatric syndrome. For a greater coverage of the somatic studies done on schizophrenia in the last fifty years the reader is referred to other works (Lewis, 1936; Bellak, 1948, 1957; Bellak and Loeb, 1969; Siva Sankar, 1969; Weil-Malherbe and Szara, 1971; Cancro, 1971, 1972; Kaplan, 1972).

Many findings reported by numerous authors do not necessarily indicate a direct etiological connection with the disorder. They may represent a greater variability of the schizophrenic in his physiological functions, relative to the general population.

It could also be that rather than the organic origin of schizophrenia, some of the reported changes indicate the psychosomatic aspect of the disorder. In fact, the psychological changes occurring in the psychosis so disrupt the usual habits of life and have such repercussion on the individual that they can presumably produce alterations of the somatic functions. These altered somatic functions in their turn may lead to organic pathology in certain cases. In other words, psychosomatic effects might be formed not only in milder psychiatric conditions but in psychoses too. In addition, some somatic changes may be compensatory mechanisms or reactions to previous changes. A chain of altered functions leading to clear-cut anatomical pathology may be engendered. Some of my studies concerning functional changes involving the nervous system have already been mentioned (Chapters 23, 24, 25). The role of the central nervous system will be further studied in Chapter 30. This chapter will be devoted to genetic studies.

Heredity has been studied in reference to schizophrenia since the early period of classic psychiatry. Genetic research is of two major kinds. The first consists of collecting statistical data from family studies and from surveys of total populations to determine whether the morbidity risk is higher than expected in certain families or other groups. By definition the disease expectancy of a person is "the risk of becoming ill during one's lifetime, if one lives long enough to pass the period of risk" (Stromgren, 1950). The period of risk must be considered that part of life during which the disease may develop. According to Kallmann (1959) the expectancy of the schizophrenic disorder in the general population is 0.9 percent. The specific genetic studies of schizophrenia aim at determining whether the incidence increases (or, theoretically, decreases) in certain families or other groups.

A second set of studies consists of investigating in schizophrenics special physical characteristics (typically, the chromosomes) that are connected with genetic characteristics.

II

Statistical Studies

Statistical studies have generally consisted not only of collecting data, but also of determining whether these data could be interpreted in accordance with Mendel's laws (and their derivatives). On Kraepelin's request, Rüdin was probably the first author to make significant attempts to prove the assumption that schizophrenia was determined by genetic Mendelian traits. Although he continued to believe in the genetic origin of schizophrenia, he had to abandon the idea that the disorder was transmitted by a single Mendelian trait. Later (1916) he advanced the theory that the disorder was caused by recessive genes.

Kallmann (1938, 1953) conducted two of the most important investigations into the genetics of schizophrenia; the first on the relatives of over 1,000 patients of a Berlin psychiatric hospital, the second on 953 twins from psychiatric hospitals of New York State. Although Rosanoff and co-authors (1911, 1931, 1934) had already studied the incidence of schizophrenia in twins, Kallmann's work was the one that inspired a large amount of similar research. Kallmann (1959) called the twin-study method a "quasi-experimental procedure." It permits the study of two genetically different types of twins—one-egg (monozygotic) twins and two-egg (dizygotic) twins. Monozygotic twins, who of course are always of the same sex, are supposed to have the same genetic sets. Kallmann concluded that single-factor inheritance of recessive type is the genetic cause of schizophrenia. However, the single recessive factor is modified by the action of other genes. Kallmann found that the full siblings of patients have a higher expectancy (11.5–14.3 percent) for the disorder than half siblings (7.1 percent), and half siblings have a much higher expectancy than step-siblings (1.8 percent). He found the highest incidence of schizophrenia in the children of two schizophrenic parents and in monozygotic twins.

Kallmann's work was criticized by Bellak (1948) on the grounds that he excluded from his studies "the schizoform psychoses," which lack hereditary traits, thus obtaining different statistical results; by Pastore (1949) on the grounds of his statistical analysis technique; and by Koller (1957) on the grounds that if simple recessivity is the hereditary basis of schizophrenia, the incidence should be higher among the sibs than the children of schizophrenics, whereas Kallmann's figures indicate the opposite.

Böök (1960), reviewing the work of many authors, as well as his own work, reports that the incidence of schizophrenia is higher in the family of schizophrenics than it is in the general population: in parents, approximately 12 percent; in siblings, 9–12 percent; in grandchildren, 3 percent; in first cousins, nephews, and nieces, 2 percent.

Slater (1951) found a concordance rate of schizophrenia to be 14 percent in dizygotic twins and 76 percent in monozygotic twins. In a recent presentation Slater (1968) reaffirmed his conviction that genetic factors play an important role in schizophrenia. According to him the increased incidence of the disorder in certain families is consistent with a genetic hypothesis.

Other authors have reported different findings. In the case of identical (monozygotic) twins studied in Finland, Tienari (1968) found a concordance rate of schizophrenia inferior to that found by other authors: 6 percent of all the cases are taken into account; 10 percent if only the diagnoses made in hospitals are taken into consideration. Kringlen (1967, 1968, 1970) found the concordance rate of schizophrenia to be 25–38 percent in monozygotics and 4–10 percent in dizygotics.

Pollin and co-authors (1969) studied a series of 15,909 pairs of veteran twins. In this large series the concordance rate of schizophrenia for monozygotic twins was found to be 3.3 times greater than the dizygotic rate. In contrast the difference for psychoneurosis was only 1.3. These results suggested—according to the authors—the presence of a genetic factor in the pathogenesis of schizophrenia and its relative absence in psychoneurosis. However, the role of the suggested genetic factor appeared to be a limited one: 85 percent of the affected monozygotic pairs in the sample were discordant for schizophrenia.

III

Studies of Specific Families

These studies have been very interesting and accurate but unfortunately inconclusive. Rosenthal (1963) reported on a set of quadruplets. All the members of the set were found to be schizophrenic, but their disorder presented various degrees of severity and different symptomatology. Swanson, Brown, and Beuret (1969) reported a family with nonschizophrenic parents and four schizophrenic children, possibly five if we include the controversial diagnosis of another child, an alcoholic. The authors feel that the occurrence of schizophrenia in at least four out of six children suggests a heterozygous or dominant transmission; but contradicting this hypothesis is the fact that neither parent was afflicted. One would have to assume that "reduced penetrance of the dominant factor could exist in one or both parents." The authors prefer to attribute the most important role to psychological environmental factors.

Scott and Ashworth (1969) have reported their studies of schizophrenics coming from families where schizophrenia had already appeared, but they give a psychodynamic interpretation to their findings rather than a predominantly genetic one. They explain a new way "in which schizophrenia may be visited upon the third and fourth generation." The authors feel that "if the parent of a schizophrenic had an experience in earlier life of psychotic illness in a close relative, this psychotic ancestor may act as a powerful aetiological factor, operating primarily through intrafamilial expectations and relationships." The authors found several cases in which a parent experienced the patient as he experienced once his mentally ill relative. In some cases the parent literally saw the patient as the "same as" the mentally ill relative and destined for the same fate. The image of the ill relative had been present as a secret fear; the parents were looking for a duplication of such image both in themselves and in their children. The parents, however, deny such fear, and this denial produces a state of depersonalization and unrelatedness that increases the psychopathogenic effect of the family on the prospective patient.

IV

Chromosomal and Other Physical Data

Barr and Bertram's (1949) accidental discovery of "chromatin satellite bodies" in the neurons of males and females was a breakthrough for many genetic studies concerning chromosomes. In 1956 new techniques (Tjio and Levan) permitted the visualization of forty-six chromosomes in men. Since then much research on chromosomes of schizophrenic patients has been carried out. Money and Hirsch (1963) studied 1,700 mentally defective patients. Among them they found two males who were the XXXY configuration with forty-eight chromosomes, and three females who were XXX with forty-seven chromosomes. Two of these five patients (one male and one female) were schizophrenic and had schizophrenic relatives. Raphael and Shaw (1963) studied cytogenetically 210 patients who were schizophrenic but not mentally defective. In this group they found one XXY male with forty-seven chromosomes and one XXX female with forty-seven chromosomes. They concluded that specific abnormalities of sex chromosomes are more frequent among schizophrenics than in the general population. They could not exclude, however, a chance association.

Kaplan and Cotton (1968) found an unusual incidence (more than 0.5 percent) of mosaicism involving X-chromosome aneuploidy in 986 female patients diagnosed as schizophrenics and institutionalized in Ohio State Hospital.

In an unpublished work quoted by Norman Brill (1969), Judd and Brandkamp (1969) failed to find "any significant or constant chromosomal abnormalities" in a series of forty adult schizophrenics, half of whom had family history of schizophrenia. As a result of their study of sixteen patients suffering from childhood schizophrenia, as well as of similar studies by other authors in both adults and children, Siva Sankar and Saladino (1969) concluded that no chromosome anomalies can be correlated with schizophrenia with any statistical significance. Sankar and Saladino pointed out that the situation in childhood schizophrenia is quite different from that of Turner's, Klinefelter's, and Down's (or mongolism) syndromes, where chromosomal anomalies were found. The authors postulate that "a molecular lesion at the ultrastructural level of the chromosome" may be responsible for the disorder.

Kallmann (1959) visualized various studies of discordant monozygotic twins (one schizophrenic and the other nonschizophrenic) to determine the factors responsible for the discordance. These studies are being carried out now by many authors. A multidisciplinary study of discordant monozygotic twins is being conducted at the Clinical Center, National Institute of Mental Health (NIMH), Bethesda, Maryland. Investigation includes psychiatric, psychological, physiological, and biochemical variables studied in each of the monozygotic twins. In one of such studies, Stabenau and others (1969) found that the lactate-pyruvate ratio and particularly the lactate production were higher for the schizophrenic than the nonschizophrenic twins. The authors thought that their findings permit distinguishing between schizophrenic and nonschizophrenic populations. They felt, however, that it was not clear as to whether the biochemical distinction derived from the presence of schizophrenia, from some metabolic process directly related to the schizophrenic process, or was influenced by circumstantial factors, such as medication, hospitalization, or diet.

V
Review of Additional Studies and Interpretations

Altshuler (1957) summarized the findings of various observers up to 1957 and came up with the following expectancy rates of schizophrenia: general population, 0.85 percent; half siblings, 7–8 percent; full siblings, 5–15 percent; parents, 5–10 percent; children of one schizophrenic parent, 8–16 percent; children of two schizophrenic parents, 53–68 percent. Taking into consideration specifically twin studies, Altshuler (1957) reported the following expectancy rate: concordance in dizygotic twins, 3.3–16.7 percent; concordance in monozygotic twins, 66.6–86.2 percent. These statistics confirm the impression held even by laymen for centuries that psychoses run more frequently in certain families.

I feel that additional conclusions can be drawn:

1. No Mendelian trait for the transmission of schizophrenia has been found.
2. The available data do not permit explanation of the incidence of schizophrenia solely on the basis of some Mendelian laws.
3. The findings obtained in the genetic studies of well-known hereditary diseases, such as hemophilia, muscular dystrophy, Huntington's chorea, and others, could not be repeated for schizophrenia.

We must, of course, keep in mind that in the statistical studies of schizophrenia we encounter special difficulties that do not exist in studying the hereditary diseases that we have mentioned. Schizophrenia is not so clearly definable or diagnosticable as, let us say, hemophilia or Huntington's chorea. The less typical cases can be confused with other personality disorders. Moreover, the various methods or facility of hospitalization and the various degrees of environmental toleration or ambulatory treatment make statistics less reliable. Even after making allowances for all these possibilities of error, which various authors have tried to correct in various ways, it seems obvious that schizophrenia cannot be explained with the traditional Mendelian laws. To find a possible explanation, some authors have advanced the idea that the hereditary genes can be altered by different degrees of "penetrance" or "expressivity." Other authors, for instance, Kallmann (1959), believe that genes, other than the one that carries the disease, may modify that gene and confer a greater or lesser degree of resistance upon the individual. Other authors believe that a set of several genetic factors is necessary to determine the disorder. Denber and Teller (1963) hypothesized a primary chromosomal failure, and alteration in nucleotide sequences in both DNA and RNA and other factors.

As a result of his statistical studies, Karlsson (1966) believes that his data are consistent with "a modified dominant inheritance" of schizophrenia. A dominant gene, associated with a thought deviation, and the recessive gene, "associated with a state of nervous tension," could together determine an incompatible situation, usually leading to schizophrenia.

Manfred Bleuler (1968) believes that heredity plays an important role but not a specific one. He cannot believe that hereditary disposition to schizophrenia "consists of the morbidity of one or two or three genes which are altered by mutation." First of all, no Mendelian law could be determined in families of schizophrenics; secondly, "the fertility rate of schizophrenics is very much reduced and, in spite of this, schizophrenia remains a very frequent psychosis." He adds, "If we assert that mutation of a gene is the main background of schizophrenia, we must conclude that the mutation rate is very high. As a matter of fact it would have to be much higher than any known mutation rate." Bleuler believes that the hereditary background of schizophrenia is most probably a disharmony, an insufficient interplay of different predispositions of the personality. In other words, the genes would transmit physical disharmonies that run parallel to disharmonies of personality. These genetic disharmonies of personality would interact with environmental factors and the combination would result in schizophrenia.

Gottesman and Shields (1966), after reviewing genetic studies, including their own, conclude, "It seems reasonable to postulate that genetic factors are largely responsible for the specific nature of most of the schizophrenics and that these factors are necessary but not sufficient for the disorder to occur." Even Slater (1968), who, as we have already seen, is one of the strongest advocates of the genetic nature of schizophrenia, states that the genetic factors are "largely responsible but not wholly responsible." Other authors, like Kringlen, believe that the genetic factors are somewhat responsible, but not largely responsible.

There are, of course, other factors to be considered. Families may transmit schizophrenia not genetically, but psychodynamically. We have seen in detail how some authors like Jackson, Lidz, and Wynne interpret this psychological transmission and how I interpret it (see Chapters 5 and 8). With particular reference to identical twins, we cannot exclude that they have an additional psychological problem—an identity problem that may predispose them to a schizophrenic decompensation (Kringlen, 1967, 1968).

In my long psychiatric career I have had the opportunity of examining accurately and treating only three pairs of monozygotic twins. Coincidentally, all three pairs involved female patients. I have also treated many other patients who were twins, males and females, concordant by sex, but not monozygotic.

The first pair was treated by me in 1943, and I reported their cases in the literature (Arieti, 1944*b*). At that time I was very much influenced by the hypothesis of the antischizophrenic defense mechanisms advanced by Kallmann and Barrera and tried to interpret why one of the sisters, Magda, made a recovery, whereas Selma remained delusional, withdrawn, and required indefinitely long hospitalization. In agreement with the theory of Kallmann and Barrera (1941) I reported that the recovery occurred in the patient who was constitutionally the more athletic and less asthenic. I added that the recovery occurred in the patient whose prepsychotic personality was definitely more extroverted, who had always shown better ability to cope with the problems of life, and whose symptomatology was somewhat atypical because of the presence of many "psychoneurotic symptoms." I also saw a connection between Magda's mild hypochondriacal symptoms and Selma's somatic delusions. Actually there was much of psychodynamic significance in this history of the patients, which I was not able to evaluate fully at that time. There were identity problems between the two girls. Until the age of 12 they were always dressed alike. They were so similar that they were often misidentified. The mother always tried to emphasize their similarity by insisting upon dressing them alike. Once I asked the mother why she wanted to do so, and she answered, "I was proud of them. I liked to see them alike." However, the two girls did not like to dress identically and always objected to this wish of their mother, although they did so unsuccessfully. They resented the fact that they were the object of everyone's attention on account of their similarity. Magda, in particular, began to consider her being a twin as something of which she was ashamed. After the age of 12, the sisters succeeded in dressing differently. At that time, according to the mother, they started to be jealous of each other, each of them being especially jealous of the other's dresses, which by now were different. Then, too, the first differences in their personalities became apparent at that time. Up to the age of 12, the patients were both vivacious and sociable children. From that age Selma became more seclusive and reserved. She preferred to be alone; when in company she was considered shy and bashful. In the major areas of life the two sisters continued to show similarities of interest and actions, Magda retaining the role of leadership. In their teens they both started to work as domestics; Magda had her first boy friend when she was 16; Selma when she was 18. Magda was the first one to leave the parental home and became pregnant without being married. Selma always repeated Magda's events of life one or two years later. But one event she did not duplicate. At the age of 22 Magda got married, but Selma remained single. She could not relish her sister's marriage and started to hate her brother-in-law. She became delusional, withdrawn, had to be hospitalized, and although treated with sixty-three insulin treatments, she remained delusional. For details of her illness, the reader is referred to the original report (Arieti, 1944*b*).

As soon as Selma was admitted to the mental hospital, Magda started to express somatic complaints. Subsequently she revealed her fear of becoming insane and repeatedly stated that because her twin sister was insane, she would become insane also. She soon presented paranoid trends against her husband, accusing him of jealousy, although there was no foundation for such belief. The episode lasted a few months. Magda made an apparent recovery, was discharged from the hospital, and there were no relapses.

The second pair consists of Edith and Barbara, identical twins who lived together for twenty years, that is, from the time they left the parental home to the time Barbara got married. Edith felt betrayed and was unable to adjust to the separation. She could not understand how the sister who had been "part of her" could become so disinterested in her now that she had a husband. Edith had always been afraid throughout her life that the day would come when Barbara would get married. The day finally came, and Edith considered Barbara cruel, sadistic. Barbara had always been the dominant one when they lived together, but now she was much worse. Edith started to express feelings of unreality and somatic delusions and had periods of intense panic and disorientation. Her saying to herself, "You are not only half you. You are you and must live independently," did not help much. Her work declined in quality, but she was able to maintain her position. Edith underwent intense psychotherapy, and hospitalization was not necessary. Barbara did not present any symptoms.

The third pair (Henriette and Paulette) has already been mentioned in Chapter 20 in relation to Henriette's artwork. Both Henriette and Paulette exhibited a quasi-schizophrenic symptomatology since their late teens. But whereas Paulette improved after her marriage, Henriette, who remained single and alone, became much worse and eventually developed a full-blown psychosis after separation from her sister.

These three pairs of twins, although not enough to be statistically significant, show very well that the state of being an identical twin engenders additional problems for the patient. At times both siblings may be affected by the disorder, or only one, but in all cases the twin who was the dominant one in the relation is also the one who suffers less from the separation and the one who is less likely to have the psychosis. If he, too, develops the psychosis, it is the milder of the two. The psychodynamic development of twins differs from that of nontwins but it acquires pathological features in disturbed families only. The Oedipal situation is altered, the dominant sibling assuming a parental role. The submissive sibling tends to remain dependent and, in pathological cases, unable to face life if deprived of the assistance and approval of the twin.

Other authors have described how the experience of being a monozygotic twin may pervade the patient's entire life. Rosenthal (1974) wrote:

> Identification with another person reaches its strongest point in such genetically identical individuals. The literature on twins is replete with all kinds of experiences and lore that bear on this intense communality or psychological bond. If one twin develops an illness, the other is likely to do so as well. This sharing of fates is an ongoing, integral part of their development and learning. Therefore, if one twin develops a schizophrenic illness, the likelihood of the second twin's developing that illness is increased inordinately, and the concordance rate for monozygotic pairs should be appreciably higher than that of dizygotic pairs.

These hypotheses are put in doubt by the work of Allen and Pollin (1970). In a sample of 31,818 male veteran twins, 1.14 percent were found to be schizophrenic. This incidence of the disorder was thus similar to that in the general population, suggesting that there is no clear difference in incidence of schizophrenia between twins and nontwins. The incidence of the psychosis in monozygotic twins was no greater than in dizygotic twins. Their data thus did not support the hypothesis that the experience of being an identical twin increases the occurrence of the disorder.

In order to separate the effect of the family as a psychodynamic factor from that of the family as a genetic factor, the incidence of schizophrenia in identical twins reared apart was studied. Slater (1968) collected data about sixteen twin pairs (monozygotic) who were separated early in life and one or both were schizophrenic. He found that of the sixteen twin pairs, ten were concordant and six discordant.

Rosenthal (1974), after having evaluated all the evidence, concludes that a hereditary factor in the etiology of schizophrenia has been sufficiently demonstrated. However, he believes that environmental factors are also important. If schizophrenia were engendered only by heredity, all monozygotic pairs would be concordant for schizophrenia, whereas in half or more of the pairs, the twin sibling, although having exactly the same genes, is not clinically schizophrenic.

Rosenthal (1963) divided the genetic theories of schizophrenia into two main groups: (1) the monogenic-biochemical, which assumes that a single pathological gene (responsible possibly for a specific metabolic error) is either necessary or sufficient to cause schizophrenia; (2) diathesis-stress theories, according to which what is inherited is a predisposition to develop the illness. A neural integrative defect may be at the basis of the diathesis.

Even such psychodynamically oriented authors as Rado attributed an important role to genetics in the etiology of schizophrenia. Rado and co-workers (1956) accepted the distinction between genotypes and phenotypes in relation to schizophrenia. Genotype is the inherited cause of development; phenotype the final outcome. The genotype, through interaction with the environment, causes the schizophrenic phenotype (called also the schizotype) to develop an abnormal organization. Similar interactions are well known in the field of pathology. For instance, an allergy, let us say, to hay may be based on a hereditary factor, but is transformed in actuality by the presence of a particular antigen in the environment: for instance, a pollen. However, environmental situations psychological in nature presumably act with more complex mechanisms than a simple antigen.

VI

Conclusions

In Part Two of this book we have seen that psychodynamic factors are prerequisites to schizophrenia. No schizophrenic who was examined psychodynamically was found to come from a well-adjusted, harmonious family and to have had no serious conflict. However, the findings reported in this chapter indicate that a genetic predisposition is necessary to channel the psychogenic factors along certain patterns and to provide the additional elements necessary to that interplay of causes and effects that eventually leads to the disorder. If this point of view is correct, we can draw the following conclusions:

1. At least two sets of factors of different origins (biological and psychodynamic) are necessary to engender schizophrenia.
2. It is sufficient to prevent or remove one set of these factors in order to avoid schizophrenia.
3. Genetic factors cannot be altered. We must thus try to alter or prevent psychodynamic or environmental factors.

There are some authors, however, who, perhaps with some justification, are alarmed about the increasing danger of genetic factors. Erlenmeyer-Kimling et al.

(1966) and Rainer (1966) report that the reproductivity rate for schizophrenic women in the period from 1934–1936 to 1954–1956 has increased from 58 percent to 87 percent. The more effective the therapeutic procedures will be, the higher will be the reproductivity rate of patients who had been diagnosed as schizophrenics. Consequently the larger will be the number of children to whom this genetic factor can be transmitted.

VII

Constitutional Factors in Schizophrenia

In 1921 Kretschmer published *Physique and Character* (the American edition in 1925), a work that remained popular in psychiatric circles for about two decades. Advancing his theories concerning personality and constitution, he divided body build into three types: (1) the leptosomatic (or asthenic), characterized by angular profile, narrowness of muscles, small shoulders, flat chest, relatively long extremities, and little muscular development; (2) the athletic type, with strong skeletal and muscular development; and (3) the pyknic type, characterized by pronounced deposits of fat on the trunk, short extremities, and gently curved profile.

Kretschmer saw a certain correlation between schizophrenia and body type. According to his studies, two-thirds of schizophrenics are leptosomatic or athletic and one-tenth dysplastic.

Sheldon, Stevens, and Tucker (1940) and Lindegarde (1953) refined Kretschmer's rather crude technique, and many authors have adopted their method generally to confirm that there is a greater incidence of asthenic constitutions among schizophrenics. Rees (1957) and several other authors, including myself, however, unlike Kretschmer, have not confirmed a lower incidence of pyknic constitutions among schizophrenics.

Kline and Tenney (1950) studied 455 hospitalized patients with the Sheldon method. Mesomorphy was generally correlated with good prognosis and paranoid type; ectomorphy with hebephrenic type and poor prognosis. Many clinicians have noted a change in the constitutional appearance of the patient, in accordance with the improvement made. Many patients tend to become more mesodermic when they get better. This is a rule of thumb and is by no means true in every case.

CHAPTER

28

The Biochemistry of Schizophrenia

I

Introductory Remarks

A large number of researchers have carried out biochemical investigations of schizophrenia, pursuing the hypothesis that a biochemical or metabolic error is at the basis of the disorder (see Himwich, Kety, and Smythies, 1966; Weil-Malherbe and Szara, 1971). Because life is characterized by an incredibly large number of metabolic processes, it has not been an easy task to isolate the hypothetical one responsible for schizophrenia. The search has so far not been successful but continues along certain directions illustrated in this chapter.

In order to demonstrate that a toxin, a by-product of a faulty metabolic process, is the main etiologic factor of the psychosis, some of the following empirical verifications are necessary:

1. The metabolite should be isolated and should be found only in schizophrenics.
2. If found also in conditions other than schizophrenia, it must be found in schizophrenic patients in quantities that are significantly different from those of nonschizophrenics.
3. The metabolite should reproduce the disorder when introduced into nonschizophrenic persons in certain quantities.
4. A greater sensitivity, allergy, or other kind of abnormal reaction to a special metabolite should be apparent in schizophrenic patients.

Many authors have indeed found biochemical alterations in schizophrenic patients. However, these findings do not seem to satisfy any of these four requirements.

Moreover, it will appear from the content of this chapter that at the present stage of research we cannot ascertain whether these alterations are (1) inherent in the basic etiology of the disorder, (2) the *result* of the physiological or psychological changes which occur in the disorder, or (3) the result of the way of living of most patients who have been the object of the biochemical studies. The vast majority of these patients have been institutionalized. Thus the alterations that they presented may have been caused by the limitations in activity of institutional life, by the diet of institutions, especially vitamin deficiency, or by drug therapy.

In the United States the person who has made one of the most extensive studies of the biochemistry of schizophrenia is Semour S. Kety. His writings (1959, 1966, 1969, 1972) will be one of our main guidelines.

II

The Transmethylation Hypothesis

In 1952 Osmond and Smythies stressed the fact that on one hand there are some similarities between mescaline psychosis and schizophrenia and on the other hand there are similarities between mescaline and epinephrine. They quoted Harley-Mason, who had stated that it was extremely probable that the final stage in the biogenesis of epinephrine is a transmethylation of norepinephrine, the methyl group arising from methionine or choline: "It is just possible that a pathological disordering of its transmethylation mechanism might lead to methylation of one or both of its phenolic hydroxil groups instead of its amino groups" (Osmond and Smythies, 1952).

In 1959 the transmethylation of norepinephrine to epinephrine was confirmed (Blaschko, 1959). Since that time many authors have tried to prove that pathological transmethylation occurs in schizophrenia. Consequently the delicate balance between the sympathetic nervous system (which is mediated by norepinephrine) and the parasympathetic nervous system (which is mediated by acetylcholine) would be disrupted. Derivations of epinephrine, such as adrenochrome and adrenolutin, or other endogenous metabolites, would cause psychotic symptoms.

The hypothesis that pathological methylation may occur in schizophrenia finds some support in the fact that known psychotomimetic substances include in their formula one or more methyl groups attached to an oxygen or nitrogen atom. When such methyl donors as methionine and betaine are given jointly with a monoamine oxidase inhibitor, they produce exacerbation of psychotic symptoms in chronic schizophrenics (Kety, 1966). The hypothesis would have obtained additional support, according to some authors, if large doses of nicotinamide, which are supposed to divert the methylating processes, would have been able to ameliorate the psychotic condition. Hoffer claims that nicotinamide has therapeutic value, but others have denied such claims. However, if Baldessarini (1966) is right that nicotinamide does not reduce s-adenosylmethionine in the brain, the transmethylation hypothesis is not ruled out.

In conclusion, although the transmethylation hypothesis suggests the possibility of a metabolic disorder in schizophrenia, it lacks as yet all four of the above-mentioned empirical verifications.

III
The Ceruloplasmin, Taraxein, and Related Hypotheses

In 1957 the Swedish biochemist Akerfeldt reported that he had discovered a new test for diagnosing schizophrenia. The test relied on the oxidation of N-N-dimethyl-p-phenylenediamine. This news aroused some enthusiasm, which soon subsided. The oxidizing substance was recognized as ceruloplasmin, a copper-protein. The hypothesis was thus that this copper-protein was increased in the serum of schizophrenics and would increase the oxidizing activity of the serum. It was soon found, however, that ceruplasmin is consistently increased in all tested institutionalized patients who had been on a diet poor in ascorbic acid. Normal diet would lower the level of ceruloplasmin.

Under the leadership of Heath, some investigators felt that the high oxidizing power of the serum of schizophrenics on epinephrine *in vitro* could not be attributed solely to a higher level of ceruloplasmin. They isolated a special type of ceruloplasmin to which they gave the name taraxein (from the Greek *tarassein,* "to disturb") (Heath et al., 1957). They reported that when this substance was injected into monkeys, behavioral changes occurred. Also electroencephalographic abnormalities in focal subcortical regions of the brain were found that, according to the authors, resembled those of schizophrenic patients. When the substance was intravenously injected into volunteer prisoners, some symptoms characteristic of schizophrenia, such as thought disorders, hallucinations, and paranoid ideas, ensued (Heath, 1963). Robins, Smith, and Lowe (1957) tried to duplicate Heath's findings but could not. Since then the hypotheses of Heath and his school have not received confirmation.

Lief (1957) reported that a volunteer in Heath's experiments was a psychiatric resident in analysis who knew that he was going to get either saline or taraxein. Lief described in detail the psychological concomitants that may have been responsible for the results. Kety (1959) concludes that the possibility exists that the reported effects of taraxein are "the result of a combination of suggestion, nonspecific toxic reactions from ammonium sulfate or other contaminants, and reinforcement of these cues by the unconscious biases of subject and observer. . . ." Heath and Krupp (1967) continue to think that taraxein is important in the etiology of schizophrenia. They have now accepted Fessel's ideas (1962) that schizophrenia might be an autoimmune disease. Taraxein would be a component of the immunoglobulin (IgG) fraction of the serum and would be an antibody specific for the brain. In their experiments Heath and Krupp (1967) used the fluorescent antibody technique of Coons and various serum fractionation methods.

Kety (1959) listed a series of experiments done to demonstrate that the serum of schizophrenia has a toxic effect (1) on larvae of *Xenopus laevis;* (2) on tadpoles; (3) on cells in tissue culture; (4) on rope-climbing speed in rats. Other experiments purported to demonstrate that certain extracts of the urine of schizophrenic patients produce behavioral changes in rats or disturbance in web construction in spiders. According to Kety all these experiments have neither been confirmed nor contradicted.

IV

The Serotonin Hypothesis

Woolley and Shaw (1954) hypothesized that mental changes may be attributed to a cerebral deficiency of *serotonin,* caused by a metabolic disorder. Serotonin is a derivative of tryptophan and is known to exist in high concentration in the brain, especially in the limbic system. It was speculated that lysergic acid had an inhibitory effect on serotonin and thus produced a psychosis.

Other experiments, however, led to contradictory results. Iproniazid is a monoamine oxidase inhibitor that causes an increase of the serotonin level of the brain, and yet it may also produce a toxic psychosis. Moreover, other psychotomimetic drugs, or lysergic acid derivatives, do not have an antiserotonin activity. Reserpine lowers the concentration of norepinephrine as serotonin; chlorpromazine instead has no effect on serotonin.

The conclusion reached by Kety is that serotonin and its metabolism play an important role in the central nervous system. What this role consists of, however, we do not know as yet. Some researchers believe that schizophrenia is due to too little serotonin, while other researchers blame too much serotonin.

V

The DMPEA Hypothesis and Serum Proteins

Friedhoff and Van Winkle (1967) reported the presence of 3, 4-dimethoxyphenylethylamine (DMPEA) in the urine of schizophrenics. Bourdillon and coworkers (1965) found a ''pink spot'' having some characteristics of DMPEA in 55 percent of tested schizophrenics. A large number of investigators have obtained contrasting results. Some authors have found an increase in macroglobulins in the serum of schizophrenics (Fessel, 1962; Kopeloff and Fishell, 1963), which other authors (Lovegrove and Nicholls, 1965) have denied. Kety (1969) concluded that up to the present time no abnormal characteristic of schizophrenia has been evidenced by the available techniques. For further studies on the biochemistry of schizophrenia in reference especially to blood proteins the reader is referred to the important works by Beckett and Gottlieb (1970) and by Frohman and Gottlieb (1974).

VI
Other Metabolic Changes

Numerous metabolic changes have been described in schizophrenia. Many early authors have proved in a convincing manner that in many schizophrenics there is a deficiency in the intake of oxygen (Hoskins, 1932, 1937). Several explanations have been given: for instance, that the blood of the patient leaves the lungs in an undersaturated condition; or that the tissues fail to absorb an adequate quantity of oxygen; or that the sluggishness, or hypoplasia, of the circulatory system does not permit an adequate oxygen supply. Other authors have tried to correlate this low consumption of oxygen with hormonal changes (Gornall et al., 1953). Here many questions come to mind. Is the low intake of oxygen what compels the schizophrenic toward low activity? Are the psychological manifestations of schizophrenia similar to those described by McFarland (1932) in state of oxygen deprivation? Or is the opposite true, that is, does the psychological condition of schizophrenia, with its withdrawal characteristics, reduce the oxygen requirements of the patient?

The carbohydrate metabolism in schizophrenia has also been studied by numerous early authors. The reader who is interested in this subject is referred to the review by Shattock (1950). Shattock states that many of the reports have been contradicted by other authors; however, the following three findings have seldom been disputed: (1) the presence of a normal fasting blood-sugar curve; (2) a tendency to sustained hyperglycemia in early or acute cases; (3) a normal intravenous glucose tolerance test in many patients who, instead, had showed prolonged hyperglycemia after oral administration of glucose. Although these findings are undisputed, their interpretation is very controversial. Frohman and Gottlieb (1974) conclude that there are indications of some abnormalities in carbohydrate chemistry in schizophrenics, but "most data suggest that these irregularities merely reflect abnormality in other phases of metabolism."

Hoskins (1946) found that the *output of urine* was twice as large in the schizophrenic as in the normal population, but he attributed this to the fact that, generally, schizophrenics drink more water than the average person. A low hippuric acid excretion, suggesting dysfunction of the liver, was found by many authors, but the Quick test, on which these works were based, cannot be considered a reliable method. Buscaino (1952), too, incriminates the liver. Buscaino is one of the staunchest European supporters of the theory that schizophrenia is the result of a metabolic disorder. In a number of papers, summarized in his report at the First

International Congress of Neuropathology, he tried to prove that there is, in schizophrenia:

1. Evidence of functional insufficiency of the liver (bilirubinemia, detoxication power impairment, as shown by deamination test, hippuric acid test, santonin test, and so on). Buscaino states that other researchers failed to get the same results because they relied on only one test, whereas, in order to study the liver properly, one must use a battery of tests (''hepatic constellation'' or ''instantaneous picture of liver'').
2. Evidence of insufficient reactivity of the hepatic and extrahepatic reticuloendothelial system.
3. Evidence of gastroenteric function, as shown by findings of gastroenteritis.

Buscaino reports that he has found pathologic amines in the blood and urine of schizophrenics and concludes that schizophrenia is an ''amino-toxicosis.'' In a recent publication (1970) Buscaino has reaffirmed his points of view. One of the disorders of metabolism investigated by Buscaino concerns aromaturia. McGeer and co-workers (1957) have also reported that schizophrenics excrete a higher than normal concentration of aromatic compounds in the urine.

In the psychiatric literature of the last part of the nineteenth century, reference was often made to an unusual odor of schizophrenic patients, particularly catatonic ones, who also presented greasiness of the skin. Recently Smith and Sines (1960) studied again this phenomenon. They felt that ''if there is a unique 'odor' in the apocrine sweat or in the sebaceous secretion of schizophrenic patients, the identification of this odoriferous substance may give a clue to an inborn error of metabolism'' in the psychosis. The authors trained rats to discriminate between the schizophrenic sweat with the strange odor and nonschizophrenic sweat without this odor. A human odor-testing panel was also able to discriminate between the same samples with greater accuracy than the rats did. According to the authors, this odor can be recognized reliably and bears some relationship to the psychosis.

Smith (1954) studied the functions of the liver of seventy-six schizophrenics and obtained consistently negative findings. Graetz, Reiss, and Waldon (1954) found that the excretion rate of hippuric acid was diminished in chronic cases of schizophrenia but not in acute cases. Persky, Gamm, and Grinker (1952) found a decreased excretion of hippuric acid in ten catatonic patients. Numerous volumes could be written on the studies of metabolism that have been carried out on schizophrenic patients. McFarland and Goldstein (1938), who reviewed the work in this field up to 1938, concluded that the results of all these investigations were almost entirely negative, so conflicting were the reports. Bellak and Willson (1947) reviewed the literature on etiology of dementia praecox and concluded the sections on the biochemical factors with the remark that the only consistent difference of biochemical findings ''from normals lies in the greater variability of values for almost any factor investigated.''

Recently Kety (1969) concluded that although substantial progress has been made in this field, "it would be difficult to demonstrate that a definitive increase in our knowledge of biochemical mechanisms in the schizophrenic psychoses has occurred in the past decade."

Perhaps it is worthwhile to mention here Horwitt (1956), who, although writing more than a decade before the last quoted work by Kety, expressed the following notes of cautiousness:

We are now entering a period of renewed interest in biological research on schizophrenia. Nothing can be more harmful to this rejuvenation of the investigation of the biology of mental health than the publication of reports based on techniques of patient selection which do not meet the minimum standards accepted by other disciplines. The manner in which the patient chooses to manifest his difficulties may not be a function of his physiological status.

Symptoms that are usually considered artifacts in other studies are often erroneously accepted as biological aberrations in the evaluation of the schizophrenic patient. Year after year, papers appear which purport to distinguish between the state of schizophrenia and that of normalcy. The sum total of the differences reported would make the schizophrenic patient a sorry physical specimen indeed: his liver, brain, kidney, and circulatory functions are impaired; he is deficient in practically every vitamin; his hormones are out of balance, and his enzymes are askew. Fortunately, many of these claims of metabolic abnormality are forgotten in time with a minimum of polemic, but it seems that each new generation of biologists has to be indoctrinated—or disillusioned—without benefit of the experience of its predecessors.

Horwitt gave the following examples of procedural mistakes made in organic studies of schizophrenia. Basal metabolism during emotional stress is not basal at all but may be a reflection of metabolism during intense adrenergic stimulation due to the stress itself. Comparing data from blood samples of schizophrenics and normal people is like comparing samples from soldiers on the battlefields and people in a relaxed, basal condition. He also stressed that the vagaries of psychotic behavior are such as to affect food intake. In many cases this abnormal food intake is responsible for nutritional disorders and metabolic changes. He wrote, "Having studied such changes in mental patients for more than fifteen years, I am at a loss to understand how some studies of urinary excretion or of blood constituents can be performed without recourse to nutritional controls." In the same excellent article he gave many more illustrations, which cannot be reported here, of mistakes commonly made in biological studies of schizophrenia.

CHAPTER

29

Endocrine and Cardiovascular Changes in Schizophrenia

I

The Endocrine Glands

Great etiological significance has been attributed in the past to the endocrine system in the etiology of schizophrenia. This occurred in an era when endocrinology was making great advances.

Many cases of schizophrenia presenting varied endocrinological disorders have been described, and each time with the implication that the mental disease may be in a state of causal relationship with the endocrinopathy. A visit to a large mental hospital would be sufficient to point out that the number of endocrine disorders is not much larger among schizophrenics than in the general population, and that an occasional endocrinopathy should be considered an accidental concomitant finding.

In my clinical experience with ambulatory schizophrenics I have not found a high percentage of any typical endocrine syndrome. In some large state hospitals one finds a slightly larger percentage of adolescent schizophrenics who are dysplastic than would be expected from the general population. In a large hospital one sees also a considerable number of cases of marked obesity in hebephrenic girls, and of the adolescent type of dystrophia adiposo-genitalis (Frohlich's syndrome) in both boys and girls who are affected by the simple type of schizophrenia. It is possible that these endocrine disorders have crippled the patients not only physically but also psychologically and have increased their anxiety and made them more susceptible to the psychosis.

Because the enthusiasm for endocrinology in psychiatric circles has vanished, it seems universally agreed that no classical endocrinological syndrome can be considered responsible for schizophrenia. Manfred Bleuler (1954), who has studied extensively schizophrenia in relation to endocrine glands, found no correlation whatsoever between the disorder and known endocrine conditions. The possibility remains that another endocrine disorder, not manifesting itself with the usual symptoms, may be incriminated eventually. Many researchers have been investigating this possibility.

The thyroid gland, for example, has been studied by many. Witte (1922), who studied a series of 815 patients, was unable to confirm the high percentage of thyroid atrophy that other authors have found. He observed, however, a tendency to accumulate colloid, a characteristic indicative of moderate functional hypothyroidism. In a minority of patients, Hoskins (1946) found a triad of symptoms: low oxygen-consumption rate, secondary anemia, and scanty, nitrogen-low urine. This minority of patients generally responded favorably to thyroid medication. Simpson, Cranswick, and Blair (1963) found evidence of hypothyroidism in only 28 percent of the cases. Dewhurst and co-workers (1969) found an increase in thyrotrophic hormone in several but not all schizophrenics examined.

Pathology of the adrenal glands has also been suggested, especially because the catatonic picture, with asthenia, low blood pressure, low oxygen consumption, and anemia, reminds one of Addison's disease. Hoskin's therapeutic experiments, however, failed to show any improvement in patients under adrenalin medication.

That the adrenal glands may be implicated was also suggested by Selye's studies (1950, 1952). According to him, any stressful condition engenders a syndrome consisting of (1) acute gastrointestinal ulcers; (2) adrenocortical stimulation, evidenced by hyperemia and discharge of secretory granules from the adrenal cortex; and (3) thymico-lymphatic involution, accompanied by characteristic hematologic changes (lymphopenia, eosinopenia, and polymorphonuclear leucocytosis). Later Selye found that the stressing situation acts upon the body directly and indirectly through the pituitary and adrenal glands. Through some "unknown pathway" the stressing stimulus travels from the directly injured area of the body to the anterior pituitary. This gland, after being stimulated, secretes ACTH hormone, which, in turn, stimulates the adrenal cortex to discharge corticoid hormones. Some of these corticoids are prophlogistic, that is, they enhance the inflammatory potentiality by stimulating the proliferative ability and the reactivity of the connective tissue. Other corticoids are antiphlogistic, inasmuch as they inhibit the production of granulomatous tissue and other facets of the inflammatory process. The total of these nonspecific reactions is what Selye called the "general adaptation syndrome."

Many authors have observed a dysfunction of the adaptation syndrome in schizophrenia. According to Pincus and Hoagland (1950) schizophrenics respond to "stress" differently from normal persons. The ingenious experiments of these two investigators prove that if the patients are given adrenocortical extracts, their responses to stress are not considerably different from those of normal control subjects. On the other hand, if the patients are given high doses of ACTH, their responses to stress are by far inferior to those of control subjects. The authors conclude that the adrenal cortices of the patients are not adequately stimulated by ACTH. ACTH may be produced normally in the schizophrenic; it is the adrenal cortex that does not respond. Although these authors do not think that this lack of response is the one and only "cause" of the psychosis, they think that it may be one of a number of important factors that are involved. Pincus and Hoagland have worked on patients who had an average duration of hospitalization of two and a half years. Gildea (quoted by Pincus and Hoagland, 1950) found an abnormal adaptation reaction in chronic patients but not in early patients. Also Parsons and coworkers (1949) obtained data different from those of Pincus and Hoagland. They found that psychotic subjects respond to epinephrine in the same way that the controls do. The degree of lymphocytopenia was practically the same as in the control subjects. Electric shock produced a degree of lymphocytopenia similar to that obtained after epinephrine. Because lymphocytopenia following stress is dependent upon a normal pituitary-adrenal system, Parsons and collaborators conclude that this functional system is not impaired in schizophrenics. On the other hand, the same authors found that psychotic patients, both manic-depressive and schizophrenic, do not respond to psychological stress with lymphocytopenia or hyperglycemia. In this respect they do differ from normal subjects. The findings obtained by the authors mentioned and by others are such that no definite conclusion is possible. They all seem to agree on one thing: psychological stress does not produce a normal general adaptation reaction in the schizophrenic.

This result is easy to understand because the psychologically stressing stimulus may not be perceived as stressing by the schizophrenic. Therefore it may never reach the pituitary gland, or, if it reaches the pituitary gland, it may have lost a great deal of stressing power. But even if the stimulus is physiological or chemical and not psychological, it must travel from the injured part of the body to the pituitary gland, and it probably travels not humorally but through the nervous system. The psychological states of the schizophrenic may indirectly alter or delay or weaken even the nonpsychological functions of the nervous system, so that the stressing stimulus may have lost power when it reaches the pituitary gland. If the pituitary gland is stimulated, however, the adrenal gland should be stimulated in turn because here the interstimulation is not through the nervous system but humorally, namely, through the ACTH hormones. Pincus and Hoagland (1950), however, found that when patients were administered a standard 25 mg dose of ACTH, they responded much less intensely than normal subjects. They concluded that the adrenal cortex of schizophrenics is much less responsive than that of normal subjects. Actually, the mechanism is more complicated than that, as Pincus and Hoagland themselves admit, because the stimulated adrenal glands also secrete hormones, which again act on the pituitary gland and perhaps on the central nervous system.

Some authors have considered the pituitary gland as being directly involved in the etiology of schizophrenia, but the evidence so far has not been convincing. More importance has been attributed to the sexual glands, especially because sexual maladjustment is one of the symptoms of the disorder.

Recently the Japanese authors Suwa and Yamashita (1972) have studied the diurnal rhythm in adrenocortical activity. In normal subjects with a normal sleep routine the cyclic plasma 17-hydroxycorticosteroids (17-OHCS) pattern consists of an early morning peak, followed by a downward trend during the remainder of the day and through the night. The authors found marked alterations of the cyclic pattern in acute and chronic schizophrenics.

Mott (1919) reported a more or less advanced atrophy of the testicles in all cases of schizophrenia and a complete arrest of spermatogenesis in the majority of them. Hemphill (1944) and Hemphill, Reiss, and Taylor (1944) confirmed these findings in biopsy specimens from patients who did not belong to the paranoid type. They saw that in the males the atrophy was limited to the seminiferous tubules and speculated that what was at fault was probably a gonadotrophic hormone from the anterior lobe of the pituitary gland. Morse criticized Mott's work (quoted by Henderson and Gillespie, 1941). She felt that the changes found in the glands of the patients might have resulted from causes unrelated to schizophrenia. For instance, the age of the patient, the state of nutrition, and the nature and duration of the terminal illness are all factors that influence the histologic condition of the endocrine glands. Forster, a pupil of Mott, confirmed her teacher's findings (quoted by Henderson and Gillespie, 1941). She noticed signs of early involution in the ovaries of schizophrenic women who had reached the age of 30.

Menstrual disorders, especially prolongation of the interval and amenorrhea, are very common in schizophrenic women and are well known to all psychiatrists. Ripley and Papanicolaou (1942) investigated the menstrual cycle of patients by means of studies of vaginal smears. They found in both schizophrenic and affective disorders a greater irregularity than in a comparable normal group. A tendency to a delay, a weakened expression, or a complete temporary suppression of the follicular reaction was found by these authors. They also frequently noticed prolongation of the menstrual interval and amenorrhea. All of these alterations were interpreted as the result of a hindered growth of the ovarian follicles. Ripley and Papanicolaou also found a correlation between the severity of the illness and the degree of abnormality of the menstrual cycle. An improvement in the psychological symptomatology was usually accompanied by a return to a more normal menstrual function. The authors could not ascertain the existence of an etiological relationship.

How is one to interpret these reports on the endocrine system in schizophrenia? Although nothing has been definitely ascertained, one may nevertheless attempt to formulate some conclusions and hypotheses:

1. An etiological relationship, proving that schizophrenia is engendered by an endocrine disorder, has not been demonstrated. On the contrary, the more we know about the syndromes caused by dysfunction of the endocrine glands, the more we depart from this assumption.

2. It seems fairly well established that in the majority of cases of schizophrenia, especially in the chronic cases, there is a diminished functionality of the endocrine system. At this stage of our knowledge, it is difficult to determine whether this diminished functionality is due to decrease in the production of hor-

mones or to the decreased responsiveness to them. This point has been well emphasized by Hoskins.

3. The authors who believe in the organic nature of schizophrenia have seen in this diminished functionality of the endocrine system another proof that their assumption is valid. Others view this diminished functionality of the endocrine system as another psychosomatic disorder of schizophrenia. According to this interpretation, the psychological syndrome of schizophrenia directly or indirectly diminishes the amount of stimulation to which the endocrine system is subjected; the resulting diminished functionality in turn engenders in the organism unusual functional compensatory mechanisms and eventually even organic damages, such as fibrosis of the testicles.

It is appropriate at this point to mention that Roizin (1938) worked with roosters that were experimentally blinded and fed artificially. In comparison with control cases, he found very marked atrophy of the testicles of the blind rooster, although the general weight was not considerably diminished. (At the end of the experiment the average total weight of control cases was 1250g., and the weight of the testicles 8.40g. In the blinded animals the total weight was 1100g., and the weight of the testicles 0.320g.)

Roizin's findings may be interpreted as indicating that lack of sensory stimulation was producing the atrophy or impairment of growth of the testicles. Blindness in normal men would not produce atrophy of the testicles, because men may become stimulated by other sensory organs or by inner images and thoughts. In many cases of schizophrenia, however, this inner or external stimulation is defective. It is important to add that testicular alterations have not been found in paranoid patients, who are in better contact with external reality than hebephrenic and catatonic patients (Hemphill, 1944; Hemphill, Reiss, and Taylor, 1944).

4. The diminished functionality of the endocrine system in schizophrenia may not be necessarily directly related to the decrease in stimulation to which the endocrine system is subjected on account of the psychological picture of the psychosis. An altered functionality of the autonomic nervous system, which controls the endocrine glands, may be responsible, even totally, for this hypofunctionality.

II

The Cardiovascular Apparatus

The cardiovascular system of schizophrenic patients, from the size of the heart to the pattern of capillaries in the nailfold, was the object of many studies up to 1955. In recent years these studies have considerably decreased in number, in spite of the fact that the findings were more consistent than in other somatic studies of schizophrenic patients. Following is a brief review of the most significant of these works.

The prevalent opinion of the authors who have studied this subject is that the blood pressure of schizophrenics is generally lower than that of the general population of similar age. Freeman, Hoskins, and Sleeper (1932) found in a series of 180 patients that the average systolic pressure was 104.5 mm Hg and the diastolic was 54.5. These values were much lower than those found in medical students examined as control cases. The highest values were found in paranoids and the lowest in catatonics. Rheingold (1939) too has found the blood pressure of 129 schizophrenics in an early stage of their illness to be lower than that of the general population (life insurance applicants). Shattock (1950) has compared the blood pressure of "refractory" patients to those of socialized patients. He found that the average systolic pressure of forty-six refractory schizophrenics was 118 mm Hg, and that of thirty-two socialized schizophrenics 131.5 mm Hg. The paranoid patients in each of the two groups had the highest blood pressure. Gottlieb (1936) and several other authors have found a close correlation between the systolic and diastolic pressure in schizophrenics. Some authors (Cameron and Jellinek, 1939) have found a rise of blood pressure in clinical remission after insulin treatment. Farrell and Vassaf (1940) have noted even an increase in the size of the heart after this treatment.

Lewis (1923), in his study on the constitutional factors in dementia praecox, found a hypoplastic cardiovascular system in schizophrenics who came to autopsy. He made it clear, however, that such hypoplastic condition was not found in paranoids. Hypertrophy of the heart was never found, even in presence of valvular lesions.

Finkelman and Haffron (1937) found the volume of circulating blood in thirty-nine schizophrenics to be diminished in comparison to that of manic-depressive patients. The intracranial blood flow has been studied by numerous authors, but so discordant are the findings that no conclusion is possible. Perhaps it is safe to say that no important deviation from normal values has been obtained in the intracranial flow of schizophrenics.

Another alteration that has interested many authors is the exaggerated tendency toward vasoconstriction found in all vessels from capillaries to large arteries. Abramson (1944) found excessive vasoconstriction in the vessels of schizophrenics exposed to cold temperatures. He found improvement in the blood circulation after insulin treatment. Jung and Carmichael (1937), Minski (1937), and others have found vasomotor disturbances leading to cyanosis. Some authors felt that the vasoconstriction was an exaggerated reaction to cold temperatures and inactivity (Stern, 1937). Others feel that there is a permanent vasoconstriction in the vessels of patients, especially catatonics.

Shattock (1950), who has studied intensely the vascular conditions of schizophrenics, found the following:

1. At room temperature, 62–65° F (16.7–18.3° C), cyanosis of the extremities, especially of the feet, was present in 43 percent of 220 female psychotics and in only 5 percent of 300 male psychotics.
2. At room temperature, 62° F (16.7° C), the average temperature of the

hands and feet of thirty female schizophrenics was significantly lower than that of thirty female affective psychotics.

3. There was no relation between cyanosis of the extremities and advancing age.

4. There was imperfect correlation between cyanosis and inactivity.

5. The effect of posture on the circulation of cyanosed extremities was shown by diminution of cyanosis after raising of the feet.

6. Temporary relief of cyanosis was obtained by any means that brings about vasodilation, like vasodilator drugs, and so on.

7. The brachial, radial, and dorsalis pedis of twenty-eight female schizophrenics who suffered from peripheral cyanosis were found to be contracted and pulseless, but these vessels were normal after vasodilation had been obtained.

Summarizing, we may state that the four main alterations found in the cardiovascular apparatus of schizophrenics are (1) decrease in the size of the heart; (2) decrease in the volume of the blood flow; (3) decrease in systematic blood pressure; * (4) exaggerated tendency to vasoconstriction and resulting diminished blood supply.

The entire circulatory system of many schizophrenics seems hypoplastic or at least in a state of diminished functionality. How are these findings to be interpreted? Do they indicate a congenital cardiovascular hypoplasia of the preschizophrenic, who, on account of this hypoplasia, will be predisposed to schizophrenia? Or are these findings not a predisposition or cause of schizophrenia, but rather one of the many by-products of this condition? In interpreting these findings, we have to take into consideration the following points:

First, these findings are not constant. Although it is true that the average blood pressure of a large number of schizophrenics is lower than the blood pressure of a corresponding number of people taken from the general population, the individual schizophrenic does not necessarily have a low blood pressure. In other words, low blood pressure or hypoplasia of the heart or other vascular alterations are not present in each case of schizophrenia or necessary for the diagnosis of schizophrenia. In the initial stage of the illness, the cardiovascular alterations are, by far, less frequent.

Second, the fact that several authors have found that these symptoms, including hypoplasia of the heart, diminish or disappear at remission seems to be a strong indication that these symptoms are functional and not based on a congenital defect.

Third, most of these studies were made on chronic schizophrenics who make relatively few demands on their circulatory system, which consequently is less active than that of a normal person. First of all, the physical activities of the chronic schizophrenic are very much reduced. Even though he may have transitory periods

* The reader must be reminded that these studies were made before the drugs with hypotensive effects, like reserpine and chlorpromazine, were developed.

of excitement, restlessness, and impulsive behavior, his activity as a whole is very much decreased. Secondly, he does not discharge his anxiety or other emotional states through his cardiovascular system any longer. The psychological stimuli of external or internal origin, which produce variations in the blood pressure of the normal person, do not affect the schizophrenic very much. Sociological factors, which complicate our modern society more and more, have an effect on the vascular system. High blood pressure and arteriosclerosis are much rarer in blacks who live in Africa than in blacks who live in the United States. The schizophrenic becomes less perceptive to the sociopsychological stimuli that act on the cardiovascular system or finds other mechanisms of response to them. Paranoid patients, who remain better socialized and more active than the other schizophrenics, maintain a higher blood pressure. Again, it is the paranoid mental condition that allows better functioning of the cardiovascular system. It is not a more efficient cardiovascular system that predisposes the individual to the paranoid type, rather than to the simple, hebephrenic, and catatonic types.

Fourth, some authors, like Lewis, have been impressed by the fact that even in cases with valvular lesions, hypertrophy of the heart was not observed. Again, I think that, although the heart was diseased, the diminished demands made on it made a compensatory hypertrophy unnecessary. Even without this compensatory hypertrophy, the schizophrenic would supply sufficient blood to his organs; however, if his heart suddenly were requested to work more efficiently, as in the sudden outbreak of an acute infective condition, the patient might succumb.

Fifth, the low blood pressure and the diminished activity make the patient more vulnerable to low temperatures. The vasoconstriction that is found in many schizophrenics seems to have the main purpose of preventing dispersion of heat. If a normal person is exposed to a cold environment, he will try to warm up by moving, doing exercises, eating, grinding his teeth, and so on. The regressed schizophrenic does not increase his activities, which, on the contrary, remain very few. If he is in a catatonic state, he may not move at all. Thus a compensatory mechanism, which does not require a voluntary act, occurs. Vessels constrict, and cyanosis may ensue. Cyanosis is found more frequently in women than in men, because in our society certain parts of the female body, such as arms and legs, are more exposed than those of men. This fact holds true even for patients in mental institutions.

Another factor increases the constriction of the vessels, especially in catatonics. The postures, which they maintain at times for whole days, one day after another, activate antigravity vasoconstrictor mechanisms. Without these mechanisms, edema due to blood stasis would be very frequent. Edemas of the ankles and feet are common in catatonics who maintain a standing position, but this would be much more frequent if these vasoconstrictor mechanisms were not present. We cannot minimize the importance of motor activity for a good blood circulation. The fact that marked vasoconstriction is found in patients who are at times restless and destructive does not invalidate this interpretation. First of all, as mentioned before, although these patients may be episodically hyperactive, they are, as a group, hypoactive. Secondly, autonomous mechanisms that have originated during long periods of inactivity may continue to function, sometimes even if such inactivity decreases, because the cardiovascular system may not become quickly adjusted to the new demands. It has to use the old mechanisms. The vasoconstriction obviously has an additional compensatory function, namely, to raise the blood pressure. It may seem strange that the blood pressure of the schizophrenic is so low, notwithstanding the vasoconstriction. The obvious conclusion is that the blood pressure would be even lower without this vasoconstriction. Such low blood pressure, although tolerable in normal circumstances, cannot be tolerated by the body when the temperature is low.

Sixth, we do not imply with the foregoing that this relative hypofunctionality of the cardiovascular system is directly due only to inactivity or to diminished cardiovascular responsiveness to emotions. Another mechanism has to be taken into consideration, which is involved either directly or through the mechanisms already mentioned. This is an altered functionality of the autonomic nervous system, which regulates the cardiovascular system.

Another fact, which in a certain way contrasts with what has been mentioned so far, has also been observed. Hospitalized paranoids seem to be in a much better state of physical health than people of similar age taken from the general population. Alpert, Bigelow, and Bryan (1947) studied fifty patients who have maintained an active paranoid state from 8 to 42 years, with an average duration of 21.36 years. Except for one patient who was diagnosed ''paranoid condition,'' the diagnosis was always dementia praecox, paranoid type. The authors found that the manifestation of arteriosclerosis, including cerebral arteriosclerosis, was less frequently encountered than in the general population. They mention the fact that repressed hostility often produces essential hypertension and possibly arteriosclerosis. The paranoid continually acts out his hostilities and gives expression to his conflicts, and so he contrasts with the person who represses and develops tension. The authors do not draw any definite conclusions. However, their noteworthy work, which they called ''preliminary report,'' should have stimulated further research. It is common knowledge that paranoids tend to deteriorate less than other patients when they reach old age. Their sensorium is much better preserved. However, in some of them the mental condition improves when they finally show signs of arteriosclerosis. They are less resentful and less concerned with their delusions.

An additional finding worth mentioning is a special capillary structure found by some authors in schizophrenic patients (Hauptmann and Myerson, 1948; Doust, 1955; Wertheimer and Wertheimer, 1955). This structure is considered an immature formation of capillaries, like that found in normal children before the capillary development is completed. More recently Maricq (1963, 1966) confirmed the works of the previous authors. She found a particular capillary pattern in the nailfold of schizophrenics, with a high plexus rating. Like similar studies on fingerprints (Raphael and Raphael, 1962) these studies of capillaries need additional research.

CHAPTER

30

The Central Nervous System in Schizophrenia

It is natural that the central nervous system should have been the object of much research in schizophrenia. Emil Kraepelin, who was the first to individualize the disorder at a clinical level, always hoped that science would one day duplicate for dementia praecox the triumphant actualization of the medical model, as it took place in reference to general paresis. Such hope has not been realized.

I

Neuropathology

The founding fathers of neuropathology, Nissl, Alzheimer, and Spielmeyer, initiated a great deal of histologic research. From their time to the present the works of neuropathologists have remained as indefinite as those of other people doing other somatic research. Many histologic alterations were found in the brains of schizophrenics, but not consistently, and their significance was uncertain. Alzheimer (1897) found a local disappearance of ganglion cells in the outer layer of the cerebral cortex. Josephy (1930) described cell sclerosis and fatty degeneration in the cortical layers. Winkelman (1952) found a diffuse loss of nerve cells. Buscaino (1921) reported grapelike formations in the brains of schizophrenics. Other authors could not confirm these findings, which were considered artifacts.

Klippel and Lhermitte (1906) described areas of focal demyelination (later denied by Adolf Meyer and by Wolf and Cowen, 1952). Bruetsch (1940) found rheumatic foci in brains of schizophrenics. He felt that the incidence of these foci was greater than in the general population and that rheumatic fever must have played an important etiologic role. (In 1952, Lidz denied the importance of this role.)

In an effort to overcome the technical defects that many authors found in neuropathological studies of schizophrenia, C. and O. Vogt adopted a refined technique that consisted of a serial study of the cerebral hemispheres in slices 8 μ (micron) thick. Quantitative computations of the alterations were made and control studies in normal people of the same age were carried out. The Vogts (1954) concluded that they were able to find anatomical alterations in all cases of schizophrenia that they studied. The localization, intensity, and histologic aspect of the lesions were found to vary considerably. The most important features were:

1. So-called wasting cells (*Schwundzelle* in German; *cellule fondante* in French). In these cells there is a progressive disintegration and disappearance of the tigroid substance, increase in fat content, and decrease in volume. The nucleus becomes pale at first and then disappears (karyolysis).
2. Alveolar degeneration. The cells lose the Nissl substance and undergo vacuolation of the cytoplasm.
3. Liposclerosis. The cells are shrunken and presumably filled with fat.

Other alterations (such as cell shrinkage, balloon cells, and senile alterations) seemed to play a less important role. This impressive work by the Vogts was not completed. All the alterations described by them are found to some degree in many pathological conditions and even in the so-called normals. The only finding that would be significant would be a quantitative difference between schizophrenics and normal persons. But again even then there would remain the problem of whether the quantitative change is part of the basic schizophrenic process or the outcome of the abnormal schizophrenic way of living, especially in patients who have been sick for a long time.

Several researchers have studied biopsy material in an attempt to avoid the artifacts liable to be found in postmortem specimens. Papez (1948) and his associates reported inclusion bodies, presumably microorganisms, for example, zoospores. The significance of these findings was disputed by Wolf and Cowen (1952) and by Alfred Meyer (1954).

Roizin (1952) made morphological and biochemical studies of biopsy specimens from twenty-four patients who had undergone topectomy and electric shock (or insulin coma, or both) prior to psychosurgery. He found several alterations in the medium-sized and large-sized pyramidal neurons. He also found changes in the activity of indophenol-oxidase, cytochrome (oxidase) peroxidases, and acid phosphatases. Roizin's work is an excellent piece of research, but, as the author himself admits, it is inconclusive because the findings might have been the results of the therapies to which the patients were subjected.

Dunlap (1928), Spielmeyer (1931), Wolf and Cowen (1952), Weinstein

(1954), Ferraro (1954), and Dastur (1959), among many distinguished researchers, reached negative conclusions about these neuropathological findings in schizophrenia, minimizing their importance on various grounds: these changes are not specific, are of mild intensity, and may be found also in control brains of normal persons; they may be the result of age, malnutrition, concomitant disease, or abnormal way of living of the patient.

Other authors feel that the relatively primitive techniques of traditional neuropathology have led to the negative findings and look forward with great anticipation to the results of new techniques, such as electronic microscopy, tissue culture, and microchemistry. An alteration affecting the brain at a molecular level is not detectable with histological procedures.

II

Electroencephalographic Findings

When Hans Berger discovered the electroencephalograph (EEG) the hope arose that EEG studies would reveal what neuropathology had failed to disclose. Such hope too was doomed to failure. The results were inconsistent and open to severe criticism. Early authors, like Berger himself (1931, 1933) and Lemere (1936), reported that the EEG was normal in schizophrenia. Davis (1940, 1942) described what she termed a ''choppy activity,'' which is a disorganized pattern of low voltage ranging from approximately 26 to over 50 cycles per second (cps). This pattern could not be related to age differences. Davis did not consider this EEG record specific for schizophrenia, but she asserted that it was much more common in this disorder than in others. In fact, she found it in 61 percent of the records of schizophrenics in contrast to 39 percent of manic-depressives. Hill (1957) found the ''choppy pattern'' in only 20 percent of schizophrenics.

Walter (1942) observed slow wave changes in catatonic stupor. He found that the alpha activity shows instability and slow activity at 2 to 6 cps. Low voltage was also apparent. These findings were not constant and could not be interpreted.

Hill, who made an excellent review of the literature on this subject up to 1957, concluded that the EEG is abnormal in a proportion of patients suffering from schizophrenia, particularly of the catatonic type, but that no specific pattern is found in these patients. Subcortical type discharges, similar to those found in some epileptics, were found, particularly in young catatonics, but were not interpreted by the author as evidence of an organic-pathological process. Hill stated that the available EEG data ''do not provide adequate evidence for a genetic progressive pathological cerebral process in schizophrenia.''

Landolt (1957) found that temporal foci and spastic potential often exist in noncatatonic schizophrenia before manifestation of the disorder; they subside when the illness manifests itself overtly, and they recur when a remission takes place.

More recently several authors have studied the EEG in the course of the schizophrenic illness. Igert and Lairy (1962) found consistent normal records in sixty-two female patients throughout the illness and in spite of the therapeutic procedures with which the patients were treated. Small and Small (1965) found that the most severe and prolonged forms of schizophrenia were among the patients who had a normal EEG. Various authors have found that the most normal EEG in cases of schizophrenia is paradoxically associated with poor prognosis.

Perhaps the most conclusive work remains the one by Colony and Willis (1956), who studied EEG in a thousand cases of schizophrenia and found the frequency of abnormal rhythm to be 5 percent, that is, even less than in their control normal cases.

Strauss (1959) corroborates the findings of Colony and Willis. He believes that schizophrenics show no significantly greater degree of abnormality than normal controls, and certainly no temporal spikes.

EEG studies of schizophrenics have also been made during sleep. Gibbs and Gibbs (1963) have described a so-called mitten pattern, which seems to be connected with psychotic conditions during the state of sleep in patients not younger than age 15. It is found in the frontal lobes, but it spreads also to the parietals. Two varieties have been described: the A mitten, in which the fast component lasts longer than 100 msec, and the B mitten, in which it lasts between 80 and 100 msec. The B mitten pattern was found to occur in 37 percent of schizophrenia patients.

Phases of sleep associated with rapid eye movements (REM) have been studied in schizophrenics (Feinberg et al., 1964, 1965; Rechtschaffen, Schulsinger, and Mednick, 1964). Nothing conclusive has been found that would convincingly show that schizophrenia is literally a dreaming state or that an alteration in the dreaming process is a basic factor in schizophrenia.

III

Schizophrenia and Epilepsy

The interest in EEG studies has renewed the old debate about the relation between schizophrenia and epilepsy. Once these two conditions were considered incompatible, and it was assumed that they could never occur together. As a matter of fact, it was because of this alleged incompatibility that Von Meduna (1937) had the idea of treating schizophrenia with an artificial convulsive chemical method, that is, with intravenous injections of metrazol. Later Cerletti and Bini (1938) replaced metrazol with electric shock.

This incompatibility now seems disproved, because several cases with the concomitant presence of the two disorders have been described. In many cases the question is the one well formulated by Tedeschi (1957): are we in the presence of a patient with epileptic psychosis or of an epileptic patient who suffers also from schizophrenia? Authors vary in preferring one answer to the other.

The authors who prefer the diagnosis of epilepsy speak of schizophrenic-like psychosis of epilepsy, for example, Beard and Slater (1962). These authors studied sixty-nine patients with a psychiatric syndrome that resembled schizophrenia. The psychosis was not related to the severity of the epilepsy. EEG changes showed that the epilepsy was of temporal lobe origin in over 70 percent of the cases. Zec (1965) speaks of a pseudoschizophrenic syndrome. According to him epileptic pseudoschizophrenic syndromes have one basic characteristic: they occur in hypnoid states, whereas idiopathic schizophrenia emerges in states of lucid consciousness.

Loeb and Giberti (1957) studied psychotic syndromes in psychomotor epilepsy. In the acute cases the psychosis was polymorphous in character. In the chronic cases the syndrome included hallucinations and resembled schizophrenia. During the acute psychotic syndrome the seizures and the EEG alteration disappeared.

Ervin, Epstein, and King (1955) made a study of forty-two patients with temporal spikes. Schizophrenia was diagnosed in 90 percent of those patients who also had temporal lobe seizures, and in seven out of nine patients who never had an overt seizure. The authors reported in their patients "disturbance in thinking and affect which have come to be associated with the schizophrenic process." They described the course of the illness as episodic. Strauss (1959), who is an epilepsy specialist, objects to putting these patients in "the wastebasket diagnosis of schizophrenia." He prefers to call them "epileptics with psychotic episodes." According to him it is a mistake to think of "acute recurrent schizophrenia" when there are positive EEG findings.

Glaser (1964) studied thirty-seven patients with psychomotor temporal lobe epilepsy, all of whom had definite psychotic episodes, with bizarre and inappropriate behavior, delusions, hallucinations, depressive mood, excessive religiosity, and paranoid ideation. One-third of the patients presented transitory catatonic features. A differential characteristic from schizophrenia was the continued effort on the part of the patient to maintain contact with reality.

After reviewing the literature and studying epileptic patients with chronic delusional psychoses, Bartlet (1957) found no evidence that schizophrenia occurs more, or less, frequently in epileptics than in the general population. His EEG findings supported the idea that psychosis following epilepsy is related to temporal lobe dysfunction.

The following conclusions can be drawn from the mentioned studies:

1. Schizophrenic symptomatology may coexist with epilepsy, whether grand mal, petit mal, or psychomotor.

2. Dysfunctions of the temporal lobes, detectable with EEG, are often accompanied by symptoms that may be classified as schizophrenic or schizophrenic-like.

3. In by far the majority of cases the schizophrenic-like or schizophrenic psychosis in epileptics occurs in the form of recurrent episodes.

I can state the following regarding the patients that I examined and who had been diagnosed as schizophrenics and had positive EEG findings of temporal lobe origin:

1. They had psychotic episodes, varying in length and recurrence.
2. They had a symptomatology of paranoid schizophrenia, often with mystical, religious, and philosophical delusions.
3. They had often presented either a rigid character structure or an angry, antagonistic, at times defiant attitude.

IV

The Possibility of Psychosomatic Involvement of the Central Nervous System in Schizophrenia

Three factors have greatly handicapped neurology in its effort to understand psychological and psychopathological problems. The first factor is shared with the rest of medical science. Physicians, trained in the scientific tradition, are reluctant to use any method that is not strictly empirical. Mental constructions, working hypotheses, are generally frowned upon as armchair speculations, more appropriate to the field of philosophy than to the field of medicine, and complete reliance has been put upon laboratory experiments and clinical observations. Obviously it would be absurd to minimize the tremendous accomplishments obtained through clinical and experimental research. Nevertheless, physicians should once more compare their research with those in the fields of physics and chemistry, where great progress has been made by a combination of experiments and a formulation of theoretical hypotheses. Such an eminent scientist as James B. Conant (1952) thinks that "the history of science demonstrates beyond a doubt that the really revolutionary and significant advances come not from empiricism but from new theories." Obviously, sooner or later it is necessary to submit any new theory to the empirical test. In spite of the predominant, antitheoretical trend, even in the field of neurology, theoretical concepts like those of Jackson (1932) and the theory of emotion advanced by Papez (1937) have been very fruitful in stimulating important work.

The second factor that has delayed neurological progress toward psychological understanding consists of the poor use of data offered by related fields. For instance, I believe that a more intense application of a genetic approach, such as the one followed by Werner (1957) in the field of psychology, and a greater use of the findings of Cassirer (1953) and Langer (1942, 1949) in their studies on the symbolic functions of the mind could enrich neurology very much.

The third factor is the relative disregard of neurology that dynamically oriented psychiatrists (with a few outstanding exceptions, for example, Roy Grinker and Lawrence Kubie) have recently acquired. Overreacting to previous positivistic approaches, most of them feel that neurology has not much to offer to the understanding of dynamic psychiatry, and they tend to ignore this field, whereas they maintain much closer relations with other branches of medicine—for example, internal medicine, allergy, dermatology, and so forth.

I am one of the dynamically oriented psychiatrists who believe that neurology has great contributions to make to psychiatry if its boundaries are enlarged.

An area where further expansion is urgently needed is the study of the central nervous system itself in the field of psychosomatic medicine. Only a historically determined trend toward disconnecting psychiatry entirely from neurology is responsible for the fact that whereas every organ or system of the body (such as skin, cardiovascular, and gastrointestinal apparatuses) has been recognized as affected by many psychosomatic disorders, the central nervous system has been given only secondary consideration. And yet the central nervous system is the organ of highest functionality; it is the organ that is first affected by psychogenic stimuli before they are channeled toward the other organs of the body. Could it not be that under a certain psychological stress a more or less specific functional disintegration of habitual neuronal patterns takes place? A psychosomatic involvement of the central nervous system would require a mechanism different from those responsible for other psychosomatic conditions. In other words, the process would not originate through the action of the autonomic nervous system upon the organs of the body. The central nervous system would be the victim of the psychological conflicts that it produces; the conflicts or turmoils themselves would disrupt the organization of complicated neuronal patterns.

We have seen in Chapter 2 that Jung was the first to advocate a psychosomatic involvement of the central nervous system. Jung felt that the brain, disturbed by its own tumultuous conflicts, would produce toxins that in their turn would further damage the nervous system. In the following pages I shall consider the possibility of a functional alteration of the nervous system in schizophrenia. This alteration will not be considered at a biochemical, or molecular, level but at a preceding level: as a disintegration of usual neuronal patterns.

I shall not start by speculating on the possibility of a primary pathology of the nervous system but, rather, by positing the problem of what parts of the nervous system are functionally involved in the schizophrenic symptomatology. In other words, I shall consider, not what parts of the nervous system are diseased, but what parts are functioning when a patient has ideas of reference, thinks paleologically, hallucinates, and so on. Then I shall discuss what type of coordination of the functions of these parts of the central nervous system is involved in the schizophrenic syndrome.

I am fully aware that the concepts expressed in this section cannot be fully proved at the present stage of our knowledge. I present them not as final conclusions but as working hypotheses, aiming to stimulate further research toward a closer integration of the psychological and the neurological.

This matter will be discussed in elementary terms. Readers who may be disturbed by the simplicity of the discussion should be reminded that this subject has led to a great deal of misunderstanding, and that therefore we should not be afraid of using too clear or simple language.

Let us start, therefore, with the most elementary question. Is there any doubt that in schizophrenia the central nervous system is involved, in the sense that many of the symptoms are mediated or produced by the nervous system, although not necessarily because of an organic pathology of the nervous system? Of course not. For instance, it is obvious that the patient would not have delusions or a bizarre way of thinking if he did not have a brain. The central nervous system is as necessary for the production of these symptoms as it is necessary for the production of mental processes in the normal man. We may go further and say that at least most of the schizophrenic symptoms are produced in the cerebral cortex. Here again, from a theoretical point of view, we do not exclude the possibility of an extracortical pathology. Someone, let us say, may conceive that some pathology of the diencephalon is responsible for schizophrenia, or that the membrane of neurons is defective, or that an enzyme is lacking or an abnormal one is produced. In these cases too, however, symptoms such as delusions, hallucinations, ideas of reference, word-salad would require a cortical participation concomitant to the mentioned alterations. Most of the schizophrenic phenomena involve the functioning of the patient in a social and symbolic world; they affect his thinking and his planned actions, and all of these activities require cortical centers. The schizophrenic symptoms require the function of the cerebral cortex, independently of whether the cortex is healthy or diseased.

The second step in our thinking consists in determining what cortical areas are involved in the pathological symptoms of schizophrenia. At this point we may make a general statement, already implied in the foregoing: all the cortical areas, whose function is well known today, do not seem to be *primarily* involved in the symptoms of early schizophrenia. For instance, it is obvious that the motor, sensory, extrapyramidal areas, and so on, are not primarily involved in schizophrenia. If a patient, as a result of a delusion, commits an absurd action, many cortical areas, such as the visual, pyramidal, extrapyramidal, are of course involved in the execution of this action, but the participation of these cortical areas is not pathological *per se*. It is the motivation, the symbolic meaning, and lack of control of the absurd action that are pathological. If we exclude the sensory and motor areas and the language centers as directly or originally involved in the psychopathology of schizophrenia, only three cortical areas are left to be considered. One is an ill-defined area including most of the temporal lobe and very small parts of the occipital and parietal lobes. We shall call this area the TOP area—from Temporal, Occipital, Parietal (Figure 47). The second important area occupies the whole prefrontal area. We shall refer to this area with the abbreviation PF. The third area consists of the archipallium and mesopallium, including the rhinencephalon, the hippocampus, the cingulate gyrus, and possibly the posterior orbital gyri. Part of this area borders on the TOP area. We shall take these three areas into consideration separately.

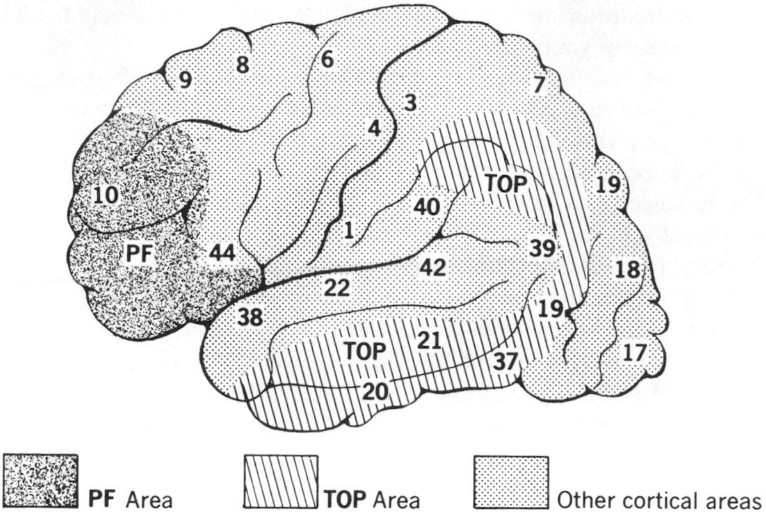

FIGURE 46. Left cerebral hemisphere showing extension of PF and TOP areas.

TOP Area

Anatomically, this area includes a large part of the temporal lobe (Brodmann's areas 20, 21, and 37) and a small part of the parietal and occipital lobes, consisting of the most central parts of Brodmann's areas 7, 19, 39, and 40. The parietal part is crossed by the interparietal sulcus. Histologically in Nissl sections it resembles the structure of the sensory associative areas. It receives projections from the lateral thalamic nucleus and from the pulvinar. The part of area 19 that is included in the TOP area possibly belongs more to the parietal than to the occipital lobe. It also has projections from the pulvinar.

Much less is known anatomically of the temporal part of the TOP area. Krieg (1947) calls this area one of the great *terrae incognitae* of the cortex. Thalamic connections to and from this part of the cortex have not been well established.

Phylogenetically the TOP area is one of the most recently evolved areas. Even such high species as *Pithecanthropus erectus* and especially *Homo Rhodesiensis* had only a rudimentary development of this area, as may be deduced from Tilney's writings (1928). Furthermore, together with other neopallic areas, it has no direct connections with the "reticular system" of the brain stem.

From a point of view of neuropathology, the TOP area is rather seldom involved in pathological conditions that could reveal its specific functions. Hemorrhages, softenings, or neoplasms are generally unilateral. In addition they either do not involve the totality of this area, or, if they do, they expand to surrounding regions.

In senile psychosis and cerebral arteriosclerosis the TOP area is involved less than the prefrontal area. Maybe this relative resistance to the senile or arteriosclerotic process is to be attributed to a different blood supply. Whereas the prefrontal area receives its supply mainly from the branches of the anterior cerebral arteries, the TOP area is irrigated by branches of all the three major arteries of the brain.

The TOP area is involved in Pick's disease, but this point will be taken into consideration later in this chapter.

From a physiological point of view the TOP area may be considered as the center of functionality of a much larger area including the whole parietal, occipital, and most of the temporal lobes. These three lobes form the part of the brain that receives stimuli from the external world and processes them into progressively higher constructs. We may divide this large part of the brain into four levels.

Before examining these four levels separately, however, we must make it clear that we do not consider them as sharply defined physiological entities. When we attribute a function to a particular cortical area, we mean only that that function is represented predominantly but not exclusively in that area. The cortex is to be conceived, not as a mosaic of distinct localizations, but as a pattern of overlapping representations, which are all more or less connected, and which also have vertical associations. These representations, however, have a relative concentration in certain areas. When we refer to levels, we refer only to these relative concentrations.

The first level consists of what Orton (1929) called the arrival platforms. It includes the borders of the calcarine fissure, Heschl convolution, and the postcentral gyrus (with other contiguous small areas of the parietal cortex and small portions of the precentral gyrus). These are the areas where crude sensation occurs.

The second level is the level of perception or recognition. It consists of area 18 for vision, a portion of the first and maybe second temporal gyrus for hearing, and an undetermined area of the parietal lobe for general sensation. If a lesion occurs at this level, the patient is not able to perceive, that is, to recognize what he experiences. He suffers from various forms of asymbolias, for instance, psychic blindness. At this level conditioned reflexes occur. This is also the level at which the symbolic activity of the mind manifests itself in the form of *signs* (see Chapter 19).

The third level (parts of Brodmann's areas 19, 22, 39, and 40) is much more complicated. Although it may exist in a very rudimentary form even in some high infrahuman species, it is only in humans that it acquires prominence. The following are some of the functions of this complicated level.

As Nielsen (1946) has described, voluntary recall of past sensations and experiences takes place at this level. This function implies some kind of primitive abstraction because in recalling one must separate or abstract a recognized experience from the other memories with which it was associated. The experience that was recognized at the second level is now abstracted from memories and is voluntarily revisualized. In order to function in this way at this level, the subject must have the ability to reproduce mentally *the image* of the external stimulus. Images are not signs, but *symbols,* inasmuch as they stand for something that is *not present* (see Chapters 5 and 19).

At this level many other functions occur. Not only images, but external stimuli (caused or not caused by the individual) start to stand for something else that is not present and, therefore, become *symbols*. Phylogenetically, symbols are preceded by *paleosymbols,* which are symbols valid only for the person who creates them. For instance, a person sees a connection between a sound and a situation or object, and that sound becomes the paleosymbol of the object or the situation. The paleosymbol becomes a symbol when its symbolic value has been accepted by at least a second person. The symbol produces in the person who pronounces it the same response that he produces in others (Mead, 1934). Verbal communication and socialization start at this level. Most probably at this level the verbal symbols denote, but have very little connotation power (see Chapters 16 and 19). Connections of this third level with the frontal lobes permit an expansion of the faculty of speech. All the language centers belong to the third level, although, as we shall see shortly, they would not have expanded without the influence of the fourth level.

Most authors follow Orton (1929) in recognizing only the three mentioned levels of elaboration. I feel that a fourth level must be differentiated, which anatomically consists of the TOP area (Brodmann's areas 20, 21, 37, parts of 7, 19, 39, and 40). This is the area where all the excitements coming from the lower levels are synthesized and elaborated into the highest mental constructs. Of course, as we have already mentioned, we must not consider this area as isolated or functioning by itself. First of all, it is associated with the corresponding area of the opposite hemisphere by means of fibers that pass through the corpus callosum. It is also connected with much lower structures through the archipallium. As we shall see shortly, it has important connections with the frontal lobes, without which it could not function at all. Furthermore, one should by no means think that only the TOP area is required for the highest mental processes. The neuronal network that mediates the highest mental processes extends to much lower levels (see engram in Figure 48). However, the highest engrams, or esthesotypes, to use a very appropriate concept proposed by Mackay (1954), need a place in the TOP area, almost as a center toward which all the associations of which they consist converge. The fact that the esthesotype extends to many lower levels has confused several researchers and has fallaciously led to conclusions that no cortical localization is possible and that what counts is only the extension of the cortical area.

But let us go back to the TOP area. In my opinion this area is needed for the highest processes of abstraction. These processes presuppose and require processes of socialization, which in simple forms have already started at the third level. As we have seen in Chapter 19, no high abstraction is possible if the individual in his development has not come into contact with other people. It is through contact with other human beings that verbal symbols continue to increase in number and that those previously acquired develop abstract meaning, that is, *connotation* or *categorical significance*. For instance, the term *mother* eventually refers not only to the mother of the individual or the mother of all the siblings, a concept that is generally connected with one visual image, but to any mother, to

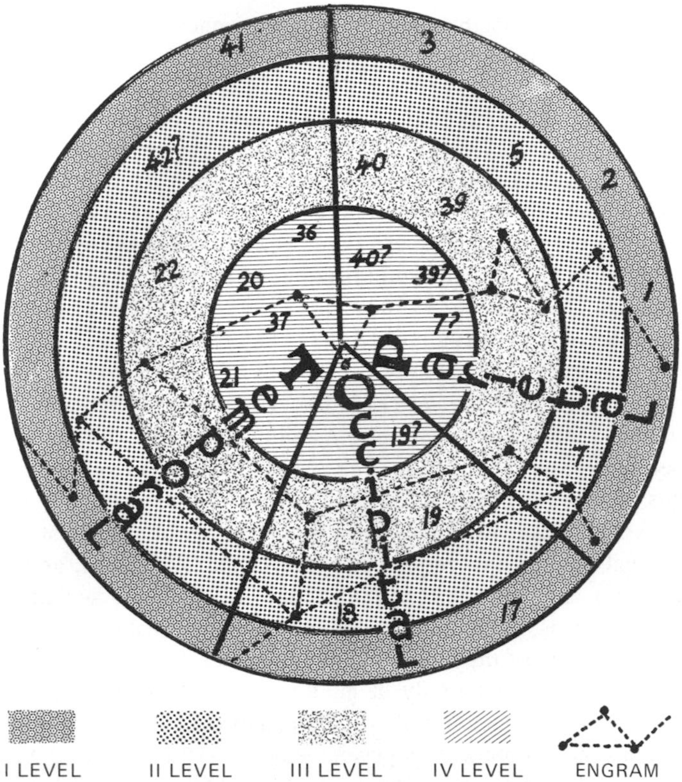

FIGURE 47. Diagram showing the four cortical levels of integration, represented schematically as four concentric areas in the temporal, occipital and parietal lobes. The numbers refer to Brodmann's areas.

mothers in general. In the TOP area, the thought processes become more and more elaborated and more distant from paleosymbols, images, and perceptions. The TOP area also facilitates or permits the full expansion of the third level. In fact, language would consist only of a few words, and only with *denoting* power, if processes mediated at the fourth level did not require a tremendous increase in vocabulary. This is another instance of the overlapping of levels (Chapter 19).

In Figure 48 the temporal (with the exception of the hippocampus and related structures), the occipital, and the parietal lobes are represented in a circular diagram. The four concentric circles represent the four different levels of integration. At the center is located the TOP area toward which all the other levels of elaboration converge. Like all diagrams, this one is intended merely as a didactical device and, as such, oversimplifies complicated neurological mechanisms. Among the important things that, for the sake of simplification, are omitted from the diagram are: (1) the associations between the different parts of the temporal, occipital, and parietal lobes; (2) the associations with other cortical areas, for example, the frontal lobes; (3) the associations between the two hemispheres; (4) the cortico-subcortical associations. Furthermore, the spatial proportions of the different areas are not exactly respected.

In my opinion there is no doubt that the functions mediated in the TOP areas are altered in the schizophrenic syndrome. We have seen in this book how in schizophrenia there is a gradual return from the abstract to the concrete, from a form of highly socialized symbolization to a form of symbolization that is decreasingly conceptual and social and more perceptual in character. Even the thought processes, deprived of abstract symbolization, abandon our common logic and become paleologic. At first the symbols lose the connotation power and denote only; then they become paleosymbols, that is, they are understood only by the patient; finally they become completely perceptualized or regressed to the levels of images or perceptions, as in the case of hallucinations. In other words, in progressive schizophrenia there is an increasing inability to use engrams or esthesotypes that need neurons located in the TOP area. At first there is a tendency to lose only the functions of the neuronal patterns that include the central parts of the TOP areas; later, as the illness progresses, there is a tendency not to use at all the functions of neuronal patterns that require any part of the TOP areas, and there is an inclination to use only the functions mediated by the first, second, and third levels. In other words, there is a reduction or simplification in the neopallic neuronal configurations of the highly symbolic mental processes.

The foregoing does not imply at all that the TOP areas of the two hemispheres are affected by some kind of organic pathology. The disintegration or loss of their functions may be viewed as psychogenic. Their functions, in fact, by permitting complicated interpersonal relations and human conflicts, may engender the greatest anxiety in human beings.

How the psychogenic mechanism brings about a dysfunction of these areas is a matter of speculation. It could be that the intensity of the emotional impact produced by these neuronal patterns is enough to make the complicated chains of these neuronal patterns disintegrate; or it could be that the rest of the nervous system learns to avoid these patterns or to do without them. Whatever the mechanism is, there seems to be little doubt that these areas do not function in the usual way or are not integrated well with the rest of the nervous system.

With this partial or complete psychogenic decline or elimination of the functions of the TOP areas, the schizophrenic does not obtain adjustment at a lower level of integration. In the process of evolution all the nervous areas readjust themselves by means of new associations every time a new area appears, changes, or extends. The entire nervous system and especially the cortex is in a state of maladjustment when the TOP areas are in a state of decreased functionality, even if this decreased functionality is psychogenic in origin. In other words, the schizophrenic regresses but does not integrate at a lower level, just as an experimental animal of a species normally provided with the cortex does not integrate at a noncortical level when the cortex is experimentally removed, because its whole organism is adjusted or attuned to the presence of the cerebral cortex. The schizophrenic's disintegration will continue. Furthermore, together with the elimination of the functions of high levels (Jackson's negative symptoms), there is a resurgence of inhibited functions (Jackson's positive symptoms), such as paleologic thinking, perceptualization, and so forth. The chronic patients who had been sick for many years, and whom we discussed in Chapters 25 and 26, presented agnosia to pain, temperature, and taste, and a syndrome not too dissimilar from psychic blindness. They also showed primitive habits reminiscent of the ones described by Klüver and Bucy (1937, 1938, 1939) in monkeys after bilateral removal of the temporal lobes. The crude sensations remained. It could be that in these patients the areas of functional impairment extended beyond the TOP areas and involved also the third level and part of the second.

PF, or Prefrontal, Area

For didactical purposes we have taken into consideration the TOP area first, but the PF areas are even more important in the psychogenesis of schizophrenia. The TOP areas elaborate the material coming from the external world, but it is the PF areas that permit this elaboration to a degree where schizophrenogenic conflicts are possible.

Increasing evidence indicates that the functions of the PF areas are very important, even if these functions are hard to define and, to a certain extent, still obscure. In addition to control of some visceral functions, at least four psychological functions of the PF lobes have so far been recognized. These four functions are certainly interrelated and are possibly different manifestations or different degrees of the same basic process.

The first function is the ability to maintain a steadfastness of purpose against distracting impulses from the environment (Malmo, 1942); in other words, it is the function of focal attention. The importance of focal attention as a prerequisite for higher mental processes has been very well illustrated by Schachtel (1954). As Schachtel wrote, each act of focal attention does not consist just of one sustained approach to the object to which it is directed but of several renewed approaches. Focal attention requires ability to suppress secondary stimuli and to delay the response.

It is obvious that the high elaborations of stimuli described in connection with the TOP areas could not take place if this function of the PF areas would not permit it.

A second function of the PF areas is the ability to anticipate the future. Whereas animals are able to anticipate events that will occur only within a very short period of time (from a few seconds to a few minutes after the stimulus takes place), man is able to anticipate mentally distant events. The importance of this faculty in the engendering of anxiety cannot be overestimated; in fact, anxiety is based on *anticipation* of danger, as Freud repeatedly wrote. Without the faculty of distant anticipation, anxiety is possible, but only a short-circuited anxiety similar to that experienced by infrahuman animals (Arieti, 1947; also Chapter 5 of this book). In animals, anxiety is experienced when the stimulus indicates a present danger or a danger that will follow shortly after the stimulus or when the animal is at the same time stimulated by two conflictful stimuli. In addition to this type of anxiety, human beings experience long-circuited anxiety, that is, an anxiety due to anticipation of distant danger. This anxiety persists even when the external stimulus has disappeared, because the external stimulus is replaced by an internal one, that is, by a chain of mental processes that permit the anticipation of distant future. Anticipation of distant future would not be possible if the individual could not receive high forms of symbols from the third and fourth levels of the posterior brain. For instance, a calf considers his mother to exist only when he perceives her, that is, when the visual stimulus of the cow or another stimulus that is simultaneously associated with the cow or follows at a very brief interval is perceived. But a man can think of his mother even when the mother is absent, because he is able to substitute mother with the symbol "mother." The symbol "mother" places mother in the three temporal dimensions: past, present, future.

A third function of the PF areas is the ability to permit planned or seriatim functions. By seriatim functions is meant the organization or synthesis of skilled acts or thoughts into an orderly series (Morgan, 1943). Although some high species, like monkeys and apes, are capable of simple seriatim series, this function expands very much in man. Seriatim functions imply ability (1) to anticipate a goal and (2) to organize and synthesize acts or thoughts in a given temporal sequence for the purpose of reaching the anticipated goal (Brickner, 1936).

The fourth function of the PF areas is the ability to make choices and to initiate the translation of the "mental" choice into a motor action.

Some experiments have proved that infrahuman animals also learn to choose; that is, they learn what choice to make in certain experimental sets and what choice not to make (Hamilton, 1911; Yerkes, 1934). These experiments are valuable in the study of "equivalent stimuli" and of a function of primitive abstraction, but they do not really demonstrate the presence of the ability to choose as it exists in human beings. Long-circuited choice as it occurs in human beings requires many steps, as we have seen in Chapter 17, section V.

These steps could not take place if the posterior brain did not provide high forms of symbolism.

There is no doubt that these functions of the PF areas are disturbed in schizophrenia. The function that comes first to our mind is the ability to anticipate the future. This function is an absolute prerequisite for long-circuited anxiety and is the basis of any complicated mental conflict. In schizophrenia it tends to be teleologically replaced by more primitive processes that require shorter circuits (see Chapter 16). The same thing could be repeated for seriatim thinking. Greenblatt and Solomon (1953) feel also that the frontal lobe circuits sustain the emotional tension of the psychotic, and Freeman and Watts (1942) have well described the importance of future anticipation in the engendering of psychoses. These functions do not seem to be very disturbed in well-systematized paranoids, possibly because at the beginning of the illness these patients resort predominantly to the mechanism of projection in the attempt to remove anxiety. At a subsequent stage, however, these functions become impaired in paranoids too. The delusions change from the persecutory to the grandiose type and are more and more related to the present time: "I *am* a king."

The other PF functions are also disturbed in schizophrenia. The ability to make choices or to translate thoughts into actions is particularly altered in catatonia. As to the ability for steadfastness or focal attention, we know that it is very much impaired in schizophrenics. Their span of attention is very limited.

Archipallium and Hypothalamus

The archipallium and the hypothalamus may be thought of as playing an important role in schizophrenia. Because great importance is attributed to these structures in the mechanism of emotions, we could even be inclined to think that an altered functionality of the archipallium could explain the affective impairment that is so pronounced in schizophrenia. One could even be induced to the hasty conclusion that the original cause of this mental condition is to be found in this part of the nervous system. At the present stage of our knowledge, such possibility cannot be denied categorically. However, such an interpretation seems improbable to me.

I do not mean that the archipallium is not involved in schizophrenia. On the contrary, a neopallic dysfunction, even if functional, is bound to have important repercussions upon the archipallium too. If we follow again Jackson's principles, we may think that the hypofunctionality of neopallic areas must be accompanied by a release and hyperfunctionality of the archipallium. Because we know so little about the functions of the archipallium and of its single parts, we cannot explain how this release is manifested. At first one would think that the release of the archipallium would increase the emotionality of the patient, but we have to remember that with the term *archipallium* we include many structures representing possible different sublevels, and that their specific action in the experience of emotions is unknown. At any rate, the release of the archipallium will increase the inhibitory power that this part of the brain exerts over lower structures, such as the hypothalamus. This inhibition of the hypothalamus may explain the hypofunctionality of the autonomic nervous system, as far as homeostatic reactions are concerned, as well as the decrease in somatic and visceral expressions of those emotions that are still experienced in schizophrenia, in spite of the neopallic-symbolic disintegration.

The interesting study by Bard and Mountcastle (1947) may support this point of view. These authors found that removal of the neocortex produces a state of placidity in cats. Anger or sham rage never occur. Nociceptive stimuli elicit mild responses. If these animals are subjected to ablation of the cingulate gyrus or to various parts of the rhinencephalon, they become angry and ferocious. These experiments suggest that the rhinencephalon restrains the hypothalamus. This action is opposed to the one exerted by the neocortex; in fact, removal of the cortex increases the inhibitory effect of the rhinencephalon.

Incidentally, the rhinencephalon may exert a restraining influence not only over the hypothalamus, but also on the thalamus, possibly through some hypothalamic-thalamic connections. We have seen that in the terminal stage of schizophrenia pain and temperature perceptions are decreased or abolished (Chapter 25). We have interpreted this phenomenon as a consequence of some possible psychosomatic dysfunction of the parietal cortex. Penfield and Rasmussen (1952) have, on the other hand, found that pain and temperature are experienced in humans at a thalamic level when the cortical areas are removed. In the terminal stage of schizophrenia an increased ability to experience pain and temperature should occur on account of a theoretically presumed release of the thalamic level. The opposite is the case. It may be that some restraining action exerted on the thalamus by the archipallium, or lack of stimulation from the hypothalamus, is involved in these processes. The fact that frontal leucotomy relieves intractable pain gives additional support to this point of view.

We have to mention that this altered functionality of cortical centers in schizophrenia also puts into a certain disequilibrium the so-called visceral brain (MacLean, 1949), that is, those cortical and subcortical centers that are now considered the highest representation of visceral functions. A dysfunction of the autonomic nervous system may be partially due to their altered functionality. Also the inhibition of the hypothalamus may reduce the excitement that normally reverberates from the hypothalamus to the cortex, and this lack of excitement may add to the dysfunction of the neocortex. Hypothalamic-thalamic and thalamic-cortical relations may also be altered as a result of this disequilibrium. Figure 49 is a diagram of these interrelations. As every diagram does, it represents an oversimplification of the processes involved.

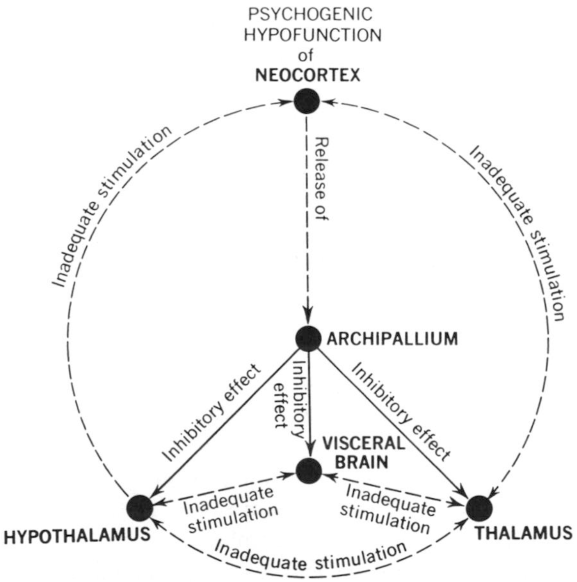

FIGURE 48. Diagram illustrating the relations between the neocortex, the archipallium and the hypothalamus in schizophrenia.

General Interpretation

We shall recapitulate now what we have mentioned about the possibility of a psychosomatic involvement of the central nervous system in schizophrenia.

Whatever is the origin of the series of events that ultimately leads to the psychosis, the overwhelming anxiety, the difficult interpersonal conflicts, and the disturbing high forms of symbolism are predominantly mediated in those cortical areas that in this chapter have been called the PF and the TOP areas. These areas are the highest in the evolutionary scale; they are the last to appear in phylogeny and the last to myelinize in ontogeny. They are probably the most vulnerable areas of the central nervous system from a functional point of view, at least in those people who have a hereditary predisposition to schizophrenia. This hereditary vulnerability may be direct, that is, immediately involving the functions of these two areas, or indirect, by disturbing another area whose normal functioning is a prerequisite for the good functioning of the PF and TOP areas. The impact of the psychological conflicts is too much to bear for a part of the central nervous system that is already genetically vulnerable. At times it may be too much to bear even if such hereditary predisposition does not exist. On the other hand, the hereditary vulnerability alone, without the psychogenic factors, would not be enough to engender the disorder. A disintegration of the neuronal patterns that involve predominantly these two areas may take place, and a reintegration or formation of simpler circuits that use these high areas less and less, and eventually not at all, may follow.

This neuronal reintegration may thus be seen deterministically and also adaptationally or restitutionally. In fact, there seems to be a psychosomatic attempt to return to lower levels of integration, levels that do not permit complicated interpersonal symbolism and long-circuited anxiety. Orton (1929) too thought that shorter circuits or crossovers are used in schizophrenia and especially in catatonia, but he thought also that the process involved was organic and affected specifically the centers connected with the longer circuits.

In my opinion, at the same time that these cortical centers or parts of them are in a state of hypofunctionality or dysfunction, other centers or some other parts of them or some lower neuronal configurations or patterns are released and cause characteristic symptoms. Jackson's concepts are valid in relation to schizophrenia too, if correlated with psychodynamic principles. For instance, when logical thinking is impaired, paleologic thinking comes to the surface. When social symbols disappear, paleosymbols replace them. Concepts become more and more perceptual, and anticipation of the future is replaced by thoughts concerning the present.

One could raise the objection that although an organic condition affecting *bilaterally* the PF and the TOP areas should give a symptomatology similar to schizophrenia, so far this occurrence has not been reported. Actually the only organic disease that would approximate a bilateral involvement of these areas, and these areas exclusively, is Pick's disease. In Pick's disease the symptomatology is similar to that found in cases of very regressed schizophrenics who have been sick for many years, but it has very little in common with the symptomatology of early cases. In both Pick's disease and schizophrenia there is an impairment of the abstract attitude described by Goldstein, that is, there is occurrence of Jackson's negative symptoms. However, in schizophrenia there is also a resurgence of many positive symptoms (paleologic thought, hallucinations, and so on) that are not present in Pick's disease. This may be due to the fact that in Pick's disease, as well as in other organic conditions, several levels are affected at the same time, and therefore a release of inferior cortical processes is prevented. We know in fact from neuropathological studies how diffuse the alterations are. In Pick's disease they involve not only association areas, but also primary centers and many subcortical structures (Ferraro and Jervis, 1936). Even when the lesions are patchy, we can hardly believe that they selectively involve only some higher neuronal configurations and respect lower ones. This state of affairs explains why Jackson's positive symptoms are not so clearly seen in organic conditions that involve the cortex.

The similarity of regressed schizophrenics to organic patients with involvement of the cerebral cortex is more pronounced than is generally assumed. For instance, Figure 50 reproduces the letter of a patient, the content of which resembles schizophrenic word-salad. Actually, this letter was written by a nonpsychotic patient suffering from motor aphasia. She was a young woman who had been shot by her irate husband. The bullet damaged her Broca's area and surrounding regions. She was not able to talk, but she understood simple spoken language. She was relearning how to write, but she could not find the right words. This letter was written to me on my last day of service at Pilgrim State Hospital. The patient, who knew I was leaving, wanted to say farewell and to thank me. In the letter, however, she seems to express ideas different from, or even the opposite of, those that she wanted to express. The result is something similar to word-salad. The difficulty may be the same one that the regressed schizophrenic presents. Each part of the mental context is equivalent to another; the patient is unable to pick up the right part. An organic patient who replies to the question, "What city is the capital of France?" with, "La Marseillaise," probably uses the same mental process as that of the schizophrenic who replied, "White House," to the question, "Who was the first president of the United States?"

Brown (1972) has stressed the similarities between some aphasics and some schizophrenic patients. According to him the type of aphasia that resembles most the language of the regressed schizophrenic is semantic aphasia, which is a midway state between anomic aphasia and Wernicke's aphasia. Semantic aphasia, first described by Head (1926), reflects an interruption of language at a prelinguistic phase in the thought-speech transition. According to Brown it is "characterized by a want of recognition of the full significance of words and phrases apart from their verbal meaning, failure to comprehend the final aim or goal of an action, and inability to clearly formulate a general conception of what has been heard, read, or seen in a picture, although many of the details can be enumerated." Brown collects from the literature cases of aphasias with semantic jargon reminiscent of schizophrenic language and thought. He quotes a patient, reported by Kinsbourne

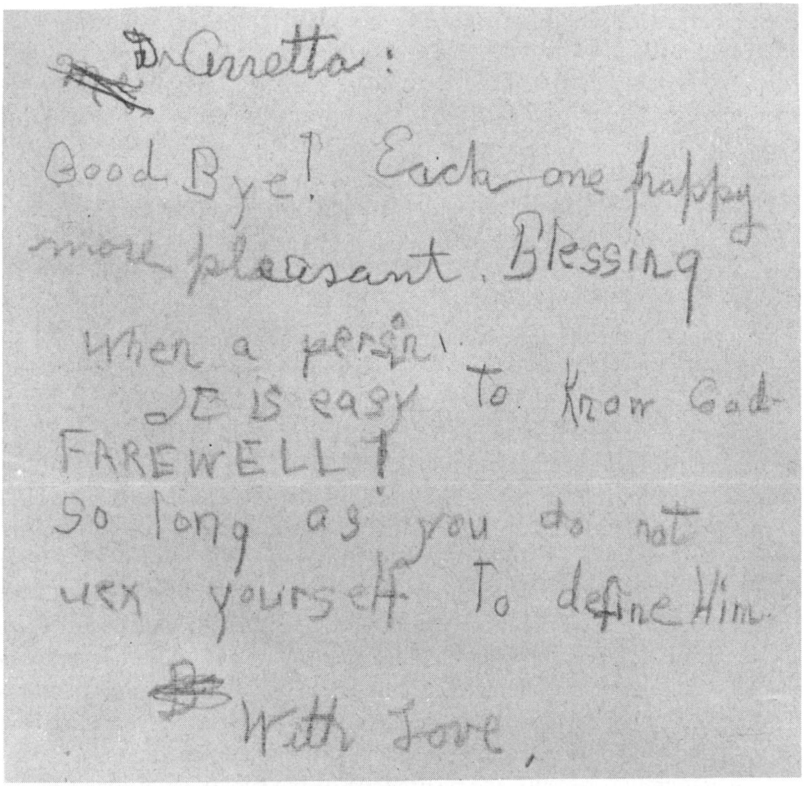
Dr. Arretta:

Good Bye! Each one happy
more pleasant. Blessing
When a persn.
It is easy To Know God
FAREWELL!
So long as you do not
uex yourself To define Him.

With Love,

FIGURE 49. Letter of a patient suffering from motor aphasia, after being shot in the left hemisphere of the brain. Notice the similarity to schizophrenic word-salad, as far as the content of the letter is concerned. The handwriting, however, differs from that of schizophrenic patients, possibly because it reflects disturbance of the motor engrams.

and Warrington (1963), who was asked to explain the proverb ''Strike while the iron is hot.'' The patient replied, ''Ambition is very very and determined. Better to be good and to Post Office and to Pillar Box and to distribution and to mail and survey and headmaster. . . .''

This sample and many others from semantic aphasics, are reminiscent of schizophrenic word-salad and at times of pseudoabstract schizophrenic language. It could be that in the semantic aphasics and in regressed schizophrenics the same cortical areas are involved, although the etiology and pathology differ.

To return to our regressed schizophrenic patients, we can state that the re-emerging primitive functions as a rule are not useful, although they include also those restitution symptoms studied by Freud. In fact, as we have already mentioned, the regressed patient does not become adjusted, but maladjusted at a level at which he cannot integrate. The hypofunctionality of the neopallic areas that we have examined must also alter associations with other areas, not only the neighboring one but also the distant, through long association bundles, commissures like the corpus callosum, the cortico-thalamic and thalamo-cortical tracts, and so on. This is a process of functional diaschisis, similar to the organic diaschisis described by Von Monakow (1914). Direct connections of these neopallic areas with the brain stem reticular system do not seem to exist (Livingston, 1955). The brain stem reticular system is of ancient origin and is more concerned with the basic physiological functions of life than with the symbolic functions. However, undoubtedly indirect connections exist through the archipallium.

We may visualize in schizophrenia also what we may call a process of functional *dysencephalization,* in a certain way the opposite of *encephalization.* It is well known that some neurologists have used the latter term to describe the shifting toward higher centers of the functions that in lower species are mediated by lower or more caudal centers. In schizophrenia the opposite takes place: not only is there a return of the functions of the released lower center but also a tendency of the function of the higher center to be mediated by the lower center. For instance, often abstract thought processes that take place in the highest centers are mediated instead at a perceptual level and become auditory hallucinations.

The three processes of the reemergence of lower functions, of functional diaschisis, and of dysencephalization determine a state of disequilibrium and of psychological splitting, which is so characteristic of this mental disorder. How does the organism defend itself from this disorganization? With further regression. The process thus repeats itself in a vicious circle that may lead to complete dilapidation. This circular process is one of the characteristics of functional regression that is lacking in the organic phenomenon of diaschisis. In organic conditions there is not complete disintegration because the resurgence of the functions of lower levels or sublevels is minimal in comparison to functional conditions. If further deterioration occurs, it is only because the organic process itself expands or produces other damages—for example, gliosis, hydrocephalus, hemorrhages, and so on. Some intoxications, however, just as those caused by mescaline, may be selective enough in their physiological action to reproduce a specific cortical hypofunctionality, and subsequent subcortical dysfunctions, similar to the ones occurring in schizophrenia.

In conclusion, at least in those cases that progress beyond a very initial phase, the schizophrenic process elicits psychosomatic attempts to integrate the highest cortical functions at a lower level. With comparatively few exceptions this attempt fails because the process engenders other self-perpetuating mechanisms that lead to regressions.

An artificial partial attempt to integrate the schizophrenic at a lower level is made by frontal leucotomy and other psychosurgical procedures. Theoretically these procedures have some validity because they remove, at least partially, the functions of such areas as the PF and do not unchain progressive regression. However, to change a disorder that is at least partially psychogenic for one that, together with symptoms, removes permanently a great part of the essence of man and reduces him to an almost infrahuman state seems more than questionable to those who today obtain an increasing number of successes with different therapeutic approaches, even in very difficult cases.

PART SIX

Epidemiology, Transcultural Aspects, and Prevention of Schizophrenia

CHAPTER

31 Epidemiology of Schizophrenia

I
Introductory Remarks

Epidemiology is a science and methodology whose object is to determine whether there is an association between a rate of illness and the changing strength of an environmental factor. For instance, if the population that smokes has a higher rate of lung cancer, then there is a positive association between lung cancer and smoking. Similarly we know that the incidence of schizophrenia is 0.85 percent in the general population. If we find that populations having a special characteristic have an increased incidence of schizophrenia, then we find a positive association. This positive association does not necessarily indicate that the characteristic in question is the cause of schizophrenia, but that it may affect in a positive way the etiology of schizophrenia. Conversely, if we find that the incidence of schizophrenia is decreased in populations having a certain characteristic, we cannot conclude that that characteristic is a cure or preventive factor of schizophrenia but that it may be part of a set of factors that are used by the individual to prevent schizophrenia. The characteristics that are studied in relation to the incidence of schizophrenia may be biological, psychological, sociological, or difficult to categorize. For instance, let us take as an example the studies relating birth order—that is, the position of an individual among his siblings—and the rate of schizophrenia. Birth order is connected with family size and with age of the parents because first born children tend to have younger parents than those born last. The sex and spacing of the siblings give a special meaning to a given position. Moreover, being the first, middle, last, or only child, or the only boy or girl, may give special meaning to the family constellation.

Needless to say, the epidemiology of schizophrenia is very much hampered by the fact that there are marked variations in the ways schizophrenic patients come to the attention of physicians, in the ways the diagnosis of schizophrenia is made, in the ways patients are hospitalized, kept in hospitals, and so forth. For instance, it is well known that American psychiatrists make the diagnosis of schizophrenia more frequently than their European colleagues, many of whom limit this diagnosis to patients with classic Kraepelinian symptomatology. Another important task is to establish the difference between the *prevalence rate* and the *incidence rate* of the condition.

The incidence rate is the number of new cases of a particular illness per 100,000 population occurring during the period of a year. The calculations of the incidence rate are susceptible to quite large errors. We have already alluded to the fact that in some psychiatric hospitals or schools many patients difficult to categorize are diagnosed as schizophrenics. The opposite is true in other hospitals and schools. In many studies the incidence has been calculated only on the basis of first admissions to psychiatric hospitals. However, we know that there is a *surplus* incidence, consisting of schizophrenic patients who are never going to be hospitalized.

The prevalence rate is the total number of cases per 100,000 population (not just the new ones) suffering from the disease during the period of a year. In the case of schizophrenia, calculations of prevalence rates are made difficult by different rates of discharge, various degrees of tolerance of the general population, and by different opinions among psychiatrists on who is to be called "schizophrenic." Some psychiatrists consider a person a schizophrenic for his whole life if he has had a schizophrenic episode once in his lifetime. Other psychiatrists, lately in an increasing number, feel that a patient can recover from schizophrenia just as he can recover from pnuemonia; in their opinion a recovered schizophrenic should no longer be called a schizophrenic. This point of view leads to a much lower prevalence rate. Thus prevalence rates are very unreliable and vary from 170 to 950 per 100,000 population (Yolles and Kramer, 1969).

II
Some Vital Statistics

Lemkau and Crocetti (1957) estimate a minimum incidence rate for schizophrenia of 50 per 100,000 population. Yolles and Kramer (1969) report an adjusted rate of 116.8 per 100,000 for schizophrenic reactions. They also report staggering figures that they have obtained from the Annual Statistical Reports issued by the U.S. Department of Health, Education, and Welfare, Public Health Service, National Institute of Mental Health. Schizophrenic patients, residents in state and county mental hospitals and Veterans Administration neuropsychiatric hospitals, numbered 289,055 at the end of 1964 and constituted half of the population of these hospitals. Schizophrenics made up 32 percent of new admissions to these hospitals, 20 percent of new admissions to private hospitals, and 15 percent of new admissions to 2,000 outpatient psychiatric clinics in the United States.

Yolles and Kramer report that the rate of first admissions to state and county mental hospitals was 15.3 per 100,000 in 1964. There was a great variation among the states, from a high of 31.1 in one state to a low of 3.7 in another.

These data do not vary very much from those that I reported for the year 1949 (Arieti, 1959). In 1949 the median first admission rate to state hospitals was 15.0, with the highest rates found in the District of Columbia (39.8) and New York (30.6) and the lowest in Kansas (4.7) and Wyoming (5.9). Yolles and Kramer report that of the total first admissions during the year 1964, 53 percent were patients between the age of 25 and 44; 20 percent were 45 or older. Patients under 15 years of age have doubled between 1950 and 1964, and the trend continues. On the other hand, from 1955 to 1964 there has been an annual decline in the resident patient population in state and county mental hospitals in the United States of 13 percent.

The marital status of the patient seems to be positively correlated with the rate of admission to state hospitals. It seems that bachelorhood, separation, divorce, and widowhood are poor risk in comparison to marriage. Yolles and Kramer report that the single male has a rate of admission to psychiatric hospitals that is six times greater than the married male; the divorced and separated male, eight times greater; the widowed, five times greater; the rate for the single female is three times greater than for the married female; the divorced and separated, five times greater; the widowed, three times greater.

The usual explanation given for the higher rate of admission in single persons is that people with psychological instability may be less fit to marry and more disposed to schizophrenia than the average person. Farina, Garmezy, and Barry (1963) added that in an industrialized society the male takes a more active role in courtship and selection. Men thus need to be more adequate than women in order to attain marital status. Consequently married men should show a lower rate of schizophrenia. As a matter of fact, statistics gathered by Farina and co-workers show that the rate of schizophrenic married women exceeds the rate for married men. There was actually no sex difference among patients who remained married, but the rate was much higher for women among the divorced and separated. The authors concluded that whereas the unstable man tends to remain single, the unstable woman tends to get married and get divorced.

Several authors (Grosz and Miller, 1958; Smith and McIntyre, 1963; Burton and Bird, 1963) have studied the association between birth order and schizophrenia but obtained negative results. Schooler (1961) found a positive relation in the rate of the disorder in siblings born last in comparison to those born first. He suggested the hypothesis that the mother's "increasing age or large numbers of previous children may affect the intrauterine environment in such a way as to leave the child with a physiologic predisposition to the disease." Contrary findings were obtained in India by Rao (1964), who determined a greater rate of schizophrenics among siblings born first or second.

Erlenmeyer-Kimling, Van Den Bosch, and Denham (1969) have reviewed the data of several authors from various cultures; they also studied data from 1,348 subjects and reached the conclusion that there is no association between schizophrenia and birth order.

Hare and Price (1968) studied the season of birth of schizophrenics and found an excess of winter births in schizophrenic patients compared with neurotic patients. To explain their findings, they advanced the following hypotheses, which to me seem indeed hard to accept: (1) protein deficiency in the mother's diet during the hot summer months of her early pregnancy or maternal ascorbic acid deficiency in later pregnancy or infectious diseases to which a winter-born child is more exposed would determine constitutional damage that in its turn would favor the penetration of a major schizophrenic gene; (2) unstable parents are less able to time their conceptions in order to avoid the less desirable winter birth. The children will have an increased liability to mental illness, not directly from their winter birth, but genetically (or culturally) from their unstable parents.

III

Schizophrenia Among Immigrants and Minority Groups

Many authors have found a higher rate of schizophrenia among immigrants than native populations.

Malzberg (1959*a, b,* 1962) has made many accurate studies that prove beyond doubt that schizophrenia is much higher among immigrants from foreign countries and also higher in migrants from one part of the United States to another. Locke, Kramer, and Pasamanick (1960) obtained similar findings. Eitinger (1959) found psychoses to be ten times more frequent among refugees from different countries than among native Norwegians. In his work he stressed the fact that the immigrants were *refugees.*

Halevi (1963) reported that in Israel the immigrants from Europe have a lower incidence of schizophrenia than the native Jewish population. Astrup and Odegaard (1961) in Norway found a lower incidence in immigrants, except for those who went to reside in the capital, Oslo. In Australian Cade and Krupinski (1962) and Schachter (1962) found psychoses more frequently among non-British immigrants than among British, possibly because the latter had less difficulty in acculturating.

The cited works are representative of a large number of studies, the majority of which demonstrate that immigration to a new country increases the risk of schizophrenia. There are two possible explanations for this increase in risk: (1) only those who are more predisposed to schizophrenia emigrate to a foreign country; (2) immigration *per se* predisposes to schizophrenia.

The first explanation seems to intimate that people who have a latent, preexisting predisposition to the psychosis emigrate more easily; that is, those more inclined to emigrate to a foreign country are the discontented, among whom there may be a higher percentage of gifted people who do not accept things as they are, as well as a higher percentage of potential psychotics. It seems more probable, however, that immigration *per se* is an important predisposing factor. The change from one culture to another, from one way of living to a different one, requires a strenuous effort. Thousands of readjustments have to be made, which may exhaust the psychic reserves of the individual and may allow deep-seated conflicts to break through. In the state of California the immigration consists mainly of people coming from other areas of the United States. The cultural readjustment thus is less marked, and this factor may explain why the rate of schizophrenia there is lower than in New York, where immigrants come predominantly from foreign countries.

However, it is impossible to isolate immigration from other, often concomitant, factors. Immigrants generally belong to special ethnic groups, constitute cultural or religious minorities, have a lower economic status, and in some cases are the victims of prejudice, discrimination, and exploitation. It is difficult to evaluate each of these variables. In Israel, where the number of immigrants is larger than the number of natives, schizophrenia is reputed to be more frequent among the natives, who constitute a minority.

Malzberg (1959*b*) found that the rate (per 100,000) for schizophrenia among Jews was lower (35.5) than the rate for Protestants (41.7) and Catholics (41.2). Malzberg (1956, 1959*a, b*) reported that the incidence of schizophrenia among blacks and Puerto Ricans was twice as high as that of the general population. Pasamanick (1962, 1964) believes that the different rates of schizophrenia among the various ethnic groups (especially among blacks) have much more to do with economics than with ethnicity.

Kramer (quoted in Yolles and Kramer, 1969) reported that in a study carried out by the National Institute of Mental Health in 1960 in thirteen states, the first admission rate for schizophrenia among blacks was 2.6 times the rate among whites.

Some authors, like Pasamanick, rightly take into consideration the importance of economic factors, but practically no author takes into sufficient consideration the factors of discrimination and prejudice in their total effect.

Sanua (1962) applies some of my ideas (Arieti, 1955) to his findings about the incidence of paranoid and catatonic schizophrenia in Jewish and Protestant patients. Sanua found more parental rejection and "consequently" more paranoid schizophrenia among Protestants than among Jews. Conversely he found more overprotection and "consequently" more catatonic schizophrenia among Jews than among Protestants.

IV

Ecology and Social Class

A few decades ago Faris and Dunham (1939) published a book on the ecology of mental disorders that for a long time was considered a classic. These authors studied the distribution of schizophrenia in Chicago and Providence, Rhode Island, and found that the incidence varied in the different areas of these cities. The findings of Faris and Dunham have been confirmed by several other authors (Green, 1939; Queen, 1940; Schroeder, 1942), who have repeated this research in other American cities. The areas with a high incidence of schizophrenia are areas of highly mobile population. They are the centers of big cities, which also have a high incidence of delinquency, crime, prostitution, and drug addiction. In other words, they are in a state of social disorganization or anomie. In these areas in which low economic classes live, the role of the family and its members is very unstable. Psychological isolation, faulty socialization, and deprivation of many sorts are common. Faris, who was the senior author of the original work with Dunham, repeated in a subsequent book (1955) that social isolation and disintegration, in the high degree in which they occur in big cities, are important determinants of mental illness.

The size of the city is also of pathogenic significance. Landis and Page (1938) found that the rate of schizophrenia increases proportionately with the size of the city. At the time of their investigation, the rate of first admissions in New York City was 28.7 patients per 100,000 population, whereas progressively smaller communities had smaller rates.

For a long time a prevailing theory postulated that schizophrenia itself was responsible for a "downward drift" or a downward social mobility among patients. Lystad (1957), for instance, studied social mobility of schizophrenic patients in New Orleans and concluded that the patients showed "less upward status mobility than matched, non-mentally ill persons." Hollingshead and Redlich's (1958) research in New Haven seems to disprove that hypothesis. According to these authors the families of schizophrenics are not more prone to move downwardly than the normal population. As a matter of fact, the authors were impressed with upward mobility in some instances. The authors found that the incidence of schizophrenic patients in the lowest class was eleven times greater than in the highest class.

Goldberg and Morrison (1963) criticized the works of Hollingshead and Redlich. They indicated the technical reasons why in New Haven studies the poorer fathers would be overrepresented and therefore wrong conclusions would be reached. Their study reconfirmed the old hypothesis of an association between high rates of schizophrenia and low occupational status.

Studies of social mobility present tremendous difficulties because they have to be matched by studies of comparable groups of nonschizophrenics. The point of origin, in terms of social status, is important. Thus if the person with a low position becomes schizophrenic, probably his mobility is less affected than that of a patient who had a prominent position.

V

Urbanism and Industrial Society

In a paper published some years ago (Arieti, 1959), I studied the rate of schizophrenic patients admitted for the first time to psychiatric hospitals in the United States and in Italy. The rates for Italy, provided by Professor Francesco Bonfiglio, who was then director of the Statistical Department of Mental Diseases in Italy, were based on the annual average of the triennium 1947–1949. The rates for the United States were calculated on the estimated 1949 population, from data obtained from *Patients in Mental Institutions, 1949,* published by the National Institute of Mental Health. Figure 50 and Table 1 show that in most of the northern industrial areas of Italy the rate of schizophrenic patients admitted for the first time to psychiatric hospitals was approximately 10 to 12 for 100,000 inhabitants. If we take regions in the south of Italy, like Puglie, Calabria, and Sicily, the admission rate was from 3.3 to 6 per 100,000. In Calabria, which is a very rural, technically backward region in the south, the incidence was one-fourth the incidence in Emilia (Bonfiglio, 1952).

These striking differences can be explained in the ways mentioned in the second section of this chapter. It may be that in the Italian regions where the admission rate of schizophrenics was low, two factors operated: (1) not all patients were admitted to psychiatric hospitals, but many were kept among the general population; (2) the proper diagnosis was not made; therefore, many patients were not recognized as mentally ill, or if they were recognized as such, the wrong diagnosis was made.

According to the first hypothesis, in certain regions people would resist hospitalizing patients for fear of stigmatizing the whole family.* I tend to believe that a different attitude toward hospitalization cannot entirely explain the differences in the admission rate. In certain Italian rural areas relatives are tolerant toward mental defectives and especially toward senile patients, for whom they retain respect. As far as schizophrenics are concerned, however, the attitude toward their hospitalization is not much different from one geographical area to another.

Undoubtedly there are many schizophrenics who are not hospitalized. But that is true for every geographical area and every country. Many of those nonhospitalized patients represent latent or nonobvious cases, persons who are not recognized as sick or who are easily tolerated. There is also a certain number of more overtly psychotic patients who, as a result of particular circumstances (for instance, the fact that they live alone), escape hospitalization. Probably they are approximately the same percentage of the total number of schizophrenics in every country or in every region.

The second explanation of the difference in rate of admission is that the

* A similar hypothesis has been advanced by American authors who thought that the increase in first admission rate occurring in New York State was due to the fact that relatives had become more willing to hospitalize patients. Malzberg (1940) analyzed this point and concluded that although this changed attitude toward hospitalization may have had some bearing on the rate of admission, it could not explain entirely the large increase in the incidence of mental patients admitted to hospitals.

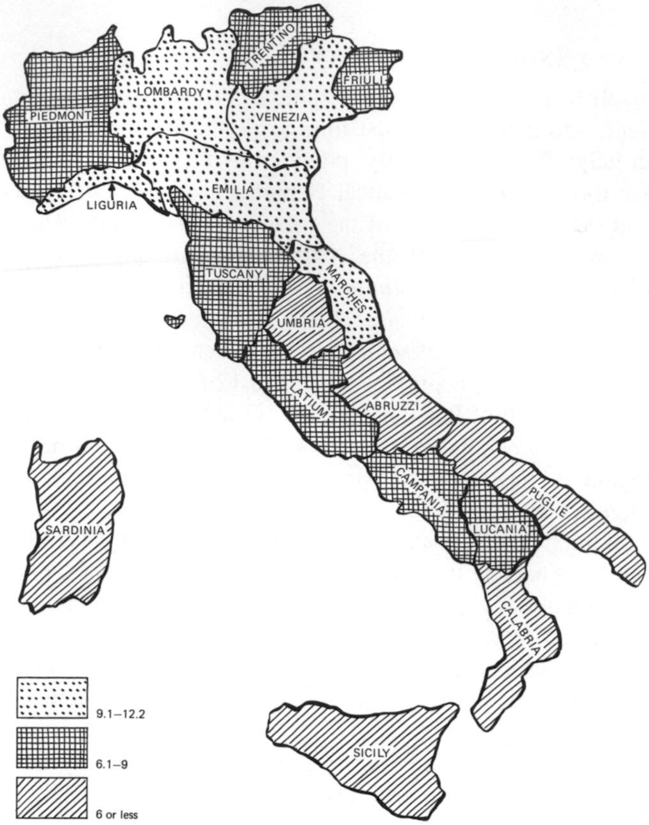

FIGURE 50. First admission rate for schizophrenia in the various regions of Italy. The rate is per 100,000 and represents the annual average of the triennial period 1947–1949.

TABLE 1

First admissions of schizophrenic patients to public psychiatric hospitals in Italy. The rate is per 100,000 inhabitants and is based on the annual average of the triennium 1947–1949.

Abruzzi	5.8	Marches	9.7
Calabria	3.3	Piedmont	7.8
Campania and Lucania	7.9	Puglie	4.9
Emilia	12.2	Sardinia	6.0
Friuli	6.5	Sicily	6.0
Latium	7.2	Trentino	8.0
Liguria	10.9	Tuscany	7.6
Lombardy	11.8	Umbria	3.7
		Venezia	9.4
	Italy	8.2	

wrong diagnosis is made, that is, that in certain regions of Italy some patients are recognized as psychotics, but are admitted under a different diagnosis—for example, they are confused with manic-depressive psychosis. Thus, where the rate of schizophrenia is low, the rate of manic-depressive psychosis should be high. This assumption is immediately eliminated by the study of the statistics prepared by Bonfiglio (1952). In Calabria, Puglie, and Abruzzi, where the incidence of schizophrenia is low, the incidence of manic-depressive psychosis is also low (3.4 per 100,000 population for Puglie, 2.8 for Calabria, 4.5 for Abruzzi). In Calabria, for instance, the incidence of manic-depressive psychosis and schizophrenia together is 6.1 per 100,000; in Emilia it is 23.3 per 100,000. From an ethnic point of view, there has been such a mixture of racial groups and interchange of population from one region of Italy to another in the course of centuries that even those who attribute this illness to a purely hereditary congenital factor cannot resort to a racial explanation. In my opinion the difference in the incidence of schizophrenia has to be explained on a cultural and social basis.

Italy, like a few other countries, from a cultural or social point of view may be divided into two parts: the north and the south. The differences between these two regions are even more marked than the differences between the North and the South in the United States. Milan can be taken as the city representing the culture of the north and Naples that of the south. Milan is like a little New York, a big urban center, highly mechanized, with an industrial population. It represents the industrial culture of the twentieth century and is not too different from American cities. Naples is entirely different. Although it is a big city, it is not nearly as industrialized or mechanized. The north of Italy is more representative of the Western industrial scientific culture of the twentieth century, whereas the south of Italy is more typical of Western culture prior to the industrial revolution. It is predominantly agricultural and rural. Even the north of Italy, however, is not as representative of twentieth-century Western culture as American cities are. I do not mean to imply here that the differences are due only to the presence or absence of industries but to all chains of cause and effect that are determined by the presence or absence of industry in society.

As seen in Table 2 and Figure 51, the incidence of schizophrenia in the United States in 1949 was greater by far than the incidence of schizophrenia in Italy (15.0 for the United States; 8.2 for Italy); also the more urban, industrial, and mechanized the milieu was, the higher was the rate of schizophrenia. Thus in the United States the highest incidence was found in the District of Columbia (39.8) and the lowest in Kansas (4.7). Highly industrialized states and large urban centers generally have a high incidence. In the District of Columbia, New York, Rhode Island, and California, with high urban populations, the rate of schizophrenia was very high (a high admission rate in Arizona and New Hampshire is difficult to explain). The greater incidence in New York and California may also be due to another sociological factor: the large percentage of people who have emigrated from other states or countries.

Malzberg (1940) found that the incidence of schizophrenia among Italian-born persons who reside in the state of New York, although considerably lower

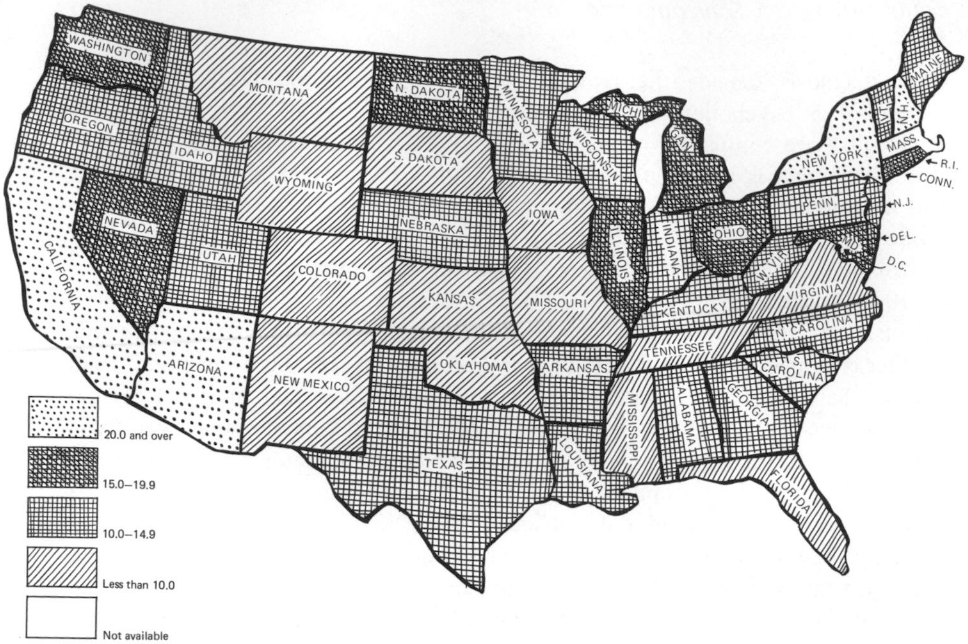

FIGURE 51. First admission rate for schizophrenia to state hospitals in the various states of the U.S. in the year 1949. The rate is per 100,000 inhabitants and is calculated on estimated 1949 population.

TABLE 2

First admissions of schizophrenic patients to state hospitals in the United States in 1949. The rate is per 100,000 inhabitants and is calculated on the estimated 1949 population, from data obtained from Patients in Mental Institutions, 1949, *published by National Institute of Mental Health.*

Alabama	13.9	Nebraska	10.6
Arizona	23.9	Nevada	18.7
Arkansas	10.5	New Hampshire	22.1
California	20.0	New Jersey	13.3
Colorado	7.4	New Mexico	9.2
Connecticut	19.0	New York	30.6
Delaware	19.2	North Carolina	10.7
Dist. of Columbia	39.8	North Dakota	16.1
Florida	8.5	Ohio	17.3
Georgia	10.3	Oklahoma	9.4
Idaho	12.4	Oregon	13.7
Illinois	18.3	Pennsylvania	14.1
Indiana	10.7	Rhode Island	23.1
Iowa	8.8	South Carolina	12.9
Kansas	4.7	South Dakota	7.5
Kentucky	11.7	Tennessee	6.9
Louisiana	13.8	Texas	12.5
Maine	13.0	Utah	10.7
Maryland	18.3	Vermont	13.5
Massachusetts[a]	—	Virginia	7.2
Michigan	16.4	West Virginia	12.8
Minnesota	12.7	Washington	17.2
Mississippi	8.3	Wisconsin	11.0
Missouri	9.4	Wyoming	5.9
Montana	6.1		
United States	15.0		

[a] No data were obtainable for Massachusetts.

than the incidence among those who emigrated from other European countries, was greater (30.4) than that of the native white population. This discrepancy is even more significant if we consider the fact that the majority of Italians who emigrate to the United States come from southern Italy, where the incidence of schizophrenia is the lowest. An Italian who emigrates from the region of Calabria to New York State increases his risk of being diagnosed a schizophrenic between nine and ten times. An immigrant from the islands of Sicily and Sardinia increases his risk five times, whereas an immigrant from Lombardy in the north of Italy increases his probability a little less than three times.

The importance of big urban centers may explain why in the south of Italy, the regions of Campania-Lucania (which are calculated together) have the relatively high incidence of 7.9 per 100,000, whereas one would expect an incidence of 6 or less. This discrepancy is due to the presence in Campania of Naples, the biggest urban center of the south.

I believe it is important to interpret why in the United States and Italy, and probably in other countries, the incidence of schizophrenia is much greater in industrial-urban centers than in rural-agricultural areas.

There is no doubt that the roles of the home and family change with the transition from an agricultural, preindustrial society to an industrial one. In a society where no industrial revolution has taken place, the home is almost the exclusive center of interest. The father works in the home or on the farm or in the shop that is nearby or within walking distance. The home provides shelter, food, and education and takes care of the physical needs of the individual as well as the psychological needs. Relatives and close friends are welcome at any time. The social function of the family strengthens the ties between its members, and the intimacy of living together is encouraged by a mass of physical activities. With the change to an industrial culture these activities are increasingly relegated to other agencies. The nursery school, the kindergarten, the school, the church, the bakery, the restaurant, the movies, the laundry, the clothing store, and many other institutions take over the functions of the home. Father has long ago stopped making tools at home for his trade; it is cheaper and more convenient to buy them when they are made by machines. Mother has to fuss less with the cooking, and even the sewing is reduced to a minimum. As we have already mentioned in Chapter 5, the family tends to become "nuclear."

In one respect, however, the family cannot change, that is, in providing for the emotional needs of the individual, which still must be satisfied. In an industrial society the satisfaction of these needs is made difficult by the lack of those activities that have been relegated to other agencies. The emotional interplay between the members of the family is sustained by a very fragile skeleton of social activities. The members of the household have relatively few contacts, do fewer things together, share fewer experiences, and are less willing to accept one another. Hostility that may exist among the members of the family is discharged during the few instances when the members meet and is therefore much more traumatic. The destructive forces of the interpersonal conflicts come to the fore with more violence and are not diluted or softened by a large number of constructive acts.

The fact that the preindustrial culture obligates members to do things for one another increases the family's solidarity and in a certain way diverts the hostility of the individual to persons outside the family, for instance, to the gossiping neighbors or, in certain cases, to the inhabitants of the neighboring town. Without reaching paranoid proportions, this extrafamily discharge of hostility protects the family from its internecine effects.

A second factor, which is implied in the first, is that in an industrial society the family does not prepare the children as well for life as it did before. The leap from the nuclear family to the big world is not easy to make. When adolescence or youth is reached and the individual has to make his first excursions into life on his own, he feels less prepared and more dependent on the family. His insecurity increases even more if he has to depend on members of the family who are incapable of giving him a feeling of emotional security.

The third factor is the change in the role of the woman in the family. We have already discussed the great simplification of the physical functions of the home in an industrial culture. These functions are largely entrusted to the woman in a preindustrial society; in an industrial society the wife has very little to do and cannot be satisfied with just being a housewife. More and more often she wants to have a business or a professional career. Because her functions have been removed by the industrial revolution, she wants to be equal to men in a still predominantly patriarchal society. She sees herself more and more in the traditional role of a man and diverts her interests from the functions of the housewife (Thompson, 1941, 1942). There is one function, however, that most women neither can nor want to dispense with—motherhood. Here, many conflicts arise as a result of the confusion in this state of transition; whereas the woman has divested herself of many functions of the housewife, she must be as good a mother as she was before, although she has been allowed to become a poor housekeeper. She will follow the trends of the time and will try to divest herself of some of the other functions of motherhood. Thus, she will resort to artificial feeding instead of nursing and to the nursery school instead of taking care of the child herself. Often she prefers to go to work and sends the child to the nursery school. If her mind has been oriented since childhood toward a career, her interests in motherhood may be relegated to a secondary role; she may actually resent the care she has to give to the child. On the other hand in the career world she feels discriminated against because of her gender. She is certainly justified in many instances, but her rancor may become hostility discharged at random.

In an industrial culture, motherhood is thus bound to lose some value, although a nostalgic longing for the old type of motherhood is strongly retained in the culture. When the mother, because of her own personal difficulties, has hostile and destructive tendencies, these will be more easily directed toward the children if she lives in a culture where motherhood does not have an almost exclusive importance in a woman's life. The father also loses some of his traditional roles and authority; he is insecure, competitive with his wife, and resentful. In this type of society, the family situations and parental attitudes that many authors have found in the majority of cases of schizophrenia (Chapter 5) may readily occur.

In a nonindustrial culture like that found in southern Italy, a hostile, neurotic mother will be more inclined to develop psychosomatic symptoms or to direct her hostility toward herself or her husband rather than toward her children. The aura of sanctity that motherhood has, and the physical needs that she must constantly satisfy in the children, make the woman less inclined to discharge hostility toward them. Obviously there are some very hostile mothers even in a nonindustrial culture, but the incidence is less common than in an industrial one. On the other hand, the same nonindustrial culture leads more easily to other difficulties. The extreme closeness with parents leads to Oedipal situations and to psychoneuroses, both of which are based to a large extent on sexual repression. A nonindustrial society may assume an inner-directed character and thus predispose to manic-depressive psychosis (Arieti, 1959). We shall state in passing here that the industrial culture corresponds in many ways to what Reisman has called other-directed (Reisman et al., 1950).

It is not very difficult now to understand also why the incidence of schizophrenia should increase in big urban centers. In fact, all the characteristics of an industrial culture become more and more accentuated with the increase in population. We have seen, however, that even in nonindustrial societies agglomeration of people in urban centers increases the percentage of schizophrenia, although not in a pronounced manner. In big cities space diminishes—children have less space in which to play, are more confined, and are more at home under the influence of their parents. In big cities, as was mentioned before, home life becomes less meaningful, and yet the child is compelled to stay at home much more than he would in rural areas. At the same time, the factors studied by Faris and Dunham (1939) also operate.

VI

Concluding Remarks

Almost all the sociological factors that we have studied in this chapter may either facilitate or make more difficult the occurrence of schizophrenia because of their direct or indirect psychological impact. Whatever is sociological must affect sooner or later the human psyche in order to favor or hinder the occurrence of the psychosis. Statistics and data remain numbers and physical facts until we are able to interpret them in terms of human suffering, aggravating circumstances, improvement, and relief.

Adverse social factors may have a psychological effect at various times in a person's life. Early in life, the psychological effect consists of a certain degree of disturbance, disorganization, or stress of the family milieu. The social factors engender, add to, or make it more difficult to compensate for, those intrafamily psychodynamic conflicts described in Chapters 5, 6, and 7. It is plausible to think that parents living in societies where inequalities, poverty, exploitation of any kind, persecution, discrimination, or false values prevail suffer in their personality structure and consequently offer poor parenthood to their children in a larger percentage than parents living in more satisfactory societies.

Throughout the life of the individual, social factors may have a psychological effect, not by eliciting special psychodynamic patterns, but merely as stress factors. In these cases the sociological factors act as adjustment hazards; that is, they represent adverse psychological pressures on the individual that cause him to be under greater strain, with the result that his psychic reserves, which might have neutralized the schizophrenogenic variables, are no longer sufficient.

When society at large engenders, adds to, or makes more probable or more virulent some destructive trends of the early family environment, the defenses against psychoses may break down more easily. On the other hand, a favorable social environment may compensate for the unfavorable psychodynamic development or even for some hereditary predisposition and make the psychosis less likely to occur. It remains more than doubtful that the social and other epidemiological factors mentioned in this book will be able to engender schizophrenia in the absence of the hereditary predisposition mentioned in Chapter 27. But this hereditary predisposition is quite common. It is also doubtful that these factors could cause the disorder in the absence of the psychodynamic processes illustrated in Part Two. But, as we have just mentioned, most of the adverse social factors make more probable or intensify these psychodynamic processes.

CHAPTER

32

Transcultural Studies of Schizophrenia

I

Introductory Remarks

Transcultural psychiatry studies whatever pertains to the field of psychiatry in relation to cultural differences. The variable in these studies is the culture. Do different cultures determine variations in the incidence, symptomatology, and course of mental conditions? If they do, why and how have they such effects? Is the uniformity of a given psychiatric syndrome or the diversity in various cultures the prominent feature? The majority of these studies take a given geographical area as the object of their research. Other studies have also given importance to time rather than geographical space because even in the same country, culture varies in different historical periods.

With particular reference to schizophrenia, we can study cultural aspects in four different ways. First, we can examine the question of whether the prevalence or incidence of the disorder changes in various cultural environments. We have already discussed this topic in the previous chapter.

Second, we can attempt to determine whether the culture facilitates, engenders, or hinders the occurrence of schizophrenia. The culture may have such effects in the following ways: (1) by its impact on the internal organization of the family, or by assigning specific roles and emotional values to its members and, more specifically, by establishing special methods of raising children; (2) by its impact on the building of the self-image and its ways of offering compensations for the injury to the self-image; (3) by offering various adverse or beneficial psychological influences on the individual (such as leisure, overwork, competitive spirit, automatization, impersonality, and so forth), so that his psychic resistance may decrease or increase.

The reader can easily visualize how difficult it is to determine the hygienic or pathogenic value of the factors mentioned in the second item in the preceding list. Some of these factors are the same social factors discussed in Chapter 31. Some others have been studied not in reference to schizophrenia but to the human psyche in general in *The Will To Be Human* (Arieti, 1972). We must keep in mind that these social factors generally exist in clusters, cannot be isolated, and therefore cannot be studied in their individual effect.

The relation between special ways of bringing up children and the vulnerability to schizophrenia has not yet been studied in a scientific manner. The incidence of schizophrenia, however, has been studied in relation to some specific cultures. Eaton and Weil (1955*a, b*) have made interesting studies of the Hutterite community. The Hutterites are a group of people of German ancestry who have settled in the Dakotas, Montana, and the prairie provinces of Canada. In a population of 8,542 people, Eaton and Weil found only nine persons who sometime in their lives had been suffering from schizophrenia and thirty-nine who had been suffering from manic-depressive psychosis. In other words, among the Hutterites, manic-depressive psychosis was 4.33 times more frequent than schizophrenia, whereas in the general population of the United States the rate of schizophrenia by far exceeded that of manic-depressive psychosis. The life of the Hutterites is very much concerned with religion, and their birthrate is very high, the average family having ten children. This type of culture corresponds to the one Riesman et al. (1950) call inner-directed. We have seen in Chapter 30 that it is particularly the type of culture called by Riesman et al. other-directed that predisposes to schizophrenia.

Third, we can study whether a given culture confers a special type of symptomatology to schizophrenia.

Fourth, we can attempt to determine whether a given culture enhances the occurrence of some syndromes, related to schizophrenia, but not generally included in the schizophrenic category.

In the rest of this chapter we shall deal exclusively with the third and fourth aspects of the relationship between schizophrenia and culture.

II

Differences in Symptomatology

Laubscher (1937) studied psychiatric disorders among the natives of South Africa. He reported that schizophrenic patients have hallucinations with magic, mythological content. The delusions are often grandiose in content (being a chief, a witch doctor). When they are of the persecutory type, they generally refer to the idea of being poisoned or bewitched.

Carothers (1947) studied mental illness in Kenya and gave a great deal of importance to acculturation as an etiologic or predisposing factor. Only 11 (6.3 percent) of 174 cases of schizophrenia were suffering from the paranoid type. The paranoid minority had attempted Europeanization and had lived in a hostile, foreign environment. Tooth (1950) studied schizophrenia among natives of West Africa and did not find acculturation to be a psychogenic factor. The symptomatology, however, changed with education and acculturation. The bush people disclosed delusions that referred to their fetish systems.

Murphy and co-workers (1963), through questionnaires filled out in forty psychiatric centers all over the world, were able to obtain reports from African countries (Kenya, Union of South Africa, Nigeria, Uganda); Asiatic countries (Formosa, Japan, Java, Hong Kong, South Korea, India, Thailand); Australasia (Australia, New Zealand); North America (Canada, United States); South America (Brazil, Colombia, Chile, Peru, Ecuador); Middle East (Kuwait, Turkey); Europe (Bulgaria, Germany, Czechoslovakia, Norway); Caribbean islands (Barbados, Martinique). Delusions of destruction and religious delusions, so frequently described in the European literature, were very infrequent in Asian countries. Withdrawal was more frequent in East Asia, where it is more acceptable than in European and American countries. However, whereas in Japanese and Okinawans withdrawal was frequently accompanied by flatness of affect and suicidal tendencies, among the Indians it was more frequently accompanied by catatonic rigidity, negativism, and stereotypy. Delusions of jealousy were more frequently reported in Asiatic countries. Simple schizophrenia was also more frequent in Asiatic countries. Catatonic signs were frequent among American Indians and mestizos; visual and tactile hallucinations were common in Arabian and African countries.

Pavicevic (1966) reported that Ethiopian schizophrenic patients are less aggressive and less dangerous to the attending personnel than European patients. Hallucinations and delusions are religiously colored; ideas of messianic mission and world recognition are also common among Ethiopian patients.

In Chapter 3 we reported that in the United States, too, the schizophrenic symptomatology has undergone noteworthy changes, presumably because of changes in the sociocultural environment. The catatonic and hebephrenic types are much less frequently observed. On the other hand, there seems to be an increase in the paranoid and undifferentiated types. There seems also to be an increase in cases with mild, marginal, or subliminal symptomatology. Whether the increase is real or is an apparent consequence of the fact that mild cases in recent years have been more easily recognized and more easily treated is difficult to determine.

A change easily attributable to environmental conditions has been noted in the content of delusions of patients in Western countries. Whereas witchcraft and magic concepts have decreased, delusions involving electricity, radio, wiretapping, radar, television, and other modern devices have increased.

Sakurai and colleagues (1964) made an interesting study of the changing clinical picture of schizophrenia in Japan. They studied the clinical records of 1,127 hospitalized schizophrenics who were admitted in the psychiatric department of Kyushu University Hospital during one of the following periods: 1939–1941; 1947–1949; 1952–1954; and 1961–1963. The authors found that there has been a marked decrease in the incidence of catatonia, but little change in the incidence of hebephrenia. There has been little change in the incidence of auditory hallucinations, but a decrease in visual hallucinations. Ideas of reference and delusions of persecution have remained at high incidence. Micromania (feeling that one's body or one part of the body is smaller), delusions of possession, metamorphosis, and expansive delusions have markedly declined. The authors suggest the following factors as the causes of such changes: changing value systems, changing family organization and parent-child relationships with consequent changes in personality, diffusion of mental health knowledge, expansion in social-welfare systems, and advances in treatment.

III

Syndromes Related to Schizophrenia occurring More Frequently in Foreign Countries than in the United States

Only a few of the related syndromes reported especially in the foreign psychiatric literature will be mentioned in this chapter. The question that promptly arises in several instances is whether we are dealing with different syndromes, different ways of classifying mental disorders, or emergence of special symptoms.

Bouffée Délirante

Bouffée délirante, or acute delusional attack, is described regularly in French textbooks of psychiatry and is also reported frequently in Haiti, where French culture (or psychiatry?) prevails. Ey, Bernard, and Brisset (1967) describe the *bouffées délirantes* as sudden explosions of transient delusional states that are polymorphic in their content and expression. The delusions may be persecutory in content, grandiose, sexual; they may refer to feelings of being possessed, influenced, having special powers, and so on. Hallucinations occur and in their content are related to the delusions.

The prognosis for the specific episode is good, but the possibility of recurrences is very strong. According to Ey and co-workers a patient who has had several *bouffées* risks becoming a schizophrenic. Ey acknowledges the fact that in many countries such syndromes are classified as "acute schizophrenia." They are indeed classified in this way in the United States. However, special *bouffées délirantes* are reported in Haiti (Mars, 1955; Sanseigne and Desrosiers, 1961; Kiev, 1961), where they acquire a particular mystical, religious symptomatology with feelings of being possessed. According to Kiev (1969), in order to understand the Haitian *bouffée délirante* it is necessary to understand the role-playing aspect of the possession phenomenon in Haitian culture and its characteristic manifestations in nonpsychotic individuals. According to Kiev (1969) some Haitian doctors, too, interpret the phenomenon in terms of spirit possession.

Capgras's Syndrome

Capgras's syndrome * is a condition that has received great attention in the European literature, especially the French and Italian. In the American literature, Davidson (1941), Stern and MacNaughton (1945), and Todd (1957) have published articles on the subject.

In 1923, the French psychiatrist Capgras, in collaboration first with Reboul-Lachaux and later with several others, started a series of articles on what he called *"L'illusion des sosies"* (1923, 1924, 1925). *Sosie* is a French word meaning "double," a person who looks exactly like another one, just as an identical twin would resemble the other twin. †

The phenomenon (or syndrome) described by Capgras is the following: the patient will claim, on meeting someone he knows well, that the person is a double or an impostor who has assumed this person's appearance. For example, the mother of a female patient comes to visit the patient in the hospital. The patient claims that this visitor is not the mother but either a double of her or an impostor who has tried to assume the appearance of the mother in order to deceive the patient. The phenomenon is thus a complicated type of misidentification, much more characteristic and specific than the usual misidentifications occurring in schizophrenia.

Although the first publications reported cases of female patients only, a few cases among males have later been described.

Is this condition, described by Capgras, a special syndrome, or just a symptom occurring in one of the well-known clinical entities? The problem is controversial. Generally the French authors tend to give to Capgras's syndrome a special place in psychiatric nosology, whereas the German authors tend to see it as a symptom. From the cases reported in the literature, however, it is obvious that, although the patients presented other symptoms, this particular delusion of the double was the center of the symptomatology.

I have seen a few typical cases in American patients and have considered them as suffering from paranoid schizophrenia or paranoid states. I am inclined to interpret also the cases described in the literature as cases of schizophrenia with a particular, unusual symptomatology. Capgras's syndrome thus should be more properly called Capgras's symptom. As a matter of fact, similar phenomena are described in the European literature in even rarer syndromes: for instance, the illusion of Fregoli, described by Courbon and Fail (1927). The patient identifies the persecutor successively in several persons—in the doctor, an attendant, a neighbor, a mailman, and so forth. The persecutor allegedly changes faces, as the

* For this section on Capgras's syndrome and for the one on latah, I have drawn liberally from the following articles of which I was a coauthor: (Arieti and Meth, 1959; Arieti and Bemporad, 1974).

† The French work *sosie* derives from Plautus's play *Amphytreon*. In this play the god Mercury assumes the aspect of Sosia, servant of Amphytreon.

famous European actor Fregoli used to do on the stage. Courbon and Tusques (1932) have also described the delusion of intermetamorphoses. The patient believes that the persons in his environment change with one another: A. becomes B., B. becomes C., C. becomes A., and so forth.

But, going back to Capgras's syndrome, several authors report that they have found the syndrome not only in schizophrenic-like or paranoid patients, but also in manic-depressives (Stern and MacNaughton, 1945; Todd, 1957).

Many patients reported in the literature have been treated with insulin or electric shock treatments, apparently with good results. Others retained their delusions and illusions or had relapses.

Even if we deny recognition as a clinical entity to the Capgras phenomenon, it deserves further study from dynamic and formal points of view. The already abundant literature seems to be preoccupied almost exlusively with classificatory controversies.

Cargnello and Della Beffa (1955), reporting an existentialistic analysis of the phenomenon, write that, in the delusional experience of the patient, three persons enter: the patient, the *alter* (the other, the person who was well known to the patient), and the *alius* (the double or the impostor). They conclude that actually it is the *alius* who is lived intensely in the *Erlebnis* (lived experience) of the patient and, although misidentified, is the closest to the ego of the patient.

A few things seem obvious in this syndrome. First, the person whose existence is denied is a very important person in the life of the patient—for instance, the mother. The patient rejects the mother, actually attributes very bad habits to her, but cannot allow herself to become conscious of this rejection because of concomitant guilt feelings or other ambivalent attitudes. What the patient feels about the mother is thus displaced to the double or impostor who allegedly assumes her appearance. Often the idea that the misidentified person is a double or an impostor occurs to the patient as a sudden illumination, or like the "psychotic insight" described in Chapter 22.

Capgras's syndrome thus may be seen as an unusual form of psychotic displacement. All gradations of displacements occur from normal states to neuroses and psychoses. In private practice we often see how the young wife's resentment toward her own mother is freely displaced and freely expressed to the mother-in-law, for whom she has no ambivalent feelings.

In Capgras's syndrome the real person is spared the hate of the patient—even becomes sanctified, a model of virtue—and the impostor made the target. But the real person, the person whom Cargnello and Della Beffa call the *alter,* becomes a pale, peripheral figure. The patient is really concerned with the *alius,* the impostor.

More difficult than the dynamic is the formal understanding of the Capgras phenomenon. We know that very often in schizophrenia the opposite process takes place: persons and things that in thinking processes should only be associated are identified. In the Capgras phenomenon, not only is there no increased tendency to identify, but a person who should be easily identified is *not*.

The real person is almost divided into two parts (the *alter* or the good part, and the *alius,* the bad part), just as often happens in dreams. In the Capgras phenomenon the persons are different, but the body has the same appearance. There is thus not only a denial of the Aristotelian first law of logic (law of identity)—*A* is *A*—but also at least an apparent denial of Von Domarus's principle. That is, in spite of characteristics in common, the visitor is not the mother but an impostor. Obviously the mother is identified with the impostor, but this identification remains unconscious.

Why Capgras's syndrome occurs (or is reported) more frequently in European countries than in the United States is a problem that still needs an explanation.

Latah

Latah is a syndrome first described in Malaya but recognized later on in many parts of the world. The etymology of the word *latah* is not known. It may derive from the Malayan words for "love-making," "ticklish," or "creeping." In Malaya this syndrome has been known for many centuries and is regarded more as an eccentricity than a disease. It occurs mostly in middle-aged or elderly women. In other parts of the world it is equally frequent in men. Sometimes it has occurred in epidemic form.

Similar syndromes have been described in Siberia under the names of *myriachit* and *tara;* in Hokkaido (northern Japan) among the Ainu as *inu;* in Thailand as *bah-tschi;* in Burma as *yuan;* in the Philippines as *mali-mali;* Madagascar as *ramenajana;* in Nyasaland as *misala;* in Congo as *banga*. It has also been reported from Somaliland, the southern part of the Sahara, and from Tierra del Fuego without any particular name.

The patient, generally a middle-aged or elderly woman of dull intelligence and compliant character, becomes increasingly fearful and seclusive. The disorder may start with a sudden fright. Among the Ainu of northern Japan, the illness often begins when the patient has actually, or imagines having, seen or stepped on a snake. The patient may at first repeat some of his own words or sentences several times; later on, he will repeat the words or sentences of other people, particularly of persons in authority. Still later, the patient, in a pantomime fashion, repeats or imitates gestures and acts of other people, even if this results in harm to himself. At other times he does the exact opposite of what other persons do. The next symptom is coprolalia. At first the patient utters incomprehensible sounds, which later become clearly obscene, or curse words that he never used before. The echolalia, echopraxia, and coprolalia are entirely uncontrollable.

Latah patients are often the butt of jokes. Adults and children may tease them until they tearfully beg to be left in peace or, less frequently, until they become violent.

In other parts of the world the *latah* syndrome acquires additional characteristics. In Africa the patients may run into the forests; in Tierra del Fuego they may climb dangerous cliffs without regard to their safety. During these fugues, the patients, who in this case are usually males, become violent and present a picture similar to "running amok."

The course of the disease is unpredicatable. Some patients have become progressively worse, ending with a severe obsessive-compulsive neurosis or with a psychosis. In other cases, the symptomatology has remained static. The disease may run a paroxysmal course, with the paroxysms lasting for weeks or months.

Various interpretations of the *latah* syndrome have been attempted (see Yap, 1952, for a good bibliography and discussion). The latah patient is a compliant, self-effacing person who, even before becoming obviously ill, had tried to solve his conflicts by blotting out all expansiveness. Latah may be interpreted as an attempt of the patient to free himself of his anxieties by surrendering himself totally to others. The compulsive utterance of obscene words may indicate that he is not wholly successful in his endeavor. Frightened children often mimic other people. The mimicking may be a primitive anxiety-relieving mechanism that is still available to children and primitive people but not to adult Western man.

I have seen a few schizophrenics and especially preschizophrenics with a symptomatology reminiscent of latah. As mentioned in Chapter 6, I have interpreted these patients as manifesting a variation of the stormy personality or other-directed personality—a variation perhaps made easier by special cultural factors. The patient is eagerly searching for object relations and identifications and tries to satisfy these tendencies in the most superficial, immature ways: identification becomes imitation.

CHAPTER

33

The Prevention of Schizophrenia

I

INTRODUCTION

To whomever is concerned with schizophrenia nothing can be more important than its prevention. In the field of psychiatry preventive medicine has made tremendous progress in at least three areas: (1) psychosis due to pellagra; (2) general paresis; (3) delirium due to infective conditions. Respectively, niamin- and thiamine-enriched diet, antisyphilitic treatment, and sulfonamides and antibiotics are responsible for these remarkable achievements. In schizophrenia the etiology is more complicated and completely different from that of the mentioned conditions. Because of our incomplete knowledge, our preventive efforts are less prominent, and what is exposed in this chapter does not achieve a degree of clarity approximating our aspirations. Nevertheless, pioneering efforts are always justifiable and deserve full consideration.

In the last few years in psychiatry, too, it has become customary to speak of primary, secondary, and tertiary prevention. Primary prevention aims at lowering the incidence (or making less probable the onset) of psychiatric disorders. Secondary prevention aims at the early recognition of the disorder in order to institute the promptest and most effective treatment. Tertiary prevention aims at reducing the defect caused or left by the disorder. Secondary and tertiary preventions are discussed in Chapters 3 and 4, dealing with the diagnosis, as well as in Parts Seven and Eight, dealing with the treatment. This chapter is devoted only to *primary prevention*.

Under the heading of primary prevention of schizophrenia I distinguish three types:

1. *Basic prevention,* which aims at the elimination of those prerequisites, either hereditary or environmental, that create a potentiality or increase the vulnerability for the disorder.

2. *Longitudinal prevention,* which aims at assisting the individual throughout his life, especially in his early life, to avoid those vicissitudes, psychogenic developments, or enduring situations that will enhance the change from a potentiality for, to a clinical actualization of, schizophrenia.

3. *Critical prevention,* which aims at avoiding those factors or specific events that will precipitate an attack or onset of schizophrenia.

What has been illustrated in this book has demonstrated that although no absolute or beyond-doubt knowledge has been acquired about the etiology of schizophrenia, the presumptive knowledge that we possess is extensive and is convincing enough to enable us to put into effect many presumably preventive measures.

II
Basic Prevention

Genetics

The studies reported in Chapter 27 have provided some evidence that a potential for schizophrenia has a hereditary basis. Schizophrenia is not inherited—only a potentiality for it. A possibility of prevention thus would consist of making impossible such genetic potentiality, so that even if individuals were exposed to the most traumatic psychological experiences, they could not develop the psychosis. However, it is almost impossible, as well as undesirable, to implement eugenic measures. In relation to schizophrenia we find ourselves in a situation quite different from that with which we are confronted in relation to the well-known hereditary diseases. In a family where Huntington's chorea, muscular dystrophy, hemophilia, and other unquestionably hereditary conditions exist, the physician can easily explain to the individual the Mendelian inheritance, either dominant or recessive, and the risk involved for possible offspring. In the case of schizophrenia similar genetic counseling is impossible. The counselor can only say that if a parent has been a schizophrenic, the potentiality for schizophrenia presumably increases ten times for children. In spite of the increased risk, the child has a 90 percent probability of not developing schizophrenia. As we have seen in Chapter 27, the potentiality for schizophrenia is presumably checked or neutralized by healthy environmental contingencies.

If it is not easy to prevent marriages of people who are carriers of definite dominant or recessive hereditary diseases, it is much more difficult to do so in the case of schizophrenia when the available literature seems to guarantee a 90 percent protection. In other words, if a person is or has been a schizophrenic, he has a 10 percent chance of being a carrier of schizophrenia. If an individual had a parent who was a schizophrenic, he also has a 10 percent chance of becoming a schizophrenic. The probability exists that if other preventive psychological measures are followed, the 10 percent potentiality will never become actuality. The fact that the statistics are not so overwhelming and the possibility that environmental factors may neutralize them completely will induce people to follow love and moral considerations rather than the genetic risk. Moreover, the individual may be strengthened in his or her determination to provide a good environment and may undergo preventive psychotherapy. Lifetime birth control, voluntary sterilization, or therapeutic abortion cannot be authoritatively recommended in the presence of such relatively little risk. Such measures should be recommended, however, when both spouses are or have been schizophrenics, because statistics indicate that in these cases the risk of offspring developing schizophrenia is very high (from 50 to 68 percent).

One must also realize that the great progress made in the treatment of schizophrenia will increase the genetic potentiality of the disorder. In fact, the more effective is the treatment and the greater is the percentage of patients who recover or greatly improve, the greater will be their reproductivity and the rate of transmission of genetic potentiality.

The following conclusions can be drawn:

1. It is difficult to counsel against marriage for people with a possible hereditary predisposition to schizophrenia unless a great risk is involved, as is the case of two prospective parents who have both suffered or are suffering from the disorder.

2. When a hereditary potentiality for schizophrenia exists, counseling should be given in order to establish a favorable family milieu and decrease the risk of the disorder.

Early Psychogenic Environment

What we have exposed in Part Two of this volume indicates that an early psychogenic environment is essential for the occurrence of schizophrenia, for transforming whatever genetic potentiality exists into an actuality. The basic function of primary prevention must consist of hindering the establishment of this early psychogenic environment (e.p.e.). As we have repeatedly stated, at the present time nothing can be suggested that is supported by unquestionable proof. What is available is only presumptive evidence.

Parents' Marriage. In my opinion the unhappy marriage of the parents is one of the fundamental determinants of the e.p.e. Needless to say, the preexisting disturbing personalities of the parents constitute original factors, but whatever is negative in the personality of each parent tends to become accentuated in an unhappy marital situation. It is true that there are many unhappy marriages and that relatively few of these have schizophrenic offspring. Not only the genetic potentiality must be there and many other circumstances, but the unhappy marriage must be pathogenic in the sense of not permitting the child to identify satisfactorily with either parent or to obtain a modicum of security and basic trust.

A survey of families of schizophrenic patients will easily reveal that marital unhappiness is more common and more pronounced than in the families of the general population (see Chapter 5). There are apparent exceptions. At times the illness of the patient confers a feeling of solidarity to the parents and reinforces their bond. These are usually late events and in most cases are more harmful to the patient than helpful. No situation that requires the patient to be ill in order to maintain itself is genuine or worthwhile.

Premarital counseling aiming at uncovering basic incompatibilities and prevention of unions based on neurotic foundations will be useful. Premarital counseling may also prevent marital unhappiness by clarifying what is expected from people who enter a marital relationship.

Parenthood. Unhappily married people may find psychological satisfaction and compensation in raising children, especially in some cultures where parenthood is considered the most important aspect of marriage. Consequently children are not seriously impaired. On the other hand, in a culture where the significance or importance of parenthood is diminished or secondary to marital harmony and kinship, unhappily married people tend also to be poor parents. From the time of the industrial revolution to the present, and especially since technological changes have taken place at a very rapid pace, our culture and society have been in a state of transition. There have been changes in the roles of mother and father that constitute threats to parenthood. When these cultural factors are reinforced by personality difficulties, the consequences may be undesirable.

In Chapter 32 we have seen that the woman has lost many traditional values and functions. At the same time she has recognized, even if until very recently she has not openly expressed, her resentment over the fact that in a predominantly patriarchal society she has often been considered a second-class citizen and has not been given opportunities equal to those given to men. In her efforts to achieve equality she now diverts some of her interests from the functions of housewife and seeks a career as a man does. She is certainly entitled and justified. But just as society failed her before for putting her in a state of submission, it fails her now for not preparing her adequately for a double role. The task is indeed difficult and sociologists should study the problem more adequately, not just along theoretical lines but with practical suggestions. Married women must have a feeling of fulfillment. Otherwise they will experience frustration and will have the compulsive need to compete with their husbands, with resulting family unhappiness.

One function that the woman cannot dispense with is motherhood. But for the sake of this function she should not be required to give up many other important aspects of life.

The reader is referred again to the description in Chapter 32 of a certain group of mothers in the urban-industrial society. In this environment many young women have not been sufficiently prepared for motherhood. Some of them see no beauty or challenge in being mothers. They state that even female animals can be mothers and raise a litter, as if raising a human child were as simple as raising a kitten. Obviously these women should not be criticized or abandoned but helped to reevaluate their role of motherhood while maintaining the possibility of a career. In our modern Western society, which aims at gender equality, the role of the father should also be redefined, and many of the functions originally assigned exclusively to women should be more fairly distributed.

Of course, focusing on a career and competing with men are not the only reasons that make preparation for motherhood more difficult. Shainess (1966) has lucidly illustrated the psychological problems associated with motherhood. She reminds us of Freud's stress on the woman's dual sexual role (Freud, 1931) and its psychological consequences: first, attracting and having a sexual relationship with a man; second, giving birth to children and assuming the mothering task. Success in one role does not necessarily imply success in the other. Some poor mothers are successful only in the first role; many poor mothers, however, are not successful in either. They enter marriage expecting a great deal and are not prepared to give in return. They assume an attitude of passivity, as if the spouse were a new parent who will take care of them. After the arrival of the child, some of these mothers experience motherhood as a stress. As Shainess writes, the ambivalence or the rejection become hatred because of the insoluble tie.

Culture as a whole should help young women to reacquire a sense of devotion toward motherhood. Young girls in high school and college and other fields should receive some counseling and education because many of them, in our transitional times, did not learn adequately by identifying with their own mothers. Courses, theoretical indoctrinations, and even counseling offered in a scholastic setup may appear dogmatic, scientific, and nonspontaneous methods of instilling love for motherhood. They can very easily be. The present state of affairs, however, is that a certain part of our female population has lost that spontaneous, pristine, natural attitude toward motherhood, which used to be transmitted from generation to generation. Until some women have recognized this socially induced situation, we must resort to any method that can help them.

Shainess states that acceptance or rejection of the child is an acting out, automatic or compulsive, stemming from unconscious sources. Unless the unconscious forces for acceptance are retrieved, society must try to find compensations for the loss of them.

Fatherhood, too, has become less satisfactory since the time of the industrial revolution. Mitscherlich (1969) and Mitscherlich and Mitscherlich (1973) have described "the invisible father" in our society. The father is no longer the teacher, the senior partner in artisanry. He has lost authority not only as a teacher of life but also as an enforcer of discipline, as a giver of examples to imitate, a person with whom the children can identify. Often he is relegated to the role of a playmate. He sees the children seldom, and when he sees them, he wants to be one of them, to play with them, to be their peer. But in doing so he soon loses his parental status. Obviously in the state of change in which present society is, fatherhood has to undergo transformation. Not all the changes described by the Mitscherlichs are necessarily negative.

However, modern fathers have not yet defined their new role, and this state of indecision may lead to conflict and family instability. Like modern mothers, modern fathers, too, need help. Help should also be provided for future fathers, similar to that suggested for future mothers.

In summary, at the present state of our knowledge it seems probable that the establishment of the e.p.e. can be avoided by all those sociological and psychological measures which (1) prevent unhappy marriages and (2) promote good motherhood and fatherhood.

III

Longitudinal Prevention

Longitudinal prevention is to a large extent to be inferred from what we have learned in Part Two about the psychodynamics of the disorder, and to a smaller degree from Chapter 32. Longitudinal prevention must aim (1) at altering the original e.p.e. and its effects and (2) at affecting social conditions in such ways that the essential needs are more easily provided to the child, adolescent, and young adult and that unusual stress does not exceed the capacity of the individual to cope with it.

Implementing longitudinal prevention is extremely difficult because of the reluctance of the family to allow professional intervention before the need is manifest and because of the attitude of indifference of society and in some environments even of the medical and educational authorities, toward psychological problems. In most schools, from nursery to postgraduate, a routine physical medical examination is required. I think that a psychiatric or psychological examination should also be required, at least in grammar schools and high schools, with the obligation of informing the parents or guardians of the results. If the examiner detects the first signs of personal abnormalities, or of an abnormal way of living, he may intervene in three ways: (1) by requesting individual psychotherapy for the student; (2) by suggesting counseling, family therapy, or therapy of the parents (these methods will reveal not only pathogenic mechanisms easily accessible but also the unconscious ones that cause or facilitate the perpetuation of faulty patterns of living); and (3) by suggesting changes in the environment of the child, adolescent, young adult, or adult. In some cases it is useful to enlarge the family circle. As we have already mentioned, in the traditional family the child was exposed to many influences: not only to parents and one or two siblings, but to several siblings, grandparents, uncles, aunts, cousins, maids, and various other persons. Today the family, especially in large cities, consists of the parents and one or two children. Thus there is no possibility of compensation for the children or of identifying with other individuals if the parents are unfit.

In many cases the examiner can recommend that the child or adolescent be under the influence of additional adults, not just of the parents. An aunt, an uncle, a maid, a good friend of the family may veer the youngster toward a good interpersonal integration. The idea that the parents must be the only ones to do the job is unrealistic when they are not willing to accept therapy or counseling or when they are unable to benefit from them. In several cases the mother may remain an important person for the youngster, but the role of motherhood must be divided with other adults and a peer group. The experience reported from the kibbutzim in Israel may give valuable suggestions. While the mother goes to work, a so-called *metapelet* (that is, "a person who takes care") is in charge of the child and exerts the functions of mothering. Bettelheim (1969) made an intense study of children born and raised in kibbutzim and reported that he encountered no schizophrenics among these children. Such a remarkable statement is unfortunately made by Bettelheim only in passing. We would like to be certain that his not encountering schizophrenics among these children really corresponds to the absence of schizophrenia among them. While I was visiting kibbutzim in Israel, I found support for Bettelheim's statements. I became convinced, although without the support of statistics, that schizophrenia was rare there. What Bettelheim says to explain his findings is very interesting and deserves deep consideration. He reminds us that a small but good amount of mothering, as that given by the real mother in the kibbutz, goes a long way. Once the breast feeding from the mother stops, it is the *metapelet* who provides food, shelter, rest, stimulation, clothing. The parents continue to provide the extras and a special warmth. That is, whereas the *metapelet* provides mostly the physical essentials for survival (and some instinctual gratification), the parent provides "love and tender care." In other words, security originates not only from the parent, but also from the several *metapelets* and the large group, the kibbutz itself, a community of peers.

What we can learn from the kibbutz experience is that a nonparental influence may be very useful. When the examiner or the counselor detects poor parenthood, he may suggest that the youngster be under diversified influence and a person acting as a *metapelet* must be found.

Separation from the family may be recommended in some instances. Whatever measure could remove the tension, the anxiety, the hostility, the conflicts of loyalty between antagonistic groups of the family, or the tyrannical attitude of some members and the submission of others, should be adopted.

The youngster can also be assisted with his feelings of frustration and defeat that come from aspirations not commensurate with his abilities, from poor interpersonal relations, lack of knowledge in dealing with the opposite sex, first romantic disappointments, inability to suppress one's homosexuality, and so forth. Such assistance is generally not given if the need for it is not discovered. Mandatory examinations would make more likely the use of counseling or therapy.

The social conditions described in Chapter 32, which generally are associated with an increased rate in schizophrenia, are difficult to change. Of course, we are all in favor of measures such as adequate housing with sufficient space and facilities, war on poverty and unemployment, fight against disease, anomie, crime, drug addiction, alcoholism, prejudice, and so on. Much more difficult to affect are such phenomena as emigration, migration to another part of the same country, social mobility, and so on. Moreover, although it is true that some of these events determine an increased rate of schizophrenia, in many other cases they strengthen the character and personality of the individual. They renew his vitality and creativity and make him rise to the challenge.

IV

Critical Prevention

Critical prevention consists of dealing with the patient in the presence of a critical situation that is likely to precipitate a schizophrenic episode. The first question is whether it is worthwhile or feasible to attempt this type of prevention. One may think that the critical and possibly precipitating event may be only the straw that broke the camel's back and that we cannot go through life avoiding or compensating for all possible straws. We have seen in Chapter 8 that this is not the case. Although it is true that the ground for the psychosis must be prepared genetically and psychologically, *any stressing event is not a precipitating event.* It must be one that is intimately related to the psychodynamic of the patient, one that will affect his special vulnerability and will injure deeply his self-image. Without a particular precipitating event the psychosis may never occur, although the patient may remain maladjusted for his span of life. To resort to a metaphorical example: a war is probably prepared by a deeply unstable political situation and social unrest or malaise, but unless a specific incident or unpleasant episode occurs, it may never be declared or waged. Some people believe that if a psychosis, especially of the acute type, is threatening, it is better to have it, endure it, and get it over with. The patient, once recovered, would be strengthened and better off than if he lived with an ever-impending psychosis or serious maladjustment. In my opinion this is fallacious reasoning. Although it is undeniable that many patients are in a much better condition after having had the psychosis and a successful treatment, we must remember that this outcome is unpredictable. Some patients do not respond fully to treatment, others retain scars, others remain crippled and incapacitated for the rest of their lives. Some who seem recovered have relapses. It would be like saying that it is a good thing to go to war because when you return, your character will be strengthened. What about those who are wounded, cripples, maimed physically or psychologically, or who do not return at all?

The second question is whether it is better to avoid the precipitating event, the challenge the patient tries to cope with. In many cases it is impossible to avoid facing the challenges. To restrict the patient's actions would mean to control the constitutional rights of the individual. To prevent him from taking certain steps would be tantamount to inflicting a demoralizing feeling that may also precipitate the psychosis. Among such events are the following: going away from home to college or to work; becoming engaged, married, or having a baby; changing school or job; going on an adventurous trip; being promoted; breaking an engagement, a marriage, a long relationship, and so forth. It is not correct to assert that these events cannot precipitate a psychosis; that is to say, that only novelists and playwrights have such viewpoints about what brings about a psychosis. Clinical experience confirms that these events may produce an imbalance between the demands of the immediate challenge and the psychological resources of the individual. It is true that had the ground not been prepared genetically and psychodynamically, the challenge would not have produced the imbalance. Nevertheless we cannot deny the effect of the challenge itself.

In some cases, like the one brought about by a promotion, the challenge may be one ordinarily considered a good event. It may thus *seem* that preschizophrenic patients are not able to cope even with good events. Good events, even those not accompanied by great challenges, may disturb the equilibrium also of partially recovered schizophrenics and may cause relapses. Anxiety about failing after having obtained success is more difficult to bear.

Using the formulation of Caplan (1964) we may say that in order to prevent life crises we must provide: (1) attenuation of hazardous circumstances; (2) services to foster healthy coping. This is generally done with interpersonal intervention.

We cannot discuss here all the situations that can precipitate a schizophrenic episode. The reader is referred to Caplan's book (1964) for a detailed study of prevention of all mental disorders in life's critical situations. Here we shall mention only: (1) the college situation; (2) pregnancy and, much more frequently, childbirth.

It is easy to understand the difficulty of the youngster who for the first time leaves home to go to a college and live on his own. He may feel deprived of the protective environment in which he grew; he has to face the challenge not only of living alone but also of increased scholastic demands. Obviously most young people take all this in their stride, and even with a sense of jubilation; but if the youngster is psychologically unstable, his anxiety may reach disturbing proportions. Although some unstable teenagers fare better away from disturbed homes, some do much worse. The early environment, although in some ways destructive, was also protective; and the protective aspect succeeded in hiding or compensating for the destructive.

At times the youngster experiences a sudden increase of anxiety and sends desperate appeals to the family by letters and telephone calls. Those appeals should not be dismissed with the formula "John will learn to grow up and to be on his own," but should be heeded. Intervention from family, friends, advisors, teachers, or whoever notices a disturbing change in the individual in question may be very helpful. The youngster who is confronted with a crisis he does not know how to deal with, at times is prone to take unusual actions in an attempt to decrease his anxiety. These actions are maladaptive and could do much harm—for example, excessive marijuana smoking, use of LSD, traveling aimlessly to different parts of the country, taking steps to change schools, and so on. Whoever notices a deterioration in the student's habits should inform the teachers or the family. Often a disintegration of psychotic proportions is preceded by several signs of minor disorganization such as inability to sleep at night, staying in bed for the whole day, inability to take action, state of starvation or excessive appetite, neglect of appearance, and so forth. If the intervention occurs before the crisis has triggered the psychosis, the prognosis is relatively good. The disturbed person is easily influenced by a stable, warm, reassuring, and, most of all, understanding and noncondemnatory person. In many instances the patient is not able to verbalize the negative experiences he undergoes. The intervening person must be patient and reassuring and must do most of the talking. Teachers and advisors should be on the alert for the mentioned signs of disorganization. Whenever doubt exists, the family should be notified and a psychiatric consultation recommended. Even after the occurrence of the psychotic episode, prompt intervention from scholastic authorities or from colleagues may be very useful (see case of Fred in Chapter 22). This intervention or vigilance on the part of scholastic authority is not always easy, because it may give the impression that a "spy system" is at work and thus may facilitate paranoid tendencies. Reassurance should be given that the rules of confidentiality will be respected.

Pregnancy and childbirth may engender crises that precipitate a psychosis. We have already dealt with this important topic in Chapter 13. Shainess's paper (1966) should also be consulted in this respect.

In his book on nonpsychotic French women who had recently given birth, Chertok (1969) describes "the choices of the negative." His clinical experience showed him that for the pregnant woman it was easier to perceive "what is wrong" than "what is right." He wrote that "the effectiveness of the integration of past conflicts and the strength and dynamic force of the ego are very difficult to assess in view of the widespread reactivation that takes place during the *state of crisis*." When what he called "the negative grid," or the constellation of all negative experiences and factors, was very marked, prophylactic therapy had a beneficial effect on the confinement. Although Chertok dealt only with nonpsychotic women, his recommendations seem even more pertinent to the prepsychotic pregnant woman. It is impossible, of course, to require from the average obstetrician a psychiatric examination of all his patients. However, when he detects a strong negative attitude toward pregnancy, motherhood, or life in general, a psychiatric examination should be recommended.

Some authors like Freeman (1951) and Wainwright (1966) have reported that the arrival of the baby precipitates mental illness (more often depression, but also schizophrenia) in the father too. The presence of an infant in the household markedly changes the lives of both parents. Reactivation of serious old conflicts in the husband of an expectant mother is sufficient reason to justify seeking counseling or psychotherapy.

PART SEVEN

Psychotherapy of Schizophrenia

CHAPTER

34

The Choice of Treatment

In the presence of a schizophrenic disorder the therapist's first duty is to choose the type of treatment. At the present stage of psychiatric development, the methods of treatment are few, and yet the choice may be difficult even among few possibilities. The psychiatrist must be aware that he is generally inclined to select, at times unwisely, the type of treatment that is in agreement with his own theoretical orientation. For instance, an organically oriented therapist may be inclined to recommend physical therapy and discard any other; a hospital psychiatrist may be inclined in the majority of cases to recommend hospitalization. Each therapist must learn to counterbalance his own biases in order to evaluate properly each individual case.

I

Hospitalization versus Ambulatory Treatment

One of the first decisions the psychiatrist has to make is whether to recommend hospitalization or to pursue a type of ambulatory treatment. Until approximately 1955, the presence of a psychotic disorder, even a mild one, was almost always followed by a recommendation for hospitalization. A long tradition was behind this practice. Kraepelin's concept of dementia praecox developed in a mental hospital setting and the equation "psychosis = hospitalization" was almost automatically made. Different critieria have lately prevailed, as our better understanding of the disorder and our techniques of prompt intervention have opened up new approaches. However, hospitalization is still to be recommended in many cases. The following are the main indications of a need for hospitalization, not listed in order of importance, which varies in each case:

1. To provide treatment that cannot be given on an outpatient basis; or when drug therapy has to be administered at dangerously high doses, or at such frequent intervals that the family cannot properly carry out the program; or when electric shock treatment or insulin is required, and so on.

2. The patient is so disturbed or so acutely ill, or his delusion may be so irrational, that he constitutes a danger to himself or to others.

3. The patient's behavior is so bizarre as to put him into conflicts with society that are of such magnitude as to have an adverse effect on the subsequent course of his illness.

4. To remove the patient from the usual environment where the conflicts are perpetuated or where a climate of hostility and rejection prevails.

5. To provide relief to the members of the family who can no longer endure the state of tension and turmoil created by the patient. This situation is keenly experienced when children are to be taken care of or when a family member is sick or pregnant.

6. When the patient who in the past had a psychotic episode from which he had a remission shows signs of decompensation or not adjusting again and seems in urgent need of a less demanding environment. We must not wait until the tenuous grasp on social life has been lost.

7. The patient is in need of a therapeutic community. Group therapy and a special type of living and working, are needed more than individual therapy, or are needed *in addition to* individual therapy.

8. The patient feels in a general state of malaise and wants the security of hospitalization. In most of these cases the psychosis is already in action. In some cases the patient feels he is falling apart, or vaguely or even distinctly persecuted, and seeks the refuge and protection of the hospital. In some of these cases by hospitalizing the patient, the psychiatrist prevents an exacerbation of the disorder.

Contraindications to hospitalization are the following:

1. The symptomatology is not severe. We must remember that the presence of such symptoms as hallucinations, delusions, or ideas of reference, or peculiar behavior is not in itself sufficient indication for hospitalization. These symptoms constitute grounds for hospitalization when they bring about the conditions that we have outlined above.

2. Psychotherapy and/or drug therapy are diminishing the symptomatology to such an extent as to remove the indication for hospitalization.

3. The symptomatology is not expected to worsen because the patient has free social contacts.

4. The patient receiving ambulatory treatment is able to work and provide for

his own treatment. Stopping work may be experienced as a defeat and should not be resorted to unless necessary.

5. The patient is able or willing to receive office or clinic treatment.

6. Environmental conditions can be changed. It is possible to make them less demanding, less traumatic, and more accepting.

The listed positive and negative variables can be subsumed under fewer categories or further divided into subclasses. It may be a difficult task for the therapist to evaluate all of them in a relatively short time and to reach a quick decision. In clear-cut cases, such as those of acutely ill patients, or homicidal and violent patients, the indications are evident. Several cases are doubtful, because indications may vary in a short period of time. Other factors at times hamper the decision of the psychiatrist. For instance, in the presence of paranoid persecutory ideation, the danger that the patient constitutes to himself or others may be very remote, and yet the therapist may be reluctant to assume even a little risk. Errors are unavoidable, because each variable can be weighed only in an approximate manner and according to criteria that often are only subjective in nature. Society must learn to accept the inevitability of some errors.

Extreme cautiousness and propensity to hospitalize or to keep patients in hospitals for a very long period of time may avoid some pitfalls but bring about many others. We have learned in Chapter 23 that hospital life promotes so-called hospitalism, a passive life without challenges, where an impersonal or even callous atmosphere and limitation of activities often prevail. Hospitalization *per se* does not *cure* schizophrenia. A form of milieu therapy is often helpful but insufficient.

II

Physical Therapies versus Psychotherapy

Such treatments as insulin coma therapy, electric shock treatment, and especially psychosurgery are no longer used today in a routine way. They are resorted to very sparingly, and only in those cases that have not responded to other types of treatment. They will be studied in Chapters 42 and 43 of this book. The cogent dilemma today is between the use of psychotherapy and drug therapy.

I have already, although indirectly, manifested my bias in favor of psychotherapy. I have tried to demonstrate that although psychodynamic factors may not constitute the total etiology of schizophrenia, they are essential or necessary elements of it and can be altered by psychotherapeutic methods. In other words, although psychotherapy cannot be considered totally specific and attacking all the etiological elements, it may attack enough of them to make the existence of the disorder impossible. Because genetic factors cannot be changed, psychotherapy seems to me a much more causative and much less symptomatic type of treatment than any other type of therapy I know of. I have obtained my best results with patients treated exclusively or predominantly with psychotherapy.

However, I hasten to state that I use drug therapy as a routine practice with some patients. It is not difficult to explain why my attitude diverges according to the case in question. In spite of the tremendous progress made in the field of psychotherapy, this type of treatment is long and, in some cases, unpredictable. It is fair to admit that some patients have not responded enough to this type of treatment even when such treatment has been given by the best specialists in the field. It is also correct to say that drug therapy is only a symptomatic type of treatment; its main or only function may lie in the reduction of anxiety. This reduction would make the symptoms, which are pathological defenses, unnecessary. On the other hand, drug therapy has the following advantages: in many cases it decreases the intensity or acuteness of the overt symptomatology; in other cases it eliminates the overt symptomatology entirely. In still other cases, even though the symptoms remain, they cause less disorganization of the personality. The patient is able to maintain a certain distance from his symptoms and becomes capable of being reached by psychotherapy. Many patients who would have to be hospitalized, interrupt work and abandon their families, can be treated outside the hospital and can continue to work and provide financially for their treatment. In a certain number of patients the therapist is able to establish relatedness with the patient only when drug therapy is administered.

The advantages of drug therapy are so many that many readers may wonder why I refrain from a total endorsement. The main reason is that in my experience drug therapy makes the patient less sensitive not only to his own anxiety but also to the treatment. Psychotherapy, although still effective, makes less of an impact on the medicated patient. Thus no instructions can be given that apply to every case. Each patient must be evaluated individually. If what we gain with drug therapy is more than what we lose, we must by all means institute drug therapy, at least for the initial stage of the treatment. If the patient cannot be affected by psychotherapy alone and especially if no relatedness can be established, drug therapy should be initiated. Another variable is constituted by the therapist himself and by the degree of experience he has with psychotherapy alone.

In many parts of the world psychotherapy is not yet available. In those cases, of course, symptomatic therapy is mandatory.

Most therapists today have solved the dilemma by accepting a mixed treatment, which consists of both psychotherapy and drug therapy. I do not see counterindications for this type of treatment in the majority of cases. As a matter of fact, the reader must be clear on one point—although I am in favor of using drug therapy in some cases, I never rely on drug therapy alone. I believe that concomitant psychotherapy is necessary if we want to obtain more than the removal of the overt symptomatology. The aim of the psychotherapist should be that of changing the patient's inner life rather than simply freeing him from his symptoms.

As already mentioned, a number of hard-core cases do not respond either to psychotherapy or usual drug therapy. Other types of treatment must be resorted to, as described in Chapter 43. Family therapy and the use of the therapeutic assistant will be discussed in Chapter 39.

III
Comparison of Different Results

Studies comparing the different methods of treatment of schizophrenia have debatable value. In most of these studies loss of overt symptoms is confused with recovery. When psychotherapy has been compared with other methods, it has generally been psychotherapy given by residents who had little experience in treating patients with intensive psychotherapy. A valuable type of comparative analysis could be offered only by a therapist who has profound experience with all the types of treatments in a statistically significant number of cases.

May (1968), in a comparative study of five methods (milieu therapy, electroconvulsive therapy, drug therapy, individual psychotherapy, individual psychotherapy plus drugs), found that drug therapy alone and psychotherapy plus drugs were the most effective treatments and also the least costly in time and money. By clinical criteria the advantage between the two was generally with psychotherapy plus drugs. However, the difference between the methods was small, "insubstantial and never impressive." May saw no antagonism between drugs and psychotherapy; on the contrary, when an effect existed, it was in the direction of potentiation of the positive drug effect. In May's study psychotherapy alone "appeared to have little effect or even a slightly adverse one." Again we must remember that in May's studies psychotherapy was done by inexperienced residents. They had supervision, but they were supervised by analysts experienced in classic Freudian analysis, which is not the most suitable for the treatment of schizophrenia.

IV
Therapies Not Described in This Book

As mentioned in the preface of this book, the very important topics of group psychotherapy, day hospital, milieu therapy, and therapeutic community will not be discussed in this volume. The omission of them should by no means be interpreted as disregard on my part for these types of therapy.

These therapeutic approaches are very important and very useful in many cases. They have to be considered as adjunct therapy. With the exception of a few cases, they cannot replace the others described in Chapters 35 to 43. The reasons why they are not mentioned in this book are several: (1) The author has made no contribution to these fields; (2) excellent reviews of the literature of these subjects exist; (3) it is not necessary for the therapist who treats the individual patient to know these techniques. On the other hand it is advisable for the therapist who practices them to have a knowledge of the subjects treated in this book.

Psychosurgery is briefly discussed in Chapter 43, not because I recommend it (as a matter of fact, I am opposed to it), but because of its theoretical implications.

For an excellent review of the literature on group psychotherapy of schizophrenics the reader is referred to the work by Schniewind, Day, and Semrad (1969). For works on day hospital the following works are recommended: Kramer (1962), Axel (1959), and Zwerling (1966). For works on milieu therapy the book by Artiss (1962) is suggested. For hospital treatment in general the following books are recommended: Stanton and Schwartz (1954), Linn (1955, 1959, 1961), and Gralnick (1969). For the therapeutic community see Jones (1953) and Kraft (1966).

CHAPTER

35

The Psychotherapeutic Approach to Schizophrenia: A Historical Survey

Although the majority of schizophrenic patients all over the world are treated with physical therapies, the number of those treated exclusively or partially with psychotherapy is rapidly increasing. At the present time, no psychiatrist can ignore individual psychotherapy of schizophrenia, nor can he escape practicing psychotherapy with schizophrenics even if he is inclined to do so. Even a psychiatrist whose practice consists predominantly in administering phenothiazines cannot help inquiring about the dynamics of the patient's anguish and conflict, cannot help observing and interpreting what happens between the patient and himself. He may not apply all the insights that people who have devoted themselves to the psychotherapy of schizophrenia have communicated, nor follow all their recommendations, but some of them have rubbed off on every psychiatrist. What Frieda Fromm-Reichmann, other pioneers, and we, their followers, have tried to do has not been ignored, but assimilated, even if at times in very diluted forms. Moreover, even those who have enlarged the field of psychotherapy to include family therapy, group therapy, and community psychiatry have built upon the foundations laid by individual psychotherapy. The study of human groups can add to, but not replace, the study of the individual.

Individual psychotherapy of schizophrenia is still in the pioneering stage, in spite of gigantic steps made in the last few decades. This treatment is not yet fully integrated and not entirely understood, because the "pioneers" and their followers have used different methods or have given different interpretations to their approaches. Generally, the fundamental premise to any type of psychotherapy of schizophrenia resides in the notion that psychological factors and psychological mechanisms constitute at least an important and necessary part of the etiology and/or symptomatology of the disorder. A collateral assumption is that even if some important aspects of schizophrenia are not based on psychological factors, a therapeutic intervention in the psychological part of the disorder will engender changes sufficient to remove or at least ameliorate the condition and in many cases prevent its recurrence.

In this chapter we shall review the main methods in their basic aspects and techniques. Space limitations will require that we omit secondary methodologies and procedures. It is possible to recognize that each method adopted in the psychotherapy of schizophrenia is the clinical expression or the therapeutic realization of one or few underlying principles held by its originator. Often the principle was deduced from the clinical experiences of the therapist; in some instances a preconeived theoretical view oriented the therapist in certain directions.

I

Freud and the Freudian School

Any review of the psychotherapy of schizophrenia must start with Freud. And yet, paradoxically, Freud, to whom we owe so much for the understanding of many aspects of this disorder, discouraged psychotherapy with schizophrenics. To be exact, as early as 1905 he did not consider the obstacles to be insurmountable in the future and did not exclude the possibility that some modified techniques would be devised that would permit the psychoanalytic treatment of the psychoses (Freud, 1905). Later, however, Freud assumed a more pessimistic attitude. He felt that the psychosis could be compared to a dream and understood as a dream, but that it could not be cured.

An underlying principle was at the basis of his pessimism. As we have seen in Chapter 2, Freud believed that in schizophrenia there is a withdrawal of libido from the objects into the self; therefore no transference can take place, and without transference no treatment is possible. He said that in "narcissistic neuroses" (that is, psychoses) "the resistance is unconquerable." The technical methods of psychoanalysis must "be replaced by others; and we do not know yet whether we shall succeed in finding a substitute" (Freud, 1924*a, b*). Several years later (1938*b*, 1940) he reiterated that in psychoses the instinctual component is too powerful to be overcome by available psychoanalytic methods of treatment.

The basic distinction made by Freud between transference neuroses (psychoneuroses) and narcissistic neuroses (or psychoses) was maintained by classical psychoanalysts, and the psychotic patient continued to be treated with the methods of traditional psychiatry. To my knowledge, Freud never treated schizophrenic patients, although he did treat some manic-depressives.

Even Abraham, the distinguished pupil of Freud, who did so much pioneering work in the treatment of manic-depressive patients, had for a long time a negative attitude toward the treatment of schizophrenia. He wrote that "dementia praecox destroys a person's capacity for sexual transference, i.e., for object love" (1908). He considered "the negativism of dementia praecox as the most complete antithesis to transference." Later Abraham (1913, 1916) changed his views and considered transference with schizophrenic patients possible. His contributions to this area, however, were modest and were by far inferior to his contributions to the treatment of depressed patients.

Another one of Freud's early and famous pupils, Paul Federn, made repeated and successful attempts to treat schizophrenic patients, in spite of the prevailing discouraging theories (1943, 1952). One of Federn's underlying principles was based on the concept of ego-feeling, or of an autonomous reservoir of libido in the ego. He felt that the ego of the schizophrenic is poorer, not richer, in this libido, contrary to what Freud's theories implied. He also felt that transference with the schizophrenic was possible; and as a matter of fact he succeeded in establishing it with several patients. Another tenet of Federn (that of the ego boundaries), however, limited his therapeutic aims. Federn believed that in the schizophrenic "the boundaries" separating the areas of the psyche (the id from the ego and the ego from the external world) are defective, so that material from the id may invade the ego and even be projected to the external world. The most important goal of therapy should be that of establishing normal boundaries. Reversing a famous sentence of Freud's, Federn said that as a result of therapy in the schizophrenic, "there where ego was, id must be." He did not mean that the id should be liberated, but that it should be put back into what he believed was its proper place, a state of unconsciousness, repression, and control. The normal resistances that the psychosis has broken down should be reestablished. To do so the classic technique has to be changed in many ways. One of the changes consists of having the help of another person, generally a woman, who takes care of the patient between sessions and especially during the periods of negative transference. The usual technical procedures (free associations, analysis of the positive transference, institution of transference neurosis) should be abandoned because they lead to a "transference psychosis" in which the analyst becomes a persecutor. The resistances that maintain repression should not be analyzed. The phobias should be left untouched "because they protect deeper fears and conflicts."

Federn relied on the healthy or mature part of the patient, on the remnants of the normal ego, to combat the sick part. He believed that at first the psychoanalyst should share

> the acceptance of the psychotic's falsifications as realities. He shares his grief and fears and on this basis reasons with the patient. When convinced that by this procedure the patient feels himself understood the analyst presents the true reality as opposed to falsification. He then confronts the patient with his actual frustration, grief, or apprehension, and connects this with the patient's deeper fears and conflicts and frustrations (Federn, 1943).

It is apparent that for Federn psychoanalytic treatment of schizophrenia should consist of a symptomatic repression of the id; of restoring the defective ego boundaries. *Render to the id what is id's.* Do not allow it to remain confused with the ego. Federn thus did not tackle the psychotic part of the patient's personality.

A nurse who was analyzed by Federn, Gertrude Schwing, applied her analyst's concepts to hospitalized patients. In a straightforward and honest, but not fully convincing book, *A Way to the Soul of the Mentally Ill,* Schwing (1954) describes the schizophrenic as a person who has been deprived of the experience of having a real mother, a person who loves her child at any cost. The psychiatric nurse must offer that love to the patient. Schwing describes several techniques that establish continuity of contact with the patient and stresses the point that the patient must have the feeling that this new mother is there and does not intend to abandon him. Schwing considers her treatment a preliminary one, to be followed by Federn's method.

Leland Hinsie is one of the American pioneers in the psychotherapy of schizophrenia. As early as 1930 he published a book devoted to this topic. He studied adolescent patients who voluntarily sought treatment and who had insight into the fact that they were sick, and were communicative and willing to follow the directions of the therapist. Thus Hinsie selected the easiest patients to treat. He relied predominantly on the clinical psychoanalytic method of "free association" and theoretically remained fatihful to the classic Freudian theory (Hinsie, 1930).

Within the Freudian school we must also mention the works of Waelder (1925), Clark (1933), Jacobson (1967), and Arlow and Brenner (1969).

The ego psychologists within the Freudian school, with the exception of Eduardo Weiss, have not followed the ego psychology of Federn, but rather that of Hartmann (1950*a, b,* 1953, 1956, 1964), Rapaport (1951, 1958, 1960), and Hartmann, Kris, and Loewenstein (1945). Although these authors have acknowledged that schizophrenia is predominantly a disorder of the ego, their practical impact on the psychotherapy of schizophrenia is not discernible so far.

II

The Kleinian School

Melanie Klein studied the earliest infantile levels of development, and her findings were soon applied to the study and treatment of the psychoses. Her writings and those of her pupils are somewhat difficult for readers not accustomed to her terminology and her general theoretical frame of reference.

According to Klein, even at birth the ego is organized sufficiently to experience anxiety, to build defense mechanisms, and to form primitive object relations both in real life and in fantasy forms. As a defense against an overwhelming anxiety of annihilation the ego develops the capacity to introject and to project. In the paranoid-schizoid position, which occurs during the first four or six months of life, anxiety is experienced as persecutory in nature. According to Rosenfeld's (1969*b*) interpretation of Klein, this way of experiencing anxiety contributes to certain defenses, "such as splitting off good and bad parts of the self and projecting them into objects, which through projective identification became identified with these parts of the self." This process is the basis of narcissistic object relationships. If the child does not proceed normally to the next phase of development, which is the depressive position, the earlier persecutory fears and schizoid phenomena return and are reinforced. This is the basis for schizophrenia later in life.

A fundamental point of view advocated by Klein's pupils Rosenfeld, Segal, Bion, and early Winnicott (1945) is that no modification of the classic Freudian psychoanalytic technique is needed in the treatment of psychotics. Winnicott later changed his views and came to attribute great importance to environmental factors. Rosenfeld, Segal, and Bion have instead maintained strict adherence to Kleinian theory and to the classic psychoanalytic technique. They continue to use the couch, rely on free association, and use frequent interpretations.

Rosenfeld has made important contributions, many of which have been collected in one book (1965). In 1947 he reported the office treatment of a schizophrenic patient suffering also from depersonalization. Rosenfeld at first found the patient's "narcissistic withdrawal and ego disintegration an insoluble problem," but then he became aware that the patient was using schizoid mechanisms against painful feelings in the transference situation. The patient had lost her feelings and believed she had lost herself. Rosenfeld interpreted her experiences as due to a process by which parts of her self were split off and projected into the analyst. The patient also felt that she was intruding inside the analyst and losing herself there. This experience made her develop projective paranoid anxieties of being intruded and overwhelmed by the analyst. Rosenfeld interpreted the patient's withdrawal as partly a defense against paranoid fears and partly a defense against closeness and intrusion.

In reporting the case of the treatment of a hospitalized acute schizophrenic, Rosenfeld (1952*a, b*), "while acknowledging the importance of the analyst's intuitive understanding of the patient's communications, . . . thought that the analyst should also be able to formulate consciously what he had unconsciously recognized and to convey it to the patient in a form that he can understand."

Later Rosenfeld (1954) reported "that the psychotic manifestations attached themselves to the transference in both acute and chronic conditions, so that what might be called 'a transference psychosis' develops." By stressing the concept of "transference psychosis" Rosenfeld did not merely reintroduce one of Federn's concepts. Contrary to Federn, Rosenfeld felt that the transference psychosis should not be avoided, is indeed analyzable, and should be worked through by means of interpretation.

Recently, Rosenfeld (1969*a*) has described a number of projective identifications that occur in the treatment of psychotic patients. He distinguished the following processes:

1. Projective identification, used by patients for communication with other objects, that seems to be a distortion or intensification of the normal infantile nonverbal relationship between infant and mother.

2. Projective identification used to rid the self of unwanted parts.
3. Projective identification aimed at controlling the analyst's body and mind.
4. Projective identification used predominantly to deal with aggressive impulses, particularly envy.
5. Patient's belief that he is living entirely inside the analyst and behaves like a parasite using the capacities of the analyst, who is expected to function as his ego.

Rosenfeld stresses that in the treatment of psychotics it is essential to differentiate these projective parts of the self from the saner parts, which are less dominated by projective identification. These saner parts are in danger of submitting to the persuasion of the delusional self. Although he stresses the fact that these saner parts are not adult but "more normal non-omnipotent infantile parts of the personality," he finally seems to get closer to the views of Fromm-Reichmann and myself in seeming to agree that the nonpsychotic parts of the patient have to be summoned in the fight against the psychosis.

Segal (1950) reported the treatment of an acute schizophrenic patient. She felt that all material, heretofore unconscious, should be interpreted to the patient at the level of the greatest anxiety. She felt that schizophrenics tolerate the conscious state of thoughts and fantasies generally kept repressed by the neurotic. They repress, however, the relations between fantasy and reality. Segal believes that by giving reassurance and sympathy to the psychotic patient, as many analysts do, the analyst temporarily becomes the good object, but at the price of enhancing the split between good and bad objects and reinforcing the defenses, so that later the negative transference will assume unmanageable proportions.

Bion made important studies on the meanings of the patient's communication (1954) and on the role of projective identification in the psychotic part of the personality as a substitute for repression in the neurotic part of the personality (1957). In describing the transference of the psychotic he said, "The relationship with the analyst is premature, precipitated, and intensily dependent" (1956).

With the exception of Winnicott, all important pupils of Klein reassert their adherence to the classic psychoanalytic method, without major alterations to fit the psychotic. Kleinian conceptions have acquired prominence in England but also in South America and especially in Argentina.

III

Sharing the Patient's Vision of Reality

Some significant psychotherapeutic methods, although originated from different theoretical premises, have the common aim of making the therapist enter and share the patient's vision of reality.

John Rosen originated his method in 1943. At the suggestion of Federn (1947) he called it "method of direct psychoanalysis." Whereas the usual or indirect psychoanalytic approach establishes communication with the patient through the ego, Rosen's treatment aims at communicating directly with the unconscious, presumably with the id or with "ego-states of infancy and childhood" (Federn, 1947).

As we have seen earlier in this chapter, Federn also thought that a transference psychosis may occur in the treatment of the psychotic, but whereas Federn felt that it had to be avoided, Rosen makes of it the major tool of therapy. Other people, like Rosenfeld and the Kleinian school in general, analyze the psychotic transference with the traditional indirect method; Rosen uses a direct method. During his early period (1943–1945) Rosen worked with severely ill patients at Brooklyn State Hospital and at the New York State Psychiatric Institute and published his first results in his book *Direct Analysis: Selected Papers* (1953). In his early writings Rosen described his technique without formulating a major theoretical foundation. He gave abundant interpretations to the patient, which were communicated in a vivid and shocking language that conveyed what Freud's early papers attributed to the unconscious. Such explanations as, "You want to screw your mother, kill your father," "You want to sleep with me" were quite frequent. During this period most of Rosen's interpretations were based on the expression of a previously repressed sexuality that was Oedipal in origin.

Repressed sexuality, however, was not the only pathogenic area. Rosen believed also that the schizophrenic is the victim of a mother who had suffered from "a perversion of maternal love," and tried to offer to the patient what he did not have. The patient must experience in the therapist a powerful, protective, benevolent person, as he wished his mother had been in his early childhood. The therapist at times must assume the role of the persecutor and try to convince the patient that he will have a beneficial rather than a persecuting effect. The analyst must spend a long time with the patient—up to sixteen hours a day—and, like Federn, must often resort to an assistant. The patient is showered or shocked with the interpretations. Such overwhelming, all-embracing treatment would often solve the acute episode in a few weeks and had to be continued by the second stage of treatment, which follows a technique more similar to classic psychoanalysis.

During the specific, or first, stage of treatment the analyst enters the psychotic world of the patient, who immediately feels better because he is finally understood. The therapist should not even avoid becoming one of the imaginary persons who appear in the delusions. Later (1953–1956) Rosen developed the theoretical view that there are no separate psychoses as disease entities but only phases of one psychosis. He wrote that "the same patient may pass from paranoia into hebephrenia or from manic-depressive psychosis into obsessive-compulsive neurosis, right before our eyes" (1964).

In what he calls the third stage (1956–1961) of the evolution of his treatment, he established in Philadelphia the Institute for Direct Analysis. Among the techniques developed there were the setting up of a treatment unit for the individual patient; the use of helpers (assistant therapists), as Federn had already done; and the establishment of the total care of the patient. During the final fourth stage Rosen published his book *Direct Psychoanalytic Psychiatry* (1962), in which he illustrated all his currently held therapeutic techniques and theoretical views.

I have witnessed a few of Rosen's therapeutic sessions, and I was impressed by the technique with which he was able to establish contact with the psychotic. The male patient who was told that he wanted to screw his mother or kill his father and the female patient who was told that she wanted to sleep with Rosen were both touched inside by these verbal shocks and unexpected attitude. They broke their barriers, started to communicate, and soon would lose their delusional thinking. I was very doubtful that the improvement would last. As a matter of fact, I heard from various sources and from Rosen himself that, contrary to his early expectations, relapses and progression of the illness occurred.

I felt, however, that to establish such a rapid contact and relatedness with a patient who was refractory to such relatedness was no little accomplishment. I felt during my observation of the way Rosen operated that somehow he succeeded in introjecting himself and almost hypnotizing the patient. In my opinion the presence of a large audience during the session was important. Somehow I felt I was participating in a primitive ritual. Rosen was the shaman or the magician. We in the audience were the clan or the tribe, giving authority and power to Rosen. The combination of the direct method and of the collective ritualistic atmosphere made the patient receptive to introjection.

I also tried to understand some of Rosen's techniques. For instance, if he said to a female patient, "I am going to sleep with you tonight," he did not want to shock her. Of course Rosen did not intend to act in accordance with his statement, nor did he intend to lie to the patient. Rosen feels that in the language of the unconscious wishes and promises have the value of reality. By making the patient wish, he was giving immediate gratification to the deprived patient. In the unconscious a wish that is not fulfilled is not necessarily a frustration, it becomes fantasied reality.

It is worthwhile to give a rapid look at Rosen's theories. After the very first period, where sexuality played the preponderant role, he developed the concept of "early maternal environment." According to Rosen, for the child "mother" equals environment. "Mother" is an entity that includes not only the mother herself and what she does or fails to do in her maternal role, but also other people and what they do or fail to do. This concept of early maternal environment expands Rosen's previous concept of the "perversion of the maternal instinct" in the etiology of schizophrenia. If this early maternal environment possesses many negative qualities, it may become the chief cause of the disorder (Rosen, 1963).

Another important concept of Rosen's is his own modification of the Freudian superego. The superego is not "the heir to the Oedipus complex" but "the psychical representation" of the whole early maternal environment. Commenting on the fact that Freud was surprised because "the superego often develops a severity for which no example has been provided by the real parents," Rosen stated that the phenomenon is not surprising at all: the total early maternal environment may be worse than the patient's parents.*

Rosen's third important concept is "You seek the Mother you knew"; that is, the individual unconsciously selects in his environment duplications of the original characteristics of the early maternal environment. He tries consciously and unconsciously to make a mother out of anybody or anything in his surroundings. "His need for 'mother' is so great that he continues to project maternal attributes upon persons or things which are manifestly not maternal in relation to him."

Rosen's fourth basic concept is that of transference, which is not interpreted in a classic Freudian way. For Rosen transference is a variety of the tendency to "seek the mother you knew." Rosen adds: "The individual cannot find the mother he knew, so he tries to make whomever is available at the moment into the one he seeks by prodding, picking, cruelty, trickery, seductiveness, and gift-bearing. And finally, if all this fails, he actually projects onto the person in question the qualities and attitudes he is seeking. Thus transference consists of a transformation of the nonmaternal into the maternal."

Whereas early in his career Rosen relied more on the shocking effects of his interpretations, later he came to see the role of the therapist predominantly as one of "foster-parent." The unit in which the patient lives during the treatment is a foster home. There the patient will find compensation for the inadequacies of the early maternal environment.

Rosen's method has been the object of much criticism. Even his admirers point out the fragility of his theoretical framework and attribute his therapeutic successes to his personal qualities: lack of hostility, perseverance, physical endurance, and so on. Others feel that the interpretations he gives the patients are arbitrary, not even necessary, and that his success was due simply to the fact that he was able in some way to establish contact with the patient. Others (Horwitz et al., 1958) doubt even his results. They state that his claims of many recoveries were exaggerated; that some of his patients were misdiagnosed; that others who were undoubtedly schizophrenic had relapses and were later treated with physical therapies.

I too feel that Rosen's early assertions, like those of any pioneer, suffered from excessive enthusiasm. Also, some of the theoretical bases of his technique are unsubstantiated. Nevertheless, it is beyond question that Rosen obtained at least temporary results and that he was able to inject faith into many workers at a time when the prevalent opinion was that psychotherapy with schizophrenics was an impossibility.

He continued to pursue some avenues opened by others: for instance, the use of the therapeutic helper, introduced by Federn. In many other ways he has been a creative innovator. Some of his theories reaffirm in different language the importance of the mother in the early life of the patient and of the early environment in

* Apparently Rosen does not attribute any role to the child in creating in his inner life an environment worse than the one of his external reality. For a different point of view see Chapter 5 of this book.

general. On a theoretical basis he has never tried to interpret why and how at a certain period in the life of the patient, "this seeking the mother the patient knew" is done through the media of the primary process.

Worthwhile works on the method of direct analysis, in addition to Rosen's, are the writings by Brody (1959), English et al. (1961), and Scheflen (1961).

The Swiss psychologist Marguerite Sechehaye also believed that the world of the psychosis can be entered by the therapist with her method of "symbolic realization" (1956). In her theory and practice she accepted much of the classic psychoanalytic and existentialistic approaches but added many innovations. In her method the actions and manifestations of the patient are not interpreted to him but *shared* with him. Of course, the therapist must formulate in his own mind interpretations of what the patient means or experiences. He resorts to his psychoanalytic experience, to his knowledge of the life history of the patient, and to his own intuition. Sechehaye's method aims at helping the patient to overcome the initial traumas of his life by offering him a level of interpersonal relations that is corrected and adjusted to the weak state of the psychotic ego. The patient is able to relive the unsolved conflicts of his early life and to solve them, or at least he becomes able to gratify some of his primitive needs. For instance, by giving her patient Renée apples (symbolic of the maternal breast) Sechehaye allowed the patient to relive an early trauma and permitted a magical gratification of an oral need. Once the meaning of the patient's symbols are understood by the therapist, he uses them repeatedly in order to establish communication and also to transform reality to a level that the patient can accept without being hurt or traumatized.

What Sechehaye tries to accomplish can be seen as the staging of a dream in waking life. As in dreams, symbols replace objects as they appear to the waking mature ego, and gratification of primitive needs takes place. Sechehaye thus enters the dream of the psychosis by creating an artificial and curative dream that eventually will lead to a healthy awakening.

Sechehaye's technique is difficult to practice. Is it really possible in the majority of cases to set up an artificial dream that uses the symbols that belong only to a specific patient? A certain capacity for intuition is necessary, and this manifests itself after contact is made with the inner core of the patient. Such capacity is not reducible to, or deductible from, rules or instructions or theoretical premises to be found in Sechehaye's method (1956).

Sechehaye devoted two books to her treatment of her patient Renée, whose case perhaps remains the best reported in the literature (1951*a, b*). She lived with the patient and spent many hours every day with her. One wonders whether the remarkable improvement she obtained was based on "symbolic realization" or on her generous giving of herself. Using Rosen's terminology we could say that certainly Sechahaye made up for the defects of Renée's early maternal environment. It is more than doubtful that such treatment is applicable on more than a very small number of patients.

Ronald Laing's method is difficult to describe because in spite of the author's many writings it has never been reported in the literature. In his first book, *The Divided Self* (1960), he insisted on examining the existentialistic despair, the division of the patient's psyche, his "ontologic insecurity." In his later writings Laing not only shares the psychotic world of the patient, but he supports it. He feels that the patient is correct in blaming his family and the environment. He had to live in an unlivable situation; he really was persecuted, was labeled "psychotic," dismissed from the human community. The method helps the patient to reassert and accept himself and to reevaluate his position within the society in which he lives. Laing relies very much on family therapy also (Laing and Esterson, 1965).

IV

Frieda Fromm-Reichmann and Her School

In contrast with the three authors that we have mentioned in the previous section, Harry Stack Sullivan and Frieda Fromm-Reichmann tried to reach the patient not by entering or sharing the psychotic world but by remaining in the world of reality.

Sullivan is very well known for his theoretical innovations in psychiatry in general and schizophrenia in particular. People who have worked under him have attested to his therapeutic successes. Unfortunately his premature death prevented him from reporting in writing his technique. Mullahy (1967, 1968) has given us not only a lucid exposition of Sullivan's theory of schizophrenia but also a succinct account of his therapeutic innovations. Mullahy reports that as director of clinical research at Sheppard and Enoch Pratt Hospital, Sullivan stressed to his assistants the importance of the first twenty-four hours on the ward for any patient. Life on the ward was more important than the daily session with the therapist, and Sullivan encouraged his assistants to spend a great deal of time with the new patient in a close and reassuring relationship. In one of his early papers, Sullivan (1931) gave a résumé of hospital treatment. He instructed the paraprofessional personnel to be aware that an extreme sensitivity underlies whatever camouflage the patient uses. The patient is immediately made to feel that he is one of the group. In this truly human environment a degree of social recovery occurs, and the patient becomes aware of his need for insight.

Mullahy writes that Sullivan attempted a direct and thorough approach chiefly by reconstructing the actual chronology of the psychosis. Sullivan impressed on the patient that whatever had befallen him was related to his life experiences with a small number of people.

Frieda Fromm-Reichmann worked closely with Sullivan. Unlike him, she became much better known for her therapeutic endeavors than for her theoretical contributions. The value of her therapy received large recognition. Fromm-Reichmann named her treatment "psychoanalytically oriented psychotherapy" and not "psychoanalytic treatment" to emphasize that it constituted a departure from the classic Freudian psychoanalytic procedure.

Fromm-Reichmann's courage in treating difficult patients, the qualities of her personality, such as her genuine warmth, humility, and exquisite psychological intuition, certainly played an important role in establishing a milieu of therapeutic acceptance of the schizophrenic and in stimulating others toward similar pursuits. In addition to a very insightful book on psychotherapy (1950) she wrote many papers (1939, 1942, 1948, 1952, 1954, 1958) that have been collected and published by Bullard (1959). Nevertheless her ideas on the therapy of schizophrenia have never been integrated into a systematic whole, perhaps because of a lack of an original theoretical system. For theoretical foundations she leaned on Freud and to a larger extent on Sullivan. Sullivan's idea (1953*a*) that some degree of the interpersonal relatedness is maintained throughout life by everyone, regardless of his state of mental health, was a basic prerequisite to her attempts to establish transference with the psychotic. Even the schizophrenic disruption is a partial one.

Fromm-Reichmann stressed that it is very hard for the patient to trust anyone, even the therapist; and if the latter disappoints him in any way, the disappointment is experienced as a repetition of early traumas, and anger and intense hostility result. Fromm-Reichmann treated the patient with daily sessions and did not make use of the couch or of the method of free association. She relied much less than other authors on the therapeutic effect of interpretations. She made a cautious use of them, however, and emphasized that the symptomatology is susceptible of many interpretations, all correct, and that at times it is useful to give even partial interpretation.

Fromm-Reichmann was among the first to emphasize that the schizophrenic is not only alone in his world, but also lonely. His loneliness has a long and sad history. Contrary to what many observers believe, the patient is not happy with his withdrawal but is ready to resume interpersonal relations, provided that he finds a person who is capable of removing the suspiciousness and distrust that originated with the first interpersonal relations and made him follow a solitary path. In order to establish an atmosphere of trust, the therapist must treat the patient with kindness, understanding, and consideration, but not with condescending or smothering attitudes as if he were a baby. There is a part of the patient that has retained an adult state and would resent being treated in a babyish way. Profession of love or of exaggerated friendship is also out of place. These would be considered by the patient bribery and exploitation of dependency attitudes.

Fromm-Reichmann tried to explain to the patient that his symptoms are ways of remodeling his life experiences in consequence of, or in accordance with, his thwarted past or present interpersonal relations. She wanted the patient to become aware of the losses he sustained early in life, but he must become aware of them on a realistic level. That is, he must not distort or transform symbolically these losses but must accept the fact that they can never be made up and that he is nevertheless capable of becoming integrated with the interpersonal world. It will be easier for him to integrate when he recognizes his fear of closeness and even more so his fear of his own hostility. Fromm-Reichmann paid great attention also to the countertransference of the therapist and especially to his anxiety in treating the schizophrenic patient.

In the course of her career, Fromm-Reichmann changed some of her ideas. Whereas in her early papers she recommended complete acceptance of the way the schizophrenic patient is, as sort of compensation for the early injuries, later she wrote that this attitude was not the only way of making the patient overcome his reluctance toward reestablishing personal contacts (1948, 1952, 1954). She emphasized more and more that the therapist must address himself to the adult part of the patient's personality, regardless of how disturbed this personality is.

Fromm-Reichmann thought that only quantitive differences exist between normal, neurotic, and schizophrenic individuals and apparently minimized the fact that quantitative differences bring about qualitative differences.

Fromm-Reichman inspired many people, not just as a therapist, but also as a teacher. Many of her pupils, although maintaining her general therapeutic orientation, have made important contributions. Prominent among them are Otto Will and Harold Searles.

Among Will's contributions is his insistence that the therapist "define his relationship with his patient, refusing the patient's attempts to avoid such definition by his withdrawal or his insistence that he can never change, that there is nothing the matter, and that the therapist is of no significance to him" (1967). In addition to reporting vivid case presentations of patients treated in a hospital setting, Will has given useful instruction about what he calls "the development of relational bond" between the patient and the therapist. Such development requires: (1) recurrent meetings of the participants; (2) contact of the participants with each other—verbal, visual, tactile, aural, and so on; (3) emotional arousal (1970).

Harold Searles has done extensive writing on the psychotherapy of schizophrenia. In his first book (1960) he showed that the concept of transference, generally restricted to human object relations, should be expanded to include the nonhuman environment. He has also written many insightful papers that have been collected in one volume (1965). It is impossible to review all of them. They make very rewarding reading, especially for some aspects of the psychodynamics of schizophrenia and of the phenomenon of transference. Searles has described the difficulties of the transference situation: how the patient fights dependence, which would compel him to give up fantasies of omnipotence. He has also shown how the transference situation leads the patient to additional projections. In an important paper (1962) he clearly differentiates between concrete and metaphorical thinking in the recovering schizophrenic patient, although he makes no use of the studies done by other authors on this important subject.

V

Miscellaneous Contributions

Bowers (1961) applied hypnosis to the treatment of schizophrenia, although the general opinion is that such treatment is not suitable for psychotics. She hypothesizes that in hypnosis the therapist rapidly establishes contact "with the repressed, healthy core of the patient." She points out that the problems of resolution of the symbiotic relationship require the utmost skill, but long remissions have been secured. A successfully hypnotized schizophrenic is moving toward recovery, because he is able to reincorporate the other, the therapist, and thus reestablish interpersonal relations.

Benedetti (1955, 1956), an Italian psychiatrist who studied with Rosen and teaches and practices in Switzerland, accepts a great deal of Sullivan and Fromm-Reichmann, as well as some existentialistic concepts. He feels that the two basic tools in the treatment of schizophrenics are sharing of the feeling of the patient and interpretation. Benedetti (1971) feels that high sensitivity, extraordinary need of love, and reactivity above the average level make the patient very vulnerable to schizophrenia. The therapist must understand the request inherent in the suffering of the patient (Benedetti, 1972). The patient wants the therapist to understand his essence, his being the way he is, even if at the same time he rejects the therapist. Society, including therapists, tends to evade the patient's request by objectifying his symptoms and by not permitting him to make claims.

From an Adlerian point of view Shulman (1968) has described very useful procedures. The therapist must help the patient to make a better rapprochement with life, to avoid the use of psychotic mechanisms, and to change mistaken assumptions. In a very human and compassionate way Shulman describes in specific details how to help the patient through these therapeutic procedures.

The Jungian school has concerned itself mostly with borderline patients or latent psychoses (Baynes, 1949). Tedeschi (1969) states that when archaic archetypal elements appear in the psychotherapy of the patient, the therapist should stimulate the patient's interest in corresponding cultural, historical, and artistic situations that contain the archetypal images. Tedeschi obtained good results by treating a schizophrenic Jewish medical student by reenacting rites from the Old Testament and correlating them to current political events.

CHAPTER

36

Establishment of Relatedness

I

INTRODUCTION

In this chapter and in the next four I shall describe psychotherapy of schizophrenic patients as I practice it. The following brief report on the origin and development of this therapeutic procedure will serve as an introduction and general orientation.

Four major roots have to be mentioned. One of them goes back to my work in Pilgrim State Hospital, at first as a resident and later as a staff psychiatrist from November 1941 to February 1946. During the period spent at that hospital I discovered that a few patients who resided in back buildings and had been considered hopeless would apparently recover or improve enough to be discharged, at times after many years of hospitalization. These were considered cases of "spontaneous recovery." I was not satisfied with this explanation and looked more deeply into the matter. I soon discovered that these so-called spontaneous recoveries were not spontaneous at all but were the result of a relationship that had been established between the patient and an attendant or nurse. I made these observations only in services of female patients, but I assumed that the same situation could take place in male services. The relationship went through two stages. In the first stage, by giving the patient special consideration and care, the nurse or the attendant had met some of her needs, no matter how primitive they were. The patient had improved somewhat and the nurse had developed attachment and deep involvement with her. The patient soon would become the pet of the nurse. In a second stage the patient had become able to help the nurse with the work on the ward. Those were war years with acute scarcity of personnel, and any help was very welcome. The patient would then be praised, and an exchange of approval, affection, and reliability was established. In this climate of exchange of warmth and concern the patient had improved to the point of being suitable for discharge. Much to my regret, however, I almost invariably observed that these formerly regressed patients would soon relapse and be readmitted to the hospital. Outside they were not able "to make it." Nevertheless I was impressed by the fact that even an advanced schizophrenic process had proved to be reversible or capable of being favorably influenced by a human contact. I thought that perhaps methods could be devised by which we could help the patient maintain, increase, strengthen the achieved amelioration, even outside the hospital environment.

The second root has to be traced in my psychoanalytic training at the William Alanson White Institute. There I learned much more about the role of interpersonal relations in every psychiatric condition, including schizophrenia. There I had the good fortune of having as a teacher Frieda Fromm-Reichmann. She influenced and inspired me greatly. Although my therapeutic approach has developed its own basic features, it has retained some of Fromm-Reichmann's characteristics.

The relevance of thought disorders in schizophrenia has been one of my basic concerns from the beginning of my psychiatric studies. Actually the origin of such interest is much more remote in time than my reading of Eugen Bleuler's writings. It goes back to my studies of the eighteenth-century philosopher Giambattista Vico while I was in college. Vico's study of the cognitive ways in which the ancients, the primitives, children, and poets conceive the world and respond to it fascinated me. It focused my interest on the many possible ways by which the mind faces, reconstructs, and experiences the universe. Vico's conceptions were among the best preparations for understanding the schizophrenic reality and the schizophrenic experience and constitute my third root. Also my discovery later of the writings of the psychologist Heinz Werner helped me to evaluate the full relevance of cognition and directed me toward a comparative developmental approach, for which Vico's writings had already prepared me.

The fourth root is to be found in the fact that either unverbalized preference, unconscious selection, chance, or other factors since I entered private practice led me to treat a large number of ambulatory schizophrenics. Office treatment of schizophrenia became my specialty at a time when even minor schizophrenic symptoms induced many therapists to hospitalize patients. Although my treatment has veered predominantly toward patients in office practice, it is applicable to hospitalized patients also, and I myself have applied it to them. There are other sources that I cannot mention, so large is their number. I cannot possibly enumerate, in distinct sequence, all I have learned from many authors and colleagues.

The reading of Parts Two and Three of this book is a prerequisite for a full understanding of the therapeutic approach that is now going to be presented. For didactical purposes my personal therapeutic approach can be considered as consisting of four aspects: (1) establishment of relatedness, which will be described in this chapter; (2) specific treatment of psychotic mechanisms (Chapter 37); (3)

psychodynamic analysis: recognition of unconscious motivation and insight into the psychological components of the disorder (Chapter 38); and (4) general participation in patient's life, in some cases with the use of a therapeutic assistant or a psychiatric nurse (Chapter 39). Although these four aspects are described and discussed separately, they occur simultaneously in various degrees.

In Chapter 40 a detailed account of the treatment of two difficult cases will be presented, and in Chapter 41 the treatment of chronic schizophrenia will be examined.

II

The Therapeutic Encounter

We must frankly acknowledge that, contrary to the other aspects of psychotherapy of schizophrenia, establishment of relatedness is still at a prescientific level of development. Szalita (1955) wrote that in this endeavor the therapist must resort to a large extent to his own intuition. On the other hand, we should not be discouraged or exaggerate the difficulties of this part of the treatment. It is important to remember that even in the sickest patient the wish to rejoin the human community is seldom completely extinguished and may help us even in the most trying phases of the treatment. When we see the patient for the first time, he may have cut all human contacts or may retain only paranoid ties with the world. He feels unaccepted and unacceptable, afraid to communicate, and at times unable to communicate, having lost the usual ways by which people express themselves. Can we really accept him when he seems so unwilling to come to terms with the human race? Can we make him feel accepted without his developing the fear that he has to pay the price of remaining dependent, compliant, or driven to do things he cannot do or does not want to do?

According to Sullivan (1953*a*) therapy must offer the patients a "relationship of security beyond what they have ever had." According to Fromm-Reichmann (1950) therapy must offer a "specific way by which they [patients] can trust the world and themselves." But how can we find this specific way? Whereas the neurotic patient in most cases wants to be helped and to be in contact with others (although in a neurotic contact), the schizophrenic seems to want to move away from the rest of mankind. He is in the process of more or less rapidly losing his grip on the world, and most attempts to establish contact with him increase his anxiety and make him disintegrate even more. How can he reestablish object relations?

The therapist's attitude must vary according to the condition of the patient. In patients who are in prepsychotic panic, or who have already entered the psychosis and are acutely decompensating, we must assume an attitude of active and intense intervention. A sincere, strong, and healthy person enters the life of the patient and conveys a feeling of basic trust. The strength of the therapist is welcomed by the patient who feels frightened and confused, but it may be also a motive for additional fear if it is not accompanied by a genuine message of concern and tenderness. The patient must be approached in very simple, at times even preverbal, ways.

As soon as he arrives on the scene, the therapist participates in the struggle that goes on; he does not listen passively to dissociated ideas. With his facial expression, gestures, voice, attitude of informality, and general demeanor he must do whatever is in his power to remove the fear that is automatically aroused by the fact that a human being (the therapist) wants to establish contact. In the confused, unstable, or fluctuating world of the patient, the therapist establishes himself as a person who emerges as a clear and distinct entity, somebody on whom the patient can sustain himself. The therapist must clarify his identity as an unsophisticated, straightforward, simple person who has no facade to put on, a person who can accept a state of nonunderstanding, a person who has unconditional regard for the dignity of another human being, no matter what is his predicament. An atmosphere of reassurance is at least attempted, and the patient recognizes it. The therapist's appeal at this moment is not to the unconscious of the patient, but to the basic and genuine part of the patient's personality. To paraphrase the words of the poet Wordsworth, it is a communication with "the naked and native dignity of man." Clarifications are given immediately. The therapist enters the picture, not as an examiner who is going to dissect psychologically the patient, but as one who immediately participates in what seems an inaccessible situation. To a male patient in panic I said, "You are afraid of me, of everybody, afraid stiff. I am not going to hurt you." To a woman who had given birth recently, I said, holding her hand, "You are going to be a good mother. I am here with you. I trust you." These are not just words of reassurance. These statements are "passing remarks" or "appropriate comments" (Semrad, 1952), but they are not detailed interpretations. They are formulations that the therapist makes at once during his first contacts with the patient. They must be given in short, incisive sentences. Their importance lies in conveying to the patient the feeling that somebody understands he is in trouble and feels with him. They should not be confused with deeper interpretations given later.

Some nonverbal, meaningful actions, such as touching the patient, holding his hand, walking together, and so forth, may be useful in some cases. The therapist must keep in mind, however, that this procedure may be dangerous with some patients. For instance, a catatonic stupor may be transformed into a frightening catatonic excitement.

This attitude of active intervention is not only not indicated in some acutely disintegrating cases but can be harmful. It may be experienced as an intrusion, and even more than that, as an attack. The patient may be scared and may withdraw, and disintegrate even more.

In these cases we have to resort to an approach similar to the one used with patients who are withdrawn or are barricaded behind autistic detachment. The therapist must be prepared to face negative attitudes and should not regard them as a rebuff. They are special ways of communicating, a special language by which the patient expresses what he experiences. For instance, the withdrawn patient finds it unbearable to look at the therapist's face. He may close his eyes or turn his face in the opposite direction. We have seen several times in this book how frightening the eyes of other people can be to the patient. The therapist should not interpret this behavior as rejection of the treatment or of himself, but as ways to reduce to a less intolerable degree the frightening aspect of the interpersonal contact. The therapist, of course, should persist in his aim of reaching the patient. Such perseverance should not be manifested by insisting that the patient talk or respond; instead, the therapist himself should make short statements that do not require answers. For instance, "I came to see you"; "I wanted to see you today and find out how you are. I know this is a hard time for you, but I am here to help you." A long dialogue or monologue is not necessary, but the patient must experience the therapist as a concrete reality, must hear the sound of his voice, and must start to distinguish him from the nebulous surrounding world.

How does one conduct a session with a mute catatonic? No repeated attempt should be made to force him to talk, for such an attempt would make him withdraw even more. The therapist should take the initiative and talk to him. The talk should be a pleasant one and should consist of neutral topics, that is, of subjects that will not increase the anxiety of the patient. This may be difficult to do, and many mistakes are possible because the catatonic spreads or generalizes his anxiety to a large number of subjects. Another frequent mistake made with catatonic patients consists of touching too soon or inadvertently on psychodynamic subjects when the patient seems somewhat improved. I have seen several cases where the mere mention of mother, wife, or husband made recovering catatonics slip back into a catatonic stupor.

While the therapist talks to the patient about a neutral subject, the patient, even if disinterested in the neutral topic, must be made to feel that a benevolent, sincere effort is being made to reach him, with no demands being made on him. At times even these one-way talks irritate the patient because he feels that they are just one-way talks or monologues and not real communications. The patient discloses his displeasure by withdrawing further. In these cases the therapist must be willing to respect the patient's desire for silence, without showing any discomfort or anxiety about it. A state of silence or of nonverbal communication will then be shared, interrupted from time to time by the firm and reassuring voice of the therapist, who will thus make his presence felt.

Equally difficult is the beginning of treatment with hebephrenics and paranoids, who are able but unwilling to verbalize. Here the tendency of the young therapist is to approach the patient with many questions in an attempt to make him talk. This attempt is understandable because there are many things that the therapist would like to know, and the therapist also tends to feel that if the patient is under pressure he will finally talk. However, from the point of view of therapy, this method should be discarded. Each question is experienced by the schizophrenic as an imposition or an intrusion into his private life and will increase his anxiety, his hostility, and his desire to desocialize. In certain respects the schizophrenic is like a young child. When a stranger visits a family and greets their young child by asking him questions, he will not be accepted by the child because the child feels that the stranger wants something from him. But later on, when the stranger is not a stranger any longer, if he asks questions that the child is capable of answering, the response will be favorable; contact will be made. The schizophrenic, too, in a later stage will be glad to answer questions that do not require an effort.

In the beginning, however, no questions shoud be asked, because every question implies an effort. This technique seems easy but is actually very difficult to follow because the therapist feels compelled to ask questions. He feels that for diagnostic and legal purposes some questions must be asked. For example, in state hospitals, the physician must ask questions that, if necessary, will prove in court that the patient is psychotic and legally detained. Whatever the diagnostic and legal requirements are, this procedure is not indicated from a therapeutic standpoint. This is a paradoxical and distressing situation for many therapists: on one side there is so much that we need to know about the patient, and on the other side there is so much that we may lose or spoil if we try to obtain the information directly from the patient. The best procedure is to obtain as much information as possible from the members of the family, friends, or the doctor who first saw the patient. If for legal reasons questions must be asked that will prove the diagnosis of psychosis or the necessity of certification, the therapist must delegate this procedure to another psychiatrist who will have just this specific function without participating in the treatment.

Some patients have reported that when they were pressured to talk or to answer, at the beginning of therapy, they felt coerced, accused, or on trial. These feelings promoted further alienation and withdrawal. At times the patient does talk somewhat and in such a way as to stimulate questions. If a patient with a tendency to withdraw says, "They are persecuting me," the psychiatrist has to refrain from asking this patient who the persecutors are. The patient often does not name them, but uses the pronoun *they*. Also, if he says he *knows* that *they* are persecuting him, that there is "something funny going on," the therapist has the urge to ask him how he knows that there is something funny going on and what this funny thing is. At the beginning of the treatment these questions may have an adverse effect. In many early cases the patient actually does not know the answers. He himself does not know who the persecutors are or what the strange feeling is. What he experiences are only vague feelings, and questions of this type may actually help him crystallize into concrete images or persons feelings that as yet have not become well-defined delusions or ideas of reference. If the therapist has patience, later on he will understand where this feeling of persecution comes from and why the patient has the need to externalize with delusions a vague feeling of hostility that the patient feels has been directed toward him.

If we do not ask questions, then what do we do with a withdrawn patient? As was mentioned in relation to catatonics, in the beginning the therapist takes the initiative and talks in a pleasant manner about neutral subjects. Sometimes I look at an art book with the patient and take the initiative in discussing the pictures in plain language. These pictures should *not* lead easily to identification, as those of the Thematic Apperception Test do. They should not arouse anxiety. At the very beginning of treatment, when the patient's suspiciousness and distrust are very pronounced, he should leave the session with the feeling that he has been given something, not with the feeling that something, even diagnostic information, has been taken from him. When the patient has gained some security in contact with the therapist, he will talk more and more and eventually will even talk about his problems and give the therapist some historical material. At times this material is collected only after an extremely long period because of the patient's distrust and difficulties in communicating. However, if the therapist is familiar with the dynamic factors of schizophrenia such as were discussed in Part Two of this book, he is prepared to expect certain things and is therefore aided in recognizing and interpreting these factors. The difficulties in understanding schizophrenic language and thought may also be overcome to a certain extent if the therapist is familiar with the mechanisms that were discussed in Part Three of this book.

In spite of his familiarity with the formal mechanisms described in Part Three, the therapist may find much material totally obscure in certain cases on account of the patient's extreme individuality and unpredictability. I am thinking especially of the productions of some paranoids and hebephrenics who are very talkative in spite of advanced regression. Their talk consists so much of word-salad that the therapist who attempts to treat them does not know how to start and is bound to feel discouraged.

The fact that the patient wants to talk is an encouraging sign; even if his talk seems incomprehensible, he still has the need to communicate, and this need may facilitate the treatment. The therapist should listen patiently; he should not pretend that he understands, because the patient detects any pretension, but should maintain a benevolent attitude and manifest a desire to communicate even in a nonverbal manner. If the therapist is willing to listen to the patient for a long time, he will be surprised to find out that even the word-salad will become more comprehensible (see Chapter 16). The therapist will detect that some themes recur often and that the patient's talk follows certain patterns. Finally, some preoccupations of the patient with certain topics will become evident and will offer important clues. The therapist will grasp the general feeling tone of what the patient says even if he does not grasp the content. The general frame of reference or the "cosmology" of the patient will be indented.

But again we must add that what is asked of the therapist is much more than it seems. Many therapists, especially those who have almost exclusive experience with psychoneurotics, are unable to endure a talk that makes no sense to them for a long period of time. The terror of lack of communication may be experienced by the therapist much more than by the patient. The therapist may experience anxiety throughout the interview, and this makes him wish to terminate the session. This menacing feeling is experienced in two disturbing ways, as threat of nothingness and threat of meaningfulness. It is experienced as threat of nothingness when the therapist finds himself inclined to accept temporarily the convenient idea that there is no content in what the patient says, that it is just nonsense. But this idea undermines his therapeutic intentions and revolts his feelings of human solidarity. Threat of meaningfulness is experienced by the therapist inasmuch as he senses that there is a meaning, a meaning that escapes him. When he finally feels that he grasps this meaning, he may not be able to repeat it. In fact, I myself and many therapists with whom I have worked, have at times felt that we had grasped the endoceptual meaning of what the patient wanted to say, but we could not repeat it to ourselves with our language or communicate it to others in meetings or during supervisory hours. We felt that the report to the supervisor would be inaccurate and that the instructions received would therefore be erroneous.

This grasping of the ineffable meaning may be considered intuitional on the part of the therapist. I prefer to say that in these cases, in order to break the schizophrenic barrier and reach the patient, the therapist has succeeded in sharing the state of desocialization and individualism of the patient. There has been no real intuition but only an unusual kind of communication at a nonverbal level or a primordial verbal communication. This may perhaps be compared to the empathic communication between the baby and the mother, to the esthetic communication that the artist establishes with the observer of his work of art, or something similar to the primordial effects that paleosymbols must have produced on people when they became social symbols (see Chapter 19). The inability to communicate the meaning to others is due to the fact that, in order to make contact with the patient, the therapist had to share his state of impaired communication and his incommunicable unique feeling. This, of course, happens in a minority of cases. Most of the time we are able to make an approximately accurate translation in our own language. At other times we go even further, and we are able to understand the patient's problems completely, as we shall see from examples given in Chapter 37.

The therapist may have several other feelings of doubt in treating the patient. Has the patient preserved the ability to understand our common language and does he understand the therapist? Does the patient understand himself when he speaks in a word-salad? It seems to me that most schizophrenics retain the ability to understand us, at least potentially. If the nonverbal communication to which we have referred and the general feeling in the therapeutic situation are such as to put the patient in a receptive attitude, he is certainly capable of understanding us. This receptive attitude may not be established for a long time, but in certain cases it may be obtained even during the first interview. Let us remember that the schizophrenic maintains his potential capacity to resume higher levels of integration and therefore high levels of communication whenever these are not accompanied by anxiety. This is demonstrated by the following observation, which has been made by almost every therapist. A regressed hebephrenic may seem unable to understand the therapist at all during an unsuccessful session, even when the therapist speaks in the most concrete language. However, when the therapist tells the patient that the session is ended, the patient rises and goes away, thus showing that he understood the meaning of this sentence. It seems almost as if the patient had allowed himself to be touched verbally by what he understood as implying a decrease in anxiety (avoidance of the unpleasant session).

Often the problem is not at all one of understanding our common language, but of misunderstanding. In other words, the personal problems of the patients make them give special meanings to what we say. That is true in different degrees for all patients, from the preserved paranoid to the regressed hebephrenic.

This impairment in exchange of meanings, which is always more or less present although the patient retains a potential ability to resume understanding of our language, is partially compensated for by the fact that the patient has increased his sensitivity to nonverbal communication, that is, to the feeling tone or to the atmospheric quality of the session. The reader should notice that we stated that the patient has increased his *sensitivity* and not his understanding, because although it is true that he may sense or recognize this feeling tone much better than a normal person does, it is also true that in many instances he attaches to it an egocentric and grossly inappropriate meaning, even if this meaning contains a grain of truth.

As to the problem of whether the patient understands himself when he speaks in a very disconnected manner, as for instance, in word-salad, the matter is controversial. We have compared some of his productions to a photographic film that has been exposed several times. The patient must be disturbed by this impairment as much as the listener is, just as the aphasic is disturbed by his own defect. The schizophrenic in a vague way is aware of what he wants to say, and he is also aware of the fact that he wishes to communicate. He experiences several feelings at the same time, as well as a desire to communicate several things at the same time, even if he is not able to formulate verbally these concomitant desires, either to himself or to the listener. The therapist may help him to understand his own productions.

Here again one is reminded of what happens in the field of art. Some modern painters have stated that when they paint they have only a dim awareness of their feelings and that they know only with a certain approximation what they are going to paint or express. At times, even when the painting is finished, they do not know what they wanted to represent. It is from the reactions that these paintings will evoke in people that the artists discover what they themselves felt and wanted to express. In the same way the schizophrenic patient may understand better his verbal productions if he is helped by the therapist, that is, when the latter is able verbally or nonverbally to communicate to him that a specific meaning has been conveyed and a given reaction has been engendered.

It is important for the therapist to be aware of his anxiety about these difficulties in communication and to be able to cope with this problem if he wants to work with regressed schizophrenics. In fact, as we shall mention again later, the patient will perceive this anxiety immediately.

It is obvious that when the impairment in communication is very pronounced, the therapeutic sessions must be very frequent, at least one a day. Of course, the number of sessions varies according to the individual patient. Some will do well even with as little as three sessions a week.

We have so far discussed patients who are rapidly disintegrating, or withdrawn and in very poor contact. There are, however, other important categories of patients: those who, although actively psychotic, with many typical symptoms like hallucinations, delusions, and ideas of reference, have the bulk of their personality well preserved, and with whom, therefore, communication can be established with less difficulty. We have also a large number of undoubtedly psychotic patients who retain a relatively intact personality and have a symptomatology that is not pronounced, consisting of a few sporadic ideas of reference and delusional trends. The more intact the bulk of the personality is, the more we can depart from the recommendations made for poorly communicating patients. We may even ask questions and direct the patient to explain his obscure experiences. In these cases, too, the dialogue between the therapist and the patient should not be diagnostic, or predominantly exploratory; the emphasis should be on giving and sharing. Free association, which was impossible with the poorly communicating patients, is also to be discouraged with these relatively integrated patients, because it can promote scattering of thoughts. Here, of course, our technique departs drastically from that of the Kleinian school. I use free association occasionally with patients who are only mildly psychotic, with no signs of regression or special areas of intense vulnerability. In these cases I believe that the tendency to repress important material is more alarming than the risk of provoking regressive features.

With verbose, well-systematized paranoids we often face a different problem. These patients may speak exclusively about their delusional complexes. In these cases I feel that some pressure has to be exerted on them. They should be encouraged to talk about something else. An indirect attempt should be made to make them see that there is something else besides their persecutors in the world; in other words, an effort should be made to circumvent their delusions. This should be done, not in order to repress the complexes, which would be impossible, but rather to enable the patients to increase their ties in the world. At the beginning, the patients' peculiar contacts with the environment are established only through their delusions. If the therapist, with his general attitude, which will be discussed later, is able to make the patients enlarge their interests, a great victory will have been achieved. In many cases of well-systematized paranoiacs and paranoids this is impossible. They remain fanatically and exclusively interested in their complexes and refuse to talk about anything else. They want only to prove to the therapist, as though to a judge, that their suspicions are well founded. Of course, it is useless to enter into any arguments with the patients. It is also inadvisable to pretend to accept their delusions or hallucinations, with a few exceptions, to be mentioned later. Tower (1947), in a very interesting paper, has emphasized the desirability that the therapist remain noninvolved in the delusions of the patients. Fromm-Reichmann (1952) recommends telling patients that the therapist does not hear or see what the patient hears or sees. They should investigate together the reasons for the difference in their experience. In many cases where the delusional material cannot be circumvented at all, ambulatory treatment is not useful or feasible, and hospitalization becomes necessary.

There is a relatively large group of schizophrenic patients, especially those who had had a stormy prepsychotic personality, with whom it is very easy to establish some relatedness. They are hungry for contacts of any kind; they ask questions repeatedly and cling tenaciously to the therapist. The contacts, however, are superficial and few. They make anxious, superficial, and self-contradictory statements. The therapist should try not to expose to a breaking point the tenuousness of these contacts; he should realize that this type of communication is all the patient is capable of at this stage. The therapist should focus only on a few elements of what was said by the patient, and through them establish communication. Contrasting with the brittleness of the world, the therapist will appear clear and distinct.

One of the reasons why some therapists have difficulty in establishing relatedness with psychotics is their adherence to some notions they have learned and professional habits that they have acquired. The therapist may need to unlearn older models of examination and treatment that otherwise almost inadvertently would creep in. Among them are: (1) the old-fashioned routine mental-status examination, purely diagnostic in aim and consisting of questions similar to those that might be asked by a district attorney; (2) strict adherence to the orthodox psychoanalytic technique, which was originally devised for the treatment of psychoneuroses. We have already mentioned in this regard that, with the exception of some well-preserved patients, the method of free association of classic psychoanalysis should be used very seldom. The same could be repeated for the use of the couch, which would interfere with the patient's need for physical closeness. Although, as we have mentioned, many schizophrenics do not want to look at the therapist's face or eyes, they do need to see him. If they do not see him, a tendency toward archaic ways of thinking may make them feel that the therapist is not present. Some patients with whom the couch was tried felt that the therapist was not there; nobody was there, or only a disembodied voice. Sechehaye (1951*a*) reported that her patient had the need to see her; when the patient could not see the therapist, she felt the therapist was not there. This feeling is reminiscent of children who close their eyes when they want to make things disappear (Fenichel, 1945).

III

Transference

What we have described in the previous section of this chapter demonstrates that we can indeed talk of transference and countertransference in the treatment of schizophrenics, but not in the same sense as in classic psychoanalysis. We must look again at these major interpersonal phenomena within the therapeutic situation before we examine them together in that more complex interpersonal exchange that we call relatedness. This section is devoted to the transferential situation of the psychotic.

As we have seen in Chapter 5, the patient never sufficiently developed a sense of basic trust; and after his break with reality, any trust is almost totally extinguished. The mistrust, unrelatedness, and hostility that he shows toward the therapist when he first meets him is no different from the way the patient feels toward the whole universe. It may appear to be directed more toward the therapist, because the therapist attempts closeness, and the patient is afraid of this closeness and is consequently suspicious and paranoid. Whenever an attempt is made by the patient to reenter social life, he perceives it as something that exerts pressure on him. The others are seen as forces, as powers that impinge on him to the point that he may lose his own existence. He finds himself in a world where the ferocious imprinting of early life and the resurgence of the primary process give monstrous shapes to whatever he experiences. At this point the therapist is also part of this world of hostility, persecution, deformity, and desolation, a world where it is better to have nothing, not even hope or some positive feeling for any other human being, because if you love them, you are bound to lose them.

Some existentialistic psychiatrists see this schizophrenic way of being-in-the-world as an unchangeable way, which ineluctably leads to disaster, as in the cases of Ellen West and Suzanne Urban reported by Binswanger (1957, 1958*a, b*). On the other hand, the psychodynamic therapist does not want to fit into this world of unrelatedness, autism, distrust, suspiciousness, no matter how much the patient tries to place him there. It is by not fitting into this world but by escaping from the category of malevolent forces that the therapist will open a window from which other vistas are seen and into and out of which the flow of society's symbolism will come and go. If such a window is opened, the whole pathological world of isolation and distrust is more likely to collapse. To a certain extent the therapist must do what Miss Sullivan did in the case of Helen Keller (1951). The therapist must have his ways with the methods outlined in the previous section and with those that we shall describe and discuss in Chapters 37, 38, and 39. The patient may change rapidly and acquire some very warm feelings for the therapist; at times he changes very slowly, at times so slowly as to make the changes almost imperceptible, especially to the members of the family of the patient. These quasi-static patients seem to live in an almost magically timeless world. Therapy makes time reenter into their life. But at first the therapist's (and the patient's) time is not society's time. It is a slower-moving time where months and in some cases years are permitted to pass by without despair, but with the vigilant and sensitive perception of what is almost imperceptible, and where the little, almost unappreciable changes are the clues that life goes on, that hope is to be retained.

After accepting the therapist, the patient generally accepts the therapeutic assistant, a nurse, or some other person. His milieu and realm of action become more diversified; the interchange less stereotyped. There is less rigidity in the psychological structure, and the patterns of behavior are less repetitive.

When relatedness is well established, the patient seems to flourish again, at times rising to unexpected heights. The period of withdrawal or incommunicability may have lasted only a few weeks, or even several years. At times a change is realized by patient and therapist with the intensity of drama. This satisfactory turn of events, which is the result not only of what we have described in this chapter but also of what we are going to illustrate in Chapters 37, 38, and 39, may have propitious effect throughout the rest of the treatment.

One fundamental point is that at the stage of treatment in which the establishment of relatedness is of primary concern, relatedness in its transference and countertransference components, has to be *lived* as a new experience in the patient's life; it should not be taken into consideration only as something to be psychodynamically interpreted. Transference and countertransference are obviously very important as objects of interpretation, but their interpretation must take place later when positive relatedness has been established.

Unfortunately, in a considerable number of cases several complications, almost opposite from each other, may arise to jeopardize the relatedness. We shall examine individually each of the most common complications, although in some cases they occur simultaneously or in mixed forms. These complications may necessitate an otherwise premature psychodynamic interpretation of the transferential situation.

In a large number of cases in which the patient tends to have a paranoid vision of the world, he will feel very uncomfortable in the new bond of warmth developed with the therapist. The patient cannot stand too much closeness; he anticipates rejection and fears that rejection after so much closeness will be more painful, and he wants to be the one who rejects and hurts. These feelings are not fully conscious or faced by him. He does not know, of course, that he wants to go again inside the hermetic paranoid structure and put the therapist too in the system of delusions. He will try to test the therapist, to show that he too is at fault, that he too does not trust the patient, that he too has a bad intention, and so on. The mistrust may cover any aspect of the relatedness. Manifestations of warmth, interest, participation, and sharing may be viewed by the patient as having ulterior motives, as proof of the therapist's intent to exploit the patient for heterosexual or homosexual gratifications or for purposes of experimentation or in order to make a profit of some kind. The patient's way of thinking and feeling undergoes what Sullivan calls a malevolent transformation. The malevolent transformation is not just hostility, freely expressed; the whole way of relating is to a greater or lesser degree structured in accordance with a paranoid model.

Whenever tendencies of this type develop, they have to be corrected immediately, before they acquire a degree of strength which may jeopardize the treatment.

Hostility is to be found sooner or later in every schizophrenic patient, but it is disguised in several forms. As Bychowski (1952) points out, it may assume the form of extreme passivity, because every act is a potential act of hostility of which the patient himself is afraid. It may assume the usual form of projection: "He hates me" instead of "I hate him." In this symbolic representation, the patient experiences the feeling "he hates me"; he seems aware now of the hostility that once was really directed toward him. However, this hostility now comes, not from the original person who was ill-disposed toward the patient, but from an imaginary substitute. Also the hostility that the patient sees in this substitute is not a reproduction of the original hostility or lack of tenderness, but a distortion of them. Whenever possible, one should explain to the patient that the hostility is misdirected and that he is acting as if situations that have long since disappeared were still in existence. We must remember that hostile manifestations are often only tests that the patient uses to probe the therapist. If the feeling of trust is maintained, the hostility will decrease, but it is very difficult to maintain this trust, because the patient is extremely suspicious and sensitive and sees signs of rejection at any moment. Fromm-Reichmann mentions a patient who went into a catatonic stupor twice when the hour of her appointment was changed. A patient of mine, also a catatonic, went into a tantrum because I answered the telephone during a session.

When it has proved to be impossible to handle the hostility, the therapist may allow another person to be present at the interview. The patient will not resent this person as an intruder if he understands that this is being done to protect him too from the expression of his own hostility. At times the patient's hostility is not obvious. The patient tries to isolate the therapist from the rest of his experiences, which are connected with hostility. The patient tries again to make the therapist an inhabitant of a planet other than the one in which the patient lives. Although this situation of nonparticipation may seem advantageous, because otherwise the transference would become a turbulent one, the consequent distant relatedness must eventually be followed by involvement.

I must repeat here what I said about the patient who becomes openly hostile. The patient who becomes again detached from the therapist does not feel strong enough to endure the new way of feeling with human beings. Seeing himself as a perennial outsider, he thinks that he is occasionally let in in order to be ousted later. More frequently, however, the patient who cuts off the affective bond that had been established in therapy feels that were he to continue social intimacy with the therapist, he would eventually have to give himself up as an individual. Even to do things or to do what others do or would like him to do is experienced as giving up his own individuality. These experiences are distortions of original situations in life and are experienced subjectively, often without the capacity to express them in words. They remain endocepts. Again I have to repeat here that in these cases of uncertain relationship the therapist must be able to be, according to the circumstances, close or distant; but always close to give, distant enough not to scare. What seems skillful navigation between two dangerous possibilities actually becomes an intuitive way of feeling one's way through the current difficulties of the patient.

Some patients, once established in some kind of elementary relatedness, develop an attitude of total dependency on the therapist. They act like babies. Lidz and Lidz (1952), who in a concise, excellent paper have discussed this aspect of therapy, felt that these patients had mothers who had an intense need to sustain in their children a parasitical attitude. A symbiotic relationship between mother and child was thus developed. The child did not live in his own right but as an appendage of mother. The reader will remember that similar problems were discussed in detail in Part Two of this book. In my opinion a decrease in self-esteem that is due to the patient's realization that he always does what mother considers wrong accompanies in several cases the belief that mother always does everything right. She must be omniscient and omnipotent, as the patient thought she was when he was a baby. He should not do things but should let her do them. As a matter of fact, that is what mother desires. The patient tends to establish not a symbiotic relation but a parasitic one, one reminiscent of the fetus completely taken care of by the mother. But here, in some cases, restitution phenomena determine those feelings of altered relatedness so well described by Lidz and Lidz. The patient feels not that he is a parasite but that he is in a symbiotic relation. In simple words, he feels that he is extremely important to mother; mother could not live without him. In addition, he believes that if mother does not allow him to do things, it is not because she is bad, but because she is good. He makes efforts to preserve the good image of the mother and to repress her bad image. Certain attitudes of the mother that are reassuring are magnified; and others that are anxiety arousing are completely obliterated (see Chapter 5).

In the therapeutic relationship, the patient may tend to resume this symbiotic attitude. This tendency may appear useful at the very beginning of treatment, when every means is exploited to make contact with the patient, but it will be harmful later if it is not combated. As Lidz and Lidz indicate, the patient must soon realize that the relationship with the therapist is not just a repetition of the symbiotic bond but a new type of close relationship: this other person can *care* for him, rather than just *take care* of him. The patient must feel and recognize that the therapist is motivated by an interest in helping him for his own sake, and not for some personal ulterior motive. Again this feeling and recognition, I believe, must come as felt experience, and not as an interpretation offered to him.

Lidz and Lidz feel that this symbiotic need may be so strong as to require a change of therapist. In my opinion this change seldom will be necessary if strong efforts have been made to combat it from a relatively early stage of therapy. If the treatment is successful, the patient comes to the realization that the therapist is not a restricting parent but permits a gradual expansion of the patient's personality as a separate entity.

The strong need to maintain the stultifying dependency will appear in different forms, but this need should always be explored. For instance, the patient may be afraid of his own improvement. When the patient looks at this progress with a feeling of achievement, he may be afraid that he will not be able to remain so independent, and at the same time he may long for the old dependent (symbiotic) attitude. The dangerous fascination that the old dependent attitude has for him should eventually be explained.

There is an additional type of transference that the patient may develop that also reveals a psychotic structure or understructure. The patient may develop a "positive" feeling for the therapist that is so profound and intense that it assumes unrealistically grandiose proportions and characteristics. The therapist becomes omniscient, omnipotent, a genius, a prophet, a benefactor of the highest rank, a superb lover, and so on. This type of relatedness is an exaggeration or psychotic distortion of what some psychoneurotic patients experience. At times it reaches comic proportions: the therapist is literally considered an angel or a divinity.

The inexperienced therapist may at times, especially if the distortions are not obviously psychotic, tolerate this relation and in some cases even enjoy it, for it may satisfy some of his narcissism. It is not difficult to understand how this apotheosis of the therapist is possible or even plausible. The therapist is the only person with whom the patient relates: he comes to represent the interpersonal world or the only person who counts in the life of the patient. If the therapist is of the opposite sex, a romantic element often enters, and this makes the relation even more intense. The patient becomes extremely dependent on this "superb human being" who becomes as necessary as "the air the patient breathes, the food he eats." The relation is obviously abnormal. Primary process cognition distorts the images that the patient had once conceived of the good mother and good lover and makes of them a grandiose and distorted mixed image that he identifies with the person of the therapist. If the relation is allowed to become so intense, severe depression or reexacerbation of the illness may occur when attempts are made to break it or decrease its intensity. This type of relation may become as difficult to handle as the hostile paranoid one. I have seen several cases in which the therapist could not handle any more the patient whose feeling had become intensely positive and had to refer the psychotic patient to another therapist, at times with serious consequences. I have even seen therapists who were considering moving to other cities in order to escape from psychotic or quasi-psychotic patients who had become so demanding in a loving way.

The proper procedure consists of correcting any tendency of this type from the very beginning. Certainly the therapist is important in the life of the patient. In some respects, especially at the beginning of the treatment, he may be as important as a good parent; but even a good parent is not the representative of the whole universe, nor has he or she the characteristics that the patient attributes to the therapist. One of my patients, during the tenth month of her treatment, told me, "The most tragic day for me will be the day when I discover that you make a mistake. My parents, my husband, every human being, I expect to make mistakes, but not you." I immediately tried to dislodge this belief by assuring her that I make mistakes, that I make them every day, and that often I catch myself in the process of making them. I also told her that I had made mistakes even in her treatment, and that yet she had improved. She began then to accept me on a more realistic plane. She did not continue to think that her recovery was based on my extraordinary powers. I suppose a patient may at times be almost hypnotized into a state of remission by believing in the magical powers of the analyst, but I wonder whether such a remission would last.

These fantasies of the patient are also pathological ways to regain self-esteem. At the beginning of therapy, the patient I have just mentioned felt that because I had such superhuman ability, I was the only person who knew that she was a good girl and, therefore, the only person who could appreciate her.

Even in fairy tales, the person who is helped by the magic supernatural being is a person who believes he deserves to be helped, a person, therefore, who has not lost his self-esteem. When the patient is made to feel that he is accepted by the therapist, in spite of the fact that the latter has no magical powers, real progress is made.

Another patient of mine was very disturbed when he heard from me that I had to take a few days off because I had to undergo a tonsillectomy. He was particularly disturbed by the fact that I needed another doctor to treat me and operate on me. In his fantasies about me I appeared self-curative. How could it be that I needed another doctor? If a physical illness were to strike the patient, would I be able to cure him? For two or three days he woke up at night with anxiety feelings, thinking that I would not be able to take care of him if something happened to him. Eventually the patient was reassured when he saw that I resumed his treatment as before, after I myself had been treated by other doctors.

Another belief that the schizophrenic often holds (and also the neurotic at times) is that the doctor knows all the answers to the problems discussed but withholds them from the patient, either capriciously or because he feels that the patient, in a certain sense, has not grown up sufficiently. This too is a resurgence of a belief that little children have about the surrounding adults, who at times are really too secretive about certain matters. When the child grows up in a normal environment, he sooner or later accepts the fact that the parents cannot answer all the questions, all the "whys," because they themselves do not know the answers. The schizophrenic, however, embraces again the belief in the omniscience of the only adult who counts. Again, the therapist must eventually convey to the patient the fact that an inability to answer all questions is a characteristic of human nature and not necessarily a handicap. In the process of improving, the patient himself will be able to answer many of his own questions; others he will answer in cooperation with the therapist; some he will never answer, and yet he will not feel less human.

Another attitude that the schizophrenic holds much more often than the neurotic is that he is the unique interest of the therapist. The therapist cannot possibly be as interested in the other patients as he is in him. I suggested a raise in the fee of a schizophrenic patient who was able to secure a remunerative employment after I had been treating him for a long time at a reduced fee. The patient was furiously insulted and almost interrupted the treatment. His faith in me was vacillating; I was treating him for money and not because I had any interest in him. Eventually he understood me when I explained to him that by intending to raise the fee, I was acknowledging his growth and the fact that he no longer required special conditions.

Another practical problem that presents itself in connection with this strong symbiotic need of the patient is how to prepare him for the vacation time of the therapist. Especially if the vacation time occurs just a few months after the beginning of treatment, the patient may experience a strong feeling of panic at the idea of being left alone. If he is a catatonic, he may actually relapse into a stupor. The situation may reactivate the patient's strong feelings of being rejected, and direct attempts to convince him that this is not the case are futile. In many instances, the therapist may avoid these complications by preparing the patient far in advance for this brief separation. He should be told a few months previously that the physician has made plans for a vacation, and that he should expect a few weeks interruption in treatment. In many cases, especially if the treatment is still at a preliminary stage, some ties have to be maintained even during the vacation time. The patient should be told that he may write to the therapist, or that if an emergency arises, he may even telephone him. In my experience, I have found that patients very seldom avail themselves of these concessions; on the other hand, they feel reassured. In the cases where the help of a therapeutic assistant is needed, this difficulty is partially removed by arranging different vacation times for the therapist and for the therapeutic assistant (see Chapter 39).

I resort to an additional technique with a minority of very anxious patients. I tape-record some salient points of sessions, during which situations that are likely to trigger anxiety and psychotic symptoms are discussed and interpreted. During the therapist's absence the patient finds reassurance in listening to the tape and hearing again the ways by which he can face and fight the symptoms. Hearing the therapist's voice promotes the feeling that the therapist is almost present and that on his return will be as involved with the patient as he was before he left.

IV

Countertransference

We have so far discussed mainly the part of the relatedness that is usually referred to as transference. We must now discuss the countertransference, which plays a very important role in the psychotherapy of the schizophrenic. Countertransference is no longer considered a negative phenomenon to be combated, as it used to be considered in early psychoanalytic conceptions in reference to the psychoneuroses. It seems obvious that the attitude of the schizophrenic patient is such as to discourage any therapist who is motivated only by the usual therapeutic feelings, or only by the desire to help, and is not moved by an unusual countertransference. Again, if by countertransference we mean, as some authors do, identifying the patient with a figure of the analyst's past life or with the analyst himself as he was in his early life, then we must admit that these identifications are important but not inclusive of all that the analyst can experience for the patient. Perhaps Eissler (1951, 1952) and Rosen (1953) referred especially to these identifications. Eissler felt that his childhood fantasy of wanting to rescue people was reactivated when he tried to save schizophrenics from the shock treatment, which he considered "a great danger" (1952). Eissler thought that the therapist must be moved and stirred; therapeutic failure must be unacceptable to him, "the whole gamut of emotionality must be at his quick command . . . he should believe in his own omnipotence." What Eissler meant probably is that the therapist should almost have that vigor, motivation, and determination that a person who believes in his own extraordinary power has. Rosen wrote that in the treatment of schizophrenics the countertransference must be similar to the feelings that a good parent would have for a highly disturbed child. Rosen expressed the idea extremely well when he said that the therapist must identify with the unhappy patient, as the good parent identifies with the unhappy child, and be so disturbed by the unhappiness of the patient that he himself cannot rest until the patient is at peace.

In Rosen's conceptions, the intensified feeling of the analyst would be a compensation for the original defective mother-child relationship. Fromm-Reichmann, however, warned that no real compensation can occur for the early uncanny experiences unless the surviving adult part of the patient is eventually summoned to help.

One of the first concerns of the therapist when he has just started treatment should be the analysis of his own feeling for the patient. If he experiences a strong feeling of empathy and interest, the chances are that he will be able to make significant contact with the patient. If, instead, he has the feeling that he is bored, or irritated, or that his patience is strained, for example, when the patient is evasive, a therapeutically significant contact will be difficult to make. Efforts of the therapist to combat or to conceal these feelings are generally of no value, because the patient will sense them anyhow. The schizophrenic personality and the schizophrenic symptomatology are such as to arouse hostility very easily in people, and, of course, in the therapist also. If at the beginning of the treatment the therapist has a feeling of hostility, or even a feeling of nonacceptance for the patient, he must try to analyze it and to solve it if treatment is to be continued successfully. The treatment will be much easier if the therapist has a positive feeling of empathy for the patient. As Eissler (1952) has emphasized, these feelings are generally experienced at the first contact with the patient.

The kind of feeling, positive or negative, that the therapist will have for the patient will depend not only on the patient's personality and psychological problems, but also on the therapist's personality and problems. If the therapist has been psychoanalyzed, he is in a better position to determine what the characteristics are in certain patients that make him react in a negative way. If the analysis has not been successful in removing these tendencies, he should avoid treating patients who have the problems to which he reacts negatively. On the other hand, some very individualistic attitudes of the therapist, which are based on the therapist's own psychological problems, may be not at all harmful but beneficial to the treatment. We have already mentioned some of them, as reported by Eissler.

If the therapist, because of his own problems, succeeds in identifying with the patient or even in seeing in the patient a psychotic transformation of his own problems, he may not necessarily be handicapped but, on the contrary, helped in his therapeutic efforts.

No matter what the origin of his feelings is, the therapist must have a sense of total commitment toward the recovery of the schizophrenic. Such a feeling of commitment is generally sensed and appreciated even by the regressed schizophrenic. The patient derives from the general attitude of the therapist the feeling that the therapist is sincere in his attempts and therefore trustworthy. The therapist should never pretend to offer love or friendship to the patient when in reality he feels differently toward him. One is reminded of the patient quoted by Fromm-Reichmann who said to the young analyst who had professed friendship during the first interview, "How can you say we are friends? We hardly know each other" (1952). However, no matter whether the analyst is overtly warm or reserved, he must be consistent, convincing, and intensely interested and, as Betz (1947, 1950) writes, must communicate to the patient his strength, his fairness, and his kindness.

Also the therapist should not refrain from giving to the patient what some therapists are reluctant to give: simple reassurance and companionship. Although we have already discussed these points in the first section of this chapter, some additional clarifications are necessary.

Reassurance has become a bad word in the field of psychoanalysis and psychotherapy in general. If by reassurance we mean patting the patient on the back or telling him, "Don't worry; everything will be all right," then, of course, we have to agree that reassurance may not be therapeutic. Our reassurance is not merely a verbal expression. It is corroborated by our actions, our devotion, participation, or, as I have already said, by our total commitment.

Is reassurance enough? Of course not. Reassurance fails even to reassure, but it has a positive effect nevertheless. Only patients with whom no positive relatedness whatsoever can be established are untouched by reassurance. The others are, to various degrees. For instance, I have received numerous telephone calls, at times in the middle of the night, from patients at an early stage of treatment who felt they were persecuted and needed protection. I always considered it a healthy sign that they called me rather than the police. Although I could not remove the delusions by telephonic magic, I was able to transmit the feeling that nothing bad was about to happen and could suggest that no action had to be taken then. Although the delusions persisted, at times even for a few years, a stronger bond with the therapist was established. The patient felt that an oasis of human contact existed and that it could be reached by telephone. As to companionship, I meant the sharing of experiences in the act of living. Many therapists have done so; some have gone shopping with their patients, some have gone to dinner to their homes, some have lived in the same household.

A group of patients very badly in need of reassurance are women in a state of prepsychotic panic after childbirth or at the beginning of a postpartum psychosis. They are overwhelmed by anxiety and not yet in a position to face in psychotherapy the clarification of the psychodynamic mechanisms described in Chapter 13. In these cases, reassurance must not be of a general type but specifically related to the birth of the baby. In many cases, I have told the patient that she is in great distress because she rejects the baby, she feels guilty about it and believes that the baby is going to suffer. I have reassured the patient by telling her that she must accept the fact that she rejects the baby and that the baby will not suffer. Adequate provisions are being made for him. We shall eventually discover why she feels this way and her feelings will change. In the meantime, she cannot feel guilty because she can't help rejecting the baby. I have found that even very disturbed women understand these explanations, partially or totally, and are relieved by them.

Wexler (1952) advocated the adoption of a general attitude for the therapist of schizophrenic patients that is different from the one suggested by me. Wexler views the schizophrenic disorganization as the result of a primitive, archaic, and devastatingly punitive superego, in the presence of urgent instinctual demands. According to him, this archaic superego is nothing more than the internalized parental figures, "the ghosts of the past." This dynamic interpretation of schizophrenia corresponds to the points of view of several other authors, as described in Part Two of this book. Wexler, however, feels that his dynamic interpretation indicates that the therapist should assume superego roles. He feels that the therapist should be harsh and strict, should forbid sexual thoughts and feelings, and should have a generally repressing attitude. He found support in Nunberg (1948), who attributed his patient's improvement to his submission to the strong, authoritarian analyst and to his belief in the analyst's magical power. I do not deny that Wexler and Nunberg obtained success with the patients they reported, but I am not sure that the good results were due to the reasons mentioned by those authors. By submitting to an authoritarian and harsh therapist, Wexler's patient apparently was able to reestablish her self-esteem and to improve. She was confident that by submitting she would obtain approval and affection from the analyst. Wexler succeeded in conveying to the patient the feeling that she could trust him, even if he was tyrannical and strict. In my opinion that was the fundamental point. In his case, in order to convey this feeling of being trusted, Wexler had to resort to assuming a strict authoritarian role. It could be that the therapists who successfully assume this strict superego role have a type of personality that conveys this feeling of trust, especially in the adoption of that role. If a therapist is successful in adopting the superego role, he does not have to contend with the guilt feelings that a permissive attitude may engender in the patient at the beginning of treatment.

Wexler and other authors stress the point that the therapeutic situation must be very similar to the old genetic situation. It seems to me that most of the improvement is due to the differences in the two situations, not to the similarities. The apparent similarity perhaps helps the treatment in the beginning, but the patient must sense the difference in the underlying feeling in order to improve. I have found it useful to interpret this difference to the patient also at an advanced stage of treatment. The same is true for the neurotic. I agree with Rioch (1943) that the therapeutic transference must expand, not repeat, the original experience and must open new vistas, which will permit the growth of the patient. As a matter of fact, it is one of the constant aims of therapy to help the patients lose distortions arising from the tendency to repeat the old situation.

Mann, Menzer, and Standish (1950) have made an interesting study of the attitudes in the therapist that have led to the deterioration of the therapeutic relationship in the psychotherapy of functional psychoses. They found that the therapist is not directed by conscious motivation in the choice of patients. The therapist tends to choose patients with problems similar to his own. Contrary to Eissler and myself, these authors see this fact as having negative results. The therapist's conflicts may be reactivated so that he may respond with "emotional flight" or with retaliation. By "emotional flight" the authors mean an unrealistic attitude of the therapist that will not permit the patient to discuss feelings related to the therapist's conflict. This unrealistic attitude of the therapist was generally brought about by the excessive demands of the patients, demands that the therapist could not or did not want to fulfill. The demands that were made on the therapist were usually either sexual or involved permission to go home.

In my own experience, I have found that one demand of the patient that may disturb the feelings of the therapist is the request that the therapist accept the delusional system, or a delusional idea of the patient. Especially well-preserved, fanatic paranoids like to put the therapist on the spot with this type of demand. In my opinion, it is better not to yield to this pressure of the patient. Rosen (1953) reports instead that in treating certain patients the therapist must accept their psychotic reality; he must act as if he accepts the fact that they are Moses, Christ, Napoleon, or some other person. We must remember, however, that there is always a part of the patient, no matter how little it is, that does not accept the psychosis. In treatment we have to rely on that part. As has been mentioned several times, we must deserve the trust of the patient at any cost, and sooner or later he will realize whether or not the therapist means what he says or not. He will develop contempt for the therapist if he acts as if he believes what even a part of the patient himself does not believe. I do not doubt, however, that if the therapist is able to identify with the patient to such a point as to share his psychotic experiences emotionally with him, this technique may be useful. This identification, however, is very difficult to accomplish. I have used the technique of allegedly accepting the patient's psychotic reality very rarely, very reluctantly, and only for reasons of expediency, when there was no other way to avoid violence or to make preparations for hospitalization. A therapist who is inclined to feel guilty if he does not fulfill the delusional demands of the patient, or one who lets himself be intimidated easily by the aggressive tendencies of the patient, should not treat defiant paranoids.

Semrad and co-workers (1952) made another study of the doctor-patient relationship in the psychotherapy of psychotic patients. They found that the libidinal and aggressive tendencies of the patients were "so intense as to mobilize immediate anxiety through the reawakening of the doctor's repressed infantile aggressive and libidinal problems." The reawakening of these problems in the doctor led to interference with the psychotherapeutic task.

There is no doubt that one of the greatest difficulties encountered in treating psychotics is the required intensity of the relationship with the therapist. This intensity is apt to bring the therapist's problems to the surface, at times with unexpected violence. As White (1952) wrote, in discussing the above-mentioned paper of Semrad and his co-workers, the psychotic gives the physician a prolonged opportunity to learn about himself. The countertransference may mobilize the anxiety of the therapist when nothing he does seems to diminish the extreme withdrawal of the patient, when he feels exasperated by the manifestations of hostility or overwhelmed by the profusion of love. The therapist's anxiety will be harmful only if excessive. A moderate amount of anxiety may even mobilize his inner resources and intuitions.

Several of my psychotic patients have been able to detect in me certain feelings and moods, at times when even I was not aware of them. This has been observed by practically everybody who has practiced psychotherapy with psychotics.

If the patients detect an unpleasant mood in the therapist, the latter should not deny it, but admit it, together with the information that such a mood has nothing to do with them. Thompson (1952*b*) reported that disturbances in the analyst's life that are revealed to the patient may have a favorable effect on the analysis.

Feigenbaum (1930) reported that during a session with a paranoid, he received by telephone the news that a close friend had suddenly died. His reaction to the sad news brought about a human response from the patient, whose analysis from that time on took a turn for the better. Thompson (1938) reported the reaction of a schizophrenic patient at the grief over the death of her analyst and teacher, Ferenczi. Her sorrow convinced the patient more than anything else that she was not a cold person as the rest of the world had been.

If the therapist does not reveal these unhappy feelings to the patients, patients may misinterpret them. They tend to react as young children do when they see their parents worried or unhappy. An egocentric distortion makes them feel that the unpleasant feeling is related to them. They react in accordance with this interpretation, that is, with a feeling of being rejected or with detachment.

In what we have just mentioned, we have another illustration of that perplexing and mixed picture that the schizophrenic presents: on the one hand, he is very sensitive and is capable of seeing through a situation and perceiving the truth even more so than a normal person; on the other hand, what he does with what he sees is so distorted that it will increase, rather than decrease, his difficulties. In some psychiatric circles, the amazement produced by the discovery of the increased power of "seeing through" of the schizophrenic has made enthusiastic therapists forget the negative side of this quality. This enthusiasm is obviously a reaction to previous psychiatric attitudes, which were pessimistic and descriptive. The fact remains that the schizophrenic cannot be considered indeed only a person of great feeling and understanding; he is much more complicated. He adds a great deal of misunderstanding to what he keenly understands. What he understands or misunderstands in relation to the therapist's countertransference is particularly important.

Incidentally, in my experience I have found that this ability to see through a situation is present not only in full-fledged schizophrenics but also in some prepsychotic stormy personalities. Schizoid personalities, on the other hand, do not manifest this characteristic prior to their break with reality.

V

Relatedness

Now that we have examined separately the two interpersonal feelings within the therapeutic situation (transference and countertransference), we must examine them together in simultaneous occurrence, in their influencing each other, merging in what is called relatedness. The feelings that the patient has for the therapist and the feelings that the therapist has for the patient elicit the feelings about each other's feelings in a self-perpetuating reciprocity. Although relatedness includes the classic psychoanalytic concept of object relationship, it views such relationship not only as a centrifugal force emanating from each of the two partners in the therapeutic situation, but as an interrelation between at least two persons, more as an I-Thou relationship in Buber's sense (1953), as an entity whose intrapsychic and interpersonal parts could not exist without the other.

At a theoretical level the ideal of any psychotherapy would be to establish among human beings a state of communion, but this state is in most cases almost impossible to achieve even among normal persons (see Chapter 5). We must be content with a state where there is an exchange of trust, warmth, and desire to share and help.

Relatedness goes through several stages, which generally succeed one another gradually, at other times abruptly. From a state of autistic alienation the patient may pass to a state of genuine relatedness. This "breaking through" may be an extremely important episode, experienced at times with dramatic intensity. In some instances it is remembered by the patient with great emotional display reminiscent of the Freudian abreaction. However, "breaking through" in this context does not have the usual psychoanalytic meaning. It does not mean the breaking of resistances and repressive forces, so that abreaction is possible and what was repressed is now remembered. It means only breaking the barrier of autism, the incommunicability and the desocialization. A human bond between two persons, important to each other, is reestablished. Geraldine, a patient whose case is reported at great length in Chapter 40, told me that during her two psychotic episodes she met at least three persons who broke through to her. The first was a nurse, who, unfortunately, was transferred to another ward; the second was a psychiatrist who was too busy with too many patients; the third was myself.

When Geraldine was far advanced in the treatment I asked her to give me more details about the "breaking through" effectuated by the nurse. She said:

> There was a reading room on the ward, with a piano and magazines. I went there and I looked at the cover of a magazine. A nurse stepped in. I had never seen her before. She started a conversation with me as if I were a normal person. I told her with tremendous emotion, "You are the first person who has broken through to me." She was not on guard. I was not on guard. She was an ordinary girl. She made me feel communication with people was worthwhile. Before that nothing was worthwhile. People were hateful.

At this point the patient burst into tears, as never before during the whole course of treatment. A little later she continued, "With most of the nurses the illness is a fault; it was not with her. I felt that the other people were on to me. She was not."

In the treatment with me during her second breakdown, this "breaking through" was not as dramatic as it was the first time with the nurse. Again, on one occasion, Geraldine expressed herself in this way: "With you I felt as confident as with the nurse. I feel it was so because you are always so relaxed and not intellectual, just as the nurse was." These words of Geraldine aroused a state of perplexity in me. I always so relaxed? That's not what my family thinks of me. I, nonintellectual? But my friends do not hesitate to tell me that I often make too much use of intellectuality in conversing with them.

To the best of my self-evaluating knowledge, I do not assume an artificially therapeutic attitude of relaxation and nonintellectuality. But my roles are different in different situations. I stress this point to indicate that although spontaneous and sincere, the therapeutic attitude cannot be the therapist's usual attitude toward life but requires the acquisition of a special role. When I am with my wife the accumulated tension of the problems of the day may find easy manifestations. With my friends I am a peer, and because intellectuality is a part of me, it soon comes to the surface. With the schizophrenic patient who is in the early stage of treatment, I am not yet a peer. My role is nutritional and maternal. Although there is an exchange between the patient and myself, I want to give more than I take. I do not burden him with my own anxiety, if I can help it; and intellectuality does not enter the immediacy of our relatedness. Incidentally, I considered Geraldine an intellectual, too, but the needs she wanted to satisfy in her relation with me were not intellectual ones. Perhaps what I am trying to describe here is the same attitude of motherliness that Schwing (1954) advocates in the treatment of schizophrenia. This motherliness, or immediate relatedness, need not be offered exclusively by a therapist or a nurse, or by a person in a maternal role. At times the encounter even with a layman in the role of a paternal or authoritarian figure has great therapeutic effect.

When the breakthrough has occurred, the patient-therapist relationship becomes a special-object relationship. Although the therapist must avoid the mistakes the parent made, the relationship must at first bear some resemblance to the parent-child relationship. Although the therapist, like a parent, is willing to give much more than he receives, an exchange takes place in attention, affection, and care. The relationship will always be threatened by the distortion of the patients. We have seen in this chapter that projective mechanisms or paranoid tendencies of all kinds, states of panic or of sudden distrust, deification or amorous tendencies toward the therapist, longing for renewal of withdrawal, will put the relatedness to hard test. But, therapeutic relatedness will be maintained if it is based on basic trust, the psychological entity that has been defective especially in the early life of the patient and after the outbreak of the psychosis. Basic trust implies trust in each other, accepting the other and hoping in each other's future and in the stability of the relatedness. The therapist is experienced as a human being who believes in the potentialities of the patient and who, with his trust, understanding, and devotion, facilitates the unfolding of such potentialities.

We have mentioned that relatedness must at first resemble a good parental situation. This similarity may engender some jealousy and resentment toward the therapist on the part of the patient's parents. However, as we shall see in Chapter 38, the recovering patient will eventually reaccept his parents and will remove the therapist from the authoritarian aspect of the parental role. The therapist eventually descends from a pedestal if he was ever put there. The two persons involved in the therapeutic situation become more and more like peers. The two persons discover that the patient's limitations decrease with his improvement, and the therapist's limitations will increase with the patient's improvement, because he is seen more in his natural dimensions. We must specify that what we call a peer relationship between therapist and patient is not a replica of a relationship between young schoolmates. We mean the peer relationship that good parents have with their children who have become adults. They are now all adults together, and they respect one another and care for one another.

Other equally important aspects of the peer relationship with the therapist will be discussed in Chapter 39.

CHAPTER

37

Specific Solutions of Psychotic Mechanisms

I

INTRODUCTORY REMARKS

Some therapists rely only on the establishment of relatedness in the treatment of schizophrenia, especially in very acute cases. The manifest symptoms disappear at times as soon as relatedness is established. In my experience, although this is true in some cases, in the majority of cases the symptoms persist or return if the patient has not acquired insight into his psychological mechanisms and has not changed his vision of himself, the others, life, and the world. Although psychodynamic interpretations are much better known, interpretations concerning mechanisms and forms are also important, especially at an early phase of treatment. We shall devote most of this chapter to this topic.

Since Jung's formulations, schizophrenic symptoms have been compared to dreams of normal and neurotic persons and have been interpreted similarly. However, whereas dreams are interpreted while the patient is awake and has reacquired the normal cognitive functions, the schizophrenic has to be treated while he is still in "the dream" of the psychosis.

In this chapter we shall see how with some special technical procedures the patient can be helped to become aware of the ways with which he transforms his psychodynamic conflicts into psychotic symptoms.* Although form and content are interrelated, a fundamental distinction remains between interpretations of con-

* For the content of this chapter I have drawn liberally from my previous writings on this subject (Arieti, 1955, 1961*b*, 1962 *a*, 1963 *a*, 1965 *a*).

tent given in accordance with more traditional psychodynamic methods and interpretations of forms and mechanisms. Whereas the benefit from traditional interpretations is due, or is believed to be due, to acquisition of insight into repressed experiences and to the accompanying abreaction and therefore is supposed to be immediate, the effectiveness of the second type of interpretation consists of the acquisition of methods with which the patient can work at his problems. They do not consist exclusively of insights passively received, but predominantly of tools with which the patient has to operate actively.

In what follows I am going to discuss this type of treatment with regard to such symptoms as hallucinations, delusions, ideas of reference, and related manifestations. Before doing so, however, we must clarify some issues.

Insistence on attacking the schizophrenic symptom at any stage of the treatment may appear a restricted and an antiquated procedure. In fact, we have learned not only in psychiatric training but even in medical school that it is not the symptom but the cause of the disease that we should be mostly concerned with. Symptomatic treatment is secondary to causal treatment. This general principle should be followed most of the time. In the most serious psychiatric conditions, however, we find ourselves in unusual circumstances. The symptom is more than a symptom. Often it is a maneuver that tends to make consensual validation impossible and to maintain interpersonal distance. What may have originated as a defense actually makes the whole situation of the patient more precarious and may enhance regression.

Secondly, the symptom stands for a great deal more, actually for what it wants to eliminate but cannot. The symptom is a symbolic barricade around the core of anxiety; it does not permit us to touch the genuine anxiety. Let us take as an example a typical and common symptom that we have already considered in previous chapters. A patient has an olfactory hallucination; he smells a bad odor emanating from his body. In this symptom a great deal of pathology is encapsulated. The patient feels he has a rotten personality, he stinks as a person. A schizophrenic process of concretization takes place and an olfactory hallucination results. This olfactory hallucination stands for, or summarizes, the whole life history, the whole evaluation of the self, the whole tragedy of the patient. We usually say that the hallucination symbolizes what the patient feels about himself. This is correct, provided we understand that the symbol is a symbol for us, not for the patient. The patient, by virtue of the symptom, stops worrying about his personality and worries only about his stinking body. What we call a symbol actually has a realistic, not a symbolic, value for the patient. It tends to replace the reality that it wants to substitute. The symptom is not, for instance, like a flag that represents a country. The flag is not the equivalent or a duplication of the country it represents. This process of concretization, as exemplified in the hallucination of the patient just mentioned, is perhaps the most common mechanism in schizophrenia and, as we have studied in this book, is related to altered cognition. Whatever cannot be sustained at an abstract level, because it is too anxiety provoking, is reduced to, or translated into, concrete representations.

At this point an important question may arise in the mind of the reader. If the symptom is a substitution for such a great part not only of the illness but also of the life of the patient, is it not true that the patient needs this substitution? He needs to eliminate so much mental pain, and the therapist, in a cruel and antitherapeutic way, wants to deprive him of his precious defense.

The point is that if an atmosphere of basic trust is developed in which the patient feels he obtains a great deal from the therapist in human relatedness, he is willing to relinquish his symptoms or to experiment with ways that convert them into less psychotic or neurotic ones. The new symptoms, like the recognition of being concerned with one's own personality and not body, may be more difficult to bear but can be more easily shared with the therapist. In other words, the therapist will be able to help the patient to bear "his cross," if this cross is a less autistic or less psychotic one.

Some people may ask, why not remove symptoms with less difficult methods; for instance, with drug therapy? Symptoms can and should be eliminated with drug therapy if psychotherapy fails. However, the patient who is able to conquer his symptoms by psychological means reacquires an active position in his life. He no longer feels victim of persecutors or of phenomena that he does not understand. He becomes more aware of the role he plays in his illness; how at times he can actually choose between the realm of psychosis and the realm of reality; how even in such apparently immutable processes, which he takes for unchangeable reality and which we call hallucinations and delusions, he can recognize that it is up to him to resist the seduction of the abnormal mechanisms. He will be able to accept the increased anxiety and increased suffering coming from nonpsychotic mechanisms and from the knowledge of the meaning of the nonpsychotic processes if he feels that the therapist is there to share that anxiety and that suffering.

In other words, whereas the intangible gift of relatedness is offered freely to the patient and at least in the beginning is received by him passively, the formal interpretations given to him become tools that he actively uses to fight his own illness. He soon recognizes what he himself does to the world of reality in order to transform it into the world of psychosis. Examination of this transformation by the therapist and the patient is a common exploration, where patient and therapist retain different mutually active roles.

II

Hallucinations

Until recently the opinion prevailed that incorrigibility was one of the fundamental characteristics of hallucinations. That is, until the symptom altogether disappeared, either through treatment or spontaneously, it would be impossible for the schizophrenic patient to become aware of the unreality of the phenomenon and to correct it. I have found that this is not necessarily so (Arieti, 1961*b*, 1962*a*). Only auditory hallucinations will be taken into consideration, but the same procedure could be applied to other types of hallucinations, after the proper modifications have been made.

Hospitalized patients approached with old, routine questions such as "Do you hear voices? Who is talking to you?" are unable to give up their hallucinations. As long as an atmosphere of unrelatedness exists, the patient cannot make an effort to see and hear things as other people do, and it is unwise to attack the problem directly. However, it is also unwise to give the patient the impression that the therapist hears his voices and shares his unusual private experiences. The therapist should simply tell the patient that he does not hear the voices and will maintain an attitude of cordiality and relatedness.

With the exception of patients who are at a very advanced state of the illness or with whom no relatedness can be reached, it is possible to recognize that the hallucinatory voices occur only in particular situations, that is, *when the patient expects to hear them.*

For instance, a patient goes home after a day of work and expects the neighbors to talk about him. As soon as he expects to hear them, he hears them. In other words, he puts himself in what I have called *the listening attitude.*

If we have been able to establish not only contact but relatedness with the patient, he will be able under our direction to distinguish two stages: that of the listening attitude and that of the hallucinatory experience. At first he may protest vigorously and deny the existence of the two stages, but later he may make a little concession. He will say, "I happened to think that they would talk, and I proved to be right. They were really talking."

A few sessions later, however, another step forward will be made. The patient will be able to recognize and to admit that there was a brief interval between the expectation of the voices and the voices. He will still insist that this sequence is purely coincidental, but eventually he will see a connection between his putting himself into the listening attitude and his actually hearing. Then he will recognize that he puts himself into this attitude when he is in a particular situation or in a particular mood, for instance, in a mood on account of which he perceives hostility, almost in the air. He has the feeling that everybody has a disparaging attitude toward him, and then he finds corroboration for this attitude of the others; he hears them making unpleasant remarks about him. At times he feels inadequate and worthless, but he does not sustain this feeling for more than a fraction of a second. The self-condemnation almost automatically induces him to put himself into the listening attitude, and then he hears other people condemning him.

When the patient is able to recognize the relation between the mood and putting himself in the listening attitude, a great step has been accomplished. He will not see himself any longer as a passive agent but as somebody who still has a great deal to do with what he experiences. Moreover if he catches himself in the listening attitude, he has not yet descended to or is not yet using abnormal or paleologic ways of thinking from which it will be difficult to escape. He is still in the process of falling into the seductive trap of the world of psychosis but may still resist the seduction.

That he is not just a passive agent, he may find out from an opposite procedure. The patient who is prone to hallucinate is told to go into another room alone and to expect to hallucinate. Soon he will realize that the voices come, just because he expected them.

I have found that if an atmosphere of relatedness and understanding has been established, patients learn with not too much difficulty to catch themselves in the act of putting themselves into the listening attitude at the least disturbances, several times during the day. At times, although they recognize the phenomenon, they feel that it is almost an automatic mechanism, which they cannot prevent. Eventually, however, they will be able to control it more and more. Even then, however, there will be a tendency to resort again to the listening attitude and to the hallucinatory experiences in situations of stress. The therapist should never tire of explaining the mechanism to the patient again and again, even when such explanation seems redundant. It is seldom redundant, because the symptoms may reacquire an almost irresistible attraction.

But now that we have deprived the patient of his hallucinations, again you can ask, how will he be able to manage with his anxiety? How can we help him to bear his burden or a heavier but less unrealistic cross? An example will perhaps clarify this matter. A woman used to hear a hallucinatory voice calling her a prostitute. Now, with the method I have described, we have deprived her of this hallucination. Nevertheless she experiences a feeling, almost an abstract feeling coming from the external environment, of being discriminated against, of being considered inferior, of being looked upon as a bad woman, and so forth. She has almost the wish to crystallize or concretize again this feeling into a hallucination. If we leave her alone, she will hallucinate again. If we tell her that she projects into the environment her own feelings about herself, she may become infuriated. She says, "The voices I used to hear were telling me I am a bad woman, a prostitute, but I never had such a feeling about myself. I am a good woman." The patient of course is right, because when she hears a disparaging voice, or when she is experiencing the vague feeling of being disparaged, no longer has she a disparaging opinion of herself. The projective mechanism saves her from self-disparagement. We must instead point out to the patient that there was one time when she had a bad opinion of herself. Even then she did not think she was a prostitute but had a low self-esteem, such as she probably thought a prostitute would have about herself.

In other words, we must try to reenlarge the patient's psychotemporal field. As long as he attributes everything to the present, he cannot escape from the symptoms. Whereas the world of psychosis has only one temporal dimension—the present—the world of reality has three: past, present, and future. Although at this point in the illness the patient already tends to live exclusively in the present, he retains a conception of the past, and such conception must be exploited. We direct the patient to face longitudinally his deep feeling of inadequacy. At the same time the therapist with his general attitude and firm reassurance and sincere interest will be able to share the burden. At this point the therapeutic assistant may be very useful, as we shall discuss later.

The realization of the low self-esteem is not yet a complete psychodynamic explanation of the symptom, but at this stage of the treatment we stop at this explanation. The matter will be pursued later, when we shall examine factors in the early family environment that led to this negative self-appraisal. We have seen, however, that any formal mechanism that is pursued to its origin discloses not purely the nature of its form but its psychodynamic counterpart. This multifaceted nature of the symptom is seen even more clearly in other psychotic phenomena that can be called at the same time hallucinatory, illusional, delusional, or referential. For instance, a patient has the idea that people laugh at him. He actually hears them laughing, and he turns his head; he looks at them and sees them smiling and ridiculing him. They may not smile at all, and he may misinterpret their facial expression. If they do smile, they may do so for reasons that have nothing to do with him. Again we must help the patient to recognize that he sees or hears people laughing at him when he expects to see or hear them. However, when the treatment is more advanced, the patient recognizes that he feels people *should* laugh at him because he is a laughable individual. He hears them laughing because he believes that they should laugh at him. What he thinks of himself becomes the cause of his symptoms. It is painful for the patient to acknowledge that that is what he thinks of himself. In this case also, the psychotic mechanism will dissolve itself when it is understood both formally and psychodynamically and when the patient, with the help of the therapist, is able to bear the unpleasant psychodynamic meaning.

Another patient cannot look into the eyes of some people because those eyes send telepathic messages with unpleasant content. The patient sees and hears the messages. He must realize that he expects to be made uncomfortable by those people, by those eyes that scrutinize and criticize, and must learn eventually from the events of his past history why he has attributed to these people the power to make him uncomfortable. Moreover, "being uncomfortable" is transformed or perceived by him as being persecuted or being the victim of telepathy. In most instances, after the symptoms have been understood formally and the patient is able to control or check them, they will be understood psychodynamically as related to the patient's self-image and to the projective mechanisms by which the patient tried to hide his self-image.

III

Ideas of Reference, Delusions, and Projective Mechanisms

What we have said about hallucinations could with the proper modifications be repeated for ideas of reference and delusions. Before the delusions or ideas of reference are well formulated, the patient must learn to recognize that he is in what I call the referential attitude. For instance, he is taking a stroll in the park on a beautiful Sunday afternoon when all of a sudden peculiar events begin to take place. People sitting on the benches start to talk with animation and to look at him with strange eyes. They make some gestures that have obvious reference to him. Children who were running all over or playing in the nearby playground now all run toward the opposite direction to avoid being near him. An American flag that could be seen from the distance, open to the wind and waving on the top of a pole, is now drooping. All this is an indication that people think that a horrible man, perhaps a pervert who attacks children and women, is in the park. The patient is supposed to be that man. The news is spreading. He rushes back home in a state of intense, agonizing turmoil.

And yet, we must ask him when he comes for the session, what happened before he went into the park? In what mood was he? Was he not looking for a certain evidence? Did he not almost hope to find it, so that he would be able to explain that indefinite mood of being thought of as a horrible creature? He had the impelling need to transform a vague, huge menace into a concrete threat, to restrict to a specific event a spreading feeling of being humiliated, disparaged, discriminated against (Chapter 16).

The direct attack on the symptom consists again in making the patient aware of his concretizing the vague threat. He must recognize how he substitutes ideas and feelings for others that are easier to grasp or to contend with in his distress. He will learn to check himself, as he may learn to check his listening attitude.

But again we made him retranslate the concrete into the abstract and reinproject what he had projected. Will he be able to do so? He will, if we share his burden with the ultimate aim of removing it altogether. The patient must become aware that he is searching for references that will corroborate the preexisting mood. Let us take another example, that of a patient who tells us that while he was in the subway he observed peculiar faces, some unusual motions that some people made, an unusual crowd at a certain station, and how all this is part of a plot to kidnap him and to kill him. It is useless to reply to him that these are imaginary or false interpretations of certain occurrences. At this point he is forced to believe that these events refer to him. We must instead help the patient to recapture the mood and attitude that he had prior to those experiences, that is, we must help him to become aware of his *referential attitude*. He will be able to remember that before he went into the subway, he looked for the evidence, he almost hoped to find it because if he found that evidence, he would be able to explain the indefinite mood of being threatened that he was experiencing. He had the impelling need to transform a vague, huge menace into a concrete threat. The vague menace is the anxiety of the interpersonal world, which in one way or another constantly reaffirms the failure of his life.

The patient is then made aware of his tendency to concretize the vague threat. The feelings of hostility and inadequacy that he experienced before the onset of the psychosis have become concretized, not to the point of becoming hallucinations, but to the point of delusions or of ideas of reference. No longer does the patient feel surrounded by an abstract worldwide hostility. It is no longer the whole world that considers him a failure; now "they" are against him, "they" call him a failure, a homosexual, a spy. This concretization is gradual. The "they" obviously refers to some human beings who are not better defined (see Chapter 8).

We make the patient aware not only of his referential and delusional attitude, but also of his *concretizing attitude* (see Chapters 15 and 16). The symbolism is often clearly understood if the patient, supported by our sharing of his anxiety and pain, is able to accept the impact of the revelation. For instance, a patient may be helped to recognize that it is easier for him to think that his wife poisons his food than to think that she "poisons" his life. He may also recognize that the feeling he has that some people control his thoughts is a reactivation and concretization of the way he once felt that his parents were controlling or trying to direct his life and his way of thinking. If relatedness is achieved, the patient becomes gradually aware of the almost incessant process of transforming the abstract part of his life into concrete representations.

Some of this active concretizing may be difficult for some patients to understand, especially in some manifestations. However, a large number of patients will eventually understand it with great benefit. One of the most apparently obscure and yet most important manifestations of this process of concretization is a phenomenon that has baffled not only patients but psychiatrists as well. A patient happens to think, let us say, that dead relatives are coming to visit him in the hospital. As soon as such a thought occurs, the thought becomes a reality! He believes that the relatives are already there in the hospital. Thoughts are immediately translated into the real facts that they represent, just as in hallucinations and in dreams they are transformed into perceptions. A thought that represents a *possibility* cannot be sustained. Schizophrenics are still capable of conceiving and even sustaining thoughts of possibilities, when they do not involve their complexes. However, possibilities concerning anxiety-provoking situations are conceived by the schizophrenic but not sustained for a long time: they are translated into actuality.

The patient is made aware of this tendency, and although at the beginning of the treatment he may not be able to arrest the process, he becomes familiar with what he himself is doing to bring about the delusional world.

In some other instances, it is through the content of the symptom that we can help the patient to recognize the concretizing attitude. A patient in her middle twenties had the delusion that she was receiving messages from a power higher than herself that were directing her life. The pulsations, of which she was aware when she was pressing her wrists, were like a Morse code that would tell her what to do or not to do. These messages were pearls of wisdom that told her which situations would endanger her life or put her in awkward positions. Because of the feeling of relatedness that already existed, it was relatively easy to explain to the patient that these commands were actually advice she gave herself. However, she would not accept them as long as they came from her. She had to believe that some important and benevolent external authority or power was sanctioning her decisions. Related to this belief was her complaint that her parents had never been able to guide her or to let her grow as an independent person.

Some patients present some symptoms that are halfway between delusions and phobias. The fears that they express are generally concrete representations of what they experience in a more abstract way. A patient says that he is afraid of certain people, and he does not know why. There is nothing in these people that should make him afraid. We must help the patient realize that these people, whom he believes he is afraid of, make him feel uncomfortable. They indeed have the power to make him uncomfortable, but he transforms or concretizes the psychological discomfort into fear. If the patient acknowledges the discomfort caused by the presence of these people, he moves much closer to reality. Of course, the inquiry should not stop here. Eventually we must determine why such people have the power to make him uncomfortable. What are the connections with the patient's past history or what are his symbolic associations?

Other patients are afraid of big crowds. The big crowd represents "the pulsating life," and the patients are afraid of life or of being defeated in life. Other patients may be afraid to go into buses or streetcars because they feel exposed. "People will find out what I am like." All these fears are obviously connected to the negative self-image. In psychotherapy the projective mechanism has to be dismantled, but the more we succeed in doing so, the more the patient has to become painfully aware of his adverse vision of himself.

The concretizing attitude is expressed not only by ideas and delusions but also by bizarre behavior. We shall use here again some examples already considered in Chapter 17. Some patients always stand close to a wall, away from the center of the room. The habit is so common and so well known that we are not liable to make mistakes if we say to the patient, "You want the wall to protect you from the threatening feelings you sense all around. I am here with you. Nothing will attack us. Nothing will injure us. We need no walls. Let's walk together."

To some patients who injure themselves to substitute a physical pain for an emotional one, we may say, "You want to hurt yourself to remove your anguish. If we talk about it, we share the pain; the pain will decrease." This explanation has to be given with some cautiousness because self-injury is not always an attempted concretization of mental pain or a way to make the pain "more real." At other times it is exclusively or predominantly an expression of need for punishment or a way to achieve change in gender or to inflict bodily disfigurations that have a symbolic meaning.

A frequent symptom is screaming; at times a loud, terrifying scream occurs abruptly. Screaming is a way of expressing sorrow, powerlessness, and protest in a more primitive way than even the crying of the sufferer. Crying, as a baby would do, has an appealing quality, which the scream does not possess. The patient feels he cannot appeal to anybody. His lifelong whimpering was never heard, and he must scream now. But the therapist must perceive the scream as a dramatic revolt against the lifetime suffering in quiet and desolate solitude. He must let the patient know that he has received the message and is ready to answer it.

Different, although related, is the apparently inappropriate hebephrenic smile or, less frequently, the almost spasmodic laughter. The patient laughs at it all, or laughs the world off. The trouble is too big, too lurid; not only must you keep distance and have nothing to do with it, you must actually laugh at it. The therapist must receive the hebephrenic's message of defiance and rejection of the world and help him to find at least a little part of this big world at which he does not need to laugh.

Fromm-Reichmann reported a female schizophrenic patient who always walked with a thumb extended and the other fingers flexed over the palm of her hand. Fromm-Reichmann did not interpret the extended thumb as a phallic symbol or as indication of penis envy. For her it meant "I am one: alone, alone, alone!" (reported in Arieti, 1968*c*).

This concrete way by which attitudes and feelings are experienced and expressed in behavioral forms has been compared by some to surrealistic art (Barison, 1948; Roi, 1953). But surrealism can be shared and appreciated and used as a partial return to realism or as an extension of reality.

IV

Awareness of the Punctiform Insight

In some delusions and ideas of reference there is an element of reality that is valid at a realistic level as well as at a symbolic level. The coincidence between psychosis and reality is exploited to make contact with the patient and to develop consensual validation in some areas. Freud (1937) also postulated that in delusions and hallucinations there is a fragment of historical truth and hoped that one day the liberation of this fragment would lead to useful therapy. In some cases of relatively mild forms of psychosis I have been able to follow Freud's suggestion, with some modifications. The fragment of truth did not refer to the past life but to the present. Moreover, the concrete event, of which the fragment of truth consisted, could be accepted both at a realistic face value and as a symbol.

When what seemed delusional is recognized as real insight, not only is the patient praised for the insight but helped to see that the insight has a larger scope because it includes not only the realistic episode but its symbolic meaning. An example will illustrate what I mean. Violet, a 35-year-old single patient, was suffering from a relatively mild form of schizophrenia that permitted her to maintain a not too inadequate social life and to keep her job in spite of her many symptoms. She had occasional hallucinations, some delusions, and numerous ideas of reference.

On her birthday she received a bouquet of roses from the company for which she worked. When she opened the package and saw beatuful yellow roses, instead of experiencing a happy feeling, she started to concentrate on the color yellow. The color is supposed to mean jealousy, and she felt that by giving her yellow roses the people in the office wanted to let her know that they knew she was jealous of the wife of the boss. The following day she heard one of the workers humming the song "The Yellow Rose of Texas," and she felt this was done purposefully to expose her.

Eventually everything that was yellow in color acquired the same meaning for her and had to be avoided. Finally she even got rid of two of her dresses, because they were yellow.

In her office there was a water cooler that was out of order and that had to be hit in order to let the water flow. When people, and especially the boss of her department, were hitting the cooler, she thought they meant to hit her. When I asked her why she thought so, she said, "I never walk. I run, like water, and I deserve to be hit!" I explained to her that when she was in a state of anxiety, she resorted to a special type of thinking to demonstrate her unworthiness, and that she attributed to others the feelings she had about herself. This explanation helped, and for some time there was considerable improvement, but then similar symptoms came back. For instance, when people in the office and especially the boss in the department were using the word *machine,* she was sure they were referring to her. She said, "I work like a machine. I am sure they refer to me."

One day Violet came to my office in an angry mood and told me that she was angry because the previous day her friend Lucy had come to visit her and had brought along her dog, a little cocker spaniel. She added, "You see! She thinks my home is a doghouse. She thinks I am a dog."

Occasionally I use some examples taken from one patient in my explanations to other patients with whom I have established relatedness, in order to make them aware of the mechanisms they are liable to use when they are in distress. It happened that I reported this episode of the dog to another very articulate and sensitive schizophrenic patient, who told me, "Your patient is probably right. Her friend probably treats her as a dog. Do you know that dog-owners own dogs because they want to treat people like dogs? A human being does not obey them easily, but a dog does. I keep away from people who own dogs."

Of course I did not accept my patient's point of view that dog-owners necessarily have those characteristics, but I remembered that a small percentage of dog-owners whom I have treated, do own dogs for the reasons mentioned by my patient. It occurred to me also that Lucy, Violet's friend, fitted that description very well. She was a domineering, aggressive person who was treating people like dogs, especially masochistic and compliant persons like my patient, who were willing to accept her behavior unconditionally. I realized then that Violet had had good insight in thinking that Lucy was treating her like a dog, but this insight was sustained not by logical thinking or convincing evidence, but by the evidence brought forth by a small, otherwise insignificant episode. I reexamined all the bizarre symptoms Violet had experienced and discussed them with her. The chief of the department who was hitting the water cooler in a forceful manner was then recognized as a hostile and demanding person who gave Violet a tremendous amount of work and showed hostility at the least provocation, taking advantage of her submissive and masochistic characteristics. It is probable that by hitting the cooler after talking to her, he was letting off hostility. Perhaps he was doing something emotionally equivalent to a desire to hit Violet when she dared not comply in an absolute manner. Most probably my patient had intuitively recognized in this apparently harmless act of the boss a gesture of displaced hostility. My patient thus had insight, but the insight was sustained by paleologic thinking and concretization. She was more intuitive than the average person in recognizing this gesture of the boss as an act of hostility directed toward her, but for her the act had become equivalent to an overt act of hostility. For the normal person, the act is not equivalent to an act of hostility but is only symbolic: at the level of reality hitting the cooler is different from hitting Violet. Continuing in her paleologic thinking, the patient then extended to all members of the firm the intention intuitively perceived in the boss.

The patient also had the conviction that when her co-workers used the word *machine,* they were referring to her. In fact, they actually were treating her as a machine, not as a person, by taking advantage of her efficiency and willingness to do a large amount of work without protest, like a machine. There is no doubt that people working in the firm had realized that her excessive work and compliance were due to some kind of abnormality in her personality, but nevertheless they took advantage of her condition. The bouquet of roses, or similar gestures, were thus acts of compensation for exploiting her, but at the same time an acknowledgement that there was something unusual with her, symbolized by her being jealous of the boss's wife.

A reconsideration of Violet's symptoms disclosed that in her ideas of reference there was always some truth—I would say at least a grain of truth. This grain of insight, however, remained a grain, a punctiform insight, and did not expand into a complete insight, for the following reasons:

1. It could not transcend the level of immediate reality that made the insight possible. Although the insight was obviously derived from a more general or abstract evaluation of the total situation, this total evaluation had become unconscious, and the patient was aware only of the significance of the concrete event, which was accepted as expression of reality, not as a symbol. Thus Violet felt hit only as the cooler was, literally treated as a dog, and so forth.

2. The patient tried to attune or accord with the symptom the rest of her life, but attempts of this kind remain incongruous with reality. In other words, instead of enlarging the insight to an abstract level, the patient generalizes it at a concrete level, actually distorting the rest of reality to fit the concreteness of the manifestation.

This partial insight can be used psychotherapeutically. The patient must be told that he has insight, that he saw some truth. When we reexamined the symptoms, I told Violet that she had unusual understanding in perceiving that the boss wanted to hit her and in realizing that Lucy was treating her like a dog, and I praised her for such understanding.

This is, of course, interpretation, but from a new slant. The interpretations we generally give the patient concern their inner reality; here it is suggested instead that we tell him how the inner reality coincides with his appreciation of the external world, and how accurate this appreciation is at times. The insight is not given as something that the patient will passively accept, but as something he has actively created. As in the case of the recognition of the listening attitude, the patient changes from a passive to an active role. In other words, we use the little gaps of reality in the realm of the psychosis, or, to put it in a way that I prefer, we use the points of agreement between psychosis and reality.

The benefit the patient receives from this method is not just the result of some kind of intellectual agreement between two debating persons, which will help therapist and patient to move toward large areas of consensus and shared experience. Violet felt much better and no longer alone with her strange symptoms. She felt I shared her feelings and ideas. I did not pretend to do so. Since then Violet started to improve; she became more socially adequate and was able to sustain relations with men. At the age of 39 she got married, and at the age of 40 she had a child.*

The method of acquiring awareness of the punctiform insight may present risks if not applied appropriately. For instance, if the patient accepts the insight only at the level of concretization, he may act out in accordance with his psychosis. The therapist must intensively help him move away from the point where psychosis and reality converge. This is possible in an atmosphere of relatedness and under the momentum generated by the conviction that some points of view are shared with the therapist.

For instance, Violet was told that it was true she was treated as a machine and what a sensitivity she had in realizing that they treated her as if she were a machine. But what could she do to change the situation? How could she change her attitude, so that she would no longer be treated as a machine?

The method of acquiring punctiform insight has unfortunately serious limitations, inasmuch as it can be applied only to a certain number of patients who present a mild form of psychosis. In this group of patients, the symptomatology is actually promoted by the reality situation, and its connections with reality are relatively easily found. In most other patients, ideas of reference, tendency toward meanings, discovering puns, and so on, have no connection with the reality shared with other people, but only with the associations of the patient's inner reality.

V

Awareness of Abnormal Cognition

Throughout this book we have seen how important is the study of abnormal cognition for the understanding of the nature of schizophrenia in general as well as of the specific symptomatology. It also permits an evaluation of the state either of regression or reintegration of the patient. It permits the therapist to understand the way the patient thinks and talks, even when at first it seems impossible to do so.

In therapy, however, a knowledge of the abnormal cognition of the schizophrenic may also be more directly useful, because it enables us to explain to the patient his faulty patterns of thinking. Actually all interpretations that we have discussed in this chapter are based on the study of abnormal cognition. At a later stage of treatment the patient may become aware of the fact that some of his interpretations are based on a special form of thinking (paleologic thinking).

* At the time of this writing the child is 7 years old. The whole family is well and happy.

The therapist must be able to recognize this form of thinking and logic and explain it to the patient. It is beyond the purpose of this chapter to repeat the characteristics of schizophrenic cognition.

If the patient is very regressed, he will not benefit from any direct explanation from the therapist. The therapist will benefit indirectly, however, because his knowledge of the formal characteristics and ways of thinking will enable him to understand the degree of regression and the hidden meaning.

There are, however, some ways of thinking used by the schizophrenic that are not too dissimilar from those used by normal persons, and these can be better explained to the patient. One of them is rationalization, which we discussed in Chapter 16. In the examples given there we saw that there is an important difference between the rationalization of normal people and the absurd rationalizations of the schizophrenic. The reader is referred to that chapter again so that he can apply to therapy the understanding of schizophrenic rationalization. In rationalizations of schizophrenics there is no congruence or concordance between the external facts, used as excuses, and the psychodynamic meanings and needs. The rationalizations become plausible only if we understand what is suppressed, substituted, or concretized, if we know the complicated experiences the patient went through. It is only when the patient is told what he is doing and when we share with him the anxiety of the knowledge of what was once repressed that he will be less likely to resort to implausible rationalizations.

CHAPTER

38

Psychodynamic Analysis

I

INTRODUCTION

Psychodynamic analysis starts to some extent at the very beginning of treatment. However, as we have seen in the two previous chapters, the early stages of therapy are predominantly concerned with the establishment of relatedness, with the phenomena of transference and countertransference as lived experiences, and with special attempts to solve the structure of some psychotic mechanisms.

Psychodynamic analysis of the schizophrenic consists of interpreting to the patient his past and present life. He is helped to become aware of his unconscious motivation and to acquire insight into the origin and development of the psychological components of his disorder. This part of psychotherapy becomes the major one when relatedness is more or less established and at least some of the prevailing psychotic mechanisms have abated or have disappeared.

There are some technical difficulties in giving a detailed illustration of this part of the treatment. In the first place we would have to repeat what was studied in the whole of Part Two of this book. In the second place, some of the psychodynamic interpretations apply also to patients belonging to other psychiatric categories and are already known to the reader. In the third place we have the problem common to every psychodynamic study: every case is psychodynamically different and is the result of a particular set of circumstances. Thus the study of previous cases has definite but only relative, not absolute, pragmatic value. In this chapter we shall discuss basic situations that are likely to occur in many cases. Again I have to draw from some of my previous writings (Arieti, 1955, 1957, 1968*a*, 1968*c*, 1971*a*).

Contrary to what is believed by many, schizophrenics do not have insight into the psychodynamic meaning of most of their symptoms. Interpretations are thus necessary when these patients are ready to accept them. As we have already mentioned, the therapist gives interpretations while the patient is still, metaphorically speaking, in the dream of the psychosis. The interpretation will be useless (1) unless it will be integrated in a context of relatedness (the patient is not alone in the psychotic dream); (2) unless the emotional content and meaning are shared by the therapist; and (3) unless it will be given in a simple and clear language that appeals to the primitive as well as to the elevated levels of the psyche.

II

Analysis of Relations with Members of the Family

The importance of the original relations with parents, parent-substitutes, and other members of the family will unfold gradually during the psychodynamic analysis. If the therapist calls his attention to it, the patient may realize even from the very beginning of the treatment that what the voices say has a strong similarity to the ideas he once attributed to the important people of his past. In the beginning of treatment the parental role is generally shifted in a distorted way to the persecutors. In a minority of cases it is displaced not to persecutors but to supernatural, royal, or divine benefactors, who, in these grandiose delusions, represent figures antithetical to the parents. In a certain type of patient, one who used to be more common in the past and may become more common again, at the beginning of the treatment the parents themselves are seen as saviors, angels, benefactors. The patient, who is frightened of the world and feels still so dependent on the parents, has the need to see them (more frequently the mother) in that extremely positive way. Any negative quality that the parent may possess is displaced to the persecutors.

The majority of psychotic patients never see their parents in this light. After the initial stage of treatment, during which the patient focuses on the persecutors or other aspects of his symptomatology and sees the parents in a neutral way, he discovers the importance of childhood and of his relations with mother and father. He then develops another attitude toward them. The original parental image comes to the surface, and he attributes to the parents full responsibility for his illness and despair. As we have seen in Chapter 5, even many analysts and psychiatrists have accepted as real insights, and as accurate accounts of historical events, these explanations given by patients. It was easy to believe in the accuracy of the patients' accounts, first of all because some parents do fit this negative image; secondly because the patients who had shifted their target from the persecutors to the parents had made considerable improvement, were no longer delusional or delusional to a lesser degree, and seemed to a large extent reliable.

The therapist must be careful. In a minority of cases the parents have really been as the patient has depicted them. In by far the majority of cases, however, the patient who comes to recognize that the parents have played a role in his psychological difficulties exaggerates and deforms that role. He is not able to see his own deformations until the therapist points them out to him. In many cases it is very difficult for the therapist, too, to distinguish what was neurotic, psychotic, or malevolent in the parents from what the patient has superimposed. The two parts often blend and coalesce. Fortunately some circumstances may help. In his newly developed antiparental zeal the patient goes on a campaign to distort even what the parent does and says now. Incidentally, this tendency is present not only in schizophrenics but also in some preschizophrenics who never become full-fledged psychotics. By being fixated to an antiparental frame of reference they may not need to become delusional and psychotic. To a much less unrealistic extent this tendency occurs in some neurotics too. At times the antiparental campaign is enlarged to include parents-in-law and other people who have a quasi-parental role.

The therapist has to help in many ways. First, he points out how the patient distorts or exaggerates. For instance, a white lie is transformed into the worst mendacity, tactlessness into falsity or perversion. These deformations are caused by the need to reproduce a pattern established in childhood, a pattern that was the result not only of what happened historically but also of the patient's immaturity, ignorance, and misperception. At times these deformations are easy to correct. For instance, once the mother of a patient told her, "Your mother-in-law is sick." The patient interpreted her mother's words as if they meant, "With your perverse qualities you have made your mother-in-law sick as you made me sick once." Another time the mother asked what the patient was making for dinner. The patient interpreted mother's remarks as criticisms. Mother intimated that she was not a good cook or did not know how to plan a meal. On still another occasion the mother spoke about the beautiful apartment that the patient's newly married younger sister had just furnished. The patient, who, incidentally, was jealous of the mother's attention for her sister, interpreted this remark as meaning, "Your sister has much better taste than you."

In the second place, the patient must be helped to realize that the negative traits of parents or other important people are not necessarily arrows or weapons used purposely to hurt the patient. They are merely characteristics of these people and should not be considered total qualities. For instance, in the remarks of the mother of the patient, which we have just reported, there might have been some elements of hostility. As a matter of fact, one may think that the patient was not only distorting but was very close to the truth, because she became particularly sensitive to her mother's hostility—hostility that the world at large wanted to deny. If the therapist also denies this hostility, he may appear to retrogress to a nonpsychodynamic approach. The situation is often reminiscent of a Pirandellian drama, in which we do not know who is right and who is wrong. The distinction is more difficult when we do not deal with definite delusions but with distortions. A distortion is based on reality, but the proportions or the various ingredients of the reality situation are altered. We must tell a patient like the one we have just referred to that we recognize that she may be correct in some particular aspects of her mother's communication. Yes, there might have been more than an element of hostility in mother's remarks, elements of which the mother might not have been aware. The patient might have acquired what in Chapter 37 has been described as punctiform insight. This insight, although important, concerns only one aspect of mother's attitude.

In every human relation and communication, in every social event, however, there are many dimensions and meanings, not only in the so-called double-bind talk of the so-called schizophrenogenic mother. But the patient focuses on this negative trend or aspect and neglects all the other dimensions of the rich and multifaceted communication. The patient is unable to tolerate any ambivalence, any plurality of dimensions. Treatment must help him to accept this plurality as inherent in human life.

Third and most important, the therapist must help the patient to decrease the impact of the parental introject. The patient is an adult now; it is up to the patient to provide for himself or to search for himself what he once expected to get from his parents. The patient shows considerable improvement when the original parental introject has been transformed, when he has understood how he came to build such negative parental images (see Chapter 5). His changed attitude toward his parents will be revealed especially by his dreams, as we shall see in the last section of this chapter. As long as the patient has not been able to solve in one way or another his conflicts with his parents, he remains vulnerable to the psychosis.

Many patients come to realize that some of the worst things their parents have said or done should not be interpreted as signs of total or constant rejection but as expression of a temporary state of exasperation, partially caused by the patient himself. Some patients shift their animosity from the parents to all adults or to society at large. At times it is difficult to recognize below a grudge that may even seem justified a need to converge hate toward other people in authority, parental role, or who somehow were conceived as hampering the spontaneous wishes of the patient.

At an advanced stage of treatment the patient will recognize not only how much he distorts now and in the past, but also how much his distortions facilitated the subsequent development of his illness. His misconceptions became additional causes of abnormalities and deviations.

III

Special Delusional Mechanisms

The mechanism of projection, to which we have referred several times in this book, is very commonly used by the patient and can be explained to him both from a formal and from a psychodynamic point of view. We may explain to the patient that he attributes to the external world certain ideas about himself that he himself entertains but is unwilling to admit. If he hears voices of persecutors calling him a spy, a homosexual, a thief, it is because *he* has or had a very disparaging opinion of himself. These accusations that he attributes to others are exaggerations or distortions of the original self-accusation. We have seen in Chapter 37, however, that this explanation of the projection mechanism is not effective unless the patient comes to see that he himself passes a negative judgment on himself and unless we help him to change this self-evaluation.

The explanation of the projection mechanism often requires reevocation of what occurred in childhood and adolescence. For instance, it is useful to explain to some paranoids, in a language that they can understand, that their feeling of persecution is also a reexternalization of the hostile feelings that they experienced in early childhood and that the later experiences of life have exacerbated. In some instances I found it useful to explain to the patients that their feeling that their thoughts were being controlled by an external force was a reactivation and a concrete representation of the feeling that they had in early childhood that their thoughts were being crushed or controlled by those of the dominant adults.

The specific content of some delusions can be easily traced to early life experiences. During a psychotic episode a patient in his early thirties believed that he had the power to control the world, make the human race perish, and replace it with a population of dogs.

This patient lost his mother at the age of three. He was brought up by two much older sisters, who resented having to take care of him, and by a father who was a ''perfectionist.'' Because of his own frustrations the father was unhappy and hard to please. In order to stimulate the patient toward constant improvement the father provoked great anxiety in his son, who came to believe he would never succeed in anything he tried. When the father remarried, the stepmother was perceived by the patient as a caring person at first, but hostile later and a source of sexual stimulation from which he could not escape. The poor communication, the inability to ventilate properly the problems and the resulting anxiety, predisposed the patient to think that the father would always find fault in him and would never love him. And yet love from the father was what the patient wanted most. Nothing could be more precious or more difficult to attain. Was there in the world a creature toward whom the father was lenient, not demanding, and on whom he bestowed love? Yes, the dog of the family, or rather the series of dogs that succeeded one another. When the patient became delusional, he changed from a state of hopelessness and worthlessness into a position from which he felt he had the power to control or transform the world. The new world would be populated not by people who withdraw love but by those who could obtain love: the dogs. When the acute phase of the episode was over and the patient was able to give a detailed personal history, he was easily helped to trace back the origin of his delusions. It was also explained to him that the original relations with the father, although unhappy and unhealthy, were already unrealistically transformed in childhood and made worse by poor communication, inability to see the totality of the picture, difficulty in finding compensations, and especially by the tendency to experience the rapport with the father in a restricted and unfavorable way. As we have already mentioned, the relation with the stepmother proved to be a difficult one and in its turn made the relation with the father even more complicated because of a new and rather late Oedipal situation.

In some cases it is difficult to explain the projection mechanism because it is connected with some realistic problems of the patient. In these instances we do not have the punctiform insight, described in Chapter 37, but a further deformation of reality because of the realistic connection. An example will serve as an illustration. Justin, a patient in his early twenties, experienced the following phenomenon: he was hearing a man (whom at times he would consider an impostor, at other times "another self") say profane things. Justin felt that this other person was using his—Justin's—mouth and his voice so that people would actually think it was just Justin who was talking. This man would utter embarrassing words with homosexual content. For instance, he would say, "I like cocks."

The fact was that Justin *was* homosexual and had had some overt homosexual experiences. As is common among homosexuals, a part of him wanted to reject homosexuality because it was unacceptable to society. Another part of him admitted frankly that he enjoyed homosexual life. He was unable to suppress or repress this latter part: he thus projected it. The impostor was divulging the news and was using the patient's mouth. Justin was told how he was divided on the issue of homosexuality and that if he would accept either his ambivalence or his homosexuality, he would not need to resort to this strange phenomenon.

The part of the patient that is determined to reject the wish is either representative of society or of the parents. Often we are successful in explaining to the patient that the negativistic or ambivalent attitude is a persistence of the original oscillation between the parental wishes and his own.*

IV

Psychodynamic Analysis of Relatedness, Transference, and Countertransference

Whereas at an early stage of treatment relatedness and transference were important almost exclusively as lived experiences and did not require interpretation, at a certain stage of the treatment they do. The fear, the mistrust, the experiencing of others as monstrous powers and of the world at large as an unbearable pressure from which the patient wants to withdraw in order not to be crushed, are discussed at an advanced stage of treatment. All these explanations have to be made with extreme cautiousness, lest they evoke a reaction that is the opposite of what we want. In fact, the patient withdrew not only physically but also emotionally, and actually developed means of desocialization (see Chapter 19) in order to avoid these unpleasant facts. At first it would thus seem that we want to make him aware of what he cannot bear, thus facilitating his desocializing and withdrawing tendencies.

* Powdermaker (1952), in her therapeutic efforts, stresses this important point, which was also discussed in this book, especially in connection with catatonics.

Again we must take into consideration that at this stage of the treatment a certain amount of relatedness and trust exists. What we offer is not just an interpretation but also a feeling of understanding and willingness to share some views of the world and to correct others. All the family situations that we have described in detail in Part Two will receive full consideration, description, and understanding. We must help the patient to become aware not only of the past but also of the present needs and psychological structure that confer a particular experiential form to his transference or relatedness in general. Whereas early in life the patient shaped his relations with the world according to deformed parental patterns, now, if treatment is successful, in relating to the world he is influenced by the transferential pattern. But the transferential pattern, in order to be beneficial, must not be distorted by psychotic trends, and only to the minimal irreducible extent should it be distorted by the old parental pattern.

The developments that we have described in Chapter 36 must now be verbalized and discussed with the patient. It would be redundant to repeat them here. We shall discuss a few more. The therapist will gradually change his attitude toward the patient as the patient improves. From being so giving and maternal he becomes more demanding and paternal. The patient may resent this attitude and may claim that the therapist has changed and is no longer so helpful. Now he is like the others; now he does not care for the patient any more; he makes excessive demands. The therapist must point out to the patient that the demands made on him are a proof of his improvement, of the faith put on him, a recognition that now he can face the world without fear, or at least with less fear.

Of course, demands must be made very slowly, especially on patients who had a symbiotic tie to the mother or mother-substitute. Growing may be experienced as cruel separation, acute realization of excessive dependency, and the end of a vital symbiosis. The therapist must restrain his desire for fast progress lest the patient's longing for the old symbiosis precipitate a relapse.

When the treatment is protracted for a very long time, two countertransferential situations may occur that are almost antithetical. The therapist may have become so used to treating the patient that he is not aware of his improvement. The routine of the treatment has become such an important part of the therapist's life that he does not recognize that sessions have to be curtailed. The therapist may not even recognize at times that the patient is ready for discharge. He must pay serious attention to any request on the part of the patient to decrease or end the treatment. Although it is true that often patients are eager to terminate treatment prematurely, it is also true that some therapists eventually believe that they are always indispensable to patients who used to be very sick. There is a part of the therapist who enjoys being a benefactor. His narcissistic needs are gratified by associating with a person who has benefited so much from his intervention. Also, it is difficult for him to face the emotional deprivation caused by not seeing any longer a person toward whom he felt very close and on whom he invested affection and devotion for a long time. In other words, the therapist must always be aware of his countertransferential feelings. If he cannot recognize them, he has to resort to the help of a colleague or of a supervisor. When the countertransferential feelings are known to the therapist, they reveal a great deal about the therapist as well as about the patient who elicited them.

The second situation we have referred to may have worse consequences. The therapist is so used to the patient after having seen him so often and for such a long time that he no longer is able to recognize the patient's pathology, especially if he has a strong liking for him. He is so used to the patient's projective mechanisms, peculiar ways of thinking and talking, that he no longer recognizes them as abnormal or strange. The result is that a patient who would immediately appear very ill to a new therapist does not seem so to the original therapist. In some instances it is difficult to evaluate whether this situation is the result purely of habituation, reminiscent of that of some relatives who are so used to the peculiarities of the patient as to be able to overlook them, or whether other factors enter. Both in the cases of the therapist and of the relatives there may be a desire not to see for different reasons.

Less frequent, but frequent enough to be considered, is another countertransferential complication. Many therapists are deeply and seriously interested in schizophrenic patients as long as the latter show schizophrenic symptoms. These therapists have a very deep scientific or humanistic interest for *folie*. When the patient no longer presents schizophrenic symptoms, he appears like a simple neurotic, and the therapist may not feel so deeply committed or interested in his complete recovery. Some patients have been able to detect this change in the therapist. Whereas at first this change seemed a projective mechanism on the part of the patient, it revealed itself to be realistic in supervisory discussions and was corrected. In some cases it was necessary to understand why only the obviously psychotic patient would be of interest to the therapist.

Needless to say, the therapist in training must be made aware of the danger of these countertransferential complications and must learn to correct them.

V

Interpretations Related to the Self-Image

Unless the patient changes his vision of himself, he is not likely to lose his psychosis or the potentiality for the psychosis. Interpretations are very useful in this respect. How the psychotic sees himself is often revealed in the most primitive, bizarre, and concrete ways by his dismorphophobic delusions or dysmorphic ideas: he is very little, his face has changed aspect, his head is flat or empty, he has lost his heart, injured his brain, his blood has dried out, his genital organs have undergone metamorphosis. He stinks, gas is emitted from his body constantly, and so forth. In most cases, however, the self-image does not receive such a clear-cut concrete representation.

The self-image is so terrible that the patient wants to hide it not only from the world but from himself. He generally tries to bargain by accepting a self-image that is also terrible, but not as terrible as the original one. We have already seen several times in this book how even some delusions and hallucinations that give the appearance of being very painful are attempts to protect the self-image (Chapter 8). As bad as it is to be accused by others, it is better than to accuse oneself.

If the therapist has succeeded in establishing relatedness and in exchanging some warmth, which is not mistrusted, the patient will have less need to keep the self-image secret from himself or projected and distorted by means of delusions and hallucinations. We must reaffirm to the patient that we agree with him that his life has been discouraging. His discouragement has been intensified by his way of seeing the world. By adopting different ways and with a feeling of hope, life may unfold in a more rewarding manner. From the way the therapist has treated him, the patient will recognize that his human dignity has been respected, that the therapist does not consider him a curious specimen in an insane asylum, one who is incomprehensible to others. It is because the patient thinks so little of himself that he has to defend himself so tenaciously. Yes, there is some truth in what he says about the others. They have minimized and belittled him. The others have not recognized his values, but he has not helped them to do so.

In discussing the establishment of relatedness in Chapter 36, we have discussed the role of reassurance. But whereas the reassurance given at the beginning of the treatment was that of a person who wants to give, understand, and share the patient's burden, the reassurance given at a much more advanced stage of treatment depends on the reinterpretation of the self-image. The patient's destructive anxiety, rooted in his early life experiences, had compelled him to see himself in a horrible way, in a way that would explain the complete discouragement about himself.

If there are particular reasons why the patient has sustained a tremendous injury to the self-esteem, of if there are particular factors in the life history that are responsible for a development of a weak self-image, they have to be discussed and clarified. Homosexuality or lack of sexual identification may be among such factors. At times the complexes have to do with special or impossible roles that the patient thought he had to play in life.

Mario, an Italian patient, was the son of a well-known patriot and writer who had been killed by the Fascists. The patient grew up in an atmosphere where the mother, overwhelmed by the tragedy in her life, had not been able to fulfill an adequate maternal role. The patient grew up with the feeling that mother did not like him and considered him inferior and unlovable. Different, however, was the feeling he received from the paternal grandmother, who thought little Mario would grow up to be as great as his heroic father. Mario would be a writer, a great painter, a great leader, and so forth. When the patient, later in life, felt unable to carry the burden of living up to being a duplication of his father and of fulfilling his grandmother's aspirations, which had become his own, he was more prone to accept the image of himself that he thought his mother had of him. These two self-images produced inconsistency and doubt in him and, either in conjunction or separately, were the psychodynamic factors that led him to psychosis. He had to be gradually helped to abandon both these images and to see himself in a different way.

VI

Dreams

Interpretation of dreams also plays an important role in the psychotherapy of schizophrenia. Of course, because the study of dreams requires a high degree of participation on the part of the patient, such study cannot occur until relatedness has been established and the symptomatology no longer interferes with the necessary cooperation.

Authors have reported contrasting findings. Noble (1951) has found primitive ideation, with free and undistorted expression of destructive and incestuous drives. Richardson and Moore (1963) have reported an interesting study. Their expectation was that the dreams of schizophrenics would reveal less distortion and less censorship than those of nonschizophrenics. Their study did not disclose that this was the case. Primitive aggressive dreams (including bodily mutilation) and undistorted sexual dreams (including incest) occurred with no more frequency in the schizophrenic than in the nonschizophrenic group. The authors felt that the first significant finding in their study was that repression (or censorship) appeared to be approximately as effective in the dream work of the schizophrenic as in the nonschizophrenic. Their second significant finding consisted of the quality of uncanniness, bizarreness, and strangeness of many (but not all) schizophrenic dreams.

Ephron (1969), reporting on studies made in collaboration with his wife Patricia Carrington, compared dreams of thirty schizophrenic and thirty nonschizophrenic women whose average age was 19 years. He reported that the nonschizophrenic dreams tended to be practical, realistic, and detailed, often relating experiences from waking life. By contrast, schizophrenic dreams seemed stark and tragic. Detail was minimal and was subordinated to tense drama. They were aggressive, bizarre, replete with mutilation, and the persons depicted in them were overwhelmingly threatening. According to Ephron, in dreams of normal people the "element of searching, of reaching for security, for the familiar territory, for an orientation to one's self, seems a paramount drive during sleep as during waking life. This search can be seen to commence at the beginning of almost any dream and work its way persistently through until the end. And it will be more or less successful according to the personality of the dreamer, the time of night, and other factors which may influence the eventual outcome of such an endeavor." There are no constructive elements in schizophrenic dreams, according to Ephron. Even when bizarre imagery, mutilations, brutality, devastating bleakness, or catastrophic danger are missing, it is possible to detect the inability of the patient to regain in the dream some reintegration. As an example of this possibility,

Ephron reports the following dream: "I dreamt about the sea all night. I kept waking up. I remember being down by the shore and building castles and having them washed away. And there were erotic dreams, also, because I also was having dreams about having intercourse." Ephron says that the patient "seems to attempt to establish a home territory during sleep, to build her own identity by constructing a fantasy castle. But like a little child, she builds her castle only of sand, and it is repeatedly washed away into an ego-less void."

Ephron goes on to say that although the patient reaches eventually for orientation in another direction—sexual contact—she does so in a strange depersonalized intimacy. The dreamer does not have intercourse with any specific person. In the dream there is only a vague sense of sexuality occurring in a void.

As a result of my work with many patients treated with prolonged psychotherapy, I can draw the rule-of-thumb conclusion that schizophrenics and non-schizophrenics differ much less in their dreams than in their waking life. This basic finding is easy to explain: in fact, the dreams of every human being are characterized by the supremacy of the primary process. However, if we examine a large number of dreams of schizophrenics, we recognize the following characteristics more frequently than in dreams of other people:

1. The element of bizarreness is more pronounced. More frequently than in dreams of other people there are transformations of persons into animals, plants, flowers, and so forth.
2. Secondary process material hides less the latent content. Thus in spite of their bizarreness, these dreams are easier to interpret than those of neurotics.
3. There is a pervading feeling of despair or a crescendo of anxiety with no resolution.

These characteristics may persist even when the patient is improving or recovering. However, as we shall describe shortly, when the patient is recovering, other types of dreams are likely to occur.

The following dream offers an example of bizarreness. "I dreamt I was a bee. A bubble of honey connected me to the queen bee so that I could suck the honey. A nasty bee came along and said to me, 'Go on your own; don't suck the queen's honey.' " The patient had been sick for many years. At the time she had this dream, she was much better and free of overt symptoms. Her previous therapist, whom she idealized as a deity or a king, and with whom she wanted to retain a symbiotic relation, had moved to another city a few months ago, and she had continued treatment with me. Many sessions had been devoted to discussing her transference with the previous therapist, for whom she had a deep feeling of subservient respect, and on whom she depended "for succor." A great deal of time was used to discuss how she could break her attachment and become less dependent on any therapist. The patient interpreted her dream by herself. She said that the queen bee was her previous therapist, Dr. X.; and that I was the nasty bee.

The dream also illustrates the second characteristic: simplicity, easy translation into language of waking life. Other examples of simple dreams will be given in Chapter 40 in relation to the case of Geraldine.

A dream of Robert, a 21-year-old male student, offers an example of the third characteristic:

I have a horse and a dog. They both run away. I steal a car to look for the dog and horse. The car catches on fire, and I run to the nearest house to call the fire department. I find out that the house is a whorehouse. There are dogs in the whorehouse that seem to act like whore-owned dogs. In the house I see a friend of my sister, and I feel funny for being here. Then I remember shaking hands with somebody and get stung through the hand. It's like a man-of-war stinging feeling.''

The patient had recovered from the acute manifestations of a paranoid episode, during which he had many grandiose delusions, one of them consisting of the belief that he was Jesus Christ. When the patient had this dream, he was no longer delusional but had to contend with two major problems: fear of the world and extremely low self-esteem. His outlook on life was very pessimistic. Rather than reference to specific events, the dream required explanations connected with these two basic feelings.

Many dreams of schizophrenic patients reveal the patients' pessimistic attitude and lack of successful resources to solve problems. However, I cannot share the deep pessimism that could be inferred from reading the authors who wrote on dreams of schizophrenics.

Schizophrenic dreams seem also to have constructive elements. Let us reexamine the dream of the patient who dreamt she was a bee. The bizarreness (being a bee) and the simplicity pointed to a schizophrenic dream style and structure. However, the patient revealed that she had acquired insight. Although I was seen as a nasty bee, the feeling was that I was right and that she should be less dependent on the previous therapist. As a matter of fact a drastic change in the transference situation took place after the occurrence of this dream. Moreover, her seeing the other bee as nasty was an indication that she tried to prevent the formation of a symbiotic transference with the new therapist.

Robert, the patient whose pessimistic dream we have examined, continued to have dreams with schizophrenic elements, even when the manifest psychotic symptomatology had disappeared. However, these dreams demonstrated a progressive ability to solve the major situations of life. Five months after the dream reported above he had the following one: ''The whole world knows that Hitler is alive again, Hitler being me. I feel like writing a book which would prove I am not against the Jews. I want the people of the world to respect, not condemn, me.'' Here the patient, who, when he was delusional, identified with the person he thought was the best (Jesus Christ), in this dream is identifying himself with the worst person he could think of (Hitler). But he really does not accept this horrid image of himself. He wants to demonstrate that he is not what people think Hitler was. Robert is not what he believed people thought of Robert. By writing a book he will show his worth.

Four months later Robert had the following dream: ''My father is in an accident and he needs a new face. He becomes very sad. I see the face that will be his. It is one of an old man, but when the face is put on, it looks like my next-door neighbor George. The next thing I know is that my father, with the new face, and I are at a high school dance. We both try to dance wildly and have fun like everybody else, but we are really not having fun dancing."

In my opinion this dream shows improvement and movement toward the solution of the patient's problems. One of his major problems, which played a major role in his psychodynamics, was his relation with his father, with whom he could not identify. Such swinging between unrealistic identifications (Jesus Christ and Hitler) were partially a result of this difficulty. During the postpsychotic period Robert, with the help of psychotherapy, made an attempt to see his father in a different, more realistic way, with "a new face." It turned out that this attempt made father look like his friend George. Father became a peer in whose company he could go to a high school dance. The patient and the father were trying to dance wildly and have fun like everybody else, but they could not. There was thus in the dream a recognition that all the problems had not been solved yet.

Solutions of psychodynamic problems in dreams of schizophrenics are the best prognostic signs. Often these dreams use material very similar to the delusional content that appeared during the acute or active phase of the illness. The similarity of the dream to the content of the psychosis may be evaluated adversely by a therapist who has little experience with psychotic patients. Actually this is, all in all, a good sign: material that was previously dealt with by the patient in psychotic ways is now dealt with by means of the physiologic psychosis that is available to every human being: the dream. The following is an example. A 23-year-old woman, from a well-to-do conservative Southern family, left her home, where she felt she could not adjust, and came to live in New York City. Soon she started to mingle with a nonconformist group of people living in Greenwich Village. She finally went to live in a common-law marital relationship with an artist, a bohemian type of person, of different religious faith and different family background. One day in 1960, during the United Nations session in which Khrushchev participated, she was caught by the police in an obvious psychotic state, wandering and screaming on the street. She was immediately hospitalized. It was found that she was hallucinating and delusional. She thought that the Russians were chasing her. As a matter of fact, the Russians had invaded the city. New York would be their first base of operation. From there they would attempt to conquer the whole world. Toward sunset, near the Hudson River, she saw the whole sky turning red from the rays of the sun. She interpreted that natural phenomenon as a divine warning that the whole world would become Red. She had to deliver the message to the people. God had chosen her to save the world.

Later on when the patient got somewhat better it was possible to find out that the episode had been precipitated by a letter received from her parents announcing that they would come for a visit to New York. She became frantic. What would they do if they discovered the kind of life she was living? Now, after having controlled her throughout her youth, they were coming to New York to invade the land where she had found freedom. Her panic intensified and finally changed into a delusional system. Now no longer the parents but the Russians were invading New York.

The patient recovered from the most obvious symptoms in about three weeks, without any physical therapy, with the exception of some sedation when she was hospitalized. A change toward more than superficial improvement, however, was announced approximately a year later by a dream. The patient dreamt that she was being chased by her parents all over New York City. She saw in this dream scenes similar to those she saw in her acute delusional state, including the scene near the Hudson River. She was afraid and kept hiding. Finally, however, she felt she did not care whether the parents caught her or not. They would not hurt her. She decided she had nothing to hide and went toward the parents to meet them.

CHAPTER

39

Other Aspects of Psychotherapy

I

Participation in Patient's Life: The Therapeutic Assistant

The treatment of the schizophrenic cannot consist only of the sessions, but an active participation in his life is necessary, as many authors have reported. The patient needs to feel that many events in his life are shared by the therapist. Rosen (1947) went to the extent of shopping with patients or of spending as much as ten hours daily with some of them. Sechehaye (1951*a*, *b*) spent practically the whole day with her only patient. These procedures are exceptional and are not compatible with ordinary practice. When the patient is very sick and his requirements are immense, I have resorted to the help of a therapeutic assistant. A psychiatrically trained nurse, or a former patient when a nurse cannot be found, is the best qualified to act as a therapeutic assistant. Federn (1952) and Rosen (1953) were the first to report this procedure. Federn used as a therapeutic assistant a nurse, Gertrude Schwing, to whom we have already referred in Chapter 35. I wish to stress that the use of the therapeutic assistant is not necessary in every case, but only in the most difficult ones, or when for some particular reasons hospitalization is not advisable in spite of the seriousness of the condition. If the patient has to be hospitalized, the therapeutic assistant may be a trained psychiatric nurse working in the hospital.

When the very ill patient is treated only with psychotherapy, he requires much attention. At times one person must be at the continuous and exclusive disposal of the patient. The therapeutic assistant stays with the patient during the day, except, of course, for the time of the psychotherapeutic session. She cooperates with the patient and duplicates the general attitude of the therapist. The assistant is there to help, to support, to share. It is particularly at a certain stage of the treatment that the therapeutic assistant is valuable. When the patient has lost concrete delusions and hallucinations, by virtue of the methods outlined in Chapter 37, he may nevertheless retain a vague feeling of being threatened, which is abstract and from which he tries to defend himself by withdrawing. The assistant is there to dispel that feeling. That common exploration of the inner life in which the patient and therapist are engaged is now complemented by an exploration of the external life made together with the therapeutic assistant.

Peplau (1952, 1959) thinks that the nurse (or assistant) helps by establishing a feeling of ''thereness.'' Somebody is *there,* available, always ready to help. There is somebody the patient can rely on, somebody whom he trusts, somebody who could dispel many fears. The therapeutic assistant, directly and realistically, paves the way to the external world. She shows that many of the things the patient is afraid of either do not exist or have no power to hurt. The therapeutic assistant is recognized not as a distant, potential, or magic helper, but as a person who is in physical proximity. She is the person who shows that by doing things together many obstacles will be overcome. For instance, the patient may not want to go to a store for fear of persecutors, but in the company of the assistant he will go. Needless to say, the therapeutic assistant would not be able to help the patient if the therapist had not prepared the ground with his inner exploration.

There is a tendency on the part of many patients who are helped by a therapeutic assistant to return to a condition of early childhood, but what is important in the treatment is not the similarity but the difference between the present and the early situation. The therapeutic assistant does not stultify the growth of the patient, who is allowed to take his own initiative whenever possible.

The patient also wants tasks to be given to him and demands to be made on him, contrary to the way he felt at the beginning of the treatment. By fulfilling these tasks, the patient will make gains in self-evaluation. As I have already mentioned in Chapter 36, I have learned this technique in Pilgrim State Hospital. At that time I noticed that in some back buildings for chronic patients, where no physical treatment or psychotherapy was given, a considerable number of patients could be discharged. I have described how I came to the realization that these discharges were a consequence of the relatedness that had developed between certain nurses and certain patients. These nurses offered the patients an image of a good mother by being warm and kind, and appearing strong at the same time. The patients responded to this atmosphere of consistent warmth by becoming more active. The nurse or the female attendant then would give the patient tasks that the patient was certainly able to perform and would then praise the patient, who felt an incentive to do more. The patient felt that he deserved the praise of the nurse, and in this way his self-esteem increased. Inasmuch as in wartime there was a serious shortage of employees, the nurses naturally had a tendency to show preference for those patients who would help. This feeling, however, was not experienced as having strings attached to it.

The relation to the nurse had the following characteristics:

1. The patient did not have conflictual areas with the nurse as he had with the parents.

2. The assignments were not out of proportion to the capabilities of the patient. The patient was asked to do what could reasonably be expected of him, and therefore his insecurity was not increased.

3. The patient would definitely and consistently get some kind of approval or preferential treatment, which increased his self-esteem.

To summarize, what I think was happening was that the nurse, a very maternal person, not at all hostile but love inspiring, with her general attitude was able to remobilize the patient. Once the patient was made to move as a result of this attitude, he became involved in a method of increasing his self-esteem. Not all patients responded to this procedure, but a fairly large number did.

When we assign tasks to patients, we must take their wishes into consideration and not try to fit them into traditional occupational therapy classes. Patients, like everybody else, are more willing to do what they like. It is useful to remember that schizophrenics, more frequently than average persons, have artistic inclinations (Chapter 20). Many of my patients, during treatment, started to study painting, music, or classical dancing, with considerable success. Quite a number of them started literary careers.

Although the artistic work of the patient may be useful to the therapist as a means of acquiring additional insight and of evaluating the psychological status of the patient, it should be assessed independently as an artistic work and as an accomplishment.

The therapeutic assistant is particularly useful with hard to mobilize or motivate patients. It is inadvisable to entrust the treatment of the very vulnerable psychotic patients to one person only, the therapist. If, for some unexpected reasons, the therapist must discontinue treatment, the patient should not feel isolated or alone. Secondly, at least two useful interpersonal relationships are needed in very difficult cases for a healthy reintegration and socialization. We should not forget that even in the original situations, there are two persons, the two parents, who help the child to introject and to grow. Thirdly, it is a physical impossibility for the therapist, in the structure of our society, to devote to one patient as much time as he may require.

It is a good practice to use as therapeutic assistants persons who have undergone psychoanalysis or intense psychotherapy. However, in my opinion, well-adjusted persons with warm, radiating, maternal personalities have done well even if they had not undergone treatment.*

Rosen has been assisted by two nurses who had previously suffered from schizophrenia and who had recovered as the result of his treatment. I have been greatly helped by my former patient Sally Lorraine, about whom I wrote in Chapter 10. A former patient who has been successfully treated and has a fresh

* Since my early experiences with psychotherapy of schizophrenia, nurse training has undergone a dramatic improvement. Now it is possible to find many psychiatric nurses who are able to do excellent work with psychotic patients.

memory of the experience he went through may have a feeling of empathy and understanding difficult to match (Lorraine, 1972).

Another main function of the nurse or therapeutic assistant consists of giving a kind push—not a total push à la Myerson, but a soft push. The feeling of relatedness for the patient, rather than preconceived ideas, planned programs, or daily activities, will tell the therapeutic assistant when to practice the soft push to combat the tendency to be inactive or to withdraw. The patient may nevertheless resent the pushing. We know that schizophrenics feel "pushed around" throughout their lives. The push will more probably be accepted and not resented if it is soft, if it is accompanied by tenderness and by a hopeful glimmer of success. The patient must be encouraged to take his own initiative whenever possible. For instance, we could tell him something like this: "The other day when you did this, you enjoyed yourself; would you like to do it again?" In this way the initiative is still on the part of the patient, but he has been helped to make a decision.

The therapeutic assistant may help the patient to overcome some harmful or disruptive habits. Unless corrected, these habits tend to perpetuate themselves, to become more ingrained and more intense. The physician may not be aware of these habits, either because he does not have the opportunity to observe them or in some cases because in the session they pass unnoticed. For instance, many therapists do not know when a patient is going to hallucinate. But some nurses know, sometimes from familiarity with the patient's facial expression or body posture, that in a few minutes or seconds the patient is going to hallucinate and perhaps act-out with impulsive behavior. The nurse gently should go to him, distract him, and involve him in other things so that he is prevented from hallucinating.

Whereas the therapist tries to interpret and make the symptoms unnecessary, the therapeutic assistant offers the patient ways to avert them. This aversion therapy has nothing to do with mechanical conditioned-reflex therapy, but has everything to do with the warm intervention of another human being. By aversion of symptoms, I mean (just as in the given example concerning hallucinations) creating situations in which symptoms are not likely to occur and avoiding situations in which they may easily occur. For instance, if the patient has the tendency to indulge in rituals when he is alone, he should be left alone as little as possible. Aversion therapy is much more than symptomatic treatment; symptoms and habits become stronger and more resistant the more frequently they occur.

Marram (1970) has described how some problems in the management of the patient consist of helping him promote social adaptation, discouraging social isolation, and decreasing overtaxing demands of the environment.

Several complications may develop in the work of the therapeutic assistant. Many of them involve the assistant as a person who undergoes feelings of countertransference similar to those described in the therapist (Chapter 38). In quite a few cases the therapeutic assistant tends to see the patient as a person who needs help very much, even when he has improved considerably. She may be unwilling to spend less time with the patient or to decrease his care. The assistant must be instructed by the therapist to recognize and acknowledge the improvement of the patient.

Another difficulty lies in the hostility that the patient in some cases develops for the assistant, either because he resents being dependent on her or because he is afraid of the warmth he has for her or because he identifies her with a figure of his past and sees her through paranoid distortions. All these situations, of course, must be reported to the therapist, who will analyze them with the patients. Another difficulty may arise on account of those triangular social processes first described by Stanton and Schwartz (1949*a, b*). They occur in ambulatory patients also, although the most intense entanglements have been reported in hospitalized patients. If the patient feels that there is a nonexpressed disagreement between the therapist and the therapeutic assistant about his own treatment, or between the therapist or therapeutic assistant and a parent, he is bound to become disturbed. This disturbance is relatively mild because the patient generally feels that the therapist is on his side in disagreements between therapist and therapeutic assistant, or that the therapeutic assistant is on his side when the patient disagrees with the parent. When the problem is openly discussed or an agreement is reached, the disturbance tends to disappear. The disturbance in some cases is caused by a reactivation of the patient's childhood feeling that he was the cause or the victim of the dissension that existed between his parents.

Federn (1943, 1952) wrote that the helper may be even a relative or a friend. This question comes up often, because in many cases it may be economically impossible to resort to a therapeutic assistant. In my opinion, a relative, especially a close relative such as a parent or the spouse, is not a good helper because he is too much involved in the problems of the patient. Even if the relative has, through his own psychoanalysis or psychotherapy, overcome his own emotional problems, the patient's problems in connection with this person will make the task a very difficult one. I have encountered a few cases where the husband acted as a therapeutic assistant, but these attempts were not successful. The patients tended to resume a symbiotic relationship with their husbands. They tended to become passive bodies that had to be taken care of completely. Of course, in these cases the hostility for the husbands was given this opportunity to express itself.

II

Advanced Stage of Treatment

At an advanced stage of treatment the patient becomes increasingly similar to a neurotic patient. The therapist should not be overly impressed with the change and should remember that the recovering psychotic remains always more vulnerable and unstable than the neurotic and that some relapses often occur. Conversely, if minor relapses do occur, the therapist should not feel unduly discouraged. The occurrence of them and the relative mildness of them in comparison to the initial attack of the illness should be explained to the patient and his family.

One of the difficulties encountered at a later stage of treatment is the fear of improvement. This fear may be caused by many factors. One of the most common is the fear of having to face life again and of not succeeding. Being healthy implies the responsibility of living with all the threats that life presents. Again life has to be reinterpreted to the patient, and the fears have to be analyzed and reduced to their normal proportions.

The patient may also feel that he does not deserve to improve, feels guilty for feeling well, and may want to live in accordance with the negative image of himself.

Another idea that may discourage him from improving is the thought of getting well for somebody else's sake, not for his own. Actually, contrary to his belief, improvement will make him freer, not more dependent, not more obligated to others. In the process of reasserting himself, the patient may reexperience the feeling that tormented him in his prepsychotic stage, when he thought that to be himself meant to be odd or queer, and that therefore it was advisable for him to be as others wanted him to be. Actually this feeling will not last a long time after its return because the patient is learning to accept himself as he is and to have respect for his own feelings, ideas, and judgment. He sees himself more and more as a person in his own right.

Some of the habits he rigidly adhered to are finally abandoned. For instance, a patient would never be seen without sun glasses. If she did not wear them, people would notice her feelings. She could survive only if she had something to hide behind. She felt she had wrecked her life. However, there was still in her the desire to save herself. Eventually she did not have to hide any more what was inside of her, and she stopped wearing dark glasses.

At an advanced stage of therapy the basic dynamic patterns are established and can be clearly formulated and related both to current behavior and general relations with the world (see case of Mark in Chapter 40).

One of the things to consider is whether at an advanced stage of treatment it is worthwhile to bring up the memories, circumstances, and characteristics of the acute psychotic episode. There are several psychotherapists who are against such a procedure. Müller (1963), for instance, believes that the amnesia for the psychotic episode not only should not be prevented, but made a therapeutic vehicle. This point of view is in line with Federn's concept that in schizophrenia, "where ego was, id should be." I do not share this point of view. If what we aim at is only a symptomatic treatment, such as, for instance, what we achieve with electric shock treatment, then amnesia is valuable. Perhaps one of the means by which electric shock treatment is effective is by producing this amnesia. However, I saw the best therapeutic results in those patients who at an advanced stage of treatment remembered the acute episode, were able to analyze its content, to interpret it, and to understand it in the context of their life history. In other words, they came to understand it as an attempt to escape from, or to cope with, the conflicts.

Of course I too think that if the patient is quickly recovering from an acute episode, he should not be pressured to remember it because the conflicts are still pathogenic and may again bring about decompensation. However, before the episode is completely forgotten, I direct the patient to reexamine it. In my experience, in the security offered by the therapeutic relationship, the exposure to the memory of the psychotic episode is useful. The patient is now in a position to free his conflicts, to understand them partially, and may even begin making some tentative steps toward the solution of them. I have almost invariably found that patients who forget their acute episode sooner or later are going to have another one.

Kelman (1973) has reported that some schizophrenics maintain a secret that they do not want to reveal to the therapist. As long as they do so, improvement is delayed. The secret that some patients safeguard does not generally concern the psychotic episode but the meaning they give to their life, the unfulfilled aspirations, the sense of defeat, the fear of others, the vision of the self.

A controversial point in the psychotherapy of schizophrenia concerns the nature of the fragility of the schizophrenic patient, to which we have already referred. Some therapists believe that the patient is very vulnerable; and some others, Searles (1965), for instance, state that the fragility of the schizophrenic is a myth. I disagree with either extreme position. When relatedness is established with the patient, he is able to accept the basic truth about his predicament in life. The truth, revealed with candor and authenticity, is less of a threat to him than artificial embellishments and beating around the bush. The schizophrenic patient, however, remains very vulnerable at the beginning of treatment concerning such events as separation from the therapist during vacation time, or because he gives a symbolic meaning of despair or utter rejection to some events or words or actions of the therapist. The schizophrenic is more ready than the neurotic to hear the truth about himself but less ready to stand duress, adversity, and drastic changes. If he is more ready to accept the truth, it is not because he is already conscious of mechanisms that are usually unconscious to the average person. This is a myth. We have seen repeatedly in this book that the schizophrenic too, either because he represses or distorts or uses primary process thinking, is not aware of many aspects of his personality and interpersonal relations.

Why, at a more or less advanced stage of treatment, is the patient not devastated by the truth? First of all, we must remember that once he knew the truth or was very close to it. When he rediscovers the truth, he has a feeling of familiarity. Moreover, now he hopes in spite of what he knows. He relates and knows and feels much more than the neurotic that the therapist shares the burden of the knowledge of the truth. Whereas a major part of his previous life—that is, the totality of his prepsychotic and psychotic mechanisms—can be seen as a gigantic maneuver to hide or compensate for the truth or experiential truth, now he is ready for a confrontation with the truth.

Whenever the therapist feels that the patient is ready for a decrease in the number of sessions, this step should be taken. The patient generally dislikes a reduction in treatment because of his dependency, which may remain great in spite of the improvement.

At an advanced stage of treatment, the patient may become distressed by typical neurotic symptoms. Rosen (1953) also has mentioned this common occurrence. One of the urges commonly found, especially in former catatonics, is the compelling necessity to do everything best and to avoid mistakes. The patient must buy the best suit, must go to the best doctor, must read numerous times what he writes for fear of having made mistakes, and so on. These symptoms are generally easy to explain. The protection of inactivity is no longer available, but the patient still wants to please the incorporated parental figure from whom he wants approval. He wants to avoid mistakes at any cost or identify with mother and do the best. The "power" to avoid the mistake is searched for also as proof of the ability to fight a feeling of powerlessness that now and then reemerges. If the patient is able to avoid the mistake or able to obtain "the best results," he feels he has power; he does not need to feel hopeless or to go back to the state of withdrawal. The patient has to hear again and again that mistakes are indicative of the human condition and not of a state of unworthiness and irreparable inadequacy.

One of the problems that must be considered at a certain point in the treatment of nonhospitalized patients who are improving concerns the separation of the patient from his family. Should he live by himself? This is always a major step. On the one hand, we may think that it is in the family that the troubles of the patient started, and there probably, that they are maintained. On the other hand, we may feel that to remove the patient from his family would not really be helpful because this would be merely a removal from the external situation, not from the introjected conflicts. As a matter of fact, one might even think that this separation might reexacerbate the symptoms. We shall see in Chapter 40 that Geraldine, a patient who was improving, started to hallucinate again when she was separated from her mother.

Actually, in my experience, separation from the family is a positive step to be considered when the other conditions, to be mentioned later, permit. It is true that the introjected members of the family will continue to act within the patient. However, the schizophrenic patient must also mature at a conscious reality level, and this process of maturation, of striving toward independence and self-reliance, is handicapped by his living with his family. Of course, minor reexacerbations of symptoms must be anticipated and coped with immediately by discussing them with the patient or even by warning him of their possible occurrence.

Separation from the spouse or a sibling has approximately the same psychological significance as separation from the mother, with whom this sibling or spouse is generally unconsciously identified.

The other problem is to determine when the patient is ready for separation. I think we must be prepared to take some risks. Again in my experience, several patients who appeared dependent and helpless proved to be able to take care of themselves much better than the members of the family or I had anticipated. Of course, in some cases we must make return possible—a return accompanied not by a sense of defeat but by the willingness to try again a little later.

The patient will be able to live by himself if he is given more than what he is deprived of; that is, if he is given by the therapist a sense of trust, confidence, and belief in the unfolding of his potentialities. The patient should also be told that he will be able to stay again for short periods of time with the members of his family when he is in a position not to be hurt any longer by what they represent.

Generally when the patient is able to live alone, another type of relatedness is established, to which we have already alluded in Chapter 36. The more the patient improves, the more he becomes a peer of the therapist. How can patient and therapist become peers? By age, sex, background, training, they are most of the time quite different. Certainly they can have common interests, but I do not believe that is enough. Therapist and patient can be peers if they share values. We hit here a crucial and controversial point. The therapist is no representative of the values of society, nor does he advocate any value that the patient does not accept. However, let us not delude ourselves, as many psychoanalysts have done in the past. An intense relatedness, like the one required for the therapy of the psychotic, and, by the way, for any healthy human encounter, necessitates the experience of sharing values. In the past the psychoanalyst in training was instructed not to invade the realm of values. Values, of course, do not need to be expressed in words; they can be sensed. A surgeon or a general practitioner can perform a service without sharing values with the patient, except those concerned with the pursuit of health and life. In the psychotherapy of the psychotic, the situation is entirely different. We must search for and find common values with the patient (Arieti, 1971*b*). We have seen in Chapter 8 that some therapists (Siirala, 1961, 1963; Laing, 1967) have found these common values in their belief that schizophrenics have an understanding of social injustice that is superior to that of the average person, an understanding that the therapist should accept. In Chapter 8 we have also seen that although the schizophrenic may be alert to realistic hostility, malevolence, and evil more than the normal person, we would do him and ourselves a disservice to accept his experience of this hostility, with the psychotic structure, deformations, and exaggeration that he has superimposed on it.

We must, however, be always aware of the possibility that the patient has positive values and that these positive values can be retrieved in their original purity once we remove the psychotic overlay. Even if we feel that the patient, in both his prepsychotic and psychotic stages, responds abnormally to the world or misinterprets the world, we should not necessarily evaluate his position in a negative way. Let us first of all become aware of the fact that normality, or what we call normality, may require mental mechanisms and attitudes that are not so healthy. At times what is demanded of us is callousness to the noxious stimuli. We protect ourselves by denying them, hiding them, becoming insensitive, or finding a thousand ways of rationalizing them or adjusting to them. We become a silent majority. By being so vulnerable and so sensitive the patient may teach us to counteract our callousness. By spending so much energy in adapting we survive and live to the best of our ability, but we pay a big price that may result in the impoverishment of a part of our personality. This impoverishment of the personality is particularly pronounced, not always but often enough, in the nonpsychotic members of the patient's family. They were able to avoid the psychosis, but often the rigidity, peculiarity, compromises, and distortions that they underwent, mutilated important parts of their personality and deprived them of some dimensions of living.*

When the preschizophrenic and schizophrenic see society as a Darwinian

* See Chapter 40, case of Geraldine.

jungle, we must remind ourselves that not the patient but Darwin himself made the first analogy in the reverse order. After having studied society in Malthus's writings, Darwin in the Galapagos Islands saw the jungle as a reproduction of society. Inequality, competition, struggle, and power prevail in the two situations. Unless checked by human will, power wins out in both society and jungle. The future schizophrenic is certainly not the fittest in any jungle. When he becomes psychotic, he is not literally a prophet but a reminder of the inimical powers that most of the time win and say, "Woe to the vanquished." He is not a prophet but a significant voice; and yet, in spite of its significance, this voice is most of the time too humble, too weak, too deprived of adaptational value to be heard. The therapist must hear this voice. At the same time he must dismantle or help dismantle the psychotic scenario that deforms the message. The philosopher, the dissenter, and the revolutionary, like the schizophrenic, lack adaptability, but they compensate for this lack with their creativity. With a few outstanding exceptions, the schizophrenic is not as creative as they are. If we want to hear his disguised voice and transmit his message to the world, we must overcome the obstacles built by the psychosis.

What is the real voice, the value that the schizophrenic tries to express before it is distorted by the disorder? It is the basic value of the human being. He wants to be the sovereign of his will (Arieti, 1972*a*). He wants to be totally himself, but he does not know how. He finds, as a matter of fact, sovereigns all over, but not in himself. He attributes to them hostile intents, and he himself harbors a great deal of hostility.

We are willing to accept and transmit his message, but this action may possibly help only future generations. We want to help the patient himself. We will be in a position to help him, to transmit to him our own message if he experiences us as human beings who share his values and as peers. When he feels that some of the real or fantastic forces that disturb him disturb us also, he will start to relate to us without distrust. By accepting his perception of hostility from a general point of view, we shall be in a position to help him later to cut or dismantle the delusional distortions of this hostility. Gradually the patient's main goal becomes not that of fighting persecutors but of fighting evil and searching for love and fulfillment. Thus, his first and ultimate values will also be our values.

When the patient realizes that we stand neither for his madness nor for that of society, but that we are his companions in both madnesses, treading cautiously but hopefully on the narrow path on which the intangible universal values of individualism reside, the prognosis is good.

III

Complications

Complications arising during the course of the treatment or existing even before the beginning of it at times make psychotherapy more difficult.

The first is the development of depression while the patient is gradually losing the schizophrenic symptoms. We have already seen in Chapter 3 that recently the number of patients changing from a schizophrenic to a depressed symptomatology is increasing. Thus we do not necessarily have to attribute this development to psychotherapy. However, it seems evident that at least in some cases psychotherapy has hastened, made more probable, or actually determined this change.

In some cases the reason for the depression seems clear. The patient has the feeling that he has lost something precious. The symptoms might have been disagreeable and painful, but they permitted a certain tie with the world and constituted an important part of the inner life. Without them the patient feels empty; he almost wishes to have the symptoms back. One of Roth's patients pleaded over and over, "Please, please, let me be crazy again" (Roth, 1970).

In some cases this type of depression manifests itself not with the usual feeling of melancholia but with a form of apathy, or apathetic nihilism. In these instances the therapist and, whenever available, his assistant must become more active in entering the life of the patient and offering those non–anxiety-producing possibilities that may fill somewhat the huge gaps.

However, a much more complicated mechanism is often at the basis of the depression sustained by the recovering schizophrenic. When he was paranoid, he projected the bad image of himself to the external world. The persecutors were accusing him, but he felt he was an innocent victim and gained in self-esteem. When, as a result of treatment, he is deprived of these paranoid mechanisms, he may tend to reintroject the bad image of himself, to consider himself worthless and guilty, and consequently he may feel extremely depressed. Generally in these cases tendencies toward retention of a bad self-image with strong depressive overtones existed even before the psychosis started. However, after the onset of the psychosis the schizophrenic projective mechanisms prevailed.

The self-accusatory tendency has to be analyzed, discussed, traced to the origin, and corrected. These cases present some risks because at times the improvement in the symptomatology of depression revamps the schizophrenic symptomatology. In other cases we do not have a recurrence of schizophrenia, but the patient retains personality defects, like emotional instability, paranoid tendencies, propensity to misinterpret.

Most authors, including myself, do not as a rule consider the occurrence of this depression in negative terms but, on the contrary, as a sign of growth and good prognosis. However, other authors have given different psychodynamic meanings to its occurrence. Spiegel (1973) advanced the daring hypothesis that the "schizophrenic response" may be a depressive equivalent. Hoedemaker (1970) considers the depression an almost appropriate response on the part of the patient to the recognition of his inner emptiness and utilization of unreal defenses. The patient sees reality for the first time, his lack of individuation, and develops feelings of desperation. For Miller and Sonnenberg (1973) depression occurs when the patient, as a result of psychotherapy, experiences an impetus to further autonomy. But the patient is afraid of functioning at a more autonomous level, especially if the end of treatment is contemplated, and such fear makes him depressed.

A second complication is the development of psychopathic traits during psychotherapy. The patient becomes very promiscuous or may even steal or refuse to pay debts. Unless the patient was originally a psychopath who also became psychotic, the outlook is not as alarming as it may seem. Psychopathic traits in recovering schizophrenics generally signify difficulties in the attempts to readjust, vindictiveness toward society, or desire to assert oneself or to make up for what the patient believes he has lost in life. As a rule they soon disappear and progress is made.

A third complication is homosexuality. The two conditions, homosexuality and schizophrenia, may have some common predisposing factors residing in the original disturbed family environments. However, the two conditions have many different characteristics and different psychological organizations. Generally, in my experience if the schizophrenic is homosexual, his chance of recovering from the psychosis decreases. Since he lives in a heterosexual society that is prone to condemn homosexuality, the patient has additional important reasons for feeling anxious, threatened, rejected. Especially in early youth, for instance, in college or at work, when he succumbs to the first homosexual seductions, he may go into a state of panic leading to a schizophrenic psychosis. Of course, the psychosis is determined not only by the anxiety that is related to the emerging homosexuality but also and especially by the anxiety of the whole life history and especially of the childhood experiences. Nevertheless homosexuality constitutes an important aggravating factor and may be responsible for precipitating and maintaining psychotic episodes. In these cases when therapy has reached the stage during which psychodynamic analysis is the main endeavor, the patient should be encouraged to recognize his conflict and to accept his homosexual orientation without anxiety. It will be impossible for him to do so if he feels that even his therapist rejects his homosexuality and would like him to be or become heterosexual. In my experience only if the patient loses his anxiety over his homosexuality can we treat his schizophrenia with any hope of success. Exceptions are those few cases where the occurrence of the psychosis had nothing to do with the patient's homosexuality. In my opinion in all these cases our goal should be that of treating schizophrenia and not homosexuality. Incidentally, in my opinion it is easier to recover from schizophrenia than to change sexual orientation. Perhaps it is not difficult to understand why. A homosexual orientation is compatible with a rich life, although in its pure forms it is not compatible with reproduction. It is also compatible with pleasure achievement and with the fulfillment of the fundamental human potentialities. Many of the problems connected with homosexuality are derived from the fact that the patient must live in a heterosexual society.

The situation is very much different in schizophrenia. In most severe cases this psychosis is not a condition compatible with life, unless, of course, the patient is taken care of by nonpsychotic members of the human species. It is fundamentally a process of progressive disorganization in spite of the organization of psychotic patterns and is not compatible in most cases with pleasure-attainment and with the fulfillment of the potentialities of man. It is thus natural for the teleologic or regenerative capacities of the psyche and of the whole organism to participate in the fight against schizophrenia but not in fight against homosexuality. Of course the foregoing does not imply that the psychodynamic mechanisms that led to homosexuality should not be examined. It also does not imply that acceptance of the goal of combating only the psychosis is a definite attitude that psychiatrists should take at all times or in all cases. I think, however, that at the present stage of our knowledge, it is in most cases an insurmountable, as well as undesirable, task to remove therapeutically both schizophrenia and homosexuality.

IV

Precautionary Measures: Legal Responsibility

A situation from which the therapist must protect himself is the possible accusation of having sexual relations with the patient. Sexual intentions are often attributed to the therapist even by neurotic patients. However, with neurotics, this is not a serious problem. It is easy to discuss these feelings and to interpret them. The situation is much more complicated with a psychotic, who, in his tendency to concretize ideas, does not speak of intentions of the therapist, but of real acts. Because the nature of the therapy is such that it does not allow for the presence of a nurse or an attendant during the session, the physician must master the situation in other ways. First of all, the young therapist is warned against taking these accusations too seriously. He should not put himself in a position of defense, but whenever possible he should interpret these sexual feelings to the patient, as he would do with a neurotic patient. Generally the psychotic patient who does not dare to have feelings of closeness has to distort anything resembling them. As Sullivan illustrated, "in a malevolent way" he transforms his own longing for closeness or the therapist's warm attitude into sexual acts initiated by the therapist. The therapist should take notes, reporting the expressions of these accusations, not out of context but in an account of the session that is as complete as possible. In the proper context these ideas will appear delusional to everybody and can be used if the paranoid patient, who cannot stand closeness with the therapist, interrupts treatment and makes legal charges against him. A record of the session would be very useful. As was mentioned before, the presence of a witness when the patient has the feeling that the therapist uses him or her sexually is not recommended. In a certain respect this recommendation is contrary to what has been suggested in cases of uncontrollable hostility.

If the paranoid patient feels that the therapist wants to abuse her sexually, the presence of another person may reinforce her belief. A young resident was attempting psychotherapy on a hospitalized antagonistic paranoid who soon accused him of some kind of sexual activity when he was alone with her in the office. The doctor asked an attendant to be present at the subsequent interviews. Such a procedure did not dispel the ideas of the patient but reinforced them. According to her, the therapist, now having a paid witness on his side, could really do whatever he wanted with her. She really believed that sexual affairs were taking place, even in the presence of the attendant. The resident then assumed a disparaging, contemptuous attitude, after which these sexual fantasies disappeared because there was no longer any fear of closeness. The rapport was lost, however, and treatment had to be discontinued.

If the patient who harbors such ideas is a minor, and if interpretations have not been successful, the therapist should inform the relatives of the existence of such ideas and should advise treatment with a therapist of the same sex. One should not forget that the relatives are often disturbed people and that in their unconscious desire to blame others for their troubles they are bound to believe the patient's allegations unless they have been informed by the therapist in advance. Revelation of such ideas to the relatives may be harmful as far as the treatment is concerned, but we cannot expect the therapist to be a masochist who does not want to protect himself.

I have not read or heard of actual physical sexual attacks being made by psychotic patients on therapists, although they have been made on nurses, attendants, and other patients. Undressing in front of the therapist to a state of complete nudity occasionally occurs. Homosexual desires generally manifest themselves in symbolic forms. As we have seen in Chapter 36, declarations of love toward the therapist of the opposite sex are not rare, especially in paranoids who express these feelings in a bizarre, generally harmless manner. These erotic feelings are different from the usual transference feelings of neurotics. They generally, although not always, indicate ways to gain self-esteem, acceptance, and protection. If the therapist would yield and have sexual relations with the patient, that fact would be proof to the patient of the therapist's acceptance of him. Incidentally, similar feelings, expressed openly by some psychotic patients, for the parents of the opposite sex seem to me often to indicate the same thing. Physical love is a concrete symbolization of what is really wanted: love and reassurance. It is true that the psychosis may uncover an Oedipus complex. But the Oedipal aims are now in the service of attempts to rebuild the self-image.

It is obvious that the treatment of a psychotic individual, especially ambulatory treatment, presents a certain risk. On the other hand, it is also evident that some therapists of psychotic patients, especially young therapists, are often afraid of the patient. First of all the therapist should try to find out why he is afraid. Often his personal problems more than the actual actions of the patient engender such fear. If the therapist is in personal analysis or supervision, he should discuss this fear with his own analyst or supervisor. If he is not in analysis or supervision, he should discuss the matter with a competent colleague. As we mentioned before, the treatment of some schizophrenics is bound to elicit in the therapist a disturbing countertransference. A colleague, by being less emotionally involved, is able at times to help the exhausted therapist. However, if, in spite of this help, the therapist continues to be afraid of the patient, he should not treat him. The patient senses this fear and becomes more hostile toward himself because he feels that he is so bad as to cause fear even in the therapist. He may also become more resentful toward the therapist and may burst into acts of violence.

At times during treatment the patient may become worse and may require hospitalization. Whenever possible the patient should be told the truth by the therapist and should be reassured that the treatment will be continued while he is in the hospital. Sometimes, however, the situation is out of the hands of the therapist because the patient, generally a defiant paranoid, refuses hospitalization. The family should be informed of the situation. In a minority of unfortunate cases the patient is so hostile and openly or potentially dangerous that he cannot even be told by the therapist that he needs hospitalization. Here, too, special arrangements have to be made with the family.

Occasionally the patient may not have appeared to the therapist to be dangerous to himself or others, and yet he may suddenly burst out in episodes of violence. Such risk cannot be completely eliminated. We must stress that in almost all cases the risk is minimal. As a matter of fact, in facing such risk more therapists tend to be rather too cautious than too liberal. However, liberality is increasing. Those instances in which the simple presence of a psychotic symptom made consideration of hospitalization mandatory are remote now, if not in time, at least in conception and outlook. On the other hand episodes of violence in unsuspected patients and, more frequently, in patients who could not be hospitalized have occurred. A few psychiatrists or members of families of the psychiatrist have been killed by patients or former patients. In the instances that have come to my attention through newspapers or even psychiatric journals, I was not able to ascertain whether the therapist had actually done intensive psychotherapy.

If the patient has paranoid ideation involving the therapist, and therapy is not able to dissolve it, the therapist should consult a colleague and should consider the possibility of referring the patient to a therapist of different age, sex, or background for whom the patient is less likely to develop these trends. Switching to physical therapy or hospitalization is to be seriously considered. No precautionary measure that we know of today can be absolutely sure of safeguarding the therapist or the patient from these fortunately extremely rare episodes.

Errors in predicting whether or not the patient will be violent or antisocial are rare, but they occur and in most cases are unavoidable. In order to eliminate them (not totally, but to some extent) we would have to be so cautious as to hospitalize or to restrict forcibly a large number of patients, thus preventing their recovery and often aggravating the symptomatology.

What is the legal responsibility of the psychotherapist of a patient who commits an antisocial act? Obviously if the act was unpredictable because the patient had shown no indication of it, the therapist has no responsibility whatsoever. The therapist seems to me also to have no responsibility if the antisocial act was mentioned as a mere, distant, or almost hypothetical possibility with no evidence of actions being carried out to implement it. Again it would be impossible and antitherapeutic to hospitalize all patients who belong in this category. The therapist also has no responsibility if he was not in a position to prevent the activity of the patient, because of the legal requirements of the place where the patient resided or other reasons.

The legal problems connected with the psychotic are numerous and complicated. They cannot possibly be discussed in this book. The reader is referred to textbooks of forensic psychiatry.

V

Further Growth of the Patient and Termination of Treatment

When treatment is successful, the patient continues to grow and eventually to blossom, actualizing some of his potentialities to a degree by far superior to that achieved during his prepsychotic period of life.

How the patient is going to be at the end of treatment is impossible to predict. It depends obviously on the inherent qualities of his total personality. In a minority of cases that have come to my attention, the patient became more of a conformist, decreased his expectations from life, increased all his capacities for adaptation, and became, I would say, what the majority of people would consider an average person. I am not including in this group the patients who had defects consequent to the psychosis, but people whom I would consider completely recovered.

I am glad to report, however, that the majority of patients who terminated treatment upon my advice disclosed clearly a great expansion of their personality, a vaster range of interest, a grasp of what is beyond the world of appearance. Recovering or almost recovered patients return to the normal use of the secondary process but retain the awareness that an important part of their life is going on in the primary process. Although in the average person this part of life eludes a cognitive grasp, it is accessible to the patient who is thus psychologically enriched. Although it is true that he too will gradually lose this ability the more he reconnects himself with the things of the world, he will continue to have at his disposal a wider spectrum of views than the average person.

When can a patient be considered ready for termination? Loss of symptoms is not enough. Even the changes in dreams that we discussed in Chapter 38 are not sufficient indication for termination.

Termination of treatment of a schizophrenic patient presents greater problems than termination with other patients. The whole philosophy of the treatment enters into the attitude toward termination. At the time when the end of the treatment is contemplated, the therapist must evaluate whether the patient has sufficiently modified his self-image and his vision of life and of the world. That is, his self-identity must be more definable and his awareness of inner worth must have increased. Reality must be experienced as less frightening and less impinging. The patient must be ready to return to the world with less fear and more understanding. If he is ready for termination, he no longer experiences a sense of enormous passivity; that is, he does not see himself any longer purely as the object of fate, chance, nature, persecutors, spouse, parents, children, and so forth, but as somebody who thinks and acts as independently as the other members of society. He must have succeeded in maintaining an active and satisfactory role in his work activities, interpersonal relations, and especially in situations of intimacy.

It is not true, as some therapists, perhaps influenced by Rado's concept of unhedonia, believe, that recovering schizophrenics and former schizophrenics never achieve a level of normal sexual relations. It is also not true that female patients can eventually achieve only clitoral orgasm. The case of Geraldine, described in Chapter 40, will disprove this point.

Attention must be stressed on another point. We often read in psychoanalytic literature that termination of treatment should occur only when the transference and countertransference are solved. But in the treatment of psychotics and former psychotics the transference and countertransference are hardly ever solved, if by these terms we mean strong reciprocal feelings. Certainly inappropriate feelings should have undergone drastic changes, but the continuation of a strong attachment is what reality demands.

The patient cannot cease to have positive feelings for the former therapist, just as a child does not cease to love his parents when he grows and does not need them any longer. The grown child has also become an adult peer of his good parents. In similar manner the therapist cannot forget or relinquish his feelings for a patient with whom he had such a long and close relation—a person with whom he shed "blood, sweat, and tears," a person with whom he reaffirmed ideas and values about life and the human predicament. Therapists remember with great pleasure the feeling of joy and the atmosphere of festivity quickly created when former schizophrenic patients come to visit them several years after the end of the treatment. Former psychotic patients never become index cards or collections of data on yellowed medical records. They remain very much alive in the inner recesses of the therapist's psyche to the end of his days.

VI

Cure and Outcome

Is schizophrenia curable? Before attempting an answer we must define the word *cure*.

If it is difficult to define *cure* in the field of medicine in general, it is even more difficult to do so in the field of psychiatry. Traditional medicine considers a cure a *restitutio ad integrum* or to the *statu quo ante,* that is, a return to the state that existed prior to the onset of the illness. This concept loses some of its significance in psychiatry because in many psychiatric conditions the so-called premorbid state was already morbid and very much related to the subsequent condition. If by cure we mean simply loss of manifest schizophrenic symptomatology, then the answer is definitely yes. But we have already seen that no psychotherapist should be satisfied with this type of recovery, with a return to the prepsychotic personality.

If by cure we mean the reestablishment of relatedness with other human beings, closeness with a few persons, love for the spouse and children, a reorganization of the personality that includes a definite self-identity, a feeling of fulfillment, or of purpose and hope—and this is the cure we want—the answer is still yes. In my experience we can obtain these results in a considerable number of cases. I have already mentioned that as a result of psychotherapy many patients achieve a degree of psychological maturity by far superior to the one that existed prior to the psychosis.

There are, however, other questions to which my answer, at the present stage of our knowledge, must be different. If by cure we mean achieving a state of immunity, with no possibility of recurrence later in life, my reply is that we are not yet in a position to make a definite statement because not enough years have passed since intense psychotherapy has been applied to schizophrenia, and the cases are not yet so numerous as to permit reliable statistics.

I believe that if we have succeeded in altering the fundamental psychodynamic patterns and have been able to effect a basic reorganization of the personality, a recurrence is much less likely to occur.

In reviewing the cases that have been treated satisfactorily with intense psychotherapy, I have come to the conclusion that my optimistic predictions proved to be accurate in by far the majority of cases, but not in all. To my regret, I remember a few patients whom I treated to a degree that I deemed satisfactory and who nevertheless had relapses. They remained vulnerable to fear-provoking situations. I must stress, however, that in most of these cases the relapses were moderate in intensity and the patients promptly recovered.

The evaluation of the recurrence of psychotic attacks in patients who have undergone psychotherapy is completely different from that given in the era prior to the advent of psychotherapy. I remember that when I was a resident in psychiatry, the third attack (or hospitalization) was considered the crucial one. The third episode meant that the patient was irreparably moving toward chronic schizophrenia. Today, in patients who have been treated with psychotherapy, second or third attacks are recognized as milder than the previous one or ones and of shorter duration. By no means do they indicate poor prognosis, and the patient and his family should be so reassured.

In cases in which we cannot obtain a complete cure, we nevertheless achieve a way of living in which social relations, conjugal life, and work activities are possible to a level superior to the one prevailing prior to the psychosis. In some unsuccessful cases the patients learn to recognize situations to which they are vulnerable. By avoiding them in most instances they are able to live an acceptable life.

Some of my patients whom I consider cured have achieved important positions in life, in the academic world as well as in other activities. If I forced myself to look for a negative common denominator in patients successfully treated by me, I would say that frequently they have married persons intellectually inferior to them. But this is hardly a negative factor (because spouses are seldom equally endowed) and reveals an intellectual bias on my part. The common positive quality that stands out in all of them is that eventually they were able to find love in life, although in varying degrees.

This statement does not imply that all the troubles of the patient are over after successful psychotherapy. We must repeat here the famous words of Fromm-Reichmann that we cannot promise a rose garden. It would be Utopian to believe that the promise of life is a promise of a life comparable to a rose garden, Utopian for the patient, and Utopian for us, his peers. But I think it is not Utopian to promise to the patient what we promise to ourselves, his peers; namely, that sooner or later in life we will have our own little garden.

VII

Relations with the Family and Family Therapy

The relations of the therapist with the family of the patients are always difficult, even when the patient is hospitalized or receiving only drug therapy. In these cases the relation consists of attempts to obtain an adequate history of the patient and of a few short exchanges of information about the present condition of the patient and his prognosis.

Much more complicated are the relations with the relatives of the patient who is in psychotherapy. First of all, the patient, especially if he is a defiant paranoid, often resents any intrusion on the part of the family. On the other hand, in the treatment of psychotics it is difficult to preserve this inaccessibility of the therapist as it is generally done in the psychoanalytic treatment of neuroses or personality difficulties. The patient is in a much more serious condition and causes great anxiety and alarm. The family wants to be kept informed. Moreover, the family members often have to receive instruction from the therapist. Should the patient live with the family? Should he be allowed to go on vacation alone, and so on?

As we mentioned in Chapter 38, the therapist too often acquires toward the relatives the same negative attitude that the patient has. His dislike may be so great that he tries, consciously or most of the time unconsciously, to make it difficult for the relative to communicate with him. Because of his deep involvement with, and empathy for, the patient, he may be afraid of not controlling himself, as he believes his professional role would require, and of showing his hostility to the relative. The therapist, of course, must be fully aware of what we have emphasized in Chapters 5 and 38, that the negative traits of the family are intensely lived by the patient, so intensely that they acquire unrealistic proportions. Galli (1963) described how the therapist may be dragged into a situation that he calls "adoption of the patient.'' ''The therapist adopts the patient and he lives the family's interventions as a father lives the strangers' interventions into his own children's upbringing.'' Galli warns against falling into this pitfall.

Whether the family or the patient himself has ''hired'' the therapist for treatment is not important from the point of view of privacy and noninterference. The point is whether the patient is able to assume responsibility for his own welfare and actions in general, or whether such responsibility is to be shared with other members of the family. In the latter case, contacts with relatives are necessary, but these must diminish or stop entirely as the patient regains his ability to assume responsibility for himself. On the other hand, the fact that the patient cannot assume total responsibility for himself may give the relative unwelcome free rein, and he may take advantage of the situation for at least two reasons:

1. He suspects that in the course of the intense psychotherapy he is often discussed. He feels threatened by some moral evaluation of himself and may rush to defend himself. He wants the therapist to know that he did not really do what he is accused of, or that at least his intentions were good.
2. The family may rush to find scapegoats for their hostility and may welcome any opportunity of contacts in order to discharge their discontent on the therapist, who may be mercilessly blamed.

In hospital therapy, of course, the use of a social worker will smooth all the problems between the therapist and the patient's family, but a social worker is not generally used for these purposes in office psychotherapy.

The role of the relative in a psychotherapeutic program for hospitalized patients has been very well outlined by Gralnick and other therapists associated with High Point Hospital. Gralnick and Schween (1966) treat the patient together with one or more family members in conjoint sessions over a period of time. The therapist continues to see the patient in individual therapy. No individual therapy has ever been discontinued in favor of family therapy. They list six indications for family therapy with psychotic patients:

1. Impasse in the patient's progress, particularly if it is the result of an unsolved conflict between him and a family member.
2. The patient cannot communicate to the relative significant material that needs to be known for the resolution of intrafamily conflicts. He can more easily do so in the presence of the therapist.
3. Presence of obvious symbiotic relationships or other severe pathological relationships.
4. Imminent and premature rupture of marital or other relationships.
5. Nonacceptance of patient's illness.
6. Distorted understanding between patient and relative that may threaten treatment.

Lefebure and colleagues (1958) found relatives useful not only as a source of information, but also because they show how distortions operate in the family.

The authors viewed the attitudes of the relatives as due to anxiety and as defensive operations against such anxiety. The authors mentioned the following as possible causes of anxiety in the relatives: the shame with regard to mental illness; "the dawning awareness that he or she is threatened with having to adjust to, or live with, a psychotic person"; financial difficulties when the family breadwinner is incapacitated by mental illness.

In my experience, predominantly with families of patients treated on an ambulatory basis, the mentioned motives for anxiety existed, but they were not the most frequent ones nor the ones that caused the most profound disturbances. The main form of anxiety, in my experience, was the family's growing feeling of having, because of realistic reasons or distortions, played a role in the patient's illness. The family member may have a strong need to defend himself either from the fear of continuing to make mistakes in his relation with the patient or from the self-accusation or patient's accusation of having played a role in his illness. He may thus assume the following undesirable attitudes: (1) he may become inaccessible, or distant emotionally or physically; (2) he may sabotage the treatment; (3) he may displace hostility on the therapist.

If the therapist, especially in the case of hospitalized patients, succeeds in making the relative feel that he is an ally in a common endeavor, somebody who could help a great deal, the family member may become a very useful person. As Gralnick (1962) says, he stops feeling like *la bête noire*. At the same time that the therapist uncovers the peculiar family styles, he enters into an understanding of the family myths.

The High Point Hospital group, under the leadership of Gralnick (1969), has studied and practiced conjoint family therapy in the hospital setting. Rabiner, Molinsky, and Gralnick (1962) state that in spite of a variety of theoretical orientations, the common aim of family therapy is that of encouraging a maximum interplay between family members, with the therapist serving (1) to decode veiled communications and (2) to provide role clarification for the involved family members while protecting the participating individuals against joint assault. In a hospital, with a majority of schizophrenic patients, Rabiner and co-workers found that as a result of family therapy the patient decreases his feeling of hopelessness in facing the world. The authors have attributed these changes to the patient's following experiences:

1. "If the therapist dares to stand up to the omnipotent parent, perhaps he or she is less formidable than I believed."
2. "If the therapist can make him or her understand me, perhaps I can too," and conversely, "If the therapist cannot understand, no wonder I can't."
3. "If he or she (family member) can accept, without falling apart or viciously retaliating, the therapist's criticism (confrontations, interpretations), then maybe I too can risk self-assertion."
4. Spontaneous remarks by relatives, for example, "I never looked at it that way before," as well as shifts in family alliances, no matter how transient, create the impression that change is possible.

To these four very well formulated possibilities I would add a fifth one that is in my opinion at least equally important: the recognition, with the help of the therapist, of the patient's own distortions and misinterpretations of the relative's actions and words. The distortion is seen immediately *in statu nascendi,* that is, at the moment of origin. If the distortion is an old one, the present example will be the prototype of a series of similar situations that thus will be clarified.

I would also add a sixth possibility: the discussion and resolution of family myths, as described by Ferreira (1963, 1967). Although I do not believe, as Ferreira does, that the psychosis is an exaggeration of the family myths, these myths (or false beliefs accepted or taken for granted as reality) are definitely important in the psychodynamics of schizophrenia, and therefore should be eliminated (see Chapter 8).

Rabiner and co-workers feel quite optimistic about the effect of family therapy in a hospital setting. They state that the involved family members can arrange to come to the hospital at least once a week. The defenses of each family member are not so fixed and desperate as to lead to decompensation upon conjoint exploration of them. Family members and the patient have an unfulfilled mutual need to relate to each other in a more gratifying way. The patient has already developed a sufficient positive transference to the therapist, and so the initial stress of joint family interview is overcome and inquiry into the hidden determinants of the patient's own behavior becomes possible in the joint setting without jeopardizing the existing rapport between him and the therapist.

VIII

Rehabilitation

In a context of intense individual psychotherapy a program of rehabilitation loses the significance and importance that it has in other types of treatment. In therapies other than intense individual psychotherapy, the planning for the patient's future is made with the help of a social worker, vocational counselor, psychiatrists who discharge the patient from the hospital, and other persons. At times a rehabilitation team consisting of a psychiatrist, a social caseworker, and a vocational or rehabilitation counselor, plans the future activities and setting of the patient. The assets and liabilities of the patient and the opportunities presented by his family and life situation are evaluated. Important in this respect are the book by Black (1963) and the article by Braceland (1966). Braceland describes in a succinct and clear way the patient's rehabilitation in relation to the therapeutic community, day hospital, halfway house, occupational rehabilitation, expatients' clubs, and family care.

The rehabilitation procedures for patients treated with physical therapies or for chronic schizophrenics who have been hospitalized for long periods of time generally investigate such problems as the ability of the patient to adjust at a behavior level, to be able to support himself or to engage in some kind of useful occupation, to socialize without difficulties. Although these goals are legitimate, they are inadequate for the patient treated with intense psychotherapy. Rehabilitation is part of the psychotherapy itself, except that instead of stopping at a managerial level, or at a level of acceptable or nonacceptable behavior, it goes deeper and examines the psychodynamic essence of the patient's difficulty or progress in his process of maturation. The tendencies to withdraw and to be passive, or to be hostile or too forward, are definitely discussed. Any interpersonal relation that becomes the source of difficulty is examined and clarified.

Termination of psychotherapy is inconceivable if the patient has not yet found his place in the community and does not yet feel reintegrated. Thus there is no need of rehabilitation at the end of psychotherapy: the patient must have been rehabilitated before therapy ends. He must have improved his personal relationships and must be able to prevent the social crises that may lead to hospitalization whether these crises occur within the family or in society at large.

The problem of whether the patient should be considered rehabilitated when he has acquired economic independence is to be solved in view of other circumstances: the age of the patient, the physical health, his previous status, the length of illness, and so on. However, if he cannot become independent, it is desirable that he become at least less dependent (Wing, 1967).

In connection with rehabilitation in the community, we must mention the very interesting book by Pasamanick, Scarpitti and Dinitz (1967). Unfortunately this book does not deal with patients treated with intense psychotherapy. The authors found that the group of patients treated with drug therapy who were returned home immediately and were not hospitalized did much better than those who were hospitalized. Thus rehabilitation was started as soon as the patient was diagnosed as a schizophrenic. This book, in my opinion, strikes a hard blow at hospitalization. The authors have demonstrated that home care for schizophrenic patients is feasible and that drug therapy was effective in preventing hospitalization. The authors state that "in all of the many specific measures, home care patients were functioning as well as or better than the hospital control cases. If counseling and appropriate utilization of community resources were used, probably the results would have been even more satisfactory." Of course one would like to ascertain whether the patients were really recovered or whether the recovery was only symptomatic. Although I am working from another angle, I myself long ago reached the conclusion reached by Pasamanick and colleagues that only part of the patients who are hospitalized actually need hospitalization.

CHAPTER

40

Two Cases Treated with Intensive Psychotherapy

In this chapter I shall report the cases of two patients who have been treated with intensive and prolonged psychotherapy. The psychodynamics and the psychostructure of the symptomatology will be interpreted, and the psychotherapeutic procedure will be described in greater detail than in cases reported so far in this book.

What follows is not a mere presentation of two cases but also a discussion of certain therapeutic issues. These two cases are not the most typical, nor the most successful. They are chosen because of the impact they had on the psychotherapeutic evolution of the author and because of their didactic value.

Geraldine

First episode. When I first saw Geraldine, she was a 32-year-old woman who was slowly recovering from an acute psychotic attack, the second in her life. She was withdrawn, thin, and looked much younger than her age.

While on vacation, far away from home, she became acutely ill and was hospitalized in the nearest state hospital. She received thirteen electric shock treatments, improved somewhat, and was discharged at the request of her family. After her discharge she was treated by me. The patient's history and symptomatology are so rich in content that it would require much more space than is available to give a very detailed account of them. In this first section only a brief history as given by Geraldine herself and a description and interpretation of her first psychotic episode will be presented, as it was reconstructed during therapy. The second episode and her psychotherapy will be described in the subsequent section.

Geraldine was born of upper-middle-class Protestant parents of Anglo-Saxon stock. Her father came from a well-to-do family that had been prominent in the social and political activities of the community. He was considered a rather eccentric man who, instead of working in the usual way, would spend all his time in impractical literary and philosophical pursuits. His writings, however, were so unappealing and difficult to understand that, although praised by several people, they were never published. He was a restless soul and forced the family to move from place to place. For a few years the whole family had to live on a boat, traveling between the Caribbean islands. The family owned, however, a big, isolated farm, where they always went after the other temporary residences. The father was quite attached to the patient and prior to his death, which occurred when the patient was 25, requested that she edit and publish his writings posthumously.

The mother was a rather passive woman who was torn by ambivalent feelings toward her husband when he was alive. On one side she professed to admire his extreme brightness, his culture, his intellectual and spiritual aspirations. On the other side she resented having to put up with his peculiarities. She resented his lack of practicality, his unwillingness to work, his wanting to live in isolation, and so on. Geraldine heard from an aunt that even shortly after her marriage her mother was unhappy and contemplated a divorce, but she was already pregnant with Geraldine and decided to stick to her husband. It was obvious from many facts that cannot be reported here that she resented Geraldine because it was on account of her that she had to stay with her husband.

When, two years later, however, she became pregnant again and gave birth to a boy, she accepted this child very well. Most probably by that time she had decided that she had to live in that marital situation and that within it she had to find a purpose to her life. She found this purpose in John, her second child. The family thus became split into two sides, as if by a schism, as described by Lidz. John was the mother's child and Geraldine was her father's child. However, the father was distant, removed, always absorbed in his philosophical pursuits; and Geraldine too had to be taken care of by her mother, who never found anything good in her and constantly criticized her. Geraldine was never made to feel sure that she was capable of doing the right thing. She could always have done better, according to her mother; she had better reveal her intentions to her mother before doing anything. Geraldine did so, but she never got any approval. The result was that she felt her mother was a useful person to have around to prevent her from making mistakes, but at the same time what a nagger, what an intruder, what a burden! Geraldine never accepted the values of her mother, her way of interpreting the world; and although she was going through the motions of obeying, she inwardly rebelled. She never accepted her mother, she never integrated her as a part of herself. John, on the other hand, always accepted his mother. Even during the time that Geraldine was in therapy, John and his mother were very close, lived together on the family's farm, went on vacation together. John did not seem to be interested in girls and gave almost the impression that after his father's death he had taken the father's place.

Geraldine's predicament was made worse because her relations with her father were not normal either. On one side, she appreciated his tenderness and consideration; she remembered with affection when he gave her a little turtle, and the long philosophical discussions she had with him, and how she could express her thoughts to him and did not need to be as humble and submissive as she was with her mother. On the other side, her father, because of his peculiarities, did not facilitate her having contacts with anybody else. When they were living on the boat, Geraldine could not even go to school; she was taught by her parents and had no playmates except her brother. It was a typical ingrown family. They were also isolated when they lived on the farm. Animals were Geraldine's childhood companions. It was interesting to see how restricted the population of her dreams was, until the third year of therapy. Only mother, father, John, and squirrels, bears, deer, porcupines, turtles, and so forth used to appear in her dreams.

The father told her his personal ideas about life, which were completely accepted by the patient. For instance, sex, according to the father, was only for reproduction. Even in her late teens and in her twenties, Geraldine was not allowed by him to wear lipstick because, as he would say, "If you wear it, men do not think of you, but only of one part of your body." Which part of the body it would be, however, Geraldine was not even sure. When she came for treatment at the age of 32, she showed a great ignorance about sexual matters. The father prescribed a very rigid, laconic, almost monastic way of living. The important fact is that whereas Geraldine resisted her mother, she was willing to accept her father and his values; but to do this would require a tremendous effort, and giving up a great part of her life. In addition, she was disturbed at times by the impracticality of her father; and occasionally she would feel that her mother was right and that her father deserved contempt.

It is easy to see that Geraldine grew up in a very confused environment. Essentially the same environmental climate prevailed in her adolescence and youth. Although she did fairly well scholastically, she always had difficulties in establishing friendship with members of either sex; and when she wanted to work, she had vocational difficulties. At 22 she obtained an M.A. degree in journalism. She had a moderate talent for writing, drawing, and painting and had several jobs, but she was never very satisfied. Her private life was characterized by several crushes on young men, but she felt they were never reciprocated. After the father's death she took a year off for the purpose of editing her father's writings. It proved to be a difficult task. When she tried to have these writings published, she met rejection all over. She started to write short stories for children, but they too were always rejected. In October 1951 she stopped all other activities and became an ardent and enthusiastic campaigner during the presidential campaign.

During the campaign activities at the party's local headquarters she met a young man, Gregory, with whom she became easily infatuated. One day, however, she became aware that Gregory was interested in another girl. During that week she had realized that all her ideas about conducting the campaign had been rejected; coincidentally during the same week some publishers had returned her manuscripts. All this rapidly put Geraldine in a state of anxiety and depression, and finally panic. She had the feeling that something strange or bad was happening to her; she moved from her room to a hotel, had the sensation that people were talking disparagingly about her, and had thoughts about dying and being reborn again.

Because she felt that she was not improving, she telephoned her mother and told her that she was very sick and that she should come to see her. Her mother and brother came and took her to the farm. For a few days the patient quieted down, but one day she became very upset, and the mother and brother decided to take her to a psychiatric hospital.

The following are certain experiences that Geraldine described to me during the treatment. As I said before, her symptomatology was so rich in content that only a few samples of it may be reported here.

While she was being taken by car to the hospital, she knew that she was going to be committed but felt that her mother, not she, was insane. As John drove, she saw him as a mad monster, a hollow shell of a man whose voice reverberated eerily in his empty skull, a mindless automaton. The first few days that she was in the hospital she felt she had died; as a matter of fact, one day she heard "the ruffled drums of a large military funeral in her honor." Lifting her hand, she waved to her admirers.

At the same time she thought that her brother was in control of the hospital. He and her mother had a little room at the top of the building, could see her through a television, and could plan tortures for her. At the same time that she was a prisoner, Geraldine felt that telepathically she could keep in contact with the world and could send messages to both presidential candidates.

One morning she looked in a mirror and saw in her face negroid features. She saw very vividly her nose as broad, her eyes and skin as dark, and her curly hair as fitting the negroid picture. Here is a verbatim account of how she experienced the episode: "Agony seems a tame word to describe my feelings at finding myself a member of a race that unfortunately is often treated despicably in this country. I saw the other patients, as well as the hospital staff, as all becoming negroid, to make up a Negro community behind bars. They seemed to change before my eyes. I found that one eye saw people dark, the other eye saw them light."

She also felt that the hospital was surrounded by Negroes. They were sitting in cars in the streets adjacent to the hospital, waiting for a signal. She did not dare look out the window, but she knew they were there. They were waiting for a signal. At a given signal they would go to the farm where her mother and John lived. The farm was a new Garden of Eden, where mother and John were living in sin. The Negroes, after receiving the signal, would go there, burn the farm, and lynch mother and John. She was extremely afraid lest the Negroes interpret anything as the signal. If a patient lit a cigarette, she was afraid that it would be interpreted as the signal to go to the farm. She made up her mind to prevent at all costs this signal from reaching the "flaming hordes."

One night, while she was locked in her cell, she stood at the window with her arms raised to make herself a target, shaped like a cross. She began to think of herself as a Christ, sacrificing herself for others, particularly for her mother and John. She thought of the shot through her head as "a shot heard round the world," an incident that would cause sorrow throughout the world. Her true nobility would be recognized at last.

One of the delusions that had remained most vividly in her mind was the following: Robert, a man for whom she had had a strong infatuation in the past, had come to the door of the hospital and had asked for her. He had a golden wedding ring in his pocket for her. This ring would be the "key" to her illness. But the door was kept closed. Robert was not allowed to come in. She "heard" him ask for her at the door. He knew that she was sick, but nevertheless he persisted in remaining and trying to save her. She heard the Negro mob opposing him, and she feared the mob would kill him, stuff him into a garbage can, and bring him to her, dead. "How about a cold Robert sandwich?" a member of the mob asked her telepathically. She replied telepathically that if someone must be dead, she would rather be taken dead to Robert.

The patient was given insulin treatment, and she made a quick recovery as far as the first acute episode was concerned.

Before proceeding with the rest of her history, we shall stop to interpret this episode.

It is not strange that the breakdown came at a culminating point, when the self-esteem was so low, the feeling of inadequacy and defeat so great, the sensation of being alone and unloved so tragic and profound. It is interesting to see how, during the acute episode, there were attempts to reproduce the early conflicts and to solve them.

But in order to solve the conflicts the patient had to resort to schizophrenic cognition. The acute episode shows abundant examples of concrete representations of feelings and thoughts. The predominant law of thought followed here is Von Domarus's principle; thoughts are then perceptualized and resemble poetic metaphors.

Gregory, the man who abandons her, is a symbolic reproduction of her father, who, first because of his uncertain loyalty and second because of his death, cannot be a reliable source of security to the patient. The patient goes for protection to the farm, but the farm is the place where all her conflicts originated. Mother and John live in sin and plot against her. But this is not completely fantastic; in a certain way it is even true. Mother and John have always been on the opposite side of the schism and have criticized her and made her feel inferior, lonely, unloved. After the acute episode and later during the first stage of the treatment, she could not understand why she had such a preposterous idea that her mother and her brother were living in sin. But to us this idea does not seem so preposterous. We do not mean that the mother and John had sexual relations, but that they were extremely close. Even the relatives had commented that the mother and John acted like a married couple. This idea of their living in sin was the culmination or dramatization of the closeness Geraldine felt they had, closeness that contrasted with the distance or hostility they had for Geraldine. Thus, although these ideas about mother and brother could be interpreted as a delusional reenactment of an early Oedipal ideation, they also had a partial basis in the current situation.

The patient felt that her mother, with the help of her brother, was controlling her thoughts telepathically from the roof of the building. This again was a concrete representation of the way she felt throughout her life when her mother, with her criticisms, disapproval, and by imposing her will, did not allow her to think freely, to make decisions, and in a certain way thus controlled Geraldine's thoughts and tortured her.

The patient actually saw John as a "hollow shell of a man whose voice reverberated eerily in his empty shell, a mindless automaton." She meant this literally, but this seems to be an accurate metaphorical description of John, the automaton put in motion by the mother.

The combined application of Von Domarus's principle and of perceptualization of the concept is seen in all these delusions (see Chapter 16). For instance, Geraldine looks at herself in the mirror and sees herself becoming a Negro. First we have the application of Von Domarus's principle: she is worthless, "like a Negro"; thus she is a Negro. Second we have the perceptualization of the concept. She thinks she is a Negro; she actually sees herself as a Negro. It is interesting that when she recovered, Geraldine did not seem to have any prejudice against blacks. But during the acute episode she borrowed the prejudices of society. The other patients were also "worthless," and they became Negroes. The hostile, revengeful world outside was also populated by Negroes. She was going to save mother and John by dying for them, and by doing so she would reestablish her self-esteem. She would be a saint, a heroine; at least, in death she would be accepted and her work would be recognized.

Robert came to the door of the hospital to save her. Who is Robert? Again he is a personification of a part of her father, the part that was perceived by Geraldine as the rescuer and as the love object. But the Negroes, that is, the horrible world, wanted to take Robert away from her and kill him, as her father was taken away. Robert had the golden ring, symbol of marriage; but in the delusion the ring was the key to her cure because it was the symbol of love. Notice here the paleologic use of the word *key*. Robert is at the door of the hospital and has the key to open the door, to set her free. There was an identification here between the key that opens the door and the key that, by being a marriage ring, will remove the illness with an act of love.

Second episode and treatment. After the patient completed a series of insulin comas, the symptoms disappeared and the patient was discharged. For a period of two years Geraldine had several jobs but did not adjust to any of them. She was doing what she was supposed to do with some resentment, but felt that she had creative possibilities and was wasting her life with trivial matters.

Finally she found a job as a secretary in a college. But there too the situation did not improve. From time to time she had the impression that the other employees were talking about her. Occasionally she had the impression that the boss was talking about her and was saying, "I want her to get out of here."

Geraldine used to go dancing at a French club, but nobody she was interested in seemed to acknowledge her presence. She was left alone, nailed to the chair or isolated in a corner of the room; or she was monopolized by a queer fellow who would not leave her alone for the rest of the evening.

During the first part of the summer of 1955 the mother and an uncle invited her to join them in a trip to the West. That trip was a torture. She felt no gratitude for the invitation. To be near her mother tired her. Mother did not openly criticize her, but Geraldine had the impression that the mother was inwardly criticizing her, even when she was not speaking. At the end of the trip she felt exhausted, as if she had been, not on vacation, but in a concentration camp.

In September she decided to go to a folk dance summer camp. It was there that her difficulties became overt. At the end of the first week she started to realize that she was becoming sick again, and she tried to resist the illness as much as she could. She could not sleep, nor could she eat. She was all alone, often walking in the woods. At times she imagined herself to be a beautiful butterfly who flew over the grass. Occasionally she had the idea that a policeman was among the guests and that he thought she was a spy. Again she had the fantasy that Henry, one of the vacationers, toward whom she felt attracted, would save her in case of need.

One day she had the impression that a camper was going to molest a little girl. She went toward him and punched him in the face. When this man reported the episode to the main office, Geraldine was examined by a doctor, who suggested immediate hospitalization in a psychiatric hospital.

The patient remembered very little about this second hospitalization. Perhaps this amnesia was due to the fact that she was treated with ten electric shock treatments, whereas during the first episode she had had insulin therapy, which generally does not leave a marked amnesia. In spite of this amnesia, Geraldine remembered some fragments of this second episode.

While, from the window of her cell, she was looking at the bushes that surrounded the hospital, she believed that some soldiers were hiding behind the bushes, ready to free her because she was their leader. She heard the soldiers give one another instructions. When the delusions became more definite, the bushes actually became soldiers, ready to fight in order to free her. Even cigarette butts that were collected in some trays near the door of the hospital were potential persons. She watched the trays, waiting for the moment when the butts would become persons and come to help her.

It is not necessary to report other details about this second hospitalization. The patient improved up to a certain point. The most acute symptoms disappeared, although hallucinations and some delusional ideas remained. The mother and the brother exerted pressure on Geraldine's doctor to have her discharged from the hospital. The doctor agreed, provided the family would make arrangements to have Geraldine treated privately.

Psychotherapy. It is at this time that I enter the picture. When I saw Geraldine for the first time, she was 32 years old. She was self-absorbed and apparently apathetic. I would have thought from her appearance that she was 25 or 26. She did not care about her appearance, was wearing no lipstick or powder, and was dressed in a peculiar, old-fashioned way. Two warts on her cheek made her face even less attractive.

Her mother and brother, who accompanied her, did not make a better impression. Although well-to-do people, they were very poorly and cheaply dressed. They appeared to me either stunned by the events or lacking in manners and savoir faire. They were tall and thin and had a strange, Byzantine look. However, at first impression they appeared to be simple people who were interested in the patient.

It was decided that I would treat Geraldine three times a week, that she would continue to live in her apartment in a town near New York, and that the mother would live with her and accompany her to my office.

When I saw the patient for the first time, I realized that she had not at all recovered from the second psychotic episode, and I wondered whether she was already a chronic schizophrenic. Against this diagnosis was the fact that in the hospital she had made considerable progress, the visual hallucinations had disappeared, as had many delusions. What still remained were auditory hallucinations, some delusional ideas, and withdrawal and apparent apathy.

In a certain way I felt she was distant, far away from me. At first I thought that the fact that she came from an environment so dissimilar to mine contributed to this feeling. She was Anglo-Saxon, from an old family of landowners. Actually what contributed to this sense of distance was not her origin but her withdrawal, her face deprived of mimic movements, almost cold. And yet her face also had an imploring, hard-to-describe quality. Behind that blank mask of apathy was fear, which I sensed and saw. I must add that I felt right away a wish to be of help to this human being.

During the first few sessions, if gently encouraged the patient answered questions, although slowly and with the fear of making mistakes every time she opened her mouth. However, I was the one who was talking most of the time, and she was listening attentively. At times in her silence, in her expression, in her attentive attitude, she seemed to say, "You rich, I poor. I want to draw from your richness, but I am so afraid. And my fear is stronger than my poverty." But in talking with her about topics of neutral character, or about myself, I tried to diminish her fear, to make her accept my presence and to make her less afraid of what the next instant or the next question would make her face. I must add that during the whole treatment of this patient no drugs at all were used.

Later in a diary Geraldine described our first meetings in her own words:

> I liked Silvano's relaxed, informal manner, and I had the feeling he knew what he was about. I was on edge and scared. I thought he would think very poorly of me as I told him about myself. I did not wish him to think poorly of me, but my wish to recover was stronger than my wish for approval. I gained confidence as I saw that he did not think me so terrible, so sinful, or so demented as I had expected. In fact, he said little that was disapproving. At first I thought he must actually disapprove of me; but as time passed, I saw that this was not so. Later on I was able to accept his telling me he thought I was making a mistake in this or that. But as I remember, in the beginning he did not particularly disapprove even in that way. I think he was wise. I have never been particularly gracious about criticism of myself.

Between the patient and me relatedness was soon established. For the first time she felt able to talk openly. And in reality she was very eloquent and expressive. At this point what she was telling me referred either to her auditory hallucinations or to her relations with her mother. For the first time she was able to reveal her animosity, hostility, and contempt for the mother. It was the mother who always had bitterly criticized her actions and her intentions. It was the mother who had not allowed her to have faith in herself. It was the mother who had always opposed the spiritual values that the father and the patient appreciated so much.

From the beginning of therapy I debated within myself whether it was advisable for Geraldine to live with her mother. How could two people with such antagonism for each other live together? Still, Geraldine was too sick to live alone; there were no relatives or friends in New York or vicinity with whom she could stay, and I was reluctant to hospitalize her. I decided that perhaps the best of the possibilities available to Geraldine was to live with her mother.

The more the therapy proceeded, the less frequently the hallucinations occurred. I became aware of an important fact. The more the patient could talk about the mother and about the criticisms that she was expecting from her, the less frequently the hallucinations recurred. Geraldine became aware that now it was she who criticized the mother. The hallucinations, which allegedly were the neighbors' voices, were more or less elaborate transformations of what she expected mother would say.

Her steaming off concerning the mother diminished the need for these hallucinations. Moreover, she found in me not only a listener, but also a supporter. For the first time in her life she had succeeded in convincing another person that there was something wrong with the way her mother had treated her and that her criticisms of her mother were not without basis, even if here and there she was altering and editing the memory of facts and events.

In a few months Geraldine lost almost all the hallucinatory phenomena, and I was jubilant over the results of the treatment.

At this point Geraldine started to say that she felt much better, that there was no need for mother to live with her. The apartment was very small. It consisted of only one and a half rooms. Mother could go back to the farm and could come to visit her from time to time. At this point I allowed myself to be convinced that I should support her desire, especially because my experience with other patients had taught me that separation from a hated member of the family is sooner or later greatly beneficial.

In this case, however, two days after the mother left the hallucinations returned more strongly than before. Now the neighbors were actually screaming that the patient was a bad woman, a whore, a worthless person. Geraldine believed in the reality of these hallucinations and tried to explain why they had occurred. For instance, the neighbors had seen her talking to a man, and now they believed that she was having sexual relations with him for monetary compensation.

In my opinion the worsening of the condition was precipitated by the separation from mother. First of all, although Geraldine hated her mother, she felt reassured and protected by her presence. This is a dilemma often to be coped with, not only in schizophrenia, but also in all serious psychogenic disorders: the person who is experienced as destructive is also experienced as the sustaining person. The mother is seen as malevolent but also as strong. The patient is weak and in need of strength from somebody else. The mother is malevolent, but without her there would be nobody; there would be interpersonal emptiness. Without mother, who will protect the patient from the malevolent replicas of the mother, who populates the world? In the second place, periods of solitude and of increased introversion facilitate the occurrence of hallucinations, just as sensory isolation experiments do. The psychological barrier of the schizophrenic and the actual isolation from other people facilitate the occurrence of hallucinatory phenomena.

In the third, and perhaps more important, place, as long as the mother was there, in her physical presence, in the act of criticizing or rather of having the intention of criticizing her, as Geraldine believed, the patient did not need fantastic voices to express those criticisms.

At this point I decided to take a step backward, and I suggested that the mother come back. When the mother returned, the hallucinations persisted, although they diminished in number. The irritation caused by the contact with the mother was even more openly experienced and was reported in the sessions.

At this point an event occurred that I would have expected to have harmful consequences, but it did not. While they were returning home from my office after a session, the patient and her mother were crossing Central Park when they were held up by a black man who stole their pocketbooks. Because I remembered Geraldine's past delusions about blacks, which had occurred during the first psychotic episode, I was afraid that this event would rekindle old complexes, but it was not so. Geraldine was shaken but not thrown. The blacks of the real world, even when it happens that among them there is a thief, are different from the fantastic Negroes who are evoked only by a symbolic need.

At this point of the treatment, in spite of the fact that the symptoms persisted, Geraldine became capable of examining and discussing her past life, and also of reinterpreting it. We thus reexamined some of the events that had preceded the first psychotic episode and those that had occurred during the episode itself, events already described and discussed in the first section of this report. It was especially at this stage of treatment that the relation with the mother was explored in detail. Geraldine's life had been an emotional desert, where the only inhabitants were the four members of the family, among whom towered the figure of the mother, like that of a monster ready to terrorize the patient, to insult her, to demolish her and undermine her faith in herself. The other members of the family were pygmies in comparison to the mother. And the only other living beings that were not frightening were not human beings: they were the bunnies, the hares, the squirrels, the little birds of the woods and farm.

As I have already expressed in this book, I have asked myself many times, not only in relation to the case of Geraldine, but to many others, whether the mother of the schizophrenic is really the monster that the patient at a certain stage of therapy portrays, or whether the image of the mother has undergone a transformation that is part of the patient's delusional experience. For instance, I had seen

Geraldine's mother a few times; and although to me too she appeared to be an unusual person, I noticed in her concern and interest, not the malevolent attitude that Geraldine had spoken about. Which was the right evaluation, mine or Geraldine's? I realized that my contacts with the mother were superficial in comparison to those she had with Geraldine. On the other hand I felt that Geraldine perceived as salient parts some characteristics of her mother and blew them up to a large degree. Also the mother became the depository of all the negative qualities that the family as a unity and in its individual members manifested.

Let us look again at Geraldine's family. The father failed in his role of father because of his peculiarities and lack of interest in the practical aspects of life. But Geraldine defended the father, and the responsibility for what was negative in him was attributed to the mother. The father, she explained, remained remote because he could not be close to such a horrible woman as mother was. John, the brother, had not been a good playmate for Geraldine, but how could he have been? He was the preferred child of the mother, a private possession of mother. In other words, everything that was negative was focused on the mother. The responsibility of others was diminished and the role of the mother was magnified. Certainly there was no equilibrium or harmony in Geraldine's family, but her seeing the family constellation in such unbalanced form increased her sensation of disequilibrium. On the other hand, a state of equilibrium had been reached by mother, father, and John. Here, in my opinion, resides one of the reasons why some psychiatrists praise to the skies schizophrenic patients. In fact, we cannot but have admiration for Geraldine for not accepting that sick equilibrium. The mother, a disappointed, frustrated woman; the father, a misfit; the brother, an appendix of mother, a man who was not interested in any woman except mother, an automaton put into motion by mother. These three people were the failures, the ones who were vanquished by life. They had avoided the visible defeats that Geraldine had undergone—if we can call the two psychotic attacks defeats—but their victories had been less than pyrrhic. They had reduced their life to the desolation of the desert.

Geraldine did not want that desert. She could not accept that immense reduction or distortion of the human experience that mother and brother had accepted.

Geraldine continued to hallucinate. It was from her that I learned many things about hallucinations and that therapeutic technique, described in Chapter 36, that since then I have applied to many patients. Before then I thought that hallucinations could not be corrected or controlled and that they could disappear only when the patient was cured.

First of all, a little episode took place. Geraldine was accepted as a member of the choir in her church. One day the director required that she sing alone. The patient tried to sing but her voice came out feeble and toneless. With the exception of a young man who was there, all the choir members seemed to whisper, "This woman will ruin us." Geraldine ran away, went home, and there she heard the neighbors talking about her bad performance. The following day by phone she gave her resignation to the director, who seemed to accept it gladly. The following Sunday in the same church she heard the voice of a man saying, "She is here again." When the choir started to sing the hymns, well known to her, she burst into tears and ran away from the church. The hallucinations about the neighbors continued.

Geraldine believed in the reality of her hallucinations. From her account of them I realized that they occurred when she expected to be criticized. For instance, in the choir she expected the director to criticize her, and the alleged voices from the choir members came to criticize her. She went home, lonely and melancholy, with the feeling of being an inferior and blameworthy person, a person lacking confidence in herself and despairing about her own life. She expected the neighbors to blame her, and there they were: she could hear them in the act of criticizing her and speaking against her. Every day, as soon as she expected to hear them, she heard them. She was putting herself in what since then I have called *the listening attitude*. Under my guidance Geraldine became capable of distinguishing two stages: that of the listening attitude and that of the hallucinatory experience. At first she strongly protested and denied the existence of the two stages, but later she made a little concession. She said, "I was thinking that they would talk about me, and there they were, talking about me."

A few sessions later, however, another step forward was made. Geraldine was able to recognize the brief interval that elapsed between the expectation of the voices and the voices. At first she insisted that this sequence was purely coincidental, but finally she saw the connection: she herself was putting herself into the listening attitude. Then she would hear. Eventually she recognized that she was putting herself into that attitude when she was in a negative mood, for instance, when she had suffered a defeat, or an alleged defeat, as in the choir; when she felt irreparably alone and lonely, abandoned and without hope. In these circumstances she was almost automatically finding ways to exchange this feeling with the feeling that she was not inferior but rather a victim, the object of the hostility and malevolence of others. In other words, a feeling that made her accuse and condemn herself was transformed into another one in which the others—the neighbors—were accusing and condemning her. When she felt condemned and surrounded by hostility, she expected an auditory proof of this hostility. When the patient became able to recognize the relation between her mood and her putting herself in the listening attitude, great progress was made. She did not envision herself any longer as a passive victim, as a recipient of malevolence coming from others, but as a person who played an active role in what she was experiencing.

Geraldine recovered from hallucinatory experiences almost completely. Occasionally a hallucination had the tendency to come back, but she succeeded in controlling it. For instance, once she went to a dance organized by a friend. Nobody asked her to dance. She felt humiliated and depressed, and at a certain moment she was almost on the point of hearing a voice that criticized her, but she controlled herself. As she used to say, Silvano had taught her to recognize hallucinations, and she could no longer indulge in the luxury of having them. As a matter of fact, once the hallucinations would start, one could never know when they could be checked. They could multiply and give vent to a full psychotic episode.

Freedom from hallucinations and other symptoms did not mean the end of Geraldine's basic conflict. As a matter of fact, as we have seen in Chapter 36, the transformation of psychotic symptoms into neurotic ones or awareness of the conflict brings about more anxiety. However, anxiety that has not undergone the psychotic transformation is more easily shared with the therapist, if relatedness has been established. Geraldine knew that I was with her to share her aloneness, loneliness, disappointments, serious doubts about herself and her future. Eventually we had to analyze the origin of these negative attitudes toward life.

Geraldine understood in reference to her personal history the psychodynamic developments that I illustrated in Part Two. She saw the intrafamily war that took place in her childhood in the conflicts of all the members of the family. She understood how she reinforced the negative aspects and came to build an extremely negative image of mother and of herself. In the second part of childhood she built a schizoid type of personality that permitted a partial repression of the suffering of the first period. She understood how in adolescence and youth she came to the conception and feeling that the promise of life was not going to be fulfilled and how she sustained repeated attacks on her self-esteem. Eventually, when the injury could no longer be sustained, it elicited a revival of the conflicts of early childhood, which had been buried and blended with the old injuries. The psychosis resulted: a need to project what she had introjected. She was at war with the world. The world underwent a transformation.

Throughout the treatment Geraldine's dreams received much consideration. Her dreams were very simple, and much easier to understand than those of neurotic patients. Quite often they reproduced the conflicts with her mother. Here are some examples. The first example is a dream that occurred during the sixth month of therapy.

I found a turtle's egg, and felt very fond of the baby turtle developing inside of it. I showed it to mother. "Break it," said mother.

"No!" I cried. "That would destroy the little turtle." Before I could stop her, she cracked it, and the poor little half-developed turtle slid out. He tried to eat the yolk and somehow to save himself. Almost crying, I ran with him to a biologist and implored him to save the little turtle. But it was no use; he would die. I felt enraged at mother's cruelty.

Another dream:

Mother, John, and I had rented a house with several acres of ground. A formal garden behind the house was, in my opinion, badly planned. I knew it would be lovely if allowed to return to nature, with rhododendrons and trees growing at random, and I said so. But mother said, "It must be kept formal." She placed furniture in it and planted straight rows of daffodils until it was a mess.

Another dream:

Mother accompanied me on a date with a very attractive young man. We were in a night club. My date said, "The music is starting. Let's dance."

"We really ought to leave," said mother.

"We were just going to dance," said I.

"Come," said mother. "It's nine o'clock!"

So he went out to the car, and I stopped to powder my nose. When I got mother into the powder room, I said furiously, "What was the idea? He had just asked me to dance! Why did you have to spoil everything? Did you see how he looked? He won't ever ask again!"

"Oh, did he ask you to dance?" asked mother, her eyes widening in surprise.

"You heard him," said I coldly. "He was sitting next to you!"

"I didn't hear a thing," said mother, leaving to go out to the car.

A moment later I arrived at the curb to find the car and its occupants gone. I guess mother couldn't wait, I decided. I was stranded. I had no money. I went back into the night club to think of what to do.

I found a little girl baby, and I picked her up. She was unhappy and wouldn't eat. You'll eat when you see your new little brother, I reasoned.

I took her into the next room. Mother was absorbed with a baby boy. Mother didn't even look up. I handed a cup of warm milk to the baby girl. The little girl wouldn't take the milk and made no response of any kind.

These dreams are so simple! The identifications, like the one with the embryo turtle in the first dream and with the little girl in the third dream, are so easy to understand, and the reproduction of life scenes is so realistic, as in the second dream, one may wonder whether the patient really dreamt in this way or whether these were fantasies in a half-awake, half-sleeping state. My work with Geraldine and other patients has convinced me that dreams of this type really do occur and are common in schizophrenics. The dream-work is often, although not always, less pronounced than in dreams of neurotic or normal people.

The state of relatedness, the direct attack of the symptoms, and psychodynamic interpretation produced progressive improvement. Geraldine changed both physically and psychologically. When I was looking at her or thinking about her, Dante's verses used to come to my mind:

> Quali i fioretti dal notturno gelo
> chinati e chiusi
> poi che il sol gl'imbianca
> si drizzan tutti aperti in loro stelo . . .
>
> As flowerets, by the nightly chill bent down and closed,
> erect themselves all open on their stems when the sun
> whitens them . . .

So did she, Geraldine.

Physically, and this is something that I have noticed in many recovering schizophrenics, Geraldine lost her youthful appearance. She started to show her age. In spite of this aging she had a much more attractive appearance. She gained weight, started to use lipstick, and had those two warts removed from her face. Her hair, which was perhaps precociously gray, was well combed and conferred a certain charm to her appearance.

The menstrual cycle, which was always delayed and lasted approximately thirty-five days, shortened and was reduced to thirty or thirty-one days. A cycle of twenty-eight days was not obtained.

Geraldine worked as a secretary in a college. Soon she started to notice that men paid attention to her and that Paul, a young engineer, had an infatuation for her, although he was a few years younger. Paul was a young man from a Protestant, traditionalist family. Intellectually Paul seemed to me to be somewhat less endowed than Geraldine. He had many good qualities, and his feelings for the patient were sincere. Geraldine experienced no anxiety in his presence. A year later Paul and Geraldine were married. I was invited to the wedding, and I accepted the invitation.

In this regard, I must say that many therapists refuse these invitations because they feel they must remain outside the real life of the patient. This stand seems to me untenable with patients who had a psychosis. The therapist is an important and intimate person, and it is artificial and harmful to maintain a professional barrier.

At this point Geraldine told me, "I connect myself more and more to the world, and I become more and more distant from mother." With the word *distant* at this point she meant "less in need of being angry at her." Actually a partial reacceptance and reconciliation with mother took place.

Contrary to what I would have expected, sexual relations were satisfactory starting with the honeymoon. The reader may have surmised that Geraldine was a virgin until her wedding night. In spite of the fact that she was 35 when she got married, she experienced vaginal orgasms immediately. Some psychiatrists, who believe strongly in Rado's theory of unhedonia, are skeptical when former schizophrenics report full sexual gratification. These therapists are inclined to believe that the orgasm did not really take place, but was a fantasy of the patient. Maybe the patient is hallucinating again. My clinical experiences with former schizophrenics have convinced me that this is nonsense. Former schizophrenics are indeed able to experience sexual pleasure fully. Some of them, including Geraldine, have ridiculed me when I have put in doubt their assertions and have given me unquestionable details.

Relations between Geraldine and Paul were excellent from every point of view. The symptoms had all disappeared. Socially and in her relation with her husband nothing abnormal was reported. I was completely satisfied with the results, except for the following facts. A year after her marriage Geraldine became pregnant. Pregnancy and childbirth were normal. However, a few days after the birth, while she was still in the hospital, Geraldine saw a group of nurses talking to the elderly chief nurse, and she heard voices again, which she recognized as hallucinatory. The chief nurse was telling the other nurses that Geraldine would not be a good mother.

For a second Geraldine chilled inside, but she was not overcome by the episode, because within a fraction of a second she realized that she had had an hallucinatory experience. The rest of her puerperal state was normal. The following summer another abnormal experience occurred. While she was vacationing in a pension, on a day that Paul had gone back to the city to work and had left her alone with the child, she felt that the landlady, the owner of the pension, was talking against her. Again she acquired insight within a fraction of a second. In spite of these episodes, which were isolated, Geraldine and Paul found satisfaction in living together; she acknowledged no new symptoms and expressed desire that treatment be terminated.

Geraldine had come to me for five years and was eager to stop. Moreover, Paul had been offered a good position in a distant state. Thus treatment was interrupted.

At this point we must attempt some conclusions. Can I consider Geraldine completely recovered and immune from future attacks? The answer is "No." Although it is true that she has acquired insight into her problems, that her personality has blossomed in many areas, and that the basic gratifications of life have been fulfilled, she still retains a certain vulnerability. When she is in treatment, she is able to recognize the pathological nature of some experiences that occasionally recur in specific situations that reproduce the old anxiety. However, we cannot be sure that if she is confronted with difficult life situations, she will not succumb again. The episode after the birth of the child and the episode with the landlady indicate that some experiences are able to reactivate in her the introjected distorted image of the mother that is easily transformed into a persecutor in the external world. Were she to continue treatment, a progressive weakening of this image and increased satisfaction with the world would seem likely to take place.

We may feel disappointed that the propensity for the disorder was not eradicated completely. Whether this is due to a presumed hereditary predisposition or to the tenaciousness of her early introjects is impossible to determine. Still, we should not minimize the accomplishments, especially because at the beginning of treatment the case appeared a very difficult one, that of a patient moving toward the chronic state of schizophrenia. Geraldine came to know the joy of fulfillment. Even if she has to live with an Achilles' heel, she has blossomed as a human being. Except for the rare and very fleeting episodes, she is in the realm of reality. I have learned a great deal from Geraldine, and I hope readers have also. Her image continues to return to my mind from time to time. She is still remembered as the floweret that the night's chill bent down and closed, but the light of dawn straightened on the stem, all open and whitened.

Mark

Mark was a 25-year-old Jewish married man when he was urgently hospitalized. As he later reported, his psychotic episode occurred acutely, when he thought he had a heart attack. He felt he had to pray to God for survival, and the way to pray to God was to spin around. Rosette, his wife, came to see what was happening to him and wanted to stop him, but he did not let her touch him because she was not God. He did not want Rosette to touch his eyes because otherwise he would become blind. He felt that his eyes were pointing in different directions because the muscles that controlled them had been mixed up in his skull and intertwined.

The patient had the feeling that he could control every fiber of his body, but not his eyes. He felt that the brain tissue as well as the muscles that sustained his brain were being torn apart. He had also many other kinesthetic delusions and hallucinations. Mark felt that his heart was going to fall down, because its ligaments could not sustain it in its natural place. He would lie down on the floor and pull up his legs and lean them against the wall so that the heart would not fall down.

If Rosette or other members of the family tried to stop him when he was spinning around, he would resist them because he thought that if he stopped moving, he would die.

When Mark had this attack, he had been in psychoanalysis with an orthodox Freudian therapist for several years. He had sought treatment because he was shy, had difficulty in making friends, and felt lonely. When the acute attack occurred, the therapist recommended immediate hospitalization.

While Mark was being taken to the hospital, he expected to die. He was waiting for the moment his heart and blood vessels would explode into a thousand pieces. He overheard the voice of his brother-in-law saying, "Let's take Mark as soon as possible to the hospital or he will die." As a matter of fact, he had the impression that the relatives were already mourning him. While he was going to the hospital in the car, he was sitting next to the brother-in-law, and he was afraid that pieces of his body would eventually soil him.

While in the hospital the same delusions continued. He also had the impression that the other patients were talking disparagingly about him. As a matter of fact, he overheard some female patients stating that he was "not masculine."

In the hospital he was withdrawn, apprehensive, and hallucinated. On admission he was given 225 mg Thorazine (chlorpromazine) and 5 mg Stelazine (trifluoperazine hydrochloride) four times daily and 2 mg Artane (trihexyphenidyl HCL) twice daily.

I was consulted and agreed to take charge of the patient after the patient and his family refused to continue with the previous therapist. The patient improved somewhat, and it became possible for a member of the family or for an attendant to accompany him to my office and to take him back to the hospital three times a week.

The patient appeared apathetic, withdrawn, and could not even express his delusions. Occasionally, however, he would make remarks that were very revealing. He could not look people in the eyes because they would find out things of which he was ashamed. He felt he could not get along with people in the hospital; they would laugh at him or make unpleasant remarks about him. They would refer to him as a "she," not "he." At times they were saying what he was thinking. Now he was understanding many things that never appeared important to him before. He also referred a few times to the fact that lately he had been fired from his job because instead of attending to what he had to do, he was calling his broker repeatedly and discussing the stock market with him. After he had been fired from his job, he went to work for his father, who was a successful businessman; but his father was never satisfied and would constantly criticize him.

I tried to reassure him and was as convivial as possible, but it took many months for the blank face of the patient to reveal mimic play or emotion of any sort. The only thing about which he talked without difficulty was the stock market. Because I understood that this was the area in which he was competent and proud of his knowledge, I let him talk about it. As a matter of fact, I learned many things from him about Wall Street, and I let him know that he had taught me something. Later on, when he would recall this first stage of treatment, Mark said:

> You made me feel at ease; you were receptive, uncritical; you accepted me with all my faults. Only two persons had been like you in my life. One was my grandfather, who died when I was 5. I loved him very much; more than anybody else. The other was my physics teacher in high school. My previous therapist could not relate to me. He was distant, not a real person. I was supposed to free associate with him, but I couldn't. I was always on guard.

Because he had improved considerably after six months of hospitalization, I decided to transfer Mark to a day hospital. In the day hospital he did not adjust well. He could not relate to people, felt he had nothing to say, and to avoid the discomfort caused by the company of the other patients he would go to the bathroom and stay there for long periods of time. Later in the treatment, reminiscing about the period spent in the hospital and day hospital, he said that at this time his mind was a blank. He could not come across to people, and they could not reach him.

Practically all the somatic delusions disappeared; as a matter of fact, they had diminished a few weeks after the beginning of the acute attack. I tried to explain to him that the feelings he had about his body were an expression of the way he felt about himself. Terrible things must have gone on in his mind; hopes and ideas about himself were disintegrating and were assuming the form of preoccupations about his body. As he told me later, he felt that I was there, willing to share his anguish and anxiety, and willing to help him, if only he would be able to talk about his inner torment. But he would not. Only about the stock market could he talk without hesitation. He would occasionally say that he was unable to be a husband and a father to his 3-year-old son. He should leave his wife and son and not ruin their lives. As a matter of fact, he refused to have sexual relations with his wife. I told him a few times that he was not in a position to make important decisions then; he had to wait until he knew that he was better.

For a long while he did not want to see anybody, relatives or friends. He was afraid people would discover that he was like a plant, that he had no feeling or emotion and did not know how to act or react. Only his wife and son were allowed to see him; and yet he wanted to abandon them too. Slowly, however, by receiving support from the therapist and the feeling that his anxiety was understood and shared by him, he became capable of establishing some interpersonal contacts. His father reinstated him in his business and he started to work again. As a matter of fact, the father gave him a certain amount of money to invest in the stock market, and to everybody's surprise Mark did so well that in a few months he more than doubled his capital. He stopped talking about leaving wife and son and resumed sexual relations.

Eventually he was able to unfold the psychodynamic factors that had affected his life. The marriage of his parents was not a happy one. When his father was a young man, he was exclusively interested in the business; he was a good provider, but nothing else. He was distant, remote, always critical of everybody else. Mark remembered that when his father and mother were fighting, he would always be on his mother's side, not because he thought mother was right or needed his help, but because mother could protect not only herself but him too from his father.

His mother depicted the world as a bad place to be, and soon Mark came to believe that the world was as frightening as his father was. Mark came to believe that there was an incompatibility between the world and himself. All the other human beings were parts of the terrible world. Mother was the only exception. Not only would she be able to protect him from the world, but she would also interpret the world for him. As he later came to realize, his mother did not really explain the facts of the world, but only her feelings about the world. But mother was the only person he could communicate with; thus mother's vision of the world was the only one he could accept. Moreover, he felt he was mother's special child or the most important person in mother's life. He owed it to her to listen and to accept her views, even when they did not agree with his experiences or with what his senses made him aware of. Mother was the only person who knew his feelings, needs, and thoughts, the only one who could prevent him from being completely lost in the woods. He remembered how scared he was the first day he went to a nursery school, at the age of 3; and since then he continued to be scared, especially until he was 10.

He remembers that the people of the world, represented by the people on the street, were considered by him as unpredictable objects, things to be afraid of, as mother had represented them. They could attack you at any minute, like wild animals in the jungle do.

Mark added later in the treatment that his was one of the few Jewish families in the predominantly gentile neighborhood. Although there had never been episodes of anti-Semitism there, and although his mother did not accuse anybody of being anti-Semitic, the awareness of belonging to a traditionally persecuted minority increased a certain vague, diffuse, uneasy feeling, which Mark perceived as danger. Although Mark's mother was never very clear or explicit in this regard, her actions and her attitudes seemed to betray the following appraisal and conclusions about society, to be taken by Mark as guidelines: ''Be aware that the world is not going to accept you. There is something threatening in everybody that cannot be easily seen. Be careful! Be careful! Be careful!''

Mark came to believe that everybody, everything was irrational, unpredictable, and uncontrollable except his mother's love. As mentioned before, his father was one of the people of the world too, and he was as terrible as everyone else was. Mark never thought that he would grow up like his father and could not identify with him. He wanted to be the opposite of his father.

The situation improved very much toward the end of childhood, and especially during adolescence and young adulthood. The patient was able to have a few friends, but he did not have meaningful heterosexual relations. Later he had occasional contacts with prostitutes. He completed college successfully, secured a job as an engineer, and at the age of 22 married Rosette, whom he had met while attending high school. When he married Rosette, a revolution occurred inside of him: he started to see the world in a new way, not just as mother had taught him. The world became a vaster arena and yet was less terrible than he had anticipated. He could live in it and prosper. He loved Rosette very much but depended on her too much. He tended now to put her in the same position in which his mother was. Rosette naturally resented that attitude; she wanted to be his wife, not his mother. Sexual relations were normal, and a child was conceived during the first year of marriage.

The situation became much worse when the patient was fired from his job, apparently because he was too slow in his work and did not get along with people. The patient's father suggested that Mark work for him; the job would be easy and Mark would make much more money. He did make more money, but the job was not easy. Mark and his father did not get along well. His father acquired again the "monstrous" aspect that the patient, under the influence of his mother, had seen in him early in childhood. Mark's father did not allow him to be free; he controlled his actions by criticizing everything he was doing and thus made him hesitant, or actually psychologically paralyzed, or more likely to make mistakes.

Mark was seeing Dr. X. but could not reveal his predicament to him. His unrest increased. He could not work, and he oscillated between feeling that he was an outsider from everything that surrounded him or was ensnared in a gigantic trap or web where his father was the spider.

By getting married he had given up mother; but Rosette resented helping him and yet she was becoming more and more demanding. His father not only did not protect him but was exposing his weakness and his inability to deal with the world. The patient felt that if his wife and father were so critical of him, they must be right: he was unfit to live in this difficult world; there was something fundamentally wrong with him. What was wrong was with him, not with other people. It is at this point that the patient became ill. As he later understood, the psychosis started with his concretizing into physical symptoms the image that he had of himself. No longer did he think there was something wrong with him as a person, but with him as an organism. The psychosis was precipitated, of course, by the recent events and feelings that had a strange resonance with the early events and feelings of his childhood.

The psychodynamic meaning of the life history, as we have so far reported, was easily grasped by the patient. He made great improvement, and the illness seemed directed toward an early complete recovery when unfortunate external events occurred and disturbed the promising picture. In 1970 the stock market fell considerably. Not only did Mark lose all his profits, but also a large part of the invested capital. But Mark lost more than money. In the attempt to reemerge from the psychosis and to rehabilitate himself, he had relied a great deal on his successes in the stock market. During the brief period of success he had also invested money for relatives, and now they were losing money too. They would have no respect for him. He would diminish in their eyes as well as in his own. The recent events had demonstrated that he was good for nothing, an inferior human being, unable to make a living or to provide for his family.

The patient was discouraged and depressed. His ability to work decreased very much, but he knew that father would not fire him because he was his son. Delusions, hallucinations, and ideas of reference did not reappear, with the exception that he believed people at times were laughing at him. A group of symptoms related to relations with other persons developed. He became more and more afraid of people. He would feel a tremendous discomfort in their presence. They would inhibit him and suffocate his life. In crowds he saw so many eyes looking; so many people talking. He felt people were malevolent, ready to laugh at him if he happened to do something wrong. If people looked into his eyes, he was afraid they would discover he was not a man; he pretended to play the role of a man. When somebody looked at him, he felt inferior; he had to drop his eyes or look elsewhere. When he was asked to explain why he did not feel like a man, he said it was because he did not feel capable with women and also because he did not feel able to compete with other men for women or for work. When he was at work, he tried to "compete," but he could not stand the competition for more than a few minutes. He could not even compete with father.

He felt that he could not be on his own, that he could not give direction to his life; and yet he was unwilling to accept the guidance of other people, including his father. A person who guides is not an intruder, but an oppressor because he tells you in what direction to go. The patient wanted to do what he decided himself to do, not what other people expected him to do; and yet he expected to fail and felt that he would not to be able to make it on his own. He was not making it. That is why people looked at him and laughed. He fooled everybody when he gave other people the feeling he was doing well in the stock market. His father too expected him to do well, but his mother did not. Mother knew better; she always knew he was not able to do anything. Mother always treated him like a prince who should not be concerned with the practicalities and dangers of life. When he was doing well in the stock market, he had the feeling he was doing things better than others. In order to feel at ease, comfortable, accepted, not laughed at, he felt he had to do things better than others. Also in playing the stock market he had no contact with people; he did all the work by reading financial reports and telephoning his broker. Thus his real feelings for people were suppressed during that time. He also had reduced to a minimum the work for his father. In order to feel free he had to reject people, to live as if people did not exist. He felt that people came across his path, cramped him, and did not let him stretch his extremities. He was afraid of them; he could not escape from them; he had to meet them every day; every day he had to renew the effort. Maintenance Thorazine therapy had no effect on these symptoms.

When I asked him what people should do to make him less afraid of them, he said it was he who had to do something. He had to convince them that he was worthy. But he did not know how. On the other hand, people behaved as if they were feeling worthy and therefore reminded him that he was not. He was weak and effeminate. When he felt weak, he even felt attracted toward men, as if he were a homosexual. If he felt attracted to men, men became less frightening. But he never had relations with men; he would not even know how; he enjoyed relations with women.

When I asked him what people should do to make him less afraid, I was remembering another patient, a teenage girl, not schizophrenic but with preschizophrenic anxiety, who was also afraid of people. When I asked her what people should do so that she would not be afraid of them any more, she replied, "They should lose their penises and vaginas."

However, in the case of Mark, the problem was not sexual. The homosexual remarks seemed to me an artifact. To be homosexual was, in his system of values, the same as to say that he was completely worthless and despicable.

If I have gone to such a length in reporting his feelings about people, it is because they illustrate very well the type of symptomatology that his illness acquired and retained for a long time. It consisted of a conscious abnormal way of relating to the interpersonal world in general.

At the time when this report was written, Mark was still in treatment, although he had made steady progress. Treatment consisted at first of attacking the symptoms directly. He soon recognized that he saw people laughing at him when he expected to see them laughing. He also promptly recognized that he felt they were laughing because he believed they should laugh at him. He understood that the fear and the feeling of inadequacy were correlated and reinforced each other in a vicious circle. The more fearful he was, the more inadequate he felt; the more inadequate he felt, the more fearful he became of others. The fear at times was experienced as a real terror.

Before the reexacerbation of the symptoms, which occurred after the market's fall, the original terror of people had been repressed and had changed into disinterest in people. When the condition reexacerbated, the terror came back, the terror experienced by him for the first time when he had to go to the nursery school and leave his mother. The role of the mother was interpreted at length. The mother was experienced by him as wanting to hold him in her protective embrace: another womb, after he left her original womb at birth. But mother was not only the protector; she was also the one who depicted the world in such ways that Mark felt he needed her desperately. On the other hand, father, especially because mother was not happy with him, had become the symbol of the menacing world. Undoubtedly Oedipal rivalry with the father made it easier for Mark to conceive this symbolization.

Mother's description of life and the world as a place reminiscent of the jungle, and father's achievements as a result of hard work and successful competition, helped Mark to see the world in Darwinian terms. As we mentioned in Chapter 8, there is some truth in this conception of some prepsychotic, psychotic, and formerly psychotic patients. However, what made the situation worse in the case of Mark was that, contrary to other patients, he felt that the competition, the arena, and the struggle were healthy parts of life: they have to be accepted. If you want to have security, you must compete and win. He was a staunch supporter of rugged individualism. He tried to win with the stock market, but eventually he lost. Losing meant for him not to be as good as his father, to be castrated by his father, to be less than other men, to be homosexual.

It was important to explain to the patient how his whole vision of mankind and his relation to mankind were based on the terrible fear that originated in the ways he interpreted mother's messages and in his profound feeling of inadequacy. It took prolonged, repeated work, going over the same material time and time again, to make the patient ameliorate his relations with people. A new team, consisting of him and the therapist, had the purpose of diminishing the fear. As Shainberg (1973) has written, the patient was helped to confront his fears in a setting where there is some hope that he need not be so afraid.

The values in which the patient believed, that you have to fight and win in order to assert your humanity and masculinity, were values that the therapist could not share. They were certainly a transformation or derivation of the patient's original experiences. This inability to share values remained for a long time. It was thus difficult to establish that situation of sharing values that I described in Chapter 39. Improvement was thus delayed by this difficulty. Eventually the patient changed his values somewhat as he began to understand that they were a derivation of his original experiences. Until then in his system of values to be worthy (and therefore worthy of mother's love, of women's love, and of society's respect) required being superior to others. Self-respect and an acceptable self-image were based on competition, for which the patient felt utterly unprepared.

This case is interesting on many counts. The shift in symptomatology deserves attention. In the initial acute attack there was a disintegration of the self and self-esteem, represented delusionally by destruction of the body. After the setback the disorder consisted mainly of an altered relatedness to the interpersonal world, whose psychodynamic origin we have retraced. The course of treatment shows clearly how ephemeral and unstable is the improvement determined only by external events (success in the stock market).

Moreover, the case shows how the specific values of the patient may have actually delayed his recovery, because they were intimately related to the original conflictful areas and could not be shared by the therapist.

Another important point deserves full consideration. With the permission of the patient I had several sessions with the parents. They did not appear to me as Mark had portrayed them. His picture of them was lopsided, because he had magnified some of their characteristics to the point of grotesque distortion. It is true that the father, especially when the patient was a child, was overconcerned with his business, but he was not the tyrant or perfectionist that Mark had portrayed. On the other hand, the father had been even more than tolerant and was desperately concerned with Mark's health and happiness. However, as chief of an important firm, he had those authoritarian ways that bring about efficiency but that, with some justification, are disliked by most subordinates who learn to live with them without experiencing deep psychological traumata.

There is no doubt that mother was an extremely anxious person and that because of her anxiety she had always been and continued to be overprotective. However, it was certainly not her intention to scare Mark as she did or to make him, consciously or unconsciously, a puppet, a pawn, or a doll at her disposal. There is no doubt that Mark incorporated all of his mother's anxiety, magnified it inside of himself, and projected it into the world in a very subjective way so that it became the terror of the interpersonal world. Whether an extreme sensitivity predisposed him biologically to this distortion or whether the Oedipal antagonism for his father was the major concomitant factor is hard to say. Incidentally, a brother of Mark had also some short psychotic attacks; but the third, and youngest, brother never had any psychiatric illness.

Other points of this interesting report require much longer analysis and discussion. It will be up to the individual reader to try to find as many of them as possible and to attempt to interpret them in order to enlarge the didactical value of what I think is an unusually interesting case. However, to start with, I suggest a few points for further consideration.

Was Mark trying to prolong throughout his life a symbiotic relation with his mother or mother substitutes? Was he seeing the world in such a terrible way in order to maintain such a symbiotic relation reminiscent of the first year of life?

From the point of view of social psychiatry, how much importance must we give to the fact that the patient's family was one of the few Jewish ones in the neighborhood? Was the ghost of anti-Semitism an excuse or was it founded on certain facts? The patient's mother was overprotective and anxious, as "Jewish mothers" have often been portrayed in contemporary fiction. The overprotectiveness of the Jewish mother has historical foundations, because in many eras and many countries her children have been exposed to harsh hostility. Neither Mark nor his mother was exposed to that hostility, but could it be that fears and other feelings are transmitted in ethnic groups from generation to generation and continue to act psychodynamically? On the other hand, most children of Jewish mothers do not become paranoid schizophrenics; as a matter of fact, as some authors have found (Malzberg, 1962, Sanua, 1962; Bastide, 1965), children of Protestant mothers are more frequently afflicted by this disorder.

One of the most controversial points concerns the value system of the patient. Did it really interfere with treatment because the patient himself was the victim of what he believed in: the competitive society? Was the fact that the therapist did not share his values a real interference to that recovery? On the other hand, the patient felt very close to the therapist and might have been afraid of recovering for fear of losing him. Did he see in the therapist another mother? Was treatment another symbiotic relation? In fact, Mark liked to see the therapist as often as possible, hopefully every day, but this wish of his was gradually curtailed.

CHAPTER

41

Psychotherapy of Chronic Schizophrenia

I

Definitions: Scope of the Problem

Before prolonging the debate over whether psychotherapy is a suitable mode of treatment for the chronic schizophrenic, we have to define the term *chronic schizophrenia*.

My point of view is that neither the severity of the symptomatology nor the long duration of the illness is the characteristic required for the diagnosis of chronic schizophrenia. Only the quality of the symptomatology is the criterion for whether a patient should be considered chronic. A patient who has been in a catatonic stupor for several months is not necessarily a chronic schizophrenic. He may still not have recovered from the acute state with which the illness started. At times even experienced therapists are unclear on the subject. For instance, Ferreira (1959) reported his successful treatment with two "severely regressed schizophrenics" whom he called chronic catatonic. It is to the credit of Ferreira to have achieved great success with these two severely ill patients. He achieved success by "accepting and, as much as possible, satisfying the patient's needs, regardless of how unrealistic they were." As each patient improved, Ferreira encouraged him to utilize his own reacquired ego functions more and more. Ferreira's merit is not decreased by the fact that these two patients, although in a severe catatonic state, were not chronic. If in the category of chronic schizophrenia we include the patients who in this book have been diagnosed as belonging to the second, or advanced, stage, the third, or preterminal, stage, and the fourth, or terminal, stage, then we must be more cautious in expressing optimistic opinions.

Even the most optimistic therapists who treat chronic schizophrenics with psychodynamic psychotherapy limit their efforts to patients who have been described in this book as belonging to the second stage. Those in the third or fourth stages are excluded. Even the patients who, as I reported in Chapter 36, were studied by me in Pilgrim State Hospital and who obtained temporary remission belonged to the second stage in spite of their prolonged hospitalization.

We shall not repeat here the symptomatology of the second stage, which has been described in Chapter 23. I shall merely repeat that the symptoms have assumed a fixed and definite form. The secondary process seems to have been defeated permanently, and the primary process prevails. At the level of interpersonal relations there is very little mobile anxiety. As a matter of fact, it is very difficult to mobilize anxiety again. The patient has to master all the resources available to him to delay or to stop the progression of the regression.

Grinspoon, Ewalt, and Shader (1967) have reported pessimistic results in chronic patients treated with psychotherapy on a long-term basis. They conclude their work with the statement that psychotherapy alone does little or nothing for chronic schizophrenic patients in two years' time. The patients were treated by residents. In answer to anticipated criticisms the authors added:

> There are those who would argue that even nearly two years of psychotherapy with exceptionally well-qualified therapists is not enough time in which to draw any meaningful conclusions about its usefulness as a therapeutic tool with this kind of patient. They would claim that it takes five or even ten years of psychotherapy with such sick patients to accomplish anything substantial, let alone to effect a cure. If this is the case, however, then intensive psychotherapy as a treatment for chronic schizophrenia would have merely academic interest since it would be available for only an infinitesimally small number of patients and would therefore have no public health value. On the other hand, if, after almost two years of intensive psychotherapy, it appears that little or no fundamental change has occurred in the patients reported on here (and in fact there was in these instances very little to suggest that any substantial working alliance had been established), then by extrapolation one might certainly question whether any number of years of individual psychotherapy would be useful to such patients, if one considers ''useful'' to mean a fundamental alteration of the patient's ego in the direction of greater health.

The authors conclude that psychotherapy for a much longer period of time is rarely feasible because of the expense and time involved. Thus, its effectiveness becomes a theoretical question. On the other hand, the authors report that ''phenothiazine therapy in conjunction with psychotherapy seems to work quite well at reducing florid symptomatology and also perhaps at making the patient more 'reachable,' more receptive to communication with the therapist and others.'' I must regrettably add to the conclusions of this important work that unfortunately a large number of chronic schizophrenics are also not affected by drug therapy or, if affected, improve too little to warrant discharge from the hospital and reintegration into the community.

II
Methods of Social Interaction

Many authors have attempted treatment of the chronic schizophrenic with methods consisting not of individual treatment but of social interaction. Several authors (Fairweather, 1964; Pace, 1957; and Sanders et al., 1962) obtained a certain degree of resocialization but no correction of the psychopathology *per se*.

Ludwig and co-workers (1967) instituted a fifteen-week treatment program with chronic schizophrenics. The treatment group consisted of five groups of four patients each (two male, two female); the control group consisted of ten other patients on the same ward. Situations were devised in each group in which the patients would be exposed to one another, would be forced to interact, and would be considered responsible for one another's behavior. By earning privileges or incurring sanctions, patients were stimulated to become involved with one another and to acquire a sense of responsibility. Increased interaction occurred, but it was not related to any overall improvement. Many patients actually got worse.

In spite of these results, a number of ideas and principles emerged that have stimulated Ludwig to conduct further research in the treatment of the chronic schizophrenic. His research deserves accurate study. Ludwig's methodology is not psychoanalytic or psychodynamic; but being psychosocial it remains in the field of psychotherapy. If we remain cognizant of the large number of chronic patients and of the magnitude of this problem in psychiatric hospitals, we must welcome studies like those of Ludwig and must evaluate them with the open-mindedness that they deserve.

Ludwig's theoretical premise is that the symptomatology of the chronic schizophrenic may be subsumed under the term "alteration in consciousness" (Ludwig and Farrelly, 1966; Ludwig, 1970, 1973). He feels that, as far as his technique is concerned, it does not matter whether chronic schizophrenia is the result of an organic disorder, institutionalization, or an unconscious desire on the part of the patient to remain sick. This altered consciousness has to be combated with a pragmatic approach. Ludwig (1970) sees four facets of the therapeutic approach of the chronic schizophrenic. The first is how to get the patient's attention. "The potency or the magnitude of the stimulus must increase proportionally to the depth of alteration in consciousness." Also, the greater the depth, the more concrete, specific, immediate, and tangible must be the transmitted message or reinforcement for the appropriate response. Second is the problem of how to sustain the attention of the patient, once it is obtained. Third is the problem of how to get the patient to internalize therapy's external alarms and arousal stimuli so that he can remain alert and attentive and provide his own "self-arousal stimulation." The fourth facet concerns what to do with the sober or intact mental state once it is attained and sustained. In fact, at this stage the patient may appear lazy rather than crazy and psychopathic rather than psychotic.

Ludwig's specific techniques presuppose the acceptance of the following general points of view: (1) patients would not play and exploit the sick role if the hospital did not provide a reinforcing atmosphere for the perpetuation of this behavior. Institutional pressures make it likely for chronic patients to indulge in such typical forms of behavior as excessive reliance on authority, fixed routines, and loss of personal dignity. (2) A treatment program for the chronic schizophrenic "must adopt and implement a value system of its own which does not reinforce the sick role and which does encourage and reinforce responsible, socially adaptive behaviors." What Ludwig fundamentally affirms is that treatment must fight not only the illness but also "institutionalism." Institutionalism is seen by him, and incidentally by many other authors, as an enduring event just as bad or almost as bad as the illness itself.

Ludwig and Marx (1969) obtained very impressive results with the "buddy system." This method consisted of pairing patients and then maximizing their exposure to each other in all daily activities, including work, eating, and recreation. Previous studies consisting of larger groups of patients had given unsatisfactory results, possibly because too much responsibility had been delegated to patients, who had become discouraged and had decompensated under pressure. This particular group, a pair consisting of one better and one poorer functioning patient, gave much better results. Each of the buddies was responsible and accountable for the other. The privileges each buddy received were contingent upon the weekly average behavior rating score of the buddy pair. The general improvement of the twenty-eight patients involved was attributed by the authors mainly to a marked improvement of twelve of them. Although the improvement was not sufficient to permit discharge of most patients, it achieved significant results. It demonstrated that a close relationship in many of these pairs was possible. It is important to mention that each pair had half an hour per day of joint psychotherapy.

Other authors have used various techniques of operant conditioning. Ayllon and Azrin (1965) have developed a "token economy." By awarding tokens for such good behavior as work, grooming, bathing, toothbrushing, and so on, patterns of good behavior were reinforced. Some improvement was noticed in a large number of patients. It is important to consider the fact, however, that almost all the studied patients were on phenothiazine medication.

If we try to evaluate these methods, we must reach some conclusions: they do not consist of attempts to change the inner self of the patient, to solve his conflicts or remove the symptoms that made him experience the world and himself in a different way. The aim is to help the patients to develop patterns of behavior that are less unacceptable and more manageable. To that extent these methods have succeeded. Inasmuch as nothing has so far been devised that would offer help to a large number of regressed patients who do not respond to drug therapy, even these minimal results are to be welcomed. They indicate that even the regressed schizophrenic is able to respond to very simple methods that invoke simple psychological mechanisms. Operant conditioning and nonsymbolic learning work also with subhuman animals, mental defectives, autistic children, and therefore there should be no great surprise if they work also with regressed schizophrenics. The mental mechanisms that involve highly symbolic processes, complicated interpersonal relations, and abstract value systems are bypassed. It is easier to bypass them in "the burned out" schizophrenic than in the less sick schizophrenic, whose symptoms are still unsettled and whose anxiety and symbolic connections may change form rapidly or spread out, even to areas involving the conditioning process.

We must praise the authors who have devised the treatments based on token economy and special interpersonal relations. These techniques involved symbolic learning, but only to a minimal degree. Perhaps the concomitant use of phenothiazine helped. All these procedures could be subsumed in the following way: even many regressed schizophrenics can learn with the method of reward and punishment.

We must be grateful to Ludwig and other authors who have tackled these almost impenetrable problems. Any experiment that could diminish the tragedy of the chronic schizophrenic has to be welcome. On the other hand, we must admit that the results so far obtained are far from satisfactory. Some of these procedures repeat partially the methods that I have observed in nurses and attendants of Pilgrim State Hospital from 1941 to 1945 (Chapters 36 and 39). They repeat the method of the good nurse to the extent that they establish a system of reward and possibly of rebuilding of self-esteem. Still, they lack what seems to me the necessary prerequisite of the good-nurse method. In the first stage of the nurse method, she satisfies the needs of the patient, no matter how immature these needs are. Thus she discloses a maternal attitude and opens up the possibility of interpersonal communion. Nothing of this is found in the methods reported in this chapter.

Sanders, Smith, and Weinman (1967) have dealt with the treatment of chronic psychoses, continuing a work, already quoted, done in collaboration with others (Sanders et al., 1962). They structure three socioenvironmental conditions that demand three different degrees of interaction—minimal, partial, and maximal. The improvement in each of the three socioenvironmental programs was evaluated in succession in reference to awareness of others, interaction in structural situations, and spontaneous social behavior.

The socioenvironmental treatment consisted of changing the social living situation programs of interaction activity and intensified group experiences.

The physical environment was changed to approximate more closely nonhospital conditions. Private rooms situated in small cottages were substituted for dormitories. Each cottage had a comfortable living room. Each patient had the key to his own room and was responsible for cleaning the room. The promotion of an attitude of therapeutic community was implemented by regular staff meetings with the nursing personnel. Special clubs and gatherings were organized. The goal of extramural living was impressed on all patients.

The interaction activity program was conducted by small, relatively closed activity groups. The intensified group experiences were obtained through four hours a week of group therapy and patient government. The authors found that this psychosocial treatment ameliorated the social maladjustment and improved the psychiatric status of some patients but exacerbated the symptomatology of others. The older patients and those who had been ill for a long time showed the most favorable social response and the most positive psychiatric adjustment in the maximally structured treatment condition. The improvement was less noticeable in less structured treatment programs. Younger male patients and those who had been ill for a short time showed less favorable response to the treatment. Although some of them benefited, many others were apparently disturbed by the intimacy of the interpersonal interaction. The results with female patients were less satisfactory. The authors concluded that chronic schizophrenia is "not a unitary entity, characterized by progressive apathy, withdrawal and alienation." Two groups of patients could be distinguished. The first group, which responded much better to treatment, consisted of patients who had undergone a reduction in drive level as a consequence of the aging process, duration of illness, and length of hospitalization. These patients were better able to tolerate and adjust to the demands of an intense social milieu. The second group, consisting of younger and more active patients, responded less favorably to appropriate social behavior. I believe that these findings are in line with what we have already said in reference to Ludwig's methods. If from the group of so-called chronic schizophrenics we remove patients whom I classify as belonging to the first stage—no matter how long ago the illness started—we are left with burned out schizophrenics who respond much better to very simple nonsymbolic or slightly symbolic methods of treatment. Their active pathology will not interfere; the treatment will not become an object of mistrust or involved in paranoid ideation, and defenses will not be established against it. On the other hand, the schizophrenic patient who is not so sick may even sustain an additional injury to his sense of human dignity in being treated with such primitive techniques, which do not involve his thinking, feeling, and willing.

Sanders, Smith, and Weinman believe that whereas a physician is required for administering drug therapy, shock therapy, or psychotherapy, no medical training is required for people who want to work with psychosocial methods. They believe that one year of hospital-based didactic and practical training given to graduates from two-year program community colleges will enable them to participate in this type of therapy.

In spite of the limitations of the social treatment of chronic schizophrenia, there seems to be no doubt that good social conditions and a spirit of therapeutic community are helpful. As early as 1961, Wing and Brown reported their study of how social conditions in a given hospital influence chronic schizophrenia. In their accurate study of three hospitals a consistent pattern was detected. Hospital A was characterized by the most personal freedom and useful occupation of patients and optimism among the nurses. This was the hospital where the least clinical disturbance was found. Conversely, hospital C was the one where there was the least personal freedom, useful occupation, and optimism. It was also the hospital with the most clinical disturbance. Hospital B had an intermediary position.

PART EIGHT

Physical Therapies of Schizophrenia

CHAPTER

42

Drug Therapy

I

Introduction and Historical Notes

It is beyond the purpose of this book to offer a detailed account of the techniques or of the neurophysiological or pharmacological background of psychiatric physical therapies. Many authors have written excellent books on this subject (see, for instance, Kalinowsky and Hippius, 1969). This chapter deals with the major aspects of drug therapy in reference to schizophrenia only. The criteria for choosing drug therapy over other types of treatment or in conjunction with psychotherapy have been discussed in Chapter 34.

At the beginning of the sixteenth century the Portuguese Garcia de Orta, physician to the viceroy, described in his *Coloquios* the effects of the drugs with which he had become familiar during the thirty years he spent in the Far East. His observations on the effect of extracts from the root of *Rauwolfia serpentina* might have been forgotten had not the French physician Charles de l'Escluse, known also by the Latin name of Carolus Clusius, diffused the findings of de Orta in a book that was published in Latin in the year 1567.* *Rauwolfia* was named after Leonhard Rauwolf, a German physician and botanist who toured the world to study medicinal plants.

In 1931 Siddiqui and Siddiqui isolated five different alkaloids from the roots of *Rauwolfia*. In 1952 in Basel, Switzerland, Müller, Schlittler, and Bein isolated a new alkaloid to which was given the name reserpine. It was soon discovered that this pharmacological agent had an important beneficial effect on psychotic pa-

* For more historical data on reserpine, see the interesting article by Belloni (1956) from which this information is taken.

tients. During the same year, Charpentier in France synthesized chlorpromazine. The French school conducted the most important early research on chlorpromazine under the inspiring leadership of Delay and Deniker (1952*a, b,* 1961). Since an early period during which reserpine was enthusiastically used, this drug has lost some ground. On the other hand, chlorpromazine and similar compounds belonging to the group of the phenothiazines have continued to gain favor among psychiatrists. The French authors continue to divide them between neuroleptics and other tranquilizers. Delay and Deniker propose five criteria for including a substance in the neuroleptic group:

1. It must not have a hypnotic effect.
2. It has inhibitory action toward excitement, agitation, and aggressivity.
3. It reduces the acute and chronic symptomatology.
4. It has important neurovegetative and psychomotor effect.
5. Its predominant action is on subcortical structures (especially on the reticular activating system and on the basal ganglia, with consequent engendering of extrapyramidal effects).

In the United States the terms *neuroleptics* and *tranquilizers* have been used synonymously.

The reasons why the phenothiazines have become more popular than reserpine (in spite of the latter's cheaper price) are the following: less delay in action and less frequent complications (such as depression and gastrointestinal hemorrhages).

A paper of historical importance is that by Brill and Patton (1957), which reported that in 1956, for the first time since 1929, there had been a reduction of the population of mental patients in New York State hospitals. Such reduction, attributed to drug therapy, continued through 1959, the time of publication of their paper. It has continued since then (Brill and Patton, 1964).

II

Chemical Structures of the Phenothiazines

Phenothiazine was used long ago as an antihelminthic for livestock and as a urinary antiseptic in man. Because of its toxicity, its use was discontinued. The phenothiazine nucleus consists of two benzene rings connected by a sulphur and nitrogen atom. According to what is substituted at R_1 we have three types of

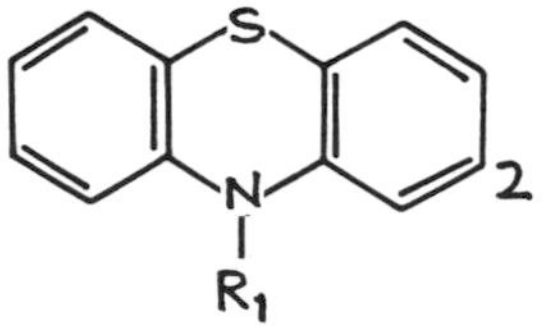

phenothiazines (Dally, 1967). A dimethylaminopropyl side chain will produce promethazine (Phenargan), promazine (Sparine), and chlorpromazine (Thorazine). A piperidine side chain will produce thioridazine (Mellaril). A piperazine side chain will produce such compounds as trifluoperazine (Stelazine), prochlorperazine (Compazine), perphenazine (Trilafon), and so on. For a more detailed report on the action of the eighteen most common phenothiazine derivatives, see Kalinowsky and Hippius (1969).

Contrary to the barbiturates, which act mainly on the cerebral cortex and on the respiratory centers in the medulla, the phenothiazines act mostly on the reticular formation, midbrain, hypothalamus, rhinencephalon, and basal ganglia. The exact mechanism by which they bring about beneficial results is still unknown.

III

CHLORPROMAZINE

This phenothiazine, which at present is the most widely used tranquilizer, will be taken as our paradigm for drug therapy. Variants concerning the use of other related drugs will be discussed later.

Chlorpromazine was introduced in the United States in May 1954 after extensive previous use in Europe. In Europe chlorpromazine is known under the name of lagtocil. In the United States it is manufactured under the trademark name of Thorazine.

Results

Chlorpromazine has been used in both acute and chronic patients. In acute cases it decreases the anxiety, the psychomotor activity, and the aggressive tendencies. There is only a minimum of drowsiness. After a varying interval, hallucinations, delusions, and ideas of reference first become less intense and disturbing; later they disappear. In some other cases there is only a partial improvement. The symptoms persist but are less disturbing and permit some kind of limited social adaptation. In acute hospital cases, generally an initial dose of 50 mg at eight-hour intervals is increased to a maximum oral dose of 500 mg every eight hours. Some patients who have shown no response to oral administration even at large doses may respond to intramuscular injections of doses as little as 25 mg three times daily. The injection should be increased if necessary but should not exceed 100 mg.

Lehmann (1965) divides the course of the acute schizophrenic episode that is treated with chlorpromazine into three stages. In the first stage (first week or two) there is reduction of excitement. In the second stage (from second to sixth weeks) there is improvement of behavior, appearance, affects, and social participation. In the third stage (after six weeks or later) there is significant reduction of major psychotic symptoms involving perceptual and cognitive processes. At times this third stage lasts two or three months. The drug should be gradually diminished in the second and third stages, at least in a tentative way. Lehmann speaks of a maintenance dose to be given once or twice a day. He writes that most studies have shown that 35 to 50 percent of schizophrenic patients in full remission relapse within about six months after they have stopped medication. On the other hand only 10 to 15 percent of patients who remain on maintenance medication will relapse.

Kalinowsky and Hippius (1969), as well as many other authors, recommend instead that treatment should always be discontinued in acute cases, at least in a tentative way, to determine whether or not the obtained results are of lasting duration. Lehmann believes that to reduce prematurely or to "discontinue the maintenance medication of a recovered schizophrenic too early means severing his lifeline to a normal existence." Lehmann is very strong on this point, because he is concerned with the fact that relapses will lead to chronicity. According to him, the principal problem will be one of management, that is, in persuading symptom-free patients to take the drug. In a more recent publication, Lehmann (1974) quotes many sources indicating that the risk of recurrence of a schizophrenic attack is at least twice as great for patients on no maintenance drug or on placebo as it is for those on active maintenance drug therapy. Lehmann recommends that during maintenance treatment the patient's drug taking be restricted to one and certainly not more than two doses. Kris and Carmichael (1957) used a single dose at bedtime of from 50 to 150 mg in patients discharged from hospitals. This dose prevented drowsiness and permitted the patient to work.

In chronic cases, too, there is a favorable response to phenothiazine therapy. Some patients who have been in back wards of hospitals for even ten to twenty years at times show an improvement sufficient to permit their discharge. The treatment is long and may be required for an indefinite period of time. In most regressed or chronic cases there is an improvement inasmuch as the basic requirements of life—eating, sleeping, defecating, and taking care of oneself—become better attended to by the patient. However, there is no improvement in the higher functions of life. The patient is quieter and more manageable. Violence persists in a few sporadic cases only. The basic symptoms and the signs of progressive regression generally remain. Brill and Patton (1964) report that chronicity has not been abolished by drug therapy, although its conditions have been vastly ameliorated. At the time of their report, chronic cases in New York were at about 75 percent of the rate that prevailed just before the introduction of drugs.

Chlorpromazine is useful also in cases of ambulatory or subliminal schizophrenia, where the symptomatology is less rich in overt manifestations. The patients are able to make better contact and in most cases respond more quickly to psychotherapy. The initial dose is 25 mg four times daily. In a few days a maximum of 75 to 100 mg is reached, still four times a day, until good contact is established and the patient is more active and better organized. The dose is then gradually diminished.

Contraindications

The contraindications are few. Patients in coma due to intake of barbiturates, narcotics, or other depressants should not be given chlorpromazine. Agranulocytosis is also another counterindication. According to Kalinowsky and Hippius (1969) pregnancy is a possible contraindication only during the first three months. Chlorpromazine crosses the placental barrier but in amounts so small as not to constitute danger to the baby. The use of it seems safe in labor and delivery.

Severe cardiovascular disease and especially marked hypotension or conditions of cardiac failures require great caution.

Some authors add to this last contraindication liver damage of any kind and extrapyramidal diseases.

Withdrawal Symptoms

There is no evidence that chlorpromazine causes dependence. It does not produce addiction and only a minimal tolerance. However, some withdrawal symptoms may develop if administration is abruptly withdrawn or reduced drastically following high doses. Dizziness, vomiting, nausea, as well as extrapyramidal tremor, do occur. These symptoms can be avoided by withdrawing the drug slowly and continuing the use of antiparkinsonian agents.

Overdosage

Overdoses are generally taken in connection with suicidal attempts. They are very seldom fatally dangerous unless taken simultaneously with barbiturates or other hypnotics.

Three general pictures result: (1) extreme somnolence—unless stimulated, the patient falls asleep; (2) severe hypotension, with unrecordable pulse, cyanosis, and so forth; (3) moderate or mild drop in blood pressure. Respiration is slow but regular. The pulse is strong but fast.

IV
Side Effects and Complications of Chlorpromazine Therapy

Cardiovascular Symptoms

Hypotension is very common, especially after intramuscular administration. Within forty minutes the pressure may drop from 30 to 50 mm systolic and 20 to 30 mm diastolic. A compensating tachycardia with complaint of palpitation may follow. To minimize the effect of the hypotension after the first injection the patient should be kept lying down, with head in low position and legs raised.

Noradrenaline rather than adrenaline is used to raise blood pressure because phenothiazine may reverse the action of adrenaline. Some EKG changes have been reported, but these are usually reversible. Their relations to myocardial damage or sudden death could not be confirmed.

Liver Functions

Jaundice occurs in a small percentage of cases, generally between the second and fourth weeks of therapy. The clinical picture is similar to that of infectious hepatitis of obstructive type, not with parenchymal damage. This complication is interpreted as a sensitivity reaction. It reverses quickly on withdrawal of the medication. History of previous liver disease does not exclude the use of chlorpromazine, but greater cautiousness is advised. Bloom and Davis (1970) made a follow-up second biopsy of eleven of twenty original patients who, a few years previously, had shown liver histopathology as a consequence of tranquilizing medication. The study revealed that three patients had worsened, three improved, and five had remained the same. The authors could not individualize the factors responsible for these changes or variations. All the patients were anicteric and asymptomatic in general.

Hematological Complications

Agranulocytosis, according to Ayd (1963), occurs at the rate of one in 250,000 cases. Eosinophilia, leukopenia, hemolytic anemia, thrombocytopenic purpora, and other blood diseases have been reported in rare cases. These complications generally occur between the fourth and tenth weeks of therapy. Patients should be observed regularly, especially during this period, for sudden appearance of sore throat. Blood counts at regular intervals should be taken. A moderate diminution of total white blood cells is not indication for discontinuing the drug. However, discontinuation is indicated if the white cell count falls below 4,000. Once agranulocytosis occurs, antibiotics, cortisone, or ACTH should be given.

Extrapyramidal Symptoms

These are very common. If an accurate neurological examination is done, minor signs of extrapyramidal involvement are found in the majority of patients who receive chlorpromazine.

Masklike face, rigidity, tremor, salivation, slow gait, lack of associated movements, and so forth, occur in various degrees. According to Ayd (1961) extrapyramidal symptoms occur in 35 percent of cases treated with chlorpromazine and 60 percent of cases treated with trifluoperazine (Stelazine). These symptoms are reversible; they discontinue when treatment is terminated or interrupted. Moreover, they respond well to antiparkinsonian agents such as benztropine mesylate (Cogentin), trihexyphenidyl HCL (Artane), and procyclidine hydrochloride (Kemadrine).

Tardive Dyskinesia

This occurs in a minority of patients who have received neuroleptics for a long time. It is more frequent in elderly patients. Involuntary movements of the lips, tongue, and face and at times chorea like movements of other parts of the body occur. These involuntary movements often appear when the drug has been reduced or discontinued and unfortunately in most cases are not reversible. However, Sato, Daly and Peters (1971) have obtained good results in treating the condition with high doses of reserpine.

Depression

This has been reported in some cases (Hoch, 1955). Hoch recommends interruption of drug therapy and switching to electric shock treatment in severe cases.

Drowsiness

This is a very common effect, especially during the early stage of therapy. Patients who drive motor vehicles or operate machinery should be warned against doing so early in therapy, and, in some cases, for the whole duration of therapy, even if the other symptoms are not counterindicating. Most psychiatrists permit patients to drive if the dosage has been reduced to 100 mg daily and if the mental symptoms do not interfere with safe driving. Individual variations are, of course, to be taken into account.

Other Miscellaneous Side Effects

Bladder disturbances requiring catheterization have occasionally been reported. Mild fever also occurs at the beginning of intramuscular therapy. Nasal congestion is a common complaint. Increase in appetite and weight gain are frequently reported. All these side effects have to be treated symptomatically.

Dermatologic allergic reactions occurred frequently before the tablets started to be coated. Different types of dermatitis have occurred since then and are easily treated with antiallergic medications.

Patients treated with phenothiazines also have an increased photosensitivity and should be warned against sun exposures. Skin pigmentation has also been reported in hospitalized female patients who had received very high doses (from 500 mg to 1500 mg daily) for at least three years. The pigmentation, which may fade after discontinuance of the drug, is probably a melaninlike complex (Greiner and Berry, 1964). Ocular opacities have also been reported in patients who have been treated for long periods of time with large doses, but Delong (1967) and Kalinowsky and Hippius (1969) remind us that lenticular opacities are relatively frequent in the general population over forty years of age.

Engorgement of the breast with lactation occurs in some female patients taking large doses. The condition disappears if the drug is reduced or discontinued. Menstrual irregularity is transient and requires no treatment. Blurred vision is caused by disturbed accommodation and may worry some patients. Reassurance should be given about the temporary character of the symptom.

Inhibition of ejaculation occurs occasionally and may disturb the patient who was not informed of its possible occurrence. Generally it disappears with a reduction of dosage.

V

Other Phenothiazines

Thioridazine (Mellaril) is of approximately the same strength as chlorpromazine. The same dosage is recommended. Side effects are less intense than with chlorpromazine. However, inhibition of ejaculation is more frequent.

Promazine (Sparine) is less effective than chlorpromazine. Perhaps it is preferable with elderly patients and with patients who are restless and agitated.

Prochlorperazine (Compazine) is according to Appleton (1967) twice as potent as chlorpromazine; according to Lehmann (1965) six times. It was the first drug of the piperazine group to be used in the United States. It is more rapid in action than chlorpromazine and produces less drowsiness.

Trifluoperazine (Stelazine) is twenty times as powerful as chlorpromazine. It has the valuable effect of activating the withdrawn, apathetic, or depressed schizophrenic. According to Lehmann and Knight (1958) it increases the capacity to organize incoming stimuli and improves the concentration power.

Chlorprothizene (Taractan) differs from chlorpromazine in having a carbon atom instead of a nitrogen atom in the central ring. Some authors have found it somewhat superior to chlorpromazine, thioridazine, and fluphenazine.

Fluphenazine (Prolixin) is from twenty to sixty times as powerful as chlorpromazine. It causes strong extrapyramidal symptoms.

Contrary to early reports there seems to be no advantage in combining various drugs in the treatment. According to Appleton (1967) no combination of phenothiazines is more effective than chlorpromazine alone. In general we could say that such symptoms as violence, aggression, excitement, hyperactivity, and delusions respond best to treatment; the symptoms that indicate regression or passivity respond considerably less well.

VI
Other Neuroleptics

Reserpine

Kline (1956) and Barsa and Kline (1956) have made important studies on this derivative of *Rauwolfia serpentina*. These authors distinguish three stages in the reserpine treatment: the sedative, the turbulent, and the integrative phases.

The sedative action of the drug manifests itself within the first few days. The patients become less disturbed, less overactive, less resistive. Their appetite usually improves. They also become more cooperative and in better contact with the environment.

At the end of the first week the turbulent phase generally starts. This phase is characterized by a reexacerbation of the symptomatology. Delusions and hallucinations become more pronounced. If they had disappeared, they return. This period varies in duration from a few hours to three or more weeks.

In the third, or integrative, period, the patients become more cooperative, friendly, and in better contact with the environment. Delusions and hallucinations disappear or become less disturbing. At first the patient tries to rationalize the manifestations of the illness, but later he recognizes that he has been ill. Kline (1956) feels that the pathological patterns are broken up and that an opportunity is given to the patient to reintegrate and reorganize.

Kline recommends an oral dose of 3 mg and an intramuscular dose of 5 mg the first day. If there are no complications, the patient is given 3 mg orally and 10 mg intramuscularly for the next three weeks. At the end of this period only the oral doses are given, unless "booster shots" are needed.

Untoward effects similar to those caused by phenothiazine treatment may occur. The most frequent is marked hypotension. The blood pressure should be taken before treatment and kept under observation. Sluggishness, tremulousness, flushing, loose stools, nasal stuffiness, increased gastric secretion, and uterine contractions have been reported. Very rarely edema of the glottis has occurred. Reversible parkinsonian symptoms may develop.

Haloperidol (Haldol)

Haloperidol, a derivative of butyrophenone, has been accepted more readily in Europe than in the United States. It is now widely used in the United States too. Haloperidol is particularly useful in handling episodes of excitement especially in paranoid and manic patients, in the treatment of the Gilles de la Tourette syndrome, and in all psychotic patients who show restlessness, hyperactivity, and involuntary movements. In acute schizophrenics doses range from 5 to 10 mg daily. In severe excitements the dose is 5 mg intravenously, to be repeated if the excitement has not subsided in twenty to thirty minutes. Additional injections could be given every six to eight hours, not to exceed a maximum of 15 mg daily.

VII

Other Types of Drug Therapy

So-called minor tranquilizers, like chlordiazepoxide (Librium), diazepam (Valium), and meprobamate (Miltown, Equanil) have no effect on schizophrenia.

Hoffer and Osmond (1957) and Hoffer and co-workers (1957) have treated schizophrenic patients with large doses of nicotinic acid and ascorbic acid (vitamin C)—megavitamin treatment. At least temporary good results have been observed by many psychiatrists. Other authors (for instance, Gallant and Steele, 1966) have not confirmed these results.

The theory on which the megavitamin treatment is based is the presumed correction of a metabolic defect by the administration of nicotinamide or nicotinamide adenine nucleotide (see Chapter 28). Whereas at first Hoffer, Osmond, and Smythies (1954) recommended 3,000 mg of niacin (vitamin B_3) per day, later Hoffer (1971) recommended doses up to 30,000 mg per day. Hoffer and collaborators also recommend at the same time ascorbic acid (vitamin C) in doses of 3,000 mg per day, and pyridoxine in doses of 150 mg. At least good results have been observed by several authors. Other authors (for instance, Gallant and Steele, 1966) have not confirmed these results. In my personal experience I have never seen good results in patients treated exclusively with this method. However, I do agree with Lehmann's following conclusions: "There does not seem to be sufficient evidence at this time to initiate megavitamin therapy on clinical grounds alone, but its possible negative effects are probably not serious enough to refuse treating a patient with megavitamins—in addition to the generally accepted physical therapeutic approaches in schizophrenia, e.g., pharmacotherapy—if the patient or his family insist on it" (1974).

Itil (1973) has tried seldom-used drugs in schizophrenics who have been resistant to the common therapy. He obtained particularly good results with thiothizene.

CHAPTER

43

Other Physical Therapies

Physical therapies other than drug therapy are not as frequently used as they used to be until the middle 1950s. However, because they remain in the therapeutic armamentarium of many psychiatrists, a brief description of them and a critical discussion of their use will be presented.

I

Convulsive Shock Treatment

Convulsive shock treatment was first applied by Von Meduna (1937) with pharmacologic methods. Von Meduna thought that there was an incompatibility between schizophrenia and epilepsy and that therefore even an artificially produced epilepsy would be beneficial to schizophrenic patients. This theoretical basis is very dubious; furthermore, convulsive therapy was soon found more effective for psychotic depressions than for schizophrenia. No matter how debatable were his theoretical premises, the introduction of convulsive therapy in psychiatry is nevertheless to Von Meduna's credit.

Pharmacologic convulsive therapy has, however, a serious drawback. The convulsion occurs not immediately after the injection but after a brief interval during which the patient retains consciousness. During this interval the patient experiences fear and unpleasant feelings of extreme intensity. Electric convulsive therapy (ECT), introduced in 1938 by Cerletti and Bini (1938), immediately replaced the pharmacologic method partly because it was technically simpler than the latter, but most of all because it produced an almost immediate loss of consciousness and therefore eliminated the above-mentioned unpleasant interval experiences. A simple machine, modeled after the original one devised by Bini, is necessary. Two electrodes are placed on the temples of the patient and a certain amount of current is allowed to pass. The amount of current and the duration are measured. The doses range from 70 to 150 volts for 0.1 to 0.5 second. Petit mal and grand mal seizures result, but only grand mal seizures are therapeutically effective. The average course of twenty treatments is generally given to schizophrenic patients.

Kalinowsky and Hippius (1969) recommend an initial dose of 70 volts for 0.2 second. An increase in time and voltage is applied if no convulsion occurs. The patient should have no breakfast prior to treatment. Dentures, hair pins, and other metal objects should be removed. Partial dentures are left in the mouth to prevent breaking of unevenly spaced teeth. All medication should be suspended. The bladder should be voided.

Although Kalinowsky and Hippius believe that the danger of treating with ECT patients who were receiving phenothiazine treatment was exaggerated, they still refrain from treating patients who are on high doses of tranquilizers. They prefer to wait two days from the time the dose was drastically reduced. On the morning of the treatment all neuroleptic drugs are suspended. Mouth gags are used to keep the patient from biting his tongue. The trunk and extremities are held gently by attendants. To obtain muscle relaxation and to avoid fracture many practitioners used curare, in accordance with a technique first described by Bennett (1940). Because this procedure is dangerous, curare has been replaced by succinylcholine. This substance is given in combination with an intravenous anesthetic and therefore the assistance of an anesthesiologist is required.

Severe cardiovascular diseases, pulmonary diseases, diseases of the bones, brain tumors, and epilepsy are contraindications to ECT.

The results obtained with ECT are very impressive, especially in patients whose illness is recent (generally no longer than a year). In many cases, the obvious symptoms—such as delusions, hallucinations, ideas of reference, catatonic postures—disappear. The patient becomes more cooperative and is soon capable of living socially. The treatment is not affective in every case; furthermore in many cases relapses occur sooner or later.

As we mentioned before, if we probe deeply enough into these patients, we see that the cause of the deep conflicts will remain or may reemerge once the effects of the treatment fade away. Nevertheless, what we obtain is of considerable worth. Generally, after ECT, the patient is able to return to society; he will no longer be a public charge and, although his functions may be curtailed, he may be able to live some kind of limited social life. In many fortunate cases, where the events in dramatic succession (acute attack → hospitalization → institution of ECT) have acted as catalytic agents on the environmental forces, the results may be much more than a removal of the immediate symptoms.

I recommend ECT especially in acute or refractory cases, when the patients do not respond to psychotherapy or drug therapy. After the course of ECT the capacity to experience anxiety is diminished and the patient is more reachable. The elimination of the gross psychopathology makes communication easier and reduces the duration and the frequency of the sessions of psychotherapy. If the patient cannot be affected psychotherapeutically after ECT, this fact must be considered an ominous sign, and a recurrence has to be expected sooner or later.

But it is my opinion that, if a complete or solid recovery is hoped for, psychotherapy is a necessity after ECT, just as it is in drug therapy. In certain difficult cases psychotherapy will make it possible to spot minor subliminal setbacks, which may then be checked and controlled. If not worked out with the therapist, these setbacks would develop into full psychotic relapses. At the same time the patient is made able to understand and to manage the conflicts or the anxiety that is bound to reappear with the gradual resumption of his normal functions of life.

How is ECT capable of producing its symptomatic therapeutic effects? Here the field is still open to the realm of speculation. Gordon (1948), in an interesting short paper, listed no fewer than fifty theories that have been advanced to explain the effect of ECT. Twenty-seven of them are somatogenic theories and twenty-three psychogenic. At the present stage of our knowledge it is difficult to ascertain which one or which combination of them is valid.

Despite the fact that ECT acts as a psychological catalyst on the relatives of the patient, and despite the fact that I consider the psychological determinants and components of schizophrenia very important, I am inclined to believe that ECT has a predominantly physiological action, not a psychological one. Although the improvement may be partially due to the fact that the patient receives some kind of care, obviously it cannot be due only to the fact of being treated, irrespective of the nature of the treatment. Some of the past physical treatments, such as hormone therapy, did not produce any effect on schizophrenics. The symptomatic improvement is also not due to the fact that the patients become more accessible to psychotherapy. Although, as we have already mentioned, it is true that they become more accessible to psychotherapy and that we should take advantage of this greater accessibility to the fullest possible extent, the fact remains that hundreds of patients have been discharged from hospitals after ECT free of overt symptoms, even though they have not received any kind of psychotherapy.

I share with many others the view that the improvement is a consequence of the reversible histological alterations produced in the central nervous system, particularly in the frontal lobes. These alterations engender those transient clinical pictures of organic disorder that Kalinowsky (1945) has described and called "organic-psychotic reactions occurring during ECT" and that are mainly characterized by impairment of memory and by confusion. In order for the patient to experience the kind of anxiety that produces a psychosis, some areas of the brain, either cortical or subcortical, must function adequately. If those areas are in an altered condition, no long-circuited anxiety is possible. There is loss of memory of the conflicts, or, if the conflicts are remembered, they are incapable of eliciting anxiety. By the time the reversible alterations have disappeared, the patient may have reoriented his life, or his life may have been reoriented for him, or the acute, precipitating factors may have disappeared, so that there may be no recurrence of the symptoms. But if these factors have not changed, sooner or later there will be a relapse.

The chief objection to this theory is the following. Why is not ECT effective in psychoneuroses? After all, we know that in psychoneuroses, too, anxiety is the basic factor. The transient damage produced by ECT is not enough to prevent the degree of anxiety that is necessary to engender a neurosis. In other words, according to this theory, to elicit the anxiety that causes a psychosis, a higher degree of functionality is necessary than for the development of the anxiety that leads to psychoneurosis. We have already learned that in order to become psychotic, the patient must have cortical centers that will permit him to experience long-circuiting anxiety, that is, cortical centers that will permit him to live in a symbolic and interpersonal world.

Thus, according to this point of view, ECT is a reductive procedure; it operates by putting the patient artificially on a lower level, where it will be easier for him to integrate. We have seen that the illness itself attempts to do so. However, with relatively few exceptions the illness fails in its teleologic attempts because, although it pushes the patient to lower levels, it does not give him the ability to integrate; on the contrary, it puts into motion a mechanism of self-perpetuating and progressive regression. ECT is successful if the patient, with the help of others, can manage to reach some kind of solid integration before the conflicts come back, so that he will be able then to repress them or to find some kind of *modus vivendi* with them. ECT, like all organic cerebral traumata, does not unchain a progressive regression (Arieti, 1956). Undoubtedly ECT has a useful effect also on the autonomic nervous system and on the reticular system, but the mechanism is unknown.

Two points must be examined on account of which ECT has been bitterly criticized: (1) does ECT produce serious damage to the nervous system? (2) does ECT hinder or make impossible subsequent psychotherapy?

ECT *does* produce some damage, but of relatively mild intensity and of reversible character. Apart from the theoretical considerations about the therapeutic mechanisms of ECT, we have clinical and pathological evidence of damage. Clinically, we have those organic reactions that have already been mentioned and that generally subside in a few weeks after termination of the treatment. The works of many authors (Winkleman and Moore, 1944; Arieti, 1941; Cerletti and Bini, 1940; Globus et al., 1943) have made it evident that histological changes produced by both metrazol and ECT are all *reversible,* unless an unusual quantity of treatment is given for a prolonged period of time.

Clinical and histological studies indicate that the damage is mild and transitory. Complete *restitutio ad integrum* is to be expected if the proper technique is used.

If physical hazards do not exist or are minimal when the proper conditions are met, then the objections of many authors to this type of treatment must concern possible psychological harm. We have already seen that some intellectual impairment and emotional liability may occur during the treatment, but that they are transitory. No patient, as a result of the treatment, has been permanently incapacitated intellectually or has developed psychopathic traits.

Finally, and this question concerns the second fundamental point to be evaluated, does ECT hinder the ensuing or concomitant psychotherapy that is necessary for a complete recovery?

Eissler (1952) speaks of "the great danger" he saw in ECT and of his great efforts to save patients from it.

My experience with many patients who, before the era of drug therapy, were treated psychotherapeutically after ECT has convinced me that this physical treatment did not hinder psychotherapy but, on the contrary, made it easier or possible in many otherwise untreatable cases. It is necessary, however, that the psychotherapist be not the same physician who administered the shock. A new reorientation, with new interpersonal contacts, is necessary for the patient.

ECT, however, should not be the first choice among various methods of treatment. It is symptomatic in nature, the effects are not lasting in many cases, and the memory of it remains painful to the patient. All in all, it remains a useful procedure, to be kept in the psychiatric armamentarium and to be used only when the other types of treatment have failed to bring about even symptomatic improvement.

II

Insulin Treatment

Insulin shock treatment was introduced by Sakel (1936). It consists of administration of insulin in progressively larger doses. One starts initially with 10 to 15 units and increases the dosage until the patient undergoes severe hypoglycemic shocks, which are characterized by comas and, less frequently, by epileptic seizures. The average coma-producing dose is 100 to 150 units. The state of coma used to be terminated in the fourth or fifth hour by administration of an adequate amount of carbohydrates. Sugar was given orally if the patient was able to drink, or through tube feeding, or through an intravenous injection of a glucose solution. Now termination is obtained through the use of glucagon, in doses of 0.33 to 1 mg intravenously or intramuscularly. Small amounts generally awaken the patient, who is then able to drink a sugar solution.

From a minimum of twenty to a maximum of eighty comas are generally produced, usually at a frequency of at least three times a week.

Many modifications of Sakel's original technique have been devised. Laqueur and La Burt (1960) devised the method of multiple doses of insulin. Treatment is started with 5 to 10 units and the daily amount is divided into three doses given at fifteen-minute intervals. In most patients comas are obtained with only 60 or 70 units of insulin.

Elderly patients should not be accepted for insulin treatment, nor should patients with cardiovascular, renal, or respiratory conditions or other debilitating diseases. Pregnancy is also a counterindication. From a pathological point of view, some researchers have found severe histological alterations (Ferraro and Jervis, 1939), whereas others have found irreversible cell damage in experimental animals *only* when the animals died in coma or when unusually high doses were injected over a long period of time (Accornero, 1939; Weil, Liebert, and Heilbrunn, 1938).

Insulin coma treatment requires a proper hospital setting; it is not a procedure suitable for office practice. Because of its relative technical difficulties, it has been replaced by ECT. However, some authorities, including Kalinowsky and Hippius (1969), feel that insulin remission is superior to that achieved with ECT.

III
Some Notes on Psychosurgery

In the first edition of this book (1955) I concluded my notes on psychosurgery with the following words:

> By doing surgery on the patient, we give up all hope. We share the pessimism and hopelessness of the patient. We are ready to make him more docile but less human, without any possibility of redemption. The irrevocability of the damage, which precludes the application of new methods, devised in the future, or additional unforeseeable opportunities, has been dramatized recently by the development of the new tranquilizing drugs. The partial amelioration obtained with psychosurgery could have been obtained shortly afterwards with these pharmacological agents. Thousands and thousands of patients, all over the world, who lost their frontal lobes could have obtained the same or greater degrees of improvement in a less dangerous, nontraumatic, and reversible manner.

I still subscribe to these remarks. Nevertheless, inasmuch as psychosurgery is still practiced in a few treatment centers for refractory chronic patients, I shall describe here a few of its modalities.

Psychosurgical treatment, forerunners of which were applied even in ancient times, was reintroduced on a scientific basis in 1935 by the Portuguese Ega Moniz (1963*a*, *b*). As Fulton reported (1951), Moniz was impressed by Jacobsen's and Fulton's experiments. Monkeys present anxiety and temper tantrums if they are not rewarded in a test situation, but they do not manifest this disturbed behavior if their frontal lobes have been removed. Moniz felt that if this result is obtained in monkeys, it could also be obtained in men suffering from anxiety. He proceeded to cut the frontal projections of twenty patients and reported favorable results. He first destroyed the white matter by means of alcohol injections but soon replaced this method with another one that consists of cutting the white matter. This procedure appeared more reliable and controllable. Leucotomy was thus originated.

Freeman and Watts (1942) introduced Moniz's method into the United States and refined its technique. Since then many types of operations have been tried and advocated in an attempt to reduce the damage and to increase the safety of the operation. After the original work of Moniz, Fiamberti (1947) introduced the method of transorbital leucotomy. A frontal cut is produced in the lower medial quadrant merely by drawing the upper eyelid away from the eyeball and inserting the transorbital leucotome, which goes through the orbital plate, penetrates the frontal lobe for a depth of three inches, and severs the basal portion of the thalamofrontal radiation. Freeman (1949), who originally preferred Moniz's operation, later became one of the chief advocates of Fiamberti's technique. This technique is relatively simple and does not require surgical skill.

Scoville (1949) advocated a technique called "selective cortical undercutting," which cuts only the orbital surface of the frontal lobes. Mettler (1952) and others have advocated another operation called topectomy or gyrectomy, which consists of the bilateral removal of Brodmann's areas 9 and 10. Thalamotomy and other operations have also been attempted. Lindstrom (1954) produced cortical destruction with ultrasonic beams, which did not produce gliosis.

It is out of place to give here a description of the various techniques or a detailed account of the postoperative handling of the patients or of the early postoperative symptoms.

Some differences have been noticed in the results obtained with the various operations, but the fundamental characteristics seem to be the same. These operations have been performed on patients suffering from a variety of psychiatric syndromes, such as severe obsessive-compulsive neuroses, involutional melancholia, and anxiety states. They have also been performed on patients suffering from intractable pain.

The largest number of patients who have been treated belong to the schizophrenic group. The results are not constant, but most authors feel that if deterioration has not occurred, improvement is likely to occur. These authors stress the fact that the patients who were unhappy or anxiety ridden before the operation seem very much relieved. They appear euphoric, gay, carefree. If they had obsessions and compulsions or disturbing hallucinations, they may lose these symptoms. More often the symptoms persist but do not seem so disturbing. According to Burlingame (1949) these patients present a "third personality"—that is, a personality that is different from the psychotic and psychoneurotic. This "third personality" is characterized by reduced affectivity and increased responsiveness to immediate stimuli and environment. The patients who are not improved enough to leave the hospital are easier to manage. They cooperate better and do not manifest destructive behavior or attacks of rage. Neurological complications, especially epilepsy, occur in some cases. The mortality rate is low.

Some enthusiastic authors have spoken even of social recoveries. Some patients are able to resume their previous occupations if these did not require too much initiative. Others adjust in a lower occupation. Many authors stress the fact also that the common psychological tests, such as the usual intelligence tests, do not reveal any impairment of the mental functions of the patients.

These views are optimistic because they give only a partial account of the results. It is enough to stay for a few hours in close interpersonal relationship with some of these operated patients in order to realize that they are not normal. Perhaps their abnormality cannot be differentiated or illustrated by the usual psychiatric examination or by the common psychological tests. This proves only the limitations of these tests. Not only is the operated patient in an abnormal state, but his abnormalities are serious. He lacks initiative, originality, foresight, moral judgment. Psychopathic behavior is prominent in many cases, because the patient is carefree, oblivious of the consequences of his acts, and interested only in satisfying his wishes. On the other hand, it is true that some patients show only minimal defects or sporadic outbursts of temper.

Many people feel that, undesirable as these postoperative symptoms are, they are still better than the ones the patient presented prior to the operation and that therefore the change is worthwhile. In other words, the difference between the preoperative and postoperative symptoms is more important than what we lose potentially. This point of view is very questionable. It is true that prior to the operation the patient was unmanageable and suffering and that after the operation he often becomes docile and easy to manage. However, as we have already mentioned, often he also becomes a ruthless extrovert, impulsive, lacking in deep emotionality, foresight, initiative, creativity, and spirituality, and manifests psychopathic behavior. These characteristics are not *secondary* undesirable sequelae. They are very important. They also prevent deep psychotherapy, which requires an awareness of long-circuited anxiety and of one's dynamic mechanisms. After psychosurgery only training toward adjustment to a limited existence is possible, nothing else.

The principle under which psychosurgery is practiced is fundamentally a reductive one. Damage is caused to the highest levels of the nervous system, so that it will not be able to mediate those functions that are necessary for the production of symptoms (see Chapter 30). Theoretically there is no objection to this principle. Many medical treatments, especially surgical ones, are of reductive nature. They diminish the functionality; they remove organs. In the field of neurosurgery, this principle is followed quite often. For example, in order to eliminate the involuntary movements of postencephalitic parkinsonian patients, cortical tracts are cut. No cortical impulses, therefore, can produce the pathological movements by acting on other centers. We have just seen that shock therapy also is reductive. But in psychosurgery the treatment is not reductive in a mild or transitory manner. Important areas, necessary for the highest processes of symbolism and interpersonal relations, are destroyed for the lifetime of the patient.

On the other hand, in the schizophrenic process itself, the damage is not necessarily permanent. As striking recoveries, at times even from very advanced cases, indicate, there is nothing in schizophrenia proving the absolute irreversibility of the process. The situation is thus different from that of postencephalitic parkinsonian patients who are treated surgically. It is a physical impossibility for them to reacquire the normal functions of the extrapyramidal centers that are diseased. It is more than questionable whether one can feel authorized in schizophrenia to barter a damage that is permanent for one that is not, especially when what we get is only a partial amelioration of dubious value, and almost always accompanied by serious complications.

PART NINE

The Larger Horizons and the Concept of Schizophrenia

CHAPTER

44

Syndromes Related to Schizophrenia

We have seen throughout this book that the scope of schizophrenia is large indeed, but it becomes much larger if we add to it the psychiatric conditions that various authors have included in a less definite conception of the disorder. This tendency to enlarge the scope of schizophrenia started with Bleuler (see Chapter 2); but it has been pursued since then by several authors. Some inclusions did not prove to be justified by the test of time. However, the three syndromes that we shall briefly illustrate in this chapter (paranoia, anorexia nervosa, and childhood schizophrenia) are probably related to schizophrenia.

I

Paranoia

In some psychiatric centers today the diagnosis of paranoia is never made; it is replaced by such classifications as the paranoid type of schizophrenia, paranoid state, and paranoid condition. Kraepelin, who was the first to give the diagnostic criteria for paranoia, divided all paranoiac-paranoid syndromes into three groups. At one extreme he put the paranoid type of dementia praecox (schizophrenia). This type includes cases that present projective and delusional symptoms together with the other regressive symptoms of schizophrenia. At the other extreme he put cases of paranoia, a syndrome characterized by well-systematized delusions, with no tendencies toward regression, remission, or recovery. Hallucinations, according to Kraepelin, may occur in paranoia, but only rarely; regression may be present also, but only to a minimal degree.

Between these two groups Kraepelin put the paraphrenias, which in American psychiatry correspond roughly to "paranoid states" or "paranoid conditions." Paranoid states are supposed to be delusional syndromes that are fairly well systematized but are not as logically constructed as paranoia. The differential diagnosis between paranoid conditions or states and the paranoid type of schizophrenia is often determined more by the diagnostic orientation of the psychiatrist than by the actual symptomatology.

The confusion between these terms is even more pronounced when adjectives and personal nouns are used. A person suffering from pure paranoia is a paranoiac, and not a paranoid, as he is occasionally called. A paranoid is a person suffering from a paranoid state or from the paranoid type of schizophrenia, not from paranoia. Just as we call a person suffering from schizophrenia, a schizophrenic, and not a schizophrenid, so we must call a person suffering from paranoia a paranoiac. Paranoid means "not quite paranoiac but similar to, or almost, a paranoiac."

Many authors (for instance, Kolb, 1968), however, put paranoid conditions and paranoia together, either because they believe that the two conditions cannot be distinguished or because paranoia or "pure paranoia" or "true paranoia" is such a rare condition that it does not deserve a separate consideration. Most authors who reluctantly recognize the existence of paranoia as a separate entity consider it a very rare disease. Paranoia is said to be much more frequent in the male sex, especially after the age of 35–40. Adolph Meyer described the prepsychotic personality of the paranoiac as characterized by rigidity, pride, haughtiness, suspiciousness or actual distrust, and disdain. A large percentage of these patients are unmarried and show little interest in sexual life; the few paranoiacs who get married are unable to establish a warm conjugal relationship. Some patients disclose indications of overt or latent homosexuality. Contrary to early psychoanalytic formulations, however, homosexuality does not seem a prerequisite for paranoia.

I feel that it is useful to retain this condition as a separate clinical entity, even if we do not understand it completely and do not know how close it is to schizophrenia. We are probably correct to exclude from this group all cases presenting hallucinations and obvious signs of regression. Even if such cases are omitted, however, paranoia is much more common than is usually believed. The diagnosis of paranoia is seldom made for several reasons:

1. Many psychiatrists are still influenced by the early descriptions of this disorder, which portrayed only its most severe forms. They adhered to Kraepelin's view that no remission or recovery was possible. Contrary to general belief, however, the majority of cases are mild.

2. Many cases are not recognized and never reach the office of a psychiatrist. The patient has no insight into his condition, and people take him for an eccentric, fanatic, or strongly opinionated person, but not necessarily a psychotic.

3. Some paranoiacs eventually act out and are occasionally labeled as psychopaths. Actual paranoiac-psychopathic mixtures do occur. In my own clinical

experience I have encountered quite a few of them, which I cannot report here because they would be easily identified. Although I cannot be absolutely sure about this point, my clinical inferences when I read the life history of some historical figures like Hitler and Stalin lead me to believe that they were at first complex psychopaths, with an underlying psychotic structure that eventually revealed itself (Arieti, 1963*c*). Some psychopathic-paranoiacs, endowed by intelligence, fluency of speech, and apparent strength of personality, find followers and satellites as easily as they find persecutors—two groups of people who are useful in enhancing the power drive.

The notion that mild paranoia is a common disease is gaining recognition. Revitch (1954) made a study of conjugal paranoia and reported four cases in detail. In this type of paranoia delusions and pathological attitudes are directed against the spouse. The pathological attitudes characterized by humiliating and destructive acts against the marital partner may precede by many years the outbreak of obvious delusions. The patient always preserves good contact with the environment, is able to conduct his affairs, and may be able to veil projections so skillfully that, not the patient, but the spouse may be considered abnormal and may become the target of indignation of the patient's immediate family. According to Revitch, homosexual conflicts and a general feeling of inadequacy aggravated by conjugal relationship are the most important factors in the genesis of conjugal paranoia. Revitch added that projective techniques do not always elicit the gravity of the clinical condition but are valuable in the evaluation of the personality structure of the patient. The best diagnostic tool, however, is an unhurried and careful interview of both spouses by the same psychiatrist. The problem of disposition is also extremely difficult, defying simple solutions, on account of the apparent lucidity and productive capacity of the patient.

Johanson (1964) reported her study of fifty-two cases of patients suffering from mild paranoia. She did her study in Uppsala and all but seven of her patients were Swedish. Of the seven foreign-born patients, three were refugees. Johanson's patients did not differ from the average population in intelligence or marital status. Twenty-seven were men and twenty-five women. Only six of them, all male, were eventually diagnosed as schizophrenic.

Psychodynamics

Difficulties with one's parents and other family situations similar to those described in Part Two in reference to schizophrenic patients are found also in the life history of paranoiacs.

The future paranoiac keeps a "chip on the shoulder" and harbors a secret desire for revenge against the oppressor. Like the schizophrenic, he generally shifts his hatred from the people who made his life uncomfortable and painful to imaginary oppressors. Endowed with superior intelligence he spends an enormously long time brooding and conceiving plans of revenge.

My clinical experiences have not revealed that homosexual leanings are important in the psychodynamics of most paranoiacs. What is prominent, however, is either a confusion in sexual identification or a sense of deep inadequacy in sexual life. The inadequacy actually manifests itself in all areas of interpersonal relations. The patient is almost compelled to live alone, aloof, in celibacy, and is indeed considered inadequate or bizarre. But he cannot accept this fate and lives for the time when he can manifest to the world his real worth. That time never comes; he feels more and more disappointed, to the point of desperation. Eventually a life experience occurs that he was consciously or unconsciously waiting for. He gives special meaning to the episode: this may be the beginning of an ever-expanding paranoiac system.

Among the events that paranoiacs have misinterpreted and used as the beginning of a delusional system I have found with great frequency the following four:

1. The patient is involved in an automobile or other accident. He starts to believe that the accident was not casual but planned, and he eventually discovers the machinery of a conspiracy behind it. If the patient was the only one to survive in the accident, or hardly escaped death, he may give to the episode a mystical resonance. He may consider himself destined to save the world.

2. The patient was really the victim of an injustice or, more frequently, of an error. For instance, he was unjustifiably accused of stealing. Subsequently he builds up a system of delusions springing from the episode. An important variation of this second possibility is the following: the patient has not been accused, but he believes he has been accused. For instance, some people seem to him to indicate that he is the one suspected of having committed a particular crime that was reported in the newspapers.

3. The patient interprets an attitude or action of a person close to him (generally the spouse or fiancée) in a peculiar way and subsequently elaborates a paranoiac system over the episode.

4. The patient has undergone a permanent change, for instance, facial plastic surgery or sterilization. Although he himself chose to be operated upon, he is not satisfied with the result and attributes evil intention to the surgeon or to any person who recommended the operation. Other changes affecting position, location, and so forth, may also act as precipitating events. This fourth type of possibility is more frequent in paranoid schizophrenia than in paranoia.

An important point to be considered is the relevance of the original episode. It is not just a precipitating event; it is a very important dynamic factor, without which the patient would have been able to check, or even compensate, his psychotic propensity.

Tolentino (1957*a, b*) reported the interesting diary of a patient who developed true paranoia after he felt that people were accusing him of having stolen a carpet. Actually nobody accused the patient, but he interpreted the words and gestures of some people in a way that sustained his convictions. The patient became sure that a colonel in the army was accusing him when actually the colonel himself was the thief. Thus he reported the colonel to the proper authorities. This action led to suit for slander, which was followed by incarceration and eventually hospitalization of the patient. In the hospital the paranoiac attitude of the patient extended to attendants and nurses, who retaliated by isolating and restricting the patient in a cruel manner. The patient's diary is reminiscent of a Kafka novel. Tolentino interpreted the case as a case of true paranoia. According to him the delusional idea was the projective reconstruction of a deep feeling of guilt. The external events, that is, the theft that really happened and the possibility that the patient would be accused, motivated and deformed the feeling of guilt. According to Tolentino the unconscious self-accusation of the patient was externalized in the following way:

1. Projection (by accusing the colonel of theft).
2. Self-punishment (with actions that led the patient to incarceration, hospitalization, and bad treatment from attendants).
3. Regression to primary narcissism. The patient at the acme of the illness could not concentrate on, or be concerned with, anything else—only his delusional system.

In the third case that we have listed (when the patient interprets in a peculiar way an attitude or action of a person close to him) it is not accurate to dismiss the point of view of the patient as merely delusional or referential. I have become convinced, and Revitch has also, that the other person (generally the spouse) is often psychologically disturbed, although not psychotic, and is given to conscious or unconscious actions that increase the vulnerability of the patient. Thus in conjugal paranoia a particular family relation explains to some degree the psychodynamics of the disorder or its perpetuation. However, it does not entirely explain its origin and the selection of the particular cognitive mechanisms necessary to sustain the delusions.

Formal Mechanisms

Once an idea becomes dominant in the mind of a paranoiac, for example, the thought that he must avenge a misdeed or uncover and openly condemn his own persecutions, he needs to demonstrate that the idea has a basis in fact. He has to transform his beliefs into certitude, in spite of what appears to others to be a lack of corroborating evidence.

I have accumulated some presumptive (but not unquestionable) clinical evidence that some psychopaths who later revealed themselves to be (or become) paranoiacs at first were aware that they were lying. Later they accepted their ideas as true in order to sustain their motivation. One is again reminded of Hitler, who at first recognized he was lying. He is the one who said that the bigger the lie, the more easily it will be believed. Later there is presumptive evidence that he too came to believe his own lies, which thus became delusions (Arieti, 1963*c*).

The paranoiac does not resort to obvious regressive phenomena in order to demonstrate to himself and to others that what he believes is true. He does not experience the psychotic insight of the paranoid schizophrenic, that sudden illumination resulting from the acceptance of paleologic forms. The paranoiac starts by accepting some premises as undeniable truths. These truths, however, have to be defended by uncovering hidden connections and by discovering a plan, a plot, or a structure that was not apparent. The patient becomes engaged in collecting material that will prove his allegations. He indulges in prolonged and elaborate investigations, and little by little he connects things to create a well-structured system, which actually consists of misinterpretations and distortions.

These distortions are so well rationalized as to give the impression to the layman, and occasionally even to the psychiatrist, that the patient is perfectly sane. As a matter of fact, he appears to be a very intelligent person who has been able to find relations between things and facts that seemed unrelated to more naïve people.

How does the patient find these relations? As already mentioned, he does not resort to paleologic thinking, or to a confusion between identity and similarity. Unlike the schizophrenic, he follows only secondary process mechanisms. In scanning the several possibilities that may account for a certain fact, he selects and accepts as true the ones that fit his overall system or his preconceived belief. He can view clues and possibilities as sure evidence, so that what should remain a hypothesis becomes a fact if it fits the preconceived notion. In this way the unconscious wish and the impelling need to believe become supported by a cognitive scheme.

To give an example, the patient happens to see X., his alleged persecutor, in the street where he himself works, and he concludes that X. has come to spy on him or to harm him. The fact that X. is there becomes a proof that X. is persecuting him, whereas it should be only a hypothetical possibility, soon to be discarded. Similar clues, of course, are studied by the police in evaluating suspects and are discarded unless supported by other facts. The scientist too conceives hypotheses and wants to determine whether they are valid or not. But for the paranoiac the possibility becomes certainty because it is "proved" retrospectively by what it purports to prove. That is, because X. is a persecutor and wants to molest the patient, his being on the street where the patient works is not coincidental but is caused by the fact that X. is there to persecute the patient. Because X. is there to persecute the patient, it is true that X. persecutes the patient. This is circular reasoning, and obviously, incorrect; but it is not paleologic.

Such paranoiac thinking, based on premises supported by secondary process mechanisms, is occasionally also found in paranoid conditions and in the paranoid type of schizophrenia, where it is mixed in with paleologic thinking and other regressive types of cognition. In my opinion, the diagnosis of paranoia is justified only when there are no traces of paleologic or other regressive types of thinking.

The paranoiac system becomes the only inner object the patient cares about. Any therapeutic attempt would have to aim at reenlarging his attachment to other inner objects. This is a difficult task because relations with the other objects increase his anxiety and enhance his desire to withdraw again into his paranoiac construction, within which he has become a very efficient manipulator. Although the most typical conditions of paranoia are chronic and progressive, many cases are characterized by episodes that alternate with periods of normal or almost normal behavior. In some instances, the delusional symptoms disappear and are replaced by hypochondriacal or even psychosomatic complaints.

The following case report is typical of the common form of mild paranoia.

Mr. Paruval

Mr. Paruval came for treatment at the age of 49. He stated that an old trouble—incomprehension with his wife—had become steady and persistent, and he wanted help. He seemed sincere and desirous of improving his marital situation. Soon it became evident that he had a need to convince somebody of how much was wrong with his wife. A psychiatrist would be a person who would understand him.

The patient had emigrated ten years previously from Europe. He was the older of two siblings in a middle-class family. His father was a weak man, completely henpecked by his wife. The mother was described as a spendthrift, almost to the point of irrationality, and as oblivious to her maternal duties. The patient and his sister, when they were in their teens, advised the father to divorce the mother, but the father did not agree. He felt that for better or for worse he had to remain with his wife. Early life seemed uneventful to the patient. He did well in school and became a professional man.

In his early twenties he became interested in Alicia, a girl whom he seriously considered marrying. Paruval said that a year after he had started to date this girl, a good friend of the family revealed to him that Alicia was promiscuous and a woman with other undesirable habits. The friend gave Paruval ample evidence that these allegations were true. The patient decided to break the friendship, felt disappointed in women in general, and was not too optimistic about ever obtaining love. He had subsequently occasional and unimportant dates, but a few years later he let himself be convinced by a matchmaker to marry Patricia, a girl who was represented to him as "immaculate," a nice girl from a good family; as a matter of fact, she was the sister of a clergyman. It is important to add that in the particular local European environment where the patient lived marriages arranged by matchmakers were not uncommon. The patient met Patricia, liked her, and decided to marry her. The date of the wedding was arranged a few months after the first meeting. About two months prior to the wedding day Patricia told her fiancé that she preferred to wear a regular dress during the wedding ceremony, not a white bridal gown.

The patient was shocked by this remark. On the best day of one's life, why not wear the white gown, symbol of purity and innocence, as brides have traditionally done for thousands of years? He tried to convince Patricia to wear the white gown, and Patricia agreed. Nothing was said any more about this little incident, and the marriage took place as arranged. But on the wedding night, the patient, who is not a physician, submitted his wife to a regular gynecological examination. He felt that Patricia's hymen had a big opening and that her vagina was so large that it seemed to indicate that she had already given birth to a few children. He felt this was incontrovertible evidence that the woman he had married was not a virgin. The matchmaker who had represented her as an immaculate girl was a cheater. Now Paruval could understand Patricia's reluctance to wear a white gown during the wedding ceremony. How could a woman who does not feel pure inside wear a symbol of purity?

During the wedding night Mr. Paruval became increasingly infuriated, beat the wife up, and in a vague way threatened more energetic actions. The wife vainly protested her innocence. Finally she suggested that she be examined by a physician, who would determine and testify whether she was a virgin or not. Two days later a doctor examined Patricia and certified that she was a virgin. This fact, however, did not reassure Paruval. He had evidence that this doctor had been a friend of Patricia's family for a long time and consequently would make statements only in her favor.

Although unconvinced, the patient "decided to forgive" his wife and even "allowed himself to have intercourse with her." During the treatment he repeatedly said that he forgot the incident that had occurred on the wedding night, but it was obvious that he not only did not forget it, but continued to brood about it and to exploit it in order to give a special coloring to his relation with his wife. Soon a child was born, and Paruval never doubted that he was the father. However, some events that occurred later on were interpreted by him in such a way as to reinforce in him the image of his wife as a woman unworthy of wearing the bridal gown.

One of the principles in which the patient believed was that wives should not go to work; only husbands. Mrs. Paruval had promised not to work; however, Mr. Paruval would occasionally call his home during the day, and if nobody answered, he would think that his wife had gone to work in spite of her promise. He did not know what kind of work the wife was engaged in. He knew that the work she would do was reputable, but that did not matter. She had broken the promise not to work. He thought she was putting the earned money in banks and then hiding the bankbooks in secret places so that he had no idea of how much money she had saved or earned. He was also sure that Patricia was spying on him. He was convinced that she was opening all the mail he received although he had told her absolutely not to do so. What evidence did he have? He had noticed that a bottle of glue that was on a shelf in the kitchen was half empty. This was convincing proof that she steamed the envelopes of the letters when they arrived, read the letters, glued the envelopes shut again, and put them back into the mailbox so that he would not be aware that the mail had been tampered with when he arrived from work.

His assumption became certainty when the wife told him that at Christmas she had given a five-dollar tip to the mailman. Why would she give such an enormous tip? They were not wealthy people. Obviously she had done so to keep the mailman silent or on her side because he had become aware of what she was doing to the mail.

The history of this case is too long to be reported in its entirety. There are many details that reveal how minor episodes were interpreted to support the atmosphere of lies and subterfuges that the patient imagined his wife was creating. On the other hand, it is possible to conceive that with her behavior the wife contributed to perpetuating her husband's doubts. As a matter of fact, further developments suggested that this was the case. With Paruval's permission I interviewed his wife a few times, and she repeated to me that all the accusations of the husband, from the wedding night to the present, were false, with one exception. She was indeed opening the letters that he was receiving from his family and regluing them again before he arrived home from work. She was doing so because those letters were detailed accounts of all the difficulties the family had. The news in these letters was disturbing him very much and would prey on his mind. She wanted to be prepared and help him. I was indeed shocked when I heard this. It became obvious that the wife too was trapped in a paranoiac setup. Obviously she was cooperating in keeping alive a paranoiac structure.

Other circumstances were difficult to evaluate. The patient complained that the wife was cold and distant. He interpreted this attitude as proof that she could not be warm when at the same time she was involved in secret machinations. But how could the wife not be distant and cold when she felt constantly accused and under investigation?

There was in Mr. Paruval's attitude also a need *not* to arrive at the truth, a need to perpetuate the atmosphere of doubt and suspiciousness. None of his investigations were carried out as a prosecuting attorney would do. For instance, when it was decided that the wife be examined by a physician to prove whether she was a virgin, he did not object to the choice of a physician who was immediately classified as a friend of the family. As a matter of fact, at that time the fact that the physician was a friend was welcome because the whole matter would be less embarrassing. Later on, the very same fact permitted the perpetuation of the doubt.

Mr. Paruval was very eloquent in his speech and at times quite convincing. He would talk with emphatic fervor and at other times the quasi-legalistic style that paranoiacs and paranoids have. He would say, "If my wife had told me she was not a virgin, if she had told me she wanted to go to work, if she had told me that she had had an irresistible impulse to open my mail, I would have tried to understand, to excuse, to forgive; but she did nothing of the sort: she lied."

One could have expected that Mr. Paruval would not want to live with a person for whom he had no trust or respect, but on the contrary he claimed that he loved her very much and that he wanted to get to understand the incredible things that she was doing. He wanted to find out why she did such strange things and tried to hurt him so much. Obviously he had the need to perpetuate the paranoiac situation.

Treatment helped the condition to some extent, but much paranoiac ideation remained. The paranoiac periods later alternated with periods characterized by hypochondriacal preoccupations.

Although the manifest illness probably started the day of the wedding, and there have been in the subsequent twenty-five years many exacerbations and remissions, there has been no regression or deterioration. On the contrary, since the onset of the illness the patient has been able to make considerable progress in his professional activities. When the political situation in Europe made him emigrate to the United States, he adjusted well to the new country, overcame external difficulties, and continued to make progress in his career. At the same time he felt inadequate, ineffective, overwhelmed by family problems, deserted, and alone. His tendency toward intellectualization and his work protected him from complete collapse. At the same time they favored in him a paranoiac structure in which he could channel his conflicts. We do not know much about his experience in childhood. We do know that, probably with justification, he never accepted his mother in his heart. On the contrary he made her the prototype of all women, whom he saw as powerful, threatening, deceitful, and potentially destructive of men. Paruval did not remember well what his mother did to him directly, but he remembered well what the father had to go through with her. Thus he lived in terror of having a fate similar to that of his father. Considering himself weaker than his father, he expected a worse destiny. What he reported as having heard when he was in his twenties about his first love, Alicia, was a forerunner of what was to come later. Of course, we do not know how much distortion was already in his own report or memory of the Alicia episode. His basic underlying philosophy or unconscious premise that any responsibility for whatever is uncertain, untrustworthy, and painful in family relations resides in women.

Although he mentioned the mother quite often in relation to what the father had to tolerate from her during the patient's adolescence and youth, he never became very vehement about the mother. He spoke of her with a sense of resignation and simplicity. "Father decided to accept. That was his life." But what the patient did not openly feel and express about his mother, he felt prone to feel and express about his own wife, whom he despised but never divorced.

What makes him a paranoiac rather than a paranoid is the way he sustained his delusionary beliefs. There were no hallucinations or paleologic thinking. He was interpreting logically, although with false premises, certain events in such a way as to prove the central themes that his wife was untrustworthy and was doing things for the purpose of hurting him. His reasoning power was used to transform a mere possibility into actuality.

Of course, we have to consider also what role the wife played. In my opinion the paranoiac structure resided in the patient himself. However, the wife enhanced and perhaps made possible the perpetuation of the disorder, thus giving a Pirandellian flavor to the family situation. Why did she open the mail? I do not believe that we have here the usual schizophrenic *folie à deux,* where one patient is the inductor and the other a passive recipient of delusions (see Chapter 11). In the paranoiac family situation generally the second member is an active participant. His or her participation, however, is not enough to explain the origin of the condition, but it is sufficient at least in some cases to explain its prolongation and its exacerbation.

Although psychotherapy of mild paranoia is successful in diminishing the intensity of the exacerbations and in preventing future attacks, psychotherapy is ineffective in cases of severe paranoia. At times the diagnosis between the mild and the severe type is impossible to make because there are many intermediary stages. This diagnostic difficulty presents one of the most serious problems in the practice of psychiatry because whereas most cases of mild paranoia cause pain only to the sufferer and his immediate family (unless, of course, the patients become politicians), cases of severe paranoia are dangerous to others. Under the effect of delusional ideas the patient may even murder the alleged persecutors.

Paranoiacs present great practical problems not only for psychiatrists but also for lawyers. Especially the litigant type consults many lawyers in the hope that they would believe his claims and help him to sue or to obtain vindication (Revitch and Hayden, 1960).

II

Anorexia Nervosa

Anorexia nervosa is a condition that is often confused or associated with schizophrenia. It affects almost exclusively girls from puberty to the late twenties. Clinical evidence suggests that anorexia is not necessarily a schizophrenic syndrome or a precursor of schizophrenia. However, inasmuch as a certain number of cases, by far superior to statistical probabilities, shows an evolvement to definite schizophrenia, we must think that the two disorders are related.

The relation between weight and psychosis has been amply studied by Bruch (1957), more in relation to obesity than anorexia. According to her, progressive obesity in youngsters may be an expression of an underlying disturbance in adaptation: "It may be the first visible manifestation of a potential psychosis; the overeating and inactivity that bring about obesity serve as defenses against unbearable anxiety and situations which might arouse new conflicts." Bruch correctly states that overeating may be a mechanism of defense, and that growing obese and maintaining the weight may be of extraordinary importance for prepsychotics until new solutions have been found. Bruch reports that many schizophrenic psychoses have been precipitated by forcing a reduction in weight.

Anorexia nervosa is an even more challenging condition as patients may literally starve themselves to death. Patients refuse to eat and some of them, unless hospitalized and tube fed, do die of inanition.

Anorexia etymologically means lack of appetite, and therefore is a misnomer. Anorexic patients have indeed a strong appetite, but in spite of it, they refuse to eat. There is a large literature on anorexia (Bruch, 1962; Meyer and Feldman, 1965; Thomä, 1967), but I shall follow the major ideas of Selvini (1963, 1970), who, in my opinion, has made outstanding contributions on this subject.

The patient reveals a determination to undernourish and emaciate herself in spite of her intense desire for food. At times she resists excruciating hunger, because she is afraid that if she eats, her body will expand, become obese, unappealing, or even monstrous and grotesque. Actually she becomes unappealing because she is very emaciated. She denies that she is very thin in spite of the evidence and in spite of keeping track of her weight regularly on a scale. That the patients knows that she is emaciated is also revealed by some drawings that she makes of herself and other people. Strangely, she states that her drawings do not portray emaciated persons. If she gains an ounce of weight, she considers this fact a great calamity and the beginning of her doom.

According to Selvini the patient is afraid of her body and of food, which once ingested becomes part of her growing body. Selvini writes that "for the anorexic patient to be a body means to be a thing. If the body grows, the thing also grows at the expense of the person. Her fight against the body-thing is her fight against being a thing. A desperate fight, because, paradoxically, though refusing to be a thing, she fights her battle not at the level of spiritual values but rather at a material level, that of the body" (1970).

According to Selvini the patient equates her body with the incorporated object, namely the bad mother. The patient attributes to her body the qualities she attributes to the mother; namely, being powerful, indestructible, self-sufficient, growing, and threatening.

Selvini posits the question of why anorexia nervosa occurs almost exclusively in the female sex and around the time of puberty. She believes that when the patient's body develops larger breasts and other feminine curves, the patient unconsciously experiences it not as her own body but as the maternal object itself, which she has incorporated. This incorporation is not an identification with the mother. The aggression that the patient used to have for her mother is now directed against her own body. The patient must fight against her own body. The body "becomes the persecutor, but a persecutor whom it is easy to spy on and control. This projection onto the body is a safeguard against interpersonal delusional ideas and thus somehow saves the capacity to socialize and to relate to the world." Schizophrenia is thus averted. Nevertheless, Selvini calls anorexia nervosa an "intrapersonal paranoia" because a delusion exists, although the projection involves one's own body rather than the external environment.

I am very much impressed by Selvini's psychodynamic analysis, which in my opinion was confirmed in the majority of cases I have treated. I doubt, however, whether we can call anorexia nervosa an intrapersonal paranoia or psychosis. Although I am convinced that the patient identifies her body with her mother and considers her body as the origin of her trouble, as a persecutor is often conceived, this mental attitude is completely unconscious. The patient would never say that her body is her persecutor. On the contrary, at a conscious level she believes that by eating she will harm her body. Thus she uses mechanisms that are more neurotic than psychotic. Nevertheless it is true that her attitude toward food and life in general are almost psychotic and may become psychotic.

In a certain number of patients who have come to my attention there had been either a suspicion of schizophrenia or an actual history of short schizophrenic episodes. In one case there was a history of a withdrawal and almost catatonic immobility for many months. In several cases there were no manifestations of schizophrenia at any time. In all my cases there was no thyroid dysfunction, but rather amenorrhea.

Another differential characteristic between my cases and those of Selvini lies in the fact that in at least half of my patients periods of anorexia were alternated by periods of overeating. Some patients, when on an eating spree, would eat incessantly for many hours in a way that is hard to believe and could gain even ten pounds in a single day. A few days later the same patients could go on a self-imposed regime of almost total fasting. This periodicity in some cases was reminiscent of that seen in typical cases of circular manic-depressive psychosis.

III

Childhood Schizophrenia

Childhood schizophrenia was first described between 1905 and 1908 by De Sanctis, who called it dementia praecocissima (De Sanctis, 1925). Many important subsequent studies of this condition have been made, such as those of Potter (1933), Bradley (1941), Bender (1947), Mahler (1952, 1968), Despert (1941, 1968), Goldfarb (1961), Szurek and Berlin (1973).

No attempt will be made here to treat fully this important topic. Our main interest is to study whether childhood schizophrenia is related to adult schizophrenia or is an independent clinical entity. The following remarks are abstracted from the major available works on the subject and are intended to be of integrative character to the main topic of this volume.

Three types of child schizophrenia are described: (1) autism; (2) symbiotic psychosis syndrome; (3) forms of psychosis similar to adult schizophrenia.

Autism is generally associated with Kanner (1944, 1946) who first described it under the name of early infantile autism. This condition is characterized by special attitude toward people and by a serious thinking disorder. From the time he has learned to walk, the child seems to run away from personal contacts. Extreme aloofness is present. Often rather than aloofness there is a denial of the existence of other human beings. The child does not seem to see or hear adults or in any way acknowledge their presence. For instance, Kanner reports that if one of these children is pricked with a pin, the child is aware of the pin, and perhaps of the hand that holds it, but not of the person who pricked him. In a later paper Kanner (1965) wrote that perhaps autism is not the proper name for this condition. Referring to autistic children he wrote:

> While they are remote from affective and communicative contact with people, they develop a remarkable and not unskillful relationship to the inanimate environment. They can cling to things tenaciously, manipulate them adroitly, go into ecstasies when toys are moved or spun around by them, and become angry when objects do not yield readily to expected performance. Indeed, they are so concerned with the external world that they watch with tense alertness to make sure that their surroundings remain static, that the totality of an experience is reiterated with its constituent details, often in full photographic and phonic identity.

These children are either mute or, if they speak, they do so in a peculiar way. One of the common characteristics is the fact that they use pronouns just as they hear them. If the child is told by his mother, "I will give you some soup," the child subsequently expresses the desire for the soup in exactly the same way. He speaks of himself as "you" and not too infrequently of the mother as "I." That is, he uses the same pronouns as his mother would use. The child does not see those reflections coming from the adults around him as related to his self. The "you" remains a "you" and is not transformed into "I"; it somehow remains a foreign body.

The expressions used by these children seem irrelevant or completely nonsensical and resemble those of some adult schizophrenics. Kanner gives many examples of these expressions, which he calls "metaphorical" in the sense that they represent "figures of speech by means of which one thing is put for another which it only resembles" (1944, 1946). Kanner reports that the transfer of meaning in these expressions is accomplished in a variety of ways: (1) through substitutive analogy, in which for example, breadbasket becomes "home bakery"; (2) through generalization, or *totum pro parte,* in which "home bakery" becomes the term for every basket; (3) through restrictions, or *pars pro toto*—such as, when the number 6 is referred to as "hexagon."

These examples given by Kanner represent typical paleologic expressions and may be reinterpreted in accordance with Von Domarus's principle, which implies substitutive analogy, generalization, and restriction (Chapter 16).

Kanner considers these children austistic and does not call them schizophrenics, in spite of certain similarities in thinking. These children present stereotyped utterances, neologisms, and withdrawal. However, they do not have symptoms like delusions, hallucinations, ideas of reference, catatonia, and so forth, as reported in many descriptions of child schizophrenia, such as those given by De Sanctis (1925), Potter (1933), Bradley (1941), and Kanner himself (1942). In addition, and this is an important point, there was no evidence that these children had reached a normal or relatively normal adjustment after the age of 2. On the contrary, since that age there had been some disturbance in their mental integration and especially in their process of socialization. In other words, there seems to be no real schizophrenic regression in these children, but there is an inability to develop interpersonally beyond the level of 1½ to 2½ years of age. Instead, children who develop a schizophrenic syndrome more or less similar to that found in adults are able to integrate or socialize better after the age of 2 and have already learned to use language normally before the mental disorder starts.

According to Mahler and colleagues (1959) and to Mahler (1968) autism is a defense of children who cannot use or experience the mother as the living primary-object. According to her, autism is an attempt at dedifferentiation and deanimation. The children behave as if they were still in the first few weeks of life, in a "normal autistic phase in which the distance receptors are not yet functionally tuned."

The parents of these children are described as generally cold, detached, obsessive, and intelligent people. Abnormalities in electroencephalogram, neurological or other physical ailments, and frequency of mental disease in the family do not seem more frequent than in the general population.

The etiology of autism has not been clarified. Eisenberg and Kanner (1957), after many years of investigation, wrote: "It is difficult to escape the conclusion that the emotional configuration in the home plays a dynamic role in the genesis of autism." Rimland (1964) believes "that there is sufficient information at hand to demonstrate clearly that early infantile autism is not the same disease or cluster of diseases which has come to be called childhood schizophrenia." Kanner (1965) states: ". . . we can state unreservedly that, whether or not autism is viewed as a member of the species schizophrenia, it does represent a definitely distinguishable disease. This disease, specific—that is, unique, unduplicated—in its manifestations, can be explored *per se*. The emotional configuration in the home plays a dynamic role in the genesis of autism." Bettelheim (1967, 1970) does not deny organicity, although he tends to give great importance to psychogenic factors. According to him, an unremitting fear for their lives compels these children to withdraw and defend themselves in the "empty fortress" of autism.

The symbiotic psychosis syndrome is also called the Mahler syndrome, because Mahler first described it. The child has reached a degree of development in which he is able to differentiate and individualize from the mother, but he cannot proceed to a full separation. Panic results whenever separation is attempted. According to Mahler, "the symbiotic psychotic syndrome is aimed at restoring the symbiotic-parasitic delusion of oneness with the mother and thus serves a function diametrically opposite to that of the autistic mechanism." According to Mahler the psychosis may be insidious and may remain undiagnosed until school age, or it may be acute and sudden. The clinical picture is characterized chiefly by catatonic-like temper tantrums and states of panic. According to Mahler some feverish attempts to recontact reality seem to perpetuate the delusional omnipotence phase of the mother-infant fusion of the first year.

Other psychotic syndromes resembling adult schizophrenia, with hallucinations, delusions, and ideas of reference, have been described by many authors, generally in children not younger than 8 years of age. If these patients were older, they would be indistinguishable from cases of adult schizophrenia.

Bender considers every type of child schizophrenia to be based on biological alterations and at least until 1953 recommended electric shock (1947, 1953). Bender found in most children whom she diagnosed as schizophrenics such conditions as disordered respirations, persistence of primitive postural and righting reflexes, as demonstrated by the "whirling test." In this test the child closes his eyes and stands with his arms extended and parallel to each other. In a positive response, when the child's head is turned as far as possible, the child turns his body in the direction in which the head turned. In a negative response the child does not turn his body.

We may conclude by stating that the three conditions discussed in this chapter—paranoia, anorexia nervosa, and childhood schizophrenia in its subvarieties—are symptomatologically and psychodynamically very much related to schizophrenia and must be taken into consideration in any study that views schizophrenia in its largest scope. Certainly they are more related to schizophrenia than such conditions as depression, hysteria, or psychosomatic gastric ulcer. Nevertheless, as long as our knowledge of psychiatric syndromes remains as unsettled as it is, it is preferable to retain the concepts of these three conditions as separate clinical entities. Psychogenic factors appear important in all of them. Organicity is suspected in childhood schizophrenia much more than in all the other syndromes, including adult schizophrenia. Paradoxically the genetic evidence for such suspicion is even more unreliable than for adult schizophrenia.

CHAPTER

45

The Concept of Schizophrenia

In this final chapter I shall pursue three aims. First, I shall discuss whether schizophrenia as a concept should be retained in spite of recent attacks. Second, I shall examine some theories which are not included or derived from the works of the six innovators discussed in Chapter 2. Obviously we cannot discuss all of them, as the number is enormous and always increasing. My discussion will be succinct and limited to three theories which have received much attention respectively in Russia, German-speaking countries, and the United States. Third, I shall give a last expression to some of my concepts, more amply formulated in the various parts of this book.

I

Attacks on the Concept of Schizophrenia

A considerable number of American authors are reluctant to accept schizophrenia as a clinical entity or as a distinct syndrome. Some of these authors have found support and inspiration in the writings of Bleuler, the very man who coined the word *schizophrenia*. In Chapter 2 we have seen that Bleuler himself delivered two blows at the concept of schizophrenia as a distinct psychosis. The first blow was inflicted when he included in Kraepelin's category of dementia praecox many syndromes that at that time nobody considered related to schizophrenia. The second blow was inherent in the concept of latent schizophrenia. However, most American authors who are critical of the concept of schizophrenia found their earliest inspiration in the writings of Adolph Meyer.

Meyer did not deny the existence of schizophrenia as a clinical entity. However, the fact that he saw a continuity, or a longitudinal sequence, between the prepsychotic state and the psychotic was interpreted by many as an obliteration of diagnostic boundaries. There would be no schizophrenia but only progressive maladjustment.

One of the most vigorous attempts to abolish the concept of schizophrenia was made by Szasz (1957*d*). Szasz called the word *schizophrenia* a *panchreston,* a term coined by Hardin to denote dangerous words that are purported to explain everything, but that actually obscure matters. Szasz wrote:

> . . . categories such as "schizophrenia" may be doubly harmful: first, such categories are unsatisfactory as readily validatable concepts for purposes of classification, and secondly, they give rise to the misleading impression that there "exists" a more-or-less homogenous group of phenomena which are designated by the word in question. If this line of thought is correct—as I believe it is—it leads to the realization that the "problem of schizophrenia" which many consider to be the core problem of psychiatry today, may be truly akin to the "problem of the ether." To put it simply: There is no such problem.

Szasz added that "a better comprehension of the 'real facts' . . . will probably lead to the gradual disappearance of this word, whose function, like that of all panchrestons, is to fill a scientific void."

Other authors have stressed the similarity of the psychodynamics of many psychiatric syndromes and have tended either to include in the concept of schizophrenia the multiple conditions with similar psychodynamics or to abolish the concept of category completely. In my opinion it is a basic error to assume that it is in the psychodynamic mechanisms that we must find the individuality or specificity of schizophrenia. The psychodynamic factors, including parental attitudes, childhood situations, development of particular personality traits, and occurrence of special events, are very important. Although without them there would be no schizophrenia, they in themselves do not constitute schizophrenia or the whole etiology of schizophrenia. We have the phenomenon schizophrenia only when the psychodynamic content is translated or channeled into a special psychotic form. For instance, an irrational feeling of self-depreciation and guilt, with special reference to the sexual area, may be evaluated in its great dynamic import and traced back to abnormal relations with the patient's mother. However, only when this conflict assumes special forms—for instance, that of a hallucinated voice that tells the patient that she is a prostitute—can we talk of the presence of schizophrenia. In the presence or absence of other factors, conflict of guilt could have been channeled in different ways, for instance, into phobic or obsessive-compulsive symptoms.

Several authors have repeatedly stressed that there is only a quantitative difference between the schizophrenic, the neurotic, and the normal. This point of view has been strengthened by the fact that in recent years clinicians have observed an increasing number of schizophrenics with such mild symptomatology as to make the traditional diagnosis quite difficult. The point is no longer made whether we are dealing with latent schizophrenia, as Bleuler did, but whether the distinctions between diagnostic categories should be retained. Whether the increase in mild cases is only apparent and connected with the availability of a large number of psychiatric facilities or whether it is real and engendered by sociocultural factors is a question difficult to answer at the present time. Kubie (1971) writes, "At last a rebellion against the concept of schizophrenia is in full swing. Recently many psychiatrists are gradually coming to realize that this combination of a misconception and a misnomer has led us up blind alleys." Kubie recognizes various degrees of psychotic disorganization, but he sees no need for a separate subcategory among psychotic disorders called schizophrenia.

Before Kubie, Karl Menninger strongly advocated the abolition of diagnostic categories. In his book *The Vital Balance* (1963) he suggested eliminating not only the concept of schizophrenia, but also all psychiatric categories. However, he recommended his own classification, which consists of grouping mental patients in five categories of "dyscontrol." In a symposium on schizophrenia (1969) he repeated his attack, stressing also that an additional reason for rejecting the term *schizophrenia* is the fact that this word has acquired a pejorative connotation. According to Menninger an additional psychological trauma is inflicted on the patient who knows he has been diagnosed as schizophrenic.

I believe that when psychiatrists examine typical cases, for example, a patient who states that he is Jesus Christ because he drank Carnation milk and therefore has been reincarnated, or who uses peculiar neologisms or metonymic distortions or typical word-salad, or who sees everywhere FBI agents spying on him, or hallucinates all the time, or is in catatonic postures, or complete withdrawal, they are confronted with a constellation or gestalt that cannot be confused. Certainly no pejorative connotation should be given to a dysfunction of the human being; but if human beings are inclined to do so, they will not refrain from attaching sooner or later a pejorative connotation to the name that replaces the old one.

As we have seen in Chapter 16, normal people occasionally become suspicious in a paranoid-like way; they misinterpret, they make slips of the tongue and unpredictable puns. But these phenomena of everyday life do not make a schizophrenic gestalt.

Even if we adhere to the continuous hypothesis and believe that psychiatric pictures may change by infinitesimal increments, that is, by steps too small to be noticeable, we must be aware of the qualitative differences that may result depending on when and where the change occurs. The difference between 34° and 33° F does not have the same significance in relation to water as the difference between 33° and 32° F. There may be only a quantitative difference between a 39 percent and a 41 percent water solution of a substance, but if the dissolved substance precipitates when the concentration is 40 percent, the two solutions will no longer be only quantitatively different. They will also become qualitatively different, because one has a precipitation and the other has not. The situation is more complicated in the field of biology, and especially in the field of psychology, where the element of subjectivity enters. There may be only a quantitative difference in wavelengths that are responsible for the fact that we see various colors, but indeed we do see a variety of colors.

A person may have symptoms similar to those of the schizophrenic, but it is only when he accepts them as part of reality, integrates them into the context of his whole life, and consequently experiences the world and himself in a different way and alters his relationship with others that the total quality changes and the psychosis emerges.

Similar remarks can be made in relation to homosexuality and heterosexuality. We may find some homosexual conflicts in many heterosexual patients, but it is only when the individual integrates his own sexuality along a homosexual orientation that we consider him homosexual. There is no doubt that in by far the majority of cases it is possible to decide whether a given individual is homosexual or heterosexual.

In reference again to schizophrenia, we must attempt in Hegelian terms to lay bare the core and significance of the psychotic event, to free it from the adventitious contingencies that, although not irrelevant accessories, are only partially causally related and of merely secondary importance.

II

Three Additional Theoretical Frameworks

Pavlov and the Pavlovian School

After his visits to the psychiatric hospital of Vdlenaja and to the Third Psychiatric Hospital of Shvortsov-Stepanon in 1918, Pavlov developed great interest in schizophrenia, especially of the catatonic type, and tried to attempt a physiological interpretation of its symptomatology.

In one of his important psychiatric papers (1919) he described two cases of catatonia. The first concerned a 22-year-old girl, and the second a 60-year-old man who had been hospitalized for twenty-two years. His catatonic illness had started around the age of 35 and had continued for many years. But when the patient approached the age of 60, there was a rapid disappearance of the catatonic symptomatology. This patient told Pavlov that during the years of catatonic stupor he was conscious of everything that was happening around him, but "that an extreme and unconquerable heaviness of his muscles" made it difficult for him to move, eat, talk, and even breathe. Pavlov compared catatonic patients to experimental animals that have been conditioned. The motor inhibition, although possibly chemical in origin, would be fundamentally functional in nature and would have to be interpreted as an irradiating inhibition spreading to the motor cortex. In a second article (1930) Pavlov interpreted schizophrenia as a chronic state of hypnosis caused by hereditary and acquired weakness of cortical cells. Social factors in critical periods of life may also contribute to exhaust the cortical cells. According to Rochlin (1969) with these statements Pavlov implied that cortical inhibition is a defense, that is, it has a protective function. Pavlov compared the negativism of the catatonic to the negativism of the conditioned dog who withdraws from the food at the beginning of the experiment and then goes toward the food when it is withdrawn. According to him the conditioned stimulus (sight of food) reaches the point of the cortical motor area whose stimulation provokes in the dog a movement toward the food. But inasmuch as the cortical point is weakened, it responds abnormally, that is, not with excitation but with inhibition. When, instead, the food is withdrawn, the cerebral area that had been inhibited and that was connected with the movement toward the food is now in excitement because of a phenomenon of successive induction. At the same time the point previously excited and connected with the movement of withdrawal from the food becomes inhibited. Thus a movement of the dog toward the food occurs. Pavlov explains in a similar way the negativism of the catatonic.

The use of the words *hypnosis* and *functional* had led some to believe that Pavlov considered schizophrenia a functional disease. However, as he remarked during a lesson given at one of his regular Wednesday lectures (December 12, 1934), and as Rochlin later clarified, Pavlov considered schizophrenia a functional disease only in the initial stages. Later the functional condition would become organic. A specific autointoxication might be at the bottom of the disorder. Pavlov also thought that the inhibition of the cerebral cortex may determine a disinhibition of the brain stem, which is no longer under cortical control.

In an open letter to Pierre Janet, Pavlov (1933*a*) described his concepts of delusional ideas, based on the notion of the contrary. Pavlov wrote that the notion of the contrary is a fundamental one in normal thinking. In delusional thinking the category of contrary is altered. The right thought and the positive affirmation are blocked; the opposite thought, which is false, instead of being excluded, starts to prevail. What should be inhibited becomes stimulated, and what should be stimulated becomes inhibited. According to Pavlov this reaction is due to "an ultraparadoxical hypnotic phase" and is at the basis of paranoiac-paranoid thinking and of schizophrenic ambivalence. In another article Pavlov (1933*b*) tried to explain in the same way the obsessions of the neurotic and the thinking of the paranoiac-paranoid, inasmuch as all these symptoms have the tendency to persist. According to him these symptoms are caused by pathological inertia of excitement of small areas of the brain. Some cortical islets would continue to remain abnormally excited and would be responsible for the persistance of the symptoms.

Among the pupils of Pavlov worthy of mention are: (1) Ivanov-Smolenskij, who demonstrated the difficulty of the catatonic patient to form conditioned reflexes (1934); (2) Protopopov, who, with many studies about conditioned reflexes, believed he had confirmed Pavlov's idea of schizophrenia as a hypnotic state of the cortex (1938); (3) Popov, who did important work, especially on catatonics (1957).

The Existentialistic School

Schizophrenia has received much attention from followers of the phenomenological-existentialistic school of psychiatry, especially in German-speaking countries, but also in France, Italy, and Japan. There is no definite phenomenological-existentialistic theory of schizophrenia, but special orientations or attitudes, which, although varying from author to author, can all be included in the phenomenological-existentialistic literature. Such people as Binswanger, Minkowski, and Boss have diversities of view that are no less important than what they have in common.

Binswanger is perhaps the best-known psychiatrist of this group. He devoted four large works to the study of schizophrenia, which consist of the detailed existentialistic analysis of four patients to whom he gave the names Lola Voss, Ilse, Ellen West, and Suzanne Urban. These works have become classics for students of existential psychiatry (1949, 1957, 1958*a, b*).

In the reports of these cases Binswanger was interested not in constitutional or psychodynamic or symbolic or characterologic studies of the patient but in the underlying *structure* that existed prior to the illness. This structure explains the way of being-in-the-world of the patient, his pathologic potentialities, and the uniqueness of his experiences.

Binswanger tried to explain the delusional world of the patient as the evolving of a theme—terror, for instance, in the case of Suzanne Urban, who is the prisoner of her own theme of terror and who becomes the prisoner of a world of terror. The theme in the case of Ellen West is fear of filling the body and becoming fat in order to compensate for an empty existence. Undoubtedly these studies enrich our understanding of the schizophrenic patient and will be useful, provided they are complemented by the psychodynamic, formal, and psychosomatic studies.

The patients that Binswanger selected for demonstration, although seriously ill, disclosed a preservation of their personality and no signs of regression. Thus the general theme of this delusional world could reveal itself to the author's analysis with not too much difficulty. Other psychiatrists might consider these patients cases of paranoia or paranoid conditions. In the case of Ellen West there is a strong possibility that the case is one of anorexia nervosa and not of schizophrenia.

Minkowski, a pupil of Bleuler, added to Bleuler's conceptions the flavor of Husserl's and Bergson's philosophies. In his major work, *La Schizophrénie* (1953), he stated that the crucial point of the schizophrenic syndrome is "the loss of vital contact with reality." He also added that such contact can be reestablished as a result of therapy, but he did not give instructions on how to reestablish such contact. In other studies he focused his attention on the alteration of the sense of time and space in schizophrenics. Whereas space expands to include the whole category of the objects that are involved in the patient's delusions, time is blocked and limited to the present.

In a later study Minkowski (1966) stated that the function of unreality is as important as the function of reality. Man can be at fault for excessive realism as well as for excessive unrealism. We need to escape from the hard reality and resort to our imagination. The human being may be in deep contact with reality, for instance, in the state of contemplation. He may also detach himself from reality, as in reflection and meditation. Whereas the imagination of the normal is within the limit of reality, the imagination of the sick undergoes *"une rupture morbide du contact avec la réalité."* Minkowski searched for the central unifying experience in the life of his patient and tried to orient the person around this experience. This experience gives meanings and structures to one's life.

Boss is a Swiss psychiatrist who has tried to reconcile psychoanalysis with existentialism (1963). According to him, the way of existence of the psychotic patient is different from that of the normal or of the neurotic. We call some experiences "hallucinatory" and "delusional," but rather than use these terms, which have a derogatory meaning, we should call them different ways of encountering the world. In the schizophrenic experience there is a deconstriction, a new way of discovering phenomena and of relating to them. Thus a patient who had undergone a setback in being badly disappointed by a friend started to represent the sun intellectually as something that was for him as important as the only friendship he had in life. Soon the thought of the sun became a hallucination of the sun itself, which he saw in his room, on the wall, during the night (Boss, 1973).

The Australian psychologist MacNab (1966) also interprets schizophrenia from a predominantly existentialistic point of view. He adopts Kierkegaard's view that objective reason should not be identified with reality. The therapist must understand the patient's being-in-the-world; must see the world through the patient's eyes. Although schizophrenia is an estrangement, a special mode of being, an unusual way of making decisions, it is predominantly "a loss of the Determining Center." MacNab follows Paul Tillich, according to whom a man who does not find his "Determining Center" in God despairs in his quest for courage to be. "In the schizophrenic the loss of courage devastates his whole being."

Schizotaxia and Schizophrenia

In his presidential address to the Seventieth Annual Convention of the American Psychological Association, held in St. Louis on September 2, 1962, Meehl advanced his theory of schizophrenia (1962). According to him some persons, whom he calls schizotypic, present four main characteristics: cognitive slippage, interpersonal aversiveness, anhedonia, and ambivalence. They are indications of a neural integrative defect, which Meehl calls *schizotaxia*. The four core behavior traits are not innate; they are learned by people with this integrative defect, in some predisposing environmental situations.

All schizotaxics become schizotypic in personality organization, but most of them do not decompensate and never develop a psychosis. A minority of schizotaxics who happen to have other constitutional weaknesses and schizophrenogenic mothers (most of whom are themselves schizotypes) are "potentiated into clinical schizophrenia." In other words, schizotaxia is a necessary but not sufficient condition in the etiology of schizophrenia. Meehl believes that a nonschizotaxic individual, whatever his other genetic potentiality and whatever his life experiences, would not become a schizotype and therefore would not become a schizophrenic. Even in the most adverse circumstances he would develop a character disorder or a psychoneurosis rather than schizophrenia.

According to Meehl the neurological defect underlying schizotaxia probably resides in the neuron's synaptic control function. Meehl borrows the concept of anhedonia from Rado, to whom we have already referred in this book. The characteristic ambivalence, which originated with Bleuler, has since been found not to be specific to any psychiatric condition. Interpersonal aversiveness is social fear or expectation of rejection. Meehl stresses cognitive slippage in preschizophrenics and in parents of schizophrenics, but cognitive slippage is common in all kinds of seriously disturbed people. Meehl correctly states that the increased interest in interpersonal *dynamics* has made people underestimate the importance of cognition in the field of schizophrenia.

III

Concluding Remarks

In this third and final section I cannot adequately summarize all the ideas that I have expressed in forty-five chapters. I feel that a well-organized outline would not do justice to the complexity of the problems that have been studied. Instead, I shall allow some ideas to emerge spontaneously as recurring themes do, or themes that want to be expressed once more, because they are deeply felt and want to be heard again in a slightly different formulation.

I believe that the concept of schizophrenia is useful and should be retained when applied to a particular psychological dysfunction of the human being that manifests itself in many varieties. The disability is real, and in almost all cases painful and harmful. The dysfunction can therefore be included in the medical model, provided this model is enlarged to comprehend those biological functions that are called psychological and are partially related to the social environment. To adhere to a medical model which followed Virchow's tenets and which was formulated before psychiatry had gained full consideration as a science, would be like following in physics a Euclidian-Newtonian system after Einstein and Heisenberg had conceived a more inclusive one.

Schizophrenia is an abnormal way of dealing with an extreme state of anxiety, which originated in childhood and was reactivated later on in life by psychological factors. It is an abnormal state inasmuch as it uses a category of specific mechanisms which belong to lower levels of integration and ordinarily play a much less prominent role in life.

What is the cause of schizophrenia? When we contemplate the fact that the average incidence of the disorder in the general population is less than 1 percent, but the concordance in monozygotic twins, even if reared apart, although variously estimated, is many times greater, we must conclude that a genetic factor plays a role. This role, however, does not explain the problem in its entirety. Otherwise the concordance in monozygotic twins would be 100 percent. What is transmitted is only a potentiality, which is transformed into clinical actuality by special circumstances of life. These circumstances of life originate in the family environment.

Perhaps the parent has a disturbed but not psychotic variety of personality that is linked biologically with being a carrier of the genetic potentiality of the disorder. Perhaps the personality of the parent is completely dissociated from any genetic factor. In either case the future patient grows in a psychologically unhealthy environment. The psychopathology occurring early in life is the result of an interplay between interpersonal and intrapsychic mechanisms. This early pathology is of crucial importance, inasmuch as it narrows the range of choices of life directions, determines basic orientations, thwarts the possibility of compensation, and facilitates abnormal sequence of events. Life patterns that may lead to the disorder start to emerge.

I have divided the life cycle of the patient into four periods, the last of which is the psychotic. Many authors see a continuity between the family disturbance and the state of the patient in his prepsychotic periods and finally in the psychotic. Since my early studies in the 1940s, I too have seen this psychodynamic continuity. However, in disagreement with the authors whose writings I have discussed in Chapters 5 and 8, within the framework of this continuity I see also a discontinuity that is equally important for a psychodynamic, psychopathological in general, and psychotherapeutic understanding. The mentioned authors believe that the family members transmit directly to the child, or teach him, irrational patterns of thinking, the same irrationality that is later manifested in the schizophrenic disorder. Because the child does not have at his disposal adequate models for identifications, he does not have the instrumental equipment for growing in a mature way.

In Part Two of this book I have shown that the child does not absorb passively this family pathology and irrationality, but that he too adds his own contribution to a pathological complex. His genetic characteristics either make him particularly sensitive and vulnerable to painful situations or elicit in him an abnormal use of maladaptive primary process mechanisms. Other factors caused by the psychological environment or by the timing or sequence of events play a role. So do sociocultural factors by acting on the parents or on the child himself. Vicious circles that consist of partially interpersonal and partially intrapsychic processes repeat themselves, accrue, and prolong a course that leads to schizophrenia, but not ineluctably. The direction can always be diverted at any period. Defenses are always built against the injury to the inner self.

During the first period the environmental pathology is not directly absorbed or mirrored by the child but distorted, magnified, and internalized in discontinuous ways. Not only do the self-image and the mother-image in most cases become grotesque representations of reality, but the same thing happens to the image of the other, any person other than the self, who comes to be experienced as a stranger, removed from bonds of human solidarity, and possibly the carrier of inimical power. The child will develop an actual or potential abnormal fear of the self, the other, life, the world.

During the second period (grammar school) the child develops as defenses prepsychotic types of personality, the most common of which are the schizoid and the stormy. Massive repression of experiences and the formation of the prepsychotic personality permit a compromise with the environment, but not a condition of basic trust or a normal dialogue with the family or a state of relatedness with the interpersonal world.

During the third period (adolescence and youth) the defenses start to be less effective. The patient finds himself in "a jungle of concepts," which attack from all sides his inner image, his inner self. He undergoes a preschizophrenic panic during which what is repressed and archaic and what is conscious and present reinforce each other and inflict a fatal blow. The psychosis, in its various types, ensues.

It is at the beginning of the fourth, or psychotic, period that a second discontinuity takes place: the break with reality, the adoption of ways not shared by society, the entrance into the world of schizophrenia.

In Part Three I have illustrated in detail the modalities of schizophrenic thought and language, action and will, work and creativity, living symbolically with oneself and others. I have attempted to individualize the basic structures that underlie the psychotic variety of the psychodynamic experience. Both the structural and the psychodynamic approaches have been applied to study the constant coupling and interplay of form and content.

How do we explain the passage from a psychodynamic frame of reference culminating in the defeat of the self to a psychostructural frame of reference that deals with such phenomena as archaic symbolism, paleologic thinking, perceptualization of the concept, concretization of the abstract, impaired volition, and so forth? It seems almost as if we have to merge two logical universes, two irreconcilable views of man and nature. With the formulation of the principle of progressive teleologic regression, presented in Chapter 15, I have tried to explain what I consider a second discontinuity in the life of the schizophrenic.

Unless the regression is stopped, it proceeds through four different stages, with specific processes described in Part Four. In Part Five, after having reviewed the major somatic studies, I discuss in purely hypothetical terms a third or psychosomatic discontinuity. It is the psychological process itself that may sooner or later bring about a disorganization of neuronal patterns.

Other etiological factors are examined throughout the book, and blueprints for the prevention of schizophrenia are tentatively drawn in Chapter 33.

But I am sure that the reader has grasped what I think is the most important of my conclusions: that even if we do not know the whole complex etiology of the disorder, what we know is a great deal and is sufficient to cure or ameliorate the condition of the majority of people suffering from schizophrenia. Physical therapies help considerably by making the patient less susceptible, less vulnerable, or less sensitive to the type of anxiety that brings about psychotic symptoms. But psychotherapy, although unable to alter the biological predisposition to the disorder, affects the psychological components that have actualized the genetic potenti-

ality into a clinical syndrome. If we remove their impact, we may remove the disorder.

In this book we have seen that it is not easy to do so, because the psychogenic patterns of living are ingrained in the distant past and the psychotic ways offer alluring secondary gains. Often the patient's remoteness looms unconquerable, and our offer of warmth rekindles his terror. But in this book I have also tried to show how in most cases the therapist can help the patient to experience the human tie more intensely than any fear, more strongly than any need for distance. To the extent that I have failed, I hope I have at least encouraged others to further this arduous task. To the extent that I have succeeded, I have helped those dedicated to relieve the sufferer. I also hope that by showing that we can learn and practice the ways of bringing trust to the distrustful, clarity to the bewildered, speech to the mute, creativity to the grotesque, confident expectation to the hopeless, and companionship to the lonely, I have suggested a larger vista for the human horizon, a larger use for the human bond, and optimism for the solution of those other conditions in health or illness that, although difficult, are not so obscure, so hard to approach, so desperate, so far from the usual reach of man's words and care.

When the person who had the habit of staring vacantly, almost into space, because he felt the world was not to be perceived, focuses on the many little things of life and recognizes sparks here and there and sees again the sun and the stars and the new leaves and hears the rustling of the branches and the children's laughter and the neighbors' greetings and the joyful noises of the street and craves for what tomorrow will bring, then we believe in greater realizations, then we envision with faith the universality of the human embrace.

Bibliography

Abraham, K., 1908, "The Psycho-Sexual Differences between Hysteria and Dementia Praecox." In Abraham, K., *Selected Papers in Psychoanalysis*. New York: Basic Books, 1953.
———, 1912, "Notes on the Psycho-Analytical Investigation and Treatment of Manic-Depressive Insanity and Allied Conditions." In *Selected Papers*. New York: Basic Books, 1953.
———, 1913, "Restrictions and Transformations of Scoptophilia in Psycho-neurotics." In *Selected Papers*. New York: Basic Books, 1953.
———, 1916, "The First Pregenital Stage of the Libido." In *Selected Papers*. New York: Basic Books, 1953.
Abramson, D. I., 1944, *Vascular Responses in the Extremities of Man in Health and Disease*. Chicago: University of Chicago Press, 1944.
Accornero, F., 1939, "L'istopatologia del sistema nervoso centrale nello shock insulinico." *Riv. di Pat. Nerv.*, 53:1.
Ach, N., 1935, *Analyse des Willens*. Berlin. Quoted by Humphrey, G., *Thinking: An Introduction to Experimental Psychology*. London and New York: Methuen & Wiley, 1951.
Ackerman, N. W., 1954, "Interpersonal Disturbances in the Family: Some Unsolved Problems in Psychotherapy." *Psychiatry*, 17:359–368.
———, 1958, *The Psychodynamics of Family Life*. New York: Basic Books.
———, 1960, "Family-Focused Therapy of Schizophrenia." In Sher, S. C., and Davis, H. R. (eds.), *The Out-Patient Treatment of Schizophrenia*. New York: Grune & Stratton.
Adler, A., 1944, "Disintegration and Restoration of Optic Recognition in Visual Agnosia." *Archives of Neurology and Psychiatry*, 51:243–259.
———, 1950, "Course and Outcome of Visual Agnosia." *Journal of Nervous and Mental Disease*, 111:41–51.
Akerfeldt, S., 1957, "Oxidation of N-N-dimethyl-p-phenylenediamine by Serum with Mental Disease." *Science*, 125:117.
Alanen, Y. O., 1958, "The Mothers of Schizophrenic Patients." Supplement No. 124, *Acta Psychiatrica et Neurologica Scandinavica*, Helsinki.
Allen, M. G., and Pollin, W., 1970, "Schizophrenia in Twins and the Diffuse Ego Boundary Hypothesis." *American Journal of Psychiatry*, 127:437–442.
Alpert, H. S., Bigelow, N. J. T., and Bryan, L. L., 1947, "Central Arteriosclerosis in the Paranoid State," *Psychiatric Quarterly*, 21:305–313.
Altshuler, K. Z., 1957, "Genetic Elements in Schizophrenia. A Review of the Literature and Résumé of Unsolved Problems." *Eugenics Quarterly*, 4:92–98.
Alzheimer, A., 1897, "Beiträge zur pathologischen Anatomie der Hirnrinde und zur anatomischen Grundlage einiger Psychosen." *Monatsschr. Psychiat. u. Neurol.*, 2:82.
Appleton, W. S., 1967, "A Guide to the Use of Psychoactive Agents." *Diseases of the Nervous System*, 28:609–613.
Arieti, S., 1941, "Histopathologic Changes in Experimental Metrazol Convulsions in Monkeys." *American Journal of Psychiatry*, 98:70.
———, 1944*a*, "The 'Placing-into-Mouth' and Coprophagic Habits." *Journal of Nervous and Mental Disease*, 99:959–964.
———, 1944*b*, "An Interpretation of the Divergent Outcome of Schizophrenia in Identical Twins." *Psychiatric Quarterly*, 18:587–599.
———, 1945*a*, "Primitive Habits and Perceptual Alterations in the Terminal Stage of Schizophrenia." *Archives of Neurology and Psychiatry*, 53:378–384.

———, 1945*b*, "Primitive Habits in the Preterminal Stage of Schizophrenia." *Journal of Nervous and Mental Disease*, 102:367–375.
———, 1946, "Histopathologic Changes in Cerebral Malaria and Their Relation to Psychotic Sequels." *Archives of Neurology and Psychiatry*, 56:79–104.
———, 1947, "The Processes of Expectation and Anticipation. Their Genetic Development, Neural Basis and Role in Psychopathology." *Journal of Nervous and Mental Disease*, 100:471–481.
———, 1948, "Special Logic of Schizophrenia and Other Types of Autistic Thought." *Psychiatry*, 11:325–338.
———, 1950*a*, "Primitive Intellectual Mechanisms in Psychopathological Conditions. Study of the Archaic Ego." *American Journal of Psychotherapy*, 4:4.
———, 1950*b*, "New Views on the Psychology and Psychopathology of Wit and of the Comic." *Psychiatry*, 13:43–62.
———, 1955, *Interpretation of Schizophrenia*. New York: Brunner.
———, 1956*a*, "The Possibility of Psychosomatic Involvement of the Central Nervous System in Schizophrenia." *Journal of Nervous and Mental Disease*, 123:324–333.
———, 1956*b*, "Some Basic Problems Common to Anthropology and Modern Psychiatry." *American Anthropologist*, 58:26–39.
———, 1957*a*, "The Two Aspects of Schizophrenia." *Psychiatric Quarterly*, 31:403–416.
———, 1957*b*, "What is Effective in the Therapeutic Process?" *Am. J. Psychoanalysis*, 17:30–33.
———, 1959, "Some Socio-Cultural Aspects of Manic-Depressive Psychosis and Schizophrenia." In Masserman, J., and Moreno, J. (eds.), *Progress in Psychotherapy*, vol. 4, pp. 140–152. New York: Grune & Stratton.
———, 1960, "Recent Conceptions and Misconceptions of Schizophrenia." *American Journal of Psychotherapy*, 14:1–29.
———, 1961*a*, "Volition and Value: A Study Based on Catatonic Schizophrenia." *Comprehensive Psychiatry*, 2:74.
———, 1961*b*, "Introductory Notes on the Psychoanalytic Therapy of Schizophrenia." In Burton, A. (ed.), *Psychotherapy of Psychoses*. New York: Basic Books.
———, 1962*a*, "Hallucinations, Delusions and Ideas of Reference Treated with Psychotherapy." *American Journal of Psychotherapy*, 16:52–60.
———, 1962*b*, "Psychotherapy of Schizophrenia." *Archives of General Psychiatry*, 6:112–122.
———, 1962*c*, "The Microgeny of Thought and Perception," *Archives of General Psychiatry*, 6:454–468.
———, 1963*a*, "The Psychotherapy of Schizophrenia in Theory and Practice." American Psychiatric Association, *Psychiatric Research Report* 17.
———, 1963 *b*, "Studies of Thought Processes in Contemporary Psychiatry." *American Journal of Psychiatry*, 120:58–64.
———, 1963*c*, "Psychopathic Personality: Some Views on Its Psychopathology and Psychodynamics." *Comprehensive Psychiatry*, 4:301–312.
———, 1964, "The Rise of Creativity: From Primary to Tertiary Process." *Contemporary Psychoanalysis*, 1:51–68.
———, 1965*a*, "The Schizophrenic Patient in Office Treatment." In *Psychotherapy of Schizophrenia, 3rd Int. Symp., Lausanne, 1964*. Basel: Karger.
———, 1965*b*, "Conceptual and Cognitive Psychiatry." *American Journal of Psychiatry*, 122:361–366.
———, 1965*c*, "Contributions to Cognition from Psychoanalytic Theory." In Masserman, J. (ed.), *Science and Psychoanalysis*, vol. 8, pp. 16–37. New York: Grune & Stratton.
———, 1966*a*, "Creativity and Its Cultivation: Relation to Psychopathology and Mental Health." In Arieti, S. (ed.), *American Handbook of Psychiatry*, 1st ed., vol. 3, pp. 720–741. New York: Basic Books.
———, 1966*b*, "Transferencia e contra-transferencia no tratamento do paciente esquizofrenico." *Jornal Brasileiro de Psiquiatria*, 15:163–174.
———, 1967, *The Intrapsychic Self: Feeling, Cognition and Creativity in Health and Mental Illness*. New York: Basic Books.

———, 1968*a*, "The Psychodynamics of Schizophrenia: A Reconsideration." *American Journal of Psychotherapy*, 22:366–381.

———, 1968*b*, "The Meeting of the Inner and the External World: In Schizophrenia, Everyday Life and Creativity." *American Journal of Psychoanalysis*, 29:115–130.

———, 1968*c*, "New Views on the Psychodynamics of Schizophrenia." *American Journal of Psychiatry*, 124:453–458.

———, 1968*d*, "Some Memories and Personal Views." *Contemporary Psychoanalysis*, 5:85–89.

———, 1969, "Current Ideas on the Problem of Psychosis." *Excerpta Medica* International Congress Series, No. 194:3–21.

———, 1971*a*, "The Origins and Development of the Psychopathology of Schizophrenia." In Bleuler, M., and Angst, J. (eds.), *Die Entstehung der Schizophrenie*. Bern: Huber.

———, *1971b*, "Psychodynamic Search of Common Values with the Schizophrenic." *Proceedings of IV International Symposium, Turku, Finland, 1971. Excerpta Medica* International Congress Series, No. 259:94–100. Amsterdam.

———, 1972 *a*, *The Will To Be Human*. New York: Quadrangle Books.

———, 1972 *b*,"Discussion of Otto Allen Will's Paper." *Contemporary Psychoanalysis*, 9:58–62.

———, 1972*c*, "The Therapeutic Assistant in Treating the Psychotic." *International Journal of Psychiatry*, 10:7–11.

———, 1973, "Anxiety and Beyond in Schizophrenia and Depression." *American Journal of Psychotherapy*, 17:338–345

———, 1974, "Psychoses." In *Encyclopaedia Britannica*.

Arieti, S., and Bemporad, J. R., 1974, "Rare, Unclassifiable, and Collective Psychiatric Syndromes." In Arieti, S. (ed.), *American Handbook of Psychiatry*, 2nd ed., vol. 3, pp. 710–722. New York: Basic Books.

Arieti, S., and Meth, J., 1959, "Rare, Unclassifiable, Collective, Exotic Syndromes." In Arieti, S. (ed.), *American Handbook of Psychiatry*, 1st ed., vol. 1, pp. 546–563. New York: Basic Books.

Arlow, J. A., 1958, "Report on Panel: The Psychoanalytic Theory of Thinking." *J. Am. Psychoanal. Ass.*,6:143.

Arlow, J. A., and Brenner, C., 1964, *Psychoanalytic Concepts and the Structural Theory*. New York: International Universities Press.

———, 1969, "The Psychopathology of the Psychoses: A Proposed Revision." *The International Journal of Psychoanalysis*, 50:5–14.

Artiss, K. L., 1962, *Milieu Therapy in Schizophrenia*. New York: Grune & Stratton.

Astrachan, J. M., 1965, "Severe Psychological Disorders in Puerperium." *Obstetrics and Gynecology*, 25:13–25.

Astrup, C., and Odegaard, O., "Internal Migration and Mental Disease in Norway." *Psychiatric Quarterly*, 34:116–130.

Axel, M., 1959, "Treatment of Schizophrenia in a Day Hospital. Preliminary Observations on an Eclectic Approach." *International Journal of Social Psychiatry*, 5.

Ayd, F. J., 1961, "A Survey of Drug-Induced Estrapyramidal Reactions." *JAMA*, 175:1054–1060.

———, 1963, "Chlorpromazine: Ten Years' Experience." *JAMA*, 184:173.

Ayllon, T., and Azrin, N. H., 1965, "The Measurement and Reinforcement of Behavior of Psychotics." *Journal of Exper. Anal. Behav.*, 8:357–383.

Bacciagaluppi, M., and Serra, A., 1963, "Sull'eredita' della schizofrenia tardiva." *Il Lavoro Neuropsichiatrico*, 33:1–7.

Balakian, A., 1970, *Surrealism: The Road to the Absolute*. New York: Dutton.

Baldessarini, R. J., 1966, "Factors Influencing Tissue Levels of the Major Methyl Donor in Mammalian Tissue." In Himwich, H. E., Kety, S. S., and Smythies, J. R. (eds.), *Amine Metabolism in Schizophrenia*. Oxford: Pergamon.

Baldwin, J. M., 1929. Quoted by Piaget, 1929.

Balken, E. R., 1943, "A Delineation of Schizophrenic Language and Thought in a Test of Imagination." *Journal of Psychology*, 16:239.

Bard, P., and Mountcastle, V. B., 1947, "Some Forebrain Mechanisms Involved in the Expression of

Rage with Special Reference to Suppression of Angry Behavior.'' *Res. Pub. A. Nerv. e. Ment. Dis.*, 27:362.

Barison, F., 1934, ''L'Astrazione formale del pensiero quale sintomo di schizofrenia.'' *Schizophrenie,* 3, 1934. Quoted by Piro, 1967.

———, 1948, ''Il Manierismo schizofrenico.'' *Riv. Neurol.* 18:1.

———, 1949, ''Dissociazione e incomprensibilità schizofreniche.'' *Riv. Neurol.,* 19:1.

Barr, M. L., and Bertram, E. C., 1949, ''A Morphological Distinction between Neurons of the Male and Female, and the Behavior of the Nucleolar Satellite during Accelerated Nucleoprotein Synthesis.'' *Nature,* 163:676–677.

Barsa, K., and Kline, N. S., 1956, ''Use of Reserpine in Disturbed Psychotic Patients.'' Quoted by Kline, 1956.

Bartlet, J. E. A., 1957, ''Chronic Psychosis following Epilepsy.'' *American Journal of Psychiatry,* 114:338–343.

Bastide, R., 1965, *Sociologie des maladies mentales.* Paris: Flammarion.

Bateson, G., Jackson, D. D., Haley, J., and Weakland, J., 1956, ''Toward a Theory of Schizophrenia.'' *Behavioral Science,* 1:251.

Baynes, H. G., 1949, *Mythology of the Soul. A Research into the Unconscious from Schizophrenic Dreams and Drawings.* London: Methuen.

Beard, A. W., and Slater, E., 1962, ''The Schizophrenic-like Psychoses of Epilepsy.'' *Proceedings of the Royal Society of Medicine,* 55:311–316.

Becker, E., 1962, ''Toward a Theory of Schizophrenia. External Objects and the Creation of Meaning.'' *Archives of General Psychiatry,* 7:170–181.

Beckett, P. G. S., and Gottlieb, J. S., 1970, ''Advances in the Biology of Schizophrenia.'' In Arieti, S. (ed.), *The World Biennial of Psychiatry and Psychotherapy,* vol. 1, pp. 505–528. New York: Basic Books.

Bellak, L., 1948, *Dementia Praecox. The Past Decade's Work and Present States: A Review and Evaluation.* New York: Grune.

———. 1957, *Schizophrenia: A Review of the Syndromes,* New York: Logos Press.

Bellak, L., and Loeb, L., 1969, *The Schizophrenic Syndrome.* New York: Grune & Stratton.

Bellak, L., and Willson, E., 1947, ''On the Etiology of Dementia Praecox.'' *Journal of Nervous and Mental Disease,* 105:1–24.

Belloni, L., 1956, ''Dall' Elleboro alla reserpina.'' *Archivio di Psicologia, Neurologia e Psichiatria,* 17:115.

Bemporad, J. R., 1967, ''Perceptual Disorders in Schizophrenia.'' *American Journal of Psychiatry,* 123:971–975.

Bemporad, J. R., and Dunton, H. D., 1972, ''Catatonic Episodes in Childhood.'' *International Journal of Child Psychotherapy,* 1:19–44.

Bender, L., 1947, ''Childhood Schizophrenia.'' *American Journal of Orthopsychiatry,* 17:40–56.

———, 1953, ''Childhood Schizophrenia.'' *Psychiatric Quarterly,* 27:663–687.

Bender, L., and Schilder, P., 1930, ''Unconditioned and Conditioned Reactions to Pain in Schizophrenia.'' *American Journal of Psychiatry,* 10:365.

Bendi, S. B., Beckett, P. G. S., Caldwell, D. F., Grisell, J., and Gottlieb, J. S., 1969, ''Nailfold Capillary Structure and Skin Temperature in Schizophrenia.'' *Clinical and Basic Science Correlations. Supplement to Diseases of the Nervous System,* 30:2.

Benedetti, G., 1955, ''Il problema della coscienza nelle allucinazioni degli schizofrenici.'' *Archivio di Psicologia, Neurologia e Psichiatria,* 16:287.

———, 1956, ''Analisi dei processi di miglioramento e di guarigione nel corso della psicoterapia.'' *Archivio di Psicologia, Neurologia e Psichiatria,* 17:971.

———, 1971, ''Ich-Strukturierung und Psychodynamik in der Schizophrenie.'' In Bleuler, M., and Angst, J. (eds.), *Die Entstehung der Schizophrenie.* Bern: Huber.

———, 1972, ''Response to Frieda Fromm-Reichmann Award Presentation.'' Meeting of the American Academy of Psychoanalysis, May 1972.

Benedetti, G., Kind, H., and Mielke, F., 1957, ''Forschungen zur Schizophrenielehre 1951 bis 1955.'' *Fortschritte Neur. Psychiatrie,* 25:101–179.

Benjamin, J. D., 1944, "A Method for Distinguishing and Evaluating Formal Thinking Disorders in Schizophrenia." In Kasanin (1944*a*), *Language and Thought in Schizophrenia: Collected Papers*. Berkeley: University of California Press.

Bennett, A. E., 1940, "Preventing Traumatic Complications in Convulsive Shock Therapy by Curare." *JAMA*, 114:322.

Berger, H., 1931, "Über das Elektroenzephalogramm des Menschen." *Arch. f. Psychiat.*, 94:16–60.

———, 1933, "Über das Elektroenzecepalogramm des Menschen." *Arch. f. Psychiat.*, 100:302–321.

Berk, N., 1950, "A Personality Study of Suicidal Schizophrenics." *Microfilm Abstracts*, 10:155.

Bernard, P., and Bobon, J., 1961, "Le 'Rînhâûzhâîrhhâûsês' neomorphisme compensatoire chez un paraphrène débile." In *Premier Colloque International sur l' Expression Plastique*. Brussels: Les Publications "Acta Medica Belgica."

Best, C. H., and Taylor, N. B., 1939, *The Physiological Basis of Medical Practice*. Baltimore: Williams and Williams.

Bettelheim, B., 1956, "Schizophrenia as a Reaction to Extreme Situations." *American Journal of Orthopsychiatry*, 26:507–518.

———, 1967, *The Empty Fortress: Infantile Autism and the Birth of the Self*. New York: Free Press.

———, 1969, *The Children of the Dream*. New York: Macmillan.

———, 1970, "Infantile Autism." In Arieti, S. (ed.), *The World Biennial of Psychiatry and Psychotherapy*, vol. 1, pp. 400–425. New York: Basic Books.

Betz, B. J., 1947, "A Study of Tactics for Resolving the Autistic Barrier in the Psychotherapy of the Schizophrenic Personality." *American Journal of Psychiatry*, 104:267.

———, 1950, "Strategic Conditions in the Psychotherapy of Persons with Schizophrenia." *American Journal of Psychiatry*, 107:203.

Bexton, W. H., Heron, W., and Scott, T. H., 1954, "Effects of Decreased Variation in the Sensory Environment." *Canadian Journal of Psychology*, 8:70–76.

Bieber, I., 1958, "A Critique of the Libido Theory." *American Journal of Psychoanalysis*, 18:52–65.

Bieber, I., et al., 1962, *Homosexuality: A Psychoanalytic Study*. New York: Basic Books.

Billig, O., 1957, "Graphic Communication in Schizophrenia." *Congress Report 2*, Intern. Congress for Psychiatry, Zurich, Vol. 4.

———, 1968, "Spatial Structure in Schizophrenic Art." *Psychiatry and Art Proceedings IVth Int. Coll. Psychopathology of Expression* 1–16. Basel and New York: Karger.

Binswanger, L., 1949, "Der Fall Lola Voss." *Schweizer Archiv für Neurologie und Psychiatrie*, 63:29.

———, 1957, *Le Cas Suzanne Urban, étude sur la schizophrenie*. Paris: Desclée de Brouwer.

———, 1958*a*, "The Case of Ellen West." In May, R., Angel, E., and Ellenberger, H. F. (eds.), *Existence*. New York: Basic Books.

———, 1958*b*, "Insanity as Life-Historical Phenomenon and as Mental Disease: The Case of Ilse." In May, R., Angel, E., and Ellenberger, H. F. (eds.), *Existence*. New York: Basic Books.

Bion, W. R., 1954, "Notes on the Theory of Schizophrenia." In Bion, W. R., *Second Thoughts*. London: Heinemann.

———, 1956, "Development of Schizophrenic Thought." In Bion, *Second Thoughts*. London: Heinemann.

———, 1957, "Differentiation of the Psychotic from the Non-Psychotic Personalities." In Bion, W. R., *Second Thoughts*. London: Heinemann.

Black, B. J., 1963, *Guides to Psychiatric Rehabilitation*. New York: Altro Health and Rehabilitation Services.

Blacker, K. H., Jones, R. T., Stone, G. C., and Pfefferbaum, 1968, "Chronic Users of LSD: The 'Acidheads.' " *American Journal of Psychiatry*, 125:341–351.

Blanshard, B., 1967, "Internal Relations and Their Importance to Philosophy." *The Review of Metaphysics*, 21:227–236.

Blaschko, H., 1959, "The Development of Current Concepts of Catecholamine Formation." *Pharmacol. Rev.*, 11:307–316.

Bleuler, E., 1912*a*, *The Theory of Schizophrenic Negativism*. Nervous and Mental Disease Monograph Series No. 11. New York.

———, 1912*b*, *Affectivity, Suggestibility, Paranoia*. Utica, N.Y.: State Hospital Press.
———, 1913*a*, "Autistic Thinking." *American Journal of Insanity*, 69:873.
———, 1913*b*, "Kritik der Freudschen Theorien." *Allg. Z. Psychiatrie*, 70:665–718.
———, 1924, *Textbook of Psychiatry*. Translated by A. A. Brill. New York: Macmillan.
———, 1943, "Die Spätschizophrenen Krankeitsbilder." *Fortschr. Neur.*, 15:259.
———, 1950 (originally in German, 1911), *Dementia Praecox on the Group of Schizophrenias*. Translated by J. Zinkin. New York: International Universities Press.
Bleuler, M., 1954, *Endokrinologischc Psychiatric*. Stuttgart: Thieme.
———, 1963, "Conception of Schizophrenia within the Last Fifty Years and Today." *Proceedings of the Royal Society of Medicine*, 56:945–952.
———, 1968, "A Twenty-Three-Year Longitudinal Study of 208 Schizophrenics and Impression in Regard to the Nature of Schizophrenia." In Rosenthal, D. and Kety, s.s. (eds) in *The Transmission of Schizophrenia:* London: Pergammon Press.
Blondel, C., 1939, "Les Volitions." In Dumas, G. (ed.), *Nouveau Traité de Psychologie*. Paris: Alcan.
Bloom, J. B., and Davis, N., 1970, "Changes in Liver Disturbance Associated with Long-term Tranquilizing Medication." *Diseases of the Nervous System*, 31:309–317.
Blum, R. A., Livingston, P. B., Shader, R. I., 1969, "Changes in Cognition, Attention and Language in Acute Schizophrenia." *Diseases of the Nervous System*, 30:31–36.
Boas, F., 1927, *Primitive Art*. Oslo: H. Aschehong e Company.
Bobon, J., 1955, "Psychopathologie de l'expression plastique (mimique et picturale). Note préliminaire sur les 'néomimismes' et les 'néomorphismes.' " *Acta Neurologica et Psychiatrica Belgica*, 11:923–929.
———, 1957, "Contribution à la psychopathologie de l'expression plastique, mimique et picturale: Les 'néomimismes' et les 'néomorphismes.' "*Acta Neurologica et Psychiatrica Belgica*, 12:1031–1067.
Bobon, J., and Maccagnani, G., 1962, "Contributo allo studio della comunicazione nonverbale in psicopatologia: Il 'linguaggio' dell' espressione plastica." *Rivista Sperimentale di Freniatria*, 86:1097–1173.
Boernstein, W. S., 1940*a* and *b*, "Cortical Representation of Taste in Man and Monkey." (a) Functional and Anatomical Relations of Taste, Olfaction and Somatic Sensibility. *Yale Journal of Biology and Medicine*, 12:719. (b) The Localization of the Cortical Taste Area in Man and a Method for Measuring Impairment of Taste in Man. *Yale Journal of Biology and Medicine*, 13:133.
Bonfiglio, F., 1952, "Considerazioni sulla morbosità per malattie mentali in Italia nel triennio 1947–1948–1949." *Lavoro Neuropsichiat.*, 10:22.
Böök, J. A., 1960, "Genetical Aspects of Schizophrenic Psychoses." In Jackson, D. D. (ed.), *The Etiology of Schizophrenia*. New York: Basic Books.
Boss, M., 1963, *Psychoanalysis and Daseinanalysis*. New York: Basic Books.
———, 1973, "The Phenomenological Approach to Schizophrenia." In Arieti, S. (ed.), *The World Biennial of Psychiatry and Psychotherapy*, vol. 2, pp. 314–335.
Bostroem, A., 1928, "Storungen der Wollens." In Bumke, O. (ed.), *Handbuch des Geisteskrankheiten*, vol. 11, pp. 1–90. Berlin: Springer.
Bourdillon, R. E., Clarke, C. A., Ridges, A. P., Shepparn, P. M., Harper, P., and Leslie, S. A., 1965, " 'Pink Spot' in the Urine of Schizophrenics." *Nature*, 208:453–455.
Boutonier, J., 1951, *Les Defaillances de la volonté*. Paris: Presses Universitaires de France.
Bowers, M. K., 1961, "Theoretical Considerations in the Use of Hypnosis in the Treatment of Schizophrenia." *International Journal of Clinical and Experimental Hypnosis*, 9:39–46.
Bowlby, J., 1951, *Maternal Care and Mental Health*. World Health Organization Monograph, Series n. 2.
———, 1960, "Grief and Mourning in Infancy." In *The Psychoanalytic Study of the Child*, vol. 15. New York: International Universities Press.
Bowman, K. M., 1935, "Psychoses with Pernicious Anemia." *American Journal of Psychiatry*, 92:372.

Boyd, D. A., 1942, "Mental Disorders Associated with Child Bearing." *American Journal of Obstetrics and Gynecology,* 43:148–163, 335–349.

Braceland, F. J., 1966, "Rehabilitation." In Arieti, S. (ed.), *American Handbook of Psychiatry,* vol. 3, pp. 643–656. New York: Basic Books.

Bradley, C., 1941, *Schizophrenia in Childhood.* New York: Macmillan.

Breton, A., 1932, *Les Vases Communicants.* Paris: Cahiers Libres.

———, 1952, *La Clé des Champs.* Paris: Sagittaire.

Breton, A., and Eluard, P., 1930, *L'Immaculée Conception.* Paris: Editions Surrealistes.

Brickner, R. M., 1936, *The Intellectual Functions of the Frontal Lobes: A Study Based upon Observation of a Man Following Partial Bilateral Frontal Lobectomy.* New York: Macmillan.

Brill, H., and Patton, R. E., 1957, "Analysis of 1955–1956 Population Fall in New York State Mental Hospitals in First Year of Large-Scale Use of Tranquillizing Drugs." *American Journal of Psychiatry,* 114:509.

———, 1964, "The Impact of Modern Chemotherapy on Hospital Organization, Psychiatric Care, and Public Health Policies: Its Scope and Its Limits." *Proceedings Third World Congress of Psychiatry,* vol. 3, pp. 433–437.

Brill, N. G., 1969, "General Biological Studies." In Bellak, L., and Loeb, L. (eds.), *The Schizophrenic Syndrome.* New York: Grune & Stratton.

Brody, M. W., 1959, *Observations on "Direct Analysis," The Therapeutic Technique of Dr. John N. Rosen.* New York: Vantage Press.

Brooks, G. W., Deane, W. N., and Hugel, R. W., 1968, "Some Aspects of the Subjective Experience of Schizophrenia." In *Supplement to Diseases of the Nervous System,* vol. 29, pp. 78–82.

Brown, J. W., 1972, *Aphasia, Apraxia and Agnosia.* Springfield, Ill.: Thomas.

Bruch, H., 1957, *The Importance of Overweight.* New York: Norton.

———, 1962, "Perceptual and Conceptual Disturbances in Anorexia Nervosa." *Psychosomatic Medicine,* 24:187.

Bruch, H., and Palombo, S., 1961, "Conceptual Problems in Schizophrenia." *Journal of Nervous and Mental Disease,* 132:114–117.

Bruetsch, W. L., 1940, "Chronic Rheumatic Brain Disease as a Possible Factor in the Causation of Some Cases of Dementia Praecox." *American Journal of Psychiatry,* 97:276.

Bruner, J. S., 1951, "Personality Dynamics and the Process of Perceiving." In Blake, R. R., and Ramsey, G. V. (eds.), *Perception, an Approach to Personality.* New York: Ronald Press.

Buber, M., 1953, *I and Thou.* Edinburgh: Clark.

Bullard, D. M., 1959, *Psychoanalysis and Psychotherapy. Selected Papers of Frieda Fromm-Reichmann.* Chicago: University of Chicago Press.

Bumke, O., 1924, *Lehrbuch der Geisteskrankheiten,* 2nd ed. Munich: Bergmann.

Burlingame, C. C., 1949, "Rehabilitation after Leucotomy." *Proceedings of the Royal Society of Medicine,* 42:31.

Burney, C., 1952, *Solitary Confinement.* New York: Coward-McCann.

Burton, A., and Adkins, J., 1961, "Perceived Size of Self-Image Body Parts in Schizophrenia." *Archives of General Psychiatry,* 5:131–140.

Burton, A., and Bird, J. W., 1963, "Family Constellation and Schizophrenia." *Journal of Psychology,* 55:329–336.

Buscaino, V. M., 1921, "Nuovi date sulla distribuzione e sulla genesi delle 'zolle di disentegrazione a grappolo' dei dementi precoci." *Riv. di Pat. Nerv.,* 26:57.

———, 1952, "Extraneural Pathology of Schizophrenia (Liver, Digestive Tract, Reticulo-Endothelial System). In *Proceedings of the First International Congress of Neuropathology.* Turin: Rosenberg & Sellier.

———, 1970, "Biologia e terapia della schizofrenia." *Acta Neurologica,* 25:1–58.

Bychowski, G., 1943, "Physiology of Schizophrenic Thinking." *Journal of Nervous and Mental Disease,* 98:368–386.

———, 1952, *Psychotherapy of Psychosis.* New York: Grune & Stratton.

Byrd, R. E., 1938, *Alone.* New York: Putnam.

Cade, J. F., and Krupinski, J., 1962, "Incidence of Psychiatric Disorders in Victoria in Relation to Country of Birth." *Medical Journal of Australia,* 49:400–404.

Cairns, H., Oldfield, R. C., Pennybacker, J. B., and Whitteridge, D., 1941, "Akinetic Mutism with an Epidermoid Cyst of the Third Ventricle." *Brain,* 64:273.

Callieri, B., 1954, "Contributo allo studio psicopatologico dell' esperienza schizofrenica della fine del mondo." *Archivio Psicologia, Neurologia e Psichiatria,* 16:379.

Cameron, D. C., and Jellinek, E. M., 1939, "Physiological Studies in Insuline Treatment of Acute Schizophrenia: Pulse Rate and Blood Pressure." *Endocrinology,* 25:100.

Cameron, N., 1938, "Reasoning, Regression and Communication in Schizophrenics." *Psychological Monograph,* 50:1.

———, 1939, "Deterioration and Regression in Schizophrenic Thinking." *Journal of Abnormal and Social Psychology,* 34:265.

———, 1947, *The Psychology of Behavior Disorders. A Biosocial Interpretation.* Cambridge, Mass.: Mifflin Co.

Cameron, N., and Margaret, A., 1951, *Behavior Pathology.* Cambridge, Mass.: Mifflin Co.

Cancro, R., 1971, 1972, *The Schizophrenic Syndrome,* vols. 1, 2. New York: Brunner-Mazel.

Cantor, M. B., 1968, "Problems in Diagnosing and Prognosing with Occult Schizophrenic Patients." *American Journal of Psychoanalysis,* 39:36–47.

Capgras, J., and Carrette, P., 1924, "L'Illusion des sosies et complexe d'Oedipe." *Ann. méd.-psych.,* 82:48.

Capgras, J., Lucettini, P., and Schiff, P., 1925, "Du Sentiment d'estrangeté à l'illusion des sosies." *Ann. méd.-psych.,* 83:93.

Capgras, J., and Reboul-LaChaux, J., 1923, "L'Illusion des sosies dans un délire systematisé chronique." *Soc. Clin. Méd. Psych.,* 81:186.

Caplan, G., 1964, *Principles of Preventive Psychiatry.* New York: Basic Books.

Cargnello, D., 1964, "Fenomenologia del corpo." *Annali di Freniatria e Scienze Affini,* 77:365–379.

Cargnello, D., and Della Beffa, A.A., 1955, "L'illusione del Sosia." *Archivio di Psicologia, Neurologia e Psichiatria,* 16:173.

Carothers, J. C., 1947, "A Study of Mental Derangement in Africans." *Journal of Ment. Sci.,* 93, No. 392:548–597.

———, 1951, "Frontal Lobe Function and the African." *J. Ment. Sci.,* 97, n. 406, pp. 12–48.

Cassirer, E., 1946, *Language and Myth.* New York: Harper and Brothers.

———, 1953, *The Philosophy of Symbolic Forms,* vol. 1. New Haven: Yale University Press.

———, 1955, *The Philosophy of Symbolic Forms,* vol. 2. New Haven: Yale University Press.

———, 1957, *The Philosophy of Symbolic Forms,* vol. 3. New Haven: Yale University Press.

Cerletti, U., and Bini, L., 1938, "L'Electtroshock." *Arch. Gen. di Neurol., Psichiat., e Psicoanal.,* 19:266.

———, 1940, "Le alterazioni istopatologiche del sistema nervoso nell' electtroshock." *Rivista Sperimentale di Freniatria,* 64:2.

Chapman, J., 1966, "The Early Diagnosis of Schizophrenia." *British Journal of Psychiatry,* 112:225–238.

Chapman, L. J., 1958, "Intrusion of Associative Responses into Schizophrenic Conceptual Performance." *Journal of Abnormal Social Psychology,* 56:374–379.

———, 1960, "Confusion of Figurative and Literal Usages of Words by Schizophrenics and Brain-Damaged Patients." *Journal of Abnormal Social Psychology,* 60:412–416.

———, 1961, "A Re-interpretation of Some Pathological Disturbances in Conceptual Breadth." *Journal of Abnormal Social Psychology,* 62:514–519.

Chapman, L. J., and Chapman, J. P. , 1965, "The Interpretation of Words in Schizophrenia." *Journal of Personality and Social Psychology,* 1:135–146.

Chapman, L. J., Chapman, J. P., and Miller, G. A., 1964, "A Theory of Verbal Behavior in Schizophrenia." In Maher, B., *Progress in Experimental Personality Research,* vol. 1, pp. 49–77. New York: Academic Press.

Chertok, L., 1969, *Motherhood and Personality. Psychosomatic Aspects of Childbirth.* London: Tavistock. Originally published in French, 1966.

Chrzanowski, G., 1943, "Contrasting Responses to Electric Shock Therapy in Clinically Similar Catatonics." *Psychiatric Quarterly,* 17:282.

Clark, L. P., 1933, "Treatment of Narcissistic Neuroses and Psychoses." *Psychoanalytic Quarterly,* 20:304–326.

Clements, S. D., 1966, *Minimal Brain Dysfunction in Children.* NINDB Monograph No. 3, Washington, D.C.: U. S. Public Health Service.

Cole, E., Fisher, G., Cole, S. S., 1968, "Women Who Kill. A Sociopsychological Study." *Archives of General Psychiatry,* 19:1–8.

Colony, H. S., and Willis, S. E., 1956, "Electroencephalographic Studies of 100 Schizophrenic Patients." *American Journal of Psychiatry,* 113:163.

Conant, J. B., 1952, *Modern Science and Modern Man.* New York: Columbia University Press.

Courbon, P., and Fail, J., 1927, "Syndrome de Fregoli et schizophrenie." *Soc. Clin. Méd. Ment.*

Courbon, P., and Tusques, J., 1932, "Illusion d'intermetamorphose et de charme." *Ann. Méd.-Psych.,* 90:401.

Courtauld, A., 1932, "Living Alone under Polar Conditions." Cambridge: *The Polar Record,* No. 4.

Crahay, S., and Bobon, J., 1961, "De la représentation naturaliste à l'abstraction morbide des formes." In *Premier Colloque International sur l'Expression Plastique.* Brussels: Les Publications "Acta Medica Belgica."

Critchley, M., 1953, *The Parietal Lobes.* London: Arnold.

Croce, B. 1947, *La Filosofia di Giambattista Vico.* Laterza: Bari.

Dahl, M., 1958, "A Singular Distortion of Temporal Orientation." *American Journal of Psychiatry,* 115:146–149.

Dali, S., 1930, *La Femme visible.* Paris: Editions Surrealistes.

———, 1935, *Conquest of the Irrational.* New York: Julian Levy.

———, 1942, *The Secret Life of Salvador Dali.* New York: Dial Press.

Dally, P., 1967, *Chemotherapy of Psychiatric Disorders.* New York: Plenum Press. London: Logos Press.

Dastur, D. K., 1959, "The Pathology of Schizophrenia." *A.M.A. Archives of Neurology & Psychiatry,* 81:601–614.

Davidson, G. M., 1936, "Concerning Schizophrenia and Manic-Depressive Psychosis Associated with Pregnancy and Childbirth." *American Journal of Psychiatry,* 92:1331.

———, 1941, "The Syndrome of Capgras." *Psychiatric Quarterly,* 15:513.

Davis, P. A., 1940, "Evaluation of the Electroencephalograms of Schizophrenic Patients." *American Journal of Psychiatry,* 96:850.

———, 1942, "Comparative Study of the EEG's of Schizophrenic and Manic-Depressive Patients." *American Journal of Psychiatry,* 99:210.

Dawson, J. G., and Burke, G. W., 1958, "*Folie à Deux* in Husband and Wife." *Journal of Psychology,* 46:141–148.

Dax, E. C., 1953, *Experimental Studies in Psychiatric Art.* Philadelphia: Lippincott.

DeJong, H., 1922, "Ueber Bulbocapninkatalepsie." *Klinische Wochenschi,* 1:684.

DeJong, H., and Baruk, H., 1930*a,* "Pathogénie du syndrome catatonique." *Éncephale,* 25:97.

———, 1930*b, La Catatonie expérimentale par la bulbocapnine; Étude physiologique et clinique.* Paris: Masson.

Delgado, H., 1922, *El Dibujo des los psicopatos.* Lima.

Delay, J., and Deniker, P., 1952*a,* "Le traitement des psychoses par une méthode neurolytique derivée de l'hibernotherapie (le 4560 RP utilisé seul en cure prolongée et continue). L. ème Cong. des Alién. et Neurol. de Langue Française, Luxemburg, 21–27 July." *Comptes-Rendus du Congrès,* 497–502. Paris: Masson.

———, 1952*b,* "38 Cas de psychoses traités par la cure prolongée et continue de 4560 RP. L. ème Cong. des Alién et Neurol. de Langue Française, Luxemburg, 21–27 July. *Comptes-Rendus du Congrès,* 503–513. Paris: Masson.

———, 1961, *Méthodes Chimiothérapiques en Psychiatrie.* Paris: Masson.

Delong, S. L., 1967, "Chlorpromazine-induced Eye Changes." Quoted by Kalinowsky and Hippius, 1969.

De Martino, E., 1964, "Apocalissi culturali ed apocalissi psicopatologiche." *Nuovi Argomenti.* Quoted by De Martis, 1967.

De Martis, D., 1964, "La Corporeità nella schizofrenia." *Rassegna di Studi Psichiatrici,* 53:412–428.

———, 1965, "Réflexions sur les délires de négation et de fin du monde." *L'Evolution Psychiatrique,* 1:111.

———, 1967, "Note sui deliri di negazione." *Rivista Sperimentale di Freniatria,* 91:1119–1143.

De Martis, D., and Petrella, F., 1964, "Le Stereotipie. Studio psicopatologico e clinico (con particolare riferimento alla stereotipia schizofrenica)." *Rivista Sperimentale di Freniatria,* 88:946–1005.

De Martis, D., Petrella, F., and Petrella, A. M., 1967, "Ricerche sull' evoluzione dell' esperienza di esordio della malattia nella schizofrenia cronica." *Psichiatria Generale e dell' Età Evolutiva,* 5:1–17.

De Martis, D., and Porta, A., 1965, "Ricerche sulla qualità della percezione del proprio corpo in un gruppo di soggetti psicotici." *Rivista Sperimentale di Freniatria,* 89:779–810.

Denber, H. C. B., and Teller, D. N., 1963, "A Biochemical Genetic Theory Concerning the Nature of Schizophrenia." *Dis. Nerv. Syst.,* 29:106–114.

Denny-Brown, D., 1960, "Motor Mechanisms. Introduction: The General Principles of Motor Integration." In Field, J. (ed.), *Handbook of Physiology,* vol. 2, p. 781. Washington: American Physiological Society.

De Sanctis, S., 1925, *Neuropsichiatria infantile. Patologia e diagnostica.* Turin: Lattes.

Despert, L., 1941, "Thinking and Motility Disorder in a Schizophrenic Child." *Psychiatric Quarterly,* 15:522–536.

———, 1968, *Schizophrenia in Children.* New York: Brunner.

Deutsch, H., 1945, *Psychology of Women,* vol. 1, 2. New York: Grune & Stratton.

Dewhurst, K. E., El Kabir, D. J., Harris, G. W., and Mandelbrote, B. M., 1969, "Observations on the Blood Concentration of Thyrotrophic Hormone (T.S.H.) in Schizophrenia and Affective States." The *British Journal of Psychiatry,* 115:1003–1011.

Diamond, S., Balvin, R. S., and Diamond, F. R., 1963, *Inhibition and Choice: Neurobehavioral Approach to Problems of Plasticity in Behavior.* New York: Harper and Row.

Diem, 1903, "Die einfach demente." *Form der Dp. A.,* 37:111. Quoted by Bleuler, 1950.

Doust, J. W. L., 1955, "The Capillary System in Patients with Psychiatric Disorder: The Ontogenetic Structural Determination of the Nailfold Capillaries as Observed by Photomicroscopy." *Journal of Nervous and Mental Disease,* 121:516–526.

Drellich, M., 1974, "The Theory of the Neuroses." In Arieti, S., (ed.) *American Handbook of Psychiatry,* vol. 1. New York: Basic Books.

Dunlap, C. B., 1928, "The Pathology of the Brain in Schizophrenia." *Association for Research in Nervous and Mental Disease, Proceedings,* 5:371. New York: Hoeber.

Easson, W. M., 1966, "Myxedema with Psychosis." *Arch. Gen. Psychiat.,* 14:277–283.

Eaton, J. W., and Weil, R. J., 1955*a, Culture and Mental Disorders.* Glencoe, Ill.: Free Press.

———, 1955*b,* "The Mental Health of the Hutterites." In Rose, A. M., *Mental Health and Mental Disorder.* New York: Norton.

Eisenberg, L., and Kanner, L., 1957, "Early Infantile Autism." *American Journal of Orthopsychiatry,* 26:550–566.

Eissler, K. R., 1951, "Remarks on the Psycho-analysis of Schizophrenia." *Int. J. Psycho-Anal.,* 32:139.

———, 1952, "Remarks on the Psychoanalysis of Schizophrenia." In Brody and Redlick, *Psychotherapy with Schizophrenics.* New York: International Universities Press.

Eitinger, L., 1959, "The incidence of mental disease among refugees in Norway." *Journal Ment. Sci.,* 105:326–338.

Ellinwood, E. H., 1967, "Amphetamine Psychosis: Description of the Individuals and Process." *J. Nervous Ment. Disease,* 144:273–283.

English, O. S., Hampe, W. W., Bacon, C. L., and Settlage, C. F., 1961, *Direct Analysis and Schizophrenia. Clinical Observations and Evaluations.* New York: Grune & Stratton.

Ephron, H. S., 1969, "Dreams of Schizophrenics and 'Normals': Do They Differ?" Paper presented at a Dream Symposium under the auspices of the Comprehensive Course in Psychoanalysis, New York Medical College, November 1, 1969.

Erikson, E. H., 1940, "Problems of Infancy and Early Childhood." In *Cyclopedia of Medicine, Surgery, and Specialties*. Philadelphia: F. A. Davis, Co.

———, 1953, "Growth and Crises of the Healthy Personality." In Kluckhohn, C., Murray, H. A., and Schneider, D. M. (eds.), *Personality in Nature, Society and Culture*. New York: Knopf.

Erlenmeyer-Kimling, L., Ranier, J. D., and Kallman, F. J., 1966, "Current Reproductive Trends in Schizophrenia." In Hoch, P. H., and Zubin, J. (eds.), *The Psychopathology of Schizophrenia*. New York: Grune & Stratton.

Erlenmeyer-Kimling, L., Van Den Bosch, E., and Denham, B., 1969, "The Problem of Birth Order and Schizophrenia: A Negative Conclusion." *British Journal of Psychiatry*, 115:659–678.

Ervin, F., Epstein, A. W., and King, H. E., 1955, "Behavior of Epileptic and Nonepileptic Patients with 'Temporal Spikes.' " *A.M.A. Archives of Neurology and Psychiatry*, 75:548.

Ey, H., 1948, "La Psychiatrie devant le surréalisme." *Evolution Psychiat.*, 3:3–52.

Ey, H., Bernard, P., and Brisset, C., 1967, *Manuel de psychiatrie*. Paris: Masson.

Fairbairn, R., 1952, *Object-Relations Theory of the Personality*. New York: Basic Books.

Fairweather, G. W. (ed.), 1964, *Social Psychology in Treating Mental Illness: An Experimental Approach*. New York: Wiley.

Farber, L., 1966, *The Ways of the Will: Essays Toward a Psychology and Psychopathology of the Will*. New York: Basic Books.

Farina, A., Garmezy, N., and Barry, H., 1963, "Relationship of Marital Status to Incidence and Prognosis of Schizophrenia." *Journal of Abnormal Social Psychology*, 67:624–630.

Faris, R. E. L., 1955, *Social Disorganization*. New York: Ronald Press.

Faris, R. E. L., and Dunham, H. W., 1939, *Mental Disorders in Urban Areas. An Ecological Study of Schizophrenia and Other Psychoses*. Chicago: University of Chicago Press.

Farrell, M. J., and Vassaf, F., 1940, "Observations on the Effect of Insulin Shock Therapy in Schizophrenia." *Arch. Neurol. Psychiat.*, 43:784.

Faure, H., 1971, *Les Appartenances du délirant*. 3rd ed. Paris: Presses Universitaires de France.

Federn, P., 1943, "Psychoanalysis of Psychoses. I. Errors and How to Avoid Them. II. Transference." *Psychiatric Quarterly*, 17:3, 17, 246. Reprinted in Federn, 1952.

———, 1947, "Discussion of Rosen's Paper." *Psychiatric Quarterly*, 21:23–26.

———, 1952, *Ego Psychology and the Psychoses*. New York: Basic Books.

Feigenbaum, D., 1930, "Analysis of a Case of Paranoia Persecutoria. Structure and Cure." *Psychoanalytic Review*, 17:159.

Feinberg, I., Koresko, R. L., and Gottlieb, F., 1965, "Further Observations on Electrophysiological Sleep Patterns in Schizophrenia." *Compr. Psychiat.*, 6:21–24.

Feinberg, I., Koresko, R. L., Gottlieb, F., and Wender, P. H., 1964, "Sleep Electroencephalographic and Eye-Movement Patterns in Schizophrenic Patients." *Compr. Psychiat.*, 5:44–53.

Fenichel, O., 1945, *The Psychoanalytic Theory of Neurosis*. New York: Norton.

Ferenczi, S., 1950, "Some Clinical Observations on Paranoia and Paraphrenia." In Ferenczi, S., *Sex in Psychoanalysis*. New York: Basic Books.

Ferraro, A., 1954, "Discussion at the Session of Histopathology of Schizophrenia." In *Proceedings of First International Congress of Neuropathology*. Turin: Rosenberg & Sellier.

Ferraro, A., Arieti, S., and English, W. H., 1945, "Cerebral Changes in the Course of Pernicious Anemia and Their Relationship to Psychic Symptons." *J. of Neuropath. and Experim. Neur.*, 4:217–239.

Ferraro, A., and Barrera, S. E., 1932, *Experimental Catalepsy*. Utica, N.Y.: State Hospital Press.

Ferraro, A., and Jervis, G., 1936, "Pick's Disease. Clinico-pathologic Study with Report of Two Cases." *Archives of Neurology and Psychiatry*, 36:739.

———, 1939, "Brain Pathology in Four Cases of Schizophrenia Treated with Insulin." *Psychiatric Quarterly*, 13:419.

Ferreira, A. J., 1959, "Psychotherapy with Severely Regressed Schizophrenics." *Psychiatric Quarterly*, 33:664–682.

———, 1963, "Family Myth and Homeostasis." *Archives of General Psychiatry*, 9:457.

———, 1967, "Psychosis and Family Myth." *American Journal of Psychotherapy,* 21:186–197.

Fessel, W. J., 1962, "Blood Proteins in Functional Psychoses: A Review of the Literature and Unifying Hypothesis." *Archives of General Psychiatry,* 6:132–148.

Festinger, L., 1957, *A Theory of Cognitive Dissonance.* Stanford, Calif.: Stanford University Press.

Fiamberti, A. M., 1947, "Indicazioni e tecnica della leucotomia prefrontale transorbitaria." *Rassegne di Neuropsichiatria,* 1:3.

Fink, M., Simeon, J., Hague, W., and Itil, I., 1966, "Prolonged Adverse Reactions to LSD in Psychotic Subjects." *Archives of General Psychiatry,* 15:450–454.

Finkelman, I., and Haffron, D., 1937, "Observations on Circulating Blood Volume in Schizophrenia, Manic-Depressive Psychosis, Epilepsy, Involutional Psychosis and Mental Deficiency." *Am. J. Psychiatry,* 93:917.

Fisher, C., 1954, "Dream and Perception. The Role of Preconscious and Primary Modes of Perception in Dream Formation." *Journal of the American Psychoanalytic Association,* 2:380–445.

———, 1960, "Subliminal and Supraliminal Influences on Dreams." *American Journal of Psychiatry,* 116:1009–1017.

Fisher, C., and Dement, W., 1963, "Studies on the Psychopathology of Sleep and Dreams." *American Journal of Psychiatry,* 119:1160.

Fisher, C., and Paul, I. H., 1959, "The Effect of Subliminal Visual Stimulation on Images and Dreams: A Validation Study." *Journal of the American Psychoanalytic Association,* 7:35–83.

Fleck, S., 1960, "Family Dynamics and Origin in Schizophrenia." *Psychosomatic Medicine,* 22:333–344.

Forrest, D. V., 1965, "Poiesis and the Language of Schizophrenia." *Psychiatry,* 28:1–18.

———, 1968, "The Patient's Sense of the Poem: Affinities and Ambiguities." In Leed (ed.), *Poetry Therapy.* Philadelphia: Lippincott.

———, 1969, "New Words and Neologisms with a Thesaurus of Coinages by a Schizophrenic Savant." *Psychiatry,* 32:44–73.

Foudraine, J., 1961, "Schizophrenia and the Family, a Survey of the Literature 1956–1960 on the Etiology of Schizophrenia." *Acta Psychotherapeutica,* 9:82–110.

Freeman, H., Hoskins, R. G., and Sleeper, F. H., 1932, "Blood Pressure in Schizophrenia." *Archives of Neurology and Psychiatry,* 27:333.

Freeman, T., 1951, "Pregnancy as a Precipitant of Mental Illness in Men." *British Journal of Med. Psychol.,* 24:49–54.

Freeman, T. (ed.), 1966, *Studies in Psychosis.* New York: International Universities Press.

Freeman, W., 1949, "Transorbital Leucotomy: The Deep Frontal Cut." In *Proceedings of the Royal Society of Medicine,* 47:8.

Freeman, W., and Watts, J. W., 1942, *Psychosurgery.* Springfield, Ill.: Thomas.

Freud, S., 1894, "The Defence Neuro-Psychoses." *Neurologisches Zentralblatt,* vols. 10, 11. Reprinted in *Collected Papers,* vol. 1, pp. 59–75.

———, 1896, "Further Remarks on the Defence Neuro-Psychoses." *Neurologisches Zentralblatt,* October 1896, No. 10. Reprinted in *Collected Papers,* vol. 1, pp. 155–182.

———, 1901, *The Interpretation of Dreams.* New York: Basic Books, 1960.

———, 1904, "On Psychotherapy." *Collected Papers,* vol. 1. London: Hogarth Press, 1946.

———, 1911, "Psycho-Analytic Notes upon an Autobiographical Account of a Case of Paranoia (Dementia Paranoides)." *Jahrbuch für psychoanalytische und psychopathologische Forschungen,* vol. 3, 1911. Reprinted in *Collected Papers,* vol. 3, pp. 387–470.

———, 1914, "On Narcissism: An Introduction." *Jahrbuch,* vol. 4, 1914. Reprinted in *Collected Papers,* vol. 4, pp. 30–59.

———, 1923, *The Ego and the Id. Standard Edition,* vol. 19, pp. 12–63. London: Hogarth. New York: Macmillan. First published as *Das Ich und das Es.*

———, 1924*a*, "Neurosis and Psychosis." *Zeitschrift,* vol. 4. Reprinted in *Collected Papers,* vol. 2, pp. 250–254.

———, 1924*b*, "The Loss of Reality in Neurosis and Psychosis." In *Collected Papers,* vol. 2, pp. 277–282.

———, 1931, "Female Sexuality." In *Collected Papers,* vol. 5, pp. 252–272. New York: Basic Books, 1959.

———, 1937, "Constructions in Analysis." Reprinted in *Collected Papers,* vol. 5, p. 358. London: Hogarth.

———, 1938*a,* "Psychopathology of Everyday Life." In Brill, A. A. (ed.), *The Basic Writings of Sigmund Freud,* pp. 33–178. New York: Modern Library.

———, 1938*b, A General Introduction to Psychoanalysis.* New York: Garden City Publishing Co.

———, 1940, "An Outline of Psychoanalysis." *Standard Edition,* vol. 23, pp. 141–208. London: Hogarth. New York: Macmillan. First published as "Abriss der Psychoanalyse."

———, 1946, *Collected Papers,* vols. 1–5. New York, London, Vienna: The International Psychoanalytical Press.

Friedhoff, A. J., and Van Winkle, E., 1967, "New Developments in the Investigation of the Relationship of 3,4-dimethoxyphenylethylamine to Schizophrenia." In Himwich, H. E., Kety, S. S., and Smythies, J. R. (eds.), *Amines and Schizophrenia.* Oxford: Pergamon Press.

Frohman, C. E., and Gottlieb, J. S., 1974, "The Biochemistry of Schizophrenia." In Arieti, S. (ed.), *American Handbook of Psychiatry,* (2nd ed.), vol. 3. New York: Basic Books.

Fromm-Reichmann, F., 1939, "Transference Problems in Schizophrenia." *The Psychoanalytic Quarterly,* 8:412.

———, 1942, "A Preliminary Note on the Emotional Significance of Stereotypes in Schizophrenics." *Bulletin of the Forest Sanitarium,* 1:17–21. Reprinted in Bullard, 1959.

———, 1948, "Notes on the Development of Treatment of Schizophrenia by Psychoanalytic Psychotherapy." *Psychiatry,* 11:263–273.

———, 1950, *Principles of Intensive Psychotherapy.* Chicago: University of Chicago Press.

———, 1952, "Some Aspects of Psychoanalytic Psychotherapy with Schizophrenics." In Brody, E. B., and Redlich, R. C., *Psychotherapy with Schizophrenics.* New York: International Universities Press.

———, 1954, "Psychotherapy of Schizophrenia." *American Journal of Psychiatry,* 111:410.

———, 1958, "Basic Problems in the Psychotherapy of Schizophrenia." *Psychiatry,*21:1.

Frosch, J., 1964, "The Psychotic Character." *Psychiatric Quarterly,* 38:81–96.

Fulton, J. F., 1951, *Frontal Lobotomy and Affective Behavior.* New York: Norton.

Gabel, J., 1948, "Symbolisme et Schizophrènie," *Revue Suisse de Psychologie et de psychologie appliquè,* 7:268.

———, 1962, *La Fausse conscience.* Paris: Les Editions de Minuit.

Gallant, D. M., and Steele, C. A., 1966, "DPN (NAD-oxidized form): A Preliminary Evaluation in Chronic Schizophrenic Patients." *Curr. Ther. Res.,* 8:542.

Galli, P., 1963, "The Psychotherapist and the Psychotic Family." Unpublished lecture.

Gelb, A., and Goldstein, K., 1920, *Psychologische Analysen hirnpathologischer Fälle.* Leipzig: Barth.

Gentili, C., Muscatello, C. F., Ballerini, A., and Agresti, E., 1965, "Psicopatologia del vissuto corporeo nella schizofrenia: studio clinico e fenomenologico dei deliri a tema somatico." *Rivista Sperimentale di Freniatria,*89:1077–1139.

Gibbs, F. A., and Gibbs, E. L., 1963, "The Mitten Pattern. An Electroencephalographic Abnormality Correlating with Psychosis." *Journal of Neuropsychiatry,* 5:6–13.

Giberti, F., De Carolis, V., and Rossi, R., 1961, "La Schizofrenia tardiva." *Sistema Nervoso,* 480–499.

Glaser, G. H., 1964, "The Problem of Psychosis in Psychomotor Temporal Lobe Epileptics." *Epilepsia,* 5:271–278.

Globus, J. H., Harreveld, A. Van, and Wiersma, C. A. G., 1943, "The Influence of Electric Current Application on the Structure of the Brain of Dogs." *J. Neuropath. & Exper. Neurol.,* 2:263.

Goffman, E., 1961, *Asylums. Essays on the Social Situation of Mental Patients and Other Inmates.* Garden City, N.Y.: Doubleday.

Goldberg, E. M., and Morrison, S. L., 1963, "Schizophrenia and Social Class." *Brit. J. Psychiat.,* 109:785–802.

Goldfarb, W., 1961, *Childhood Schizophrenia.* Cambridge, Mass.: Commonwealth Fund–Harvard University Press.

Goldman, A. E., 1960, "Symbolic Representation in Schizophrenia." *Journal of Personality*, 28:293–316.

Goldstein, K., 1939, *The Organism*. New York: American Book.

———, 1943*a*, "The Significance of Psychological Research in Schizophrenia." *Journal of Nervous and Mental Disease*, 97:261–279.

———, 1943*b*, "Some Remarks on Russel Brain's Articles Concerning Visual Object Agnosia." *Journal of Nervous and Mental Disease*, 98:148–153.

———, 1959, "The Organismic Approach." In Arieti, S. (ed.), *American Handbook of Psychiatry*, vol. 2, pp. 1333–1347. New York: Basic Books.

Goldstein, K., and Gelb, A., 1920, *Psychologische Analyse hirnpathologischer Fälle*, vol. 1, pp. 1–43. Leipzig: Barth.

Gondor, L., 1963, "The Fantasy of Utopia." *American Journal of Psychotherapy*, 17:606–618.

Gordon, H. L., 1948, "Fifty Shock Therapy Theories." *The Military Surgeon*, 103:397–401.

Gornall, A. G., Eglitis, B., Miller, A., Stokes, A. B., and Dewan, J. G., 1953, "Long-Term Clinical and Metabolic Observations in Periodic Catatonia. An Application of the Kinetic Method of Research in Three Schizophrenic Patients." *American Journal of Psychiatry*, 109:584–594.

Gottesman, I. I., and Shields, J., 1966, "Contributions of Twin Studies to Perspectives on Schizophrenia." In Maher, B. A. (ed.), *Progress in Experimental Personality Research 3*. New York: Academy Press.

Gottlieb, J. S., 1936, "Relationship of the Systolic to the Diastolic Blood Pressure in Schizophrenia. The Effect of Environmental Temperature." *Archives of Neurology and Psychiatry*, 35:1256.

Graetz, B., Reiss, M., and Waldon, G., 1954, "Benzoic Acid Detoxication in Schizophrenic Patients." *J. Ment. Science*, 100:145–148.

Gralnick, A., 1942, "Folie à Deux. The Psychosis of Association." *Psychiatric Quarterly*, 16:230–263, 16:491–520.

———, 1962, "Family Psychotherapy: General and Specific Considerations." *American J. of Orthopsychiatry*, 32:515–526.

———, 1969, *The Psychiatric Hospital as a Therapeutic Instrument*. New York: Brunner-Mazel.

Gralnick, A., and Schween, P. H., 1966, "Family Therapy." *Psychiatric Research Report*, No. 20:212–217.

Grassi, B., 1961, "Un contributo allo studio della poesia schizofrenica." *Rassegne di Neuropsichiatria*, 15:107–119.

Green, H. W., 1939, *Persons Admitted to the Cleveland State Hospital, 1928–1937*. Cleveland: Cleveland Health Council.

Greenblatt, M., and Solomon, H. C., 1953, *Frontal Lobes and Schizophrenia*. New York: Springer.

Greene, M. A., 1962, "The Stormy Personality." *Psychoanalysis and Psychoanalytic Review*, 49:55–67.

Greenson, R., 1974, "The Theory of Psychoanalytic Technique." In Arieti, S. (ed.), *American Handbook of Psychiatry*, 2nd ed., vol. 1. New York: Basic Books.

Greiner, A. C., and Berry, K., 1964, "Skin Pigmentation and Corneal Lens Opacities with Prolonged Chlorpromazine Therapy." *Canadian Medical Association Journal*, 90:663–664.

Grinspoon, L., Ewalt, J., and Shader, R., 1967, "Long-Term Treatment of Chronic Schizophrenia." *International Journal of Psychiatry*, 4:116–128.

Grosz, H. J., and Miller, I., 1958, "Siblings Patterns in Schizophrenia." *Science*, 128:30.

Guntrip, H., 1961, *Personality Structure and Human Interaction*. New York: International Universities Press.

———, 1966, "The Object-Relations Theory of W. R. D. Fairbairn." In Arieti, S. (ed.), *American Handbook of Psychiatry*, vol. 3., pp. 230–235. York: Basic Books.

———, 1968, *Schizoid Phenomena, Object Relations and the Self*. New York: International Universities Press.

———, 1973, "Science, Psychodynamic Reality and Autistic Thinking." *Journal of the American Academy of Psychoanalysis*, 1:3–22.

Gutheil, E. A., 1951, *The Handbook of Dream Analysis*. New York: Liveright.

Guttmacher, M. S., 1960, *The Mind of the Murderer*. New York: Farrar, Straus and Cudahy.

Guze, S. B., Goodwin, D. W., and Crane, J. B., 1969, "Criminality and Psychiatric Disorders." *Archives of General Psychiatry,* 20:583–591.

Haley, J., 1959, "The Family of the Schizophrenic. A Model System." *Journal of Nervous and Mental Disease,* 129:357–374.

Halevi, H. S., 1963, "Frequency of Mental Illness among Jews in Israel." *Int. J. Soc. Psychiat.,* 9:268–282.

Hamilton, G. V., 1911, "A Study of Trial and Error Reactions in Mammals." *Journal of Animal Behavior,* 1:33.

Hamilton, J. A., 1962, *Postpartum Psychiatric Problems*. St. Louis: Mosby.

Hanfmann, E., and Kasanin, J., 1942, *Conceptual Thinking in Schizophrenia*. Nervous and Mental Disease Monographs Series No. 67. New York.

Hare, E. H., and Price, J. S., 1968, "Mental Disorder and Season of Birth: Comparison of Psychoses with Neurosis." *British Journal of Psychiatry,* 115:533–540.

Harlow, H. F., Wehling, H., and Maslow, A. H., 1932, "Comparative Behavior of Primates: Delayed Reaction Tests on Primates." *J. Comp. Psychol.,* 13:13.

Harrow, M., Tucker, G. J., and Bromet, E., 1969, "Short-Term Prognosis of Schizophrenic Patients." *Archives of General Psychiatry,* 21:195–202.

Hartmann, H., 1950*a*, "Psychoanalysis and Development Psychology." In *The Psychoanalytic Study of the child,* vol. 5. New York: International Universities Press.

———, 1950*b*, "Comments on the Psychoanalytic Theory of the Ego." In *The Psychoanalytic Study of the Child,* vol. 5. New York: International Universities Press.

———, 1953, "Contribution to the Metapsychology of Schizophrenia." In *The Psychoanalytic Study of the Child,* vol. 8, pp. 177–198. New York: International Universities Press.

———, 1956, "Notes on the Reality Principle." In *The Psychoanalytic Study of the Child,* vol. 11, p. 31. New York: International Universities Press.

———, 1964, *Essays on Ego Psychology*. New York: International Universities Press.

Hartmann, H., Kris, E., and Loewenstein, R. M., 1945, "Comments on the Formation of Psychic Structure." In *The Psychoanalytic Study of the Child,* vol. 2, p. 11. New York: International Universities Press.

Hauptmann, A., and Myerson, A., 1948, "Studies of Finger Capillaries in Schizophrenic and Manic-Depressive Psychoses." *Journal of Nervous and Mental Disease,* 108:91–108.

Head, H., 1920, *Studies in Neurology*. London: Oxford.

———, 1926, *Aphasia and Kindred Disorders of Speech*. New York: Macmillan.

Heath, R. G., 1957, "Effect on Behavior in Humans with the Administration of Taraxein." *Am. J. Psychiatry,* 114:14–24.

———, 1963, *Serological Fractions in Schizophrenia*. New York: Hoeber.

Heath, R. G., and Krupp, I. M., 1967, "Schizophrenia as an Immunologic Disorder." *Archives of General Psychiatry,* 16:1–33.

Heath, R. G., Martens, S., Leach, B. E., Cohen, M., and Feigley, C. A., 1958, "Behavioral Changes in Nonpsychotic Volunteers following the Administration of Taraxein, the Substance Obtained from the Serum of Schizophrenic Patients." *American Journal of Psychiatry,* 114:917–920.

Hebb, D. O., 1954, "The Problems of Consciousness and Introspection." In Delafresnaye, J. F. (ed.), *Brain Mechanisms and Consciousness*. Springfield, Ill.: Thomas.

Hemphill, R. E., 1944, "Significance of Atrophy of Testis in Schizophrenia." *J. Ment. Sci.,* 90:696.

———, 1951, "A Case of Genital Self-Mutilation." *British Journal of Med. Psychol.,* 24:291.

Hemphill, R. E., Reiss, M., and Taylor, A. L., 1944, "A Study of the Histology of the Testis in Schizophrenia and Other Mental Disorders." *J. Ment. Sci.,* 90:681.

Henderson, D. K., and Gillespie, R. D., 1941, *A Text-Book of Psychiatry*. 5th ed. New York: Oxford University Press.

Henderson, J. L., and Wheelwright, J. B., 1974, "Analytical Psy." In Arieti, S. (ed.), *American Handbook of Psychiatry,* (2nd ed.), vol. 1. New York: Basic Books.

Henle, M., 1962, "On the Relation between Logic and Thinking." *Psychological Review,* 69:366–378.

Heron, W., Bexton, W. H., and Hebb, D. O., 1953, "Cognitive Effects of Decreased Variation in the Sensory Environment." *Amer. Psychol.,* 8:366.

Heron, W., Doane, B. K., and Scott, T. H., 1956, "Visual Disturbances after Prolonged Isolation." *Canadian Journal of Psychology,* 10:13.

Higgins, J., 1964, "The Concept of Process-reactive Schizophrenia: Criteria and Related Research." *J. Nerv. Ment. Dis.,* 138:9025.

———, 1969, "Process-Reactive Schizophrenia." *Journal of Nervous and Mental Disease,* 149:350–472.

Hill, D., 1957, "Electroencephalogram in Schizophrenia." In Richter, D., *Schizophrenia.* New York: Macmillan.

Hill, L. B., *Psychotherapeutic Intervention in Schizophrenia.* Chicago: University of Chicago Press, 1955.

Himwich, H. E., Kety, S. S., and Smythies, J. R. (eds.), 1966, *Amine Metabolism in Schizophrenia.* Oxford: Pergamon.

Hinsie, L. E., 1930, *The Treatment of Schizophrenia.* Baltimore: Williams and Wilkins.

Hinsie, L. E., and Campbell, R. J., 1960, *Psychiatric Dictionary.* New York: Oxford University Press.

Hinsie, L. E., and Shatzky, J., 1950, *Psychiatric Dictionary.* New York: Oxford University Press.

Hoch, P., 1955, "The Effect of Chlorpromazine on Moderate and Mild Mental Emotional Disturbance." In *Chlorpromazine and Mental Health.* New York: Lea Febiger.

Hoch, P., and Polatin, P., 1949, "Pseudoneurotic Forms of Schizophrenia." *Psychiatric Quarterly,* 23:248–276.

Hoch, P., and Zubin, J., 1966, *Psychopathology of Schizophrenia.* New York: Grune & Stratton.

Hoedemaker, F. S., 1970, "Psychotic Episodes and Postpsychotic Depression in Young Adults." *American Journal of Psychiatry,* 127:606–610.

Hoffer, A., 1966, "The Effects of Nicotinic Acid on the Frequency and Duration of Re-Hospitalization of Schizophrenic Patients; A Controlled Comparison Study." *International Journal of Neuropsychiatry,* 2:334.

———, 1971, "Megavitamin B3 Therapy for Schizophrenia." *Canadian Psychiatric Association Journal,* 16:499.

Hoffer, A., and Osmond, H., 1964, "Treatment of Schizophrenic with Nicotinic Acid. A Ten-Year Follow-Up." *Acta Psychiat. Scand.,* 40:171.

Hoffer, A., Osmond, H., Callbeck. M. J., and Kahan, I., 1957, "Treatment of Schizophrenia with Nicotinic Acid and Nicotinamide." *J. Clin. Exp. Psychopathol.,* 18:131–158.

Hoffer, A., Osmond, H., and Smythies, J., 1954, "Schizophrenia: A New Approach." *J. Ment. Sci.,* 100:29–54.

Hollingshead, A. B., and Redlich, F. C., 1954, "Schizophrenia and Social Structure." *American Journal of Psychiatry,* 110:695–701.

———, 1958, *Social Class and Mental Illness.* New York: Wiley.

Hollister, L. E., 1968, *Chemical Psychoses LSD and Related Drugs.* Springfield, Ill.: Thomas.

Horney, K., 1937, *The Neurotic Personality of Our Time.* New York: Norton.

———, 1945, *Our Inner Conflicts.* New York: Norton.

———, 1950, *Neurosis and Human Growth.* New York: Norton.

Horwitt, M. K., 1956, "Fact and Artifact in the Biology of Schizophrenia." *Science,* 124:429.

Horwitz, W. A., Polatin, P. Kolb, L. C., and Hoch, P. H., 1958, "A Study of Cases of Schizophrenia Treated by 'Direct Analysis.' " *Am. J. Psychiat.,* 114:780.

Hoskins, R. G., 1932, "Oxygen Consumption (Basal Metabolic Rate) in Schizophrenia. II. Distributions in Two Hundred and Fourteen Cases." *Archives of Neurology and Psychiatry,* 28:1346.

———, 1937, "Oxygen Metabolism in Schizophrenia." *Archives of Neurology and Psychiatry,* 38:1261.

———, 1946, *The Biology of Schizophrenia.* New York: Norton.

Huizinga, J., 1924, *The Waning of the Middle Ages.* Garden City, N.Y.: Doubleday, 1956.

Hunt, R. C., 1958, "Ingredient of a Rehabilitation Program." In *An Approach to the Prevention of Disability from Chronic Psychoses.* New York: Milbank Memorial Fund.

Hunter, W. S., 1913, "The Delayed Reaction in Animals and Children." *Behavior Monographs,* 2:86.
Igert, C., and Lairy, G. C., 1962, "Prognostic Value of EEG in the Development of Schizophrenics." *Electroenceph. Clin. Neurophysiol.,* 14:183–190.
Itil, T. M., 1973, "Drug Treatment of Therapy-Resistant Schizophrenic Patients." In Arieti, S. (ed.), *The World Biennial of Psychiatry and Psychotherapy,* vol. 2, pp. 246–264. New York: Basic Books.
Ivanov-Smolenskij, A., 1934, "The Various Forms and the Neurodynamics of Catatonic Stupor." *Archives of Biological Sciences,* 36:85–106. Originally published in Russian.
Jackson, A. P. Comments in Whitaker, C. A., *Psychotherapy of Chronic Schizophrenic Patients.* Boston: Little, Brown, 1958.
Jackson, D. D., 1960, *The Etiology of Schizophrenia.* New York: Basic Books.
———, 1967*a,* "The Transactional Viewpoint." *International Journal of Psychiatry,* 4:453.
———, 1967*b,* "Schizophrenia. The Nosological Nexus." In Romano, J., *The Origins of Schizophrenia.* Amsterdam: Excerpta Medica Foundation, 1968.
Jackson, J. H., 1932, *Selected Writings.* London: Hodder and Stoughton. Reprinted by Basic Books, New York, 1958.
Jacobi, J., 1943, *The Psychology of Jung.* New Haven, Conn.: Yale University Press.
Jacobson, E., 1967, *Psychotic Conflict and Reality.* New York: International Universities Press.
James, W., 1950, *Principles of Psychology.* New York: Dover Publications, Inc.
Jamieson, G. R., 1936, "Suicide and Mental Disease." *Archives of Neurology and Psychiatry,* 36:1.
Janzarik, W., 1957, "Zur Problematik Schizophrener Psychosen im Höheren Lebensalter." *Nervenarzt,* 28:535.
Jaspers, K., 1946, *General Psychopathology.* Reprinted in English by University of Chicago Press, Chicago, 1964.
Johanson, E., 1964, "Mild Paranoia. Description and Analysis of Fifty-Two In-Patients from an Open Department for Mental Diseases." *Acta Psychiatrica Scandinavica Supplement 177,* pp. 1–100.
Johnson, A. M., Giffin, M. E., Watson, E. J., and Beckett, P. G. S., 1956, "Studies in Schizophrenia at the Mayo Clinic. II. Observations on Ego Functions in Schizophrenia." *Psychiatry,* 19:143–148.
Jones, E., 1938, *Papers on Psycho-Analysis.* Baltimore: Wood.
Jones, J., 1953, *The Therapeutic Community: A New Treatment Method in Psychiatry.* New York: Basic Books.
Josephy, H., 1930, "Dementia Praecox (Schizophrenie)." In Bumke, O., *Handbuch der Geisteskrankheiten.* Berlin: Springer.
Jung, C. G., 1910, "The Association Method." *American Journal of Psychology,* 21:219–269.
———, 1917, "The Content of the Psychoses." In *Collected Papers on Analytical Psychology.* London: Tindall & Cox, 1917.
———, 1918, *Studies in Word Association.* London: Heinemann.
———, 1920, "A Contribution to the Study of Psychological Types." In *Collected Papers on Analytical Psychology.* London: Baillière, Tindall & Cox.
———, 1921, *Psychology of the Unconscious.* Translated by B. M. Hinkle. New York: Moffat, Yard.
———, 1933, *Psychological Types.* New York: Harcourt, Brace.
———, 1936 (originally 1903), *The Psychology of Dementia Praecox.* Nervous and Mental Disease Monograph Series No. 3. New York.
———, 1939, "On the Psychogenesis of Schizophrenia." Lecture given at the Section of Psychiatry of the Royal Society of Medicine, London, 1939. *Journal of Mental Science.*
———, 1959, "The Archetypes and the Collective Unconscious." In Jung, C. G., *Collected Works.* New York: Pantheon.
Jung, R., and Carmichael, E. A., 1937, "Uber Vasomotorische Reaktionen und Warmerregulation im Katatonischin Stupor." *Arch. f. Psychiat.,* 107:330.
Kagan, J., 1972, "Do Infants Think?" *Scientific American,* 226(3):74–83.
Kahlbaum, K. L., 1863, *Gruppierung der Psychischen Krankheiten.* Danzig: Kafemann.
———, 1874, *Die Katatonic oder das Spannungsirresein.* Berlin: Hirschwald.

Kalinowsky, L. B., 1945, "Organic Psychotic Syndromes Occurring During Electric Convulsive Therapy." *Archives of Neurology and Psychiatry,* 53:269.
Kalinowsky, L. B., and Hippius, H., 1969, *Pharmacological, Convulsive and Other Somatic Treatments in Psychiatry.* New York: Grune & Stratton.
Kallmann, F. J., 1938, *The Genetics of Schizophrenia.* Locust Valley, N.Y.: August.
———, 1953, *Heredity in Health and Mental Disorder.* New York: Norton.
———, 1959, "The Genetics of Mental Illness." In Arieti, S. (ed.), *American Handbook of Psychiatry,* vol. 1, pp. 175–196. New York: Basic Books.
Kallmann, F. J., and Barrera, E., 1941, "The Heredo-Constitutional Mechanisms of Predisposition and Resistance to Schizophrenia." *American Journal of Psychiatry,* 98:544.
Kanner, L., 1942, *Child Psychiatry.* Springfield: Thomas.
———, 1944, "Early Infantile Autism." *J. Pediat.,* 25:211.
———, 1946, "Irrelevant and Metaphorical Language in Early Infantile Autism." *Am. J. Psychiat.,* 103:242.
———, 1965, "Infantile Autism and the Schizophrenias." *Behavioral Science,* 10:412–420.
Kantor, D., and Gelineau, V. A., 1969, "Making Chronic Schizophrenics." *Mental Hygiene,* 53:54–66.
Kantor, R. E., and Herron, W. G., 1966, *Reactive and Process Schizophrenia.* Palo Alto, Calif.: Science and Behavior Books.
Kaplan, A. R., 1972, *Genetic Factors in "Schizophrenia."* Springfield, Ill.: Thomas.
Kaplan, A. R., and Cotton, J. E., 1968, "Chromosomal Abnormalities in Female Schizophrenics." *Journal of Mental and Nervous Disease,* 147:402–417.
Kaplan, E. H., and Blackman, L. H., 1969, "The Husband's Role in Psychiatric Illness Associated with Childbearing." *Psychiatric Quarterly,* 43:396–409.
Karlsson, J. L., 1966, *The Biologic Basis of Schizophrenia.* Springfield, Ill.: Thomas.
Karpov, P. I., 1926. Quoted by Volmat, 1955.
Kasanin, J. S., 1933, "The Acute Schizoaffective Psychosis." *American Journal of Psychiatry,* 90:97–126.
——— (ed.), 1944 *a, Language and Thought in Schizophrenia: Collected Papers.* Berkeley: University of California Press.
———, 1944*b,* "The Disturbance of Conceptual Thinking in Schizophrenia." In Kasanin, J. S. (ed.), *Language and Thought in Schizophrenia: Collected Papers.* pp. 41–49. Berkeley: University of California Press.
———, 1945, "Developmental Roots of Schizophrenia." *American Journal of Psychiatry,* 101:770.
Kay, D. W. K., and Roth, M., 1961, "Environmental and Hereditary Factors in the Schizophrenia of Old Age (Late Paraphrenia) and Their Bearing on the General Problem of Causation in Schizophrenia." *Journal Ment. Sci.,* 107:649–686.
Keller, H., 1951, *The Story of My Life.* New York: Doubleday.
Kellogg, W. N., and Kellogg, L. A., 1933, *The Ape and the Child.* New York: McGraw-Hill. Quoted by Langer (1942), *Philosophy in a New Key.* Cambridge, Mass.: Harvard University Press.
Kelman, H., 1973, "Chronic Analysts and Chronic Patients: The Therapist's Person as Instrument." *Journal of the American Academy of Psychoanalysis,* 1:193–207.
Kelsen, H., 1943, *Society and Nature: A Sociological Inquiry.* Chicago: University of Chicago Press.
Kety, S. S., 1959, "Biochemical Theories of Schizophrenia. A Two-Part Critical Review of Current Theories and of the Evidence Used to Support Them." *Science,* 129:1528–1532, 1590–1596.
———, 1966, "Current Biochemical Research in Schizophrenia." In Hoch, P. H., and Zubin, J., *Psychopathology of Schizophrenia.* New York: Grune & Stratton.
———, 1969, "Biochemical Hypotheses and Studies." In Bellak, L., and Loeb, L. (eds.), *The Schizophrenic Syndrome.* New York: Grune & Stratton.
———, 1972, "Progress in the Psychobiology of Schizophrenia: Implications for Treatment." Paper presented at a Symposium on "Treatment of Schizophrenia. Progress and Prospects," March 18, 1972. The Neuropsychiatric Institute, UCLA.
Kiev, A., 1961, "Spirit Possession in Haiti." *American Journal of Psychiatry,* 118:133–141.
———, 1969, "Transcultural Psychiatry: Research Problems and Perspectives." In Plog, S. C., and

Edgerton, R. B. (eds.), *Changing Perspectives in Mental Illness.* New York: Holt, Rinehart & Winston.

Kimmins, C. W., 1937, *Children's Dreams.* London: Allen and Unwin.

Kinsbourne, M., and Warrington, E., 1963, "Jargon Aphasia." *Neuropsychologia,* 1:27–37.

Klein, H. R., and Horwitz, W. A., 1949, "Psychosexual Factors in the Paranoid Phenomena." *American Journal of Psychiatry,* 105:697.

Klein, M., 1948, *Contributions to Psycho-Analysis.* London: Hogarth.

Kline, N. A., 1956, "Clinical Applications of Reserpine." In Kline, N. S., *Psychopharmacology,* No. 42 of the American Association for the Advancement of Science, Washington, D. C.

Kline, N. S., and Tenney, A. M., 1950, "Constitutional Factors in the Prognosis of Schizophrenia." 107:434.

Klippel, R., and Lhermitte, J., 1906, "Ruckenmarksläsion bei Dementia Praecox." *Neurolog. Zentralbl.,* 25:735.

Klüver, H., 1933, *Behavior Mechanisms in Monkeys.* Chicago: University of Chicago Press.

———, 1936, "The Study of Personality and the Method of Equivalent and Non-Equivalent Stimuli." *Character and Personality,* 5:91–112.

Klüver, H., and Bucy, P. C., 1937, " 'Psychic Blindness' and Other Symptoms Following Bilateral Temporal Lobectomy in Rhesus Monkeys." *American Journal of Physiology,* 119:352.

———, 1938, "An Analysis of Certain Effects of Bilateral Temporal Lobectomy in the Rhesus Monkey with Special Reference to 'Psychic Blindness.' " *Journal of Psychology,* 5:33.

———, 1939, "Preliminary Analysis of Functions of the Temporal Lobes in Monkeys." *Archives of Neurology and Psychiatry,* 42:972.

Köhler, W., 1925, *The Mentality of Apes.* New York: Harcourt, Brace.

Kolb, L. C., 1959*a,* "Disturbances of the Body-Image." In Arieti, S. (ed.), *American Handbook of Psychiatry,* vol. 1, pp. 749–769. New York: Basic Books.

———, 1959*b,* "The Body Image in the Schizophrenic Reaction." In Auerback, A. (ed.), *Schizophrenia. An Integrated Approach.* New York: Ronald Press.

———, 1968, *Noyes' Modern Clinical Psychiatry.* 7th ed. Philadelphia: Saunders.

Koller, S., 1957. Quoted by Roth, M., "Interaction of Genetic and Environmental Factors in Causation of Schizophrenia." In Richter, D. (ed.), *Schizophrenia: Somatic Aspects.* New York: Macmillan.

Kopeloff, L. M., and Fischel, E., 1963, "Serum Levels of Bactericidin and Globulin in Schizophrenia." *Archives of General Psychiatry,* 9:524–528.

Korzybski, A., 1933, *Science and Sanity: An Introduction to Non-Aristotelian Systems and General Semantics.* International Nonaristotelian Library Publishing Co.

Kraepelin, E., 1919, *Dementia Praecox and Paraphrenia.* From 8th German ed. Edinburgh: Livingston.

Kraft, A. M., 1966, "The Therapeutic Community." In Arieti, S. (ed.), *American Handbook of Psychiatry,* First Ed., vol. 3, pp. 542–551. New York: Basic Books.

Kraft, D. P., and Babigian, H. M., 1972, "Somatic Delusion or Self-Mutilation in a Schizophrenic Woman: A Psychiatric Emergency Room Case Report." *American Journal of Psychiatry,* 128:893–895.

Kramer, B., 1962, *Day Hospital.* New York: Grune & Stratton.

Kretschmer, E., 1925, *Physique and Character.* New York: Harcourt, Brace.

———, 1934, *A Text-Book of Medical Psychology.* London: Oxford University Press.

Kreig, W. J. S., 1947, *Functional Neuroanatomy.* Philadelphia: Blakiston.

Kringlen, E., 1967, *Heredity and Environment in the Functional Psychoses: An Epidemiological-Clinical Twin Study.* London: Heinermann.

———, 1968, "An Epidemiological-Clinical Twin Study on Schizophrenia." In Rosenthal, S., and Kety, S. S., 1968. *The Transmission of Schizophrenia.* New York: Pergamon Press.

Kris, E. B., and Carmichael, D. M., 1957, "Follow-up Study on Thorazine Treated Patients." *American Journal of Psychiatry,* 114:449.

———, 1970, "New Studies on the Genetics of Schizophrenia. In Arieti, S. (ed.), *The World Biennial of Psychiatry and Psychotherapy,* vol. 1, pp. 476–504. New York: Basic Books.

Kubie, L. S., 1971, "Multiple Fallacies in the Concept of Schizophrenia." *Journal of Nervous and Mental Disease,* 153:331–342.

Laing, R. D., 1960, *The Divided Self.* London: Tavistock.

———, 1967, *The Politics of Experience.* New York: Pantheon Books.

Laing, R. D., and Esterson, A., *Sanity, Madness and the Family.* Vol. 1, *Families of Schizophrenics.* New York: Basic Books, 1965.

Landis, C., and Page, J. D., 1938, *Society and Mental Disease.* New York: Rinehart.

Landolt, H., 1957, "Elektroenzephalografische Untersuchungen bei nicht Katatonen Schizophrenien. Eine Vorlanfige Mitteilung." *Schweiz. Z. Psychol.,* 16:26–30.

Langer, S. K., 1942, *Philosophy in a New Key.* Cambridge, Mass.: Harvard University Press.

———, 1949, "On Cassirer's Theory of Language and Myth." In *The Philosophy of Ernst Cassirer.* Evanston, Ill.: Library of Living Philosophers.

Langfeldt, G., 1939, *The Schizophreniform States.* London: Oxford University Press.

———, 1969, "Schizophrenia: Diagnosis and Prognosis." *Behavioral Science,* 14.

Laqueur, H. P., and La Burt, H. A., 1960, "Coma Therapy with Multiple Insuline Doses." *Journal of Neuropsychiatry,* 1:135.

Laubscher, B. J. F., 1937, *Sex, Custom and Psychopathology.* London: Routledge.

Layman, W. A., and Cohen, L., 1957, "Modern Concept of Folie à Deux." *Journal of Nervous and Mental Disease,* 125:412–419.

Lefebure, P., Atkins, J., Duckman, J., and Gralnick, A., 1958, "The Role of the Relative in a Psychotherapeutic Program: Anxiety Problems and Defensive Reactions Encountered." *Canadian Psychiatric Association Journal,* 3:110–118.

Lehmann, H. E., 1965, "Drug Treatment of Schizophrenia." In Kline, N. S., and Lehmann, H. E. (eds.), *Psychopharmacology.* International Psychiatric Clinics, Vol. 2, No. 4, October 1965. Boston: Little, Brown.

———, 1974, "Physical Therapies of Schizophrenia." In Arieti, S. (ed.), *American Handbook of Psychiatry,* Second Edition, vol. 3. New York: Basic Books.

Lehmann, H. E., and Knight, D. A., 1958, "Psychophysiologic Testing with a New Phrenotropic Drug." In *Trifluoperazine.* Philadelphia: Lea and Febiger.

Lehrman, N. S., 1961, "Do Our Hospitals Help Make Acute Schizophrenia Chronic?" *Diseases of the Nervous System,* 22:1–5.

Lelut, 1846, *L'Amulette de Pascal; pour servir à l'histoire des hallucinations.* Quoted by Morgue, 1932.

Lemere, F., 1936, "The Significance of Individual Differences in the Berger Rhythm." *Brain,* 59:366–375.

Lemkau, P. V., and Crocetti, G. M., 1957, "Vital Statistics of Schizophrenia." In Bellak, L., *Schizophrenia, A Review of the Syndrome.* New York: Logos Press.

Levin, M., 1932, "Auditory Hallucinations in 'Non-Psychotic' Children." *American Journal of Psychiatry,* 11:1119–1152.

———, 1938*a,* "Misunderstanding of the Pathogenesis of Schizophrenia, Arising from the Concept of 'Splitting,' " *American Journal of Psychiatry,* 94:877.

———, 1938*b,* "On the Causation of Mental Symptoms." *Journal Ment. Sci.,* 82.

Levy, S., 1966, "The Hyperkinetic Child—A Forgotten Entity. Its Diagnosis and Treatment." *International Journal of Neuropsychiatry,* 2:330–336.

Lévy-Bruhl, L., 1910, *Les Fonctions mentales dans les sociétés inférieures.* Paris: Alcan.

———, 1922, *La Mentalité primitive.* Paris: Alcan.

Lewis, N. D. C., 1923, *The Constitutional Factors in Dementia Praecox.* New York and Washington: Nervous and Mental Disease Publishing Company.

———, 1925, "The Practical Value of Graphic Art in Personality Studies. 1) An Introductory Presentation of the Possibilities." *Psychoanalytic Review,* 12:316–322.

———, 1928, "Graphic Art Productions in Schizophrenia." *Proc. A. Research Nerv. & Ment. Dis.,* 5:344–368.

———, 1933, 1934, "Studies on Suicide." *Psychoanalytic Review,* 20:241, 21:146.

———, 1936, *Research in Dementia Praecox.* New York: The National Committee for Mental Hygiene.

———, 1944. Unpublished lecture, Inter-State Hospital Meeting, October 1944, New York.

Lidz, T., 1952, "Some Remarks Concerning the Differentiation of Organic from So-called 'Functional' Psychoses." In *The Biology of Mental Health and Disease.* New York: Hoeber.

———, 1969, "The Influence of Family Studies on the Treatment of Schizophrenia." *Psychiatry,* 32:237–251.

———, 1973, *The Origin and Treatment of Schizophrenic Disorders.* New York: Basic Books.

Lidz, T., Cornelison, A. R., Fleck, S., and Terry, D., 1957*a,* "The Intrafamilial Environment of Schizophrenic Patients: II. Marital Schism and Marital Skew." *American Journal of Psychiatry,* 114:241.

———, 1957*b,* "The Intrafamilial Environment of the Schizophrenic Patient: The Father." *Psychiatry,* 20:329.

Lidz, T., Cornelison, A., Terry, D., and Fleck, S., 1958, "Intrafamilial Environment of the Schizophrenic Patient: The Transmission of Irrationality." *A.M.A. Archives of Neurology and Psychiatry,* 79:305.

Lidz, T., and Fleck. S., 1964, "Family Studies and a Theory of Schizophrenia." Paper presented at 1964 Annual Meeting of American Psychiatric Association. Reprinted in Lidz, Fleck, and Cornelison, 1965.

Lidz, T., Fleck, S., and Cornelison, A. R., 1965, *Schizophrenia and the Family,* New York: International Universities Press.

Lidz, R. W., and Lidz, T., 1952, "Therapeutic Considerations Arising from the Intense Symbiotic Needs of Schizophrenic Patients." In Brody and Redlick, *Psychotherapy with Schizophrenics.* New York: International Universities Press.

Lidz, T., Parker, B., and Cornelison, A. R., "The Role of the Father in the Family Environment of the Schizophrenic Patient." *American Journal of Psychiatry,* 113:126.

Liebert, R. S., Wapner, S., and Werner, H., 1957, "Studies in the Effects of Lysergic Acid Diethylamide (LSD-25). Visual Perception of Verticality in Schizophrenic and Normal Adults." *Arch. Neurol. Psychiat.,* 77:193–201.

Lief, A., 1948, *The Commonsense Psychiatry of Dr. Adolf Meyer. Fifty-Two Selected Papers.* New York: McGraw-Hill.

Lief, H. I., 1957, "The Effects of Taraxein on a Patient in Analysis." *Archives of Neurology and Psychiatry,* 78:624–627.

Lilly, J. C., 1956, "Mental Effects of Reduction of Ordinary Levels of Physical Stimuli on Intact, Healthy Persons." *Psychiat. Res. Rep.,* 5:1–28.

Limentani, D., 1956, "Symbiotic Identification in Schizophrenia." *Psychiatry,* 19:231–236.

Lindegarde, B., 1953, *Variations in Human Body Build.* Copenhagen: Ejnar Munksgard.

Lindstrom, P. A., 1954, "Prefrontal Ultrasonic Irradiation—A Substitute for Lobotomy." *Archives of Neurology and Psychiatry, 72:399.*

Linn, L., 1955, *A Handbook of Hospital Psychiatry.* New York: International Universities Press.

———, 1959, "Hospital Psychiatry." In Arieti, S. (ed.), *American Handbook of Psychiatry,* vol. 2, pp. 1829–1839. New York: Basic Books.

——— (ed.), 1961, *Frontiers in General Hospital Psychiatry.* New York: International Universities Press.

Livingston, P. B., and Blum, R. A., 1968, "Attention and Speech in Acute Schizophrenia." *Archives of General Psychiatry,* 18:373–381.

Livingston, R. B., 1955, "Some Brain Stem Mechanisms Relating to Psychosomatic Medicine." *Psychosomatic Medicine,* 17:347.

———, 1962, "How Man Looks at His Own Brain: An Adventure Shared by Psychology and Neurophysiology." In Koch, S. (ed.), *Psychology: A Study of a Science.* Study II, vol. 4, pp. 51–99. New York: McGraw-Hill.

Locke, B. Z., Kramer, M., and Pasamanick, B., 1960, "Immigration and Insanity." *Public Health Report,* 75:301–306.

Loeb, C., and Giberti, F., 1957, "Considerazioni cliniche ed elettroencefalografiche a proposito di sindromi psicosiche in suggetti epilettici." *Sist. Nerv.*, 9:219–229.
Lombroso, C., 1880, "On the Art of the Insane." Later (1888) included as Chapter 2 of *The Man of Genius*. English edition, London: Scott, 1895.
Lorraine, S., 1972, "The Therapeutic Assistant in Treating the Psychotic Case Report." *International Journal of Psychiatry*, 10:11–22.
Lovegrove, T. D., and Nicholls, D. M., 1965, "Haptoglobin Subtypes in a Schizophrenic and Control Population." *Journal of Nervous and Mental Disease*, 141:195.
Lu, Y., 1961, "Mother-Child Role Relations in Schizophrenia." *Psychiatry*, 24:133–142.
Ludwig, A. M., 1968, "The Influence of Nonspecific Healing Techniques with Chronic Schizophrenics." *American Journal of Psychotherapy*, 22:382–404.
———, 1970, "Chronic Schizophrenia: Clinical and Therapeutic Issues." *American Journal of Psychotherapy*, 24:380–399.
———, 1973, "New Treatment Methods for Chronic Schizophrenics." In Arieti, S. (ed.), *The World Biennial of Psychiatry and Psychotherapy*, vol. 2, pp. 232–245. New York: Basic Books.
Ludwig, A. M., and Farrelly, F., 1966, "The Code of Chronicity." *Archives of General Psychiatry*, 15:562–568.
Ludwig, A. M., and Marx, A. J., 1968, "Influencing Techniques on Chronic Schizophrenics." *Archives of General Psychiatry*, 18:681–688.
———, 1969, "The Buddy Treatment Model for Chronic Schizophrenics." *Journal of Nervous and Mental Disease*, 148:528–541.
Ludwig, A. M., Marx, A. J., Hill, P. A., and Hermsmeier, G. I. 1967, "Forced Small Group Responsibility in the Treatment of Chronic Schizophrenics." *Psychiatric Quarterly Supplement*, 41:262–280.
Lukianowicz, N., 1958, "Autoscopic Phenomena." *A.M.A. Arch. Neurol. & Psychiatry*, 80:199.
———, 1967, "Body Image Disturbances in Psychiatric Disorders." *British Journal of Psychiatry*, 113:31–47.
Lystad, M. H., 1957, "Social Mobility among Selected Groups of Schizophrenic Patients." *American Sociological Review*, 22:288–292.
Maccagnani, G., 1958, "L'Arte psicopatologica." *Rivista Sperimentale di Freniatria*, vol. 82, supplement to No. 2:3–126.
MacCurdy, G. G., 1926, *Human Origins. A Manual of Prehistory*. New York: Appleton.
Mackay, R. P., 1954, "Toward a Neurology of Behavior." *Neurology*, 4:894.
MacLean, P. D., 1949, "Psychosomatic Disease and the 'Visceral Brain.' Recent Developments Bearing on the Papez Theory of Emotion." *Psychosomatic Medicine*, 11:338.
Macmillan, D., 1958, "Hospital-Community Relationships." In *An Approach to the Prevention of Disability from Chronic Psychoses*. New York: Milbank Memorial Fund.
MacNab, F. A., 1966, *Estrangement and Relationship. Experience with Schizophrenics*. Bloomington, Ind.: University Press.
Mahler, M. S., 1952, "On Child Psychosis and Schizophrenia: Autistic and Symbiotic Infantile Psychoses." *In The Psychoanalytic Study of the Child*, vol. 7, pp. 286–305. New York: International Universities Press.
———, 1958, "Autism and Symbiosis: Two Extreme Disturbances of Identity." *International Journal of Psycho-Analysis*, 39:77–83.
———, 1968, *On Human Symbiosis and the Vicissitudes of Individuation. Vol. 1, Infantile Psychosis*. New York: International Universities Press.
Mahler, M. S., Furer, M., and Settlage, C. F., 1959, "Severe Emotional Disturbances in Childhood: Psychosis." In Arieti, S. (ed.), *American Handbook of Psychiatry*, vol. 1, pp. 816–839. New York: Basic Books.
Mahler, M., Ross, J. R., Jr., De Fries, Z., 1949, "Clinical Studies in Benign and Malignant Cases of Childhood Psychosis (Schizophrenic-like)." *American Journal of Orthopsychiatry*, 19:295–305.
Malmo, R. B., 1942, "Interference Factors in Delayed Response in Monkeys after Removal of Frontal Lobes." *Journal of Neurophysiology*, 5:295.

Malzberg, B., 1940, *Social and Biological Aspects of Mental Disease.* Utica, N.Y. State Hospitals Press.
———, 1956, "Mental Disease Among Puerto Ricans in New York City." *Journal of Nervous and Mental Disease,* 123:262–269.
———, 1959*a,* "Statistical Data for the Study of Mental Disease among Negroes in New York State." Albany Research Foundation for Mental Hygiene and New York State Department of Mental Hygiene.
———, 1959*b,* "Important Statistical Data About Mental Illness." In Arieti, S. (ed.), *American Handbook of Psychiatry,* First Edition, vol. 1, pp. 161–174. New York: Basic Books.
———, 1962, "Migration and Mental Disease among the White Population of New York State: 1949–1951." *Hum. Bio.,* 34:89–98.
Mann, J., Menzer, D., Standish, C., 1950, "Psychotherapy of Psychoses: Some Attitudes in the Therapist Influencing the Course of Treatment." *Psychiatry,* 13:17–23.
Maricq, H. R., 1963, "Familial Schizophrenia as Defined by Nailfold Capillary Pattern and Selected Psychiatric Traits." *Journal of Nervous and Mental Disease,* 136:216–226.
———, 1966, "Capillary Morphology and the Course of Illness in Schizophrenic Patients." *Journal of Nervous and Mental Disease,* 142:63–71.
Marram, G. D., 1970, "Problems in the After Care Management of the Schizophrenic Patient." *Journal of Psychiatric Nursing,* 8:13–16.
Mars, L., 1955, *La Crise de possession.* Port-au-Prince: Imprimerie de L'Etat.
Masserman, J., 1943, "Experimental Neuroses and Psychotherapy." *Archives of Neurology and Psychiatry,* 49:43–48.
Matte-Blanco, I., 1959, "Expression in Symbolic Logic of the Characteristics of the System UCS." *International Journal of Psychoanalysis,* 40:1–5.
———, 1965, "A Study of Schizophrenic Thinking: Its Expression in Terms of Symbolic Logic and Its Representation in Terms of Multi-dimensional Space." *International Journal of Psychiatry,* 1:19–26.
May, M. R. A., 1968, *Treatment of Schizophrenia. A Comparative Study of Five Treatment Methods.* New York: Science House.
May, R., 1969, *Love and Will.* New York: Norton.
Mayer-Gross, W., 1950, "Psychopathology of Delusions. History, Classification and Present State of the Problem from the Clinical Point of View." In Morel, *Psychopathologie des Délires.* Paris: Hermann.
McFarland, R. A., 1932, "The Psychological Effects of Oxygen Deprivation (Anoxemia) on Human Behavior." *Arch. Psychol.,* Monograph 145.
McFarland, R. A., and Goldstein, H., 1938, "Biochemistry: Review." *American Journal of Psychiatry,* 95:509.
McGeer, P. L., McNair, F. E., McGeer, E. G., and Gibson, W. C., 1957, "Aromatic Metabolism in Schizophrenia. 1) Statistical Evidence for Aromaturia. 2) Bidimensional Urinary Chromatograms." *Journal of Nervous and Mental Disease,* 125:166.
McGhie, A., 1966, "Psychological Studies of Schizophrenia." In Freeman, T. (ed.), *Studies in Psychosis.* New York: International Universities Press.
———, 1972, "Attention and Perception in Schizophrenia." In Cancro, R. (ed.), *Annual Review of the Schizophrenic Syndrome,* vol. 2, pp. 99–134. New York: Brunner-Mazel.
McGhie, A., and Chapman, J., 1961, "Disorder of Attention and Perception in Early Schizophrenia." *British Journal of Medical Psychology,* 34:103–116.
Mead, G. H., 1934, *Mind, Self and Society.* Chicago: University of Chicago Press.
Mead, M., 1958, "Cultural Determinants of Behavior." In Roe, A., and Simpson, G. G. (eds.), *Behavior and Evolution.* New Haven, Conn.: Yale University Press.
Mednick, S. A., 1958, "A Learning Theory Approach to Research in Schizophrenia." *Psychological Bulletin,* 55:316–327.
Mednick, S. A., and Freedman, J. L., 1960, "Stimulus Generalization." *Psychological Bulletin,* 57:169–200.

Meehl, P. E., 1962, "Schizotaxia, Schizotypy, Schizophrenia." *American Psychologist,* 17:827–828.

Meerloo, J. A., 1954, *The Two Faces of Man.* New York: International Universities Press.

Menninger, K., and Mayman, M., 1956, "Episodic Dyscontrol: A Third Order of Stress Adaptation." *Bulletin of the Menninger Clinic,* 20:153.

Menninger, K. (with Mayman, M., and Pruyser, P.), 1963, *The Vital Balance: The Life Process in Mental Health and Illness.* New York: Viking Press.

Meth, J. M., 1974, "Exotic Syndromes." In Arieti, S. (ed.), *American Handbook of Psychiatry,* vol. 3. New York: Basic Books.

Mettler, F. A., 1952, *Psychosurgical Problems.* Philadelphia: Blakiston.

———, 1955, "Perceptual Capacity, Functions of Corpus Striatum and Schizophrenia." *Psychiatric Quarterly,* 29:89–111.

Meyer, A., 1906, "Fundamental Conceptions of Dementia Praecox." *British Medical Journal,* 2:757. Reprinted in Lief, 1948.

———, 1910, "The Dynamic Interpretation of Dementia Praecox." *American Journal of Psychology,* 21:385 (July 1910). Reprinted in Lief, 1948.

———, 1912*a, The Role of Habit-Disorganizations.* Paper read before the New York Psychiatric Society, Jan. 3, 1905; Nervous and Mental Disease Monograph Series No. 9. New York. Reprinted in Lief, 1948.

———, 1912*b, Substitutive Activity and Reaction-Types.* Nervous and Mental Disease Monograph Series No. 9. New York. Reprinted in Lief, 1948.

Meyer, A., Jelliffe, S. E., and Hoch, A., 1911, *Dementia Praecox, A Monograph.* Boston: Badger.

Meyer, Alfred, 1954, "Critical Evaluation of Histopathological Findings in Schizophrenia." In *Proceedings of the First International Congress of Neuropathology.* Turin: Rosenberg & Sellier.

Meyer, J. E., and Feldman, H. (eds.), 1965, *Anorexia Nervosa.* Stuttgart: Thième.

Miller, J. B., and Sonnenberg, S. S., 1973, "Depression Following Psychotic Episodes: A Response to the Challenge or Change?" *Journal of the American Academy of Psychoanalysis,* 1:253–270.

Minkowski, E., 1933, *Le Temps vécu.* Paris: d'Artrey.

———, 1953, *La Schizophrénie.* Paris: Desclée de Brouwer.

———, 1958, "Findings in a Case of Schizophrenic Depression." In May, R., Angel, E., and Ellenberger, H. F., *Existence.* New York: Basic Books.

———, 1966, *Traité de psychopathologie.* Paris: Presses Universitaires de France.

Minski, L., 1937, "Note on Some Vasomotor Disturbances in Schizophrenia." *J. Ment. Sci.,* 83:434.

Mishler, E., and Waxler, N. (eds.), 1968, *Family Processes and Schizophrenia.* New York: Science House.

Mitscherlich, A., 1969, *Society without the Father. A Contribution to Social Psychology.* London: Tavistock.

Mitscherlich, M., and Mitscherlich, A., 1973, "Fathers and Fatherhood in Our Time." In Arieti, S. (ed.), *The World Biennial of Psychiatry and Psychotherapy.* New York: Basic Books.

Mohr, F., 1906–1907, "Über Zeichnungen von Geisteskranken und ihre Diagnostische Verwertbarkeit." *J. f. Psychol. u. Neurol.,* 8:99–140.

Money, J., and Hirsch, S. R., 1963, "Chromosome Anomalies, Mental Deficiency, and Schizophrenia." *Archives of General Psychiatry,* 8:242–251.

Moniz, E., 1936*a,* "Les Possibilities de le Chirurgie Dans le traitment de certaines psychoses." *Lisboa Med.,* 13:141.

———, 1936 *b, Tentatives Opérationes Dans le Traitement De Certaines Psychoses.* Paris: Masson.

Morgan, C. T., 1943, *Physiological Psychology.* New York and London: McGraw-Hill.

Morgenthaler, W., 1921, "Ein Geisteskranker als Künstler." *Arbeit. angew Psychiat.,* 1:1–126.

Morselli, G. E., 1955, "Ce qui Demeure et ce qui est périmé dans la 'Schizophrenie' de Bleuler." *L'Evolution Psychiatrique,* 645–651.

Mott, F. W., 1919, "Normal and Morbid Conditions of the Testes from Birth to Old Age in One Hundred Asylum and Hospital Cases." *British Medical Journal,* November 22, 29, and December 6.

Mourgue, R., 1932, *Neurobiologie de l'hallucination*. Brussels: Lamertin.

Mowrer, O. H., 1946, "An Experimental Analogue of 'Regression' with Incidental Observations of 'Reaction Formations.' " *Journal of Abnormal and Social Psychology,* 35:56.

Mullahy, P., 1948, *Oedipus. Myth and Complex*. New York: Hermitage Press.

———, 1949, *A Study of Interpersonal Relations*. New York: Hermitage Press.

——— (ed.), 1952, *The Contributions of Harry Stack Sullivan*. New York: Hermitage House.

———, 1967, "Harry Stack Sullivan's Theory of Schizophrenia." *International Journal of Psychiatry,* vol. 4, pp. 492–521.

———, 1968, *Psychoanalysis and Interpersonal Psychiatry*. New York: Science House.

Müller, C., 1962. Personal communication.

———, 1963, "Psychotherapy of Schizophrenic Patients." Lecture presented to Department of Psychiatry, New York Medical College.

Müller, J. M., Schlittler, E., and Bein, H. J., 1952, "Reserpine, der sedative Wirkstoff aus Rauwolfia serpentina Benth." *Experientia,* 8:338.

Murphy, H. B. M., Wittkower, E. D., Fried, J., and Ellenberger, 1963, "A Cross-cultural Survey of Schizophrenic Symptomatology." *International Journal of Social Psychiatry,* 9:237–249.

Naumburg, M., 1950, *Schizophrenic Art: Its Meaning in Psychotherapy*. New York: Grune & Stratton.

Neale, J. M., and Cromwell, R. L., 1972, "Attention and Schizophrenia." In Cancro, R. (ed.), *Annual Review of the Schizophrenic Syndrome,* vol. 2, pp. 68–98. New York: Brunner-Mazel.

Nielsen, J. M., 1946, *Agnosia, Apraxia, Aphasia. Their Value in Cerebral Localization*. New York: Hoeber.

Niskanen, P., and Achté, K. A., 1971, "Prognosis in Schizophrenia. A Comparative Follow-up Study of First Admissions for Schizophrenic and Paranoid Psychoses in Helsinki in 1950, 1960, and 1965," *Psychiatria Finnica. Year Book 1971,* pp. 117–126.

Nivoli, G., 1973, *Le Schizophrène Meurtrier*. (In preparation. Private communication.)

Noble, D., 1951, "A Study of Dreams in Schizophrenia and Allied States." *American Journal of Psychiatry,* 107:612–616.

Norris, V., 1959, *Mental Illness in London*. New York: Oxford University Press.

Nunberg, H., 1948, "The Course of the Libidinal Conflict in a Case of Schizophrenia." In *Practice and Theory of Psychoanalysis,* Nervous and Mental Disease Monograph Series No. 74. New York.

Ogden, C. K., and Richards, I. A., 1947, *The Meaning of Meaning*. New York: Harcourt, Brace.

Orton, S. T., 1929, "The Three Levels of Cortical Elaboration in Relation to Certain Psychiatric Symptoms." *American Journal of Psychiatry,* 8:647.

Osmond, H., and Smythies, J., 1952, "Schizophrenia: A New Approach." *J. Ment. Sci.,* 98:309–315.

Pace, R. E., 1957, "Situational Therapy." *Journal of Personality,* 25:578–588.

Papez, J. W., 1937, "A Proposed Mechanism of Emotion." *Archives of Neurology and Psychiatry,* 38:725–743.

———, 1948, "Inclusion Bodies Associated with Destruction of Nerve Cells in Scrub Typhus, Psychoses and Multiple Sclerosis." *Journal of Nervous and Mental Disease,* 108:431.

Parsons, E. H., Gildea, E. F., Ronzoni, E., and Hulbert, S. Z., 1949, "Comparative Lymphocytic and Biochemical Responses of Patients with Schizophrenia and Affective Disorders to Electroshock, Insulin Shock, and Epinephrine." *American Journal of Psychiatry,* 105:573–580.

Pasamanick, B., 1962, "A Survey of Mental Disease in an Urban Population. VIII. An Approach to Total Prevalence by Race." *American Journal of Psychiatry,* 119:299–305.

———, 1964, "Myths regarding Prevalence of Mental Disease in the American Negro: A Century of Misuse of Mental Hospital Data and Some New Findings." *Journal Nat. Med. Assoc.,* 56:6–17.

Pasamanick, B., Scarpitti, F. R., and Dinitz, S., 1967, *Schizophrenics in the Community*. New York: Appleton-Century-Crofts.

Pastore, N., 1949, "Genetics of Schizophrenia: A Special Review." *Psychological Bulletin,* 46:285–302.

Pavicevic, M. B., 1966, "Psychoses in Ethiopia." Addis Ababa, typescript, 6 pp. Reported in *Transcultural Psychiatric Research,* 3:152.

Pavlov, I. P., 1919, "Psychiatry as Auxiliary Science of Physiology." *Russian Journal of Physiology,* 2:257. Printed in Russian.

———, 1930, "Digression of a Physiologist in the Field of Psychiatry." *Izvestija,* 122 (3969), May 5. Printed in Russian.

———, 1933*a,* "The 'Sentiments d'Emprise' and the Ultraparadoxal Phase." Open letter to Professor Pierre Janet. Last Communications on the Physiology and Pathology of the Superior Nervous Activity, 2:5–11. Leningrad. Printed in Russian.

———, 1933*b,* "Tentative of a Physiological Explanation of Obsessive Neuroses and Paranoia." Last Communications on the Physiology and Pathology of the Superior Nervous Activity, 2:13–24. Leningrad. Printed in Russian and reprinted in English, *Journal of Mental Science,* 80:187–197 (1934).

Payne, R. W., 1958, "Some Aspects of Perception and Thought Disorder in Schizophrenic Subjects." *Swiss Rev. Psychol. Its Applic.,* 17:300.

———, 1961, "Cognitive Abnormalities." In Eysenck, H. J. (ed.), *Handbook of Abnormal Psychology.* New York: Basic Books.

———, 1962, "An Object Classification Test As a Measure of Overinclusive Thinking in Schizophrenic Patients." *British Journal Soc. Clin. Psychol.,* 1:213.

Payne, R. W., Mattussek, P., and George, E. I., 1959, "An Experimental Study of Schizophrenic Thought Disorder." *Journal of Mental Science,* 105:627.

Penfield, W., and Rasmussen, T., 1952, *The Cerebral Cortex of Man.* New York: Macmillan.

Peplau, H. E., 1952, *Interpersonal Relations in Nursing.* New York: Putnam.

———, 1959, "Principles of Psychiatric Nursing." In Arieti, S. (ed.), *American Handbook of Psychiatry,* First Edition, vol. 2, pp. 1840–1856. New York: Basic Books.

Persky, H., Gamm, S. R., and Grinker, R. R., 1952, "Correlation between Fluctuation of Free Anxiety and Quantity of Hippuric Acid Excretion." *Psychosomatic Medicine,* 14:34–40.

Petiziol, A., and Sanmartino, L., 1969, *Iconografia ed espressivita' degli stati psicopatologici.* Milan: Feltrinelli.

Petrella, F., 1968, "Implicazioni psico e sociodinamiche di una particolare condetta instituzionale: La Tendenza ad accumulare oggetti." *Rassegna di Studi Psichiatrici,* 57:767–785.

Pfeifer, R. A., 1925, *Der Geisteskranke und sein Werk: Eine Studie über Schizophrene Kunst.* Leipzig: Kröner.

Pfister, O., 1923, *Expressionism in Art: Its Psychological and Biological Basis.* Translated by B. Low and M. A. Mügge. New York: Dutton.

Phillips, R. H., and Alkan, M., 1961*a,* "Some Aspects of Self-Mutilation in the General Population of a Large Psychiatric Hospital." *Psychiatric Quarterly,* 35:421–423.

———, 1961*b,* "Recurrent Self-Mutilation." *Psychiatric Quarterly,* 35:424–431.

Piaget, J., 1929, *The Child's Conception of the World.* New York: Harcourt, Brace.

———, 1930, *The Child's Conception of Physical Causality.* New York: Harcourt, Brace.

———, 1948, *The Language and Thought of the Child.* London: Routledge & Kegan Paul.

———, 1952, *The Origins of Intelligence in Children.* New York: International Universities Press.

Pincus, G., and Hoagland, H., 1950, "Adrenal Cortical Responses to Stress in Normal Men and in Those with Personality Disorders. Part I. Some Stress Responses in Normal and Psychotic Subjects. Part II. Analysis of the Pituitary-Adrenal Mechanism in Man." *American Journal of Psychiatry,* 106:641.

Piro, S., 1967, *Il Linguaggio schizofrenico.* Milan: Feltrinelli.

Plokker, J. H., 1964, *Art from the Mentally Disturbed.* London: Mouton.

Polyakov, V. F., 1969, "The Experimental Investigation of Cognitive Functioning in Schizophrenia." In Cole, M., and Maltzman, I. (eds.), *A Handbook of Contemporary Soviet Psychology.* New York: Basic Books.

Pollin, W., Allen, M. G., Hoffer, A., Stabenau, J. R., and Hrubec, Z., 1969, "Psychopathology in 15,909 Pairs of Veteran Twins: Evidence for a Genetic Factor in the Pathogenesis of Schizophrenia and Its Relative Absence in Psychoneurosis." *American Journal of Psychiatry,* 126:597–610.

Popov, E., 1957, "Some General Problems in the Pathogenesis of Schizophrenia." In *Actual Problems of Neurology and Psychiatry,* 150–157. Printed in Russian.

Potter, H. W., 1933, "Schizophrenia in Children." *American Journal of Psychiatry,* 12:1253–1270.

Pötzl, O., 1971, "Experimentell erregte Traumbilder in ihren Beziehungen zum indirekten Sehen." *Ztschr. f. Neurol. e Psychiat.,* 37:278–349.

Pötzl, O., Allers, R., and Teler, J., 1960, *Preconscious Stimulation in Dreams, Associations, and Images.* Psychological Issues, 11 (3). New York: International Universities Press.

Powdermaker, F., 1952, "Concepts Found Useful in Treatment of Schizoid and Ambulatory Schizophrenic Patients." *Psychiatry,* 15:61.

Prinzhorn, F., 1922, *Bildnerei der Geisteskranken.* Berlin: Springer.

Pritchard, R. M., 1961, "Stabilized Images on the Retina." *Scientific American,* 204:72–78.

Pritchard, R. M., Heron, W., and Hebb, D. O., 1960, "Visual Perception Approached by the Method of Stabilized Images." *Canadian Journal of Psychology,* 14:67–77.

Protheroe, C., 1969, "Puerperal Psychoses: A Long-Term Study 1927–1961." *British Journal of Psychiatry,* 115:9–30.

Protopopov, V., 1938, "Physiopathologic Characteristics of the Activity of the Central Nervous System in Schizophrenia." *Works of Central Psychoneurologic Institute,* vol. 10, pp. 14–26. Printed in Russian.

Queen, S. A., 1940, "The Ecological Study of Mental Disorder." *American Sociological Review,* 5:201.

Rabiner, E. L., Molinsky, H., and Gralnick, A., 1962, "Conjoint Family Therapy in the Inpatient Setting." *American Journal of Psychotherapy,* 16:618–631.

Racamier, P. C., 1959, "Psychoanalytic Therapy of the Psychoses." In Nacht, S. (ed.), *Psychoanalysis Today.* New York: Grune & Stratton.

Rado, S., Buchenholz, B., Dunton, H, Karlen, S. H., and Senescu, R., 1956, "Schizotypal Organization. Preliminary Report on a Clinical Study of Schizophrenia." In Rado, S., and Daniel, G. E., 1956.

Rado, S., and Daniel, G. E., 1956, *Changing Concepts of Psychoanalytic Medicine.* New York: Grune.

Rainer, J. D., 1966, "New Topics in Psychiatric Genetics." In Arieti, S., (ed.), *American Handbook of Psychiatry,* 1st ed., vol. 3. New York: Basic Books.

Rao, S., 1964, "Birth Order and Schizophrenia." *Journal of Nervous and Mental Disease,* 138:87–89.

Rapaport, D., 1951, *Organization and Pathology of Thought.* New York: Columbia University Press.

———, 1958, "The Theory of Ego Autonomy: A Generalization." *Bulletin of the Menninger Clinic,* 22:13.

———, 1960, *The Structure of Psychoanalytic Theory.* New York: International Universities Press.

Raphael, T., and Raphael, L. G., 1962, "Fingerprints in Schizophrenia." *American Medical Association Journal,* 180:215–219.

Raphael, T., and Shaw, M. W., 1963, "Chromosome Studies in Schizophrenia." *American Medical Association Journal,* 183:1022–1028.

Rausch, H. L., 1952, "Perceptual Constancy in Schizophrenia." *Journal of Personality,* 21:176–187.

———, 1956, "Object Constancy in Schizophrenia: The Enhancement of Symbolic Objects and Conceptual Stability." *Journal of Abnormal Social Psychology,* 52:231–234.

Rechtschaffen, A., Schulsinger, F., and Mednick, S. A., 1964, "Schizophrenia and Physiological Indices of Dreaming." *Archives of General Psychiatry,* 10:89–93.

Reed, J. L., 1970, "Schizophrenic Thought Disorder: A Review and Hypothesis." *Comprehensive Psychiatry,* 11:403–432.

Rees, L., 1957, "Physical Characteristics of the Schizophrenic Patient." In Richter, D., *Schizophrenia: Somatic Aspects.* New York: Macmillan.

Reichard, S., and Tillman, C., 1950*a,* "Patterns of Parent-Child Relationships in Schizophrenia." *Psychiatry,* 13:247–257.

———, 1950*b,* "Murder and Suicide as Defenses against Schizophrenic Psychosis." *Journal of Clinical Psychopathology,* 11:149–163.

Reitman, F., 1951, *Psychotic Art. A Study of the Art Products of the Mentally Ill.* New York: International Universities Press.
———, 1954, *Insanity, Art, and Culture.* New York: Philosophical Library.
Relfer, M. I., and D'Autremont, C. C., 1971, "Catatonia-like Symptomatology." *Archives of General Psychiatry,* 24:119–120.
Rennie, T. A. C., 1941, "Analysis of One Hundred Cases of Schizophrenia with Recovery." *Archives of Neurology and Psychiatry,* 46:197.
Revitch, E., 1954, "The Problem of Conjugal Paranoia." *Diseases of the Nervous System,* 15:2–8.
Revitch, E., and Hayden, J. W., 1960, "The Paranoid Marital Partner: Counselor's Client, Psychiatrist's Problem." *Rutgers Law Review,* 9:512–527.
Rheingold, J. C., 1939, "Autonomic Integration in Schizophrenia; Autonomic Status Determined Statistically, Thyroid Factor, and Possible Thyroid-hypothalamus Mechanisms." *Psychosomatic Medicine,* 1:397.
Ribot, T., 1899, *Les Maladies de la volonté.* Paris: Alcan.
Richardson, G. A., and Moore, R. A., 1963, "On the Manifest Dream in Schizophrenia." *Journal of the American Psychoanalytic Association,* 11:281–302.
Richter, D. (ed.), 1957, *Schizophrenia: Somatic Aspects.* New York: Macmillan.
Riesen, A. H., 1947, "The Development of Visual Perception in Man and Chimpanzee." *Science,* 106:107–108.
Riesman, D., Glaser, N., and Denney, R., 1950, *The Lonely Crowd.* New Haven: Yale University Press.
Rimland, B., 1964, *Infantile Autism.* New York: Appleton-Century-Crofts.
Rioch, D. McK., and Stanton, A. H., 1953, "Milieu Therapy." *Psychiatry,* 16:65–72.
Rioch, J., 1943, "The Transference Phenomenon in Psychoanalytic Therapy." *Psychiatry,* 6:147.
Ripley, H. A., and Papanicolaou, G. N., 1942, "Menstrual Cycle with Vaginal Smear Studies in Schizophrenia." *American Journal of Psychiatry,* 98:567–573.
Ritter, C., 1954, *A Woman in the Polar Night.* New York: Dutton.
Robins, E., and Guze, S. B., 1970, "Establishment of Diagnostic Validity in Psychiatric Illness: Its Application to Schizophrenia." *American Journal of Psychiatry,* 126:983–987.
Robins, E., Smith, K., and Lowe, I. P., 1957. In Abramson, H. A. (ed.), *Neuropharmacology,* pp. 123–136. Transactions of the Fourth Conference. New York: Josiah Macy, Jr., Foundation.
Robinson, E. S., 1932, *Association Theory Today.* New York: Century.
Rochlin, L., 1969, "La Concezione pavloviana della schizofrenia." In Pavlov, I. P., *Psicopatologia e Psichiatria,* edited by E. Popov and L. Rochlin. Rome: Editori Riuniti.
Roi, G., 1953, "Analisi fenomenologica dell' assurdo schizofrenico nei rapporti col surreale dell' arte." *Archivio di Psicologia, Neurologia e Psichiatria,* 5:605–625.
Roizin, L., 1938, "Organi di senso quali generatori di riflessi neuro-endocrino-vegetativi della regione diencefalo-ipofisaria." *Rassegna di Neurologia Vegetativa,* 1:338.
———, 1952, "Histopathology of Schizophrenia." In *Proceedings of the First International Congress of Neuropathology.* Turin: Rosenberg & Sellier.
Rosanoff, A. J., Handy, L. M., Plesset, I. R., and Brush, S., 1934, "The Etiology of So-called Schizophrenic Psychoses with Special Reference to Their Occurrence in Twins." *American Journal of Psychiatry,* 91:247–286.
Rosanoff, A. J., and Orr, I., 1911, "A Study of Heredity in Insanity in the Light of Mendelian Theory." *American Journal of Insanity,* 63:221–261.
Rosanoff, A. J., and Rosanoff, I. A., 1931, "A Study of Mental Disorders in Twins." *J. Juv. Res.,* 15:268–270.
Rosen, J. N., 1947, "The Treatment of Schizophrenic Psychosis by Direct Analytic Therapy." *Psychiatric Quarterly,* 2:3.
———, 1953, *Direct Analysis: Selected Papers.* New York: Grune & Stratton.
———, 1962, *Direct Psychoanalytic Psychiatry.* New York: Grune & Stratton.
———, 1963, "The Concept of Early Maternal Environment in Direct Psychoanalysis." Doylestown, Pa.: The Doylestown Foundation.
———, 1964, "The Study of Direct Psychoanalysis." In Solomon, P., and Glueck, B. C. (eds.),

Recent Research on Schizophrenia. Report 19, Psychiatric Research Reports of the American Psychiatric Association.

Rosenfeld, H. A., 1947, ''Analysis of a Schizophrenic State with Depersonalization.'' *International Journal of Psycho-Analysis,* 28:130–139.

———, 1952*a,* ''Notes on the Psychoanalysis of the Superego Conflict of an Acute Schizophrenic Patient.'' *International Journal of Psycho-Analysis,* 33:111–131.

———, 1952*b,* ''Transference-phenomena and Transference-analysis in an Acute Catatonic Schizophrenic Patient.'' *International Journal of Psycho-Analysis,* 33:457–464.

———, 1954, ''Considerations Regarding the Psycho-analytic Approach to Acute and Chronic Schizophrenia.'' In Rosenfeld, 1965.

———, 1965, *Psychotic States: A Psychoanalytic Approach.* New York: International Universities Press.

———, 1969*a,* ''Contribution to the Psychopathology of Psychotic States: The Importance of Projective Identification in the Ego Structure and the Object Relations of the Psychotic Patient.'' In Doucet, P., and Laurin, C. (eds.), *Problématique de la Psychose,* vol. 1. Amsterdam: Excerpta Medica Foundation.

———, 1969 *b,* ''On the Treatment of Psychotic States by Psychoanalysis: An Historical Approach.'' International Journal of *Psycho-Analysis,* 50:615–631.

Rosenthal, D., 1963, *The Genain Quadruplets.* New York: Basic Books.

———, 1974, ''The Genetics of Schizophrenia.'' In Arieti, S. (ed.), *American Handbook of Psychiatry,* Second Edition, vol. 3. New York: Basic Books.

Roth, S., 1970, ''The Seemingly Ubiquitous Depression Following Acute Schizophrenic Episodes, A Neglected Area of Clinical Discussion.'' *American Journal of Psychiatry,* 127:51–58.

Rubino, A., and Piro, S., 1959, ''Il Mutamento pauroso e la schizofrenia.'' *Il Pisani,* 83:527.

Rüdin, E., 1961, *Zur Vererbung und Neuentehung der Dementia Praecox.* Berlin: Springer.

Russell, B., 1919, *Introduction to Mathematical Philosophy.* London:

Sakel, M., 1936, ''Zur Methodik der hypoglykämiebehandlung von psychosen.'' *Wien. Klin. Wchnschr.,* 49:1278.

Sakurai, T., Shirafuji, Y., Nishizono, M., Hasuzawa, T., Kusuhara, G., Yoshinaga, G., and Hirohashi, S., 1964, ''Changing Clinical Picture of Schizophrenia.'' *Seishin Igaku,* 6:369–373. Reported in *Transcultural Psychiatric Research,* 2:97–98, 1965.

Sanders, R., Smith, R. S., Weinman, B. S., 1967, *Chronic Psychoses and Recovery.* San Francisco: Jossey-Bass.

Sanders, R. Weinman, B., Smith, R. S., Smith, A., Kenny, J., and Fitzgerald, B. J., 1962, ''Social Treatment of the Male Chronic Mental Patient.'' *Journal of Nervous and Mental Disease,* 134:244–255.

Sankar, Siva D. V., 1969, *Schizophrenia. Current Concepts and Research.* Hicksville, N.Y.: PJD Publications.

Sankar, Siva D. V., and Saladino, C. F., 1969, ''Chromosome Studies in Childhood Schizophrenia.'' *Schizophrenia,* 1:260–270.

Sanseigne, A., and Desrosıers, M., 1961, ''The Evaluation of Psychopharmaceuticals in an Underdeveloped Country.'' In Kline, N. S. (ed.), *Psychiatry in the Underdeveloped Countries.* Washington: American Psychiatric Association.

Sanua, V. D., 1962, ''Comparison of Jewish and Protestant Paranoid and Catatonic Patients.'' *Diseases of the Nervous System,* 26:1.

Sartre, J.-P., 1969, *Being and Nothingness.* New York: Citadel Press.

Sato, S., Daly, R., and Peters, H., 1971, ''Reserpine Therapy of Phenothiazine-Induced Dyskinesia.'' *Diseases of the Nervous System,* 32:680–685.

Schachtel, E. G., 1954, ''The Development of Focal Attention and the Emergence of Reality.'' *Psychiatry,* 17:309.

———, 1959, *Metamorphosis.* New York: Basic Books.

Schachter, F., 1962, ''A Study of Psychoses in Female Immigrants.'' *Med. J. Australia,* 49(2):458–461.

Scheflen, A. E., 1961, *A Psychotherapy of Schizophrenia: Direct Analysis.* Springfield, Ill.: Thomas.

Schilder, P., 1918, *Wahn und Erkenntnis: eine psychologische Studie*. N. 15 Monog. Ges. Neurol. Psychiat. 1–115.

———, 1931, *Brain and Personality*. New York and Washington: Nervous and Mental Diseases Publication Company.

———, 1935, *The Image and the Appearance of the Human Body. Studies in the Constructive Energies of the Psyche*. London: Kegan Paul.

———, 1953, *Medical Psychology*. New York: International Universities Press.

Schipkowensky, N., 1938, *Schizophrenie und Mord*. Berlin: Springer.

———, 1967, "Les Champs de force des homicides schizophréniques." *L'Évolution Psychiatrique*, pp. 89–113.

Schniewind, H. E., Day, M., and Semrad, E. V., 1969, "Group Psychotherapy of Schizophrenics." In Bellak, L., and Loeb, L., *The Schizophrenic Syndrome*. New York: Grune & Stratton.

Schooler, C., 1961, "Birth Order and Schizophrenia." *Archives of General Psychiatry*, 4:91–97.

Schroeder, C. W., 1942, "Mental Disorders in Cities." *American Journal of Sociology*, 48:40.

Schwing, F., 1954, *A Way to the Soul of the Mentally Ill*. New York: International Universities Press.

Scott, R. D., and Ashworth, P. L., 1969, "The Shadow of the Ancestor: A Historical Factor in the Transmission of Schizophrenia." *British Journal of Medical Psychology*, 42:13–32.

Scoville, W. B., 1949, "Selective Cortical Undercutting." *Proceedings of the Royal Society of Medicine*, 47:3.

Searles, H., 1958, "Positive Feelings in the Relationship Between the Schizophrenic and His Mother." *International Journal of Psychoanalysis*, 39:569–586.

———, 1959, "The Effort to Drive the Other Person Crazy—An Element in the Aetiology and Psychotherapy of Schizophrenia." *British Journal of Medical Psychology*, 32:1–18.

———, 1960, *The Nonhuman Environment in Normal Development and in Schizophrenia*. New York: International Universities Press.

———, 1962, "The Differentiation between Concrete and Metaphorical Thinking in the Recovering Schizophrenic." *J. American Psychoanal. Ass.*, 10:22–49.

———, 1965, *Collected Papers on Schizophrenia and Related Subjects*. New York: International Universities Press.

Sechehaye, M. A., 1951*a*, *Symbolic Realization*. New York: International Universities Press.

———, 1951*b*, *Autobiography of a Schizophrenic Girl*. New York: Grune & Stratton.

———, 1956, *A New Psychotherapy in Schizophrenia*. New York: Grune & Stratton.

Segal, H., 1950, "Some Aspects of the Analysis of a Schizophrenic." *International Journal of Psycho-Analysis*, 31:268–278.

Seitz, P. F. D., 1951, "A Dynamic Factor Correlated with the Prognosis in Paranoid Schizophrenia." *Archives of Neurology and Psychiatry*, 65:604–606.

Seitz, P. F. D., and Molholm, H. B., 1947, "Relations of Mental Imagery to Hallucinations." *Archives of Neurology and Psychiatry*, 57:469–480.

Selvini Palazzoli, M., 1963, *L'Anoressia Mentale*. Milan: Feltrinelli.

———, 1970, "Anorexia Nervosa." In Arieti, S. (ed.), *The World Biennial of Psychiatry and Psychotherapy*, vol. 1, pp. 197–218. New York: Basic Books.

Selye, H., 1950, "Stress (The Physiology and Pathology of Exposure to Systemic Stress)." Montreal: *Acta Med. Publ.*

———, 1952, "The Story of the Adaptation Syndrome," Montreal: *Acta Med. Publ.*

Semrad, E. J., 1952, "Discussion of Dr. Frank's Paper." In Brody, E. B., and Redlich, F. C. (eds.), *Psychotherapy with Schizophrenics*. New York: International Universities Press.

Semrad, E. J., Menzer, D., Mann, J., and Standish, C., 1952, "A Study of the Doctor-Patient Relationship in Psychotherapy of Psychotic Patients." *Psychiatry*, 15:377.

Serieux and Capgras, J. Quoted by Mayer-Gross, 1950.

Shainberg, D., 1973, *The Transforming Self. New Dimensions in Psychoanalytic Process*. New York: Intercontinental Medical Book Corporation.

Shainess, N., 1966, "Psychological Problems Associated with Motherhood." In Arieti, S. (ed.), *American Handbook of Psychiatry*, vol. 3, p. 47. New York: Basic Books.

Shakow, D., 1963, "Psychological Deficit in Schizophrenia." *Behavioral Science*, 8:275.

Shattock, M. F., 1950, "The Somatic Manifestations of Schizophrenia. A Clinical Study of Their Significance." *Journal of Mental Science,* 96:32–142.
Sheldon, W. H., Stevens, S. S., and Tucker, W. B., 1940, *The Varieties of Human Physique.* New York: Harper.
Shenkin, H. A., and Lewey, F. H., 1944, "Taste Aura Preceding Convulsions in a Lesion of the Parietal Operculum." *Journal of Nervous and Mental Disease,* 100:352.
Shulman, B. H., 1968, *Essays in Schizophrenia.* Baltimore: Williams and Wilkins.
Siddiqui, S. S., and Siddiqui, R. H., 1931, *J. Ind. Chem. Soc.,* 8:667. Quoted by Müller, Schlitter, and Bein, 1952.
Siirala, M., 1961, *Die Schizophrenie–des Einzeln und der Allgemeinheit.* Göttingen: Vandenhoeck & Ruprecht.
———, 1963, "Schizophrenia: A Human Situation." *American Journal of Psychoanalysis,* 23:39.
Silberer, H., 1909, "Report on a Method of Eliciting and Observing Certain Symbolic Hallucination-Phenomena." Reprinted in Rapaport, D. (ed.), *Organization and Pathology of Thought.* New York: Columbia University Press, 1951.
———, 1912, "On Symbol-Formation." Reprinted in Rapaport, D. (ed.), *Organization and Pathology of Thought.* New York: Columbia University Press, 1951.
Silverman, J., 1964, "The Problem of Attention in Research and Theory in Schizophrenia." *Psychol. Rev.,* 71:352–379.
———, 1967, "Variations in Cognitive Control and Psychophysiological Defense in the Schizophrenias." *Psychosomatic Medicine,* 29:225–251.
Simon, M., 1876, "L'Imagination dans la folie: Étude sur les dessins, plans, descriptions, et costumes des aliénés." *Ann. Méd.-Psychol.,* 16:358–390
———, 1888, "Les Écrits et les Dessins des Aliénés." *Arch. Anthrop. Crim.,* 3:318–355.
Simpson, G. M., Cranswick, E. H., and Blair, J. H., 1963, "Thyroid Indices in Chronic Schizophrenia." *Journal of Nervous and Mental Disease,* 137:582–590.
Singer, M. T., and Wynne, L. L., 1965, "Thought Disorder and Family Relations of Schizophrenics." *Archives of General Psychiatry,* 12:187–212.
Slater, E., 1951, *An Investigation into Psychotic and Neurotic Twins.* London: University of London Press.
———, 1968, "A Review of Earlier Evidence on Genetic Factors in Schizophrenia." In Rosenthal, D., and Kety, S. S. (eds.), *The Transmission of Schizophrenia.* London: Pergamon Press.
Slocum, J., 1901, *Sailing Alone Around the World.* New York: Dover, 1956.
Small, J. G., and Small, I. F., 1965, "Reevaluation of Clinical EEG Findings in Schizophrenia." *Dis. Nerv. System,* 26:345–349.
Smith, R. B., 1878, *The Aborigines of Victoria.* Quoted by Werner, 1957.
Smith, S., 1954, "Problems of Liver Function in Schizophrenia." *Journal of Nervous and Mental Diseases,* 120:245–252.
Smith, C. M., and McIntyre, S., 1963, "Family Size, Birth Rank, and Ordinal Position in Psychiatric Illness." *Canadian Psychiatric Association Journal,* 8:244–248.
Smith, K., and Sines, J. O., 1960, "Demonstration of a Peculiar Odor in the Sweat of Schizophrenic Patients." *Archives of General Psychiatry,* 2:184–188.
Soby, J. I., 1946, *Salvador Dali.* The Museum of Modern Art. Distributed by Simon and Schuster, New York.
Spiegel, R., 1973, "Gray Areas Between the Schizophrenias and the Depressions." *Journal of the American Academy of Psychoanalysis,* 1:179–192.
Spielmeyer, W., 1931, "The Problem of the Anatomy of Schizophrenia." *Proceedings of the Association for Research in Nervous and Mental Disease,* 10:105. Baltimore: Williams and Wilkins.
Spitz, R., 1945, "Diacritic and Coenesthetic Organization." *Psychoanal. Rev.,* 32:146.
Stabenau, J. R., Pullin, W., Moshe, R. L. R., Froman, C., Friedhoff, A. J., and Turner, W., 1969, "Study of Monozygotic Twins Discordant for Schizophrenia. Some Biologic Variables." *Archives of General Psychiatry,* 20:145–158.
Staercke, A., 1920, "The Reversal of the Libido Sign in Delusions of Persecutions." *International Journal of Psychoanalysis,* 1:120.

Stanton, A. H., and Schwartz, M. S., 1949*a*, "The Management of a Type of Institutional Participation in Mental Illness." *Psychiatry*, 12:13.
———, 1949*b*, "Observations on Dissociation as Social Participation." *Psychiatry*, 12:339.
———, 1954, *The Mental Hospital*. New York: Basic Books.
Stein, W. J., 1967, "The Sense of Becoming Psychotic." *Psychiatry*, 30:262–275.
Steinen, K., 1894, *Unter den Naturvölkern Zentral-Brasiliens*. Quoted by Werner, 1957.
Stern, E. S., 1937, "Acrocyanosis." *Journal of Mental Science*, 83:408.
Stern, K., and MacNaughton, D., 1945, "Capgras Syndrome, a Peculiar Illusionary Phenomenon, Considered with Special Reference to the Rorschach Findings." *Psychiatric Quarterly*, 19:139.
Stierlin, H., 1956, *Der gewalttätige Patient*. Basel: Karger.
———, 1965, "Bleuler's Concept of Schizophrenia in the Light of Our Present Experience." In *International Symposium on the Psychotherapy of Schizophrenia*, pp. 42–55. New York and Basel: Karger.
———, 1967, "Bleuler's Concept of Schizophrenia: A Confusing Heritage." *American Journal of Psychiatry*, 123:996–1001.
Storch, A., 1924, *The Primitive Archaic Forms of Inner Experiences and Thought in Schizophrenics*. New York and Washington: Nervous and Mental Disease Publication Company.
Stransky, 1903, "Zur Kenntniss gewisser erworbener Blödsinnsformen." *Jahrb. f. Psych.*, 24:1.
Strauss, H., 1959, "Epileptic Disorders." In Arieti, S. (ed.), *American Handbook of Psychiatry*, 1st ed. vol. 2, pp. 1109–1143. New York: Basic Books.
Strecker, E. A., and Ebaugh, F., 1926, "Psychoses Occurring during the Puerperium." *Archives of Neurology and Psychiatry*, 15:239.
Stromgren, E., 1950, *Statistical and Genetical Population Studies with Psychiatry. Methods and Principal Results*, vol. 6. Paris: Hermann. Quoted by Kallmann, 1959.
Sturm, I. E., 1965, "Overinclusion and Concreteness Among Pathological Groups." *Journal of Consulting Psychology*, 29:9–18.
Sullivan, H. S., 1924, "Schizophrenia: Its Conservative and Malignant Factors." *American Journal of Psychiatry*, 81:77–91.
———, 1925, "Peculiarity of Thought in Schizophrenia." *American Journal of Psychiatry*, 5:21–86.
———, 1929, "Research in Schizophrenia." *American Journal of Psychiatry*, 9:553–567.
———, 1931, "The Modified Psychoanalytic Treatment of Schizophrenia." *American Journal of Psychiatry*, 11:519.
———, 1953*a*, *Conceptions of Modern Psychiatry*. New York: Norton.
———, 1953*b*, *The Interpersonal Theory of Psychiatry*. New York: Norton.
———, 1956, *Clinical Studies in Psychiatry*. New York: Norton.
———, 1962, *Schizophrenia As a Human Process*. New York: Norton.
———, 1964, *The Fusion of Psychiatry and Social Science*. New York: Norton.
Suttie, I. E., 1952, *The Origins of Love and Hate*. New York: Julian Press.
Suwa, N., and Yamashita, I., 1972, *Psychophysiological Studies of Emotion and Mental Disorders*. Sapporo, Japan: Hokkaido University.
Swanson, D. W., Brown, E. M., and Beuret, L. J., 1969, "A Family with Five Schizophrenic Children." *Diseases of the Nervous System*, 30:189–193.
Szalita, A. B., 1955, "The 'Intuitive Process' and Its Relation to Work with Schizophrenics." *Journal of the American Psychoanalytic Association*, 3:7.
———, 1958, "Regression and Perception in Psychotic States." *Psychiatry*, 21:53–63.
Szasz, T., 1957*a*, *Pain and Pleasure*. New York: Basic Books.
———, 1957*b*, "The Psychology of Bodily Feelings in Schizophrenia." *Psychosomatic Medicine*, 19:11–16.
———, 1957*c*, "A Contribution to the Psychology of Schizophrenia." *A.M.A. Archives of Neurology and Psychiatry*, 77:420–436.
———, 1957*d*, "The Problem of Psychiatric Nosology: A Contribution to a Situational Analysis of Psychiatric Operations." *Am. J. Psychiatry*, 114:405.
———, 1961, *The Myth of Mental Illness*. New York: Harper and Row.

Szurek, S. A., and Berlin, I. N. (eds.), 1973, *Clinical Studies in Childhood Psychoses*. New York: Brunner-Mazel.

Tanzi, E., 1909, *A Text-Book of Mental Diseases*. New York: Rebman.

Tedeschi, G., 1957, "Psicosi epilettica o schizofrenia in epilettico?" *Lav. Neuropsichiat.*, 21:35–48.

———, 1969, "Analytical Psychotherapy with Schizophrenic Patients." *Journal of Analytical Psychology*, 14:152–162.

Terzuolo, C. A., and Adey, W. R., 1960, "Sensorimotor Cortical Activities." In Field, J. (ed.), *Handbook of Physiology: Section 1, Neurophysiology*, vol. 2, pp. 797–835. Washington: American Physiological Society.

Thomä, H., 1967, *Anorexia Nervosa*. New York: International Universities Press.

Thompson, C., 1938, "Development of Awareness of Transference in a Markedly Detached Personality." *International Journal of Psychoanalysis*, 19:299.

———, 1941, "The Role of Women in This Culture." *Psychiatry*, 4:1.

———, 1942, "Cultural Pressures in the Psychology of Women." *Psychiatry*, 5:331.

———, 1950, *Psychoanalysis, Evolution and Development*. New York: Hermitage House.

———, 1952*a*, "Sullivan and Psychoanalysis." In Mullahy, P., *The Contributions of Harry Stack Sullivan*. New York: Hermitage House.

———, 1952*b*, "Counter-Transference." *Samiksa*, 6:205.

Tienari, P., 1968, "Schizophrenia in Monozygotic Male Twins." In Rosenthal, D., and Kety, S., The Transmission of Schizophrenia, 1968. London: Pergammon Press.

Tilney, F., 1928, *The Brain from Ape to Man*. New York: Hoeber.

Tinbergen, N., 1951, *The Study of Instinct*. Oxford: Oxford University Press.

Tjio, H., and Levan, A., 1956, "The Chromosome Number of Man." *Hereditas*, 42:1–6.

Todd, J., 1957, "The Syndrome of Capgras." *Psychiatric Quarterly*, 31:250.

Tolentino, I., 1957*a*, "Diario di un paranoico considerazioni psicopatologiche e psicodinamiche. 1) Il Diario." *Rassegna di Studi Psichiatrici*, 46:681–715.

Tolentino, I., 1957*b*, "Diario di un Paranoico (1) Considerazioni, Psicopatologiche e Psicodinamiche (2) Considerazioni Psicopatologiche e Psicodinamiche." *Rassegna di Studi Psichiatrici*, 46:716–730.

Tooth, G., 1950, *Studies in Mental Illness in the Gold Coast*. Research Publication No. 6. London: H.M.S.O.

Tower, S. S., 1947, "Management of Paranoid Trends in Treatment of a Post-Psychotic Obsessional Condition." *Psychiatry*, 10:157.

Tyhurst, J. S., 1957, "Paranoid Patterns." In Leighton, A. H., Clausen, J. A., and Wilson, R. N., (eds.), *Explorations in Social Psychiatry*. New York: Basic Books.

Ungerleider, J. T., Fisher, D. D., Goldsmith, S. R., Fuller, M., and Forgy, E., 1968, "A Statistical Survey of Adverse Reactions to LSD in Los Angeles County." *American Journal of Psychiatry*, 125:352–357.

Vaillant, G. E., 1967, "The Prediction of Recovery in Schizophrenia." In *Current Issues in Psychiatry*, vol. 2. New York: Science House.

Vetter, H. J., 1968, "New-Word Coinage in the Psychopathological Context." *Psychiatric Quarterly*, 42:298–312.

Vico, G., 1725, *Principi di Una Scienza Nuova*. Naples.

Vinchon, J., 1926, "Essai d'analyse des tendances de l'art chez les fous." *L'Amour de l'Art*, 7:246–248.

———, 1950, *L'Art et la Folie*. Paris: Stock.

Vogt, C., and Vogt, O., 1954, "Alterations anatomiques de la schizophrenie et d'autres psychoses dites fonctionelles." In *Proceedings of the First International Congress of Neuropathology*. Turin: Rosenberg & Sellier.

Volmat, R., 1955, *L'Art Psychopathologique*. Paris: Presses Universitaires de France.

Von Domarus, E., 1925, "Uber die Besiehung des Normalen zum Schizophrenen Denken." *Arch. Psychiat.*, 74:641.

———, 1944, "The Specific Laws of Logic in Schizophrenia." In Kasanin, J. S. (ed.), *Language and*

Thought in Schizophrenia: Collected Papers, pp. 104–114. Berkeley: University of California Press.
Von Meduna, L., 1937, *Die Konvulsionstherapie der Schizophrenie.* Halle: Marhold.
Von Monakow, C. V., 1914, *Die Lokalisation in Grosshirn und der Abbau der Functionen durch Korticale.* Wiesbaden, Herde: Bergmann.
Von Monakow, C. V., and Mourgue, R., 1928, *Introduction biologique à l'étude de la neurologie et de la psychopathologie.* Paris: Alcan.
Von Senden, M., 1960, *Space and Sight. The Perception of Space and Shape in Congenitally Blind Patients Before and After Operation.* London: Methuen.
Vygotsky, L. S., 1934, "Thought in Schizophrenia." *Archives of Neurology and Psychiatry,* 31:1036.
———, 1962, *Thought and Language.* Cambridge, Mass.: M.I.T. Press.
Waelder, R., 1925, "The Psychoses: Their Mechanisms and Accessibility to Influence." *International Journal of Psychoanalysis,* 6:259–281.
Wainwright, W. H., 1966, "Fatherhood as a Precipitant of Mental Illness." *American Journal of Psychiatry,* 123:40–44.
Wallace, M., 1956, "Future Time Perspective in Schizophrenia." *Journal of Abnormal Social Psychology,* 52:240–245.
Walter, W. G., 1942, "Electro-Encephalography in Cases of Mental Disorder." *Journal of Mental Science,* 88:110.
Waring, M., and Ricks, D., 1965, "Family Patterns of Children Who Became Adult Schizophrenics." *Journal of Nervous and Mental Disease,* 140:351–364.
Warnes, H., 1968, "Suicide in Schizophrenics." In *Toward a Definition of Schizophrenia,* Supplement to Diseases of the Nervous System, 29 (5).
Watzlawick, P., 1963, "A Review of the Double Bind Theory." *Family Process,* 2:132–153.
Weckowicz, T. E., 1957, "Size Constancy in Schizophrenic Patients." *Journal of Mental Science,* 103:432.
———, 1960, "Perception of Hidden Pictures by Schizophrenic Patients." *Archives of General Psychiatry,* 2:521–527.
Weckowicz, T. E., and Blewett, D. B., 1959, "Size Constancy and Abstract Thinking in Schizophrenic Patients," *Journal of Mental Science,* 105:909.
Weckowicz, T. E., and Sommer, R., 1960, "Body Image and Self-Concept in Schizophrenia." *Journal of Mental Science,* 106:17–39.
Weckowicz, T. E., Sommer, R., and Hall, R., 1958, "Distance Constancy in Schizophrenic Patients." *Journal of Mental Science,* 104:436.
Weil-Malherbe, H., and Szara, S. I., 1971, *The Biochemistry of Functional and Experimental Psychoses.* Springfield, Ill.: Thomas.
Weil, A., Liebert, E., and Heilbrunn, G., 1938, "Histopathologic Changes in the Brain in Experimental Hyperinsulinism." *Archives of Neurology and Psychiatry,* 39:467.
Weiner, I. B., 1966, *Psychodiagnosis in Schizophrenia.* New York: Wiley.
Weinstein, M. R., 1954, "Histopathological Changes in the Brain in Schizophrenia." *Archives of Neurology and Psychiatry,* 71:539–553.
Werner, H., 1956, "Microgenesis and Aphasia." *Journal of Abnormal Social Psychology,* 52:347–353.
———, 1957, *Comparative Psychology of Mental Development.* New York: International Universities Press.
Werner, H., and Kaplan, B., 1963, *Symbol Formation: An Organismic-Developmental Approach to Language and the Expression of Thought.* New York: Wiley.
Werry, J. S., 1968, "Studies on the Hyperactive Child. An Empirical Analysis of the Minimal Brain Dysfunction Syndrome." *Archives of General Psychiatry,* 19:9–16.
Wertham, F., 1937, "The Catathymic Crisis." *Archives of Neurology and Psychiatry,* 37:974.
Wertheimer, N., and Wertheimer, M., 1955, "Capillary Structure: Its Relation to Psychiatric Diagnosis and Morphology." *Journal of Nervous and Mental Disease,* 122:14–27.
West, L. J. (ed.), 1962*a*, *Hallucinations.* New York: Grune & Stratton.
———, 1962*b*, "A General Theory of Hallucinations and Dreams." In West, 1962*a*.
Wexler, M., 1952, "The Structural Problem in Schizophrenia: The Role of the Internal Object." In

Brody, M. W., and Redlich, F. C., *Psychotherapy with Schizophrenics*. New York: International Universities Press.

Weygandt, W. 1902, *Atlas und Grundiss der Psychiatrie*. Lehmanns Atlantin. Quoted by Bleuler, 1950.

White, M. J., 1952, "Discussion of Paper by Semrad, Menzer, Mann, and Standish." *Psychiatry*, 15:384–385.

Will, O. A., 1967, "Schizophrenia: Psychological Treatment." In Freedman, A. M., and Kaplan, H. I., *Comprehensive Textbook of Psychiatry*. Baltimore: Williams and Wilkins.

———, 1970, "The Psychotherapeutic Center and Schizophrenia." In Cancro, B. (ed.), *The Schizophrenic Reactions*. New York: Brunner-Mazel.

———. 1972, "Catatonic Behavior in Schizophrenia." *Contemporary Psychoanalysis*, 9:29–58.

Wilson, G. C., 1968, "Suicide in Psychiatric Patients Who Have Received Hospital Treatment." *American Journal of Psychiatry*, 125:752–757.

Wing, J. K., 1967, "Social Treatment, Rehabilitation and Management." In Copper, A., and Wall, A., *Recent Developments in Schizophrenia*. Ashford: Headley.

Wing, J. K., and Brown, G. W., 1961, "Social Treatment of Chronic Schizophrenia: A Comparative Survey of Three Mental Hospitals." *The Journal of Mental Science*, 107:847–861.

Winkelman, N. W., 1952, "Histopathology of Mental Disease." In *The Biology of Mental Health and Disease*. New York: Hoeber.

Winkelman, N. W., and Moore, M. T., 1944, "Neurohistological Findings in Experimental Electric Shock Treatment." *Journal of Neuropathology and Experimental Neurology*, 3:199.

Winnicott, D. W., 1945, "Primitive Emotional Development." In Winnicott, D. W., *Collected Papers*. London: Tavistock, 1958.

Witenberg, E. G., 1974, "The Interpersonal and Cultural Approaches." In Arieti, S. (ed.), *American Handbook of Psychiatry*, Second Edition, vol. 1. New York: Basic Books.

Witte, F., 1922, "Uber Anatomische Untersuchungen der Schildrüse bei der Dementia Praecox." *Ztschr. f. d. ges. Neurol. u. Psychiat.*, 80:1901.

Wolf, A., and Cowen, D., 1952, "Histopathology of Schizophrenia and Other Psychoses of Unknown Origin." In *The Biology of Mental Health and Disease*. New York: Hoeber.

Wolman, B. B., 1966, *Vectoriasis Praecox or the Group of Schizophrenia*. Springfield, Ill.: Thomas.

Woolley, D. W., and Shaw, E., 1954, "A Biochemical and Pharmacological Suggestion about Certain Mental Disorders." *Science*, 119:587–588.

Wynne, L. C., Ryckoff, I. M., Day, J., and Hirsch, S., 1958, "Pseudomutuality in the Family Relations of Schizophrenics." *Psychiatry*, 21:205–220.

Wynne, L. C., and Singer, M. T., 1963, "Thought Disorder and Family Relations of Schizophrenics. I. A Research Strategy. II. A Classification of Forms of Thinking." *Archives of General Psychiatry*, 9:191–206.

Yap, P. M., 1952, "The Latah Reaction: Its Pathodynamics and Nosological Position." *Journal of Mental Science*, 98:515.

Yerkes, R. M., 1934, "Modes of Behavioral Adaptation in Chimpanzees to Multiple Choice Problems." *Comp. Psychol. Mono.*, 10.

Yerkes, R. M., 1943, *Chimpanzees. A Laboratory Colony*. New Haven, Conn.: Yale University Press.

Yolles, S. F., and Kramer, M., 1969, "Vital Statistics." In Bellak, L., and Loeb, L., *The Schizophrenic Syndrome*. New York: Grune & Stratton.

Zec, N. R., 1965, "Pseudoschizophrenic Syndrome." *Psychiat. et Neurol.*, 149:197–209.

Zeigarnik, B., 1965, *The Pathology of Thinking*. New York: Consultants Bureau Enterprises.

Ziferstein, I., 1967, "Psychological Habituation to War: A Sociopsychological Case Study." *American Journal of Orthopsychiatry*, April.

Zilboorg, G., 1928, "Malignant Psychoses Related to Childbirth." *American Journal of Obstetrics and Gynecology*, 15:145–158.

———, 1929, "The Dynamics of Schizophrenic Reactions Related to Pregnancy and Childbirth." *American Journal of Psychiatry*, 8:733–767.

———, 1941, *A History of Medical Psychology*. New York: Norton.

Zwerling, I., 1966, "The Psychiatric Day Hospital." In Arieti, S. (ed.), *American Handbook of Psychiatry*, 1st ed., vol. 3, pp. 563–576. New York: Basic Books.

Name Index

Subject Index